THE PEOPLE'S BIBLE COMMENTARY

Acts

15 The Chambers, Vineyard
Abingdon OX14 3FE
brf.org.uk

Bible Reading Fellowship is a charity (233280)
and company limited by guarantee (301324),
registered in England and Wales

ISBN (boxed set) 978 1 80039 093 5
First published 2006
This edition published 2022
10 9 8 7 6 5 4 3 2 1 0
All rights reserved

Text © Loveday Alexander 2006
This edition © Bible Reading Fellowship 2022
Cover images: detail of window, St Paul's Church, Dosthill, Staffordshire,
photo © Aidan McRae Thomson; background © iStock.com/petekarici;
gold texture © AmadeyART/stock.adobe.com

The author asserts the moral right to be identified as the author of this work

Acknowledgements
Scripture quotations marked with the following abbreviations are taken from
the version indicated. NRSV: The New Revised Standard Version of the Bible,
Anglicised Edition, copyright © 1989, 1995 by the Division of Christian Education
of the National Council of the Churches of Christ in the United States of America,
and used by permission. All rights reserved. RSV: The Revised Standard Version
of the Bible copyright © 1946, 1952, 1971 by the Division of Christian Education
of the National Council of the Churches of Christ in the United States of
America, and used by permission. All rights reserved. NIV: The Holy Bible, New
International Version (Anglicised edition) copyright © 1979, 1984, 2011 by Biblica.
Used by permission of Hodder & Stoughton Publishers, a Hachette UK company.
All rights reserved. 'NIV' is a registered trademark of Biblica. UK trademark
number 1448790. NEB: New English Bible copyright © 1961, 1970 by Oxford
University Press and Cambridge University Press. KJV: The Authorised Version
of the Bible (The King James Bible), the rights in which are vested in the Crown,
reproduced by permission of the Crown's Patentee, Cambridge University Press.

Extract from *The Book of Common Prayer* of 1662, the rights of which are vested
in the Crown in perpetuity within the United Kingdom, are reproduced by
permission of Cambridge University Press, Her Majesty's Printers.

Every effort has been made to trace and contact copyright owners for material
used in this resource. We apologise for any inadvertent omissions or errors, and
would ask those concerned to contact us so that full acknowledgement can be
made in the future.

A catalogue record for this book is available from the British Library

Printed and bound by CPI Group (UK) Ltd, Croydon CR0 4YY

THE PEOPLE'S BIBLE COMMENTARY

Acts

Loveday Alexander

Photocopying for churches

Please report to CLA Church Licence any photocopy you make from this publication.
Your church administrator or secretary will know who manages your CLA Church Licence.

The information you need to provide to your CLA Church Licence administrator is as follows:

Title, Author, Publisher and ISBN

If your church doesn't hold a CLA Church Licence, information about obtaining one can be found at **uk.ccli.com**

PREFACE TO THE 2010 EDITION

I have been delighted with the response to this commentary since it was first published. It seems to be striking chords with readers all around the world, and study notes and workshop resources based on this commentary have found their way into a variety of settings, from parish groups to missioners' conferences to working groups on Fresh Expressions of church. I find it hugely encouraging that readers are prepared to meet the challenge of wrestling with the biblical text in ways that do justice both to its original context and to where we are today, and pray that this new edition will continue to awaken enthusiasm for dynamic and engaged study of the Bible.

Loveday Alexander

ACKNOWLEDGEMENTS

My thanks are due to Richard Burridge, Naomi Starkey and the editorial board of The People's Bible Commentary for their support, encouragement (and patience!) with this project, and to all my colleagues and students in the world of Acts scholarship with whom it has been a pleasure to engage in this fascinating study. But this volume is really addressed to all my friends outside the university with whom I have tried to discover what Acts might mean for 21st-century Christians, and I would like to dedicate it to Canon Brian Young and the congregation of St Philip's, Alderley Edge (especially the ecumenical Bible study group), in whose company I have learnt more than I can say of what it means to read God's living word in today's world. Keep on studying – and keep on asking awkward questions!

CONTENTS

Introduction 9

1	Act One: Jerusalem 18	29	The hand of fellowship..... 79
2	On the holy mountain 21	30	A convert in trouble 81
3	The missing apostle.......... 23	31	Beside the seaside 83
4	The Spirit comes............... 25	32	Seaside lodging 86
5	'This is that'....................... 27	33	Peter's challenge............... 88
6	'This Jesus'........................ 29	34	Strangers and guests........ 91
7	Getting through 31	35	A sermon and its aftermath 93
8	The church begins to grow 33	36	The Jerusalem church reflects................................ 96
9	Lame man leaping............ 35	37	A tale of two churches 98
10	It's your call 37	38	The apostle and the king............................. 100
11	None other name.............. 39	39	Act Three: Paul the missionary........................ 103
12	Boldness under fire 41
13	Everything in common 44	40	Mission in Cyprus............ 105
14	Living in an open universe.............................. 47	41	Antioch of Pisidia............ 107
15	We must obey God............ 49	42	'We bring you the good news'....................... 109
16	Dare to be a Gamaliel 52
17	Hebrews and Hellenists ... 54	43	Seek the Lord 111
18	A deacon in danger........... 56	44	The word of grace 113
19	A vision and a promise 58	45	Miracle at Lystra.............. 115
20	Israel in Egypt.................... 60	46	Closing the circle 117
21	A Saviour rejected............. 63	47	Controversy at Antioch... 119
22	Your God is too small........ 65	48	The apostolic council 121
23	The first Christian martyr................................ 67	49	James intervenes 123
		50	The apostolic decree 125
24	Act Two: Judea and Samaria 69	51	Paul the missionary: phase two........................ 127
25	Mission in Samaria 71	52	The roads not taken........ 129
26	Magic and money 73	53	A seller of purple dye...... 131
27	Show me the way 75	54	Exorcism and arrest........ 133
28	The road to Damascus...... 77

55	Prison and earthquake... 135		71	Paul meets James........... 168
56	Anatomy of a riot............ 137		72	Riot in the temple........... 170
57	From Beroea to Athens... 140		73	Paul the Jew.................... 172
58	The unknown God 142		74	Status games 174
59	Tentmaking in Corinth ... 144		75	Before the Sanhedrin 176
60	Church-planting in Corinth............................. 146		76	Plots and counterplots... 178
61	Leaving Corinth................ 148		77	Trial in Caesarea 180
62	Apollos and Paul.............. 150		78	Courtroom drama........... 182
63	Paul in Ephesus................ 152		79	'I appeal to Caesar'......... 184
64	Magic and miracle 154		80	Power politics 186
65	Being church in Ephesus....................... 156		81	The heavenly vision........ 188
66	Diana of the Ephesians... 158		82	Almost persuaded 190
67	Act Four: Paul the prisoner........................... 160		83	Down to the sea in ships 192
68	Farewell at Miletus.......... 162		84	Storm and shipwreck 194
69	I have finished my course 164		85	Desert island hospitality 196
70	Towards Jerusalem 166		86	And so to Rome............... 198
			87	In my end is my beginning 200

Notes... 202

INTRODUCTION

Bilbo often used to say that there was only one Road; that it was like a great river: its springs were at every doorstep, and every path was its tributary. 'It's a dangerous business, Frodo, going out of your door,' he used to say. 'You step into the Road, and if you don't keep your feet, there is no knowing where you might be swept off to.'

J.R.R. Tolkien, *The Lord of the Rings: The Fellowship of the Ring*.

Welcome to the journey!

'This book will make a traveller of thee,' says John Bunyan at the beginning of *The Pilgrim's Progress*, and the same could well be said of the Acts of the Apostles. The book of Acts is the story of a journey. It tells the story of the birth of the church, and its journey outwards and across the world from where it all began, in an upstairs room in Jerusalem. Woven into this story are the journeys of a whole host of individual travellers, apostles and others, moving back and forth across that Mediterranean world and spreading the word wherever they go. But it's also the story of the journey of faith, a journey to which every reader is invited: it's no accident that one of Luke's favourite metaphors for discipleship is 'the Way'.

As so often in the Bible, the journey starts with a vision, which empowers and controls the travellers and to which they constantly revert. The story begins on a mountaintop, the classic location for vision in the Bible, where the heavens open and angels and mortals speak face to face (ch. 1). Then comes the communal visionary experience of Pentecost, when the empowerment of God's Spirit becomes something visible even to the crowds in a Jerusalem street (ch. 2). Further into the narrative, the two controlling visions are Peter's rooftop trance (ch. 10) and Paul's encounter with the risen Christ on the Damascus road (ch. 9); each is recounted over and over again, as the characters in the story are challenged to unravel the true significance of what God is saying to them (chs. 11; 15; 22; 26). And vision provides not only the starting point for mission but also its content: 'We cannot but speak of the things which we have seen and heard' (4:20; 26:19).

Journey into outer space

Like any road movie, Acts contains a strong geographical element. It's the one book in the New Testament where you really need to keep an eye on the map. Most Bibles include a map of 'The journeys of St Paul', and there are excellent maps available in Bible atlases and other guides. (Tip: a modern physical map of the eastern Mediterranean will often give you a much better flavour of the terrain covered in the book.) More than any other book of the New Testament, Acts conveys a sense of the excitement and romance of travel. It's a cosmopolitan book, moving with ease from the narrow streets of Jerusalem to the classical elegance of Athens, from the high passes of the Turkish-Syrian border to the back streets of Rome. And on the way we meet a variety of deftly drawn characters, from the Ethiopian court treasurer (ch. 8) to the friendly Roman centurion Julius (ch. 27). Acts reminds us that there's a big wide world out there – a daunting prospect to the Galilean disciples on the Mount of Olives, as Jesus gives them their marching orders (1:8). But gradually, as we read, we come to share with them the unfolding excitement of finding that God is out there too, waiting to meet them and surprise them in this strange world that is also God's world.

Journey into inner space

There's also a more hidden journey, a journey of discovery in which the familiar turns out to be more surprising than we thought. 'Who will show me the way?' asks the Ethiopian, sitting in his chariot on the Gaza Road and poring over an ancient scroll (8:31). It's not a road map he's asking for but a new way to read the age-old scriptures, and that's what Philip provides (8:35). Acts conducts its characters (and therefore its readers) into an inner journey of exploration under the guidance of God's Holy Spirit, working out how the 'this' of personal experience corresponds with the 'that' of God's revelation. This is not always an easy thing to do. Often it means facing up to the puzzlement and hostility of our closest compatriots. Even harder, it means confronting our own prejudices and facing up to our own persistent refusal to recognise God's Spirit at work. So there's a lot of conflict built into the story of Acts; and some of the shortest journeys in the book, geographically speaking, turn out to be some of the longest and most significant in terms of inner space.

A guide for time travellers

This commentary is designed as a kind of interactive travel guide for readers of Acts, helping you to relate to Luke's story on three levels.

My first priority is to describe the journey itself from the point of view of the author and his first readers, taking pains to listen carefully to the story as he tells it, to pick up the clues he has laid for informed readers, and to try first of all to understand the story in its own terms. This is a basic courtesy we owe to any book, especially to a book written 2,000 years ago in a very different culture from our own. That means trying to experience the journey from the viewpoint of the characters in Luke's story, hearing the conversations and debates from inside, trying to understand both sides before jumping to conclusions about what's going on. It also means trying to hear Luke's story through the ears of his original readers, asking about the literary echoes or political resonances that would be picked up by a first-century audience.

Second, we can take a step back and ask how Luke's story relates to other stories we know of from that time and place. This means filling in some of the historical information we need, to understand the significance of Luke's story: who was this emperor or that official? What else was going on at the time? How does Luke's version of events tie in with other evidence – Paul's letters, for example? I have tried to indicate what the main historical questions are and where you can find out more if you want to.

And third, we need to move back into the 21st century (which of course we never really left) and ask how Luke's story relates to our own stories. There are many different kinds of travel guides, but most of them fall into two categories: those that offer an armchair substitute for travel, and those that incite you to get out there and sample the real thing. My hope and prayer is that readers will find this guide provoking in many different ways, and that you will be able to use it to inform and inspire your own journeying on the Way, whether individually or as a group. So each reading ends with a question, a quotation or a prayer, suggesting ways to link up with some of the stories that belong to our lives today – things that are happening in the newspapers, in our churches or in our own spiritual lives. Use these any way you want, and treat them as a springboard to make your own connections between Luke's world and ours – or simply as a framework for your own prayers.

Basic orientation

The rest of this introduction will deal with the basic information and equipment you need for the journey. You may like to read it all before starting, or you may prefer to save it up and refer back to it as the need arises.

The author

Like most New Testament scholars, I use the name 'Luke' as shorthand for 'the author of Acts – whoever that was'. This is the name that has been attached to the third gospel and Acts from earliest times, both in the manuscript tradition and in the early church writers who quote him. But it's worth pausing at the outset to ask what we know about the person who put this crucial story together – and what kind of detective work has gone into piecing the story together.

First, we know from Acts 1:1 that the author has already written a book about Jesus – and it doesn't take much detective ability to work out that this 'former treatise' is the third gospel, which is dedicated to the same person, Theophilus, and is written in very much the same style. So 'Luke' is actually the author of two books, which together make up almost a quarter of the whole New Testament. And our author tells us a bit more about himself in the preface to the gospel, at Luke 1:1–4. This preface doesn't give the author's name (although the masculine participle used in verse 3 does tell us that he was male). In some ways the preface tells us more about who Luke was not than who he was: he wasn't the first to write down the story of Jesus (v. 1); he wasn't an eyewitness (v. 2). But the whole way he writes tells us quite a bit about the sort of person he was: rational, business-like, reassuringly pragmatic, full of words like 'carefully', 'accurately', 'thoroughly', 'in an orderly fashion' (vv. 3–4). It's as if Luke wants to reassure his readers that the extraordinary story they're about to read is one that belongs in the real world, a world of people like Theophilus who like to check out the reliability of what they're told (v. 4) – in other words, a world of people like you and me.

Nevertheless, this sober, rational author is not standing outside the story he tells, like an investigative journalist. He has a personal stake in it. The 'we' of the preface to Luke's gospel aligns the writer with the whole Christian tradition, with all those who have received the testimony of the original eyewitnesses (v. 2). In fact, he's part of the community in which the whole extraordinary business has come to pass (v. 1). And towards the end of his second volume, the 'we' slips in again in a way that implies that the author is actually part of the story he narrates (Acts 16:10–17; 20:5–15; 21:1–18; 27:1—28:16). It sounds as if our author was one of those who accompanied Paul on his travels, including the last, fateful trip to Rome. If so, all we need to do is to work out from Paul's letters which of Paul's many friends and co-workers is the most likely candidate for the job. It seems safe to assume that the author isn't any of the people he mentions in the third person (Barnabas, Timothy, Gaius and so on – you can work it out for yourself if you want to). That still leaves quite a few options: Paul had a lot of friends! (Look at Romans 16, for example.) But as far back as we can see (as early as Irenaeus, writing around AD180), the favoured candidate is the attractive if shadowy figure of the beloved physician of Paul's prison epistles, the co-worker who sends greetings to the house churches in Colossae, the faithful Luke who sticks with the apostle in prison: look up Philemon 24; Colossians 4:14; 2 Timothy 4:11.

Not all scholars accept that this detective work has come up with the right answer. Some would argue that the 'we-passages' of Acts are just a literary device or that the author has incorporated some genuine diary entries from one of Paul's companions. Many find it hard to believe that a close companion of Paul could have written Acts, on the grounds that the Paul whom Luke portrays is actually rather different from the Paul who comes across from his letters. That's an issue we shall look at from time to time in the second half of Acts, but for my part (in common with a number of other recent commentators), I find that on balance the traditional authorship is the simplest way to account for all the data. Not that Luke's viewpoint is identical with that of Paul's letters in every respect. Luke hardly ever calls Paul an apostle, for example, and (as we shall see) he has certainly been selective in the story he tells. But then, which of our closest friends would portray any of us exactly as we would like to portray ourselves?

Ultimately, I don't believe that the name of the author is what really matters. Much more important is to work out why the author has shaped his story in the particular way he has. For that, it is highly significant that the author (let's stick with calling him Luke) has chosen to align himself with the first-hand experience of Paul's travelling companions. And that, I believe, provides a vital clue to the distinctive viewpoint that gives his story its shape.

The shape of Luke's story

It's helpful to think of Luke's story as a drama in four acts. The first three correspond roughly to the threefold geographical plan outlined in Jesus' commission in 1:8: Jerusalem (Act I: chapters 1—7); Judea and Samaria (Act II: chapters 8—12); 'to the ends of the earth' (Act III: chapters 13—19). Act IV (chapters 20—28) brings Paul back to Jerusalem, and tells how he eventually ended up travelling to Rome as a prisoner.

Looking forward, in other words, the story proceeds like a series of chain reactions (Pentecost; persecution; mission), each one triggering the next. As we watch each explosion, it's impossible to predict where the debris will end up: the potential is global (2:9–11), and Luke doesn't attempt to tell all the stories that his narrative opens up. (What happened to all the other apostles, or the other deacons?) But unrolling the story backwards, it's quite easy to see how each step links back to the one before. Starting out from the Mount of the Ascension, there's no way you could predict Paul's imprisonment in Rome, but if you begin at the end you can trace the causal links all the way back. And the wonderful thing that Luke wants to impress above all on his readers is how each step – even the apparent disasters – is under the guidance of God's Holy Spirit. Like Joseph, Paul could have said, 'It was God who brought me here to preach the life-giving gospel of salvation' (compare Genesis 45:5).

So in many respects the easiest way to understand the shape of the drama is to begin at the end. 'And *that's* how we got to Rome!' says Luke triumphantly, after all the excitement of the shipwreck (28:14) – as if the whole point of his story is to explain how Paul comes to be arriving in Rome, accompanied by a Roman centurion, charged with disrupting the peace and generally causing mayhem back in Jerusalem. In fact, I believe that is precisely Luke's point. The whole last quarter of the book tells the long and complicated story of the riot in the temple that triggered it all off and the series of trials in which Paul has to defend himself before the Jewish and Roman authorities. But of course we want to know how he came to be in the temple in the first place, and why he got people so wound up: so that takes us back into Act III, which tells the extraordinary story of Paul's mission, and how he kept trying to give his message to Jewish audiences around the Mediterranean world and then finding that he was being pushed into giving it to the Gentiles too. But Paul wasn't acting just under his own steam: Act II takes us further back, to the heavenly revelation that stopped Paul in his tracks and made him a follower of Jesus instead of a persecutor of Jesus' disciples, and shows how Paul's story ties in with the stories of other people following this Way that people call 'the sect of the Nazarenes' (24:5, 14). And that takes us, finally, to Act I (chapters 1—7), which tells the story of how the sect originated and its links with the hidden substratum of Acts, the good news that God has sent salvation for the whole world in Jesus, the Christ (compare Luke 1:68–79; 24:44–47).

Journey's end

The final scene of Acts also provides a vital clue to Luke's original audience and situation. Luke tells us a lot about Paul the missionary, preaching to the Gentile world (in Act III), and Paul the prisoner, making his defence before the Roman empire (in Act IV). In the final scene of the book, however, Paul is neither of these. His final words are addressed to the leaders of the Jewish community in Rome, who ask him (in surprisingly neutral tones), 'Tell us about this sect.' In essence, I believe that Luke's whole story is the answer to that question – although my hunch is (along with most scholars) that Luke is actually writing after Paul's death and after the destructive and futile rebellion against Rome that left the temple in ruins.

The final scene of Acts is a kind of freeze-frame that encapsulates a key moment in the long, fraught history of Jewish–Christian relations. Acts records three decades of dialogue, debate and division – sometimes violent – over 'the Way' within the Jewish community. Much of this dialogue takes place on the margins, in the border zones where different groups within the Jewish family are jostling for position, each at times trying to edge the others out. So there are times when Luke speaks of 'the Jews' as outsiders, and times (much more often) when Paul and Peter address their fellow Jews as insiders in impassioned, prophetic appeal. That's the time warp Acts is caught up in, a freeze-frame that's hard to recapture from where we stand today. But I believe it is essential that we give full weight to all the voices in that dialogue, within and outside the church, refusing to foreclose the debate – which in many ways foreshadows the debates going on in the church today between continuity and innovation, 'traditional' and 'emerging' patterns of church life. In our ready identification with one side or the other, with the prodigal or the elder brother, it's all too easy to shut out the voice of the Father who says to both brothers, 'Son, you are always with me, and all that I have is yours' (Luke 15:31).

For information and further reading

Because this dialogue within the Jewish community is so important as a framework for Acts, we need to draw on a range of contemporary sources to understand what is going on in first-century Judaism and how that fits into the wider world of the Roman empire. I have included a minimum of source references in the notes, but you may like to follow up some further reading to get the flavour of Luke's world. All the books listed here will provide a portal for further exploration of current Acts research if you are so inclined. If you're not, just ignore them!

- Probably the most accessible single resource for reading Acts in its historical context is the splendid five-volume set on *The Book of Acts in Its First-Century Setting*, edited by Bruce Winter and Andrew Clarke (Paternoster/Eerdmans, 1993–1996). This contains summaries of recent findings on such matters as house churches, Roman roads, magistrates and 'God-fearers', as well as essays by leading scholars on literary and theological issues in Acts.

- One of the most significant finds for enlarging our understanding of first-century Judaism is the Dead Sea Scrolls. The Scrolls, and the Qumran community that read them, throw a fascinating light on some of the practices of the Jerusalem church, such as the casting of lots and the community of goods. The Scrolls are easily available in English translation – see Geza Vermes, *The Complete Dead Sea Scrolls in English* (Penguin, 1998). There are many good scholarly introductions: I recommend Jonathan G. Campbell, *Deciphering the Dead Sea Scrolls*, second edition (Blackwell, 2002), George Brooke, *Qumran and the Jewish Jesus* (Grove Books, 2005) and George Brooke, *The Dead Sea Scrolls and the New Testament* (SPCK, 2005).

- Much of the argument of Acts turns on the interpretation of scripture. Luke and his contemporaries in the Greek-speaking diaspora read the Bible not in Hebrew but in Greek, following a translation made by Jewish scholars over the last few centuries before Christ. This Greek Bible is often referred to as the Septuagint (LXX for short), from the Greek word for '70'. The name derives from the legend that the translation was made by 70 scholars working independently but coming up (miraculously) with identical results. Jennifer M. Dines, *The Septuagint* (T&T Clark, 2004) provides an excellent short introduction.

- Outside the Bible, our main historical source for events in first-century Palestine is the Jewish historian Josephus, who took part in the great Jewish war against Rome in AD66–70, and wrote up his memoirs in Rome at the end of the first century. Josephus' great history of the Jewish War is available in English in the Penguin Classics series, as are Roman writers like Tacitus, Suetonius and Pliny.

- Commentaries on Acts are numerous. The 'big four' reference commentaries at the time of writing were: C.K. Barrett, *The Acts of the Apostles*, International Critical Commentary, two volumes (T&T Clark, 1994, 1998); Joseph A. Fitzmyer, SJ, *The Acts of the Apostles*, Anchor Bible (Doubleday, 1998); Luke Timothy Johnson, *The Acts of the Apostles*, Sacra Pagina (Liturgical Press, 1992) and Ben Witherington III, *The Acts of the Apostles: A socio-rhetorical commentary* (Eerdmans, 1998). Of the shorter, more accessible commentaries, I'd recommend especially Beverly R. Gaventa, *Acts*, Abingdon NT Commentary (Abingdon, 2003). More recently, Steven Walton, *Acts*, Word Biblical Commentary 37A (W Publishing Group, 2008) has been published, while a collection of my own essays on the literary world of Acts appears in my *Acts in Its Ancient Literary Context: A classicist looks at the Acts of the Apostles* (T&T Clark, 2005). My own commentary, part of the Black's New Testament Commentaries series, is due to be released in 2023.

- Finally, there are some exciting publications dealing with the theological issues raised by studying Acts within the life of today's worldwide church. I have benefited enormously from the work of Justo Gonzalez, *Acts: The gospel of the Spirit* (Orbis, 2001); Luke Timothy Johnson, *Scripture and Discernment: Decision making in the church*, revised edition (Abingdon Press, 1996); and Anthony B. Robinson and Robert W. Wall, *Called To Be Church: The book of Acts for a new day* (Eerdmans, 2006). Robert Gallagher and Paul Hertig (eds), *Mission in Acts: Ancient narratives in contemporary context* (Orbis, 2004) also suggests some imaginative connections between the world of Acts and the worldwide church today, as does the introduction to James Alison, *On Being Liked* (Darton, Longman and Todd, 2003).

1

Acts 1:1–5

Act One: Jerusalem

When the Lord restored the fortunes of Zion, we were like those who dream. Then our mouth was filled with laughter, and our tongue with shouts of joy; then they said among the nations, 'The Lord has done great things for them.' The Lord has done great things for us; we are glad.
PSALM 126:1–3 (RSV)

The opening chapters of Acts capture something of the dream-like quality of the psalmist's vision of the restoration of Zion. Restoration, and the fulfilment of the age-old promises, is very much what the first quarter of the book is about. But restoration is also about repentance, and that is what is on offer for the people of Jerusalem and their rulers.

The story so far

Like the preface to Luke's gospel (Luke 1:1–4), the opening verse of Acts is essentially a kind of label stuck on to the front of the book, in which the author momentarily speaks in his own voice and addresses the reader direct. The practical reason for putting the label here is that each of Luke's two volumes is about the right length for a scroll, so this point marks the break. Because a scroll has no spine or dust jacket, ancient authors normally used the first sentence to supply the essential information that readers needed to identify what they were reading. The effect is rather like changing reels halfway through the film in an old-fashioned cinema. For a few moments we slip out of the narrative world and back into the real world of authors and readers.

Volume two

The first thing we learn as we open the book is that it's the second volume of a diptych, the second half of a book that describes 'all that Jesus did and taught from the beginning' (v. 1). And it's not just a loosely connected sequel. It's easy to see from the first verse that Luke expects his readers to know what has happened in the gospel. He makes very few concessions to new readers: there are no footnotes or helpful glosses to tell them who John or the apostles were. Everything in the second volume, Acts, presupposes the story of the first (that is, the story of Jesus) and there are all sorts of links and connections that observant readers can pick up between the two.

Captain and crew

The preface also lays the groundwork in important ways for the second half of Luke's story. It introduces the key characters of Acts, beginning with Jesus himself. Luke's story of Jesus is shaped in a particular way, focused on the actions and teachings of a holy man (v. 1), just as many Greek biographies described the actions and teachings of a philosopher. That story is directed towards the ascension (v. 2), which creates the centrepoint for the whole two-volume work. For Luke, the ascension of Jesus is not an afterthought, tacked on to tidy up the end of the narrative: the passion, resurrection and ascension are a unit, beginning as far back as Luke 9:51. But the story doesn't end with Jesus' departure to heaven: the opening scene of Acts creates a double overlay with the last chapter of the gospel (Luke 24), both describing in different ways the captain's final instructions to his crew. In a sense, everything in Acts stems from this moment. In the chapters that ensue, we shall follow the apostles' attempts to carry out the mission Jesus has entrusted to them.

The apostles and the Spirit

The apostles (v. 2) are therefore the next most important characters. We shall hear much more about them as the story progresses, but this brief introduction already tells us that they were chosen by Jesus and instructed by Jesus – companions who shared table-fellowship with him (the meaning of 'staying with them' in v. 4, NRSV). The essence of their commission lies precisely in being entrusted with the unique experience of seeing Jesus alive after his passion (v. 3), witnessing the 'many convincing proofs' of his resurrection life. Transmitting this experience to an unbelieving world, offering living proof of Jesus' continued (but hidden) resurrection life, is what they are about. They are not alone: Jesus' instruction is 'in the Holy Spirit' who has been with him since the beginning of the gospel story (Luke 1:35; 3:22; 4:14). And more is on its way: the promise of the Father (compare Luke 24:49) is about to be realised not many days from now (vv. 4–5). There's a sense of expectancy here which takes us right back to the beginning of the gospel.

Prayer

Lord Jesus, as we read the story of the apostles, help us to catch a glimpse of what it means to be your disciples, and to take our place in your mission in the world.

2 Acts 1:6–12

On the holy mountain

Most prefaces of this type move rather prosaically from 'What I've just told you' to 'What I'm going to tell you' in a matching sentence. Luke gives his readers a much more dramatic and vivid preview of the book we're about to read. Already in 1:4 he has drawn us in unexpectedly to eavesdrop on Jesus' conversations with his disciples in those last 40 days. Now we find ourselves standing beside them, in the mountaintop vision that powers the whole of the narrative of Acts.

Restoring the kingdom

First, Jesus has to redirect the apostles (and, with them, ourselves) from looking back to looking forward, and to a rather different kind of future from the one they (and perhaps we) expect. The air of expectancy that pervades this opening scene rekindles the eschatological expectations of the coming kingdom in Luke 3 – but God's future is very different. The disciples ask, 'Is this the time to restore the kingdom to Israel?' (v. 6). 'Yes,' is the answer: God is about to act, and Israel is being offered restoration – but with a difference. Its timing is not something we need to worry about (v. 7). The Christian is to live in a constant state of alertness and expectancy, without knowing exactly when the end will be. What we do have is empowerment for the present task (v. 8) – 'You will receive power when the Holy Spirit has come upon you' – and with the promise comes a glimpse of the immense and daunting task ahead. This is the first hint that travel is going to be important in the apostles' story: verse 8 gives a threefold geographical shape to the story of Acts, which we shall see gradually unfolding in the mission to Jerusalem (chs 1—7), to Judea and Samaria (chs 8—12), and 'to the ends of the earth' (chs 13—28).

On the mountaintop

It is only in verse 12 that we learn that the ascension takes place on a mountain. As mountains go, the Mount of Olives is a relatively insignificant height overlooking the city of Jerusalem, but it is the only mountain mentioned in Acts (apart from Stephen's reference to Mount

Sinai in 7:30), and, like Mount Sinai, it is a place of immense theological significance. Traditional icons of the transfiguration show Jesus at the top of a sharp and pointy mountain, with the disciples prostrated in attitudes of awe and wonder at his feet – a classic attempt to fix in paint the intersection of the eternal with time, a moment with no before and after. But (as in a cartoon) some versions of the icon also show Jesus and the disciples precisely in those 'before' and 'after' moments, with Jesus leading the disciples up the mountain on the left-hand side, and shooing them down again on the right. That, to me, is how Luke's picture of the ascension works. Right at the heart of his two-volume narrative is a mountaintop scene, where Jesus is seen in his glory and taken up into heaven. It's a moment of vision (note the four different words for 'seeing' in verses 9–11), where the disciples (eleven of them this time) are finally vouchsafed a glimpse of the true nature and destination of this person whose company they have been sharing over the last three years – before the cloud tantalisingly hides him from their sight (v. 9).

Down the mountain

Acts is also the narrative of a journey. Ever since Luke 9:51, Jesus has been leading his disciples along the way that leads to his 'taking up', teaching them, bearing with their failings and leading them to an end that seems progressively darker – until the single moment of revelation comprised in the double action of resurrection and ascension. Now the way leads down the mountain again, downwards and outwards from the defining moment of revelation, back into the mundane world of argument and doubt. It's not an easy transition to make: it's much easier to stand 'gazing up towards heaven' (v. 10). On the mount of transfiguration, Peter had insanely proposed setting up a campsite (Luke 9:33), until the cloud faded and they found themselves alone on the misty mountainside, with only Jesus there to show them the way back down to earth. This time, they won't have that consoling human presence: they will have to discover new ways of experiencing his presence. At the moment, all they can feel is absence. Yet, there's a task to perform – and a promise to hold on to (v. 11).

Prayer

Lord Jesus, help us to follow wherever you lead, and to know your presence every step of the way.

3

Acts 1:13–26

The missing apostle

This whole scene has an air of the interim about it, an air of focused expectancy, waiting obediently for… what? There is some unfinished business to be resolved before the narrative proper gets under way: the problem of the apostle who wasn't.

Retracing steps

When you have no guidance over where to go next, the sensible thing is to stay put (compare Luke 24:49). For the disciples who had come up from Galilee those few short weeks before, the upstairs room (v. 13) must have seemed like a sanctuary in a suddenly hostile and empty city, a room full of memories of a vivid and urgent presence, now bafflingly withdrawn. Luke gives us here a strategic reminder of the names of the original disciples from Galilee (compare Luke 6:14–16), minus one. But the eleven disciples are not the only members of this fledgling community. In fact, we learn from verse 15 that there are up to 120 people in that first fellowship, all persevering in prayer (v. 14). When there's no way forward, that's always a good idea!

Sisters and brothers

Luke singles out two other groups here (v. 14). The 'women' could refer to the wives of the disciples, but more probably means the band of women supporters who had followed Jesus from Galilee (Luke 8:1–3) and who, in all the gospels, play an important role in the resurrection narratives (Luke 23:55—24:11). This particular group has no role in Luke's ongoing story (he makes it clear that only men can act as witnesses to the resurrection), but women, named and unnamed, will continue to play a significant part in the development of the early church (5:1–11; 6:1; 8:3; 9:36–42; 12:12–16; 16:11–15; 18:1–4, 26; 21:5).

Then there are Mary the mother of Jesus and his brothers. This is the first and last mention of Mary in Acts. The brothers of Jesus also are not mentioned again as a group, although James will play a significant role later on (see comment on 15:12–21; 21:18–30).

Luke goes out of his way to stress the togetherness of the three groups (the eleven, the women and Jesus' family) at the outset, and the fact that they acted in concert in the choice of a replacement apostle.

The twelfth apostle

The list of names in verse 13 ends with a yawning gap – Judas, named as the betrayer in Luke 6:16 (compare Luke 22:21). Judas is both an embarrassment and a theological conundrum. Peter, taking his first steps into a leadership role here (v. 15), doesn't balk the issue. Judas was 'numbered among us' and 'was allotted his share in this ministry' (v. 17): in other words, he *was* an apostle, sent and commissioned just like the others. Luke is realistic about the possibility of failure within the holy community (see the story of Ananias in ch. 5). In fact, he adds a footnote at this point (vv. 18–19 is clearly Luke speaking, not Peter), which highlights Judas' fate as an awful warning to the later community. Nevertheless (and this is the first appearance of a recurrent theme in Acts), Judas' failure was 'foretold by scripture'; in other words, it was part of God's purpose (vv. 16, 20). The scriptural verses that Peter cites to make his point (v. 20, citing Psalms 69:25; 109:8) are essentially descriptions of a life alienated from God; but Peter uses them to highlight the fact that the 'office' Judas held, the ministry he shared in, is more important than the individual and can survive his failure.

There is, then, a vacancy, and it is the job of this assembly to fill it. The qualifications are clearly described (vv. 21–22): being with Jesus from the beginning, plus the willingness to 'become a witness'. In other words, witness-ship does not depend simply on what you've seen but also on your willingness to speak out about it. This last point may explain why women are disqualified from the position: women were not legally accepted as witnesses in Jewish law.

There is no shortage of qualified candidates (v. 23), so a mechanism has to be found for making a choice. Casting lots (v. 26) is a nice combination of human action (something must be done) and divine will. The casting of lots never appears again in Acts as a mechanism for selection, but it was a recognised means of discovering the divine will both in ancient Judaism (especially at Qumran) and in the Greek civic process. This is not a resort to mere chance, however: the essence of the process is prayer (vv. 24–25).

Prayer

Father, teach us to persevere in prayer when we can't see the way forward.

4

Acts 2:1–8

The Spirit comes

The denouement, when it comes, is as dramatic as it is unexpected. After the preliminaries, the sense of expectancy in chapter 1, this scene makes the beginning of the drama proper, the first 'big' scene of Acts. It follows a threefold pattern that we shall see more than once: a theophany, a dramatic revelatory event in which God acts directly to make himself known; followed by diverse reactions, for and against; followed by explanation in which the characters go back to the Hebrew scriptures to make sense of what is happening.

The day of Pentecost

First comes the event itself, described with dramatic ceremony and in richly scriptural language. Pentecost (v. 1) comes 50 days after Passover, so this date fixes the outpouring of the Spirit precisely to ten days after the ascension (1:3) and seven weeks after the crucifixion (Luke 22:1), details which would eventually determine the shape of the Christian liturgical year. Pentecost was originally a harvest festival, the feast of Weeks (Hebrew: *Shavuot*), thanking God for the first grain of the new harvest (see Deuteronomy 16:9–10; Leviticus 23:15–16). By Luke's time, however, it had also come to be associated with the giving of the law on Mount Sinai and with the renewing of the covenant at Qumran. The Temple Scroll from Qumran speaks of three successive 'Pentecost' feasts of new grain, new wine and new oil. So, for Luke and his first readers, this is a day rich with symbolic resonances. It is the day when God chooses to 'fulfil' everything that this multilayered festival points to: thanksgiving and celebration for the outpouring of God's blessings on the life of his people, and the renewal of God's covenant with his people and of their commitment to living as God's people in the world.

Wind and fire

What happens exactly? Luke uses several words to stress the togetherness of Jesus' followers on this occasion (v. 1), which makes it look as if he means to include all the 120 believers of 1:14–15 (including Jesus' family and the women), not just the twelve. What they heard must have been frightening to an indoor gathering, busy trying to keep themselves quiet. It sounds like the noise of a powerful, dynamic blast of wind (not a gentle breeze!), filling the house (v. 2), a blast that brings to mind the biblical evocations of God's wind buffeting the mountaintops (1 Kings 19:11; compare Psalm 29:9) or God's breath blowing life into dead bodies (Genesis 2:7; Ezekiel 37): the words for 'spirit' in Hebrew and Greek (*ruach*, *pneuma*) mean both 'wind' and 'breath'.

There's fire, too – another indicator of God's active presence (cf. Exodus 3:2; Psalm 104:4; Ezekiel 1:4) – not the terrifying fire of judgement (Luke 3:17), but tongue-shaped flames distributed around each head (v. 3), the fire of the Holy Spirit that the Baptist had promised (Luke 3:16). The thing about a flame is that the more you divide it, the more there is to go round: split a flame in half and you get more, not less. So the coming of the Spirit is a gift of new life to the community, which brings out the individual gifts of each member, a gift that brings God's living word to articulate expression in a host of individual tongues (v. 4).

The word on the street

This is not something you can keep behind closed doors! Jerusalem is packed with pilgrims, jostling through the city's narrow streets and full of the excitement of the festival (v. 5). They come from 'every nation under the sun', and they create a ready-made crowd which 'flows together' (v. 6), drawn magnetically to the confused sound coming from behind the shutters, and hearing, mysteriously, not the Galilean Aramaic you would expect (v. 7), but each person's native language (v. 8). The crowd's words in verse 8 could mean 'in our own dialect', suggesting that what they hear is the many different dialects of Aramaic spoken across the Middle East, but in verse 11 they repeat the exclamation with the word 'tongue'.

The nations listed in 2:9–11 cover a much broader language-range than the Aramaic-speaking East, and it's clear that Luke means us to understand this event as a miracle of language. How it relates to the more common association of the Spirit with 'speaking in tongues' (see 10:46; 19:6; 1 Corinthians 14) is unclear, but modern studies have shown that those present often have the sensation of hearing real languages.

Prayer

Come, Holy Spirit. Blow away the cobwebs from our minds; blow us out on to the streets and kindle our hearts with the fire of your love.

5 Acts 2:9–21
'This is that'

Who was present in that polyglot crowd? Luke's list of nations (possibly taken from a list of diaspora nations) gives a marvellously cosmopolitan dimension to the revelation of God's Spirit, opening up our geographical horizons and preparing us for a story that is going to take us to the ends of the earth (1:8). It's a list that spans the boundaries of Rome's empire, centred not on Rome but on Jerusalem. At Pentecost, pilgrims pour into Jerusalem from all directions: from the east, from the ancient Jewish exilic communities in the old Persian empire (Parthia, Media, Elam, Mesopotamia: v. 9); from the provinces of Asia Minor and the Black Sea coast in the north; from Egypt and north Africa in the south (v. 10); across the sea from Rome (which marks the furthest western boundary on this map), via Crete; and not forgetting the desert caravans of Arabia (v. 11). At the centre, though, is Judea (v. 9), and it may be the locals who are so notably unimpressed by the miracle of languages that all they hear is a drunken babble (v. 13). Miracles by themselves produce wonder, but not conviction (v. 12): Peter has got some serious explaining to do.

Men of Israel

Despite its cosmopolitan nature, this is a Jewish crowd, a crowd of pilgrims gathered in from the scattered nations of the diaspora to worship at the emotional centrepoint of Jewish life (v. 5) – a symbolic foretaste of the gathering in of the diaspora and ultimately of the Gentiles, but at this stage no more than that. When Peter gets up to speak, he addresses the crowd as 'Men of Judea and all you residents of Jerusalem' (v. 14), addressing particularly the sceptics among the local inhabitants (v. 15) and, as will become clear, all the residents, locals and pilgrims who have been in Jerusalem over the festival period and have witnessed the events of Passover (2:22–23). The argument of his speech is quintessentially Jewish, drawing on techniques of biblical exposition known from the Dead Sea Scrolls, leaning on the Jewish scriptures to explain what is actually happening in front of their eyes. You want to know what this is all about? No, they haven't been at the new wine – it's only nine o'clock in the morning (v. 15). To understand what's going on here, you have to look further than that – look back, in fact, to what God has already promised in scripture.

This is what Joel meant

This style of exegesis, known as *pesher* in the Dead Sea Scrolls, is fundamental to the whole argument of Acts and indeed to the biblical understanding of how scripture works. It starts with 'this' (vv. 14, 16) – with the inbreaking revelation of the living God, active in the most unexpected people and places – and then goes back to scripture to match it up with 'that' (v. 16): God's self-revelation in the past. And that may well involve, as it does here, a radical rereading of the scriptures we thought we knew. In fact, as we shall see, the whole of Acts is a plea to read the Bible in a new way in light of the new things that God is doing in the present. So here in verses 17–21 Peter's quotation from Joel 2:28–32 is subtly reshaped to heighten the theological parallels between Joel's prophecy and the events of Pentecost.

I will pour out my Spirit

Joel's prophecy announces the 'great and glorious day of the Lord' (v. 20), a time of judgement for Israel and the nations, accompanied by signs and portents in earth and sky (Joel 2:30–31). The shock comes in Peter's insistence that the 'last days' are happening *now*. The Pentecostal fire and the sound from heaven (Acts 2:2–3) are two of the signs and portents that Joel prophesied (v. 19) – the first but not the last prophetic 'signs' in Acts (cf. 4:30; 5:12; 6:8; 7:36; 15:12). And this babble of prophetic speech, giving speech to the inarticulate, empowering men and women alike, matches wonderfully Joel's vision of an outpouring of God's prophetic Spirit on God's people, an inclusive vision that breaks down the barriers of age, class and gender (vv. 17–18). In its original setting, however, Joel's prophecy was about the restoration of Judah and Jerusalem and judgement for the nations of the world (Joel 3:1–8), so Peter's audience (and Peter himself) would not necessarily hear a promise of universal salvation in Acts 2:21 (as Paul does in Romans 10:12–13). The significance of that particular bit of rereading will unfold gradually as Peter's journey takes him out into God's world.

Prayer

Father, help us to be open to the surprise and challenge of seeing your word fulfilled in ways that explode our narrow horizons.

6

Acts 2:22–32

'This Jesus'

Peter's speech begins with his own and his friends' experience of God's inrushing, overwhelming presence (2:15–16): that's what has pushed them out on to the street, and that's what has attracted the attention of the passers-by (2:1–5). But his priority as an apostle (and the priority of any church that claims to be apostolic) is to redirect that attention from the emissary to the one who sent him, from the gift to the giver. So here Peter wastes no time in linking the community's experience to the person of Christ (v. 22): Jesus is the interpretive key to everything that happens in Acts.

This Jesus whom you crucified

That also means tying the new events in with a shared recent experience of the audience. Jesus of Nazareth is someone they will all have heard of, and many of them will have seen him preaching and teaching in street and temple in that last week before his death, only seven weeks ago (Luke 19—22). He was a public figure: Peter can assume that his audience will all know of the amazing things God did through Jesus right in their midst (v. 22). So it is clear that Peter is now addressing a very particular audience on a very particular occasion. Acts gives no warrant for the disastrous tendency to blame all Jews everywhere for the death of Jesus, which has blighted Christian history and contributed eventually to the Holocaust. When Peter speaks of 'this Jesus whom you crucified' (vv. 23, 36), he means precisely *this* Jerusalem crowd, the crowd who were part of a very specific series of events just a few weeks before. This is the hard part, but this audience has to face it. We can't move forward into God's future without facing up to our past.

The Jesus whom God raised up

The place of greatest shame and failure, humanly speaking, is the place where God's grace breaks in and transforms the situation. Even at the lowest moment, the moment of the triumph of human sin and failure – the power plays of the politicians, the fickleness of the crowd and the cowardice of the disciples – even then, Jesus was never outside God's plan (v. 23). Sometimes God allows human action to create a disaster. The crucifixion is about God's passivity, about God in the person of Jesus accepting the worst that humans can do to one another. To suffer is to allow oneself to become an object, to be acted upon: the same Latin word gives us both 'passive' and 'passion'. But that is never the end of the story, because what God does (even in the passive) is always the action of love, and the next event is pure grace (v. 24): resurrection, life that cannot be defeated by death.

David the prophet

Now this whole complex of events, the key to the whole story of Acts, has to be located in scripture and related to the preconceptions of the audience (both Peter's audience and Luke's) about how God acts in the world. The quotation from Psalm 16:8–11 (in vv. 25–28) forms part of a series of classic proof texts that runs through the sermons and speeches in Acts and, in total, summarises the key points in the Jewish–Christian debate over the next 200 years. The Psalms play a key role in this debate (see Luke 20:42; 24:44; Acts 1:20; 13:33), especially those (like this one) where the tradition names David as the speaker. Psalm 16 is a great outpouring of hope and faith in the God who sustains his anointed king and one of the few Old Testament passages that clearly looks forward to a future hope. Ancient interpreters liked to fit the words of the Psalms into the events of David's life, but here David is looking beyond the horizon of the grave to a hope which was not fulfilled in his own lifetime (vv. 26–27).

Taking the words of the psalm literally, Peter points out that when David died, his flesh was subject to the normal processes of bodily decay. The tomb of David is visible proof that he died and was buried in the normal fashion (v. 29). But the words of a prophet cannot be untrue (v. 30), so David must have been referring to somebody else, his divinely appointed descendant (vv. 30–31). Easter proves that Jesus is the Messiah, the anointed successor to David (v. 36). But proof texts are no good without proof people: the real witness to the resurrection is its effect in the lives of Peter and his friends (v. 32).

Prayer

Father, give us the courage to face up to our past and to move forward into your future.

7

Acts 2:33–39

Getting through

At Catterick Camp there's a poignant painting from World War I showing a young signaller 'lying dead in no-man's land. He had been sent to repair a cable broken down by shellfire. There he lies, cold in death, but with his task accomplished: for beside him lies the rejoined section of cable. Beneath the picture stands one pregnant word – THROUGH.'[1]

The promise of the Father

Now Peter comes back to the Pentecost event. It isn't enough to show that there is a precedent for our spiritual experience in scripture (2:16–21). To understand what is really going on, he has to show how it relates to the central event of all God's self-revelation to the world, to the living key who unlocks the meaning of the whole of scripture (Luke 24:27) – that is, to Jesus himself. So Peter moves seamlessly from resurrection to ascension to Pentecost, from the promise that God's Holy One will be welcomed with joy into the very presence of God (2:28) to the outpouring of the Spirit (v. 33). Only after his death did Jesus win the right to ascend to God's right hand and pour out the Holy Spirit on his followers. Peter last saw Jesus disappearing into a cloud at the top of the Mount of Olives (1:9), and he has only the angels' word to tell him where his Lord has gone. The gift of the Spirit is the proof that Jesus has in fact 'got through' and reconnected the channels of communication between heaven and earth.

Preaching for a result

The effect of Peter's first sermon is electrifying: no scoffers this time! 'What are we to do, brothers?' (v. 37). The question captures the groping confusion that is the prelude to true liberation. In this moment of disorientation, there is a need to hold on to the only people who seem to know their way in this strange new world: the Galileans previously laughed at (2:7, 13) have become 'brothers'. There is a radical shift of perception going on here, a shift of authority and leadership from centre to margins – or, rather, a sudden perception that 'out there' on the margins is the only place we can find salvation.

Peter's hearers also know instinctively that they need something to do, something to seal and solidify the profound changes that are going on in the heart. And that's what Peter goes on to provide, in a fourfold action that has become a pattern for Christian initiation in churches around the world.

Repent and be baptised

Repentance – the basic discipline of admitting 'I was wrong' – is the first and most fundamental response to the challenge of God's word (v. 38). In fact, all the different audiences in Acts are called to repent in one way or another, pagan and Jewish alike (see 3:19; 8:22; 11:18; 17:30; 20:21; 26:20; compare Luke 24:47). This is something that each one in the crowd has to do for themselves, to face up to the challenge of recognising Jesus as the heart of what God is doing in the world today. But the internal change of heart needs to be accompanied by an external act of public commitment. 'Be baptised in the name of Jesus the Christ,' Peter says: tie your destiny in with his; hitch your wagon to his star.

Forgiveness and the Spirit

From that act of public commitment come the twin benefits of Christian baptism. First, there is the promise of forgiveness, the liberation of the past. For this Jerusalem audience, this means that even the sin of failing to recognise God's Messiah is not unforgivable: it needs to be repented of, like all sin, but there is a way back. Then comes the gift of the Spirit, the liberation of the future. Like John the Baptist in Luke 3:1–18, Peter stands at the threshold of the book of Acts, preaching good news to God's people and reoffering John's baptism – but with a difference: the gift is now on offer to all, just as the prophets had said. Peter's final words glance back at Joel 2:32, and open up wider horizons with the link to Isaiah 57:19. But for now, the important message for Peter's audience is, 'It's for you!'

Reflection

Without forgiveness and reconciliation there can be no future. It is this that lies beneath the hurt and anger of our memories that invade the present, hindering us from moving forward.
Stuart Ware

8

Acts 2:40–47

The church begins to grow

The day of Pentecost is the birthday of the church – not of any particular church, but of the one worldwide church, the glorious fellowship of all who are baptised into the name of Christ. So this chapter ends, fittingly, with a cameo portrait of what being church means, looking back to that momentous day when it all began and forward to the whole yet-to-be-written story of the church down the ages.

Growth and perseverance

The offer is on the table, but there's a choice to be made, and, although plenty do respond (vv. 41, 47), there's always the possibility that some will not accept it. The task of exhortation is never complete (v. 40). Perseverance is mentioned twice in the Greek text (vv. 42, 46), and it is going to be essential for these new Christians – so new that there isn't even a name for what they've joined. But baptism is the beginning of a new lifestyle, and Luke gives us here the four pillars that mark out and nourish that lifestyle (v. 42).

- **The teaching of the apostles:** The new disciples will need to learn from the Twelve what they had learnt from being with Jesus (1:21–22) and what Jesus had entrusted to them in those 40 precious days between Easter and ascension (Luke 24:44–49; Acts 1:3–4). This is the foundation for the Christian life, and there is no substitute for it. It also means keeping up the habit of discipleship, realising that students never stop learning – not just from the words of their teachers, but from their actions as well.

- **The fellowship:** Students learn from each other just as much as from their teachers. Being a Christian is about acquiring a new allegiance, following a new Lord, but that is not just a private matter between ourselves and God. There is also a horizontal aspect to this new allegiance: whether we like it or not, we are part of something bigger. We are setting out on the journey with a band of fellow pilgrims – and we're there to sustain and support each other, just as Frodo's companions supported him in J.R.R. Tolkien's *The Lord of the Rings*. Trying to be a Christian on our own is asking for trouble.

- **The breaking of bread:** In Paul's letter to the Corinthians, 'breaking bread' together is the quintessential expression of Christian fellowship, a practical way of building community and an act of remembrance of Jesus' death (1 Corinthians 10:16–17; 11:20–34). 'Breaking bread' is clearly something distinct from 'taking nourishment' (v. 46), although both happen together in believers' homes, and both are expressions of Christian fellowship.
- **The prayers:** The church's regular life of prayer (v. 42) continues as the ground bass behind all these early chapters, something that goes on all the time even though we only occasionally get a glimpse of it (compare 4:24–31). As we see in the next chapter, the temple is the natural place to go to pray (3:1), the focus for the worshipping life of all God's people. There are also set hours for prayer, times when all God's people will be setting aside 'time to be holy' – something that Luke expects his readers to appreciate (since he doesn't bother to explain) as the standard pattern of the spiritual life.

Fellowship in action

The result of all this is, literally, awesome. 'Fear' in Acts (v. 43) is the right and proper reaction to the presence of the living God. That presence continues to be experienced in 'signs and wonders' that embody the life-transforming power of God's kingdom: we shall see an example in the next chapter. It is lived out in the life of the community too, a life that takes 'sharing' seriously (vv. 44–45). The Greek words translated 'possessions and goods' here imply that Luke is talking about disposable property rather than personal homes and possessions. This is practical charity in action, ensuring that no one in the community is needy, rather than the monastic surrender of personal property which was practised at Qumran (see further comment on 4:32–35). The overwhelming impression that comes across from this first phase of the church's existence is grace (v. 47): a lifestyle characterised by 'rejoicing and simplicity of heart' (v. 46), overflowing in praise to God; a community of grace, at peace with itself and thus enjoying the grace and favour of the wider community. It's no wonder that people kept wanting to join them!

Prayer

Father, keep us faithful in the teaching of the apostles, and help us to live out your grace in the world.

9

Acts 3:1–13

Lame man leaping

Luke's storytelling alternates between telling and showing, so Acts contains a series of 'summaries' that tell us what's happening in the church, interspersed with big set-piece 'scenes' that show particular actions in a much more dramatic fashion. Here, in the first big action scene after Pentecost, Luke shows us a specific example of two individual apostles, Peter and John, acting out in their lives some of the general features of the apostolic life. We shouldn't suppose that these were the only examples; Luke selects this story as a typical example of the general pattern of what life was like in those early days after the coming of the Spirit.

Signs and wonders

Peter and John's visit to the temple (v. 1) is part of a standard pattern, a discipline of observing regular times for prayer, but what happens on this particular afternoon is anything but standard. The lame man (v. 2) is also on his regular route, being carried (as he was every day) to a profitable spot for begging, ready to catch the worshippers on their way into the temple. Two paths intersect in an apparently chance encounter, and two sets of lives are changed forever. Luke's whole tone in this story conveys a sense of breathless awe (v. 10) as we see the first clear demonstration that the apostles now, since the coming of the Spirit, have the same miraculous healing power that Jesus had.

Taking a proper look

Peter looks intently at the lame man, then gets the man to look him in the eye (v. 4). That's what turns a routine, embarrassed transaction, avoiding eye contact, into a place of real encounter. As it happens, the apostles don't have the silver and gold that the lame beggar wants (v. 5). They have only one thing to offer, and only in the name of Jesus Christ of Nazareth (compare v. 12). The apostles don't wield any kind of miraculous power in their own right, only as agents of Jesus Christ. So the beggar doesn't get what he wanted, but he does get something better. The word Luke uses for 'almsgiving' is the standard Jewish-Greek term *eleemosune*, 'mercy', which perhaps here turns out to be truer than anyone expected. Peter gives the man a hand to raise him up (v. 7: the same word that the New Testament uses for resurrection). The result is new life, coursing through feet and ankles wobbly from disuse – a dramatic and visible sign of the effects of an encounter with the living God.

Awe and wonder

The healing of the lame man is visible for all to see and has a dramatic effect on the crowd (vv. 9–10): they are stunned and amazed. This is the correct and expected reaction to seeing the divine life in action, a sense of numinous awe. But this dramatic effect is never an end in itself in Acts: awe and wonder have to be channelled; the sensational has to be put in its theological framework. So the swirling crowd comes to a halt around the centre of the dust storm, where the once-lame man is holding desperately on to the only people who can help him make sense of the bewilderment and confusion of his new life (v. 11).

In the name of Jesus

This gives Peter his second opportunity for an unscripted sermon (v. 12). His first priority is to direct their focused attention ('Why are you staring at us?') to its proper goal. The miracle was not due to some special power or piety on our part, he says: it was the action of God himself, the God of the Bible, the God of our shared heritage and history (v. 13). Peter quotes Exodus 3:6 here, and the familiar formula reminds his audience that the God they believe in is a God who acts in history, who comes down to save his people. Putting God at the beginning of the sentence is essential – but the sequence is less expected. It is God's power that has healed the lame man (that's the underlying message), but that power is channelled through God's servant Jesus. The essential message of the apostles throughout Acts is that all the miracles they perform are done only in the name of Jesus and testify to the saving power of faith in his name. The apostolic witness always points to Jesus.

Reflection

Jesus said, 'Freely you have received; freely give' (Matthew 10:8, NIV).

10 Acts 3:14–26

It's your call

The word Luke uses in 3:13 (*pais*) can mean both 'child' and 'servant' (like the 'boy' of colonial English), and recalls the mysterious 'suffering servant' of Isaiah 52—53 whom God has glorified. But the servant has to suffer before he can be glorified (Isaiah 52:13–14). The terrifying part of Peter's message is that 'you' – that is, the Jerusalem crowd who were caught up in the collective madness that had seized the city only weeks before – have rejected God's holy and righteous servant (v. 14). Peter's words are painfully ironic. The prince of life, the one whose very name is an agent of physical healing (v. 16), is the very one you killed, he says (v. 15). It's a shocking indictment, but the sermon doesn't end there. Telling people they're sinners is *not* the good news! Facing up to what we do to God when he comes among us is not the end of the story, by any means. In fact, it's only the beginning.

Who's to blame?

There are several ways, of course, in which we can evade the indictment: 'We didn't know' is always a good one, or 'We were only obeying orders.' The people of Jerusalem acted in ignorance, Peter says (v. 17), as did their rulers. Peter will confront the ruling authorities later in this episode; here he is directly addressing the crowd. So Peter is quite happy to accept both of these excuses. In fact, he even adds another way out: it was God all the time. Everything that happened to Jesus, Peter says, was part of God's plan, something already revealed by the prophets (v. 18). Interestingly, however, none of this makes the slightest bit of difference to the question of responsibility: you did it, Peter says; you were there, so you need to turn your life around.

It's easy to claim that we were just caught up in the actions of the crowd or to blame peer pressure or society or our culture or a particular set of social conditions. But that doesn't absolve us as individuals from taking personal responsibility for our own actions: social psychology may be able to tell us why we behave as we do, but (as any teacher knows) we can't change without accepting responsibility for who we are.

What next?

This might seem unfair if Peter was administering punishment. But in fact, he's much more interested in effecting a positive change. What the people need to do is to repent (literally, a change of mind or heart) and turn to God (a complete change of direction). The future, in other words, is more important than the past. The preaching of the gospel can never stop at inducing guilt, focusing on past failings: it's all about opening ourselves to God's future. Repentance opens up the way to the wiping out of sins (v. 19), and the world-changing results are not only individual but communal. Repentance will unleash showers of blessings (v. 20) and even – oddly enough – the return of the Christ (v. 21). Pentecost is simply a foretaste of the real restoration stored up in heaven when all God's promises will be fulfilled. To treat this speech simply as an indictment of 'the Jews' is to miss the point. Luke is much more concerned with repentance than with guilt.

Free gift – act now!

There is also a note of warning, however: the free offer has to be accepted (v. 23). What Peter is offering is nothing more or less than an invitation to take possession of your whole inheritance: it's all there for you. This is what all God's promises are about; it's what all the prophets were saying (v. 24), including Moses himself (vv. 22–23; compare Deuteronomy 18:15–20). In fact, it goes right back to old father Abraham himself (v. 25). What's happening now is part of the original covenant, God's promise of blessing to all the families of the earth (Genesis 12:3), but you have the choice of accepting or rejecting it (v. 26).

Prayer

Lord, have mercy on our failures, both corporate and individual. Help us to recognise the new ways of living in the world opened up through Jesus Christ our Lord.

11 Acts 4:1–12

None other name

To readers familiar with the stories of the prophets, the next twist in Luke's story will come as no surprise. Prophets proclaim God's word: they get into trouble. The Old Testament is full of such stories, and Luke has already pointed up the moral in his gospel (Luke 13:33–34). But there is also a familiar political pattern to what happens here. The apostles are proclaiming God's word to the people (v. 1), with the result that the ruling classes start to get worried. The pattern is repeated throughout history, from the Wycliffites in 13th-century England to the liberation theologians of 20th-century Latin America.

Who controls the temple?

In fact, you could say that this whole story is about power and control. It's about who controls the temple. Peter and John treat it as a holy space, a place where anyone can go to pray and where God's healing power can be encountered. But the temple authorities regard it as a space that they police, a place where they have the right to control everything that is said. Jesus had similar problems with the temple authorities (Luke 20:1–8). But this isn't a problem unique to the first-century temple authorities. All religious authorities have the tendency to act like this, inside the church as well as outside. The story is also about who controls teaching (v. 2). The Sadducees were the most theologically conservative group in first-century Judaism. They regarded the popular doctrine of the resurrection as unscriptural (see comment on 23:8), and here they are determined to ensure that it is impossible to teach that kind of doctrine within their holy space. Finally, it's about who controls the people. The way Luke tells the story, it looks suspiciously as if the real reason for the arrest is that Peter and John are teaching the people (v. 1), and the point of throwing them into custody (v. 3) is not so much to punish them as to silence them. The incidental note that it is now evening reminds us how much has been packed into this one day: it was already afternoon when Peter and John set out for the temple in 3:1.

Who's really in control?

Events show that neither the temple authorities nor the Sadducees are really in control. Like seed blown from a dandelion clock, the word of God has its effect, despite the authorities' attempts at weed control. The contrast in verse 4 is piquant: even the arrest doesn't stop 5,000 people believing. That's something to hold on to as events unfold and the massed forces of law and order assemble to confront the apostles.

We should not underestimate the social contrasts implied in verses 5–7. The Sanhedrin was the highest court in the land, the apex of political and religious power in first-century Jerusalem, and, of course, the court that had condemned Jesus in Luke 22:66–71. Their question in verse 7 highlights the real point at issue here: 'In what power or in whose name – that is, in whose authority – did you do this?'

Peter's testimony

It is just at this point, when Peter is faced with the question of his life, that Jesus' promise comes true (Luke 21:12–15). The last time he came to the high priest's house, Peter crumbled into denial at a slave girl's question (Luke 22:54–62). This time, he can face the high priest himself with a fearless proclamation inspired by the Spirit (v. 8). Peter asks, 'You want to know who has the real power in this situation? I'll tell you: it's not us, and it's not you either. It's the one you tried to destroy, the very same Jesus Christ of Nazareth whom you crucified. It was his name that brought salvation to the powerless (v. 9). The fact that this man is standing before you whole and sound (v. 10) is proof that Jesus is far from dead, that God has raised him from the dead. And the final proof is that God has already showed us this pattern in his word (v. 11).'

The rejected stone of Psalm 118:22 (another favourite text in early Christian polemic) underlines the dynamic of reversal in God's kingdom, in which the powerless, the despised and those the world considers 'nothing' become the key to God's salvation. One way or another, we all have to come back to this point: the crucified Christ is either the ultimate stumbling block or the cornerstone of our salvation (cf. 1 Corinthians 1:18–25).

Reflection

Many Christians feel powerless in face of the overwhelming imbalance of power in our world. Faith in 'the name' often seems ridiculous. Pray for them, and for ourselves, that we may hold on to the faith that God is really in control of our world.

12 Acts 4:13–31

Boldness under fire

Empowered by the Spirit, Peter has found words to convince the crowds in street and temple, but the Sanhedrin is a much harder nut to crack. There is no easy conviction here, but a reluctant and grudging admiration from an elite group of men to whom the Galilean apostles are simply illiterate outsiders with no professional training or status (v. 13). What impresses the council is their *parrhesia* or 'boldness' (NRSV). This should be understood not so much in terms of physical courage (although that is implied) as of intellectual and political integrity. That was what struck the council members about Peter and John – that, and the recognition that they had been with Jesus. To the council members, the events we have been witnessing over the past few chapters were simply a confused rumour of street-level disturbance. It is only now that they make the connection with the crucifixion of a Galilean troublemaker some six weeks earlier.

Control order

Admiration can only go so far. The council is not prepared to face up to the implications of what has happened, despite the undeniable public healing of this very public character, who appears to have been thrown into overnight custody with the apostles (vv. 14, 22). So the real problem for this group is not truth but public relations (v. 16), a problem that affects corporate and political life all over the world. This is precisely where *parrhesia* is a necessary civic virtue, and it includes having the spiritual and intellectual integrity to perceive when the normal civic duty to obey those in authority is overridden by a higher duty (v. 19). Ultimately, when the decision is put in those terms, there is no choice (v. 20). This is what apostolic witness boils down to, in the end: simply doing what you've got to do. The verdict could be counted as some kind of moral victory. The apostles are saved by public opinion and let off with a caution (v. 21). It's still the honeymoon period.

The church at prayer

Reporting back to their friends (v. 23) seems an obvious response but it reflects the need for consolidation (after all, they only left to go to afternoon prayers). The community's response might well have been a cautious reassessment: better keep our heads down. Instead, it's a united recourse to prayer (v. 24). True prayer always begins with who God *is* before focusing on our present needs. So this prayer begins by setting out three facts about God. It starts with a cosmic vision of God which puts everything else in proportion: God is the one who created the heaven, the earth, the sea and everything in them. But God is also the living voice of the Holy Spirit (v. 25), linked to a continuous human history of revelation. Through this history, God enters into relationship with human beings: the Lord of creation is also the God who spoke through the mouth of our father David.

Searching the scriptures

The quotation in verses 25–26 is another in the series of key texts used by the early Christians as they sought prayerfully to understand what was happening in their lives. It comes from Psalm 2, which plays a major role in New Testament reflection on Christ, recognising the 'this' of immediate experience ('in this very city', v. 27) already foreshadowed in the 'that' of God's self-revelation in scripture. It's a royal psalm about 'the Lord and his anointed' (*Messiah* in Hebrew, *Christos* in Greek). The 'kings and rulers' who oppose the king in the psalm are identified with Herod and Pontius Pilate in the passion narrative, joining in unholy alliance with the nations and the people of Israel. There is no mention of Israel in the original Hebrew, but the Greek translation uses the two words *ethne* and *laoi* ('nations and peoples') in parallel. For Luke, the *ethne* are always the Gentiles, and *laos* always means the people of Israel. So the psalm text legitimates a new vision of the world order in which everyone is briefly united against the Christ – although none of this is outside the divine plan (v. 28).

Here and now

The third element of prayer is relating our story to God's story, so what is happening now to the apostles can be read as part of this wider history. But note what the apostles ask for: not protection, not safety, but more boldness and more signs (vv. 29–30). The response is, literally, earth-shaking (v. 31), an overwhelming affirmation by God's Spirit of the apostolic witness.

Prayer

Lord Jesus, may our lives reflect the fact that we have been with you.

13 Acts 4:32–37
Everything in common

Here Luke shows us the power of God's Spirit at work on two fronts simultaneously. On the external, visible front, the apostles continue to exercise their task of public testimony to the resurrection of Jesus. It's a task that they tackle firmly – affirmed by their renewed experience of God's invigorating presence in 4:31 – but not aggressively or rudely. Everything is done with 'great grace' (v. 33; compare Colossians 4:6).

Luke also gives us a glimpse behind the scenes into the invisible, internal life of the community (v. 32). It is just as important that the whole inner life of the church and its ordinary, bog-standard members (that's you and me) should also show the power of God's Holy Spirit at work. Otherwise, the testimony of the apostles will be fatally undermined. Luke's picture of the infant church (still in its first weeks of life) is one in which the life of the Spirit is visible in the way Christians relate to each other. This is, in many ways, the most basic function of the Spirit (much more basic than 'gifts'). Paul calls it the *koinonia* or 'fellowship' of the Holy Spirit (2 Corinthians 13:13), and it has profound implications for the way Christians are called to live out their lives together in the actual realities of congregational life (see Philippians 2:1–5).

Koinonia in action

Luke has already described one practical outworking of *koinonia*: it means that Christians hold everything in common (*koina*) for the relief of those in need (2:44), and here he returns to the theme (v. 32). Luke's language here evokes the ideal picture of the wilderness community in Deuteronomy 15:4–11 (and might also remind some of his readers of the Greek philosophers' vision of a utopian community where all property was held in common for the good of all). We know that the Qumran community operated some form of monastic pooling of property, and this provides corroboration that such practices were part of the world of the early church. But Luke probably doesn't mean an early form of communism so much as a willingness to put everything at the disposal of others. Believers held their private property as a trust to be used by God.

The details become clearer in verse 34: those who could afford it sold their possessions as need arose, and what people sold was not their own homes but any disposable property that they happened to have (2:46 and 12:12 make it clear that believers still kept their own homes). The object is not to disadvantage themselves but to use their surplus assets to raise money for those in need. The apostles thus find themselves acting as middlemen in a sort of ad hoc centralised distribution system, which will soon become too much (see ch. 6). But already there is a suggestion that the numbers in the church have grown since 2:45, when the distribution to needy members of the community happened directly without involving the apostles. (See comment on 2:44–45.)

The son of consolation

Moving from the general to the particular, Barnabas enters the story (vv. 36–37) simply as a positive, concrete example of the general picture that Luke is painting. This is an affectionate portrait of one of Luke's most attractive characters, one who is going to provide an important link between Jerusalem and Antioch (11:25–26) and between the Jerusalem apostles and Paul (9:27). The tribe of Levi, which performed certain liturgical duties in the temple, was not supposed to own property within Israel (Deuteronomy 10:9), which probably means that the farm Barnabas sold was in Cyprus (v. 37).

The *koinonia* challenge

It's easy to dismiss Luke's picture of the early church as utopian. The fact is, however, that the interactive social care practised by the early churches for their poorer members made a huge impression on outsiders and played a vital part in the mission and survival of the church in the early centuries. As late as the second century, the satirical Greek writer Lucian notes that Christians in Syria believed in holding their property in common.[2] It's an idea that rather frightens us in the affluent West today, and it's worth wondering why; but it is a fact that sitting light to personal property and seeking to resist the tyranny of the acquisitive society has always lain close to the surface for those who seek to follow Jesus. (Luke's gospel has some pretty tough things to say about personal wealth, too: see Luke 1:53; 3:11; 6:24–25; 12:13–24; 16:19–31; 18:18–30).

Reflection

*'I can't hear your words because your actions are shouting too loud!'
All too often it's the inner, private behaviour of Christians towards one another that prevents people from hearing the gospel message.*

14 Acts 5:1–16
Living in an open universe

What is it about money that brings out our worst instincts? Following on from the description of the 'community of goods' in 4:32–34, Ananias and Sapphira provide a negative counterweight to the positive example of Barnabas (4:36–37). Maybe, as astute businesspeople, they thought they could put one over on the gullible Galilean apostles, with their naive ideas about sharing property. Whatever way you look at it, this is a most uncomfortable story, and it raises two kinds of question.

Does it make historical sense?

Many readers wonder what all the fuss is about. What exactly was the process that Luke is describing? What did Ananias and Sapphira do wrong? There are irresistible parallels with the Qumran community, where new members were expected to put their whole property at the community's disposal. But that doesn't seem to be quite what Luke is describing here: Peter stresses that the gift is voluntary (v. 4). Ananias and Sapphira were quite free to disagree with the principle of *koinonia*, or to withhold any amount of their own property that they liked.

The language of verse 2 provides a better clue to the cultural framework of the story. The rare word *enosphisato* ('kept back', NRSV) recalls the story of Achan in Joshua 7, where it is used of embezzling funds placed in sacred trust. The same word turns up in 2 Maccabees 4:32, in a story designed to show the numinous, supernatural power invested in a holy place which is under threat. For Luke, this is a story about the holiness of the *ecclesia* (v. 11). This primitive *koinonia*, which doesn't even have a building of its own to meet in, is the dwelling place of God's Holy Spirit and has the same kind of scary holiness as the temple itself (compare 1 Corinthians 3:16–17).

Does it make moral sense?

We can begin to see why the story had a point for Luke's first readers. Luke is talking about a tiny, persecuted church, and the message of the story is both an encouragement to its members and a warning to anyone who tries to mess with it. God does care what happens to this apparently insignificant group. Most of us still find it morally repugnant now:

the death penalty seems a bit extreme for anyone embezzling church funds. But it's worth pondering the underlying significance of the story. What Luke gives us here is a dramatised representation of an important truth about the integrity of the church. The church is more than the human institution we see, with all its human foibles and failings. It's the dwelling of God's Holy Spirit: like Moses at the burning bush (Exodus 3:6), we stand on holy ground, and on that ground nothing less than utter truthfulness will do. Nothing destroys community quicker than equivocation in interpersonal relations. It is not disagreement that destroys Christian community so much as a failure to acknowledge the truth before each other and before God's Holy Spirit (vv. 3–4, 9).

Danger – God at work

Fear (v. 11) is a natural reaction to these events. In the world of the Bible, fear – or, perhaps better, awe – is seen as a wholly appropriate reaction to the visible manifestation of God at work. Note that it is not our job to induce fear by hellfire preaching or puritanical discipline, but where God is at work there is a sense in which the right and proper response is one of awe, mingled with a rather wary and distant respect (v. 13).

Nevertheless, people are still joining the church, which is now so large that it has taken over one of the city's public spaces (v. 12). The sense of awe that God is at work here in an extraordinary way is reinforced by the healing power displayed by the apostles, especially Peter (vv. 15–16). God has answered the apostles' prayer in 4:29–30 in a dramatic and incontrovertible way. This is part of the proof that Jesus is not dead: his Spirit is carrying on his healing ministry in the work of his church. An apostolic church is a church in which God is visibly at work, a church carrying on the mission of Jesus and empowered by the life of his Spirit.

Reflection

If then our common life in Christ yields anything to stir the heart, any loving consolation, any sharing of the Spirit, any warmth of affection or compassion, fill up my cup of happiness by thinking and feeling alike, with… a common care for unity.
PHILIPPIANS 2:1–2 (NEB)

How does 'the fellowship of the Spirit' actually show itself in our life together as Christians?

15 Acts 5:17–32

We must obey God

In this scene we glimpse another side of the apostolic persona. The apostles have real authority, real spiritual power, but real vulnerability and pain too. 'You have stood by me in my trials,' said Jesus in Luke 22:28, and here we see a Peter who has learned from his failures, who has now been 'strengthened' so that he can strengthen his brothers by example (Luke 22:32). As Latin American theologian Justo Gonzalez remarks, the preaching of marginality sounds rather different to poor churches who are already marginalised.[3] They need to hear the underlying message of strength and hope in the living God.

A hand on the shoulder

The church is winning popular support (5:13), but predictably the authorities are going to be less pleased (v. 17). The group is growing in size, attracting huge crowds to its public meetings in the temple. The right to free speech and public association only goes so far, even in a modern democracy: sooner or later, you're going to be 'moved on'. The authorities' motives are not necessarily bad in themselves. 'Zeal' (v. 17: NRSV 'jealousy') can be a positive thing (see comment on 13:45 and 17:5), but, from Luke's point of view, it's misdirected. The tragedy in this story is that both sides believe they are doing God's will. For Luke and his readers, though, there is no room for doubt: the angel's message (vv. 19–21) makes it quite clear that preaching the 'words of this life' in the temple is precisely what the apostles ought to be doing.

The great escape

Luke's gift for dramatic irony is evident in this scene, which is not without a touch of slapstick humour. The council convenes in all its official splendour (v. 21), only to discover that the jail is empty (vv. 22–23). Luke's carefully drawn picture, with all the different elements precisely described, brings out the irony of a situation in which the powerful, those in control of the judiciary and all the vested interests of church and state (the Establishment, if you like), find out that they are not in control at all. In fact, they are completely at a loss (v. 24). Meanwhile, the powerless – those who have no resources except their own integrity and their obedience to God – have escaped from prison and are unconcernedly pursuing their God-given task of 'teaching the people' (v. 25), who have a much better instinct than their leaders for where the real authority lies (v. 26).

Civil disobedience

The humour underlines dramatically the real issue that Luke is highlighting in this episode. The apostles have embarked on a campaign of civil disobedience: they have knowingly ignored a court injunction imposed by the legally constituted judicial authority of their country. Thus far, the court has right (as well as might) on its side. This was a situation often experienced by Jews seeking to remain faithful to their religious identity in a world where secular power was held by the pagan empires. Daniel 6 provides the classic template. Like Daniel, the apostles have only one defence: that the legal duty of all law-abiding citizens to obey the courts is overridden by a higher duty to obey God. This is a dangerous claim (and Luke is no political radical), but everything in this narrative – the miracle of the escape, the angel, the power of the apostles' preaching, the testimony of the Holy Spirit (v. 32) – bears out their words. Luke's message is that God is not on the side of the big battalions. As the prophet Elisha said to his petrified servant Gehazi, 'There are more with us than there are with them' (2 Kings 6:16).

How do you tell?

Apostles also need the gifts of wisdom and discernment, however. It takes an enormous amount of courage and faith in a real-life situation to hold on to the apostles' perception. Standing up against the forces of law and order – even against the spiritual leaders of one's own people – does not come easily to naturally law-abiding citizens. It takes perception to see when the forces of law and order have been subverted and must be resisted in God's name. The apostles' words in verse 29 appear on the tomb of Cardinal-Archbishop Galen of Münster, one of the very few churchmen to resist openly the growing domination of Nazism in German political life in the 1930s, and they have inspired many Christians (and others) in the courageous decision to say 'No' to a corrupt exercise of power.

Prayer

Father, give us the humility to obey, the courage to resist and the wisdom to know the difference.

16 Acts 5:33–42

Dare to be a Gamaliel

Luke now draws us into an unusual behind-the-scenes peep into the council's private deliberations, thus giving us the chance to exercise a bit of empathy by looking at the whole sequence of events from the point of view of the authorities.

Behind closed doors

Inside this slightly farcical narrative is a surprisingly sympathetic dramatisation of the real dilemma facing the council – the same dilemma that faces anyone called to a position of authority in church or state. Yes, it takes courage to 'dare to be a Daniel', but it's too easy to assume that Daniel is always right. Look at Romans 13 for a powerful exposition of the classic view that the authority of the state (even the pagan state) is God-given and must be respected. 'Pray for the peace of the government,' said the later rabbis, 'for without it, we would have eaten one another alive.'

The problem of Theudas

Gamaliel was one of the great Pharisaic sages of his day, and a man deeply respected for his wisdom and integrity. But there is a real problem about taking this passage as a transcript of an actual speech. Theudas (v. 36) was a real historical figure, mentioned by the contemporary Jewish historian Josephus alongside Judas the Galilean.[4] Judas (v. 37) was the ringleader in the first stirrings of Jewish revolt against the Romans at the time of the census in AD6, but Theudas was active in the 40s, a decade after the dramatic date of Gamaliel's speech. Josephus mentions Theudas and Judas in the same paragraph and in the same order as Gamaliel does – which is odd, because it is the reverse of the historical order.

The problem of the speeches

More generally, this passage illustrates the historical problem of the speeches in Acts. It's clear that they cannot automatically be treated as actual transcripts of the words spoken on any given occasion (especially in Jerusalem). There are really two possibilities: either they are totally fictitious (Luke made up the occasion and the words) or the occasion is genuine and Luke gives the gist of the argument but adds circumstantial detail of his own. The latter would be in line with the normal practice of ancient historians like Thucydides. Either way, it is important to remember that Luke's speeches are written *post factum* and serve a rhetorical function, addressing Luke's own readers as much as the dramatic audience in the story. In other words, Luke is telling this story not just to explain what happened in the past, but as a part of an active debate that is still going on.

Don't fight with God

The real point about this speech is the theological warning that it gives to Luke's readers, then and now. For his first readers, the message is, 'Beware! Watch what you're doing' (v. 36). There is still a real decision to be made about this 'new thing': the nation's future hangs on a knife-edge. This, in many ways, is the underlying question of the whole of Acts: what's going on, and is it of God? (v. 38). Any reader familiar with the Jewish scriptures would be able to bring to mind prophetic warnings that were heeded or not heeded, and Gamaliel's message is just as relevant to the church today. The Gamaliel principle can be dangerous if it becomes a way of avoiding making decisions and allowing injustice to continue unchecked,[5] but in many ways his question is the real question we need to be asking ourselves when any 'new thing' threatens our security, our comfortable patterns of faith and worship. Where is God in all this? Is God here with us, cowering behind the bastions of 'what we've always done'? Or is God out there too, nudging and surprising us into new ways of seeing the world? It needs faith, discernment and the ability to wait humbly on God.

Prayer

In a world of change, Father, thank you for your unchanging truth. Help us to meet you both in the stability of tradition and in the excitement of change.

17 Acts 6:1–4

Hebrews and Hellenists

Chapter 6 marks a transition to the next phase of the church's life, a phase that will see the apostles, and the church, begin to broaden their horizons in unexpected ways. It begins (as so often) with a problem – a church beset by a groundswell of grumbling (v. 1) that finally reaches the ears of the apostles. In such a situation, it's often helpful to do a SWOT analysis: what are the strengths, weaknesses, opportunities and threats for this church?

Strengths

It is, of course, a nice problem to have – a problem caused by the church's continual growth in numbers (v. 1). We don't know exactly when this growth happened, but we must assume that God has continued to add to the church daily those who are being saved (2:47), and we must be looking now at a church numbering several thousands. Moreover, it is an increasingly varied congregation, drawing on the two main groupings of the Jewish community in Jerusalem: the 'Hebrews' (Aramaic-speaking Jews) and the 'Hellenists' (Greek-speaking Jews). It is also a strength that the disciples have continued their commitment to pooling their surplus assets and dispensing charity to the needy.

Weaknesses

Size creates its own problems, however. The church has begun to outgrow its original structures, and the old, individual sense of being in a community where everyone matters is getting lost. This is partly a matter of administrative systems. What worked for a group of 120 (1:15) would hardly work for a group of over 5,000 (2:41; 4:4), without any central building or paid administration. The simple and expressive act of laying contributions at the apostles' feet (4:35–37) is placing an intolerable burden of administration on the apostles: no wonder some people are feeling overlooked! And it sounds as if the multicultural variety within the body of believers is also creating its own problems, with the language of 'us' and 'them' and 'It's not fair' creeping in. Was there also a sense that the original believers had become some kind of 'in group', with the newer converts feeling left out? Did the older church members feel threatened by these brash new arrivals? What had they done to integrate the newcomers and make them feel welcome?

Opportunities

There is always a temptation for church leaders to treat 'grumbling' as a threat to their own authority, but the apostles treat it as an opportunity to listen to what God is saying to them in this situation (v. 2). When someone says to us, 'You're doing too much', it's easy to feel defensive about 'my ministry' (look at Moses in Exodus 18), but actually it's an opportunity to take stock, and to realise that God has other people out there who have gifts and ministries too. So we see the first indications here that being an apostle is only one of a variety of ministries within the whole body (1 Corinthians 12; Ephesians 4). The apostles spot the opportunity not only to delegate (v. 3), but also to decentralise, resisting the temptation to keep all forms of power, financial as well as spiritual, in their own hands. That creates opportunities for other people to act as benefactors, to have the joy of ministering to people's needs, to realise that they too can be filled with God's Spirit and have a ministry to fulfil.

Threats

One person's opportunity is another person's threat! Multiculturalism – even growth, the arrival of new faces – can be seen as a threat by some communities. Collaborative ministry and the need to recognise the gifts of others can be a threat to many church leaders. And it isn't only leaders who suffer from this problem. Church members too can feel threatened by the gifts of others and spend their time trying to denigrate them (look again at 1 Corinthians 12). Equally, though, church members can feel threatened by leaders who treat them as autonomous adults and say, 'Here's the problem – you sort it out' (v. 3). Peter and the apostles are effectively treating the body of believers here like a civic assembly, saying, 'This isn't our church – it's yours too, and it's just as much your responsibility as ours to be open to the Spirit's guidance and responsive to the needs of the world.'

Prayer

Father, help us to see opportunities for you in place of threats, and to call on your strength in our weakness.

18 Acts 6:5–15

A deacon in danger

The election of Stephen and his fellow deacons is like dislodging a pebble on a mountain path and triggering a landslide – a small action, but one with enormous consequences for the narrative of Acts and for the history of the church. It's amazing what happens when you trust the Spirit!

Varieties of service

The gift of the Spirit isn't just for the visible, up-front tasks in the life of the church: backroom administration and balancing the books need prayer too. In fact, this story isn't so much about delegation as about trust. The apostles have to trust the people – trust their choice, and trust that there are others out there already 'full of the Spirit'. Both apostles and people then have to trust that the Spirit will continue to call and empower people for service in God's church. This is not 'top-down' management – or, rather, the apostles are not the ones at the top!

Luke never actually calls the seven 'deacons' – all who serve in God's church are engaged in *diakonia* (ministry) of one kind or another (6:4) – but the word *diakonia* came to be used especially of practical service to the local congregation, in which the administration of charity was always important. Since that implies the identification of local needs, deacons came to be assigned a special role (which they still have in the Orthodox churches) of presenting the offerings of the people and voicing their prayers.

The laying on of hands

This scene also gives us the prototype for the ordination of ministers for specific service in God's church. Note that Stephen and his colleagues already have the gift of the Spirit (6:3); the laying on of hands (v. 6) is both a confirmation of the gift and a commissioning for a new task. Discerning someone else's vocation is always a risky but exciting task, calling for sensitivity to what God is already doing, and lots of prayer.

The result for the Jerusalem church surpasses all expectations, with the growth pattern apparently unstoppable (v. 7). Most of the group ordained as 'deacons' here disappear from Luke's story after this chapter, but Philip and Stephen are going to be very important in the next few chapters, and they quickly grow out of the limited role originally assigned to them (v. 8). That little spot of 'grumbling' (6:1), along with the apostles' willingness to extend their ministry, has unwittingly (and under the guidance of God's Spirit) brought two new players on to the scene.

Stephen the Hellenist

Who was Stephen? It seems clear he was one of the 'Hellenists' of 6:1. His name is Greek (it means 'crown'), as are all the names in verse 5, and he has his own personal network in the Greek-speaking synagogues of diaspora Jews settled in Jerusalem (v. 9). It is not clear how many congregations Luke is talking about here, but they come from all the great cities of the empire. Alexandria, Tarsus (Cilicia) and Ephesus (Asia) are all known to have had major Jewish communities, and Rome is where the Libertini (a Latin term meaning 'freed slaves') came from. The gospel is starting to engage in conversation with new dialogue partners – a small but highly influential grouping in Jerusalem, and one which is going to play an increasingly important role in Acts. This group has a strong theological commitment to the law of Moses, which is the most important badge of identity for Jews living in pagan countries (v. 11), but it also has wider horizons and a broader vision of God's scattered people.

Stephen the disciple

The most important thing about Stephen, for Luke, is that he is full of the Spirit (v. 5). Someone who had (probably) never met Jesus in person finds Jesus' words in Luke 21:15 a living reality in his life: no one is able to withstand his wisdom and Spirit (v. 10). Like the apostles, he finds quickly that the call to follow Jesus leads him into violent confrontation (v. 12), and from there into direct imitation of his Lord in suffering and death. The stage is set for a dramatic confrontation.

For reflection and prayer

There are varieties of services, but the same Lord.
1 CORINTHIANS 12:5 (NRSV)

Whatever the service we are called to, help us to remember that we are gifted by the same Spirit and serve the same Lord.

19 Acts 7:1–16
A vision and a promise

Stephen's speech is the longest in Acts, and it introduces a new set of themes. It continues the apologetic started by Peter, but in a different style, retelling the Bible story rather than appealing to proof texts and drawing on different scriptures. At first sight, it seems to have little relevance to the charge of speaking 'against this holy place and the law' (6:13–14), but in fact it is highly pertinent. Stephen focuses on texts from the law of Moses (the first five books of the Hebrew scriptures), on the figure of Moses himself, and (right at the end of the speech) on 'this place' – that is, the temple. In effect, what Stephen is doing is to undercut the charge of abandoning the Mosaic law by appealing to a higher authority.

The vision

What Stephen gives his audience (and what Luke gives his readers in this speech) is a whistlestop tour of the whole of biblical history, from Abraham to Joshua. But the significance lies in what he selects and what he leaves out. It is a powerful retelling of Israel's past, addressed to people who share that past ('brothers and fathers', v. 2) but realigned to recall them to their roots. Stephen begins with Abraham, the starting point of Israel's experience of the living God, which is also the beginning of Israel's existence as a people (Genesis 12:1; compare Hebrews 11:8–12). Right from the start, it's a story that has the God of glory as its subject (v. 2). Following the Greek translation of the Bible, Stephen rephrases the call of Abraham into the language of vision – a constant theme in Acts. Behind the condensed storyline (vv. 3–5) lies careful study of the complicated story of Abram's call in Genesis 11:31—12:9, a two-stage process that adds up to a single experience of God's calling (Genesis 15:7).

The promise

God's call is to 'come out' (v. 3). It's all about leaving present certainties and committing ourselves to an uncertain future – but a future with God in it. But what is Abraham called to come out to? Stephen's potted history emphasises the coming out more than the eventual destination, the letting go of certainties more than the acquisition of new possessions. The land to which Abraham was called is the land that we (Stephen reminds his audience) are now living in (v. 4), but Abraham was not given so much as a foot's length in it. The promise was not for him but for his descendants (v. 5, literally 'seed') – a seed that didn't even exist when the promise was made. Before coming into the promised inheritance, Abraham's progeny would have to endure exile and slavery (v. 6). The covenant looked ahead to the exodus (v. 7), focusing not so much on the promised land (Genesis 15:18–21) as on the creation of a worshipping people (Exodus 3:12; compare Luke 1:74). Circumcision (v. 8) was especially important as an identity marker to diaspora communities: Stephen reminds his hearers that it is part of the covenant with Abraham, not the law of Moses.

A feuding family

Stephen assumes a basic knowledge of the patriarchal narratives (v. 8), but focuses on the part of the story closest to diaspora experience. Joseph (v. 9) was (like Daniel and Esther) a prototype diaspora hero, prospering in exile and bringing salvation both to his host country and to his own people. But this part of the story also highlights the long history of fratricidal feuding within the patriarchal family. Stephen reminds his audience that the history of God's people is a history of jealousy and rejection within the family, a story of exclusion and betrayal. So Joseph becomes a kind of prototype for Jesus himself, rejected by his brothers but honoured by outsiders because God is with him (v. 10; compare Genesis 39:2), and God enables him to become a saviour to his own people (vv. 11–14; compare Genesis 45:7–8). The final summary brings the Genesis story down to the death of Jacob and his sons (v. 15) and their burial in Shechem (v. 16) – a detail which seems to be a confusion of two burial stories in Genesis (compare Genesis 23:15; 33:19; 50:13; Joshua 24:32).

Prayer

Father, give us the faith of Abraham, to leave behind our comfortable certainties and journey out with you in obedience and trust.

20 Acts 7:17–34

Israel in Egypt

It's all about timing. At the exact moment when all seems lost, God acts to save his people. It's not always easy to recognise God's saving acts, however, when your eyes are blinded by the tears and sweat of struggling with a hostile world.

In the nick of time

Stephen's story moves on to the exodus, to the time of the promise (v. 17). Time is of the essence here as two storylines converge: the prolonged sojourn of Jacob's descendants in Egypt, and the promise given to Abraham 400 years before. The time of promise is also the time of greatest danger. God had warned of exile and ill-treatment (7:6–7), and the quotation from Exodus 1:9–11 (v. 18) underlines the precariousness of 'diaspora' existence – how much it depends on having somebody at the top of the system who knows you and remembers why you are there. But it's precisely at this time of greatest danger that God sends a saviour for his people (v. 20), a baby whom his parents recognise as beautiful before God (*asteios*).

This whole story is told in words taken from the exodus narrative in the Greek Bible, though with some subtle alterations that focus the narrative on the tiny scrap of life on whom the safety of God's people hangs. Stephen misses out the courage of the midwives (Exodus 1:15–21) and the faith of Moses' mother and sister (Exodus 2:1–4; see Hebrews 11:23), and implies that Moses was being exposed (v. 21), that is, left out to be taken by wild animals or rescued by passers-by. This was a common method of disposing of unwanted babies in Egypt and the Greco-Roman world, and one that Jews and Christians consistently refused to follow. This adds a sobering touch of realism to the well-known story of the baby in the bulrushes, but also a fairy-tale quality which would not have been lost on Luke's Greek readers. Greek myth and legend were full of tales of babies (like Oedipus) who were exposed at birth and returned in adulthood to claim their rightful inheritance.

The unknown prince

So Moses is brought up in the palace (v. 21), inheriting and surpassing all the wisdom the pagan world could offer (v. 22) – a privileged existence that lasts for 40 years (v. 23). This detail is not in Exodus: Stephen is part of an ongoing Jewish tradition working out the chronology of the whole story (compare v. 30). But Moses' return to claim his place among his own people has a paradoxical quality. As the letter to the Hebrews puts it, for Moses it means a descent from the privileged cocoon of palace life to the harsh realities of life among an oppressed and marginalised people (v. 24; compare Hebrews 11:24–26). In such conditions, the oppressed can easily turn on their fellows, venting their frustration and impotent rage on each other or on the person trying to help, rather than on the system that causes the oppression (vv. 26–28). Moses has the humiliation of wanting to be recognised as a God-sent agent of salvation (*soteria*), but totally failing to convince the people he is trying to help (v. 25). The question, 'Who sent you?' (v. 27) is deeply ironic, as 7:35 shows; but it is also perhaps a salutary warning to Moses. He has good intentions, a vague idea that something needs to be done, but he hasn't yet been into the desert to discover himself and receive his call (v. 29). He doesn't really know himself who has sent him.

A vision in the desert

Before he can save his people, Moses has to experience the precariousness of *paroikia*, living as an alien, for himself – and also to find himself as a man, a human being, a father. It is all too easy for missionaries (and charities) to come in from outside and offer solutions without knowing what it's like on the ground. But identification is not enough (otherwise the Hebrews could have saved themselves). Moses also needs a vision (v. 30), recalling the foundational vision of Abraham (v. 32) as God calls out his people anew. However well-intentioned our desire to save the world, it will run into the sand unless it is grounded in attentiveness and obedience to what God is doing. God (as always in the Bible) is the real hero of this story, the one who has heard and seen what is happening to his people and is determined to rescue them (v. 34). Before anything else, Moses has to turn aside from his daily work (v. 31) and realise with awe that he stands on holy ground (v. 33).

Prayer

Father, lead us out into the desert to meet with you face to face. Then send us back to work for the salvation of your world.

21 Acts 7:35–43
A Saviour rejected

This encounter with God and obedience to God's call makes it possible for Moses to go back to Egypt and save his people. He returns to his task as someone sent by God, but that doesn't make life any easier for him.

This Moses

There is a deep irony (underlined in the word order in the Greek) in the fact that it was *this* Moses, the same one whom his people had denied and rebuffed, who was in fact sent and called by God to be their ruler and redeemer (v. 35: 'this one' [*houtos*] comes in an emphatic position five times in verses 35–38). The words Stephen uses deliberately point up the parallel with Jesus, the Saviour sent by God but rejected by his own people. This is the one who has the God-given power to bring his people out of slavery and to perform signs and wonders in the wilderness (v. 36), and it was this same Moses who prophesied that God would raise up another prophet 'like me' (Deuteronomy 18:15). Far from denying the importance of Moses, in other words, Stephen argues that Moses himself pointed forward to God's salvation in Jesus, both in his words and through the paradigm of his life.

The golden calf

From verse 39 onwards, the focus moves from Moses to the people he led, with the emphasis on rejection and a shift from 'us' to 'them'. The pace of the story quickens as Stephen links the events in the wilderness with the ultimate tragedy of exile. The essential seeds of the tragedy are already there in the exodus narrative of the golden calf (Exodus 32), a story that was a sore point to contemporary Jewish exegesis (Josephus leaves it out altogether in his rewriting of biblical history[6]). How could God's redeemed people, at the foot of Mount Sinai itself, indulge in this blatant piece of idolatrous worship? Stephen identifies the fateful steps that led to disaster: disobedience, hankering for the past life (v. 39), loss of confidence in their leader (v. 40), then the making of the golden calf itself (v. 41). Stephen's language highlights the fact that the people had fallen into nothing less than the pagan sin of idolatry (see Exodus 20:4–6).

From idolatry to exile

Finally comes the chilling verdict (v. 42): the people had turned away from God, so God turns away from them and hands them over to the worship of the host of heaven (compare Isaiah 63:10, where the same verb is used). The 'host of heaven' is a reference to the star gods of neighbouring cultures, a development foreshadowed in Deuteronomy 4:19 and frequently denounced in the later prophets (see, for example, Jeremiah 8:2; Zephaniah 1:5). Stephen is able to link it to the wilderness period through the mysterious text from Amos 5:25–27 which he cites in verses 42–43. This text is hard to interpret even in the Hebrew, and may refer to a tradition (also preserved in Jeremiah 7:21–26) that Israel did not offer animal sacrifices in the wilderness. But Stephen focuses on the word *moi* ('to me') at the end of the first line of the quotation, and implies that the house of Israel did offer sacrifice in the wilderness (as we know from v. 41), but not to the God who had redeemed them.

Rereading the Bible

These verses provide a nice illustration of the way ancient exegetes, both Jewish and Christian, adapted the text of the Bible to their own circumstances. Amos was writing in the eighth century BC, and the Greek translators of the Hebrew scriptures, working some 600 years later, could not understand all the allusions in Amos's rather obscure Hebrew. That's why the text that Stephen quotes is rather different from what we find in an English Old Testament, although the end result is well in accord with Amos' fierce description of the 'day of the Lord' (Amos 5:18–27). The Hebrew *sikkut* in Amos 5:26 was probably the name of an Assyrian god (Sakkut), but in the Greek Bible (and thus also in Acts 7:43) it becomes 'tabernacle' (*sukkat*). The Hebrew *melech*, 'king', is reread with different vowels as Moloch, the name of a pagan deity (compare Jeremiah 39:35). The mysterious Kaiwan (or Raiphan) defeated the ancient scribes completely. The only substantial change in Stephen's quotation, however, is the change from Damascus to Babylon: Syria was the enemy when Amos was writing, but later readers inevitably assimilated the old prophetic warnings to the more famous exile in Babylon.

Prayer

Father, as we journey with you across the wilderness, keep us mindful of the cost of our salvation and faithful to the one who calls us.

22 Acts 7:44–53

Your God is too small

If the worship of gods made with human hands is idolatry, what of the construction of a sanctuary made with human hands? This seems to be the underlying theme that links the two final sections of Stephen's speech, both almost certainly derived from centuries of reflection and preaching in the synagogue. We can see traces of this debate in the patterns and links made in contemporary Jewish exegesis, both Hellenistic and rabbinic.

From tabernacle to temple

Stephen crashes through the final stages of salvation history very fast: Joshua's conquest of the promised land (v. 45) does not really interest him. What does concern him is the shift between the tabernacle (v. 44), the sign of God's grace to a pilgrim people, and the temple – the more permanent dwelling place for God that David longed to build and Solomon completed (vv. 46–47; compare Psalm 132:5). His final answer to his accusers picks up again on a well-established biblical theme: the inadequacy of all attempts to pin God down. The passage he quotes from Isaiah 66:1–2 expresses one side of a deep-rooted ambivalence in biblical tradition about the location of worship in the temple, an ambivalence brought out in the story of Nathan (2 Samuel 7) and by Solomon himself (1 Kings 8). It expresses one of the fundamental insights of the book of Acts – that the temptation to idolatry, the temptation of limiting God to inadequate human conceptions of the divine, is prevalent in all human societies, Jewish or pagan.

The parting of the ways

Stephen's final words (vv. 51–53) crackle with the pain of the 'parting of the ways' between church and synagogue. Seen from the other side of that divide, it's a despairing indictment of the failures of God's chosen people to recognise the work of the Holy Spirit, tracing a damning line of rejection from the wilderness generation right through to the sufferings of Israel's prophets – a theme echoed in Luke's gospel (see Luke 13:33–35; 19:41–44), in Hebrews 11, and in other Jewish and Christian writings of the Second Temple period. In the early church's apologetic, this prophetic rejection was linked with the prophetic witness to Christ. The rejection of the Holy Spirit who speaks through the prophets thus becomes a way of explaining (or simply expressing) the puzzling fact that the scriptures which, to Christians, self-evidently prophesy the coming of Jesus are read in a very different way by Jewish readers (2 Corinthians 3—4 is another way of expressing this puzzle). The fact is that there is no 'neutral' way of reading the Bible. Throughout their history of mutual incomprehension, Jews and Christians have appealed to the same texts but interpreted them very differently.

Reading after the Holocaust

It is important for us, reading in a post-Holocaust world, to keep a hold on the dramatic setting of Stephen's words. Stephen is addressing the Sanhedrin in Jerusalem within weeks of Jesus' death. In this context his words have a particular sense, and they emphasise that his quarrel is not with the law of Moses but with those who fail to keep it. Many of Stephen's contemporaries at Qumran would have said the same (though for different reasons): the Dead Sea Scrolls contain even more chilling indictments of the Jerusalem leadership. Even in the rhetorical setting in which Luke is writing, some decades later, we are still far from a definitive split between Judaism and Christianity. This is part of a sectarian controversy, a ding-dong argument between rival Jewish interpretations of the Bible that will rumble over the next few centuries. We cannot transfer Stephen's bitter denunciation of a particular group in his own context to a post-'parting' perspective, as if what Stephen says here is meant to be true of all Jews everywhere. Luke never says this (as we shall see), and in a post-Holocaust world it is not a stance that Christians can accept.

Prayer

Father, we ask your forgiveness for the bigotry and prejudice that have soured relations between Jews and Christians over the centuries. Help us to work together for the restoration of your kingdom.

23 Acts 7:54–60
The first Christian martyr

I write these words on the anniversary of the terrorist attacks on the World Trade Center in New York in September 2001, an event etched on the minds of millions around the world who watched in horror as it unfolded on our TV screens. For many people, those events have problematised the very concept of martyrdom. Post-9/11, many would see 'martyrs' simply as religious fanatics with a reckless disregard for life, both their own and other people's. But it would be wrong to let this parody of martyrdom tarnish the biblical paradigm of martyrs as witnesses to their faith, prepared to stake their own lives – not the lives of others – on the truth they believe in. Stephen remains a challenge and an example for Christian witness in a world where many Christians are called to stake everything on their faith.

Paul's words in Acts 22:20 suggest that Stephen was already seen as the first Christian 'martyr', in the sense of someone who is prepared to die for his or her faith. But the word *martus* in Greek means first and foremost a witness – not an exhibitionist, not a spiritual athlete drawing attention to their own endurance capacities, but a witness pointing to a truth beyond themselves – and that is part of every Christian's calling. 'You will be my witnesses,' said Jesus to the eleven (1:8), and later he called Saul to be 'a witness to what you have seen and what you will see of me' (26:16). In other words, what we are here for is to provide living testimony to the transformative presence of God in his world. The witnesses at Stephen's lynching 'laid their coats at the feet of a young man named Saul' (v. 58), who thereby became implicated in the deed (as Paul himself implies at 22:20). But who can calculate what effect the manner of Stephen's death had on that young man?

Eyes fixed on the Lord

Alone in front of a hostile crowd, it would have been easy to see nothing but hostile faces and gestures, but Stephen looks steadfastly upward (v. 55) and sees the glory beyond the pain. He sees the human figure of the crucified and rejected one standing in the place of ultimate honour and acceptance (v. 56). In the hour of extreme need, the martyr is sustained with a vision that sees further into reality than anyone else in the story has done so far. Where the apostles on the mountain saw only the cloud (1:9), Stephen sees right into the heart of heaven, to the centre of the universe. Without that vision there is no witness, only defiance: it is a risen and victorious Lord whom we serve.

This enables Stephen to put a proper value on his life. He was young (at least, we always assume so), vigorous, full of the Spirit (6:5), passionately engaged in life. He had a job to do (6:8), and the ability and spiritual gifts to do it. A martyr is not a person who is tired of life or has nothing better to do; but when that life is put at the service of another, it can be laid aside. It ceases to take centre stage. Preserving 'my' life, 'my' calling, 'my' work, is not the prime object any more.

Caught in the crossfire, following Jesus

Being a martyr takes courage: it is all too easy to duck out of conflict situations. There are times in all our lives when we have to stand up and be counted, when our witness to Christ has to face up to peer-group pressure, to society's expectations, to what's going on around us. Knowing when and how to do it is tricky, though. Christian witness isn't about courting trouble for its own sake or about 'making a martyr of ourselves' in a kind of virtuous self-righteousness that won't win anyone to Christ.

Stephen's death, like his life, is modelled on that of his Lord. Just as Jesus committed his spirit to the Father (Luke 23:46), so Stephen entrusts his spirit to the Lord Jesus whom he has seen standing at God's right hand (v. 59). Even more strikingly, Stephen's last words are words of forgiveness for his persecutors (v. 60) – words paralleled by Jesus' own prayer from the cross (Luke 23:34). This is the final, costly realisation of the principles that activated Jesus' life: 'Love your enemies... pray for those who abuse you' (Luke 6:27–28). Stephen's speech is polemical, passionate and at times harsh: here we see into his heart.

Prayer

Grant, O Lord, that in all our sufferings here upon earth, for the testimony of thy truth, we may steadfastly behold the glory that shall be revealed; and, being filled with the Holy Ghost, may learn to love and bless our persecutors, by the example of thy first Martyr Stephen, who prayed for his murderers to thee, O blessed Jesus, who standest at the right hand of God to succour all those that suffer for thee, our only Mediator and Advocate. Amen

Collect for St Stephen's Day, *The Book of Common Prayer*

24 Acts 8:1-4

Act Two: Judea and Samaria

In Luke's four-act drama, Stephen's death marks the beginning of 'Act Two', the point where the gospel begins to move out from its first phase in Jerusalem and slowly, tentatively, becomes a worldwide mission. This is phase 2 of the original mission charge in 1:8, and it forms an essential bridge to the planned missionary journeys of phase 3 (chs 13—28). Witness in 'Judea and Samaria' (8:1-25; 9:31) opens up surprising and unexpected horizons, as far afield as Ethiopia (8:26-39), down to the coastal towns of the Mediterranean (8:40; 9:32—10:48), and up to Syria and Cyprus (11:19). Slowly, painfully, the apostles and the Jerusalem church begin to face up to the questions, 'Exactly who is God speaking to? Who is the gospel for?' This initial expansion is anything but planned. In fact, what we see here is God's Spirit gradually moving the original witnesses out of their comfort zone, nudging them to raise their sights and broaden their horizons.

Introducing Saul

The new phase begins with an event that appears to be nothing short of a disaster. Verse 2 adds the final touch to the story of Stephen: despite his execution for blasphemy, pious men gave him proper burial – perhaps a hint that not everyone in the Jewish community agreed with the council's decision. Verse 1, on the other hand, introduces a new storyline, carrying the gospel out far beyond the confines of the city – and a new hero, who is going to dominate the story from chapter 13 onwards. Up to this point, Saul is merely a hidden presence, lurking ominously in the background of Stephen's story as a witness to Stephen's death (7:58). Now Luke brings him a little more into the foreground, telling us that he was fully in agreement with the execution. He is not taking part, apparently – just holding the coats – but something about that event propelled Saul to become active in persecution, ravaging the church in a classic portrayal of intolerant and out-of-control religious fanaticism.

Luke's picture is close enough to Paul's own description of this phase of his life to make sense (see Galatians 1; Philippians 3; 1 Corinthians 15). The detail that he was a young man (7:58), coupled with Paul's own half-shamefaced, half-boasting admission that he had outclassed his contemporaries in zeal (Galatians 1:14), adds up to a familiar type on the contemporary religious scene. Saul was a radical young fundamentalist, top of his class and busting to change the world to his own way of thinking, irrespective of the cost to himself or to anyone else.

Exile – or mission field?

Perhaps one of the things that spurred Saul on to get actively involved in the mission to wipe out the new sect was its surprising success: verse 3 provides the first confirmation in Acts that this rapidly expanding movement included women as well as men. But Jerusalem is no longer a safe haven for the believers. Stephen's confrontation with the Sanhedrin seems to have stirred up so much anger and bitterness that it sparked off a concentrated attempt to root out the whole of this troublesome sect – although the fact that the apostles were able to remain in Jerusalem (v. 1) may suggest that it was particularly the 'Hellenists' who were affected.

Being scattered (vv. 1, 4) is not necessarily a bad thing, however. At least some of those who are expelled from Jerusalem see it as an opportunity rather than a threat, and start preaching the word as they go about through the countryside of Judea and Samaria. So the church begins to fulfil the mission charge laid upon the original disciples in 1:8, although, humanly speaking, it happens more or less by accident. Also (as so often in Acts), what Luke doesn't tell us is as interesting as what he does. Who was responsible for this momentous development? Clearly not the apostles, who were left behind in Jerusalem (v. 1). The inference is that it must have been ordinary believers, acting under the Spirit's guidance and without any express instructions from the leadership of the church. So often, we find that the only way the church begins to grow is when we allow ourselves to be forced out of our comfort zone and begin to trust the Spirit.

Reflection

Declare God's praise before the nations, you who are the children of Israel: For if our God has scattered you among them, there too has he shown you his greatness.
TOBIT 13:3–4 (RSV)

25

Acts 8:5–13

Mission in Samaria

Like Stephen, Philip has a Greek name, so was probably one of the 'Hellenists' from the Greek-speaking Jewish community in Jerusalem (6:5). Like Stephen, too, he was originally commissioned to serve at table (6:2–3), but finds himself entrusted with a wider vocation.

Our friends in the north

Restoration is the first of the two major underlying themes in Luke's account of Philip's mission in Samaria. In the geographical schema of 1:8, Samaria holds a special place. It is not just an intermediate stage, one step further out from Jerusalem; it is also part of greater Israel, the old northern kingdom. Philip's mission symbolically reunites the old northern and southern kingdoms of Israel and Judah in the new kingdom era ushered in by God's anointed Messiah (compare 1:6). So there is a definite eschatological (end-time) dimension to Luke's geography here, with undertones of the restoration and reconciliation of long-sundered branches of God's people.

Exactly where Philip's mission takes place is not clear. Some manuscripts read 'the city of Samaria' in verse 5, recalling the ancient capital of the northern kingdom, but in Philip's time Samaria was an ethnic region, not a city. Luke is more concerned to portray a mission to the Samaritan people, who lived not in the rebuilt Greek city of Sebaste but in scattered villages across the uplands, so it probably makes sense to go with the alternative reading, 'a city of [the region of] Samaria' (as in John 4:5). Either way, Luke uses geographical names in a way that brings out the theological significance of the events he describes.

Magic and miracle

This is also a story about power – different kinds of spiritual power, and its use and abuse. Philip's one object was to preach Christ to the Samaritans (v. 5), and he found in so doing that the signs and wonders that had accompanied Jesus' mission in Galilee and Judea were now spilling over into Samaria. People paid attention to what Philip said (v. 6) because they could see as well as hear the effective presence of God's energetic Spirit in his words (v. 7). Just as in the gospel, the effect of an encounter with the living Christ is an outpouring of wholeness and joy (v. 8).

Christians, though, are not the only ones who can exercise spiritual power in Luke's story, and the Samaritans already had their own miracle worker. Simon (v. 9) had already established a nice line in wonder-working, and had the reputation of embodying 'the power of God that is called Great' in his community (v. 10). Amazement, not joy, is the result of his activity, which Luke labels 'magic' – a label that identifies Simon not as a charlatan but as a rival. Later Christian tradition knows Simon Magus as the first heretic, founder of a Samaritan cult that is seen as a forerunner of Gnosticism and comes to a dramatic confrontation with Peter in Rome.

The real thing

On the surface, the contest between Philip and Simon looks like a competition between two rival manifestations of spiritual power – a contest between magicians, we might say, rather like the contest between Elijah and the prophets of Baal in 1 Kings 18. On the face of it, it's not obvious how we are to choose between them: is it the one that shouts loudest or the one who performs the most impressive wonders? This is a problem that preoccupies Luke, and he will return to it in chapters 13, 19 and 28. So part of what Luke is doing here is to set up the first of a series of confrontations which explore the nature of spiritual power and the boundaries between magic and miracle.

The simple fact is that there is no contest. Simon, as well as his audience, instinctively realises that what Philip is offering is the real thing, not just bigger and better miracles but something qualitatively different that demands a real commitment to spiritual transformation. Philip's message is about the kingdom of God and the name of Jesus Christ (v. 12). One cannot be attained without the other, and there is much more involved than the immediate gratification of sensationalism. That's why baptism is the logical response (v. 13): it means a fundamental change of heart ('repentance', 2:38), and a personal commitment to becoming part of God's kingdom-plans through faith in the person of Christ ('in the name of the Lord Jesus', 8:16).

Prayer

Father, help us to recognise that true spiritual power comes from following in the footsteps of the one who laid down his life for others.

26

Acts 8:14–24

Magic and money

Now the twelve in Jerusalem hear rumours that Samaria has accepted the word of God, preached in the name of Jesus. Given the history of bad blood between Samaria and Jerusalem (see Luke 9:51–56; John 4), it is perhaps not surprising that they send Peter and John to investigate.

The apostles and the evangelist

Luke, like Paul, takes a strategic view of the economy of mission: a successful mission in one Samaritan town means that 'Samaria has received the word of God' (v. 14). This is not so much exaggeration as *pars pro toto*, a manner of thinking that sees the whole as implied in the part (compare 19:10, or Paul in Romans 15). It implies that the job of the evangelist is to plant the seeds in a region and let God do the rest. But there is one more thing needed before Philip can move on. Philip has baptised his converts in the name of the Lord Jesus, but they have not yet received the Holy Spirit (v. 16). They have been incorporated into a larger whole, but (like many Christians today) they do not yet realise the full implications of what has happened to them. The full process of Christian baptism in water and Spirit (Mark 1:8) involves both a turning away from the old life and a turning towards the new, both saying 'No' to the sins and failures of the past (*metanoia*, repentance) and saying 'Yes' to the new life that God has on offer. The gift of the Holy Spirit is what gives Christians the power to stand on their own two feet and grow in the spiritual life. It is an essential part of all Christians' experience (compare 2:38–39), not just of those called to a particular ministry (6:3–5).

The gift of the Spirit

Instead of calling down the fire of judgement, then, the apostles find themselves calling down the fiery presence of God's Holy Spirit on the Samaritans (v. 15). Here Luke makes the baptism and reception of the Spirit a two-stage process, with the apostles coming down from Jerusalem to 'confirm' the new believers by the laying on of hands (v. 17). This is the biblical model for the practice of 'confirmation' by a bishop in many churches (a similar pattern can be seen at 19:1–7). Churches in the Pentecostal/charismatic tradition work with a rather different two-stage model, seeing 'baptism in the Spirit' as a distinct experience. But, as we shall see, Luke does not always present a consistent pattern in Acts (compare 8:36–38, where the Spirit is not mentioned, or 10:44–48, where the Spirit comes first). What is important is not the order or the manner in which they are experienced, but that both are essential to the Christian life.

The apostles and the magician

As we have seen, Luke is careful all along to distinguish the miraculous power of the Spirit from magic. This story progressively unfolds some of the essential differences. Simon claims a name for himself (8:9), while Philip and the apostles do everything in the name of Jesus (8:5, 12, 16). Simon basks in the admiration of his community, using his powers to advance his own status (8:9–10); Philip fades quietly into the background when the apostles arrive (vv. 14–25) and moves on when his work is done (8:26), trusting his converts to their Lord. Simon seeks to attach people to himself; Philip and the apostles aim to integrate them into a community. Simon sees spiritual power as a force to be manipulated and controlled (vv. 18–19); the apostles see it as a gift from God (v. 20).

Money in Acts frequently functions as a touchstone for distinguishing true from false in the realm of the Spirit (cf. 3:6; 5:3). What God gives is pure gift: it transcends our value system, so it cannot become part of a commercial transaction. Peter's rebuke to Simon underlines how important it is for this fledgling community to put a proper value on a gift which is literally 'priceless' (vv. 20–23). You cannot calculate the financial value of ministry. Being allowed to participate in God's dealings with his people is both above and below the profit/loss accounts of human financial systems.

Prayer

Remember, O Lord, what you have wrought in us, and not what we deserve; and as you have called us to your service, so make us worthy of our calling: through Jesus Christ our Lord.
Leonine Sacramentary

27 Acts 8:25–40
Show me the way

What has Philip been doing all this while? Luke does not tell us, but Philip's role is becoming more clearly defined as that of an evangelist (see 21:8) rather than a church-builder. The apostles themselves briefly become itinerant missionaries on their way home (v. 25), but for Philip, itinerancy is the essence of what he does. He is attuned to God's guidance (v. 26), ready to take off at the drop of a hat and journey into the emptiness of a desert landscape, to await whatever encounter God has in store.

Hitting the road

This is a story of intersecting journeys. Philip's route-map is precise: head due south to intercept the Jerusalem–Gaza highway, and then wait and see. What he sees, just as he arrives at this desolate spot, is a chariot bowling along the road. It bears perhaps the last person he would have expected to see – an African pilgrim from the ancient and romantic kingdom of Ethiopia. 'Eunuch' (v. 27) could be a physical description, or it could simply describe an official function at the court. ('Candace', incidentally, is a royal title, not the name of an Ethiopian queen.) So the eunuch is a court official, used to authority and luxury. He is also a pilgrim: he has been up to Jerusalem to pray in the temple. On the mental map of the ancient Mediterranean world, Ethiopia is part of the 'ends of the earth' (1:8). But in religious terms, the Ethiopian is a figure of the borderlands, halfway between Jew and Gentile, either a God-fearer or (more likely) a full convert to Judaism.

Reading and understanding

The eunuch is not only wealthy but also learned, learned enough to be able to read Isaiah (apparently) in Hebrew (v. 28). God has been preparing the way for this most improbable of encounters, but Philip doesn't know this until he gets close enough (v. 29) to hear what the distinguished foreigner is reading aloud to himself. Philip's question (v. 30) perhaps reflects some surprise that this non-Jewish pilgrim should be able to read the Hebrew text with understanding. For a high court official, literacy was a necessity. Nevertheless, many (if not most) Jews in first-century Palestine needed the help of an Aramaic paraphrase to understand the Hebrew text.

Preaching the good news

Underlying this apparently mundane conversation is a fundamental principle of Lucan exegesis. Quite apart from language problems, scripture is not self-interpreting: Spirit-inspired guidance is required to unpack the true significance of the Hebrew scriptures. The Isaiah scroll is open at one of the key texts of early Christian apologetic, part of the great Servant Songs of Isaiah 53, which portray God's 'servant' as a despised, wounded, rejected figure, the very antithesis of the victorious messiah of Jewish expectation (vv. 32–33). But who is this mysterious 'servant'? The Ethiopian's question (v. 34) is a reasonable one, which continues to puzzle students of the Hebrew Bible, but for Philip the evangelist there can be only one answer. The Isaiah passage holds a vital clue to the paradox of a suffering Saviour, wounded for his people's transgressions and suffering before entering into his glory. This is not the anticipated messiah of popular expectation, but nevertheless a figure firmly rooted in scripture. So the Hebrew text, properly interpreted, becomes a vehicle for preaching the good news (v. 35), a Way that leads straight to baptism (vv. 36–38).

On the Way

And then? We can speculate about what happened next (in Ethiopian tradition, the eunuch went home and founded the Ethiopic church). In Luke's story, though, what is important is the roadside encounter itself, a point of intersection with no before and after – or rather, where the before and after are known only to God. Philip is caught up by the Spirit (vv. 39–40) and disappears from the story at this point until chapter 21; and all we know (and need to know) of the Ethiopian is that this is the beginning of a new journey, a journey suffused with joy (v. 39).

For discussion and prayer

You search out my path and my lying down, and are acquainted with all my ways.
PSALM 139:2 (NRSV)

Pray for the people you will encounter on your journey today.

28 Acts 9:1–9

The road to Damascus

This is a story that meant a lot to Paul. He refers to it several times in his letters, and Luke has him retell it twice when he is on trial for his life (Acts 22; 26). This is the memory he turns to when he has to explain, 'Who am I? How did I get here?' The key moment in his life was his meeting with Jesus on the Damascus road, a meeting of enormous significance not only for Paul but for the whole history of the church. But we can also read this story from the personal angle, as a story of God's call and how it changes real human lives.

A change of direction

We call this event Paul's 'conversion', but actually the word is rather misleading. We generally use it to describe a change from unbelief to belief or a change from one religion to another, but Paul already believed in God, and it is much too early at this stage to think of Judaism and Christianity as two separate 'religions'. Paul himself describes the event as an encounter with the risen Jesus, the last of the resurrection appearances (1 Corinthians 15:8–10). He also uses the language of 'vision' (1 Corinthians 15:8; Acts 26:19) and of a prophetic 'calling' (Galatians 1:15, echoing Jeremiah 1:5). But Luke's very concrete account highlights that it was, above all, a dramatic change of direction. Saul was the top student of his year, full of zeal, busily engaged in serving God – but going the wrong way (v. 1). He was on a journey, going after a bunch of idiots who called themselves 'the Way' (v. 2), a way that Saul had no intention of following. His idea was to turn them round, by force if need be, and bring them back into the fold. Unfortunately for Saul's plans, the opposite happened. The 'Way' that looked all wrong turned out to be the right way, and it was Saul who had to change direction.

Called by name

There is a voice, calling Saul by name (v. 4). All Luke's three accounts of this event stress the double naming: 'Saul, Saul'. This was Paul's Hebrew name, the name that established his family tree and national identity (Philippians 3:5), the name (doubtless) in which he took all his academic awards at the university in Jerusalem (Galatians 1:14). God's call is always directed to the real person. It's easy to say, 'No, Lord, you've got the wrong person', but God's call says, 'No, it's you I want, you with all that history and genetic make-up, all the things you're proud of as well as the things you wish hadn't happened – all that goes to make up the real you.'

A reversal of perceptions

There is also a heavenly light (v. 3): the call comes in such a way that Saul cannot doubt that it is from God. Saul, who is trying so hard to serve God, can only say, 'Lord, I don't know who you are'; and the answer comes, 'I am Jesus, the one you are persecuting' (v. 5). Saul was convinced that Jesus was the wrong Way, the one who was leading all these other poor souls astray, and now he speaks with God's authority, is standing (as Stephen had claimed in 7:56) at the right hand of God. This was precisely what Gamaliel had warned his fellow councillors of (5:39), and it is a terrifying discovery.

Learning dependence

There is a tradition in paintings of this story that Saul was riding a horse on his way to Damascus. There is no horse in Luke's story, but the dramatic fall is there (v. 4): the arrogant persecutor who knows what's right for everyone else becomes humiliated (literally 'on the ground'). Moreover, he is blinded, has to be led by the hand (v. 8) and will spend three days in the dark (v. 9), waiting to be told what to do (v. 6). There could hardly be a better way to dramatise the complete revaluation that Saul experienced. Before he could work for God, he would have to learn dependence on God's grace. Paul himself puts it this way in Philippians 3:7: 'Whatever gain I had, I counted as loss for the sake of Christ.'

Prayer

Lord, we find it so hard to hear your call. Help us to accept our complete dependence on your grace.

29 Acts 9:10–19

The hand of fellowship

There's a story of the newly appointed minister who stood up to preach in his new church and announced, 'My job is to find out what God is doing here – and get in on the act.' Acts is all about finding out what God is doing out there in the world. But it can be disconcerting to discover when and how God is at work: God's horizons are always so much wider than ours.

A disciple called Ananias

Ananias only has a walk-on part, yet he plays a pivotal role in the drama of Acts. He was the person whom God chose to release Saul from his imprisoned and blinded state into full and active faith. He is not an apostle, simply a disciple, one of the many unsung heroes and heroines of Luke's story. But the essence is that, like Samuel and Isaiah (1 Samuel 3:10; Isaiah 6:1–8), he was ready to say, 'Here I am, Lord' when God spoke to him. Like Philip, he receives precise directions (v. 11), but unlike Philip, he is told whom he is going to meet: a man called Saul, who is praying. That's all he needs to know, all that matters to God. Time and time again in Acts, when believers muster up the courage to speak of their faith, they discover that God has got there first. When we left Saul, he was being led, sightless and fumbling, into a safe house somewhere in Damascus (9:8). Now we discover that he wasn't doing nothing during his three-day fast: waiting in the darkness, he was learning to listen, waiting on God.

You cannot be serious!

It may be enough for God – but it isn't enough for Ananias! He knows a lot about Saul, none of it reassuring. He knows exactly why Saul has come to Damascus (vv. 13–14). So we have the slightly comic picture (but haven't we all done it?) of Ananias arguing with God, trying to tell God his business: 'Lord, you don't know this guy!' But God does know Saul – knows the very worst about him – and still chooses him. It's a paradox that Paul, when he looks back on his life years later, sees only too well: election and grace go hand in hand (see 1 Corinthians 15; Philippians 3; 1 Timothy 1:12–16).

To reveal his Son in me

Precisely what God has in mind for Saul's future becomes clearer in subsequent retellings of this story (see chs. 22; 26). Looking back, we can see that the seeds of the future mission to the Gentiles are here already, but it will take Saul/Paul quite some time to work out exactly what his vocation means. For the moment, all he needs to know is that it's a call to testify and a call to suffer (v. 16).

The privilege of vocation cannot be divorced from the privilege of suffering. If God chooses to 'reveal his Son in me' (Galatians 1:16), it's my whole life that's on the line, not just my words. There is a robustness about this view of vocation which at least has the merit of being realistic. Nobody ever said that the Christian life would be easy, and perhaps it's just as well that we don't know quite what lies around the corner. But there is reassurance here too: the way may be hard, but Christ will be a part of it.

Brother Saul

Ananias' capitulation, once he gets the point, is unreserved. There's no grudging welcome for the black sheep, no 'I'll be keeping an eye on you.' Nor does he attempt to ration out the privileges of being a believer ('Wait till you've been here a few years'). For Ananias, whatever the convert's past, once he's accepted, he's in – welcomed as a brother, sharing all the blessings of physical healing and spiritual reorientation.

Formally speaking, the laying on of hands here (v. 17) is not apostolic. Ananias was not one of the twelve, and there is no record that he himself was ever commissioned by the Jerusalem apostles. He acts simply as a believer, responding directly to the vision out of the conviction that he too has been sent (v. 17) by the same Lord Jesus who appeared to Saul on the road. For Luke (as for Paul: see Galatians 1:12), Paul's apostolic commission came not from Jerusalem but direct from the Lord himself. So Saul's Damascus Road experience leads him into a transformative encounter with the risen Christ. Its results are vision restored, rising to new life, baptism and filling with the Holy Spirit (vv. 17–18), and renewed strength (v. 19).

Prayer

Say a prayer of thanksgiving for all the anonymous, 'unimportant' people who helped you along the road to faith.

30 Acts 9:20-30
A convert in trouble

No half measures for Saul! The apostle Paul (as he was to become) later described his early years as full of 'zeal': a consuming ambition to do better than any of his classmates in seminary, a passionate commitment to putting the world right for God and eradicating those who were getting God wrong, a burning zeal for the interpretative tradition that showed how God's revelation was to be read in the world (Galatians 1:13–14). As he later testified of his fellow Jews, he bore 'a zeal for God – only it was not enlightened' (Romans 10:2).

Testifying to the Christ

That zeal is immediately turned, with all the enthusiasm of the convert, against his former allies and employers (v. 20). Saul now spends his time in synagogue arguing vociferously that Jesus is the Son of God and Christ (v. 22). Not surprisingly, this sudden volte-face meets with a stormy reception: amazement and wonder (v. 21), confusion but no conviction (v. 22). Saul's Damascus journey, which started with such grand ambitions, ends in an ignominious escape over the wall in a basket (vv. 23–25). This was probably not as precarious as it sounds: basketware slings are still used today in the Middle East for hoisting bricks and timber on building sites. Paul himself describes this episode in 2 Corinthians 11:32–33 in tones suggesting that he saw the whole thing in a distinctly anti-heroic light. He also gives a slightly different spin to the story: Luke focuses on the hostility of 'the Jews' (v. 23), while Paul attributes the problem to the ethnarch (NRSV 'governor') of the Nabatean King Aretas.

This incidentally gives us a chronological framework for the episode, which suggests that a longer period has elapsed than we might think from the account in Acts. (Luke is supremely uninterested in dates, and his 'after many days', v. 23, is not a great deal of help.) Aretas was ruler over the kingdom of Nabatea from 8BC to AD39/40, and seems to have been given some kind of political control over Damascus by the emperor Gaius Caligula after the death of Tiberius in AD37. The Nabateans drew a large part of their revenues from the caravan trade, and there was a colony of Nabatean merchants resident in Damascus.

The ugly duckling

The fact is, however, that Saul the convert is still in a very raw and unfledged state, marginalised not only by his old allies but also by his new 'brothers'. Although the disciples in Damascus (following Ananias' example) are prepared to accept him (v. 19), the community in Jerusalem is highly suspicious (v. 26). Anthropologists speak of a period of 'liminality', a 'wilderness experience' essential to the integration of any religious vision or vocation at a deep personal level. Maybe the disciples in Jerusalem thought that his zeal was doing more harm than good (vv. 29–30), but in fact Saul needed time alone with his God before he could begin to learn what it would mean for God to reveal his Son in his life (compare v. 16).

Enter Barnabas

The role of an advocate and protector is vital in this precarious state, and Barnabas is the crucial catalyst, the friend and 'godfather' who welcomes the new convert, introduces him to the apostles, tells his story (v. 27) and sends him away for a period out of the limelight (v. 30). In Galatians 1:17, Paul speaks of a period in Arabia before returning to Damascus, and stresses the brevity of his visit to Jerusalem in order to emphasise his independence of the apostles (Galatians 1:18–20). Both accounts agree that after visiting Jerusalem, Saul went home to Tarsus in the province of Cilicia (v. 30; Galatians 1:21), to wait quietly (maybe some years) before Barnabas came to find him and bring him back to play an active role in the life of the church in Antioch (11:25–26). But that is still in the future. Saul has met Christ, he's begun his journey, there are hints of great things to come, but for the moment he has to watch on the sidelines, waiting for the full significance of his vocation to unfold in God's good time.

For discussion and prayer

How difficult is it for new converts to become integrated into the life of your church? Who plays the Barnabas role there?

31 Acts 9:31–42
Beside the seaside

Luke's storyline in this middle section of the book looks rather randomly arranged, but in fact there's a clear progression, leading up to chapter 10, where Peter will meet the Gentile Cornelius. First, though, Peter has to be winkled out of Jerusalem so that he can be in the right place to discover what God is doing out in the rest of the world.

The church in Judea

Luke marks the bridge to a new scene with a summary verse (v. 31) which links back to 1:8, showing us that everything in this section is part of the witness in 'Judea and Samaria'. The dispersed believers have done their job well: working outwards from Jerusalem, the church is now well established in the whole of Judea and Galilee and Samaria. There are no hints here of continued persecution or of the controversy that dogged Saul's visit to Jerusalem. This is a picture of peaceful consolidation as the church learns to 'walk in the fear of the Lord' (an Old Testament phrase expressing the ideal of an ordered society: see Psalm 19:9; Proverbs 1:7) and is filled with the comfort of the Holy Spirit (not just a one-off experience, but a characteristic of the ongoing life of the renewed people of God).

An itinerant ministry

This section shows how the apostolic role is changing in a rapidly expanding network of believers. First comes the realisation that their own special charism within the people of God is the ministry of word and prayer (6:4); others can be trusted, under the guidance of the Spirit, to handle administrative and charitable work. In chapter 8 they discover that they do not have a monopoly on evangelisation: here, too, others can be trusted to preach the word and baptise new believers. So the apostles begin to move into an oversight role, integrating new communities into the wider network and ensuring the continuity of their ongoing spiritual life with the Pentecost experience (8:14–17). This is the role that Peter continues here, moving about among them all (v. 32), visiting the tiny enclaves of God's people ('the saints') in Lydda and Joppa (vv. 32, 38), leaving his base in Jerusalem and moving into a more mobile role.

A healing ministry

In so doing, Peter rediscovers the essence of apostolic ministry in following, and imitating, his master's lifestyle. Ministry 'on the road', ministry bringing real lives into a healing encounter with the power of God, is exactly how Jesus spent his time, and the healings of Aeneas and Tabitha show Peter following Jesus' example and taking the healing power of the kingdom out from Jerusalem and right down to the coastal plain. The difference is that Peter does nothing in his own name or by his own power. It is the healing power of Jesus Christ that brings wholeness and new life (v. 34) and brings another whole region to turn to the Lord (v. 35). Lydda (modern Lod) is on the very edge of the hill-country of Judea; the Sarona (Hebrew *Sharon*) refers to the wooded area on the coastal plain between Joppa (modern Jaffa) and Caesarea. It's a marginal region in every respect: coastland, facing out across the Mediterranean, much more open to the cosmopolitan influences of the Hellenistic and Roman world and largely settled by Greeks.

Down to the coast

God's next move brings Peter himself right down to the coast. Joppa was not in his travel plans: the impulse comes from the disciples in Joppa, distraught at a death within the community. Amazed to hear that Peter is as close as Lydda, they send a small deputation to beg him to come (v. 38). 'Do not hesitate' is a polite form of request, but it suggests that Peter might have had reason to hesitate before going as far as the coast. For a Galilean fisherman, this was unknown territory. Tabitha's name (v. 36) means 'gazelle' (Luke gives the name in both Hebrew and Greek), and she was obviously a gentle and much-loved member of the community, expressing her discipleship (Luke uses the feminine form *mathetria*) forcefully and effectively by using the traditional women's skills of weaving and making garments to benefit the needy (vv. 36–37, 39). Once again, Peter brings the healing power of his master into a hopeless situation and finds life renewed and faith reinvigorated (vv. 40–42).

Prayer

Pray for all whose ministry leads them into an oversight role: for strength and sustenance on the road, and that they may never lose sight of the master, whose lifestyle they seek to follow.

32

Acts 9:43—10:8

Seaside lodging

All this apparently random wandering – responding to a call here, taking a few days' rest there – brings Peter to the right place at the right time for one of the most momentous scenes in the book, a scene so important that it gets told three times over, once by Luke as it happens (ch. 10), and twice by Peter as he reflects on it (chs 11; 15).

At the house of the tanner

Small narrative details underline the precariousness of Peter's position. He is lodging, staying as a guest, accepting hospitality, with Simon the tanner in his house beside the sea in Joppa (9:43; 10:6). Hospitality is going to be a major theme of this episode: watch out for who offers it, who accepts it and what are the difficulties and implications of accepting it.

The Greek word *xenos* means both 'guest' and 'stranger', and there is a hint that Peter is very much a stranger in town. He is already taking a risk by staying with a tanner. The craft of the tanner was a necessary one in the ancient world, but the smelliness of its processes meant that tanneries tended to be sited on the edge of town, preferably downwind (you can see this in the Roman city of Barcina, beneath modern-day Barcelona). So it is natural that the tanner's house would be beside the sea, but the detail is significant for a story that wastes very little time on incidental detail and for an author who chooses his words as carefully as Luke does. In Luke's gospel, the 'sea of Galilee', where Peter grew up and worked as a fisherman, is called a lake (*limne*). For Luke, the real sea (*thalassa*) is the Mediterranean, a lurking menace on the edge of Hebrew nightmare, a place of storm and sea-monster, opening up horizons to the wider world. Peter doesn't get to travel on the sea in Luke's story – only Paul does – but here is Peter, beside the seaside, about to have his horizons dramatically enlarged.

Cornelius the centurion

First, we have to meet a new character, important enough to have a personal introduction and a whole scene to himself. Cornelius lives in Caesarea (10:1), a coastal city that embodies all the ambiguities of Jewish identity. It is the seat of Roman government for the province of Judea, a port and trade centre, but also a thriving Greek city where Herod located the baths and hippodrome that he didn't dare build in more conservative Jerusalem. The name Cornelius is a good patrician Roman name which he (or his family) probably got from a patron, and he is a centurion in the Italian cohort. Suddenly we're in another world, the brusque military world of the Roman empire, a reminder of the huge and complex imperial framework that encloses Peter and his small community. As a centurion, Cornelius wouldn't be top-brass himself – centurions were the senior warrant officers of the Roman army – but he would be a considerable swell in the eyes of the natives.

A man who fears God

Yet Cornelius is also a pious and God-fearing man, one who (like the centurion of Luke 7:1–9) is respected by the local Jewish community and finds himself drawn to the high spiritual and charitable ideals of the synagogue. This is the first mention in Acts of a group that is going to play an important role in the story. The 'God-fearers' were righteous Gentiles who attended synagogue worship and supported the Jewish community in vital ways, both financial and political (see comment on 13:16). Luke depicts him as fulfilling all the demands of Jewish piety (v. 2) except one: he is a Gentile.

A soldier's vision

As so often in Acts, the key moment in this story is a moment of vision (10:3), a vision that is repeated three times as the story unfolds (10:22, 30–32; 11:13). Cornelius is faithful in observing the regular hours of prayer (10:30). It's a moment when God takes the initiative, speaking to the outsider by name (long before Peter is even aware that such a person exists), and giving him precise instructions which Cornelius has no hesitation in taking seriously.

Prayer

God of surprises, thank you that your horizons are always so much wider than ours.

33 Acts 10:9–20

Peter's challenge

By running two narrative threads at once, Luke makes it abundantly clear that the action in this story is happening on two fronts simultaneously: God is at work both inside and outside the church. This is going to be a crucial point in the argument later on, when Peter and James have to justify this encounter to the church at large. It was God who took the first step (15:7, 14).

Lunch break

Cornelius' messengers have started on their fateful journey (v. 9); the next step is to ensure that Peter is prepared to make them welcome. Peter, of course, has no clue what is about to happen. He just goes up to the roof of the tanner's house about midday to say his prayers. Having regular times for prayer is something that Luke takes for granted as a normal feature of the apostles' lives. Maybe Peter also wanted a breath of fresh sea air above the reek of the tanning-vats. He was not deliberately fasting, but he was extremely hungry (v. 10), perhaps listening with half an ear for the sounds of dinner being prepared down below. (Praying doesn't prevent our normal human responses to hunger!)

In this state of heightened anticipation, Peter falls into a trance (Greek *ekstasis*, literally 'standing outside oneself') and has a vision (v. 11). It's a vision of food, but a bizarre and disgusting one. He sees the heavens opened – a remarkable event in itself, one that normally portends a moment of significant revelation (see Luke 3:21; Acts 7:56). But what comes down is almost bathetic. It's a huge sheet held up over the earth by its four corners, and bulging with a motley collection of animals, reptiles and flying creatures (v. 12). Then Peter hears a heavenly voice (v. 13), which says, 'You're hungry – so get up and help yourself.'

Unknown waters

'No way,' says Peter. 'I have never yet eaten anything common or unclean' (v. 14). The words highlight his sense of standing on the brink of unknown waters: I'm safe, I know my values, I've always worked within fixed boundaries. And, rhetorically speaking, this is the answer that an orthodox Jewish community would respect and approve. Up to now, nothing in Acts – at least in Peter's experience – has transgressed the purity laws. This makes the response of the heavenly voice all the more shocking: what God has cleansed, *you* (emphatic pronoun in the Greek) must not 'soil' (v. 15). The word is hard to translate. It can mean either to 'make something unclean' or to 'call something unclean'. So is it about labels, or about reality? The answer is both, because, in a purity context, labels create reality. The next question is: whose labels? Who actually has the right to label some parts of God's creation 'pure', fit for human consumption, and others not? Who gets to decide?

Making distinctions

The vision happens three times (v. 16), and each time the vessel with its bizarre, indiscriminate cargo is taken up into heaven – the same words that Luke had used of Jesus' bodily ascension (1:2, 11). And, like the ascension (how can a human body ascend to heaven?), it leaves us – with Peter – wondering (v. 17) if heaven is a stranger (and perhaps more interesting) place than we had thought. What are all these creatures doing up there? Is heaven perhaps less discriminating than we are?

This, it turns out, is precisely the question Peter has to wrestle with. It's not really about food (although food will come into it), but it is about discrimination, making hard and fast distinctions between people and labelling some as okay, insiders, and some as outsiders, unclean. Now the real test of Peter's discrimination is standing below, knocking at the door (vv. 18–19), even as he rubs his eyes and scratches his head and wonders what the vision was all about (v. 19). 'Go down,' says the Spirit, 'and go with them without making distinctions [v. 20], because I [emphatic pronoun] have sent them.'

Whose problem?

What is at the heart of Peter's problem? Most readers of this commentary are probably (like me) Gentile Christians, so it's easy to label Peter's problem as a Jewish thing, something to do with 'the Jewish law' or Jewish dietary regulations. But labels create artificial lines here, lines between 'them' and 'us'. To understand how it looks from Peter's viewpoint, we have to ask, 'Who told him that certain foods were unclean?' The answer is, the Bible – God's revelatory word (see Leviticus 11).

For discussion and prayer

It's not difference that creates the problem, but discrimination.
Desmond Tutu (1931–2022)

34

Acts 10:21–29

Strangers and guests

One of the remarkable things about this story is the way Luke slows down the narrative pace by giving us all sorts of unnecessary detail about travel and hospitality that he doesn't normally bother with. It has the effect of filming in slow motion – another way to highlight how important this episode is for the whole story of Acts. It's Luke's way of saying, 'This is a God moment: something is happening here, so pay attention.' It's worth taking time to read the whole thing in slow motion, not skipping over the detail but savouring it and using it to get inside the characters' skins. For a group, that could mean doing a dramatic reading, using different characters in different parts of the room.

A knock at the door

From this point on, Peter is in unknown waters, trying to be attentive to what God is revealing in the situation as it unfolds. The first step is to go down (v. 21), down from the place of vision into the confusion of everyday life, down to meet the three men knocking at the door and accept the God-given role that they are pushing him into: 'Yes, it's me you're looking for.' Who knows what that action cost Peter? But everything else flows from that initial acceptance. Then he can begin to ask questions, to listen, to hear the other side of the story.

His question allows the visitors to tell their own story – which we know, but Peter doesn't – in their own words, adding some significant details (v. 22): Cornelius is a righteous man, vouchsafed for by the Jewish community. All of this only serves to underline the inescapable fact that he is a Gentile, not 'one of us'. Nevertheless, he has been visited by an angel, a divine messenger, who sent the human messengers on their mysterious errand. So what have they come for? In a sense, they don't know either. They've come for a word that nobody in the story can yet envisage, a word that Peter himself doesn't yet know.

Come on in

Hospitality is the next step (v. 23). The strangers have to be welcomed in – but at first on Peter's own terms. From Peter's point of view, it's not too difficult to invite Gentile visitors in to share table-fellowship in a Jewish home, to share what he has and become part of his way of life. The next step is bolder: to go out with them and allow his strange guests to lead him somewhere new, to become a guest (and therefore a stranger) himself. It is a sensible precaution for Peter to take some of the brothers with him, as an escort, as a guarantee of safety, as witnesses (compare 11:12). But it is also an added risk. It means trusting the strangers enough (or trusting God enough) to risk taking others with him on a journey into the unknown.

Crossing the threshold

The sense of heightened anticipation on Peter's arrival in Caesarea is palpable (v. 24). Cornelius is expecting him: he has even got a houseful of friends and relatives there as a reception committee (a leap of faith if ever there was one!). What were they thinking? Did they wonder if their friend had taken leave of his senses? Who were they waiting for? Hence the extravagant gestures when (against all odds) Peter finally appears on cue (v. 25). Cornelius tries to kneel to Peter, to treat him as a messenger of the gods – only to be gently rebuffed. So the meeting starts (as all such meetings must) with the fundamental recognition that both parties are human beings, a recognition that creates a crucial platform for what follows. 'I'm here in God's name,' Peter says, 'but that doesn't put me on a different plane from you. I'm here because God is calling me – but so are you.' In that confidence, he can take the momentous step of crossing the threshold (vv. 27–28).

Receiving hospitality, becoming a guest, is often much more difficult than giving it. We are not on our own turf; we have to learn to live by somebody else's rules. There's no neutral territory here, no 'safe house' where we can get to know one another. Either you are my guest, or I'm yours: either you learn to live by my rules, or I learn to live by yours. Or is there another way? That's essentially what Peter is on a quest to discover.

For discussion and prayer

Peter's story is a challenge to come down from our isolated rooftops and come out from behind the barricades we build up between ourselves and the 'other'. How far are we prepared to travel to meet the strangers outside our churches on their own ground?

35 Acts 10:30–48
A sermon and its aftermath

It's a strange feeling to be the answer to someone else's prayers! The multiple retellings of this story allow Luke to highlight the impact of Peter's vision on three different groups: on Peter himself, on Cornelius and finally (ch. 11) on the Jerusalem church. So far, we've been experiencing the event through Peter's eyes. Now, in this face-to-face encounter with Cornelius, the stranger to whom God has already spoken, we begin to experience its significance for Cornelius, for those 'outsiders' who lurk on the edges of our religious life, fascinated and yet repelled by what they see inside our churches.

First, Cornelius tells his story in his own words (v. 30). Again, this is a recap of what Luke has already told us, but that bit more vivid: 'Four days ago, about this time, I was praying in my house… and behold!' The wonder of that shining visitor is still with him – along with the incomparable sense of being heard and remembered (v. 31). Cornelius concludes, 'So I did what I was told, and the rest is up to you' (vv. 32–33). As we might expect of a soldier, his words ('commanded', NRSV) have a military feel: he has a sense that both he and his visitor are under orders (compare Luke 7:8).

The God of all

Peter's sermon (the first we've heard outside Jerusalem) is a remarkably vivid evocation of a gospel message that is thoroughly trinitarian, and thoroughly universal. Peter begins with God (vv. 34–35). There is only one God, and that God is (in the old phrase) 'no respecter of persons': he does not discriminate or make distinctions between people on grounds of class, gender or race. Peter's rather quaint language here picks up an Old Testament phrase (compare Deuteronomy 10:17); Paul uses similar language in Romans 2:11. It's a familiar phrase, but the force of it is that Peter has suddenly seen what it means for the real person standing in front of him. And that has implications not just for Cornelius but for people of every nation (v. 35).

The Lord of all

What does this God want Peter to say to these people, though? What is the word that Peter has been so elaborately summoned to give them? 'You want a word? Well,' he says, 'I only know one word, the word that God sent to Israel [v. 36], preaching peace through Jesus Christ. Is that what you want to hear?' We can almost hear Peter feeling his way through the broken syntax of his opening sentences. 'Preaching peace' echoes a prophetic phrase (Isaiah 52:7), connected with preaching to the Gentiles in Ephesians 2:17, just as the phrase 'far off' is linked with the worldwide preaching of the gospel in Ephesians 2:13, picking up Joel 2:32 and Isaiah 57:19 (compare Acts 2:39). Whatever God is offering Israel through Jesus, Peter suddenly sees, is offered to all – and that's worth saying, even if he can't yet quite see how the theology works.

So the story of Jesus, the only story Peter knows how to tell, is precisely what needs to be told in this new setting. He can assume that the story is known in outline, even as far off as Caesarea, and verses 37–43 give a good summary of the gospel story. Jesus' ministry comes across as a power struggle between two rival forms of kingship, a mission to rescue those over whom Satan was seeking to exercise illegitimate control (v. 38). But Satan, whatever he may claim, has no right to control any human being, Jew or Gentile: it is Jesus of Nazareth who is 'Lord of all' (v. 36). So the familiar story takes on a new significance. The crucifixion of God's Anointed One (vv. 38–39), the witness of the disciples to his ministry and resurrection (vv. 39–42), the warning of judgement and the offer of forgiveness of sins (vv. 42–43): we have heard all this as a message for Israel, but now we can begin to see that it has a wider, more universal significance. This is a message for the whole world.

The Spirit of all

The result of preaching is (mercifully) in God's hands, not Peter's. The Spirit comes, dramatically and unmistakably, on this group of Gentiles (vv. 46–48), reversing the order of 8:14–17 (where baptism comes first). This is the climax of the episode, the public event which convinces Peter that God is really at work in this unlikely setting (see 11:16).

Reflection

We have to be careful not to fall back into the trap of acting as if the church were only for people 'like us'. When in any of our churches people are rejected because 'they are not decent' or... because they do not share our political ideology, it is time for us to... ask ourselves what it means to declare that 'God shows no partiality'.

Justo Gonzalez, *Acts: The gospel of the Spirit* (Orbis, 2001), p. 136.

36 Acts 11:1–18
The Jerusalem church reflects

'Can anyone withhold the water for baptising these people?' Peter asks in 10:47. The Ethiopian asks the same question in 8:36, and in both cases it carries a touch of irony. As we see here, there are plenty of people who would like to put barriers in the way of receiving these outsiders into the church. Peter's momentous journey is not finished yet.

Centre and periphery

Back in Jerusalem, rumours are beginning to circulate – either exciting or disquieting, depending on your point of view (vv. 1–2). Where has Peter been all this time? What's going on, out there at the margins, down by the dangerous sea? Is it a time for reasserting centralised control? Or for allowing the margins to change how the centre thinks? Up to this point, 'the church' in Acts has effectively meant the Jerusalem church, with the apostles exercising a regional oversight over the fast-growing bands of believers in Judea and Samaria. Peter and John, in 8:14, act as delegates of the whole body of the twelve in Jerusalem, acting on behalf of the Jerusalem church as a whole, and it is natural to think that this delegated authority was behind Peter's role when he set out on his journey in 9:32. So this debate is partly about the patterns of authority that direct the ongoing life of the church. Are the apostles answerable to an organisation called 'the church', or to someone else?

Why did you do it?

The whole church has heard the news (v. 1); the question comes from one section of that by now large body of believers, 'those of the circumcision' (v. 2). The phrase is odd, given that all believers at this date (apart from Cornelius and his friends) were Jews. It recalls Paul's phrase in Galatians 2:12, and it may be that Luke, looking back on these early discussions, has unconsciously cast them along the party lines of the later debate. What these believers are doing is 'making distinctions' – exactly what the Spirit told Peter not to do in 10:20. But the question is innocent enough, touching on a matter of fact and on a perception that Peter himself had shared (10:28), which must have been troubling more than one of his fellow apostles. Peter has travelled a long way since his rooftop vision in Joppa, but his fellow believers haven't had that experience, so now he needs to lay it before them for a process of joint discernment, retracing his steps and testing every link in that extraordinary chain of events by telling his story 'step by step' (v. 4, NRSV).

Action and reflection

The questioners started with the negative, concerned about rules being broken. But Peter starts with the positive, with the vision of God (v. 5). One approach asks, 'If these are the rules, what does that tell us about God?' The other asks, 'If God is like this, what does that tell us about how we should behave?'

'Take another look at my creation,' says the heavenly voice; 'it's more varied than you think' (vv. 6–7). Peter stresses that his initial reactions were just the same as his hearers': 'I can't, it doesn't make sense, it goes against everything I believe' (vv. 8–10). So Peter needs to hang on to the conviction that it was the voice of God's Spirit, not just a personal whim, that told him to go against God's revelatory word (vv. 12–14). This is not an action that any of us take lightly, and the questioning of our fellow believers will always make us wonder, 'Was I right?' But as Peter retells the story and reflects on it, new connections start to pop up that help to make sense of this new journey led by the Spirit.

Thinking back, the action of the Spirit seen in other people's lives (v. 15; 10:44) is part of what gives Peter confidence that his journey to Caesarea was right – that and the generosity to accord others' spiritual experience equal importance with his own. But only now, reliving the experience with his brothers, does he give us his considered reflection on how it all ties in with the Jesus story (v. 16), the familiar tale now seen with new significance. What this means is nothing less than earth-shaking: it means that the Spirit is not something we earn by keeping the rules, but is God's free gift, for Jew and Gentile alike. And all anyone has to do is to believe in the Lord Jesus Christ (v. 17) – just as the first disciples did. Stop them being baptised? You might as well try to stop God!

Reflection

Stuckness shouldn't be avoided. It's the psychic predecessor of all real understanding. An ego-less acceptance of stuckness is the key to an understanding of all Quality, in mechanical work as in other endeavours.

Robert M. Pirsig, *Zen and the Art of Motorcycle Maintenance* (Morrow, 1974), p. 286.

37 Acts 11:19–26
A tale of two churches

Meanwhile, the Spirit is busy getting on with things, out there in the world. After the slow-motion ruminations of the Cornelius episode, the pace begins to speed up in this summary section – a reminder of the constant dialectic between reflection and action that characterises the mature Christian life.

Gossiping the gospel

Back in chapter 8, Luke told us that many of the disciples (probably 'Hellenists', Greek-speaking Jews) were 'scattered' in the persecution that arose after the lynching of Stephen (8:1, 4). It is these anonymous believers who now take the next momentous step in the 'scattering' of God's word. Timing is crucial here: Luke is keeping a number of diverse storylines in play at this point, and it is impossible to be sure of the correlation between the various events in chapters 10—11. From Luke's point of view, however, it is significant that Peter's life-changing encounter with God's Spirit at work in the Gentile Cornelius is placed right in the narrative centre of the book, between the dispersal from Jerusalem and its unexpected harvest – and that the Jerusalem church has accepted the principle of including the Gentiles (11:18) before the next phase begins in earnest.

The distances covered here are huge (v. 19), although it seems probable that many of these Greek-speaking believers (like the Cypriote Barnabas, 4:36) were returning home to their roots. On the way they are 'gossiping the gospel', 'chatting' (NRSV 'spoke') the word. This is mission not as centralised campaign but as real people out on the roads of the empire, sharing the news that is too good to keep to themselves. Initially, the news is shared only with fellow Jews, but some of them, men from Cyprus and north Africa (a long way from home!) come to Antioch and start talking to Greeks as well (v. 20). Imperceptibly, the distinction between Jew and Gentile starts to melt away in cosmopolitan Antioch, and, Luke tells us, 'the hand of the Lord was with them'. This is Pentecost all over again, with 'a large number' believing and turning to the Lord (v. 21; see 4:4; 6:7). The preaching of Jesus as Lord produces exactly the same results as in Jerusalem: against all expectations, this one word that Peter had thought was only for the chosen people allows the Gentiles to discover that they are part of God's kingdom too.

Jerusalem investigates

Word gets back to the church in Jerusalem, already prepared by the events in Caesarea (v. 22). The contact between centre and periphery needs to be kept open, and this time it is Barnabas who is chosen as intermediary. He was a good choice, as it turns out – after all, encouragement is his middle name (4:36)! Barnabas has just the right gifts to nurture this fledgling work of the Spirit: discernment, encouragement and a selfless ability to rejoice at the grace bestowed on others (v. 23). There's an air of gratitude about Luke's report here, and a timely reminder that being 'full of the Spirit' is as much about discerning and nurturing the work of the Spirit in other people as it is about doing the frontline work (v. 24).

Saul joins the team

Verse 25 brings Saul back into Luke's narrative. After his abortive attempt to join the Jerusalem church, he had gone home to Tarsus (9:30). Barnabas, finding himself not too far away, remembers the passionate, fiery young convert, recognises his potential gifts as a teacher, wonders if he is still in Tarsus, finds him and brings him back to Antioch. This fits in with what Paul says in Galatians 1:21 and with the importance of Barnabas in the early phases of Paul's mission (cf. Galatians 2:1, 9). Looking back on those early years, Paul only sees God's hand at work – but God uses human beings to act for him. Bringing Saul to Antioch as a teacher for this fledgling church (v. 26) was a momentous step in the history of the church. What if Barnabas hadn't had his brainwave?

Just in passing, Luke records another significant moment in the life of the church: it is in Antioch that this ever-expanding group of 'disciples' first acquires (probably as a nickname) a distinctive identity. Whose followers are they? Not Saul's or Barnabas's: they are known as *Christianoi*, people who belong to Christ.

Prayer

Father, help us to rejoice in your gifts to others and to nurture them with love and encouragement.

38 Acts 11:27—12:23
The apostle and the king

Chapter 12 forms a kind of interlude in a story whose centre is shifting imperceptibly from Peter to Paul, from Jerusalem to Antioch. While Barnabas and Saul are visiting Jerusalem (11:30; 12:25), the focus swings back briefly to Peter and a dramatic prison break.

Spirit-inspired prophecy (11:28) was an important aspect of ministry in the early church, and many of the early prophets were itinerant; Agabus reappears briefly at 21:10–11. Contemporary Roman historians refer to several famines in the eastern Mediterranean in this period, and Luke dates this one to the reign of Claudius (AD41–54). Josephus speaks of a severe famine in Judea in AD46–48. Saul and Barnabas' visit to Jerusalem must belong to the time of the actual famine, not to the time of the prophecy. Luke may not have had precise dates for these long-ago events: more important to his narrative is the lively network of teaching, prophecy and reciprocal charity that continues to link Antioch with Jerusalem.

Herod the king

The Herod of chapter 12 is Agrippa I, the grandson of Herod the Great (of Matthew 2) and nephew of Herod Antipas, who was ruler of Galilee during Jesus' ministry (Luke 3:1). Agrippa is well known from contemporary Roman and Jewish historians, and the events Luke describes fit the general character of his reign. If the 'precise moment in time' (*kairos*) of 12:1 means the time of the famine (11:28), it would be consistent with the behaviour of despots down the ages to try to deflect attention from ecological disaster by identifying a scapegoat within the population. But there is a chronological problem: the death of Agrippa, which Luke links with Peter's imprisonment, can be dated to AD44, three years into the reign of Claudius but well before the famine described by Josephus in 46–48. Either Luke is thinking of an earlier famine (which is possible), or he has put together separate (undated) items of tradition in a theological rather than chronological sequence.

A miraculous escape

The execution of James is described with stark brevity (12:2), but Peter's imprisonment is told with much more narrative detail and an element of humour. The link with the Passover (12:3–4) explains why Peter was kept in prison: prison in the pre-modern world was normally not a punishment in itself but a holding area pending trial or execution. The problem was (as Paul was to discover: see 24:27) that such 'temporary' custody was outside judicial control and could last indefinitely. All of this, though, is just background to the vivid scene that Luke paints of the apostle in prison, fully expecting to meet the same fate as James, assigned like a dangerous terrorist to four squads of soldiers, chained to his guards – and peacefully sleeping while the church prays for his release (12:4–6). Once again, God's timing gives the story its punch. On the very night before Herod had planned to parade Peter before a hostile crowd, the angel appears and, step by careful step, leads him through mysteriously open doors to the fresh night air of the street (12:7–10).

It's a sensational story: the dazed apostle who doesn't believe what's happening to him; the doors opening 'of their own accord' (12:10); the slave-girl who leaves him knocking at a closed door in the excitement of discovering – beyond all expectations – that God really does answer prayer (12:13–16). God's saving power is always so much greater than we consider possible. Stories like this serve a serious theological function in communities facing the harsh realities of persecution, then and now. Peter's miraculous escape from prison, like Daniel's escape from the den of lions (a favourite theme in early Christian art), provides dramatic demonstration of God's protective power for his persecuted people.

Death of a tyrant

It's also important to know that God does judge evildoers – and that is what Luke shows in the second part of the chapter (cf. Daniel 4). There is consternation among the guards at Peter's disappearance, although the fate of the soldiers for their dereliction of duty is anything but funny (12:18–19). Not long afterwards, Agrippa himself comes to a bizarre and gruesome end in Caesarea (12:20–23). Josephus tells a version of the same story, treating Agrippa's death as a fitting punishment for a mortal monarch who accepted the kind of worship due only to God (again, an underlying theme of the Daniel cycle: see Daniel 3).

Prayer

Pray for all prisoners and captives – and for those who have to guard them.

39 Acts 12:24—13:3
Act Three: Paul the missionary

This point marks a watershed in Acts, the beginning of a momentous journey which will lead eventually to Rome. The mission now has a new base, Antioch, and a new hero, Saul (aka Paul), who will occupy centre stage in virtually every episode from now to the end of the book.

From Jerusalem to Antioch

First, though, Luke interweaves the different threads of his story with some typically deft narrative footwork. In 12:24 there is a pointed reminder that even the Herods of this world cannot prevent the relentless forward progress of God's saving word. Verse 25 picks up the narrative at the point where we left it at 11:30, with Saul and Barnabas completing their mission in Jerusalem and returning to Antioch with a new team member, John Mark. In passing, Luke tells us that significant changes have been happening in the Jerusalem church. The sudden appearance of 'elders' (11:30), the new role of James the Lord's brother and the departure of Peter to 'another place' (12:17) all raise intriguing questions for the historian. But Luke is not attempting to write a complete history of the early church (or even of all the apostles). His task is to explain the steps by which God's Spirit is preparing the way for the Gentile mission. From this point on, the Jerusalem church is effectively off stage except when Paul revisits the city in chapters 15 and 21.

'The church that was in Antioch'

This formal-sounding phrase (v. 1) recalls the openings of many of Paul's letters, and gives a certain weight and dignity to this fledgling church, which is going to launch the next phase of mission. Suddenly we're in a different world, far more cosmopolitan than Jerusalem. Antioch is a vibrant city which straddles the eastern borders of the Roman empire and controls the trade networks linking east and west. It is appropriate that the church there should be introduced with a certain amount of ceremony. It has its own patterns of ministry: 'prophets and teachers' are mentioned here together for the first time, and (like the Jerusalem church) it has its own leaders, who are carefully introduced by name.

Two of these names are familiar: Barnabas, a link back with the apostles and the first, heady days of the Jerusalem church – a trusted, safe pair of hands – and Saul. Three are new: Simeon Niger, a Jewish name with a Latin nickname meaning 'black'; Lucius of Cyrene, another Latin name, pointing to well-established trading and business links between Antioch, Cyprus and north Africa; and Manaen (a Greek form of Menahem), who provides an intriguing link with the Herodian court and a reminder that the Herodian family was also one of the major business empires of the East. 'Herod the tetrarch' is the Herod of the gospels, a generation back from Agrippa, so Manaen, who had been his youthful companion, must be an older man.

The Spirit's call

It is appropriate too that this next stage in the mission of the church should be marked with spiritual solemnity and ceremony – as in the parallel passage at 6:7–11, which likewise marked the beginning of a new phase in the church's history. Both are formally marked with prayer and the laying on of hands (13:3) in response to the direct guidance of the Holy Spirit, presumably utilising the prophetic gifts of Antioch's church leaders (13:2). The statement that this happens in the context of worship and fasting gives us a tantalising glimpse into the spirituality of the early church. The details here all serve to underline that the start of Paul's mission was undertaken within the worshipping life of the church and under the explicit guidance of the Holy Spirit who 'sends them out' (13:4) as they head in a westerly direction, heading initially for Barnabas' old stamping ground – the Jewish communities of Cyprus.

Reflection and prayer

'For the work to which I have called them' (13:2) – but what work? Sometimes we have to head out in faith, like Abraham, without knowing where God is calling us or what God wants us to do. As a friend said to me when I was ordained, 'Sometimes the Lord leads us into strange places; but where he leads, he always provides.'

40

Acts 13:4–12

Mission in Cyprus

The journey begins – tentatively at first, following well-trodden pathways, but gradually gaining in confidence and learning to trust God's Holy Spirit. Luke delicately points up parallels between Paul's public ministry and that of his master, so the first major 'scene' on this voyage shows Paul victorious in conflict with Satan (compare Luke 4:1–13).

Partners in mission

Verse 5 forms a bridge between two sections and sets the pattern for all Paul's missionary journeys. Saul is not yet the leader: he has learnt an immense amount from Barnabas, and the essential pattern of teamwork which undergirds the whole Pauline mission is a pattern set by Barnabas at the start. Their aim is to announce the word of God (not themselves), and their objective is 'the synagogues of the Jews'. In other words, they are using the established networks of Jewish community life in the diaspora. Many Jewish communities did not have dedicated synagogue buildings at this date, but (like the Christians) they did have regular community gatherings, often in people's homes, for prayer and Bible study. The mission on which Saul and Barnabas set out from Antioch was first and foremost a mission to the Jews, a prophetic proclamation of God's word to God's scattered people. True, the church in Antioch (like many Jewish synagogues) has its Gentile adherents as well, and they are starting to find that word relevant to them in unexpected ways, but the full implications of that discovery are still around the corner.

Encounter with a proconsul

We have to assume that Luke's summary sets the general pattern for proclamation throughout the island (v. 6). But now we move to the exceptional event (v. 7), a triangular encounter with rival gurus battling for the soul of the proconsul. Sergius Paulus was the most powerful political figure on the island and the representative of Roman colonial power. Like many high-status Romans of his day, he was clearly fascinated by the battling cults of the eastern Mediterranean and inspired (by curiosity?) to invite the two representatives of this latest spiritual fad to his residence for a consultation, perhaps to see if there was anything in it for him. Luke notes that he was an intelligent man, and his interest is initially on the intellectual level ('to hear the word', v. 7); but for Elymas (Luke here gives his Greek name, about which there is some confusion) this is a matter of personality control, and he has no intention of losing his position of influence (v. 8). So the word has to be backed up by deeds, and what Sergius Paulus gets is not a reasoned intellectual discourse but a display of spiritual pyrotechnics.

A change of name

Is it coincidence that the Hebrew Saul switches to his Roman name Paulus at this point in the story? Clearly the Roman name was more user-friendly as he began to move west and north, away from the frontier zones and deeper into imperial territory. But Luke also emphasises the continuity between Saul and Paul. This is the first scene in which we have had a chance to see what has happened to Saul since his own conversion: there are numerous links back to chapter 9, as well as strong verbal parallels with Peter's story. Paul, like the Jerusalem apostles, is 'full of the Holy Spirit' (v. 9) and has that powerful, intent gaze when confronting a spiritual challenge that Peter had at the Gate Beautiful (3:4). The danger with the magical perversion of spiritual power is precisely its power to deceive, the corruption of God-given gifts in the service of spiritual control (v. 10), so it has to be confronted head on (v. 11).

Perhaps Paul recognised Elymas' opposition to the gospel as a mirror image of his own self-righteous zeal. Certainly, what Elymas suffers is a parallel to Saul's own experience, a temporary but paralysing blindness that leaves him groping around for guides. The proconsul is impressed by the whole package: the 'teaching of the Lord' (v. 12) makes its effect by deed as well as word. There is a dual message here for Luke's first readers: for outsiders, 'Don't mess with these people – they've got the living God on their side'; for insiders, 'Don't get the gospel mixed up with magic'.

For discussion and prayer

This is a disturbing story! Is this the best way to impress the world with the power of the gospel? Or is it the only way to deal with the perversion of the gospel?

41

Acts 13:13–25

Antioch of Pisidia

Travel itself becomes an integral part of the story in Luke's account of Paul's voyages. In this second major scene of the mission, Paul, like Jesus, is offered the opportunity to set out his prophetic vision before an attentive synagogue audience (compare Luke 4:16–30).

Who and where?

Perga in Pamphylia (v. 13) is on the south coast of modern Turkey, one of the few ports of call on this precipitous section of coast, and a major access point for the interior. A paved Roman road, the Via Sebaste, links Perga with Antioch of Pisidia (v. 14), and that is probably how the party reached their next stop. The mission is moving on into unknown territory – although it is worth remembering that Paul was brought up in Tarsus and could have known Antioch as an important staging-post on the trade routes across the interior of Asia Minor. It is also a fact that Antioch was the home town of the proconsul Sergius Paulus, who may well have suggested it to Paul as a strategic base for the evangelisation of central Asia Minor (and could have given Paul valuable letters of introduction). The team is gradually changing its focus, too. Luke does not say why John Mark left them at this point (maybe the sight of the mountainous wooded slopes behind Perge put him off!), but the decision will have repercussions later (see 15:37–38).

An impromptu sermon

For Jewish visitors to a strange town, the sabbath-day gathering of the synagogue is the natural meeting-place. Luke assumes that his readers will be familiar with synagogue practice, with the main reading from the Torah followed by a reading from the prophets (v. 15). Paul and Barnabas were probably instantly distinguishable as strangers in town, but may also have been distinguished as visiting scholars from Jerusalem by their dress. A later rabbinic source records a saying of R. Huna: 'Wherever a Jerusalemite went in the provinces, they arranged a seat of honour for him to sit upon in order to listen to his wisdom.'[7]

The 'officials of the synagogue' were not rabbis but local benefactors who made major contributions to the fabric of the synagogue and undertook a supervisory role in its meetings. They would be the obvious ones to identify the strangers as scholars and send a message to ask if they have a 'word of encouragement' for the people, linked with the scriptural texts that had just been read. And that is how Paul addresses the congregation, after 'motioning with his hand' (like a Greek orator) to secure their quiet attention (v. 16). They are 'men of Israel', the gathered people of God, no less here than in Jerusalem. There is also an additional element which is going to become increasingly important in the story of Acts: 'you who fear God', the Gentile 'god-fearers', like Cornelius, who are attracted to the philosophical purity of Jewish religion and attend sabbath services regularly.

Reclaiming the past

Paul's sermon picks up the history of God's dealings with his people at the point where Stephen's left off in chapter 7, so that for Luke's readers the two together dovetail into a complete account of salvation history. As in Stephen's retelling, Israel's history begins with the action of God (v. 17): election (the choice of a people), divine grace (the exodus narrative) and exaltation. Note that exaltation is something that happens to God's people 'in exile' – appropriate in an address to a group who are also in some kind of exile. Paul summarises the years of wilderness wandering and conquest (vv. 18–19), using a patchwork of Old Testament quotations, but his main focus is on God's election of the line of David, heralded by the prophet Samuel (v. 20) and the abortive election of Saul (v. 21). It is David, and the scriptural promises to David, that form the basis of Paul's proclamation here. Jesus, the Saviour who comes of the seed of David 'according to promise', is the culmination of Israel's history (v. 23), with John the Baptist saluted as the forerunner and the final episode in the prophetic witness to the coming of the Christ (vv. 24–25).

For discussion and prayer

What do you see when you look back over history – human failure or divine grace?

42

Acts 13:26–41

'We bring you the good news'

The prophetic appeal to God's people encapsulated in Isaiah 55 is very much at the heart of what is happening here. When God's word goes forth, we expect a result. God's word never comes back fruitless (Isaiah 55:10–11). The offer is there, and it is totally genuine: living water instead of cracked cisterns, the peace and cosmic rejoicing of God's everlasting covenant (Isaiah 55:12–13). But the prophetic word carries a health warning too. Once it is issued, it must be either accepted or rejected.

You, them and us

That was then, this is now: in the second part of his sermon, Paul turns from history to the present tense, from God's encounters with his people in the past to the salvation that is on offer now. This synagogue audience is a typical diaspora mixture of Abraham's descendants (ethnically Jewish) and 'those among you who fear God' (emotionally and ideologically Jewish). Paul addresses both as 'my brothers' (v. 26), reciprocating the same warmth of welcome that he has received (13:15). The boundaries of 'brotherhood' in Acts are elastic and fluid: Luke does not limit the term to followers of Christ. The horizons of Paul's message are equally fluid: 'It is to us,' Paul says (pronoun in emphatic position) that 'the word of this salvation has been sent'. Some of our earliest witnesses read 'to you' here (a single letter change in the Greek, which would have sounded identical in dictation) – a reading that picks up the inclusive nature of this appeal: it's for all of us gathered here today, you and me both.

The message of salvation

The words of verse 26 have a distinctly biblical feel without being an exact quotation. God's word here is both judgement and salvation: salvation for those who recognise the fulfilment of God's promise; judgement for those who do not. For Paul, it was not 'the Jews' as a nation who had rejected God's promised Saviour but 'those living in Jerusalem and their rulers' – a specific group, clearly distinguished from this diaspora congregation (v. 27). But this failure to recognise the Messiah is also a failure to recognise the voice of God in scripture. The Jerusalemites and their rulers thus became the fulfilment of the scriptures that they failed to hear (although Pilate was the actual agent of execution: v. 28). None of this was outside God's control (v. 29; compare 3:17–18), but what happened next was pure grace, pure divine initiative (vv. 30–31).

Witnesses to the people

The role of the witnesses is carefully defined: the witnesses are 'those who came up to Jerusalem with him from Galilee' (v. 31; compare 1:21), and their role is to bear witness to the Jewish people in their homeland. Paul's job is to bring this same good news 'to you' (v. 32), the good news that the promise made to 'our fathers' (13:23) is now fulfilled in God's action in raising Jesus from the dead (v. 33). That's the point of this visit and the fulcrum of the whole sermon. This is not just a piece of abstract history or Bible study: it is about God entrusting his word to his messengers and sending it out to 'you', just as it was earlier sent out to the inhabitants of Jerusalem. Now is your chance; *you* are going to have to decide whether to accept it or to reject it.

The testimony of scripture

This solemn moment of appeal is reinforced by the testimony of scripture. For Luke's readers, this sermon completes the catalogue of testimonies supporting the messianic reading of scripture that runs through all the sermons in Acts, right from chapter 2. Here the focus is appropriately on the two key Davidic texts: Psalm 2 and Psalm 16. What was not fulfilled in David himself comes true in the death and resurrection of David's greater Son (vv. 34–37). What is new here is the link with Isaiah 55:3 (v. 34), linked with Psalm 16:10 by the keyword 'the sure mercies of David'. Finally (and marked by another direct address), the appeal itself: *this* is what I want you to take in, brothers, this is what's in it for you (v. 38). The public proclamation of 'remission of sins' goes back to the roots of the gospel (see Luke 1:77; 3:3), and it is at the heart of the worldwide proclamation, both for Jesus (Luke 24:47) and for Paul (compare Galatians 2:16; Romans 3:28).

Reflection

Your holy hearsay is not evidence. Give me the good news in the present tense.
Sydney Carter (1915–2004)

43

Acts 13:42–47

Seek the Lord

Paul's sermon and the sharply polarised reactions to it are described in some detail. This is a paradigmatic scene for the diaspora, just as Peter's sermon in chapter 2 was for Jerusalem. The central event is the proclamation of the word, and we then watch the double helix of belief and unbelief unravelling (just as Simeon predicted in Luke 2:34–35) before our eyes.

Positive reactions

Initial reactions are favourable (v. 42), and many of the congregation, both Jews and 'god-fearing proselytes', throw in their lot with Paul and Barnabas (v. 43). The 'grace of God' is the foundation for the future life of those who become believers (see 1 Corinthians 1:4–9), but Luke is not concerned at this stage with the founding of a new community. What interests him is the wider reaction: on the next sabbath, virtually 'the whole city' (typical Lucan exaggeration!) is agog to hear more of Paul's preaching (v. 44). The 'word of the Lord', which started with John the Baptist's mission to Israel (Luke 3:2), is reaching out to wider and wider circles.

Negative reactions

At this point, however, the insiders react in panic to protect their privileged position (v. 45). 'The Jews' here (as in v. 50) means the unbelievers – possibly the synagogue authorities, certainly those who are not convinced by Paul's arguments and start to argue against his interpretation of scripture (another fulfilment of Simeon's prophecy: see Luke 2:34). 'Jealousy' (NRSV) may be unfair: the Greek word *zelos* can also be translated 'zeal'. Paul's opponents here show the same quality of energetic opposition to God's enemies that he had shown in his pre-conversion days. Paul uses the same word of himself in Philippians 3:6, so there is no need to imagine that the synagogue authorities were 'jealous' over Paul's success with proselytes or God-fearers. What we have here is a highly coloured and one-sided description of what must actually have happened time and again in Paul's ministry, as he goes 'to the Jew first' (1 Corinthians 9:20; Romans 1:16) and seeks to win over not just a few individuals but a whole community for Christ.

Turning to the Gentiles

This explains, I think, a slight artificiality about the next step, as Paul and Barnabas formally turn on the host community and announce that they have rejected God's prophetic word and judged themselves to be 'unworthy of eternal life' (v. 46). Luke is trying to describe a pattern of formal rejection by Jewish communities in the diaspora, which then justifies Paul's decision to 'turn to the Gentiles'. Rhetorically, this is close to the whole focus of this episode (and therefore of Luke's presentation of the Pauline mission). The word of salvation is sent by God 'to the Jew first'. The Jewish community as a whole has a chance to accept the message (and some do), but the community as a whole rejects it and thus disqualifies itself. So, finally, Paul turns to the Gentiles.

At one level, Luke is defending Paul against the charge of gratuitously abandoning his own people to preach to the Gentiles. ('Far from it,' he says, 'they pushed me out.') But at a deeper level the whole episode is, like Romans 9—11, a prolonged meditation on the mystery of unbelief which was a fact of life in early Christian experience. Why did Israel not believe? Luke (like Paul) keeps coming back to the problem like a sore tooth (cf. especially ch. 28). For the present, the point is made: this is what is happening, and therefore it cannot be outside God's sovereign will (vv. 46, 48). Hence the need to find prophetic warrant, both for the process of rejection and for the alternative mission that begins to open.

Isaiah 49:6 is a key text in Paul's emergent understanding of his own vocation (v. 47), and links both backwards to Simeon's prophecy and forwards to the end of the book. But note that there is no corresponding turning away *from* Israel. Israel exercises its freedom of choice in rejecting Paul's message, but Paul (as we shall see) keeps returning time and time again to win over the Jewish communities of the diaspora.

Reflection

Pray for those who need to forget the God they do not believe in and meet the God who believes in them.

Wild Goose Worship Group, *A Wee Worship Book* (Wild Goose Resource Group, 1999), p. 62.

44 Acts 13:48—14:6
The word of grace

Inclusion and exclusion are two sides of the same coin. Paul's words signal a new, more positive attitude to Gentiles in his mission, a new recognition that Gentiles are entitled to hear God's word in their own right, not simply to overhear a message addressed to Jews. The expelled word goes out and, as in Luke's parable of the great banquet (Luke 14:15–24), the act of expulsion itself becomes the means of inclusion. Quite what that word will sound like when spoken to Gentiles, though, we have still to hear.

Expelled from Antioch

For the present, the narrative continues to trace the self-destructive spiral of rejection. Preaching to the pagan inhabitants of Antioch proves to be a fruitful experience (v. 48), and the word of the Lord begins to spread outside the city into the surrounding countryside (v. 49). The role of 'women of high standing' (v. 50) fits with what we know of the attraction of highly placed women to Judaism, here used (as often in Roman history) as a shortcut to the sources of civic power. Paul and Barnabas are formally escorted across the borders of Antioch. In their turn, they enact the ritual of protest against the city laid down in Jesus' mission commands (Luke 9:5; 10:11) and move on to Iconium (v. 51), leaving behind a small but vigorous cell of disciples, 'filled with joy and Holy Spirit' (v. 52).

On to Iconium

Exactly the same pattern is repeated in Iconium (v. 1) – another indication that the Antioch episode is a type-scene setting the pattern for subsequent mission. Once again, Paul conducts a successful mission in the synagogue, resulting in a mixed crop of Jewish and Gentile believers. Once again, however, he is unable to win over the entire Jewish community to his viewpoint. Not everyone is persuaded, and those who are not stir up hostile feeling against 'the brothers' among the city's Gentile population (v. 2). Mission here is a matter of staying put in a difficult situation as long as one can, doing one's own part in 'speaking boldly for the Lord' – and, much more importantly, watching in awe to see what God is doing (v. 3). As with the Jerusalem apostles, the mission of Paul and Barnabas is supported and authenticated by the 'signs and wonders' that go along with the faithful proclamation of God's word. The 'word of grace' (and if it isn't that, it isn't the good news of Jesus) is matched by deeds of grace, healing and mending God's broken world.

Division in the city

The scandal of division can't be evaded (v. 4): the whole city is forced to take sides between 'the Jews' and 'the apostles'. This (with 14:14) is the only place where Luke calls Paul and Barnabas apostles. Normally he reserves the term for the twelve. It may reflect a different source, one with a more distinctively anti-Jewish stance than most of his narrative. Alternatively, it could simply reflect a wider and older usage, in which *apostolos* means 'delegate', as it does in 2 Corinthians 8:23. Paul and Barnabas here are acting as delegates of the church in Antioch from which they were sent out (13:4) and to which they will in due course report back (14:26–27). Eventually, the situation gets out of control (v. 5): the only solution is to recognise the inevitable, move on and start again (v. 6).

A narrative of exclusion

We need to be very careful when reading texts like this. Luke is not attempting to write a neutral, objective account. Like Paul, he has experienced persecution, and knows at first hand the bitterness of rejection by his own community. Christians in these first generations were always a small, precarious minority, dependent for their survival on the goodwill of the civic authorities. Luke's narrative is designed to instil courage and endurance in communities facing more official persecution. Yet, for us in the 21st century, it is impossible to read these narratives without an awareness of the centuries of Christian ascendancy that reversed the power structures and made Jews, not Christians, a persecuted minority in Europe. Luke could not have imagined the situation that led to the Holocaust, but we have to be careful not to perpetuate any reading of his narrative that demonises 'the Jews' as the enemies of 'the apostles' and allows Christians to ignore or even support persecution of Jews.

Prayer

Father, help us to speak your word with grace and to meet rejection with love.

45 Acts 14:6-18

Miracle at Lystra

Once again, Luke moves from a generalised summary of Paul's evangelistic activity (vv. 6-7) to a sharply focused, vivid scene that brings the story to life. This episode gives Paul a miracle to match Peter's healing at the temple gate in Jerusalem (ch. 3), and allows us a rare chance to overhear what Paul actually said when he was preaching to Gentile audiences.

Saving faith

Paul is imperceptibly getting deeper and deeper into foreign territory here. Lycaonia (v. 6) is a distinct region of southern Asia Minor, with its own language (v. 11) – not a dialect of Greek – and its own distinctive patterns of religious belief. In Paul's world, the countryside is always a different world from the city, more conservative and less assimilated to the international patterns of Greco-Roman culture. But the man sitting at the town gate of Lystra as Paul and Barnabas approach (v. 8) suffers from a problem that transcends culture. Unable to walk from birth, he is simply classed as *adunatos*, powerless, with no recourse but to sit and watch the world go by, relying on family and passers-by for charitable handouts.

There's nothing wrong with his ears, though, and in fact there's quite a bit of intent listening and watching on both sides here. Paul clearly has the feeling that at least one member of the crowd is really listening (v. 9), and in turn (like Peter at the Gate Beautiful, 3:4) fixes his attention firmly on the one person who has grasped what's on offer in this chance encounter. The good news that Paul brings is all about salvation through faith, and here is one man who longs for healing, wholeness, all that is comprised in the biblical concept of salvation – and clearly has faith that he can find it in Paul's God. That takes faith on Paul's side too. There's no room for whispering in corners here. Paul simply has to shout aloud the offer of resurrection life in Christ: 'Get up and stand straight on your feet' (v. 10).

The gods have come down to earth

Miracles are not self-interpreting: they need a framework of interpretation, and the townspeople naturally call on their own mythology to help them unpack what is going on here. A famous local story tells of the gods Jupiter (Zeus) and Mercury (Hermes) coming down to earth, knocking on door after door and failing to find a welcome, until a humble old couple named Baucis and Philemon open the doors of their cottage and offer them the best of their poverty-stricken fare.[8] Ironically, the crowd here identify Paul, the speaker, as Hermes, the messenger and mouthpiece of the gods, and the quieter Barnabas as Zeus, the king of the gods himself (vv. 11–12). It's a timely reminder that Greek religion has not only its own gods but its own value system, one in which the word plays a much less prominent role than it does in the Bible.

The living God

The joke pales when the apostles suddenly realise what is going on – the Lystrans are not just using a figure of speech. These pagans understand well that there is only one proper response to the presence of the divine, and that is worship (v. 13). Paul and Barnabas' reaction is swift and dramatic (v. 14). The prophetic action of tearing their clothes arrests the crowd's attention and holds it long enough for Paul to try – somewhat haltingly – to explain why he is so horrified at their natural desire to offer sacrifice to these messengers of the divine. The impromptu sermon that follows (vv. 15–17) illustrates the dangers of relying on 'signs and wonders' without a common theological frame of reference. We get a glimpse here of what that frame of reference might look like: an orthodox condemnation of idolatry based on the appeal to a common humanity (v. 15), a proclamation of good news which does not mention Jesus at all, but concentrates on the living creator God revealed to 'all the nations' (v. 16) in an outpouring of providence and grace (v. 17).

We shall see in chapter 17 a more fully developed version of Paul's message to the pagan world. Here there is just a hint of judgement (v. 16), but the major emphasis is on the appeal to turn away from idols to serve the living and true God (compare 1 Thessalonians 1:9) who showers us (v. 17) with gifts.

For discussion and prayer

How do we set about preaching the gospel in a post-Christian world that has never read the Bible and does not share our frame of reference?

46 Acts 14:19–28
Closing the circle

Lasting results in mission are built not just on the dramatic and miraculous, or even on the heroic and prophetic. Now Paul has to take steps to ensure the survival of the tiny fledgling Christian communities he has planted. In this final section of the first missionary journey, Luke gives us a rare glimpse of Paul in consolidation mode, an essential aspect of his ministry that forms the underlying concern of Paul's own letters.

Death and resurrection

We never get a chance to find out how Paul's sermon went down with its intended audience. The hostility and division that Paul had left behind him in Iconium come back to dog his footsteps (v. 19), and the pagan crowd (crowds are generally fickle in Luke's eyes) is quickly persuaded to abandon its awestruck posture and join in an act of violent expulsion. Being stoned and left for dead is the most violent thing that has happened to Paul so far, and it illustrates how thin is the line that separates adulation from rejection in the sensationalist world of the wonder-worker. Having thrown in his lot with Stephen and the followers of the Persecuted One (9:5), Paul is now really beginning to experience what life is like on the other side of the tracks. But he is not alone: the 'disciples' encircle him (v. 20) in a touching gesture of solidarity and protectiveness, enabling him to get up and walk back into the city that has thrown him out.

Strengthening and encouragement

It is time to move on: first eastwards to Derbe, then back westwards to Lystra, Iconium and Pisidian Antioch (v. 21). Note the sequence of events so economically described in Derbe: preaching the gospel has to be followed by making disciples, the essential next step for survival. These tiny churches cannot rely on their apostolic founders always being there. They have to have the seeds of their own survival built in from the start. Precisely how they survived, here and across the Mediterranean world, is an astonishing story, largely untold, but in the next few verses Luke gives us the essential clues. The task of the itinerant apostles is to strengthen the hearts of the local congregations and encourage them to remain in the faith, and one aspect of this encouragement is the warning that the experience of persecution is built into the job description of being a Christian (v. 22). 'Don't lose heart when this happens,' says Paul; 'I warned you beforehand.' Knowing what to expect is half the battle; and the other half is keeping our eyes on the goal, never losing sight of the glorious vision of what it means to belong to God's kingdom (v. 22).

Patterns of ministry

The other plank in Paul's survival plan for local congregations is strong local leadership. Probably this should be taken as a type-scene for the later missions too. Using the familiar synagogue pattern of a body of 'elders' for each congregation (v. 23), Paul creates a strong dual ministry structure of local elders linked in a network whose mobile agents (as we shall see) are the itinerant apostolic ministers. Fundamental to both, however, is the action of the living God: the one who inspired their loyalty and devotion in the first place is the one to whom Paul can safely commit them for the future.

Back to base

The last few verses of this chapter (vv. 24–28) detail the route that Paul's party takes back home to Antioch in Syria, travelling through Pisidia to Pamphylia, preaching the word in Perga and then dropping down to Attalia (modern Antalya) on the coast. Then it's home to Antioch by the shortest sea route, back to the community that had 'committed them to the grace to God for the work that they had completed' (v. 26). There's an indescribable sense of achievement in those words. There is nothing quite like the feeling of having launched out in faith, taking the risk of trusting God – and finding that God is with you, opening doors and acting in this world which is God's world (v. 27). It's quite sufficient for a period of rest and rejoicing (v. 28).

Prayer

Now to him who by the power at work within us is able to accomplish abundantly far more than all we can ask or imagine, to him be glory in the church and in Christ Jesus to all generations, forever and ever. Amen.
EPHESIANS 3:20–21 (NRSV)

47 Acts 15:1–3
Controversy at Antioch

Paul has every reason to relax for a bit: he has a new name, a new vocation, a new mission field. But he's forgotten the folks back home.

The circumcision debate

Just when everything seemed to be going so well – a growing, bustling church in Antioch sending out missionaries in an act of faith, learning to trust the Holy Spirit, planting churches in unexplored territory and discovering a whole new mission field among the Gentiles – controversy rears its ugly head. 'Certain people' (Luke is careful not to give them any kind of official status) come down to Antioch from Judea (v. 1) to say, 'You're doing it all wrong. You can't just bypass the Sinai covenant and sign people up to faith in Jesus – it doesn't make sense. God has revealed once for all in the scriptures the means of salvation. How can you just set it aside?'

It is important to listen to both sides of this controversy. We get a slightly different perspective in Galatians 2, which gives us Paul's personal view on the controversy at the time it was all happening. There is a long and complicated scholarly debate over the relationship between Luke's account of the apostolic council here and the events described in Galatians. It is difficult to reconcile the two accounts, and it seems most likely that Luke, writing some 40 years later, didn't have access to precise timings (who would remember all this after the protagonists had all passed on?), and has conflated two events to give a general impression of the way the controversy worked. Either way, Paul's letter gives us a good idea of the way the controversy blew up, and of what Paul himself would have said to justify his own position (Galatians 2:15–20).

What's at stake?

The other side in the debate has a theological viewpoint too, however – a viewpoint based on fidelity to God's revealed word in scripture. This is the viewpoint represented by Peter's anguished and tentative deliberations over the call to meet Cornelius in chapter 10 – the beginning of the story to which this chapter effectively forms the coda. In fact,

Paul doesn't get a chance to speak in Luke's version of the story: it is Peter who has the decisive word, as we shall see. And it is important for us, reading the story now as 21st-century Christians, to be prepared to hear both sides. It is much too easy to dismiss Paul's opponents as 'the Judaisers' or 'the circumcision party', as if the problem was all to do with 'them' and not 'us'. At one level, this controversy is about holiness – about what it means to be living as God's called and chosen people in God's world. More broadly, we could see it as a debate about inclusion and exclusion, about the terms on which we are prepared to welcome strangers into our religious communities. Do they have to change to become like us, or are we prepared to let them change the nature of our community? This is not simply a controversy from the past, but one that is reflected time and time again in the history of God's people – not least in current controversies over sexuality or medical ethics. All of us, Jew and Christian alike, have to wrestle continually with the tension between law and grace, between preserving the tradition and moving forward in the Spirit, between God's revealed will in scripture and the work of the Spirit in God's world.

Argument and debate

Acts 15 is also about how to deal with dissension and debate within God's people, about how the church acts to tackle a potentially destructive conflict. Jerusalem here assumes, for the first time in Acts, a mediatorial role, with both sides sending delegates to argue their case before the apostles and (also for the first time) the elders of the Jerusalem church, assuming implicitly the role of the Sanhedrin as an arbiter and repository of traditional wisdom in Jewish society. The delegates' route through Phoenicia and Samaria (v. 3) assumes the character of a triumphal procession, giving Paul and Barnabas an opportunity to relate the conversion of the Gentiles to the Christian communities all along the road.

Reflection

The story begins with the experience of two individuals and expands step-by-step into a debate and decision of the church as a whole. In the process, the church discovers new dimensions of what 'we believe'.

Luke Timothy Johnson, *Scripture and Discernment: Decision making in the church*, revised edition (Abingdon Press, 1996), p. 107.

48

Acts 15:4–11

The apostolic council

It's easy for the old, traditional centres in church life to think they have all the answers, and for those who have traditionally been recipients of 'mission' to think they have nothing to contribute. This passage encourages both sides to see matters in a different light.

Learning to listen

Listening is essential to any genuine process of trying to discern God's will, and there is a remarkable amount of both listening and silence going on in this passage – but that takes time to establish. The first step is a warm welcome (v. 4) from the whole church in Jerusalem, giving Paul and Barnabas the opportunity to tell their story, together with their own reflection on it. It is about what God has been doing (not about what the missionaries have been doing) among the Gentiles. The first reaction to his account, though, is negative (v. 5): bringing in Gentile converts is fine, but they have to be real converts. In other words, they have to be circumcised and keep the Mosaic law. Note that this is not a dispute between insiders and outsiders but between fellow Christians with different views of what it actually means to make a commitment to Christ.

Peter's testimony

The next step is to convene a formal apostolic conclave of the apostles and elders (v. 6) to discuss the matter. The first impression is nothing but a confused noise of argument and debate (v. 7). The key to unlocking the whole sterile controversy and moving it forward lies in Peter's willingness to give his own testimony. Being willing to stand up and say 'I was wrong' testifies to a rare breed of courage and honesty in a church leader. God is the subject of all the verbs in these opening verses: it was God who chose Peter to speak to the Gentiles (v. 7); it was God who gave the Gentiles the visible testimony of the Spirit 'just as to us' (v. 8); it was God who 'made no distinction between us and them', cleansing their hearts through faith (v. 9). Here we are right back in Cornelius' front parlour, watching with bated breath as God's action in sending the gift of the Spirit (10:44) confirms Peter's internal hunch that it was right to go with the strangers, right to cross over into their territory.

It is only now, though, that we can hear Peter making the final theological connection between his vision of clean and unclean animals (10:11–15) and the visit to Cornelius. How did God 'cleanse' the Gentiles' hearts? Not by righteous deeds (which is what we might have expected from 10:35) but by faith – 'just it was as for us' (v. 9). Here we have proof that God does not discriminate between Jews and Gentiles. How do we know? Because of the gift of the Spirit. And because of that visible gift, we can make deductions about the invisible inner person, the 'heart' that only God sees (v. 8). This same fundamental point of God's refusal to discriminate underlies verse 11: we believe that salvation comes through the grace of the Lord Jesus, and so do they.

The yoke of the commandments

The practical conclusion comes in verse 10, with a direct appeal to the assembly: 'Why do you put God to the test?' This is emotive language reminiscent of Gamaliel's appeal to the Sanhedrin (5:39), and it expresses one of the central dilemmas of Acts. Are we capable of discerning the new things that God is doing, or are we so determined on maintaining our own loyalty to past ways of interpreting God's will that we end up fighting against God? The issue here, though, is a practical one: what are Gentiles committed to when they enter the community of the Messiah? In traditional Jewish thought, accepting circumcision meant (gladly and willingly) 'taking on oneself the yoke of the commandments', that is, taking up Israel's privilege of trying to keep the whole of God's law. But, says Peter, this is a yoke that neither we nor our fathers were able to shoulder, so why put it on the necks of Gentile believers?

Reflection

The place where we are, at this apparent edge, is where God is doing new things. And those who daily see the new things that God is doing in the world have the obligation toward God and toward the rest of the Christian world to go back to the old centers, which often have lost much of their vision, taking to them our renewed vision of what God is doing today.

Justo Gonzalez, *Acts: The gospel of the Spirit* (Orbis, 2001), pp. 179–80.

49 Acts 15:12–18
James intervenes

Testimony and silence go together in this delicate debate. Peter's testimony creates the silence that finally allows the testimony of Paul and Barnabas to be heard (v. 12). Then it's their turn to be silent to hear a new voice (v. 13).

James of Jerusalem

James has not been properly introduced up to now in Acts (apart from the brief note in 12:17), and even now Luke seems to assume that his readers will know who he is. He is one of the brothers of the Lord mentioned briefly at 1:14 and has clearly come to play an important role in the Jerusalem church. It is typical of Luke's lack of interest in church governance that he does not trouble to explain what has been going on in the Jerusalem church while the narrative focus has been on Antioch and Paul's mission. Paul calls James one of the 'so-called pillars' of the Jerusalem church (Galatians 2:6–9) and believes that the troublemakers of Galatians 2:12 came from James (although James denies this in Acts 15:24, or at least implies that they had exceeded their brief). Later tradition makes James the first bishop of Jerusalem, but the letter issued by the council and the decision it records (vv. 22, 23) come from the group, not from the individual.

An authority of listening

What is important about James is that he has the moral authority to comment on what has been happening and to command the attention of the whole assembly (v. 13). It is an authority based first of all on listening. James has been silent all this time, listening to Peter's account of his experience in Caesarea (15:7–11) and listening to Paul and Barnabas (v. 12), the centre being prepared to listen to what is going on at the margins. Within those stories, there is a process of listening to God, discerning the signs that God is at work in unexpected ways and places.

For James, the point that emerges most clearly from Peter's story is 'first God' (v. 14): God's action out there in the world comes first. It seems clear that James is referring to Peter's story here, using formal, biblical-sounding language that echoes God's original choice of his people from among the nations of the world in such Old Testament passages as Deuteronomy 14:2 (cf. Exodus 19:5; 23:22; Deuteronomy 7:6). The verb *epeskepsato* (NRSV 'looked favourably') is the same as that used in the Benedictus at Luke 1:68, 78, and conveys the sense of 'God's decisive, liberating action on behalf of the persons concerned'.[9] What happened in Caesarea, James implies, is the liberation of a new people as exciting and dramatic as the exodus story, and it is happening before your very eyes.

The authority of scripture

The second essential component in James' authority is his ability to listen to the word of God in scripture and to discern how the 'this' of God's action now corresponds to the 'that' of the prophetic witness. Theological discernment means holding together the new and the old, the action of the living Spirit with the revealed words of the eternal God (v. 15). The passage James chooses to provide the scriptural warrant for the Gentile mission (vv. 16–17) is from Amos 9:11–12. It is not the most obvious one to our way of thinking, and the argument depends on the ancient Greek translation of the Hebrew Bible. Jewish biblical scholars believed that only the consonantal text of the Hebrew Bible was inspired, so in Hebrew it is easy to read 'the remnant of Edom' (Amos 9:12, NRSV) as 'the rest of humanity' (reading Adam in place of Edom). That gives us the sense 'all other peoples' (Acts 15:17, NRSV), a minimal verbal alteration of the Hebrew that completely reverses the sense of the text. In the Greek Bible, 'humanity' becomes the subject of the sentence instead of its object, so that the text becomes a prophecy of the Gentiles 'seeking the Lord'. This passage probably formed part of an early Christian collection of *testimonia* or proof texts. James uses the exegetical techniques of his own day in the service of an apostolic fidelity to God's revelation to the past that includes adaptation to God's revelation in the present.

Reflection

The basic decision, after all, is to let God be God, to say 'yes' to the work of the Lord, which goes before the church's ability to understand or even perceive it.

Luke Timothy Johnson, *Scripture and Discernment: Decision making in the church*, revised edition (Abingdon Press, 1996), p. 107.

50 Acts 15:19-29
The apostolic decree

James' solution is a neat compromise. Gentile Christians do not need to be circumcised, and are not bound to keep the whole Mosaic law (vv. 19, 28). Note that this is a ruling *for Gentile Christians* (v. 23). There is nothing in it to prevent Jewish Christians from continuing to keep the law if they so desire; in fact, that is almost certainly James' unexpressed premise. But this does not mean that Gentile believers are under no moral constraints at all – heaven forbid (as Paul would have said: Romans 6:2)! In fact, all the New Testament epistles seek in a variety of ways to define the moral code under which Christians now live. They are subject to the 'law of Christ', which means the law of love (Romans 13:8; 1 Corinthians 13; Galatians 5:14; 6:2) – and, as Paul shows in Romans 14 and 1 Corinthians 8—10, one of the things this means is prioritising the needs of my brother or sister in Christ above my own 'rights' to express my freedom in Christ.

James' solution seems to focus on this area, the area thrown into relief by the Antioch controversy (Galatians 2) and hinted at in Acts 11:1-10: that is, the practical issue of maintaining table-fellowship between two different groups of Christians living by different dietary regulations.

The Noahide laws

There are two suggestions as to what precisely is meant by the restrictions proposed by James (v. 20) and circulated in the apostolic decree (v. 29). One is that this is a version of the moral laws which, in Jewish tradition, were part of God's covenant with Noah and his descendants after the flood (Genesis 9:1–17). Jewish thinkers regarded these as constituting a basic 'natural law' binding on all humanity. The traditional number of the Noahide laws is seven, but contemporary lists vary from three to 30, focusing on the core areas of idolatry, sexual immorality and bloodshed. 'Pollutions of idols' (v. 20) is a more general term for impurity derived from contact with pagan worship, and is glossed more specifically as 'idol foods' at verse 29 (cf. also 21:25): that is, food that has been sacrificed to a pagan deity. This was the most likely form in which Jews or Christians might come into contact with this form of impurity.

The law of the alien

The other possibility is that the list is derived from the prohibitions binding on 'the alien who sojourns among you' in Leviticus 17—18, which includes these three with the addition of 'things strangled'. This fourth prohibition ties the restrictions more closely to the dietary restrictions of observant Jews and makes it easier to read 'from blood' as a dietary rather than a moral restriction. This would fit in with the Antioch incident as described in Galatians 2:11–14, and could be seen as a move designed to make it easier to maintain table-fellowship between Gentile and Jewish believers. But some early manuscripts omit this clause and add in its place a negative version of the Golden Rule ('And not to do to others whatever they do not wish to be done to them'). This turns the list more obviously into a list of fundamental ethical rules, with 'blood' meaning 'bloodshed' – that is, murder.

The council decrees

James gives his considered opinion (v. 19), but it is the whole assembly – the apostles and elders plus the whole church – who make the final decision (v. 22). Luke uses the language of a formal civic decree, familiar from countless inscriptions and imperial edicts across the Mediterranean world. The decree is then translated into a formal letter (vv. 22–23), sent back with Paul and Barnabas and two official delegates from Jerusalem to the church in Antioch which had requested a ruling, and to 'the brothers in Syria and Cilicia' (v. 23, Paul's home province). The letter throws a fascinating light on the processes of decision making in the early church: the decision is the result of a formal conclave and has the seal of the Holy Spirit (v. 28). It gives an implied reprimand to the unauthorised zealots who were trying to impose unnecessary restrictions on new converts, and gives a formal seal of approval to Paul's mission (vv. 25–26).

For discussion and prayer

What happens when the needs of Christian fellowship seem to conflict with Christian freedom – or with the desire to impose a strict moral code on new believers?

51 Acts 15:30—16:3

Paul the missionary: phase two

This episode marks a decisive break for Paul in more ways than one, and changes his relationship both with Antioch and with Jerusalem. He returns to Antioch with two new colleagues and an endorsement of the Gentile mission initiated by the church in Antioch, but his own vision embraces wider horizons.

Mission accomplished

The immediate task is to take back the council's decision to Antioch, where the problem first arose. A formal meeting of the body of believers is convened (v. 30), and the decision is received with joy as an affirmation of this frontline church's sense of the Spirit's leading (v. 31). Judas and Silas (v. 32) were clearly well chosen for their task of mediating between the centre and the margins – congenial to the believers in Antioch, equally open to the Spirit and able to encourage and strengthen the church. There is some confusion in the manuscripts about the Jerusalem delegates' return to base (vv. 33–34): did they both go back? If so, how did Silas come to be available for Paul's next mission (v. 40)? Luke is notoriously vague about chronology, and the periods covered in verses 33–36 may be a matter of months rather than days.

A break with Barnabas

The initial result of the delegation to Jerusalem is a period of affirmation and consolidation in Antioch (v. 35), but Paul's restless vocation will not leave him content to stay in one place for long. He has not forgotten the fledgling communities that sprang into being on his first missionary excursion (v. 36).

First, though, Paul breaks with his long-standing friend and mentor Barnabas (vv. 37–39). This must have been painful: verse 39 uses strong language indicating profound irritation or exasperation. The immediate cause was poor John Mark, Barnabas' cousin (as we discover from Colossians 4:10), the young man who had left them at the beginning of the journey to Pamphylia (13:13). Did Paul feel this desertion as a lack of personal loyalty? Or did he simply doubt John Mark's roadworthiness for another long trip? Luke does not tell us, but the split must have been significant for him to mention it at all. This is the last time Barnabas appears in the story of Acts, although he is mentioned affectionately by Paul in 1 Corinthians 9:6. John Mark's tracks reappear at intervals across the later Pauline letters (see Colossians 4:10; 2 Timothy 4:11; Philemon 24) and also at 1 Peter 5:13. Later tradition treats him as Peter's companion and secretary in Rome.

A new team

The split with Barnabas heralds the first steps towards building a new team. Paul's vision of ministry was always collaborative, and we can see from his letters that he has an astonishing capacity to deploy a complex team of delegates from a constantly mobile base. Two of the new team who meet us in the later epistles are introduced here. Silas (vv. 32, 40) is almost certainly the same as Paul's later companion Silvanus: Paul always uses the Latin form of his name, Luke the Greek. He will be Paul's major partner in the next phase of his mission (see 2 Corinthians 1:19; 1 Thessalonians 1:1; 2 Thessalonians 1:1).

Timothy (vv. 1–3) is different. Hand-picked from among the firstfruits of the first mission, the son of a mixed marriage, this is a young man who has already shown his survival capacity in the testing conditions of the frontier church in Lystra. Timothy's mother (Eunice), along with his grandmother Lois, are described in 2 Timothy 1:5 as women of faith – the same characteristic that Luke singles out here (v. 1). As a Jewish woman married to a Greek, Eunice is rather typical of the earliest Christian converts: belonging by faith and heritage to the Jewish community, but marginalised by marrying out. Timothy is one of the first 'second generation' converts of the new faith, a welcome sign that discipleship can pass from one generation to another (2 Timothy 3:15). Having a Jewish mother, Timothy was legally Jewish, so Paul's decision to circumcise him (v. 3) is perfectly consistent with Paul's own policy in 1 Corinthians 9:20, and equally with the decision not to circumcise Titus (Galatians 2:3), who was not Jewish.

Prayer

When we fail you, Lord, help us not to despair. Give us the confidence to come back to your love and the humility to pick ourselves up and try again.

52 Acts 16:4–10
The roads not taken

It's not always easy when the Spirit says 'No', especially when we are busting with new ideas, new projects, new glimpses of great works to do for God. But Paul and his party need time for foundation-laying: travelling together, learning to trust one another, learning to trust God and to seek God's direction together.

An episcopal visitation

From this point on, Paul becomes more and more a freelance operator, learning to trust the Spirit for himself, but increasingly divorced from HQ. Back home in Antioch, all his friends can do is to entrust him to God's grace (15:40). The new journey begins as a pastoral visit to the churches founded on the first missionary journey in chapters 13—14. Paul's vision of the apostolic office already includes a commitment to 'oversight' (15:36), the continuing duty to care for an ever-expanding flock that was to take up so much of Paul's energies in the years to come. He finds the congregations flourishing, growing both in numbers and in the strength of their faith (v. 5). Paul takes the land route this time, up through northern Syria and Cilicia, then through the mountain passes of the Taurus to link up with the Via Sebaste leading westwards towards Asia. Was this area included in the 'Cilicia' of the apostolic decree (15:23)? Paul clearly considers it part of his brief to convey the decisions of the apostolic council to this region as well (v. 4).

A change of plan

So far, so good; but Paul has no intention of stopping there. The Lycaonian-speaking population of Lystra had been temporarily impressed by the miracle of 14:8–18, but there was not much scope for sustained evangelisation in the non-Greek villages of these upland areas. Paul's natural route would have been to make directly for the prosperous Greek cities of the Aegean coast and to open up the Roman province of Asia for the gospel. But, at a fork in the road (probably somewhere around Antioch of Pisidia), a fateful decision is taken and the party decides to head north, not west (v. 6).

Galatia was a huge province which included Lycaonia and the cities of Derbe, Lystra, Iconium and Antioch in its southern region. Phrygia (technically within the province of Asia) lies along its western border. The old trade route through Antioch runs north through Phrygia towards Bithynia and the populous Greek settlements of the Black Sea coast (v. 7). But again, the Spirit says 'No'; so, cutting down past the mountainous region of Mysia, the puzzled and frustrated little party find themselves in the busy port of Alexandria Troas, the natural embarkation point for crossing over into Europe (v. 8).

Journeying with the Spirit

By the time they get to Troas, Paul and his party have travelled almost as far north as they will travel south in chapters 16—18. Was this all a completely fruitless journey? Not entirely: next time Paul passes this way, there will be 'disciples' to be strengthened and to offer fellowship, both in Phrygia and Galatia (18:23) and in Troas (20:6–12). Wherever Paul travels, the seed is sown, one way or another. Nevertheless, there is a mounting sense of frustration in this journey as the Spirit balks Paul's plans in one place after another. Ever since his acrimonious split with Barnabas, there is a sense that Paul is striking out on his own, moving into a territory without signposts. This mission, unlike the first, is not planned and directed by the home church. Nevertheless, Luke makes it plain that the whole journey is under the guidance of the Holy Spirit (who is also the 'Spirit of Jesus', vv. 6, 7).

Silas, we should not forget, had prophetic gifts, as did Paul himself. And the final step, too, there in the harbour town backed by Mount Ida, where the only way out is by sea, comes as the result of a revelatory vision in which Paul sees a man from Macedonia pleading for help (v. 9). It is a dream shared with his companions: verse 10 shows that this is a team decision, based on a team discernment. It's the clue the party has been waiting for. Finally, after all the 'No's, there is an unambiguous 'Yes'. It's time to take to the sea.

For discussion and prayer

How do we look for the guidance of the Spirit in our own journey (or as a church)?

53 Acts 16:11–15

A seller of purple dye

The 'we concluded' of 16:10 tells us that the team has acquired a new member – either Luke himself or somebody whose diary he had access to. Either way, there is a new vividness and immediacy about the next phase of the story, especially in relation to travel.

Over to Macedonia

The party's new diarist speaks as a business-like and experienced traveller, someone who knows his way around the shipping routes of the Mediterranean seaboard and relishes the circumstantial details of the journey. The first leg of this new phase of the journey is by sea over to the island of Samothrace, then across the Saronic Gulf to Neapolis (New City) on the Macedonian coast (v. 11). Then it's back to the Roman road – a relief, probably, after trekking across the high plateaux of Anatolia – a road with a sense of direction. The Via Egnatia led from the Aegean coast straight across Macedonia to the ports of the Adriatic, and then to Brundisium (Brindisi) and Rome. It was the obvious route to follow into this new territory, and it leads straight to Philippi, a city with a strong sense of its own importance and of its place in the imperial economy.

Luke tells us that Philippi was a colony (v. 12), a little bit of Rome on Macedonian soil, populated by civil war veterans from the Roman army and imbued with a distinctively Roman identity. It must have presented a distinctive challenge to Paul, faced with a blank wall of imperial indifference and a gratuitous display of Roman military power, very different from the cosmopolitan eastern cities of Tarsus and Jerusalem or from the remote upland villages of the Anatolian plateau. But all roads lead to Rome, and the milestones along the Via Egnatia would make it clear just how close the city was getting – no further, overland, than Paul had already travelled from Antioch. Was this where Paul first began to form his desire to see Rome (19:21)? Perhaps, but he is certainly not going to get there by the direct route.

The women by the river

The party spend a few days in the city (v. 12), looking for an entrée. Paul's usual strategy of connecting with the local Jewish community is frustrated by the fact that he cannot find a synagogue. Perhaps the community was too small to have its own meeting place, or perhaps the Roman magistrates here were strict in applying to this little bit of Rome the rules enforced in the capital, which at this period forbade the cultivation of foreign worship within the city boundary. That makes it difficult to engage in public evangelism, too: you can't just turn up in an ancient city and take over the streets. Outside the city walls, however, on the banks of the river that provided running water for ritual baths, they find a group of women assembling for prayer on the sabbath (v. 13), and there a series of informal conversations bear their first fruit. Paul's strategy is based on finding common ground, sitting down and talking – not megaphone evangelism, but 'gossiping the gospel'.

A house church is born

Lydia (v. 14) in many ways epitomises the profile of these early Pauline communities. She is an independent businesswoman, obviously mistress of her own household and able to offer hospitality to a group of visiting scholars. Like dyers everywhere, she will tend to base her business by the riverside, on the city's margins, and in Philippi she is doubly marginalised. As an immigrant from Thyatira in a Roman city (and a woman into the bargain) she will be tolerated and taxed but hardly integrated into the civic life of the colony. As a god-fearer or 'worshipper of God', she will be similarly tolerated but not fully integrated into the life of the small Jewish community. Nevertheless – perhaps because of this marginality – she is receptive to the gospel and becomes the founding member of a new community, baptised along with her entire household (v. 15). Her house, hospitably offered as a base for Paul's operations, becomes the nucleus of the new house church. Hospitality was and remained the key to the establishment of church life in the cities of the empire. Patrons like Lydia offered a vital service to the church, not only through making physical space available for the church to meet in but also by offering some kind of political protection. The next episode, though, will make it clear how precarious their position is.

Prayer

Father, we thank you for Lydia, and for all who offer their homes as a base for the work of the gospel.

54 Acts 16:16–24
Exorcism and arrest

In the unfolding story, the narrator and his readers see the whole picture and have a broad idea of what is going on. If these Bible stories are familiar, it's even easier for us to take each development for granted, to see it as inevitable. But none of the characters inside the story has that privileged knowledge, and in real life we are the characters, not the narrator. A dramatic story like this is a good opportunity for an exercise in empathy: pick one of the characters and try to get under their skin. Then read the story again, slowly, and try to experience it from the point of view of your character. Forget what everybody else (including the reader) knows: just think about what your character knows.

The slave-girl

The slave-girl is even more marginalised than Lydia. She doesn't even have a name. She is just a female slave (v. 16) with a gift for divination – somebody who would probably be classed as mentally ill in modern Western society, but with a distinct potential for commercial exploitation. A 'Python' spirit is a spirit like the famous prophetic spirit that inspired the priestesses of Apollo at the Delphic oracle. Luke takes it for granted that such spirits exist and have their place in the divine economy. As with the demon-possessed people in the gospels, everything the girl says of Paul and his companions is true (v. 17), though couched in terms that make sense in a pagan environment. Numerous inscriptions from this area make it clear that devotion to 'God Most High' was common in this area, possibly as a result of Jewish influence. So what we have, in this unlikely form, is a prophetic message from the local divinities to the people of Philippi – and the message is that the gospel-gossip that Paul is sharing with the Jewish women at the riverside is a 'way of salvation' for the whole city.

The missionary

To Paul and his party, the slave-girl and her owners are initially just part of the colourful crowd of market vendors milling around the narrow streets leading out of the forum and impeding their way through to the river-gate. But somehow she's always there, following Paul and shouting after him, day after day: it's getting embarrassing (vv. 17–18). Of course, Paul could have taken her prophecy as an unsolicited testimonial and exploited it for his own ends, but that would be to treat her the same way as her masters do. Instead, he treats her the way Jesus did – as a real person who deserves to have control of her own life (v. 18).

The slave owners

To the slave owners, this is a gratuitous act of commercial vandalism. Slaves in ancient law were chattels – 'living tools', as the Greek philosopher Aristotle put it – possessed of certain physical or mental skills which could be used at will by their owners. And this was a pretty profitable one, a nice little earner, suddenly gone without trace. Looking into her eyes, they knew that they would never be able to manipulate her in quite the same way again. Their response is that nothing must be allowed to stand in the way of business interests (v. 19).

The magistrates

It's not too difficult for the slave's owners to exploit Paul's precarious position as a Jew in a Roman city (vv. 20–21), and magistrates and crowd readily concur (v. 22). In the Roman empire, you could preach what you liked as long as it didn't interfere with trade: then it became political. There is irony in the fact that Paul and Silas are accused of teaching unlawful Jewish customs, which Paul makes no attempt to deny. Jews were allowed to practise their own religion as long as they did not try to proselytise others. Because it was not comfortably polytheistic like most religions, Judaism was seen as antisocial by contemporary Roman writers: being Jewish (or Christian) meant detaching yourself from the normal civic religious practices of the empire, and that was always seen as dangerous. The punishment is being 'beaten with rods' (v. 22), a technical term for corporal punishment administered by Roman magistrates. Paul uses the same term at 2 Corinthians 11:25. Throwing them into jail (v. 24) is simply a way of asserting control, making sure they can't continue to peddle this mischievous superstition.

Reflection

Believing in God is okay as an add-on, as long as it doesn't interfere with the rest of my life, with business or with politics. Where have we heard that one before? What modern parallels can you think of for the characters in this story?

55 Acts 16:24–40
Prison and earthquake

Most Westerners take for granted the freedom to travel around the world on business or holiday trips, but many non-Westerners could tell us that international travel is a very different experience if you have the wrong kind of passport – or the wrong colour skin.

Paul the prisoner

Becoming a victim of the Roman judicial system was no joke. Paul and Silas are stripped of all human dignity, manacled to a beam in the innermost cells – hot, foetid, dark and smelly (v. 24). Finding the ability to pray in this situation (v. 25) is a mark of spiritual maturity. Having taken the step of faith, crossed over to Europe after that long fruitless trip north and made one convert, most of us would want to ask, 'Where is God in all this?' Yet Paul and Silas find the courage not only to pray (privately, desperately, silently) but to sing hymns – an act of public fellowship and defiance that reaches the ears of the jailer. Feeling the first tremors of an earthquake must have seemed at first like the last straw to the prisoners trapped in that airless cell (v. 26). But it is (literally!) an act of God, revealing God's presence in no uncertain terms, leaving the doors gaping open and the manacles broken. The messengers of the gospel can't be so easily constrained: there is a greater power than the emperor's at work here.

The jailer

We already know that the jailer is a conscientious town official, taking extra care to keep his prisoners safe in the innermost cells. Those special orders must mean that these prisoners must not be allowed to escape at any cost. So his first thought, on being jerked out of sleep by the earthquake, is that he has failed in his charge: the doors are open and the prisoners must have escaped (v. 27). Paul, though, has more at stake than his own personal safety. The jailer is not just a political symbol but a real person poised between disaster and salvation (v. 28), and Paul's intervention brings him back from despair to a glimpse of hope (v. 30). So the jailer, calling for light to illuminate that black pit of despair, becomes a paradigm for the readers' response to Luke's story, moving from despair and guilt to fearful trembling at the revelation of divine grace (v. 29), then to faith, to salvation, to baptism into a new community (vv. 30–33). Finding the light of grace in the pit of darkness rebuilds the bonds of humanity between the jailer and his charges. As he washes the prisoners' wounds, takes them home and puts a meal in front of them, his whole household is suffused with joy (v. 34). So when, in the morning, word comes down that Paul and Silas are to be released, the jailer's relationship with his prisoners is totally transformed (v. 36).

Let these men go

This was Paul's first real experience of being on the wrong side of the Roman legal system. To a Roman citizen on the road, Rome represented peace and stability, good roads and protection for travellers. But here in Philippi, Paul experiences Roman power from the underside, and it's not a happy experience. So when the magistrates, having left their prisoners to cool their heads overnight, send word to let them go, the curt formal message (v. 35) is met with a surprising refusal (v. 37). Paul is acutely conscious of the public degradation he has suffered and is determined to reverse it. He is not an object but a person, someone with a status that should actually mean something in the Roman world (v. 38), and especially in Philippi, where citizenship meant being 'Roman' in a particularly conscious way (see 16:21). As countless prisoners have found, the only answer to the attempt to dehumanise is to refuse to allow it: the dogged assertion of human worth is an essential response to tyranny in any form. So Paul leaves Philippi (v. 40), but on his own terms (v. 39) and after re-establishing contact with Lydia and the little group of 'brothers' (which must include sisters!) – the marginal group in that Roman colony which has the only citizenship that really matters (compare Philippians 3:20).

Prayer

Where can I go from your spirit? Or where can I flee from your presence? If I ascend to heaven, you are there; if I make my bed in Sheol, you are there… If I say, 'Surely the darkness shall cover me, and the light around me become night', even the darkness is not dark to you; the night is as bright as the day.
PSALM 139:7–8, 11–12 (NRSV)

56 Acts 17:1–9
Anatomy of a riot

Paul's missionary odyssey unfolds in a series of vivid vignettes, strung along the relentless plod of the journey. Luke's narrative gives little feeling for the passing countryside but conveys a strong sense of the road itself.

To Thessalonica

The next two staging-posts, Amphipolis and Apollonia, pass without incident. Paul's goal is Thessalonica, an ancient port city with a flourishing commercial centre. Here, there is a strongly established Jewish community with its own 'synagogue' (NRSV) or 'assembly' (v. 1) – not necessarily a building, but a formal weekly meeting for prayer and study of the scriptures. This is Luke's clearest statement yet that it was Paul's custom to attend the synagogue (v. 2), using the sabbath community gatherings as the obvious forum to expound his message (v. 3).

The crucified Messiah

There are twin strands to Paul's preaching (v. 3): it is grounded in scripture ('It was necessary' – that is, part of the divine plan), and it is based on personal experience ('This Jesus whom I proclaim to you'). It's the second strand that brings the message alive, with an unexpected slide into the first person. And the focus of the message itself has begun to shift. The bone of contention, the double helix that has to be held together at all costs, is the Messiah who both suffered and was raised from the dead. The magnetic centre of Paul's preaching is the crucified-and-risen one, the Jesus who suffered an ignominious death on the cross: this is the 'this' for which he has to find a 'that' in the scriptures. What texts he used, Luke does not tell us. Perhaps he expects us to remember the key text from Isaiah 53 that Philip used to 'preach Jesus' to the Ethiopian pilgrim (8:32–35). But he has already shown us Peter preaching that 'all the prophets' bear witness to this (3:18), and this is the heart of the teaching of the risen Christ (Luke 24:26, 46).

Varied responses

The response is slow but initially positive. Some at least of the Jewish community find Paul's words persuasive (v. 4) and throw in their lot with Paul and Silas, together with a significant number of Greek 'God-fearers', including not a few of the city's leading ladies. But (in what is now becoming a familiar pattern), Paul's message creates as many enemies as friends, and the fault lines in the community begin to show. 'The Jews' in verse 5 means effectively the rest of the community, all those who were not convinced by Paul's arguments. What binds them together is not jealousy (as in NRSV) but 'zeal', the fundamentalist conviction of righteousness that flies to the defence of a holy God – the same zeal that had driven the young radical Saul to persecute the church.

What follows is Luke's clinical analysis of the makings of a street riot. It's not hard to find troublemakers among the marketplace hangers-on, and once a crowd develops they need to find a scapegoat on which to vent their anger. Luke does not explain who Jason was, although we discover as the story unfolds that he has been acting as host to Paul and his friends (v. 6–7). If he is the same as the person mentioned in Romans 16:21, he was a relative of Paul.

Turning the world upside down

Did Jason realise what he was letting himself in for? There are times when even a simple act of hospitality becomes a political act. Failing to find Paul at the house, the mob leaders drag Jason and some other believers before the civic authorities. Thessalonica was not a Roman colony but a Greek city, governed by its sovereign *demos*, represented by elected magistrates known locally as *politarchs* (v. 6). The overarching rhetoric of loyalty is the same, however: to maintain even this much-prized degree of autonomy, the Greek cities had to demonstrate their loyalty to the emperor, and nobody wanted to get a name for harbouring political agitators. Precisely what 'decrees of the emperor' were in question here is unclear, but the implication is that Paul's preaching of the crucified Messiah was in effect advocating 'another king' (v. 7) whose lordship challenged Caesar's claims to absolute world authority. It seemed best, therefore, to play safe by extracting surety from Jason, presumably for Paul's good conduct (v. 9).

Reflection

Paul and Silas are accused of 'turning the world upside down' (v. 6). Could that be said of the church today? Should it?

57 Acts 17:10–21

From Beroea to Athens

Whatever the conditions of Jason's bond, he clearly couldn't undertake to stop Paul preaching the gospel, and presumably didn't want to. So the logical step is to send Paul on his way, a hurried departure by night (v. 10), but in the company of loyal friends who know the way and know, perhaps, that he can expect a better reception when he gets to the next town.

Reception in Beroea

Two cities; two very different faces of the gospel proclamation. Beroea is a kind of reverse image of Thessalonica – same synagogue (v. 10), different reaction to the gospel. Again, Paul goes straight to the Jewish community and finds a receptive audience, willing and eager to listen to his message and (more importantly) to check it out for themselves, searching the scriptures on a daily basis (v. 11) to see if what Paul says is true. The assumption is that if this message is God speaking, there must be something about it in God's word. Beroea is a model of a responsive community: not just 'some' but 'many' of the Jewish community believe, together with a number of Gentile women of good social standing and quite a few men (v. 12).

Paul has no time to enjoy or consolidate his gains, though. Delegates from Thessalonica turn up and repeat the same rent-a-crowd tactics that had proved so successful there. Having the volatile crowds of the city stirred up (v. 13) is just what these small Jewish communities want above all to avoid: as the situation in Philippi shows (16:20–22), their own position is precarious enough. So their understandable reaction is to get rid of Paul as quickly as possible – although Silas and Timothy, less high-profile and perhaps less inflammatory, remain behind (v. 14). For Paul, it's time to head back to the coast and find a passage to Athens (v. 15).

Waiting in Athens

Paul didn't waste his time in Athens 'just waiting'. This wasn't quite what he had planned, but it was an opportunity to use his eyes and ears to take the measure of this exciting and immensely varied place to which God had brought him. Athens wasn't a bad spot for a bit of enforced leisure! By Paul's time, Greek culture had become international, a near-universal means of communication all over the eastern Mediterranean. Athens, though, remained its emotional heartland, a site immortalised by the poets and dramatists that every Greek-educated child studied at school, and still home to the philosophical schools (like a combination of Oxford, Cambridge and Stratford-upon-Avon). This is the only place in all Paul's journeys where Luke gives us a visual perspective, a tourist's-eye view of the city (v. 16) – but Athens is still described very much through the eyes of a Jewish tourist, someone who sees the city not as a treasure-house of art but as 'full of idols'. It's the beliefs that animate people's lives, not the glories of the past, that interest Paul.

Talking to philosophers

Maybe because of Athens' iconic status, we see a change of tactics here. Paul continues to dialogue with Jewish residents and God-fearers in the synagogue (v. 17), but for the first time he is also prepared to join the more relaxed discussion in the marketplace, a long-standing Athenian tradition going back to the days of Socrates. In this city, the philosophers were still part of public life: the Stoics and Epicureans were the most popular exponents of philosophy in the Roman world, not so much cosmologists as lifestyle gurus. But the shadow of Socrates still haunts even this bastion of free speech. Socrates was executed by the good citizens of Athens in 399BC for introducing 'new deities' (*kaina damonia*) that the city did not believe in. The echo would not be lost on Luke's readers when Paul, in this same city, is charged with introducing 'strange deities' (v. 18, *xena daimonia*) and is summoned to explain himself in the ancient assemblage point of the Areopagus (Mars Hill), the place where philosophers were tried (v. 22). There is more than a hint of menace in the polite invitation (vv. 18–20).

Reflection

Active waiting means to be present fully to the moment, in the conviction that something is happening where you are and that you want to be present to it. A waiting person is someone who is present to the moment, who believes that this moment is the moment.
Henri Nouwen, *Seeds of Hope* (Darton, Longman and Todd, 1989), p. 103.

58 Acts 17:22–34
The unknown God

It's a breathtaking invitation, when you think of it. 'Can we know what you're talking about?' (17:19): literally, 'Is it possible for us to understand this? Can you explain it in words that make sense to us? Or is it just for insiders, the religious people who already talk your language?'

Building bridges

There is a maturity and breadth of vision in Paul's Areopagus speech that is light years away from the stammering, panic-stricken sentences of 14:15–17. In Lystra, Paul was reacting to an immediate situation. He was taken by surprise, not expecting outsiders to be interested in his message. Here, he has had time to reflect, to listen and observe, and to look more deeply at his audience. He can stand on the outside of the culture and denounce it as 'full of idols' (17:16) or he can look at the people and realise that the city is full of seekers (v. 22), full of people made by God, loved by God and reaching out to find God (vv. 24–27). Other ancient Greek writers speak of an Athenian custom of dedicating altars to 'unknown gods' (v. 23), but Paul's chance observation is more than just a clever pretext for a sermon. It shows an evangelist prepared to take seriously the reality of the human quest for God. Worship in ignorance (v. 24) is still worship; it deserves respect, not ridicule.

The God beyond

So where do we begin? Accepting the reality of our audience's conceptions doesn't mean being bound by their limitations. Paul has to start by expanding his listeners' view of God. 'I'm not talking about just any old unknown god,' Paul says. 'I'm talking about the God behind the gods, the creator of the universe' (v. 24). This is the God none of us can claim to 'know', because God is beyond human conception, beyond the most beautiful visual images and temples, beyond the most venerable sacrificial traditions, beyond religion itself (vv. 24–25). This God does not belong to any particular nation or culture. Nations and cultures are part of the world God made (v. 26), so God can't be owned by any one of them. The real God is far above the religious and ethnic divisions of the human race, beyond the furthest reaches of the human imagination (v. 27).

The God beside

Yet this God is also unimaginably close, closer than breathing, closer than family (v. 28). The quotation in verse 28 is from the great evocation of the universal deity of Zeus by the Stoic poet Aratus. And with closeness comes responsibility: this is a God who is not content to be passively sought by humanity, who seeks to evoke a response, who cares enough to nudge us out of our woefully inadequate ways of conceiving God (v. 29). The coming of the Christ means the dawn of a new era, not just for the Jewish people but for the whole of humanity. For both, though, this is a critical moment, a moment of judgement (v. 31, *krisis*; compare John 3:19–21). For the Gentile world, it means that the time of blissful ignorance is past (v. 30). The unknown God wants to be known, and that – for all humanity – involves repentance, a change of heart, being faced with the inescapable demands of a God who cannot be contained in the structures of human religion but only in the person of the risen Lord (v. 31).

We will hear you again

That, for this occasion, is as far as Paul gets. When it comes to the idea of a human being rising from the dead, the philosophers of the Areopagus are frankly incredulous (v. 32), although one or two are convinced (v. 34). As long as Paul stays on the level of philosophical generalities, he's safe; it's the person of Christ that's the stumbling-block. So this great set-piece speech falls short of setting out precisely how the Jewish Messiah is also good news for the Gentile world. It is noticeable, however, how closely the agenda of this speech follows the gospel that Paul himself claims to have preached to the Gentile converts of Thessalonica: see 1 Thessalonians 1:9, and compare the theme of judgement that dominates 1 Thessalonians, a letter written from or very soon after a visit to Athens, according to 1 Thessalonians 3:1.

Reflection

The mission and evangelism of the church would be much more effective if we were better able to build upon that instinct for God… which is so widely dispersed in our society.
Peter Forster

59 Acts 18:1–3
Tentmaking in Corinth

A change of venue, a change of pace and a chance to settle down for a while after the hustle and hurly-burly of Macedonia and Athens. Corinth was one of the great cities of the ancient world, a cosmopolitan Roman colony and a busy commercial centre straddling the Isthmus. Its twin ports, Cenchreae and Lechaeum, commanded the shipping routes of the Aegean and the Adriatic, and the Diolkos or Portway across the Isthmus created a valuable short cut between eastern and western Mediterranean.

Tentmaking

Here for the first time we get a glimpse of Paul's long-term missionary strategy. The (chance?) meeting with Aquila and Priscilla (v. 2) gives him a more secure base, an opportunity to earn his keep and an entrée into the city's commercial life. The life of a travelling artisan (v. 3) in many ways provided an ideal vehicle for the travelling evangelist. Such artisans were mobile (the tools of the trade could be easily packed up), and they had their own networks of business contacts across the Mediterranean. Paul's own ability to deploy a complex network of co-workers may well owe something to his business experience. Travelling artisans had a recognised place in the life of the city, without the special privileges of citizens but accepted (and taxed) as resident aliens. The workshop of Aquila and Priscilla provides a long-term base for Paul's operations, and solves the problem he had experienced in Philippi, Thessalonica and Athens. No one could just turn up in a Greek city (especially if it's also a Roman colony) and start preaching, but the shopfront of a typical workshop, opening directly on to the marketplace, could provide an ideal location for engaging in conversation with passers-by. The shop also gave Paul financial independence, something that was to prove useful in later years in his somewhat stormy relationship with his Corinthian hosts (see 1 Corinthians 9:6).

Aquila and Priscilla

Did Paul already know Aquila and Priscilla? It's not clear from Luke's narrative, but they were to become two of his most trusted associates (Acts 18:18, 26; 1 Corinthians 16:19; Romans 16:3; 2 Timothy 4:19). The name *skenopoios* (v. 3) is usually translated 'tentmaker', but could be used more widely of leather-workers. Tents, shop awnings, ships' sails or booths for the biennial Isthmian Games could all have provided good trade opportunities in Corinth.

Claudius' edict expelling the Jews from Rome (v. 2) should give us a date for this episode, but things are never as simple as they seem. The Roman writer Suetonius, writing in the early second century AD, mentions in his biography of the emperor Claudius that Claudius 'expelled the [or, some] Jews from Rome, because they were constantly causing disturbances at the instigation of Chrestus'.[10] This could be a garbled reference to riots within the Jewish community in Rome caused by the preaching of Jesus as Messiah (*Christos* would sound the same as *Chrestos* in first-century Greek). If so, this would be the earliest known reference to Christian activity in Rome, and would increase the possibility that Aquila and Priscilla were already Christians when they came to Corinth. A much later historian, Orosius, dates this event to the ninth year of Claudius' reign, AD49, which would fit well with the date of Gallio (see next section) and with other data of New Testament chronology. But this apparently insignificant detail also sounds a warning note: Rome is becoming an ominous presence in the wings of Paul's Aegean journey.

For discussion and prayer

If this world really is what the church has always said it is, the place and the vehicle of God's activity, and if therefore the world's activity displays all of the signs by which we have learned to recognise God (disfigured but never destroyed by the dirty marks which we make), then our ministry 'out there' becomes much clearer... We are to proclaim the word which was before the church began and which is in all the work of the world... Repentance and forgiveness, being God's properties, are also properties of all well run carpenters' shops.

Michael D. Ranken, 'A theology for the priest at work', in James M.M. Francis and Leslie D. Francis (eds), *Tentmaking: Perspectives on self-supporting ministry* (Gracewing, 1998), p. 281.

60 Acts 18:4–11
Church-planting in Corinth

The workshop in the marketplace provides a fruitful base for church-planting. Corinth was to prove one of Paul's most vibrant and challenging foundations, a church that gave him more heartache than all the others put together – or so it would appear from the letters he wrote to the Corinthians. But little of that appears here. Luke takes us back to the very foundations of the church.

To the Jew first

The initial pattern of evangelisation is familiar from Pisidian Antioch (ch. 13) and Thessalonica (ch. 17). Paul begins by getting involved with the local Jewish community and its weekly worship, engaging in dialogue with Jews and with Gentile sympathisers (v. 4). When Silas and Timothy arrive from Macedonia, they find Paul already fully engrossed in the business of the word, busy testifying to the Jews that the Christ, the life-changing and world-changing Messiah of Jewish expectation, is Jesus (v. 5). Once again, though, he fails to persuade the whole community (v. 6). The action of shaking out the garments is a prophetic action that indicates absolution from a spiritual responsibility (see 13:51). Like Ezekiel (Ezekiel 3:18–20), Paul is acutely conscious of his prophetic responsibility to proclaim God's word to his own people (compare 1 Corinthians 9:16–23). Only after he is convinced that the Jewish community has rejected his message does he feel free to turn to the Gentiles.

It is important not to confuse Paul's words in verse 6 with the so-called 'blood libel' of Matthew 27:25. This is not about assigning responsibility for the death of Jesus (neither Luke nor Paul ever implies that all Jews everywhere bear that responsibility); it is about the individual hearers accepting responsibility for their own response to the Christ. If prophets fail to preach the word assigned to them, then they must bear the heavy responsibility of failing to warn those to whom they are sent. But if they have delivered their message faithfully, the responsibility for accepting or rejecting it lies with the listener. Even so, Paul's decision to go to the Gentiles is not a decision for all time but a decision for Corinth: the drama of 'to the Jew first' will continue to be played out in each place he visits (see 18:19).

And also to the Greek

Once again, the preaching of Jesus as the Christ provokes a crisis, a double effect of rejection and acceptance. The move from Jew to Greek is described with some ceremony as a physical move from one building to another (vv. 6–7: 'synagogue' here must mean a building, since Luke speaks of it as 'adjoining' the house of Titius Justus). There is a sense here of a real community, probably known both to the author and to his first readers. Titius Justus (v. 7) is not mentioned anywhere else in the New Testament, but Crispus (v. 8) is named in 1 Corinthians 1:14 as someone baptised by Paul. Both names are Latin, reflecting Corinth's close links with Rome as a colonial foundation. As a synagogue official, Crispus would have been a wealthy patron of good standing in the city, a significant loss to the synagogue and a catch for Paul's splinter group. Titius Justus, too, as a house owner, would have been a valuable acquisition with the facilities to act as host to the church (which may be why Luke mentions him and Crispus).

I am with you

However (as John Wesley used to say), 'the best of all is, God is with us': whatever qualms Paul may have felt at leaving the Jewish community, a dream gives him the assurance of God's presence (vv. 9–10). The message is not only 'I will be with you' as you step into an uncertain future, but also 'I am already here.' Like Peter in Caesarea (ch. 10), Paul finds that God is already at work in this confusing pagan city: there is no territory outside the purview of the living God. So there's a sense of relief about the verb 'stayed' (NRSV) in verse 11. Eighteen months is longer than Paul has stayed anywhere for some time, and it enables him to do real foundational work in Corinth, teaching the word and building up the church. This is bread-and-butter stuff that Luke assumes but does not tell us about, except in this summary form.

Reflection

'Dialogue' and 'testimony' are two of the key words in Luke's description of Paul's church-planting. How important are they to us today?

61

Acts 18:12–22

Leaving Corinth

This period of settled expansion was not to last. Paul, in Luke's narrative, is not destined to settle anywhere for more than a couple of years. We are coming to the final stages of the drama, with the looming presence of the imperial city beginning to exert its pull over Paul's journey.

The new governor

Corinth was the administrative capital of the province of Achaea and the seat of the proconsul. The arrival of a new governor from Rome for his one-year tour of duty gives Paul's opponents in the synagogue an opportunity to get rid of him (v. 12). Gallio was the brother of the philosopher Seneca, and by chance we can date the year of his proconsulship from an inscription discovered at Delphi, which fixes his appointment to the twelfth year of Claudius' reign: AD51/52. The confrontation with Gallio serves as a foretaste of Paul's coming confrontation with the imperial power of Rome, and it brings the apostle face to face with the representative of the emperor who had just expelled the Jews from Rome.

Before the tribunal

Paul has left a trail of civic disturbance behind him on his unruly progression through Macedonia and damaging charges have been laid at his door: teaching un-Roman customs (16:21), acting against the emperor's decrees and advocating another king (17:7). These serious political accusations are so far unanswered, and the confrontation with Gallio gives Luke an opportunity to quote a ruling that Paul's teaching, however troublesome it may be for the Jewish community, is not in contravention to Roman law. The Roman empire was not a totalitarian state in the modern sense, and Rome had neither the desire nor the means to regulate the empire's myriad ways of worshipping God. The only 'law' that has been infringed by Paul's teaching, Gallio declares, is the law of the Jewish community – and that is purely an internal affair (vv. 14–15). Gallio's ruling thus identifies Paul's messianic Judaism as a legitimate sect within the broad spectrum of first-century Judaism, and establishes the important point that this Roman official at least sees no legal or moral fault in the activities of the church.

Luke does not tell us who Sosthenes is (v. 17), but if he is the same person as Paul's co-writer in 1 Corinthians 1:1, this is another synagogue official who has gone over to Paul's party.

Moving on

Despite his vindication at the tribunal, Paul takes this fresh outbreak of hostility as the signal to depart. It is more than three years since he left Antioch and he clearly feels that it is time to touch base again, so, after taking some time to tidy up his affairs, he takes ship for Syria (v. 18).

The visit to the barber's in Cenchreae is a tantalising note. Paul's vow should probably be understood in light of the nazirite vows of the Old Testament (see Numbers 6:2, 9), where the shaving of the head is one of the marks of a life dedicated to God's service, and it may be linked with Paul's planned return to the Jewish heartlands. He is not leaving alone, however, and does not make directly for Syria. Aquila and Priscilla (perhaps reflecting on their earlier experience of being hounded out of Rome as Jews) decide to move on too. This may be the point at which they became Paul's active co-workers in his ongoing mission, but they had no business in Syria, and Ephesus seemed as good a place as any to set up shop again – both in business and (as we shall see) in the gospel. Paul is not yet ready to settle down in Asia. He can't resist testing the waters, however, with a visit to the synagogue (v. 19) and finds a favourable response (v. 20), enough to make him promise to return (v. 21).

Touching base

So, finally (and much more quietly than on his return at the end of the first mission in 14:26–28), Paul slips back home to Antioch via Caesarea and Jerusalem. (The unexplained 'going up' in verse 22 probably indicates a visit to Jerusalem, perhaps to fulfil the vow undertaken in Cenchreae.) Paul's mission 'is not only preaching the gospel, converting people, and founding churches, but also creating and strengthening the ties among Christians and between churches'.[11]

Reflection

In the biblical vision, to believe in Jesus Christ implies and requires joining the community of the faithful… To believe in Jesus Christ is indeed a very personal matter, but not a private one.
Justo Gonzalez, *Acts: The gospel of the Spirit* (Orbis, 2001), p. 214.

62 Acts 18:23–28
Apollos and Paul

Luke's story in the second half of Acts is very much focused on Paul, but the next two episodes serve as a salutary reminder of the variety and diversity of early Christianity, and of the many criss-crossing storylines that Luke can only hint at.

Travelling up-country

Paul himself spends some time in Antioch (v. 23), perhaps waiting for the travelling season to open up the high passes of the Taurus again. Then it's back up through the Cilician Gates to make a systematic visitation of the disciples in 'the region of Galatia and Phrygia'. This is a variant of the phrase in 16:6 but probably means exactly the same – that is, the churches in Derbe, Iconium, Lystra and Pisidian Antioch founded by Paul and Barnabas on the first journey. Thus begins what is often referred to as Paul's 'third missionary journey', although, as we can see, Luke does not mark it as a significant new beginning in comparison with the first (13:1–3) and second (15:36—16:10) journeys. It's more helpful to think of it as 'phase 3' of the Pauline mission, which takes us down to Acts 20:38. This is the period of Paul's most intense letter-writing activity (1 and 2 Corinthians were written from Ephesus), the period when Paul describes himself as consumed by the daily pressure of 'the care of all the churches' (2 Corinthians 11:28). Luke never mentions Paul's letters (one of the many minor puzzles in his portrait of Paul), but on this trip we see Paul engaged as much in consolidation and encouragement as in mission, busily trying to keep in touch with an ever-expanding network of churches.

Apollos

In Ephesus, however, things have been moving on in Paul's absence: the church in Luke's story is never dependent on its 'stars' to make progress. Aquila and Priscilla, while still attending the synagogue (v. 26), are part of a circle of 'brothers' (v. 27): compare 1 Corinthians 16:19, where Paul sends greetings to Corinth from the church in their house.

Meanwhile, a new voice arrives from a totally unexpected quarter. Apollos was a Jew from Alexandria (v. 24), a member of the largest and most prosperous Jewish community in the Mediterranean diaspora. Alexandria was a sophisticated university city (home to the famous museum and library founded by the Ptolemies), and a major forum for interchange of Greek and Jewish culture at the highest level. Apollos was, Luke tells us, an eloquent man: good with words, highly educated and sophisticated, a man with all the verbal dexterity that impressed the Greek world (which Paul, by his own account, lacked: see 1 Corinthians 2:1–5). But Apollos was no mere academic or flashy speaker. He was also learned in the scriptures, able to combine the best of Jewish and Greek culture. More surprisingly, he was also 'instructed in the way of the Lord', and is able to draw on a fund of stories and teaching about Jesus, although he 'knows only the baptism of John' (v. 25).

Collaborative ministry

Had Apollos visited Judea and encountered John the Baptist's preaching there? We shall never know, but we have no warrant for doubting that Apollos was a genuine believer, even though there was something missing in his teaching, which Priscilla and Aquila notice when they hear him in the synagogue. Rather than issuing a public corrective (which would be humiliating) or telling him that he is not qualified to teach at all (which would be discouraging), Priscilla and her husband take him aside privately to share their own understanding of the Way (v. 26) – a brave step, considering the differing educational and social levels of the tentmakers and the scholar from Alexandria. The tiny group of brothers in Ephesus welcomes the newcomer with generosity, recognising his gifts and encouraging him to use them in the Lord's service and follow his own vision of mission to Corinth (vv. 27–28). Apollos then disappears from Luke's story, although Paul mentions him in 1 Corinthians 16:12 as a trusted colleague who had built on the foundation that Paul laid in Corinth (1 Corinthians 3:4–22). If Apollos' Corinthian fan club were inclined to set him up as a rival to Paul (1 Corinthians 1:12), Paul is careful not to blame Apollos himself.

For discussion and prayer

How quick are we to welcome God's gifts in others?

63 Acts 19:1–12

Paul in Ephesus

Paul, meanwhile, has been working his way down towards Ephesus by the upland route (v. 1), coming overland from Phrygia. This is the same journey he had attempted to make at 16:6 – and this time there is no impediment. Ephesus presents a new challenge to Paul. The challenge of the unknown always appealed to Paul's adventurous instincts. Ephesus is different, though: Paul is not the first to preach the gospel there, and he has to work out how to follow his own vision and vocation while respecting the vision that God has given to others. Ephesus raises the question: when our vision differs from somebody else's, how do we know what is right? What makes discipleship *Christian*?

The baptism of John

We already know that there is a small fellowship group in Ephesus, working with Aquila and Priscilla (18:26–27). It is more of a surprise to encounter another group of disciples who have links with John the Baptist (v. 3). Quite how the Baptist's message reached Ephesus is not clear, but it is important to remember that there were many trading and community links between Palestine and the major cities of the diaspora, and similar groups such as the Qumran sect had adherents in a variety of city locations. Are these people Christians? Luke doesn't attempt to define them except as 'disciples' (v. 1), which in Acts normally means disciples of Jesus (9:26; 11:29; 13:52). The key question for Paul is, 'Did you receive the Holy Spirit when you came to faith?' (v. 2) and the answer sheds light on the deficiencies of John's baptism. It is a baptism that looks backwards, a genuine movement of the soul leading to repentance (v. 4). It expresses a repugnance for everything in our lives that separates from God, and it's an essential part of the divine plan in preparing a people cleansed from sin (see Luke 1:17, 76).

The gift of the Spirit

Looking back, though, is not enough. The message of the gospel is about looking forward to the one who is coming, that is, Jesus (v. 4). And baptism in the name of Jesus (v. 5) means baptism not just in water but also in the Holy Spirit (Luke 3:16). Christian baptism comes with a promise attached: it's not just about lamenting our sins and letting go of the past, but also about accepting the invitation into God's future, into a community empowered by God's indwelling Spirit. Sometimes, as here, that indwelling is manifested visibly and audibly through identifiable charismatic gifts like speaking in tongues and prophesying (v. 6), but Paul's letters make it clear that that is only half the story. All Christians are promised the gift of the Spirit, as God's life-giving, transforming initiative for changing lives from the inside (see Acts 2:38–39; Romans 12:1–2; Galatians 5:16–23). There are many baptised Christians today who have 'not even heard that there is a Holy Spirit' (v. 2) – or, at least, don't realise that the Holy Spirit is for them.

Peter and Paul

Several aspects of this story remind us of Peter's role earlier in Acts. Like Peter, Paul has the power to release the gift of the Holy Spirit through the laying on of hands (v. 6; compare 8:17). Like Peter, Paul performs extraordinary miracles, so much so that spiritual power even leaks out from his person at one remove (vv. 11–12, compare 5:15), although Luke is careful to stress that the source of this power is not Paul but God. And, as with Peter, the net result is a whole population awestruck with 'fear' – that is, the proper response to the numinous presence of God (compare v. 17 with 5:12–14).

Yet Paul's mission is not primarily about impressing the crowds with a demonstration of spiritual power. His bread-and-butter of mission is the careful, patient, person-to-person work of dialogue and persuasion (v. 8), working within existing community structures for three months before deciding to make a break (v. 9). Unusually, here in Ephesus Paul moves from the synagogue not into a house but into a school. The school of Tyrannus (v. 10) was probably a private building used for lectures during the morning but available for hire when it was not in use for regular classes. It's a reminder of the continuing importance of 'going public' with the gospel, communicating the good news not just inside the church but in a place – and in a language – that is accessible to all.

Prayer

Father, confirm and strengthen in us the promise of our baptism, that we may daily increase in your Holy Spirit more and more, until we come to your everlasting kingdom: through your Son, our Saviour Jesus Christ.

64 Acts 19:13–20
Magic and miracle

Right from the beginning of the gospel, Jesus and his followers have had to answer the persistent charge that the spiritual power seen at work in them is not heavenly but demonic (compare Mark 3:20–30). Paul's active missionary career began with a confrontation with a magician (13:6–12), and it ends with a scene that makes clear the radical difference between magic and miracle. Luke wants to make quite sure that his readers won't confuse the two.

The sons of Sceva

Luke's account of Paul's extraordinary charismatic power (19:12) highlights the ever-present danger, for those to whom God entrusts such power, of worship becoming attached to the individual's name and not to the true source of all spiritual power. When spiritual power becomes a commodity that can be carried by inanimate objects, we are in dangerous waters. The cult of saints and their relics has always been a part of Christian history. It's a testimony to the spiritual reality located in certain individuals, but (as all the saints are aware) that reality always has to be referred back to the God who gives the gift. Quite who the 'sons of Sceva' were (v. 14) is not clear: the 'high priest' himself could not have operated in Ephesus, but (as we have seen) Ephesus had a large and vigorous Jewish community with many links with Jerusalem, and Jews had a name in the ancient world as powerful healers and magicians. We know from the ancient magical papyri that such magicians operated all over the ancient Mediterranean, drawing cheerfully and indiscriminately on any name that held the promise of power – pagan, Jewish or Christian.

Who are you?

The underlying message of Luke's story is clear: don't mess about with spiritual powers, good or bad (v. 16). There are real spiritual forces at work here, and no parrot-fashion recitation of magic formulae will control them: 'Jesus I know, and Paul I know; but who are you?' (v. 15). The power Paul wielded was real, but it was bought at deep personal cost, and sprang out of an encounter with the self-giving love through which Jesus won the ultimate victory over evil on the cross (see 2 Corinthians

12:1–10; Galatians 6:14–17). On the field of spiritual conflict, shortcuts are dangerous. It is never a matter of simply finding the right words to say. The spirit 'knows' Paul – recognises his name as one that has currency in the spiritual realm – Luke implies, because Paul's own identity is defined by his relationship with the Lord Jesus, 'whose I am, and whom I serve' (19:17; 27:23).

There is no room for second-hand faith here (v. 13). Knowing Jesus as Lord provides the only safe answer to the question, 'Who are you?' The true path to spiritual integrity, or spiritual power, may lead through gifted individuals to whom God has given exceptional gifts of leadership, teaching or healing, but the ultimate question of spiritual identity can only be answered by each of us alone, face to face with the unknown God.

Bonfire of books

The experience of the exorcists carries a sharp warning for anyone inclined to use the name of Jesus as a shortcut to spiritual power. Ephesus had a name in the ancient world as a centre for the production of magic books, and there must have been a number of believers who saw the name of Jesus as a useful addition to a successful spiritual portfolio. But Jesus can never be just one name among others. Christian discipleship means making choices, and in this passage we see the dawning realisation (it doesn't happen all at once!) that these magic practices were incompatible with their newfound faith. Hence the slow process of inner acknowledgement (we have to admit these things to ourselves first), followed by public confession (v. 18), and then the very necessary renunciation of the visible and material (not to say expensive) expressions of that other life (v. 19). Faith is not only about initial commitment. It's also about the slow and painfully honest process of discovering what the lordship of Christ really means. But when believers are prepared to do that – and do it publicly – then the power of God's word becomes visible to all the world (v. 20).

Reflection

The demon sees that it knows Jesus. Why? Because Jesus faced evil, entered its dwellings, walked with the sick, the lame, and the sinners, was criticised, insulted, and eventually killed by the powers of evil, and through all this he came out victorious.

Justo Gonzalez, *Acts: The gospel of the Spirit* (Orbis, 2001), p. 227.

65

Acts 19:21–28

Being church in Ephesus

This chapter brings together in a vivid and dramatic way many of the different perceptions of what it means to be church in the urban world of the first century. To insiders, it means being part of a dynamic and diverse network of autonomous house churches. This is the world we glimpse in Paul's letters. But Acts also shows what the church looks like to outsiders: Jewish splinter group, philosophical school, wonder-working cult. Here it's beginning to look alarmingly like a rival to the powerful local trade guilds, and it is this confrontation that forms the climax to Paul's stay in Ephesus.

God's plans and ours

We are beginning to move into the final phase of Paul's story. It's a story that will end with Paul's arrival in Rome as a prisoner (ch. 28), but Paul doesn't know that yet, and what we see in chapters 19—21 is Paul's gradual realisation of the new direction in which God is calling him – and of what it will cost. The first stirrings are here, in the bustle of making plans and getting ready to move on.

Paul's stay in Ephesus (more than two years, 19:10) is the longest stay that Luke records anywhere, and we know it as one of the most fruitful periods of Paul's letter-writing activity. Acts doesn't mention the letters or the conflicts in Corinth that occupied so much of Paul's attention in Ephesus. Even more mysteriously, Luke doesn't mention the 'collection for the saints' that motivated Paul's final trip to Macedonia and Achaea (see 2 Corinthians 8—9). Perhaps, writing with hindsight, he finds it too painful to record this abortive project, which Paul conceived as a way of holding together the Gentile churches and the mother church in Jerusalem, a project about which Paul himself records his hopes and misgivings in Romans 15:25–32. What he does tell us is that Paul is getting ready to hit the road again (v. 21), preparing a pastoral visitation of the churches founded in the second phase of his mission in Macedonia (Philippi, Thessalonica, Beroea) and Achaea (Corinth, Cenchreae and perhaps others we don't know about). The plan is to do a round trip across Greece before returning to Jerusalem – not as crazy as it sounds, given that a sea voyage direct from Corinth to Jerusalem would cut out the long overland trek across Asia. Somewhere in there, too (as we see in Romans 15:22–24, which was written from Corinth on the last stage of this round trip), is a conviction that God is calling him to go further west, to Rome itself (v. 21). 'Must' is one of Luke's codewords for what God has planned, although the manner and final destination of Paul's last voyage to the imperial city was to turn out very differently from what the apostle himself envisaged (Romans 15:24).

Demetrius the silversmith

First, though, Ephesus has a final surprise in store – which perhaps makes it clear to Paul that it's high time to leave! As in Thessalonica, Luke sets out the anatomy of this riot very carefully (v. 23). It surfaces as a face-off between Paul's uncompromising preaching of monotheism ('Real gods are not made with hands', v. 26) and the city's most famous cult, the worship of Diana (Greek Artemis) of the Ephesians. Any good illustrated Bible dictionary will show you a picture of the famous many-breasted cult image of Artemis, the centre of the civic cult at Ephesus and a major reason for the city's wealth (v. 27). Archaeologists have found silver mini-shrines of the type Luke describes (v. 24), manufactured in their thousands for the tourist/pilgrim trade. But as Luke tells the story, the underlying motive for the disturbance is not religious but commercial: Demetrius and his co-workers are frightened by the prospect of losing their trade (vv. 24–26). This concern is echoed half a century later by Pliny the Younger, the Roman governor of Bithynia in AD111, who complains that the success of Christianity is having a negative impact on the sales of sacrificial animals at all the local shrines.[12]

To any pagan reading Luke's story, the message is clear: the preaching of God's word is making serious inroads into one of the major cult centres of the eastern Mediterranean. To Jewish readers, it sends an equally clear message: Paul is faithfully proclaiming the worship of the living God.

Reflection

If the preaching of the gospel is having any real effect, sooner or later it will start to touch the political and economic structures with which our lives are entwined – and then, watch out for fireworks!

66 Acts 19:29–41

Diana of the Ephesians

Demetrius succeeds in whipping up a full-scale religious demonstration, which erupts into the theatre, one of the biggest public spaces in the city (vv. 28–29). Two of Paul's travelling companions are caught up in the excitement – Gaius and Aristarchus from Macedonia. This is the first time Luke has mentioned these delegates from the Macedonian churches, who have become part of Paul's mobile team. We discover later that Aristarchus comes from Thessalonica (20:4) and is probably the same person who accompanies Paul on his final voyage to Rome (27:2) and who later sends greetings as a companion of Paul from prison (Philemon 24; Colossians 4:10). Gaius was a common Roman forename, and there are at least three of Paul's associates called Gaius, one from Corinth (Romans 16:23; 1 Corinthians 1:14), one from Derbe (Acts 20:4) and this one from Macedonia.

The wild-beast show

Paul sees this as a golden opportunity to address the whole civic body in the theatre (v. 30), but his friends know better. Ephesians are not philosophers, and this is no Areopagus. Passions are running high (v. 32): think of a cross between a football crowd and a political rally. The 'officials' (v. 31, NRSV, literally 'Asiarchs') were responsible for the maintenance of the emperor-cult for the whole of Asia. Ephesus was the provincial centre for this politically sensitive cult, and although there was no formal conflict between the imperial and civic cults, it may be that the Asiarchs too were keeping a wary watch on this violent display of public attachment to the city's more traditional cult.

Silent witness

Unusually, Paul has hardly a word to say in this episode, yet it highlights the courage and endurance needed to witness to the one God in a pagan city. The whole scene speaks volumes about the delicate positioning of 'the Way' in the religious maelstrom of the great cities of the eastern empire. Historians have argued in the past that Christianity made an impact because people were becoming disillusioned with the old gods – but this is simply not true. In Ephesus, civic pride and identity were integrally bound up with the cult of 'the great Artemis' (v. 34), believed locally to have chosen the city as her official 'temple keeper'. The ancient cult-image was believed to have fallen from heaven (v. 35), and was probably a meteorite. Jews in these pagan cities maintained a precarious position.

It is not clear whether Alexander (v. 33) was put up to speak by people in the crowd, by Paul's friends or by members of the Jewish community, anxious to distance themselves from Paul and his message. In any case, he gets no chance to speak (v. 34). Jews were normally accepted members of the city's polyglot commercial community, but in this highly charged atmosphere no one who looked like an outsider was going to get a hearing.

Political pressures

This story also subtly distances Paul and his message from the rioting crowd. It reveals the overwhelming concern of the city authorities to maintain law and order. The 'town clerk' (v. 35) has only one thing in mind – to dissolve this illegal assembly and peacefully disperse the chanting crowd. In his eagerness to keep the peace, the town clerk unwittingly makes an important statement in Paul's defence: he is not a 'temple robber' and has not directly blasphemed the city's patron goddess (v. 37). Both Jews and Christians were often charged with being 'atheists' and bad-mouthing other people's religious beliefs, but Luke is keen to show that this is no way to bring people to belief in the one God. And, finally, Luke's story chillingly reveals the hidden pressure exerted by Rome on the Greek cities. Anything that might attract the censure of the governor (and riots and illegal assemblies certainly would, v. 40) has to be suppressed or channelled into a more legal format (v. 39). Rome encouraged the cities to keep up the forms of local self-government and provided an outlet for litigation through the local assizes run by the Roman proconsul on his annual tour of duty in this province (v. 38). The implication for Luke's readers (who should remember what happened last time Paul was brought before a proconsul, in 18:12–17) is that, in a legal court, no charges against his message would stand.

Prayer

Lord, teach us to approach other people's beliefs with respect, and to witness with courage to you, the living God.

67 Acts 20:1–12
Act Four: Paul the prisoner

So the final stage of Luke's drama begins. Ephesus (although Paul does not know it) marks the end of an era of church-planting and missionary preaching, and the beginning of Paul's transformation from missionary to prisoner. The Greek word for witness (*martus*) also gives us our word 'martyr', and this is the point at which Paul begins to understand that being a witness is not only about talking but also about being prepared to lay your life on the line.

To Troas via Corinth

The story begins innocuously enough, with the long-planned trip to revisit the churches of Macedonia and Achaea (v. 1; see 19:21). It is intended as a trip of encouragement and consolidation (v. 2), but Paul's reappearance triggers a sharp counter-reaction in the Jewish community (presumably in Corinth), and the original plan to take ship from Corinth to Jerusalem is abandoned (v. 3). Instead, the whole group will return via the overland route, up the coast to Thessalonica and then across to the coast of Asia Minor.

The party is looking more and more like a formal delegation (v. 4), with representatives from three of the areas in which Paul has worked: Macedonia, Galatia and Asia. Sopater may be the same person as the Sosipater of Romans 16:21. Tychicus turns up again in the later Pauline letters (see Colossians 4:7; Ephesians 6:21; Titus 3:12; 2 Timothy 4:12); Trophimus must be the Gentile mentioned in Acts 21:29. Intriguingly, there is no delegate from Achaea, but we must not forget the old friend who now rejoins the party, as the 'we-narrative' resumes in Philippi, just where we left our mysterious companion on the second phase of Paul's mission (v. 6; see 16:16).

Before there was a Sunday

The Asian members of the party may well have gone straight to Troas to wait for Paul there (v. 5). Paul himself lingers in Philippi to celebrate the feast of Passover with his friends (v. 6), then crosses over to Troas to spend a week with the community there. As a starting point for a fateful trip to Rome, Troas would have had interesting resonances for Roman readers. Ancient Troy was the ruined city from which Aeneas set out, in Virgil's great epic poem *The Aeneid*, for a voyage of tragedy and shipwreck that culminated in the founding of the city of Rome. But instead of epic grandeur, Luke gives us a vivid vignette of the worshipping life of these first Christians. Before there was such a thing as Sunday, Christians had to squeeze their meetings into whatever time was available, even if it meant staying up all night on the first day of the week before going off for a day's work or travel (v. 7). So, just as Pliny, the Roman governor of next-door Bithynia in AD111, tells of Christians meeting 'before dawn' to sing hymns to Christ,[13] Luke gives us this charming domestic scene of the night-time meeting in the third-storey room of a tenement building (v. 9), lit by smoky lamps (v. 8).

Unlucky Eutychus

The meeting is for the breaking of bread (v. 7) in memory of Jesus' last Passover meal with his disciples, but Paul also has a lot to say to this precious little group whom he may never see again. That's one reason why unlucky Eutychus falls asleep (v. 9). His name (which means 'Lucky') is often a slave-name, and he may already have had a long day's work, but the fumes from the lamps could also have had a soporific effect. It's not clear from Luke's story whether the fall left him dead or merely unconscious, but either way Paul's prompt action (which recalls the prophet Elijah in 1 Kings 17:17–24) saves the boy's life (vv. 10, 12). Like the widow of Zarephath, Luke's readers will recognise the life-giving power at work in this man of God. It's entirely appropriate that the episode closes with Paul 'breaking the bread' with this tiny group of disciples (v. 11), in the memorial meal with which Christians down the ages have gathered on the first day of the week to celebrate the victory of life over death.

Prayer

Thanks be to God, who gives us the victory through our Lord Jesus Christ.
1 CORINTHIANS 15:57 (NRSV)

68

Acts 20:13-21

Farewell at Miletus

The narrative becomes a ceremonial progression down the west coast of Asia Minor (vv. 13-16), listing the islands and ports of call on a typical island-hopping Aegean coastal voyage. Paradoxically, this creates a sense of suspense as we move slowly down the coast, stopping to pick up Paul in Assos, since for some unexplained reason he had decided to do the first part of the journey on foot (v. 13). We come to share Paul's sense of frustration at the slowness of the voyage (v. 16); after celebrating Passover in Philippi, he is anxious to get to Jerusalem within 50 days in time for Pentecost – and we've already spent a week in Troas (20:6). But coastal traders follow their own timetables, and a few days' enforced delay at Miletus gives Paul the opportunity to summon the leaders of the Ephesian house churches for a farewell discourse.

The elders from Ephesus

It is only a few months since Paul left Ephesus (20:3), but we seem to have shifted into a different time frame altogether. The 'elders' of the church (v. 17) were never mentioned in chapter 19, but we should not forget that Paul was not involved in setting up the church in Ephesus. It was already well established before he got there, and we can reasonably infer that Priscilla and Aquila would have followed the same pattern of church structures that Paul had instituted in 14:23. Diaspora synagogues normally had a governing body of local 'elders', and the early church seems to have followed this pattern. It's a timely reminder that while Paul was acting as a kind of evangelistic front-man in his public lectures in the school of Tyrannus (19:9-10), the day-to-day work of the local church was going on behind the scenes.

Paul the pastor

Now, however, in this long valedictory speech, Luke gives us a rare insight into Paul's pastoral concerns for the leaders of the local church. He has told us often enough of Paul's continued determination to build up and encourage the churches he founded (14:22; 15:32; 20:2). Now we get a chance to eavesdrop on Paul the pastor in action – not necessarily a real speech, but (as Luke's speeches often are) a paradigmatic composition putting together the kinds of things Paul would have said in so many different places and on so many different occasions. Not surprisingly, this speech is the closest of all Paul's Acts speeches to the sort of thing he says in his letters, which are dealing with the same kinds of issues. But, rather than dealing with particular problems in a church situation, this speech gives a general impression of Paul the pastor as Luke feels he should be remembered.

Looking back

As so often in his letters, Paul begins by looking back over a life dedicated to his Lord's service (vv. 18–21; compare Philippians 1; Galatians 1; 1 Thessalonians 2). It's a life in which there is no hiding place: 'You know how I was with you the whole time' (v. 18). What we are says just as much about the gospel as what we say. As a pastor, Paul had to make his whole life available to the people he worked with as a testimony to the gospel, a life defined not by success but by enslavement to his Lord (v. 19). This is the relationship that defines all others in Paul's life: see Romans 1:1; Philippians 1:1; Galatians 1:10; 2 Corinthians 4:5. The pastor's life has to be a Christlike life, a life of humility (Philippians 2:3, 8), of tears and trials and persecutions (1 Thessalonians 1:6–7; 2:14–16; Philippians 1:12–17, 27–30). But none of this has deflected Paul from his prime task of announcing and teaching the gospel message of repentance and faith in Jesus, both publicly (in the synagogue, in the school of Tyrannus) and from house to house (vv. 20–21), a good summary of the Pauline mission.

Reflection

Do I define my service to Christ in terms of 'my ministry', or do I define my ministry in terms of service to Christ?

69 Acts 20:22–35

I have finished my course

And now? There's a note of foreboding as Paul describes his present state, still technically a free agent but 'bound in the Spirit' (v. 22) – a chilling glimpse of what lies ahead, even though we have as yet no hint of the events that will lead to Paul's eventual imprisonment. For Paul, the future at this moment is opaque, full of prophetic hints of bonds and persecution in store (v. 23). The powerful metaphor of a race almost finished (v. 24) echoes the prison epistles (cf. Philippians 3:14; 2 Timothy 4:7). Yet Paul refuses to let the future's darkness deter him from carrying out the ministry with which he has been entrusted, the marvellous mission of making God's grace known in the world. This is what's in his mind as he writes to Rome from Corinth before setting out for Jerusalem (Romans 15:15–24); and here too he has the conviction, looking back, of having fulfilled the task entrusted to him, of having 'fully proclaimed' the gospel (Romans 15:19). Even if these people never see him again in this life (v. 25), he knows that he has discharged his duty, making full use of every opportunity to pass on every insight into God's purposes (vv. 26–27).

Tend the flock

This leaves the elders, humanly speaking, on their own. They won't be able to rely on Paul's leadership any more. So there's a sober note of warning in verses 28–31: take care, be alert, there are wolves about. You can expect attacks both from outside the community and (perhaps more alarming) from inside. Isn't Paul worried about leaving such an inexperienced local team to carry on in his absence? No, he says, you don't need to worry, because your confidence, like mine, rests not on yourselves but on God. It is God who has put you where you are and given you a ministry to fulfil there, a distinctive ministry entrusted to you directly by God's Holy Spirit (v. 28).

Being 'local' is no more and no less important in the divine economy than having a worldwide itinerant ministry like Paul's. You are *episkopoi*, Paul says – 'guardians' or 'overseers' – a term which later meant 'bishop' but here is another name for the local elders (20:17). That means being entrusted with the enormous responsibility and privilege of shepherding the flock which is God's (not yours or mine), a flock that God has acquired at enormous cost. Put simply: if God thought it was worth dying for, you'd better take good care of it! So don't be surprised if you have a few sleepless nights (v. 31). Your ultimate resource, like mine, is the infinite reserves of God's grace, a grace which has the power to build you up and bring you through to the inheritance that God has in store for all his saints (v. 32). The key word here is 'commend', a word that appears again in a different form in 2 Timothy 1:12 to express the double paradox of Christian ministry. It's something that God commits to us, but we can only do it insofar as we commit it (and ourselves) to God.

Remember the little things

'Remember the little things that I taught you,' said the sixth-century Welsh saint David on his deathbed, and Paul too closes with a list of 'little things'. Ultimately, the gospel of grace has to be lived out in real lives. That's what people remember, and that's what apostles are for. Discipleship in the ancient world meant, above all else, watching your teacher's lifestyle like a hawk so as to learn what wisdom really meant, so the most important task of the apostles was to model in their own lives what they had learnt from their own Master.

Like Peter (3:6), Paul has learnt that ministry is not about money-making (v. 33); on the contrary, he has worked with his own hands to support himself during the three years he was in Ephesus (v. 34; 18:1–4). And this pattern of self-support, even though it looks contrary to the apostolic lifestyle authorised by Jesus (compare Paul's discussion in 1 Corinthians 9), can be directly linked with Jesus' teaching on giving (20:35; Paul draws a similar parallel from the self-giving pattern of Jesus' life in 2 Corinthians 8:9). Interestingly, this is a saying of Jesus which is not recorded in the gospels; it is a salutary reminder that the gospel writers could only record a fraction of all Jesus' sayings (see John 20:30; 21:25).

Reflection and prayer

I thank my God every time I remember you, constantly praying with joy in every one of my prayers for all of you... confident of this, that the one who began a good work among you will bring it to completion.

PHILIPPIANS 1:3–4, 6 (NRSV)

70 Acts 20:36—21:17

Towards Jerusalem

Contrary to popular belief, Paul wasn't all head and no heart! This passage shows us the deep affection in which he was held, and goes some way to revealing the real person behind his pastoral ministry.

Miletus to Tyre

We don't normally think of Paul as inspiring affection, but the Miletus speech dissolves into an emotional farewell scene (vv. 36–38), which forms a fitting climax to Paul's pastoral ministry. Now the voyage resumes (21:1), with the same loving and leisurely evocation of the passing scene. This is a working ship, probably a coastal trader, but its passengers, after all the emotion of Miletus, have an unexpected period of leisure with nothing to do but watch the unfolding panorama from the ship's deck. Patara means a change of ship, finding a boat heading east to Phoenicia (v. 2); and then, with Cyprus slipping below the horizon on the port side (lots of nautical language here: Luke clearly enjoys sailing), a quiet, unmarked landing in Tyre, where the boat is to discharge her cargo (v. 3).

Tyre to Ptolemais

There is an increasing sense that this voyage is in God's hands. Mysterious, unexplained disciples appear to offer hospitality for a few days in Tyre (v. 4: Luke hasn't told us before that there is a church here). But now the warnings begin again (see 20:23), and we have another affecting seashore farewell (v. 5), with tearful women and children. Then it's back on board (v. 6) as the boat resumes the next stage of her voyage, described in equally loving, lingering detail, before meeting and greeting a new set of brothers in Ptolemais (v. 7). It's fascinating in these last stages of Paul's journey to see how the Way has been spreading like an underground root system in all sorts of unexpected directions. Luke clearly doesn't expect us to conclude that the story he tells is the whole story of the early church (although we often read it that way).

Ptolemais to Caesarea

The next day, it's round the Carmel headland to Caesarea, the main port of debarkation for Jerusalem (v. 8). Here we meet an old friend, Philip the evangelist, one of the 'seven' (6:5; 8:5–40). Philip has four daughters, all prophets (v. 9), although it is not they who provide the conclusive prophecy for Paul. Agabus, another old friend (v. 10; 11:28), calls in from Judea and is inspired by the everyday sight of Paul's belt (v. 11) to a symbolic action of the type familiar from the Old Testament prophets. The theme is binding – tying up hands and feet, taking away the power of independent action – surely a personal nightmare for the much-travelled and independent Paul. To his friends, Agabus' prophecy is a warning, a timely hint to keep away from danger, to turn and make off in the opposite direction (v. 12). But this personal sense of being 'bound' has been with Paul since 20:22, and he knows, obscurely but ineluctably, that it comes from God. So, gently but firmly, he has to ask his friends to stop crying (v. 13) and let him remain faithful to his calling, even if that means death. For Paul, as for his Master, only one thing matters in the last analysis – that God's will be done (v. 14; compare Luke 22:42).

Caesarea to Jerusalem

The party have their own preparations to make for this last visit to Jerusalem (v. 15). Even their friends in Caesarea seem to be affected by Paul's sombre mood and make sure that Paul is delivered to a safe house in Jerusalem (v. 16). Mnason, a Cypriot with a Greek name, must have been a 'Hellenist', perhaps one of the original Hellenist converts who had left Jerusalem after Stephen's death and so inconspicuously launched the Gentile mission (see 11:19–20). So, for the moment, it's good just to be there and enjoy a warm welcome from these sympathetic friends (v. 17).

Prayer

Father, keep us faithful to your will, even when the way is dark.

71 Acts 21:18–26
Paul meets James

Things have changed since Paul was last in Jerusalem – changed radically since the council met in chapter 15 to find a central platform to hold together Jewish and Gentile Christians in the church.

A change of leadership

Peter, who had faced the struggle to accept his own vision of God's work among Gentiles, and had worked so hard to accommodate the new insights Paul was bringing, has moved on: Luke doesn't mention him after chapter 15. James is now (although Luke never tells us exactly how) in a leadership position in Jerusalem, and it is to James and the elders (v. 18) that Paul brings his delegation, the day after his arrival, to make his report, blow by blow, about what God has been doing through his ministry among the Gentiles (v. 19). There is a clear sense here that Paul has to render account of himself, explain what he has been up to all these years. To understand James' caution, we need to remember that Paul has been effectively a freelance evangelist since his split with Barnabas (15:39), trusting the Spirit's guidance (hence the importance of chapter 16), and (apart from hurriedly touching base in 18:22), setting up his own independent missionary networks. So does he return as hero or loose cannon?

A change of mood

Formally, James and the elders are full of praise for what God has done through Paul (v. 20), but it becomes clear that the precarious balance held by Peter and James in chapter 15 has been destabilised. Christian opinion has begun to polarise; the church in Jerusalem has been growing, and many of the new believers are deeply suspicious of Paul and everything he stands for. The suspicion is fuelled by 'zeal for the law' (v. 20), a radical fundamentalist stance prepared to impose its will on others, by force if need be. Paul had shared this position in his student days, but that was 20 years ago, and we know from the Jewish historian Josephus that Felix's period of office in Judea saw a massive build-up of fundamentalist fervour and an impassioned rejection of anything that looked like political or religious compromise with Rome. It is also fuelled by misinformation: word has been spreading that Paul's mission is not so much a mission to bring the Gentiles into God's people as a mission to take the Jews out, to persuade Jews to commit apostasy from their ancestral religion (v. 21).

Paul and the law

Watching Paul's progress around Greece and Asia Minor, you could understand how people might think these things about him. Preaching in the synagogue, then engineering a split and walking out with half the congregation, is not a recipe for popularity with community leaders. But what were Paul's converts joining? The apostolic council had established the principle that Gentiles who became Christians did not need to keep the law of Moses (15:19–21), and James has no intention of going back on that pledge (v. 25). But nowhere in Acts does Luke imply that Jews who accepted Jesus as Messiah had to give up keeping the law. In fact, he implies the contrary: Paul's decision to circumcise Timothy (16:3), his continued insistence on visiting synagogues, his keenness to keep Passover and Pentecost (20:6, 16) and the vow at Cenchreae (18:18) all build up to a picture of a Paul who is happy to be regarded – at least when it suits him – as a faithful, Torah-observant Jew (cf. 1 Corinthians 9:20).

Building bridges

Now, in order to make it absolutely clear that the charge of teaching apostasy is false, James suggests a neat solution which will demonstrate at a stroke Paul's own devotion to Torah and temple (v. 24) and show his support for the ultra-zealous in a practical way. Undertaking the voluntary piety of a nazirite vow was an expensive business, and it was common for eminent visitors to make this charitable gesture. James suggests that Paul should pay for the necessary sacrifices for four Christian nazirites (v. 23), and accompany them to the temple while undertaking the ritual purification for himself that was expected for a pious Jew returning from the lands of the Gentiles (v. 24).

Prayer

Father, as I look back, help me to see not my own successes or failures, but what you have done in and through and in spite of them. And thank you for being with me.

72 Acts 21:27–40

Riot in the temple

He almost gets away with it! Paul's desire to build bridges with the hardliners of the Jewish-Christian community puts him in a dangerous position, right in the fomenting heart of the city, visiting the temple over a seven-day period (v. 27). It's on the very last day that trouble strikes – trouble that will take Paul eventually to the opposite end of the world.

The Jews from Asia

Agabus had prophesied that Paul would be handed over to the Gentiles by 'the Jews' (21:11), but which Jews? The previous section has shown that the Jerusalem church is not to blame, even if it also reveals a frightening level of hostility there to Paul's mission. One thing Luke's narrative has made clear, though, is that 'the Jews' are not a monochrome group. Here a new group comes into view, the 'Jews from Asia' (v. 27), who see Paul in the temple and jump rapidly to the wrong conclusion. Paul is on dangerous ground now. Bringing Gentiles into the inner court of the temple (v. 28) was a capital offence in Jewish law that was upheld by Roman law. An inscription found in the temple precincts marks the boundary of the Court of the Gentiles and warns that Gentiles may not pass this barrier on pain of death. So Luke is careful to tell us that this part of the charge is simply not true (v. 29). Trophimus of Asia had been seen with Paul in the streets of the city, but Paul had not brought him into the temple. But nobody in this crowd is really interested in finding out the truth. The real charge, far harder to answer, is the charge of 'teaching everyone everywhere against the people, the law and this place' (v. 28). The immediate result is that Paul is physically ejected from the centre of worship and 'the doors were shut' (v. 30) – a note of finality, marking the end of an era in Paul's life, and a moment of deep irony for this visionary preacher who had dedicated his life to breaking down the barriers that religious people put up around their faith.

The tribune of the cohort

Paul has no time to reflect on the irony of his situation. He is within an ace of receiving the same kind of summary execution he had seen meted out on Stephen (7:54—60) when word gets back to the Roman military commander in charge of policing the temple area (v. 31). Romans were not allowed inside the inner courts of the temple, but they were very concerned to keep an eye on this volatile spot, especially at festival times, and had built a fortress, the Antonia, right on the corner of the temple precinct to give them a commanding position over what was happening inside. Here is another irony: by locking Paul out of the inner courts, the rioters have brought him into the domain controlled by the imperial power of Rome (v. 32), and it is this power that now takes charge of Paul.

The young officer who clatters down the steps of the Antonia with his squaddies undoubtedly saves Paul's life (vv. 33—36), but the chains they place on Paul will not come off (except briefly when Paul is facing his accusers) for the rest of the book.

A citizen of no mean city

There's a nice John Buchan touch about the next scene. To the bored young tribune on temple guard duty – just as to the young British or US soldier in the Middle East – all orientals look the same. The man at the centre of the riot has got to be some kind of terrorist. The 'Egyptian' (v. 38) was just one of the many religious agitators who were giving Rome grief in those unsettled years leading up to the Jewish war with Rome. According to Josephus, an Egyptian claiming to be a prophet had recently led a mob to the Mount of Olives to watch the walls of Jerusalem fall.[14] The governor Felix dispersed the mob with the aid of soldiers, but the ringleader escaped. Not unnaturally, the tribune here thinks he's struck lucky. So when this dishevelled figure addresses him politely in faultless Greek (v. 37), the effect is something like the whirling dervish in a John Buchan novel speaking in an impeccable Oxford accent. There's a serious side to the exchange, however. Faced with the brutality of empire, Paul displays a calm dignity that impresses the tribune. The momentary respite gives Paul the chance to make his last formal address to the people of Jerusalem, standing on the steps like a Greek orator (v. 40).

Prayer

Father, teach us to find our dignity and status only in you.

73

Acts 22:1–21

Paul the Jew

There is a certain farcical element in Paul's position here, pinned down outside the sanctuary, halfway up the steps of the fortress, brandished aloft by Roman soldiers with the mob clutching at him below. But the farce also underlines Paul's marginal status, not only physically but politically and culturally. It was perhaps part of the secret of his success as a missionary that Paul was able to move effortlessly between the three aspects of his identity – Jewish, Greek and Roman. In the next few scenes he will need to deploy all of those – and remain true to his underlying calling as a disciple of Jesus Christ.

Brothers and fathers

Paul the Jew comes first (21:39), proudly stated at this focal point of Jewish identity. As a Jew, he has a right to be in the temple, and to address the crowd in their own language (21:40, 22:2), which the Roman tribune can never share. Paul may have been raised in a Greek city, but he is determined to show that his Hebrew credentials are second to none (compare Philippians 3:4–6). This is the first of Paul's defence speeches in Acts, but it is not the kind of self-defence we might expect. There is no reasoned, point-by-point rebuttal of the charges laid against him in 21:28. Instead, he goes right back to his own starting points, seeking to make his audience understand the whole life-journey that has brought him to where he is now. So the speech begins by laying out in relentless detail how much Paul shares with his audience (vv. 1–5): Jewish first and foremost, born in Tarsus, educated in Jerusalem at the feet of one of the century's most revered saints and scholars, and sharing the same zeal that fires up his audience.

Who are you, Lord?

The key to understanding his present predicament, though, lies in a moment of vision on the Damascus road, that encounter with the living Lord that turned his life around forever (v. 6). It was precisely the same 'zeal' that the audience shares that made him a persecutor (vv. 4–5) and brought him face-to-face with the crucified Jesus, surrounded by the bright light of heaven (vv. 7–8). If we compare Paul's retelling here with chapter 9, we can see that different details are emphasised for the different occasions. Here the story is told from Paul's viewpoint, so we don't see Ananias' personal doubts and prevarications (9:10–16). Paul simply stresses Ananias' piety and his good standing in the Jewish community (v. 12). What is important is that Paul's Lord is not some new deity but 'the God of our fathers' (v. 14), who has chosen Saul for a purpose (v. 10).

I will send you far away

What that purpose is becomes clear only gradually. The fundamental shape of this experience for Paul – as for Isaiah and all the prophets – is an encounter with the living God. It's about being chosen to know God's will, to see God's Righteous One, to hear a voice from his mouth (v. 14). The commission grows out of that encounter: you can't be a witness (v. 15) unless you have first seen and heard for yourself, experienced something of the glory of heaven (v. 11) and let it knock you off your high horse (v. 7). Everything else stems from that initial encounter: first, incorporation into a new community (v. 16), a letting go of the past and a humble acceptance of a new identity, then repeatedly being drawn back to worship and prayer (vv. 17–18), a need to be in God's presence simply because God is worth it – which is what worship is about. Then (and only then) comes a new direction, a step at a time: first recognising the impossibility of going on any further, then facing up honestly to the past (vv. 19–20) and finally a new direction for the future (v. 21).

Reflection

Evangelism is useless unless it is the work of one devoted to God, willing and glad to suffer all things for God, penetrated by the attractiveness of God.
Evelyn Underhill (1875–1941)

74 Acts 22:22-29
Status games

Paul has done very well so far, travelling around the empire and using its resources without drawing official attention to himself (apart from a few local skirmishes). Here, however, on the temple steps, he has finally run out of options. He has to play the only trump he's got, and trust God for the outcome.

Away with him!

Up to this point, the crowd has been listening in spellbound silence. The zealot who unexpectedly meets his God, the heavenly voice, the prophetic call – all this can be fitted into the mould of preconceived ideas. But the word 'Gentiles' (v. 21) acts like a red rag to this bullish, militant crowd. The idea that God should reveal himself to his faithful followers is conceivable; that the revelation in some way includes the Gentiles is not (v. 22) – not, that is, to this particular brand of fundamentalism. It was not inconceivable to first-century Judaism in general that God's revelation to Israel should be for the sake of the outside world. In fact, the burden of Acts is that Paul's vision is not only consistent with scripture but is an organic outworking of God's self-revelation to Israel. But alongside the argument (which is worked out in detail in this series of trial scenes), Luke also shows us a progressive rejection of that insight by successive groups, culminating in the expulsion of Paul's message from the heart of his own tradition.

Out of the frying pan into the fire

The Roman officer has been standing by all this time, unable to understand Paul's speech but carefully watching the body language of the crowd – which suddenly erupts (v. 23). Now he decides it's time to intervene. He hasn't a clue what Paul was talking about, but it was obviously inflammatory, so the squaddies are ordered to interrogate the prisoner to find out what's going on (v. 24). Given the routine brutality of army interrogation of foreign nationals, Paul's 'rescue' is rather like falling out of the frying pan into the fire. So he decides to play his trump card, and reveals to the horrified centurion that he has arrested a Roman citizen

(vv. 25—26). This is a bit like having a suspected terrorist suddenly whipping out a US passport. There's a touch of farce about the whole scene, as the embarrassed tribune falls back from the forcible interrogation (v. 29) – but still does not release Paul.

This man is a Roman

We might perhaps ask why Paul has waited till this moment to reveal his Roman citizenship to the tribune. Things have been happening rather fast, though, and outside, on the steps before the hostile crowd in the temple, it was more important for Paul to focus on his Jewish identity. In private, inside the Roman fortress, things are rather different, and Paul has to face up to the fact that he is now, for good or ill, in Roman custody. That situation has to be played with care. The empire could function quite usefully to protect its citizens from local injustice, but its legal machinery was relentless, and no one would want to get into it unless they were sure they had a way out. For provincials, being a Roman citizen (a comparatively rare privilege at this date) meant two things: they could not be beaten, bound or executed without a fair trial, and their accusers had to appear in person to lay charges against them. It also meant that they had the right to appeal to have their case heard before the emperor in Rome – and, as we shall see, this is the right that Paul will eventually invoke when he stands before Festus (25:9—12).

Born or bought?

There is a nice irony in the exchange with the tribune in verse 28. For Paul, the privilege of citizenship could be taken for granted as part of his family history, whereas the tribune has to confess that his own citizen rank is of much more recent origin. So the status levels of officer and prisoner are in one sense reversed, although the prisoner remains in custody. The exchange has sown enough doubt in the tribune's mind to leave him seriously worried (v. 29). Detaining a citizen without formal charge could be a very serious mistake, which could have repercussions in the highest quarters. On the other hand, failing to detain a terrorist could have equally serious repercussions.

Prayer

Pray for soldiers, police officers, prison guards and all whose jobs give them control over the lives of others.

75 Acts 22:30—23:9

Before the Sanhedrin

From the rioting zealots in the temple to the heart of a corrupt colonial administration: Luke shows us here a Paul who is poised between the two extremes of pre-war Jerusalem, desperately trying to offer both sides a vision of a different future.

Judicial enquiry

The tribune's next step is logical enough. Paul must have done something illegal to have caused so much disturbance, so, since there is clearly no hope of getting a rational answer from the temple crowd, he needs to get the prisoner examined by the Sanhedrin, the ruling council of Judea and the only native body with which the Roman government could do business (v. 30). This is not, strictly speaking, a trial. It is a judicial enquiry on the tribune's behalf, set up to ascertain if there is actually any charge to answer. The effect, for Luke's readers, is twofold. It underlines the parallels with the trials of Jesus (cf. Luke 22:66; 23:13), and it ensures that Paul gets his chance to make a second *apologia* or defence speech before a different Jerusalem group – the chief priests and other leaders who had made such a dramatic impact on the Jerusalem apostles 20 years before (see 4:6, 23; 5:24). Like other contemporary writers, Luke speaks of 'high priests' in the plural because, although there was only one high priest in office at a time, retired high priests retained their title and much of their influence until their death.

Before the council

The atmosphere of the council chamber should have been very different from that of the temple mob. Paul addresses the council as 'brothers' (v. 1) – that is, as equals – and begins his speech by stressing how much he and they have in common. He has nothing to be ashamed of: everything he has done to date has been done in good conscience as a loyal and observant Jew, conducting his life in a way that is loyal to God. It is a bold claim, and the high priest regards it as provocative (v. 2). Ananias was a controversial figure who earned a name for exceptional wealth (and exceptional greed) in the turbulent years leading up to the outbreak of the Jewish War, and was eventually assassinated by rebels on the outbreak of war in AD66.[15] For Luke's readers, as for Paul himself, Ananias would have been an ambivalent figure, representing by virtue of his office the highest and holiest religious authority in Judaism, yet widely known for venality and corruption – a 'whitewashed wall' (v. 3) concealing inner depths of corruption.

Allies and enemies

The action of ordering Paul to be struck on the mouth tips what should have been an orderly debate over the edge into an undignified fracas. Paul reacts with anger, but takes the opportunity to claim the moral high ground and shows himself well-trained in legal argumentation (vv. 3–4). Ananias' action could have no legal justification, and so he shows himself unworthy to be regarded as a 'ruler of the people' (v. 5, quoting Exodus 22:28). Almost inevitably, then, Paul looks around and decides he has no chance of getting a fair hearing from this council. His only hope is to appeal over the heads of the priestly hierarchy to other members of the Sanhedrin (and beyond them, perhaps, to the wider community) by aligning himself with his natural allies, the Pharisees (v. 6).

Pharisees and Sadducees differed on many points of interpretation of the scriptures. The Sadducees were conservatives who held that only a literal interpretation of scripture was acceptable. They held to Torah only, devalued the Prophets and Writings, and regarded the idea of resurrection (which was a commonly held belief in first-century Judaism) as a new and unscriptural doctrine. But we should not regard Paul's appeal to the resurrection simply as a cynical ploy to divide the assembly. It allows Paul to swing the argument back to his own agenda (cf. 26:8), and reminds his audience – and Luke's readers – that there is a real theological issue at stake here (v. 9). The Pharisees believed (unlike the Sadducees) that God was still revealing himself to his people. The real question was, were they prepared to accept that the apostolic testimony to Christ was part of this continuing self-revelation?

Prayer

Pray for lawyers, judges, court officials and all to whom the administration of justice is entrusted.

76 Acts 23:10–30

Plots and counterplots

The scene is confused and confusing – but it must have been even more confusing for Paul, kept in the dark and knowing nothing of what was going on. Luckily for him, Someone else did…

Take courage

Paul's outburst has the effect of splitting the council into factions and starting a major riot. Certainly that's what it sounds like to the tribune, listening outside (v. 10), so he sends the troops down to rescue Paul and take him back to the fortress.

It's precisely at this point of maximum confusion, in the darkness of uncertainty, danger, instability and the loss of personhood, that 'the Lord stood by him' (v. 11). Paul must have been wondering whether his predicament meant that God had abandoned him. Was he wrong to come back to Jerusalem? Was it crazy to go along with James' proposal and carry out the temple ritual – which is what he'd been doing only 36 hours before? More importantly, was his whole mission based on false premises? Bravado is all very well (and Paul was obviously the kind of person who thrived on confrontation), but in the long, slow reaches of the night, it's easy to wonder if we've got it all wrong. So this is a crucial reassurance from the Lord, both for Paul and for us as readers: 'Don't worry; everything that's happening is part of *my* plan.'

As the action speeds up, Luke really slows down his narrative pace in this section, so we can follow every twist in an increasingly convoluted plot and overhear every whispered conversation. It's as if he's saying, 'How on earth is God going to get Paul out of this one? Just watch and wonder!'

Ambush in the temple

The first step in getting Paul out of Jerusalem is an apparent disaster, but disasters in Acts have a way of furthering God's own plan. As long as Paul is in the Antonia fortress, he's safe, but he can't stay there forever. So a small group of conspirators (vv. 12–13) make a plan to ambush Paul and take summary action the next time the Romans bring him down through the temple precincts to meet the Sanhedrin. The plotters are worryingly close to elements in the council itself (vv. 14–15), some of whom could have seen this as a useful strategy to circumvent the Roman legal stranglehold that prevented them from carrying their own legal processes to their logical conclusion. There is clearly a strong element in Jerusalem who are convinced that Paul is an incurable apostate who must be removed for the sake of Israel's purity. But not all the young radicals milling around in the crowd are hostile to Paul, and he has a young nephew who overhears the plot and spills the beans to the tribune (vv. 16–22). This is the first time we've heard that Paul has a sister, but this could partly explain the constant pressures that keep drawing him back to Jerusalem.

From Jerusalem to Caesarea

Now matters are in the tribune's hands, and his duty is clear. As a Roman citizen, Paul is entitled to a fair trial, and it is becoming clear that he won't get that in Jerusalem. The only option is to get him out of the city, fast, with an armed, mounted escort (vv. 23–24). The tribune's nervousness is palpable, as is his determination to get Paul off his own patch and safely into Roman custody. The Antonia is little more than a fortified police station, and the last thing he wants is a mob trying to storm his gates. But the prisoner must be accompanied by a letter of explanation (vv. 25–30), and this has to be composed with some care: no need to mention that unfortunate business about trying to flog Paul before he let on that he was a Roman (v. 27). The letter formally proclaims Paul's innocence under Roman law (v. 29), although it acknowledges that he may still have a charge to answer under Jewish law (v. 30).

The tribune (now identified as Claudias Lysias) is evidently convinced that there is no substance in the original charge of violating the sanctity of the temple precincts by bringing a Gentile into the Court of Israel (21:28). In any case, under Roman law a citizen could not be brought to trial unless his accusers were there in person to lay charges, and there is no sign that anyone is prepared to do that. What remains is the more general charge of teaching against the law and the temple (21:28), and that is the case Lysias is transferring to the jurisdiction of Felix – provided Paul's accusers are prepared to travel to Caesarea to make their case before the governor (v. 30).

Prayer

Pray for all who feel abandoned by family, friends and society.

77 Acts 23:31—24:9
Trial in Caesarea

Now the stage shifts from the explosive atmosphere of Jerusalem to the seat of Roman provincial government in Caesarea. Felix (unlike Claudius Lysias) is on his home ground, hearing the case before his own tribunal, and the burden of proof has shifted to the accusers – hence the change of tone.

Down to Caesarea

The amount of detail in this story is extraordinary. God's rescue mission now enlists (unwittingly) not only the tribune but two centurions, 200 soldiers, 70 cavalrymen and 200 spearmen (23:23), all clattering down to Antipatris at dead of night (v. 31). This is the only place in his travels where Paul is described as riding (which rather implies that it was unusual). Antipatris was a day's march from Jerusalem on foot, so the foot-soldiers return to Jerusalem the next day (v. 32). But it's an easy ride for the cavalrymen, who act as an escort to deliver Paul safely to Felix the governor in Caesarea (v. 33). This is a significant move, down from the uplands of Judea to the Mediterranean coast, out from the political control of the temple hierarchy (where even the tribune has to move circumspectly) to a more public arena, and securely into colonial territory. Caesarea Maritima was a cosmopolitan Greek city, where Jews were a vocal but not dominant segment of the population. More importantly for Paul, it was also the seat of the Roman administration's provincial HQ, so Paul is coming closer and closer to the seat of Roman power.

Meet the governor

The first step is for the escort to hand Paul over, complete with attached letter, to the Roman magistrate in whose hands (humanly speaking) his future lies (v. 33). On the face of it, it is a rather dubious prospect. Felix (23:24) was a slave in origin, who, with his brother Pallas, became a confidant and favourite at the imperial court. As a mark of favour, the emperor Claudius made him procurator of Judea (around AD52–60), much to the disgust of the later Roman historian Tacitus, who described

Felix as wielding the power of a king 'with all cruelty and lust, and with the mentality of a slave'.[16] It was during Felix's procuratorship that the province of Judea began to move inexorably towards revolt against Rome.

Felix's first question is, on the face of it, an odd one: 'What province are you from?' (v. 34). The answer might have given him the option of transferring the case to the prisoner's home province, but Paul's home province of Cilicia, like Judea, falls under the ultimate jurisdiction of the legate of Syria, so there is no easy way out there. Felix will have to hear the case himself (v. 35).

The case for the prosecution

The accusers have to present their case in person, and in five days' time, a deputation from the Sanhedrin duly arrives, together with a carefully briefed Greek orator (no expense spared!) to ensure that the case is presented to the governor in the most advantageous way possible (v. 1). Tertullus' speech (vv. 2–8) is couched in the best rhetorical style, nicely calculated to win friends and influence people. In fact, almost half the speech (as Luke reports it) is taken up with flattery, stressing (against all the evidence, it must be said) Felix's record of peaceful political reform, his political sagacity and his excellent reputation. Tertullus then moves to setting out the charges against Paul in terms designed to impress a Roman governor: provoking civil riots (*staseis*) among Jews throughout the inhabited world (v. 5), and being a ringleader of the Nazarean sect. Then comes the more specific charge of profaning the temple by taking Gentiles past the permitted limits (v. 6). That's the capital charge; that's the one that should stick – apart from the minor technicality that it wasn't the Sanhedrin who originally apprehended Paul, and the Asian pilgrims who raised the original hue and cry in the temple are not here to press the charge.

Prayer

Pray for all prisoners and captives, all refugees and asylum seekers, all who feel confused, outmanoeuvred and overwhelmed by the forces of officialdom.

78 Acts 24:10–21
Courtroom drama

All the speeches in Acts address two audiences: the immediate audience inside the dramatic scene as it unfolds, and the wider audience of Luke's readers. This one is no exception. Paul is making his *apologia*, the speech for the defence (v. 10), using all the wits God gave him to talk his way out of trouble. But he is also offering a defence of a whole way of life, a Way that some people call a 'sect' (v. 14), but which for Paul (and for Luke) is simply the logical outcome of his ancestral faith. So, like all the speeches in this final section of Acts, this one serves both as legal defence and as the affirmation and confirmation of the gospel itself (cf. Philippians 1:7, 16). As we watch and listen to the courtroom drama, Luke is asking us to do two things: to weigh up an argument, and to empathise with a person – a person facing the greatest challenge of his life.

The case for the defence

On the one hand are the men in suits: official deputations, expensive barristers, the best that money can buy. On the other, there is just the prisoner, wearing the clothes he stands up in (he didn't expect to be arrested the day he set out for the temple), speaking (as was normal in a Roman court) in his own defence. Paul knew that you had to treat the Roman governor with respect if you were going to get anywhere. Tertullus' speech in verses 2–4 was a piece of unabashed flattery. Paul plays the same game, but plays it by his own rules. 'I understand,' he begins (with all the dignity of an outraged citizen of cosmopolitan Tarsus), 'that you have been judge over this nation for many years' (v. 10). It's hardly fulsome, but it fulfils the protocols of politeness and allows Paul to move on to a careful statement of the facts, which just as carefully avoids engaging with the accusation except on his own terms.

Let's get the facts straight

Can it really be only twelve days (v. 11) since Paul travelled up to Jerusalem, back in 21:15? It was, Paul maintains, a perfectly legitimate journey, made for the entirely pious and proper purpose of worshipping in Jerusalem and with no intention of getting into disputes or rabble-rousing either in the synagogues or in the city (v. 12). Paul is, of course, being quite truthful here (if a little economical). He has done plenty of disputing in synagogues across Asia, Macedonia and Achaea, but not in Jerusalem; and under Roman law the original plaintiffs have to be present to press the charge (vv. 13, 19).

The Way that they call a sect

All I have done, Paul says, is to follow my ancestral religion according to this Way, a Way that makes me more faithful, not less, to the scriptures we share (v. 14). Some people call it a 'sect', but that just means 'choice'. First-century Judaism was not monolithic: it offered choices, different party allegiances, different emphases in the interpretation of the common heritage. One of the main differences, we already know: Pharisees and Sadducees differed in their interpretation of the scriptural witness to resurrection (vv. 15, 21; 23:6–8). But these are choices to be made within Judaism, legitimate ways of being Jewish – and so, Paul implies, is the Way I have chosen, the Way that sharpens my conscience and makes me ever more acutely aware of the duty I owe both to God and to my neighbour (v. 16). So it is a logical outcome of this shared faith that brings Paul back to the temple after many years (v. 17) and leads to his being found there, not desecrating the temple but completing a rite of purification (v. 18).

The reference to 'offerings' (v. 17) would not have made much sense to Felix; Luke seems here to be combining the story of the nazirite vow (which Paul took on after his arrival in Jerusalem: 21:23–24) and the collection for the Jerusalem church, which we only know of from his letters (see Romans 15:25–28).

Reflection

Do not fear what they fear, and do not be intimidated, but in your hearts sanctify Christ as Lord. Always be ready to make your defence to anyone who demands from you an account of the hope that is in you; yet do it with gentleness and reverence.
1 PETER 3:14–16 (NRSV)

79 Acts 24:22—25:12
'I appeal to Caesar'

And after all the drama? Nothing but the worst kind of waiting, waiting with no end in view, waiting on the whim of an official bureaucracy over which we have no control whatever. Waiting can sap our reserves of faith and courage like nothing else can.

Procrastination of a procurator

Felix is intrigued, but undecided. He already knows a bit about this Way, Luke tells us (v. 22: we have to wait till verse 24 to find out why), but he has received two conflicting accounts of the temple riot, and he won't make a legal decision till Lysias the tribune comes down to give a full report. Presumably the deputation from the Sanhedrin is allowed to go back to Jerusalem, but Paul remains in custody in the *praetorium* of Herod (23:35). At first, it probably doesn't seem too bad: Paul is given some liberty within the prison, and his friends and family are allowed to minister to him by providing food and clothing (v. 23). Within a few days, Felix is back, this time with his wife Drusilla, who was the younger daughter of Herod Agrippa I. Drusilla's knowledge of Jewish affairs could well account for Felix's interest in Paul's case and for his frequent visits to converse with Paul (v. 26). But the couple's interest is strictly limited: when religion gets up close and personal, it's time to back off. Paul's talk about the moral demands of religion (v. 25) is much too close for comfort for Felix. So the case remains unresolved. Bribery would have been one (strictly illegal) way out, but Paul won't play that game (v. 26). Meanwhile, the days and weeks are ticking away.

New man in town

Paul has been in prison for a full two years when Felix's term of office comes to an end. He leaves Paul in prison (v. 27), and it is left to the new governor, Porcius Festus, to clear out his predecessor's filing cabinet. Porcius Festus succeeded Felix as procurator about AD60, and vainly did his best to reverse the slide into anarchy that had begun under Felix. An early meeting with the ruling council in Jerusalem would have been a good way to start (v. 1), and listening carefully to a long-standing complaint would make a good impression (v. 2). But Festus is careful not to get too closely identified with the interests of the temple hierarchy, and insists that if the case is to be reopened it will be heard in Caesarea (vv. 4–5).

The second hearing in Caesarea

Once again, Paul and his accusers are summoned to appear at the governor's tribunal (v. 6), not so much to hear the case as to determine if there is a case to answer and, if so, who should act as judge. Once again, the prosecution and defence state their cases (vv. 7–8). Now Festus sees an obvious way of clearing his backlog and ingratiating himself with the provincials at a stroke: why not send the case to be tried in Jerusalem (v. 9)? This means removing the case from Roman jurisdiction and treating it as a problem under Jewish law – although Festus intends to retain some kind of presence in the process. Because Paul is a Roman citizen, though, Festus cannot make this decision for him. He has to ask if Paul is willing to be tried in Jerusalem. If Paul had accepted the jurisdiction of the local court, he would have been bound by its verdict. But no governor had the power to compel him to accept its jurisdiction. That was one of the privileges of the citizen.

To Festus, it must have looked straightforward enough: the temple riot was a long way in the past. But Paul knows that the passions roused by his visit to Jerusalem are still seething just under the surface (v. 3). Sending him to Jerusalem would be, effectively, to sign his death warrant. So he has only one option left: to appeal to have his case heard in Rome, at the tribunal of Caesar himself (v. 11). This is not about appealing against a verdict (as in modern English law) but about the fundamental right to decide where and under what system of jurisdiction his case will be heard. The outcome is still very much in the balance: 'You have appealed to Caesar: to Caesar you shall go' (v. 12).

Reflection

The big courage is the cold-blooded kind, the kind that never lets go even when you're feeling empty inside, and your blood's thin, and the trouble's not over in an hour or two but lasts for months and years... I reckon fortitude's the biggest thing a man can have... [And] the head man at the job was the Apostle Paul...

John Buchan, *The Four Adventures of Richard Hannay* (Hodder and Stoughton), pp. 631–32.

80

Acts 25:13-27
Power politics

Luke takes a lot of trouble here, setting the scene for the last big speech in Paul's protracted self-defence. It's like a stage setting, with the bustle and buzz of the actors assembling for the last big courtroom scene, and Luke the master storyteller makes the most of it. But the story has its place in history too, and we need a few programme notes at this point to explain things that would have been familiar to Luke's first readers.

Paul and the Roman citizenship

The whole story turns on Paul's claim to be a Roman citizen, which provides the mechanism (humanly speaking) for getting Paul out of Jerusalem and off to Rome. Paul does not mention his Roman status in his letters, but there is no obvious reason why he should mention this fact of family history in his letters to fellow Christians. It was only relevant, as here, in a dispute over identity before a Roman magistrate.

How did someone prove their citizen status? Recently enfranchised citizens, like the veterans who regularly received their citizenship on discharge from the Roman army, would be given a *diploma* to prove it, a folded bronze (or lead) tablet that could be easily carried around. But for second- or third-generation citizens, like Paul, the question of proof was less likely to arise in the normal circumstances of provincial life, and the record would simply be kept in the citizen lists of the citizen's native town, which were updated every five years for tax registration purposes. But given that magistrates could be sued for mistreating a Roman citizen, someone in Paul's position could simply rely on the magistrate's constant fear of litigation. Court cases from disgruntled citizens could do a lot of damage to a rising political career, and it was always wiser to play safe.

Festus, Agrippa and Bernice

Who are the players in this final scene? Festus, the new governor, is busily putting his house in order and energetically clearing his desk for the new administration. The case of *Paul v. Sanhedrin* has to be transferred to Rome, and he will have to provide some paperwork to send with the prisoner (vv. 26-27). Meanwhile, all the protocols of political politeness have to go on – and here come the local royalty, King Agrippa and his consort Bernice, paying a courtesy call to welcome the new governor (v. 13). There is a nice touch of court scandal about these new arrivals, which would not have been lost on Luke's first readers. Agrippa II was the son of Agrippa I (the 'Herod' of Acts 12). He had an uneasy relationship with the Jerusalem hierarchy in the years before the war, and ended his days in Rome. Bernice was his sister (and also the sister of Felix's wife Drusilla) and caused a scandal by coming to live with her brother after the death of her previous husband, their uncle Herod of Chalcis. Nobody was quite sure of the relationship between Agrippa and Bernice, although most people thought the worst. To Festus, the royal couple was an important part of the local political scene, with the potential to become valuable allies or dangerous antagonists.

Conversations in court

Luke gives the impression that Festus is trying desperately to find something to entertain his visitors when Paul's case comes up in conversation (v. 14). Whatever the reason, it attracts Agrippa's attention (v. 22), and it is entirely plausible that the incoming governor, new to Jewish politics and politely puzzled by Jewish religious rivalries, should enlist the aid of this local potentate in drafting his letter to the emperor (vv. 26–27). It gives him the chance to make a good propaganda point about Roman standards of justice and fair play (v. 16). But Festus' conversation also gives us, as readers, a behind-the-scenes glimpse of the Roman view of the whole proceedings (vv. 18–21, 24–25). Like Gallio before him (18:14–15), this Roman governor cannot see that Paul has committed any offence against Roman law. It's all a matter of academic disputes about the native superstition (*deisidaimonia*, a very dismissive term) and about some dead guy called Jesus whom Paul maintains is alive (v. 19). This is not a bad summary of what Paul's life was all about!

Reflection

It is my eager expectation and hope that... by my speaking with all boldness, Christ will be exalted now as always in my body, whether by life or by death. For to me, living is Christ, and dying is gain.
PHILIPPIANS 1:20–21 (NRSV)

What's the one sentence by which you would like an observer to sum up your life?

81 Acts 26:1–16

The heavenly vision

The scene is set; the audience is assembled; the performance is about to begin. All we need is the soloist, summoned from prison to give the performance of his life. That's precisely what this is: Paul's last big speech in Acts, the final aria into which Luke pours his own summing-up of what Paul's mission – Paul's whole life – adds up to. And it all goes back to that Damascus road encounter, to the vision of Christ that gives meaning to the whole.

The prophet and the king

Festus has had his say, and the Roman viewpoint now fades into the background. Luke's narrative spotlight focuses all our attention on the two central players, Paul and Agrippa (v. 1). Paul makes it very clear from the outset that he is addressing his longest and most impassioned defence speech to 'King Agrippa' (v. 2), and he reiterates the address at key points in the speech (vv. 7, 13, 19, 26–29). Agrippa was a political ally of Rome, but he is also and more importantly invoked as an expert in Jewish law (v. 3), with a good record of support for Jewish political interests in Rome. In his official capacity, he has ultimate responsibility for the running of the temple and the appointment of the high priest, so he is a significant player in Jewish affairs, both in Jerusalem and in the diaspora. So, with Festus looking on, Paul's argument is predominantly a conversation within the Jewish community. In that context, Paul adopts the biblical stance of the prophet, acting out of faithfulness to God's call, issuing a disturbing personal challenge to the king. Prophets who talk that way to kings need one characteristic above all: *parrhesia* (26:26), a word we often translate as 'boldness' but which carries with it all the overtones of Athenian free speech and the integrity of the philosopher confronting the wielders of absolute power with a few home truths (see comment on 4:13–31).

Following the Way

'Tell us about yourself,' says Agrippa (v. 1), and that is precisely what Paul does. It's all about 'my way of life' as an observant Jew growing up in Jerusalem (v. 4). Tarsus and Rome recede into the background; this is what really counts. That life, says Paul, is its own testimony, publicly known and uncontested (v. 5) – the life of a Pharisee, devoted to the most stringent interpretation of the Jewish heritage. And it's that shared heritage, not some alien outside influence – that biblical treasury of promise and hope – that underlies where he is today. There is a real continuity, Paul is arguing, between the Pharisee and the apostle, and the thread that ties them together is the shared hope in the resurrection of the dead. In theory, Paul implies, we are all committed to the belief that God raises the dead (v. 8). The trouble is, we seem very reluctant to admit that what we believe in might actually be true.

Who are you, Lord?

Now we're coming to the point – that foundational vision to which Paul keeps returning and which gives meaning to his whole life. We know the story already (chs. 9; 21), but note the extra vividness in this description, the visual detail ('brighter than the midday sun') that we haven't heard before (v. 13). It's as if Paul, forced into inactivity in prison, has been drawn further and further back to reliving the ground-breaking encounter that has brought him to where he is today. He has been reflecting on its deeper meaning: 'It is hard for you to kick against the ox-goad' (v. 14) was a proverbial saying in Greek, expressing the futility of resisting the divine imperative. This is the central challenge of Acts, expressed in a variety of ways by characters from all sides of the debate (see 5:39; 15:10): how can anyone resist the inbreaking activity of God's Spirit?

For Paul himself, the challenge came with the profoundly destabilising realisation of precisely whom his violent, intolerant zeal was really directed against (v. 15). Yet that moment of truth formed the ground – the only ground – on which he could stand (v. 16) and face the future. Moreover, this vision wasn't a one-off, but an introduction to a living presence (v. 16). Witness isn't just about looking back, but about looking forward to what God is going to go on revealing in our lives.

Prayer

Thanks be to thee, my Lord Jesus Christ, for all the benefits thou hast won for me, for all the pains and insults thou hast borne for me. O most merciful Redeemer, friend and brother, may I know thee more clearly, love thee more dearly, and follow thee more nearly, day by day.
Richard of Chichester (1197–1253)

82 Acts 26:16–32

Almost persuaded

Light to the Gentiles

Paul's vision isn't a punishment or even just a warning, but a commission and a promise (v. 16) – the clearest statement yet that Paul saw his vision on the Damascus road as a prophetic call to bring the gospel to the Gentiles (cf. Galatians 1:15–16). The calling is couched in the language of Isaiah (see Isaiah 42:7, 16; 49:6) and, for Luke's readers, echoes the prophetic vision of Simeon in Luke 2:32. Here Paul expresses (with hindsight, surely) the comprehensive and unambiguous vision into which his whole life's work has been leading, extending to the Gentiles – that is, to the whole world – what was already on offer to Israel: light, the kingdom of God, the remission of sins and a share in the world to come (v. 18). The offer is the same for everybody, Jew and Gentile alike. And the conditions are exactly the same, for Gentile as for Jew: repentance and faith in the name of Jesus, the Persecuted One who speaks from heaven. So Festus was right. It is all about this dead guy called Jesus (25:19), whom Paul had experienced as a living presence.

Here I stand

'After that, King Agrippa, I was not disobedient to the heavenly vision' (v. 19) – and that, of course, is the crunch. As Agrippa knows (and as Greek philosophers like Socrates knew), you don't just walk away from that kind of revelation. Looking back, Paul sees his whole missionary enterprise, the story unfolded by Luke step by step through the second half of Acts, springing from that moment (vv. 19–20). That's what brought him to the point of arrest in the temple (v. 21); that's the ground on which he makes his stand (v. 22). And that's the final note of *apologia* from this very undefensive defendant: 'However you cut it, this is my testimony; this is what I have to say to great and small alike.' There's nothing outlandish about this testimony, nothing alien to what Moses and the prophets have led us to expect. If we read them properly (that is, if we read them in the way Luke's narrative has trained us to do: see Luke 24:26, 46; Acts 3:18; 17:3), the scriptures reveal a Christ who accepts the burden and fragility of human suffering, and in doing so releases life and light both to the Jewish people and to the rest of the world (v. 23).

Do you believe?

As a legal defence, this speech is a washout. Its only effect is to convince Festus that Paul is a harmless nutcase (v. 24) – which may be no bad thing in legal terms (vv. 31–32), but hardly constitutes a serious *apologia* to the Roman emperor.

The real issue is not self-defence, but faith, and in the vivid dialogue that closes the scene (vv. 26–29), Paul's passionate conviction almost leaps off the page. This is a direct, prophetic appeal to the king, which at the same time breaks down the barriers between the dramatic audience (the 'on stage' audience listening to Paul's speech) and the real-world audience of the readers. Suddenly, this isn't just an entertaining way to pass the afternoon: it's a story that has the potential to change lives. Paul appeals to Agrippa to consider the real, personal import of the story he has just heard, a double appeal to the publicly known facts of the story (v. 26) and to the scriptural framework that unlocks the events' true significance (v. 27). Its object is clear: Agrippa is right, Paul is doing his best to make him a Christian (v. 28) – him and anyone else who hears (or reads) this remarkable story (v. 29). This is surely as broad a hint as we could hope for of Luke's underlying purpose in writing: narrative and speech combine to show us the unfolding events and to spell out their hidden significance. The ultimate aim of studying the scriptures is persuasion – persuasion leading to faith.

Reflection

We proclaim Christ crucified, a stumbling-block to Jews and foolishness to Gentiles, but to those who are the called, both Jews and Greeks, Christ the power of God and the wisdom of God.
1 CORINTHIANS 1:23–24 (NRSV)

83

Acts 27:1–6

Down to the sea in ships

After the long build-up of tension, the charge and counter-charge of courtroom rhetoric and the frustrations of two years' imprisonment, it's a relief to be on the move again. This final voyage to Rome is a journey long planned (19:21) and underwritten by God's promise (23:11), but not at all the way Paul had envisaged it. Paul is still in chains, in the grip of forces outside his control, shipped from place to place like a parcel (v. 1) – very different from his earlier voyages as a freewheeling traveller. But he has the reassurance that the real power controlling his movements is not the imperial bureaucracy but the plan of God.

Under way

Even in human terms, he is not alone on this final voyage. Look at the dynamic interplay of verbs in verse 1: first, the impersonal language of bureaucracy ('it was decided' – by Them Upstairs, by the unknown forces that control our destiny); then, the warmth of companionship ('that we should sail' – don't worry, you've got friends coming with you). Companionship makes all the difference (compare the poignant notes in Paul's prison letters: Colossians 4:14; 2 Timothy 4:11). God's guiding hand can be seen even in the detail. Julius the centurion, evidently a decent professional soldier trying to do a decent job, provides a human face within the system (vv. 1, 3). Aristarchus of Thessalonica (v. 2) has been one of the party since 19:29 (see Colossians 4:10). But we can also recognise the distinctive voice of the we-narrator (probably Luke himself) in the description of the voyage (27:1—28:16), and he is an ideal travelling companion, with an innate sense of adventure awakened by the mechanics of the voyage itself, and a positive relish for the nautical details of ships and ports, winds and waves.

Coastal waters

The first stage means revisiting familiar waters along the southern coast of Asia Minor (modern Turkey: you'll need a map to get the full flavour of this voyage). Most shipping in the Roman empire was privately owned merchant shipping, taking on a few passengers to supplement the time-honoured business of transporting merchandise between the busy ports of the Mediterranean seaboard. So Julius' first task is to find a coastal trader to connect with the Roman shipping lanes further west (v. 2). Did the little ship from Adramyttium strike a homely note for the traveller who had first joined Paul at nearby Troas (16:10–11)? Then it's a matter of threading their way between island and shore, sailing in the lee of Cyprus to avoid contrary winds (v. 4), watching Cilicia and Pamphylia slip by, perhaps reflecting on all that had happened there – and finally disembarking at Myra (v. 5), where the boat from Adramyttium turns north up the Aegean coast and Julius has to find a ship to take the party west, across the open sea.

The Italian job

Greek seamanship drew on an age-old expertise in sailing coastal waters, but was much less confident in crossing the open sea towards Italy. There was, however, a regular trade supplying the voracious imperial city with its luxuries and its basics – top among which was grain. Enormous grain-ships from Egypt regularly made the hazardous crossing from Alexandria via the ports and islands of the southern Aegean. The emperor Caligula described them as 'crack sailing craft, their skippers the most experienced there are; they drive their vessels like race horses on an unswerving course that goes straight as a die'.[17] This was the type of ship Julius found to transport his little group of prisoners to Italy (v. 6). Such a ship could take up to 1,000 passengers (probably camping on deck), as well as a hold stuffed with grain (27:38), so there would be plenty of room for the 276 passengers that Luke mentions on this sailing (27:37). The real voyage is about to begin.

Reflection

Some went down to the sea in ships, doing business on the mighty waters; they saw the deeds of the Lord, his wondrous works in the deep.
PSALM 107:23–24 (NRSV)

84

Acts 27:7–38

Storm and shipwreck

A sea-voyage quickly takes on its own momentum. The ship becomes a microcosm, its own little world cut off from other kinds of reality – one in which the true dimensions of the physical and spiritual world assert their priority over the social and political structures that dominate life on land. Certainly, the authority of the physical world is very evident in Luke's description of this voyage into the unknown.

Running before the storm

First, we feel the contrary winds that keep the ship desperately beating against the wind (vv. 7–8), making heavy weather of a stage that should be a straight run to Crete. There is almost a sense of a physical force keeping Paul back from his divinely ordained destination, with the Fair Havens (one of the few natural harbours on the southern coast of Crete) a welcome shelter from the hostile forces of nature. Then comes the deceptive light wind (v. 13) that entices the ship's master to nose out from the relative safety of this shallow and exposed cove in a risky attempt to scuttle round to the north coast to find a safer shelter from the winter storms (v. 12) – only to be caught by the vicious blast of 'the typhoon known as Euraquilo' (v. 14) and swept out into the nameless horrors of the open sea, out of sight of land, without sun or stars to navigate by (v. 20).

Whose I am, and whom I serve

Life on board ship also shows up the true dimensions of spiritual authority. Paul has already shown himself a better judge of wind and weather than the professional sailors (vv. 9–10), although we can hardly blame Julius for trusting the professional expertise of the ship's master and his helmsman (v. 11). As the storm takes hold, there is a panic-stricken sense of the powerlessness of human skill and resource in the face of the relentless forces of nature (vv. 15–19). Gradually, Paul the prisoner emerges as the true leader of the beleaguered crew (vv. 21–32), but only by virtue of the fact that he too is a servant (v. 23).

Land ahead

Sailors often have a sixth sense that tells them there is land ahead, even in the dark (v. 27). That, however, brings a new danger. In the open sea, the preoccupation of the ship's crew is to keep the ship afloat and the right way up: hence the priority of getting rid of unnecessary gear (vv. 17–19). But with land – and a totally unknown land – ahead, the first priority is to prevent her running blindly aground (vv. 27–29). Taking soundings (v. 28) is done by the traditional method of swinging a line with a weight at the end to touch bottom. They are close enough, clearly, to run out four anchors from the stern (v. 29), and close enough for some of the sailors to think of making off to shore in the ship's dinghy, under the pretence of putting out anchors from the bows (v. 30). But the passengers will be helpless without the crew, and the ship's company must stay together (vv. 31–32). There is nothing to do but wait and see what day will bring (v. 33).

Jonah in reverse

There is a nice reversal here of the Jonah story. There, the whole ship's company is endangered by a prophet running away from his God (Jonah 1:7–16); here, the whole ship's company is saved by the presence of a prophet who is acting in obedience to his God (v. 24). In that context, there is a peculiar piquancy in the act of breaking bread and giving thanks to God on the swaying ship's deck, listening to the waves crashing on the reefs ahead (vv. 34–35). This is a powerful demonstration of moral authority coming from the most expendable person on board. The prisoner's calmness and refusal to panic have a beneficial effect on the whole crew (vv. 36–38). But Paul's action is also, in the deepest sense, sacramental, a celebration of Eucharist – the thanksgiving of the whole created world to its creator, enacted by the faithful remnant in the midst of and on behalf of the unbelieving micro-world with whom its fate is inextricably entwined.

Reflection

Then they cried to the Lord in their trouble, and he brought them out from their distress; he made the storm be still, and the waves of the sea were hushed. Then they were glad because they had quiet, and he brought them to their desired haven. Let them thank the Lord for his steadfast love, for his wonderful works to humankind.

PSALM 107:28–31 (NRSV)

85 Acts 27:39—28:6

Desert island hospitality

Here, finally, is the emissary of the gospel, washed up on a desert island, bearing the signs of God's active presence with him – and finding unexpected hospitality from the island's inhabitants.

All safe to land

The ship's final traumatic moments are described in fascinated detail. The sailors abandon all attempts to control the ship by anchors or rudder, and trust that the onshore wind will bring her safely ashore on the sandy beach glimpsed beyond the breakers (v. 40). But the shallow bay has a deceptive 'double sea', a place of contrary currents caused by the underlying configuration of the seabed, and the ship finds herself trapped, bows rammed aground and stern being broken up by the force of the waves (v. 41). It's a moment of epic drama that calls forth echoes of the sea stories of Homer's *Odyssey*, known to every Greek schoolboy – but, for the prisoners, the chief danger comes from the soldiers (v. 42). Julius the centurion has to exert his authority to prevent Paul being summarily executed (v. 43), so there is a real sense of having escaped 'by the skin of our teeth' in the final words of this dramatic chapter (v. 44).

An island called Malta

But where are they? In Luke's story, this is an island in the farthest west, reached after storm and tribulation – an island peopled by 'barbarians' (v. 2), the patronising Greek word for anyone who did not speak Greek. But Malta is home to one of the oldest civilisations in the world, and had been settled over the centuries by a variety of incomers. The native language was in fact a form of Punic, a relic of the centuries-old Phoenician colonisation of the western Mediterranean. So the shipwrecked party find themselves surrounded by native islanders speaking an unintelligible language – a potentially hostile crowd, but still part of God's world and capable of mediating God's grace to the shipwrecked passengers and crew. Kindling a fire is the obvious priority for the soaked, shivering survivors (v. 2). It's raining (the only place in Acts where the weather is mentioned), and it's cold – not only because it is still early dawn (27:39), but because it was already autumn when the ship left Crete (27:9) – only two weeks ago – which means that winter is getting closer.

Bonfire night

In the flickering half-light, with unaccustomed bodies barging about in the undergrowth, it's no wonder the startled adder fastens on to Paul's hand as he gathers brushwood (v. 3), under the terrified gaze of the locals, who expect Paul to swell up or drop dead (v. 6). Like the pagan sailors on Jonah's ship (Jonah 1:7–10), they are only too ready to make connections between natural disaster and divine displeasure. It looks to them like a surefire proof that this particular prisoner was not meant to survive the shipwreck (v. 4). But their expectations couldn't be more wrong: Paul shakes the adder off, completely unharmed. There's now an instant switch from execration to hero-worship. In the public imagination, you're either a criminal or a god.

In the midst of the disaster, there is a wry humour about this episode, but Luke is making a serious point too. Paul is on trial for his life, his whole mission under scrutiny. We know from Paul's own letters that many of his fellow Christians were questioning his motives and doubting his divine calling when he was in prison (see Philippians 1:12–20). Many people today are equally ready to jump to conclusions when a star or public figure is overtaken by accident or illness, lurching from adulation to vilification. So Luke's story subtly conveys a deeper and more powerful verdict on Paul's mission than Caesar could ever do. God's servant is neither a criminal nor a god: he's a vulnerable human being, subject to the same winds and waves as the rest of us, but someone who has placed his life in the hands of the one who is utterly trustworthy (27:23).

Reflection

By awesome deeds you answer us with deliverance, O God of our salvation; you are the hope of all the ends of the earth and of the farthest seas… You silence the roaring of the seas, the roaring of their waves, the tumult of the peoples. Those who live at earth's farthest bounds are awed by your signs; you make the gateways of the morning and the evening shout for joy.

PSALM 65:5, 7–8 (NRSV)

86 Acts 28:7–15

And so to Rome

Islands play a peculiar role in the Greek imagination, evoking both fear of the unknown and idyllic visions of a natural paradise. There is an element of that mixture in Paul's winter on Malta – a time out of time, making space for rest and restoration, a momentary glimpse of creation reunified and made whole.

Paul the healer

Malta is not a desert island: it has a 'first man' (local governor) with the very Roman name of Publius (v. 7). He has a country estate near to where Paul and his party are washed up, and he offers hospitality for three days. Luke doesn't explain how this came about. 'Us' probably means not the whole crew but Paul the Roman citizen and his friends and fellow prisoners, an introduction probably effected under the watchful eye of Julius the centurion, who wastes no time in getting himself and his charges safe under a civilised Roman roof. Here at the ends of the earth, Paul finds hospitality – and Luke highlights the parallels with other hosts and other healings, right back to the beginning of the gospel story. Jesus' mission began with the prophetic proclamation of God's creation order restored (Luke 4:16–21), and his healing ministry in Capernaum began with the healing of his host's mother-in-law (Luke 4:38–39). Even as a shipwrecked prisoner, Paul is still an agent of that healing power (vv. 8–9). Here is further confirmation (if we needed it) that Paul's God is still with him and a reminder that the healing that Jesus proclaimed was never confined to Israel (see Luke 4:24–27).

Romeward bound

This idyllic island life isn't where Paul's story ends, however. God has work for him to do in Rome. Rather incongruously, just over the island are the busy shipping lanes leading across to the ports of Sicily (vv. 12–13) and on to Italy. Generously supplied for the voyage by their new island friends (v. 10), all they have to do is to wait for the sailing season to open again in March and take the first ship heading across the straits to Rome (v. 11). This is another Alexandrian vessel, over-wintering on the island and sailing under the figurehead of the *Dioscuri* or 'Heavenly Twins' ('Gemini' to modern astrologers). They were the patron deities of sailors and frequently appear in shipwreck stories, but Paul has no need of their protection. Our nautical diarist is enjoying the sense of being on the move again and relishing the details of ports and winds (vv. 12–13), but also, perhaps, marking with some nervousness every stage of the prisoner's journey to Rome to face again the problems he had been able to forget at sea. From Rhegium, the ship sails up the west coast of Italy to Puteoli, one of the major disembarkation points for the city (v. 13), and meets an unexpected grace: there are 'brothers' in Puteoli, Christian friends who offer hospitality and encouragement as the party pauses for another week (v. 14).

Journey's end

There is a real sense of achievement about the end of Paul's epic voyage: 'And that's how we got to Rome!' (v. 14). We have tracked across the Mediterranean, battling our way against contrary winds, battered by everything the sea can throw at us, and survived storm and shipwreck. So have we reached the 'ends of the earth' (1:8)? In a way, yes. Certainly Rome seems a long way away from Jerusalem (2:10), and the long sea-voyage of chapter 27 reinforces that impression. But there is also a surprising sense of homecoming about these last stages of the voyage, coming up the Appian Way past the Forum of Appius and the Three Taverns (v. 15), the final staging-posts on the road maps of the empire in which all roads lead to Rome. Word has got back from Puteoli about Paul's arrival, and there is a welcoming party coming to greet and escort the prisoner to Rome with all the ceremony of a visiting dignitary. We have got to the ends of the earth – but God is there before us.

Prayer

If I take the wings of the morning, and dwell in the uttermost parts of the sea, even there thy hand shall lead me, and thy right hand shall hold me.
PSALM 139:9–10 (RSV)

87 Acts 28:16–31

In my end is my beginning

The emissary of the gospel has finally reached Rome, but this final scene is not quite what we might expect. Rome already has a flourishing Christian community (28:15), and Paul arrives not as a missionary but as a prisoner, with the ever-watchful presence of a soldier to keep him in mind of the restrictions on his freedom (v. 16).

Meeting the Jewish community

The final scene of Acts shows Paul defending his position for the last time, not (as we might expect) before the emperor, but before the leaders of the local Jewish community (v. 17). They are the ones he is most concerned to meet and explain his position to – insisting that nothing he has done was intended to harm the interests of his own nation (vv. 18–19). Paul's underlying motivation, he insists (as he has done all through the trial chapters in Acts), is not treachery but loyalty – loyalty to Israel's deepest hopes and aspirations (v. 20). Equally interesting is the response of the community leaders (vv. 21–22): a measured neutrality regarding the actions of the Jerusalem authorities, and a genuine open-mindedness towards Paul's theological claims. Tell us about this sect, they say, for we have had no ruling about you from Jerusalem (v. 21); all we have is contradictory rumours about a sect that seems to attract bad publicity wherever it goes (v. 22). In a sense, that is the question to which Luke's whole narrative seeks to provide an answer: 'Tell us your story, tell us what this Jesus business is all about.'

Famous last words

The final scene of Acts (vv. 17–28) leaves us effectively where Luke's story of Jesus began, with the messenger of God's kingdom pleading, arguing, debating, testifying to his fellow Jews, seeking by every means possible to persuade his listeners about Jesus (v. 23) – but finding, just as John the Baptist did, that some are persuaded while others are not (v. 24; cf. Luke 3:7–20). This is the tragedy that Luke's story ultimately faces: not a total rejection of the gospel, but a failure on the part of the community as a whole to grasp the opportunity on offer.

Like the Baptist and Jesus himself (Luke 3:4–6; 4:16–25), Paul finds himself falling back on the words of the prophet Isaiah to identify what is happening here, picking up those chilling words from Isaiah 6:9-10 that seem to suggest that some of God's people are simply incapable of hearing the word of God's salvation (vv. 26–27). This is another example of the early church's habit of using the 'that' of scripture to throw light on the 'this' of what is actually happening, to find scriptural precedent for the unfolding pattern of events (cf. Luke 8:9–10). Although most of the first Christians were Jews, it is a fact that the churches failed to convince Israel as a whole to adopt their messianic view of history. We can see Paul wrestling with the same problem in Romans 9—11. This is not a judgement on Israel, much less a final 'turning away' from preaching to the Jews. It is Paul's justification for extending the preaching of God's kingdom to the Gentiles (v. 28), saying in effect, 'I've given you your chance; now you can't complain if I give them theirs too.' The bringing in of the Gentiles doesn't mean that God has rejected his people. By no means (Romans 11:1)!

Light to the Gentiles

That is the note on which Luke chooses to end his story. Acts doesn't come to a grand climax or a triumphalistic conclusion. Paul is still a prisoner, still awaiting a trial that may end in his death. The journey that began on the mountaintop, with the heavens opened and angels pointing the way, ends in a hired lodging in a back street in Rome (v. 30), where even the words of God's messenger are open to doubt and debate. It's the end of the story – but not the end of the journey. 'The story of God's purpose has not drawn to a close, but, quite the contrary, is manifestly still being written in the life of Jesus – then in Acts, in the life of the early Christian communities, and is now ongoing'.[18] The word is loose: it's out on the street – and nothing can stop it (v. 31).

Reflection

> *'Lord, now lettest thou thy servant depart in peace, according to thy word: for mine eyes have seen thy salvation, which thou hast prepared before the face of all people; a light to lighten the Gentiles, and the glory of thy people Israel.'*
> LUKE 2:29–32 (KJV)

NOTES

1 Peter Jackson and Chris Wright, *Faith Confirmed* (SPCK, 1999), p. 23.
2 Lucian, *Peregrinus* 13.
3 Justo Gonzalez, *Acts: The gospel of the Spirit* (Orbis, 2001), pp. 86ff.
4 Josephus, *Antiquities*, 20.97–98.
5 Gonzalez, *Acts*, p. 85.
6 Josephus, *Antiquities*, 3.93–102.
7 Lam.R. 1.1.4.
8 Ovid, *Metamorphoses* 8.620–724.
9 C.K. Barrett, *The Acts of the Apostles*, International Critical Commentary, two volumes (T&T Clark, 1994, 1998), vol. 2, p. 724.
10 Suetonius, *Life of Claudius* 25.
11 Gonzalez, *Acts*, p. 213.
12 Pliny, *Letters* 10.96.
13 Pliny, *Letters* 10.96.
14 Josephus, *Antiquities* 20.169–72; *Jewish War* 2.261–63.
15 Josephus, *Jewish War* 2.429, 441–42.
16 Tacitus, *Histories* 5.9.
17 Lionel Casson, *Travel in the Ancient World* (George Allen and Unwin, 1974), p. 158.
18 Joel B. Green, *The Theology of the Gospel of Luke* (Cambridge University Press, 1995), p. 28.

The Bible is at the heart of BRF's work, and this special anniversary collection is a celebration of the Bible for BRF's centenary year. Bringing together a fantastically wide-ranging writing team of authors, supporters and well-wishers from all areas of BRF's work, this resource is designed to help us go deeper into the story of the Bible and reflect on how we can share it in our everyday lives. Including sections which lead us through the Bible narrative as well as thematic and seasonal sections, it is the perfect daily companion to resource your spiritual journey.

The BRF Book of 365 Bible Reflections
With contributions from BRF authors, supporters and well-wishers
Edited by Karen Laister and Olivia Warburton
978 1 80039 100 0 £14.99

brfonline.org.uk

Prayer is at the heart of BRF's work, and this special illustrated anniversary collection is a celebration of prayer for BRF's centenary year. It can be used in a range of different settings, from individual devotions to corporate worship. Including sections on prayers of preparation, seasonal prayers, and themed prayers for special times and hard times, it is the perfect daily companion to resource your spiritual journey.

The BRF Book of 100 Prayers
Resourcing your spiritual journey
Martyn Payne
978 1 80039 147 5 £12.99

brfonline.org.uk

'Lord Jesus Christ, Son of God, have mercy on me.' This ancient prayer has been known and loved by generations of Christians for hundreds of years. It is a way of entering into the river of prayer which flows from the heart of God: the prayer of God himself, as Jesus continually prays for his people and for the world he loves. Simon Barrington-Ward teaches us how to use the Jesus Prayer as a devotional practice, and opens up the Bible passages that are crucial to understanding it.

The Jesus Prayer
BRF Centenary Classics
Simon Barrington-Ward
978 1 80039 087 4 £14.99

brfonline.org.uk

The BRF Centenary Prayer

Gracious God,
we rejoice in this centenary year
that you have grown BRF
from a local network of Bible readers
into a worldwide family of ministries.
Thank you for your faithfulness
in nurturing small beginnings
into surprising blessings.
We rejoice that, from the youngest to the oldest,
so many have encountered your word
and grown as disciples of Christ.
Keep us humble in your service,
ambitious for your glory
and open to new opportunities.
For your name's sake
Amen

Friends of BRF

I never fail to be amazed by the generosity of our supporters.

BRF is a remarkable charity, but we can only do what we do with the help of our faithful supporters: volunteers, people who pray for us and spread the word about our work, and people who support us financially, both individuals who give donations and legacies, and charitable trusts.

Many of our supporters have become 'Friends of BRF', choosing to make a regular monthly gift to help ensure that our work can be sustained and developed in the coming years. Every single donation, whether occasional or regular, small or large, makes a huge difference and I, along with all my colleagues here at BRF, thank God for each one.

If you'd like to help support Living Faith and our wider ministry, please visit **brf.org.uk/give**, contact a member of the fundraising team by email at **giving@brf.org.uk** or call **01235 462305** to speak to one of us direct.

With heartfelt thanks

Julie

**Julie MacNaughton,
Head of Fundraising MCIOF(Dip)**

 *Enabling all ages to grow in faith*

Anna Chaplaincy
Living Faith
Messy Church
Parenting for Faith

100 years of BRF

2022 is BRF's 100th anniversary! Look out for details of our special new centenary resources, a beautiful centenary rose and an online thanksgiving service that we hope you'll attend. This centenary year we're focusing on sharing the story of BRF, the story of the Bible – and we hope you'll share your stories of faith with us too.

Find out more at **brf.org.uk/centenary**.

To find out more about our work, visit
brf.org.uk

THE PEOPLE'S BIBLE COMMENTARY
John

15 The Chambers, Vineyard
Abingdon OX14 3FE
brf.org.uk

Bible Reading Fellowship is a charity (233280)
and company limited by guarantee (301324),
registered in England and Wales

ISBN (boxed set) 978 1 80039 093 5
First published 1998
This edition published 2022
10 9 8 7 6 5 4 3 2 1 0
All rights reserved

Text © Richard A. Burridge 1998, 2008, 2010
This edition © Bible Reading Fellowship 2022
Cover images: detail of east window, chapel of Manchester College, Oxford, photo © Fr Lawrence Lew, OP; background © iStock.com/petekarici; gold texture © AmadeyART/stock.adobe.com

The author asserts the moral right to be identified as the author of this work

Acknowledgements

Scripture quotations taken from The New Revised Standard Version of the Bible, Anglicised Edition (NRSV), are copyright © 1989, 1995 by the Division of Christian Education of the National Council of the Churches of Christ in the United States of America, and are used by permission. All rights reserved.

Scripture quotations taken from The Revised Standard Version of the Bible (RSV) are copyright © 1946, 1952, 1971 by the Division of Christian Education of the National Council of the Churches of Christ in the United States of America, and are used by permission. All rights reserved.

Every effort has been made to trace and contact copyright owners for material used in this resource. We apologise for any inadvertent omissions or errors, and would ask those concerned to contact us so that full acknowledgement can be made in the future.

A catalogue record for this book is available from the British Library

Printed and bound by CPI Group (UK) Ltd, Croydon CR0 4YY

THE PEOPLE'S BIBLE COMMENTARY

John

Richard A. Burridge

Photocopying for churches

Please report to CLA Church Licence any photocopy you make from this publication. Your church administrator or secretary will know who manages your CLA Church Licence.

The information you need to provide to your CLA Church Licence administrator is as follows:

Title, Author, Publisher and ISBN

If your church doesn't hold a CLA Church Licence, information about obtaining one can be found at **uk.ccli.com**

PREFACE TO THE 2010 EDITION

So much has happened since I wrote the first edition of this commentary in 1998. Then it was one of the first to be published in a new series for BRF to be called *The People's Bible Commentary*, of which I was also privileged to be one of the three general editors. It is a joy that within ten years we were able to complete the project for the whole Bible in 32 volumes, including scholars from a wide range of countries, different backgrounds and various Christian denominations. Yet the format of each volume has remained the same, providing double-page readings of each book, passage by passage, either for daily use or to assist with study groups, talks or sermons. It has been a delight as I go around the country taking study days and training sessions to find that my commentary and the series as a whole has become greatly appreciated by clergy and lay people alike. Indeed, over the last decade, I have found myself regularly turning to many volumes in the series, either for my own personal Bible study or as part of my preparation for preaching.

I was honoured that the Archbishop of Canterbury and the planning group, led by Professor Gerald West from Pietermaritzburg, South Africa, should have chosen this commentary as preparatory reading for the Lambeth Conference 2008. Accordingly, we produced a slightly updated second edition, which was then sent to all the Anglican bishops throughout the world with a daily reading plan for the six months February to July 2008. Archbishop Rowan himself began the Conference by leading the bishops in three days' retreat with addresses on St John, while the rest of the Conference started each day with study of John's gospel in small groups. I hope and pray that we may follow the bishops' example in our own reading of the fourth gospel.

I remain deeply grateful to Richard Fisher and Naomi Starkey at BRF, and to our colleagues at Hendrickson for the American version, and I pray that this new edition may help us love Jesus and each other more.

Richard A. Burridge

ACKNOWLEDGEMENTS

I learned so much while I was writing this book, despite my years of preaching and teaching it in universities and churches. The list of books at the back contains the key works to which I have been indebted for so much of the material in this commentary.

I am also grateful to my undergraduate students at the University of Exeter and King's College London for their encouragement and ideas, as well as to various postgraduates for their stimulation. Congregations in Exeter University Chapel, King's College Chapel and St Andrew's Church, Whitehall heard quite a lot of this preached over the years. While I was writing the commentary, I delivered the daily key note Bible readings on John for the Diocese of Rochester's 'Forward in Mission' conference in October 1997; my thanks to all who participated, especially the Bishop of Rochester and Canon Gordon Oliver.

Revd Shelagh Brown of BRF invited me to write this and was very encouraging at the beginning; her sudden death in July 1997 left us all the poorer. I am grateful to Naomi Starkey for her editorial assistance and the way she took over the project, as well as to my colleagues as editors, David Winter and Henry Wansbrough as we completed the commentaries on the entire Bible. Many people acted as 'trial readers' of these studies while they were being written, but I am particularly grateful to Jane Pendarves and Betty Jeffery for all their time, interest and helpful suggestions.

As always, it was my wife, Sue, and our daughters, Rebecca and Sarah, who put up with author's stress and preoccupation at the computer. Without their continuing love and understanding, it would not have been possible.

I am grateful to Professor Raymond Brown for the constant inspiration of his writings on John and for his personal warmth and interest in the first edition of this commentary. Following his sudden death when it was just about to be published, I gladly dedicated this book to his memory.

CONTENTS

Introduction 9

1 In the beginning................26
2 Light in the darkness........28
3 Acceptance or rejection?..30
4 The Word became flesh ...32
5 Questions and answers....35
6 The witness of John the Baptist 37
7 Come and see 40
8 Follow me 42
9 The wedding at Cana 44
10 Water into wine.................46
11 House cleaning..................48
12 Destroy this temple 50
13 Realising and believing....52
14 Nicodemus by night 54
15 The teacher is taught heavenly things 56
16 God so loved the world 58
17 Jesus and John the Baptist 60
18 Jesus – the one from above.........................62
19 A Samaritan woman at a well............................64
20 Living water 66
21 Prophet or Messiah?.........68
22 Food and harvests.............70
23 Healing an official's son ...72
24 Do you want to be healed?..............................74
25 The sabbath and Jesus' claims................................76
26 The Son gives life and judges 78
27 Bearing witness 80
28 The scriptures and Moses 82
29 Feeding the 5,000 84
30 Who is this? 86
31 More questions and answers......................88
32 I am the bread of life 90
33 Bread from heaven...........92
34 Eat my flesh and drink my blood 94
35 The parting of the ways....97
36 Times and places............100
37 Teaching in Jerusalem ...102
38 Jesus' authority and identity....................104
39 Come to me and drink....106
40 No one ever spoke like this man 108
41 The woman taken in adultery......................110
42 I am the light of the world.........................112
43 Who are you? 115
44 The truth will make you free 117
45 Who is your Father?........119
46 Before Abraham was, I am.................................122
47 The light comes to a blind man...............125
48 The blind man is healed 127
49 Healing brings opposition......................129
50 I was blind but now I see 131

51	Jesus brings both sight and blindness	133
52	I am the door	136
53	I am the good shepherd	138
54	Tell us plainly	140
55	The Father and I are one	142
56	The one you love is ill	144
57	Lazarus is asleep	146
58	Your brother will rise again	148
59	I am the resurrection and the life	150
60	Lazarus, come out!	152
61	One man must die for the people	155
62	Anointing at Bethany	157
63	What sort of king?	159
64	We want to see Jesus	162
65	Lifting up the Son of Man	164
66	Belief, blindness and fear	166
67	Light sent to save the world	168
68	Jesus washes the disciples' feet	170
69	I have given you an example	172
70	Beloved or betrayer?	174
71	Love one another	176
72	I am the way, the truth and the life	178
73	Show us the Father	180
74	The promise of the Spirit	182
75	A parting gift	184
76	I am the vine	187
77	Abide in love	189
78	Not of the world	191
79	The Spirit of truth	193
80	Returning to the Father	195
81	The task of the Spirit	197
82	Sorrow will turn to joy	199
83	Going to the Father	201
84	Father, glorify your Son	204
85	Jesus prays for his disciples	206
86	Sanctify them in the truth	208
87	Jesus prays for the church	210
88	Betrayed in a garden	212
89	From garden to courtyard	214
90	Jesus before the high priest	216
91	Rebukes and denials	218
92	Accused before Pilate	220
93	Are you king of the Jews?	222
94	Hail, king of the Jews!	225
95	No king but Caesar!	227
96	The king is crucified	229
97	The king's last words	231
98	The death of the king	234
99	The king is buried	236
100	They have taken away the Lord	238
101	I have seen the Lord!	241
102	Sent out in the Spirit	243
103	Thomas: from disbelief to faith	246
104	Gone fishing	248
105	Breakfast with Jesus	250
106	Do you love me more than these?	252
107	Follow me	254

Glossary ... 256
For further reading ... 257

INTRODUCTION

A book in which a child may paddle but an elephant can swim deep.

Welcome to all those who cannot wait to get in the water

Whenever we go to the beach, my children rush to take off their shoes and socks and go paddling immediately – and I was the same at their age. So this is a quick word of encouragement and safety warning to those who want to jump straight into the text. John's gospel is a lovely story. It can be enjoyed by those who know little of Jesus and nothing of the background, which is why it is often given out at churches and meetings to those who are enquiring about the Christian faith. So, go ahead and splash around in it! You can jump about and dip in here and there, because these little studies are all separate in themselves. On the other hand, you might want to use it for your early morning bathe and exercise, and take one or two sections each day for meditation and prayer. If you have the stamina, you can immerse yourself in reading it straight through, for each part flows into the next.

But, as that little saying above about John notes, it is also a book in which the real heavyweights, the mystics and the theologians, have been drowning for centuries! Beneath that placid surface run powerful undercurrents and eddies which will circle you around and bring you out some way forward or back from where you went in. I have tried to chart some of these as we go along, but if you get into difficulties, you might find it helpful to get out, sit on the beach and read these notes. And of course, if you want to do some serious wallowing in John, a little bit of preparation is always a good idea.

You will need a Bible, New Testament or gospel text open as you read. Each study is on a small section and we shall usually work through it verse by verse. Quotations tend to be from the RSV or NRSV, but often I will paraphrase the meaning of the original Greek. You should be able to follow it with any translation, and try several for variation.

What is this book?

It is called a 'gospel', or *eu-angelion* in Greek, which means a 'good message' or 'good news', connected with the word 'angel' or messenger. In the Old Testament this means the 'good news' of God's peace and salvation, brought to poor and hurting people trapped in pain or oppression (Isaiah 52:7; 61:1). In the Greco-Roman world, it was used for the latest proclamation from the local government or the emperor. But what it is called does not tell us what it is. In its form and content it describes a couple of years of the life and work of Jesus of Nazareth, a preacher, teacher and wonder-worker in the Roman province of Judea, concentrating particularly on his trial and execution by the political and religious authorities and the rather strange things which happened afterwards. It is not what we would expect from a biography today.

On the other hand, it is very like many ancient accounts of teachers, philosophers, generals and statesmen. They tended to be quite short; John is just over 15,000 words, or about a sixth of this book. It was the amount which could fit on a single scroll of papyrus and be read aloud in a couple of hours. Because they were relatively short, such works could not cover all of a person's life. So they would focus on some significant stories from someone's public life in society, including a concentration on their death, to show what they were really like. These books were not meant to be accurate historical reporting, nor were they fiction or legend; they would include stories about the person and the kind of things they said and did, to interpret their significance. So John makes it clear that he has made a similar selection from the 'many other things Jesus did' to show the reader who Jesus is, 'the Christ, the Son of God' (20:30–31; 21:25). Therefore we must expect to find both story and interpretative reflection, both history and theology.

This explains why the book is structured in two main sections. The first describes Jesus' ministry, from his baptism and meeting his first followers through his teaching and miracles as some people come to believe and accept him while the opposition of others, particularly the authorities, grows over a couple of years (1:19—10:42). It is sometimes called the 'Book of Signs' because of the way Jesus' miracles are used to show who he is. The second half covers only his last few days, teaching his disciples and his trial, death and resurrection (13:1—20:31), often known as the 'Book of Glory' because John uses 'glory' to describe what happens to Jesus. From these two parts emerges a clear picture of who Jesus is and what happened to him. Around these sections, the writer has arranged a prologue, like an overture to set out the main themes (1:1–18), an interlude at half-time to help change gear (11:1—12:50) and an epilogue to tie up some loose ends (21).

How was it composed and produced?

This book is called 'the gospel according to John'. It does not say it was written *by* him, but is 'according to' his teaching and interpretation. In fact, even this description is not original, but dates from the second century when the four gospels were collected together and given these titles to distinguish them from one another. Furthermore, John is never mentioned in the text. There is an unnamed disciple described as 'the one Jesus loved' who is present at the last supper, the trial, the cross and the resurrection (see on 13:23; 18:15–17; 19:26–27; 20:2–8 below). In the epilogue, he is claimed as the 'witness' who caused it all to be written but who may have since died (see on 21:24). Since the only possibilities in that chapter are the 'sons of Zebedee and two others' (21:2), he has been traditionally identified as the apostle John, son of Zebedee.

It was quite common in the ancient world for the followers of a great man to write up his ideas and teachings, as Plato did for Socrates. If John had led this particular early church for many years, it might be better to think of him as the 'authority' rather than the 'author' of the gospel 'according to John'. Since we do not know who actually wrote the book, in this commentary we shall use 'John' to refer to the 'writer', 'author' or 'evangelist', and sometimes even to describe the text itself in the traditional manner.

Whoever wrote it seems to have worked independently of the other three gospels. Matthew, Mark and Luke are often called the 'synoptics' because when you 'see' them 'together' (*syn-optic-* in Greek), it is clear that the texts are related, probably with Matthew and Luke using Mark as a source. While John has some of the same people and similar stories, he uses different words and writes in a completely different style with many individuals, events and teachings occurring only in this gospel.

Because of the interlude and the epilogue, and the way the story jumps around between Galilee and Jerusalem, some scholars think the gospel may have gone through several editions before reaching its final form. Certainly it seems to show the effect of years of theological reflection and teaching. However, the attempts to reconstruct earlier versions vary so much that it is probably impossible. Furthermore, with the one exception of the woman taken in adultery (see on 7:53—8:11 below), all the ancient manuscripts have the gospel in the form we have it today. So we shall take the gospel as we find it and work through it verse by verse.

How does it read?

This gospel is written in a very distinctive style, which seems to have emerged through years of teaching and prayer, meditation and theological reflection. Furthermore, the whole gospel uses this style and vocabulary. Punctuation marks were not put into manuscripts until a thousand years later, and sometimes it is difficult to see where they go. Thus it is not clear whether the most famous verse, 'God so loved' (3:16), is spoken by Jesus or is a comment from the writer; the same difficulty makes it unclear whether 3:31–36 is spoken by John the Baptist or another narrative comment (see on 3:9–36 below).

Style and vocabulary

In fact, we could all probably write in John's style after spending a while immersed in the gospel. It has a limited vocabulary with a number of key words repeated over and over again, such as look, see, witness, know, believe, have faith, world, glory, abide, remain, hour, send. Other words are in contrasting pairs: light and darkness, truth and falsehood, life and death, above and below, love and hate, father and son. The sentences tend to be short, but they build on each other in steps and stairs and spirals, connecting and reconnecting. Someone has said these words over and over and over again in prayer and teaching. It is ideally suited, therefore, for use now in contemplation and the little prayers and suggestions at the end of each section in this commentary are designed to help you reflect on the passages and let them soak into you.

Time

Time also seems to behave in a similar way for John. Unlike the other gospels, which seem to relate only one season of ministry leading to a Passover, John has a logical sequence over several years with three Passovers (2:13; 6:4; 12:1). But time seems to go round and round, to speed up and slow down. The first half of the gospel occupies at least two years, while the second half is little more than a week. Little references like 'now', 'already', 'recently', 'day' abound. At first, Jesus' 'hour' has 'not yet come' (2:4; 7:30; 8:20), but when it arrives it is both the 'hour of glory' and the Passion (12:23, 27; 13:1; 17:1). There are 'flash backs' and 'flash forwards' which connect parts of the narrative: for example, 7:50 and 19:39 refer back to Nicodemus' visit by night in 3:2, while 11:2 looks forward to Mary's anointing in 12:3. There are even references out beyond the story to the disciples' later reflections (2:22; 7:39; 21:23).

Levels of meaning

Like many in the ancient world, John tends to see the world in different levels, with earthly things reflecting or foreshadowing heavenly realities. This is also true of the way he writes. To go back to our opening analogy, the surface looks placid, but underneath flow ever deeper currents of meaning. Most of Jesus' conversations begin with natural things, like birth (3:3), water (4:7), bread (6:25), sight (9:1), but questions and misunderstandings soon follow. As Jesus takes his questioners deeper, John invites us to look beyond earthly things to spiritual realities, to the true bread or true vine. If we look closely at what is happening, some of the stories and images, like the manna in the desert or the figure of the good shepherd and the sheep, are being played out in Jesus' life and eventual death. There is tremendous irony below the surface, so that Jesus' talk of 'being lifted up' actually means a cross (3:14; 8:28; 12:32) or the soldiers' mocking someone who really is the 'king of the Jews' (19:1–3, 19–22).

Signs and discourses

While John narrates several of Jesus' miracles, he never calls them this. They are 'signs', which 'reveal his glory' (2:11). People believed in him because of the signs (2:23; 7:31; 10:41). The writer tells us that Jesus did many more of them of which these are only a selection to help us believe in him (20:30–31). Most analyses of the gospel suggest that there are seven signs:

- changing water into wine (2:1–11)
- healing the official's son (4:46–54)
- healing the paralysed man (5:1–15)
- feeding the 5,000 (6:1–15)
- walking on the water (6:16–21)
- giving sight to the blind man (9:1–7)
- raising Lazarus from the dead (11:17–44)

In addition, there is the huge catch of fish in the epilogue (21:1–11). In order to include this one but still keep to the perfect number seven, some remove one of the others, like the walking on water, because it does not seem to 'sign' anything. Certainly, some of the signs lead naturally into Jesus' debates and discourses, which draw out the meaning of the 'sign', and some are linked to the seven 'I am' sayings. Thus the feeding leads to the debate about the 'bread of life' (6:25–59) and the blind man is connected to 'the light of the world' (8:12; 9:5). However, other signs, like the water into wine or the official's son, do not lead to a discourse, and John never mentions the word 'seven', so perhaps we should be careful about trying to be too clever sometimes!

These notes on John's style and way of writing might help us in our studies ahead. The levels of meaning suggest that we should start by reading each passage as a whole at the surface level, but then be ready to go back over it looking more deeply. Use any connections John makes by word echoes or references to time to see how it all links together and to the rest of the gospel. Meditate upon the words he uses and let the simple style and vocabulary sink into you in prayer as you use each section as a 'sign' to reveal God's glory in Christ.

What was the situation?

Whoever was involved in writing and producing this gospel was very familiar with the multifaith, multicultural world of the eastern Mediterranean in the first century. It was a real melting pot because of the Romans' deliberate policy of bringing all the countries and peoples together in one empire of peace and easy communications. Probably nothing was seen like it again until today's 'global village'. Just like today, lots of ideas and beliefs were circulating and being mixed together and their effect can be seen in the gospel.

The Greek background

The dominant Greek philosophical tradition from Socrates and Plato was essentially dualist, contrasting the real but invisible realm of the intellect, the soul and the gods with our material physical universe. In addition, Stoicism stressed the logical stability and rationality (called *logos* in Greek) behind the cosmic order which made ethical demands on people's lives. Meanwhile, religious cults and sects abounded with stories of divine figures who came from the realm of light above to save us from this dark world, and they often had initiation ceremonies into the 'mystery' or 'secret knowledge' which could set people free. The influence of all this can be clearly seen on this gospel, both in the prologue and in the way John portrays Jesus coming into the world to bring salvation. This need not imply that the writer had ever belonged to or studied any of these groups in particular detail. The ideas saturated the culture, and like any good evangelist, John is trying to present Jesus in a way that people will understand.

The Jewish background

At the same time, he is obviously steeped in the Hebrew scriptures and Jewish beliefs. Many of the stories are set against the background of the great Jewish festivals, such as the sabbath (5), Passover (6), Tabernacles (7—8), Hanukkah (10) and Passover again (13—20), and draw their themes from the rituals and beliefs at each feast. Many of the events take place in and around the temple in Jerusalem. The debates between Jesus and his opponents are conducted according to Jewish customs about witnesses and evidence (see on 5:30-47 below) and great heroes like Moses and Abraham are brought in. The themes of the law, the prophets and the scriptures run constantly just below the surface, and particular quotations and prophecies are used through the Passion (see on 12:15; 19:24, 28, 36). Furthermore, modern study of other groups, like the Essenes and the Qumran community near the Dead Sea, and of the development of the rabbinic traditions has all shown many links with the ideas and beliefs described in this gospel.

This Jewish background is not surprising. After all, with the exception of a few Samaritans, Greeks and Romans like Pilate (4:7, 39; 12:20; 18:28) everyone in the gospel is Jewish – Jesus, the disciples, the crowds, the leaders, the priests. Jesus is explicitly called 'a Jew' and he says that salvation is 'from the Jews' (4:9, 22). John uses the phrase 'the Jews' nearly 70 times, in contrast to only a few mentions in the other gospels. So it is a shock to discover that it often describes Jesus' opponents, particularly among the religious leaders (see on 1:19 below) – so we shall denote this with inverted commas. People are frightened of 'the Jews' in case they are put 'out of the synagogue', *aposynagogos* (9:22; 12:42; 16:2). While people could be punished by being barred from the synagogue for a week, or a month, or even totally excommunicated in the Old Testament (see Ezra 10:8), this does not seem to have happened to Jesus and his disciples, who went to synagogue as good Jews regularly in the gospels and Acts. Of course, there was opposition and conflict (Luke 6:22), but this technical term, *aposynagogos*, seems to belong to a later period.

After the Jewish War and the destruction of Jerusalem and the temple by the Romans in AD70, the surviving rabbis regrouped Judaism around the synagogue and study of the Torah. A prayer called 'the blessing against the heretics' was put into the synagogue liturgy, probably at the Council of Yavneh in AD85, asking that the '*nosrim* and the heretics perish quickly'. If the *nosrim* mean 'Nazarenes' this would make it very difficult for Jewish Christians to attend synagogue and pray against themselves. Regrettably, the split between the early churches and the synagogues developed rapidly after this.

Thus it is possible that John's gospel is being written in the late first century after the war, in the period leading to the Council of Yavneh or even after it, and John's use of the phrases 'the Jews' and *aposynagogos* reflects that unhappy time. Perhaps he is aware that some of his readers may have suffered the traumatic experience of excommunication. So he relates their current painful situation to the conflict and opposition from the leaders in Jesus' own day. This is important to remember as it shows John's careful attempt to make his story of Jesus relevant to the people he was writing for. It does not give any justification for the anti-Jewish way the gospel has sometimes been used in later centuries, particularly most recently by the Nazis (see on 8:44 below).

So John is probably writing for a mixed group of people, reflecting the multicultural situation of that period. They would know something of Greek philosophy and Near Eastern religious cults, as well as recognise the allusions to Jewish beliefs and practices. Some might be converts from Hellenistic religions or Jews who have found their faith fulfilled in Jesus as Messiah.

John the Baptist

Another possible group would be followers of John the Baptist. The Jewish historian, Josephus, refers to the Baptist's ministry of preaching and baptising people. Some people may have been baptised while on pilgrimage or visiting Jerusalem and then taken their new faith back to the cities of Asia Minor or Greece. Thus Paul finds disciples of John the Baptist in Ephesus (Acts 19:5). John shows that some of Jesus' early followers had also been disciples of the Baptist (1:35–37). Whenever John the Baptist appears in this gospel, he directs people to Jesus. It is made clear that he is 'not the light' himself, but a witness 'to the light' (1:8). His 'witness' is then repeated and expanded (see on 1:24–34). He does not even mind when his followers complain that Jesus is baptising more people, saying 'He must increase and I must decrease' (3:30). Some scholars have interpreted this material as an 'attack' on the Baptist, seeing it as an attempt to persuade his followers to join the new Christian church. Certainly, John is keen to encourage everyone to find life though faith in Jesus as Christ, but this need not imply a particular attack on anyone, especially not the Baptist. Later Jesus pays him the compliment of 'bearing witness to the truth' as 'a burning and shining lamp' (5:33–35).

Peter and the beloved disciple

If the 'disciple Jesus loved' is the 'authority' behind the gospel, it is interesting to consider his relationship with Peter. They always seem to appear together and the beloved disciple usually goes one better than Peter. Thus he is next to Jesus at the supper and asks Peter's question for him; he gets Peter into the high priest's courtyard; he is at the foot of the cross when Peter is nowhere to be seen; he beats Peter to the empty tomb and is the first to believe; he tells Peter that the stranger on the lakeside is the risen Jesus; and he will live long when Peter is martyred (13:23–25; 18:15–17; 19:26–27; 20:2–8; 21:7, 22). Some scholars read this as a game of 'anything you can do, we can do better'; so they argue that John is promoting his church and attacking the churches linked with Peter.

On the other hand, there is a lot of positive material about Peter: Simon is one of the first to follow Jesus and is renamed Peter, the 'rock', by him; he is the one who makes the confession of faith when others are leaving; he wants to be washed all over by Jesus; he tries to defend Jesus; there is no cursing, swearing oaths or bitter weeping at his denial; the beloved disciple waits to give him the honour of being first into the tomb and the first to meet Jesus at the lakeside; finally he is restored by the good shepherd to the pastoral care of his flock (1:42; 6:68; 13:9; 18:10, 27; 20:6; 21:7, 15–17). This is all too much for an 'attack' on him. Peter is just another human being who tries to follow Jesus, who sometimes gets it wonderfully right and other times horribly wrong – but he is forgiven and restored by Jesus, so there is hope for us also. The anonymity of the beloved disciple makes him almost an 'ideal figure' – and we are all encouraged to fill in the blank with our own face and name and become a 'disciple Jesus loved'.

John and other early Christian groups

In recent decades, it has been fashionable to reconstruct the 'community of the beloved disciple', the church within which and for which the gospel was written. Some have even read the gospel as a kind of symbolic history of John's community, taking Jesus' encounters with people as allegories of the church being started from disciples of the Baptist and some Jerusalem Jews with missions to the Samaritans and the Greeks leading to its eventual expulsion from the synagogue. All of these people may well have been found in the communities which read John's gospel. However, if he had wanted to write recent church history for them, it would have been easier to do it like the book of Acts. The variety of reconstructions and the lack of any external evidence has meant that such approaches are less common now. There is clearly a long process of prayer and reflection behind the gospel over many years, but all we have is the finished text.

Others have tried to relate the gospel to the epistles of John and the book of Revelation, calling them all 'Johannine' books. The epistles are certainly written in a similar style and share John's vocabulary. They are also involved in a situation of splits and conflicts, especially against early Docetic heretics, so called because they thought Jesus only seemed (*docein* in Greek) to be human (1 John 4:2–3; 2 John 1:7). This fits in with John's stress that the 'Word became flesh' (1:14). Revelation has many similarities to this gospel, but also differences of style, vocabulary and content.

Without any further evidence it is difficult to be sure about all of this, and going much further into these complex issues would take us away from our task here of studying the gospel. What this brief survey has shown is how John does not write in a vacuum. Like all those who wrote ancient biographies, he is trying to tell people about his subject, Jesus, and to interpret him afresh for their situation. As we study his gospel today we can have no better aim.

What does it teach?

John is not just a beautiful writer who is clever enough to fit his message to the situation facing his initial readers; he is also the sublime theologian of the early church. Debates raged about the meaning of his apparently simple words as ever deeper levels were explored. He was used by all sides in the various controversies over the formation of the creeds during the next few centuries, and he was loved by groups in the mainstream, at the fringes and way outside what came to be seen as orthodox Christianity. Equally, over the last two millennia and all around the world he has provoked an extraordinary output of homilies, sermons, statements, books, lectures, courses, papers, essays, dissertations and so forth. Here we can only sketch out briefly a few key aspects of his theology.

Christology

John is clear at the end of the gospel that his purpose is that we might believe that 'Jesus is the Christ, the Son of God' (20:31). He has perhaps the highest Christology, or understanding of Jesus, in the whole of the New Testament. At the same time, we must be careful about reading the arguments of later debates back into his text. John stresses that we see the 'glory of God' in the 'Word become flesh' against the philosophical and religious background of his own day; but the later arguments about the nature of Jesus and the Trinity were based on a much more complex philosophy. These debates were really about *ontology*, the nature of 'being' within the Godhead and *how* Jesus could 'be' both human and divine. John just asserts that he *is*; he is more concerned for *function* – what Jesus said and *did* then, and still does now, for human beings. It is no accident that John's style is a lot more full of verbs and 'doing' things than 'static' nouns of 'being'.

As we shall see in the prologue, he draws upon the rich philosophical tradition of the 'Word', *logos*, behind the cosmos to explain who Jesus really is as that Word becomes flesh and dwells among us (1:14). He also uses the Jewish tradition about the Word of God, which he combines with the figure of God's Wisdom, who was with him at the creation and comes among men and women to teach them the way of God (Proverbs 8:22–31).

He uses a number of *titles* to describe Jesus. The gospel opens with debate about who the Christ might be (1:20); John the Baptist says that it is not him. Soon Jesus is called 'Christ' by the first disciples, some Samaritans and other believers (1:41; 4:25, 29; 11:27). 'Christ' is the Greek form of the Hebrew 'Messiah' and both words mean God's 'anointed one'. In the Hebrew scriptures priests, kings and prophets were all anointed as a sign of God's special task for them. Later there emerged a longing for someone who would be *the* Messiah, God's anointed person to bring in his kingdom. When Jesus enters Jerusalem to be hailed as 'king' (12:13) the authorities are worried and he is executed as 'king of the Jews', which is also a messianic claim. John makes it clear that Jesus lived and died as the 'Christ'.

However, John's reason for writing connects 'Christ' with 'Son of God' (20:31). God is called Father over 100 times and Jesus is identified as the 'Son' about 50, so John is making a clear statement about his relationship to God. The name of God was linked in the Old Testament with ultimate Being, 'I am who I am' (Exodus 3:14). In John's gospel,

Jesus makes seven 'I am' statements, claiming to be the bread of life, the light of the world, the door to the sheepfold, the good shepherd, the resurrection and the life, the way, truth and life, and the true vine (6:35, 41, 51; 8:12, 9:5; 10:7, 9; 10:11, 14; 11:25; 14:6; 15:1, 5). Not only do these hint at the divine name, 'I am', but the descriptions are all central images of the Jewish faith and law being now fulfilled in Jesus.

John also depicts Jesus being aware of his unique relationship with God, knowing that he was pre-existent with God and is going to return to him in glory. He is the source of all life and all judgement is committed to him (3:16–21; 5:19–29). The Father inspires and indwells all he says and does so much that to see him is to have seen the Father, for 'the Father and I are one' (14:9–10; 10:30). At the same time, 'the Word became flesh' (1:14), so John shows Jesus' humanity: he gets tired and thirsty in Samaria; he weeps at his friend's grave; he is tempted to shrink back from being crucified; and on the cross he is thirsty and really dies a human death (4:6–7; 11:33–38; 12:27; 19:28, 34).

This is indeed a highly developed Christology and shows how much John has thought and reflected on the meaning of Jesus over many years. And yet, it is only the logical outworking of the picture of Jesus in the other gospels who taught us to call God *Abba*, our Father, and who was bringing in the kingdom of God through his parables and miracles. At the same time, John's understanding of Jesus was to set the tracks on a course which would lead to the later debates and creeds.

Eschatology

We have already noted John's interest in time. The Hebrew prophets looked forward to the 'last day', the 'day of the Lord', when God's justice would finally be revealed at the end of time. The Greek word for 'end' is *eschaton*, so the study of things to do with 'the end' is called 'eschatology'. In the other gospels, Jesus says that the end, the 'kingdom of God', when God's kingship will be recognised by everyone, was breaking into our time here and now through his teaching and miracles (Luke 11:20). However, they also each contain long sections of Jesus' teaching about the end, when he will come again on the clouds of glory to judge everyone (Mark 13:3–37; Matthew 24—25; Luke 21:5–36).

John does not have anything quite like these blocks of teaching about the coming of the end. Instead, Jesus talks as though his coming into the world has brought the end here already. So, although God did not send his Son to condemn the world, but to save it, the coming of light into darkness inevitably creates shadows; the arrival of Jesus has brought about the judgement, the 'critical moment' when some people reject the light and prefer to remain in the shadows (3:16–21). So we say that John sees eschatology as 'realised', made real in the present in our decision here and now. As people accept and believe in Jesus so they come into eternal life now, so much that Lazarus can even be raised from the dead now without having to wait for the end of time (see on 11:17–44 below).

On the other hand, Jesus still talks of 'the last day' (e.g. 6:39–40; 12:48). While all the benefits of eternal life and knowing God can be received as we accept Jesus, there is still inevitably a future dimension to judgement. Perhaps the best section about John's understanding of eschatology is 5:19–29. Here Jesus says that all judgement and authority to give life has been granted to him by God the Father. In 5:19–24 this seems to be happening now in the present, while in 5:25–29 it is all repeated in the future tense. The two sections are linked by 'the hour is coming, and now is' (5:25). This is the heart of what John is trying to say: 'the hour is coming' when there will be judgement and eternal life, but it 'now is' available to us in Jesus, here, already.

Church and sacraments

Perhaps no topic so divides scholars as John's understanding of the church and the sacraments. On the one hand, scholars of a more Protestant background point out that there is little about this in the text of the gospel. In reply, those from a more Catholic tradition see images of the church and sacraments all over the gospel. In part, this situation arises from John's habit of writing on several levels at once; two commentators can look at the same passage and see different things depending on how deep they look.

On the surface, the first group are right to point out that none of the key words about the church are ever used in John; there is little emphasis on the twelve apostles, but lots of stories about various people, most of whom are never heard of again – the Samaritan woman, the woman taken in adultery, the blind man and so on. It is all very individualistic, with individuals coming to Jesus, but not through the church or the community of faith.

In response, the other group look more deeply at Jesus' great images of the shepherd and the sheep, or the vine and the branches and notice how corporate these are. Part of the problem is that English does not distinguish between 'you-singular' (the old 'thee' and 'thou') and 'you-plural'. It is thus easy to take all the wonderful promises of Jesus at the last supper in an individualistic way as addressed to each believer personally. However, closer inspection of the Greek reveals that these are all 'you-plurals'; we experience the promises of Jesus and the presence of the Spirit all together as the community of believers. We shall try to point out these 'you-plurals' in these studies. Furthermore, it is John's gospel where Jesus gives us the example of washing each other's feet and the 'new commandment' to 'love one another as I have loved you'. The mark of the church by which people will know we are his disciples is if we love one another (13:1–11, 34–35; 15:12–13). It is hard to have a higher understanding of the church than that!

Unfortunately, mention of the last supper causes the more Protestant scholars to jump up again. They note that it is curious that there is no institution of the Holy Communion at the last supper, just the foot washing (13:1–11). What is more, there is no account of Jesus actually being baptised either, but it is just passed over briefly in a mention by John the Baptist (1:32–33). There is no command to baptise or to 'do this in remembrance of me' for the Communion. Instead, there is a great stress on the Word and on Jesus' teaching; we should get rid of our altars and fonts and build bigger pulpits!

The sacramentalists have to admit that the omission of Communion and baptism is rather embarrassing, on the face of it at least. But, if we look below the surface, suddenly we are awash with sacramental references. Water is in nearly every chapter at the start, from the Baptist, to water into wine, to being born of water and the Spirit, to living water, to healing by water, to streams of living water, and so on through to Jesus washing the disciples' feet (1:26–33; 2:1–11; 3:5; 4:10–15; 5:1–9; 7:38; 9:7; 13:1–11). Equally, water is turned into vast quantities of wine, Jesus calls himself the 'true vine' and there is lots of bread around, even at the last supper (2:1–11; 15:1; 6:1–14, 31–35; 13:26–30). The feeding of the 5,000 looks like an open-air Communion and it is difficult to interpret the debate about eating his flesh and drinking his blood as anything other than the Eucharist (6:1–14, 50–58).

This is an excellent example of how the way we read John's style and manner of writing can affect our view of his theology, particularly with regard to the deeper levels of meaning. Are these things really there below the surface, or are they merely reflections of our own views? We will point out the main passages for the debate as we go through the gospel, and you will have to think about it and ask the Holy Spirit to help you decide.

Truth, theology and history

Clement of Alexandria said towards the end of the second century that John was a 'spiritual gospel' written later to supplement the 'physical facts' described in the other three gospels (according to Eusebius, *Ecclesiastical History* VI:14:7). This came to represent how John was viewed up to this century – that John knew the synoptics and wrote later to provide spiritual reflection upon their historical accounts.

The development of modern scholarship and literary criticism tended to confirm this approach to John. For most of this century, scholars thought that John was written at the end of the first century, or even into the early part of the second; his philosophical awareness seemed very Greek and to have lost touch with the Jewish background of Jesus and the early disciples; everything was seen to have a theological purpose or spiritual meaning and none of his events or conversations were thought to have any basis in history. The only possible historical material John had would have come from the synoptic gospels. One example of such an approach is that the five porticoes at the pool of Bethesda were interpreted from St Augustine onwards as symbolising the five books of the law of Moses – identifying the sick but not able to heal them; then Jesus does what the old law could not and makes the man whole (5:1–9). Obviously, in this view, the porches had no historical existence; Jerusalem was destroyed a generation or more before the gospel was thought to have been written, so neither the writer nor the first readers would have known anything about what it had looked like.

Over recent decades, however, this approach has been seriously challenged. First, most scholars now consider that John was written independently of the other gospels, and they are therefore no longer the yardstick by which he is to be judged. Certainly he shares some old material with them which was passed on through the oral tradition, which may or may not have an historical basis; each must be assessed on its own merits. Furthermore, we have become more aware of the amount of theological interpretation in the other gospels which makes them more like John. Like other ancient biographies, all the gospels set out to explain and interpret their subject and his significance.

While the synoptic gospels are now seen as more theological, conversely John has been shown to be more historical. Research on the

Dead Sea Scrolls and on the beliefs of the Essenes and other Jewish groups of the early first century has revealed lots of ideas and thoughts which are quite similar to John's approach. These groups were all destroyed in the Jewish War of 66–70 and their beliefs were lost. Without them, John's ideas used to look quite late and Greek. Now we know that they were not so different from other earlier, Jewish writings. Similarly, developments in archaeology in Israel and Palestine over recent decades have revealed a lot more about Jerusalem and Judea before the Jewish War – and John's awareness of places and geography now seems quite good. Even the Pool of Bethesda has been excavated and we can now walk among its five porticoes! Of course, this cannot prove the historicity or otherwise of any miracle or conversation Jesus or anyone else may have held there – but it does caution us against assuming that everything is only symbolic and theological.

This all means that the process by which John's gospel came to be written is a lot more complex. Both the previous extreme views are too simplistic. John's awareness of Greek philosophy and the painful separation of the early churches from the synagogues in the latter part of the first century mean that this gospel is not meant to be a straightforward eyewitness accurate record of what a Galilean fisherman heard and saw Jesus say and do. On the other hand, his knowledge of early Aramaic terms, like 'Messiah' or 'Cephas' for Peter (1:41–42), his use of ideas common to Jewish groups wiped out – and awareness of places destroyed – in the Jewish War of 66–70 suggests that the gospel contains a good historical foundation dating back to the first half of the century. If the 'witness' behind the gospel, identified as 'the disciple Jesus loved', was John son of Zebedee some of it will have come from him. It is not just a later Greek symbolic invention.

As Pilate says in John, 'What is truth?' (18:38). To us today, truth is about recordings of what an American President might or might not have said – and even then the truth is hard to discover! On the other hand, we consider 'myth' to be 'untrue', a fairy story. The people of Jesus' and John's day, however, had different ideas and we must not impose our concepts of truth on to first-century texts like the gospels. To the ancients, 'myth' was the medium whereby profound truth, more truly true than mere tape-recorded facts could ever be, was communicated – hence John's use of the words 'true' and 'truly' nearly 50 times. John's gospel has an underlying basic level of historical information about the sorts of things Jesus said and did and the places where they happened, leading up to his trial and death. Over that are laid levels of awareness of the complex melting pot of the first century, including Jewish beliefs from before the destruction of Jerusalem and Greco-Roman religious and philosophical systems. In writing his brief account of Jesus, he is trying to get from one level to the other. He has prayed and reflected on 'the many other things Jesus did' and makes a selection under the guidance of the Holy Spirit in order to 'bear true witness' in the situation of his first readers about the *truth* of who Jesus *truly* is and *really* means for them – 'so that you may believe that Jesus is the Christ, the Son of God, and that through believing you may have life in his name' (20:30–31; 21:24–25).

The kids are splashing about, and the elephants are enjoying wallowing; the children of God are enjoying new life in Christ, and the theologians are plumbing ever greater depths. Breakfast on the beach is over, and it is time for us to immerse ourselves in John's living waters. Enjoy it!

Richard A. Burridge

1

John 1:1–2

In the beginning

The opening of John's gospel is one of the most magnificent pieces of religious literature ever written. Not surprisingly, it has inspired vast amounts of analysis and interpretation. And yet, we are not even sure quite what it is. Is it an introduction, a hymn or a poem? Arguments rage over whether it extends from verse 1 to verse 14 or to verse 18, whether or not the passages about John the Baptist belong here (1:6–8, 15), and how its structure might be analysed.

It is usually called 'the prologue', although it is more like an overture, for it introduces some key themes and particular words which the writer will use over and over in the gospel. On the other hand, some of its ideas and phrases never appear again, including the central idea of 'the Word'. Therefore scholars have wondered whether it was written by the same author as the rest. Some suggest that it may have been an early hymn, which already existed and which the evangelist adapted for his purposes. Others think that it was composed later and added to the already completed gospel. Indeed, I wrote the rest of this commentary first and came to the prologue last!

So, read it now as the introduction to the gospel and these studies. It will give you a flavour of the great journey we are about to undertake, and you will hear some of the major themes. Don't worry if some ideas are difficult or the motifs too grand at this stage. Come back and study it again after you have finished the whole gospel – and see how all the things you have learned and friends you have made are hinted at here.

Begin at the beginning

So we begin, as John does, at the beginning. Mark starts his gospel with Jesus being baptised by John the Baptist, Matthew begins with Jesus' birth, while Luke takes us back to the birth of John the Baptist as the one who prepared his way. John is traditionally symbolised by an eagle, and he certainly takes the high-flying perspective here! Jesus cannot be introduced in terms of time, place and human ancestry: he existed 'in the beginning' (1:1). This phrase would remind his readers immediately of the opening words of the Hebrew scriptures, 'In the beginning' (Genesis 1:1). Indeed, while *genesis* is the Greek word for 'beginning' or 'origin', the Jews called the first book of the Bible by its opening Hebrew words, 'In the beginning.' Yet John goes even further, for Genesis starts with the creation of everything *at* the beginning; John takes us back *before* then, when only God existed.

The Word

John does not actually name Jesus until the end of the prologue (1:17). Instead, he calls him 'the Word'. The Jews thought that God's word was alive and active (Isaiah 55:11) from the creation – when God had only to say, 'Let there be…' for things to come into being (Genesis 1:3, 6, 9, etc.) – to God's word coming through all the prophets. In Greek philosophy from early thinkers like Heraclitus to the Stoics, who were also popular among the Romans, the 'word', *logos*, was used for the logical rationality behind the universe. In later Jewish beliefs, this masculine principle was complemented by the feminine figure of Lady Wisdom, who was present with God at the creation (Proverbs 8:22-31). This idea was developed in the writings between the times of the Testaments, as can be seen in the book of Wisdom in the Apocrypha (7:22—10:21). There was further speculation in Jewish mysticism about the role of both wisdom and the law with God.

But it is John who pulls all these threads together with the amazing idea that the Word was not only pre-existent with God but also personal. In 1:1-2 he states that 'the Word was with (the) God', including the definite article 'the' to stress how the Word existed with the creator Father God of Jewish monotheism – for there is no other god. Furthermore, 'the Word was God' without any article. He does not say 'the Word was *a* god', with the indefinite article, implying that Jesus was some sort of lesser divinity, as some groups believe who have split away from orthodox Christianity both in the past and today. Nor does he say 'the Word was *the* God', for that would imply that Jesus was all there is to God. No, he carefully writes 'the Word was God', divine, personal, existing in the unity of the Godhead and yet somehow distinct – for 'the Word became flesh and dwelt among us' (1:14). That is the wonderful story which John is setting out to tell us.

Prayer

God our Father, inspire our study of these written words that we may know your living Word, Jesus Christ.

2

John 1:3–8

Light in the darkness

Greek philosophy and many eastern religions had an essential 'dualism', a separation between the material world and the spiritual realm. God exists in brilliant light in the world above, while we live in the darkness of created matter. Therefore God can have nothing to do with the physical level. At best, this material universe is but a pale shadow of divine reality; however, many saw our world as positively evil, containing nothing good. Human beings were seen in a similar dualistic fashion: the physical body is sinful flesh or meaningless matter, inhabited by the soul which pre-existed in the divine light and strives to return there. Thus ancient philosophy from Socrates and Plato onwards sought 'enlightenment' or 'knowledge' to set the soul free into the bright intellectual realms, while many eastern religions offered 'salvation', often through 'initiation' into mysteries to enable the soul to leave the body after death and ascend back to the divine. As a child of his time, John shares some of this. Thus he depicts the Word pre-existing with God in light, but descending into our dark world to bring salvation, before returning to the Father. John uses the separation of the divine 'above' and the world 'below' frequently, so the overture has introduced his first theme. However, he has also been nourished in the Jewish tradition that the world is the good creation of a loving God: 'the earth is the Lord's and all it contains' (Psalm 24).

Thus he affirms the world's goodness and the Word's involvement in creation in a way abhorrent to a thoroughgoing dualist.

Life and light

First he asserts that 'all things came into being' through the Word and nothing exists without him (1:3). At a stroke, John inspires the great Christian involvement in the arts *and* the sciences. Scientific enquiry is possible if the world is not some malicious fantasy but the result of a creator's love – to study the laws of physics is to search out the mind of God, as many great scientists like Kepler and Newton believed. Equally, rather than trying to escape the material body, our humanity can be explored in sculpture and paint, poetry and prose, dance and drama, music and song – because 'in him was life' (1:4).

Suddenly two great fanfares burst out of John's overture to announce the major themes of light and life, two words which he uses twice as often as the other gospels. Here all 'life' is found in the Word and he balances this neatly at the end with his purpose in writing that we 'might have life in his name' (20:31). Because 'God so loved the world', he gave his Son so we 'should not perish but have eternal life' (3:16). His life is also 'the light of all people' (1:4). The presence of the Word is the 'light come into the darkness' (3:19), and John uses light and darkness as a contrasting pair throughout, together with the images of night and day. Now, 'the light shines in the darkness and the darkness cannot master it' (1:5). The English 'master' reflects the double meaning of the Greek, both to 'understand' or 'comprehend' and to 'overcome' or 'extinguish'. The coming of light into darkness inevitably creates shadows, so there will be conflict and judgement.

A witness to the light

Next, John introduces two more themes – 'sending' and 'witness'. John the Baptist was 'sent from God' (1:6). Unlike the dualist God who has no contact with the world, John stresses that the nature of God is to 'send'. He uses the verb 'send' about 60 times, nearly twice as frequently as the other gospels – and God does most of the sending. First he sends John the Baptist, and then Jesus. Finally, Jesus sends us into the world, 'as the Father sent me' (20:21).

John is sent as a 'witness to the light' (1:7). The Greek word for witness, *martur-*, gives us the English 'martyr' for a witness even to death. John uses the noun and its verb 'to bear witness' or 'to testify' more than the other three gospels put together, so it is another key idea. It recurs throughout as Jesus is constantly put on trial and asked for 'witnesses' for his claims, and with another careful balance the gospel ends with the witness of the writer himself (21:24). John the Baptist had many devoted followers, but the evangelist stresses that 'he himself was not the light', but came as a 'witness to the light' (1:8). The relationship of John the Baptist and Jesus will be explored in the first few chapters; for now, the writer states simply that John came to witness to the light 'so that all might believe through him', introducing another important theme – 'believe' – into this overture.

Prayer

Lord Jesus, shine your light into my life, that I may be a witness for you.

3

John 1:9–13

Acceptance or rejection?

The overture is now in full swing, moving from its magnificent opening about the Word with God in the beginning to what happens when the Word enters into the world. This introduces many of the gospel's key themes. As God 'sends' the 'light' into the 'darkness' to bring 'life', some 'believe' and 'witness'. Unfortunately, this is not the only reaction possible and the gospel's main story is about the acceptance or rejection of the Word which the overture now introduces.

First, John distinguishes the Word as 'the true light' (1:9) from John the Baptist, whom many thought was the light, while actually he was only a reflection or witness to it (1:7–8). Another key motif, the words 'true' and 'truth' feature nearly 50 times in this gospel, three times the total in the others. Here too, John turns the dualists' ideas around. Greek philosophy stressed how true reality was only in the realm above, and everything in our world merely pale shadows and reflections. So for John, Jesus is 'the truth', foreshadowed by Jewish festivals, beliefs and ideas about the law. But while dualists thought we had to leave this world to find truth, John announces that the 'true bread' and the 'true vine' has come to find us (14:6; 6:32; 15:1).

The Hebrew prophets looked forward to God's light coming in glory (Isaiah 9:2; 42:6; 60:1). That light, says John, is personal – as he breaks grammar from the neuter 'light' to the personal pronoun 'he' – and available, 'coming into the world'. We do not leave the world to find enlightenment; he 'enlightens everyone'. The scale of John's insight is staggering: what is true and good in all philosophies and religions, thought and culture, arts and science – all of it comes from the enlightenment of the Word.

The world

John's stupendous claim, which no dualist would dare contemplate, is that the divine Word, the true light, has come 'into the world' (1:9). To them 'the world' was negative and evil. John is more subtle: he uses 'the world' nearly 80 times, over five times as often as in the synoptics. Sometimes it is simply neutral, meaning 'the earth' or 'everyone', like the French *tout le monde* (e.g. 12:19). Essentially the world is positive, the good creation of the loving God, which he sent his Son to save (3:16). On the other hand, when the world rejects Jesus, it becomes negative, the source of opposition, especially later in the gospel (see on 15:18–19 below). All three usages are here: 'he was in the world [neutral], and the world was made through him [positive], yet the world did not know him [negative]' (1:10).

His own

The dualists thought that 'knowledge' was a way out of the world. Some who split away from Christianity were called Gnostics from their stress on 'knowledge', *gnosis*, to get us back to the divine realms. 'Knowledge' and 'knowing' are used by John over 140 times – but it is often Jesus' knowledge of everything (e.g. 13:3; 18:4). Eternal life is 'to know God and Jesus Christ whom he sent' (17:3) and such knowledge comes through 'believing', which occurs nearly 100 times, three times its usage in the synoptics. The Word, the true light, came into the world 'to his own', a neuter phrase for his own possession, realm, or home. While 'the whole world' belongs to God, Israel was his 'special possession' (Exodus 19:5) and the Jews 'his people' (Deuteronomy 7:6; 14:2). But John moves from the neuter to the personal pronoun to say that 'his own people did not accept him'. So 1:11 is a summary of the first half of this gospel, as Jesus comes to his own people but many, especially the religious leaders, reject him.

Alongside that theme of rejection, the overture plays the counterpoint of 'all who received him, who believed in his name'. Thus 1:12 is the summary of the second half of the gospel. Although 'his own people' do not accept him, Jesus calls together a group who 'know' that he was sent by God and who 'believe in him'. These become 'his own sheep' who 'know his voice'; at the last supper, he gathers together 'his own in the world' and loves them 'to the end' (10:4, 14; 13:1). To these he gives 'the authority to become children of God', who are born not by natural means, but a spiritual rebirth 'of God' (1:13). As the gospel unfolds, watch for people like Nicodemus, coming out of darkness to believe in Jesus, and to become 'his own', born of the Spirit (3:1–8).

Prayer

Light of the world, help me to know and believe in you and make me a child of God.

4

John 1:14–18

The Word became flesh

Like an overture, the prologue introduces the gospel's major themes. First, John arranged his composition against a cosmic backdrop of the realm of divine light above and our dark world below. Then John's middle section challenged this dualistic system as the Word from above enters into our world. In this final movement, he takes his themes more from the Old Testament, leading to a final climax which confronts Greek philosophy and Jewish beliefs alike.

The incarnation

'The Word became flesh' (1:14) sounds four crashing chords to make any dualists listening jump out of their seats! The Word 'coming into the world' was bad enough, but for the divine to enter something as physical, messy and downright sinful as human flesh was outrageous. Even some early Christians (called Docetics) had problems with this, believing that Jesus only 'seemed' (*docein* in Greek) to be human. Of the four gospels, John has the clearest emphasis on the divinity of Jesus. As the story unfolds, Jesus knows all things, is aware of his pre-existence with the Father, and goes to his death serenely in control, confident of his return to the divine realm. Some scholars suggest that John stresses this so much that he risks going Docetic himself. Against this are all the places where John describes Jesus' humanity in the gospel itself, and this ringing declaration in his overture.

If the incarnation of the Word was difficult for Greeks, the next phrase would have startled Jews. 'He lived (*eskenosen*) among us' means literally 'dwelt in a tent', like the tent of the tabernacle (*skene*) where God resided during the Israelites' desert wanderings (Exodus 25:8–9). The prophets longed for God to 'pitch his tent' among his people again (Ezekiel 37:27; Joel 3:17; Zechariah 2:10). This, declares John, is what has happened in Jesus. The consonants of 'tent', *s-k-n*, are linked to the Hebrew *s-k-n*, to 'dwell', from which comes the *shekinah*, the glorious cloud of God's presence on Mount Sinai, which then filled the tent and later the temple (Exodus 24:16; 40:34–35; 1 Kings 8:10–11). So John says, 'We have seen his glory.' The other gospels depict the glory of God coming upon Jesus at the transfiguration. John does not relate this event, for he sees the *shekinah* glory of God in Jesus in all he says and does; supremely the hour for Jesus to be glorified and 'lifted up' is the crucifixion (12:23; 13.32; 17:1).

Furthermore, Jesus shares God's glory as an only son resembles his father. This is John's favourite description for the relationship of Jesus and God. Jesus is frequently called 'the Son', and God is 'the Father' over 110 times, twice as often as in the other three gospels combined. As the proverb goes, 'Like father, like son.' In the Old Testament God is always 'abounding in steadfast love and faithfulness' (Exodus 34:6). So here John translates this into Jesus being 'full of grace and truth'.

This is an astounding verse. In one sentence John breaches the dualistic divide of Greek philosophy, counters early Christian heresy about Jesus' humanity and divinity, and gathers together Jewish ideas of the presence, glory, mercy and love of God – all of this, he says, can now be seen among us in Jesus!

The revelation

So now we hear a reprise of the theme of John the Baptist, the last Jewish prophet, to 'bear witness' again to Jesus (1:15). Many thought the Baptist was fulfilling all the Jewish hopes, but he never appears in this gospel without 'witnessing' that it is Jesus who does this, not him. John uses two words frequent in Paul but occurring only here in the gospel – 'fullness' and 'grace' (1:16). We saw that 'grace' represents the 'steadfast love of the Lord' so common in the Old Testament. As the Baptist witnessed to Jesus, so the evangelist shows throughout the gospel how all the Jewish beliefs and practices are fulfilled in Jesus – and even surpassed. Moses will be another important witness (see on 5:39–47; 6:25–50). Now John notes that 'the law was given through Moses, but grace and truth came through Jesus Christ' (1:17). No one has ever seen God (1:18). Even Moses was not allowed to see God's face (Exodus 33:18–23). But Jesus, the Word, who was with God in the beginning, the only Son who exists 'in the Father's heart' – he has revealed him and 'made him known'.

So the prologue has come full circle, the overture has introduced all the themes, and it climaxes with a loud cry that Jesus is God come among us. That is why the story we are about to read is so important.

For reflection and prayer

Read the whole prologue slowly and meditate upon it phrase by phrase. What does Jesus show you?

5

John 1:19–23

Questions and answers

After the magnificent heights of the prologue, the overture is over and a sense of hushed expectancy falls upon the audience as the curtain rises and the story begins. As so often in any great drama, John's opening scene introduces some key themes – but the star, the person at the centre of the story, is curiously offstage. However, the way is being prepared for his entry because the characters actually on stage are discussing the central question, 'Who is the Christ?' Messengers from the religious authorities have been sent to question the person at the centre of the action as the story begins, thinking, not unreasonably, that he might be the star: 'Who are you?' So let us consider this man and his questioners.

'The Jews'

The messengers are priests and Levites who have been sent by 'the Jews' from Jerusalem (1:19). This is the first appearance in John's story of 'the Jews'. While this phrase occurs in the other three gospels only a few times, mostly in their accounts of Jesus' trial and death, it appears in John's gospel some 70 times: a few times in each chapter from 2 to 12, and then 20 times at the trial (chapters 18—19).

This statistic should make us pause for a moment and ask what John means by the phrase. 'The Jews' appear here at the beginning as questioners, and the questions get sharper as they are directed away from John the Baptist to Jesus himself. The conflict builds until both Jesus and 'the Jews' accuse each other of being demonic (8:44, 48). Here the phrase refers to priests and Levites from Jerusalem (1:19, 24), and it is used particularly of the Jewish leaders, especially when they bring about Jesus' trial and death (18—19). However, we cannot read this phrase today without thinking of the persecution of the Jews, particularly by the Nazis who used the accusation of 'being of the devil' as a justification for the Holocaust.

Yet Jesus is a Jew (4:9), and he tells a Samaritan that 'salvation is from the Jews' (4:22). In this gospel, all those who come to believe are Jews, just like those who do not believe. Jesus came into conflict with the Jewish religious authorities in his own day, which led to his death.

This conflict continued 'within the family', between Jews who believed in Jesus as Messiah and Jews who did not – until, as the believers grew and included non-Jews among them, eventually they split away from the synagogue to the formation of the church. Such events do not happen without some bitterness and pain on both sides, and this is reflected in John's use of the phrase 'the Jews' for Jesus' opponents.

So we must always bear in mind when reading this gospel that the phrase 'the Jews' refers to the religious leaders who rejected what God was doing at that time in Jesus, rather than the Jewish people down through the ages. How often do *we* question what is happening and fail to recognise the activity of God?

John the Baptist

On the other hand, other Jews are portrayed throughout this gospel looking for the coming of the Christ, including the first disciples and others like Nicodemus, Martha and Mary. The first of these is John the Baptist. We know from the Jewish historian Josephus that John was seen by many as a prophet: he came out of the wilderness, preaching and baptising people as a sign of their repentance. No wonder the religious authorities wanted to question him and find out who he was.

His answer at first is negative. In response to their questions, he states three times who he is not: he is not the Christ (1:20), nor Elijah, whom some expected to come before the Messiah, following the prophecy of Malachi 4:5, nor he is the prophet like Moses promised in Deuteronomy 18:15–18 (1:21). Understandably, the questioners want a more positive answer to take back to Jerusalem, so John declares that he is 'the voice of one crying in the wilderness, "Make straight the way of the Lord"' as prophesied by Isaiah 40:3. Thus the evangelist depicts John the Baptist as a 'witness' (1:19) who prepares the way for the main star still to step on stage. He is not an opponent like 'the Jews' but a proponent who will direct others to Jesus.

Prayer

Lord, make me a voice crying in the wilderness, not one who misses or opposes what you are doing, but a true witness.

6

John 1:24–34

The witness of John the Baptist

John the Baptist's response to his questioners was to direct their attention away from himself to the 'star' of the show who has been offstage, waiting in the wings. Now, on 'the next day' after the questioners have departed, Jesus makes his arrival upon the scene (1:29), the first mention of him since the end of the prologue (1:17). Modern biographies usually begin with their subject's birth, family, upbringing and education; ancient accounts of people's lives would often start straight in with their public debut, as John does here. Unlike the accounts in the other gospels, there is no narrative of the actual baptism itself. John the Baptist says he saw the Spirit descend upon Jesus as a dove (1:32), but in this gospel his role is less about being the one who baptised Jesus and more that of a witness to him: note how his 'witness' in 1:19 leads to what he says (1:32, 34). Here the Baptist declares four things about Jesus.

Jesus is greater than John

Before the questioners withdraw, John the Baptist tells them of the coming of one who is greater than himself. John is not worthy to untie his sandals, which is the work of a slave when his master enters the house (1:27). Perhaps this helps to explain why this gospel has no account of the actual moment of baptism, for this might imply that the baptiser is greater than the one baptised. Matthew also grapples with this problem by describing Jesus having to persuade John to baptise him (Matthew 3:14–15). This gospel consistently points out that the Baptist sees Jesus as greater (see on 3:22–30). In its own day, when the ancient Mediterranean was full of religious leaders and prophets, John's gospel stressed the pre-eminence of Jesus – and it proclaims the same message in our pluralistic society today.

Jesus is the Lamb of God

When Jesus appears, coming towards John, the Baptist points him out: 'Behold, the Lamb of God, who takes away the sin of the world!' (1:29). The 'lamb' immediately recalls the Passover story when the ancient

Israelites wanted to leave slavery in Egypt: when all the firstborn of Egypt were killed, the Israelites were saved because they had sacrificed a lamb and smeared its blood on their doorposts, causing God to pass over their houses (Exodus 12). John the Baptist has already quoted the prophet Isaiah to describe himself as the voice in the wilderness (1:23; cf. Isaiah 40:3). Now he uses Isaiah also to describe Jesus, the suffering servant of God who bears the sins of the people like a 'lamb to the slaughter' (Isaiah 53:4–7). In the literature written between the time of the Old and New Testaments, the image of a lamb is also used of the one who will destroy evil. Now the Baptist draws on all these images to describe not just who Jesus is, but what he will do – he will take away the sin of the world.

Jesus baptises with the Holy Spirit

In John the Baptist's third description of Jesus, there is another contrast – between his own baptism in water and the baptism with the Holy Spirit which comes through Jesus. Even though John is forever identified as 'the Baptist', yet even here, Jesus' baptism is greater than his. As a prophet, John would have experienced the inspiration of the Holy Spirit on various occasions, particularly for his preaching. But the Spirit has descended from heaven and remains on Jesus. Because he possesses and is possessed by the Holy Spirit of God, Jesus is the one who can baptise others with that same Spirit (1:33).

Jesus is the Son of God

John the Baptist answered the religious leaders' questions by describing himself as the voice preparing the way (1:23). Now we see how great is the one who comes after him: he can take away the sin of the world and baptise with the Holy Spirit because he is nothing less than the very Son of God himself – another term with a rich Jewish background. The reason God wanted Pharaoh to let his people go was that 'Israel is my firstborn son' (Exodus 4:22). God's promise to David was that from his line there would come someone to rule Israel: 'I will be a father to him, and he shall be a son to me' (2 Samuel 7:14).

Thus the testimony of John the Baptist to Jesus is a rich tapestry, weaving together several strands from the Jewish scriptures to witness to the greatness of Jesus, the Son of God.

Prayer

Lord Jesus Christ, Son of God, have mercy on me; take away my sin and fill me with your Holy Spirit.

7

John 1:35–42

Come and see

Once again, this scene begins with John the Baptist declaring that Jesus is the Lamb of God (1:36). Two of John's disciples hear what he says, and, realising that he is pointing away from himself to Jesus, leave John to find out about Jesus. It is very likely that Jesus' first disciples came from among followers of John the Baptist. John's preaching of repentance as preparation for the kingdom would encourage his disciples to look for the next step. So here we have the origin of the community of faith, the church. A couple of people start following Jesus because someone else has pointed them that way. Verses 36–37 use the key word 'follow' twice. Probably what they were doing, to begin with at least, was tagging along behind Jesus to see what he was up to and where he was going or staying (1:38) rather than the technical use of 'following', meaning like a disciple committed to a master. But, as so often, the one leads to the other. Why did we first start to follow Jesus? Was it because someone told us about him or pointed us in his direction – a parent or grandparent, a teacher or minister – or because we tagged along just to see what was happening?

The invitation

The first words spoken by the main character are very important in a play. Now we hear Jesus' first words in this gospel, and they are a question: 'What are you looking for?' (1:38). This theme of seeking or looking for someone or something becomes quite important through this gospel. Many seek Jesus, some because they want to kill him, and others because they want to know about him and his teaching. On other occasions, Jesus asks, as here, 'What do you want? What are you seeking?' Even when he knows the answer, he graciously allows the other person to express their desire – even in the garden asking the temple police who they are looking for (18:4). When Mary Magdalene is crying so much outside his tomb that she cannot recognise the risen Jesus, he will gently repeat this question: 'Whom are you looking for?' (20:15).

The two new followers stammer a reply about finding out more about him, so Jesus follows up his open question with an invitation: 'Come and see' (1:39). He does not force himself upon them – but asks what they are looking for and offers them the chance to find out the answer to their questions. As we read John's gospel, we are also asked the same question – what are we looking for? And we receive the same invitation from Jesus – come and see.

Inviting others

When someone has pointed you to Jesus and you have responded and seen him for yourself, you have to go and tell others and bring them also to 'come and see'. The news is too good to be kept to yourself. So it is here. Andrew and the other disciple stay with Jesus for the rest of the afternoon and evening – and then Andrew goes to find his brother, Simon, and tell him the good news, 'We have found the Messiah', using the Hebrew word which is translated into the Greek 'Christ', which means 'the anointed one' (1:40–41).

Andrew seems particularly good at bringing others to Jesus. At the feeding of the 5,000, it is Andrew who finds the little boy with the loaves and fishes and brings him to Jesus (6:8–9); later when some Greeks want to see Jesus, it is to Andrew that Philip brings them so Andrew can introduce them all to Jesus (12:22). In each case the consequences of these simple acts of bringing people to Jesus were significant: the hungry get fed; new peoples hear the gospel – and here, Simon becomes a disciple. Andrew could not have known the significance of what he had done in bringing his brother to the Lord – but Jesus looked at him and saw through the rough exterior to the enduring qualities of the man: so, he calls him *Kephas*, which means the same in Aramaic as the Greek, *Petros* – 'Rocky', the foundation upon which so much will be built. We may not all be missionaries or famous evangelists, but perhaps there are people we could direct towards Jesus or who need us to bring them to him – and who knows what the result may be?

Prayer

Lord Jesus, thank you for your invitation to come and see; help me to accept your call and to follow you.

8

John 1:43–51

Follow me

The invitation 'Come and see' leads to the command 'Follow me'. In the other gospels, this is the first thing Jesus says to Andrew and to Simon Peter (Mark 1:17), and in John's gospel, Jesus repeats it to Peter as his last word (21:22). Here, though, Jesus goes to Galilee to find Philip and give him this invitation (1:43). Philip comes from Bethsaida, where the Jordan flows into the Sea of Galilee in the north, in the territory of Philip the tetrarch (see Luke 3:1). The gospel writer tells us that it is also the city of Andrew and Peter (1:44), although Mark 1:21–29 suggests that they now live in Capernaum, a few miles to the west along the shore of Galilee. Like Andrew, Philip has a Greek name and he is often mentioned with Andrew (6:5–8; 12:20–22). Philip also shares Andrew's readiness to go immediately and tell someone else about Jesus – Nathanael, whose Hebrew name means 'God has given'. And so, in this cosmopolitan seaside area the good news of what 'God has given' in Jesus begins to spread.

From disdain to faith

Unfortunately, like many others who think they are 'God's gift', Nathanael is not impressed. Philip tells his friend that they have found the one prophesied throughout the Hebrew scriptures and identifies him as Jesus of Nazareth, son of Joseph (1:45). Nathanael comes from Cana (21:2), a village up the road from Nazareth, and he is quite clear about the likelihood of God giving anything of value to his local rivals: 'Can anything good come out of Nazareth?' (1:46). Nathanael's disdain reflects our natural human expectations. If God is going to give something special, it will come in a special way, not from a carpenter's shop up the road! While this gospel opened with Jesus' cosmic origins with God (1:1), it recognises that Jesus' human origins are humble – and will prove a stumbling block to many (see 6:42; 8:40–43). Philip does not try to argue his friend out of his prejudice, but rather he shares his own experience of Jesus and issues the same invitation as the others received – 'Come and see.'

Jesus' knowledge of us

So Nathanael tags along with Philip, expecting his prejudices to be confirmed. Jesus, however, surprises him by taking the initiative and welcoming him as an Israelite in whom there is no guile (1:47). This is a compliment: all Israelites knew of the guile of the patriarch, Jacob, who stole his brother's blessing (Genesis 27:35); only one in whom there is no guile can serve the Lord (Psalm 32:2; Isaiah 53:9). Nathanael is taken aback: it is a shock when God lets us know that he believes in us more than we do in him! Jesus says that he saw Nathanael sitting under the fig tree. This may suggest he was studying the law: some rabbis used to teach under fig trees, while the prophets used sitting under a fig tree as an image of the peace of the day of the Lord (e.g. Micah 4:4; Zechariah 3:10). Later, Augustine says that he was reading beneath a fig tree when he heard the call of Jesus to 'pick up and read' the New Testament (*Confessions* 8.28–29). Jesus sees us and brings his welcome and his invitation into the midst of our ordinary daily activities.

Greater things

It is not clear how Jesus knew him under the fig tree, but Nathanael is impressed and moves from provincial scepticism to a declaration of messianic faith: 'Rabbi, you are the Son of God! You are the king of Israel!' (1:49). Jesus' somewhat amused response at this sudden turn around is in the best tradition of B-movie actors: 'You ain't seen nuthin' yet, kid!' Following Jesus is not about being impressed by his superior knowledge or his ability to do supernatural things – but something much greater than these things (1:50). It is nothing less than the connection of God with all his creation. In the midst of his guile, Jacob received a vision of a ladder between heaven and earth upon which the angels ascended and descended (Genesis 28:12). So now to follow Jesus is to witness the bridge between the divine and the human, the means by which heaven is opened (1:51). From start to finish, this gospel is clear that Jesus is the way to God the Father, as Jesus explains to Philip later at the last supper (14:6–11).

For meditation and prayer

Do I despise my local Nazareth or can I find God there? 'Rabbi, you are the Son of God! You are the king of Israel!' (1:49).

9

John 2:1–8

The wedding at Cana

'There was a wedding at Cana in Galilee.' For a little town nestling in the hill country above the Sea of Galilee a few miles from Nazareth, Cana has become remarkably well known down through the ages and across the world by being mentioned at the start of the wedding liturgies of many churches. Some couples save up for years to visit Cana to renew their marriage vows on significant anniversaries, and the little church there today is full of images of love and marriage. It is little wonder, then, that some people, particularly from Catholic traditions, interpret this story as being about the sacrament of marriage. Yet we are told nothing of the marriage itself or the happy couple – just about the disaster of the wine running out at the party! The wedding serves merely as the backdrop for the occasion of Jesus' first miracle in this gospel. For the evangelist, the important thing is not the event, but the fact that Jesus was there (2:2). The Word made flesh, the God who dwells among us, goes to wedding parties, joins in our everyday activities and gets involved with human affairs.

When resources run out

It is so embarrassing: the guests are here, the party is going well and then you realise that the special item for the dinner menu must have been left behind at the supermarket check-out or a miscalculation of amounts per person has left you short. Given the tendency of ancient Near Eastern weddings and parties to go on for days, supplies must have run out occasionally – but it would still have been a disgrace for the family. And so Mary turns to Jesus for help. It is futile to speculate why she does so or to surmise that they are related to the wedding couple or that Jesus has caused the shortage by bringing his friends along. None the less, Mary clearly expects that simply explaining the situation to her son will lead him to do something about it. When we come to the end of our human resources, and we simply have nothing left to say, do or give in a situation, so too we can turn to God in prayer and tell him what has happened.

Jesus' initial response is not encouraging. The address, 'Woman', is not as brusque in Greek or Aramaic as in English, and indeed he uses it to his mother again while on the cross (19:26). However, 'What is that to you and me?' does not suggest that he is going to do anything, because his 'hour has not yet come' (2:4). John uses the word 'hour' about 25 times. Twice more we are told that Jesus' 'hour had not yet come' (7:30; 8:20). When it does arrive, it refers to Jesus' death and glorification (12:23; 13:1; 17:1) – the very hour when Mary again stands at her son's side and is addressed as 'woman'. Thus we have a link in John's account between the beginning of Jesus' ministry when Mary turns to him when resources run out and the end when Mary watches his human life ending.

Do whatever he tells you

Mary, however, is not put off by Jesus' response. She tells the servants to do whatever he tells them. This motif of someone persisting despite an apparent initial rebuff from Jesus recurs later with the official who wants his son to be healed (4:47–50). Sure enough, Jesus now acts. He turns to the large stone jars holding the water used for purification, for washing people's feet when they came into the party or for their hands before eating and even between courses (see Mark 7:3–4). Jesus tells the servants to fill the jars, and not only do they obey, but they fill them 'to the brim' (2:7); then he tells them to take what is apparently water to the person in charge of the feast – and they take it, without protest. So the miracle happens through the persistence of Mary and the obedience of the servants. It is as though the evangelist is saying that simply expecting Jesus to take over when human supplies fail is not enough: persistence in faith is needed, together with the willingness to do whatever he says. God in Jesus dwells among us in times of joy, like that of bridegroom and bride, and of need at the end of our resources – but in both he desires our co-operation to grant us his grace.

Prayer

Lord, when resources run out and things seem hopeless, grant me the faith to trust in you and the willingness to do whatever you say, that your abundance may be shed on this world.

10 John 2:9–12

Water into wine

John describes the events at Cana as the first of Jesus' 'signs' and thus it stands at the start of his ministry as a foretaste of what is to come and an introduction to the rest. So what is the meaning of this miracle, apart from merely saving the blushes of the wedding family whose supplies had run out? After all, the sheer quantity of the water turned into wine is remarkable. The evangelist notes that each jar held 'two or three measures'; a measure – a *bath* or firkin – was between 20 and 30 gallons, so six jars works out around 150 gallons, or 800 bottles of the best-quality wine! It was clearly going to be quite a party...

This prodigious amount has invited comparisons between Jesus and the Greek god of wine, Dionysus. Various stories are told of bowls being miraculously filled with wine in his temple at Elis or of a fountain flowing with wine in his temple at Andros. In fact, we do not need to go so far afield for inspiration. The prophet Amos uses the image of 'the mountains dripping with sweet wine and the hills flowing with it' for the great day of the Lord to come, and similar examples of wine as a sign of so-called 'messianic abundance' can be found in other Hebrew prophets (Amos 9:13; Hosea 14:7; Jeremiah 31:12). Isaiah looks forward to the Lord giving a huge party, 'a feast of rich food, a feast of well-aged wines' (Isaiah 25:6) and likens God's rejoicing over his people to a wedding (Isaiah 62:4–5). Jesus uses this image of a wedding banquet for the kingdom of heaven in his parable of a marriage feast and those who refused the invitation (Matthew 22:1–10; Luke 14:15–24), and he likens himself to the bridegroom in Mark 2:19. All of this, says the fourth evangelist, is being inaugurated in the here and now as Jesus begins his ministry at this wedding feast in Cana.

New for old

Christians, of course, look forward to the heavenly wedding feast of God with his people every time we celebrate the Holy Communion, and so it is not surprising that some have seen an allusion to the sacrament of the Eucharist as well as marriage here. But in the absence of any mention of bread, or of blessing, this seems unlikely, except in the sense that John sees everything as sacramental: he fills his gospel with symbols of the grace of God being found in bread and wine, water and light. The great richness of this gospel is that so many levels of understanding can be found, but at the surface level of the story, the climax is the proclamation of the master of ceremonies that the best has been saved until last (2:10). Here at the start of his story of Jesus' activity, the evangelist says that we 'have seen nothing yet', that all which has gone before in the writings and prophecies, the hopes and beliefs of God's people, is now being made new in Jesus. The old order is passing away, as the new is inaugurated among us – and we should celebrate.

A sign to reveal his glory

This is the whole point of the miracle – it is not so much about what was done as who did it. As we saw in the Introduction (see p. 13), John uses the word 'sign', *semeion*, for Jesus' miracles, rather than 'mighty act', *dynamis*, more common in the other gospels. This, 'the first of his signs', points to Jesus; it 'revealed his glory, and his disciples believed in him' (2:11). The purpose of the sign is not for public display; apart from the servants, no one knew what had happened and so the person in charge compliments the bridegroom (2:9–10). For the disciples, however, the miracle of changing water into wine is the sign which moves them on from their call in chapter 1 to putting their faith in Jesus. At the end of the gospel, the evangelist tells us that he has selected these signs from the many done by Jesus 'in the presence of his disciples' that we might believe that 'Jesus is the Christ, the Son of God' and so have life in him (20:31). So, as Jesus brings life to the wedding party when things ran out, so he comes to us with the superabundance of his grace to make all things new.

For reflection and prayer

What are the 'signs' around you where God is changing the ordinary things of life into the new wine of his kingdom?

Lord, thank you that you have kept the best until now; grant me insight to see your signs and courage to believe in you.

11

John 2:13–17

House cleaning

Many signs in this gospel are followed by a debate to explain the sign's purpose – as the story of the feeding of the 5,000 leads into the discourse about Jesus as the bread of life (see on chapter 6 below). However, the first of Jesus' signs, the changing of the water into wine, has no such dialogue. Instead the scene shifts a hundred miles south to Jerusalem for the incident in the temple, which the other gospels use to introduce the final week of Jesus' life and the crucifixion. In these next studies, therefore, we will consider why the temple incident comes here in John, and how it is connected to the water into wine story.

The Passover in Jerusalem

'The Passover of the Jews was near, and Jesus went up to Jerusalem' (2:13). In the other gospels, only one Passover is mentioned, that during the final week of Jesus' life. However, John mentions three Passovers, introducing them each time with this phrase, 'the Passover of the Jews was near' – this Passover in 2:13; another a year later at the time of the feeding of the 5,000 (6:4); and the final Passover introduced in 11:55 and 13:1, upon which Jesus dies (19:14). John's dating gives us the traditional chronology of Jesus' ministry lasting three years. We have already noted John's interest in time with the mention of Jesus' 'hour' in the previous story (2:4). In fact, this gospel abounds in references to time, with words like hour, day, time, moment, now and already occurring frequently.

We also note that it is the Passover of 'the Jews'. Festivals of 'the Jews' punctuate this gospel: in addition to three Passovers, we have the Feast of Tabernacles in chapter 7 and the Dedication in chapter 10, with an unspecified festival in chapter 5. In each case, Jesus goes up to Jerusalem for the feast, like any pious Jew. This portrayal of Jesus the Jew is important in the light of John's use of the phrase 'the Jews' to denote his opponents. The other gospels concentrate on Jesus' ministry in Galilee and show him going to Jerusalem only once to die at Passover time – indeed Luke structures the whole of his account around Jesus' journey to Jerusalem (Luke 9:51—19:27). In contrast, John shows Jesus visiting Jerusalem regularly over several years.

This incident in the temple must come at the end of Jesus' ministry in the other gospels since it is the only time he is in Jerusalem, but historically that makes good sense also, since it precipitates the events of Holy Week leading to his arrest and death. Even today, the temple site in Jerusalem is heavily policed and any demonstration quickly attracts the authorities' interests! Since it is unlikely that Jesus could have done this twice, we must assume that John places it here at the start for theological rather than chronological reasons. So what are they?

A good clean-out

The common description of Jesus' removal of the traders and animals as the 'cleansing of the temple' suggests that it is some form of protest about its system. The other gospels' use of Jeremiah's phrase 'you have made it a robbers' den' (Jeremiah 7:11) implies a protest at the financial trading and exploitation of people through money changing and the sale of sacrificial animals (Mark 11:17; Matthew 21:12; Luke 19:46). Others have inferred from the reference about a 'house of prayer for all nations' (Isaiah 56:7; also in Mark 11:17, etc.) that Jesus' action in the Court of the Gentiles was a protest about the exclusion of women and Gentiles from worship in the inner courts reserved for Jewish men, especially the priests. But there is none of this here. Jesus does drive out the traders and money changers, even using a whip, but the saying is simply a pun about making 'my Father's house' into a 'trading house' (2:16). There is no reference to robbers or financial exploitation. It is almost as though the temple itself and its whole use is the focus of Jesus' action as he begins his ministry.

John would have known the prophecy at the end of our Old Testament canon that the messenger of the Lord would suddenly come to his temple, like a refiner's fire (Mal. 3:1–4). This may be why John places the temple incident here, almost as programmatic for Jesus' ministry. Now it makes the same point as the story of water into wine – the replacement of the old order by the new, for the Lord has come. Everything is changed as Jesus fulfils the festivals and the very temple itself – if only they would recognise him.

Prayer

Lord, may I recognise when your time comes and may the 'inner courts' of my life be ready for you.

12 John 2:17–20

Destroy this temple

It is not only in his placing of the temple incident at the start of Jesus' ministry that John differs from the other gospels. He also has this story concerning a saying of Jesus about the destruction of the temple. We have already noted that sometimes a sign or action in John's gospel is explained by a dialogue afterwards, so this next incident, acting as a counterbalance to the water-into-wine story, can further illuminate the meaning of the temple event placed between them.

Zeal for the temple

It is introduced by the disciples remembering a verse from Psalm 69:9, 'Zeal for your house will consume me' (2:17). The early Christians often saw messianic prophecies in this psalm, and John will refer to it again for Jesus' thirst at the crucifixion (19:28, quoting Psalm 69:21). This gives a different atmosphere to the story, moving the attention away from a protest *by* Jesus about the temple to a concentration on Jesus himself, telling us of his zeal for God's house and warning us that it will lead to his death. Thus the temple event becomes a foreshadowing of the crucifixion.

The response by the religious authorities, identified again simply as 'the Jews', is to question Jesus' authority. The old prophets, such as Jeremiah, prophesied in and against the temple and were questioned by the authorities (see Jeremiah 7:1; 19:14; 36:5), and Mark records a similar challenge to Jesus' authority after his account of the temple incident (Mark 11:28). So here, 'the Jews' ask Jesus, 'What sign can you show us for doing this?' (2:18). The prophetic word could be accompanied by an action, such as Ezekiel's dramatic acting out of the siege of Jerusalem as a sign (see Ezekiel 4:3). However, we have already noted that 'sign' in John's gospel (*semeion*) is used for a miraculous action which reveals something about Jesus – and this happens here too.

Destruction and the temple

However, instead of giving them a confirming miracle, Jesus replies with a *mashal*, a riddle, about destroying the temple and raising it up in three days (2:19). The second part alludes to Hosea 6:2, 'after two days he will revive us, on the third day he will raise us up', which should warn the hearers that something prophetic is being suggested. However, in this gospel, John often makes use of ironic misunderstandings between Jesus and his hearers, where he tries to explain something on a more spiritual level to someone who can only (mis-) understand it on a literal level. So here 'the Jews' interpret the comment literally as a rebuilding of the temple in three days and curtly dismiss such a preposterous idea! After all, Herod had begun to rebuild the temple during 20BC and after 46 years it was still under construction. It would be finished finally in AD63, only to be destroyed by the Romans a few years later in the Jewish War in 70.

Forty-six years from the start of construction would bring us to AD26, when Jesus was about 30 years old. This is probably a little too early for the actual temple demonstration leading to Jesus' death. However, if Jesus' ministry lasted three years, AD26 could have been around its start, so John may be right to place the *saying* here. It is also interesting that various versions of this saying about destroying the temple are quoted against Jesus by the false witnesses at his trial (Mark 14:58; Matthew 26:61; see also Acts 6:14) and at the cross (Mark 15:29; Matthew 27:40). If John is correct in placing the debate about the temple right at the start of Jesus' ministry, it would explain why the witnesses disagree about the saying several years later.

Thus this saying reinforces the point from the previous section by directing our attention away from interpreting this incident in the temple as a protest about particular abuses and back to Jesus himself. In the new order, when water is turned into wine, a prophecy about the destruction of the temple actually refers forward to Jesus' own death. The temple sacrifices will be replaced by his sacrifice on the cross.

For reflection and prayer

What are the practices in my life and my ways of worshipping God which need to be replaced by the new order in Jesus?

Father, give me a proper 'zeal for your house,' renewed in the death of your Son, Jesus Christ.

13   John 2:21–25

Realising and believing

We have seen that the evangelist is carefully linking the incident in the temple with the changing of water into wine, so that both stories reveal the arrival of the new age with Jesus. Of course, this is only realised with the benefit of hindsight, as the early Christians prayed and reflected upon the events of Jesus' life and death. As John makes clear in 2:22, it was only after the resurrection that the disciples remembered and finally understood what had been said and done – and in the light of the resurrection, they began to see how God's new life in Jesus transformed everything, even prophecies about the temple.

Resurrection and the temple

If 'zeal for your house' would lead to Jesus' death, and the saying about the temple be quoted at his trial, the evangelist is keen to point out that the rest of the saying refers to his resurrection. After the three Passovers and the three years, the phrase 'three days', with its roots in Hosea 6:2, would instantly remind any early Christian reader of Jesus being raised from the dead. We have noted John's interest in time, and he will often refer ahead to what is still in the future in the story-time, but which is now in the past from the point of view of the time of the writer and the reader. Thus Jesus' death and resurrection, which are still three years in the future in the story, dominate everything for the evangelist. So everything is all brought together in this story about the temple, which is placed at the start of Jesus' ministry but which looks ahead to the consummation of it all in his death and resurrection.

Now we really see the meaning of the whole chapter and how John likes to order events more for their theological significance. This whole incident is not about a prophetic cleansing of the temple, nor an anti-racial or financial protest; rather it reveals John's understanding of Jesus. The link with the water into wine is now clear – the new and better for the old. Just as the water became the abundant new wine, so this incident looks ahead to the replacement of the temple and its sacrifices by Jesus' sacrifice and his new life. The temple may have been destroyed only a few years after its final completion, and never rebuilt, but Jesus rose again after his death. Something beyond the physical level is happening and to argue about the timing of this event or that saying is to make the same mistake as the Jewish leaders who were so concerned about construction timetables that they could not understand who was standing before them, challenging them with his actions and his words.

Believing and trusting

John tells us that Jesus did many other signs, but that he has selected certain ones to describe so we may believe that Jesus is the Christ (20:31). This is clear here since, in between the 'first of his signs' of water into wine (2:11) and the 'second sign' (4:54), we are told about people believing in Jesus' name because of the signs he was doing (2:23). But belief which is based upon miraculous signs is not enough – hence Jesus' refusal to give one to 'the Jews' to prove his authority (2:18). While the disciples can 'believe' or 'trust' (*pisteuein* in Greek) his word after the resurrection (2:22), and others similarly 'believe' because of the signs (2:23), Jesus will not 'entrust' himself to them, as John uses the same word *pisteuein* here in 2:24 as in the preceding verses. He knows what people are like (2:25). His supreme knowledge of all is stressed throughout this gospel, from knowing Nathanael under the fig tree in 1:48 to knowing 'all things' at the end (13:3; 21:17).

This is the one who has come from being with God in the beginning to call disciples in chapter 1. So in chapter 2, this is the one who makes all things new, who can change water into wine and temple worship into resurrection faith. Both stories point clearly to Jesus and challenge us to respond, either with the questioning of the authorities, the following of the crowd or the dawning belief of the disciples. This challenge will become clearer and sharper in the next few chapters as more and more people come face to face with Jesus.

Prayer

Lord Jesus, teach me to see all things in the light of your resurrection and to believe the word you have spoken.

14 John 3:1–8

Nicodemus by night

In the last chapter, Jesus did not 'trust' himself to people who 'trusted' in him because of his signs (2:23–24). Over the coming chapters, many people come to Jesus because of his signs – the Samaritan woman (4:29), the official whose son is healed (4:47), the paralytic (5:9), the crowd who were fed (6:14), the blind man (9:25) – who all need to move on from trusting in the signs to faith in Jesus himself. The first is Nicodemus, a Pharisee and 'a ruler of the Jews', a member of the Sanhedrin, the Jewish council (3:1). He is a man of influence and wealth (he buys spices in 19:39), whom Jesus calls 'a teacher of Israel', a theologian perhaps!

He comes 'by night', which may be caution arising from his fear as one of the authorities of being seen talking to Jesus (3:2). However, the rabbis also saw the night as a quiet time for study of the scriptures. Whether it is out of fear or that he wants to talk to Jesus undisturbed, the evangelist depicts Nicodemus as someone still in the dark – but who comes to the light. In due course he will come out into the open to speak for Jesus (7:50) and to bury him (19:39); at this point he simply wants to ask questions.

You must be born again

We have noted John's habit of using the way people misunderstand Jesus to get at deeper levels of meaning. This happens in Jesus' conversation here. Jesus responds to Nicodemus' trust in the signs (3:2), by telling him that he must be born over again, *anothen* (3:3). Just as 'the Jews' misunderstand Jesus to mean literally rebuilding the temple, so Nicodemus interprets this as a man trying to climb back into his mother's womb (3:4). So, what does *anothen* mean? Some Bible translations will have 'born again' and others 'born from above'. In fact, *anothen* can have both meanings, in the way our phrases 'start over' or 'from the top' use language from 'above' to mean 'again'. The evangelist probably intends both meanings. Jesus has come from above, with God (1:1ff) and wants his followers to be with him there (17:24). However, both Jews and Greeks used the idea of rebirth to mean starting again in a new life, for Gentiles wanting to follow Judaism and for initiates in the Greek mystery cults. So Nicodemus' misunderstanding allows Jesus further explanation.

Water and the Spirit

Jesus replies to this misunderstanding by explaining that we have to be 'born of water and the Spirit' to enter the kingdom of God (3:5). There is a lot of water in this gospel: John baptises in it (1:26), and Jesus turns it into wine (2:9), offers it to the woman at the well (4:14), heals by a pool (5:7), walks on it (6:19), offers it again to the thirsty (7:37) and uses it to heal (9:7) and to wash the disciples' feet (13:5). There is something cleansing, healing and satisfying about it all. Little wonder, then, that many have interpreted 'born of water' as referring to Christian baptism, seeing 'of the Spirit' as meaning confirmation or a Pentecostal second blessing or baptism in the Spirit. The paradox of this gospel is that although John's theology is supremely sacramental in the way ordinary things like water, bread and wine are used to convey great spiritual truths and meanings, he never actually describes the sacraments of baptism and Communion, or indeed any others. It is thus unlikely that he has any reference to any 'two stages' of Christian initiation here.

Instead, he is contrasting Nicodemus' literal understanding of getting back into the womb with the spiritual rebirth from above offered by Jesus. When my wife's waters broke at the birth of our daughters, I was amazed by how much water had protected them in the womb – but now they had to take their first breaths of air. So too we must move from our physical natural birth through a new spiritual birth to enter the kingdom of God. 'That which is born of the flesh is flesh' but to be born of the Spirit is to be like the wind, which comes and goes at will, invisibly (3:6–8). The Greek word, *pneuma*, which gives us words like 'pneumatic tyres', means wind, breath and spirit, from the air in our lungs to the Holy Spirit of God. Nicodemus has to come out of the darkness, be born again, take a big breath and let himself be carried on the winds of God.

For reflection and prayer

What are the darknesses and misunderstandings out of which we need to be born again? Do we have the courage to launch out in the Spirit?

Lord Jesus, grant me God's Holy Spirit that I may be born again to your new life.

15 John 3:9–15

The teacher is taught heavenly things

After Jesus' comparison of the Spirit with the wind, poor old Nicodemus has to ask for yet further explanation (3:9). As 'a teacher of Israel' (3:10), he should have known the old prophecies about God giving his people 'a new heart and a new spirit' (Ezekiel 18:31; 36:26) and writing his covenant on their hearts (Jeremiah 31:33). In response to his question, Jesus embarks on a section of teaching introduced by the phrase 'Amen, amen I tell you' (3:11), variously translated as 'Truly, truly' or 'Very truly'. While the other gospels use only one 'Amen' to introduce Jesus' teaching, John stresses it by using this doubling effect some 25 times.

Furthermore, something strange happens in verse 11, for Nicodemus disappears from view: the first 'you' in the verse is singular, still addressing Nicodemus, but after that the speech moves into plural pronouns, 'we' and 'you-plural'. Also, it is not clear when Jesus' speech ends. Since ancient manuscripts had no punctuation marks, which were only put into the text centuries later, modern editors have to work out where to put inverted commas around someone's speech. Usually it is clear where someone stops speaking and the narrator restarts – but not in John. Some Bible translations end the quotation in 3:15, while others run it right through to 3:21, since both the narrative and Jesus' speech use the same style and words. It is as though the quiet night-time conversation between Jesus and Nicodemus has been replaced by Jesus speaking through the evangelist and the early Christians to the rest of the Jews and, indeed, to the whole human race, asking them to 'receive our testimony' (3:11).

Earthly and heavenly things

The misunderstanding of 'the Jews' about the temple saying and by Nicodemus about the new birth arose because they interpreted Jesus just on a literal or earthly level, when he wanted to direct them to a higher, heavenly one (3:12). This happens regularly throughout this gospel. So here Jesus has been speaking of earthly things like a birth or the wind, but uses them to refer to the heavenly things of a new beginning with God and his Spirit.

In fact, John often distinguishes a heavenly divine realm from the earthly world we inhabit. The problem is that we cannot ascend from our level to God's. Jesus, however, is the Son of Man who has descended from heaven to our lowly depths (3:13). We saw this in chapter 1, in the great prologue describing Jesus as the Word with God in the heavenly realm (1:1–14), and also in Jesus likening himself to Jacob's ladder connecting the two levels in his conversation with Nathanael (1:51). We should not assume that John held a primitive two- or three-tier view of the physical universe; rather, this distinction between a 'superior' level of the world of ideas and the divine over an 'inferior' realm of the physical universe of material bodies runs right through ancient writings from the Greek philosophy of Plato to Jewish prophecy. Thus we must expect to find it often in this gospel.

Moses' serpent and the Son of Man

Next, the Old Testament allusions move away from the prophets and Jacob's ladder to Moses and the Israelites in the wilderness. In Numbers 21:4–9, we find the story of the Israelites grumbling against Moses and God, and being punished by a plague of poisonous snakes. As a remedy God told Moses to make a bronze snake and lift it up on a pole – and anyone who looked at it was healed (Numbers 21:9). The bronze snake itself was eventually smashed as an idol by Hezekiah (2 Kings 18:4). However, the later Book of Wisdom, which was written in intertestamental times and can now be found in the Apocrypha (see Glossary), described it as a 'symbol of salvation' (Wisdom 16:6). This is exactly how John uses it here. He seizes on another word capable of several levels of meaning – the verb *hypsoun*, to 'lift up'. Of course, it has the positive meaning of to raise or exalt, but when Jesus talks here and in 8:28 and 12:32–4 of the Son of Man being 'lifted up', we know that it will be on a cross. Once again, we are asked to look beyond the earthly level to spiritual things. Like the dying Israelites looking to the snake 'lifted up' for healing, we are to see in Jesus' broken body 'lifted up' on an instrument of torture our means of healing and the source of eternal life (3:14).

Prayer

Lord Jesus, give me grace to see beyond earthly things and to receive your salvation as you are lifted up.

16 John 3:16–21

God so loved the world

As we saw before, this passage can be read either as the end of Jesus' conversation with Nicodemus or as a separate comment by the evangelist. Who says it is less important than what it says, for it is one of this gospel's supreme passages, full of John's favourite vocabulary and themes, including, of course, probably the most famous verse in the Bible, 3:16. But this verse, rich in the love of God, is set within a whole series of contrasts. John is fond of balancing sets of opposites, such as above and below, life and death, truth and falsehood. Such pairings are also found in Greek philosophy and within Judaism, notably in the Dead Sea Scrolls found at Qumran. Again we see how John explains the gospel in words and ideas accessible to his own day, but which also have had a profound influence upon human history ever since.

Eternal life or perishing

John's use of contrasting pairs and his portrayal of the heavenly realm as opposed to the earthly could lead to accusations of dualism. Certainly, the dualism of Greek philosophy valued the heavenly above the earthly, seeing the physical, material world as something from which to escape. While John does sometimes use 'the world' in a negative sense for those opposed to God, especially in the last supper discourses, this section shows us that the world can never be seen totally negatively. 'For God so loved the world' tells us that it is the *world*, for all its sin and shortcomings, which is the object of God's love, which has a universal scope. Sometimes Christians act as if John 3:16 read, 'For God so loved the *church*…' in their neglect of the world! Yet this gospel makes it abundantly clear that God acts for the whole world in sending his 'only Son'.

This phrase recalls another Old Testament story, where Abraham is told to take 'your son, your only son, Isaac whom you love' up the mountain for sacrifice (Genesis 22:2, 12). While Abraham was spared this ultimate sacrifice, God did not spare his Son, Jesus, but gave him so that the world should not perish. For this is the ultimate choice John puts before his readers: to perish apart from God or to receive his gift of eternal life in his Son. There is no other option – and for this reason 'God sent his Son into the world.'

Belief or condemnation

This idea of God 'sending' Jesus is one of John's most frequent, occurring over 50 times in this gospel. But he is also clear why God sent the Son – not to condemn the world but to save it (3:17). The Greek verb *krinein* means to judge or to condemn, and it gives us the English words 'crisis' and 'critic'. The coming of Jesus provokes a crisis both for the world and for all who dwell upon it, a 'critical moment' of judgement and decision. It is not that he comes as judge, to condemn the world, for those who do not believe are already lost in their darkness and evil deeds (3:18–19). Instead, he comes to save, that they might turn to him and receive eternal life. It is often thought that judgement is something which happens at the end of all time and space on judgement day. But John makes it clear that this deciding, this judgement is already happening in every 'critical moment' in the here and now. As we saw in the Introduction (see p. 20), for John 'eschatology' (things to do with the end, *eschaton* in Greek) is made real in the present, as Jesus comes into the world to save us.

Light or darkness

Of course, the coming of light into darkness creates shadows, and this, says John, is the crisis, the judgement, because some prefer to remain in the shadows (3:19). Thus we have another contrast, between those who practise what is true, who come to the light, and those who do evil, who hide (3:20–21). But since Jesus comes not to condemn the world but to save it, it is not the case that only those who do truth may come forward. Those who do not know how to live truly, or who stumble in the darkness, may come to the light as Nicodemus does by night and find love and acceptance. Later in the gospel, as Nicodemus comes more out into the open, we will also read of Judas, who leaves Jesus to go out into the darkness of the night (13:30). The options, the opposing contrasts are always before us at each critical moment, which is why God sent his Son into the world, that we should not perish but have eternal life.

Prayer

Lord Jesus Christ, may I recognise the 'critical moment'; let me come to you out of my darkness to receive your eternal life.

17 John 3:22–30

Jesus and John the Baptist

The next scene gives us a glimpse of the ministry of Jesus and his disciples baptising, in much the same way as John the Baptist and his followers. It was a good job there was 'much water there' (3:23)! This reminds us of how similar their ministries were at first, before John was put in prison (3:24). In fact, this is the last appearance the Baptist makes in this gospel, although he is mentioned in comparison with Jesus later (e.g. 4:1; 5:33–36; 10:41). Such comparisons were bound to raise the possibility of rivalry between the two men and their respective groups. Disciples of John the Baptist were known around the Mediterranean for some time later, as is shown by the apostle Paul's baptising some at Ephesus in the name of Jesus (Acts 19:5). Thus it would not be surprising if there was debate among the Jews about these rites of purification, and whether Jesus' or John's was better (3:25). Even more understandable is the complaint of John's disciples that Jesus is doing better business: 'All are going to him' (3:26). What is not perhaps expected is John's reaction.

Bearing witness

Even John the Baptist's disciples who are complaining know perfectly well that Jesus had been with John 'across the Jordan' and that John had borne witness to him (3:26). This gospel shows John the Baptist as satisfied to accept the success or otherwise of the ministry given to him by God (3:27). He reminds his followers that he had denied any claims to be the Christ, but was only the one sent before him (3:28, referring back to 1:20–23). He has given his fourfold witness to Jesus being greater than himself as the Lamb of God and Son of God who baptises in the Holy Spirit (see on 1:24–34). While this understanding of Jesus is more theologically developed than John's questioning of Jesus in the synoptics (see e.g. Matthew 11:3; Luke 7:19), it need not be interpreted solely as a later 'attack' by the early Christians against the followers of the Baptist. John the Baptist's ministry is clearly attested in all the gospels and in the writings of the Jewish historian Josephus as preaching and baptising for forgiveness in preparation for the coming of the kingdom of God. Thus he was looking forward to something greater to come.

He must increase, but I must decrease

Matthew makes this point by showing John as reluctant to baptise Jesus at first, recognising him as greater than himself (Matthew 3:14). In this gospel, John uses the analogy of the bridegroom and his friend (3:29). It is a bit like our custom of having a 'best man' at a marriage – and the old joke about the bride not marrying the best man at her wedding! In Jewish weddings of the time, the bridegroom would be assisted by one or two friends who would make the arrangements and escort the bride to the groom, and eventually to the bridal chamber. The reference to rejoicing at 'the bridegroom's voice' may refer to the friend standing guard at the chamber and only admitting the groom, whose voice he recognises, or to hearing his voice calling out joyfully when the marriage had been consummated – the sign for the friend to slip away quietly, his duty done. Of course both the Baptist and the evangelist, as well as their readers, would have been very familiar with all the bridal imagery used to refer to the people of God in the Hebrew prophets: 'as the bridegroom rejoices over the bride, so shall your God rejoice over you' (Isaiah 62:5; see also Isaiah 49:18; 54:6; Ezekiel 16:8–14; Hosea 2:16–20). The same idea recurs later in Revelation (19:7; 21:2, 9–10).

Thus with this imagery, the Baptist is saying that his task is done and it is time for him to disappear: 'He must increase, but I must decrease' (3:30). I remember as a best man enjoying all the festivities and basking in the reflected joy of the happy couple – and there is sometimes the same temptation in the Christian life and ministry, especially when God is blessing our work. But while it is perfectly right to rejoice at such times, we must always remember that we are not meant to be centre stage, only the groom and his bride – and like John the Baptist, slip away quietly, happy as God is magnified.

Prayer

Lord Jesus, teach me to follow the example of John the Baptist that I may bear witness to you and decrease while you increase.

18 John 3:31-36

Jesus – the one from above

This last section is 'free floating' like 3:16–21; again it is unclear who is the speaker. John the Baptist started talking in 3:27 and some translations continue his speech through to 3:36, while others make this a comment by the evangelist. Some scholars even see this as a separate speech by Jesus. Since both the Baptist and Jesus speak in the same style of the evangelist and quotation marks had not yet been invented, it is not vital. Far more important is how it sums up this chapter's themes by redirecting our attention, as John the Baptist does, back once again to Jesus.

The origins of Jesus

The section begins by using the phrase 'the one from above' to refer to Jesus (3:31) and this picks up the earlier conversation with Nicodemus where Jesus described himself as the one who has descended from heaven (3:13). We saw how this dualism of the heavenly realm above and the world of earthly things below dominates John's thought (see on 3:12), so this recapitulation is not surprising. From the heights of the prologue through to when Jesus ascends to return to his Father, John makes it clear that he is the one who has come down from heaven into our world. It is so central to John's view of Jesus that he does not even name him in this passage at all – the phrase 'the one from above' is quite sufficient to refer to Jesus. Here, 'from above' is *anothen* once again, the word Jesus used when he told Nicodemus that he needed new birth 'over again, from above' (3:3, 7). This is why we need to be born over again, so that we can participate with Jesus in the realm where he belongs with God.

The mission of Jesus

If Jesus has come down from above, then we next need to ask the question why and what for? As John the Baptist constantly bears witness to Jesus, so too Jesus testifies to what he has seen and heard in the presence of God (3:32). Again, this picks up his conversation with Nicodemus, where the transition to the more general statement happened with 'We bear witness to what we have seen' (3:11). Throughout this gospel, Jesus is identified as 'the one whom God has sent' (3:34), which reminds us that the expression of how much God loves the world is that he sent his Son into the world (3:17). Jesus is well aware of this, and his favourite description of God in this gospel is 'the one who sent me' (e.g. 7:28; 8:26–9). His mission is to speak 'the words of God' as the one who 'gives the Spirit without measure', abundantly (3:34). This also reminds us of how Jesus taught Nicodemus about being born of water and the Spirit, the Spirit which blows where God wills like the wind (3:5–8). Jesus warned Nicodemus that some will not accept his testimony (3:11) and this is reinforced here in 3:32. But, thanks be to God, there are those who do accept it, who are prepared to put their names to it, to sign up and 'certify that God is true' (3:33).

The Father of Jesus

If Jesus is the one who bears witness to God, the Father is the one who loves the Son and gives all into his hands (3:35). This stress on God's love for Jesus and his entrusting of everything to him is common in this gospel. If, however, God has made Jesus the centre of everything, then the consequences of any response to him are great. As well as John's typical dualism of above and below here, we also find another one of belief and disbelief or disobedience, which brings either life or death (3:36). This recalls the themes of the previous teaching section about the coming of Jesus as a crisis, a critical moment of decision and judgement (3:15–21). In both sections it is clear that whoever believes in Jesus has eternal life (3:36, cf. 3:15–18). However, the alternative must also be true, that rejection of Jesus leaves us under God's wrath (3:36). This is not some temper tantrum of a malicious deity, for God so loved the world that he sent his Son to bring us into his light. But if men and women choose to remain in the darkness (3:19), the God of love cannot force them out. The late Bishop Lesslie Newbigin has expressed this sober truth well in his commentary on John, aptly entitled *The Light Has Come*, thus: 'If we turn our backs upon light, where shall we go but into darkness?' (p. 48).

Prayer

Lord Jesus, help me to accept your testimony that God has sent you, and give me your eternal life.

19 John 4:1–9

A Samaritan woman at a well

This gospel's geographical setting moves between north and south, from Jesus calling disciples in Galilee (1:43) and the wedding in Cana (2:1) to the temple in Jerusalem (2:13) and Nicodemus' night visit (3:1). Now, after the debate about Jesus' baptism compared with John's (4:1), Jesus leaves Judea and heads back to Galilee. The hundred-mile journey takes about three days in a straight line north, which goes through Samaria, an area Jews would prefer to avoid. However, the alternative route going up the Jordan valley to the east needs twice the time, so Jesus sets off through Samaria (4:4), and this becomes the scene for yet more contrasts and meetings of opposites.

Jews and Samaritans

Jesus arrives at the city of Sychar, or Shechem, a place with a history stretching back to the patriarch Jacob (4:5). This immediately recalls 1:51, where Jesus described himself as the connection between the heavenly realm and the earth just like Jacob's vision of a ladder with angels ascending and descending. It was the same Jacob who bought this land on his return (Genesis 33:18–9), and then gave it to Joseph before he died in Egypt (Genesis 48:22); the Israelites later buried Joseph's bones there after the occupation of Canaan (Joshua 24:32).

Centuries later, after the kingdom of David split following Solomon's death, King Omri made it the capital of the northern kingdom around 870BC (1 Kings 16:24). It was captured by the Assyrians in 721, who settled non-Jews there; their intermarriage with the locals offended later ideas of Jewish purity (2 Kings 17:6, 24). The southern kingdom also fell, and the people were deported to Babylon in 586BC. Those who returned from exile 50 years later prided themselves on their purity. Those in Samaria offered to help the exiles rebuild the temple in 520BC since they shared the same sacrificial worship of God, but this was spurned (Ezra 4:1–3). So the Samaritans built their own temple. From these roots came the bitterness still so strong in Jesus' day. The irony is that ancient Samaria is now the West Bank, occupied by modern Israeli soldiers locked in continuing conflict with its inhabitants – and so the ancient troubles persist, despite their shared history going back to a patriarch who dreamed that even the gulf between heaven and earth could be bridged.

Men and women

So Jesus, the bridge between heaven and earth, arrives in this place and immediately confronts yet another division. He is tired and sits down by the well in the noonday heat (4:6). A woman comes to draw water, which reminds us of how the patriarchs met their wives by wells. Jacob himself met his future wife Rachel by a well (Genesis 29:1–20), which was also where his mother Rebecca met the servant searching for a wife for his father Isaac (Genesis 24). Moses met Jethro's daughters at a well (Exodus 2:15–21). After a wedding with no mention of the happy couple in 2:1–11, and Jesus likened to a bridegroom in 3:29, we might expect this woman coming to a well to be the bride. The problem is that she is a Samaritan. Furthermore, the barriers of race and creed were complicated by gender divisions in Jesus' day. The rabbis taught that a man should not talk to a woman in the street. Some even refused to acknowledge their wives in public, while certain Pharisees sported bruises from bumping into things when their eyes were shut to avoid looking at a woman! What is more, this woman has come in the hottest part of the day, which can only be to avoid others, implying that she is immoral as well.

If Nicodemus was the representative Jew with whom Jesus debated (3:1–11), this woman is the representative Samaritan. But now we have a real meeting of opposites – of a Jew with a Samaritan, a man with a woman, a rabbi with a sinner, the one 'from above' confronting the lowest of the low. It sums up all the bitterness of human separation by race, creed, class, sex, profession, status – yet Jesus, alone, without even his disciples to protect him, asks her for a drink (4:7–8). No wonder there follows her disbelieving, even sarcastic reply: 'Are *you* talking to *me*?!' (4:9). Yet this is what it means for him to be the ladder at Jacob's well, bridging not only the gulf between God and the world, but also all the barriers human beings put between themselves. It was for this reason that God sent his Son into the world, and for this reason there is hope for us all, from modern Samaria on the West Bank to our daily petty differences.

Prayer

Lord Jesus, great bridge-builder and ladder into heaven, forgive us our divisions and reconcile us to God and one another.

20 John 4:10–19

Living water

The woman is surprised that Jesus, a Jewish man, should talk to someone of her gender, race and status – but talk he continues to do. As the conversation unfolds, a dynamic develops similar to that with Nicodemus, as Jesus gently leads her through levels of misunderstanding from the earthly and the literal to the heavenly and spiritual. As this happens, she gradually becomes more aware of who Jesus is. At the moment she thinks he is simply a Jewish man who ought to know better than to talk to her, or can only be doing so for some ulterior motive (4:9). So he teases her by hinting at 'a gift' and suggesting that she does not know who he is; if she did, she would have asked him and would receive 'living water' (4:10). The English translation hides the pun and the beginning of the shift of level, for *zon*, living, with water means 'running, moving' as opposed to the still or even stagnant water found in a well. Jesus has aroused her interest, and she addresses him with respect, 'Sir'. But he does not even have a traveller's skin bucket – so how is he going to get 'running/living' water (4:11)? Who does he think he is? Even the great patriarch, Jacob, had to dig the well very deep to provide for his family (4:12). How is this man going to get to its actual source?

Wells and springs

Jesus' reply suggests that despite Jacob's greatness, the water in the well cannot satisfy, but people will be thirsty again – which is why the woman has to come to draw water (4:13). However, if people drink the water he is offering, they will never be thirsty again; the still water of the well will be replaced by a 'spring welling up for eternal life' (4:14). This contrast between ordinary water and a leaping fountain reminds us that water is a key theme in this gospel (see on 3:5). The use of water as a spiritual metaphor is common in the Old Testament scriptures, where the psalmist's soul is as thirsty for God as a deer for flowing streams (Psalm 42:1–2) and God calls all who are thirsty to come and drink freely (Isaiah 55:1). A century or so before Jesus, the phrase 'the well of living waters' is used in the Dead Sea Scrolls to describe the Jewish law, while the wisdom writers used water as a symbol of wisdom itself: 'Those who drink of me will thirst for more' (Ecclesiasticus 24:21). Jesus' offer goes even beyond that, with the promise of never thirsting (4:14). In the new order where water turns into abundant wine and the temple is replaced by Jesus, even wisdom and the law itself must give way to the superior gift of God in Jesus.

Not surprisingly, however, the woman again misunderstands it literally; if what Jesus says is true, he is to be respected as someone to save her work and the trouble of carrying water: 'Sir, give me this water, so that I may never be thirsty or have to keep coming here to draw water' (4:15).

Husbands and gods

If the woman has to keep drawing water, she must have a family to care for, so Jesus tells her to call her husband (4:16). After the betrothal hints in the story so far of Jesus, the bridegroom, asking for water from a woman at a well, her reply that she has no husband (4:17) is only to be expected – does this mean she is available? Now the conversation moves into another level, as the gentle teasing is replaced by the blunt truth, that she has had five husbands as well as her current man (4:18). The Jews permitted three marriages at most, and so this is why she is slinking around the well in the quietest, but hottest part of the day. As with Nathanael under the fig tree (1:48), so now Jesus demonstrates his knowledge of all things and everyone. He confronts her with herself so that her impurities can be cleaned out and the living water run freely.

Some interpreters see in the five husbands a reference to the five non-Jewish groups brought in to intermarry with the remaining members of the northern kingdom after the fall of Samaria in 721BC, as listed in 2 Kings 17:24, each with their own gods and worship. Thus the woman becomes an allegory of the racial impurity of the whole Samaritan people. However, since seven gods are mentioned in 2 Kings 17:30–31, this is unlikely. What is more, the woman now reacts in a very human way. Her estimation of Jesus goes up another notch; for him to know the truth about her, he must be more than 'Sir' – he must be a prophet, and what better way to move him off her private life than to throw a theological conundrum at him (4:19–20)?

Prayer

Lord, give me this water, that I may never be thirsty.

21 John 4:19–30

Prophet or Messiah?

As the story unfolds, Jesus has gently led the woman to a greater understanding of who he is, from her initial ignorance (4:9) to calling him 'Sir' (4:11, 15); as he confronted her with the facts of her life, she began to wonder if he might be greater than Jacob. Now Jesus must take her further.

The place of worship

When Jesus reveals that he knows all about her sex life, the woman thinks he must be a prophet. If he knows all these things, perhaps he knows the answer to the theological question which divided Jews and Samaritans – where should we worship (4:20)? We suggested that she throws this 'hot potato' at him to deflect him away from her personal difficulties. We too sometimes avoid the embarrassing truth about ourselves by debating knotty problems or church politics! Alternatively, since the place of worship is where sacrifice for sin was made, the woman's question might not be a diversionary tactic but a response to the truth Jesus has revealed: yes, you are right about my life, so where can I go to find forgiveness?

The woman is correct that the patriarchs worshipped on this mountain in Samaria, not only Jacob (Genesis 33:20) but also Abraham (Genesis 12:6–7). Of course, Mount Gerizim, as it was called, was later eclipsed by the great temple built by Solomon on Mount Zion in Jerusalem. However, after the Samaritans' offer to help rebuild the temple was rejected (Ezra 4:1–3), they built their own temple here around 400BC. Relationships deteriorated further when some Jews led by John Hyrcanus destroyed it in 138BC. No wonder this Samaritan wants to ask this Jew where she should go with her sinful life to find God (4:20).

Jesus says that the place is not important, as the time is coming when neither mountain will have a temple (4:21). As we saw in 2:13–22, the earthly temple will be destroyed and replaced by Jesus himself. Furthermore, as in the conversation with Nicodemus, suddenly the verbs move into 'we' and 'you-plurals' (4:22, cf. 3:11). Although John uses the phrase 'the Jews' to describe Jesus' opponents among the religious authorities, he is clear that Jesus himself is a Jew ('we') and 'salvation is from the Jews' (4:22). However, while salvation may come *from* the Jews, who have worshipped God faithfully in the temple for centuries, and *through* the Jew Jesus, it is not solely *for* them. 'The hour is coming and now is' for worship to be not tied to a place but open for all. John uses this phrase to show how God's heavenly future is breaking into our earthly realm now (see also 5:25). As was made clear to Nicodemus, only through the Spirit can we enter into God's kingdom, for 'God is spirit, and those who worship him must worship in spirit and truth' (4:23–24, cf. 3:5–9 above).

Who is this?

Now it has become too much for the woman and she wistfully repeats her trust that one will come to explain all this (4:25). The Samaritans revered the first five books of the Hebrew scriptures, and so were waiting for the 'prophet like Moses' foretold in Deuteronomy 18:15, which they called the *Taheb*, the restorer. The term 'Messiah' used here means 'the anointed one' in Hebrew, as does 'Christ' in Greek. Jesus realises that the woman has now progressed as far as she can, so the moment has come to reveal himself (4:26). Again, however, John's language works on two levels: on the surface Jesus says, 'That's who I am', but the verb *ego eimi*, 'I am', on its own in the sentence recalls the name of God revealed to Moses, 'I am who I am' (Exodus 3:14; see also Isaiah 41:4; 43:10). This is the first time this phrase appears in the gospel, but it will become a very important way of understanding who Jesus is.

Meanwhile, the disciples have returned from their shopping expedition and are amazed to discover their rabbi talking with a Samaritan woman (4:27). The woman realises that it is time to go and return into the city, extraordinarily forgetting to take her water jar with her – an indication of how flustered and excited she is by what has happened perhaps, or even a sign that she intends to return (4:28). But she has changed; she came to the well in the hottest, quietest part of the day to avoid people – but now she goes to find them and tell them what has happened to her. Now the fact that Jesus knows all she has done is not something to be avoided with a theological hot potato – but the hottest news to be shared: 'Can this really be the Christ?' (4:29).

Prayer

Lord Jesus, help me to worship you in Spirit and truth and to know you as Messiah.

22 John 4:31–42

Food and harvests

The woman has gone, but her abandoned water-pot is a silent reminder to the disciples that their rabbi was talking with a woman, a Samaritan and a sinner, openly in the middle of the day. But too embarrassed to mention it directly, they can only stammer two words, 'Rabbi, eat' (4:31). In their confusion, they concentrate on simple necessities. But Jesus will not allow them to deflect him like this, any more than he let the woman divert him with questions about the place of worship. So he teases them that he has food which they do not know about (4:32). Just as the woman misunderstood the living water for a labour-saving spring, so the disciples, tired from their shopping, wondered why they bothered: 'Who has given him something to eat?' (4:33). You can almost hear the scandalised whisper – it cannot have been that woman, can it?! Like both 'that woman' and Nicodemus, the disciples are stuck on the earthly, literal level of meaning, while Jesus is talking about heavenly nourishment, simply to do the work of the one who sent him, his heavenly Father (4:34). Now it is the disciples' turn to progress to a deeper understanding.

Lift up your eyes

In the other gospels, Jesus frequently uses images from farming in his parables – a sower, seeds growing secretly, the harvest (see Mark 4). Remarkably, John has no parables in his gospel, but this little section uses the same imagery, like a parable. Jesus begins with a common saying, that there are four months between the sowing, in January or February, and the harvesting, in May and June. He then invites them to look around at the fields, 'white for harvesting' (4:35). If the story is set around harvest time, reapers may have been working in the fields; certainly this plain of Samaria on the west bank of the Jordan is one of the few open expanses of arable land. At harvest time, the sowers and the reapers, those who began and those who ended the process, can rejoice together in their success (4:36–37). The disciples, still clutching the bread they have brought from market, look at the fields and wonder what the point of this agricultural lesson is.

By now we have learned to expect that they will interpret Jesus' words on the literal, earthly level. But perhaps, as they look at the white-flowering fields surrounding the well, they begin to notice instead the white robes of the Samaritan villagers who have been listening to the woman's testimony and are now on their way to see Jesus (4:30). Here again, the level shifts, from shopping for food to sowing and harvest, and then on to the spiritual meaning. The conversation between Jesus and the woman is where the sowing took place (4:37), 'others' have laboured (4:38) – but the seeds sown by Jesus the sower and disseminated by the woman have not needed four months to come to harvest. If only the disciples could 'lift up their eyes' beyond the ordinary level of worrying about food and prejudice against women and Samaritans, they would see that the work of God, the one who sent Jesus, is being done. Now they are invited to the joyful climax, reaping the fruits of that little talk by the well in the noonday heat. So this section comes full circle: the disciples were embarrassed about Jesus talking to a woman – but he not only explains what he was doing, but also corrects their prejudice and invites them into God's work.

The Samaritan harvest

In fact, the woman has been doing the work of a disciple – giving her testimony, her witness, through which others are coming to faith for themselves (4:39). The short cut through Samaria ends up taking as many days as the long way round, since the Samaritans invite Jesus and his disciples to stay with them (4:40). First, the woman wondered who this person able to tell her all she ever did might be, then others came to faith through her, but now many believe because of Jesus' words (4:41). The testimony of others may enable us to see how God acts in each of our lives individually, but in the end we all have to hear and believe for ourselves that Jesus is indeed 'the Saviour of the world' (4:42). And so, Jesus' real identity is finally revealed: he is not just a Jewish man talking to a woman, or a rabbi, nor even the prophet or the Christ – but the Saviour, a term reserved in the Hebrew scriptures for God alone: 'For I am the Lord your God, the Holy One of Israel, your Saviour' (Isaiah 43:3; see also, Isaiah 45:15; 49:26).

Prayer

Lord of the harvest and Saviour of the world, feed me with your Father's will, that I may sow your seed.

23 John 4:43-54

Healing an official's son

After all the excitement in Samaria, Jesus finally returns to Galilee (4:43). Although the Galileans welcomed him, it was only because they had seen what he had done at the festival in Jerusalem (4:45). Once more the evangelist notes that Jesus was aware of how fickle such a welcome could be, especially in his home locality (4:44). This reminds us of his previous comments about Jesus' knowledge of human hearts in 2:23-24. The move to Cana also takes us back to chapter 2 with the reminder about the changing of water into wine (4:46). Thus chapters 2 to 4 form a little section from Cana to Cana with this passage balancing 2:23-25 like a pair of bookends.

Unless you see signs

The story concerns a 'royal official' who asks Jesus to heal his son. Such an official would have worked for Herod, perhaps as a soldier or as an administrator, and could be Jewish, Greek or Roman. In a similar story in Matthew and Luke he is a centurion (Matthew 8:5-13; Luke 7:1-10). If this man is a Gentile, he balances Nicodemus the Jew and the Samaritan woman. However, John does not tell us his nationality, just that his son is ill in Capernaum. Jesus' response is rather brusque, turning to address the crowd, 'Unless you [plural] see signs and wonders, you will not believe' (4:48). The official does not have time for all this debate and presses Jesus harder, 'Sir, come down before my little boy dies' (4:49). This reminds us of the other miracle in Cana, where Mary's request to Jesus for help at the wedding also seemed to receive a rebuff at first. Her persistence then was rewarded by Jesus telling the servants to fill the water jars and take it to the top table; through their obedience it became wine (2:1-11). So too here, as the official believes Jesus and obeys him when told to go, so he meets his servants who bring him the good news that the fever had left his son (4:50-52). This same basic structure in both of the signs at Cana of request-rebuff-persistence-obedience-miracle cannot be coincidental. This is John's answer to human fickleness and sensation seeking: Jesus responds to those who persist in their prayerful request.

Your son lives

Throughout the fourth gospel, the evangelist stresses Jesus' authority and power. Capernaum, where the little boy is sick, is 20 or 30 miles from Cana – but when Jesus tells the official 'your son lives', the fever leaves him straight away (4:50–53). Jesus has only to speak and it happens, regardless of the distance, which will take the official most of a day to cover. To stress this, John repeats the phrase 'Your son lives' no less than three times – when Jesus tells the official, when the slaves meet him with the good news; and when he reflects on when Jesus said it (4:50, 51, 53). No wonder not only the man himself but also his whole household came to believe, not just in the sign but in Jesus (4:53).

Signs in John's gospel

John ends this section by pointing out that this was the second sign Jesus did (4:54), in the same way that he began it by noting that the water into wine was his first (2:11). This careful numbering, which does not take into account the other signs Jesus did in Jerusalem which impressed the Galileans (2:23, 4:45), has fascinated biblical scholars. John's statement at the end of his gospel that he has selected these signs to convince his readers that Jesus is the Christ (20:31) has stimulated much discussion. It is usually noted that there are seven main signs in this gospel: water into wine (2:1–11); this boy's healing (4:46–54); the lame man (5:1–15); feeding the 5,000 (6:1–15); Jesus walking on water (6:16–21); the blind man (9:1–11); and the raising of Lazarus (11:1–44). Some signs are linked to discourses, such as that about the bread of life in 6:25–58 and the light of the world in 8:12–59. There is no obvious discourse for these two signs in chapters 2 and 4, but we have seen how Jesus' actions in the temple pick up the idea of 'new for old' in the water into wine. Similarly, Jesus' discussions with Nicodemus about being born again to eternal life and with the Samaritan woman about living water are brought to a climax here as Jesus gives this little boy new life, even at a distance. It is easy enough to promise life, says John – but Jesus actually brings his promises into the reality of our pain and suffering.

Prayer

Lord Jesus, help me to persist in my praying and bring your new life to us all.

24 John 5:1–9a

Do you want to be healed?

This new chapter begins with the mention of 'a feast of the Jews' (5:1). Various Jewish feasts provide the backdrop for the next chapters: we have already seen one Passover in 2:13, and the next Passover happens in 6:4. Then the Feast of Tabernacles is the background for chapters 7—8, with Hanukkah or the Dedication for 10, before we come back to Passover again in 11:55. It is thus curious that John does not identify this feast. This may be because he wants to draw attention not to an annual feast but to the weekly festival of the sabbath which dominates this chapter. Whatever the feast is, Jesus once again goes to Jerusalem. Some scholars suggest that chapters 5 (in Jerusalem) and 6 (back in Galilee) should be swapped around to give a more coherent flow to the story. However, all ancient manuscripts have them in this order. It gives us a sequence of each sign being followed by a visit to Jerusalem: so the changing of water into wine is followed by the temple incident in chapter 2 and the feeding of the 5,000 in chapter 6 is followed by the Tabernacles visit in chapter 7. This visit to Jerusalem in chapter 5 not only follows the sign of the official's son (4:43–54) but includes the healing of this lame man. Both signs then lead into discussion with the Jews and a discourse from Jesus about his authority and identity.

The healing pool

The healing takes place at a pool, variously called in the manuscripts Bethesda or Bethzatha, which had five porticoes (5:2). Since so many things in this gospel have symbolic meanings, these five porticoes have often been interpreted as representing the five books of Moses – Genesis, Exodus, Leviticus, Numbers and Deuteronomy – known together as the Pentateuch. There are other references to Moses and the exodus in this chapter, but more recently a double pool near the Sheep Gate in Jerusalem has been excavated which does have four porticoes around the sides with a fifth down the central divide between the two baths. The site also contains the old church of St Anne, a cool, peaceful building with a marvellous acoustic, quite suited to a place of healing!

Once again we notice the presence of water. After baptism in chapter 1, water into wine in chapter 2, being born of water and Spirit in chapter 3, being thirsty at a well in chapter 4, now we find that water is also a source of healing. The best manuscripts do not contain the story of the waters being troubled by an angel (5:3b–4), but it is assumed in the lame man's later comment (5:7). Spas have been very important throughout history where waters stirred up by a bubbling spring have often contained curative minerals. The Roman baths at Bath are a very good example, where patients at the Hospital for Rheumatic Diseases are still helped into the waters. No wonder so many invalids lay in the porticoes around these pools (5:3).

Wanting to be healed

However, the image of 'troubled waters' is often more one of mental distress than physical, of getting agitated as something disturbs us, even at an unconscious level. When Jesus realises how long the man has been there, he confronts him with the key question, 'Do you really want to be made well?' (5:5–6). After all, 38 years is a long time, as long as the main wanderings of the Israelites in the wilderness (Deuteronomy 2:14), another link back to Moses. There are lots of other people here, but this man is alone – and he has his answer ready: 'I am all abandoned and helpless. Even when the water bubbles, I cannot get there. Someone else always enters first' (5:7). The word used here for paralysed (5:3) is *xeron*, which means all dried up, 'withered' in the AV. The man has withered into his loneliness and isolation, and hope has all dried up; it is not fair, he complains.

But Jesus cuts straight through the man's prepared speech with a direct command. He does not need the troubled waters, just to stand up, pick up his simple mattress and walk away – healed. It is an extraordinary idea which leaves us all wide-eyed with gaping mouths, astonished and asking why this one was healed and not the others. Yet something of the waters of Jesus' new life which we have seen in the previous chapters pour into this man's heart and wash through his body – and off he goes, healed and carrying his mat!

For reflection

What causes the 'troubled waters' around me? Which parts of my life have dried up and withered? Do I really want to be healed? Can I trust Jesus' word of life?

25 John 5:9b–18

The sabbath and Jesus' claims

This day is not only 'a festival of "the Jews"', but also a sabbath (5:1, 9b). So 'the Jews' notice the man carrying his bed on the sabbath and accuse him of doing something unlawful (5:10). Since the man who was healed and Jesus who healed him were both Jews, as were all those attending the festival, it is curious to find the phrase denoting a separate group – especially since we have just been told that 'salvation is from the Jews' (4:22). Once again, this phrase seems to denote the Jewish authorities, who questioned both John the Baptist and Jesus himself (1:19–22; 2:18–20). Now they move on beyond mere questioning, as their opposition to Jesus starts to gather momentum.

The first complaint is that it is not lawful for this man to carry his mat on the sabbath. Observance of the sabbath is central to the Jewish way of life. It was a day which God had made holy after he finished his work of creation (Genesis 2:2–3), setting it aside for worship and a rest from work. The problem is how to define what constituted 'work'. In the collection of rabbinic teaching about the sabbath, compiled just after New Testament times, 39 types of activity were prohibited (*Mishnah Sabbath* 7:2). Even today in some cities with a large Jewish population, some of the Orthodox would like to link the houses and streets together into one residential area within which they are allowed to carry objects on the sabbath without breaking the law. Certainly, for this man to carry his bed, even if it were only a simple mat, would have been seen by some as 'work'. Once again, however, he has his answer ready: it is not my fault, I am only doing what I was told by the man who healed me (5:11).

Jesus found him

However, this attempt to 'pass the buck' runs into problems because the man does not know who Jesus was. Jesus' ability, especially in Jerusalem, to appear in public to do or say something and then to merge back into the crowd happens frequently in this gospel (5:13). On the other hand, it is also typical that he seeks out and finds those in need and those whom he has helped. So now, while 'the Jews' are looking for him, Jesus takes the initiative and finds the man in the temple. First, he points out that he is now well, and then warns him to 'sin no more, so that nothing worse happens' (5:14). This need not imply that Jesus shared the common belief that sickness and suffering were results of, or even punishments for, someone's sin. Actually he denies that view later (see 9:2-3). But if such a simplistic cause and effect is rejected, the biblical idea is still that we are a unity of body mind and spirit, that what we say or believe, think or feel affects who and how we are – and this is borne out by the 'psychosomatic' approach of much modern medicine. Perhaps Jesus is warning the man about lapsing back into his old self-centred attitude developed in so many years by the pool side; if so, he does not seem to heed the warning, for he promptly goes off to tell the authorities that it was Jesus who had healed him on the sabbath (5:15)!

At this point, 'the Jews' move from questioning Jesus to actively opposing him – not just because of this one incident, but because he made a habit of it, as is shown by John's use of the continuous imperfect tenses in 'doing such things on the sabbath' and 'breaking the sabbath' (5:16, 18).

My Father is working

Jesus' response was to draw attention to the fact that God was still working on the sabbath (5:17). The rabbis and theologians soon realised that God could not be completely idle on the sabbath, since it still rained and crops grew, still people were born and died. Thus God did not cease from giving life and declaring judgement, for that is his very nature as ruler of the universe. But Jesus' offence was now something worse than merely breaking the sabbath. To call God his Father and to connect his healing activity with the giving of life and judgement by the Father was a claim they could not ignore. In fact, this is not actually 'making himself equal to God', as the next verse makes clear Jesus' total dependency upon God and his inability to do anything without him (5:18-19). None the less, the whole of Jesus' ministry and teaching could be seen as acting in the place of God, as his representative or agent, in giving life and proclaiming judgement. No wonder they sought 'all the more to kill him' (5:18).

Prayer

Lord Jesus, thank you that you have made me well; grant that I may sin no more, but rather work with you and your Father.

26 John 5:19–29

The Son gives life and judges

We now come to the first of the 'discourses' common in this gospel, sections of teaching delivered by Jesus. Speeches were used not just in ancient biography, but also in history writing to help readers understand the true meaning of what was happening, rather than as an exact account of what was actually said. As we have seen punctuation marks were not added until a thousand years later. So too, John, drawing on his years of meditation under the guidance of the Spirit on what Jesus said and did, connects these discourses to the signs to explain their significance. In these two signs Jesus gave life to the official's son and to the paralysed man; to the latter, he also spoke a word of warning and judgement. In the Old Testament, both of these activities belong supremely to God (see e.g. Deuteronomy 32:35–41; 1 Samuel 2:6). The giving of life and death in judgement is also ultimately connected with the end of all things (see Introduction, p. 20, on 'Eschatology'). We have already noted John's interest in time with words like 'hour' and 'day' (see on 2:4 and 2:13 above). Now he shows how the end is breaking into time in Jesus' deeds and words.

The Father and the Son

If Jesus is giving life and acting in judgement, this is a claim to be acting for God here on earth. Thus we begin with the relationship of Jesus with his Father. Far from 'making himself equal with God', in fact he can do nothing on his own. Although John has no parables, this saying is like a parable when read without the capital letters: a son can only do what he sees his father doing, and whatever the father does, so does the son, because the father, out of love for his son, shows him everything he is doing (5:19–20). It reminds us of a child watching his father, in a carpenter's workshop perhaps. Yet in this gospel no other description says more about Jesus. John uses 'the Father' to describe God over 100 times, with the corresponding 'Son' for Jesus about 50 times – much more often than in the other gospels. This elucidates perfectly Jesus' relationship with God in which he has equality and identity with God as he speaks and acts for God here on earth, but yet he is totally dependent on his Father who loves him to show him all things.

Judgement now

In the light of that relationship between Father and Son, the next few verses explore how Jesus gives life and acts in judgement in the present, as the events of the end, the *eschaton*, are made real among us. God raises the dead and gives them life, as in Ezekiel's vision of the valley of dry bones (Ezekiel 37:1–14). Now he shares this with Jesus who 'gives life' to whomever he wishes (5:21). Judgement has also been given to Jesus, since people's reaction to the Son now is a reaction to the Father who sent him (5:22–23). Thus anyone who hears Jesus and believes him has already passed from death into eternal life; there is no judgement to come (5:24). Eschatology is not about 'pie in the sky when you die'; it is realised – made real – in the here and now. In the last two signs, the official's son received new life as soon as his father believed Jesus and the paralytic got up and walked immediately upon Jesus' command. Unfortunately, the opposite is also true, that those who refuse Jesus are rejecting God the Father who sent him (5:23).

Future judgement

And yet, the end can never be totally realised in this life, so now we get the same themes repeated with a future dimension. Thus the time is coming when the dead and those 'in their tombs' *will* hear Jesus' voice (5:25, 28). This is because God has given him the authority to execute judgement, now and in the future. Those who have done good will rise from death to life, while evildoers will come to judgement (5: 27, 29). Jesus can do all this because of the relationship of the Father and the Son: only God is totally self-sufficient, with 'life in himself', but he shares this with his Son (5:26). Thus those who have received the Son's life, like the official and the paralytic, will come into eternal life, while those who go on opposing him risk judgement at the end.

In other words, we can never escape the inevitable tension between the present and the future, the 'now' and the 'not yet'. In Jesus the Son, the end is breaking into our present, so the two passages are linked with the phrase 'The hour is coming and now is' (5:25; see also 4:23). This is what his signs point towards.

Prayer

Lord Jesus, grant that I may hear your voice and receive your life now, and forever.

27 John 5:30–38

Bearing witness

So far Jesus has made some claims through his signs, which have then been challenged by 'the Jews'. He has repeated the claims directly through this discourse, arguing that he shares in God's activity of giving life and judgement both in the present now and in the future at the end. The obvious question must then be – where is the evidence for this claim? When people claim today that God has told them to do something, it needs careful examination; some seem quite right, but others end up being looked after in prison or hospital. Similarly, the next few chapters examine the evidence for Jesus' claims. It is as though Jesus is on trial before 'the Jews', long before the formal proceedings which lead to his crucifixion. This is why the word 'witness' or 'testify/testimony' is so important in this gospel. It occurs about 35 times, especially with John the Baptist and in debate between Jesus and 'the Jews' (as here and in 8:13–18).

Witnesses were important in any ancient trial. Without our modern techniques of forensic science and evidence gathering, the testimony of witnesses was the main way to discover the truth. Thus the Jewish law did not allow anyone to be convicted on the statement of a single witness, but only if their evidence was corroborated by one or two others (Deuteronomy 19:15). In order to deter malicious or false accusations, judges had to subject witnesses to a thorough investigation. If the witness was found to be false, he would suffer the fate intended for the person he accused. In this way, others would be deterred from making such false claims (Deuteronomy 19:16–20). Paul also requires two or three witnesses for any charge (2 Corinthians 13:1). So, in these chapters where Jesus is on trial for what he claims, the issue of his witnesses is crucial.

Jesus' own witness

First, Jesus states once again that his claim to exercise judgement is not based on his own authority. He is only doing the will of God, who sent him (5:30). Therefore, the discourse moves away from Jesus' claim to the evidence for it. As a good Jew, Jesus accepts immediately the point of law that his witness to himself is not enough (5:31). However, he argues that there is another witness on his behalf whose testimony is true (5:32). So, let us call this next witness.

The witness of John the Baptist

So the discussion moves to John the Baptist. Jesus reminds 'the Jews' that they had already questioned John and heard his testimony to the truth (5:33; see 1:19–28). Even in the prologue to his gospel, the evangelist described the Baptist's role as to 'bear witness to the light' in Jesus (1:6–8) and John the Baptist made this clear to his disciples (3:28–33). Now Jesus returns the compliment by bearing witness to him. If John was not the light, he was at least like an oil lamp with its wick burning and shining bright. What is more, even 'the Jews' were grateful for his light (3:35). But Jesus' claim will need more than the human testimony of John to be upheld, however much the questioners may need to be reminded of it to avoid becoming false accusers (3:34).

The witness of the Father

So Jesus now calls something greater than John's testimony to the witness stand. He appeals to the works he is doing, such as the healing of the paralysed man which started this debate, as well as his other miracles. Thus this gospel calls such works 'signs' since they bear witness on Jesus' behalf that God has sent him (5:36). Even one of 'the Jews', Nicodemus, accepted that such miraculous signs indicated that God was with Jesus (3:2). But in appealing to the evidence of his works, Jesus is actually calling God as his final witness. The problem is that the opponents have 'never heard his voice nor seen his form' as God used to appear in the Old Testament (5:37). Nor indeed, do they have his word, the prophecy which was the other way God communicated with their forebears. Ultimately, this is because they have not believed in Jesus, whom God has sent as his supreme word (5:38). So, who is on trial here? Is it Jesus, who must call these witnesses to prove his claims – or his questioners, who refuse to recognise and accept the evidence God gives them? We need to find a judge to decide this, which takes us into the final section.

Prayer

Lord Jesus, give me grace to accept your testimony and to believe in the one who sent you.

28 John 5:39–47

The scriptures and Moses

Chapter 5 has given us a good example of how John weaves together signs, dialogues and discourse to develop his story of Jesus. The sign of healing the paralysed man on the sabbath led to accusations about Jesus' work and his claims, which have then been tested through the dialogue and the discourse. In his defence, Jesus has called to the witness stand himself, John the Baptist, his miraculous signs and God his Father. So who will judge the witnesses and decide whether the accusation is correct? The ultimate arbiter for Jews is always Moses and the law. After all, it all began with Jesus being charged of violating the law of Moses by breaking the sabbath with his work of healing.

The witness of the scriptures

The accusers have appealed to the scriptures for their witness, namely the commandments about the sabbath and keeping it holy, as evidence that Jesus is wrong. What Jesus does is to claim that their witness actually testifies to him, to bring the 'hostile witness' on to his side. He compliments them on the way they search the scriptures; the word used for 'search', *ereunan*, implies proper rigorous study and analysis (5:39). Unfortunately, this detailed search has missed the main point, which is to find life in God and Jesus whom he has sent (5:40). It can often be like that for us in our Bible reading. Rigorous detailed study is vital, but not so that we cannot see the wood for the trees and end up missing the main point, which is to bring us to life in Christ. This is particularly important when studying the gospels, whose primary focus is the life and work, death and resurrection of Jesus of Nazareth. They were written to testify to Jesus, that we might come to him and have life (5:39–40).

Receiving glory

Jesus makes it clear that he is not interested in being judged by human beings' opinion of his work (5:41). Their inability to understand the scriptures and to believe the witnesses he has called, in addition to their failure to recognise God at work in his healing signs, all show that the accusers do not have the love of God in them (5:42). To make matters worse, he suggests that they will accept others who come in their own name (5:43). There were many messianic claimants in the first century, each with their various supporters. In any group or society, those who work within the system are likely to be praised by the others. This is as true of any 'mutual admiration society' today as it was then. Does our searching of the scriptures, our preaching, teaching or writing, merely lead to human praise, to receiving 'glory from one another' (5:44)? To go beyond 'You scratch my back, and I'll scratch yours' to seek the glory from God alone is difficult. Jesus implicitly denies the charge of claiming 'equality with God', since there is 'one who alone is God' (5:44). He has simply come in his name, dependent upon God for everything, and to accept or reject him is to accept or reject 'the one who sent me'.

Judgement by Moses

So we come to the end of this first round of trial by witnesses. Jesus has been accused of breaking the law of Moses by violating the sabbath, but he is more than happy to appear before Moses. For Moses is the judge who will turn the tables and accuse the accusers (5:45). If we search the scriptures, we will find that the commandments and the law point towards Jesus, in whom God's people are to find their sabbath rest and their healing (5:46).

So here all this chapter's themes come together. The story of the paralysed man spending 38 years in the five porticoes was full of allusions to Moses, the five books of the law and the years of the exodus. Those hints continue through the discourse about judgement and witness, asking us some questions as we search the scriptures. Who is actually on trial here – Jesus, his accusers, or those of us who read this chapter today? Will what we trust in actually come back to accuse us? Do we seek glory from the only true God, or merely each other's approval? These are vital questions, since the final judgement breaks into our present here and now in Christ, according to this whole chapter. If we respond to what God has done in Jesus whom he has sent, then we pass from death to life (5:24).

Prayer

O God our Father, grant that we may so search the scriptures and seek your glory, that we may find life in the one you have sent, Jesus Christ our Lord.

29 John 6:1–13

Feeding the 5,000

Jesus' miraculous feeding of a vast crowd is such a well-known story. This is the only miracle narrated in all four gospels – indeed, it is the only incident from Jesus' ministry before his last week which they all include. The synoptic gospels each describe the feeding of 5,000 people (Mark 6:31–44; Matthew 14:13–21; Luke 9:10–17), and a feeding of 4,000 occurs in Mark 8:1–9 and Matthew 15:29–38. Here, we shall concentrate on the details unique to John, especially its link with the 'bread of life' discourse with its eucharistic overtones.

The story begins back in Galilee, as Jesus goes to the other side of the lake (6:1). John alone tells us that the crowd followed Jesus because 'they saw the signs he was doing' (6:2). This recalls the last few chapters, especially the signs done in Cana. More importantly, only John tells us that Jesus went up a mountain at the time of the Passover (6:3–4). Chapter 5 hinted at the Israelites in the wilderness and appealed to Moses; now we are reminded of Moses who began the Passover and who went up the mountain to meet God. So what will Jesus do on this mountain?

How to feed so many?

In all the accounts, Jesus sees the crowd coming to him, but as so often in John, here Jesus is the one in control, and he takes the initiative. He begins by questioning Philip (6:5), of whom we have heard nothing since his call in chapter 1. Since then, Philip has seen Jesus at work in the miraculous signs – but he does not seem to have learned much from them. After all, where did the 'good wine', the 'living water' and Jesus' food come from (2:10; 4:10, 33)? It is also typical of this gospel that Jesus knows what he is going to do and is only testing Philip. Philip fails the test by suggesting that 200 denarii would not buy enough for everyone to have even a little (6:6–7). A denarius is a day's wage (according to Matthew 20:2) so this sum is about six or seven months' wages.

Every little helps

Next the evangelist brings Andrew into the story. Andrew and Philip came from the same town and often feature together in John (see

1:40–44). In his last appearance, Andrew brought his brother Simon Peter to Jesus (1:42). Now, keen as always to help, Andrew goes beyond Philip's despair by bringing a 'little boy' to Jesus. Only John's gospel mentions this lad and, in addition, tells us that the loaves are 'barley loaves' and the fish are dried. Barley loaves were the food of the poor, a third of the price of wheat (see Revelation 6:6), while the word *opsarion* means a small dried or pickled fish. In the other gospels, the word is *ichthys*, used for fresh fish as we might expect so near the lake. John stresses how meagre is this offering of a poor little boy's packed lunch. No wonder Andrew is tempted to follow Philip's despairing attitude, 'but what is this among so many people?' (6:8–9). But Jesus accepts it, however small it is, and tells everyone to sit down to eat (6:10).

When he had given thanks

In the other gospels' accounts, Jesus says grace, that is, he blesses (*eulogein*) both the bread and God for it. But John says he 'gave thanks' over the bread – *eucharistesas*. This is the very word which gives us 'Eucharist', which is rather curious, considering that there is no account of the institution of Holy Communion in this gospel (see on 13:1–20). Equally, while the people pick up the fragments in the other gospels, here Jesus specifically instructs the disciples to do this 'so that nothing may be lost' (6:12). This may anticipate Jesus' concern that no one should be lost, in 6:39, but it could also reflect the tradition of consuming all the consecrated bread at Communion.

So if we pull all these hints together, we can see how John has carefully told this story so that it goes beyond just an account of a miraculous feeding, amazing though that might be. The references to the mountain and Passover remind us of how Moses fed people in the wilderness, just as Jesus does now. But to do so, he wants our cooperation. What we have may be meagre, but like Andrew or the boy, we are to offer it to Jesus. When he has given thanks for it (*eucharist*) and shared it around in Communion, then everyone is satisfied and all can be gathered together. These hints about Moses and the Communion are developed further in the events and discourse which follows.

Prayer

Lord Jesus, give us courage to offer the little we have to you that you may use it to satisfy all your people.

30 John 6:14–24

Who is this?

After this amazing sign, it is hardly surprising that people wonder who such a person can be, which gives us the theme of this next section. People seek, Jesus hides; Jesus finds, people seek. The miraculous feeding of a multitude in the mountains would make people think of Moses and remind them of Moses' promise: 'The Lord your God will raise up for you a prophet like me from among your own people' (Deuteronomy 18:15). After all, John the Baptist was asked if he was this prophet right at the start (1:21), and the Samaritan woman wondered if Jesus was the prophet (4:19, 25). No wonder the crowd concluded that Jesus was the prophet they were expecting and would have sought to acclaim him (6:14). But Jesus does another of his disappearing acts and withdraws up into the mountains, perhaps to be alone and pray. The writer explains that this was because the crowd would not stop at prophet but would make him king as well, whether or not he wished it (6:15).

Walking on water

The disciples seem to have taken the hint as well, and keep out of the crowd's way by going back down to the shore (6:16). The Sea of Galilee is about four miles across at its northern end, and they set out back to Capernaum by boat. The lake is surrounded by the mountains, and as evening draws on and the hills cool, so the wind springs up and it can get rather strong, making rough seas (6:17–18). As the disciples are struggling to row back, they see Jesus coming towards them (6:19). It has been noted that the phrase translated 'on the sea' can also mean 'by the sea' on the shore, as is the case when it is used of Jesus on the beach in 21:1. On this reading, the disciples have almost rowed back across the lake, and then they see Jesus walking around it alongside them. However, their reaction of fear suggests that here John intends us to understand that Jesus is walking on the water to find them. After the allusions to Moses in the wilderness, now we are reminded of crossing the Red Sea. After the suggestions that Jesus might be the prophet and king, now we have hints about him acting like God: as the psalmist referred to the exodus crossing, 'Your way was through the sea, your path through the mighty waters' (Psalm 77:19). So who is this person coming across the waves now?

I am

Jesus' reply is simple: 'It is I; do not be afraid' (6:20). Except nothing in John is as simple as it seems. Even on the lake, we find deeper waters underneath the surface! While it is true that the Greek phrase, *ego eimi*, can be used to identify the speaker in this way (see e.g. 9:9), its literal translation is 'I am.' As we saw when Jesus used it to introduce himself to the Samaritan woman (see on 4:26 above), it reminds us of the divine name revealed to Moses and used in the prophets (e.g. Exodus 3:14; Isaiah 41:4; 43:10). Jesus uses it about 35 times to refer to himself in this gospel, often with a description like bread or light; on other occasions, his use of it on its own as the divine name will invite stoning (8:58–59). Here too it stands alone; whether the disciples take it as his simple self-identification or hear the resonance of the name of God is unclear – but it is enough to calm their fears and bring the boat to land immediately (6:21). Like those who 'went down to the sea in ships', who called to the Lord in the midst of a storm, they have been brought to the safety of the harbour (Psalm 107:23–30). The one who can feed them in the mountains can also bring them home afterwards.

Seeking Jesus

While the disciples have been safely found by Jesus, the crowd of would-be kingmakers are having less success. When day dawns, they find that the disciples, the boat and Jesus himself have all gone (6:22). They are still at the place where 'the Lord had given thanks', again using the *eucharist* word to identify the feeding (6:23). Therefore they have no option but to get into boats and go 'seeking Jesus' (6:24). Only when he lets them find him, will they be able to discover what this has been all about and who he really is.

Prayer

Lord Jesus, my prophet, my king, my God, come and find me when I struggle through the storm and bring me safely to your rest.

31 John 6:25–34

More questions and answers

We have seen how John likes to move from signs into a dialogue between Jesus and others which ends with a discourse. So here, we start with three questions from the crowd, each answered by Jesus, which pick up the signs and begin to explore the themes they raise. Like Jesus' dialogue with Nicodemus and with the Samaritan woman, we progress through different levels from the obviously physical to the deeper spiritual meaning.

Perishable or eternal?

After the games of hide and seek earlier in the chapter, the crowd are surprised finally to find Jesus on the other side of the lake. Their question 'When did you come here?' probably includes 'How?' and 'Why?' as well. In other words, they are still at the stage they were after the feeding; they call him 'Rabbi' (as did Nicodemus) and still want to follow him on their terms, to hail him as prophet and make him king (6:25).

Jesus ignores their question, preferring to go straight to the heart of why they are seeking him. He suggests that it is nothing to do with his teaching as rabbi or his signs, but because they were getting free food (6:26). In other words, like Nicodemus or the Samaritan woman, they are stuck at the physical level. Jesus has to lead them on to the spiritual level, just as he did with the others. Like Isaiah calling people to stop working for bread which does not satisfy (Isaiah 55:1–2), so Jesus reminds them that the multiplied bread, like manna, is merely perishable – which is why they want some more. Instead, they need to work for food which leads to eternal life. The word 'food', *brosis*, is the same as the food which nourished Jesus at the well when he had no bread (4:32). As Jesus told the woman to ask for the water of life instead of a physical well (4:10), so now he tells this crowd to work for the living food he offers (6:27).

The works of God

Like the woman, they are interested enough to ask what they must do 'to work the works of God' (6:28). Jesus' reply is brief: the work of

God is not something we have to do, but someone we are to believe in. Throughout this gospel, Jesus is the one who does the works: they are his 'food' (4:34) and they are a witness that God has sent him (5:36), because in the end his works are those of his Father (5:17; 10:37–38). All we have to do is to believe in Jesus as the one God has sent (6:29). It is so simple, and yet so demanding. We can do no work to earn it, yet it will cost us everything. The crowd found it hard then, as we do today. Such is the life of faith.

Bread from heaven

If the work of God is that we should believe in Jesus, then again we need some evidence. So the crowd's immediate response is to ask what sign or work Jesus will do as proof for them (6:30). We have had several signs already and the last chapter introduced various witnesses, including Jesus' works and Moses as the judge. Now the crowd again remind us of Moses by referring to his work of providing manna in the wilderness. The text they quote, 'He gave them bread from heaven to eat' (6:31), is from Psalm 78:24 mixed with allusions to the manna story in Exodus 16:4, 15.

Jesus could have replied by saying that this is exactly the sign which he has worked by feeding them in the mountains. Instead, he interprets the text as a rabbi would correct someone's understanding, by saying 'It's not this, but that', in three points. First, it was not Moses but God, identified as 'my Father', who fed them; second, it is not about the perishable manna, but the true heavenly bread; third, it refers not to a single event in the past, 'gave', but God '*gives* life to the world' now in the present (6:32–33).

After this succinct exposition, the crowd are even more eager for this bread. If God is giving out bread from heaven, this is much easier than going to the baker's all the time! It is hardly surprising that they want 'this bread always' (6:34). But like the woman who thought that 'living water' was better than coming to the well (4:15), they have not realised yet that Jesus is offering something beyond physical bread, or even magical provisions: it is nothing less than the very life of God.

For reflection and prayer

Do I work for that which is perishable or eternal?

Father God, help me to believe in Jesus as the one you have sent.

32 John 6:35-40

I am the bread of life

After the miraculous feeding and Jesus walking on the water and the discussion about bread, attention is now focused on Jesus by his direct claim, 'I am the bread of life' (6:35). Since the gospels are a form of ancient biography, the focus will be constantly redirected at the person of Jesus. The evangelists are trying to tell us about him, who he is and what he is doing, what it means and how it can change our lives. So what does it mean to identify Jesus with the bread of life? This phrase, 'I am the bread of life', is so well known from our liturgies, hymns and songs that we take it for granted – but what is it telling us about Jesus?

We saw in the walking on water story that the phrase 'I am' on its own recalls the name of God (see 6:20 above). However, in this gospel, 'I am' is also linked to seven well-known predicates or descriptions of who Jesus is: the bread of life (6:35, 51); the light of the world (8:12; 9:5); the door (10:7, 9); the good shepherd (10:11, 14); the resurrection and life (11:25); the way, truth and life (14:6); the true vine (15:1, 5). Some of them are linked to signs, as with bread here and the feeding, or light with the healing of a blind man (9:7), and resurrection with the raising of Lazarus (11:43). Some of them also include the word 'life' or 'living', which we know is a key theme of this gospel. But what all these images share in common is a strong Jewish background. We have seen that this section of the gospel is structured around the Jewish feasts, in which Jesus takes the key aspect of the feast and goes beyond it (see on 5:1 above). In these 'I am' sayings, something similar is happening, as these key Jewish ideas – of bread and so forth – are taken and reapplied to Jesus and identified with him. In each case, we will need to explore their background and meaning and see what this tells us about Jesus.

The bread of life

According to Deuteronomy, Moses told the Israelites that God fed them with manna to make them realise that 'one does not live by bread alone, but by every word that comes from the mouth of the Lord' (Deuteronomy 8:3). Over the years, the Jews often used manna and bread as images of the word of God, for the Law and for divine wisdom. Thus Wisdom invites people, 'Come, eat of my bread and drink of the wine

I have mixed' (Proverbs 9:5). The Wisdom of Jesus son of Sirach (written around 190BC) says that Wisdom feeds those who fear the Lord and hold to the law 'with the bread of understanding'; therefore those who eat of her 'will hunger for more' and those who drink of her 'will thirst for more' (Ecclesiasticus 15:3; 24:21). But this Jesus, the son of his Father who sent him (6:37–38), is even better than that. Just as he promised the Samaritan woman that those who drink his living water would never thirst again (see on 4:14 above), now, as the bread of life, he is superior to the bread of the law and wisdom. Whoever comes to him 'will never be hungry', and whoever believes in him 'will never be thirsty' (6:35). As Jesus offers more than the Jewish feasts, so 'I am the bread of life' is saying that he is better than the very centre of Jewish devotion, the law itself. It may only be a simple phrase, but it is a staggering claim!

The Father's will

Thus it is not surprising that people could see Jesus, but not believe (6:36). It is one thing to be miraculously fed by him and even to want to make him prophet and king – but quite another to accept that he is superior to all you have ever believed. We may claim to want to do the work of God and to want the bread (6:28, 34) – but to come to Jesus on these terms demands everything we are and have ever been. He, however, is clear that he is not interested in exalting himself; his only purpose is to do the will of God who sent him, which reminds us of John's theme of Jesus' dependency upon his Father (6:38). All that the Father gives him will come to him so that nothing may be lost (6:37, 39), any more than any of the 'eucharisticised' bread was to be lost after the feeding (6:12). Because Jesus is the bread of life, to see him and believe in him is to receive eternal life, to become a fragment which he will gather up on the last day (6:40). This phrase means nothing more, and nothing less, than that.

Prayer

Lord Jesus, thank you that you reject none who come to you; feed me now and raise me up on the last day.

33 John 6:41–51

Bread from heaven

Jesus and the crowd have been debating the meaning of the feeding and the last section concentrated on the issue of Jesus' identity. Suddenly it is no longer a matter of whether he is 'the prophet like Moses' who can feed people in the mountains as Moses did. His claim to be 'the bread come down from heaven' has taken the debate to a much higher level where Jesus is portrayed as superior to the whole of Jewish faith and practice; acceptance of this and faith in him are necessary for eternal life.

It is no wonder that such a claim leads to 'murmuring' or 'grumbling' introducing the wonderfully sounding word, *gongusm-*, which will feature regularly over the next chapters (6:41, 43, 61; 7:12, 32). Until now Jesus' hearers have been simply called 'the crowd'; but now they are identified as 'the Jews'. We have noted before that, although Jesus and his disciples are all Jews, this term is used here to denote Jesus' opponents. The murmuring of the crowd has now brought them into conflict with Jesus. Their dissent has been growing through the chapter, from their desire to make Jesus their kind of king, through chasing him around the lake, to asking for a sign (6:15, 24–25, 30). Grumbling is also what the Israelites did in the wilderness; in fact, it was as a result of their complaining that God sent them the manna (Exodus 16:2–15). Thus we have another link between Jesus' feeding of the crowd and the experiences of Moses and the Israelites in the wilderness.

Who is Jesus' Father?

The complaint centres around how Jesus can make such grand claims for himself in the light of his origins. Once again John gives us one of his typical contrasts between two levels, the earthly and the heavenly. The crowd know Jesus' earthly origins – he is the son of Joseph. And they know not only his father, but his mother also. Who does he think he is to start making claims about coming down from heaven (6:42)? As at the start of this dialogue (see 6:25–26), Jesus chooses not to answer the question asked, but goes to the heart of the matter. He warns them not to grumble and complain (6:43). If he has only an earthly origin, then no one will pay him any attention, in the way that we are cautious about claims to divine revelations from people who are mentally ill. No one will come to him unless 'drawn' by his real Father, the one who sent him (6:44). The prophets knew all about the attractive power of God's love. Hosea says that God has 'drawn' us with cords of love (Hosea 11:4), while the Greek version of Jeremiah 31:3, 'I have drawn you with an everlasting love', uses the same word for 'drawn' as here in John. These prophets looked forward to a time when everyone would learn about God and this, says Jesus, is what is happening now (6:45). His claim is not blasphemy or self-seeking megalomania; the initiative always remains God's, whom no one has ever seen. Even Moses could not see God and live, but had to be hidden in a cleft of rock as he passed by (Exodus 33:18–23). But if Jesus is the bread come down from heaven, then he has seen the Father (6:46).

Death or life

This is no debate merely about different interpretations of the story of the Exodus. Just as the claim that Jesus is 'the bread come down from heaven' is staggering, so the consequences of acceptance or rejection of him are vital. Thus it is restated with the solemn introduction, 'Truly, truly I tell you' (6:47). To call Jesus the bread of life means that belief in him brings life, the eternal life of the age to come (6:47–48). Because the Israelites in the wilderness grumbled, God fed them with manna; but their grumbling also led to their death, as they wandered around for years and none came into the promised land (6:49; see Numbers 14:26–35).

Thus we reach the final contrast in this section. All the comparing of Moses with Jesus, of manna in the wilderness with the feeding of the crowd, of earthly and heavenly origins, of complaining or believing – all come down eventually to the simple choice of death or life (6:50). As he offered 'living water' to the Samaritan woman, now Jesus offers the crowd 'living bread'; whoever eats this bread will live forever, for this bread is none other than his own flesh, his body given in sacrifice for us. Because he feeds us with living bread, we need not die; because he died for us, we can live forever with him (6:51).

Prayer

Lord Jesus, draw me with the cords of your Father's love, and give me the living bread from heaven, that I may eat of it and not die.

34 John 6:51–58

Eat my flesh and drink my blood

The debate between Jesus and the crowd since the miraculous feeding and walking on water has been exploring the text, 'He gave them bread from heaven to eat' (6:31). Like a rabbi preaching on the text, Jesus has taken each word or phrase in turn. First he stressed that it was God who 'gave' and still gives the bread (6:32–37) and then that the 'bread from heaven' is nothing other than himself (6:38–51). This only leaves the last part of the text, 'to eat', as the subject of this final section. It was introduced at the end of 6:51, where the bread was identified as 'my flesh'. Having begun with the overtones of the Eucharist in the feeding through Jesus 'giving thanks' (6:11, 23), now we come back to Communion themes again.

This explains why there has been little mention of such sacramental allusions in the earlier section, which focused on Jesus, using the material about wisdom in the Old Testament and later Jewish writings. Because of this, some scholars think the two sections are separate, with 6:35–50 describing Jesus as the word and wisdom of God in an almost anti-sacramental way, and then 6:51–58 put in later to make everything more sacramental. Once we realise that the dialogue is working its way through this text, we would expect the central section to concentrate on Jesus coming 'from heaven' like God's word and wisdom, while 'to eat' would bring in more sacramental material at the end. Furthermore, the last section picks up the themes of the rest of the chapter beautifully and helps to round it all off.

The bread is my flesh

The middle section concludes with 'The bread that I will give for the life of the world is my flesh' (6:51). Two things immediately remind us of the words of Jesus at the institution of Holy Communion. First, the Greek word for 'flesh' is a literal translation of the Hebrew word *basar* which is used with bread in Exodus 16:8, 12 and at the Passover *seder* meal. To say 'This (bread) is my flesh' is the same as 'This is my body.' Second, it is 'for the life of the world'; the word 'for' or 'on behalf of', *hyper*, also comes in the eucharistic words 'This is my body, which is given *for* you' (see Luke 22:19; 1 Corinthians 11:24). No wonder this direct statement produces a strong reaction from Jesus' hearers. Once again they are called 'the Jews' and now they 'dispute among themselves' – the Greek word is actually 'fought' (6:52! This was, and still is, a frequent reaction about Holy Communion – how can Jesus give us his flesh to eat? Quite apart from the general abhorrence of cannibalism, Jewish food laws specifically forbade eating flesh with the blood still in it, because the blood was considered to contain the animal's life (see Leviticus 3:17; Deuteronomy 12:23).

Yet the discourse continues with exactly this point, that if we want to have Jesus' life in us and be raised on the last day, we must eat his flesh and drink his blood (6:53–54). This picks up Wisdom's metaphorical invitation to eat and drink from the earlier section (Proverbs 9:5, see on 6:35) and goes beyond it. The words are very vivid: 'flesh and blood' are given up in a sacrifice and the word for 'eat', *trogo*, literally means to chew or munch – stressing that Jesus' flesh and blood are 'really', 'truly' food and drink (6:55). This is strong stuff! Some early Christians could not accept that Jesus really came in the flesh, in human form (see 1 John 4:2), while others saw Jesus as the word and wisdom of God in a non-sacramental way. Against both of these positions, this passage stresses that God sent Jesus to us in the flesh, and that he gives himself to us in his body and blood at the Eucharist.

Live in me

It is through eating his flesh and drinking his blood that we abide in Jesus and he in us – in other words, Holy Communion is a way to union with him (6:56). After Jesus' words earlier about coming to him and not being rejected (6:37), now we see that we come to him and he feeds us so that we may live and abide in him. God the Father who sent Jesus is the source of all life, and even Jesus himself only lives because of the Father; thus any who receive his flesh and blood take the life of God into themselves (6:57). And so this whole discourse after the feeding of the multitude climaxes with one final contrast. The manna in the wilderness could not prevent the Israelites from dying ultimately; even those who are devoted to the law and who eat of wisdom will hunger and thirst again. But those who eat the true bread from heaven, the bread of life in Jesus, will live forever (6:58).

Prayer

Bread of heaven, feed me now and ever more.
William Williams (1717–91)

35 John 6:59–71

The parting of the ways

This chapter's setting has moved from up in the mountains for the feeding, across the storm-tossed lake to a crowd in Capernaum. The last part of this discourse at least has been Jesus' teaching in the synagogue at Capernaum (6:59). The impressive remains of the synagogue still visible there today date from a bit later than the time of Jesus, but there was an earlier building for study of the scriptures. This background of synagogue teaching explains why the debate has taken each part of the chosen text in turn for discussion, in the light of its context of Moses and the exodus. We saw in 6:52 that 'the Jews disputed among themselves' and the subject of this chapter was hotly debated in synagogues across the Mediterranean during the second half of the first century, between Jews who accepted Jesus as Messiah and other Jews who did not. Central to the debate were the kind of claims made here about whether Jesus really had been sent by God from heaven, and whether he replaced the Jewish feasts, customs and laws. The 'parting of the ways' between the synagogue and the early church was happening gradually over these years (see Introduction, p. 15; also on 9:22; 16:2 below). However, Jesus' teaching and miracles led to argument and conflict even in his own day.

The hard saying

Thus it is not surprising that 'many of his disciples' said that this teaching was 'a hard saying' (6:60). These disciples are a larger group than the twelve, who are mentioned separately later (6:67). They may have witnessed Jesus' healings and miraculous signs, like the feeding, or heard him teach and joined in the debates. After all the dialogue and discourse in this chapter, the teaching is not difficult to understand, for it has been rigorously clarified section by section. On the contrary, its stark clarity makes it all the harder to believe and accept. As Mark Twain is reputed to have said, 'It is not the parts of the gospel which I do not understand which cause me difficulty – it's the demand of that which I do understand.'

Jesus is aware that the grumbling and murmuring is taking place even among disciples who follow him and asks them why they are 'scandalised' or offended (6:61). If they find difficult all this talk about him having descended from heaven to bring us life (6:38, 41, 51), what will happen when he goes back (6:62)? The word 'ascend' here has John's typical levels of meaning. At the simple level it refers to Jesus 'going up' to Jerusalem, where he will be 'lifted up'; but that lifting up on a cross will also be how he is exalted and ascends back to his Father. This will force a final decision on his grumbling disciples; for some, it may demonstrate that his claims are true, while for others it will be the final straw. Again he contrasts the natural life of the flesh with the supernatural life of the Spirit (6:63; see on 3:6 above). Jesus can give his flesh for people and speak the words of life, but unless they are drawn by the Father to believe, it is of no avail. Once more, John stresses Jesus' knowledge of all things and all people, including those who would not believe and even his betrayer (6:64–65).

Will you also go away?

The result is a parting of the ways even within Jesus' followers as 'many of his disciples turned back and no longer went around with him' (6:66). In a wistful verse, Jesus tests the resolve of the twelve, asking them if they (the 'you' is plural) also wish to leave him (6:67). Peter answers with a rhetorical question: there is nowhere else to go – this whole chapter has demonstrated that Jesus is superior to everything else with the 'words of eternal life' (6:68, see 6:63). Then Peter speaks for them all with his confession of faith that Jesus is the 'Holy One of God' (6:69). This is another way of declaring that Jesus is the Messiah and may be compared with the story of Peter's confession in the other gospels (Matthew 16:16; Mark 8:29; Luke 9:20). Whether this is a version of that story or a separate occasion, it makes a good conclusion to the debate among the Jews and the disciples about the significance of the feeding and Jesus' claims. It ends with another reminder of Jesus' knowledge in calling all of them, including Judas Iscariot, who will 'hand him over' (6:70–71). Among the crowds who seek Jesus, there will always be those who want to make him king on their own terms, those who murmur and complain, those who question or oppose him, followers who turn back or betray him, and those who realise that he is their only hope of life and receive his body and blood.

For reflection and prayer

Where do we stand in the crowd who seek Jesus?

Lord, where else can we go? You have the words of eternal life.

36 John 7:1–10

Times and places

This chapter begins with Jesus 'walking about' in Galilee (7:1). The verb, *periepatei*, describes the 'peripatetic' life Jesus lived as a wandering teacher and preacher. In John, Jesus moves between Galilee and Jerusalem frequently, especially in the sequence of chapters which we are following, rather than swapping chapters 5 and 6 around to bring the Jerusalem episodes together. In John's sequence, Jesus' times and places go like this. His first year of ministry begins with gathering disciples in Galilee and his first sign at Cana (1:35—2:12); at Passover time in the spring, he goes to Jerusalem for the temple incident and the conversation with Nicodemus (2:13—3:36). He then leaves Judea and travels through Samaria back to Galilee for his second sign at Cana (4:1–54). At the end of this year, or early in the second, Jesus goes up to Jerusalem for an unnamed feast where he heals the lame man on the Sabbath (5:1–47). Because of this, 'the Jews' wanted to kill Jesus (5:18), which is why he is now back home in Galilee (7:1). The second year was marked by the springtime feeding of the crowd at Passover and the subsequent dialogue (6:1–71). Now it is autumn and the Feast of Tabernacles is coming, so Jesus' brothers assume he will be going up to Jerusalem again (7:2–3).

There is no opening sign here, like the water into wine, the healing or feeding, to get things underway – just the reference to the Feast of 'Succoth'. This is celebrated at the harvest in September or early October. In a week-long celebration, people lived in temporary dwellings, called huts, tents, booths or tabernacles, as a reminder of their wanderings in the wilderness and coming into the promised land to settle down and harvest crops (Leviticus 23:33–43). John may be suggesting that the 'peripatetic' wanderings of Jesus are also coming to an end; it is time for him to go to the heart of the promised land, to Jerusalem, to settle there until the final harvest of his ministry at the crucifixion. This is confirmed perhaps by the way the central drama of this festival uses water and light, two of John's key themes which will dominate the next chapters (see 7:37–39 and 8:12).

Telling Jesus what to do

The water into wine, the healing of the official's son, the feeding and the walking on water have all been done in Galilee, with only the healing of the lame man described in Jerusalem, which led to the death threats (7:1). Now Jesus' brothers encourage him to go to Judea so that his followers can see his signs and he can have more success (7:3–4). John mentions Jesus' brothers, while Mark even names them (Mark 6:3). Because of the later tradition of Mary's perpetual virginity, some commentators suggest that these are half-brothers or cousins. Whichever interpretation is adopted, clearly Jesus' family did not believe in him and are challenging him to make a public demonstration of his power (7:4–5).

When Mary encouraged him to use his power to help the wedding couple, she was told, 'My hour has not yet come' (2:4). Similarly, Jesus tells his brothers now that his *kairos*, which means a special time, has not yet come (7:6, 8). He knows that this moment will come, because it is not only 'the Jews' who seek to kill him, but the world itself which hates him (7:7). We have noted how Jesus is somewhat elusive in this gospel, playing games of hide and seek. He is not yet ready for an open demonstration to provoke the final crisis, and so he avoids the caravans of pilgrims, remaining for a while in Galilee (7:9).

And yet the odd thing is that he does eventually go up by himself, not in public with the others (7:10). For this will be his final journey to Jerusalem, from which he will not return. After Tabernacles, he will stay through the winter for the Feast of the Dedication (10:22–23), and on to the spring for the third Passover (11:55; 13:1) at which he will die. The paradox is that what the brothers asked for will happen: Jesus does go up to Jerusalem and, when the time is right, he will reveal himself. But the times and the places, the festivals and the results will be different, beyond their imagining. In John, Jesus is always serenely in control; others may think they are, or make suggestions to him – but he knows the right time and place for what he has come to do. This should be a warning when we seek to tell God the best thing to do, or the right time and place for everyone to see his power.

Prayer

Lord, help me to trust that times and places are in your hands.

37 John 7:11–18

Teaching in Jerusalem

Jesus' brothers were not the only ones who were expecting him to make a public showing at the festival. 'The Jews' were looking for him and speculating about him, which picks up the theme of seeking which we saw in the previous two chapters (7:11; see 5:13–14; 6:24–25). Also the 'muttering' or 'complaining', *gongusmos*, about him in the crowd here in Jerusalem reminds us of the reaction of those in Galilee in the previous dialogue with all the echoes of the Israelites grumbling in the wilderness (6:41). As there was in Galilee, so here again there is division about Jesus: some think he is a good man, but others believe that he is deceiving them, leading people astray (7:12). This is a serious charge. According to the law, anyone who leads others astray, away from the worship of God, must be killed (Deuteronomy 13:1–11). In fact, during the debate between Jews and Christians in the next couple of centuries, this became a common Jewish allegation. The writings of the Talmud state that Jesus had 'led Israel astray' and this is why he was crucified (*On the Sanhedrin*, 43a).

This explains the odd comment that people would not discuss Jesus openly 'for fear of the Jews' (7:13). Once again, we must remember that both Jesus himself and all those discussing him are all Jews. Here again, then, the phrase 'the Jews' of whom people are afraid must mean the authorities. This is the first mention that others are afraid of them, but this will become more prominent as the gospel progresses.

Learning and authority

During the middle of the festival, Jesus decides to come out of his self-imposed privacy and goes into the temple to teach (7:14). After his previous reluctance, we might ask why he chooses this moment. It may be that, as we will see below, the festival's ceremonies of water and light gave him a good starting point (see 7:37–38). Whatever the reason, John reminds us again that Jesus is in control and he chooses when and where he wants to appear.

The courts of the temple were large and offered many shady porticoes where rabbis might teach any who chose to sit at their feet to listen. Clearly, people did stop to hear Jesus. The reaction of 'the Jews' is astonishment. They have questions about what and how he is teaching. The usual pattern was for a young man to attach himself to a rabbi to learn the law and the traditions for several years as a disciple or pupil. He might even attend a rabbinic school to further his education. When eventually he came to teach himself, he would cite other teachers as his authorities, those who had taught him, or quoting precedent from other rabbis: 'Rabbi X said this, but Rabbi Y said that' and so on. In the same way, although I have studied and taught John's gospel for many years, even now I am writing surrounded by some of the great commentaries which I consult constantly to see what these authorities have said before me. I do not write at my own whim. But not Jesus; he had never been a pupil, never 'learned his letters' and did not quote the authority of his respected predecessors (7:15).

Jesus' response to the crowd is typical: because his teaching is not his own, his authority is that of the one 'who sent me' (7:16). In both his previous debates after healing the lame man on the sabbath and feeding the crowd, Jesus had stressed his utter dependence on God who sent him (see 5:30; 6:29). He is not interested in quoting others; to some this may seem like teaching his own ideas, but those who want to do the will of God will recognise the truth of what he is saying (7:17). He picks up both previous debates by this stress on doing the will of God (see 6:38) and seeking not other people's respect for his teaching, but only the glory of his Father (7:18; cf. 5:41–44). The way this chapter builds on the last two is another good reason for following the traditional sequence, for it shows how attention is increasingly focused on Jesus himself. The mixture of reactions to him directs our attention to the central question of his identity: who is this man who does not need others' authority? Where has he come from and what is his purpose?

Prayer

Lord Jesus, I would sit at your feet; teach me the will of the one who sent you.

38 John 7:19–31

Jesus' authority and identity

Having answered the question about why he does not quote other authorities for his teaching, Jesus goes on the offensive by directing his hearers' attention back to the ultimate authority – Moses himself (7:19). We saw in chapter 5 how Jesus was accused of lawbreaking by healing on the sabbath, but was content to have Moses as the judge in his case (see 5:30–47). Now he accuses his opponents of not keeping the law themselves by wanting to break the fifth commandment, 'Thou shalt not kill' (Exodus 20:13). This refers back to the opponents wanting to kill him after he had healed the lame man (5:18). The crowd, watching the debate between Jesus and the authorities, interject that he is mad to think that people want to kill him (7:20). So Jesus reminds them of his 'one work', the healing on the Sabbath which so amazed them (7:21).

Next, this 'uneducated' teacher shows that he is quite capable of proper theological debate by using an argument 'from the lesser to the greater', used by the rabbis. He notes that they are perfectly happy to perform one work on the sabbath, namely to circumcise a baby boy. The rabbinic authorities are all clear that the command to circumcise infants eight days after they are born takes priority over the sabbath command, particularly as this is to enable the child to fulfil the law. Circumcision only affects one of the 248 members of a man's body according to Jewish reckoning; therefore, says Jesus, making his 'whole body' well, in all its members, must be even more permissible (7:23).

Then Jesus sums up his argument: healing on a sabbath might have had the appearance of work, but when it is assessed with a proper judgement, it can be seen as fulfilling the law (7:24). The problem is that this summary opens up further debate, for the one who will judge not by appearances, by 'what his eyes see, or his ears hear' but who will give a right judgement 'for the poor and for the meek of the earth' is none other than the Christ, the shoot from Jesse (Isaiah 11:3).

Can this be the Christ?

Thus Jesus' comment about the ability to judge aright makes the lame man's healing, like the miraculous feeding, into a messianic claim. So the people of Jerusalem begin to speculate even more about Jesus' identity. After all, here he is, teaching openly in the temple, and the authorities seem to do nothing (7:25-26). The way the Jewish crowd refer to those who oppose Jesus as 'the authorities' confirms our interpretation of the phrase 'the Jews', when used of his opponents, as indicating such leaders.

Furthermore, Jesus' identity and origins were well known: in a culture without surnames, places of origin, like fathers' names, were important as a way of identifying people – hence 'Jesus of Nazareth'. There was a Jewish tradition that the origins of the Messiah would be unknown, and he himself unrecognised until the moment of his revelation. This may have been based on Malachi's prophecy that the Lord would come to his temple 'suddenly' (Malachi 3:1). So Jesus *of Nazareth* cannot be the Christ (7:27). Like Nathanael (1:46), the Jerusalemites would never think that God might come into our world in such an ordinary way; are we any different?

Jesus' reply, which is best translated as a statement rather than a question, accepts the point that they do know about him – at the earthly level at least (7:28). But as always, there is a deeper level beyond earthly things. John has made it clear time after time since the heights of the Prologue that Jesus' true origins are to be found in the God who sent him (7:28). This has been the constant theme throughout the dialogues of the last two chapters, and now it is summarised in stark simplicity: 'I know him, because I am from him, and he sent me' (7:29). By now the pattern is clear: such a claim is followed by another attempt to arrest him which is not successful because 'his hour had not yet come' (7:30). While this may be the moment, *kairos*, for him to make such a public claim as his brothers wanted (see 7:6), the final hour, *hora*, of both glory and passion still lies several months in the future (see 2:4 and 13:1). For the present, we have a division among the people again; while the authorities plot and scheme, 'many in the crowd' do believe and accept him as Christ because of the signs he is doing (7:31, cf. 2:23).

Prayer

Jesus of Nazareth, grant me a right judgement that I may know your true origins and believe that you are the Christ.

39 John 7:32–39
Come to me and drink

Jesus chose his moment to start teaching in the middle of the Feast of Tabernacles. He provoked mixed reactions, with some seeking to arrest him while others believe (7:30–31). John describes the debate within the crowd as 'complaining' or 'muttering', using *gongus-* again (7:32, see 7:12; 6:41). Jesus' opponents are identified as the Pharisees, who were centred around the law and the synagogue, and the chief priests, who were responsible for the ritual sacrifices and the temple; the two groups were not natural allies. However, right from their early questioning of John the Baptist (1:19, 24), they have been united in their opposition to this Christ-movement; now they send the temple police to arrest Jesus. Down through the church's history, and even in our own day, it is as remarkable as it is lamentable how often opponents from different ends of the ecclesiastical spectrum seem to unite only in their desire to stop something new happening – and how often that new thing turns out to be of God!

Seeking and finding

John stresses Jesus' control of times and places. Now he says that he will only be there 'a little while' before returning to the one who sent him (7:33). In fact, the 'little while' will be about six months from this autumn's Tabernacles to next spring's Passover when he will return to his heavenly Father through the crucifixion and resurrection. Over this time, Jesus repeats this phrase to warn both the crowds and the disciples that time is getting ever shorter (8:21; 12:35; and throughout chs. 13—16). Now is the time to search for him, not to arrest him, but to find out what he has to say and to offer; the time will come soon enough when they will not be able to follow where he goes (7:34). This enigmatic comment is greeted with typical misunderstanding. Just as they think they know Jesus' origins, but actually know only the human level (7:27–29), so now they speculate that his destination is among the Jews dispersed in the Greco-Roman world and do not understand why they cannot follow him there (7:35–36). The deeper level is that he has come from his Father and soon will return there. Ironically, by the time the gospel is written, Jesus' followers will have spread far and wide among the Greeks, while the temple and the priests will have been destroyed. How easy it is to miss God's 'little while'; we must seek him 'while he may be found' (Isaiah 55:6).

Rivers of living water

Having chosen his moment to go to the festival, and to teach in its middle, now Jesus picks the last day, when people were packing up their booths, to make his proclamation. Water, so important in this gospel, was central to the festival. The harvest celebrations included prayers for rain; the rainy season began soon afterwards and it was believed that if rain fell during the festival it would continue abundantly. Every day water was taken from the Pool of Siloam in a golden flagon in solemn procession through the Water Gate into the temple, as the people sang, 'With joy you will draw water from the wells of salvation' (Isaiah 12:3) and chanted Psalms 113—118. In the temple, the water was then poured around the altar. Now Jesus no longer sits down to teach; he stands up to issue his ringing invitation for the thirsty not to go to the ceremony, but to come to him (7:37).

Some Bibles punctuate 7:38 differently, but the invitation to come to Jesus and drink is clear. However, the scripture quotation could mean that rivers of living water will flow from the heart of Jesus or from the believer's heart. The quotation's source is unclear. Psalm 78:24 was behind the text about 'bread from heaven' debated in 6:31–59; the same psalm describes how God 'made streams come out of the rock, and caused waters to flow down like rivers' (Psalm 78:16). The waters will flow out of his heart or belly, *koilia*; Jerusalem was thought to be the *koilia*, the centre of the world, from which living water would flow (Zechariah 14:8). Nicodemus used the same word when he misunderstood being 'born again' to mean climbing again into his mother's *koilia*; then Jesus told him to be born of water and the Spirit (3:4–5). Now this living water is identified with the Spirit, to be poured out after Jesus is glorified through his Passion (7:39).

As Jesus was superior to the healing water and the sabbath in chapter 5 and to the bread and the Passover in chapter 6, so now he transcends the temporary booths and the water ceremony of Tabernacles with his offer of the living water of the Spirit.

Prayer

Lord Jesus, let your living waters flow from my heart to a thirsty world.

40 John 7:40–52

No one ever spoke like this man

Jesus' claims to transcend the sabbath and feasts like Passover and Tabernacles and to replace their perishable bread and water with his living bread and water have provoked speculation among his hearers. Throughout this chapter, some people have believed him (7:31), while others have been dismissive (7:27); the authorities, however, have tried to arrest him (7:32). All these reactions are now repeated, following his climactic invitation to come to the living waters at the end of the festival.

Prophet or Christ?

Some who heard him concluded 'This is really the prophet' (7:40). When the Pharisees and the priests questioned John the Baptist at the start, he denied being 'the prophet' (1:21, 25). Both the woman of Samaria and the 5,000 recognised Jesus as the prophet (4:19; 6:14). Since the prophet was expected to be like Moses (Deuteronomy 18:15), it is not surprising that Jesus' offer to give bread and water, as Moses did in the wilderness, should be so acclaimed.

Others go still further and decide 'This is the Christ' (7:41). This stimulates the third debate about where Jesus is from: there has already been discussion about his parentage (6:42) and his origins, contrasting them with the supposedly unknown origins of the Christ (7:27). Now Jesus' background in Galilee is debated (7:41–42). Micah 5:2 (quoted in Matthew 2:6) suggests that the Messiah would come from Bethlehem. However, for John both places are still only on the earthly level; throughout his gospel, he stresses Jesus' real origins with his heavenly Father who sent him.

This debate produced yet another division in the crowd about Jesus. This has been happening through all the recent dialogues (6:52; 7:12, 30–31). This time John uses the Greek word *schisma* (7:43). The 'schism' between the early church and the synagogue centred around exactly the same questions as here: whether Jesus was an ignorant law-breaker or an authoritative teacher from God; the contrast between his humble origins and the messianic claims being made for him; whether he replaced or fulfilled Jewish faith and worship or had been rightly executed for 'leading the people astray'. Once again, this division leads to another futile attempt to arrest him (7:44).

Acceptance or rejection?

The arresting party now return empty-handed to the chief priests and the Pharisees and their report shows again the division of reactions to Jesus. The temple police, like the crowd, are amazed by Jesus' different way of teaching; they stress that no human being, *anthropos*, has ever spoken the way this person does (7:46; cf. 7:15). The Pharisees, however, are so convinced of their view that they miss the hint that Jesus might be more than human and simply dismiss the police report; anybody who differs from them must have been 'led astray' (7:47; cf. 7:12). After all, they assert with supreme self-confidence, none of the authorities nor the Pharisees have believed Jesus (7:48). It is only the rabble – the crowd, who know nothing of the law (7:49). The disdain of the religious leaders for the ordinary 'people of the land' is well documented at that time, and often enough since in our own history, regrettably. Since those who do not uphold the law are accursed (Deuteronomy 27:26), the truly religious would avoid them.

In fact, they do not all take this view. Nicodemus, described as one of the authorities and a Pharisee when he 'went to Jesus before', is still called 'one of them' (7:50; see 3:1). He refutes both their points by showing that some of the authorities have been to Jesus and that they do not have sole control of the law. Far from the people being ignorant of the law's demands, the Pharisees are acting against the law in judging Jesus without a fair hearing (7:51). Earlier, Jesus had suggested that his accusers did not keep the law by wishing to kill him (7:19); now one who had previously only talked to him 'by night' redirects their attention to the law's provision for a proper hearing with witnesses (see on 5:30 above). But Nicodemus' point is dismissed even more contemptuously than that of the police; the absurdity of taking Jesus' side must indicate that he is a Galilean too! Their metropolitan self-confidence that no prophet, still less a Messiah, could come from Galilee is such that they conveniently forget that Jonah came from only a few miles north of Nazareth (7:52; see 2 Kings 14:25; Jonah 1:1).

For reflection

What is our response to Jesus? Are we so convinced of our point of view that we dismiss or despise what others tell us about him?

41 John 7:53—8:11
The woman taken in adultery

This famous story is not without problems. Some Bible versions put it in a footnote, while others include it, but note that it interrupts the flow of the story. In 7:53 'they all go home', only to return in the morning with the woman (8:3); in 8:9 they all leave except the woman, who also then departs (8:11). Thus Jesus is left on stage alone, but in 8:12 he starts speaking 'to them' again and carries on with the interrupted debate at the Feast of Tabernacles. It looks as though 7:52 should run straight into 8:12. This is what we find in most early manuscripts and in the earliest gospel commentaries by the Fathers. Later manuscripts include it here, but mark it separately, while others place it after 7:36, 7:44 or at the end of John, or even after Luke 21:38, since there is some evidence of different style here, not unlike Luke's.

John 20:30 refers to other things Jesus did which were not included because of space. Perhaps God wants this one in the Bible somewhere, even if we are not sure where! Certainly, the story reflects John's account of Jesus being sent not to condemn the world but to save it. Furthermore, it fits John's motif of Jesus being on trial and yet still in control. Its position here illustrates Jesus' statement 'I judge no one' (8:15).

The trap is set

Early in the morning, Jesus is sitting down to teach in the temple in the outer Court of the Women, where 'all the people' could come to him (8:2). The Pharisees enter, with their scribes. As experts on the law, they call Jesus 'Teacher' and make a woman stand 'before all of them' (8:3). Presumably, the poor woman is rather dishevelled, having been 'caught in the very act of committing adultery' (8:4). This means that Jesus cannot give her the 'benefit of the doubt', as the law allowed for someone raped where no one could hear her shout for help (Deuteronomy 22:25–27). No, the law is clear: both she, and the man, must die (Deuteronomy 22:22–24). But where is the man? People do not normally commit adultery in public view, and to have caught her 'in the very act' suggests a trap with the man being allowed to escape, hopping around Jerusalem half-clad!

Our suspicions are confirmed when these lawyers ask for Jesus' opinion, appealing as so often to Moses and the law as judge (8:5). It is not so much the woman who is on trial here, as Jesus himself, as they seek to test and trap him (8:6). The legal and political trap is that if Jesus forbids stoning her, he is breaking the law of Moses, while if he encourages stoning, he is breaking Roman law, which reserved the death penalty to Roman courts. Then there is the religious trap: if he decides against Moses' law of stoning, Jesus would forfeit any claim to be a teacher in the temple, whereas to advocate killing would contradict all his teaching about receiving and saving people. The woman is just a pawn, being used more than any sexual act can have used her.

The trap is sprung

Jesus averts his eyes and begins to write in the sand, like a teacher with a blackboard (8:6). Many speculate about what he may have written; a list of their sins, perhaps, or a text like Exodus 23:1, prohibiting false witness. When pressed further, he suggests that the one 'without sin' should throw the first stone (8:7) – the task of the witnesses (Deuteronomy 17:6–7). But Jesus writes again in the sand, maybe continuing with Exodus 23:7, warning people not to join a false accusation. As he writes, the older ones, conscious of their own sin and their implication in this trumped-up charge perhaps, slip away, until the woman is left alone with the only one who is 'without sin', Jesus himself (8:9). Instead of throwing stones, Jesus asks where her accusers are; are none left to judge (8:10)? In reply, this woman is remembered for two brief words, 'None, Sir' (8:11). Then the one to whom the Father has given all judgement (5:22), but who was himself accused by this charade, delivers his verdict: there is neither condemnation nor commendation; she is to go, but not to 'keep on sinning'. The use of the present continuous here is a challenge to her, and to us, to lead a new life.

Like all the passages around this story, once again Jesus has been put on trial, only for his accusers to be judged and found wanting, while we who read it are forgiven and invited to respond to God's love letter written in the sand of our lives.

For reflection

Recreate the scene in your imagination – and join in. Are you one of the accusers, an onlooker or the woman? What does Jesus say to you?

42 John 8:12–20

I am the light of the world

Jesus chose his moment to go to Jerusalem and teach at the Feast of Tabernacles. During that Feast's ceremony of drawing water, he announced that he is the source of the living water. His claims have provoked arguments about his authority and identity. As the discussion continues from 7:52, another of the symbols from the festival intensifies the debate further.

As well as the water procession recalling drinking from the rock in the wilderness, Tabernacles also included a light ceremony. On the first night, four large golden lamps were lit in the Court of Women, where both men and women could gather – and where the woman taken in adultery would have been brought to Jesus. It is said that this light was so bright that every court and area around was reflected in it. Then, led by some exuberant priests, the people danced all night. Once again, this ceremony recalls the wilderness wanderings when the Israelites were led by a pillar of fire at night 'to give them light' (Exodus 13:21). Just as Jesus claimed to be the real bread and water, so now he takes over this symbol of light with his second 'I am' statement: 'I am the light of the world' (8:12). Light was another central image for the Jews. Not only did God lead them with light at night, but it could describe his very self: 'the Lord is my light' (Psalm 27:1). As with bread, light could also be a symbol for the law: 'Your word is a lamp to my feet and a light to my path' (Psalm 119:105). Light was also an image for the divine wisdom, while Israel's enemies were kept in darkness (Wisdom 7:26; 18:1–4).

Electric light means that we have too easily forgotten what darkness meant to ancient people. It never really gets dark in cities like London, because of so-called light pollution. We have to go deep into the hills or moors to find thick darkness for star gazing. The darkness of wandering in the wilderness was very real for the Jews, so Jesus invites his hearers not to walk in darkness, but to follow him in the light of life as he fulfils and surpasses another symbol, central to both Judaism and John's thought (8:12; cf. 3:19).

A witness to the light

This claim leads us into a difficult chapter as the conflict between Jesus and his opponents becomes more intense, with abuse on both sides. It is a chapter which has been much misused, especially in the Nazi persecution of Jews. But John is not 'anti-Jewish', since he himself, Jesus, and all those involved are Jews. For him, it is the battle of light against darkness, with those who think they are in the light gradually going into darkness after the healing of the blind man (see on 9:39–41).

Thus we find ourselves in debate about familiar themes again. Jesus' opponents, identified as Pharisees as in the previous chapter, reject his statement about himself as the light on the grounds of self-witness (8:13). This reminds us of the previous discussion about the need for two other witnesses (see on 5:31 above). But, as the incident with the woman taken in adultery showed, witnesses can be fixed. So this time, Jesus is not afraid to admit his own self-witness, because he knows it is true and valid, arising out of his own knowledge of his true origins and his eventual destination (8:14). Although his opponents think that they know about him over the last chapters, in fact they only 'judge by human standards' (8:15), by the appearances he warned them against in 7:24. When asked about the adulterous woman, Jesus refused to judge, even though his judgement is true and supported by the Father (8:16). The law's requirement for two witnesses is met by the testimony of Jesus and of his father (8:17–18). Significantly, for the first time here we have the phrase 'your law' as the polarity between Jesus and the Jewish authorities deepens.

Since Jesus has appealed to his father as a witness, his hearers want to know where he can be found to cross examine him. This is another typical 'misunderstanding'. They are thinking at the earthly level, by 'human standards'; if they realised the truth about Jesus, they would know his father also (8:19). This introduces another topic into the debate for the rest of this chapter: who is Jesus' father, and who is the father of the Jews?

But first we are reminded that Jesus is teaching by the temple treasury, in the Court of the Women, where the great lamps are burning. The true light of the world teaches in the light, and none can arrest him, for his hour has still not come (8:20).

Prayer

Light of the world, grant that I may not walk in darkness, but rather know you and your Father in the light of life.

43 John 8:21–30

Who are you?

Jesus' claim to be the light of life has sparked another round of debate about his identity, his origins and parentage. Now we move to his final purpose and destination. It is the end of the festival and people are packing up to go home; so too Jesus announces that he is 'going away' (8:21). He had already warned his hearers that the time would come when they would not be able to find him since they do not know where he is going (7:33–36; 8:14). This theme of seeking is repeated now with a stronger warning that time is running out. To refuse the light is to stay in darkness; since Jesus offers water which is 'living' and the 'light of life', to not accept life leads to dying in sin and not being able to follow him.

As before, the conversation proceeds on several levels. We know that Jesus means that he is going back to the Father. Last time, his hearers mockingly suggested that he might be going to the Greeks, with the irony that the gospel would indeed spread there (7:35). Now they pick up the hint about death and wonder if Jesus is going to kill himself to stop them following him (8:22). Of course, as readers, we know that Jesus will die. This time the irony is that it is not Jesus, as a suicide, who will go below, under the earth. Quite the reverse: it is his accusers who are the ones 'from below'; throughout all these dialogues, Jesus' origins 'from above' have been stressed consistently (8:23; cf. 3:31; 6:38). He is not 'of this world', but has been sent by his Father into this world. The repeated 'I am' from above and 'I am' not of this world prepares the way for the stronger use of this phrase without any description: his hearers will remain in darkness and death 'unless you believe that I am' (8:24). With John's usual levels of meaning, we, as readers, notice the divine claim which is being implied, but it is not yet obvious to Jesus' hearers.

The Father who sent me

Thus, they ask for the description – 'I am who?', 'I am what?' – and so we are back to the fundamental question of Jesus' identity: 'Who are you?' (8:25). Jesus' reply is difficult to translate. Some versions, such as the RSV, NIV and AV, interpret it as an answer to the question – 'I am... what I have been saying from the beginning.' Others, like the NEB and NRSV, see it as an exasperated question: 'Why do I bother?' Whichever we read,

Jesus' frustration with their failure to understand is clearly growing. He has more to say, which will result in judgement as he seeks to declare to the world the words of the one who sent him, who is true (8:26). But even this repeated stress on Jesus' dependency on his Father is again misunderstood, as the evangelist makes clear to the reader (8:27).

Final realisation will have to wait until Jesus has been 'lifted up' (8:28). The earlier use of this phrase compared Moses, lifting up the bronze serpent in the wilderness to bring life to the dying Israelites, with Jesus being 'lifted up' (3:14). Even this has a double meaning, referring both to Jesus' exaltation and to the way he will be exalted, through his death on the cross (12:32–34). His hearers' earlier guess was partly right; they will not be able to follow him, for he will die, but it will not be a suicide. These opponents will bring it about when they lift him up on the cross. This will be the moment when people will 'realise that I am' – and again the 'I am' phrase stands alone (8:28). Yet Jesus stresses that this is no claim to divinity in himself. He can do nothing on his own; he is totally dependent on his Father for all he does and says. His relationship with the one who sent him is such that God is always with Jesus and Jesus always does what is pleasing to his Father (8:29). A closer relationship than this is hard to imagine.

So the question 'Who are you?', with all the issues about Jesus' identity, origins and purpose, is answered with several claims of 'I am', together with an emphasis that his identity and purpose are only to be found in his dependency upon his Father who sent him. This is a clear response and so 'many believed in him' (8:30). This debate will soon become more polarised. As John has frequently pointed out, Jesus is causing a division among his hearers, with some believing and others opposing him.

Prayer

Lord Jesus, help me to realise who you really are, that I may live in the light of your relationship with your Father.

44 John 8:31–38
The truth will make you free

The debate at the end of the Feast of Tabernacles continues between Jesus and 'the Jews'. As often, his hearers are divided. Many of them have come to believe in him, and he now addresses those believers (8:30–31). As the dialogue continues, it becomes clear that not all his hearers are believers; some question him and become more opposed as the chapter progresses. Some commentators try to explain this apparent change by distinguishing between those 'who believed *in* him' in 8:30 and those who simply 'believed him' in 8:31 but then lapse into opposition later. The distinction in the Greek is hard to maintain, and most translations do not note it. The situation is better explained by a mixed crowd of believers and opponents – and probably a good number of observers waiting to see how things turn out! John has noted such a divided context frequently in previous dialogues. Jesus' words, then and now, elicit a reaction in people, which can be either faith or rejection.

This point is amplified by the comment that it is those who 'continue in my word' who are truly his disciples (8:31). This means to remain or abide, *menein*, and the same word is used for abiding in Jesus the true vine (15:4–10). Discipleship is not a single event, an instant reaction to someone speaking; it is a life of constant listening and learning. Such a life will enable us to know the truth and 'the truth will make you free' (8:32). This would have been recognised both by Jews, who believed that the truth seen in the law made people free, and by Greeks, who were liberated by truth discovered through reason and philosophical debate.

Descendants of Abraham

Thus, Jesus' hearers do not see why they need to be set free. Indeed, they take great pride in being 'descendants of Abraham' (8:33). After all the appeals to Moses in recent chapters, this shift back to the father of Judaism is significant. It was through God's promise of descendants to Abraham that their nation came into being (Genesis 22:17–8) and they used his name to define themselves (Psalm 105:6). But the proud boast of freedom is somewhat hollow. Years after Abraham, they were slaves in Egypt and needed the light of the pillar of fire to guide them to freedom across the wilderness. Centuries of independence may have followed, but this ended in the captivity in Babylon. More recently, they had been absorbed into various near eastern empires, of which Roman rule was only the latest.

Slaves, sons and fathers

But Jesus has a different slavery in mind, the bondage to sin (8:34). He illustrates this with an image which is like a parable, the difference between a slave and a son where only the son 'abides' in the father's house (8:35). It is the same word as 'continuing in my word' (8:31). After the mention of Abraham, this image would remind his hearers of the contrast between Ishmael, the son of Hagar the slave-woman, and Isaac the legitimate son (Genesis 17:20–21). Only the freeborn son could stay in father Abraham's house forever (Genesis 21:9–21). Thus, says Jesus, 'If the son makes you free, you will be free indeed' (8:36). The move from 'the son' in the story to 'the son' who sets us free is one of John's typical shifts of level. The Greek words are the same, with no different punctuation or capital 'S' as in our translations. But the meaning has changed to a deeper level, as 'the Son' – one of John's favourite ways of referring to Jesus – claims to 'make you free' in a way superior to both Jewish law and Greek reason.

Jesus initially accepts his hearers' claim to be 'descendants of Abraham' (8:37). However, a son should reflect his father's character, but these 'descendants of Abraham' seek to kill him. Instead of 'continuing in my word', his word finds no place in them. Relying on the past is never enough. No matter how illustrious our spiritual parentage or how wonderful the time when we first 'believed in Jesus', it is the reality of our present action which reveals whose children we are. Jesus speaks what he has seen with 'the father', and his opponents do what they have heard from 'the father' (8:38). It is the same phrase in Greek, with no capital 'F' or possessive pronoun 'my' or 'your' to indicate that they have different fathers. But the separation of the two is revealed by their different characters and activity, saving life or seeking to kill, just like two children growing up in the same family but revealing different paternity by their contrasting appearances.

Prayer

Lord Jesus, set me free by your truth that I may live in your house forever and reflect our Father's glory.

45 John 8:39–47

Who is your father?

The debate between Jesus and his opponents has moved beyond Moses to the father of Judaism, Abraham. A son remains in his father's house forever and his paternity is revealed in his actions. Thus the opponents' desire to kill Jesus conflicts with their claim to be descended from Abraham. After all, Jesus only says and does what he has learned from his Father – so where have his opponents learned what they say and do? The debate shifts away from Jesus' origins to those of his hearers: who is their father as revealed by their actions?

Abraham

Jesus' hearers are confused by his comments about doing what they heard from the father (8:38); so they assert once again, 'Abraham is our father'. Jesus says that, if so, they would do 'what Abraham did' (8:39). In fact, they want to kill him even though he brings a true message which he 'heard from God' (8:40). This is not behaviour to be expected from Abraham. In the famous story at the beginning of the Jewish faith and nation, God visited Abraham with three messengers. Abraham fed and received them so well that God promised him a son and debated his intentions about Sodom with Abraham (Genesis 18). Thus their rejection of Jesus as the one sent by the Father must reveal that his hearers are following the example of a different father (8:41a).

God

Their immediate response is that they cannot have a different father because they are not illegitimate (8:41b). This may be an allusion to doubts about Jesus' paternity. The crowd wondered whether the one who feeds multitudes and makes such claims could be the 'son of Joseph, whose father and mother we know' (6:42; see 1:45). John does not mention anything about the virgin birth or Jesus' earthly paternity. Later Jewish debate with the early Christians quickly included the charge that Jesus was illegitimate, born of Mary and a Roman soldier called Panthera, and this may be the first hint of this claim.

However, if Jesus is right to suggest that they have another father and not Abraham, they claim it must be God (8:41c). The Hebrew scriptures are full of this idea, from God calling Israel his firstborn son out of Egypt (Exodus 4:22) to Isaiah's assertion that even 'though Abraham does not know us… you, O Lord, are our Father' (Isaiah 63:16). Jesus replies that if God were their father, they would love Jesus, since he has been sent from God (8:42). The fact that they do not understand him and cannot accept his word implies that they must have a different father (8:43).

The devil

Because they seek to kill Jesus, the awful reality must be that their father is the devil, for they are doing what he desires (8:44). As a 'murderer from the beginning', he inspired Cain's murder of Abel, which John's first letter contrasts with Jesus' sacrificial death (1 John 3:12–16). Later Jesus will stress that it is really the devil who wants his death (12:31; 14:30). As well as being a murderer, there is 'no truth in him'. The word 'devil', *diabolos*, means slanderer. His lies from the time of Eve and the serpent (Genesis 3:1–5) speak 'from his own nature' as a liar. Jesus, however, does not speak from himself, but only what God has sent him to say, the truth to make us free (8:45). No one can convict him of sin (8:46). He has rebutted the charges of Sabbath-breaking and their other accusations and avoided the trap with the adulterous woman. Unlike the others who went away, aware of their sin, he was the only one to remain with her (8:7–9). He speaks the truth, the words of God. Those who are of God recognise him, so the only conclusion must be that these opponents are not of God (8:47).

The use of this passage, especially 8:44, by the Nazis to claim that all Jews were of the devil is clearly false. The section began with 'the Jews who believed', while both Jesus and John are Jews, like the rest of the disciples. The chapter describes an internal 'family feud' between two Jewish groups, one that accepts Jesus and another that rejects him. Jewish or Irish jokes can be funny when told by their own comedians, but seem racist when repeated by others. This debate, however, is no joke, for family feuds and civil wars are always the most bitter. There is no doubt that there was real conflict between Jesus and the authorities of his day, but some of the strong language here also reflects the pain and bitterness of the Jewish believers in Jesus who were thrown out of the synagogue later (see Introduction, p. 15).

For prayer and reflection

What do my actions reveal about my spiritual parentage?

46 John 8:48–59

Before Abraham was, I am

This dialogue is set at the end of the Feast of Tabernacles, with its ceremony of light and Jesus' claim, 'I am the light of the world' (8:12). Debate has concentrated on Jesus' identity and authority, his origins and destination, which he says come from the Father who sent him. Some Jews have believed, but others have become more opposed. This led to speculation about their origins since the desire to kill Jesus indicated that their father is neither God nor Abraham, but the devil himself. Now it climaxes with three questions from the opponents back on Jesus' claim and identity.

You are a Samaritan and have a demon

'The Jews' respond to Jesus' suggestion that the devil is their father in similar terms (8:48). To call him 'a Samaritan' was to go beyond the hint that he was illegitimate; the Samaritans were seen as the illegitimate offspring of Jews and pagan oppressors and religiously impure (2 Kings 17:24–41; see on 4:4). Thus it is Jesus who is inspired by the devil, not themselves. Again, all these charges were part of later argument between Jews and those who accepted Jesus, when, as here, the insults went both ways. Jesus replies that he cannot be a demon because he is honouring God, which demons could never do (8:49). The insult dishonours him, but since he does not seek his own glory, it does not matter to him. It is God who matters as he has maintained throughout the chapter. But God is concerned about his Son's glory (see 8:18), and he is the ultimate judge (8:50). However, those who keep Jesus' word need not worry about judgement since they will not see death (8:51; cf. 8:31). All his sayings about the bread of life, living water and the light of life have been offers of life, not death.

Are you greater than Abraham?

'The Jews' repeat the charge of demon possession and interpret Jesus' offer of not seeing death on a literal level as usual. After all, even Abraham died and all the prophets likewise (8:52). Jesus' statement is preposterous, pretending to be greater than Abraham. Previously, they asked Jesus, 'Who are you?' (8:25); now this claim makes them ask, 'Who do you think you are?' (8:53).

Jesus responds again that what he thinks about himself does not matter. He glorifies the Father, not himself. As always, he is totally dependent on his Father who in turn glorifies his Son (8:54). As we know, this glory will be through his suffering and passion (see 12:23, 28; 13:31). Jesus' opponents may claim his Father as their God, yet they do not know him. Jesus has constantly stressed his knowledge of God through this debate and does so again (8:55; see 7:28–29; 8:19). To deny it now would make himself into a liar like them (see 8:44). This reference back to the earlier debate recalls their claim to be children of Abraham; if Abraham is their father, they should know that he rejoiced to see Jesus' day (8:56). This may allude to rabbinic belief that Abraham's vision of Genesis 15:12–16 showed him all his future descendants, including the Messiah. Alternatively, it suggests that Abraham is in the presence of God now, rejoicing at Jesus' ministry.

I am

Once again, 'the Jews' misunderstand his comment at an earthly level: a young man like him cannot have seen Abraham (8:57). 'Not yet 50' does not tell us anything about Jesus' actual age. Since 50 was the age when the Levites retired (Numbers 8:24–25), it means in his prime. (Luke 3:23 suggests Jesus was about 30.)

Jesus' reply is truly staggering: 'Before Abraham was, I am' (8:58). This balances how the debate began with his claim 'I am the light of the world' (8:12). After the other 'I am' sayings here with their hints and levels of meaning (see 8:23, 28), this time it is an absolute and unmistakable claim to exist in the eternal being of God. The attempt by his opponents to pick up some of the stones lying around for the building work on the temple to stone him is itself recognition of what he has said (8:59). It is not about stoning an adulterous woman any more, but someone guilty of the much more serious blasphemy, according to the penalty in Leviticus 24:16. Jesus' accusation that they wish to kill him is thus proved true. Yet, somehow, Jesus leaves the temple, hidden 'in secret' as he came to the temple 'in secret' at the start of the Feast (7:4, 10). After this debate, the hour for his suffering is much closer, but it is still not yet.

Prayer

Eternal 'I am', search my heart that I may rejoice in your day and glorify the Father.

47

John 9:1–5

The light comes to a blind man

The story of how the light of the world comes to heal a blind man is beautifully written. Although it is self-contained in chapter 9, its part in the development of the gospel is significant. Chapters 7 and 8 take place during the Feast of Tabernacles, with its rituals of water and light. Both of those symbols recur here also. Jesus' claim to be the 'light of the world' (8:12) led to debate about his origins and identity, causing divisions and antagonism. The accusations and counter-claims culminated in charges of demonic inspiration and an attempt to stone him. Now those symbols of darkness and light are translated into physical terms as a blind man is healed. It happens 'as Jesus passed by' (9:1); in the narrative, Jesus has just left the temple (8:59), so perhaps he passes the blind man at the temple gate, a favourite spot for the sick and the destitute to lie, beseeching help from entering pilgrims (see Peter and John at the gate, Acts 3:2).

The stress on light at the Feast of Tabernacles and Jesus' claim to be even greater as the light of the world are reflected in this chapter's key words which are repeated many times, such as 'blind' (9:1, 2, 13, 17, 18, 19, 20, 24, 25, 32, 39, 40, 41), 'eyes' (6, 10, 11, 14, 15, 17, 21, 26, 30, 32) and 'to see' (7, 8, 11, 15, 18, 19, 21, 25, 37, 39, 41). The actual healing from blindness to seeing happens early (9:7), but it leads rapidly to another debate about Jesus' identity which causes division. As the blind man comes more fully into the light, so we discover that 'there are none so blind as those who will not see'. As the blind man journeys not just out of physical darkness, but also from ignorance to a growing faith, Jesus' opponents travel from certainty through increasing doubt to rejecting the light. And all the while others are watching – the disciples, the man's parents, the bystanders, and even us, the readers. What will be our journey be, into light or darkness, healing or rejection?

Sin and suffering

In the Old Testament, to 'open the eyes of the blind' is the work of God (Psalm 146:8), a sign of his coming (Isaiah 29:18; 35:5) or of his anointed servant (Isaiah 42:7). It is remarkable therefore that no one blind is cured anywhere in the Old Testament, yet now Jesus comes to this blind man.

What is more, he has not gone blind recently, but was born like that (9:1). Jesus' disciples ask their rabbi, 'Why?' (9:2). It is a common human reaction to suffering, especially of the innocent, to ask, 'Why me? Why her?' In fact, the disciples assume it is *not* undeserved and want to know whose fault caused it, the man's or his parents? Faced with this situation, they see not a person in need, but a theological problem – is this the result of sin? The Old Testament suggests that the sins of parents could be visited upon their children (e.g. Exodus 20:5), and some rabbinic commentators also thought it possible for a foetus to sin (when discussing Esau and Jacob's behaviour in the womb, Genesis 25:22). Belief in the reincarnation of souls, which would have been known in first-century Palestine among followers of both Greek philosophy and Eastern religions (and which is increasingly common today), also suggests that people can be punished in this life for their former sins. Against all these views, the book of Job argued that suffering is not necessarily caused by sin, and Jesus endorses this here.

Darkness and light

Where the disciples see a problem, Jesus sees a person in need and an opportunity for works of God 'to be revealed', to be made manifest in the light (9:3). In this gospel, Jesus' miracles are 'signs', pointers to the glory of God. His comment does not mean that this is the reason for the man's suffering, but that his situation can result in God's work. Jesus must 'work the works of him who sent me' while he can, 'while it is day' (9:4). Jesus knew his time was limited, and he had to 'seize the day', *carpe diem*, as the Latin proverb puts it, for night, the time of darkness, was soon coming. Here John picks up the theme from the Feast of Tabernacles, that Jesus is the 'light of the world' (9:5; see also 8:12). The man has spent his existence in darkness, but now he meets the one 'in whom was life, and the life was the light of men', as the prologue made clear (1:4). Regrettably, there is still much death and darkness in our world, which we struggle to understand; but if we are to 'work the works of God', we must never just discuss it, but seek to bring light and life.

Prayer

Jesus, light of the world, shine in our darkness and bring us your healing life.

48 John 9:6-12
The blind man is healed

As with Nicodemus, the Samaritan woman and the paralysed man, so the blind man is led by Jesus away from understanding things on a simple physical level to a deeper spiritual reality. In particular, there are a lot of links to the story of the paralysed man in chapter 5. Both have been suffering for many years (9:1; 5:5) but are healed by Jesus by a pool in Jerusalem (9:7; 5:2) on a sabbath (9:14; 5:9). This causes problems with the authorities (9:16; 5:10, 16), who question the men (9:15, 24; 5:12). Jesus is absent (9:12; 5:13), and the men do not know anything about him (9:12, 25; 5:13), but he comes to find them and reveal himself to them (9:35; 5:14). This similarity is not accidental, but part of John's artistry in painting his picture of Jesus to reveal his loving concern and divine identity through his miracles, the 'signs'. In both cases, the physical healing must lead on to a revelation of who Jesus is.

'Sent' for healing

True to his comment about doing the works of God while there is time (9:4), Jesus turns his words into action for the man's healing. As soon as he finished speaking, he spat on the ground and mixed his saliva with the earth to form a clay to put on the man's eyes (9:6). Some early church Fathers link this action to God's creation of Adam (whose name in Hebrew means 'earth') out the dust of the ground in Genesis 2:7; other commentators compare the use of saliva by the emperor Vespasian to cure a blind man at Alexandria, described in Tacitus' *Histories* IV:81. Saliva was highly regarded in the ancient world, and it certainly makes a better eyesalve than the honey and cock's blood a blind Roman soldier called Aper wore on his eyes for three days at the instruction of the healing god Aesculapius! (Dittenberger's *Greek Inscriptions* 1173:15-18).

Whatever the reason for Jesus' impromptu eye ointment, he tells the blind man to go and wash in the Pool of Siloam (9:7). This is the pool from which water was drawn for the procession at the Feast of Tabernacles (see on 7:37 above). It is a marvel of ancient Jewish engineering. The Gihon spring is one of Jerusalem's main water supplies, but it was in the Kidron valley outside the old fortified city. Therefore, when Jerusalem was threatened with attack in 701BC, Hezekiah cut a tunnel through the solid rock for over 500 metres to 'send' the water to a basin inside the walls, called Siloam or 'sent' (see 2 Kings 20:20; 2 Chronicles 32:2–4,30; Isaiah 22:9–11). Now this man is sent to the pool of 'Sent' by the one who is himself sent by God to bring light and healing. Because the man is healed of being blind from birth by washing in the pool, many in the early church saw a reference to baptism in this story, and it would often be depicted as a baptism in art in the catacombs, as well as in the writings of people like Tertullian and Augustine. Whether John intended an allusion to baptism is not clear, but what is vital is that, unlike Naaman refusing to wash in the Jordan (2 Kings 5:10–12), the blind man obeyed his instruction: he was told to go and he went – and as a result he came back seeing (9:7).

Who, how and where?

The miracle, however, is not the end of the story – merely its beginning. Now the questions really start. The first is, 'Who is this man?' The blind man has been so changed, even transformed by his encounter with Jesus that his old neighbours are not sure if it is him (9:8–9). People do not expect change – and those who have been brought out of darkness through baptism into Christ are sometimes not recognised by their former acquaintances.

Some, though, will keep asking how it happened: 'How were your eyes opened?' (9:10). All the man can do is to tell his story of being anointed with mud and told to go and wash, and how his obedience led to receiving his sight (9:11). He does not know anything about his healer yet, as is shown by his reference to him as 'a man called Jesus'.

Naturally, people want to know where someone who can do this can be found, but the man is not afraid to admit, 'I don't know' (9:12). He has much to learn, but all he can do now is bear witness to what happened to him and confess his ignorance. Jesus has slipped quietly away again, and will not reappear until 9:35. In the meantime, as so often after a new spiritual experience, the man will have to face some questioning and opposition, yet through this he will grow in understanding what has happened to him.

Prayer

'Man called Jesus', let me obey your instructions, and wash me in your love, that I may see.

49 John 9:13–23
Healing brings opposition

The blind man's healing is only the start of this story. More important is what happens next and everyone's reactions. After the bystanders' initial questioning, 'they lead him to the Pharisees' (9:13) as Jesus himself will be led to the authorities later (18:13). Their investigation forms the centrepiece of the whole story.

The man is now described as 'formerly blind' (9:13), but the problem is that he was healed on 'a sabbath day', as when Jesus healed the paralysed man (9:14; see 5:9). The paralytic's offence was to carry his mat on the sabbath, and Jesus' was the work of healing. This time not only did Jesus heal, but his actions breached various regulations. Ancient Jewish writings on the sabbath forbid many things, including kneading, carrying water, anointing eyes and using saliva. Jesus' mixing of earth with saliva (a form of water), making clay and putting it on the man's eyes would all have been unacceptable. So the Pharisees investigate carefully which rules were broken. The man, however, sticks to the simple facts of his story: 'He put clay on my eyes, I washed and I see' (9:15).

Division of opinion

Unfortunately, the 'simple facts' cause an immediate division. For those who concentrate on the importance of keeping the sabbath, such unlawful actions show that Jesus cannot be 'from God' (9:16). Others look not at the sabbath, but at the miraculous sign and disagree, using Nicodemus' earlier logic (see 3:2), for a sinner cannot do such things. Earlier there was a division, *schisma*, among the people at the Feast (7:43); now the same word appears, with a schism among the religious leaders (9:16). They ask the blind man's opinion, given that his eyes have been opened. He has moved from seeing his healer as 'the man called Jesus' to describing him as 'a prophet' (9:11, 17), like the Samaritan woman at the well when Jesus correctly identified her situation (4:19).

Out of the synagogue

While the man is making progress in his faith, the authorities are going the other way: 'The Jews did not believe' (9:18). The Pharisees are called 'the Jews', as so often in John for Jesus' religious opponents. While they seemed to accept the healing (9:17), now they 'do not believe' and even doubt his blindness. Perhaps he was never blind or is lying – and so they check the story with his parents (9:19). There are indeed 'none so blind as those who will not see'. When our cherished views are threatened we will believe anything to avoid the terrifying consequences of change. The man's parents seem curt and frightened by the question; they confirm that he is their son and was indeed born blind (9:20), but they have 'no comment' on how it happened. They pass the buck: 'He's a big boy now – ask him' (9:21).

The writer explains that 'they were afraid of the Jews' (9:22), which is curious since the parents, the man, Jesus and everyone else involved are all Jews. Furthermore, these frightening 'Jews' have 'already agreed' that anyone who 'confesses Jesus as Christ' should be put 'out of the synagogue'. This word, *aposynagogos*, occurs only here and in John 12:42 and 16:2 in the New Testament. Yet it did not stop Jesus and his disciples going to synagogue regularly in the gospels and in Acts. The threat makes more sense after the Jewish War and the destruction of Jerusalem and the temple by the Romans in AD70. After Jewish faith and practice was regrouped around the synagogue at the Council of Yavneh in AD85, 'the blessing against the heretics' in the services made it difficult for Jews who confessed Jesus as the Christ (see Introduction, p. 15).

Some scholars believe that John (like Matthew) is writing for people who have suffered the traumatic experience of being excommunicated, perhaps while their parents or families stood aside. This followed the opposition to Jesus and his followers in his own day (see Luke 6:22). Perhaps, therefore, John is using this later technical term here to console those who have been healed by Jesus and come to faith in him – and who, like their master, suffer rejection from family, friends or religious community. This explains why this interrogation is at the centre of this story: as Christ was rejected so will all those like this man who were blind, but now can see.

Prayer

Jesus, who suffered rejection for our sake, bless all who are rejected by their families or friends because of faith in you.

50 John 9:24–34

I was blind but now I see

The Jewish leaders' interrogation of the blind man's parents has not given them any answers, but it has confirmed their suspicion and doubts. Now, therefore, they call the man in for a second interrogation. It begins with their opening statement, 'Give glory to God' (9:24). In fact, they are not interested in giving glory to God for the man's healing. It is like Joshua's cross-examination of Achan: 'My son, give glory to the Lord God of Israel and make confession to him. Tell me now what you have done; do not hide it from me' (Joshua 7:19). In other words they are ordering the man to tell the truth, and stop lying about being blind and having been healed. Instead of being divided (9:16), now they are sure: the man is a liar, and 'we know' that Jesus is 'a sinner' (9:24).

The paradox of this chapter is that the more they push the man, the more he seems to understand about Jesus and what has happened in his healing. He has already moved from calling him a man to 'a prophet' (9:11, 17). Now he refuses to be drawn into a theological argument with them. He may not know much – but he wants really to give glory to God: 'One thing I do know: though I was blind, now I see' (9:25). This simple statement is the testimony of Christians down through the ages and across the world.

Whose disciples?

Faced with the man's continuing assertion of his healing, they go back to the same questions – what happened and how (9:26)? They follow the age-old police method, getting him to repeat his story in the hope of catching him out. The man, however, gets exasperated and refuses to tell the story again, replying instead with some wonderfully sardonic comments. He pretends not to understand why they want to hear it again, unless it is because 'you want to become his disciples' (9:27). Not surprisingly, this suggestion leads them to abuse him but in their opposition they inadvertently take him a step further in his pilgrimage: it's you who are that fellow's disciple – the 'his' is very dismissive (9:28). They contrast his poor discipleship with their pride as 'disciples of Moses'. The argument about Jesus' healing of the paralytic soon became a contrast between Jesus and Moses (see on 5:45 above), and the same happens here. After all, they note, 'we know' that God spoke with Moses (9:29), as the Old Testament says, 'face to face, as one speaks to a friend' (Exodus 33:11; see also Numbers 12:8). In contrast to what 'we know' about Moses, they know nothing about Jesus, not even where he comes from, as in the previous debate about Jesus' origins at the Feast of Tabernacles (7:27; 8:14).

Cast out

As the opponents' view of Jesus goes down even further, so the man grows in both faith and confidence. With marvellous irony, he applauds this 'astonishing thing' – that Jesus can open a blind man's eyes and the religious authorities don't even know where he comes from (9:30)! He reminds them of what he and they both know, that 'God does not listen to sinners' but only to those who worship him and obey his will (9:31). This is common right across the Old Testament: 'the Lord is far from the wicked, but he hears the prayer of the righteous' (Proverbs 15:29, see also Psalms 34:15; 66:18; 145:19; Job 27:9; Isaiah 1:15). What has happened is unique; as we saw on 9:2 above, no one in the Old Testament heals blindness from birth (9:32). Therefore, reasons the man, 'the man called Jesus' is not just 'a prophet' (9:11, 17), but must be someone 'who worships God and obeys his will' (9:31). And so he concludes, 'If this man were not from God, he could do nothing' (9:33). This is all too much for the leaders; they are quite certain about what 'we know', and are not about to tolerate lessons in basic theology from someone like this. In their downward journey, they have reached the position the disciples assumed at the start (see 9:2), that the man was 'born entirely in sin' – thus tacitly admitting that he is not lying and was born blind. As such, they refuse to be taught by him, but reject him and cast him out from the synagogue and community of faith (9:34).

So this blind man becomes an example for John's original readers, who may have suffered a similar fate, and a challenge to us. Are we prepared to stand up for what Jesus has done for us – even under hard questioning and threats of rejection?

Prayer

Amazing grace, how sweet the sound, that saved a wretch like me I once was lost, but now am found, was blind, but now I see.

John Newton, converted slave trader (1725–1807)

51 John 9:35–41

Jesus brings both sight and blindness

The extraordinary thing is that Jesus has been missing for most of the story, ever since he told the man to wash in the Pool of Siloam (9:7). But, although Jesus has been offstage, his presence has been very real as the characters on stage – the Pharisees, blind man and parents – have all been discussing him. Now that is all over, and the blind man is left alone, abandoned at the edge of the empty stage – precisely when Jesus chooses to reappear, having heard that the man had been excommunicated, 'cast out' (9:35). Someone 'cast out' should be shunned and ignored by others for the punishment to work – but not by Jesus. In his divine compassion, he comes and finds the man rejected by his community and abandoned by his parents (cf. Psalm 27:9–10).

In this way, Jesus fulfils his earlier promise that 'anyone who comes to me, I will not cast out' (6:37), where the words 'cast out' are the same as what the religious leaders did to this man (9:34). This, too, is the testimony of others rejected for Christ – such as the Romanian pastor Richard Wurmbrand in solitary confinement in a Communist prison, or Dietrich Bonhoeffer in a Nazi camp – that Jesus comes to find those who remain loyal to him. He did exactly the same for the paralysed man after he had been investigated for carrying his mat on the sabbath (5:14). However, after Jesus came and revealed himself to that man, he promptly went and 'shopped' Jesus, telling the authorities who he was (5:15). The blind man, however, has had more than enough of them already – and now he is ready for the final stage of his journey into the light of faith.

Lord, I believe

When he has found him, Jesus asks the man if he believes 'in the Son of Man' (9:35). Again, the verb, *pisteuein*, does not mean 'believe in the existence of', but to trust in Jesus. The man has progressed towards faith, but now needs more explanation to believe and trust – who is he (9:36)? He can see physically and is beginning to make out spiritual things – but he is not quite able to see spiritually yet.

This time Jesus does not need to 'send' him anywhere else to open his eyes, but only to reveal himself. In fact, the man has seen him with his newly opened eyes – it is 'the one speaking to you' (9:37). This phrase is the same as Jesus used to reveal himself to the Samaritan woman (4:26). As she progressed from seeing Jesus as 'a prophet' to wondering if he might be the Christ (4:19, 29), so now the blind man finally realises who has healed him. From calling Jesus 'a man' (9:11), through 'a prophet' (9:17) to 'a worshipper of God' who has come 'from God' (9:31–33), now he proclaims 'Lord, I believe', and he worships him (9:38). Here is the real miracle, the real giving of sight. Physical sight may have come at the pool, but spiritual insight comes from the one who created eyes in the first place.

Light and darkness

After Jesus revealed himself to the paralytic, the debate centred on judgement (see on 5:19–29 above). So now Jesus warns that his coming into the world brings judgement (9:39). The divisions among the authorities are only a foretaste. Jesus' coming may enable those who do not see to be able to see, but the inevitable corollary is that those who refuse to see become blind. Some Pharisees wonder about this: 'Surely we are not blind, are we?' (9:40). The Greek construction is a question expecting the answer 'no'. They may be being sarcastic, but perhaps it is a genuine enquiry. If so, says Jesus, then they have no sin or guilt. Genuine blindness can be excused – but a deliberate, perverse refusal to see is culpable (9:41). To claim to see, to keep stressing, as they have done, that 'we know' everything while refusing to see what is front of our eyes is to put ourselves beyond help, for only those who know they are blind can receive healing, and only those who admit their sin can accept forgiveness.

In many ways, this encounter sums up all the others with Nicodemus, the Samaritan woman, the paralytic, the crowd – for here we have a full response, unlike the partial ones so far. To the ignorant and blind, Jesus can bring light. The more 'we know', the more we cling to our way of seeing the universe, the deeper into darkness we fall. The coming of light into darkness creates shadows. It is not his purpose, for Jesus was not sent to condemn the world, but it is an inevitable result when people love darkness rather than light (3:17–19).

Prayer

Lord Jesus, I believe; heal my blindness and bring me into your light.

52 John 10:1–7

I am the door

The first half of John's gospel, chapters 1—10, covers Jesus' miraculous 'signs', his teaching and the debates which followed in Galilee and Jerusalem. After an interlude at Bethany (11:1—12:11), Jesus comes to Jerusalem for his last week, arrest and death (12:12—20:31). This chapter draws together the threads from the first half and prepares us for the shift towards Jesus' passion.

Since John the Baptist first identified Jesus (1:29), Jesus has met various people – the first disciples, people in Cana and in the temple, Nicodemus, the Samaritan woman, the lame man, the hungry crowd in the desert, the worshippers at the Feast of Tabernacles in Jerusalem, the woman taken in adultery and the blind man. Sometimes these meetings have been accompanied by signs, but they have all discussed who Jesus is. The people Jesus met and the bystanders have had differing reactions, with some believing and others dismissing him, but increasingly these discussions have brought him into conflict with the religious leaders. In the last story, the blind man came to full faith in Jesus, but the authorities have excommunicated him.

Is this what true leadership of God's people means – casting them out? Who are the right leaders anyway, those who believe in Jesus or those who oppose him? As events have unfolded, we have gone through various Jewish feasts, and now the Feast of the Dedication is near, when the Jews celebrated the leadership of the Maccabeans (see on 10:22). The typical Old Testament image for the people and their leaders is that of sheep and shepherds (e.g. Ezekiel 34). So this chapter picks up this image as its theme to bring to a climax all the issues of the first half about Jesus' identity, his witnesses, and what it means to believe in him.

Most of ancient Israel-Palestine was rough stony pasture land, rather than rich agricultural fields, so the wandering shepherd and his flock was very common. Sheep were kept more for their wool than for meat, and the shepherd would herd them over several years, caring for them, feeding them and protecting them from dangers. All of these images appear here.

The door to the sheepfold

We begin with a 'figure of speech' (10:6), an image involving a door or gate, some sheep and a shepherd in 10:1–5, each of which will feature in turn through the chapter. It is more of a word-picture than a story but it is the nearest John has to the parables in the other gospels, which often feature sheep and shepherds. In our society, the shepherd and his flock is not a common sight, yet pastoral imagery is used a lot, especially in caring professions such as the church and social services, and in 'pastoral care' found in universities, colleges and schools.

We begin with the entrance to 'the sheepfold', the *aule*, a yard or enclosure where the sheep are kept, especially at night. Doors and gates are for those who have the right to enter, as when the psalmist sings of the 'gates of righteousness… the gate of the Lord' through which 'the righteous shall enter' (Psalm 118:19–20). However, thieves and robbers do not use the door, but climb in some other way (10:1–2). The door of a sheepfold admits only sheep and shepherds.

Protection from danger

The door thus gives protection for the sheep. The gatekeeper only opens it to the shepherd and the sheep are not frightened by his entry. They know his voice. Because he kept them for years, the shepherd would identify them by names like 'Black ear', 'Whitey' and so on. Even today, travellers tell stories of shepherds calling their sheep by name and by the sound of their voice out from a fold where several different flocks are together. Also, in the east, the sheep follow the shepherd, rather than being driven from behind (10:4). Like good schoolchildren, they will not 'go with strangers', but only those they know (10:5). The blind man, who could not see at all, had to respond to the voice of Jesus and follow what he said, but the religious leaders thought Jesus was just a stranger whom they did not know (9:7, 29). Not surprisingly, therefore, they do not understand this figure of speech (10:6). So Jesus has to spell it out, 'I am the door of the sheep'; he is the way to safety and salvation (10:7). Unlike the thieves and robbers, and the false leaders, he will not cast out, but save and protect all those who hear his voice and respond.

Prayer

Lord Jesus, door to salvation, may I hear your voice; call my name and enter through you to eternal life.

53

John 10:7-18

I am the good shepherd

In a pastoral society like ancient Israel, sheep and shepherds were used to describe the relationship of God with his people: 'The Lord is my shepherd' and 'We are his people, the sheep of his pasture' (Psalms 23:1; 100:3). Good leaders were 'shepherds of the people', such as David (2 Samuel 5:2; Psalm 78:71), but when he had Uriah killed and took his wife, he was exposed as a bad shepherd by Nathan the prophet (2 Samuel 12:1-7). The prophets denounced Israel's leaders as bad shepherds who do not care for their sheep (e.g. Ezekiel 34; Jeremiah 23:1; 50:6; Zechariah 11).

Pasture and life

So when the Jewish leaders treat people as they did the blind man, casting them out rather than caring for them, Jesus turns to the image of the shepherd. At Passover he used the bread of life (6:35, 51) and at Tabernacles, the living water and the light of life (7:37-38; 8:12). In this 'I am' saying, he calls himself the door for the sheep (10:7). 'All who came before me', the religious leaders, 'are thieves and bandits', and the sheep, like the blind man, will not listen to them (10:8). Thieves and robbers come to steal, but Jesus comes to provide: whoever enters through him as the door will find safety inside and they can go in and out to feed (10:9). A shepherd would lie across the entrance to a fold, to allow only his sheep to go in, and to watch them when they came out. So Jesus is the entrance to life, to 'preserve your going out and your coming in forever' (Psalm 121:8). While thieves come to kill the sheep and destroy life, Jesus comes to bring life 'in all its abundance' (10:10). The leaders rejected the blind man, destroying his hopes of life within their community, but Jesus gave him new life of physical sight and faith.

The shepherd's sacrifice for his sheep

The focus moves from the door to the shepherd, as the next 'I am' follows immediately: 'I am the good shepherd' (10:11). The word for good, *kalos*, included notions of beauty and loveliness. The good shepherd not only gives life instead of stealing it, but the life he gives is his own, laid down for the sake of the sheep. This is a contrast with the behaviour of a hireling: since he does not own the sheep, he does not care about them when danger threatens (10:12–13). The behaviour of the leaders to the blind man when they were threatened by his healing shows that they are only hirelings at best, not shepherds.

Jesus, however, is the good shepherd, who knows his own sheep as they also know him (10:14). Shepherds called their sheep out of the fold by their names and the flock followed their voice (10:3–4). The Greek word for church literally means 'called out', *ec-clesia*, from which all our 'ecclesiastical' words are derived. Jesus' knowledge of his sheep is rooted in his knowledge of his Father and his Father's knowing him as his Son. And because the nature of God's love is always self-giving, the good shepherd lays down his life for his sheep (10:15). What is more, God's love is universal, so the shepherd must also be concerned for 'other sheep… not of this fold', who also will hear his voice and be brought together into one flock (10:16). In contrast to the religious leaders' concern to maintain their pure group and throw the blind man out, the good shepherd wants to include all people. While Jesus' debate has been mostly with 'the Jews', the Samaritans have already realised that this is 'the Saviour of the World' (4:42) and the universal implications of the death of the shepherd will soon be stressed (11:52; 12:32). As we move towards the Passion, the inevitable result of his clash with the authorities, Jesus emphasises that he lays down his life willingly, out of sheer love for his people, a love which flows even from the heart of God (10:17–18).

This is a challenge to all involved in the pastoral care of God's people. It takes time and effort to know everyone individually, even as God knows us, and caring for them as Christ laid down his life for us may demand the ultimate sacrifice. The ordination charge for priests in the Church of England says: 'As servant and shepherd… set the Good Shepherd always before you as the pattern of your calling… to search for his children in the wilderness of this world's temptations… the treasure now to be entrusted to you is Christ's own flock.' This is true whether we are an archbishop, a Bible study group leader, a minister or just visiting an elderly person around the corner – we love others as the good shepherd loves us.

Prayer

Good shepherd, bless all those in pastoral care, that they may live out your self-sacrificial love for your sheep.

54 John 10:19–30
Tell us plainly

The words of the good shepherd once more cause a 'division' among 'the Jews' (10:19). Again we have the word for *schism*, which happened first to the people and then the leaders (7:43; 9:16). And so this division sums up so many attitudes throughout the first half of this gospel. On the one hand, some oppose Jesus and accuse him of having a demon and being mad, so people should not listen to him (10:20). This accusation of demon possession has been made both by the people and by the Jewish leaders (7:20; 8:48, 52). On the other hand, others point out that neither his words nor his miraculous actions are demonic (10:21). This argument from what Jesus says and does was first noted by Nicodemus, and repeated by the Samaritan woman, by the 5,000, by the crowd in Jerusalem, by some Pharisees and by the blind man (3:2; 4:29; 6:14; 7:31; 9:16, 33). The two sides are clear – so now the question must be answered plainly.

Dedication and light

The showdown takes place as we come to the Feast of the Dedication, or Hanukkah (10:22). While all the other feasts reflect the early history of the Jews, this was relatively recent. During the Greco-Syrian control of Israel in the second century, Antiochus Epiphanes desecrated the temple in 167BC with a pagan altar and sacrifices of pigs in his attempt to impose Hellenistic culture and end Jewish faith and practice. After the successful rebellion led by Judas Maccabeus, the temple was rededicated with proper sacrifice on 25 Khislev 164BC, and the Feast of the Dedication was thus instituted (see 1 Maccabees 4:36–59; 2 Maccabees 10:1–8). It was kept for eight days at the winter solstice and the custom of putting eight lights in the window, still observed by Jews today, gives it its other name of the Festival of Lights.

The festival's stress on the zeal of good leaders, like the Maccabees, contrasts with the bad shepherds' treatment of the blind man (9:34), while the lights remind us of Jesus, the light of the world (8:12; 9:5). The setting in the temple porticoes (10:23) recall the other debates in the temple (2:13–22; 7:14–44; 8:12–59), as well as the healing of the paralysed man and the woman taken in adultery (5:14; 8:1–12). In this final confrontation, John brings all that has happened to a climax. In the darkness of winter, Jesus, the light of the world and the good shepherd, the true leader of God's people, comes to the temple, not just to rededicate it, but to replace it as he offers the ultimate sacrifice of laying down his own life. Later, this connection was strengthened by celebrating the birth of Jesus on 25 December, the same month as Khislev.

The identity of Jesus

The stage is set: 'the Jews' can stand the suspense no longer and want to know if Jesus is the Christ (10:24). 'Tell us plainly' uses the same word, *parresia*, as Jesus' brothers' request to show himself 'openly' (7:4). The debate about Jesus' identity has been going on from the Pharisees' first questions to John the Baptist (1:19–28) to their discussions of 7:25–31, 40–42. In fact, Jesus has revealed himself to the Samaritan woman and the blind man (4:25; 9:35). However, in answer to the authorities' direct questions (8:25, 53), he referred them to how his works witness to who he is (see on 5:30–47; 7:14–44; 8:12–59). He reminds them of this now; if only they had had faith, they would have believed and realised who he is (10:25). That they do not know him or recognise his voice shows that they do not belong to his sheep, picking up the earlier shepherd image (10:26–27).

Those who hear Jesus' voice follow him and receive the gift of eternal life (10:28). In the figure of the shepherd and the door, Jesus offered protection to his sheep (10:3, 9). He demonstrated this by shielding the woman taken in adultery from stoning and by going to find the blind man when he had been cast out (8:7; 9:35). Thieves and robbers come to destroy life and wolves 'snatch' sheep (10:10, 12), but no one can 'snatch' Jesus' sheep or cause them to perish (10:28; see 6:37–39). This is because their security is based on the greatness of God the Father himself, and none can snatch anything from him (10:29). Thus the sheep's protection is rooted in the relationship of Jesus and his Father, as was his knowledge of them (see 10:15 above). And that relationship is so close that it alone can provide the answer to the question of 'the Jews' about Jesus' identity, as he finally replies 'plainly': 'the Father and I are one' (10:30).

Prayer

Lord Jesus Christ, revelation of the Father, help me to hear your voice and keep me safe in your hand.

55 John 10:30-42

The Father and I are one

The debates between Jesus and 'the Jews' about his identity have revealed much about his relationship with God. After healing the paralysed man, Jesus called God his Father, saying that he could only do what his Father wanted; in turn, the Father shares with the Son his authority to give life and exercise judgement (5:18-47). Similarly, during the bread of life discussion, Jesus stressed his origins with God the Father (6:37-40). The argument at the Feast of Tabernacles concerned whether Abraham, the devil or God was the Father of either Jesus or 'the Jews' (8:39-59). The desire of the good shepherd to lay down his life for the sheep comes from his Father (10:17-18). Thus it is no surprise that the first half of the gospel comes to a climax with Jesus' ringing declaration, 'the Father and I are one' (10:30).

The word 'one' is the neuter pronoun, *hen*, implying something like 'the Father and I are a unity' – in action, purpose, power, authority – rather than the masculine personal pronoun, *heis*, meaning 'one and the same person'. This interpretation is borne out in 10:38, 'the Father is in me, and I am in the Father'. This verse was used in the third and fourth century controversies about the exact nature of the relationship of the Father and Son, but philosophical debate was not John's concern here. At the end of the first half of his gospel, he stresses the unity of the Father and the Son as the basis for all Jesus says and does. In the second half of the gospel, this unity will be the basis for the relationship of believers with each other and with Jesus himself, 'even as we are one' (see on 15:9-10 and 17:11, 21-23). The sheep's relationship with the good shepherd depends totally upon the shepherd's relationship with God his Father (10:29-30).

Stoning for blasphemy

Having asked for 'plain speaking', 'the Jews' find this revelation of Jesus' relationship with God too much, and they 'took up stones to stone him' (10:31). Previous debates also ended in attempts to kill Jesus (5:17-18; 7:19-20; 8:59), so this response to a direct claim is predictable. Nonetheless, the good (*kalos*) shepherd asks which of the many 'good' (*kala*) works he has done 'from the Father' has prompted this response (10:32).

Before, Jesus' offence, officially at least, has been things he has done, and when he has done them, on the sabbath (5:16; 9:14–16). 'The Jews' reply that things have moved beyond that, from what he has *done*, to who he claims to *be*: for 'a human being to make yourself God' is to commit blasphemy (10:33). The penalty in the law is death by stoning (Leviticus 24:16), so they have no alternative.

Jesus' defence against the charge

Jesus' defence is in two brief parts. First, he notes that other human beings are called 'gods', 'written in your law' (10:34). Human judges are called 'gods', even though they are unjust and failing in their task (Psalm 82:6). If they can be termed 'gods' by the 'word of God' because judgement is entrusted to them by God, how much more can one whom the Father has sent into the world? Second, Jesus is not 'making himself God'; it is God, who has 'consecrated' him. At this Feast of the Dedication, is it blasphemy for the 'dedicated one' to call himself 'the Son of God' (10:35–36)? Of course, words are easy, but his actions, the works of the good shepherd in protecting, healing and feeding God's people, show his relationship with God, which can only be described as 'the Father is in me and I am in the Father' (10: 37–38). The works witness to Jesus' identity *and* his relationship with God.

Withdrawal across the Jordan

The previous attempts to arrest or kill Jesus failed because 'his hour had not yet come' (7:30, 44; 8:20, 59). So now, this final stoning comes to nothing, as Jesus slips away (10:39). However, the time for his arrest is drawing near, and now that his public ministry has reached its climax, he withdraws 'across the Jordan', back where it all started (10:40). This balances the beginning of the gospel with John the Baptist (1:28; 3:26) and brings the first half to a close. John did no miraculous signs, but through all these intervening chapters, Jesus has demonstrated that the Baptist's witness was true. Despite the 'schism' in the people, nonetheless many do believe (10:42). After all the opposition of the authorities, the last note is one of faith, that Jesus and the Father 'are one'.

Prayer

Father God, may I believe 'all that John said is true' and share in your unity and love with your Son.

56 John 11:1–6
The one you love is ill

Chapter 10 finished Jesus' public ministry back across the Jordan, where it all began with John the Baptist, and ended all the debates with the religious leaders. Since the division between those who believe and those who oppose Jesus is clear, we might expect to go straight into the Passion narrative, Jesus' last week in Jerusalem, his arrest, trial and death. In the other gospels, this is exactly what happens, as the temple episode provokes the hostility of the leaders.

John, however, has already used the temple incident at the start of Jesus' ministry to show him replacing Judaism (2:13–22). Instead, therefore, he has an interlude at the centre of his gospel, a 'hinge' around which everything turns from the ministry to the Passion, with one final sign to add up to the perfect seven. So far we have had six: water into wine; healing an official's son; healing the paralysed man; the miraculous feeding; walking on water; and healing the blind man (2:1–11; 4:46–54; 5:1–14; 6:1–14, 16–21; 9:1–12). This seventh sign has links to the others, especially the first, but it is also different. Unusually, the person is named, while all the others are anonymous. The miracle only happens at the end of the story, and any discussion takes place en route, unlike the usual pattern of the sign described briefly first, leading into debate about its meaning and Jesus' identity. All of that is now taken for granted. Instead, John gives us his longest single story before the Passion narrative itself – a beautiful preparation which raises the question of death. As the use of the story in funerals shows, it has the theme of life from death, but only at the cost of Jesus preparing to move from life to death, to lay down his life for his sheep.

God is my help

After all the unnamed people, the names Lazarus of Bethany are significant. Lazarus is the Greek version of the Hebrew Eleazar, meaning 'God is my help' (a son of Aaron, see Exodus 6:23–25), while Bethany means 'house of affliction'. The affliction is that Lazarus is ill (11:1). John expects his readers to know Lazarus' sisters, Mary and Martha. Mary is identified in a 'flash forward' as 'the one who anointed the Lord with perfume', but that story is yet to come (12:1–3). The sisters send a simple message for 'God to help': 'Lord, the one whom you love is ill' (11:3). It is enough to identify their brother, and the evangelist stresses this love (11:5). Some commentators identify Lazarus with 'the disciple Jesus loved', mentioned several times later (see 13:23; 19:26; 20:2; 21:7, 20). This is unlikely, since Lazarus is named and appears only here, while the unnamed disciple is part of Jesus' central group (21:2).

Notice how they simply tell Jesus the problem, that Lazarus is ill, and leave it at that. No requests are made, nor instructions given, just as the mother of Jesus told him 'they have no wine' (2:3). Many of us find it difficult in prayer just to tell Jesus the situation – and how easily we instruct God what to do! Jesus' response is again unexpected, like the apparent rebuff he gave his mother (2:4). Now he states that this illness is not fatal, but 'for the glory of God' (11:4). This does not mean that God is sadistically causing it for his glory, but that his Son will be glorified through it, as happened with the blind man (9:3). However, for Jesus 'to be glorified' entails suffering and death (see 7:39), and this phrase will recur several times (12:16, 23; 13:31).

Love and absence

Finally, John says that 'Jesus loved Martha and her sister and Lazarus' (11:5), which is necessary because of what happens next. Our reaction to such news would be to rush straight there – yet Jesus delays for another two days (11:6). John even connects these two verses with a 'therefore', which many translations omit because it seems so strange to wait when someone we love is ill. Some scholars explain this delay by referring either to Jesus' own three days in a tomb or to the rabbinic belief that the soul waited around the body for three days before finally departing, but this does not help much. What John shows is that, as with Mary's request about the wine (2:4) or Jesus' brothers' suggestion about revealing himself in Jerusalem (7:2–10), so here too Jesus takes his own initiative in his own time and acts when he is ready, hard though that may be for us to understand. How do we cope when someone we love is ill? Can we find the courage to tell God about them, and then be patient when he seems to do nothing?

Prayer

O God our help, when those we love are ill give us courage to pray and patience to wait with you.

57 John 11:7-16
Lazarus is asleep

After the unexplained delay for two days, Jesus tells his disciples that they are returning to Judea (11:7). Not surprisingly, they are rather taken aback by this – they have all just escaped from there. As they remind Jesus, 'the Jews were just now trying to stone you', referring to the outcome of the final debate with the religious leaders (11:8; see 10:31, 39).

Walk in the day

Jesus' reply seems rather odd at first since it has nothing to do with Lazarus. It is another 'figure of speech', about walking in the day or in the night. Jesus said something similar to the disciples when they asked him about the blind man's condition; then he reminded them that he had work to do as the 'light of the world' (9:4-5). The ancients divided the day from sunrise to sunset into twelve hours. Jesus says that this gives plenty of light to walk in and no need to worry about stumbling; it is those who walk around at night, in the pitch darkness of a society without street lighting, who trip over (11:9-10). This is all very well, but how does it answer their concerns about being stoned? At the surface level, Jesus is reminding them that God's timing is sufficient. The fact that there are twelve hours means there is no need to rush or panic, but also that there is only a fixed time, with none to waste for God's work. At the spiritual level, however, the disciples are still blundering around in darkness of not understanding what is going on, while Jesus is walking in the light of God's day and sees all too clearly the darkness of his final struggle with evil coming soon. He must act, and act now.

Sleep, death or life?

Therefore he explains why they must leave the safety of their refuge across the Jordan and go back into the dangers of Judea: 'Our friend Lazarus has fallen asleep' (11:11). Here Jesus is using a euphemism for death which was common in the ancient world, and is still used today. The Greek word used here gives us our word 'cemetery', the 'sleeping place', for those who sleep in Christ (see 1 Corinthians 15:6; 1 Thessalonians 4:14). As so often in John, the disciples take this simply at the surface level; if Lazarus is asleep, he does not need Jesus to wake him, for he will recover by himself (11:12). Once again we are reminded of previous misunderstandings like Nicodemus talking about wombs (3:3–8), the Samaritan woman asking about buckets for water (4:10–15) or the multitude wanting bread from heaven (6:32–34). In each case, they were thinking on the surface at the physical level, and had to be helped by Jesus through to the deeper, spiritual meaning. This is only the first of several misunderstandings in this chapter, and so Jesus has to spell it out for them 'plainly', using the same word as he was asked to speak by 'the Jews' in 10:24: 'Lazarus is dead' (11:14).

To die with him

After breaking the news of their friend's death first euphemistically, then bluntly, Jesus seems to fall back into the apparent callousness which made him wait two days when he first heard of Lazarus' illness: 'For your sake I'm glad I was not there' (11:15). The obvious reason for this is that he would have then been asked to cure Lazarus when he was ill, whereas now the bigger miracle of raising him from death will help the disciples to 'believe'. Hard though this may be for us to understand, let alone the disciples, we seem to be back to the mystery of God's timing again.

However, the disciples have not even got that far. They are still thinking that to return to Judea is simply suicide, as Thomas' remark demonstrates (11:16). Thomas' character as the one who wants it all explained at the basic level before he will believe will emerge more and more through the next few chapters (see 14:5; 20:24–29). For the moment, he sounds more like a donkey, depressed and stubborn – like Winnie the Pooh's friend Eeyore: 'Let's go and die with him.' At least this wonderfully morose comment shows that he is committed to the end – even if he thinks it is to die. The irony, of course, is that only Jesus will die – and his death will mean that they will all live, including Thomas and Lazarus and all who 'sleep in Christ'.

Prayer

Lord, when I am asleep wake me, and when I misunderstand, tell me plainly.

58 John 11:17-24

Your brother will rise again

It would probably have been a two day journey back across the Jordan to Bethany, a small village on the edge of Jerusalem. Jesus' delay of two days plus the journey means that when he arrives Lazarus is not only dead and buried, but has been in his tomb for four days (11:17). This may be another allusion to the rabbinic idea that the soul would wait for three days until it saw from the change in colour of the face that decomposition had started, and then depart. The evangelist is making sure that there is no doubt about Lazarus being really dead – no nonsense about him having been ill and merely revived in the cool of the tomb!

The two-mile journey from Jerusalem to Bethany is quite easy, and today many pilgrims and tourists travel to this little village, now called El 'Azariyeh, after Lazarus. Lazarus would have been buried on the day of his death, as is the custom in hot climates, and the usual mourning rituals would have followed. Thus 'many of the Jews' came to console Mary and Martha (11:19). Here the phrase does not mean the religious opponents of Jesus, but probably inhabitants of Jerusalem, given its proximity. After the processions to the tomb with public displays of grief and the burial, the family would keep the practice of sitting in the house mourning, accompanied by friends and well-wishers.

Martha confronts Jesus

Now John gives us a little glimpse of the two bereaved sisters. They are known also from Luke 10:38–42, where Martha was busy with her domestic tasks while Mary sat at Jesus' feet listening like a disciple. So now, Mary is 'sitting in the house' keeping the mourning. Martha, the active one here also, wants to do something and as soon as she hears of Jesus' approach, she stops sitting mourning to go and meet him (11:20). However, it is not so easy to leave her loss behind and her first words are typical of someone in grief: 'If you had been here, my brother would not have died' (11:21). 'If only I hadn't...' and 'If only she had...' are common comments from the bereaved. In the initial stages of the shock, we still cannot believe it and want it all to have been different. This may manifest itself as guilt, blaming oneself for doing or not doing something. Alternatively, it may be anger, blaming someone else instead, as here.

Martha rushes not to greet Jesus but to reproach him. Why didn't he come earlier and cure Lazarus? Perhaps she has even worked out that he must have delayed somewhere (11:6). In her pain, her first words are those of anger and criticism.

Resurrection – now or then?

As so often with grief, her mood quickly changes, to a wistful expression of hope or even faith; 'even now', she believes, whatever Jesus asks, 'God will give you' (11:22). We are reminded again of the wedding at Cana and the instruction of Jesus' mother to the servants, despite his rebuff, that they should do 'whatever he says' (2:5). Jesus gives no answer to Martha's reproach, but offers her the promise 'Your brother will rise again' (11:23). As often in John, it can be understood on at least two levels. Is this answering her half-expressed wish for a miracle, offering her some hope now, or is it just the sympathetic consolation of a conventional belief in a future resurrection which any Jew might offer?

John's usual multilevel approach would lead us to expect the conventional surface meaning to be understood first and then the other only later, and this is what happens. Martha certainly takes it as conventional sympathy and gives the automatic religious response, 'I know he will rise again in the resurrection on the last day' (11:24). Such a belief in a future resurrection on the last day begins to appear towards the end of Old Testament times (see Daniel 12:2) and was commonly held by groups like the Pharisees in Jesus' day, although not by the Sadducees (see Mark 12:18; Acts 23:6–9). But behind her resignation in what is almost a platitude, we can almost hear her screaming, 'But what about *now*? It hurts too much to wait to the last day!'

For many of us, when faced with a grieving person's pain or anger, the temptation is strong to assuage it with conventional beliefs and expressions of sympathy when perhaps we should just be quiet. But it is much more worrying when God seems to offer some hope for us *now* in response to our prayers. Can we open ourselves to that possibility – or do we quash the idea quick with a religious platitude?

Prayer

Lord Jesus, help me to hope in you for the future and open my life to you here and now.

59 John 11:24–33
I am the resurrection and the life

Martha expresses her belief in the conventional view, that her brother 'will rise again in the resurrection on the last day' (11:24). According to this, everything to do with eschatology – judgement, death, life – all are in the future at the end of time. Such 'future eschatology' is clearly expressed in passages such as 5:25–29 (see notes above). Jesus' response both confirms and challenges that. In this magnificent saying, all the other 'I am' sayings now come together: Jesus can claim to be the 'bread of life', 'light of life', the 'door' and the 'good shepherd' who brings 'life in all its abundance' (6:35; 8:12; 10:7, 10–11) only because he can also say, 'I am the resurrection and the life' and thus give Martha some hope (11:25). The two words are not synonymous: the 'resurrection' is what will happen at the end, and 'life' is what we will be raised to, as well as what we experience now.

Suddenly, Martha's conventional belief in a future resurrection at the last day is turned inside out. The resurrection and the end are here, now, in this person before her. Any resurrection in the future will be through Jesus – and will depend on people's belief in him: 'Those who believe' in him will live, 'even though they die', and what's more, 'everyone who lives and believes in me' will have something even more amazing, they 'will never die' (11:26). All the verbs are still future – 'will live' – yet there is a daring hint about the present with 'will never die'. Jesus has already promised that anyone who believes in him 'will not come to judgement, but has passed from death to life' and 'will never see death' (5:24; 8:51). This is a stupendous claim when death is all too present, with Lazarus four days in his tomb.

Yes, Lord, I believe

After this extraordinary statement, Jesus asks Martha, 'Do you believe this?' (11:26). Martha's confession of faith picks up all the key descriptions of Jesus so far. After the gradual progress towards faith made by the other individuals leading up to the blind man's 'Lord, I believe' (9:38), now we have the full set: 'I believe that you are the Christ, the Son of God, the one coming into the world' (11:27). John began with the Pharisees' questioning John the Baptist to see if he is the Christ (1:19) and continued with Jesus' revelations to the first disciples, the Samaritan woman and the blind man (1:41; 4:26; 9:37). Equally, the phrase 'Son of God' has recurred regularly from John the Baptist's original witness and Nathanael's first steps of faith to the final debate with the religious leaders (1:34, 49; 10:36). The light and the prophet which were both 'coming into the world' (1:9; 6:14) are now here, Martha says. It is a most comprehensive expression of faith in all that Jesus is, the female version of Peter's confession (see on 6:69).

Mary at Jesus' feet

Mary, however, is still back in the house, sitting at her mourning ritual; Martha tells her 'privately' of Jesus' arrival, so that she can go for a quiet word with him (11:28). In Luke's story, Mary was sitting at Jesus' feet (Luke 10:39); now she gets up from sitting alone in her grief and comes to fall at his feet (11:29, 32). Jesus is not yet at the house, or even the village; he is still where Martha met him, out on the road where the tombs would have been, since they were not allowed in towns or villages (11:30). When the Jews see her leave the house and the village, they follow, assuming she is going to the tomb 'to weep', to undertake yet more mourning (11:31). There will be not much chance of Mary's quiet word with Jesus! Undeterred by their accompanying stares, Mary comes to Jesus and 'kneels at his feet'. Perhaps she is taking up the disciple's position at the master's feet she adopted before, or maybe it is in an attitude of supplication or worship? Whatever is implied by her action, her words are the same as her sister's – the reproach of faith, 'If you had been here, my brother would not have died' (11:32). This time, Jesus does not respond with conventional expressions of sympathy or probing questions of faith, as he did with Martha. Mary's distraught position at his feet answers all those already. When he sees her grief, all Jesus can do is also to be 'deeply moved in spirit and troubled' (11:33). Sometimes, 'to weep with those who weep' is not only all we can do, but also the best we can offer.

Prayer

Lord Jesus Christ, Son of God, the resurrection and the life of all who put their trust in you, let me come to kneel at your feet and worship you.

60

John 11:33–44

Lazarus, come out!

When Jesus saw them weeping, his only response was to weep, as anyone who cared about Lazarus and his family might (11:33). Yet the words used to describe his emotions are much more than that. The first, *en-brimo*, is used in Greek of horses, 'snorting in the nostrils'. Elsewhere in the New Testament it conveys anger and indignation, when rebuking someone (Matthew 9:30; Mark 1:43; 14:5). Some scholars wonder who Jesus can be angry with, and suggest he is rebuking the Jews or the others for a lack of faith or even angry at death itself. Yet anger is part of grief, as we saw with Mary and Martha's reproach of Jesus (11:21, 32). The other word here, *tarasso*, means to be disturbed or troubled (used also of Jesus in 12:27; 13:21). Together, this phrase conveys the strength of Jesus' feeling; he was 'shuddering, shaking with emotions', grief, anger, pain, hurt and a desire to do something. Like many bereaved people, he wants to see 'the one he loved', and asks where he has been laid (11:34). Then comes the Bible's shortest verse, 'Jesus wept' (11:35). Christians do not believe in a remote God, on a cloud where all is sweetness and light, without passions or feelings, as the Greeks did and many today still do. In Jesus, God has experienced the depths of the human condition, including pain, grief and love. Even the onlookers are amazed, saying, 'See how he loved him!' (11:36). Yet others of 'the Jews' doubt him; if he really cared, the Jesus who 'opened the eyes of the blind man' could have prevented Lazarus dying (11:37). Even here we have the usual division between those who believed Jesus and those who rejected him.

Roll away the stone

Jesus, still 'greatly disturbed' (*enbrimo* again) comes to the tomb, which like most Palestinian graves was a cave cut into the rock with a stone across it (11:38). He asks them to 'take away the stone', and the reader who knows the end of the story will think of a different tomb and another Mary coming to find another stone rolled away (20:1). Martha, however, despite her earlier confession of faith, is still thinking at the surface level. Presuming that Jesus wants to view her brother's body, she is afraid of the corruption inside and the 'stench from four days'. She has not realised that her faith that 'even now God will give' whatever Jesus asks (11:22) will be answered, that the future resurrection in which she believes is breaking into the present. The future belief that 'those in the tombs will hear his voice and come forth' (5:28-29) is about to happen now. But if Jesus is to bring new life, we must face the corruption within and roll away the stone for him.

The glory of God

Jesus gently reminds her of their conversation, and repeats his comment that this would all result in the 'glory of God' (11:40; see 11:4). As the first sign in Cana 'manifested his glory' (2:11), so now will this seventh sign in Bethany, the 'house of affliction'. And so they take away the stone, while Jesus turns to prayer (11:41). He addresses his Father, the God with whom he is one (10:30). As with the loaves and the bread of life, it is a prayer of thanks, *eucharisto* (see on 6:11). The only petition is for the sake of others, those watching, 'that they may believe you sent me' (11:42). So we see clearly at last the christological nature of this miracle, the 'sign to God's glory' hinted at by Jesus' opening words, the delay and conversations on two levels (11:4, 6, 15, 23) – which have all brought us to this extraordinary moment.

Unbind him and let him go

Finally, Jesus shouts in a voice to wake the dead three words in Greek with not even a verb, 'Lazarus! Here! Out!' (11:43). At this incredible climax to all the grief and tears, the tragedy almost turns to comedy, as the former corpse shuffles to the opening, still bound with the linen cloths which held the limbs to the body and the headcloth which covered the face and held the jaw (11:44). Unlike Jesus' resurrection, when the cloths are simply left behind (20:5-7), Lazarus shuffles into new life still all tied up. Jesus, exhausted perhaps by his emotions and the miracle, seeks others' help: 'Unbind him and let him go.' The last word, *aphete*, 'release', is the same word as to 'forgive our sins as we forgive' in the Lord's prayer (Matthew 6:12-15). When we too hear the Lord's voice and shuffle into new life, what are our grave clothes that still bind us, the things we need to forgive or be released from? Who are the people Jesus tells to release us, or whom we need to forgive?

Prayer

Lord Jesus, when I am dead in sin and darkness call me to come out, unbind me and release me.

61

John 11:45-57

One man must die for the people

In a paradox typical of John, this chapter about giving life ends with the threat of death. In chapter 9, Jesus took the blind man out of darkness to see the light, while the religious leaders went from seeing into self-imposed darkness. Jesus then described himself in chapter 10 as the good shepherd in contrast to their bad leadership of God's people. Now all this is borne out as Jesus gives Lazarus the gift of life, but the leaders respond by plotting Jesus' death. The wonderful miracle, the 'sign' of God's glory, once again produces division. First many of 'the Jews' believed 'therefore', i.e. because of what they saw Jesus do for Lazarus (11:45). However, as with the blind man's healing, others go to tell the Pharisees (11:46; see 9:13).

Cynical scheming or true prophecy?

At this time, the Pharisees were only one group in Judaism, interested in interpreting and keeping the law. Much of the power, both political and religious, was held by the chief priests, the Sadducees, who controlled the temple sacrifices at the heart of Jewish practice and cooperated with the Roman authorities. Both groups, with their scribes and elders, belonged to the Sanhedrin, the council, which they now convene (11:47). Their concerns are immediately obvious. They accept that Jesus is doing 'many signs' which lead people to believe in him. While that alone would worry the Pharisees, the Sadducees are anxious about the possible consequences, if they 'let him go on like this' (11:48). Provided there was internal peace and stability, the Romans allowed local leaders, like the chief priests and Sadducees, to administer their own religion and home affairs. However, if there was unrest or trouble, they would intervene quickly. The leaders' concerns here reveal their true priorities. They are frightened that 'the Romans will take away our holy place and our nation' (11:48). They are not concerned about whether what Jesus says is true, or if God's glory is really with him, but with their own control. The temple of God has become 'our place' and the people of God are 'our nation'. The irony is that John began his account of Jesus' ministry with the prophecy that the temple would be destroyed and replaced with Jesus' body (2:19-21), while the good shepherd's self-sacrificial love for his sheep has exposed the leaders' treatment of God's flock as 'our nation' (10:11–14). Ultimately, their fears are realised in the destruction of Jerusalem and the temple by the Romans in AD70; with no temple and no power the Sadducees disappear, and the Pharisees are left to regroup Judaism around the law.

Caiaphas, high priest from AD18 to 36, accuses them of 'knowing nothing' (11:49) – but then, neither does he. In his political scheming, he suggests that it is 'better for you' that Jesus should die than that 'the whole nation perish' (11:50). Again, John is writing on two levels: on the surface, Caiaphas' comment is just cynical plotting, but at the spiritual level it is a true prophecy. At another time when the people of God could have become 'like sheep without a shepherd', Moses brought Joshua as his successor before the high priest Eleazar (the Hebrew for Lazarus) for God's guidance (Numbers 27:16–23). After the good shepherd has given life to another Lazarus, this high priest is unwittingly guided by God to prophesy how Jesus will lay down his life for the sheep (11:51). Nor will it be just for 'our nation'; the good shepherd cares for his 'other sheep not of this fold' (10:16) and his death will bring all the 'children of God' together into one (11:52; see 1:12). It is amazing how God can even take our cynical comments and turn them into his good purposes for the whole human race!

Hide and seek

Now, therefore, the leaders' plans for Jesus' death takes the gospel into its final stages (11:53). Jesus can no longer go around 'openly', 'plainly', as John uses *parresia* again (see 7:4; 10:24; 11:14). He withdraws briefly to Ephraim (11:54), a small town about 12 miles north of Jerusalem, near Bethel (2 Samuel 13:23; 2 Chronicles 13:19). But soon the third Passover comes and everyone goes up to Jerusalem (11:55; see 2:13; 6:4). As with previous feasts, such as Tabernacles (7:11), the crowd debate about Jesus: 'Surely he will not come to the feast, will he?' (11:56). And as they debate, so the two groups of religious leaders, the chief priests and the Pharisees, are planning his arrest (11:57).

Prayer

Lord God, thank you that you can speak through our cynicism and turn even our scheming to your purpose; grant that we may seek the good not just of 'our place' and nation, but of all your people.

62 John 12:1–8

Anointing at Bethany

The Passover is at hand, and people come to Jerusalem to prepare (11:55). Six days before the feast, Jesus also arrives, for dinner back at Bethany, now identified as 'the home of Lazarus'. 'Six days' implies that this is Saturday evening, the end of the sabbath at the start of this holy week leading to Passover, a week which will be Jesus' last. That hint of death is confirmed as John reminds us that Lazarus was the one 'whom Jesus had raised from the dead' (12:1). Jesus, the giver of life to those in the tomb, is setting out on the journey to his own death and burial.

At the end of this week, his crucified body will be anointed (19:39). To balance that event, it begins with a story of Jesus being anointed. Mark 14:3–9 and Matthew 26:6–13 describe Jesus being anointed on his head in Bethany two days before Passover at the house of Simon the leper by an unnamed woman; in Luke 7:36–38, he is anointed on his feet earlier in Galilee in the house of Simon the Pharisee by a sinful woman who wipes his feet with her hair. Whether these accounts describe two different events, or two versions of the same anointing, John's story has elements from both, while at the same time setting the scene beautifully for his account of the Passion.

Extravagance and fragrance

The story begins with dinner (12:2). Lazarus reclines at table with Jesus; the conversation between the one who had come out of the tomb and the other on his way to the tomb must have been interesting! Meanwhile, Martha is active, serving once more, while Mary again heads for Jesus' feet which she had clasped outside her brother's tomb; in both cases, they reflect the story in Luke 10:38–42 (see on 11:20 and 32 above).

Mary has 'a pound of costly perfume of pure nard' (12:3). The word 'pure', *pistikos*, occurs only here and may be connected with *pisteuo*, to believe or have faith, which has recurred throughout recent chapters; if so, it means 'faithful' or 'genuine' in quality, reflecting Mary's genuine faith and love for Jesus. Nard is an oil derived from the root and spike of the nard plant, and the best examples were imported from as far east as India, hence its extreme expense. A 'pound' is an extraordinarily extravagant amount, recalling the vast quantity of wine created in Jesus' first sign at another dinner party (2:6). Yet she pours all this ointment, not on Jesus' *head*, where people wore perfume and kings were anointed, but on his *feet*, where the preparation of a corpse for burial would start. No wonder the whole 'house was filled with the fragrance'. Finally, she undoes her hair to wipe his feet. Jewish women kept their hair tied up in public and only let it loose when undressing for a husband or as a sign of distraction in mourning. Mary would have had her hair loose when she fell at Jesus' feet in her grief (11:32); now she does so again, in her unabashed love for him – but the hints of burial and grief are impossible to ignore.

Protests and the poor

Judas, however, has other thoughts. He protests at the waste: so much good perfume might have realised '300 denarii'; if a denarius was a worker's daily wage, this is a year's salary, even more than the cost of bread for the 5,000 (see on 6:7 above). He claims to want to give it to the poor, perhaps in the Passover almsgiving as the group's treasurer. He has already been identified as the betrayer (6:70–71) and now he is called a 'thief', because he used to 'carry' the group's purse, a euphemism for 'steal', like the English 'lift' (12:6). The 'thief comes only to steal and destroy' and is recognised by the good shepherd (10:10), who now rebukes him and protects his sheep: 'Leave her alone' (12:7). Jesus picks up the hints of the burial ritual in what Mary has done and reminds them of the death threats against him. Yes, Passover is a good time to remember that 'the poor are always with you' and obey scripture's instructions to be generous (Deuteronomy 15:11). But it is also the week when 'you will not always have me', as Jesus heads resolutely towards his own death (12:8).

For reflection and prayer

This is a good passage for meditation in prayer. Imagine the scene at the dinner party with everybody there – and join them. Where are we? Perhaps we are sitting with Jesus like Lazarus or serving with Martha; do we show our love for Jesus at his feet or complain with Judas? What does Jesus have to say to us?

63 John 12:9–19

What sort of king?

Although Mary's anointing Jesus' feet hinted at a burial, rather than anointing the head as for a king, the next scene looks like a coronation. Once again, John tells it differently from the other gospels with a particular focus on what it means to call Jesus king. In the synoptics, it is Jesus' first visit to Jerusalem, his 'entry', while John has shown him at all the major feasts there over several years. Thus he is well known and his appearances usually provoke division among the people and the leaders. The crowd has been looking for Jesus since 11:56; when they heard that he had returned to Bethany, they came out to see him, but also to see 'Lazarus, whom he had raised from the dead' (12:9). So the chief priests plot Lazarus' death as well, partly out of fear of the Romans' intervention, but also to remove this embarrassing theological evidence. As Sadducees, the priests did not believe in the resurrection, so they need to prove that Lazarus would stay dead! Lazarus' new life was causing 'many to believe in Jesus', 'deserting' them and their religious control (12:11).

Hosanna to the king of Israel

Next comes 'Palm Sunday', although only John tells us about the day and the palms. 'The next day', after the Saturday evening dinner at Bethany, is the Sunday before Passover and 'the great crowd that had come to the festival heard that Jesus was coming' (12:12). Josephus says that over two million people would come to Jerusalem for Passover each year; no wonder the priests and the Romans were anxious about crowd control! Here, John refers to a crowd within Jerusalem who go out to welcome Jesus coming in from Bethany, waving 'palm branches' and shouting 'Hosanna' (12:13). The words for 'palm' (*phoinix*) and 'branches' (*baia*) are rare, but they occur in the accounts of greeting the successful Maccabean leaders. At the rededication of the temple after Judas Maccabeus' successful revolt in 164BC, the people greeted him with 'palm branches' (*baia*, 2 Maccabees 10:7); when his brother Simon conquered Jerusalem's citadel in 142BC, the people entered it carrying 'palms' (*phoinix*, 1 Maccabees 13:51). This recalls the Feast of the Dedication and the debate about good and bad shepherds (see on

10:22). The implication that the crowd is greeting a conquering hero is unmistakable. They sing Psalm 118, with its cry of 'Hosanna', meaning 'Save us, Lord', to the conquering Messiah 'coming in the name of the Lord' (Psalm 118:25–26). After Jesus performed the messianic sign of feeding people in the wilderness, they wanted 'to make him king by force' (6:15). Now comes the coronation victory parade, and it all looks political, military and exceedingly dangerous.

In lowly pomp ride on to die

Jesus, however, has consistently refused political kingship and withdrew into the desert last time to hide from them. Now he finds, not the conqueror's mighty horse, but a young donkey, a symbol of peace and lowliness (12:14). John uses Zechariah 9:9, about a king on a donkey, but he omits Zechariah's shout of triumph 'rejoice greatly', and replaces it with 'Fear not, O Zion', a promise that God will save Jerusalem from disaster (Zephaniah 3:16). Yes, Jerusalem's king is coming, and can 'ride on, ride on in majesty' as the Palm Sunday hymn puts it. However, he comes not to conquer by military revolt, but 'in lowly pomp ride on to die'. Jerusalem need not fear disaster from the Romans, for this one man comes to die 'for the sake of the people'.

The response

This amazing drama of the people's offer of a revolutionary kingship turned into humility by Jesus provokes different responses from four groups. The 'disciples did not understand at first', but John has a flash forward to their look back after he had been 'glorified', crucified; only then did it make sense (12:16; see also 2:22). Then there are the two crowds: the crowd coming in from Bethany with Jesus continue to 'witness' to Lazarus' raising (12:17). The mob which came out of the city to greet the conquering hero react to what they heard about the sign (12:18). The Pharisees are exasperated and can only say to one another in resignation that 'all the world' has gone after him (12:19). At the surface level they just mean 'everyone', like the French *tout le monde*; but the deeper spiritual reality is that, far from a military campaign for one nation against another, the good shepherd is bringing his sheep from all the world into one flock.

Prayer

Lord Jesus, lowly and suffering king, grant that 'all the world' may renounce violence and seek your peace.

64

John 12:20-26

We want to see Jesus

John's account of Jesus welcomed into Jerusalem by the crowd showed how he rejected violent revolution for just one nation, responding with a humility which caused 'all the world' to go after him. Both universalism and humble suffering are developed further in these next sections.

Greeks come to Jesus

First, John says that among the Jerusalem crowd 'were some Greeks' (12:20). Many Greek-speaking Jews would return to Jerusalem from all over the Mediterranean for festivals, but these are usually called 'Hellenists' (e.g. Acts 6:1). Thus, these 'Greeks' are not Jews; they might be proselytes, non-Jews interested in the Jewish faith, but they may just be visitors. The Greeks were renowned for their inquisitive nature, travelling around in search of something new. At Jerusalem, they would have been allowed into the Court of the Gentiles in the temple. Here, they are part of 'the world' which has gone after Jesus (12:19), some of the 'other sheep not of this fold' who hear the good shepherd's voice (10:16). As they watch this procession welcoming Jesus, the Greeks too want to see Jesus. They find Philip, a disciple with a Greek name (meaning 'horse lover') from a mixed Greek–Jewish town, Bethsaida (see 1:43–44). Philip goes to find Andrew, from his home town with a Greek name also, and together they go to Jesus, thus repeating what happened with the little boy with the loaves and fishes (12:22; see 1:40–42; 6:5–8). If Philip and Andrew's behaviour provides a pattern for all who wish to bring others to Jesus, the Greeks' request is the classic text for all who speak, teach, preach or listen: 'We want to see Jesus' (12:21). It is so easy to be seduced by our own eloquence, but the message is more important than the messenger and the one spoken about is greater than the speaker. The Christian's task is to communicate such that people see Jesus.

The interest of Gentiles helps Jesus realise the moment has come. After his ministry in Galilee, Judea, Samaria and Jerusalem, now 'the world' is seeking him. He told his mother and the Samaritan woman that his 'hour is not yet' but 'coming' (2:4; 4:21–3), and he has often evaded capture because 'his hour had not yet come' (7:30, 8:20). But now 'the hour has come for the Son of man to be glorified' (12:23). The whole story has been leading towards this – and we might expect it to be glorious.

A grain of wheat must die

However, as he tried to show the welcoming crowd, Jesus' glory is not human triumph. He uses another 'figure' – the 'grain of wheat', reminiscent of the other gospels' seed parables. It is a simple truth that a grain of wheat must fall into earth and be buried; its external husk has to be broken open for the life within to come out. Only if it 'dies', will it bear 'much fruit' (12:24). Lazarus' death and burial is now bearing fruit as the celebrations attract the attention of the world. But supremely Jesus is talking about his own forthcoming death. It would be so easy to avoid it, to choose the path of human glory and follow the crowd to revolution. But if the seed is not placed in the earth, 'it remains alone'. If one seed reproduces itself 40-fold in the ear of corn which grows from it, and these are all replanted, and so on each year, it would only take just over six years before that one seed results in as many seeds as there are human beings on this planet – all from one seed buried in the ground. Jesus' path to glory will also put him in the ground before he can bring his fruit to his Father.

As far too many human conflicts show, those who fight to preserve their lives end up losing them. Jesus teaches that those who sacrifice their lives in this world will find eternal life (12:25). The good shepherd is on his way to lay down his life for the sheep, and those who serve him must follow him. The paradox is that in such self-denial we find that we are with Jesus, being honoured by his Father (12:26). Although this is all expressed in John's distinctive language, it is exactly the same message found at the heart of the other gospels (see Mark 8:34–35; Matthew 10:38–40; Luke 17:33). Jesus taught consistently and repeatedly that the way to life is through self sacrifice and the path of glory found only in crucifixion. The Greeks coming 'to see Jesus' means that now is the 'hour to be glorified', the time to put the words into action.

Prayer

Father God, we want to see Jesus, to lose ourselves in him that we might find ourselves in you.

65 John 12:27–36

Lifting up the Son of Man

The coming of the Greeks to see Jesus meant that the 'hour for the Son of Man to be glorified' had finally arrived. Jesus is clear that the way to glory lies only through his self-sacrificial death. No one can face imminent death without some pause. Jesus may have been the Son of God, but he was also incarnate fully as a human being, and here John gives a brief insight into Jesus' human emotions: 'Now is my soul troubled' (12:27). The word 'troubled' is *tarasso* again, as in his feelings at Lazarus' grave (11:33). Jesus' prayer reflects how the psalmist often describes his inner turmoil (e.g. Psalms 42:6; 55:4). In the other gospels, such agony in prayer happens in the Garden of Gethsemane before Jesus' arrest. John, however, has no agonised prayer at that point, when Jesus is in control and heading for his destiny. In many ways, then, this passage serves as the Gethsemane experience for John.

As in Gethsemane, Jesus' first thought is to pray for God's deliverance: 'Father, save me from this hour.' Yet after so many times when the 'hour was not yet', how can he avoid its final arrival? He has come for this hour and the whole story has led to this point (12:27). He must remain true to his purpose: 'Father, glorify your name' (12:28). His miracles have been 'signs' of God's glory, such as the water into wine, healing the blind man or raising Lazarus (2:11; 9:3; 11:4, 40), and he has refused to exchange it for 'glory from men' (5:41–44).

The voice from heaven

In response to Jesus' decision to put the glory of God ahead of his own apprehension comes 'a voice from heaven'. Not only does John not describe Gethsemane, but also he has no account of the transfiguration. He prefers to show how Jesus reflects and shares God's glory not just on one occasion, but always. Here, we get a voice from heaven as in the other gospels' accounts of the transfiguration, as God confirms that he is being glorified in Jesus. The crowd is divided as usual, as some think it is merely 'thunder', while others assume it is an 'angel' (12:29). In the *Chronicles of Narnia* by C.S. Lewis, the voice of Aslan, the great lion, seems only a terrifying roar to those who oppose him, but gentle words and strength to the children who love him. So now, Jesus says the voice is not for his benefit, but for the bystanders'; whether they understand it or not, it is a sign to them that God is with him (12:30; see also 11:42).

Cast out and lifted up

This moment is also 'the judgement of this world' (12:31). In the raising of Lazarus we saw how the future resurrection could happen now; judgement also takes place, as the end breaks into the present. John describes the devil, or Satan, as the 'ruler of this world' (see also 14:30; 16:11). It has been the 'rulers' in this world, Caiaphas, the priests and Pharisees, who have been opposing Jesus, to keep their power here and now. But behind them is the 'ruler of this world' who will now be 'cast out', suffering what the human rulers did to the blind man (12:31; cf. 9:34). However, as Satan is cast down and out, so Jesus is 'lifted up' (12:32). We have already seen the double meaning of this word, *hypsoun*, to 'exalt' and to be 'lifted up' on a cross (see on 3:14 and 8:28), and its use for death by crucifixion is now made explicit (12:33). Also, the universal implications of the 'other sheep' and the Greeks coming to Jesus are brought out; Jesus' death on the cross will be how he will draw 'all people' to himself (12:32).

The Son of Man and the light

The crowd, however, are confused by these hints of death. They are still caught up in the messianic fervour aroused by the welcoming demonstration. Scriptures like Psalm 89:29–37 or 110:4 suggest that the Christ will 'remain forever'. So what does Jesus mean about the Son of Man being 'lifted up' (12:34)? Jesus gives to them the same response as to the disciples about the blind man and Lazarus, to 'walk while you have the light' (12:35; see 9:4–5; 11:9–10). Light and darkness have been key words since 3:19–21, but now Jesus' warning of judgement is more urgent: 'the light' is with them for only 'a little longer' (12:35). The hour has come and time is short for them to become 'children of light'. They must believe while they still have the light, and with this saying he departs from the crowd for the very last time (12:36).

Prayer

Father, glorify your name and draw me to your Son lifted up on the cross to make us all the children of light.

66 John 12:36–43
Belief, blindness and fear

We have suggested that John's gospel is a two-act drama, with this section as an interlude (see on 1:19 and 11:1 above). The central actor, Jesus, is working very hard! He was not merely on stage for most of Act One, but at the centre of the action. A couple of times he disappeared briefly into the wings while the other characters discussed what to do about him, as in the story of the blind man (Jesus offstage from 9:7 to 9:35). Now this final dialogue with the people in Jerusalem after their procession of welcome has brought the interlude almost to an end. Warning that they will only have the light for 'a little while longer', Jesus left the stage and 'hid from them' (12:35–36). He will not appear in public again until the crucifixion. The light is temporarily eclipsed.

The evangelist, as narrator, turns to address his audience directly for the first time since the prologue. Here, he reflects on what has happened, and tries to understand and explain it. Throughout the first act, Jesus has done seven great 'signs', discussing their significance with the people and the authorities. The problem is that so many still do not believe in him (12:37).

Blind eyes and hard hearts

The early Christians found it difficult to understand why the people of God did not believe the one God sent to them. It was not a new problem. Even Moses, with whom Jesus is often compared in this gospel, experienced something similar and complained that although the people saw 'signs and great wonders', they did not understand, see or hear, despite having minds, eyes and ears (Deuteronomy 29:2–4). John has wrestled with this since the prologue, when he warned us that, although Jesus came to his own people, they did not receive him (1:10–12). Now he quotes from one of Isaiah's poems about the servant of God, which had such an influence on the early church's thinking about Jesus. This fourth 'servant song' describes how the servant is 'despised and rejected... wounded for our transgressions' and how he bore the sin of all who 'like sheep have gone astray' (Isaiah 52:13—53:12). John quotes from the start of this song (Isaiah 53:1) to show that no one has 'believed our message', despite 'the arm of the Lord being revealed' (12:38).

Having noted the fact of unbelief in Isaiah, the evangelist looks at its start for an explanation. In his vision of the glory of God in the temple in the 'year King Uzziah died', Isaiah describes how he responded to God's call to go to his people. Like Moses, however, he had to realise that people's eyes could be so blinded that they could not see and their hearts so hard that they would not understand (Isaiah 6:10). In their attempt to understand why the people of God could not see what God was doing in Jesus, the early Christians recognised their experience in Isaiah's words. So now John quotes this verse here to explain why Jesus has not been accepted (12:40). This verse is similarly used to explain people's blindness in the other gospels (Matthew 13:13–5; Mark 4:12; Luke 8:10) and to conclude the book of Acts (28:26–27).

The glory of God or human praise?

Neither John, nor Isaiah, endorses a naked determinism where human beings have no choice but are condemned in advance not to believe. This is seen in John's earlier idea of 'none so blind as those who will not see' after the opening of the blind man's eyes was met with disbelief from the Pharisees, who thought they could see (9:39–41). The blind man's parents were afraid of being put 'out of the synagogue', and now John suggests that the same fear holds back even those leaders who believed (12:42; see on 9:22 above). He has already shown that one of them, Nicodemus, having come to Jesus first 'by night', has begun to travel to the light (3:1; 7:50) and he will be joined by at least one other, Joseph of Arimathea (19:38–39). But the others, says John, are held back by the fear of what people might say or think. Isaiah's vision in the temple of the glory of God included seeing Jesus' glory as well (12:41), but these leaders prefer the glory which comes from other human beings to the glory of God (12:43; see also 5:44). We cannot come to the new life when still wrapped up in our old ways. Like Lazarus shuffling out of the tomb, we need to be set free from all that binds us and holds us back. For many of us, says John, fear of what others might say or do blinds our eyes, hardens our hearts and keeps us trapped in death.

Prayer

Lord, open our eyes and melt our hardened hearts that we may behold your glory and reveal you to others.

67 John 12:44–50
Light sent to save the world

The 'hour' has arrived. Jesus has been anointed for burial and welcomed with great rejoicing. He refused the path of violent revolution, but stressed instead that he will be glorified through a self-sacrificial death for everyone, including non-Jews. While his soul may be troubled, he has been strengthened by the voice from heaven and he has made his exit from public view. As the stage cleared, the narrator addressed the audience about the inability of God's people to see what he is doing. Everything is ready for Act Two, when suddenly we have this short section of Jesus' teaching. John provides no setting for it; it stands free and independent. Some scholars provide a context by moving it elsewhere in the gospel. Yet, curiously, it fits well here, even without any context. It summarises the key themes of Jesus' teaching and prepares us for the next act. It is introduced simply by 'Jesus cried out in a loud voice' (12:44). Using our image of the theatre, it is like a reprise of the main melodies from the first half before the curtain goes up for Act Two.

The one who sent me

The first melody is 'the one who sent me'. For John, God is the God who sends. The gospel begins with 'a man sent from God', John the Baptist (1:6). However, he is only the one who has been 'sent ahead' (3:28). Now Jesus declares that 'whoever believes in me, believes not in me, but in him who sent me' (12:44). Whoever sees Jesus, sees 'him who sent me' (12:45). Jesus calls God 'the one who sent me' over 30 times in John. His awareness of being sent by God is the heart of all he says and does. It is, literally, meat and drink to him as he explained after talking to the Samaritan woman: 'My food is to do the will of him who sent me' (4:34). As the bread of life, he has come down from heaven 'to do the will of him who sent me' (6:38). His teaching at the Feast of Tabernacles is not his own 'but his who sent me' (7:16). His concern for the blind man was to 'work the works of him who sent me' (9:4), and he prayed that the raising of Lazarus would enable the crowd to 'believe that you sent me' (11:42). John ended his prologue before Act One with 'no one has ever seen God' (1:18); in this reprise before Act Two he declares that to have seen Jesus is to have seen the God who sent him (12:45).

Light and judgement

The second theme is now introduced. Jesus, whom God has sent, has come 'as light into the world' (12:46). The prologue called Jesus 'the light of men, shining in the darkness' (1:4–5). At the Feast of Tabernacles, with its light ceremonies, Jesus proclaimed, 'I am the light of the world' (8:12), which he demonstrated by healing the blind man (9:5–7) and raising Lazarus (11:9–11). No one need remain in darkness, for Jesus came not to condemn the world, but to save it (12:47). This is a reprise of the marvellous passage after Nicodemus came to Jesus 'by night' and learned that God so loved the world that he sent his only Son (3:16–17). But the coming of light into darkness creates shadows, and 'this is the judgement, that the light has come into the world and people loved darkness rather than light' (3:19). Over the intervening chapters, Jesus' opponents moved more and more into darkness by refusing to accept his light (e.g. 9:40–41). He came to save, but his coming brings judgement even now for those who reject him, a judgement which will be confirmed on the last day (12:48).

The Father and the Son

The third motif in this recapitulation is the relationship of the Father and the Son. Jesus has consistently insisted that 'I can do nothing on my own' but only the will of his Father who sent him (5:30). His stress on his relationship with God as his Father was even more unacceptable to his opponents than his healing on the sabbath, and made them want to kill him (5:18). All the debates about Jesus' identity and origins in chapters 5—8 centred around this claim, building to a climax with 'the Father and I are one' (10:30). Now he declares that all this teaching has not been his own, but what the Father commanded him 'to say and speak', and this alone brings eternal life (12:49–50).

Thus in these few verses, John reminds us of the key themes throughout the first half, that God the Father sent Jesus as light to save the world. The reprise dies away, the audience are quiet and the curtain is ready to rise on the second half.

Prayer

O God our Father, thank you that you sent your Son as light to save the world; open our eyes that we may do your will.

68 John 13:1–11

Jesus washes the disciples' feet

The curtain rises on Act Two of John's drama, yet slowly. Now that the 'hour' has finally come, time slows down. Act One and the interlude (chs. 1—12) have taken over two years, with two previous Passovers (2:13; 6:4). Act Two (chs. 13—19) covers just 24 hours: John is making a meal of it – literally! The dinner lasts until Jesus' arrest, so it is the last supper on Thursday night before the crucifixion. The other gospels imply that it was a Passover meal, but 18:28 suggests Passover is not eaten until the next day. John portrays it like an ancient dinner party or *symposium* (literally 'drinking together'), where people discussed ideas over food and drink, which gives us 'symposium' to mean an academic gathering for debate.

Jesus, knowing that the hour has finally come, gathers 'his own' to show them the 'full extent of his love' (13:1). Jesus came to 'his own', but 'his own did not receive him' (1:11); the good shepherd, however, knows 'his own' sheep, and calls 'his own' out of the fold (10:3–4). Now that Jesus has been rejected by 'the Jews', he calls 'his own' out to nourish them for the difficulties ahead. Not only will their shepherd return to his Father, but 'the thief' who comes to destroy is a disciple, Judas Iscariot (13:1–2; see 10:10; 12:6). Unlike the unwitting disciples, the author and his readers know what will happen and we have several warnings of the devil inspiring Judas' betrayal, like a funeral bell tolling somewhere in the background.

The servant

The start of the Passion narrative, when Jesus 'suffers' (the meaning of 'passion'), has nothing 'passive' about it. Jesus knows everything, including his origins and destiny, that 'he had come from God and was going to God' (13:3). Jesus' knowledge has been stressed (e.g. 1:48; 2:24–25; 6:6; 8:14) and, secure in that knowledge, he can undertake what the insecure disciples would not. He rises from table and 'lays down his clothes', like the good shepherd 'laying down his life' (10:11–18). With those clothes, he lays down his dignity and takes up the role of the servant (13:4). Walking in open sandals on unsurfaced roads, dusty or muddy in wet weather, made everyone's feet dirty. Water would always be provided for new arrivals to wash their feet, and, if you were lucky, a servant to do it. However, so menial a task could not be required of a Jewish male servant, only from women, children or non-Jews. On special occasions, it might be done as a sign of great love and respect to a superior, such as a disciple for his rabbi, or a wife for her husband. But in Jesus, the usual order is reversed. Jesus does for us what none of us are prepared to do for each other. Like someone nursing a dying spouse for whom even the most menial tasks are an act of love, so Jesus takes the water basin and the towel and starts to wash the disciples' feet (13:5).

Washing Peter

Jesus comes to Peter, who is flabbergasted and splutters a protest all out of order in the Greek, 'Lord, you – my – wash – feet?' (13:6). It is bad enough to be shown up for not having done the menial task – but ten times worse if your master does it for you! Often we hold back because we are too proud to let Jesus do something for us. It is all right for us to serve God, but to let him serve us costs our total surrender; sometimes we can only understand it later, as Jesus tells Peter (13:7). With his characteristic bluntness Peter refuses ever to let Jesus do this lowly task (13:8). Jesus gently explains that this is necessary if Peter is to have any 'share' in him. Impetuous as ever, the old 'Simon' comes out and wants the total experience – feet, hands and head (13:9)! Simon has always been 'all or nothing'. Jesus reminds him that people bathe all over before leaving home, and just need their feet washing from walking (13:10). Both ancient and modern commentators see hints of baptism here. Through baptism, we are 'made clean' and given a 'share' in the body of Christ. Walking in the world, we all get dirty feet through sin, but we cannot be re-baptised over and over again; we need simply to let Jesus cleanse us and forgive us, and let him feed us at his table. But some will accept Christ's loving ministrations while still plotting against him. Jesus would have washed even Judas' feet, despite knowing that he would soon betray him – and we hear another clang from the funeral bell (13:11).

Prayer

Lord Jesus, servant king, thank you that you laid down so much for me; give me grace to lay aside my pride and let you make me clean.

69 John 13:12–20

I have given you an example

Jesus has washed the disciples' feet and returned to the table (13:12). From our experience of church services and the other gospels we expect the institution of the Holy Communion next – but it is completely missing. Instead, Jesus explains things to his disciples and continues through the long discourse of chapters 14—17. Some argue from this curious absence that John was not interested in Communion or even opposed sacraments altogether. However, we noted that John used the '*eucharist-*' word when Jesus 'gave thanks' over the loaves and fishes (see on 6:11) and that the discourse which followed talked of eating his flesh and drinking his blood (see on 6:51–59). Not only does chapter 6 look forward to the last supper, but this section has several links back to chapter 6. So John could not have been uninterested in Communion and its omission here is even stranger.

One answer may be that John assumed that his audience already knew about the institution of the Communion, so he took it for granted. If the gospel was originally read aloud at Communion services, the account of its institution would be heard later, so was not needed here. However, his audience may not have known the other gospels, and the gospel would have been read on other occasions. Another possibility involves the practice of keeping 'holy knowledge' secret from the uninitiated. In the early church, people who were not baptised left after the readings and sermon, before the Communion; there was even speculation outside the church about what exactly happened at the Eucharist. Thus, the Communion seems absent on the surface level of John, but for those 'in the know' who look deeper, there are hints and allusions everywhere. Whatever the reason, here the foot washing is followed by a typical 'farewell speech', looking ahead to what will happen when the speaker has gone, with hopes for the future, warnings about betrayals or fighting, and prayer for the disciples' success without their leader (see the farewells of Jacob in Genesis 49; Moses, Deuteronomy 31; Joshua, Joshua 23—24; David, 1 Kings 2).

The master's humility

As earlier 'signs' led into dialogues to explain them, so now Jesus moves from the sign of foot washing to ask his disciples if they understand what he has done (13:12). He is their master: they came to him first as a teacher but then realised that he is also their Lord, and Jesus does not refuse those titles (13:13). What he does reject is the 'pecking order', equally beloved of chickens and human beings! If our Lord and master treats his followers like this, we cannot stand on our dignity, but must treat each other similarly (13:14). He challenges all human systems of management, control and hierarchy. The religious leaders have proudly expected service and obedience in this gospel (1:22; 7:47–49; 8:33, 39; 9:34). But Jesus, the humble good shepherd of the people has been out seeking the shunned Samaritan woman, the abandoned paralysed man or the rejected blind man. The foot washing is not just a symbolic action, but a way of life which Jesus' example expects us to follow (13:15). We may act this out at a Maundy Thursday service, but such humble service must characterise all Christians' lives, doing good and helping others (see 1 Timothy 5:10).

Masters, servants and messengers

If Jesus is our 'lord and teacher', his servants cannot act as if we are greater than our master. Equally, messengers, those who run errands, are not greater than 'the one who sent' them (13:16). 'The one who sent' reflects Jesus' understanding of God as 'the one who sent' him, while the word for 'messengers' in Greek is *apostles*, those who are sent. 'Apostles' are not 'top of the Christian tree'; they, and we, are just God's messengers – and when we really understand this and are set free from jockeying for position, then we are truly blessed (13:17). Of course, there will always be at least one person who wants to play it differently, and so we hear another clang from the funeral bell, as Jesus looks ahead to Judas' betrayal (13:18). What is worse, he is one who 'ate my bread', quoting Psalm 41:9, which uses the same word, *trogo*, to 'munch' Jesus' flesh, as in the bread discourse (see on 6:55). That discourse also ended with Jesus' knowledge about his betrayer (6:70–71), so now he gives them another warning (13:19). Finally, the apostles, 'messengers', are told that people who receive those he sends, not only receive Jesus himself, but also God his Father, 'who sent me' (13:20, see 5:23; 12:44).

Prayer

Lord Jesus, thank you for feeding me and washing my feet, give me courage to follow your example.

70 John 13:21–30

Beloved or betrayer?

After Jesus has explained the footwashing as an example of humility, the hints of 'eating the bread' and knowing the betrayer cause him to be 'troubled in spirit' (13:21). This is *tarasso* again; so far, Jesus has been 'troubled' by the death of Lazarus and by the prospect of his own death (see 11:33; 12:27 above). Now, however, the constant tolling of the bell through the supper has become too much to ignore, so he explains the previous allusions: 'One of you will betray me' (see 13:2, 10–11, 18). Despite the hints, the disciples are shocked, looking at each other uncertainly and wondering.

The disciple Jesus loved

Before we come to Judas, John draws our attention to the person reclining at dinner next to Jesus (13:23). He identifies him as 'the disciple Jesus loved', lying 'close to Jesus' bosom', as he earlier told us that Jesus was in 'the bosom of the Father' (1:18). Being next to Jesus might suggest that he is the host, the owner of the house, who has invited Jesus to hold his meal here; but he is clearly personally close to him also, a 'bosom friend' – yet he is unnamed. This 'beloved disciple', as he is usually called, is also entrusted with Jesus' mother at the cross (19:26–27); outruns Peter to the empty tomb (20:2–8) and recognises the risen Jesus on the shore (21:7). He may also be the 'other disciple' who knows the High Priest and gets Peter into his house (18:15–17). The description 'whom Jesus loved' reminds us of Lazarus (11:3, 36), but since he has already been named, he cannot be this anonymous disciple. The gospel concludes that he has been the authority, if not the author, behind the story (21:20–24). This clue has traditionally identified him with John son of Zebedee, who was in the boat at Jesus' final appearance (21:2) and so John is thought to be the founder of the church behind this gospel. While that is the most likely identification, we must take seriously the anonymity of the beloved disciple. He is like an 'ideal' disciple, close to Jesus and staying loyal, even outdoing Peter, who now asks him to find out who the traitor is (13:24). Given the author's liking for levels of meaning, whoever he was at the physical level, we are all invited to become disciples 'whom Jesus loved' and to stay close to him.

Judas goes into darkness

To answer Peter's enquiry, the beloved disciple 'leans back' to ask Jesus, 'Lord, who is it?' (13:25). Jesus identifies the traitor as the one to whom he will give some bread which he has dipped in the sauce on the dish (13:26). This is a mark of respect, used by Boaz to invite Ruth to his meal (Ruth 2:14). It would be easy to do if Judas, perhaps in his capacity as the group's treasurer, were sitting in the other place of honour, on Jesus' left. Yet the left side is also where the good shepherd will put the goats and the lost at the end, according to Matthew's parable (Matthew 25:33, 41). So it is here also, for after Judas has received the bread from Jesus, 'the Satan', the deceiver who inspired the betrayal (13:2), 'entered into him' (13:27). This does not absolve Judas of responsibility. At the human level, there have been several appeals to him during this meal, the tolling of our symbolic bell. But now the inner conflict of considering betrayal while letting Jesus wash his feet and feed him, proves too much for Judas, who has a spiritual breakdown. Similarly, those who are washed in the waters of baptism and fed with the bread of the Eucharist cannot plan to betray Jesus without being in grave danger of spiritual darkness.

Recognising what has finally happened, Jesus tells him to do it quickly. Once again, John writes on two levels: the others at the table misunderstand why Judas is leaving and assume he is going out as their treasurer for supplies or to undertake the Passover almsgiving, after his protest about Mary's ointment (13:28–29; see 12:4–6). This may have been the surface appearance, but the spiritual level is tersely described: having received the bread, he went out – 'and it was night' (13:30). The hour of darkness, which Jesus has warned about when people stumble (9:4; 11:10), has finally arrived. Nicodemus came to Jesus 'by night', but he has gradually journeyed out of the darkness (3:2; 7:50). Judas, however, despite having been chosen to sit with 'the light of the world', is going the other way. 'And this is the judgement, that the light has come into the world, and people loved darkness rather than light because their deeds were evil' (3:19).

Prayer

Lord Jesus, lover of all your disciples, grant that I may be fed by you and give me the courage never to betray you.

71

John 13:31—38

Love one another

When Judas has 'gone out' to begin the events leading to Jesus' arrest and death, Jesus starts talking to his disciples. This introduces several themes which will recur through the farewell discourse of chapters 14—17. There is no clear structure, but the themes are mixed together, returning and repeating as the conversation progresses. It is more like a symphony, weaving several motifs together than a logical sequence. As often in John, we have misunderstandings and levels of meaning which develop what he is saying. So it is better understood through prayerful meditation than by analysis. As it progresses, several parts of a farewell speech emerge again (see on 13:12). However, the main point is crystal clear: Jesus is going away and he wants to comfort and prepare the disciples, warning them and reassuring them that everything will be all right in the plan of God.

Judas has gone out and it is now 'night', but the hour of darkness is also the hour of glorification. Jesus begins with how he and God are glorified in each other (13:31). Jesus' signs and words have revealed God's glory (1:14; 8:54; 11:4, 40). John has used 'to be glorified' to refer to Jesus' passion and his return through death to his Father (see 7:39; 12:16, 23). So if God has been glorified like this in Jesus, then, in response, Jesus will be glorified in God himself (13:32). Jesus knows that his departure and death will be a great shock to his disciples, but stresses right at the start that he is on his way to glory. This motif will be developed further in his prayer at the end of the discourse in chapter 17. After this reminder of glory, Jesus breaks the news gently to his 'little children'; this is a farewell speech because 'I will be with you only a little longer' (13:33). They will look for him, but as he told 'the Jews', now he tells the disciples that they cannot come with him (see 7:33–34). 'The Jews' did not understand what he meant (7:35–36; 8:21–22), nor will the disciples, so this theme will also reappear later.

A new commandment

If the first two themes reveal that Jesus' way to glory involves going away, then, third, the disciples need a new way of living without him physically present, to love each other 'as I have loved you' (13:34). The chapter began with Jesus loving his disciples 'to the end' and demonstrating this by washing their feet (13:1-5). In one sense, this is not 'a new commandment' at all. The heart of the Jewish law is to 'love your neighbour as yourself' (Leviticus 19:18) and it forms part of most moral codes. On the other hand, it is also a universal human experience that it is not so easy to put into practice, such is our selfishness. What is 'new' is that Jesus gives us a new motive and power. We do not love others simply to fulfil an ethical demand, but in response to Jesus, 'as I have loved you'. 'God so loved the world that he gave his only Son', and he loved the disciples to the extreme of washing their feet and going to die for them. Such extreme love is the mark of the Christian life, by which others will know 'you are my disciples' (13:35). In the centuries of poverty and persecution which followed, this was one characteristic which the world could not ignore: 'See how these Christians love one another', says Tertullian (*Apology* 39.7). Today, when we truly follow Jesus' example, people say the same. Unfortunately, these words are all too often hurled as a sarcastic taunt at churches when we fight among ourselves! It all depends on whether we keep the new commandment, which Jesus introduces here and which will be replayed in the next chapters.

Death or denial?

The three themes of the symphony have been introduced but Peter is still trying to grasp the basic point: what is Jesus talking about? 'Lord, where are you going?' (13:36). Jesus gently repeats that Peter cannot come with him now; Jesus' hour has come, but not Peter's yet. A second-century story (turned into a Hollywood epic) describes how Peter, fleeing Rome to avoid being killed, meets Jesus going towards the city. Peter repeats his question, 'Lord, where are you going?' – *Quo vadis?* in Latin. Jesus' reply, that he is going to Rome to die for Peter, makes the apostle turn around and face his own martyrdom. The impetuous Peter, as at the foot washing, wants to go the whole way now, to do the same as the good shepherd and lay down his life (13:37). Jesus' answer shows how little Peter is really ready to die; before cock crow he will have denied his master three times (13:38).

Prayer

Thank you, Jesus, for loving us even to the extremes of the cross; grant that I may love others and so come to be with you.

72 John 14:1–7
I am the way, the truth and the life

People often start reading the farewell discourse here, but this section runs straight on from chapter 13. Starting here misses those opening themes about glory and loving each other, because Jesus is going away. Peter wanted to know where he is going and the disciples began to panic. Jesus rebuked Peter and warned him of his denial, so they are bound to be troubled and upset. As Jesus reassures them, there is a crucial change in the verbs. He began speaking to them all as 'you-plural' with 'little children' (13:33), but dropped into 'you-singular', thee/thou, when talking to Peter alone. Now Jesus returns to 'you-plurals' to address all the disciples, and most modern translations (unlike the AV) have 'your hearts' here to make the point (14:1). There is a constant temptation to apply all these wonderful promises of the farewell discourse to an individual believer's relationship with Jesus. However, remembering that the promises are to 'you-plural' enables us to appreciate better the corporate nature of our life together in Christ.

In my father's house

Jesus looks at the worried faces around the table, wondering what all this talk of going away means, and moves to comfort them: 'Let not your hearts be troubled' (14:1). Again the word is *tarasso*, recalling Jesus being troubled at Lazarus' grave and his feelings about his own death (11:33; 12:27; 13:21). Thus it is appropriate to use this passage at funerals. We comfort each other in bereavement as Jesus comforted his disciples, that there is hope in death because of Jesus' own death for us. Therefore he tells us to 'believe in God, believe also in me'. Both verbs could also be translated as statements, 'You believe', but the sense is clear: we can comfort our troubled hearts through our belief in God and so believe and trust in Jesus also.

Then comes the much-loved image of 'many mansions in my Father's house' (14:2). The word, *monai*, comes from the verb *meno*, to abide or remain, which occurs often here. So it means 'abiding-places', rooms to stay in a travel lodge, stopping places on our way to God. Its Latin equivalent is *mansio*, giving us the English 'mansions'. Jesus is going to 'prepare a place for you-all (plural)'; the word 'place', *topos*, was used by the priests for 'our place', the temple (11:48). Through Jesus, his disciples find rest and a place in the eternal worship of God. This is why he will 'come again' for us, 'that where I am, you may be also' (14:3). Does this 'coming again' mean when he returns to them after the resurrection, after each Christian's death or his final coming at the end of time? Since they all bring us to be with Jesus, probably all are included. He has made it clear that the 'way to the place where he is going' is through his glorification on the cross (14:4, see 12:23, 32–33; 13:31).

The way to the Father

Again, Thomas misunderstands, thinking at the earthly level. When Jesus was going into Judea to wake Lazarus, Thomas morosely went to 'die with him' (11:16). Again, he has not realised what Jesus means, and does not know the way to this wonderful place (14:5). Jesus replies that we do not have to *go* anywhere – we have to be with him: 'I am the way, the truth and the life' (14:6). As with the other 'I am' sayings, these are all key Jewish terms which Jesus is claiming to fulfil. To be the 'way' is similar to 'I am the door' (10:7–9), while the 'truth' is what Jesus has been talking about throughout the gospel. All the other 'I am' sayings involve 'life', 'bread of life', 'resurrection and life' and so forth. Now they all come together. As the Jewish law and scriptures brought people to God, now Jesus is claiming to be the way to the Father, where all truth and life is to be found.

The exclusive claim of 'No one comes to the Father except through me' (14:6) is much debated. What does this mean for people of other faiths? Certainly, no other religious teacher claimed actually to *be* the way, the truth and the life, but rather to have pointed people *to* the way, the truth and the life of God. Only one who has come from God, from the infinite, can become the bridge whereby finite human beings come to God. Whenever anyone, of whatever belief, finds truth and life in God they come through the way of Jesus, whether they realise it or not. But those who do know it and know Jesus as the way, do not just find God, but they know him as Jesus reveals him, as our Father: 'If you (plural) know me, you will know my Father also' (14:7).

Prayer

Lord Jesus, grant me to walk in your way, to know your truth and to experience the life you share with your Father.

73

John 14:8–14

Show us the Father

Thomas misunderstood Jesus' claim to be 'the way, the truth and the life' as a physical way to God. Jesus took him deeper into the spiritual relationship between himself and his Father, so that to know Jesus is to know the Father (14:6–7). Now Philip responds superficially. One of the first disciples, he brought others like Nathanael and the Greeks to Jesus (1:43–48; 12:21–22). He tends to look at the physical level, as in his pessimism that feeding the 5,000 would cost over half a year's wages (6:5–7). To such a literal thinker, Jesus' comment that 'you know and have seen the Father' (14:7) would seem odd. If only Jesus would 'show us the Father', then we would all be satisfied and life would be clearer (14:8).

Seeing God in Jesus

The desire to see God is a basic religious instinct. Moses, the 'friend of God', asked to see his glory, but had to be content with a view of his back (Exodus 33:18–23). The psalmist longs to behold the face of God (e.g. Psalms 13:1; 27:8; 42:1–2). However, as John's prologue put it, 'No one has ever seen God' (1:18). Philip's request is so simple, yet so profound – but it also reveals how little he has understood what he has seen. There is resigned sadness in Jesus' reply that even one of the first he called still does not see, as he addresses Philip directly: 'Have I been with you-all [plural] so long, Philip, and yet you [singular] still do not know me?' (14:9). 'How can *you* say...' and 'Do *you* not believe?' continue as you-singular. It is incredible that Philip, who brought others to Jesus, can still talk like this and not realise that 'whoever has seen me has seen the Father... I am in the Father and the Father is in me' (14:9–10). John depicts the incarnation as the Father 'dwelling' or 'abiding' in Jesus (using *meno*, the word which gave us 'dwelling places', 14:2). To see Jesus heal the paralysed and blind men and to raise Lazarus was to see God at work; to watch Jesus turn water into wine and feed the crowd was to marvel at the abundance of God; to hear Jesus speak was to see God pleading with his people. So Jesus changes back to the you-plural and appeals to them all: 'Believe me that I am in the Father and the Father is in me' (14:11). And if that is too hard, they should believe 'because of the works themselves', not because they are magic but because they are 'signs' that Jesus has come 'from God' (see 3:2; 9:33; 10:37–38).

Greater works

In farewell speeches, the person about to leave looks ahead to what will happen when they have gone. So now Jesus lifts his horizon beyond Philip's lack of insight to describe what those 'who believe in me' will do in the future. They will not only 'do the works that I do', but also do 'greater works' (14:12). What does this promise of 'greater works', also mentioned earlier (5:20), mean? The early church did many miracles, as is seen in Acts and the lists of spiritual gifts (e.g. 1 Corinthians 12:7–10). All our great spiritual reawakenings, from founding the monasteries to Wesley and beyond, have been accompanied by such 'works'. In recent years, a renewed expectation that God is active through his Holy Spirit has brought a resurgence of belief in miracles, and some people seek to do the 'greater works' than Jesus. Whenever someone is healed or prayers are answered and God is glorified, we should rejoice, but this verse does not mean that we should 'outperform' Jesus.

The 'greater works' are 'because I am going to the Father', and from his Father he poured out his Holy Spirit to send the church out in mission. In the incarnation, Jesus was limited by his human form; he could only travel within one locality and touch so many people. Since his return to the Father, he has sent his disciples across the whole world, to touch and heal millions. These are the prayers he longs to answer when we 'ask in my name' (14:13). The 'whatever' and the 'anything' (14:13–14) are sometimes understood that all our prayers can answered. Yet they have to be 'in my name'. This is not a magic formula, tacked on to the end of any outrageous request. Jesus could do nothing 'on my own' but only because the Father was dwelling in him (14:10). Similarly, we pray in his name only when we so dwell in Jesus that through the answer to our prayers, 'the Father may be glorified in the Son' (14:13). Then not only will we, and Philip, see the Father, but so will all the world, and 'be satisfied'.

Prayer

Christ has no hands but our hands to do his work today. He has no feet but our feet to lead men in his way.
Annie Johnson Flint (1866–1932)

74 John 14:15–21

The promise of the Spirit

Jesus continues to reassure his disciples as several farewell themes are woven together in this next section. He reinforces the main point that he is going away, and yet will still be with them; this leads into a discussion of the relationship of the Father and the Son, which picks up Philip's question about 'seeing the Father'. Because of the love of the Father and the Son, not only will we see God, but he will dwell with us. This is all made possible through the coming of the Holy Spirit, a new theme introduced here and repeated and developed in the coming sections.

First, Jesus moves from talking about granting the believers' prayers to how we keep his commandments (14:15). The word for 'keep' could be a future tense – 'If you love me, you will keep my commandments' – so that obedience flows naturally out of our love for him. Alternatively, it may be a command – 'If you love me, keep' – so that we show our love by striving to obey him. Either way, the connection of loving Jesus and doing what he says is clear.

Another helper

As a result of this, Jesus says that he will ask the Father to give us 'another *paraclete*' (14:16). This is the first use of an important term in these discourses. The Greek word, *paraclete*, means 'someone called alongside' to help or assist. Its direct translation into Latin gives us the word 'advocate'. It is often used in the law courts to mean someone who is 'called in' to speak for someone on trial, either as their defending counsel or to intercede with the judge on their behalf. Thus two possible English translations are 'counsellor' or 'intercessor', both of which can be found in some Bibles. The second idea of interceding can be seen in 1 John 2:1, where Jesus is our 'advocate (*paraclete*) with the Father'. Another much-loved translation is 'comforter'. This gives us the image of someone 'called in' to console someone in need or grief, as the disciples are here; but the original meaning of 'comfort' through the Latin is to give strength or courage. The Bayeux tapestry has 'Bishop Odo comforteth his men', where the good bishop is encouraging them by prodding them with a spear from behind! Thus the Paraclete is our counsellor, advocate, intercessor, comforter, strengthener – an all-round helper.

He is further identified as 'another *paraclete*', where the word 'another', *allos* in Greek, is another of the same sort, like the last one, rather than 'another, different one'. Since everything said about the Paraclete is also said of Jesus elsewhere in this gospel, he is 'another Jesus' to be with the disciples as Jesus goes away. Then he is finally identified as 'the Spirit of truth' (14:17). This description of the Holy Spirit as both Paraclete and Spirit of truth will be developed later (14:26; 15:26; 16:7; 16:13). At this point, Jesus stresses that the Spirit is coming for the disciples, to replace Jesus when he is taken from them. The 'world cannot receive' him; that which is opposed to God cannot recognise him, cannot see or know him. But if we know him, we will find that he 'abides' in us, using the word, *meno*, to dwell, linking us back to the 'many abodes' of 14:2.

I will come to you

Jesus will be with those first disciples and all who love and keep his commandments through the Holy Spirit, the Paraclete. Thus he can give us the marvellous promise 'I will not leave you desolate; I am coming to you' (14:18). The word here is literally 'orphans' and was used of children without parents or of pupils without a master, such as the followers of Socrates when he was executed. Again we note that, while this promise is to each individual Christian, the 'you' is still plural. It is in our relationship all together that we find Jesus coming to us. In 'a little while', the world will see him no longer; but we will see him: 'Because I live, you also will live' (14:19). Jesus has already answered Philip's desire to see the Father by reassuring him that 'the Father is in me and I in the Father' (14:10–11). Through the Holy Spirit, Jesus will also be one with those who love him: 'You in me and I in you.' And so we are caught up into the very life of the Godhead (14:20). Thus not only are those who keep Jesus' words loved by him, but by his Father also and through this he is able to reveal himself to them, even when he has physically departed from them (14:21).

Prayer

Lord Jesus, thank you that you do not leave us desolate; pour out your Spirit to strengthen, comfort and advise us that the world may know you live in us and we in you.

75 John 14:22–31

A parting gift

Jesus explains to his disciples that, although he is going to leave them, he will still be with them through the Holy Spirit, revealing himself to them (14:21). Each time he has talked of going away, one of the disciples has asked a question for further clarification – Peter, Thomas, Philip (13:36; 14:5, 8). Now it is the turn of Judas, who is identified as 'not Iscariot', not the betrayer, who has gone out into the darkness of the night. We know nothing else about him, although Luke also mentions a 'Judas, son of James' different from Iscariot (Luke 6:16; Acts 1:13). This Judas asks why Jesus will reveal himself to the disciples, but not to the world (14:22). Jesus' reply recalls his previous theme of loving him and keeping his commandments (14:15). Only those who love him and keep his word, which is not his anyway, but 'from the Father who sent me', can accept his revelation; those who do not love or obey him, will not recognise him or his Father (14:23–24). Yet to those who do love him, not only will Jesus reveal himself, but he and his Father will come and 'dwell' with them. Jesus and his Father will 'make our home with them', using *mone* for 'home', like the many 'dwelling places' in the Father's house (14:2). Not only does Jesus prepare a place for us in God, but he also makes a place for God in us.

The counsellor will teach you

This mutual indwelling of God in us and us in God is wonderful, but not easy to grasp. So Jesus reminds the disciples that he says all this to explain it to them, 'while I am still with you', before he goes away (14:25). This theme is repeated frequently (15:11; 16:1, 4, 6, 25, 33). But Jesus does not expect them to comprehend it all now. The task of the Paraclete, the Holy Spirit who will be sent by the Father, is to 'teach you everything and remind you of all that I have said to you' (14:26). 'Disciples' means learners, and they have called Jesus their rabbi, teacher. Now the Holy Spirit will be their rabbi, 'another' Jesus teaching them. Christians need to go on lifelong learning as we grow in our faith and discipleship. But the teaching we learn cannot be different from Jesus' words. The Spirit comes 'in my name', as we respond also 'in my name' in prayer (14:13). This is the test when someone claims a new revelation from the Spirit: is it consistent with Jesus' words and commandment, and can it be done in his name?

Peace I leave with you

Jesus returns to his central theme of reassurance as he gives them his parting gift of peace (14:27). It is customary in a farewell to bequeath something 'to remember me by', like an inheritance in a will. Jesus' bequest, however, is 'not as the world gives', where peace is merely the absence of conflict. The Hebrew concept of 'shalom' includes peace, health and well-being. It is a regular greeting and leave taking: live long and prosper. The 'shalom' of God is often promised in the Old Testament as a mark of God's coming in his glorious kingdom. Such a leaving gift of peace from Jesus means that the disciples must not let their 'hearts be troubled', as the word, *tarasso*, recalls the beginning (14:1). Why would they still be troubled? Jesus suggests that it is because they heard him say 'I am going away' (14:28). The grief this causes them shows that their love is possessive, concerned for themselves. If they really understood and loved Jesus, they would rejoice because 'I am going to the Father'. While they may be sad for their sake, they should be pleased for his sake as he returns to God. Since 'the Father is greater than I', Jesus can leave in perfect trust that God knows what he is doing. In later Christological controversies, the Arian heretics argued that this verse implied that Jesus is less than God. But the whole point of the discourse is that to have seen Jesus is to have seen the Father (14:9).

The end is very near

Actually, the Father's greatness is what Jesus is returning to, and so he seeks again to reassure them: 'I have told you this before it happens' (14:29). This is to build their faith, so that his death is not a destructive disaster, but helps them to believe because Jesus has warned them about it. Time is very short for talking, for 'the ruler of this world' is coming, a phrase describing the devil (12:31). This would terrify the disciples, so we get more reassurance – 'He has no power over me' (14:30). This final section weaves four key themes of going, obeying, knowing and loving together as Jesus goes to obey his Father 'that the world may know' his love. So it is time to be on their way (14:31).

Prayer

Lord Jesus, calm our troubled hearts and grant us your peace.

76 John 2:9–12

I am the vine

The various themes introduced in chapter 13 were developed through chapter 14, including the key elements of a farewell speech. Finally, Jesus said, 'Rise, let us go from here' (14:31). However, they do not do this until 18:1. Some scholars suggest that chapters 15— 17 were inserted later. However, even if 14:31 originally led into 18:1, the gospel as we have it today, and in every ancient copy, includes these chapters here. Others suggest that they set out at 14:31 and these three chapters are delivered by Jesus on the way to Gethsemane. Since these chapters develop many of the key themes, it is better to see Jesus' comment as giving some urgency to the discourse. After all, it is not unusual at dinner parties to say 'We really must be going' several times before actually departing, such is the interesting conversation!

The true vine and the farmer

Jesus now introduces the last 'I am' saying: 'I am the true vine' (15:1). The vine, from which wine comes, reminds us immediately of the institution of the Holy Communion in bread and wine in the other gospels, but absent here. This may be a hint for those who are 'in the know' to look beyond the words to the deeper spiritual level, as Jesus prepares his disciples for his death.

He gives them another 'figure', or *mashal,* like the door and the shepherd (10:1–6). In the other 'I am' sayings, Jesus applied the great Hebrew images of bread, light, shepherds and so forth, usually used for the law, to himself. Here he takes the vine – the supreme image, not just of the law or faith, but the very people of God themselves. Israel was a 'vine brought out of Egypt' and planted by God (Psalm 80:8). Regrettably, most references suggest a lack of fruitfulness. Isaiah speaks of a 'vineyard on a very fertile hill... which only yielded wild grapes' (Isaiah 5:1–4; see also Jeremiah 2:21). None the less, the vine was an emblem on the coins of the Maccabean leaders, which recalls the good and bad shepherds (see on 10:22).

In contrast, Jesus is the 'true vine'. The eucharistic discourse after the miraculous feeding said that his flesh is 'true food' and his blood 'true drink' (6:55). He has been called the 'true light' and the 'true bread from heaven' (1:9; 6:32), other key Jewish images. Now, as the 'true vine', he is nothing less than the 'real' Israel. God his Father is the vine grower, *georgos*, the farmer who planted the vine. Again, Jesus is dependent on his Father: as the one who sends precedes the one who is sent, so the vine grower precedes the vine. And it is the farmer, 'George', who prunes the barren branches from the vine (15:2). He 'cleans out' the small shoots budding with growth and using up precious nutrients, but not producing fruit. To have something 'nipped in the bud' can be painful, but it is the only way to promote healthy growth. The verb used for 'pruning', *kathairo*, means to 'clean out'; so Jesus remarks that the disciples need not fear since they have been 'made clean', *katharos*, by his word (15:3). This refers back to the foot washing when they were all made 'clean', *katharos*, except for Judas, who, like a dead branch, has fallen away (13:10).

Abide in me

Branches can only survive as an intimate part of the vine. So Jesus tells them, 'Abide in me as I abide in you' (15:4). The word 'abide', *meno*, links us to the 'abodes' in the Father's house and the way the Father and the Son dwell in each other and make their home in believers (14:2, 10, 23). Now this word occurs ten times in these few verses. The lesson is applied both negatively, that branches cannot bear fruit by themselves (15:4), and positively, that branches remaining on the vine bear 'much fruit' (15:5). When branches are pruned from a fruit tree, they can remain lodged in the tree, looking as healthy as the others; but as time goes by they turn brown, fall out and are fit only for the bonfire (15:6). Christians who have severed their connection with Christ may remain caught up in the church, but eventually they fall away, fruitless. To keep our life rooted in Christ's, we must protect time for prayer and worship. If we do this, we will so abide in Jesus that we will only pray that which is his will (15:7; see 14:13–14). When such prayers from our abiding in Christ are answered, they produce not just fruit, but also glorify God the Father (15:8; see 13:31–32; 14:13).

Prayer

You are the vine and we are the branches; keep us abiding in you and prune us clean that we might bear much fruit to your glory.

77 John 15:9–17
Abide in love

Jesus uses the image of the vine to describe his relationship with his disciples, even when he is physically absent. He is the 'true' or 'real vine', and we are branches which must remain in the vine to bear fruit, the fruit of love, one of John's key themes. Jesus has been dependent upon his Father in everything. Now he shows that the Father is the source of all love: 'As the Father has loved me, so I have loved you' (15:9). The Greek tense of these verbs is aorist, depicting definite and concrete events in the past, affecting us now. Jesus was so secure in his Father's love that he could show his love for his disciples by washing their feet (13:1–5).

We are to 'abide' in Jesus' love, using *meno* again, just as he 'abides' in his Father's love, by keeping his commandment (15:10). The earlier theme of remaining in love through obedience (see 14:15, 21, 23–24) is now linked to joy. Jesus is explaining all this so that 'my joy may be in you' and our joy might be 'fully complete' (15:11). He has already told the disciples that they should rejoice at his going to the Father (14:28), and this theme of joy will be developed later (16:20–33). Since the fruit of the vine is wine, which brings joy to 'gladden our hearts' (Psalm 104:15), we may have another hint of Communion here.

Love one another

As the Father has loved Jesus, and Jesus has loved us, so we are to abide in his love (15:9). Thus the church is to be a community of love where the new commandment is lived out. Jesus reminds them of the foot washing: 'This is my commandment, that you love one another as I have loved you' (15:12, picking up 13:34). The past tense of 'I have loved you' is to result in our present love for one another. Jesus' specific act of love is his self sacrifice, to lay down his life 'for his friends' (15:13). This was foreshadowed in the good shepherd laying down his life for the sheep (10:11) and now he prepares them for his sacrificial death. The word, 'for', *hyper*, means 'on behalf of', that his death is for our benefit. The same word comes in the institution of the Communion, 'this is my body, given *for* you' (Luke 22:19–20; 1 Corinthians 11:24), so here we have another hint of the Eucharist. If we are to love each other as Jesus has loved us, we must be ready to pay the ultimate sacrifice. Peter offered to lay down his life, and although only Jesus is to die now, we know that Peter's time will also come (13:37; 21:19).

Beloved friends

Talking of laying down his life 'for his friends' moves Jesus to call his disciples not 'servants' but 'friends', *philoi*, which comes from the verb 'to love' and indicates 'dear ones', 'beloved'. We show that we are his 'beloved' by our love for him, in keeping his commandment as was seen earlier (15:14; see on 15:10). There is, of course, nothing wrong in being 'God's servant'. Many Old Testament prophets, priests and kings were glad to be called this, including Joshua and David (Joshua 24:29; Psalm 89:20). Jesus himself took the servant's role when he washed their feet but, as their master, accepted them as his servants (13:13–16). But now he calls them his 'loved ones', as Moses was the 'friend' of God' (Exodus 33:11). The Roman emperor's inner circle of 'friends' were his principal advisers. So Jesus wants to 'make known' everything to his beloved disciples (15:15). Christians are often so busy being God's servants, 'working for Jesus', that we forget he wants us to be his friends, to love him and to be loved by him.

Rabbis did not usually look for disciples. Young people seeking a teacher would 'shop around', visit several and choose the one they wanted. But not Jesus, who reminds his disciples that he chose them, and did so for a purpose, that they should 'go and bear fruit' (15:16). This fruit is to 'last', 'abide' (*meno* again) and results in the Father answering their prayers, picking up another theme (14:13; 15:7). Then he repeats his final command, 'love one another' (15:17). Farewells typically include some last words or instructions, and we take them very seriously and try to do them. Thus Jesus' disciples are his 'beloved', loved by him as he is by his Father and he wants them to be a community of love, loving each other. This is not in order to be an introverted, cosy warm church but so that we might 'go and bear fruit that will last', reaching out in love to the world around us.

Prayer

Lord Jesus, thank you that you call us your beloved friends inspire us to love one another as you have loved us and send us out to bear much fruit that will last.

78 John 15:18–21

Not of the world

In a farewell speech the speaker may talk of the terrible things which will happen after they have gone: as Madame de Pompadour put it before the French Revolution, *'après nous le déluge'*. Jesus' teaching about the coming end times includes the persecution of his followers in the other gospels (Mark 13; Matthew 24—25; Luke 21). Here in John, Jesus looks ahead to the persecution and opposition coming for the disciples, first from 'the world' and also from 'the Jews'. This is an important new theme for the next chapters.

First, however, we must consider how the phrase 'the world' is used in this gospel. Already in these discourses the 'Spirit of truth' is not seen or known by 'the world' and Jesus' parting gift of peace is 'not as the world gives' (14:17, 27). Over the next few chapters, 'the world' will be increasingly portrayed as 'hating' and opposing Jesus and his disciples, until finally Jesus tells Pilate 'my kingdom is not of this world' (18:36). So some scholars accuse John of being 'other-worldly', and some Christians withdraw from the world into isolationist sects to follow this teaching. The 'world' is seen as evil, the domain of thieves, robbers and wolves, while the good shepherd's followers are to save as many individuals as possible and protect them in the sheepfold of the church. While this is an exaggeration, it is not an unreasonable inference from some verses about the world in these chapters.

The word 'world' occurs nearly 80 times in 60 verses of John's gospel (see on 1:10). But only about 20 verses have this negative connotation, mostly occurring in these farewell chapters. Nearly another 20 verses use 'the world' in a neutral way, to mean 'everyone', as the Pharisees complain that 'the world' had gone after Jesus (12:19). Finally, a third group of verses treat 'the world' positively as the object of God's love into which he sent his only Son (3:16). Jesus is the 'Saviour of the world', the living bread for 'the life of the world' and the 'light of the world' (4:42; 6:33, 51; 8:12; 9:5). Most of these 'positive' uses occur in the first half of the gospel where Jesus is calling the world to himself through his words and his miraculous signs. The 'world' only becomes negative in these final chapters after it has rejected Jesus – and the phrase now describes the human structures which oppose God.

The hatred of the world

John has stressed the intimate link of Jesus and his disciples: they are loved by him as he is loved by the Father and, as he was sent by the Father, so they are to go and bear fruit. Now we find the corollary is also true: the disciples will be hated by the world, as it hated Jesus (15:18). Jesus' identification with his persecuted church is also seen in Paul's vision on the Damascus road: 'Saul, Saul, why do you persecute *me*?' (Acts 9:4). In fact, the Greco-Roman world was remarkably tolerant of different religions. Their belief in many gods meant that any new faith could be included in their pantheon, provided that believers were prepared to sacrifice in reverence to the emperor – worship which was important in binding so many different peoples into one empire faithful to Rome. To stand out against that, as the early Christians had to, and declare that God alone is worthy of our allegiance was to be disloyal. Thus Jesus says that the world loves 'its own' (15:19). Jesus came to 'his own' and was rejected (1:11); the disciples became 'his own' whom he loved to the uttermost (13:1). He chose them (15:16) – and took them out of the world. The consequence is that the world hates them, as it does him.

Servants follow their master

The intimate relationship of Jesus and his disciples leads him to remind them that he said at the foot washing that 'servants are not greater than their master' (15:20; see 13:16). If they persecute the master, Jesus, then they will do the same to his disciples. But even here it is not all gloomy and negative. There is also the possibility that those who obey him, will also do what the disciples say. It all depends on their reaction to Jesus' name. 'Jesus' means 'Saviour', a title used by the Romans for the emperor and by the Jews for God; to call Jesus 'Lord' would offend both groups for similar reasons. So this is the motive for their opposition 'on account of my name, because they do not know him who sent me' (15:21). Because the world does not know God, they cannot recognise Jesus whom he has sent, nor his disciples who come in his name.

For reflection and prayer

Pray for all the places in the world where Christians are persecuted because of Jesus' name. If it were a crime to be a Christian in your country, would there be enough evidence to convict you?

79 John 15:22–27
The Spirit of truth

So far the opposition and the hatred has been predicted from 'the world' – every human system and structure opposed to God, anything or anyone who wants to be in the centre where only God can be. Into this world of darkness, God sent his only Son to bring light by his words and works, both of which testified that the Father had sent him. As we have seen, the coming of light into darkness inevitably brings shadows, and for those who will not see nor listen, the mission of Jesus and the disciples brings a *crisis*, a turning point of judgement.

'The Jews' reject Jesus' words and works

Jesus now moves from talking about 'the world' to discuss the fate of the people to whom he came and spoke. The first thing they have ignored is his words. Jesus was sent into the world not to condemn it but that it might be saved through him (3:17). However, there is another, awful consequence of Jesus' mission; if he had not 'spoken to them, they would not have sin'. But, since he has given them his words which they have chosen to ignore or reject, 'now they have no excuse' (15:22). This reminds us of the Pharisees who cast out the blind man while claiming that they were able to see; it was their wilful blindness to what Jesus was doing that caused their sin or guilt (9:41).

The links between the Father, the Son and the disciples in John usually means that whoever loves the disciples loves the Son, and whoever loves the Son loves the Father. Here we have the reverse: Jesus has already warned that the world will hate them because it hates him. Now it follows that those who hate him are also hating the Father who sent him (15:23).

Proof of their hatred was seen in their refusal to accept Jesus' words (15:22). Now he moves on to his 'works', the miracles which 'no one else had done'. John has called them 'signs' because they 'manifest his glory' (2:11). Jesus has appealed to both 'the Jews' and the disciples to believe in him because of his works (10:37–38; 14:11). But once again, the converse is also true: since they have refused to accept his works as signs of God's activity, they have no excuse for their sin. To see his works and reject them is the opposite of love, as was shown in their treatment of the blind man. Therefore 'they have seen and hated' both Jesus and his Father who sent him (15:24).

It has been obvious from Jesus' appeal to his words and works that he is not referring here to 'the world' in general, but to those who have seen and heard him, 'the Jews' who opposed him. Now that is made explicit as he cites the Psalms as predicting that 'they hated me without a cause' (Psalms 35:19; 69:4). The sense of rejection is such that he can even talk of the Jewish scriptures as 'their law', despite being himself a Jew who revered these holy books. This picks up his earlier debates with 'the Jews' where Jesus called the scriptures 'your law' (8:17; 10:34).

The witness of the Spirit

All this talk of hating and opposing brings back the court room imagery and the themes of witness from the debates of chapters 5—8. These arguments were like mini-trials of Jesus in advance about how to interpret his words and works. The crucial issue turned on what were his witnesses to prove that he was sent from God (see on 5:30–47). We have already noted that the 'Paraclete' is a legal term for either a defending counsel or for someone to speak or witness on a defendant's behalf, and the first mention of the Paraclete identified him as 'the Spirit of truth' (14:16–17). In a situation of accusation, defence and witness, one who can speak the truth is absolutely vital. So now Jesus says that he is sending the Spirit of truth to 'testify on my behalf' (15:26). The Spirit is described here as one who comes 'from the Father', yet also one 'whom I will send to you'. This verse caused endless debates in the early church, resulting in the phrase in the Nicene Creed that the Holy Spirit 'proceeds from the Father and the Son'. However, John was thinking more of the mission and witness of the church than eternal relationships within the Trinity! Not only will the Spirit witness to Jesus, but as the encouraging comforter he will stir up the disciples also to testify what they have seen having been 'with me from the beginning' (15:27).

Prayer

Holy Spirit of truth, comforter and advocate grant me courage to witness to the words and works of Jesus.

80 John 16:1–7
Returning to the Father

Throughout these farewell discourses, Jesus has been preparing the disciples for his departure. He has made it increasingly clear that there will be a major division after he has gone. On his side there will be those who remain in his love and in the Father's by abiding in the vine and loving one another with the Spirit as their 'helper'. On the other side, there will be opposition – from the world in general, from the Romans and from 'the Jews'. These same themes recur in this chapter as the discourse comes to an end, but in the reverse order: it begins with the certainty of opposition, and then moves through the assistance of the Spirit to Jesus' going away to his Father.

Out of the synagogues

Like most people trying hard to convey a difficult message, Jesus repeats himself. He has already said twice that the purpose of these discourses is to tell them these things while he is still with them (14:25; 15:11) and this refrain 'I have said these things' will repeat throughout this chapter (16:1, 4, 6, 25, 33). He is particularly concerned to stop them 'stumbling', or being 'scandalised', as the Greek puts it (16:1). The only other time this verb occurs in John is when Jesus asks if his teaching 'scandalises' them when some disciples give up and fall away (6:60–66). So now he is trying to stop them 'stumbling' and 'falling away' when he is no longer there and opposition comes. None of us knows how we may react under persecution. Unfortunately, the history of the church has many periods where the pressures have been so great that some have given up while others have paid the ultimate sacrifice.

Here we have the painful separation of the followers of Jesus from their Jewish roots (16:2). The problem is once again being put 'out of the synagogue', *aposynagogos*, as was threatened to the blind man and the authorities who believed (9:22; 12:42). Even if this technical term refers to action taken at the time the gospel was being written, severe opposition was waged against the early church, as the former persecutor Paul testifies (see Galatians 1:13; Philippians 3:6; Acts 26:9). Here, Jesus warns that in some cases it will even bring martyrdom, as happened to Stephen and James (Acts 7:60; 12:2). The irony is that the persecutors think they are offering a 'service' to God. The irony of people killing others as a 'service to God' when the real worship is offered by the death of the martyr has regrettably happened all too often, not just for some early Christians at Jewish hands, but also as Christians have killed Jews and most often, their fellow Christians. In all these cases, says Jesus, they may think they are doing it for God, but such actions reveal how little they know God or Jesus (16:3). Then he repeats that he is saying it now, so that when it does happen, they will not be surprised, but remember his warning (16:4).

To your advantage

With this warning, Jesus reminds them of why and where he is going, returning to 'the one who sent me' (16:5). They are so sunk in their concern about this, that Jesus notices that this time no disciple pops up to ask, 'where are you going?', the *quo vadis?* question. Of course, both Peter and Thomas asked this earlier (13:36; 14:5). So some commentators suggest that these discourses are from separate sources, or delivered on separate nights. However, in the flow of the overall narrative, it is their lack of questioning now, in the present, which shows how they are too wrapped up in grief to ask about his joy at returning to his Father. Despite his repeated stress that their hearts should 'not be troubled' (14:1), 'sorrow has filled' them now (16:6).

Jesus makes another attempt to enable them to understand. It is 'to your advantage', using the same word as Caiaphas' prophecy that it was 'expedient' or 'better' for one man to die for the nation (11:50; 18:14). Jesus' departure means that he will be able to send them the Helper, the Paraclete, already promised earlier (14:26). If Jesus does not face death and 'go away', the Spirit cannot come (16:7, see also 7:39). Jesus is still limited in space and time by his physical body, but when he has returned to his Father, he will send the Spirit, 'another helper' to be alongside them, just as he was, but not so limited. This is indeed to their advantage, but at the moment the disciples are too absorbed to realise it.

Prayer

Lord Jesus, send me your Holy Spirit, to comfort me and keep me from falling away and to stop me from being too wrapped up in my own anxieties that I miss what you are trying to tell me.

81 John 16:8–15
The task of the Spirit

In this final farewell discourse, Jesus has described the two sides, those who are abiding in love with him and his Father and those who are opposed to them all. Although he is going away, this will enable the Holy Spirit to be 'called alongside', as the Paraclete, to continue the work of Jesus. He has a particular task to do with regard to both sides.

The conviction of the Spirit

The first area relates to the world, which we have seen means here those opposed to Jesus (see on 15:18–19 above). If the Spirit is 'another' Jesus, he will do what Jesus did. Jesus came into the world to save it, not condemn it; but when the light came into the darkness, there were those who refused him, preferring to stay in the shadows lest their evil deeds were 'exposed' (3:16–20). In a verbal echo of that passage, now the Spirit's task is the same: he will 'convict' the world (16:8). In both verses the word is *elencho*. As *paraclete* is used for a legal counsel, so *elencho* means to 'prove wrong', 'convict', 'reprove', the work of cross-examination in a trial. The three things the Spirit will 'convince' the world of are also legal words meaning 'crime', 'justice' and 'sentence or verdict' at this human level. As always with John, if we look closer, we will see that they have a spiritual meaning also.

The first word, *hamartia*, can mean 'mistake', or 'crime', which at the spiritual level means 'sin'. In the cross-examination of Jesus after those who were going to stone the woman taken in adultery went away aware of their own sin, Jesus asked, 'Which of you convicts [*elencho*] me of sin [*hamartia*]?' (8:46). At his coming trial, they will 'convict' him and sentence him to death. It is the task of the Spirit to 'convince' the world that this was wrong; instead, they are guilty of the most basic sin, that God has come among them and they 'do not believe' in him (16:9). Jesus has already said that they are 'without excuse' for this sin because of their claim to be able to see (9:41; 15:22–24). It is still the first work of the Spirit to convince men and women of their sin and lack of faith in Jesus.

Second, he will convict them of 'justice' or 'righteousness', *dikaiosune*. This is the only time this favourite word of Paul's appears in John. At the human level, the Spirit will convince the world that Jesus' death was not a 'just' condemnation of a criminal. But what was a human injustice, God has made his 'righteousness'; through it Jesus has returned to his Father and his presence with God now is the final proof (16:10).

Finally, the Spirit will 'expose' the 'verdict', *krisis*. It looks as though evil has triumphed and Jesus has been condemned. In fact, the coming of Jesus brought the 'critical moment', the 'judgement' that people loved darkness rather than light (see on 3:19). So the third task of the Spirit is to convince the world that Jesus' death on the cross is actually the 'judgement' when the 'ruler of this world' is condemned (16:11; see 12:31).

Guidance into all truth

If the Paraclete comes as a cross-examining counsel to convince the world of the truth, so he comes also to the disciples to 'guide you into all truth' (16:13). As Jesus was their teacher, so now the Spirit will be also. But what he teaches will not be his own teaching; instead he will continue the teaching of Jesus. Jesus still has 'many things to say' to the disciples which they are not yet ready for (16:12). We must always beware of thinking that we know it all, or even are ready for all that Jesus longs to show us. Christian discipleship is a journey of lifelong learning in the guidance of the Spirit of truth. It is his task to speak 'whatever he hears' from Jesus and the Father, to 'declare what is to come' (16:13). As Jesus glorified the Father by doing the will of the one who sent him, so the Spirit will glorify Jesus, by taking 'what is mine' and declaring it to us (16:14). And because of the unity of love within the Holy Trinity, 'what is mine' is actually 'all that the Father has' (16:15). Thus we are back to our key themes of glory given and received within the Father, the Son and the Spirit in the unity of love into which we are invited by the Paraclete to share and abide.

Prayer

Come Holy Spirit, convince the world of sin, righteousness and judgement and guide us into all truth.

82 John 16:16–24

Sorrow will turn to joy

Now that Jesus has warned his disciples of the coming persecution and the presence of the Spirit to convince the world and guide them into truth, he returns to his main theme. The whole point of these farewell discourses has been to prepare them for his departure – but they are still having problems grasping it.

A little while

So Jesus repeats again that 'a little while' and they will not see him, but after 'a little while' they will (16:16). He used this phrase to warn the crowd and 'the Jews' that his ministry among them would only be for a limited time (7:33; 12:35). Equally, the disciples have been told twice that in 'a little while' he would be leaving them (13:33; 14:19). Now this phrase is repeated seven times in these few verses. No wonder it eventually stirs up the disciples, who have not said a word since Judas' question in 14:22, to discuss it with one another. What is Jesus talking about? What is all this about 'a little while and 'going to the Father' (16:17–18)? Obviously Jesus means that he is leaving – but because that is so unthinkable, they cannot grasp it. When pupils or students are having problems understanding something, a good teacher will let them bounce it around between them. So Jesus lets them debate it for a while, and then asks them what they were discussing (16:19). Earlier, the questions of Peter, Thomas, Philip and Judas helped to move the discussion on. Now their general questioning brings us to the final section and its key point of Jesus' departure.

Birth pangs

Since Jesus is trying to warn them about his coming death, now he says that they will 'weep and mourn'. We noted the ancient customs of loud weeping at Lazarus' death (11:31, 33, 35), and, apart from here, John uses 'weep' only there and for Mary weeping at Jesus' grave (20:11, 13, 15). This is the strongest suggestion that Jesus is going to die, reinforced by 'the world will rejoice' after his opponents' previous attempts to arrest and kill Jesus (16:20). This will cause the disciples the pain of grief, but there is the comfort that their 'pain will turn into joy'. It is unclear when this joyful transformation is meant to take place. Is the 'little while' when they will see him again at the resurrection appearances? On the other hand, much of this discourse has interpreted Jesus' coming back to the disciples as the arrival of the Spirit as Paraclete, to be with them and guide them as another Jesus. Third, it could mean the joy at his final coming on the last day at the end of all things.

These possibilities of pain being turned into joy are developed by the image of a woman in labour, experiencing birth pangs when 'her hour comes'. However, the outcome of bringing a new human life into the world gives her great joy (16:21). It is not that the 'anguish' is forgotten; I still remember the difficulties of the births of my children and the physical effects on my wife afterwards. But it is outweighed by the joy of the new life. So, says Jesus, the disciples will have pain now – the pangs of grief and the anguish of persecution by the world – but 'I will see you again', and the joy of that new life will fill their hearts with rejoicing. Furthermore, it will be a joy which 'no one can take away' (16:22). Such a joy will be experienced by them both at the resurrection and when the Spirit comes upon them, and it will fulfilled at the end – and it is likely that John, with his use of many levels of understanding, intends all three here.

Asking questions and praying

'On that day' of great joy all their questions will cease as they finally understand (16:23). But now, instead of asking all these questions, Jesus would prefer them to turn to the Father in prayer, as is shown by the change in Greek to a different verb of asking. The disciples have been used to asking things of Jesus. Now that he is leaving they need to 'beseech the Father in my name' and he will grant it. This is why throughout the discourse Jesus has encouraged them to pray (14: 13–14; 15:7). However, they have not done so yet; they need to look up from their grief and beseech the Father, so that he might answer their prayers and their joy may be 'completely full' (16:24). How often do we miss out on joy, because we are too wrapped up in our concerns even to pray about them to our heavenly Father in Jesus' name?

Prayer

Father God, draw close to all who suffer pain and persecution; bring your new life out of our birth pangs, and grant us all the fullness of your joy.

83 John 16:25–33
Going to the Father

The disciples are still discussing among themselves what Jesus means by all his allusions to 'a little while'. At the end of the discourse the time has come to be blunt.

Plain speaking

Jesus says that he has been speaking to them 'in figures of speech', the word used to describe his image of the door and shepherd (10:6). We noted then that this was the nearest John has to the parables so frequent in the other gospels. There was also the riddle, or *mashal*, about destroying the temple as a way of referring to himself (see on 2:19). In these discourses, we have had the image of the vine and the branches, and finally the recent passage about the woman giving birth. The time is coming, says Jesus, to put aside such 'figures' and talk 'plainly of the Father' (16:25). His brothers wanted Jesus to show himself 'plainly' to the world, and 'the Jews', frustrated by the 'figure' of the shepherd, asked him to speak 'plainly' (7:4; 10:24). The disciples got equally confused by Jesus' way of speaking: he had to tell them 'plainly' that Lazarus was dead (11:14) and he uses the same bluntness now for his own death. After years of asking him for what they wanted, now they must ask the Father 'in my name'. Through his death, they will have direct access to the Father who loves them. Such will be their relationship with the Father that Jesus does not need to be a *paraclete* for them, interceding on their behalf (16:26). Special pleading is not needed, for 'the Father himself loves you', because of their love for Jesus and their faith in him (16:27).

The disciples' relationship with the Father is a direct result of the whole of Jesus' mission, which is summed up sublimely in a single sentence: Jesus came from his Father into the world, and now that he has achieved the purpose for which the Father sent him, he is leaving the world to go to the Father (16:28). You could not get much plainer speech than this nor a clearer summary.

I have overcome the world

The disciples think that they have finally got it, clearly, 'plainly', not in a 'figure of speech' (16:29). His knowledge of what they were discussing and the way he answered their question without waiting for Peter or Thomas or anyone to ask him is proof enough for them: 'By this we believe that you came from God' (16:30). Now they are buoyed up with renewed enthusiasm – which just shows how little they have understood, particularly of the 'figure' of the woman in birth pangs. Jesus' reply has a hint of exasperation about it: 'So *now* do you believe?' (16:31). His return to the Father is not a matter for complacency; it will mean a lonely death for him, while the disciples will all 'be scattered, each to his own', abandoning Jesus (16:32). This echoes the prophecy of Zechariah: 'Strike the shepherd, that the sheep may be scattered' (Zechariah 13:7). Interestingly, John does not record the desertion of the disciples in his account of Jesus' arrest and death, and the beloved disciple will be at the foot of the cross (19:26). Nonetheless, Jesus will be abandoned by all human support; but the Son can never be completely alone, for his Father is always with him, as he had previously told 'the Jews' (see 8:16, 29).

After such a dire warning of desertion, Jesus' final word is to renew his parting gift of peace. He will not be surprised at their falling away and assures them of his knowledge now so that they may not be troubled when it happens, but find his peace (16:33). In the world there will be persecution, 'anguish', the same word as the birth pangs of the woman (16:21). In that anguish they are to 'be of good cheer', to 'take courage'. So the discourse which began with 'let not your hearts be troubled' (14:1) ends with similar reassurances, because, although Jesus is going to his death, this will be how he finally overcomes the world.

Like all good composers, John has ended these discourses with the same theme which opened his final symphony. As the chapters have progressed, he has deftly woven together motifs about how abiding in love for each other and for God gives confidence in prayer, under the guidance of another helper, the Spirit of truth, who will encourage them through the various trials and persecutions – and over it all the main theme is still heard: the 'hour' has finally come for Jesus to leave them and return to his Father.

Prayer

Lord Jesus, thank you that you have overcome the world; speak to me plainly and give me your peace, that I may abide in love with you and your Father.

84 John 17:1–5
Father, glorify your Son

We now come to one of the most sublime passages of the New Testament. It was common at the end of a farewell speech to pray and pronounce a blessing over the listeners. Thus Jacob blesses his sons after his farewell, and Moses breaks into a song of praise and prays for each of the tribes (Genesis 49:28; Deuteronomy 32—33). So now, after his farewell discourses, Jesus prays to his Father. This chapter reveals years of prayer and reflection by the evangelist under the guidance of the Holy Spirit, but at its heart there are three simple petitions all addressed by Jesus to God his Father:

'Father, glorify your Son' (17:1).
'Father, protect them in your name' (17:11).
'Father, may they be with me' (17:24).

These three simple prayers are developed into the three sections of this chapter when Jesus prays for himself (17:1–5), for his disciples (17:6–19) and for the whole church (17:20–26).

It has been known since the early Fathers as a 'high priestly prayer', referring to the intercession the high priest made before God for the whole people, or as a 'prayer of consecration', reflecting the way Jesus consecrates both himself and his disciples. At the same time, it echoes the Lord's Prayer: it is addressed to our 'Father', whose 'name' is stressed throughout the prayer (17:6, 11, 12, 26); his work 'on earth' has been done as he returns to heaven (17:4–5), praying that the disciples would be 'delivered from evil' (17:15).

The key themes of the prayer, which weave around the simple three petitions, are the same as in the farewell discourses, since it is praying for those same disciples Jesus has just been trying to encourage and teach. Therefore we will not be surprised to hear Jesus stress the unity of the Father and the Son with all those who believe; that Jesus is going to be glorified, but only through his death; that it is in knowing God and keeping his word that we find life; that as God sent Jesus into the world, so he sends us, but we must expect opposition from the world; and that through and over it all is the song of love.

Glory and eternal life

The time for Jesus' talking to his disciples is finished, so now 'he looked up to heaven' and addresses God with a simple 'Father', just as at Lazarus' grave (17:1; 11:41). The 'hour' so long expected has finally come (see 12:23, 27; 13:1). There is no doubt or hesitation, but just a prayer for God to be glorified in his Son, as he had prayed before (12:28; 13:31). In Jesus, God's word became flesh and 'we have beheld his glory' (1:14). All his signs have shown the glory of God, from the water into wine to the blind man and Lazarus (2:11; 9:3; 11:4, 40). Isaiah looked forward to when the glory of God would be revealed to 'all flesh', to everyone – and now not only will 'all flesh' see God's glory in Jesus, but he has authority to give them eternal life (17:2; see 1:12 and Isaiah 40:5). Then we have the famous definition of 'eternal life', the life 'of the ages', referring to its quality as much as to its quantity, 'to know you, the only true God' (17:3). To know is such an intimate word in the Bible, involving not just intellectual knowledge, but a physical, sexual, emotional, spiritual, total relationship. The prophets longed for when 'the earth shall be filled with the knowledge of the glory of God as the waters cover the sea' (Habakkuk 2:14; see also Hosea 6:3, 6). If we want to know the 'only true God', it involves knowing 'Jesus Christ whom you have sent' – John's typical phrase for the one in whom God's glory is revealed.

Returning to the Father's presence

So now Jesus can pray that he has 'finished the work on earth you gave me to do' (17:4). Because he has been sent by God, Jesus has always insisted that he has been doing the Father's work, not his own (4:34; 5:36; 9:4; 10:37–38) – but now this has been completed. All that remains for him is to return to the glory he had in God's presence 'before the world existed' (17:5). The gospel began with the wonderful prologue showing how Jesus existed with God 'in the beginning' (1:1–4). Its whole story has been about how Jesus brought that glory of God into our world through his words and works; now therefore he prays to be glorified again in his Father's presence.

Prayer

Father God, may all people see your glory in Jesus Christ whom you sent and come to have eternal life in him with you.

85 John 17:6-12

Jesus prays for his disciples

Having prayed to be with God in glory, Jesus turns to pray for his disciples who will be left behind. They are only a small frightened group, who still do not really understand what he is saying. At one level, it is not much to show for the fruits of three years of Jesus' labour. Yet these are the ones who will have to do the job and turn the world upside down.

Manifesting God's name

First, Jesus describes what he has done and to whom. The disciples originate from God, 'they were yours' but he gave them to Jesus 'out from the world' (17:6). God knows us and makes us his own, long before we think of coming to him. Jesus has manifested God's 'name' to them. Names were very important in ancient beliefs. To know a god's name gave you a certain power, to get what you were praying for. Altars to 'unknown gods' (as Paul found in Athens, Acts 17:23) were an 'insurance policy' against offending gods by not knowing their names. Names convey something of the character and nature of both gods and human beings. The Hebrew scriptures stress the importance of knowing God's name; it enables people to trust in him (Psalms 9:10; 20:7) and God dwells where he has put his name (Deuteronomy 12:5). God revealed his name to Moses as 'I am who I am' (Exodus 3:13-14), but the Jews considered it a blasphemy to pronounce his name. Thus the consonants YHWH are written in the scriptures with the vowels a-o-a, taken from *adonai*, 'the Lord' which was read instead. The mixture of Y(J)HW(V)H with a-o-a produced 'Jehovah' in early English Bibles.

The Lord's Prayer begins with 'hallowed be thy name'. In John's gospel, Jesus has used the phrase 'I am' – the bread, the light, the vine – not just to recall the great images of Judaism, but also to refer to the name of God. When he pronounced it by itself, 'before Abraham was, I am' they tried to stone him (8:58-59). Jesus has not just revealed God's name, 'I am', but also he has shown the disciples the nature and character of God. Now that the disciples have heard the farewell discourses, they 'have come to know' that everything Jesus has is from God (17:7). For all their inadequate understanding, their comments show that they realise that Jesus has come from God (16:30). Jesus has passed on God's words and truth to them; now 'they have believed that you sent me' (17:8).

Keep them in your name

Therefore, Jesus is now praying 'not for the world', but for those 'you gave me' (17:9). This does not mean that Jesus has no concern for the world. We have noted how 'the world' in John means those who oppose Jesus but is also the object of God's love (see on 15:18-21). At this point, Jesus' concern is for his disciples in the midst of a world which will oppose them as it opposed him. But his prayer is for them as he sends them into that world, which still shows his care for it. This verse cannot justify a sectarian, isolationist withdrawal from the world.

The unity of Father and Son means that 'all mine are yours, and yours are mine' (17:10). Thus as God was glorified in Jesus, so Jesus is glorified in his disciples. It is extraordinary that God is glorified in our stumbling attempts to live for him in this world, yet that is what Jesus says here. If this is to happen, his disciples need protection, so we come to the heart of his prayer. Since Jesus is no longer to be in the world with them, but is going back to his Father, he prays that God will 'keep them in your name' (17:11). This word 'keep' means to 'protect', literally to 'watch over' like a loving parent seeing their children about to launch into the world; they have to let them go, yet they are concerned to watch over them and save them from harm. So Jesus does not just call God 'Father' here, but also 'Holy'. To be 'holy' is to be set apart for God; we are to be holy as he is holy (Leviticus 11:44). This also entails being 'one as we are one', picking up a major theme of the discourse and anticipating Jesus' final prayer for the unity of all his disciples (see 13:34; 14:20; 15:9; 17:22-23).

Jesus has protected them in God's name, which is a safe refuge (Proverbs 18:10). The good shepherd has been concerned that 'none be lost' (17:12; see 6:12, 39; 10:28). However, this gives us a final clang from the funeral bell, as Jesus remembers Judas, the one who went out into the night to be lost; but even this fulfilled scripture (see 13:18 quoting Psalm 41:9).

Prayer

Holy Father, thank you that you have revealed yourself in Jesus protect and watch over us that we may glorify your name.

86 John 17:13–19
Sanctify them in the truth

In his prayer, Jesus has described how he manifested the name of God to his disciples and has prayed for their protection in the world which he is leaving as 'I am coming to you' (17:13). Before he leaves, however, he speaks this prayer still in the world 'so that they may have my joy made complete in themselves'. Twice in the farewell discourses, Jesus said that he wanted the disciples' joy to be 'full' or 'complete' through his words and their prayers (15:11; 16:24). Their joy alone, in their sadness at his death, will not do this; Jesus must pray for *his* joy to be fulfilled in them.

In the world, but not of the world

Through the farewell discourses, the division between those who refused Jesus and those who received him has been increasingly clear. So now, the disciples are the ones to whom Jesus has 'given your word', while the world responds by hating them (17:14). Jesus repeats in his prayer the connection between himself and his followers which he made throughout the discourses. Since a disciple is not greater than their master the world would persecute them as it persecuted him (15:20). Now we see that the disciples 'do not belong to the world, just as I do not belong to the world'.

The obvious temptation both for the church and for individual Christians is to withdraw from the world. When a small light is flickering in the darkness, the shadows can appear menacing. But removing the light consigns the place to total darkness. Instead, the light needs to know that the darkness cannot overcome it (1:5). So Jesus will not pray for God 'to take them out of the world' but asks rather for their protection from evil (17:15). In both the Lord's Prayer and here, the word is often translated in the neuter: 'Deliver us from evil.' However, it could also be the masculine pronoun, meaning 'from the evil one', the source of evil, the devil. Because 'they do not belong to the world, just as I do not belong to the world' (17:16), all that is opposed to God – the world, the flesh and the devil – will seek to lure Jesus' disciples into one of two responses. On the one hand, there is the call to be pure, to come out from the world, to avoid being tainted. This leads to isolation – to be 'so heavenly minded' that we are 'no earthly use'. On the other, we can try so hard to avoid this mistake that we fall into the opposite extreme, so identifying ourselves with the world that we become 'worldly', and no different from everyone else. Either way, the light has been so withdrawn or quenched, that the darkness is unaffected. To be 'in the world, but not of the world' is a difficult balancing act for churches and individual Christians alike. How can we maintain that difficult balance?

Consecrated for mission

The answer is to be consecrated for mission. Jesus prays that God will 'sanctify them in the truth' (17:17). The 'truth' reminds us of 'the Spirit of truth' and 'sanctify' picks up the description of the Father as 'holy' (14:7; 17:11). To 'sanctify' or to 'consecrate' means to 'make holy', to set something or someone apart for God. It was used in the Old Testament as much of priests and prophets like the sons of Aaron or Jeremiah (Exodus 28:41; Jeremiah 1:5) as of animals for sacrifice (Deuteronomy 15:19–21). To be made 'holy', to be set apart like this, is not for your own benefit, as some kind of reward or preferment. It is always for the sake of others. As the animals were sacrificed for the sake of the people, and as the priests and prophets were to serve the people, so Jesus sanctifies himself 'for their sakes' (17:19). The word 'for their sake' is *hyper* again, as when the good shepherd lays down his life 'for the sake of the sheep' and Jesus must die 'for the sake of the nation' (10:11; 11:51). It is the 'greater love' when someone dies 'for the sake of their friends' (see on 15:13). As Jesus 'consecrates' himself to die for our sakes, so we are made holy, 'sanctified in the truth' that, as God sent him into the world, so he can send us (17:18). Jesus could never have been accused of 'other-worldly' isolationism in his ministry to outcasts and sinners, but nor was he so identified with the world that his mission to save them was lost. This is what it means for his followers to be sent into the world, as he was, but not to be of it. It is indeed not easy to maintain that balance – but then, since it cost Jesus everything, even death on a cross, should we expect it to be any different?

Prayer

Lord Jesus, take us not out of your world, but protect us from the evil one; sanctify us in your truth that we may give our lives for the sake of others.

87 John 17:20–26

Jesus prays for the church

Jesus has prayed to return to the glory he shared with God his Father before the creation (17:1–5). He has also prayed for his disciples whom he will leave behind in the world, although they are not of the world; the key to this balancing act is found in being 'consecrated for mission' (17:6–19). As Jesus reminded his disciples earlier, 'You did not choose me, but I chose you and I appointed you to go and bear fruit' (15:16). Now, Jesus looks beyond his immediate disciples to the result of that consecrated mission, to the fruit that they will bear. So he does not pray just on their behalf (*hyper* again), but for 'those who will believe through their word' (17:20). The good shepherd spoke of 'sheep of another fold' which he had to bring into 'one flock with one shepherd' (10:16); equally Caiaphas' ironic prophecy meant that Jesus was to die 'not just for the nation only, but to gather into one the dispersed children of God' (11:52). This desire for all to be brought into one is the concern of this final section of his prayer.

That they may all be one

So Jesus prays that all those who come to believe in him 'may be one'. Such unity is rooted in the life of God: 'As you, Father, are in me and I am in you, may they also be in us' (17:21). Jesus answered Philip's desire to see the Father with 'I am in the Father and the Father in me' (14:10). This unity between the Father and the Son is to be shared through the indwelling of the Spirit with all who love him (14:23; 15:9). Thus the command to 'love one another' is 'new', because it is no mere moral exhortation, but a sharing in the life of God, 'as I have loved you' (see on 13:34). Now Jesus brings together the unity he has with the Father and the love of the disciples for one another – but it is not just to generate warm feelings of togetherness. The purpose is for the continuing mission, 'that the world may believe that you have sent me'. The world does not naturally ponder the internal relationships of the Holy Trinity, but when it sees Christians living this self-sacrificial love, then it is challenged to think again.

Jesus shares the glory he has received from his Father with all his followers (17:22), and we obscure the world's view of that glory by the divisions and separations within the church. Not surprisingly, this phrase 'that they may all be one' has become the watchword of the ecumenical movement and the title of innumerable church reports, commissions and encyclicals. Unfortunately, there is little here about institutional or structural unity. The unity of the Father in the Son and the Son in the Father is a unity of relationship, a way of life lived in love. A disunited church is a scandal to the gospel and a stumbling block for the world, but the path to unity will be found more in loving and living and working together than in ecclesiastical reorganisation. The world will know 'that you have sent me and have loved them even as you have loved me' only as Christians seek a unity arising out of 'I in them and you in me' (17:23).

That they may be with me

Finally, Jesus' prayer expresses his longing that all Christians might come to 'be with me where I am' (17:24). The prayer began with Jesus praying for himself to be glorified in the Father's presence with the glory he shared before the world was made (17:5). Now he wishes to share that glory with us as he draws this prayer – his last will and final wishes – to a climax, summing up his whole message and mission. He calls God 'righteous Father', the one in whom he has trusted throughout (17:25). It was because 'the world does not know you' that Jesus came into our world. As the one who does know the Father, he called disciples who came to know that he was sent by God. Because they accept that 'you have sent me', Jesus has made God's name known, revealing his very nature and character to them (17:26). What is more he continues to make it known, now and in the future, so that we may all share this unity of love, 'that the love with which you have loved me may be in them, and I in them'. In the end, therefore, we love each other not for our own sakes, nor even so that the world may believe, but because this is how we share the very life of God and come to be with him and in him forever and ever, Amen.

Prayer

Holy and righteous Father, grant to your church such love and unity that the world may believe and all your children come to dwell in your glory with your Son, Jesus Christ.

88 John 18:1–9

Betrayed in a garden

Jesus has finally finished 'speaking these words' of the farewell discourses and his prayer, and so now he takes his disciples out across the Kidron Valley to a garden (18:1). We notice immediately that John's account of the Passion is both similar to the others' and yet different. Here the garden is not named Gethsemane, neither is there sleep for the disciples nor agonised prayer for Jesus. Throughout the next chapters, John omits some bits well known from the synoptics, but features other aspects. We must concentrate on his account and his particular emphases. Since he stresses how Jesus knows all things and is in control of everything, there is no place for agonised doubting now; it was hinted at earlier (see on 12:27), but now all is under control. Only John mentions the *wadi* of the Kidron, where a stream flowed alongside the temple, sometimes used to wash away the sacrificial blood. Also, only John says they 'enter' a 'garden', which reminds us of the struggle with evil in the Garden of Eden and of the walled enclosure of the sheepfold.

Judas and the forces of the world

The slopes across the Kidron from the temple still contain walled enclosures with olive trees; 'Jesus often met there with his disciples', so Judas 'also knew the place'. After the tolling of our funeral bell earlier, now the event it foreshadowed happens: Judas is identified twice as 'the one who betrayed him' (18:2, 5). While the other gospels say he brought a 'crowd', only John says it included a 'detachment of soldiers' and 'officers from the chief priests and Pharisees' (17:3). The first word, *speira*, denotes a Roman 'cohort', usually 600 or 1,000 men; sometimes it refers to a 'maniple', a unit of 200 – either way a significant force. The 'officers' are the temple police which the Pharisees and priests – not known for working together – sent to seize Jesus at the Feast of Tabernacles (see on 7:32, 45–46). Thus John shows how all the forces 'of the world' – the political authorities, those in charge of the temple sacrifices and the interpreters of the law and scriptures – all united to arrest Jesus.

Furthermore they come with 'lanterns and torches', although the full Passover moon would make the night very bright in Jerusalem. But they want to arrest the 'light of the world' and no amount of lanterns will illuminate the spiritual darkness foretold by Jesus into which Judas had gone (11:10, 12:35; 13:27, 30).

I am

Although Judas is 'standing with them' (18:5), no betrayer's kiss is needed in John. Jesus, who knows 'everything which is to happen' (cf. 13:1), steps forward to take the initiative (18:4). As the good shepherd, he sees Judas the 'thief' (12:6) and the armed bandits coming and protects his sheep, behind him in the walled enclosure; force is not needed to take him – he offers his life of his own volition (see 10:18). When they say that they are seeking 'Jesus of Nazareth', Jesus replies 'I am'. Previously they have had difficulties arresting him (7:30, 44; 8:20; 10:39). Therefore they should have grabbed him after he identifies himself – but instead they are literally 'floored' and 'fell to the ground' (18:6). At the superficial level, this may be a result of their initial shock after the previous difficulties and the amount of force they have brought this time. Certainly they recover quickly enough to arrest him after he again asks them what they want and identifies himself (18:7–8). However, as so often in John the deeper level indicates that falling prostrate is the proper reaction to a divine appearance or the pronouncement of God's name (see Daniel 10:9; Revelation 1:17). After all the uses of 'I am' in this gospel to describe Jesus as something, 'bread of life', 'the true vine', and so forth, here it stands alone in the Greek, without even the 'he' supplied in most English translations (see also on 8:58 and 17:6). After asking God to protect the disciples 'in your name' (17:11), Jesus demonstrates the power of the name 'I am' here.

In serene control, Jesus tells them to let the others go. John says that this was 'to fulfil his word', making Jesus' words like scripture to be fulfilled (18:9; see also 18:32). In his prayer Jesus said that he had not lost any except Judas, fulfilling his earlier comment about 'the will of him who sent me that I should lose nothing he has given me' (17:12; 6:39). Judas, the 'thief' cannot 'snatch sheep' out of the hands of the good shepherd (10:28). Jesus offers himself willingly, that his disciples might live.

Prayer

Lord Jesus, when the world comes to extinguish your light, may I stand safe with you, protected by the name of God.

89 John 18:10-18

From garden to courtyard

When Jesus warned the disciples after washing their feet that they could not follow where he was going, Peter offered to lay down his life for Jesus (13:37). Despite Jesus' warning that he was more likely to deny him and everything in the farewell discourses about why and where Jesus is going, Peter still has not learned. All the gospels mention an attack on the high priest's slave, but only John says that it was Peter who drew his sword, and names the slave, Malchus, which comes from the Hebrew for 'king' (18:10).

Jesus tells Peter to put away his sword in words similar to Matthew's account (Matthew 26:52). The reason, however, recalls Jesus' prayer in the other gospels' accounts of Gethsemane: 'Am I not to drink the cup that the Father has given me?' (18:11; see Mark 14:36). So John is familiar with the story of the agony, even if it does not fit into the way he is narrating things. Jesus' willingness to 'drink the cup the Father has given' reflects his serene control in John, while the metaphor of the 'cup' hints at the suffering and sacrifice of Jesus' death remembered in Holy Communion.

The disciples and the garden fade from view as the Romans soldiers and the Jewish police arrest Jesus; John uses the technical term *chiliarch* for the 'officer' in charge of a cohort of a thousand men (18:12). The use of so much superfluous force is also seen as only John says that they 'tied him up'; at the human level, the authorities think they are in control, but John is telling us all is really in the hands of God.

Annas and Caiaphas

They take Jesus to the house of Annas, who was high priest from AD6 to 15. Although the Romans then deposed him, he was followed as high priest by his four sons – and now by Caiaphas, his son-in-law! The wealth and power of this family, gained from their control of the temple animals and sacrifices, was notorious. Although he was officially 'retired', it is not surprising that Jesus is taken to Annas' house to 'assist the police with their enquiries'! After all, it was his son-in-law Caiaphas who advised that it was better for Jesus to die 'on behalf of the people' (18:14; see 11:52) and Jesus will be sent on to him next (18:24).

Peter by the fireside

John says that 'Simon Peter and another disciple followed Jesus' (18:15). Since the disciple was 'known to the high priest', some suggest that he must be one of the authorities who believed in Jesus, like Nicodemus or Joseph of Arimathea. However, as these are both named elsewhere (e.g. 7:50; 19:38–39), anonymity here would be strange. Another possibility is Judas, who would have been allowed in, but is unlikely to have been accompanied by Peter. The obvious unnamed person, often linked with Peter, is the 'disciple Jesus loved' (see on 13:23). Whoever he is, he gains access into the courtyard, the *aule*, used only here and for the sheepfold (10:1, 6). Equally, Peter is left out at the 'door', mentioned for the first time since 'I am the door' (10:1–9). So the other disciple talks to the woman 'doorkeeper', *thuroros*, which is used only here and for the 'gatekeeper' to the *aule* in 10:3. None of this is in the other gospels, where Peter just wanders into the courtyard alone. These verbal echoes of the 'figure' of the door and the good shepherd are another example of John's multilevel writing; on the surface, it is just an ordinary courtyard, but at the spiritual level we see the good shepherd going to lay down his life for the sheep.

The doorkeeper seems to know that the 'other disciple' is a follower of Jesus, since she asks Peter as he comes in, 'You are not one of this man's disciples as well, are you?' (18:17). The question expects the answer 'no', and, almost before he realises it, that is Peter's reply. He is not yet under scrutiny or close questioning, but just wants to blend in quietly and get to the fire. But his reply, 'I am not' is the opposite of Jesus' ringing declaration in the garden, 'I am'. We wonder how Peter could move so quickly from protestations of being ready to die with Jesus one minute to denying him the next. In fact, it is a path we can all travel so easily, and it begins not with a great crisis but an off-the-cuff remark for a quiet life. Once denial has begun, however, the way back is all the more difficult when the pressure comes, as it soon will. No wonder Peter suddenly feels cold and warms himself alongside the very police officers whom he was attacking with his sword only a short time before (18:18).

Prayer

Lord Jesus, you know how quickly my faith can move from zeal to wanting the warmth of a quiet life, have mercy and grant me your trust in God our Father.

90 John 18:19-21

Jesus before the high priest

Jesus was taken into the house of Annas, but before we could learn what happened, we were taken out into the courtyard to see how Peter was admitted and his first quiet denial of Jesus. We know from Jesus' warning to Peter that two more denials are to come (13:38). But before these, the scene shifts back into the house for Jesus to be questioned by the high priest. This oscillation between different scenes – what is going on inside and outside the same building – is common in films or drama to heighten the tension. John would win an Oscar for his narrative artistry as we switch between Peter out in the courtyard and Jesus inside the house – both being questioned, but reacting very differently. It is as though there are two trials going on and Peter's understandable panic and fear makes Jesus' serene composure all the more remarkable.

Jesus on trial before the Jews

Jesus is still in the house of Annas; he is sent on to Caiaphas in 18:24, but nothing is said about what happens there before he is passed on again from Caiaphas to Pilate (18:28). Thus this hearing in Annas' house is Jesus' only appearance before Jewish authorities – and even this is unofficial. Jesus has no trial before the Sanhedrin in John's final chapters. And yet, in many ways, much of the first half of this gospel was like a trial. After he healed the paralysed man on the sabbath, Jesus was cross-examined by 'the Jews' about his witnesses – John the Baptist, God the Father, the scriptures and Moses (5:30-47). His teaching was debated at the Feast of Tabernacles (7:16-24), and the attempt to make him judge the woman taken in adultery actually put him on trial, leading into an argument about whether he or his opponents came from God or the devil (8:1-11, 21-59). The healing of the blind man caused both the man and his parents to be investigated under the threat of excommunication (9:12-34), followed by an examination of Jesus' claim to be 'one with the Father' (10:22-39). Finally the Sanhedrin met after the raising of Lazarus and have already decided to put Jesus to death 'for the sake of the nation' (11:47-53).

This treatment of the trial reminds us of John's 'omission' of the institution of the Holy Communion; it is missing here, where we expect to find it in these last chapters, yet the whole of the gospel is shot through with sacramental things like bread, water and wine. Equally, the whole story of Jesus' ministry, of his words and works, the 'signs' pointing to his glory, has shown Jesus constantly on trial in his discussions and debates with 'the Jews'. An account of the formal hearing now is not needed. Far more interesting to John is the contrast between Jesus inside the house and Peter outside in the courtyard.

Annas' questions

John still calls Annas the 'high priest', even if his son-in-law Caiaphas is that officially. The close connection of the two is also seen in Luke (Luke 3:2; Acts 4:6). The wily old arch-schemer has not built his family empire up on the sacrifice trade to have it brought down by preacher boys from up north, especially one responsible for unfortunate demonstrations in his temple! So Annas has two areas of questioning – about Jesus' disciples and about his teaching (18:19). The authorities' anxiety about the growing numbers of disciples has already been mentioned (11:48; 12:19) and Annas is concerned that a threat to public order might be bad for business. Second, he wants to know if Jesus' teaching could make him a false prophet, for whom death was the penalty (Deuteronomy 13:1–10).

John shows Jesus always in control, so now he appears to be in charge of his own interrogation. Jesus answers nothing about his disciples in order to protect them, and he refuses to discuss his teaching. He points out that he has spoken in synagogues (6:59) and in the temple (2:19; 7:14, 28; 8:20; 10:23), places where 'all the Jews gather'. He has said 'nothing in secret', but 'openly' – *parresia* again – 'to the world' (18:20; see 7:26; 10:24–30). Therefore there is no need to ask him; there are plenty of witnesses who heard what he said (18:21). It was against Jewish law to convict a person on their own testimony, as in the modern right to refuse to answer questions in court for fear of incriminating yourself. In the other gospels, Jesus is quiet and passive under examination, but John shows him rebutting the charges, serenely and confident.

Prayer

Lord Jesus, thank you that your whole life bore witness to God; grant that we too may speak openly to the world and stand alongside us when we are on trial for faith in you.

91 John 18:22–27
Rebukes and denials

The scene has moved from the garden to the house of Annas, the old high priest. We have seen that John is building the tension by oscillating between events out in the courtyard and the preliminary hearing taking place in the house. Annas wanted to question Jesus about his disciples and his teaching. Jesus, however, has refused to 'assist with enquiries'. He has said nothing about his disciples and has denied that any of his teaching was in secret. If the high priest wants to know about it, he should question the witnesses, not the defendant.

This reply is essentially a rebuke to the high priest for trying to get Jesus to incriminate himself, and it is taken as insolence by one of the police who hits him in the face (18:22). Cursing one of the leaders was forbidden by the law (Exodus 22:28), and so Jesus should not answer a high priest like this. Jesus maintains his position: if he is wrong, then let them bring on the witnesses to testify to his crime. On the other hand, their immediate recourse to violence just suggests how right he is (18:23). Frustrated, Annas has no alternative but to send him off to Caiaphas, still all 'tied up' (18:24).

Peter's denial

The oscillation between Jesus and Peter continues: while Jesus is being taken to Caiaphas and questioned there, the director turns the cameras back into the courtyard to see how Simon Peter is getting on. Peter is where we left him, still feeling the chill and standing by the charcoal fire trying to get warm (18:25). Peter's denial of Jesus is often represented as a sad tale of cowardice or disloyalty, but actually it has been an act of courage and bravery so far. When Jesus, hurt by some of his followers giving up, asked if the disciples also wanted to leave him, it was Peter who blurted out his faith: 'Lord, where can we go? We believe you are the Holy One of God' (6:66–69). Equally, at the last supper first he would not allow Jesus to wash his feet, but then he went to the other extreme of wanting to be washed all over (13:6–9)!

In his typically foolhardy manner, Peter put up the resistance in the garden and followed Jesus and the arresting party right into the lions' den. Gaining entry had been the problem, but with the help of the unnamed disciple he managed it – at the cost of a little white lie in agreeing with the doorkeeper's assumption that he was not a disciple. Now he is standing around with the police and the officials he was fighting not long ago. They also ask him the question inviting a negative answer: 'You're not also one of them, are you?' Having denied it once already, quietly to the doorkeeper, Peter cannot go back now and this more public denial takes him in deeper as again he replies, 'I am not.'

Even worse, a relative of Malchus, the slave he wounded, thinks he recognises him. For the first time, the construction of the question in Greek changes to expect a positive answer, yes: 'I saw you in the garden with him, didn't I?' (18:26). Suddenly there is no way out, and Peter is trapped where his rash devotion to Jesus has led him. He has no alternative but to deny it again, but, unlike the other gospels, John records no cursing or swearing of oaths here.

The breaking of the dawn

Then 'the cock crew' (18:27). Some intrepid commentators have conducted all night research on when cocks crow in Jerusalem, while others have noted that some texts forbid keeping cockerels within the holy city. This expression may even refer to the Roman early trumpet call at three in the morning, the *gallicinium*, to mark the start of the final watch of the night. Significantly, John omits any reminder here of Jesus' warning nor does Peter go out into the dark to weep. The cockcrow has signalled that the time of darkness – the night into which Judas disappeared to fetch troops with lanterns – is ending. It will soon be the start of the momentous day which will eventually bring forgiveness for all the insults and denials. Peter's love for Jesus took him into the courtyard where his courage failed him and he fell into denial. But Jesus' love for Peter will take him to the cross and beyond to another charcoal fire where it will all be put right (21:15–19). The enquiries will be answered, the insults forgiven and the fallen restored, not only for Peter but for Annas and the whole world.

Prayer

Lord Jesus, be with all those tempted to deny you in the heat of the moment or the fire of persecution and come again in your love to forgive and restore us.

John 18:28-29

Accused before Pilate

It is 'now early in the morning', *proi*, the end of the last watch from 3.00 to 6.00 am which has been spent at Caiaphas' house. We are not told what happened there. At daybreak Jesus is taken from Caiaphas' house to the Roman headquarters. After the oscillation between inside and outside Annas' house, John starts a new sequence of inside and outside the headquarters.

Entering the praetorium

John gives it the proper term, the 'praetorium' (18:28). Originally, in the field, this was the tent of the commanding officer, but by this time it is used for a Roman governor's residence. Usually, the governor of Judea lived in the port of Caesarea, named after the emperor, on the Mediterranean coast. But at sensitive times like festivals, he would come with reinforcements to stay in Jerusalem in case of disturbances. The headquarters at this time would have been either the Antonia fortress on the East Hill overlooking the temple from the north or the Herodian fortress on the West Hill on the west side of the temple overlooking the whole city by what is now called the Jaffa Gate. They bring Jesus to whichever of these Pilate was currently using – but stayed outside.

'They themselves' would not enter such a Gentile building to avoid 'ritual defilement' which would prevent them participating in the Passover sacrifices and eating the lamb. Jewish law was cautious about impurities within a Gentile's house, not least that leaven may be there which was prohibited during the fast. There is an extraordinary irony here about religious leaders conducting barely legal hearings at night and plotting cynically to execute one man 'for the sake of the people', but drawing the line at dietary regulations. They want to eat the Passover lamb, but will kill the true lamb of God who will take away the sins of all people (1:29; 11:50). It is easy for us to criticise, but how often are we so concerned for religious minutiae that we miss the more important matters of God?

Pilate

The governor has got used to these rituals, so 'Pilate went out to them' (18:29). He is so well known to both Christian and Jewish readers that the evangelist needs only to name him. Pontius Pilate was a Roman knight (the second rank, below senators) and governor of Judea AD26–36; as a lesser imperial province, it merited only a prefect or procurator. Pilate is attacked in Jewish writings for his greed, murder and inhumanity. He tried to bring the Romans' standards, adorned with 'graven images' of the emperor, into Jerusalem on his first visit, and votive shields on another; he raided the temple treasury to pay for a new aqueduct and finally crushed a revolt in Samaria so severely that he was recalled.

Outside and inside

This powerful man is now reduced almost to a messenger boy, darting in and out of the headquarters. John has constructed the Roman trial in seven carefully balanced scenes oscillating between Pilate interrogating Jesus inside the praetorium and his conversation with the Jewish leaders outside:

1 **Outside – 18:28-32** The Jews demand death
 2 **Inside – 18:33-38** Pilate and Jesus discuss kingship
  3 **Outside – 18:38-40** Pilate says Jesus is innocent
   4 **Inside – 19:1-3** Soldiers mock Jesus as king
  5 **Outside – 19:4-8** Pilate says Jesus is innocent
 6 **Inside – 19:9-11** Pilate and Jesus discuss power
7 **Outside – 19:12-16** The Jews obtain death

The balance of these scenes reveal that the trial is about power and kingship. In addition to Jesus' and Pilate's discussions, everything hinges around the middle scene where Jesus is scourged and mocked as king. There is also a contrast between the confusion outside and the calm debate with Jesus inside – and as Pilate runs between the two, he gradually moves from declaring Jesus' innocence to accepting the Jewish leaders' demand for his death.

Prayer

Lord God, forgive us when we become so entangled in our religious observances that we lose touch with your grace; grant that we might honour Jesus as our true king.

93 John 18:29–40

Are you king of the Jews?

The trial oscillates between Pilate's own interrogation of Jesus inside and those outside the headquarters. The first three scenes develop the theme of kingship, starting with Pilate's questions.

1 What is the charge?

Pilate begins outside with a reasonable request, to know the accusation; as governor, he should hold his own trial (18:29). The Jewish leaders are discomfited; the Sanhedrin decided that Jesus should die some time previously (11:53), a Roman cohort was involved in the arrest and they have done their own questioning. Petulantly they reply, 'If he were not an evildoer, we would not have handed him over to you' (18:30). In other words, 'We are working with you; trust us and do what we want'! The word 'handed him over' is the same as Judas' 'betrayed' (18:2, 5), which hints that all is not quite right. Slightly annoyed by their impertinence in using him as a rubber stamp, Pilate agrees that if they want to do it their way, they can use their own law and leave him out of it (18:31). But there is one difficulty: they do not have the power of the death penalty. Jewish sources say that they lost this right around AD30. The traditional Jewish execution was stoning, as the mob tried for the woman in adultery and for Jesus himself (8:5, 59; see Leviticus 24:16; Deuteronomy 17:7). But that is not what they need here. They want it done officially, by the Roman method of crucifixion. To the Jews, this would make Jesus accursed (Deuteronomy 21:23); to the Romans it suggests a serious political offence – but to John, this is actually fulfilling Jesus' prophecy that when he was 'lifted up' he would draw everyone to himself (18:32; see 12:32–33; 3:14; 8:28).

2 Are you a king?

Mention of the death penalty sends Pilate back inside. That can only mean that they have brought him a revolutionary wanting to be a messianic king. He looks at Jesus, but the Greek word order expresses his surprise: 'You – *you* are king of the Jews?' (18:33). The emphasis is full of irony: at the real level Pilate is right, since Jesus is the king of the Jews;

but he could not be more wrong at the ordinary human level. Jesus is not overawed by the governor's interrogation, but starts asking the questions himself, as though putting Pilate on trial. He does not admit or deny being king, but wonders whether Pilate worked it out himself, or did others ('the Jews' perhaps?) tell him (18:34).

Pilate responds with more questions: 'I'm not a Jew, am I?' (18:35). It is 'your own nation' (the word in Caiaphas' prophecy, 11:50) and chief priests who 'handed you over', again the word for Judas' betrayal: 'What have you done?' Finally, questions cease as Jesus replies, 'My kingdom is not of this world' (18:36). In fact, it is not a 'kingdom', or any place, at all; 'kingship' is a better translation. If Jesus wanted to be king in this world's terms, his disciples would be fighting on the streets for him, like many other groups at that time. Pilate does not really understand this, but he heard 'king': 'So you are a king then?' Jesus replies that these are Pilate's words and way of thinking, not his. Instead, he came into this world 'to witness to truth; everyone who belongs to the truth listens to my voice' (18:37). John's key themes like 'truth' and 'witness' here reveal his theological reflection on the meaning of this trial.

3 What is truth?

Unfortunately, like most politicians, Pilate does not have time for theology, asking, 'What is truth?' (18:38). Is he being cynical, sardonically dismissive – or perhaps wistfully wondering where truth can be found? Ironically the one who said 'I am the truth', the 'true bread' and the 'true vine', is standing before him, but he does not wait for an answer. He just turns around and goes outside again, declaring that he finds 'no case' against Jesus. All the gospels mention a custom of releasing someone at Passover, which is not otherwise known. Pilate seizes upon this to be able to release 'the king of the Jews' (18:39). But those gathered outside are not so easily satisfied and refuse, calling for Barabbas instead (18:40). In yet more irony, *bar-abbas* means 'son of the father' and John says he was a 'bandit', like those who come to steal and destroy the sheep (10:1, 8). Perhaps he was a zealot freedom fighter, but John says no more about him. In later Christian imagination, he is portrayed as standing at the foot of the cross, a free man, realising that the good shepherd dies as much for the thieves and the robbers, for Judas and Barabbas, as for the sheep.

Prayer

Lord Jesus Christ, true king and Son of the Father, thank you that you died for me; help me to live for you.

94 John 19:1–8

Hail, king of the Jews!

We have had three trial scenes so far: outside 'the Jews' have demanded the death penalty; inside Pilate discussed kingship with Jesus; and then Pilate came outside again to declare his innocence in an attempt to release him. The rejection of this offer sends Pilate back inside the headquarters for the middle scene in which Jesus is mocked as king.

4 A crown of thorns and a purple robe

Pilate has Jesus 'flogged' (19:1). The Romans had several levels of corporal punishment, ranging from a beating to 'teach them a lesson' through to scourging with a whip of leather thongs and metal spikes which would rip the flesh from someone's back and might even kill them. Matthew and Mark suggest that Jesus received the full scourging in preparation for crucifixion (Matthew 27:26; Mark 15:15). Since Jesus has not yet been condemned, John seems to be thinking more a beating for 'wasting police time', to prove to the Jews that he is a pathetic king and no threat to Rome. So the soldiers plait a crown of thorns, like an emperor's wreath (19:2). The sun god was depicted with a crown radiating light, like that on the Statue of Liberty; the spikes of the date palm would provide a painful parody of this effect. Jesus is also clad in purple, the imperial colour, and greeted with a parody of the *Ave Caesar!* – 'Hail, king of the Jews!' – except that their hands are offered not in salute, but a slap (19:3). At the human level, it is pathetic and ridiculous – but at the spiritual level, John hints at the irony that the true king is being crowned on his way to glory.

5 Behold the man

Pilate comes back outside for the fifth scene, which balances the third to stress Jesus' innocence again. The Jewish leaders outside still have not answered Pilate's original question about what the charges are (18:29). Pilate has investigated their request for the death penalty and can find 'no case against him' (19:4). To prove his point, he brings Jesus outside, still dressed as 'the king of the Jews'. A sorry sight he must have looked, and Pilate exclaims, *ecce homo*, 'What a man!' (19:5). At the human level, he is clearly just a poor chap, deluded perhaps, but certainly no threat to Rome, nor needing to be crucified. Nobody is going to follow someone in this state. And yet we can hear John's upper resonances echo, 'What a man indeed!' *The* man, 'wounded for our transgressions, beaten for our sins and by his stripes we are healed', the good shepherd suffering for 'the sheep who have gone astray' (Isaiah 53:5–6).

If Pilate thought that this pitiable spectacle would convince them to let him release Jesus, he was sadly mistaken. Infuriated by the parody of a 'king of the Jews' and outraged by the suggestion that Jesus might be '*the* man', the eschatological 'Son of Man' who would bring the kingdom of God, the chief priests and the temple police all shout out, 'Crucify him! Crucify him!' (19:6). In exasperation, Pilate gives vent to his frustration by suggesting that they should take him and do it themselves. They all know, of course, that it is not a serious proposal, since only the governor can do this – and Pilate repeats for the third time (like Peter's threefold denial, perhaps) that he can find 'no case against him'.

The Son of God

'The Jews' have no alternative but finally to admit that Jesus is not a revolutionary and reveal instead that the real charge is an offence against their law of blasphemy (19:7; see Leviticus 24:16). They allege that Jesus has claimed to be 'Son of God'. Instead of Pilate referring it back to them as an internal matter, as he previously threatened (18:31), he is much more frightened by this (19:8). The beliefs of the Greeks and Romans were full of stories of 'sons of gods', semi-divine figures with miraculous powers appearing on earth – and he had just scourged this one! Perhaps he was superstitious and afraid of retribution. Alternatively, he may have been afraid that the Jewish authorities would report him to Rome yet again for not respecting the local laws and customs. Or perhaps his fear was simply the dawning realisation that these people were not going to give up and let him get away with this, and so he has no choice but to go back inside for further investigations.

For reflection and prayer

'What a man! The king of the Jews!' Imagine the figure of Jesus, beaten and dressed up. What is your reaction and what are you going to do with him?

95 John 19:9-15

No king but Caesar!

Pilate had thought it was all over; Jesus had been whipped and the idea that he was a king duly mocked, so everything was all set for his release, when those wretched religious leaders brought the gods and their offspring into it! Unsettled by this mention of semi-divine sons, he goes back inside for the sixth scene, which balances the second, when Pilate and Jesus discussed kingship.

6 Where are you from?

The kingship discussion arose from Pilate's question, 'What have you done?' (18:35). His argument with 'the Jews' showed Pilate that the central issue is not what Jesus has *done*, but who he might *be*. So now he starts with a much better question: 'Where are you from?' (19:9). The origins of Jesus have been debated throughout John. Nicodemus recognised he was 'from God' (3:2), although his colleagues denied this (9:29; see also 3:31–36; 8:21–59). Jesus has spent most of the gospel explaining where he is from, but now he is strangely silent. After all, Pilate did not wait for an answer to 'What is truth?' (18:38), so does he really want to know about cosmic origins?

Like most people in authority faced with a silence, Pilate starts to throw his weight around. He tells Jesus, 'I have power to release you and power to crucify you' (19:10). The word for 'power' is *exousia*, or authority, and we are straight into some heavy irony. Pilate can bluster about his authority, but the bedraggled prisoner before him is the one to whom God has given 'authority over all people', authority to 'give eternal life', to 'execute judgement' or make them 'children of God' (17:2; 5:27; 1:12). Pilate might think he has 'power' over Jesus, but the good shepherd knows that no one can take his life; only he has the 'power to lay it down and the power to take it up again' (10:18).

So Jesus breaks his silence to tell Pilate that the only power he has comes *anothen*, 'from above' (19:11). At the human level, he reminds Pilate that he depends upon the emperor's favour, but at the spiritual level, 'from above' answers Pilate's question about where Jesus comes from. He is 'the one from above' (see on 3:31 and 3:3). Pilate may appear in charge but 'the one who handed me over' is more responsible. The word 'hand over' is used for Judas the 'betrayer', who 'handed him over' (13:21; 18:3, 5) – yet more recently the priests 'handed him over' to Pilate (18:30, 35). This careful reply makes Pilate pause; someone with such a sense of his proper place and understanding of authority is not a hot-headed revolutionary.

7 Here is your king

Pilate goes out for the seventh and final scene, balancing the first requesting the death sentence. Despite his efforts to release him, the cries of 'the Jews' are too much. They too realise that his power is from 'above', from the emperor. If Pilate releases Jesus, he is not 'Caesar's friend', a formal title (19:12; see on 15:14). Tiberius Caesar was emperor, a paranoid recluse on Capri, from where he considered everyone against him. In AD31, he even deposed his chief minister, Sejanus, a friend of Pilate. The early 30s, around the time of the crucifixion, was no time to have your loyalty to Caesar questioned.

Therefore, Pilate brings Jesus out to sit at his judgement seat and the irony continues. The Greek could mean that Pilate sits Jesus on the judge's bench – where he belongs since 'the Father has given all judgement to the Son' (5:22). But at the human level, Jesus stands before his judge on the Stone Pavement (19:13). A massive stone paved area has been excavated in the Antonia fortress with soldiers' dice games scratched on its surface. Since we are not sure which fortress was Pilate's headquarters or when this pavement was built, its identification with the stones on which Jesus was sentenced is not as clear as tour guides assume – but to stand there today is a moving experience.

At noon on the Friday of Preparation, when the Passover lambs were slaughtered, the lamb of God is sentenced (19:14; see 1:29). Pilate makes one last attempt, offering Jesus' broken figure to the Jews, 'Here is *your* king', accepting their charge for execution. But they do not want him, repeating, 'Crucify him!' Pilate replies, 'Crucify your king?' Their cry of 'We have no king but Caesar' passes their own sentence. Their only king was supposed to be God (Judges 8:23; 1 Samuel 8:7) or his 'anointed' (Psalm 2:2). In accepting the pagan emperor, they were not just refusing Jesus, but any messiah and ultimately God himself, renouncing his rule and breaking his covenant. Judgement has been given.

Prayer

Lord Jesus, Lamb of God and true judge, may I have no king but you.

96 John 19:16–24
The king is crucified

Through these seven balanced trial scenes, Pilate moved from mocking Jesus to a grudging respect for his kingship, while 'the Jews' rejected the rule of God, preferring Caesar. Now Pilate 'hands him over to them', using the word for 'betray', after the actions of Judas and the priests (19:16; see on 19:11). 'To them' means 'the Jews' who have finally got their way and so the soldiers take him for crucifixion.

The cross on Calvary

Jesus 'carried the cross by himself' (19:17). There is no mention here of Simon of Cyrene who helps in the other gospels, since John stresses that Jesus is in control throughout the Passion. He is taken to the 'place of the skull', probably a skull shaped rocky outcrop on the edge of the old city, called Golgotha in Hebrew or Calvary in Latin. The traditional site is now enclosed within the Church of the Holy Sepulchre, with two altars built over the rock which pilgrims can touch underneath. 'There they crucified him' (19:18). It is easy today to miss the horror which John's terse comment would have communicated to the ancients. Being roped or nailed in an upright position with your arms outstretched makes the body fluids collect in the chest. Death is caused eventually through 'drowning', or suffocating as breathing becomes difficult. It could take days, unless the person died earlier of the wounds from flogging, heat exhaustion or heart failure from the traumatic stress. Temporary relief for breathing could be obtained by sitting on a small 'saddle' half way up the cross, but this only prolonged the agony. The physical horror and the public humiliation was such that it was expressly forbidden for Roman citizens to be crucified; it was only used for slaves or local criminals. Jesus is crucified 'with two others'; John does not tell us if they were thieves or zealot fighters, nor of Luke's account of one repenting (Luke 23:39–43). His focus is totally on Jesus in the centre.

Jesus of Nazareth, king of the Jews

The title INRI on depictions of the crucifixion comes from the Latin for 'J(I)esus of Nazareth, King of the Jews' (*Rex Iudaeorum*), the inscription which Pilate had written in all three ancient tongues (19:19-20). Hebrew was the language of the Jewish faith, Greek was the language of culture, spoken by everyone and containing the beauties of literature and philosophy, and Latin was the official political language of the state. Proclaiming Jesus as king in the religious, intellectual and social realms fulfilled Jesus' prophecy that he would draw everyone to himself when he was 'lifted up from the earth' (12:32). Flushed by their success in the trial, the chief priests are horrified that Jesus should be officially proclaimed like this. After resisting all Jesus' 'I am' statements earlier in this gospel, now they want to insert 'I am' into the charge to undercut its absolute claim: 'This man said, "I am king of the Jews".' (19:21). But this time Pilate is obdurate, refusing with the pithy 'What I have written, I have written' (19:22). They brought the prisoner on a capital charge and rejected him even when he was crowned in purple, stating their loyalty to 'no king but Caesar'. It is too late for word games now; Jesus' kingship stands and the cross declares it for all Jews and Gentiles to read. Jesus reigns, even from the wood of the cross, as in crucifixes of him in regal robes as *Christus Rex*. Such is John's account of Jesus still in control.

Parting his garments

Part of the humiliation was being executed naked in public view. The soldiers would keep the person's clothes as a 'perk' for the messy job. John shows that the crucifixion party was a *quaternion*, a four-man unit, who divided Jesus' clothes between them. His tunic, however, was 'seamless' (19:23). Josephus says that the priest's tunic (see Leviticus 16:4; Exodus 39:27) was seamless, made from a single thread because of the law's prohibition against mixing different sorts of cloth. Some commentators have suggested that Jesus' robe was 'priestly' therefore; an old legend says that Jesus' mother Mary made 'the robe' herself, while Cyprian said that his clothes' four shares represent the four corners of the earth and the seamless robe is the undivided church! John has none of these, preferring his theme of fulfilment, as the soldiers cast lots for it (19:24; Psalm 22:18). The world gambles over cast-offs while 'God reigns from the tree', offering life in every language.

Prayer

Jesus our king, crucified for all nations, pour out love from your cross over all the corners of the earth.

97 John 19:25–30

The king's last words

The soldiers have finished crucifying Jesus and shared out his clothes; there is nothing left now, but to wait for death to come. John's focus moves to the foot of the cross, where there are four women: the mother of Jesus; his mother's sister; Mary wife of Clopas; and Mary Magdalene (19:25). Jesus' mother is not named, nor is her sister; comparison with the other gospels suggests that she might be Salome, the wife of Zebedee, mother of James and John (Mark 15:40; Matthew 27:56). A condemned man's family and friends could witness an execution, and people had to be near to read the charge written over the cross. The soldiers would ensure no one attempted to rescue anyone from the cross! Hearing a dying person's last words can be difficult no matter how close you are, and each gospel represents Jesus' end differently, reflecting their interpretations. Mark has one dark cry of desolation (Mark 15:34), which is answered by a supernatural earthquake in Matthew 27:52; Luke, however, has three profound sayings of forgiveness and trust (Luke 23:34, 43, 46). John also has three sayings, continuing his theme that Jesus is still in control.

Woman, behold your son

First, Jesus sees his mother and the unnamed 'disciple whom he loved'. As the eldest, Jesus would have provided for his mother, brothers and sisters since Joseph's death; but his brothers do not believe in him (7:5). If the 'beloved disciple' is John son of Zebedee and if Mary's sister is his mother Salome, then John would be Mary's nephew and Jesus' cousin, which may be why Jesus entrusts his mother to John (19:26–27). Neither is named: Jesus calls her 'woman', as he did at the wedding in Cana when his 'hour' had not yet come (2:4). Now the 'hour' has arrived (13:1; 17:1); from 'that hour', the disciple takes her 'to his own', as Jesus came 'to his own' and made the disciples 'his own' (1:11; 13:1). At the surface level, John shows Jesus still in control, ensuring that his mother and friends were cared for after he was gone. At the deeper level, some Catholics interpret Mary as the mother of the church, symbolised by the disciple. On the other hand, since the mother is given into the disciple's care, she may represent Judaism being entrusted to the church. Yet others see them as a new Adam and Eve, beneath another tree and being obedient this time.

I thirst

Once more, John stresses Jesus' knowledge. Having known that all was under control and loved 'his own' disciples 'to the end' (13:1–3), now Jesus knows that everything has 'ended', 'All was now finished' (19:28). The same word is used for 'end' as he 'finishes' scripture: 'Knowing all was fulfilled, said to fulfil scripture.' Hanging on a cross in the Mediterranean heat would make anyone thirsty. But Jesus says 'I thirst' more to fulfil scriptures like Psalm 69:21 and his own desire to 'drink the cup that the father gave me' (18:11). The soldiers had a jug of 'sour wine' to help them with their thirsty work, and so they put a sponge full on hyssop and hold it up to him (19:29). Because hyssop is not a very strong plant, some scholars prefer the reading 'javelin', *hyssos*, found in some late manuscripts. It is more likely that John was thinking of how hyssop was used to put the lamb's blood on the door frame so that God would 'pass over' his people (Exodus 12:22–23), thus making another link with Jesus as the true Passover lamb.

It is finished

Jesus has received the wine and knows that 'all was now finished' (19:28). So when he cries out 'It is finished' (19:30), it is another of John's typical two-level statements. On the surface, it looks like it is all over, Jesus is finished and everything has been a failure. Yet John's theme of Jesus being in control invites a further look: 'It is accomplished', 'fulfilled', all brought successfully to the proper conclusion. The word is also used to settle a bill; the price has been 'paid on the nail'. Then 'Jesus bowed his head', like someone going to sleep, and 'gave up his spirit'. He is still in control, with these active verbs; there is nothing passive about John's Passion; no one takes the life of the good shepherd, but he gives it up (10:17–18). When Jesus died, he 'handed over' his spirit, breathing his last over the beloved disciple, Mary and the others at the foot of the cross. As he promised, it is 'to your advantage that I go away' so that he could pour his parting gift of his Spirit upon them (see on 14:16, 26; 16:7).

Prayer

Lord Jesus, thank you for all you accomplished on the cross; make me your beloved child and pour your Spirit upon me.

98 John 19:31-35
The death of the king

The Romans would usually leave a crucified body hanging on the cross to be picked clean by animals and birds, as a warning to others, like the old gibbets for hanged highwaymen at crossroads. According to John, it is the Day of Preparation for the Passover, when the lambs were sacrificed (19:14). The priests would not even enter Pilate's headquarters in case they became ritually impure (18:28). It was even more important, as both the Sabbath and Passover approached at sunset, not to defile such a special day with bodies hanging around (19:31). Jewish law considered that 'anyone hung on a tree is under God's curse' and therefore 'the corpse must not remain all night upon the tree; you shall bury him that same day; you must not defile the land' (Deuteronomy 21:22-23; see Joshua 8:29). A crucified man died from suffocation as the body fluids collected in the chest, and he could get temporary relief by hauling himself up to breathe. Therefore, death could be hastened by breaking the legs, so that he would sag down and die more quickly. The priests ask Pilate to do this, not out of compassion for the dying, but so that their religious festival would not be spoiled by messy corpses! Once more, how easy it is for us to be so concerned with our rituals that we miss both human compassion and what God is doing.

Blood and water

The Roman soldiers smashed the legs of the other two to stop them prolonging the agony and to hasten their deaths (19:32). But when they come to Jesus, it is unnecessary, since he is already dead (19:33). To make sure, a soldier thrusts his spear into Jesus' side and 'at once blood and water came out' (19:34). This simple statement has provoked enormous comment from the early Fathers to modern medical investigations. Since John stresses its importance (19:35), we might expect to find his usual levels of interpretation here. At the surface level of human physiology, both the flogging and crucifixion would cause the body fluids to collect in his chest. Some doctors say that the blood would separate out from the more colourless fluids, which would look like water when the spear opened the bottom of the chest cavity. Others suggest that the blood came from his heart being ruptured, suggesting that Jesus died of a broken heart – literally! John stresses at the physical level that Jesus was really human and died a real human death. Because of the ancient Greek 'dualism' between the physical world and the divine realm, the idea that God could become human was ridiculous – and that he might die even more outrageous! The Docetics (from the Greek *docein*, to seem or appear) argued that Jesus only seemed to be human and just appeared to die, while actually he was rescued by God. Muslims also believe that Jesus did not die, but only a likeness was crucified (*The Qur'an*, sura 4:156–9). But John is clear: Jesus died, and blood and water came out of his side.

New life from death

As often, there are many interpretations of John's deeper meaning for the blood and water. Since Jesus dies as the true Passover lamb, blood recalls how the lamb's blood was sprinkled by the priests (2 Chronicles 35:11). On the other hand, water recalls Jesus' promise that out of his *koilia*, heart or chest, will flow 'streams of living water', which John interpreted as the giving of the Spirit after he had been glorified in death (7:38–39). Some early Fathers saw here the twofold baptism of water and baptism of blood, or martyrdom, faced by their people in the persecutions. Others interpret it as the Lord's gift of the two sacraments: water for baptism, and blood for the wine of Communion. We have noted the connection of water with baptism and the Spirit before (e.g. 3:5; 7:38–39), while blood comes only in the discourse about eating his flesh and drinking his blood (6:53–56). After the hints of bread and wine, vines and cups through John's account of Jesus' last night and day, another reference to the sacraments here is very possible.

The mystery of Jesus' death on the cross for us is so deep that none of these interpretations will ever fully exhaust it. We can only stand at the foot of the cross, like the disciple who witnessed it (19:35) – and marvel. From that messy, all too human death pours a flood of spiritual benefits of forgiveness and new life in the Spirit, freely given to us and to all God's people.

For reflection and prayer

Rock of ages cleft for me, Let me hide myself in thee;
Let the water and the blood, From thy riven side which flowed
Be of sin the double cure, Cleanse me from its guilt and power.
A.M. Toplady (1740–78)

99 John 19:35-42

The king is buried

After describing Jesus' three last sayings and the flow of blood and water from his side, suddenly John inserts a narrative comment with two of his key words both used twice, 'witness' and 'truth' (19:35). John the Baptist was a 'witness' to Jesus at the very start (1:7, 19, 32) and many of the informal trials between Jesus and 'the Jews' were about which witnesses were 'true' (e.g. 5:30-38); Jesus has also claimed to be 'the truth' and 'the true vine' (14:6; 15:1). Both words are linked to the 'Spirit of truth' who will 'bear witness' with the witness of the disciples (15:26). The use of these words here suggests that we were right to see hints of the Spirit in Jesus' 'handing over his spirit' and in the flow of water and blood (19:30, 34). The witness' testimony to the truth is repeated at the end of the gospel, where the witness is clearly the 'disciple Jesus loved' (21:24). Here he is present at the foot of the cross with Jesus' mother and now reports what he saw (19:26). At the end of the gospel, John stresses that he is writing 'that you may believe' and he states the same purpose here (19:35; 20:31). At this crucial moment of the crucifixion, the writer wants us to understand both the truth and the significance of what he is saying.

Scripture is fulfilled

Further corroboration comes from the fulfilment of scripture. John has not used this idea much until the cross, when both the dividing of the garments and Jesus' thirst were to 'fulfil scripture' (19:24, 28). Now the fact that he died before the soldiers could break his legs fulfils the requirement that the Passover lamb should not have any bones broken (19:36; see Exodus 12:46; Numbers 9:12). So John's deeper level continues the irony that the priests have sacrificed Jesus as the true Passover lamb. He may also recall the psalmist's belief that God protects his righteous people, ensuring that their bones are not broken (Psalm 34:20).

The final scripture quoted comes from Zechariah, whose themes have recurred so often recently. His prophecy that 'your king comes to you, humble riding on a donkey' was fulfilled in Jesus' entry into Jerusalem (12:15; Zechariah 9:9). His 'worthless shepherd' who did not care for God's people was behind Jesus the good shepherd's criticism of the religious leaders' lack of care for people like the blind man (10:12–14; Zechariah 11:16). The scattering of the disciples after they lost the good shepherd also picked up his prophecy (16:32; Zechariah 13:7–8). Yet Zechariah looks forward to a 'fountain which will cleanse Jerusalem' (Zechariah 13:1) reminding us of the flow of water and blood from Jesus' side. Now John quotes Zechariah's lament of Jerusalem mourning for a firstborn son as 'they look on the one whom they have pierced' (19:37; Zechariah 12:10). The king who came riding humbly in peace laid down his life like a good shepherd, pouring out the fountain of life from his side. As Jesus prophesied, when he is 'lifted up' on the cross, he draws everyone to him; some look at the 'one pierced' and oppose him even in death – but for all who 'look on him' and believe, his death brings eternal life.

Burial in another garden

Jesus' death brings two of the Jewish authorities more fully into the light. Joseph of Arimathea has been a disciple 'in secret… out of fear of the Jews' (19:38; see 12:42). Now he requests Jesus' body from Pilate; if Jesus really was guilty as a king against Caesar, his body should be left exposed as an example, while the Jews only buried criminals in a common grave. By granting Joseph's request, Pilate again implies that Jesus is innocent. Equally, Nicodemus, 'who had come to Jesus by night', finally comes out into the open, bearing lavish gifts fit for a king (19:39). Josephus describes the vast amount of spices used at the burial of King Herod the Great. Now the 'king of the Jews' is buried with a 'hundred pounds' of spices and linen – all in accordance with Jewish burial customs (19:40). He was betrayed in a garden, and is now buried in a garden nearby (19:41; see 18:1). No communal criminals' grave is used, but 'a new tomb in which no one had ever been laid'. Jesus receives a right royal treatment. Because time was short on the Day of Preparation, 'they laid Jesus there' (19:42). In fact, what was being prepared for them would be beyond their wildest imaginings…

Prayer

Lord Jesus, you were laid in the tomb and sanctified the grave to be a bed of hope to your people; grant that our dying may be so done that we live in you forever.

100 John 20:1–10
They have taken away the Lord

The arrival of the sabbath caused Jesus to be brought down from the cross and buried in a nearby tomb (19:42). Now it is early on Sunday, *proi* again, just before dawn, the time when they took Jesus from Caiaphas to Pilate on Friday morning (18:28). Mary Magdalene comes to the tomb 'while it was still dark' (20:1). Like Nicodemus coming to Jesus by night, or Judas going out into the night (3:2; 13:30), Mary is still in darkness, the black despair of grief and desolation. We saw with another Mary the custom of visiting a tomb for three days to lament, waiting for the person's spirit to depart as the body decomposed (see on 11:17, 31). Today was Mary's first opportunity, so she is up early. As she arrives, she sees that the covering stone has gone. We who know the story must remember that she would not deduce that Jesus had risen. Rather, she would assume that either the authorities had been unable to leave Jesus' body alone and had taken him off, perhaps to a communal grave, or, even worse, that tomb robbers had been lured by the rich spices and cloths.

A race to the tomb

So she ran to get help from Simon Peter who is still seen as the leader, despite his denial of Jesus. As so often, he is with the 'other disciple', who got him into the high priest's courtyard (18:15). He is now identified as 'the disciple Jesus loved', who was present at the last supper and the crucifixion (13:23; 19:26). To these two, she pours out her story: 'They have taken the Lord out of the tomb, and we do not know where they have laid him' (20:2). Like many in grief, she wants to tell the story of her loss, a story which will be repeated like a cracked record to anyone who will listen. Both disciples dash to the tomb, but the beloved disciple 'outran Peter, and reached the tomb first' (20:3–4). If he is the witness behind this gospel, he would have been younger than Peter. In the early light of dawn, he can see 'the linen grave cloths lying there', probably on a shelf cut into the rock, but he does not enter, as he waits respectfully for the elder disciple (20:5).

The grave cloths

Simon Peter arrives out of breath, all huffing and puffing – and goes straight in (20:6). This is the impetuous Peter who hit Malchus the high priest's slave in the garden and followed his master with the other disciple even into the courtyard where his rash actions led to denying Jesus only a couple of days ago (18:10; 15–27). So now, he does not stop, but enters immediately to find the linen grave cloths still lying there (20:6). Obviously, the authorities are not responsible, for they would not have undressed the body; tomb robbers might – but only to take the spices and cloths, and leave the corpse. The cloth or napkin for the head was 'rolled up by itself' (20:7). When Lazarus came out of his tomb, he still had this cloth around his face, with his body so wrapped up that he could only shuffle out (11:44). Yet Jesus' body has gone and left these cloths. What could have happened?

The beloved disciple believes

The other disciple finally enters – and goes beyond Peter, in three terse verbs: he 'entered', he 'saw', he 'believed' (20:8). Somehow the cloths suggested that the body had passed through them. His insight invites comment about this disciple and Peter. After all, he always goes one better: he leans against Jesus at the last supper and Peter asks a question through him, just as he gained access for Peter to the high priest's courtyard (13:23–25; 18:16). Now he 'outran Peter', arrived first and was the first to believe (20:4, 8). Some suggest that he represents a 'superior' church, perhaps Gentile Christians against Peter's Jewish Christians, or the evangelist's community against the mainstream church under Peter (see Introduction, pp. 17–18). Yet this gospel consistently shows Peter as the leader of the disciples; if the beloved disciple is an 'ideal figure' going beyond even Peter, that is the calling John issues to all his readers. Despite his belief, both disciples still did not understand the scriptures which suggested resurrection (20:9; see e.g. Psalm 16:10; Hosea 6:2). Therefore something very strange happens: they see all this and then – 'They went home' (20:10)! If only they had waited with Mary at the tomb, their questions would have been answered by Jesus himself, but 'they went home'. It is not enough to see like Mary, to enter like Peter or believe like the beloved disciple, if all we do is go home afterwards and carry on regardless.

Prayer

Christ is risen! He is risen indeed! Lord give us the eyes of faith to see, and believe, that you are alive.

101 John 20:11–18

I have seen the Lord!

After Peter and other disciple have gone home, Mary stays outside the tomb, frozen in her grief (20:11). She has been through the desolation of watching Jesus die on the cross; at least she was there, unlike Peter (19:25). But now she suffers a second grief with the loss of his body. She wanted to weep for him, to have something to hold on to in her pain – but even that has gone.

Messengers in white

Bent double in her agony, she peers into the tomb and sees two figures in white, keeping watch at the head and foot of where Jesus had lain (20:12). John says they are 'angels', which means 'messengers'. Mary is so locked into her tears that she does not realise who they are, since she does not react as people in the Bible usually do when they see angels. She is too wrapped up in her own concerns to be frightened or awestruck. She just wants to be left alone in her grief. Instead, they question her: 'Woman, why are you weeping?' (20:13). On the surface this is a silly thing to ask someone at a grave; the answer is obvious and the question intrusive. Yet at a deeper level, they are right to ask – for if Mary only knew what we know about Jesus, she would be weeping tears of joy. But she replies with almost the same words she told Peter and the beloved disciple (see 20:2). It is the cracked record of a bereaved person, telling the same story over and over and over again, becoming ever more personal; Jesus is now '*My* Lord' and 'I do not know where they have laid him', not 'we'. Engrossed in her grief, she does not wait for a reply, but turns away.

The gardener?

As she turns around, she becomes aware of someone else standing behind her, whom she was too occupied to notice before; even now she does not recognise that it is the very person she is looking for (20:14). So great is her desire to mourn alone, she looks away again, since she does not face him until he calls her name (20:16). Jesus, too, will not leave her alone, but repeats the angels' question, 'Woman, why are you weeping?'

For the moment he calls her 'woman', as he did his mother long ago in Cana and from the cross (2:4; 19:26). In another 'echo', he adds the first words he spoke in this gospel, which he repeated to those who came to arrest him in the garden: 'Whom are you looking for?' (20:15; see 1:38 and 18:4, 7). Mary misses these allusions and mistakes him for 'the gardener'. Impervious in her grief, she repeats her story; if he has moved the body, 'tell me where you have laid him and I will take him away'. She just wants to find Jesus' body, to hold on to it and grieve in peace. So the cracked record goes round and round, and only a miracle will change it. And that is exactly what happens, as Jesus moves from 'woman' to gently whispering her name, 'Mary.' The sheep know their shepherd's voice when 'he calls them by name and leads them out' (10:3). Recognising the good shepherd's voice, she turns again to face him, 'Rabbouni', My master (20:16)! The heart of this personal encounter with the risen Jesus is encapsulated in those two names: Mary and Master. 'They' have not taken him anywhere; there was nothing passive in the Passion, and he is still in control now: he has risen from the dead!

A new relationship for a new message

But Mary is still the same, she wants to cling on to him, to possess him as before. Jesus explains that in their new relationship she cannot 'hold on' to the risen Christ. Instead, she has a task, to be the apostle of the resurrection. Jesus sends her to go and tell the news to the disciples who would have met him themselves if only they had not 'gone home'. In this gospel, everyone gets a new task after meeting Jesus, as he brings a new covenant relationship: we are brothers and sisters with Jesus, children of 'my Father and your Father, my God and your God' (20:17; see Leviticus 26:12; Jeremiah 31:33; Ruth 1:16). Having seen God's messenger angels, Mary becomes one herself: she goes *angellousa*, 'announcing' to the disciples how Jesus has replaced her cracked record with a new song: 'I have seen the Lord' – and declaring all the wonders he had told her (20:18).

This is the heart of every Christian's story, that the risen Jesus meets us and calls us out of our selfish concerns to become an angel, announcing to everyone, 'I have seen the Lord.'

Prayer

Lord Jesus, speak through my tears, call me by my name and give me a new song to sing – that you are risen and alive forevermore!

102 John 20:19–23
Sent out in the Spirit

Mary saw some angel-messengers at the tomb, but through meeting the risen Jesus she became a 'messenger' herself. The same happens now to the disciples in a climactic scene which draws threads together from throughout the gospel. In the farewell discourses, Jesus explained that it was to the disciples' 'advantage' that he went away, so that he and the Father could send the Holy Spirit as 'another *paraclete*', an advocate or comforter (16:7). While the Spirit's role includes some 'comfort' in Jesus' leaving gift of peace in a hostile world, he comes not primarily for our benefit but to teach us and to witness to the truth for the sake of the continuing mission (14:26–27; 15:26). Through the resurrection of Jesus and the gift of the Spirit, the mission of God the Holy Trinity is passed on to us.

Peace be with you

On that Sunday evening, the disciples are all gathered together, perhaps where they had the last supper, behind locked doors out of 'fear of the Jews' (20:19). But no locked doors can prevent Jesus keeping his promise, 'I will not leave you desolate; I will come to you' (14:18). So he comes and stands among them and says, 'Peace be with you.' At the last supper he left them his parting gift of 'shalom', a peace 'not like the world gives' so that their hearts need not be 'troubled' (14:27; 16:33). Like all bequests, the disciples receive this gift after the giver has died – but unusually, he brings it in person! He had also promised that although they would feel pain as sharp as childbirth, they would rejoice when they saw him again (16:22). Now he shows them his hands and side and 'the disciples rejoiced when they saw the Lord' (20:20).

As the Father sent me, so I send you

Jesus has repeatedly stressed that he had been sent into the world by God his Father, 'the one who sent me'. In the farewell discourses, he was preparing the disciples for their mission of being 'sent'. Apostles, 'those sent', are not greater than the one who sent them, and they should expect to be treated as the master was (13:16; 15:20). But the converse is also true – that 'whoever receives one whom I send receives me; and whoever receives me receives him who sent me' (13:20). Jesus prayed for those he would send into the world 'as you have sent me into the world' (17:18). Now that moment has arrived. First, he gives them his gift of peace and then follows it with his mission charge: 'Peace be with you. As the Father has sent me, so I send you' (20:21). The apostles, the 'ones sent', are not given a new task to do; they are to carry on Jesus' mission. The Father 'sent' Jesus in the past, but Jesus 'sends' them on a continuing mission in the present and the future. An old Jewish proverb says 'a man's representative is as the man himself'. We are the 'body of Christ' here on earth; if the world receives us, then it receives Jesus who sent us, and in receiving him, it receives God the Father, the source of all mission.

Receive the Holy Spirit

To carry out someone's commission you need the power to act, and the authority to speak, on their behalf. First these frightened disciples, huddled in a locked room, need power to go anywhere, so Jesus 'breathed on them' (20:22). It is like God breathing 'the breath of life' into Adam or breathing upon the valley of dry bones (Genesis 2:7; Ezekiel 37:1–14). C.S. Lewis depicts it well as Aslan breathes upon the children in Narnia whenever they need strength for the tasks he gives them. So now Jesus fulfils his promise of sending them the Holy Spirit (16:7) – except he makes a delivery in person as he breathes upon them and says, 'Receive the Holy Spirit'.

Having fulfilled his promises to be with them and bring peace and joy, Jesus now gives them not just the power to go into the world, but also his authority. As the Father sent Jesus, so he sends his disciples. As the Father 'gave authority to execute judgement to the Son' (see 5:19–29), so Jesus gives them the task of forgiving and retaining sins (20:23). The work of liberation involves forgiving, letting go and releasing – the same word is used to 'unbind' Lazarus' bandages (11:44). The other word, 'retain', 'hold on' appears only here in John – but throughout Jesus has warned that the coming of light into darkness produces shadows, the 'critical moment' when some prefer to remain in their sin and blindness. To be sent into the world as Jesus was sent inevitably brings the possibility of acceptance or rejection.

Prayer

Risen Lord Jesus, breathe your peace upon us and send us out in the power of your Spirit.

103 John 20:24–31
Thomas: from disbelief to faith

Thomas is immortalised as 'Doubting Thomas', an unfortunate nickname which does not do him justice either in this story or earlier in John. He is first mentioned when Jesus is returning to Judea to raise Lazarus – and Thomas says, 'Let's go and die with him' (11:16). He is not really a doubter, more of a depressed donkey, the loyal pessimist, like Eeyore, who looks at ground level and sees the thistles. At the last supper, he did not understand what Jesus was saying and wanted to know the way physically (14:5). Yet this is the apostle who, according to tradition, went all the way to found the church in India. Something must have happened to get him to look up from the physical level!

I will not believe

Thomas was absent when the risen Jesus first came to the disciples behind the locked doors (20:19, 24). As the pessimist down at the physical level, perhaps he withdrew into his pain and grief. It is totally understandable, something many of us do. The problem is that we keep away from church when we need it most – and then we miss the fun when Jesus turns up! Being told what a good time everybody else had when you were absent only compounds the problem. Now the disciples all repeat Mary's message: '*We* have seen the Lord' (20:25). Thomas again wants the physical level – literally: 'unless' he can physically touch Jesus' wounded body, 'I will not believe.' At least he is honest. He is not an agonised doubter, wrestling in an effort to believe. He is an honest sceptic who just wants some physical evidence.

Be not faithless, but believe

On the next Sunday evening, the community are gathered together again perhaps to break bread in Communion. Thomas is with them this time: he may be a pessimist, but he is a loyal one who was ready to go with Jesus to die. Despite his scepticism, he is still here. The doors are locked as before, but Jesus again comes and stands among them greeting them with the same gift: 'Peace be with you' (20:26; cf. v. 19).

Jesus knows about our questions. So he gives Thomas his answer, inviting him to touch him at the physical level (20:27). Jesus told Mary not to touch him because she was clinging on to the old way of life. For Thomas, the chance to touch Jesus is the way to a new life. People progress differently spiritually; what will help one might hinder another. Everyone comes to faith differently in this chapter: the beloved disciple believes from empty grave cloths; Mary when Jesus calls her name; the disciples from seeing him come and stand among them; and now Thomas from touching him. Except that we are not told that Thomas actually touches Jesus; perhaps the appearance and the invitation are enough for him. So Jesus tells him, 'Do not be faithless, be faithful.' Nothing is said about doubt. It is about getting faith where there was none – and Jesus' word is enough. Thomas replies with a full confession: 'My Lord and my God' (20:28). This echoes the claim of the emperor Domitian to be called 'Dominus et Deus noster'. Thomas moves from the surface to the summit of Christian faith. 'My God' recalls the prologue (1:1) while Jesus echoes Thomas' 'believing' and 'seeing'. The blind man came to see and believe, while the religious leaders became blind by not believing (9:38–41). As in his high priestly prayer, Jesus lifts his eyes beyond the disciples to the wider church and blesses 'those who have not seen yet believe', which includes you and I who read the gospel today (20:29).

That you may believe

Now John addresses us directly with his purpose in what sounds like the original ending of the gospel. The first half ended with a summary about Jesus' signs echoing the beginning with John the Baptist (10:41–42). Thomas' declaration has taken us back to the prologue, while the writer reminds us of the 'signs' (see 2:11). But 'Jesus did many other signs' of which these are a selection; John had so much material that he had to choose which fitted his purpose, 'that you may believe that Jesus is the Christ, the Son of God' (20:30–31). Those titles take us from John the Baptist denying that he was the Christ through all the other expressions of faith like Martha's (1:19–20; 11:27). But faith is not an end in itself; through faith John wants us to 'have life in his name', like Thomas and all who met the risen Jesus.

For reflection

My Lord and my God! Imagine you are in the room when Jesus appears. What do you want to see, hear, touch or ask? What is your reaction? Are you like Peter, Mary, Thomas or are you the unnamed disciple?

104 John 21:1–7
Gone fishing

After the climax of Jesus' resurrection and appearances to Mary, the disciples and to Thomas, the last verses handed the baton on to the reader in what seemed like the end of the gospel. Most scholars consider this chapter to be a later addition, perhaps written in a slightly different style. Also, it is difficult to fit the story into the sequence of chapter 20 and the early church in Jerusalem. On the other hand, the story recalls many key themes from the gospel and no manuscript is without it. It deals with some 'loose ends' from the gospel, especially about Peter and the beloved disciple and their relationship. So it may be better to see it as an epilogue, balancing the prologue at the start. Jesus is always in control in John, even through his trial and death.

The same is true at the resurrection as he called Mary by name in her grief and gave peace to the disciples locked in by fear and brought faith to Thomas. The one person not sorted out is Simon, brought by his brother Andrew and called Peter, 'the rock', by Jesus (1:42). He is impetuous, the one who is quick to state his faith, and then at the last supper, moves from not letting Jesus wash his feet to wanting to be washed all over (6:68; 13:6–10). Yet Peter has been decidedly 'rocky' and wobbly lately: in the garden he lashed out at Malchus, and in the courtyard his rashness led to his denial (18:10, 15–27). His impetuosity made him rush to the tomb, behind the younger beloved disciple, and he was first to enter it (20:6–7). Then he 'went home'; presumably he was with the disciples when Jesus appeared, but he was not mentioned.

Old ways

Now he really has 'gone home', back to 'the old place', the Sea of Tiberias or Galilee (21:1; 6:1). He is also with old friends, Thomas the loyal pessimist and Nathanael of Cana who does not think anything good can come from Nazareth (1:45–51). In addition to this gloomy pair are the sons of Zebedee and two others. The beloved disciple must be one of them, hence his traditional identification with John, son of Zebedee (21:2, 7).

In the old places with old friends, Peter returns to his old way of life: 'I'm off fishing' (21:3). He is still the leader; going fishing is his idea, but the others follow him – and it is 'night'. This may be a good time to go fishing on the Sea of Galilee, but night has been used symbolically for the hour of darkness in John, what Nicodemus came out of and Judas went into (3:2; 13:30). So it is not surprising that they return to their old ways at night. But, of course, we cannot go back: it is fruitless, and they catch nothing all night. When we have done something bad or something has gone wrong in our lives, the temptation is to retreat back to old friends, old places, old habits to try to forget, yet it does not work.

The stranger on the shore

Now Jesus arrives, in control as always, taking the divine initiative at just the low point, when everything is fruitless. Every morning, the new light of God comes into the darkest hour. Once again it is daybreak, *proi*, the time when Peter had committed his threefold denial and Mary found the tomb empty (18:27–28; 20:1). Jesus comes and stands on the seashore, but they are so sunk in the old ways that they do not even recognise him (21:4).

So Jesus takes the initiative, with a friendly shout, 'Hi, guys!' or 'Lads!' It is a pleasant enquiry, but he already expects a negative answer: 'You have caught no fish, have you?' and they sadly agree (21:5). Then he gives them a simple instruction to try the right-hand side, where they catch too large a shoal to haul the net into the boat (21:6). Commentators debate whether this is meant to be a miracle and further evidence of Jesus' divine knowledge, or just reflects a trick of the light whereby people on the shore can see below the surface more easily than those on top of it in the boat. Certainly, John's gospel is all about learning to look below the surface for the deeper meaning – and, not surprisingly, the 'disciple Jesus loved' did just that. The vast number of fish is typical of Jesus, the super-abundance like turning 150 gallons of water into wine or feeding the 5,000. So, as at the tomb, this disciple has a flash of insight: 'It is the Lord!' (21:7). Peter's response is equally typical: his first impulse is to gird his clothes around him to cover his nakedness, jump straight in and swim to greet Jesus.

Prayer

Lord Jesus, when we are tempted to go back to the old ways, call out to us to look more deeply, that we might see you.

105 John 21:8–14
Breakfast with Jesus

Fishing was Peter's idea but he has abandoned ship, leaving the others lurched over the side dragging the net in (21:8). When they come ashore, they find 'a charcoal fire'. The use of *anthrakia* for the fire immediately recalls the high priest's courtyard, where Peter warmed himself at the *anthrakia* there (18:18) – the only two places the word is used in the New Testament. Peter does not need reminding: the evocative smell of charcoal would provoke all too strong a memory of that night and a hint of the conversation to come. The fire already has bread and fish on it, another verbal echo (21:9). While the fish in the net are the common *ichthys*, the fish on the fire is *opsarion*, dried fish, which appears in the New Testament only here and in the little boy's lunch at the feeding of the 5,000 (6:9–11). Since that miraculous feeding is the only other event in John to take place near the sea of Tiberias (6:1; 21:1), the link is unmistakable. So the writer cleverly pulls the threads together in this final scene.

153 fish

Before Jesus can deal with Peter's denial, he has to warm him by the fire and feed him breakfast. So he tells them to 'bring some of the fish you have just caught' (21:10). Peter springs into action – impetuous as ever, or perhaps trying to be helpful to make up for his lapse – and hauls the net ashore singlehandedly with 153 fish (21:11). The figure 153 is very precise. It is not impossible that one of them, amazed at the catch, sat down and counted them to be able to tell fishermen's tales! But after all the deeper meanings in John, this number has given commentators a field day. Since the letters of the alphabet were also used as numerals in Hebrew and Greek, some have tried to use *gematria*, adding up the numerical values of the letters, just as 666 makes the 'number of the beast' in Revelation 13:18. Thus some have reckoned that the Greek for 'Simon' equals 76, plus 'fish' *ichthys* equals 77, giving a total of 153.

The Fathers had many symbolic interpretations. Cyril of Alexandria took it as 100 (for the Gentiles) plus 50 (the Jews) plus 3 (for the Trinity). Augustine noted that 153 is the sum of all the numbers from 1 to 17, and 17 can be made up from a full 10 for the commandments plus a perfect 7 for the gifts of the Spirit. Likewise, 153 dots can be arranged into an equilateral triangle with 17 along each side; the ancients believed that such 'triangular numbers' stood for completion. Finally, Jerome thought there were 153 types of fish species in the world. So this catch represents the universal haul of all people brought to Jesus, in a net which is 'not torn'. Since 'torn' is the verb from *schism*, the 'division' we saw among 'the Jews' (7:43; 9:16; 10:19), the unbroken net signifies the undivided church, hauled in by Peter, representing the clergy or even the Pope! The variety and ingenuity of these solutions, each reflecting the commentators' interests rather than the original readers', should make us pause this time in the search for John's deeper meaning. Perhaps all we can say is that 153 is a large number, which may represent universality or completeness.

Come and eat

Meanwhile, back at the fireside, Jesus is serving breakfast (21:12). John stresses the reality of the resurrection – hallucinations or ghosts do not cook fish! The disciples 'knew it was Jesus', yet they must have been full of questions. All the resurrection appearances suggest that Jesus was recognisable, eventually, yet somehow different. His old ways and habits are still there – yet transformed. So Jesus answers their questions with a familiar action: 'He took bread and gave it to them, and did the same with the fish' (21:13). These words recall how he fed 5,000 by this same lake (6:11). We saw then that 'taking' and 'giving' are eucharistic and the reflection of the Communion is below the surface here. Pictures in the catacombs and early churches use images of fish and bread for the Communion as often as the cup of wine. So this 'third appearance to the disciples' (21:14) is a lovely picture of the risen Jesus coming to find Peter and the others when they have gone back to their old ways. He makes a meal for them, as he did in the good old days. But the smell of the charcoal fire and the bursting net hint that it is all different since the denial in the courtyard and the empty cross and tomb. They should be out fishing for people, bringing the whole universe to be completed in Jesus who feeds them with his risen life through loaves and fishes, bread and wine.

For reflection and prayer

Go and have an 'early breakfast' with Jesus at a church service near you.

106 John 21:15–19
Do you love me more than these?

Breakfast is finished, but the lingering smell of the charcoal fire is a potent reminder that something is still hanging around. Peter showed willing by jumping into the sea to greet Jesus and leaping to get more fish. But Jesus has to take the initiative after he has cared for Peter physically, warming him at the fire and feeding him. So the two of them go for a stroll after breakfast, as we see when the other disciple turns up later (21:20). Along the water's edge, Jesus starts his gentle, but firm questioning. He addresses him formally, 'Simon, son of John' – as he did when they first met (1:42). Then he nicknamed him 'Peter', but recently he has been more 'rocky' than 'solid rock'! Now is his chance to put it right. Interpreters are divided about 'Do you love me more than these?' Perhaps Jesus waves his hand at the boat and the net and the fish; Peter has gone back to the old ways, to his old business – but does he love Jesus more than that? Or maybe Jesus indicates the other disciples; at the last supper, Peter wanted to follow him even to death (13:36–38); he got further than everyone else except the 'other disciple' – but then denied him three times.

Lord, you know everything

So Jesus asks him three times if Peter loves him, once for each denial. Jesus uses *agapao* for 'love' in the first two, while Peter replies consistently with *philo*, which Jesus adopts the third time. Some suggest that Jesus is asking for a higher love, *agape*, but Peter can only offer friendship, *phile*, which Jesus settles for. However, most ancient and modern commentators argue that there is little difference in these words elsewhere in John and so not too much should be made of it here.

It is the threefold questioning which causes Peter to be 'hurt', literally 'grieved' (21:17). He has not yet dealt with his feelings about his loss of nerve in the courtyard, the loss of Jesus on the cross and losing his position among the disciples – and now Jesus asks three times. Yet it is the healer's knife, cutting out the old wound, to let Peter to affirm his love three times. He can only fling himself on Jesus' knowledge: 'You know everything.' When our pain and shame is so near the surface, we have to rely on the Lord's full understanding which looks deeper at our love beneath. Under Peter's denial was a love which followed Jesus almost to the end.

Feed my sheep

Having dealt with the painful stuff about the past, Jesus helps Peter move to his present ministry and his future destiny. When the 'good shepherd' was betrayed by Judas 'the thief', Peter may have ran away like 'the hireling' (10:10–12), but now he is to be a shepherd too. His threefold profession of love receives three commissions: 'Feed my lambs'; 'Tend my sheep'; 'Feed my sheep' (21:15–17). The good shepherd gives us the task of caring for the sheep, but they remain his, '*my* sheep'. He sends us as the Father sent him (20:21). So Jesus reinstates Peter not for his own sake, to make him feel better, but for his task of caring for the church. So often we talk about 'my ministry', 'my job', 'my decision for Christ' – but it is never mine at all. It is always *his* calling for *their* sake; it is Jesus who calls us and others who are to benefit.

The cost of being a shepherd

Finally, Jesus warns Peter of the cost of this love (21:18). The 'hireling' may run away but the 'good shepherd lays down his life for the sheep' (10:11–12). Peter has gone back to the old ways of his youth, girding up his belt and going fishing when he feels like it. Later he would write that pastoral care does not mean 'lording it about over those in your charge' (1 Peter 5:1–6); it involves 'humility', sacrificing yourself and letting others make demands. Eventually it will crucify him. When he is older, 'you will stretch out your hands and someone else' will help him dress; but the deeper meaning is that he will stretch out his hands as someone ties him to a cross beam. Jesus used similar hints 'to indicate the kind of death' he would die (12:33; 18:32); now he suggests the same fate for Peter, whose death will also 'glorify God' (21:19). Again, we think of the *Quo vadis?* legend of Peter fleeing Rome but returning to be crucified upside down after meeting Jesus carrying a cross. Like Peter, we all want to be restored when we let Jesus down, and we are all called to care for others, whether our vocation is to be Pope or unnoticed in a back pew. But are we prepared to follow all the way?

Prayer

Lord, you know everything; you know that I love you. Grant that I may feed your sheep and follow you to the end.

107 John 21:19–25
Follow me

Jesus warmed and dried Peter by the fire, fed him with fish and bread; then he restored him to his pastoral care of God's people and hinted at his glorious martyrdom to come. Only one thing remains to be said, 'Follow me' (21:19). It is Jesus' last word, yet also his first. After Andrew brought his brother Simon to Jesus at the start and he renamed him Peter, Jesus' first words were 'Follow me' (1:42–43). At the last supper, Peter asked Jesus, *Quo vadis?*, 'Where are you going?' When Jesus said that Peter could not follow then, Peter declared that he was ready to follow to death (13:36–37). So now Jesus reminds him of all that with the same two simple words, 'Follow me.' It is the call at the very start of our Christian journey, but the call is also to lifelong discipleship, repeated every day until we die.

Yet, how easily we are distracted! As they are walking along, Peter makes the typical mistake of looking back over his shoulder. He sees the 'disciple Jesus loved' also 'following' him and Jesus (21:20). Just to be clear who this is, the evangelist reminds us of his first appearance, reclining in the special place next to Jesus at the last supper and asking Jesus Peter's question about the betrayer (13:23–25). Ever since, he always seems to be with Peter, yet usually going that little bit further (see 18:15–17; 19:26–27; 20:2–8; 21:7).

Lord, what about him?

'When Peter saw him', he could not resist it. It is all very well for Jesus to put Peter through such painful questioning, giving him instructions for leading the church and his future martyrdom – but what about the next chap? So one final time Peter opens his mouth and puts his foot straight in it: 'Lord, what about him?' (21:21). The lifelong journey of following Jesus is one every individual must make – but we do so in community with others. Therefore there is always the temptation to compete, to want to know what they are doing or even to try to control them. But that is how the bad shepherds treated the blind man (9:24–34). Christian pastoral care is not about dictatorship or even interference. We are more like sheep dogs than shepherds, bringing people to Jesus the good shepherd, and their destiny is with him, not us. Thus Jesus' reply to Peter is rather brusque, essentially 'Mind your own business'! The other disciple's future is 'between him and me; your job is to follow me' (21:22).

The problem is that the Christian community are also interested in what Jesus says to the others, and so 'the rumour spread that this disciple would not die' (21:23). The writer points out carefully that Jesus did not say this; he simply told Peter it was not his business 'if it is my will that he remain', using the word for 'abide', *meno*, so beloved of the farewell discourses (see 14:2, 10, 17; 15:4–10). The obvious inference is that people were expecting Jesus to return before this disciple's death; if he had recently died, this would explain their anxiety and why the writer wants to put the record straight.

Bearing witness

The call to follow for Peter involved bearing witness even to death. The Greek for 'witness' is *martur-*, which gives us the English 'martyr'. In the end, Peter and the other disciple are always together in their witness. Peter witnesses by his martyrdom, but 'this disciple is the one who bears witness to these events and has written them down and we know his witness is true' (21:24). These last two verses appear to be an authentication by some early church leaders (after his death?) that the unnamed disciple has been the eyewitness, the authority behind the story. Furthermore, by using his key words like 'witness' and 'true' they show how much they have made his witness their own (see on 19:35 above). And so this epilogue ends as the last chapter of the gospel did, reminding us of the vast number of things Jesus did of which these are only a selection (21:25).

For reflection

Think of a time when you were impetuous and regretted it, spoke or acted first and thought later; have you slipped into denying your faith, or worked all night with nothing to show for it and envied another Christian who seems better? The risen Christ comes in the new light, tells us where to catch new resources, invites us to breakfast, gently questions and restores us and wants us to care for others.

Hear Jesus calling 'Follow me.' What is your response?

GLOSSARY

In accordance with the purpose of the series, technical terms have been kept to a minimum and we have tried to explain them where they have been used in the studies. Several important terms are collected together here for ease of reference.

Apocrypha Literally the 'hidden' books; other 'scriptures' written mostly in intertestamental times and placed in some Bibles between the Old and New Testaments; Catholic and Orthodox tradition accept them as more authoritative than do Protestants.

Christology The study of the person of Jesus, especially in relation to God; thus a 'low' Christology may treat him as a prophet, while a 'high' Christology sees him as divine and explores his place within the Trinity.

Eschatology The study of the end (*eschaton*) of everything – death, judgement, end of the world, heaven and hell, eternal life.

Intertestamental The period between Old Testament and the New Testament times, usually taken from Alexander the Great's conquest in 331BC to the early first century AD.

Maccabees The family of a priest Mattathias who led the resistance to Seleucid emperors who controlled Judea in the second century BC. Three of his five sons became important leaders – Judas Maccabeus, Jonathan and Simon. Simon's son, John Hyrcanus, secured the future for the Hasmonean dynasty in the new independent Jewish state.

Mashal A 'riddle' or figurative saying, often given by rabbis in answer to a question to provoke the listener to further thought.

Mishnah Jewish oral traditions about the law, collected together and written down during the second century AD; usually forms the first part of the Talmud.

Synoptics The first three gospels, Matthew, Mark and Luke, so called from the custom of 'looking at them together' (*syn-opt-* in Greek) to look at how they compare in the use of their material.

Talmud The collection of Jewish laws and traditions.

FOR FURTHER READING

I suppose the world itself could not contain the books that could be written.
JOHN 21:25

The evangelist's final despairing comment about the possible books on Jesus has certainly been borne out in the number of books about John. I have learned so much from so many scholars and commentators. This annotated list is only a selection, but I hope it will be helpful if you have enjoyed this commentary.

General introductions

John Ashton (ed.), *The Interpretation of John* (second edition, T&T Clark, 1997) – a collection of significant essays on John from 1923 to the last decade.

Richard A. Burridge, *Four Gospels, One Jesus? A symbolic reading* (revised and updated second edition, Eerdmans, 2005) – a general introduction to studying all four gospels, including John.

Warren Carter, *John: Storyteller, interpreter, evangelist* (Hendrickson, 2006) – a helpful introduction, drawing on John's biographical genre, with useful suggestions for discussion and reflection.

Ruth Edwards, *Discovering John* (SPCK, 2003) – an eminently sensible, sensitively written, thoroughly well-read assessment of the key issues, coming to wise conclusions.

Barnabas Lindars, SSF, *John*, JSNT Study Guide (Sheffield Academic Press, 1990) – a brief and easy-to-read introduction to all the main issues.

D. Moody Smith, *The Theology of the Gospel of John* (Cambridge University Press, 1995) – a more detailed coverage of the gospel's setting and theology and the issues raised.

Mark W.G. Stibbe, *John's Gospel* (Routledge, 1994) – an introduction to a literary reading looking at hero, plot, genre, style and polemic.

Shorter commentaries

These are all a few hundred pages in length and take the gospel in sections, including application for preaching and devotional use.

William Barclay, *The Gospel of John*, Daily Study Bible (St Andrew Press, 1955) – the classic daily commentary packed with spiritual insights and undergirded with good scholarship; still essential reading today, although some of the illustrations are now dated.

Diarmuid McGann, *Journeying Within Transcendence* (Collins, 1989) – a fascinating reading which mixes Catholic spirituality with a Jungian psychological perspective.

Lesslie Newbigin, *The Light Has Come* (Eerdmans, 1982) – a marvellous exposition which draws on Newbigin's experience in India and applies it all to modern Western culture.

William Temple, *Readings in St John's Gospel* (Macmillan, 1945) – a classic spiritual reader written in the late 1930s, when Temple was Archbishop of York.

Stephen Verney, *Water into Wine* (Collins Fount, 1985) – an interesting set of studies drawing on nearly 50 years of study as a soldier in World War II and subsequently a priest and bishop.

Tom Wright, *John for Everyone*, 2 volumes (SPCK, 2002) – provides a fresh, new translation, with commentary based upon each passage, making modern scholarship very accessible.

Detailed commentaries

These are more extended treatments of the gospel verse by verse dealing with all the academic and critical issues. Many are volumes within larger series dealing with the whole Bible.

George R. Beasley-Murray, *John*, Word Biblical Commentary vol. 36 (Word, 1987) – a good, steady treatment following a traditional approach with useful general comments.

Raymond E. Brown, *The Gospel According to John*, Anchor Bible Commentary vols 29 and 29A (Doubleday, 1966; 1970) – still the classic extended commentary, over 1,200 pages of articles, notes and comments on every verse and issue, yet packed with helpful observations for preachers and teachers.

Raymond E. Brown, *An Introduction to the Gospel of John*, edited by Francis J. Moloney, SDB (Doubleday, 2003) – was to have been the new introduction to an updated version of his commentary; unfortunately Brown's death in 1998 robbed us of that pleasure, but the introduction is an interesting insight into his assessment of the changes since his first edition came out.

D.A. Carson, *The Gospel According to John* (IVP, 1991) – a careful scholarly treatment from an evangelical perspective.

Craig S. Keener, *The Gospel of John: A commentary*, 2 vols. (Hendrickson, 2003) – over 1,600 pages with an enormous introduction, providing detailed coverage of every aspect, with well-documented evidence about the Jewish and Greek background of the ancient Mediterranean.

Andrew T. Lincoln, *The Gospel According to Saint John*, Black's New Testament Commentaries (Continuum/Hendrickson, 2005) – highly readable yet scholarly treatment, with helpful introductory essays, a new translation, organised passage by passage in a narrative approach, dealing with all the key issues in a balanced manner.

Barnabas Lindars, *The Gospel of John*, The New Century Bible Commentary (Marshall, Morgan and Scott, 1972) – helpful analysis drawing on years of teaching and scholarship.

John Marsh, *Saint John* (Pelican, 1968) – a lot bigger and fuller than it looks (700 pages) and still very useful.

Mark W.G. Stibbe, *John* (JSOT Press, 1993) – an interesting approach; shorter (224 pages), taking the gospel section by section in the light of modern literary analysis.

Ben Witherington III, *John's Wisdom* (Lutterworth, 1995) – a good commentary with insightful sections on how to preach and teach the gospel in church life today.

Commentaries on the Greek text

E. Haenchen, Hermeneia, 2 volumes, 1984.
C.K. Barrett, SPCK 1955; 1978 2nd edition.
J.H. Bernard, ICC, T and T Clark, 1928.
B.F. Westcott, Murray, 1919.

The Bible is at the heart of BRF's work, and this special anniversary collection is a celebration of the Bible for BRF's centenary year. Bringing together a fantastically wide-ranging writing team of authors, supporters and well-wishers from all areas of BRF's work, this resource is designed to help us go deeper into the story of the Bible and reflect on how we can share it in our everyday lives. Including sections which lead us through the Bible narrative as well as thematic and seasonal sections, it is the perfect daily companion to resource your spiritual journey.

The BRF Book of 365 Bible Reflections
With contributions from BRF authors, supporters and well-wishers
Edited by Karen Laister and Olivia Warburton
978 1 80039 100 0 £14.99

brfonline.org.uk

Prayer is at the heart of BRF's work, and this special illustrated anniversary collection is a celebration of prayer for BRF's centenary year. It can be used in a range of different settings, from individual devotions to corporate worship. Including sections on prayers of preparation, seasonal prayers, and themed prayers for special times and hard times, it is the perfect daily companion to resource your spiritual journey.

The BRF Book of 100 Prayers
Resourcing your spiritual journey
Martyn Payne
978 1 80039 147 5 £12.99

brfonline.org.uk

The BRF Centenary Prayer

Gracious God,
we rejoice in this centenary year
that you have grown BRF
from a local network of Bible readers
into a worldwide family of ministries.
Thank you for your faithfulness
in nurturing small beginnings
into surprising blessings.
We rejoice that, from the youngest to the oldest,
so many have encountered your word
and grown as disciples of Christ.
Keep us humble in your service,
ambitious for your glory
and open to new opportunities.
For your name's sake
Amen

Friends of BRF

I never fail to be amazed by the generosity of our supporters.

BRF is a remarkable charity, but we can only do what we do with the help of our faithful supporters: volunteers, people who pray for us and spread the word about our work, and people who support us financially, both individuals who give donations and legacies, and charitable trusts.

Many of our supporters have become 'Friends of BRF', choosing to make a regular monthly gift to help ensure that our work can be sustained and developed in the coming years. Every single donation, whether occasional or regular, small or large, makes a huge difference and I, along with all my colleagues here at BRF, thank God for each one.

If you'd like to help support Living Faith and our wider ministry, please visit **brf.org.uk/give**, contact a member of the fundraising team by email at **giving@brf.org.uk** or call **01235 462305** to speak to one of us direct.

With heartfelt thanks

Julie

**Julie MacNaughton,
Head of Fundraising MCIOF(Dip)**

 *Enabling all ages to grow in faith*

Anna Chaplaincy
Living Faith
Messy Church
Parenting for Faith

100 years of BRF

2022 is BRF's 100th anniversary! Look out for details of our special new centenary resources, a beautiful centenary rose and an online thanksgiving service that we hope you'll attend. This centenary year we're focusing on sharing the story of BRF, the story of the Bible – and we hope you'll share your stories of faith with us too.

Find out more at **brf.org.uk/centenary**.

To find out more about our work, visit
brf.org.uk

THE PEOPLE'S BIBLE COMMENTARY

Luke

15 The Chambers, Vineyard
Abingdon OX14 3FE
brf.org.uk

Bible Reading Fellowship is a charity (233280)
and company limited by guarantee (301324),
registered in England and Wales

ISBN (boxed set) 978 1 80039 093 5
First published 1998
This edition published 2022
10 9 8 7 6 5 4 3 2 1 0
All rights reserved

Text © Henry Wansbrough 1998, 2022
This edition © Bible Reading Fellowship 2022
Cover images: detail of Millennium window, St Agatha's Church,
Brightwell-cum-Sotwell, Oxon, photo © Rex Harris; background
© iStock.com/petekarici; gold texture © AmadeyART/stock.adobe.com

The author asserts the moral right to be identified as the author of this work

Acknowledgements
Unless otherwise stated, scripture quotations are taken from the New Jerusalem
Bible, published and copyright © 1985 by Darton, Longman and Todd Ltd and
les Editions du Cerf, and by Doubleday, a division of Bantam Doubleday Dell
Publishing Group, Inc. Used by permission of Darton, Longman and Todd Ltd,
and Doubleday, a division of Random House, Inc.

Scripture quotations marked AV are taken from the Authorised (King James)
Version of the Bible, the rights in which are vested in the Crown, reproduced by
permission of the Crown's Patentee, Cambridge University Press.

Scripture quotations marked RSV are taken from The Revised Standard Version
of the Bible, copyright © 1946, 1952, 1971 by the Division of Christian Education
of the National Council of the Churches of Christ in the United States of America,
and are used by permission. All rights reserved.

Scripture quotations marked NIV are taken from The Holy Bible, New
International Version (Anglicised edition) copyright © 1979, 1984, 2011 by Biblica.
Used by permission of Hodder & Stoughton Publishers, a Hachette UK company.
All rights reserved. 'NIV' is a registered trademark of Biblica. UK trademark
number 1448790.

Every effort has been made to trace and contact copyright owners for material
used in this resource. We apologise for any inadvertent omissions or errors, and
would ask those concerned to contact us so that full acknowledgement can be
made in the future.

A catalogue record for this book is available from the British Library

Printed and bound by CPI Group (UK) Ltd, Croydon CR0 4YY

THE PEOPLE'S BIBLE COMMENTARY

Luke

Henry Wansbrough

Photocopying for churches

Please report to CLA Church Licence any photocopy you make from this publication. Your church administrator or secretary will know who manages your CLA Church Licence.

The information you need to provide to your CLA Church Licence administrator is as follows:

Title, Author, Publisher and ISBN

If your church doesn't hold a CLA Church Licence, information about obtaining one can be found at **uk.ccli.com**

PREFACE

Each of us has a favourite gospel. Mine varies – now one, now another. Augustine was right when he said that looking at Jesus through the gospels is like looking through a prism: you need all four individual angles to gain an adequate picture. Two of the ways in which Luke looks at the good news of Christ are especially important to me.

For Luke Jesus is the Saviour. Yes, of course, Jesus saves in all the gospels; the very name 'Jesus' means 'Saviour'. But it is only in Luke that he is called the Saviour, and that from the very beginning. The angels at Bethlehem bring this news of great joy: 'To you is born this day a Saviour who is Christ the Lord' (see Luke 2:11). In the temple the aged Simeon echoes them, 'My eyes have seen the salvation which you have prepared in the sight of every nation' (see v. 30). At the end, too, the passion and death of Jesus are scenes of healing, forgiveness and salvation. Jesus heals the ear of the high priest's servant. He forgives those who are nailing him to the cross. He welcomes the penitent thief into paradise, and all depart from the scene beating their breasts. Throughout the gospel Jesus not merely accepts sinners and forgives the penitent; he goes out to find them. He calls that inquisitive crook Zacchaeus down from his sycamore tree in Jericho to be a disciple. In the parables there is joy in heaven when the man searches and finds the sheep he has lost, and the woman the coin she has lost, not to mention the wholesale celebration when the father finds the prodigal son he has lost. For the great feast the Master positively forces and squeezes the guests into his banquet.

The other aspect is the ever-present Spirit. Luke had experienced the Spirit at work in the churches of Paul, the Spirit-filled chaos at Corinth. In his second volume, Acts, Luke describes the Spirit active in the earliest days of the Christian movement, guiding and gently coaxing the enthusiastic followers in the right direction. Shining his light further back he shows us the Spirit again at beginning and end of Jesus' own story. The whole explosion is ignited when the Holy Spirit comes upon Mary and the power of the Most High covers her with its shadow. Jesus is filled with the Spirit when he goes out into the desert to ponder his mission and confront his demons. When he sets out his programme in the synagogue at Nazareth, the Spirit of the Lord is upon him. When the risen Christ finally departs from his bewildered followers, he sends them back into Jerusalem to await the signal for the start of their own mission, the coming of the Spirit at Pentecost. Luke reassures us of the presence of the Spirit in Christ's Church to this day.

You must experience the good news of Luke for yourself, and I pray that these pages may help you to appreciate and love it.

Dom Henry Wansbrough OSB

CONTENTS

Introduction 9

1. The prologue 12
2. Zechariah and Elizabeth 14
3. The message to Zechariah 16
4. The annunciation to Mary 18
5. Mary's visit to Elizabeth 20
6. The Magnificat 22
7. The birth of John the Baptist 24
8. The Benedictus 26
9. The birth of Jesus 28
10. Jesus in the temple 30
11. Jesus in the temple again 32
12. Community of repentance 34
13. The Baptist's message 36
14. The coming of the Spirit 38
15. Testing in the desert 40
16. Jesus at Nazareth 42
17. A day at Capernaum 44
18. The call of four disciples 46
19. Two miraculous cures 48
20. A feast with sinners 50
21. Sabbath controversies 52
22. The choice of the twelve 54
23. The beatitudes 56
24. Demands of discipleship 58
25. Parables 60
26. Two prophetic cures 62
27. Reflections on John the Baptist 64
28. The woman who was a sinner 66
29. The women with Jesus 68
30. The parable of the sower 70
31. The calming of the storm 72
32. The Gerasene demoniac 74
33. The woman with a haemorrhage, and Jairus' daughter 76
34. The mission of the twelve 78
35. The feeding of the 5,000 80
36. The first prophecy of the Passion 82
37. The transfiguration 84
38. The disciples' failure 86
39. Journey to Jerusalem 88
40. The mission of the 72 90
41. A final blessing 92
42. The good Samaritan 94
43. Martha and Mary 96
44. The Lord's Prayer 98
45. Parables on prayer (I) 100
46. Reactions to Jesus 102
47. Jesus' counterattack 104
48. Courage in the face of persecution 106
49. The danger of possessions 108
50. Waiting for the return 110

51	A call for decision	112	76	The resurrection of the dead ... 163
52	Time for repentance	114	77	Christ not only Son but Lord of David ... 165
53	Healings on a sabbath	116	78	The scribes and the poor widow ... 167
54	Jesus sets his face to Jerusalem	118	79	An apocalypse (I): the destruction of Jerusalem ... 169
55	Guests for dinner	120	80	An apocalypse (II): the coming of the Son of Man ... 171
56	The great supper	122	81	Judas betrays Jesus ... 173
57	Lost sheep and lost coin	124	82	Preparations for the Passover supper ... 175
58	The prodigal son	126	83	The institution of the Eucharist ... 177
59	The crafty steward	128	84	Parting instructions (I) ... 179
60	The rich man and Lazarus	130	85	Parting instructions (II) ... 181
61	A challenge to disciples	132	86	The Mount of Olives ... 183
62	Two stories about gratitude	134	87	The arrest ... 185
63	The day of the Son of Man	136	88	Peter's denials and the mockery of Jesus ... 187
64	Two parables on prayer	138	89	Jesus before the elders ... 189
65	Two approaches to Jesus	140	90	Jesus before Pilate ... 191
66	A prophecy of the Passion	142	91	Jesus before Herod ... 193
67	Jesus heals Bartimaeus	144	92	The way to Calvary ... 195
68	Zacchaeus	146	93	The crucifixion ... 197
69	The parable of the pounds	148	94	The crucified Jesus ... 199
70	Jesus' royal entry into Jerusalem	150	95	The death of Jesus ... 201
71	Lament over Jerusalem	152	96	The burial of Jesus ... 203
72	Jesus in the temple	155	97	The empty tomb ... 205
73	A challenge to the authority of Jesus	157	98	The message to the eleven ... 207
74	The parable of the wicked tenants	159	99	The road to Emmaus ... 209
75	On paying tribute to Caesar	161	100	Jesus appears to the eleven ... 211
			101	The ascension ... 213

INTRODUCTION

The evangelist Luke wrote nearly a quarter of the New Testament – one of the longest of the gospels and its companion volume, Acts. So on any count he is an important witness to the Christian message and to its development in the early church. Some scholars think he was responsible also for adding touches to other writings of the New Testament. Who was this important writer? There is no suggestion that he was one of the twelve, the original companions chosen by Jesus, or indeed that he knew Jesus during his lifetime; but tradition has it that he accompanied Paul on some of his journeys, for certain passages in Acts are written in the first person plural: 'We travelled… We embarked…' Tradition also holds that Paul mentioned this Luke, 'the beloved physician', as his only faithful companion in prison (Colossians 4:14; 2 Timothy 4:11). 'Luke' is, of course, one form of 'Lucius', a very common name in the Roman world. So to know that the author was called Luke does not of itself tell us very much.

Luke's world

More important than knowing the identity of the author in the sense of 'Luke Who?' is to know that he received the apostolic tradition about Jesus from the early communities. Not himself an eyewitness of the life of Jesus, he listened to the reports handed down in the Christian communities about the Master. He stresses that he did his research among the previous accounts of the good news. He obviously drew heavily on Mark, the first gospel to be written, and on another source, either Matthew or a collection of the sayings of the Lord commonly known as Q and now lost. He also had his own sources, on which he drew for such events as the stories of Jesus' infancy or the appearances after the resurrection, and especially the parables. The language of these is so thoroughly Lukan that they are most likely to have been received by him in oral form; he was the first to commit them to paper. He himself was thoroughly familiar with Judaism, but he does not expect his readers to know the Jewish tradition too well. From the way he writes, it is clear that he moved in a more sophisticated society than Mark, and a more Gentile society than the very Jewish Matthew. His courtly vocabulary and style (from 'Theophilus, your Excellency' onwards) places him within literary circles. The subtlety and wit of his writing suggest an educated background. The ease with which he handles financial and economic affairs similarly places him in moderately affluent society. It is all the more remarkable that Luke misses no opportunity to underline the responsibility and danger of being wealthy, and the need for generosity, and to stress that Jesus came to bring the good news first of all to the marginalised and wretched.

Luke the person

In reading a gospel it is a joy to get to know the author. It is, after all, through his (unlikely in that day to be 'her') eyes that we see Jesus and hear his message. Luke is a gentle and sensitive person, very aware of the importance of little touches of affection. He explains the grief of the widow of Nain by telling us that her son was her only son. When Peter denies Jesus, he is brought to repentance because Jesus just turns silently to look at him. Luke has a gentle wit too, and can quietly make fun of the rich fool in the parable, showing the man's self-importance by his repeatedly talking about himself. The characters in his parables are not like those in Matthew's parables, pure villains or pure heroes; they are mixed characters like the rest of us, with good and bad points, often doing the right thing for the wrong reason, so that we can become quite attached to rascals like the crafty steward or the lazy householder. One thing Luke stresses above all is that we are all sinners, in need of repentance on our part and forgiveness on God's. He portrays with particular tenderness the difference between the proud Pharisee and the humble tax-collector at prayer, and with particular warmth the joy at the repentance of a single sinner, or the delicacy of Jesus' silent welcome for the woman who was a sinner. His word-painting, too, is brilliant, so that the stories of the infancy of John the Baptist and Jesus, before their mission begins, breathe the atmosphere of the Old Testament: we are still living in that world and awaiting the coming of the Spirit at the baptism of Jesus.

Four faces of a prism

One of the most enriching advantages of studying the gospels is the possibility of seeing Jesus through the eyes of the four different gospel writers. Each is different, each puts the message differently, each stresses different aspects of Jesus. Down the ages, writers have likened the aspects portrayed by the four gospels to four different portraits of the same person. Augustine of Hippo called them four facets of the same prism. They complement one another and, through this interplay, all together add up to a richer and more profound picture of the Master than each separately could provide. From the earliest time they were all accepted by Christians as a valid record of what Jesus did, taught and suffered. Other versions of the Jesus story were rejected by Christians. Such versions have survived in a few copies, or been recently rediscovered in single copies by researchers, after being lost or hidden for centuries. Others presumably – perhaps including some of the accounts mentioned by Luke in his preface – are still lost. Obviously they were not felt by the first Christian generations to render an acceptable or reliable picture of their Lord and Master, or – as other theological traditions have it – to be inspired. The Christian community did not recognise in them the face of Jesus.

How to read this book

Like the other books in this series, this book is not meant to be a technical commentary, discussing the views of scholars, putting forward many possibilities and assessing them all. In most cases I have simply chosen the interpretation which seemed to me best. All reading should, of course, be done with a critical mind, but criticism is not the purpose of this reading. The purpose of reading the gospel is to come closer to the Lord, the Lord God in the Lord Jesus. I suggest that you read the passage given, slowly and prayerfully, then read the comment (or part of it) till you have enough thoughts for reflection. There is no need to read a whole section at one sitting. If part of a comment provides you with enough material for thought, stop; then start again on another occasion. It may be useful to have a gospel text beside you, so that you can refer to it while you read the comment. The comment is only a means to an end, and the end is a loving understanding of the gospel itself. While I have been writing this commentary, Luke has become a gentle friend. Let him lead you to the Lord and Saviour he portrays.

1

Luke 1:1–4

The prologue

The good news of salvation

There is always an excitement in starting to read a gospel. This is the good news of salvation! Even those last four familiar words introduce a couple of concepts which seemed special for Luke, 'good news' and 'salvation'.

The Greek word translated 'good news' was familiar round the Mediterranean world, which was all part of the Roman empire. The expression was used of special items of good news about the emperor and his family, such as a victory or the birth of an heir. This 'good news' was flashed round the world (it took about four days from Rome to Alexandria by ship), and the different communities sent back congratulatory gifts to the emperor. Luke does not use the noun 'good news', but only the verb 'proclaim the good news'. This has a link to the fine passage in Isaiah 61, 'He has sent me to bring the news to the afflicted, to soothe the broken-hearted, to proclaim liberty to captives.' And indeed Luke is always mindful of Jesus' announcement precisely to such underprivileged people.

The preface to the gospel

Many short scientific treatises have survived from the first century: works on astronomy, medicine, arms manufacture, navigation, as well as little historical booklets, of about the same size as Luke's work. This formal preface – and Luke is the only gospel to have such a preface – identifies his work as a short scientific monograph. He clearly wants to introduce his two-volume work (Acts is the second volume) as just such a scientific historical treatise.

Both volumes are addressed to Theophilus, with the complimentary title ('your Excellency') which suggests that he was a high-ranking official. This again adds dignity to the work, though we can never know whether Theophilus was a real person. His name means 'Friend of God'. Whether or not he was a real person, the name suggests the attitude needed for reading the gospel. It is no use reading the gospel as simply a scientific or historical work. It must be approached with prayer and openness to God, a willingness to listen to a friend, to accept the message and respond to it.

Luke the historian

Luke stresses that the teaching he conveys is 'well-founded' or 'safe'. He has checked it carefully with eyewitnesses and ministers of the word. He does not want to leave his readers in any doubt about the reliability of his message. Yet there are ways in which his gospel differs from the gospels of Mark and Matthew which came before him. What about these differences? When the evangelists differ from one another, is one right and the other wrong?

Luke certainly rearranges his material to make it an attractive and well-told story. Matthew collected together much of the teaching of Jesus and presents it as the sermon on the mount; Jesus is teaching on a mountain, as Moses did, giving his new law as Moses gave the old law. Luke has a similar collection, but it is a sermon on the plain, and much shorter, as though Luke thought there was too much to digest at one sitting. Some of the same sayings of Jesus are placed by Luke in Jesus' great final journey to Jerusalem. Jesus is going up to Jerusalem to die – as all prophets must die at Jerusalem – and gives much of his most important teaching in the course of that journey.

The sermon anyway occurs later in Luke. Instead, Luke puts early in Jesus' ministry the incident when Jesus' own townsfolk try to throw him off the cliff. It looks in Mark and Matthew as though this incident happened later, after the call of the first disciples. But Luke brings it in at the beginning and makes it the occasion when Jesus gives his important opening proclamation, 'The Spirit of the Lord is on me' and he will bring healing not to his own compatriots but to the Gentiles, beyond the frontiers of his people.

Prayer

Open my eyes and ears, Lord, to your good news of salvation. Help me to listen to your historian, Luke, as he tells the story of how you save the world through your Son, Jesus Christ.

2

Luke 1:5–7

Zechariah and Elizabeth

Luke's story begins in Jerusalem, in the temple, and this is no accident. We are being told that God's promises were first and foremost to Israel, and that they were fulfilled in Jesus. So the story starts in an atmosphere of the best piety of the Old Testament. Zechariah was a priest, and his wife too was of the line of Aaron; so they both belonged to the most sacred part of the sacred people. Both, also, were 'upright in the sight of God', observing the law in all its details.

The law was no tiresome, restricting force, but a liberating, joyful gift. 'Your Law, O God, is my life,' cries the psalmist so often; 'Your Law is a light to my eyes.' Its detailed prescriptions helped to bring every moment of life into conscious association with the Lord. I remember an Israeli Jew picking me a banana from a tree in the Plain of Sharon. Before he ate his own banana, he blessed God for it, and explained to me the joy of thanking God for even such a little gift. The law was the proof of God's special love for Israel, God's special closeness to his people that he should want their life to accord with his, their life to be lived according to his principles. It was also the law which made sure that every individual was kept free to serve God, could stand tall and proud before God, dependent only on God rather than on any human master.

The temple of Jerusalem

Jerusalem plays an important part in Luke's story. The gospel begins and ends there. The second half of the gospel consists of Jesus' great journey to Jerusalem, where he takes possession of the temple and uses it as his own platform for his teaching. It is at Jerusalem that the great events of the Passion are played out, and in Luke's account Jesus appears after his resurrection in and around Jerusalem. The first Christian community, which Luke paints in such inspiring colours in Acts, is at Jerusalem. It is from Jerusalem that the gospel spreads to the nations.

The centre of Jerusalem was the temple. It was this that made Jerusalem, says the Roman author Pliny, 'far the most distinguished city of the East'. The temple itself was an amazing building, as one can still today guess from the huge esplanade on which it stood, the size of twelve football fields. There were ten gilded gates, each of which was closed every evening (on rollers) by a team of 20 men. The biggest of the great stones which the disciples admired ('Master, look at the size of these stones!') is the size of a modern motor coach and weighs 400 tons. Salisbury Cathedral would fit comfortably twice into one of the colonnaded porticoes round the perimeter. It was thronged by Jewish pilgrims who came gratefully from their exile in the Diaspora, especially at the great feasts such as Passover or Pentecost, for this was the place of God's presence on earth, the meeting place between God and his people, gathered from all over the world. One can understand why love for the temple played such a part in every Jewish heart.

Barrenness

Devoted to the temple and the service of God though they were, this old couple seemed condemned to be childless. God seemed to have neglected their dogged fidelity to him. On every level this was a disaster. No lively family to keep them young. No grandchildren to spoil. No support in old age, in an era when only children could be expected to provide support for the elderly. No hope for the future. And especially for a Jewish couple a full family was (and is) the sign of a special blessing. Most of all in such an age of expectation, no possibility that their child would be the promised Messiah, the hope of every Jewish mother. 'Elizabeth was barren and they were both advanced in years.' It seemed like the end. No one familiar with the Old Testament could fail to think of Abraham and his wife Sarah, who were nomads without hope in their childless old age when Abraham received the promise of God. So the stage is set for the loving and merciful intervention of God to save his faithful servants.

Prayer

Lord, you leave me sometimes in a situation where I can see no way out. Keep me trusting in your love, however dark the horizon. Help me to know that I am always in your presence, and that you prepare for me greater blessings than I could ever hope.

3

Luke 1:11–25

The message to Zechariah

Two panels

These two chapters of the infancy stories are built on a comparison: John the Baptist is compared to Jesus. In each comparison, the importance and sanctity of John serves to show the even greater importance and sanctity of Jesus. John and Jesus in these stories look to each other, comparable but with a difference. First we see how John is the climax of all the hopes of the Old Testament; then we see how Jesus is even greater than John.

First there are the two annunciations, to Zechariah and to Mary. In each case an angel comes to tell that a son will be born against all hope and all natural means. In each case the birth is an occasion for celebration of those around. In each case the moment of religious dedication is the occasion for a prophecy of the future greatness and role of the child. The visitation joins the two panels together.

In each scene the contrast also goes into detail. Zechariah and Elizabeth are 'upright in the sight of God', but Mary 'enjoys God's favour'. The one child will be called John (most Hebrew names have a meaning, and this means 'the grace of God'), but the other will be called Jesus, 'Saviour'. John will be 'great in the sight of the Lord' and will be dedicated to God as a Nazirite ('He must drink no wine, no strong drink'), but Jesus will be called Son of the Most High. John will prepare a people fit for the Lord, but Jesus will rule over the house of Jacob forever. Zechariah doubts the angel's message and loses the power of speech, but Mary believes and receives a blessing.

A biblical scene

The story of this pious couple is the final stage in the process of God preparing a people for himself. The angel's appearance to Zechariah reminds the reader of the appearance of an angel to the mother of Samson in Judges 13. She also was barren when an angel of the Lord God appeared to her and told her she would conceive and give birth to a son. The son should be dedicated to the Lord, and even while he was in the womb his mother should drink no wine or fermented liquor. The Spirit of God was upon him, too, for his mission.

Abraham also received a similar visit from the angel of the Lord to promise that his barren wife Sarah would bear him Isaac (Genesis 18). The purpose of these stories is not merely to relate miraculous happenings. It is to underline two lessons: first, that God furthers the history of his own people with tireless watchfulness, sending his own Spirit on his chosen leaders. Second, God does not rely on human ability, skill or achievement, but chooses the most unlikely person to be his envoy and further his purposes. In the more ordinary circumstances of our daily lives, one never knows when a dazzling insight or a valuable correction may come from the most unlikely source, which one can afterwards see to have been a message from the Lord. In the case of Zechariah and Elizabeth, they were 'has-beens', ready to sink into decrepitude and oblivion. Then they received the dazzling mission of rearing John to prepare a people fit for the Lord.

Scenes in a drama

Luke is such a neat artist with words! He tells these stories in the language of the Old Testament, imitating the formulas of the Greek Old Testament ('In the days of X', 'It came to pass that' and so on) to remind us that we are witnessing the climax of that long preparation. But also each scene of these two chapters of the infancy stories is neat and well-wrapped in itself. Each begins with an entrance ('There appeared to him the angel of the Lord') and concludes with an exit ('And when he came out…'). Each scene contains a lively dialogue between the two chief characters to convey the message which is the point of the scene. The contrast with Matthew's infancy stories is marked: there, no human being speaks to any other, Joseph never even explains to Mary why he is dragging her off to Bethlehem or Egypt! Matthew has no memorable characters like Zechariah and Elizabeth or Simeon and Anna.

Prayer

Lord, grant that I too may have some part in preparing the way of the Lord, in making ready a people fit for you. Help me to realise that any work of mine for you is empty unless it is built on my own full dedication to you.

4

Luke 1:26–38

The annunciation to Mary

If the biblical backcloth to Zechariah's message is the annunciation to Samson's mother, to Mary's annunciation the backcloth is the message to Samuel's mother in 1 Samuel 1. Hannah seems destined to remain childless, when she receives a message of assurance from Eli the priest that her prayer for a son will be answered. She presents the longed-for child to Eli with a song of joy very similar to Mary's Magnificat. But the prophecies about Mary's son take us straight back to the prophecies Nathan made to David: 'the Lord God will give him the throne of his ancestor David' forever. He will be Son of the Most High, just as Nathan promised David that his descendants would rule forever, and that God would always treat them with the gentleness of a father.

Mary

What was Mary's reaction to all this? The normal age for a girl's betrothal in those days was soon after the twelfth birthday (for boys four years later). We certainly do not have to think of a scene like a Fra Angelico painting, Mary kneeling piously at a prie-dieu, while a feather-winged angel addresses her. The angel need not have taken any physical form at all, and no audible word need have been spoken. It was a message from God, and the gospel – though it delights in visual and imaginable details – is careful to give no physical description of God's messenger. The angels are the powers of God and need no feathers.

I like to imagine this young Galilean girl, intrigued by the budding of her own sexuality, excited at the prospect of marriage, daydreaming while she feeds the family chickens or brings water from the well. At a certain moment she knows that God is calling her (we can use only physical terms, as though she heard a sound!) to bear a son by the power of the Most High. What was that son to be? To a people who knew the Bible, the best way of describing his future greatness was in terms of the promises made to David about the special favour which God would show his royal line. Mary's child would fulfil these promises of a son who would reign forever. God would be a father to him, and he a son to God. How much did Mary understand about her son? It is not necessary to suppose that she already understood his divinity. How much do the words of the dialogue owe to Luke's later understanding and formulation? They certainly accord better with the disciples' understanding and language after the resurrection than with their first puzzled and wondering reactions.

Mary's consent

The two clues to Mary's spirituality as Luke sees it come at beginning and end. At the beginning comes the greeting, 'You who enjoy God's favour.' Jerome, who translated the gospels into Latin, read this as 'full of grace', which suggests a fluid-filled receptacle, and grace has often been represented as a divine fuel or a current of divine power for good action. Rather, it is the unmerited favour of an all-powerful ruler, who needs to justify his deeds to no one; he simply chooses his favourites unpredictably and showers his gifts upon them as he will. Primarily it is the personal relationship, the choice and the love, and only secondarily the gifts, the graces which follow. So God simply fixed his choice upon Mary, quite arbitrarily, not for any merits of hers.

At the end comes Mary's reply. 'Behold, the handmaid of the Lord,' may be rendered in more modern terms, 'You see before you the Lord's servant.' Absolute consent, without conditions. The meaning may be deeper yet, if we see an allusion to Isaiah's songs of the servant of the Lord. The four songs depict a servant who yields absolutely to the Lord's will, to end in suffering and humiliation, before final vindication. Jesus certainly spoke of himself in these terms, and it is attractive to see his mother also using this terminology to signify her utter, unconditional assent to God's call. Amid all the excitement, the young girl will have realised that no great task is easy. Luke shows her pledging in these terms the suffering and endurance which her consent implied. In this, as elsewhere in Luke's gospel, Mary is the first and most faithful model for her son's disciples.

Prayer

Lord, you sometimes give me tasks which I do not understand. Let me take your mother as my model in willingness to respond to your call and in gentle courage and endurance through difficulties.

5 Luke 1:39–45

Mary's visit to Elizabeth

Mary's kindness

There are several dimensions to the story of Mary's visit to Elizabeth. It is the first story in Luke of human kindness and affection, qualities which are so important in this gospel. It is a week's walk from Nazareth to the territory of Judah, an expedition into a different world, and yet Mary goes to support her ageing relative and share with her the excitement and worries of pregnancy. From a literary point of view it is thoroughly satisfying that the two separate annunciations should be so linked before the two separate birth-stories. The two panels are here brought together. But there is also a touching appreciation of the human dimension: the delight of the two mothers-to-be in their babies and their concentration on them comes to delightful expression in their conversation. There is something especially charming in the way the older woman bows to the younger and addresses her with a formal, biblical beatitude, 'Blessed is she who believed', to which the younger replies with the youthful outpouring of her heart in the Magnificat. Luke's writing always has great delicacy, which comes to full expression here.

Fulfilment

There is never any doubt that the process taking place is guided in detail by God's plan. Of this Luke gives us little indications, and especially of prophecies made in the course of the gospel story and fulfilled later within the story. In the annunciation to Zechariah we had heard of John that 'even from his mother's womb he will be filled with the Holy Spirit'. To anyone who knows the Bible this was a hint that he would be a prophet like Jeremiah, whose prophecies begin, 'The word of the Lord came to me saying, "Before I formed you in the womb I knew you, before you came to birth I consecrated you".' Now we see John fulfilling the angel's word, silently prophesying by his movement in the womb. The movement itself is charmingly described: the word used for 'leapt' is normally used for a dance of joy or the skipping and gambolling of lambs, and the word translated 'joy' indicates thrill, delight and excitement.

'Mother of my Lord'

Elizabeth's greeting slips out so easily that one can easily miss its import. The title 'Lord' has already been used in the infancy stories a dozen times, each time signifying the Lord God, the initiator of the whole chain of events. Now for the first time it is used of Jesus. This one word is an excellent measure of the gradually deepening understanding and appreciation of the person of Jesus during the development of the New Testament. It was the word used in the Greek Bible to translate the unpronounceable Name of God, Yahweh. The Name is full of awe and dignity. In the earliest gospel (Mark), 'Lord' is used of Jesus only by people speaking to Jesus, calling him 'Lord!', in which sense it can mean no more than 'Sir!' Apart from this it is used only of the Lord God. Matthew advances on this only at the empty tomb, speaking of 'the place where the Lord lay' (28:6, AV). By the time of Luke, faith in the divine status of Christ shines through in the almost careless way in which 'Lord' may be used either of the Lord God or of Jesus the Lord: 7:13, 'When the Lord saw her he felt sorry for her', etc. Here truly it is the Lord God, walking upon earth. So the import of Elizabeth's greeting to 'the mother of my Lord' is staggering.

Now here not only is the baby John 'filled with the Spirit from his mother's womb' as Zechariah had already been told, but his mother too as she is inspired to bless Mary.

A Spirit-filled world

Luke is constantly reminding us that every movement in the advance of the gospel is guided by the Spirit. This is less evident when Luke is following Mark's gospel (roughly from the baptism of Jesus till the story of the empty tomb), but more when he is writing more freely on his own, in these infancy stories, in the resurrection appearances, and above all in Acts.

Reflection

Of all women you are the most blessed, and blessed is the fruit of your womb.

6

Luke 1:46–56

The Magnificat

One of the most attractive features of Luke's infancy narratives is the three lovely and joyful canticles sung over the two children. A well-known scripture scholar has said, 'As soon as Jesus is born, everyone bursts into song.' Indeed, it happens even before the birth of Jesus. These songs, Mary's Magnificat, Zechariah's Benedictus and Simeon's Nunc Dimittis, now taken over into Christian liturgy, express wonderfully the joy and gratitude of the three principal adults in these stories, drawing Christians to share in their feelings. One can imagine the overflowing joy of the young girl at meeting her elderly relative. At last she can fully share on intimate terms the secret and the pent-up feelings of approaching motherhood which she has been cherishing since she gave her consent at the annunciation.

The song of Mary falls obviously into three parts, the first five lines telling of what the Lord has done for Mary herself, the last seven drawing the wider consequences for the world – all these built on verbs of action. They are jointed together at the centre by a couplet reflecting on the generosity of God: 'Holy is his name, and his faithful love extends age after age to those who fear him.'

The poor of the Lord

The song echoes most closely the song of Hannah at the birth of her son, Samuel. Hannah had been considered barren, and, though loved by her husband, this was the tragedy of her life until the Lord gave her a son, whom she dedicated to the Lord. The similarity with Mary's situation is obvious.

The spirit of the song is, however, more widely applied than to just one individual. Mary expresses the sentiment of all Israel, and in this way too is the spearhead of the whole people. Ever since the exodus from Egypt, Israel had relied on God's protection for its very survival. In Egypt the Hebrews had been a depressed, hated and alien minority. In the desert they had felt themselves utterly dependent on God – and the lonely starkness of the desert is a great place for anyone to experience the presence and power of God. After the settlement in Canaan the

Spirit of God, descending upon the 'judges', had rescued his people from repeated foreign dominations. As the wealth of the nation increased, so did oppression of the poor and helpless. Accordingly, at the Babylonian exile, the remnant of the people as a whole saw themselves as the wretched and oppressed, dependent for their existence on the generosity of the Lord. This became a central theme in their spirituality, and the later prophets and the psalms see God above all as the deliverer of the oppressed.

With the coming of the Romans, and the increasing poverty and oppression which this brought, the domination of many people by very few, a longing for deliverance grew ever stronger and more vocal. So throughout the infancy stories we are made aware of the helplessness of those to whom the Lord sends his salvation. Old Zechariah and Elizabeth are childless. Mary can find no house to give birth. Hireling shepherds are the first to hear the good news. Mary and Joseph can afford only the offering of the very poor.

Mary thanks the Lord for the answer she has received to her own perfect gift of herself to God, and for the response which this implies to the prayers of all those who depend on God. The phrases of her prayer are drawn almost entirely from the grateful pleas of the poor in the prophetic literature. She personifies the remnant of Israel.

Faithful love

The theme of her song is, in effect, 'his faithful love', an expression which comes twice in the hymn, as it does also in Zechariah's song. 'For his faithful love endures forever' is the continuous refrain of Psalm 136. Matthew three times repeats the phrase of Hosea, 'What I want is faithful love, not sacrifice.' So this idea of faithful love is at the very centre of Israel's concept of God. It was first proclaimed by God himself in the desert of Sinai as the meaning of his name. It remained in the forefront of Israel's mind, alluded to constantly in the scriptures. God is a God not of anger but of generous and enduring forgiveness. And human beings must show this quality too.

Prayer

The more helpless I am, Lord, the more I throw myself on your faithful love. Help me to avoid all arrogance, pride and pomposity. Let me remember that all my hope is in you, O Lord.

7

Luke 1:57–66

The birth of John the Baptist

The birth of a son

The stories of these two chapters form two panels, comparing and contrasting the two families, and principally the two boys. The two stories have been linked together at the visitation, and now they separate again. The overwhelming impression of this first scene of birth is bustle and joy, family and neighbours fussing around to share in Elizabeth's joy at the son she had never expected to bear. The contrasting factor at the birth of Jesus will be joy in heaven: at John's birth the joy is on earth, from the neighbours and relations. At the birth of Jesus the angels in heaven, as well as the shepherds on earth, will rejoice.

What's in a name?

Names are always significant to the Hebrew mind. It was felt that they somehow constituted the person. So when God brought all the wild animals to Adam and he named them, he was in a way giving them their nature, constituting them as themselves and asserting his God-like sovereignty over them. There are many stories in the Old Testament which explain the names of characters: 'Isaac' in Hebrew means, or is close to meaning, 'will smile/laugh' (originally an abbreviation for 'God will smile on him') and this element of smiling recurs frequently in the stories: Sarah smiling in the tent, Isaac laughing with Ishmael. 'Jacob', more ominously, means 'will supplant', which is realised in his supplanting his brother Esau. When Jacob has finally abandoned his trickiness and become respectable, God gives him a new name, 'Israel', as a sign of approval and adoption. So, later in the gospel story, Jesus will give a new name to Simon, 'Peter', and so create him 'Rock' of foundation. (It must surely originally have been a nickname which was soon found to have special significance.)

The name John is a combination of the shortened divine name Yahweh, or Ja, and the word for grace or favour. So 'God will show him favour'. This provides one more link between the two families, reminding the reader of the angel's greeting to Mary, 'you who enjoy God's favour'. The name itself has a nationalistic ring to it, ever since the

Maccabean leader John, who had led the Jews in the second century. The Maccabees had been the spearhead of resistance to Greek attempts to dissolve the Jews and their religion into the common culture of the eastern Mediterranean. So the name John itself proclaims that Israel is the special object of God's favour, for whom God has a special regard and special plans.

Obedience

Luke is constantly aware of the importance of obedience to God's commands. Mary is the first disciple and model of disciples by her obedience and acceptance of God's word through the angel. So now Zechariah wins back his voice by insisting on obedience to the angel's choice of a name for his son, flying in the face of family tradition. The angel said he would be John and John he shall be! It is also an example of Luke's constant care to show his reader the fulfilment of prophecies made in the course of the gospel, reminding the gospel reader of God's constant guiding hand in this vital moment of history: what he promises he brings to fulfilment.

Prayer

Lord, the birth of a child is always a sign of your favour, a pledge of your continuing gift of life, now and hereafter. We thank you for the children born today, and pray that they may be loved. May they be guided to recognise and respond to your love. May they also in their lives show your love to others.

8 Luke 1:67–80

The Benedictus

God's promises fulfilled

Zechariah's joyful song of praise falls into two halves, the first looking back to the promises of God which are now fulfilled, the second looking forward to the prophetic role of the child so recently born.

Zechariah (and through him the evangelist) sees these events as the fulfilment and culmination of the whole of the Old Testament. This is clear from the mention of those two central historical figures, David and Abraham. They stand for the two major periods of Israel's history, the time of the patriarchs and the time of the kingdom. Mention of the promises to Abraham immediately brings to mind the promise that his descendants would be as the stars of the sky or the sands on the seashore. Mention of the promises to David brings to mind the promise that David's descendants would inherit a throne forever, and that God would consider them as his sons, correcting them as a parent corrects children. These were the two pillars on which Israel's hope was built during the dark days of the exile and the subsequent oppression of the impoverished and powerless remnant.

Matching these two significant figures are two evocative concepts, the covenant and God's faithful love. The covenant was the basis of Israel's existence. The group of escaped slaves around Moses were at their lowest ebb: they had been oppressed in Egypt and subjected to ethnic cleansing as the hated remnant of a dominating foreign power. Escaping, they were pursued into the wastes of Sinai where only the most experienced small group can survive, and even complained that they longed to return to the fleshpots, the leeks and the garlic, of Egypt. At this moment God created them a people, and his own people, a people closer to their God than any other people had been; he made with them a covenant, promising them his own protection. This was an agreement, like an alliance between two powers, or an overlord and a subject people. Israel was to be God's people: he would protect them and they would be faithful to him. This was the basis of their life, of their very existence as a people.

And then, when they had so quickly deserted him by worshipping the golden calf (or bull), he proclaimed the meaning of his name as faithful love. The prophet Hosea gave a new intensity to the concept by his imagery of this love as the passionate and unshakable love of a man for his unfaithful wife. Another dimension is the family love of siblings who stand by each other in ultimate distress and disaster. This was the love which God showed by bringing his promises to their fulfilment. It is the key to the first part of Zechariah's canticle.

Freedom

God has visited his people and set them free, proclaims Zechariah. Free from oppression or from sin? The domination of the Romans was certainly hated, but just how oppressive it was remains disputed. There was financial and economic distress, and the distress of uncured sickness. But there is no firm evidence that there was widespread dire penury and want. In this canticle it is more likely that Zechariah has in mind primarily the freedom to serve the Lord.

Prophet of the Most High

John is to be a prophet preparing the way for the Lord, as will be seen when his ministry begins. He is to proclaim forgiveness and repentance for salvation, paving the way for Jesus' own message of forgiveness. As such he is the prototype also of the Christian apostle, for the apostles in Acts in the same way are filled with the Spirit. The apostles, too, proclaim forgiveness in their call to repentance at the end of each of their sermons in Acts.

He is to 'guide our feet into the way of peace'. By so doing he begins the mission which will continue into the mission of the disciples. In Luke Jesus characteristically brings peace by his miracles. The angels sing 'Peace on earth' at Jesus' birth. The crowds proclaim peace in heaven at Jesus' entry into Jerusalem. Missioners are told by Jesus to bring peace where they go, and to Cornelius Peter describes Jesus' message as the good news of peace. Peace, reconciliation and forgiveness are the watchwords of Luke's Christian message.

Prayer

The rising sun from on high has come to visit us, to give light to those who live in darkness and the shadow dark as death.

9 Luke 2:1–20

The birth of Jesus

Luke the popular historian

Luke is a historian, and is careful to show that Jesus' birth is an event in world history. So he dates the birth of Jesus in relation to the great Roman Emperor Augustus and the census of tribute. The provinces of the empire paid tribute to Rome, but during much of King Herod's reign as a dependent sovereign, Palestine had been exempt. It was only after Herod invaded a neighbour and excited the emperor's anger that tribute was imposed. The first assessment of resources to be taxed roused great opposition and petty revolts and was remembered years later. However, Quirinius is now known to have been governor of Syria in AD6/7, and it is also highly unlikely that all the populace would have had to register in the town of their remote ancestors. Luke was not a modern research historian; he simply uses well-known figures and events of about that time to link his story to world history. We do not know exactly when Jesus was born. For the believer, this ignorance itself has a message as part of Christ's reversal of values: the Son of God was born not in the capital city of an empire but in a tiny hill village of an obscure country. We do not know his age or his birthday (25 December was chosen later because it was the pagan feast day of the rebirth of the sun after the winter solstice). As the people of Jerusalem say in John's gospel: 'When the Christ appears, no one will know where he comes from.' In fact, the place is better known than the time: the one firm element about the tradition (in both Matthew and Luke) is that he was a Nazarene, but was born in Bethlehem.

A poor and obscure birth

Luke goes out of his way to emphasise that Jesus was born in poor circumstances, with none of the advantages of position, despite being of the line of David. His parents were migrants, friendless in the town, and could find no place for the mother to give birth. There was no space for them in the *kataluma*. This Greek word does not mean 'inn' as the old Latin translation goes. So the Christmas images of inhospitable innkeepers have no place in the story. We need to imagine a large open dwelling room, on two levels. The humans are on one level, the animals at a slightly lower level. As the level for the humans is too crowded even for a precious newborn baby, Mary leans over to place her baby in the hay-filled feeding trough of the cattle. And so our Christmas crib-scene is completed by the ox and the ass. They are not mentioned in the gospel, but in Isaiah 1 the devotion of the ox and the ass to their master is contrasted with Israel's infidelity.

In Matthew Jesus' first recorded visitors are oriental sages. In Luke they are simple shepherds. Later rabbinic tradition regarded shepherds as unclean. Though this was not yet in force, night-shift shepherds were surely low on the social scale. But the shepherds also remind us that the child will be the shepherd of Israel.

The song of the angels

Jesus may be born the son of a homeless migrant, but his true significance is proclaimed by the angels. There may not be an extended family to rejoice around the newborn (as there was for John), but there is joy in heaven. The canticle is spoken not by Zechariah but by God's own messengers. The good news is announced not just to Zechariah but to the people, to Israel as a whole. The three titles they give to the baby are full of awesome promise. The Christ or Messiah, born in the city of David, is the fulfilment of all human hopes, but 'Saviour' and 'Lord' are properly divine titles. Previously these had always been applied to God, never to a human being.

The waves of praise, song and joy succeed one another: the great army of heaven, the shepherds as they bustle along, all those who heard their news, and the shepherds again as they disappear back into the night.

Prayer

Lord, with your birth as a human child you transformed the world. You became one of us so that you could take us to yourself and give us a share in your divine life. Let me treasure this honour and realise my dignity.

10 Luke 2:21-38

Jesus in the temple

The faithful of Israel

The first incident told after the birth of Jesus stresses the lesson we have already heard, that Jesus is the fulfilment of God's promises, coming to the faithful of Israel. The parents of Jesus fulfil the law rigorously, first by circumcision, then by the purification – indeed overzealously, for Joseph goes up to fulfil it too when in fact by the law only the mother is purified. Still it is underlined that they are among the poor, for they can afford the offering only of the very poor. According to Leviticus, 'if she cannot afford a lamb, she must take two turtledoves or two young pigeons' and offer their life as a symbol of recognition that all life comes from God.

There they are welcomed by the two representatives of Israel, Simeon and Anna. They represent the patient faithful, for their great age and their joy denote their patient waiting. The life of both is centred on the piety of the temple. Simeon is already so full of the Spirit that the Spirit prompts him to come forward at the exact moment. Anna also has spent her life 'serving God night and day with fasting and prayer', the two traditional good works of the law. The fact that the third traditional good work, almsgiving, is omitted shows that she is one of the faithful poor of the Lord, too poor to exercise this good work. She has no canticle of her own, but as a prophetess spreads the good news of the child 'to all who looked forward to the deliverance of Jerusalem'. Both of them are full of that lively praise of God which makes the infancy stories so positive and enthusiastic.

The canticle of Simeon

With Simeon a new vista opens up. His joyful song welcomes the child as the 'glory for your people Israel' but also as 'a light of revelation for the Gentiles', the first indication of a theme which will be so important to Luke. Writing for an audience formed in the culture of the Greco-Roman world, he points out again and again that Jesus brings salvation to all nations, not only to Israel. Again the wonderful symbol of light is used. Zechariah had sung that the child was the rising sun come from on high to visit us, those who sit in darkness. Now the light spreads to the Gentiles.

However, salvation is first for Israel, as Luke has shown us throughout these two chapters. But the first note of sadness creeps in with the hint of rejection. The child is destined for the fall as well as the rise of many in Israel, a sign that will be opposed. Both division and sadness will be the lot of Mary herself, by the piercing of her heart with a sword. Already the shadow of the cross hangs over the tender child and his mother. One may surmise also that the rejection of her son by so many of her own people was itself a sadness to her, a cause of division in her heart.

Sexual equality

The meeting and prophecy in the temple is the first really clear instance of the careful representation by Luke that men and women have equal value before the Lord, an insistence that runs through his work. Already we have had the two annunciations, to Zechariah and to Mary. Here we have Simeon and Anna. Later, Jesus will point out that the prophet brought salvation to the widow of Zarephath and the man Naaman. Two miracle stories open, respectively, 'There before him was a woman' and 'There in front of him was a man' (13:11; 14:2). Two models of persevering prayer are the friend at midnight and the persevering widow. In other lessons on prayer the contrast between the Pharisee and the tax-collector is balanced by the contrast between Martha and Mary.

In the spread of the gospel in Acts the same equality continues. Ananias and Sapphira are both punished for their sin. Aeneas and Tabitha are both healed in the neighbouring towns of Lydda and Joppa. At Athens the man Dionysius and the woman Damaris are both mentioned as coming to faith.

Prayer

Lord, grant me to wait for the coming of your salvation in the joyful hope of Simeon and Anna. Help me to welcome it as it is fulfilled in me in whatever way you will, by happiness or by sorrow. Let me see both happiness and sorrow as your light dawning from on high.

11

Luke 2:39–52

Jesus in the temple again

Jesus among the teachers of the law

This incident has captured the imagination of artists through the ages, who show the twelve-year-old Jesus teaching the teachers. This is not what the gospel says. He was sitting among the teachers, listening to them and asking them questions. It was his replies and his intelligence – the clarity and directness of the child – which astonished them, rather than his precociousness.

The background to the scene is the devoted practice of pilgrimage. Jerusalem was a real centre of pilgrimage, a sort of holy holiday. The biblical custom was three annual pilgrimages to Jerusalem for three great feasts. For the Passover it became so crowded that the theoretical limits of the city, within which the Passover must be celebrated, were extended to include the Mount of Olives. So there was a fair amount of thronging and celebrating crowds.

Didn't you know?

For me the most endearing feature of the scene is a touch typical of any twelve-year-old, which Luke has captured perfectly. Anyone who has dealt with children of that age will know their infuriating and worrying habit of disappearing, wrapped up in their own exciting preoccupations, worries or explorations. When the distracted parents have torn their hair, searched every corner, probably rung the police, the child will reappear, innocent and bright-eyed, to say, 'Didn't you know? I only went frog-hunting.' It is perfectly clear to the child that this activity was the most obvious thing in the world to do, that anyone of any sense would know exactly where this particular child was to be found, and there was nothing to worry about. This is just what the twelve-year-old Jesus does. Luke is showing us that he was human through and through. Mary, the wise mother, reacts calmly after her three-day worry, and accepts his answer without complaint or cavil. She does not understand all the implications; she merely obediently takes him for what he is, an inquiring youngster.

At the same time, of course, the reader sees where Jesus' centre of gravity lies. The English language does not allow the indefiniteness of the Greek – 'In my Father's realm, in his territory, about his business, among his friends', all are included. I am tempted to translate by a phrase which would fit in the gospel of John – 'At my Father's side.'

The adolescent

The visit to the temple is sandwiched between two brief and sober references to Jesus' hidden life at Nazareth. They contain little information. Both before and after, two elements are repeated, his growth in wisdom and the favour of God. Other factors are mentioned: he lived under his parents' authority, and he grew in maturity and in stature.

The later 'infancy gospels', documents of the second century, embroidered with Christian devotion and imagination, fill out the hidden years with the child Jesus moulding clay pigeons and breathing life into them, or – less edifyingly – withering up companions who beat him at games. These were not accepted by the early church as true accounts. The silence of the gospels is more valuable, for silence has its own worth. The mention of growth is enough to remind us that he was a real boy, youngster, young man. He went through the enquiries, daydreams, doubts, bewilderment, enthusiasms, tenderness and vigour of every growing child. He will have discovered his own sexuality, too, with all its excitements and heartache. At the base of his consciousness must have been the growing awareness of his own personality and of his union to his Father, growing in just the way that every child becomes, in unsteady leaps and bounds and unexpected gulps, aware of personal identity. The growth in wisdom did not mean that he was always serious. Many a child shows an almost awesome wisdom and then immediately bursts into inconsequent impishness or laughter.

Prayer

Jesus, you discovered yourself. You grew in wisdom and maturity. You knew what it was to obey. No doubt some of the orders of your elders were unjust and hurtful. You came to share our humanity, its joys and trials. Grant me always to be open with you and confident, and to share my humanity with you.

12 Luke 3:1–6

Community of repentance

The historical context

Luke prefaces his account of Jesus' ministry with a roll-call of worthies. Each suggests a different aspect of the world history into which Jesus was plunged. Emperor Tiberius Caesar ruled the known world, with its clanking foot-gear of battle. The Romans were engineers, whose drains, straight roads, aqueducts and theatres can be seen in Carthage, Constantinople and Cirencester, making one single, worldwide culture. The same plan of defensive wall and military camp lies visible on the shores of the Dead Sea and the banks of the Tyne. A Roman soldier in York had an inscription carved on his tombstone in his native Aramaic. Tiberius himself was a tough general – as a young man he once rode 200 miles in 24 hours – but by this time was leaving most of the affairs of state to his slimy minister, Sejanus. Locally the Roman power was represented by Pontius Pilate, the longest-serving Roman governor of Judea. His job was to guard the peace and Roman interests in the country, to keep under control the incomprehensible Jews with their odd eating habits, their waste of one day in seven, their contempt for the Olympian gods. Despite the bad press he gets from later Jewish apologists, he must have been a skilled operator, with at least some human qualities, to last so long. Pilate's opposite number on the Jewish side was the high priest.

Caiaphas worked with Pilate for nearly a decade. Pilate mostly kept his watching brief from Caesarea on the coast, while Caiaphas presided over the nation and its seething religious squabbles from his palace in Jerusalem. Annas was his father-in-law, and together they formed the centre of a powerful clan of priestly families. With his council, and no doubt his informers, he will have picked up on this charismatic figure who appeared at the crossing-point where the road to the east forded the Jordan. In the neighbouring territories (where Jesus' ministry began) an insecure dependent sovereignty was held by the three mediocre sons of that hated tycoon, King Herod the Great.

The mere mention of the rulers' names serves to sketch a world of real people going about their own businesses, with their bustling concerns and preoccupations. This was the cauldron of conflicting interests in which John and Jesus appeared.

John the Baptist's role

In Mark's gospel the Baptist simply appears at the Jordan, dressed as the prophet Elijah, describing himself in Isaiah's words as a voice crying out in the desert and offering a baptism of repentance. He is a figure heralding the end of time and God's decisive intervention in world history, warning and offering a chance to shelter from God's wrath in his community of repentance. At the same time he looks forward to a greater figure who is to come, and points this out as Jesus when he arrives on the scene. The shock waves caused by his call come to expression long after his murder in prison: the crowds have such respect for him that the temple authorities dare not upset them by denying that John was a prophet.

By the time we get to this point in Luke, we know far more about John. John's vocation and sacred quality have served as a basis on which Jesus' vocation and far greater sacred quality are built. He is not an Elijah, announcing the end of all things, but is the forerunner of Jesus. So his message prepares for that of Jesus and, later, of the disciples in Acts, for he emphatically preaches repentance and forgiveness. Throughout Luke these are the prerequisites for any approach to Jesus. Although it is stressed that John's career comes to an end before Jesus' public ministry begins, Luke tells us in Acts that John still had disciples years later in Ephesus. So John's ministry, too, had its lasting international flavour, spreading over the Jewish communities of the Mediterranean world. Was it from a Baptist community that the Alexandrian preacher Apollos came to Ephesus? Certainly Luke indicates that the concerns of John himself stretched beyond Judaism: '*All humanity shall see the salvation of God,*' he adds to the quotation from Isaiah.

Prayer

Let every valley be filled in, every mountain and hill be levelled, winding ways be straightened and rough roads made plain. Lord, help me to see in myself those valleys, those humps, those corners and roughnesses which need to be corrected if you are to come and make me your own.

13 Luke 3:7–18

The Baptist's message

In Luke, the Baptist's message is given in a much fuller form than in Mark. It has three components: a warning to repent; a warning about the use of money; and pointing to Jesus.

A warning

The Baptist warns that the axe is being laid to the root of the trees, that the Messiah, Christ, is coming, his winnowing fan in his hand to separate the wheat from the chaff. These are warnings that the moment of judgement is at hand. The people would recognise these images as threats of the day of the Lord. Since the time of the prophets, and particularly of Amos, the people had constantly been warned that the day of the Lord was approaching. This was to be a visitation from God which would set right the wrongs in the world. The wicked would be punished and the oppressed released from the oppression. At first this was seen on the individual level: the rich who oppressed the poor would be toppled from their comfortable lifestyle. Then it broadens to the national level: Israel as a whole would be punished for its infidelity, a punishment which was seen as fulfilled in the sack of Jerusalem and the dispersion of the nation to Babylon and beyond. Once this has occurred, Israel is in the place of the oppressed, and the day of the Lord will, at the end of time, re-establish Israel and punish the nations which oppress Israel.

This was the central element in Israel's expectation of the Messiah, or the Christ ('Christ' is a Greek word, meaning 'anointed', the meaning also of the Hebrew word 'messiah'). The Messiah would establish God's sovereignty, rule or kingship on earth. This would include fulfilling his promises to Israel, his chosen people. John's warning is that it is not enough simply to be members of that people, children of Abraham. Some of the trees may be dead wood which needs to be cut out. In the final harvest there will be chaff fit only for burning, as well as good grain. For the chaff it will be a day of disaster. This warning against complacency is still relevant for Christians today.

A community of repentance

John goes 'through the whole Jordan area' preaching his message of repentance. Mark and Matthew place his preaching 'in the desert', alluding to the passage in Isaiah, 'Make straight in the desert a highway for our God.' But the whole Jordan area, well below sea level, is barren desert apart from the narrow strip of the Jordan River itself. Christian tradition has narrowed the focus of John's preaching to the point where the great road to the east crosses the Jordan itself, a ford which would daily be thronged with travellers and traders of all kinds.

John describes the fruits of repentance in practical terms, and above all in terms of the use of money and resources. He addresses various classes of people, focusing on the temptation which lies nearest to hand for them. Luke is acutely aware of the danger of wealth and of the need to use wealth responsibly and generously. In the biblical world excess of wealth was expressed in terms of clothing and food. 'Festal robes' feature frequently among lists of grand gifts given by powerful people to each other, and excess of food has been a temptation in every age. Tax collectors and soldiers are warned not to exercise their own particular opportunities for exploitation.

John points to the Christ

John is already the perfect example of the Christian teacher. His message of repentance will be that also of the apostles after Pentecost. Another striking element is his humility. He refuses any acclaim for himself and points always to Christ. No Hebrew slave could be obliged to undo his master's sandals (foot-washing was not a frequent occupation in those days!), and yet John says he is not worthy even to do this for the Christ. This has even greater poignancy if Jesus had once been John's disciple – an intriguing possibility, which cannot be established. The Baptist's words in John could be the motto of any Christian teacher, priest, parent or educator: 'He must grow greater, I must grow less' (John 3:30).

Prayer

Lord, save me from complacency and self-importance. Keep me always aware that the greatest Christian dignity is to be a channel of your grace, to bring others to the appreciation of your love and to help them embrace your vision.

14 Luke 3:19–38

The coming of the Spirit

John the Baptist imprisoned

In Mark and Matthew we have a full story of the arrest and execution of the Baptist, rather further on in the story. Luke gives a brief mention here of his arrest, and that is the last we hear of him. Luke is keen to show that John's ministry is only preparatory and that it comes to an end just as Jesus' ministry is about to begin. History is thus divided into three periods: the preparation for Jesus (the Spirit at work in the preparation, as we have seen in the account of Jesus' birth and the events leading up to it); the lifetime of the earthly Jesus; and the life of Jesus through the Spirit in the work of the apostles as they spread the message of Jesus to the ends of the earth. As we shall see, Luke is at pains to show that the life of the church echoes and mirrors that of Jesus: in the power of his Spirit the apostles preach the same message, work the same miracles and undergo the same trials of martyrdom.

John does not even appear at the baptism of Jesus. It seems to have been an embarrassment to the early church that Jesus submitted himself to baptism at the hands of his inferior, John. Mark merely relates the occasion, but Matthew gives a little dialogue between the two. The import of this dialogue is to show that it is not an action of John upon Jesus, but is a joint action of the two: 'It is fitting that *we* should, in this way, do all that righteousness demands,' says Jesus. Luke solves the problem by not telling us who baptised Jesus.

The coming of the Spirit

Indeed, in this gospel the event can hardly be called the baptism of Jesus. The baptism is hardly more than a timing-device for the coming of the Spirit. Just as the beginning of the mission of the apostles is marked, kicked off, by the descent of the Spirit at Pentecost, so the mission of Jesus is marked by the descent of the Spirit on him, 'while Jesus after his own baptism was at prayer'. The reality of the event is stressed by its physical character: the Spirit descends not only 'like a dove', as in the other gospels, but 'in a physical form'.

In Luke, Jesus is at prayer before all the important events of his life – the transfiguration, the choice of the apostles, the teaching on the Lord's Prayer, in Gethsemane before the Passion. The same importance of prayer at crucial moments is shown also in the life of the early Christian community gathered together in Jerusalem in Acts. Particularly the disciples turn to prayer before the beginning of a mission – before the appointment of the twelfth apostle, before the appointment of the seven 'deacons', before Paul is sent out on his mission by the community at Antioch. We will also find many lessons in Luke on the quality of prayer and how to pray.

What can be meant by 'heaven opened'? This again is scriptural language. At the beginning of the first chapter of Ezekiel, the heaven opens to reveal the scintillating vision of the chariot of God. This is the nearest the Bible gets to giving us a vision of God in person: 'The sight was like the glory of the Lord.' At the baptism this prepares us for the full divine majesty and authority of the voice proclaiming Jesus as his authorised messenger, the Son of God. So is the stage set for Jesus to begin his mission of bringing God's message to the world.

The ancestry of Jesus

The genealogy of Jesus given by Matthew at the beginning of his gospel goes back to Abraham. That was the Jewish ancestry of Jesus, son of David, son of Abraham. Here, on the other hand, the ancestry goes back further to Adam himself, the progenitor of the whole human race. The details – and their differences from Matthew's account – are unimportant. The point being made is that Jesus is of universal significance, not just to Jews but to all people of all races descended from Adam. Salvation is to be proclaimed to them all.

Prayer

Lord Jesus, the voice from heaven at your baptism assures us that you set out on your mission in the full Spirit and power of your Father. You fill your followers too with this Spirit. Grant me confidence in that Spirit, not in myself, so that I may respond sensitively to your direction through your own Spirit living in me.

15 Luke 4:1–13

Testing in the desert

Preparation

Mark gives us a short account of this incident. Jesus was put to the test by Satan in the desert. But the only details are, 'He was with the wild animals and the angels looked after him.' It is the peace of the time of the Messiah, as foretold by Isaiah (11:6): 'The wolf will live with the lamb, the panther lie down with the kid'. And the angels are fulfilling God's promise in Psalm 91, 'to guard you wherever you go'.

Luke concentrates much more on the details of the testing. Through his eyes we can see that in the 40 days in the desert Jesus, the Son of God, is undergoing the same testing as Israel, God's son, underwent in the 40 years of wandering in the desert after the exodus from Egypt. Only, where Israel so often failed and complained, Jesus remains faithful and true to his Father. The number of 40 is often used in the Bible for a period of preparation: not only the 40 years of Israel's wanderings while it was being forged into a nation under God's care, but Elijah's 40 days and 40 nights of preparation in the desert for his encounter with God at Horeb (1 Kings 19:8). The closest parallel of all is the 40 days of preparation between the resurrection and the ascension, when the risen Christ is preparing his disciples for their mission. Just as the mission of Jesus begins with a preparation period of 40 days, so does the mission of his disciples. The dialogue between Jesus and the devil is also a reminder that Jesus is undergoing the same testing in the desert as that undergone by Israel in the desert.

The dialogue is like a religious discussion between rabbis, each participant setting Bible text against Bible text, as we know from countless rabbinic discussions preserved in contemporary Jewish writings. The first two texts which the devil produces are drawn from Deuteronomy; the third text is from a psalm, but Jesus neatly replies with a text from Deuteronomy, turning the discussion back upon the tempter. The link with the testing of Israel in the desert is that Deuteronomy, the last book of Moses, describes the wanderings and murmurings of Israel in the desert.

The messianic mission

After the declaration of the beginning of his mission with the coming of the Spirit, Jesus withdraws into the desert to prepare. It is a profound occasion of grace, for he is 'filled with the Holy Spirit'. What was his mission to be? How was he to fulfil his task as Messiah? There were many different aspects of the hopes for the Messiah. The gospel here shows us Jesus being presented with some of them by the devil. They are false trails, and so temptations which must be resisted.

The first, to turn stones into bread, represents the temptation to material plenty. One hope for the messianic times was a time of perpetual feasting, all play and no work – the easy way out, a shortcut to contentment and physical luxury.

The second temptation, to have power over all the kingdoms of the earth, represents the notion of a powerful kingship, a dictatorship by force. Domination by brute force is often an easy way out. It comes from the thrust in everyday life to dominate and exploit without regard for the rights and feelings of others. As in the story of Adam and Eve, perhaps the basic temptation for all humanity is the temptation to exercise power and independence, without caring for the consequences. This is why it results in falling down and worshipping the spirit of evil. Christ's kingship is utterly different from this, a kingship over the heart, which must be won.

Jesus' third temptation, to throw himself down from the temple, represents the power of showing off with 'flashy' miracles and self-aggrandisement, very different from the humility and gentleness of Jesus. Jesus worked his miracles in response to need, healing the sick and comforting the disabled, not showing off his own power and the divine protection he might have enjoyed – particularly in the lonely agony of his Passion.

These temptations, given here in a neat and rather formal mode, no doubt recurred for Jesus throughout his life. In the fourth gospel one can see Luke's second temptation occurring, for instance, in the temptation to accept the offer of kingship (John 6:15). The way of the Son of God was far from luxury, royalty or popular acclaim.

Prayer

Lord, help me to see what is your way and what is only mine. Grant me the wisdom to distinguish your will from my self-deceptions. Grant me the courage to follow your path.

16 Luke 4:16–30

Jesus at Nazareth

After the descent of the Spirit at his baptism, and a period of withdrawal and assessment in the desert, Jesus at last begins his public ministry with what would today be called a keynote address. Again there is a careful parallel in Acts: after the descent of the Spirit at Pentecost, Peter makes a great speech, a sort of manifesto. Both speeches begin by explaining the presence of the Spirit in the terms of the ancient prophets. The scene at Nazareth is painted with all Luke's skill and artistry: the dramatic reading from scripture, the calm exposition, the angry response. Jesus throws down a challenge – only to be immediately rejected. The scene is a fuller and more explicit version of the rejection of Jesus by his own people at Nazareth recounted by Mark.

First, he declares that the time of the Spirit has come: 'The Spirit of the Lord is on me,' as in the prophet Isaiah. Jesus himself is seen as a prophet. The prophet's ministry in the power of the Spirit is not to foretell the future but to bring the people back to God's path, and this is what Jesus proceeds to do. There are two particular directions in which his message here points.

Good news to the poor

The quotation from Isaiah concentrates on captives, the afflicted, the poor and the oppressed. Throughout his gospel Luke will stress that these are the favoured children of God, to whom Christ's message is primarily addressed. The shepherds at Bethlehem, Lazarus covered with sores at the rich man's gate, the outcast tax collectors, the executed criminal are all in different ways the special object of God's care. Luke seems generally more at home in a richer world than do either Mark or Matthew: he uses larger sums of money in his imagery; he mentions bankers, loans, interest rates and other such high financial matters, which would have left Mark's audience utterly puzzled. Writing to a rich audience, it makes more sense for Luke to underline the danger of wealth and the need to use it rightly, and especially God's care for the poor. In Luke the beatitudes promise blessedness to the poor now and to those who hunger and thirst now, while Matthew's envisage the poor *in spirit* and those who hunger and thirst *for righteousness*. So Luke concentrates on the material need, on those who do not know where their next meal is coming from, while Matthew concentrates on moral and spiritual qualities.

Nor is Jesus' message in Luke confined to the financially underprivileged. He has special care for the outcasts and sinners, all those marginalised by polite society. This is one reason why Luke is always careful to show that Jesus' message comes to women equally with men: Anna as well as Simeon; Mary as well as Zechariah; the widow of Nain (and her son) as well as Jairus (and his daughter); the woman who lost a coin as well as the man who lost a sheep; the woman who was a sinner as well as the prodigal son.

Good news to the Gentiles

Jesus' prophetic proclamation makes clear that his message is for the other nations of the world as well as for Israel. Indeed, more than that, he stresses that the chosen recipients of the miracles of the great prophets Elijah and Elisha were Gentiles *rather than* Jews: Naaman the Syrian rather than any leper in Israel; the widow of Zarephath, 'a town in Sidonia', rather than any widow in Israel. Especially in the gospel of Luke we see Jesus paying special attention to non-Jews. In Mark and Matthew he has little contact with them. In Luke we find the parable of the good Samaritan (and the Samaritans were hated by the Jews) and the one Samaritan leper who came to thank Jesus after ten lepers were healed. In the parable of the great supper, the messengers are sent to invite the outcasts in the city (representing Jerusalem or Judaism); but there is still space and they are sent outside the city to compel the outsiders to come to the feast. The reader is made aware that after Pentecost, the second volume of Luke's work will deal with the spread of the gospel to all the nations of the known world. The ground is already being prepared for this.

Prayer

Lord, you came to bring the good news to all the nations. The whole world is to be transformed by your message of peace. Enable me to welcome that message and to spread it even – and especially – to the harmed and handicapped members of society.

17 Luke 4:31–44

A day at Capernaum

Immediately after Jesus' proclamation of his mission he goes down to Capernaum, the lakeside village which will be his home now that he has been rejected by his own townsfolk of Nazareth. There we see a sort of sample day of his ministry, consisting of the cure of a man in the synagogue, the cure of Simon's mother-in-law and an unspecified number of other cures. In Mark the day at Capernaum comes considerably earlier than the incident at Nazareth, and this is obviously the original historical order. Luke arranges the events in an order which gives prominence to Jesus' first public appearance during his mission at Nazareth. There Jesus makes the keynote sermon which is a sort of manifesto of the programme of his ministry and mission.

A word of authority

The dominant impression of Jesus' miracles on the day at Capernaum is one of authority. The authority of his teaching makes a deep impression on the people in the synagogue. Then Jesus confirms this by expelling the unclean spirit merely by his word. It is the authority of his word that makes the deep and astonishing impression: he merely rebukes the unclean spirit. Later Jesus rebukes the fever which has gripped Simon's mother-in-law, and again his word alone suffices to cure her. In the other gospels he takes her by the hand and raises her up, but in Luke no physical gesture is needed. Again, in the last group of cures, Jesus rebukes the evil sprits and prevents them speaking: no word is to rival his own. Even though they cry out that he is 'the Son of God', their proclamation is forbidden, for no one but Jesus and his followers may spread the message.

It is the word of preaching and the message which are being stressed, and indeed at the end of the series of incidents Jesus says he must go to proclaim the good news elsewhere. So it is the force and authority of the proclamation of the good news which is responsible for all these cures. In Acts the word of Jesus spoken by the disciples in his name will have the same effect of authority and healing. One cannot but reflect on the power which the word of God should have in the preaching of the church today. It must be a healing word as well, curing disorders and driving out evil.

Evil spirits

The gospels show many people going around Galilee in the grip of demonic possession. It would be brash to maintain that such possession does not and could not occur. However, in a world of primitive medicine, grave physical distortions and profound mental disorders were primarily attributed to the influence of evil spirits. Anyone who has seen a dear friend in the grip of such agony can sympathise with this description.

Mental disorders are today sometimes cured by prolonged courses of therapy. It may be that what the gospel describes as an evil spirit yielding to Jesus is the encounter of such a tortured personality with the healing presence of Jesus. So great was his authority and so healing his presence that his word could instantly bring peace and restore the victim to normality. No human personality can have such wondrous, instant effect. But most of us will have met extraordinary people whose personalities can provide a glimmer of understanding of such an experience and of the astonishment which it would cause.

Son of God

The demons here call Jesus 'Son of God', the first time this title has been used in the ministry of Jesus. The angel at the annunciation had declared that Jesus would be Son of God, and the devil had taunted him with this expression during the temptations in the desert, 'If you are the Son of God…' Here we begin to see what it means. But this is only a beginning, and its full sense will become gradually clearer. Angels and judges, rulers and Israel itself are also called 'sons of God', and it will be long before human beings acknowledge Jesus as Son of God in a full sense. But to Christians the title has a profound meaning, and Luke is writing for those who already believe in the fullness of Jesus as Son of God.

Prayer

Lord, grant me to see and treasure the wonder of your healing power in all the distressful situations of life.

18 Luke 5:1–11

The call of four disciples

There must have been several stories circulating in the early Christian communities about the call of the first disciples. In Mark, Jesus calls Simon, Andrew and the two sons of Zebedee as they are tending their fishing nets on the shore of the lake. He just walks along, calls them to follow him, and they go after him, simply drawn by his personality. In the fourth gospel, John the Baptist (presumably in the Jordan valley) points out Jesus to Andrew and another disciple, who approach Jesus and are won over to believe in him as the Messiah. Then they are joined individually by Simon, Philip and Nathanael. Luke's story here has a close similarity to the story of the miraculous catch of fish after the resurrection in John 21. There also they fish unsuccessfully all night and then are guided by Jesus to net a huge haul; the climax of the scene is Jesus' appointment of Peter to feed his sheep. Three times the risen Christ asks Peter whether he loves him and elicits a protestation of loyalty which must surely correspond to Peter's three denials a few days earlier. Luke's story here contains the same hint of admission of failure, when Peter falls on his knees to Jesus and confesses that he is a sinner.

The Lake of Galilee

The Lake of Galilee (or Gennesaret, as Luke here calls it) is a placid inland sea, some eight miles long and five miles wide at its broadest point. It lies several hundred metres below the level of the Mediterranean Sea, in a bowl, surrounded by high hills. There are little villages dotted round its shore; Capernaum is one of them. The River Jordan, a slow and muddy little stream, flows into it at the north end and out of it at the south, down towards the Dead Sea. Being so low, the lake is always warm and has an abundance of fish. It has always been the centre of a thriving fishing industry, carried on by small boats working in family or small village community partnerships. The traditional place of this catch of fish and Peter's call is a couple of miles from Capernaum, at a spot where some warm springs flow into the lake. The fish congregate there, especially in the early spring (which would fit especially the story in John 21, just after the resurrection), and the canny fisherman would know this. The story of the abundant catch of fish is in both cases surely symbolic of the huge catch of fish which the guidance of Jesus will enable the apostolic 'fishermen' to make. These warm springs are hardly a mile along the shore from Magdala, the home of Mary Magdalene. The whole shore is studded with memories of Jesus and his ministry.

'I am a sinner'

Peter's reaction to the wonderful catch of fish is awe and amazement, expressed in a sense of his own unworthiness to be in the presence of this personality. This is just like the prophet Isaiah, at his call in the temple, when he experiences the vision of God filling the temple and crumples in awareness of his own sinfulness. Especially Luke draws out the truth that awareness and acknowledgement of sin is a primary prerequisite for being called to be a follower of Jesus. So the tax collector Zacchaeus acknowledges that he must return his ill-gotten gains as Jesus calls him. It is only after the good thief has twice admitted that he is getting his just deserts that Jesus promises to take him into paradise. Most Christian rituals and services begin therefore with an admission of sin, by which the Christian is put in the frame of mind to accept Christ again.

'They left everything'

In Mark and Matthew, when the first disciples are called, they leave their father, their nets, their boat and their livelihood. But it is only Luke who stresses that they left *everything*. Luke's awareness of the danger of wealth is such that he underlines that the true disciples of Jesus must be wholly free of this distraction. His parable of the rich man and Lazarus shows the dangers of selfishness with wealth. In the parable of the great supper it is the fascination with possessions which distracts the invited guests from taking up the invitation. Again and again the warning is given, so Peter and his companions leave everything to avoid any possible danger from possessions.

Prayer

Lord, how often is my pride a barrier to your work! Yet I know that I am prepared to trust others as your representatives precisely because they know their faults and have no pretensions. Help me to remember that I am a sinner, yet safe and secure in your mercy.

19 Luke 5:12–26

Two miraculous cures

The terrible thing about 'leprosy' was the separation from society which it involved. The term is used much more widely in the Bible than in modern medicine. It was not confined to the disease which results in the leper colonies of Africa to which Father Damien and Albert Schweitzer gave their lives, a disease which has almost died out with the advance of medicine. It embraced a whole group of contagious skin infections, and the Bible prescribed that sufferers from these diseases should be isolated from society until they were officially pronounced clean. The rules for diagnosis given in Leviticus 13—14 are impressively careful and thoughtful, though of course they lack the exact analysis of modern medicine. In many cases the separation from society must have been more painful than the disease itself. It is moving that Jesus' compassion for the victim of the disease is such that he fearlessly touches him, deterred neither by the risk of infection nor by the biblical rules.

Then, as so often in Luke, there is the little note that he went off to pray. This prayer of Jesus comes between the two miracle stories, as a reminder of what Jesus is really about. The acclaim of the crowds is not the mainspring of his action. Jesus returns constantly to prayer, as the background of all his actions. This is the more striking as Luke here recounts it: amid all the acclaim and the spread of the message, there is only one relationship which is of real importance to Jesus. He turns his back on the popular success to return to the Father in prayer.

Healing and forgiveness

Luke has taken over the story of the healing of the 'paralytic' from Mark. Again the 'paralytic' is not exactly paralytic in the modern sense of someone unable to move; rather, the word means bedridden. There are two cures, which reflect on each other, a physical and a spiritual cure. The combination of the two, side by side, or rather intertwined, shows that Jesus could heal the one ailment as easily as the other. The two are put together at several levels. In the messianic renewal, the Messiah will come to abolish all evil and bring back the peace and blessedness of paradise, when both these evils are to be abolished together. So Jesus' miracles are prophetic signs of the beginning of that renewal. At another level, in the primitive pre-scientific world sin was often thought to be the cause of illness, a connection which Jesus explicitly rejects in the case of the man born blind (John 9:3), but which no doubt remained strong in the popular mentality. Both are signs that Jesus is acting with the sovereign power of God, for God alone can forgive sin and God alone has free power over human life.

The power of the Lord

Luke adds a particular awe to the story by his statement 'The power of the Lord was there so that he should heal.' It is not clear who 'the Lord' is in this case. Is it God or Jesus? Who does the healing, God or Jesus? One of the special marks of Luke's use of 'the Lord' is that one cannot tell whether it is God or Jesus; the ambiguity shows the growing understanding of the mystery of Jesus in the Christian community during the course of the first generation of Christians. At the conclusion of the story of the Gerasene demoniac in Luke's version, even more explicitly than in Mark, 'God' and 'Jesus' seem to be the same: '"Go back home and report all that *God* has done for you." So the man went off and proclaimed throughout the city all that Jesus had done for him.' In whose power is this miracle done? Jesus' awesome power is given particular respect by Luke, without making clear whether it is Jesus' own power or divine power in him. It almost seems a sort of *mana*, a kind of supernatural power: everyone tries to touch him and be healed because 'power came out of him that cured them all' (6:19). When the woman with a haemorrhage touches him, Jesus says, 'I felt that power had gone out from me' (8:46). It is a power which he passes on to his followers when he sends them out: 'He gave them power and authority over all devils and to cure diseases' (9:1).

Prayer

Grant me an appreciation of your power. You became a man to show us the power and the caring love of God in human form. You can make me whole again if only I will give myself to you.

20 Luke 5:27–39

A feast with sinners

Luke now welds together three scenes: the call of Levi; a meal with tax collectors; and the question about fasting. Immediately after his call, Levi makes a great feast for Jesus in his house. It is part of Luke's cheerful style that he loves a party with plenty of lively dialogue. There can, of course, be good and bad parties, as we learn especially from Luke's parables. The rich fool who had to enlarge his barns, and the rich man who neglected Lazarus both feasted every day, but got little joy of it in the end. On the other hand, the shepherd who sought out his lost sheep and the woman who found her lost coin each invited friends and neighbours for a merry party to celebrate. Another parable warns that a party is not simply an occasion for inviting friends who will repay the hospitality; it must be an occasion for generosity and winning friends in heaven. For the guests a party can be an occasion of humility, in not choosing the best places but waiting to be called up higher. Luke often uses a dinner as a scene for teaching, not least the last supper, where he gathers together several important teachings of Jesus.

The call of Levi

The brevity of this call narrative is important. Its very starkness is the most striking feature: Jesus simply summons the tax collector, and the tax collector follows, leaving everything. There is no introduction, no preparation, no reasoning. Capernaum was the first town inside the province of Galilee after crossing the border (the River Jordan) on the main road from Syria and the east. It was, no doubt, an important customs post, and there would be entry taxes to pay. But we are left on our own to imagine Levi sitting at his customs table beside the dusty road. All Luke shows is that the personality of Jesus is such that the call is compelling. This must be another illustration of that extraordinary authority of the word of Jesus which we have seen healing the sick and curing the possessed.

There is another aspect of Jesus' fearless authority here too. Tax collectors were outcasts from society, especially from decent, religious society. Tax collectors are, from the nature of their job, not popular; the job requires a certain unyielding severity. Taxation itself was a fairly recent innovation in Palestine and the institution itself would still have been disliked. Under the Roman system it was worse, for they worked on something similar to a commission basis: once they had filled their quota, the rest went into their own pockets. Worst of all, they worked for the hated Roman oppressors. So, all in all, to call a tax collector into the group spreading the good news of God's kingship was a bold gesture. One can imagine the gasps of astonishment from the rest of the group. One can imagine also the thrilled gratitude of the tax collector at breaking out of the vicious circle into which he had bound himself.

The shocking nature of what has happened is underlined at the party which follows. The Pharisees were the conventional representatives of a devoted search for God. Nowadays we may be critical or even mocking of their methods of seeking God, of their arrogance and hypocrisy, and (most of all) of the superstitious exactitude of their observance. But there is ample evidence in rabbinic stories that they were aware of all these dangers and could even laugh at themselves.

Conversion

This whole section in Luke demands that we reflect on the nature of something that Luke emphasises in all his call narratives – conversion. Levi leaves 'everything' to follow Jesus; in an instant he gives up his whole way of life. In the conversation at the supper, Jesus adds that he has come not just to call sinners, but to call sinners *to repentance*. The Greek word means 'a change of mindset'. It consists in the adoption of a whole new set of values. This is illustrated by the abandonment of such conventional ways to holiness as fasting; Jesus wants to emphasise the joy of coming to him. So he uses such images as the merriment of a wedding feast and the joy of harvest time. This is reinforced by the other images: you cannot patch an old piece of clothing with new cloth or put new wine into skins already soaked in old wine.

Prayer

Lord, grant me to re-examine my values, the ways in which I think I am seeking you. Lead me to a true conversion, so that my whole way of life flows from the joy in your kingship.

21 Luke 6:1–11

Sabbath controversies

Luke now gives us two stories of Jesus' confrontation with the Jewish authorities about the sabbath. In each the point of the story is Jesus' authority. Just as his teaching with authority amazed the onlookers, so his action expresses the same authority. Luke's audience was not primarily interested in the Jewish law, and for him the special purpose of these stories is to illustrate the personality of Jesus.

Plucking corn on the sabbath

There was nothing wrong with walking through a cornfield and plucking a few ears of corn to eat. The law allowed plucking corn by hand in a neighbour's field, but not use of a sickle; the difference presumably is between satisfying passing hunger and garnering corn. The tricky point in this instance was the sabbath, for threshing was forbidden on the sabbath, and rubbing the corn in their hands was construed by the Pharisees as threshing.

Luke's view of the incident can best be seen by a comparison of his telling of it with Mark's and Matthew's. Mark gives here Jesus' saying, 'The sabbath was made for man, not man for the sabbath.' It is an argument within the Jewish law. For Luke's Gentile audience such a controversy had little relevance. So he omits this saying; his Gentile audience were not interested in the relative importance of the Jewish sabbath observance. Luke's interest is in the supreme authority of the Son of Man. Luke inserts 'took' into the way Mark describes David's action in the house of God, and so stresses David's commanding authority: 'He went into the house of God and took the loaves of the offering and ate them and gave them to his followers.' For Luke, David is the precedent for Jesus' right to override petty rules of the law. One is reminded of the story in Acts when in a vision Peter sees clean and unclean food together let down in a sheet from heaven. To Peter's indignant surprise, he is told that there is no such thing any longer as clean and unclean food: all food created by God is clean. So now, Jesus does not ask permission. He does not have to justify his actions. He is simply the lord of the sabbath.

Cure of a man with a withered hand

The second story pairs with the first. The parallelism (and Luke likes parallels) is already suggested by the openings, 'One sabbath… On another sabbath…' The original issue in this second story must be whether it was legitimate to cure on a sabbath. This could be construed as being work, and therefore against the command of keeping the sabbath free for the Lord. Mark puts it very simply: it is a matter of Jesus' sympathy and pity for the sufferer. He is angered and grieved at the hardness of heart of his opponents, who just sit there, waiting for him to put a foot wrong, and impervious to the man's plight. Matthew, who is always concerned about the law, and keeping within its bounds, makes the incident into a legal controversy by introducing a statement of principle: if it is legal to pull an ox out of a pit on the sabbath (and not all authorities agreed that it was), it must be legal to heal a human being.

Luke, as we have seen, was not interested in the Jewish law. He retells the story, changing a few details. No doubt these changes were unconscious, and all accord with his conception of Jesus' imperious authority. First, Luke adds that Jesus went into the synagogue to teach; he was not there as a simple worshipper. Then he adds that Jesus knew the thoughts of those who were watching to catch him out. The mention of Jesus' anger and grief at their attitude has disappeared; to Luke Jesus is above getting upset about such things. On the contrary Luke adds a slight touch which makes the man's plight worse: it is his right hand, his working hand, which is withered.

The grandeur of the occasion is also stressed by the man's stance. In Mark Jesus merely tells the man to get up into the middle. In Luke Jesus tells the man to get up and take his stand in the middle, adding 'and he came forward and stood there' out in the middle of the synagogue, so that we can have no doubt about the public nature of the miracle. So all this shows another occasion of the power of the Lord being there to work miracles.

Prayer

Lord, as a human being you showed an awesome power of command over all creation, human and animal, natural and beyond nature. Grant me to appreciate that this gives hardly an inkling of your divine power, always present and always at work.

22 Luke 6:12–19

The choice of the twelve

The prayer of Jesus

Always, before some specially important occasion in his life, Luke shows Jesus going off to pray. This time he spent the whole night in prayer, an indication of the importance of this moment. But it cannot be a mere exterior event which leads him to prayer, like the panic prayer at the last minute before an examination, an interview or a driving test. The prayer of Jesus is a return to his Father, a moment of peace, when he can be truly himself, and linked to the 'ground of his being'. Following Jesus, every Christian yearns for this moment, when passing worries are put aside, and we face in awe and wonder the deepest of all realities, whom we call God. It is a moment of reverence and fear, but a moment also of confidence and trust, a moment of losing self and of finding self again, enriched and enhanced.

The twelve

We do not know very much about the twelve, not even all their names, for the names of the twelve (though always twelve in number) vary slightly in the different lists. Peter is the spokesman and leader, but otherwise, apart from James and John, the sons of Zebedee, none of them plays any individual part in the first three gospels. From their names it has been deduced that some of them were nationalists, for Simon, John, Matthew and Judas are names of the great leaders of the Maccabean revolt against the Syrian monarchy in the second century before Christ. The Syrian king had tried to replace Jewish religious belief and customs with the Greek conventional religion which prevailed all over the rest of his empire, only to encounter fierce opposition roused by these leaders. It may have been that the names of these leaders continued in the Galilean families as a sign of religious fidelity, and that this was what made them responsive to Jesus' call.

Many attempts have been made over the centuries to probe into the mind of Judas 'who became a traitor'. One interpretation sees the name as a sign that he first became a disciple in the belief that Jesus was a nationalist leader like Judas the Maccabee, and would lead a rebellion to throw off the Roman yoke. On discovering that he had misjudged Jesus' messianic claims, he became disillusioned and betrayed him. More poignant is the truth that Judas is the symbol of the tragedy of Jesus. The tragedy of the cross is that Jesus dies alone, deserted even by his chosen followers, his attempts to found God's kingdom seemingly in tatters. From the human point of view he has failed. He failed to convert the crowds in Galilee. The twelve chosen supporters on whom he relied all deserted him. Worst of all, one of them actually turned him in. The mustard seed appeared to have rotted to nothing in the ground. He could boast no human success at all. He could rely only on his fidelity to his Father's will. It is this love and faithfulness which is the secret of the cross.

Apostles

The twelve are the twelve foundation stones of the new Israel, corresponding to the twelve tribes of Israel. Matthew tells us that they will sit on twelve thrones, judging the twelve tribes of Israel. The mere existence of this body of twelve is one of the most important signs that Jesus meant to found a new Israel, a new people of God. Chosen from the larger body of Jesus' disciples, their name means 'sent out', and later tradition ascribes to each of them a separate region of the world to which they each brought the message of Jesus. So there is a strong tradition, for instance, that Thomas was the apostle to India. When it comes to the appointment of a substitute for Judas in Acts 1, the qualifications are that he should have been with Jesus right through his ministry and that he should be a witness to the resurrection. We cannot today be apostles in the sense of the original twelve, but if we would do the work of Christ and bring the message of Jesus to others we must first and always spend ample time in prayer with him.

Prayer

Lord Jesus, if I am to be your apostle, grant me to know you. Grant me the love to come close to you in prayer and the devotion to persevere in that prayer, buoyed up by the joy of knowledge of you and of your resurrection.

23 Luke 6:20–26

The beatitudes

Both the gospel writers who have an extended sermon early in Jesus' ministry begin with a series of beatitudes. Matthew so starts his great sermon on the mount, and Luke the corresponding 'sermon on the plain' (so called because 'he stopped at a piece of level ground' to give the instruction, 6:17). The beatitude is a well-known biblical formula, used frequently in the Old Testament, to pronounce God's blessing on certain classes of people or on certain achievements, a sort of divine congratulation: 'How blessed the nation whose God is the Lord.'

In Matthew the eight beatitudes provide a list of spiritual attitudes required for the kingdom of heaven. They form almost a checklist of conditions of entry, virtues any Christian must strive for who wishes to live under the sovereignty of God. The beatitudes in Luke are shorter, fiercer and more paradoxical. There are only four, instead of eight; but they are balanced by four 'woes', threats against those who disregard them and lack the qualities mentioned. They are phrased more piercingly and directly: not 'blessed are *those* who…' but straight to the reader or audience, 'blessed are *you* who…'. They are blows between the eyes, direct and challenging. The most important difference is that in Luke's version Jesus does not praise spiritual qualities ('blessed are the poor *in spirit*… who hunger and thirst *for uprightness*') but paradoxically pronounces blessed by God those who seem most unfortunate and most deserted of society, those who are poor, those who are hungry *now*, those who are weeping *now*. God's special regard is on those whom the world most rejects and who are worst treated by their fellows and by circumstances. On the other hand the 'woes' give a warning to those who are normally considered the most fortunate of society, those who enjoy the good things of this world.

Reversal of values

The background of much of Luke's gospel must be a comfortable society which needs to be shaken out of its comfort. They are satisfied with their wealth, their plenty and their laughter. Again and again in the gospels we are given the disturbing message that God's values are not the same as human values. There is just a different scale.

Two other consequences flow from this presentation of the beatitudes. First, a reassurance to the unfortunate that they have the special care and regard of God. The poor, the hungry, the deprived, the bereaved may seem to be deserted by God, but in fact they enjoy special favour. It is not easy to see how this is so, especially when one is personally in this position. Is this favour of God just a promise of 'pie in the sky' in the future? Is God testing out these favourites? Is God pruning them to make them bear more fruit? If we trust the teaching of John, that the Christian already enjoys eternal life, that Christ dwells in us now, there must be more to the favour of God than just a promise for the future. The trials must be the strengthening of a present personal relationship. It often needs a very strong faith to see this.

The second consequence is a warning which also comes often in the gospel: wealth and resources are a dangerous responsibility. The parable of the dishonest steward is clear enough that money must be used to make friends in heaven – in whatever way that may be done.

Persecution

The two gospels agree over the final beatitude, that persecution brings blessedness to the follower of Christ. Following the thrust of their other beatitudes, one may see that the angle is slightly different: Matthew is encouraging the Christian to see perseverance in persecution as a virtue, while Luke is reassuring the Christian that the persecuted will have their reward. Persecution – wild beasts and burning at the stake – was not only for the early church. We have known enough martyrs in Africa, China and Europe in the past century. Even short of bloodshed, to live by Christian principles often draws mockery, taunts and even material disadvantage.

For meditation

For Christ I have accepted the loss of all other things, and look on them all as filth if only I can gain Christ.
PHILIPPIANS 3:8

24 Luke 6:27–38

Demands of discipleship

The beatitudes have given a basic outline sketch of those who are and are not included in God's kingdom. There follows a commentary and expansion on the demands of discipleship, with a repeated insistence that it is not enough to repay others what they give to you. This was the golden rule, a moral principle which existed long before Jesus and was well known in both Greek and Hebrew literature. It occurs in a popular rabbinic story about two first-century sages, Shammai and Hillel. A prospective follower came to Shammai and asked to be taught the whole law while he stood on one leg. Shammai, insulted at this absurdity, sent him off with a flea in his ear. Next he went to Hillel and made the same request. Hillel replied with the golden rule, 'What is hateful to yourself, do not do to your neighbour.' For Luke, though the golden rule is included, this is not enough.

Fours

What seems at first a random collection of sayings takes shape if we realise that Luke is thinking in fours. There were four beatitudes and four woes. Now there comes a whole series of fours expressing the excessive demands of Christian discipleship. It is no good pretending that Christianity is merely reasonable, good behaviour.

First come four paradoxes (love, do good, bless, pray for) on returning good for evil. These are quiet, interior intentions and attitudes. But they soon spring into action and are reinforced by another four (to anyone who slaps, to anyone who takes, to everyone who asks, from someone who takes). All these involve abandoning natural human rights, and human nature shrieks out against them. Of the four, the first pair demands that Christians positively cooperate with those who infringe their human rights, while the second pair instructs followers of Christ to not seek to put right wrongs done to them. These four simply wipe out any claim that Christianity is a reasonable religion: following Christ goes far beyond that.

Yet it is after this quartet that Luke throws in the reasonable and less demanding golden rule, as though for good measure. This is an interesting instance of the different arrangement of material in the two sermons: Matthew gives the golden rule at the beginning of his summing up at the conclusion of the sermon on the mount; in Luke's arrangement it comes in as an extra after the far more demanding previous reactions to abuse of human rights.

Beyond reason

As if the lesson had not been sufficiently stressed, Luke next gives a trio of ways in which the generosity of a Christian must exceed the calculations of the reasonable person who expects a return for a favour. 'You scratch my back and I'll scratch yours' obtains in many spheres, from calling in political or business favours to lending clothes for a party. In Luke's world his teaching would have struck at the heart of the regular system of patronage and *amicitial* (literally 'friendship', but in fact more like bargaining) on which politics in the civilised Roman world were built: every 'boss' had his 'clients', and the 'big bosses' traded 'favours' with each other. This parity of bargaining is not the way of Christ. Luke drives this home by three verses similarly constructed (v. 32 on love, v. 33 on doing good, v. 34 on lending), pulled together by the final three-in-one of v. 35 (love, do good, lend).

The section ends with the most devastating demand of all, to be compassionate as the Father is compassionate – but here there is a reward attached. The meaning of this demand for absolute compassion can be learnt from a comparison with the way Matthew expresses it, 'Be *perfect* just as your heavenly Father is perfect.' Luke sees the Father's perfection as lying in compassion, and indeed this kind of generous and overflowing love comes to expression time and again in his gospel as the most important of all ideals. The Father is always forgiving, always welcoming back, always seeking what is lost. Luke explains what is meant by means of another quartet, two negative and two positive: do not judge; do not condemn; forgive; and give. At any rate there is a crumb of natural comfort that these have their reciprocal reward!

Prayer

So this, my God, is the meaning of your Son's generosity. I cannot take my stand on human rights, but must be unreasonably generous as you yourself are generous, ludicrously compassionate and forgiving.

25 Luke 6:39–49
Parables

The sermon on the plain concludes, as does Matthew's sermon on the mount, with a clutch of parables, imagery to drive home the lesson and the inspiration which lies behind them, the example of Jesus himself. The sermon on the plain is less a blueprint for various activities of a Christian's life than a challenge to go beyond conventional natural morality. The 'do-as-you-would-be-done-by' principle of the golden rule is no more than a rule for conduct which natural good sense could formulate, the product of fairness and educated self-interest, neat and well-balanced. If you follow this principle, you comfortably know the limits which can be placed on the demands made on you. The devastating challenge of the generosity demanded by the sermon on the plain is that its basic principle is a negation of self-interest. Jesus' saying in Luke, 'Be compassionate as your Father is compassionate,' like Matthew's 'Be perfect as your Father is perfect,' destroys all comfortable limit. There can be no limits to a compassion which is modelled on that of the Father, just as there can be no limits to the forgiveness prayed for and promised by 'Forgive us our trespasses as we forgive those who trespass against us.'

Two images of criticism

Of the four parables which conclude Luke's sermon the first two discourage criticism of others. The image of the blind leaders is used by Matthew to attack the Pharisees, and possibly Luke has the same meaning, envisaging the blind leaders as Pharisees without actually saying so. Is he implying that those who criticise Christians for deserting Pharisaic practices are leading their disciples to disaster? This may be also the context of the next saying, that the disciple is not above his master. In Matthew this is applied to persecution: if the master is persecuted, the disciple should expect to be persecuted also, and Luke may envisage the same application.

The second parable, the splinter and the log, with its cheerful exaggeration and neatly reversed order (splinter/log // splinter/log // log/splinter) also discourages criticism of others. The contrast of the two original words increases the wit of the saying: the 'splinter' is hardly more than a wisp of straw, whereas the 'log' is really a main weight-bearing beam of a house roof, a massive piece of timber. But we all know how easy it is to criticise the faults of others, and that it is often the faults to which we ourselves are most prone which annoy us most in others. Indeed, noticing a particular fault in a companion is almost a reason for looking out for that fault in oneself.

The fruit of the trees

Luke applies the contrast between the fruit of the trees rather differently from Matthew. In Matthew's context it is a means of judging whether the message of a prophet is true and of eliminating false prophets. In Luke it may be another warning against uncharitable and judgemental speech. Alternatively it may be a pair with the final parable, an encouragement to take action on the principles outlined in the sermon.

The two houses

The contrast of the two houses is attractively painted by Luke, with much more vigour than Matthew; he always depicts work imaginatively. The man goes digging industriously away, right down to the rock – perhaps too enthusiastically: is it really necessary to put down another foundation-stone once one has hit the rock? The rain and the winds described by Matthew have disappeared, perhaps because in the Near East no rain and no wind is really strong enough to knock down a house. However, a river in flood (in Luke's version) could certainly do this. A flash flood after rains could easily wash away a house incautiously built during the summer in a sandy riverbed. I once nearly experienced the same in a car on the barren shore of the Dead Sea as a flash flood came hurtling down a wadi from the hills behind.

Prayer

Help me, Lord, to avoid the hypocrisy of claiming high standards and then not bearing their fruit in action. Let me always seek your standards and be straightforward in trying to put them into action.

26 Luke 7:1–17

Two prophetic cures

In his keynote speech at Nazareth, Jesus had reminded his audience of Elijah's cure of Naaman, the Syrian army chief, and of Elisha's visit to the widow of Zarephath, and had promised to fulfil such a prophetic mission. These two miracles, for the Gentile military man and the widow, show just that.

The centurion's servant

This is an especially important event in Luke's gospel, a contact between Jesus and a non-Jew which was the first of many. In Mark's gospel there is little contact between Jesus and Gentiles, only the celebrated encounter with the Syro-Phoenician woman whose faith wins her daughter's healing (Mark 7:24–30). The story given here by Luke does not occur in Mark, but is given also by Matthew. It has close links also with the 'second sign at Cana' in John, when Jesus cures the sick son of a royal official at Capernaum – also without going near the sick boy, but simply rewarding the faith of the father, who believes Jesus' word. Again, in that case, the boy was cured at the moment Jesus' promise was given.

All these stories may well be based on the same oral tradition of a sick child who is brought to health by Jesus' response to the faith of their Gentile parent, without Jesus ever going near the sufferer. The slight variations between the different versions would give a fascinating glimpse into the way the stories were handed down by word of mouth in the primitive Christian communities. The circumstances varied and developed, but the essentials remained the same.

Luke was also aware of the parallel between this approach of the first Gentile to Jesus and the approach to Peter of the first Gentile to join the Christian community after the resurrection. Both are centurions, both send messengers, both have deserved well of the Jewish people, both are congratulated and receive a favourable response, Jesus and Peter (in their respective stories) going back with the messengers. In bringing out these parallels Luke is showing the great significance of this first meeting: it is the beginning of the approach of the Gentiles to Christ. But it is surely also significant that Jesus does not yet go as far as Peter: he does not enter the Gentile centurion's house.

There is one interesting difference in the versions of Jesus' reply given by Matthew and Luke. In Matthew Jesus says, '*In no one* in Israel have I found faith as great as this.' According to Luke he says, '*Not even* in Israel have I found faith as great as this.' In Greek the difference is only two letters. In the build up of Matthew's gospel, from Herod's massacre of the children of Bethlehem onwards, the Gentiles are as responsive as the Jews are unresponsive. Luke, on the other hand, is at pains to show that at least some of the Jews responded with faith. Jesus (and later, Paul) turns to the Gentiles only after some of the Jews have been received into the new people of God, and so have brought fulfilment to the promises of God to Israel.

The son of the widow of Nain

The story ends with Jesus being hailed as a great prophet. 'God has visited his people' shows the excitement of the people at their renewed experience of prophecy after centuries of absence, when God seemed to be silent among them. Jesus is recognised as a second Elijah, for there is an extraordinary similarity between this story and the story of Elijah raising the only son of the widow who befriended him at Zarephath (1 Kings 17). The suggestion is strengthened by Jesus' mention of this widow in his speech at Nazareth.

It would, however, be a great mistake to think of Jesus going round Galilee looking for neat parallels to the Old Testament. Jesus travelled round, spreading the good news of the kingdom and responding with love and pity to the needs of the people and situations he met. Luke also emphasises this point by the warmth with which he tells the stories. It was the disciples afterwards who saw the significance of his actions in terms of the biblical forbears and who told the stories in such a way that these parallels would be perceived.

Prayer

Lord, no matter how desperate the trouble I am in, you always have the solution. Let me turn to you in confidence and wait in hope for your solution.

27 Luke 7:18–35

Reflections on John the Baptist

This passage is crucial for the understanding of Jesus' miracles. The early preaching of John the Baptist had made clear that he was expecting a messiah of fire and judgement, one who would put an axe to the root of the tree that needed cutting down, who would separate the wheat from the chaff and burn up the waste. Now he is off in prison on the far side of the Dead Sea, in Herod's remote fortress of Machaerus. He is troubled at the news of Jesus, for Jesus does not seem to be acting as 'the one who is to come' should act. No fire and judgement, no axe to the root, no winnowing-fan. So he sends messengers to ask Jesus what is going on.

In reply to the messengers Jesus quotes Isaiah, from two passages, Isaiah 35:5 or 61:1. The burden of the quotation is to show that Jesus' activity does in fact fulfil the prophecies, not perhaps the prophecies of which John was thinking, but other parts of the prophets. The expectation of the Messiah varied considerably; the story of the temptations of Jesus in the desert shows him being presented with one after another of the views of the Messiah which he rejects as not the way of the Lord. 'The one who is to come' was pictured quite differently by different groups of the Jews. A warlord? A priest-king? A liberator? A custodian of the law? A figure appearing mysteriously in the desert? The usher of the final cataclysm? Jesus' answer here shows John the Baptist what the Messiah was truly to be. His actions were prophetic symbols of the end of death, pain, sickness, misery and poverty. This was the good news brought by Jesus.

Summary on John the Baptist

John the Baptist is here shown as the greatest of the prophets, and more than that: he was the messenger (the Greek word is the same as 'angel') preparing the way for the Lord. The identity of this Lord is left deliberately ambiguous: it could be either the Lord God or the Lord Jesus. But, by narrating John's arrest before the baptism of Jesus, Luke has insisted that the age of the Baptist was over before the age of Jesus began. He prepared a people of repentance for the Lord, but concluded his mission before the kingdom itself began to be manifested. This is why the least in the kingdom of God is greater than he.

In another sense there is continuity between John and Jesus and the disciples. All are prophets, filled with the Spirit. The message of repentance is preached by both Jesus and John, and then again by the apostles in the early speeches of Acts. The parallelism between John and Jesus had been stressed in the infancy narratives. It is made clear again in the application of the short parable of the children in the marketplace: 'We played the pipes for you, and you wouldn't dance; we sang dirges, and you wouldn't cry.' They are satisfied by neither merriment nor mourning, but cavil at each equally. The singing of dirges corresponds to John's ascetic lifestyle, and the merriment to Jesus' feasting with tax collectors and sinners.

Luke does, however, make the distinction which will be increasingly important as it comes to the Passion. All the people (and for 'people' Luke carefully uses the Greek word which indicates not just a large crowd but the people of God, the true Israel) responded to John's message of repentance by accepting baptism. It was only the Pharisees and lawyers who thwarted God's plan by refusing. In fact the Jewish historian Josephus tells us that Herod Antipas arrested John precisely because he was afraid of John's influence with the people, fearing that John would stir up a movement of rebellion among the people. This popularity – or perhaps reverence would be a better word – is seen when the temple authorities challenge Jesus' high-handed action in the temple. He replies by challenging them to explain the origin of John's authority. They dare not deny that his authority was from God, for fear of repercussions from the people.

The same distinction between the leaders and the people will be seen in Jesus' case at the crucifixion, when the leaders alone will jeer at Jesus, while all the people go home, beating their breasts in penitence.

Prayer

Lord, teach me how to combine repentance with cheerfulness, since you call for both. Help me to know that my weakness is made strong with your strength.

28 Luke 7:36–50
The woman who was a sinner

This first of Luke's wonderful stories of repentance shows us what to make of the distinction between the Pharisees and sinners. Simon the Pharisee, though he has invited Jesus, has neglected even the decencies of hospitality: not only has he failed to provide the normal comforts of the cloakroom (in a hot and dusty country a footwash was a necessity, not so much to remove dust as to make a deodorant oil superfluous!); he has not even greeted Jesus properly. By contrast, the woman lavishes every care on him: not mere water, but expensive ointment in an expensive jar; not his head, but his feet; not a kiss to the face, but his feet covered with kisses.

Jesus himself shows a lovely delicacy. First, he accepts patiently the neglect from his host. Second, he does not protect his own good name or his person by thrusting aside contact with the sinful woman. He does not interrogate the woman, ask her her sins or humiliate her in any way; he simply accepts her devotion and her love.

Jesus the prophet

The reality of the prophet contrasts markedly with what the onlookers expect from a prophet. It is already important that they are expecting him to behave as a prophet, for Luke presents Jesus as a prophet, and more than a prophet. A prophet is one who sees the reality of things as God sees it, through – so to speak – God's spectacles, and communicates this reality to human beings. The prophet sees into reality more deeply than ordinary people, judging what the real issues and values are. Humanity being what it is, more often than not this message involves correction, so that the prophet's message is seldom welcome or expected, but strikes a chord in the depths of the conscience. The prophet's message is self-authenticating: once it is pronounced it is seen to be correct. So on this occasion the onlookers expect the prophet to see through the outward appearance to the human reality behind it. And this is just what Jesus – to their surprise – does; but he sees deeper than they expect or like.

The parable of the two debtors

The kernel of the story is found in the dialogue. This centres on the parable of the two debtors. The message of the incident is that the woman's generous love earns her forgiveness; she is forgiven much because she loves much. This is complemented by the message in the parable. There the greater generosity of the creditor's forgiveness earns greater love from the man who is more deeply in debt. The love and the forgiveness are the other way round. However, this lack of balanced logic has itself a message: in fact the two, love and forgiveness, are intertwined: love leads to forgiveness and forgiveness leads to love. Each intensifies the other.

Behind the story

There has been considerable discussion about whether this story is based on the same incident as the story of the anointing of Jesus at Bethany. There is the same anointing with precious ointment by a woman at a supper, with a rebuke from Jesus to the onlookers. The three gospels of Matthew, Mark and Luke also all agree that the host was named Simon and that the jar was made of precious alabaster. There are one or two oddities in Luke's story: anointing the head was the normal custom, as in Mark and Matthew, but anointing the feet has distinct drawbacks: it makes them sticky, so that the dust adheres all the more! Did the original of the Lukan story present the woman only as washing Jesus' feet with her tears, and then the anointing and the precious alabaster jar slip in from the anointing at Bethany as a further sign of her loving attentiveness?

Traditionally the woman has been regarded as a prostitute, on the grounds that she 'had a bad name in the town'. In fact the reason for her bad reputation is nowhere stated. Nor in the gospel story is she identified as Mary Magdalene.

Prayer

Lord, increase in me that love which brings your forgiveness, and by your forgiveness increase in me that love still further.

29 Luke 8:1–3

The women with Jesus

Luke is about to give us one of the two major parables he takes over from Mark: the parable of the sower. In Mark this is the dividing line between Jesus' preaching to the masses and his more private instruction and preparation of his little group of disciples. It is preceded by an extended Markan passage which shows that Jesus was widely rejected: the Pharisees accused him of casting out evil spirits by being in league with Beelzebul, the prince of devils; even his own family failed to understand him and thought he was out of his mind. In Mark the parable of the sower is a reflection on this rejection.

In Luke the situation is quite different, and this will affect the meaning of the parable for Luke's readers. Both immediately before and after the parable Luke shows us a loyal audience, so that the parable is enveloped in a favourable atmosphere. Before the parable comes the little notice that Jesus went round the towns and villages proclaiming the good news – presumably with the same success as we have already seen. He is accompanied by two groups of disciples, the central group of the twelve, and the women, who will also witness his death and burial. Two of them, the Magdalene and Joanna, will also be the first to receive the news of his resurrection. Now we are told that they ministered to him, and the same verb is used as in Acts 6, where it refers to the seven who minister to the needs of the poor of the young community.

Women in Luke

This is another instance of Luke's quite deliberately pairing up women with men. In Christianity women have equal standing with men. The subjects of the miraculous cures by Jesus, and later by the apostles in the early chapters of Acts, are equally women and men. Women just as much as men receive the divine message and call; indeed, in the parallel of Zechariah and Mary, Mary is the clear winner! Parables are about women as well as men: a man loses his sheep; a woman loses her coin. In the early community of Jerusalem, women are constantly mentioned and brought into prominence. Women as well as men are inspired by the Spirit to prophesy. As Paul journeys round, women are often the leaders of the group or community who receive him. (This is reflected in the greetings at the end of Paul's letters, especially to the Romans. There women stand at the head of the household in which the Christians meet for worship. Paul even calls a woman, Junia or Julia, an apostle.) At Ephesus both Priscilla and Aquila, a woman and a man, instruct the teacher Apollos.

Particularly in the Jewish world, but also in the Hellenistic, this would have been a striking novelty. The respect and legal protection accorded to women in the Old Testament may not be enough to be politically correct by modern standards. But, measured against the countries and civilisations round about, it stands out. Similarly, the leading role for women which is evident in the situation just outlined for the first generation of Christianity is unparalleled in the Greco-Roman world. Admittedly, in the generation after Luke's writing, when the pastoral letters to Timothy and Titus came to be written, the situation seems to have changed. There is less confidence, and women are relegated to a subordinate position. Luke shows us that it was not so in the first beginnings of the Christian community.

Jesus' confidence and freedom with regard to women was the beginning of a revolution. More than striking, indeed rather shocking, would have been the note that these women followed Jesus around to minister to him, leaving their own families and homesteads. One can imagine the scandal that this would have created. But Jesus is not afraid of public opinion.

Name dropping

A striking sideline about Luke is his propensity for name-dropping. He is always keen to show that Christianity has a certain status. So here we are told that one of the women was wife to Herod's steward.

Prayer

Lord, help me to grant equal respect to all people, men and women, rich and poor, whatever their status in society. Help me to remember that you created each one of us. Each one of us has infinite value in your eyes, and you love us as we are, with all our infuriating faults.

30 Luke 8:4–21

The parable of the sower

The parables are not always easy to understand, because we lack their original context. The basic meaning of 'parable' is 'comparison', 'image' or 'riddle'. Riddles and images can have different applications in different situations. Often the gospel parables have come down to us without their original contexts, and without the original situation their exact force is often difficult to discern.

The parable

This is one of the great turning points in Jesus' ministry, when he turns away from the fickle crowds to instruct his chosen disciples. One can easily imagine him reflecting on the failure of his preaching with one group after another, but coming finally to dwell on the great fruitfulness of the few who did respond. He had tried one expedient after another, but all to no avail till he picked on the small group of the twelve. So, in the short quotation from Isaiah which comes before the allegorical explanation, all receive the message, but some fail to understand. All are given the chance, but not all take it.

The allegory

The temptations which prevent the seed from bearing fruit are those which we find throughout the gospel. First, the devil comes and takes away the seed. During Jesus' ministry the devil is significantly absent: at the end of the temptations in the desert the devil leaves him. No more is heard of the devil until Satan enters into Judas in Luke 22:3, and Jesus announces that now is the hour of darkness (22:53). The second failure of the seed is in those who lack perseverance and give up in time of temptation, for Luke is acutely aware of the pressures on Christians and the need for perseverance under persecution. Even their initial joy will not carry them through. The third failure is through those temptations and distractions which are stressed so often in this gospel, especially wealth and luxury. Faith is not a momentary response, but demands generosity and perseverance over a long period, despite distractions and temptations.

The same is clear from Luke's alterations to the short parable of the lamp, which follows. The light of faith must shine brightly so that others may see it, not from the outside but 'when they come in'. It is to aid the understanding of those who believe. And instead of 'Take notice of *what* you are hearing' (Mark), Luke concentrates on the mode of hearing and believing: 'Take care *how* you listen' – just to hear the message is not enough.

The true family of Jesus

There is a subtle change in Luke here also. In Mark we find a sharp division between Jesus' family outside and 'the crowd sitting round him' inside. Jesus rather brushes off his family, indicating those around him as he says, 'Here are my mother and brothers', in contradistinction from his own natural family. Such a separation is obviously unthinkable to Luke, after he has painted Mary's faith and response in such glowing colours at the annunciation and throughout the infancy narrative. So in Luke there is no separate group of family; they do not stand outside and send in a message, they continue to try to get to him. And Jesus responds with almost the same words but a different emphasis, praising them as the first examples of acceptance of the message, 'My mother and my brothers are those who hear the word of God and put it into practice.' Again Mary is the perfect example of the disciple, obedient and attentive to the will of God. This is reinforced by the change in position of the incident. It comes not as part of the hardening distinction between believers and unbelievers, but by being placed after the parable it makes Mary and the others the first hearers of the message of the parable, forerunners of all who accept and put into practice the message of Jesus.

Prayer

Lord, keep me aware of the need to respond ever more deeply to your message, to grow in appreciation of it, despite the distractions and temptations of the world, and so to reach finally to full understanding of your revelation with you.

31 Luke 8:22–25

The calming of the storm

This is Luke's only story of Jesus mastering the sea. The other synoptic gospels have also the story of Jesus walking on the waters of the Sea of Galilee. Luke, however, is careful to avoid what he considers might be duplication. He has only one story of a miraculous feeding – the 5,000 – and omits the other story of the feeding of the 4,000, probably because he thinks it (probably correctly!) to be a duplicate of the other. He is a careful historian. It is most likely for the same reason that he omits the Mark-Matthew story of Jesus walking on the waters, although there is considerably more difference between the two stories in this case.

In both Mark and Luke, this is the first of a little group of wonders witnessed by the disciples after the parables and before the disciples are sent out on their mission (Luke 9:1), which serves to strengthen their belief in Jesus and his powers. In Mark, the fright of the disciples leads them into sarcasm, 'Teacher, do you not care? We are lost!' (Mark 4:39). Jesus, for his part, is severe in his double rebuke, 'Why are you so frightened? Have you still no faith?' Luke 8 gives a gentler version of the exchange. 'Master! Master! We are lost!' (v. 24) already implies that Jesus can do something about their predicament, and Jesus' reply, 'Where is your faith?' (only a single question), implies that they do have faith, although it has temporarily failed them. Matthew also is less harsh on the disciples, for they appeal confidently to Jesus in the decidedly Christian phrase, 'Save us, Lord' (Matthew 8:25). After calming the storm, Jesus reproaches them not as entirely faithless, but as having little faith.

Perhaps, at a later stage of the development of the church and its leaders, the later evangelists were hesitant to show this abrasive exchange between the Lord and the future leaders of his church in all its Markan roughness. This is not the only occasion when Matthew and Luke soften the failure of the twelve and Jesus' firm rebukes to them (often couched in Mark's characteristic style of double question). In Mark, all the disciples flee at the beginning of the Passion, 'every single one of them' (Mark 14:50), whereas Luke omits this verse, and even seems partially to contradict it with 'All his friends stood at a distance' (Luke 23:49). They may not have been all that close, but at any rate they had sufficient courage and concern to be present.

A significant action

The significance of Jesus' action is enormous. Critics of Jesus at the time denounced his healings as exorcisms carried out by the power of Beelzebul, the prince of demons. In the primitive knowledge of medicine at the time, it was common to regard illness as the work of an evil power or possession by a demon. Similarly in Africa today, the first question asked is often not 'What caused the sickness?' but 'Who caused the sickness?', the sickness being regarded as imposed by a curse. More sophisticated modern critics may dismiss many of Jesus' healings as psychosomatic – the astounding effect on an unbalanced person of Jesus' holy and inspiring (but not divine) personality. No such explanation can be given of his calming the elements. The story must either be regarded as a mere expression of faith rather than the account of an event or accepted as evidence of Jesus' control of the elements of the weather.

To people brought up on the Bible, the significance is even greater. For Israel, the sea was always a frightening element. The world was envisaged as a flat plate resting on the waters below, while the waters above were blocked off by the vault of the skies. If the Lord should ever cease to hold back these waters, they would rush together and engulf all creation. The Lord alone can control the might of the seas: 'You calm the turmoil of the seas, the turmoil of their waves,' cries the psalmist (Psalm 89:9). Even more apt to our passage: the sailors 'cried out to the Lord in their distress, he reduced the storm to a calm and all the waters subsided' (Psalm 107:28–29). It is no wonder that the disciples' awestruck response to Jesus' action was, 'Who then is this, that he commands even the winds and the water, and they obey him?' (Luke 8:25).

Prayer

O Lord, you hold all creation in being from moment to moment. Give me trust in your control of the winds and the seas that buffet my little world. Give me courage to face any flecks of foam that may fly in my face, and thank you for the reminder of your guidance.

32 Luke 8:26–39

The Gerasene demoniac

The location of this miracle has caused plenty of trouble. The difficulty is that Gerasa is some 30 km south-east of the Lake of Galilee. Some versions of the gospel avoid this difficulty by reading the place as Gadara, whose territory reaches to within 10 km of the lake. The place name is not so important. The main point is that this seems to be Jesus' only visit to the Decapolis, the territory which lies to the south-east of the Lake of Galilee. This was not Jewish territory, but was marked by (and named after) ten fine Greek cities. Their remains still show a trace of their splendour – streets lined with noble colonnades; theatres ready for the classical Greek dramas; temples of Zeus, Diana and the nymphs. The significance of the incident is that it is Jesus' only brush with the great Greco-Roman civilisation which still marks our own culture. To this, too, he brings salvation and healing.

The main point of the story is the contrast between the pitiable state of the man in his deranged condition and the calm contentment as he sits at Jesus' feet. The fate of the pigs at the end of the story is a visual flourish which serves to underline the strength of the power which gripped the poor madman. The spirits beg not to be sent into the 'Abyss', which is classical Greek language for the mythical abode of demons. They want to continue their mischievous and destructive reign above ground. Their return to the place of torment where they belong is a forceful demonstration of Jesus clearing evil and destruction from the world. On his one incursion into pagan territory, Jesus immediately makes inroads against the superstitions and idolatry of that culture.

The gospel gives us an expressive picture of the poor victim. He is exiled from all civilisation, living in the haunted abodes of the dead and not even properly dressed. His strength is daunting and uncontrollable, and as soon as he has broken his bonds he rushes off into the hideous desert, the eerie home of evil spirits. What makes it almost more tragic is that the attacks seem to have been periodic, presumably with periods of lucidity in between. It was only when the attacks came on that people would fetter him in an unsuccessful attempt to restrain him. But he always ended up in the wilds. Such periodic derangements to a friend whom one thinks one knows are easily ascribed to possession by a powerful and evil spirit alien to himself.

Salvation

Luke sees in the miracle more than the merely physical or psychological significance of the cure. He characterises the miracle as 'how the man who had been possessed came to be *saved*' (v. 36), a phrase not present in the accounts of the other evangelists. This happens in other Lukan stories too, as in the following story of Jairus' daughter: 'only have faith and she will *be saved*' (v. 50). For Luke Jesus is above all the Saviour, as in the Old Testament God had been the Saviour of Israel. By these subtle touches Luke reminds the reader that Jesus' work of healing, curing sickness, suffering, poverty and misery is in fact a series of prophetic actions. The actions are important in themselves, but are also signs of something beyond themselves. Jesus' work is to save the total human being.

A further touching hint of Jesus' work and quality comes right at the end of the story: Jesus tells the man to go off home and report all that *God* had done for him. In fact he goes and proclaims all that *Jesus* had done for him. Are we to assume that Jesus is God, or just that he is doing God's work? In any case, this is already a strong hint, early in Jesus' ministry, of the divine quality of Jesus.

Discipleship

This salvation which Jesus brings turns the man into a full disciple. This is implied by his sitting at the feet of Jesus, a position of gratitude, obedience and learning. Further, he also asks to stay with Jesus, and the disciples were originally chosen 'to be with Jesus'. Instead, he is sent off with the mission to spread the news of what God or Jesus has done for him, the first and only mission during Jesus' lifetime into this Greek region of the Decapolis.

Prayer

Lord, you care for the whole person, everything about me. I can trust you with all my worries, for your one purpose is to save me.

33 Luke 8:40–56

The woman with a haemorrhage and Jairus' daughter

Stories are often interwoven in the gospel. This shows up the significance of the two components by setting one off against the other. So Mark's account of the cleansing of the temple is set off on either side by the story of the cursing of the fig tree – the fig tree is the symbol of Israel, and so its cursing shows the barrenness of Israel, the meaning also of Jesus' prophetic action in the temple. The sending out of the disciples and their return is separated by the account of the death of John the Baptist – this emphasises that preaching the gospel inevitably involves suffering and persecution. In the case of the two cures here, the story of the woman with a haemorrhage certainly increases the tension: and indeed, while Jesus is delayed by the woman with a haemorrhage, Jairus' daughter dies.

The story of Jairus' daughter is also linked, in one of the most remarkable of Luke's pairings, with the raising of the widow's son at Nain. There it is the male child of a female parent; here, the female child of a male parent. Each is an only child, which makes the prospect of the loss all the more tragic for their parents. The crossover is another expression of the insistence in this gospel on the equality of the two sexes before the Lord. The president of the synagogue was an important personage in the town. He ruled the synagogue, which was the centre of religious life, and probably also civic life, in the village. There would be a board of elders, with a president elected for a fixed period. For such a man to be childless would be a tragedy indeed. For such a man to fall at Jesus' feet and do him reverence was an extreme token of putting trust in him. Luke underlines the sadness for Jairus, not only by telling us that his daughter was an only child, but also by stating at the beginning that she was only 12 years old. Mark mentions her age only at the end, when she has been cured and starts prancing around.

The woman with a haemorrhage is presumably suffering from a gynecological disorder. This disorder would not only have had its inherent difficulties, but would also have made her ritually unclean (according to the rules of Leviticus 15) and so forbidden to associate with normal society. Her desperate bid, amid the stiflingly close crowd, to touch simply the fringe of his cloak, would have incurred the utter disapproval of the religious authorities. It must have been a last resort; she had already spent all her money on unsuccessful treatment. To say that the cure changed her life is an understatement. (Mark makes the wry remark that medical treatment had in fact only made her worse. Luke omits this remark, and many have seen in this omission a confirmation of the tradition that the author of the gospel was 'my dear friend Luke, the doctor' mentioned by Paul in Colossians 4:14. He omitted the remark out of loyalty to the medical profession!)

Faith and mission

These two miracles are the last of four which immediately precede the mission of the disciples in 9:1, just as a series of four miracles immediately preceded the call of the disciples in 5:1. Both of these are demonstrations of the authority of Jesus in word and action. The same authority is seen in the ability to control the elements and heal as is seen in the teaching of Jesus and his chosen apostles.

In both these miraculous cures the faith of the recipients is underlined. In close proximity Jesus speaks to both his suppliants, first to the woman, 'Your faith has saved you,' then to the man, 'Only have faith and she will be saved' (vv. 48, 50). In both cases the same open-ended word is used; she is or will be 'saved'. From her death, from her disability, or more totally? The one is a sign of the other. In the case of the little girl to be restored to life, and in the case of the older woman restored to normal life, these are potent signs of salvation of the whole person, the salvation which Jesus came to bring to the world.

Prayer

Lord Jesus, as God made man you were alert to every human need of those around you, responding with love and generosity. Keep me aware that you are still present to us when we are in need, still protecting and cherishing us.

34 Luke 9:1–10

The mission of the twelve

It was a world where itinerant preachers were not unknown, and the instructions given by Jesus resemble those given to the wandering teachers of various popular philosophies, except that they are stricter. The task of these teachers is both more immediate, so that no distractions may enter in, and more powerful: their needs will be supplied. No staff to lean on or to use for beating off stray dogs or animals. No money, which especially to Luke is a dangerous distraction. (It is interesting that Luke uses the word 'silver' for 'money', whereas Mark uses 'copper'; Mark moves in a world where copper coins are common, whereas in Luke's world more expensive silver coinage is the norm.) No spare clothes or food. This is an ideal of poverty and reliance on the power of the task itself. There is a directness and confidence about this mission which is almost frightening – it brooks no compromise, allows no preparation, leaves room for no weakening. Preaching the kingdom is not an occupation for those who seek personal comfort and security. All this shows the nature and power of the kingdom which is being preached. It is a kingdom with authority: they are sent to preach and to heal – both works of authority – and that is what they do.

There is no compromise either in the reception of the message. If it is not received, the envoys are to employ the prophetic gesture of shaking the dust off their feet. This is a natural gesture of disgust and dissociation: 'I will have nothing more to do with this place, getting rid of even the dust from the road.' Luke is always keen to show fulfilment of prophecy. He shows us Paul and Barnabas doing just this when opposition is stirred up against them at Antioch and they are hustled out of the town.

A renewal of prophecy

It was widely accepted that prophecy had ceased in Israel. The great period of the prophets was before the exile. After the exile there had been one or two prophets, like Haggai and Zechariah, but now not for many hundreds of years. Now there was only a longing for the return of God's word, both for the guidance it would give and as a sign of God's affection for his people – however challenging and corrective this prophetic message had always been. The prophet Jeremiah was greatly revered as the champion of his people. A century and a half before Christ there was a tradition that Jeremiah would return as champion (2 Maccabees 15:11–14); a very similar story is told of Jeremiah protecting his own tomb during the 1948 Israeli War of Independence. There was a tradition also (Malachi 3:23) that Elijah would return 'before the great and awesome day of the Lord comes'. The scrolls of Qumran, the fullest evidence we have for Jewish thought in Jesus' own century, show that the community on the desert shores of the Dead Sea were awaiting a prophet, 'a voice crying in the desert'.

All this testifies to a popular longing that God would return and speak to his people. It explains the immediate response to the Baptist and his message: he spoke into a void ready to receive his word. Even the temple authorities had to admit to themselves that his message had struck a chord with the people. Even the Jewish historian Josephus records that the Baptist was so influential that Herod took him into custody to prevent any possible uprising. The messengers could expect a response among the people, though perhaps durable results would be more difficult!

Herod the jackal

Later in Luke (13:32) Jesus calls Herod 'that jackal'. This Herod was the tetrarch of Galilee and other territory, though he did not inherit the full kingdom of his father, King Herod the Great. Jesus' name for him may stem from his activities in the Palestine area as a spy for the central Roman government. Luke does not want to bring the Baptist back into the picture by here telling the story of his execution by Herod, as Mark and Matthew do. Herod's curiosity here prepares for his reappearance in the story of the Passion. It also serves to put in a nutshell the amazement and wonder at this spreading movement.

Prayer

Lord, give me the single-mindedness which you asked of your apostles. Let me enjoy what you give me, but not be distracted from concentration on the lasting values of your kingdom.

35 Luke 9:10–17

The feeding of the 5,000

The story of the miraculous feeding must not be taken on its own in Luke. It is closely joined to the return of the apostles from their preaching journey and to the short summary, at the beginning of the story, of more teaching and healing by Jesus. So it comes as the climax of these and sums up various themes which have been present to mind. First, it must still be attached to the instructions given to the apostles as they set out on their journey, taking no food in their haversacks: it shows definitively that there is no need to fuss about provisions, for Jesus can provide food for his people, not merely for the apostles, but for vastly greater numbers. Second, it is the fulfilment of the beatitude, 'Blessed are those who are hungry now, for they shall be filled,' which we see being accomplished in the ample food provided for the hungry crowds. Third, in this context, the disciples play an important part: it is the disciples rather than Jesus who act responsibly towards the crowds by taking pity on the multitudes. In Mark the crowds are 'like sheep without a shepherd' and Jesus himself takes the initiative. In Luke, on the other hand, the twelve have already begun to take responsibility for the people – they come up to Jesus and ask him to take action with regard to the hungry crowd; then, spurred on by him, they themselves sit the crowds down and distribute the food to them. This is in sharp contrast to the behaviour of the disciples in Mark, where they reply to Jesus' command by some pretty sharp sarcasm, 'Are we supposed to go and spend two hundred denarii on bread for them to eat?' Of this sarcasm there is no sign in Luke's account; now the disciples are willing, if puzzled, helpers. Thus Luke uses the narrative to express the theme of the kingdom and of the little band of disciples which is already beginning to develop in so many ways.

The miracle of feeding

The meaning of the miracle in its original version in Mark was that Jesus was shown to be the messianic shepherd, feeding his sheep, as in the psalm, on pastures green. He was also acting as the prophet Elisha had acted. The story has not lost this meaning in Luke. The prophet Elisha provided bread for his followers in the desert, just as Moses had done for his people. The process of the narrative is so similar to the Elisha account in 2 Kings 4:42–44 that there can be no doubt that the evangelist intends to show that Jesus is acting in just the same way as Elisha. There is the same process of dialogue, the same distribution, the same plenty, the same satisfaction and the same leftovers. Only, the miracle done by Jesus is many times greater, for Elisha feeds 100 men with 10 loaves, while Jesus feeds 5,000 with 5 loaves. Jesus is thus seen to be acting in the line of the prophets, but also to be the greatest of the prophets, greater even than Moses.

A messianic celebration

The plenty provided ('they all ate as much as they wanted'), and again demonstrated by the abundance of scraps left over, is a sign of the plenty of the messianic banquet. The number of twelve, featuring in the group of the twelve and the twelve baskets of scraps, suggests that Jesus' community is the new Israel, corresponding to the twelve tribes of ancient Israel. The twelve represent the foundation stones of the new Israel. The whole scene, therefore, shows in many ways the feast of the Messiah with his new people of God, which has come to fruition at the end of time.

When it comes to the blessing and distribution of the food, we are reminded of the meal at the Last Supper, when Jesus again, with his disciples round him, took bread, said the blessing, broke the bread and handed it to his disciples. The feeding near Bethsaida is, then, also a foretaste of the eucharistic celebration.

Prayer

Lord, your delight is to be with your disciples at the eucharistic meal. Grant that I may there welcome you into my heart with the overflowing joy of your generosity, eager to be your willing disciple, zealous to do your work.

36 Luke 9:18–26

The first prophecy of the Passion

On the whole Luke has been following the order of incidents in Mark's gospel. Now he does something quite remarkable, cutting out a considerable number of incidents given in Mark 6:48—8:26. This is either because he thinks them unnecessary or uninteresting to his audience or because he wants to press on to use this scene as part of his developing picture of the disciples.

The growing understanding of the disciples reaches a new stage with the confession of Peter that Jesus is the Christ of God, or God's Messiah. Till now we have had a series of hints laid down that Jesus is a prophet and a series of questions raised. The demons have acknowledged Jesus as Son of God, but human beings have simply been puzzled, astonished and awestruck at his miracles and his teaching, as Simon and his companions in the boat, as the people of the territory of the Gerasenes, as Jairus and his wife were. People have asked, 'Who is this man, that even forgives sins… that gives orders even to winds and waves and they obey him?' Jesus has been repeatedly greeted as a prophet. He has himself given the meaning of his miracles to the envoys from John the Baptist as fulfilling the messianic prophecies of Isaiah; he has sent his followers out on a messianic mission; on their return he has provided food for them and others, just as Elisha had done.

Now, in response to Jesus' questioning, the other disciples tentatively put forward the opinions of others that Jesus is various of the ancient prophets. For centuries there had been a dearth of prophecy. Although the message of the prophets was normally critical of society and often uncomfortable, the Jews felt acutely that these messengers of God were a sign of God's love for them – like the guidance or even the scolding of a loving parent. So they felt the silence of prophecy and longed for its renewal. So clearly many hoped that Jesus was at least the renewal of prophecy. But Peter goes further and comes straight to the mark with 'the Messiah of God'. At the time of Jesus this could have many shades of meaning – a warlike leader who would liberate Israel from the Romans; a king; an anointed priest. At the very least it is God's chosen messenger, who is to bring God's will to fulfilment at the end of time. By his actions and his teaching, Jesus has been showing what this means. Now, in reply to Peter's declaration, he begins to show that it must mean suffering also.

Discipleship and persecution

A striking difference from Mark's account, which must be deliberate on Luke's part, is that there is no mention of failure on the part of the disciples. In Mark's account Peter rejects out of hand any idea of Jesus suffering, and is sternly rebuked, 'Get behind me, Satan.' At each of the three prophecies of the Passion in Mark, the disciples misunderstand or reject the idea of suffering and have to be told forcefully by Jesus that any followers of his must share his sufferings. In Luke the solidarity between Jesus and his followers is considerably stronger. There is taking place, so to speak, a crescendo of bonding between Jesus and his followers. Not only is there no objection from Peter, and so no rebuke to him, but also the need to share in Christ's suffering is addressed not merely to the chosen group of disciples, but to all disciples, future as well as present: 'Speaking to all he said…' Luke has in mind a lesson not just for the twelve but for all who will set out to follow Jesus. He stresses that it is not a one-off event which is in view, but the daily challenge of discipleship, by adding 'take up the cross *daily*'.

It is often questioned whether the expression 'take up the cross' can stem from Jesus. Could he have used the expression before his own crucifixion? The ugly sight of crucified bodies rotting on gibbets by the roadside, and the process of dragging the execution beam to the place of execution, can hardly have been unknown. But the expression clearly takes on massive added significance after Jesus' death and resurrection.

Prayer

Grant me, Lord, to join more fully with you in your sufferings. Help me to realise the privilege of joining you in your passion, through the crosses you send to me in daily life, both great and small.

37 Luke 9:27–36

The transfiguration

The story of the transfiguration of Jesus is knit into Luke's developing narrative. It comes as a climax of the process which we have seen developing, as the disciples understand more and more who and what Jesus is. This experience of Jesus transfigured comes as a high point of this understanding. It is also the continuation and development of the message of the approaching suffering and Passion of Jesus, which is just beginning to impinge on the consciousness of the disciples: the three figures speak together 'of his passing which he was to accomplish in Jerusalem'.

One important element in the scene is that it starts with an ascent of 'the mountain' to pray. We have no means of knowing which mountain, though Christian tradition has localised the scene at Mount Tabor, an awesome, rounded mountain, rising isolated from the fertile Galilean plain. The important thing is that a mountain is the favoured place for an encounter with God. Just as the first prophecy of the Passion, a few verses previously, had emerged from Jesus' prayer ('he was praying alone, and his disciples came to him…'), so at the transfiguration he is praying. Luke is insistent that the knowledge of God and of his will must be founded on prayer. There is no approach to God without first yielding oneself to God in prayer.

The imagery and symbolism of this experience of Jesus, before he begins his journey up to Jerusalem and to the Passion, is rich with Old Testament allusions. His sparkling white clothing can mean only that he is seen as a heavenly being. The support of Moses and Elijah is difficult to evaluate, for it can have many overtones. Perhaps Moses and Elijah stand respectively for the law and the prophets of the Old Testament. Perhaps they are figures who were expected to return at the end of time, for Jesus is frequently represented both as a second Moses and as an Elijah figure. Alternatively, they may be being presented as prophets who themselves received an experience of God on mountains, namely Sinai and Horeb, respectively.

The climax of the experience is, however, of the glory of God. The vision of the three heavenly figures is bathed in the glory of God, which persists as a sort of afterglow in the glory of Jesus when the disciples rouse themselves. It has a fascination and a terror, so that Peter says, 'It is wonderful to be here,' and yet as they enter into the cloud (another symbol and expression of God's glory) they are rightly afraid. It is a reminiscence of the glory of the Lord which was shown to Moses on Mount Sinai, a terrifying, awesome experience, the nearest a human being can get to experiencing God, 'whom no man can see and live'. The vision of God in the temple reduced even Isaiah to quaking, terrified awareness of his own sinfulness, so that 'the Holy One of Israel' remained his slogan and inspiration throughout his message. Peter's strange and baffled suggestion that they should make three shelters is perhaps an idea that they should make three shrines so that the experience might remain permanent.

This climax of this awesome experience of God is the divine voice confirming the authority of Jesus as God's chosen messenger. To contemporaries this would have been clearer still, for there are other contemporary stories of a voice from heaven which confirms the authority of a teacher, underpinning his message with God's own authority. Further, Luke already has his eye on the proclamation of the gospel message when he carefully says, 'The disciples kept silence and *at that time* told no one what they had seen.' There is a direct line between the message of God, the message of the disciples and the reception of the gospel.

Thus the disciples are strengthened at the beginning of the preparation for the final prophetic act of the journey up to Jerusalem and the Passion.

Prayer

Lord, grant me devotion in prayer, grant me even to glimpse your glory and to long for the full vision of your presence. May I be inspired particularly at moments of trial at least by the knowledge that your glory is there, infinitely superior to any human power, and even to the power of my own sinfulness and incompetence.

38 Luke 9:37–50

The disciples' failure

It is staggering and yet obviously deliberate that now, immediately after this vision of divine glory which was the transfiguration, the weakness and incomprehension of the disciples should be drummed in by a series of incidents. These form a whole group between the transfiguration and the beginning of the journey to Jerusalem. Luke seems to have welded together into one unit several incidents, the scene of the epileptic child, the second prophecy of the Passion and finally the dispute about greatness.

The incomprehension of the disciples is a striking feature of the gospel. In the first half of the gospel, leading up to the eventual confession of Peter at Caesarea Philippi, they are several times rebuked by Jesus for their slowness to understand, and are even reproached for 'hardness of heart', like the Pharisees themselves. On more than one occasion they treat Jesus to quite unpleasant doses of sarcasm. When Peter has finally recognised that Jesus is the Christ, they still cannot stomach the idea that he is a suffering Messiah. Every time he foretells the Passion they show their incomprehension by turning a deaf ear to his lessons on the ministry of service and by squabbling about their own precedence in the kingdom.

On the whole Luke softens this criticism of the disciples and stresses their close companionship with Jesus and their responsiveness to him. This was especially clear, as we have seen, in the lead up to the transfiguration. But now their failure to share with Jesus comes through with all the more force.

The epileptic boy

Despite having been given earlier the power over all evil spirits, the disciples now fail to drive out the spirit which is tormenting the young man. In this context it must be the disciples who are envisaged in Jesus' exasperated rebuke to the 'faithless and perverse generation'. The inability of the chosen disciples to help contrasts unfavourably with the obviously heartfelt prayers of the boy's father. Luke increases the father's plight by pointing out that the sufferer is an only son. The contrast between the failure of the disciples and Jesus' power is made all the more striking by the effortless way in which Jesus triumphs over the spirit of epilepsy. There is none of the graphic description of struggle as given in Mark's account, nor of the father's desperate faith: 'I believe; help my unbelief! (Mark 9:24, RSV). Jesus restores the boy by his simple, overriding authority. It is all over in a flash, and the crowds are left goggling at the greatness of God. At the end of the passage the ineptitude of the disciples is again underlined by the fact that others are succeeding in driving out evil spirits in Jesus' name, while the disciples both fail to do this themselves and attempt to prevent others doing it. Is it that they lack faith? Or is it that they are too preoccupied with their own position and status, as the dispute in verse 46 suggests?

The second prophecy of the Passion neglected

The disciples again show their insensitivity by completely disregarding Jesus' prophecy of his approaching suffering. Throughout this journey up to Jerusalem he clearly has the coming Passion in mind. So much was made clear by the discussion about his 'passing' during the scene of the transfiguration. It breaks the surface again in the three prophecies of the Passion and in such remarks as 'It would not be right for a prophet to die outside Jerusalem' (13:33). This is enough to show that the prospect of his fate and its inevitability was constantly before his mind. Yet all this the disciples fail to understand. Instead of asking what it means they seem to turn away and block it out of their minds. Instead, they straightaway fall to arguing about their own positions, till Jesus gives them a counter-demonstration by means of the little child. Children are not really any more innocent or straightforward than adults – only less experienced and so less skilled in deception. Perhaps the quality which Jesus puts forward is rather dependence and willingness to receive. Whatever it is, the disciples have a lot to learn on the road up to Jerusalem.

Prayer

Lord, you have chosen me to be your follower and disciple. Often I fail to understand your ways and close my ears to your message. Make me more sensitive to your guidance and responsive to your will.

39 Luke 9:51–62

Journey to Jerusalem

Now begins the great journey to Jerusalem, full of presage and omen for the Passion of Jesus, full of presage also for the resurrection and the worldwide mission of the apostles which will result from it. Jerusalem is, for Luke, the hinge: there Jesus dies and is raised; from there the word spreads to the ends of the earth. So Luke deserts the Markan structure which he has followed in at least close outline since the baptism of Jesus. He rearranges the material and brings in more from other sources, focusing the whole on the goal of Jerusalem. All other distracting geographical references are suppressed, so that the reader is not diverted from the intention of Jesus who now 'resolutely turned his face towards Jerusalem'.

The Old Testament atmosphere and regular reference to the prophets again and again remind us that Jesus is fulfilling the whole movement of the Old Testament. The journey is put under the sign of Jesus being 'taken up'. Superficially this may mean only his 'going up' to Jerusalem. But on a deeper level a hint is already being given of the ascension, when Jesus will be 'taken up' into heaven. This in its turn already reminds us of Elijah, who was taken up into heaven at his death, and perhaps also of Moses, who was last seen before his death on Mount Nebo, and whose tomb was unknown. The gospel of John gives a still fuller meaning to this 'being taken up', regarding the 'lifting up' of Jesus on to the cross as his exaltation or lifting up to heaven, where he would draw all people to himself and also come to share in the heavenly glory of the Father; the lifting up is interpreted as the glorification of Jesus.

The apostolic journey

Another reminder of Moses is the appointment of the '72 others' whom Jesus sends out ahead of him. In just the same way Moses had appointed 72 elders to assist him in his task. The background of journeying is surely significant in all this. For Luke journeying is a way of life. The people of Moses were on the move for 40 years in the desert, and similarly the apostle of Jesus is always on the move. According to one calculation, Paul journeyed 10,000 miles in the course of his mission, a extraordinary feat of endurance in a world where 10 miles a day by road was a dusty and exhausting average. Luke, too, must have been acutely conscious of journeying from his own travels in the apostolic cause. This is why journeying is the background of so much of his double volume.

A sign of contradiction

There are no illusions that the journey is easy or has a happy outcome. Some scholars have seen a balancing pattern in all the incidents of the journey, by which (like onion skins progressively peeled off) the first balances the last, the second balances the penultimate, the third balances the antepenultimate and so on. How general this pattern is may be doubted, but at least the first and last incidents balance each other. Each of them is a rejection: at the beginning Jesus is rejected by the Samaritans (and the suggestion of calling down fire from heaven again reminds us of Elijah calling down fire from heaven on those who come to arrest him in 2 Kings 1). At the end Jesus is rejected in Jerusalem, so the first rejection provides a sort of premonition at the start of the journey which has its fulfilment at the end.

Much of the teaching on this journey – and the material on the journey is overwhelmingly sayings of Jesus rather than actions – is about discipleship. Accordingly, it starts with three stern sayings on the demands of being a disciple of Jesus, as though to say, 'Let there be no illusions: you are entering on a tough course.' The fact that none of them records any reply shows that the evangelist is more interested in the saying than in any story in which it occurred; the lesson is general, not limited to any particular person. The first demands total homelessness. The second puts the claims of the kingdom above the most sacred of human ties. The third requires ceaseless and concentrated dedication: if you lose concentration for a moment with a handplough the whole endeavour goes to pieces.

Prayer

Give me strength, Lord, to follow you on your journey, even though it is a hard road. Give me your company and your inspiration on the way.

40 Luke 10:1–20
The mission of the 72

The first question is why Luke gives us a second account of mission, when 9:1–6 has already given the instructions to the twelve for their mission. Luke seems to dislike doublets (this may be why he omits the second miraculous feeding of the 4,000 after the 5,000, and the walking on the water after the calming of the storm), but he does not mind repeating really important teaching. After all, he tells the story of the conversion of Paul three times in Acts, and – as here – with some slight variations for elegance and to avoid boredom. The differences are probably more for literary variation than for theological significance: on the first mission they are forbidden staff and bread; on the second they are forbidden sandals and greetings on the way. The same message of urgency and single-mindedness lies behind both.

The answer to a second question also throws light on the first: is it 70 or 72 disciples? The original Greek text is hard to establish; some manuscripts give 70, some 72, and it is difficult to decide between them. There is an important parallel to this in the Old Testament. In Genesis 10 the nations of the earth are enumerated. In the Hebrew text there are 70 of them, in the Greek 72. When Moses chose the elders to help him, there were also 70, and by tradition these were one for each nation of the world. Whatever the solution to the numerical problem, the importance of this muddle is that it suggests that Luke had in mind the mission of the apostles to all the nations of the world, sent out two by two, but nevertheless one for each nation.

Then the two missions make sense, the twelve being sent in chapter 9 to the tribes of Israel and the 70 (or 72) sent in chapter 10 to the non-Jewish nations. The same two-stage mission comes again in the parable of the great feast, where the messengers are sent first to the outcasts within the city (that is, Israel) and then to those outside the city (the Gentiles). This is also, of course, the pattern of Luke's two volumes – the first describing the message to Israel; the second (Acts) that to the nations. On this wider mission perhaps the most notable variation is the threat of danger and rejection.

A gospel of peace

The first words of the missioners are to be 'Peace be to this house', and they are to bring peace to those who will receive it. This is more than the conventional Jewish greeting (still used today) of *Shalom*. Luke sees the gospel importantly as 'the good news of peace', as Peter announces to Cornelius and his household in Acts. Right from the beginning of the gospel, the angels at the nativity sing 'On earth peace' and Zechariah's canticle starts 'Now, Master, you are letting your servant go in peace' when he has received the child Jesus. The sinful woman who weeps on Jesus' feet is told to 'go in peace' with her sins forgiven. The gospel of John will give this concept an even greater depth, for the peace of Christ is part of the indwelling of Christ in his followers: 'My peace I bequeath to you, my peace I give you.' Peace is the final blessing of Jesus in the discourses at the last supper and again his greeting to them in the upper room after the resurrection. In a world of unrest, turbulence, malice and aggression, the Christian gift of peace is beyond value. So each of Paul's letters begins with the greeting of 'Peace' and many of them end with it too. Peace must be founded on respect for others and their needs, avoiding the temptation to domineer or insist on one's own interests.

The cities of the lakeside

It is in contrast to this offer of peace that the fate of the lakeside cities is so daunting. The words of the curse, 'Did you want to be raised high as heaven? You shall be flung down to hell' are an allusion to the fate of proud Babylon in Isaiah 14. The city which aspired to rule the world, like Lucifer, would, for its pride, be consigned to the lowest depths.

Prayer

Lord, as your apostles were the agents of peace, let me too bring your peace to others. Take from me all worry and insecurity, in the knowledge that if I trust in you rather than my own strength, you will give me your own peace to abide with me forever.

41 Luke 10:21–24

A final blessing

This long section on disciples and discipleship ends with a double blessing: Jesus blesses his Father in gratitude and blesses his disciples for the revelation that has been given to them, and which they are to spread to others. Between these two blessings he pronounces one of the deepest reflections in the synoptic gospels on the relationship between Father and Son.

The eagerness of children

The blessing begins with Luke's characteristic theme of reversal. Mary's hymn of praise in the Magnificat centred on gratitude that God had 'pulled down princes from their thrones and raised high the lowly'. The beatitudes promise the kingdom of God to those who are poor now and laughter to those who weep now. Now the reversal concerns revelation: it is not the learned and clever who receive the secrets of revelation but 'mere children'. This comes close to Paul's insistence, writing to the Corinthians, that God's folly is wiser than human wisdom, that human wisdom was unable to recognise God and that 'it was God's own pleasure to save believers through the folly of the gospel' (1 Corinthians 1:21).

The preference for children is no romantic idealisation of childhood, about their supposed innocence or guilelessness; rather, it gives the clue to why Jesus earlier set a child among the disciples as a model. One real universal characteristic of children is willingness to learn, an appreciation that they are an empty canvas on which there is still much to be drawn. Imitation is a feature of childhood from the very beginning. Adults hate being corrected; for children it is an inevitable part of life and something on which to grow. The eagerness to grow in mind is as keen as the longing to grow in body, and a child realises that, while it can do nothing to speed bodily growth, it can do much to speed mental development. It is this eagerness to receive and to learn that Jesus here praises as the prerequisite of revelation.

The 'Johannine thunderbolt'

Between the two blessings at beginning and end of this little section comes the stunning statement about the relationship of the Son to the Father. Nothing else like it exists in the synoptic gospels, but it is amply filled out in the gospel of John. The basic theology is that of the '*shaliah*'. This is a Hebrew term in rabbinic writings for an envoy, sent with specific powers. The envoy is regarded as having the same powers, deserving the same respect, holding the same position as his principal. He is sent out by and reports back to the principal. In his turn he can appoint envoys to extend his work. This is clearly the concept which stands behind much of John's expression of the relationship of the Son to the Father, who shows him everything he himself does, who gives all judgement to the Son: 'As the Father has life in himself, so he has granted the Son also to have life in himself' (John 5:26).

The importance of this statement comes from the fact that the Hebrew mind defines in dynamic rather than static terms. The later Trinitarian theological definitions of the great councils are given in static terms. That is, instead of describing the relationship of Son to Father in the Greek terms of essence and nature, as did the early church councils (dominated by Greek thought), the Hebrew mind describes in terms of powers and action, what a person does rather than what a person is. So here the Son reveals the Father, and to know the Son is to know the Father. Just as in John judgement has been entrusted to the Son, so here 'everything' has been entrusted to the Son, so that the Son is the plenipotentiary of the Father and stands in the place of the Father.

Prayer

Father, you reveal yourself to us in your Son. Teach me to pray and meditate over this revelation you give, and draw me ever closer into company with your Son and so with you.

42 Luke 10:25–37

The good Samaritan

The great commandment

This little dialogue is the only scene where Luke on his own gives the classic form of Jesus dialogue, common in Mark and possibly remembered as typical of Jesus' own challenging method of teaching. It happens in four moves: someone comes up and asks Jesus a question; Jesus does not answer but replies with his own question; the original questioner gives an answer, usually unsatisfactory (but here wholly satisfactory); Jesus gives his own solution.

There is a fascinating difference in Luke's account from Mark's. In Mark the questioner asks which is the first command, and Jesus gives the reply. There could never really be any doubt about which was the first commandment of the law. It was incorporated into the great monotheistic creed of Israel in Deuteronomy 6:4–5, which every faithful Jew still recites in the daily prayer: 'The Lord our God is the one, the only Lord. You must love the Lord your God with all your heart, with all your soul, with all your strength.' In Mark the punch of Jesus' answer is that he adds, unasked, the second commandment of love of neighbour. This is typical of Jesus: he was always going deeper than the questioner wanted him to and making fuller demands than were expected! This happens also with the tribute coin: 'Pay Caesar what belongs to Caesar [that is harmless enough], *and God what belongs to God.*'

In Luke's account the two are joined together, and the speaker is the lawyer. He is duly praised by Jesus, but then nearly spoils things by his blustering question, 'anxious to justify himself'. With one deft touch of pompous bluster Luke brings the lawyer to life! On the other hand, the whole dialogue is neatly sewn together by the idea of 'life' at beginning and end: 'What must I do to inherit eternal life?... Do this and life is yours.' This is one of only two occasions in Luke when the concept of eternal life appears – the other being the story of the rich aristocrat who comes to Jesus with the same question. In John the concept is frequent, and sums up all the benefits brought by Jesus, much the same as the concept of the kingship of God.

The parable

Luke adds one of his well-loved stories. The old path from Jerusalem to Jericho runs down the Wadi Qilt, a deep, twisting canyon with rocky sides and blistering heat, some four hours' smart walk. Today you can round a corner and find yourself in the middle of a flock of goats, herded by a Bedouin boy and his noisy dogs. Just as easily it could be the bandits of Jesus' tale. There is a certain wit about the story: the priest and Levite are in a nasty moral dilemma. They could not miss seeing the traveller, even by passing by 'on the other side': the bottom of the canyon is never more than 20 metres wide. It is not simply that they pass by unfeelingly. If the huddled victim of the bandits turns out to be dead, they could be defiled by contact with a corpse and disqualified from their sacred duties (and deprived of the income from them!).

The hero of the story turns out to be the Samaritan. It is the first time (apart from a brief mention in 9:52) we have come across that people whom the Jews disliked so much. They were descended from an amalgam of peoples deported by the Assyrians, centuries earlier, to the territory north of Judea. They were near enough to the Jews, both territorially and in religion, to be felt as a threat, with all the dislike engendered by rivalry. Yet Christianity spread to them early enough, and Jesus himself unforgettably drew the Samaritan woman at Jacob's Well to be his follower. For Luke they are therefore the paradigm of the foreigners who are invited by the call of Jesus to share the privileges of the Jews. To counter the exclusiveness of the Jews, Luke shows the Samaritans being more responsive than the Jews to the message of Jesus. The traveller shows open-hearted generosity at a chance meeting with a total stranger.

So here the Samaritan fulfils the commandment of love which the two Jews neglect. There is one of those little logical knots which we have occasionally encountered in Luke: the story is supposed to show who is my neighbour to whom I should show love. Instead, it illustrates who the neighbour is who shows love to me.

Prayer

Lord, you call on me to show the same love to all as you yourself show. Make me open-hearted and generous to those in need, help me to see them all as my own brothers and sisters.

43 Luke 10:38–42

Martha and Mary

Geographically, Martha and Mary have no right to appear here. According to John's gospel they belong in Bethany, less than a half-hour's walk from Jerusalem, where they lived with their brother Lazarus. In Luke the great journey up to Jerusalem has hardly begun. But one of the features of the journey is that Luke suppresses geographical details which would distract from the sense of going up to the Passion. Geography is not his principle of arrangement, and perhaps the story comes here as part of a series on hospitality (in which it fits with the story of the good Samaritan), particularly hospitality to those who bring God's message (in which it fits well after the instructions to and mission of the disciples).

The story is told with the liveliness typical of the characterisation in Luke's parables, Mary's tranquil composure vividly contrasting with Martha's busy fussiness. It is so typical of the activist, who likes to fill every available moment and would be miserable at having nothing to do, to complain of lack of help. Not content with fussing around, Martha is obviously the type who blurts out everything, even family secrets, even in front of important guests. They were not children and must have lived together for some years, so Mary's behaviour can have come as no surprise to Martha – yet still she scolds her or rather even asks the guest to scold her. One does not have the impression of a happy household, if the sibling rivalry was such that Martha needed to go about correcting her sister through a third party! There is surely a deliberate contrast in the manner of speech between Martha, who does not even have the courtesy or warmth to name her sister, and Jesus, who softens his correction by affectionately using her name twice, 'Martha, Martha.'

Jesus' reply is typical also of Luke's emphasis on detachment from possessions. There is no need for them, and the one thing necessary is to listen to the Lord. So much has been clear since the annunciation stories, and especially since the presentation of Mary and the disciples as the ones who listen. At the base of this is the simple lesson of human courtesy in hospitality: the personality of the guest is more important than any entertainment, and attention to the guest is the prime compliment to be paid. When the guest is a teacher this is even more obviously the case.

Contemplation and action

In Christian ascetical tradition the two sisters have become the symbols of the contemplative and active life, the lives centred respectively on prayer and on translating prayer into action. This builds on the assumption that the parable is contrasting two ways of prayer; in fact it would be more accurate to see it as contrasting two ways of attentiveness. Luke does not suggest that Martha's service is wrong. To begin with, he uses the same word for her service as that used for the service of the seven who are appointed to serve the poor of the faithful in the early community ideally described in Acts. Furthermore, when the Greek literally has 'Mary has chosen the *good* part', this does not imply that Martha's part is bad. It is simply that comparatives ('better', 'worse', etc) are rare in gospel Greek. Jesus' language was stark and uncompromising.

There may be another dimension to the story. The answer to the lawyer's question about eternal life (at the beginning of the previous section) was the double commandment, love of God and love of neighbour. The command to love one's neighbour as oneself was illustrated by the story of the good Samaritan. Now the command to love God above all things is illustrated by the story of Martha and Mary. Jesus is not only addressed as 'Lord!', which happens in Mark, and may mean no more than 'Sir!'. He is also described (v. 41) as '*the* Lord', which strongly suggests the Lord God. So Mary's love of Jesus is an illustration of love of God with the whole heart.

Prayer

Lord, let me listen to your word. Do not let your message be clouded over or crowded out by my own preoccupations and busyness. Give me the tranquillity and openness to hear your message in my head and in my heart.

44 Luke 11:1–4

The Lord's Prayer

This is the first of three short sections in a collection of teachings on how Jesus' disciples should pray. But it is prefaced by the notice that Jesus was praying when his disciples came asking him to teach them how to pray. Here again, as often in Luke, Jesus is at prayer, which was the wellspring of his being and his activity, and here again Jesus is the model for the disciples, teaching them to pray as he himself prays. The followers of Jesus imitate him in his prayer, his miracles, his suffering and his passion.

Luke's version of the Lord's Prayer is simpler than the more familiar version taken from Matthew's gospel. The first striking difference is the stark 'Father!' with which it opens. Matthew's 'Our Father in heaven' is more courtly and more Jewish. Luke's version has the directness and immediacy of Jesus' own prayer in the garden and elsewhere, in which he addressed God warmly and simply as 'Father'. This 'Abba' became so treasured among Christians that the Aramaic phrase was retained as a sort of talisman even in the Greek letters of Paul. It must have been regarded as the guarantee and reassurance that Christians could use this address as adopted children to their Father.

The coming of the kingdom

In Luke's version there are only two petitions in the first part of the prayer, concerned with God. Luke omits Matthew's third petition, 'May your will be done.' Perhaps he thought it was adequately voiced in the two prayers which he does have. There are other occasions also when he omits references to God's will when they occur in Matthew's gospel.

Luke's first petition is identical with that of Matthew, 'May your name be held holy.' It is a prayer that the holiness of God may be recognised. It must remind one of the call of the prophet Isaiah in Isaiah 6, when he saw the Lord enthroned in the temple, his train a sort of cloud of smoke, filling the sanctuary. So awesome was this vision that even the seraphs covered their faces to cry, 'Holy, holy, holy!' Isaiah's reaction is terror and awareness of his own and the people's sinfulness, needing to be cleansed by fire before he can announce the Lord's message. Henceforth he will always call God 'the Holy One of Israel'. No human being can stand before God; it is this holiness and total otherness from all creation that must be recognised.

The second petition, 'May your kingdom come,' touches the heart of Jesus' message. It cannot be described shortly, for it sums up the whole of his activity. He brought the kingdom (or perhaps better, the kingship) of God by the prophetic actions of his miracles of healing and forgiveness, by his teaching and the response in human hearts, by the loving obedience to his Father on the cross in which his whole life was crystallised. Yet in another sense Jesus' activity on earth was only the beginning of the establishment of the kingship of God, and we can still pray that God's kingship be fully accomplished. It is all too clear that the evils of malice, suffering, pain and death continue in the world, and God's kingship is not fully realised till all these have been abolished. The vision of the return to paradise is far from fulfilment.

Human needs

The second set of petitions is concerned with human needs. Again Luke's version is more direct: he omits the final 'but save us from evil (or the Evil One)'. The first of these three petitions is concerned with humdrum human needs. Luke makes the request more insistent than Matthew's calmer version, so that it should be translated literally, '*Go on* giving us our bread *every day*.' Just so, Luke insists that the Christian must take up the cross every single day. Of course 'bread' stands in biblical language for food in general, not necessarily the produce of corn. It is equally applicable to pasta, rice or salsa!

The next petition is the dangerous one. We blandly and unthinkingly say (in Matthew's version) 'Forgive us… as we have forgiven'. Can we really be easy in our minds at asking God to mete out to us no more than the forgiveness we mete out to others? Luke challenges the follower of Christ to assert boldly, 'For we ourselves forgive each one who is in debt to us.' Do we?

Prayer

Father, may your kingdom come. Forgive us our sins, whatever they are.

45 Luke 11:5–13

Parables on prayer (1)

The selfish householder

This is another of Luke's lively parables with his brilliant characterisation. Luke does not insist on allegory. If it were an allegory, the householder would stand in the place of God. In an allegory, such as the parable of the sower or (in Matthew's gospel) the parable of the wheat and the tares, each element in the story has a corresponding element in the meaning. For an allegory a sort of key can be provided, as it is in the case of those two parables, explaining the correspondences. Not every parable is an allegory; sometimes, as here or in the parable of the dishonest steward, there is just one point of comparison.

In any case, Luke is not afraid to make the householder act – like most of us – from mixed motives. His characters often do the right thing for the wrong reasons. Like most of us, they are mixed characters, neither plaster-cast saints nor utter blackguards. The scenario for this story is a small village and a one-roomed house. The master of the house sleeps in the inner recesses, furthest from the door. If he is to get up and answer the door, he will have to climb over his sleeping children, stretched out over the rest of the floor. So he makes the sleeping children his excuse. However, the battering on the door persists, and in the end, rather than be shamed by the whole village being woken up and hearing of his refusal to offer hospitality, he climbs over the children and gives the traveller whatever he wants (a hint of desperation or exasperation, not just 'what he wants', but 'whatever he wants'!). There are other occasions in the parables when shame is a motive for action: the crafty steward would be 'too ashamed' to beg. Human respect is often a powerful motive in our lives, and one of the encouraging aspects about the parables in Luke is how like ourselves the characters are.

One may question the origin of this short isolated parable, which comes in no other gospel. Luke is a master storyteller (was this the reason why his community commissioned him to write the gospel?), and can turn Matthew's stiff contrast of the two sons into the vibrant tale of the prodigal son, or a single remark in the book of Proverbs into the parable of the unjust judge. Perhaps this story of the selfish householder is no more than an expansion of the sayings which follow it.

Effective prayer

There follow three little sayings which Luke shares with Matthew. All three are imperatives, followed by the result. To express the result, the 'theological passive' is used. The Jews, out of reverence, avoided using the name of God. At this time the personal name of God, YHWH, was held too sacred ever to be pronounced, and 'Adonai' or 'Lord' was used in its stead. In present-day Judaism this too is avoided, and 'the Name' is substituted in its place. But one way of avoiding even that is to use the passive. What is here meant, then, is 'Ask, and God will provide. Knock, and God will open the door.'

This brings us starkly up against the problem of our unanswered prayer. The Father may not give a snake instead of a fish or a scorpion instead of an egg, but he certainly does not always give the fish or the egg! Again, it is important that the parable of the selfish householder is not an allegory. The householder gives the traveller whatever he demands; God does not. It is possible only to suggest the beginning of an answer. It is like a human father and his children – the father knows best, and the child trusting in his love can only yield to that love and wisdom of the father. We cannot understand the wisdom of God. Like Job, we cannot demand an explanation. We can only ask and trust. The battering on the door is only a sign and expression of our trust that the householder will not leave us benighted.

Prayer

Lord, you give us your Holy Spirit as your best gift, the Spirit of love and trust. You know our needs, and you know how best they can be fulfilled. I know that you will not give me a scorpion, but do sometimes give me the egg for which I ask!

46 Luke 11:14–28

Reactions to Jesus

Jesus and Beelzebul

How does this controversy get here? In Mark it comes much earlier in the gospel (Mark 3:22–27), forming the boundary between Jesus' teaching to the crowds and his turning to instruct the disciples. Luke's change of position for the episode makes two important points. First, it shows that Luke is concerned in this section to show different reactions to the message of Jesus; all the incidents round about form a study of the various ways in which Jesus' message can be accepted or rejected. Second, the shift demonstrates a rich point about the tradition behind the gospels and how that tradition was regarded: the stories which go to make up the gospels were handed down in the early Christian communities as independent units, each one carefully transmitted for itself, before they were joined together 'like pearls on a string' to form a continuous gospel. The stories would be repeated for a particular purpose, to make a particular point or settle a particular question which was relevant to the life of the community at the time. When the gospels came to be written, each evangelist arranged the pearls on the string in his own order.

That the evangelists arranged the incidents in their own order does not cast doubt on the historicity of the incidents themselves. In fact in the search for the bedrock of the Jesus tradition this controversy is an example of one important principle, sometimes called by scholars the 'friend-and-foe criterion': something accepted by Jesus' foes as well as his friends is especially strongly grounded in history. By attributing his miracles to Beelzebul, Jesus' opponents implicitly accepted that his miracles did in fact happen and needed explanation.

Beelzebul was a name for a popular evil spirit (meaning 'Lord of the Frontier', but often distorted by opponents into the mocking Beelzebub or 'Lord of the Flies'). The fact that Jesus replies with a reflection on the kingdom suggests that the original context was not merely a gibe about his exorcisms, but a wider accusation against the kingdom that he was proclaiming. His opponents must have claimed that this was not the kingdom of God at all, but the kingdom of an evil spirit. This too is an important friend-or-foe consequence: both sides accept that the central point of Jesus' activity is not isolated exorcisms but the wider implication of those exorcisms, that Jesus has come to announce the blossoming of the sovereignty of God in a new way.

Luke and the three-piece suite

The little parable about the evil spirits taking over a house has plenty to tell us about Luke and his circumstances. Mark's version is very simple: a robber enters a house to steal some tools and ties up the muscular owner. It is simply a pair with the previous parable, to reinforce that a household or kingdom can have only one master. Luke shows us an owner (representing any human being) standing guard, armed to the teeth to protect his possessions; now it is a question of what you value in life, where your heart is. The confrontation is such that the stronger man can be said to have 'won a victory'. Then he takes away the weaponry on which the householder was relying and scatters around all the cherished possessions. It is not a simple burglary of a few tools but the systematic devastation of a comfortable residence. And when the seven spirits, worse than himself, join the original tough guy, one can imagine them lounging with their dirty boots on the sofa, stubbing out their cigarettes on the carpet. If possessions are so important to Luke's audience, one can see why he needs to warn against being distracted by them from the more important concerns of God's kingdom.

The blessed mother

This preoccupation with possessions receives a stark contrast with the simplicity of the blessing on the womb and breasts of Jesus' mother, a touching emphasis on the normality of his humanity. Yet Jesus replies that the blessing on a mother is not to be compared with the blessing on those who respond to the word of God. This is not to be read as any disrespect for his mother on Jesus' part, but rather as an expression of the central task of the disciple: to hear the word of God.

Reflection

Who is master in my house? Ambition, possessions, sex, comfort, my good name, my next holiday – or the word of God?

47 Luke 11:29–54

Jesus' counterattack

The sign of Jonah

The attack of the opponents had been double, the accusation of alliance with Beelzebul and the demand for a sign. Jesus has already answered the first, and now proceeds to the second: the only sign to be given is the sign of Jonah. There seem to have been different points of view about the sign. In Mark 8:12 (surely the earliest version) Jesus gives an entirely negative response, abruptly and with an oath refusing any sign from heaven. They were perhaps wanting a direct intervention from God, in the form of a pronouncement or voice from heaven, such as was given at the baptism. In Matthew 12:40 Jesus reverses this by promising a sign, the resurrection: 'For as Jonah remained in the belly of the sea-monster for three days and three nights, so will the Son of Man be in the heart of the earth for three days and three nights.' Between these two positions falls Luke. There is no mention of the three days in the sea monster as an interpretation of the resurrection after three days, but rather the sign of Jonah is understood as his preaching of repentance. Jesus' own preaching of repentance is compared to that of Jonah. The difference lies in the response: the men of Nineveh responded to the preaching of Jonah, by contrast to the present generation. Similarly the Queen of Sheba responded with her admiration to the wisdom of Solomon. Both (note Luke's usual pairing of male and female) will come forward at the judgement in witness against those who failed to respond to the one who was greater than the wisdom of Solomon and more forceful than the preaching of Jonah.

Parables of light

Three short parables on light follow. The general idea of the first must be that the preaching of Jesus is a lamp which can be clearly seen. The second is about clarity of vision in the beholder, and so is a reflection on the acceptance of the message. It makes use of the physiology that the eye is a receptor of light by which light penetrates the body, provided that the eye does not contain a blockage. The third saying combines the two, linking the idea of a lamp shining with that of the body penetrated and transformed by light.

Rebuke to the Pharisees and lawyers

Finally Luke builds the conventional Hellenistic scene of a meal as an occasion of conversation and teaching to give a general tableau of criticism of the Pharisees and lawyers. He uses much of the material which comes in the indictment of the scribes and Pharisees in Matthew 23, but instead of lumping them together, Luke separates the charges appropriately. First come three charges against the Pharisees – they fuss about ritual cleansing rather than generosity; they are concerned with paying the tithe on minute herbs while neglecting the love of God; they are avid for human recognition and important seats in the synagogue. These are personal faults in the way they live.

Then attention turns to the lawyers, those who teach how the law should be observed; against them there are also three charges. They are charged with teaching others to carry burdens they themselves would not touch and with taking away the key of knowledge, that is, of preventing even the well-intentioned from embracing this knowledge. But the weightiest of all the charges against the teachers of Israel is the central one of persistently refusing to recognise the prophets. This is applied to the past, the present and – with the addition of 'apostles' – the future. With all solemnity 'the wisdom of God' pronounces that this generation will pay the penalty. Luke is thinking both of the failure to recognise the prophets of the Old Testament, and especially of the failure to recognise Jesus the prophet and his apostles.

The letter of James says, 'Only a few of you… should be teachers'; to be a teacher of religion (and we all teach by example and in countless other ways of which we are unaware at the time) is a dangerous occupation. It demands especial sensitivity to the wisdom of God.

Prayer

Lord, help me to see not whether but how all these charges apply to me in various ways. Open my eyes and give me courage to change what should be changed.

48 Luke 12:1–12

Courage in the face of persecution

In the teaching of Jesus which Luke so cleverly disposes in his travel narrative he constantly has his eye on the church of the future and its apostolate. Here he first puts forward a dramatic contrast between the authorities of the Jews who lie in wait to catch Jesus out (11:54) and the crowds who are so enthusiastic that some of their number get trampled (12:1). There is a steady contrast between the positive response of the populace and the negative response of their leaders. This is mirrored in the Passion narrative, where the leaders deliver Jesus up, while the people engage in an act of sorrow which almost amounts to a liturgy of repentance. In Acts, too, the opposition of the leaders becomes ever stronger, while increasing thousands of the people join the new movement.

An apostolate under persecution

As a prophet, Luke's Jesus is clearly speaking about the task of the apostles after his death and resurrection. The first point he makes is that they are his friends: 'To you my friends I say…' Nowhere else in Luke are they so addressed. The address immediately recalls John 15:14: at the last supper, Jesus is speaking of the future of the church and of their need to remain united to him as branches to the vine, when he says, 'You are my friends, if you do what I command you. I shall no longer call you servants, because a servant does not know the master's business; I call you friends, because I have made known to you everything I have learnt from my Father.' It is as the trusted friends of Jesus that his apostles are sent out.

The second important point is that Jesus sends them out in the full knowledge that they will be persecuted and killed. This foreknowledge is constantly stressed. They will be taken before synagogues and magistrates and (somewhat vaguer) authorities, as indeed in Acts the apostles are taken before the synagogue rulers and Paul is taken before magistrates in Philippi and Corinth and before the Roman authorities at Caesarea. The same sort of prediction is made by the prophet Agabus in Acts 21:11 as Paul prepares to go up to Jerusalem towards his imprisonment. Despite this, Jesus assures them of their value and the protection they will receive. Of all the qualities he recommends, perhaps Luke puts most emphasis on perseverance, the ability to hang on in the face of persecution.

A touching little parallel to this is the saying of the Galilean teacher Rabbi Simeon ben Yohai when threatened with capture by the Romans half a century later: 'Not even a bird perishes without the will of heaven. How much less a son of man.' Not only is there a parallel with the care of five sparrows worth only two bronze coins, but also a parallel in the mysterious expression (which seems to have been characteristic of Jesus' speech, for in the New Testament it comes only on his lips), 'the Son of Man', as referring to himself.

Blasphemy against the Spirit

The saying about blasphemy against the Holy Spirit is truly puzzling. In Mark 3:29 and Matthew 12:32 it comes as part of Jesus' reply to the accusation that he cast out evil spirits by Beelzebul. Why the distinction between the two kinds of blasphemy (possibly to be understood as 'abuse')? Is Jesus less sacred than the Spirit? However, by putting the saying into this context Luke does perhaps suggest a particular sense: the failure of many to recognise Jesus during his earthly ministry may be forgiven, and even the failure of the disciples at the Passion. The preaching of Acts is under the close guidance of the Spirit – it has been called the era of the Spirit – and by this preaching all are given a second chance, which many accept. It is the refusal to accept this preaching which can have no forgiveness.

Prayer

Give me courage, Lord, to persevere in the face of hostility, mockery and indifference. Give me the conviction that your message is worth persecution and death, that you never desert your messengers. Help me to remember how many sparrows I am worth.

49 Luke 12:13–34

The danger of possessions

This whole section of the journey to Jerusalem is centred on discipleship. Luke has just given us the teaching of Jesus about facing persecution without fear. Now he warns against taking false refuge in the material security of possessions, a subject to which he often returns. Luke is the most insistent of the evangelists on God's special care for the poor and on the danger of riches: these are a constant distraction from the true purpose of the disciple. The only way such danger can be removed is by using this apparent wealth to store up true wealth in heaven.

The teaching is introduced by a question from the crowd. The question about inheritance is stunningly insensitive after Jesus' previous teaching, but it forms a dramatic device often used by Luke, a question out of the blue, simply a starting point for the answer.

The rich fool

The parable of the rich fool has been described as the most terrible of all the gospel parables: retribution is swift and absolute. The story is typical of Luke's parables. First, several of Luke's parables seem to be formed out of a short allusion in the Old Testament wisdom literature, and this parable has a close parallel in the Book of Ecclesiasticus (11:18–20). Luke's story is a superb dramatisation of this little vignette:

> Others grow rich by pinching and scraping,
>   and here is the reward they receive for it:
> although they say, 'Now I can sit back
>   and enjoy the benefit of what I have got,'
> they do not know how long this will last;
>   they will have to leave their goods to others and die.

Many of Luke's parables have this sort of anti-hero instead of a hero, a disreputable character, who nevertheless sometimes does the right thing for the wrong reason. Here Luke presents his anti-hero in a lifelike and witty manner, giving him a little monologue (another feature of Luke's anti-heroes) about how he should get out of his comfortably tiresome situation of superfluity. The lip-smacking self-preoccupation is expressed in his referring to himself eight times in two verses! 'What am *I to do? I* have not enough room to store *my* crops.' Then he said, 'This is what *I will do: I* will pull down *my* barns and build bigger ones, and store all *my* grain and *my* goods in them, and *I will say to my* soul: "*My* soul, *you…*".'

This is followed by a typically Lukan four-barrelled salvo, 'Take things easy, eat, drink, have a good time,' just like the four different barrels to come in 14:21, 'The poor, the crippled, the blind and the lame,' or in 21:16, 'Parents and brothers, relations and friends.'

Trust in the Father

The word 'storehouse' links the parable to the teaching on trust which Matthew gives in the sermon on the mount: ravens have no use for storehouses. In contrast to the rich man's preoccupation with his possessions, the natural world of ravens and flowers has no such worry but has equal splendour. Luke shares this lovely appreciation of nature with Matthew, but intensifies it in two ways. He stresses the fatherly care of God: the Father will give not only natural existence and growth but the kingdom as well.

He is also more radical and extreme than Matthew about dispossession. Matthew carefully covers his back with, 'Seek *first* the kingdom,' which does not exclude attention to other things, though of course in second place. Luke is more absolute, 'Seek his kingdom and these things will be added to you,' with no suggestion of a secondary search. Indeed, Luke encourages Christians positively to get rid of possessions. Possessions for Luke are a disadvantage and a danger: 'Sell your possessions and give to those in need.' It is attractive to see the 'purses that do not wear out' as the beneficiaries of this giving, the poor who by their gratitude will function as treasure in heaven.

Prayer

Lord, keep me alert to the danger of possessions, of attachment to unimportant things which distract me from the true search. Help me to share the pain of those in need and to help them in whatever way I can.

50 Luke 12:35–48

Waiting for the return

The third major section of this collection of instructions for disciples – after a major section on perseverance under trial and another on the danger of possessions – concerns continual alertness.

Paul makes clear, particularly in his early letters, 1 Thessalonians and 1 Corinthians, that the first generation of Christians vividly expected the risen Christ to come again like a victor in a triumphal procession, to gather Christians and take them with him to present the kingdom to his Father. Paul taught that Christ had overcome death, and that, for those who by baptism had united themselves to Christ's death and resurrection, death was no more. His argument in 1 Thessalonians 4:13–18 implies that some of the Thessalonians had understood this to mean that anyone who did die had lost the chance of joining Christ in his resurrection – an interpretation which Paul is eager to correct. Paul's later letters, and especially Colossians and Ephesians, show much less interest in the return of Christ and more interest in the transformation of the Christian which has already taken place through the Spirit. Similarly the fourth gospel focuses on the enduring presence of Christ's Spirit among his disciples rather than on a future coming. The immediacy of the expectation waned as the second coming did not occur.

It is generally accepted that Luke is the latest of the synoptic gospels, written when it was becoming clear that the second coming was not to be so immediate as had originally been envisaged. So it is often said that he was at pains to deflect attention from the second coming in order to concentrate on the presence of the Spirit, now guiding the church in all its activity and decisions, as is so fully apparent in the narrative of Acts. There is little sign of this tendency in this section of the gospel; it falls into two parts.

The watchful servants

The first section is directed towards all disciples and is centred round two little images, the first illustrating endurance and the second unexpectedness. The first of the two makes an interesting combination: the servants must be ready for energetic action when the master of the house comes home from a wedding. It is perhaps slightly surprising that the master then sits the servants down and proceeds to serve them a meal, even though he comes well after midnight! Nevertheless, it is a warm testimony of his affection for them and his response to their wakefulness. In the second image the master of the household is himself on the watch, and this time for burglars, digging through the mud-brick wall of his house – or rather if he had been on the watch he would have prevented the burglar.

The trustworthy steward

The second section turns attention to those with authority in the community, as Peter's interjection suggests. It presents two opposing pictures – the steward of the household who sees his office as service and is duly rewarded with promotion, and the steward who takes the opportunity of his master's delay to domineer and terrorise the junior members of the household and to make free with his master's goods. The gentle act of service offered by the former is surely reminiscent of Jesus himself at the last supper. The behaviour of the latter resembles that of the rich fool, though rather worse; at any rate the rich fool stopped short of drunkenness!

Finally comes a careful little codicil, unique to Luke, giving a graded scale of punishment. The more you know, the worse your punishment; the greater the gift, the greater the penalty. Whom does Luke envisage? Is it a warning to the leaders of the Christian community or a threat to the leaders of the Jews? The final saying has a distinctly Semitic ring, which could stem from Jesus, literally, 'To everyone to whom much has been given, much will be asked [theological passive, avoiding use of God's name] from him [again a Semitic construction]; to whom much has been entrusted, they will ask [impersonal plural] more from him.'

Prayer

Lord, keep me alert to your coming and aware that I must render to you an account of my stewardship. Give me a true conception of service to those whom I reach. Keep me from the easy tyranny of bullying those whom I should serve.

51 Luke 12:49–59

A call for decision

Fire on the earth

At the end of this long series of teachings on the conditions and consequences of being a disciple comes the challenge for decision. The challenge is presented in a series of images, only two of which (division in households and the lawcourt scene) come also in Matthew.

When Jesus says that he has come to throw fire on the earth it could mean that he is reverting to the message of John the Baptist. His message was one of purifying fire which would burn away the impurities. Or is the saying to be related to the fire of the Holy Spirit? At Pentecost the Spirit is represented by tongues of fire, and the baptism with the Spirit is a baptism with fire. In the Bible fire is often the symbol of the presence of God, as at the burning bush or the pillar of fire in the desert. Inevitably this is a fire which purifies as well as filling with enthusiasm and ardour.

Baptism also has a natural symbolism, clarified by the saying of Jesus to the sons of Zebedee in Mark 10:38, 'Can you drink the cup that I must drink and be baptised with the baptism with which I must be baptised?' Literally baptism means 'being dipped' in water. To the Hebrew mind water was the abode of evil spirits and evil, uncontrollable passions. To be dipped in it was a kind of death and dissolution, inevitably painful; to rise from it was to rise to a new and purified life. However Jesus understood his death under this image, the saying must show that he is eager to complete his task. To the evangelist this means the advance to the life of Christ in the Christian community.

Division

It is only too clear that not all will accept the call to follow Christ. Elsewhere (Luke 14:26) Jesus says that loyalty to him must exceed even those natural family loyalties which are most dear and cherished. Here he is perhaps more extreme in promising actual strife in the household, a strife which the cumbersome English expressions make to sound even more chaotic! And this is not just during a short family visit for Christmas. In the Palestinian household no doubt all these family members lived permanently together, so that the strife between those who chose to follow Christ and those who did not was a permanent condition of existence. The price of discipleship must be faced squarely.

Warning signs

The two concluding images of weather and lawcourt are quite puzzling because they are never explained. By their position, however, it is clear that they must be challenges to decision while there is still time. The signs of change in weather are considerably more reliable in Palestine than in Britain, so that any skilled and careful countryman can read them. But why the charge of hypocrisy? It suggests that the opponents of Jesus were perfectly aware of the meaning of the signs and simply chose to ignore them.

The lawcourt challenge is not a challenge to take the law into one's own hands. Rather it must be seen as a challenge to accept what is inevitable, instead of blinding oneself by hoping against hope that it will never happen. The long-drawn-out process of being passed from one official to another merely introduces to the scene the impression of a slow-motion inevitability, not any hope that it will not happen in the end. Matthew applies a slightly shortened version of this lawcourt scene in the literal sense of the need to be reconciled with neighbours. Luke, however, may have retained the original sense of the need for decision in time of crisis. Perhaps the original challenge was to recognise the coming of Jesus as the time of decision, which is applied by the evangelist to each disciple's personal decision.

Prayer

Lord, you have warned me. To follow you is demanding. You demand that my whole life should be focused on you. You take away from me all the evasions of comfort and luxury. You demand that I serve all those around me, as you served your disciples. You warn me of strife and division. You want a decision now and every day. You offer me the fire of your Spirit and the life of your baptism, and you promise finally to claim me for your own before your Father.

52

Luke 13:1–9

Time for repentance

The specific section on the demands and tensions of discipleship is finished, and Luke now turns attention to a subject which applies more generally, the need to recognise guilt and to repent of it. First come two historical examples of sudden death without chance to repent. These may have been well-known and standard examples at the time, but which have left no other trace in history. Then comes the example of the fig tree, representing a breathing space left for repentance. Both situations show the need for a radical change of direction in the lives of most of us in order to embrace Christ wholeheartedly. The Hebrew word means simply 'to turn back', the Greek 'to change one's mind, attitude or mindset'. The follower of Christ sees all things differently and strives to act accordingly.

Pilate

The mention of Pilate here, besides giving a useful historical example, is surely an allusive preparation for his appearance later in the Passion narrative. The incident here mentioned is otherwise unknown, but the way it is described, mingling their blood with that of their sacrifices, suggests an unfeeling brutality, even sadism. This is certainly the picture of Pilate provided by Jewish historians, but then it is in the interests of Josephus and Philo to represent the Roman governors of Judea as tyrannical beasts who goaded even the placid, well-intentioned Jews to revolt. Pilate disappears from the stage of history when his superior, the governor of Syria, sends him to Rome to explain his excessive severity in putting down a messianic revolt in Samaria in AD36. Any number of reconstructions of this case is possible, and any number of studies of Pilate's psychology and history has been made. From the evidence offered by Josephus it can certainly be argued that the politically adept leaders of the Jews repeatedly made a fool of him by the skilled manipulation of their incomprehensible religious taboos. For Luke's example of sudden death Pilate's motivation and behaviour are, in any case, unimportant.

Nor is anything more known about the collapse of the tower at Siloam. The pool of Siloam still exists in the ancient city of David, the oldest part of Jerusalem. Water is carried to it from the only spring of Jerusalem, by an amazing underground tunnel in the rock, over 600m long, chiselled out 2,600 years ago. The slopes of the hill around Siloam are steep enough for the collapse of a tower not to be surprising, and the habitations are so densely packed that such a collapse could well have wreaked considerable damage.

The barren fig tree

The story of the barren fig tree again takes us forward to the Passion. In Mark the episode of the cleansing of the temple is sandwiched between Jesus' curse on a fig tree which has no fruit and the observation by the disciples that it has already withered. The fig tree is therefore the symbol of the barrenness of Israel, serving to point the moral of Jesus' action in the temple. In Luke the incident provides material for this parable. The meaning of the fig tree is reinforced by its being placed (somewhat incongruously) in a vineyard, for the vineyard also is a symbol of Israel; we have, therefore, a double symbol of Israel. The lesson of the story is, however, in this case less specifically attached to Israel than generalised to show that the Lord offers time for repentance.

Three years

This is the only mention of three years in the gospel, and it is fascinating to speculate whether it was this which gave rise to the widespread tradition that Jesus' ministry lasted three years. The only other evidence which enters into discussion is the three mentions of the Passover in the fourth gospel. In fact, this evidence is quite unclear: these need not have been separate Passovers, and there may have been others during Jesus' ministry that are not recorded. The fact is that we do not know how long his ministry lasted; it could have been more than three years or less.

Prayer

Lord, you have given me time to repent and to change my priorities to accord with yours. Help me to see how I should change my mindset, how I need to turn back to your welcoming embrace.

53 Luke 13:10-17; 14:1-6
Healings on a sabbath

These two healings form a pair. This is not unexpected in Luke, who so often pairs men and women. They are the more striking in that they are the only healing miracles to occur in this part of the gospel. The clue is given because each is introduced by the same phrase: 'There before him was a woman...'; 'There in front of him was a man...' Each occurs on a sabbath, each includes a dialogue with the Jewish authorities about whether it is legitimate to heal on a sabbath in which Jesus uses the classic rabbinic argument *a fortiori*: if it is legitimate to help a beast of burden on a sabbath it is allowable to help a human being. Each ends with the discomfiture of Jesus' opponents. Matthew has a similar story in 12:9-14, but in his equivalent to that story Luke (6:6-11) follows Mark and gives no carefully wrought legal argument.

The question which arises from these stories is what Jesus was aiming to do. The careful form of argumentation remains within the acceptable bounds of legal debate. Jesus is merely putting forward one interpretation which might or might not be accepted, but would certainly not count as rejection of the whole legal system. How radical was Jesus? Matthew 24:20 ('Pray that you will not have to make your escape... on a sabbath') suggests that the sabbath was still kept in his community, and the dispute over observance of the food laws in the early church (especially the fierce altercation at Antioch between Peter and Paul) suggests that at first they were retained. On the other hand, other actions of Jesus, such as his purging of the temple and his removal of the limited permission to divorce, do suggest that his renewal of the law was radical. Again other sayings, such as 'The Son of Man is master even of the sabbath', suggest that his mastery and renewal of the law were personal and that he was chiefly asserting his personal authority. It is difficult to make a definite decision between these points of view. Each is supported by reputable contemporary scholars.

For Luke the emphasis of the story of the woman is on Jesus' pity for her, contrasting with the niggardliness of the president of the synagogue. This must be the meaning of the double emphasis on her symptoms ('bent double and quite unable to stand upright'), the gentle description of her as a 'daughter of Abraham' and again the double mention of being set free (v. 12, 16). It is also a means of glorifying God, as both the woman and the crowd do. The story of the man is much shorter and more skeletal, so that the only real impression one gets is of the sullen stubbornness of Jesus' opponents, watching him silently and refusing to offer any answer either to Jesus' arguments or to the miracle itself.

Parables of the mustard seed and the leaven

These two short parables, again pairing male and female ('mustard seed which a man took…'; 'yeast a woman took…'), are placed by Luke in a different context to Mark and Matthew. Mark does not have the parable of the leaven; it is added to the mustard seed by Matthew, who likes to emphasise the point by giving parables in pairs. Their original meaning in Jesus' mouth fits one of two possibilities. Either they could be in answer to opponents who mock a claim that such an unimpressive group could be the overwhelming kingdom of God. Or the context could be disappointment and depression on the part of the disciples at their seeming lack of success. To each situation Jesus replies with the image of paradoxical growth: just wait and see! These two parables of promise and progress conclude the first part of the travel narrative with a hopeful and positive image. They make the point that the kingdom is even now spreading as Jesus passes on his journey. There follows immediately the second mention of Jerusalem (v. 22), the first geographical indication we have had since 9:51.

Prayer

Lord, as we travel through life on the way to our Jerusalem, many things happen to us in seemingly haphazard sequence. I cannot follow all that you are planning for me. Grant that I may stop every now and then to reflect that the mustard seed you have planted and the leaven you have hidden are both growing silently towards the completion you design for them.

54 Luke 13:22–35

Jesus sets his face to Jerusalem

By contrast to the geographical 'weightlessness' which is characteristic of the great journey to Jerusalem, here we set foot on solid ground with the mention of Jerusalem three separate times. It is a thorough reminder, at the mid-point stage, of the purpose of the journey. The whole section is full of foreboding, becoming more and more tragic as it progresses. This group of first warnings against Israel prepares for the great laments over Jerusalem and its failure to respond, which Jesus pronounces as he arrives in and finally leaves Jerusalem.

Warnings to Israel

Luke here groups several warnings which come separately in Matthew. The section comprising vv. 22–30 is bound together by the idea of the difficulty of salvation. First comes the warning about the narrow door. Then, for Luke, the idea of the narrow door leads on to that of the closed door. The scene is made more touching by the pleas of those who are shut out: 'We once ate and drank in your company; you taught in our streets' (note Luke's interest in parties, and his stress on Jesus' role as a teacher). Of course, in trying to persuade the Lord of their close relationship to him, they only succeed in making matters worse. If they have shared table fellowship with him and listened to his teaching, it makes their failure to respond even more blatant. In a later age Christians might reflect on the listening to the word of God and the table fellowship which occur in the Eucharist. The Lord's reply is all the sterner: he repeats (v. 27) the phrase in verse 25, 'I do not know you.'

Finally comes a warning Luke has reserved from the story of the centurion's boy (Luke 7), where he omitted a couple of verses given in Matthew 8:11–12. But there is an important difference. One theme of Matthew's gospel is that the kingdom will be taken away from the Jews and given to a new people of God, so there Jesus says, 'The children of the kingdom will be thrown out into the darkness outside'. Luke does not want to condemn the Jews to such wholesale failure. He always makes a sharp distinction between the leaders and the people as a whole; the former fail to respond, but the latter are sympathetic to Jesus. So it is only 'all evildoers' who are excluded. The main point is the more expansive one of admitting those who come from east and west, from north and south. The time has come for the admission of the Gentiles, and it is more important to include than to exclude.

Herod the jackal

'That jackal', says Jesus. According to the Jewish historian Josephus, Herod the Tetrarch, ruler of Galilee, worked as an informer for the Romans, keeping the authorities abreast of what was going on. This would not have increased his popularity among his own people. However, the main point of this little passage is twofold: we are informed once more that Jesus knows clearly the fate that lies in store for him, and it is as a prophet that he goes up to Jerusalem to perish there. On every level Jesus' move to Jerusalem was no chance journey. He had to fulfil his prophetic mission to Judaism at its centre, at the temple. Otherwise it would be incomplete. It was only at Jerusalem that he could make the definitive prophetic gesture to lay bare the barrenness of the temple and its cult.

Lament for Jerusalem

Jesus' love for and care of Jerusalem elicit two laments, one now at the halfway point of the journey and one immediately after the entry to Jerusalem (to which he now alludes, for it is then that they will say, 'Blessed is he who is coming in the name of the Lord!'). But such yearning for Jerusalem lies deep in every Jewish heart.

It is valuable to point out that the feminine and motherly affection of the hen is not out of place in the mouth of the man Jesus. God's own love can be expressed in the same terms: 'As a mother comforts a child, so shall I comfort you' (Isaiah 66:13).

Prayer

'How often have I longed to gather your children together, as a hen gathers her brood under her wings!'
LUKE 13:34

55 Luke 14:7–14

Guests for dinner

Now, after another story of healing on a sabbath (discussed a little earlier, under section 52), Luke gives three parables about invitations to dinner. This framework would be, perhaps, too formal for Mark's rustic world, but in Luke's more cultured Hellenistic world a dinner is often used as an occasion for teaching. Luke has used it importantly already in the house of Simon the Pharisee (7:36–50), and will so use it again at the last supper, where he places important teaching of Jesus about the leadership of the future community and the perseverance which will be needed. The present parables are about invitations, rather than about the scene of a supper itself. The heavily critical tone, however, fits the present scene: the host is 'one of the leading Pharisees' (v. 1), and Jesus is speaking to 'lawyers and Pharisees' (v. 3).

Places at table

The first parable is on humility, or knowing one's place, a condition of discipleship. This is an important quality; the parable of the Pharisee and the tax collector will suggest that it is important especially as a precondition of repentance.

This is another occasion of the genius so often demonstrated in Luke's parables of picking up a hint and turning it into a brilliant little story. Matthew (23:6) contents himself with the bare comment that the scribes and Pharisees want to take the places of honour at banquets. As the parable of the rich fool is related to a saying in the wisdom literature, this parable too may well be linked to Proverbs 25:6–7: 'Do not take a place among the great; better to be invited, "Come up here", than be humiliated in the presence of the prince.' As so often in the Old Testament wisdom literature itself, there is a certain worldly wisdom about the story. Luke's characters are certainly not above doing the right thing for the wrong reason! Christians will benefit from the lesson in knowing one's place, but it is a lesson which applies beyond the circle of Christian discipleship. There is even a neat and slightly crafty lesson on how to get on in the world, as often in the wisdom literature. It is only the final stark sentence – with its two 'theological passives' to avoid using the name of God – that hammers home the specifically Christian message about which conduct will finally win its reward, and shows that the story really is a parable rather than a straight piece of advice about how most safely to get the best places: 'Everyone who raises himself up will be humbled, and the one who humbles himself will be raised up.'

It is also characteristic of Luke to make much of this motif of shame and honour. So the crafty steward is prevented by shame from relying on begging; the friend at midnight gets what he wants by shouting out shamelessly and so shaming his friend. The incautious tower-builder is made fun of (14:29). Here the parable builds on the model in Proverbs, painting both humiliation and honour with characteristic liveliness.

The neglected are privileged

Besides the lesson to the guests there is also a lesson for the host, and this time not one about spiritual dispositions but a practical message of inviting those who cannot repay. As so often the gospel message is socially firmly subversive, the more so because the lame, the blind and the crippled are excluded from the community meal in the regulations of the scrolls of Qumran. The poor, the crippled, the lame and the blind form another Lukan set of four, who will occur also in the next parable (v. 21).

The cosy closed circle of reciprocal invitations is deeply engrained also in our modern social conventions, but Jesus' instructions here are not merely not to perpetuate it but deliberately to shatter it: do not make a habit of inviting your friends, etc, *in case they* return the invitation. The circle must be kept open by a deliberate act of avoidance of the return invitation. There is a nice touch of wit in the final sentence: the return invitation comes only to the heavenly banquet!

Prayer

Lord, keep me clear of any covert self-seeking in what I pretend to be generosity. Let me truly give without hope of reward. Give me real affection and tenderness for those who lack the good things of the world, remembering that they are your privileged friends.

56 Luke 14:15–35

The great supper

The third parable about a dinner is that of the great supper. One interest of this story is that the basic form is shared with Matthew, though the details and the use are very different. It is from a comparison of the details that Luke's purpose may be discerned, for both Matthew and Luke show their emphasis by making some details (different in each case) allegorical.

We start with Matthew. For Matthew the story is of a marriage feast for the son of the king. This is an obvious allegory, for the prophets had long looked forward to the wedding feast at the end of time when the marriage between God and Israel would finally be celebrated with carefree merriment and plenty of all kinds. Now the wedding feast has become that of God's son, a clear allegory for Jesus. The invited wedding guests are the Jews, who at the last moment refuse the invitation which had long been destined to them. They insult and kill the messengers – quite unnecessarily, except that the messengers stand for the prophets of Israel, who were traditionally maltreated. The king's over-reaction in sending armies to burn their city (odd that they all lived in the same city!) makes better sense in the application to Jerusalem than it would in a more realistic story. The overall meaning suits exactly Matthew's message, that the kingdom is to be taken away from Israel and given to another nation.

Luke's story is slightly but significantly different. There is only one messenger, who, not being a prophet, does not need to be maltreated and killed. The invited guests do not simply slope off wordlessly to their field and their shop. Instead, they have a little dialogue, full of urbane oriental courtesy. The explicitness of their excuses enables us to see more clearly that it is the distractions of possession which block their acceptance of the invitation. Luke also adds a third blockage, marriage, which is several times represented as danger in Luke.

The really significant change, however, is in the replacements. In Matthew anyone will do to fill up the place. Luke is more specific; for him there are two groups. First come Luke's favoured quartet, the poor, the crippled, the lame and the blind. So the first guests at the banquet of the kingdom are to be the underprivileged on earth: 'Blessed are you who are hungry now: you shall have your fill.' Equally significant is the second group, for which the slave has to go outside the city into the open roads and hedgerows. The city must, of course, represent the chosen people, and the sending of the messenger outside the city represents an extension of the pressing invitation to include the Gentiles. Unlike Matthew, who sees the Jews as having been totally replaced by a new nation, Luke insists that some of the Jews respond to the call and that it is extended from them to the Gentiles.

Counting the cost

After the parable Luke makes clear just how demanding is the call. This is perhaps the toughest formulation in all the gospels. Matthew's version is gentler in two respects: he has 'whoever *loves* father or mother, son or daughter more than me…' (RSV), whereas Luke goes further: 'anyone who comes to me *without hating*…'; and Matthew does not include 'wife'among the relations, whereas Luke does. We cannot accept that Christian discipleship actually demands hate within the family. To 'hate' a wife is the most paradoxical of all demands.

A step towards understanding this awesome demand may be that Semitic thought-forms and language are weak in the comparatives, 'more' and 'less' and tend to express preferences in absolute terms. The lesson must be that even the warmest and closest of all human ties of affection must give way before loyalty to Christ. Rather than a way of weakening human family ties, it takes the most vibrant of bonds to show that the bond to Christ must be even stronger.

The warning is reinforced by the two parables of calculation before setting out on a task. They are paralleled in no other gospel text and could well be parables of popular wisdom. At the end of them Luke again repeats his demand of total abandonment of possessions (v. 33). It is only in Luke's gospel that we are carefully told at the call of each disciple that they give up 'everything'.

Prayer

Lord, you don't help me to count the cost, for how can I know what the cost will be? You just demand simply that I put you before everything, that nothing at all may count besides you. No bargaining. No calculating. Give me the strength and courage to render you this fiercest of loyalties.

57

Luke 15:1–10

Lost sheep and lost coin

Now Luke has three parables of repentance, the first two of which form a pair. Again the comparison with Matthew is illuminating. To begin with, Matthew has only one to Luke's two. Luke's are similar to each other, even in language. It may be that the doubling up has two purposes – first to emphasise by repetition; and second to pair man and woman (a man loses the sheep, a woman the coin).

The lost sheep

Matthew's parable of the lost sheep comes in his chapter 18 on the community and the duties of its members to one another. So the emphasis is on the duty of every member of the community to go to look for a lost sheep. In Luke the emphasis is on the shepherd's enduring search: he goes on looking till he has found the missing sheep. The shepherd, of course, is God, who is repeatedly represented in the Old Testament as the shepherd of his people. The very search itself is an expression of desperation: it can hardly be considered good husbandry to leave 99 sheep free to wander off over the hills and fall down the precipices so frequent in Palestine. In desperation logic comes second! (In John's parable of the good shepherd there is a similar fault of logic: a good shepherd has no business getting himself killed, even if he is sacrificing himself for the sheep.) The affection of the shepherd is already seen in the contrast with Matthew: in Matthew the sheep wanders off, whereas in Luke the shepherd loses his sheep. Once the sheep has been found, the overwhelming reaction is delight, as the shepherd shows his affection for the sheep and calls his friends and neighbours together – with a typical little bit of Lukan direct speech.

The lost coin

The story of the lost coin runs on the same lines. A small Palestinian sugar-lump house would be ill-lit, perhaps with no entrance for light except the doorway. Lighting a lamp was not enough! The best way to find anything on the uneven, mud-lined floor would be to sweep it. Again the woman's joy is out of all reasonable proportion. A drachma was the Greek equivalent of a Roman denarius, so a day's wage of a casual agricultural labourer. The party for all these friends and neighbours would be bound to cost more than the drachma she had found. But the point of the two stories is precisely to show that the joy in heaven (again, a way of avoiding using the name of God) cannot be calculated according to any scale of reason.

Repentance

The two parables illustrate well the precise point which must have annoyed the Pharisees and scribes who murmur at Jesus welcoming sinners and eating with them: nothing seems to be said about repentance as a precondition. They seem to be still sinners when he eats with them. Just so, in the stories, there is no possibility of interrogating the sheep or the coin about repentance before it is brought back to the party in triumph. Is it pressing the imagery too far to maintain that the sheep and the coin remain merely passive and unchanged? It cannot be that the sinners continue forever as sinners, and repentance and conversion have a crucial part to play. This is another vital difference between the stories in Matthew and in Luke: in Matthew the emphasis is so strictly on the duty of brothers to look after one another that there is no mention of change of heart, and the conclusion is, 'It is never the will of your Father in heaven that one of these little ones should be lost.' In Luke the repentance is stressed in each story. But it is important that Jesus is prepared to eat with them while they are still sinners. He does not wait for their conversion before going to join them; the conversion comes only when he is with them. He does not avoid the company of sinners, and his presence must transform them. This is an illustration not of his tolerance of sin, but of his love for sinners. The joy of the two finders contrasts forcefully with the niggardly grumpiness of the Pharisees and scribes.

Prayer

Lord Jesus, help me to respond to your openness and welcome. You do not demand immediate perfection, but by your affection draw me gently back to your fold. Enable me, too, to show the same encouragement to others.

58 Luke 15:11–32

The prodigal son

This third parable of repentance and forgiveness has had difficulty finding a title. Should it be 'the prodigal son', 'the forgiving father' or even 'the powerless father' (because he is so helplessly affectionate)? Luke's story is told with all the delicacy and character of his artistry. The story is told with a fine balance, the geographical movements away and back neatly parallel to each other, and symbolising the breaking and mending of the relationship. The son is lost – the son is found. The son loses everything – the son receives everything. In the centre of all is the son's repentance.

The younger son

The audacity of the younger son is breathtaking. He treats his father as virtually dead already. Not only the insult, but the financial loss: presumably the father has to sell up half his property to provide the wastrel with his cash. The lowest point to which he sinks is of course tending unclean animals and even envying them. Luke is a realist and knows the usefulness of some such jolt towards repentance. This is a classic case of the Lukan anti-hero doing the right thing for the wrong reason. It is then that he is forced to take stock, and breaks out into that feature of so many of Luke's parables, a little puzzled speech to himself about what he should do (just like the rich fool, the crafty steward or the unjust judge).

The elder son

The portrait of the elder son is also masterly. His resentment after all his years of loyal labour is utterly justified on any ordinary human level. No doubt he had had to work all the harder both for lack of his brother's labour and to make up for the sale of half the property. And, after all, the calf *we* had been fattening (yes, I've been working at that too) was part of his own share of the property. So he refuses even to acknowledge his brother; he calls him 'this son of yours'. Quite without justification he introduces 'loose women' into the equation, though there has been no indication that they were among the wastrel's excesses. This detail is due entirely to the elder brother's own malice and jealousy. But then his anger is so well justified that the slight exaggeration of a carelessly chosen word is not surprising.

The father

Well, perhaps he was a bit too indulgent at the beginning. He accepts the insult and the impoverishment – but then most parents and superiors have to learn when to bite their tongues. It is not always helpful to tell home truths to the young. (Paul agreed: 'Everything is permissible, but not everything builds people up' – 1 Corinthians 10:23.) When the first dust of the son's arrival appears on the horizon, the father *runs* to meet him, affection overcoming the demands of dignity in an oriental gentleman who is no longer young. He embraces the son and will not even listen to the nice little prepared speech, which is interrupted in the middle, no doubt smothered in the embrace. He reassures the wastrel that all is forgiven and that trust is restored by even giving him the authority of a ring, so that he can sign away the rest of the property if he likes.

Nor is the resentful elder brother neglected: the celebration has begun when the father even leaves his place at the head of the table, deserting his guests and new-found son, to go out and try to coax away his resentment. He has the generosity to acknowledge (and it takes courage to give ground to an angry man) that 'all I have is yours'. To the hurtful gibe 'this son of yours' he replies gently with 'your brother'. A less generous story would have finished with a sharp contrast in the father's attitude to the two brothers and would have left the self-righteous elder brother to swelter in his own resentment. But this father's affection is so limitless that even such behaviour must be drawn back into love.

Prayer

Father, I have the faults of both the brothers. Coax me always back into your love.

59 Luke 16:1–8

The crafty steward

The previous parables have been addressed to a combination of tax collectors and sinners, with Pharisees and scribes looking over their shoulder (15:1). Now Jesus turns to the other audience which he has in the travel narrative, namely the disciples.

The parable of the crafty steward has often been a shocking puzzle. Surely the master stands for God; how then can he praise the steward's astuteness? Here it is important to distinguish between parable and allegory. In an allegory each story detail has significance for the meaning. In a parable this is not the case, but there is only one point of direct comparison. Anyway, *is* the steward really dishonest in this case?

One explanation of the parable is that the steward simply remits to the debtors his own 'cut', thereby earning their gratitude and friendship, which would be worth more to him than the short-term financial gain. It is a neat little move, and the master has the decency to approve; after all, he has himself lost nothing on the deal.

An alternative explanation is more complicated and specialised, relying on a knowledge of regional conditions. According to this, a clue to the wit of the parable is given by the different reductions of debt arranged by the steward. The debt of oil is halved, whereas the wheat is reduced only by one-fifth. The significance of this is that in some regions these are the standard interest-rates charged. Oil is obviously easily adulterated with cheaper and undetectable liquids, so that a lender presumes that it will be adulterated and charges accordingly. Wheat is less easy to adulterate unobserved, so has a lower rate of return. In this case the steward is merely remitting the interest to the debtors. But as lending at interest is against the law of Moses, he is cleverly forcing his master to observe the law, and the master can hardly complain. He should have acted more quickly and dismissed the steward in one swoop, rather than giving him time to make his arrangements.

In either case the steward behaves as a typical Lukan anti-hero, doing the right thing for the wrong reasons, and incidentally indulging in the little musing speech to himself as he wonders what he should do. The purpose of the parable is then to illustrate that the keenness with which we pursue our material objectives is often far more zealous than that devoted to 'spiritual' ones.

Sayings on money and possessions

Appended to the parable are various sayings about money and possessions, not having any close connection with the parable itself, but rather tacked on at the end, linked only by the general subject matter. Luke has earlier given us one illustration of how money can be used to win friends, by the generosity of inviting those who cannot repay or reciprocate invitations (14:14). The conduct of the rich man towards Lazarus will soon give a counter-illustration of failure to use money to win friends in the right way.

The three sayings on trustworthiness seem to be rather wisdom sayings about business life than part of the proclamation of the kingdom of God. The link to the parable is through the untrustworthiness of the steward. Further illustration of the reward of trustworthiness will be given later in the parable of the pounds. However, each of these sayings has the characteristic Lukan mistrust of money, 'that tainted thing', which runs throughout the gospel. It is the 'little thing' contrasted with 'great', and also presumably considered alien in the contrast of 'what is not yours' with the power which transforms the self, 'what is your very own'.

Finally the saying on 'mammon' has given rise to speculation that Mammon was the name of a deity, a god of money. There is nothing to support this, apart from the mention of two masters, which could suggest that Money and God can be put in rivalry to each other. But the whole meaning and derivation of the word are obscure. The word does not occur in the Old Testament, but appears sometimes in the Qumran literature in the normal sense of 'money' or 'wealth'.

Prayer

Lord, the variety of the sayings and warnings about money in the gospel passage provides a mirror for the variety of ways in which money can prove a distraction or an insidious trap. Grant me to see the dangers of being seduced by the attractions of money and to keep myself free to serve you.

60 Luke 16:14–31

The rich man and Lazarus

Various sayings

It is not easy to see a pattern in the sayings of 16:14–18. The charge against the Pharisees of avarice links well to the previous section. It has been suggested that the link to the other sayings is provided by the words 'loathsome [an abomination] in the sight of God' (v. 15); this could be a response to the jeering of the Pharisees at Jesus. The expression is used in the Old Testament for financial exploitation and for divorce, so it may provide a link between the two sayings in verses 15 and 18.

This would leave the two central of the four sayings (vv. 16–17). The first of these announces that the kingdom is no longer confined to those envisaged in the law and the prophets, for since John the Baptist '*everyone* is forcing their way into it'. After this the saying on the continuance of the law provides a counterbalance to retain the sanctity of the law. The continuing relevance of it will be illustrated in the following story, in which Abraham refers to it explicitly.

The rich man and Lazarus

The parable is told with a sparkling use of language typical of Luke's stylish writing. The rich man's invariable clothing ('He used to dress in…') is especially rich festal garb and his daily meal a glittering banquet, described in the words used for a rare and special feast. By contrast the poor man has been 'thrown down' at the gate; the word used suggests that he has been dumped and cannot move. As dogs are unclean, the dogs licking his sores are intended to increase the disgust rather than (as a nation of dog-lovers immediately assumes) to substitute for the human sympathy denied by the rich man.

The story is the perfect illustration of the reversal proclaimed in Luke's beatitudes and woes: 'Alas for you who are rich: you are having your consolation now.' This is made explicit in verse 25, when Lazarus has the consolation promised in the beatitudes. The exact meaning of the story is made clearer by comparison to a similar ancient rabbinic story. In the rabbinic story, the rich man is a tax collector, so inherently bad, and the poor man a student of the law, so inherently good. Luke does not need these moral characteristics after his repeated lessons on the danger of wealth and the need to use it rightly; wealth and lack of it are enough to give the story its point. When both men get to the far side – note: the poor man's name means 'God is my help' – the rich man is splendidly unrepentant. He still claims to be part of the chosen people by calling out blithely, 'Father Abraham', forgetting that John the Baptist has told us that it is not enough to claim Abraham as father (3:8). He still treats Lazarus as a servant who can be summarily sent as a messenger to render small services, and he actually has the effrontery to use the word for 'pity' which forms part of the word for the 'almsgiving' (*eleeo* and *eleemosyne*) which he had so signally failed to do.

When Abraham says the rich man's brothers can listen to the warnings of Moses and the prophets, he is referring to their constant teachings. One of the principal emphases of the moral teaching of the law was the preservation of human dignity: every human being must be dependent on God alone, without the humiliation, financial or legal, of being subject to another human. The prophets also, from Amos and Hosea onwards, ceaselessly speak out against the exploitation of the poor by the rich. One entirely sympathises with the sentiment that one more repetition of the warning would be useless. The irony of the rich man's final request is delicate: the Christian reader will immediately think of the resurrection proclamation of the apostles in Acts (and the failure of the rich man's brothers to respond), whereas it is still possible that the rich man himself is thinking in pre-resurrection terms of a messenger from the dead, such as Samuel, who brought a warning message to Saul in 1 Samuel 28.

Prayer

Lord, I am not destitute. I run the risk of your condemnation for failure to use properly the resources you have given me. Grant me discernment in my use of them. Above all let me listen to your warnings and keep in mind the responsibility I bear.

61 Luke 17:1–10

A challenge to disciples

Throughout the narrative of the great journey there has been an alternation between instructions to the crowds or Jesus' opponents and instructions to the disciples. Now, as we approach the end of the journey, comes a series of instructions to the disciples which concern closely personal beliefs and attitudes. It is almost a sort of spiritual programme, and has affinities with the discourse on behaviour in the community in Matthew 18.

Scandals

First a reflection on scandals in the community. The way the expression 'scandal' has developed is itself a commentary on human nature. In current usage it means something disgraceful and much talked about, a subject of gossip: 'That couple's behaviour is a public scandal.' The commentary on human nature is that regrettably most of us enjoy talking about the major failures of others (not our friends) and broadcasting them to anyone who has been unfortunate enough to miss them. The original meaning of 'scandal' is, however, importantly different. It is an obstacle, such as a stone in the way, a catch or a tripwire, which causes someone to fall over. In this sense my example may be a scandal to a single person without becoming at all public knowledge. Even a quiet suggestion will do, or anything which leads another to fail or defect from Christian behaviour. 'Little ones' is a standard gospel expression for the helpless and vulnerable, which explains why the dire and irretrievable punishment of the millstone is appropriate.

Forgiveness

In Matthew 18, the chapter on relationships within the community, it is taken for granted that there will be offences and hurts. Such is the stuff of human beings living and working together. What is specific about the Christian community is not that these do not occur, but that efforts are to be made to mend them, heal them and put them right. It is far easier to write off an offensive or hurtful colleague – often with a certain pleasurable conviction that he or she will get a millstone round the neck in the end – than to set about mending the breach. Correction will require thought, tact and timing, and certainly forgiveness in the heart. Correction and criticism administered in anger may often benefit through the home truths blurted out, but will hardly heal the wounds of community. Matthew has a whole succession of legal processes about correction within the community. Luke is more informal, merely linking it closely to forgiveness.

Similarly with forgiveness itself: Matthew, thinking more of formal structure in the community, gives the question about forgiveness to Peter, and so links forgiveness to authority in the community. Luke again leaves it more informal. In Matthew Jesus demands forgiveness seventy times seven, in Luke only seven times, but seven times daily. There can be no limit to forgiveness. It is anybody's calculation which of the two is the more demanding, but in any case the number seven denotes perfection.

Faith

There is a double confusion over the form of this saying. Matthew 17:20 has 'If your faith *is*… you *will* say', a provision for the future. Luke gives the muddled 'If you had faith… you could say', which leaves it unclear whether the disciples are presumed to have faith or not. The second confusion is over the mulberry tree: the original saying in Mark 11 concerns the transfer of a mountain into the sea, but occurs after the withering of the fig tree. Luke by confused reminiscence has a mulberry tree transferred into the sea, where it would hardly flourish! The confusion shows the importance of the saying and its frequent use. It must have been handed down and repeated widely in the oral tradition before it came into fixed and written form.

The content of the faith is not detailed. If the saying comes from the pre-Easter Jesus, as it does in the Markan and Matthean stories, it cannot concern resurrection faith. It must mean more generally concentration upon, trust in and reliance on Jesus as bringing God to us. This indeed is the foundation of all Christian living.

Prayer

'Lord, I believe. Help my unbelief!'
MARK 9:24 (RSV)

62 Luke 17:7–19

Two stories about gratitude

The servant's wages

This forceful parable of the useless servants can seem surprising after the praise of service which has been such a feature of Jesus' message. The Son of Man came not to be served but to serve, and the dignity of the Christian consists in echoing that service. How does the parable square with 'Blessed are those servants whom the master finds awake when he comes. In truth I tell you, he will do up his belt, sit them down at table and wait on them' (12:37)? There is no real contradiction. The point being made is that it is impossible to earn favours or gratitude from God. Everything God gives is pure gift, an unearned blessing, from the favour bestowed on Mary onwards. The servants of God have no rights and can have no complaints. Matthew teaches the same hard lesson with his parable of the payment of the vineyard workers, which seems so unfair. No human being can enter into reckoning with God. So, if any reader feels inclined to say, 'Behave like this and you won't get far in today's labour market,' that reflection is itself quite important. You can't sue God or quote contracts of employment at him. God is not in today's labour market. There can only be gratitude on our part, and gratitude all flows in the other direction.

The ten lepers

The story of ten lepers is unique to Luke, without parallel in Mark or Matthew. In style and language it is typical of Luke. It has two features which are favourites with Luke – Samaritans and gratitude to God. As in the story of the good Samaritan, Samaritans in Luke represent non-Jews who are open to the message of Jesus and respond to his call. All the ten lepers show faith in Jesus. They call him 'Master!' They have so much faith that they start to go off to show themselves to the priests to record their cure before it has even occurred. They were already on the way when they found themselves cured. But there the praiseworthy behaviour of the other nine ceases; in their joy and relief they simply go off and neglect him whom they have so recently called 'Master'. Presumably the other nine cured lepers were Jews, so that there is a deliberate contrast in their behaviour: this Samaritan, the only beneficiary to show a response to Jesus' action, is the forerunner of the Gentiles who will enter the Christian community in Acts.

It is a strange thing that human gratitude as such is expressed in the gospels hardly at all. The normal word for 'thanks' appears only in the story previous to this, of the master who does not thank his slave. The more formal word for 'thanks', used for the Eucharist, occurs outside a eucharistic context only in Luke. But there is plenty of its equivalent in Luke, for it is Luke especially who shows us people praising or glorifying God in gratitude after a miracle; this imparts an air of cheerfulness and celebration to the whole gospel. This praise starts as soon as Jesus is born, the angels, then the shepherds praising God (2:13, 20). The joyful canticles of Zechariah, Mary and Simeon are perfect expressions of their gratitude and recognition of God's gifts. Praise and delight are often the natural expression of thanks, as one sees in a child, delighted with a present, who shows it off with enthusiasm to anyone on the scene, praising the giver of the present. Just so, in another story, the healed paralytic goes off home praising God, with a joy that spreads to the onlookers (5:25–26). The healed Gerasene demoniac 'proclaimed throughout the city all that Jesus had done for him' (8:39). This becomes so regular after the miracles that the curmudgeonly 'other nine' in this story are rather the exception than the rule, though the racket made by the Samaritan does seem to be exceptional!

Prayer

Lord, I need to know my position. You owe me no thanks and I owe you infinite thanks. Let me enumerate just some of the things for which I need to thank you (life, health, intelligence, movement, love, your friendship, eternal life) and give you joyful praise for your generosity.

63 Luke 17:20–37

The day of the Son of Man

The earliest Christian hopes

Possibly the most pressing question of all left by Jesus' proclamation of the kingdom/kingship of God was 'When?' Had it come already? Would it come soon? What part in it did the death and resurrection of Jesus play? Mark, followed by Matthew, had concluded the account of Jesus' ministry with an extended discourse by Jesus on the future of his followers. Mark 13 ends with a promise that the Son of Man will come on the clouds of heaven to gather his chosen ones. Matthew 24—25 includes the same and ends with the great scene of the last judgement.

Both these gospel writers show just how vivid was the expectation of the coming of Jesus in triumph to take his followers with him in his victory procession, an expectation shared by Paul in his early letters to the Thessalonians and the Corinthians. Luke must have written some years after this. The expected coming simply had not happened, so his perspective and his message are entirely different.

All around you

The Pharisees open the discussion with one of those useful Lukan foil-questions, simply a hook on which to hang the answer: 'The coming of the kingdom of God does not admit of observation… the kingdom of God is among you.' These two elements will be developed, so it is important to understand them. The word translated 'observation' is used only here in the New Testament, but it must have recalled Exodus 12:42, where it was used to describe the vigil of the Passover night. But it is no use keeping vigil, watching for the kingdom to come. On the contrary, the kingdom is all around you. Luke does not mean that the kingdom is hidden in individual hearts. He means, as his stress on the ideal community of the church in Acts shows, that the kingdom is all around you in the community. Our task is not to keep vigil and watch for the coming of the kingdom, but it is to further God's kingdom in our daily lives.

The remainder of Jesus' explanation expands on this point. It is a discouragement of risking distraction and wasted energy by looking for visible manifestations of the kingdom: however much you long to see, you will not do so. Quite possibly Luke is stressing the point because Christians saw various historical events, such as the destruction of Jerusalem in AD70, as moments of the coming of the kingdom, when what is all important is the life of the Christian community.

He is determined also to prevent Christians from becoming engrossed in the preoccupations of the world. So he repeatedly stresses that, when the moment does come, it will be sudden and dire for those who are engrossed in the pleasures of eating and drinking, the preoccupations of marrying, and business interests such as marketing, agriculture and construction. He uses the stock Old Testament examples of destructive judgement, namely the eras of Noah and Lot. Destruction then was sudden and unpredictable: there was no warning of the flood, nor of the engulfing of Sodom and Gomorrah. There will be no possibility of salvaging anything, as the dire consequences of even the backward glance of Lot's wife showed.

The end of the world?

To many Christians today any idea of the end of the world is as meaningless as a literal understanding of stars falling from heaven and the Son of Man coming on the clouds. It is a piece of imagery culled from the Hebrew pre-scientific world view, which must now be discarded. But the gospel message expressed in these terms cannot be disregarded. At the very least it is a proclamation, enshrined in ancient imagery, that there is a forward thrust to history, and at the end of history (personal or cosmic?) an account must be given. The perils of absorption in the pleasures and affairs of human life, to the detriment of concern for the kingdom, remain as real as ever.

Prayer

Lord God, whatever your plans for the world and its completion, help me to keep working for the fulfilment of your kingship. Do not let me become engulfed in the attractions of life, but keep always your values and your vision clear in my sight.

64 Luke 18:1–14

Two parables on prayer

The unjust judge

This is a typical Lukan parable, teaching perseverance in prayer. There is the little monologue by the chief character, reflecting on how to get out of his difficult situation, just like the rich fool or the crafty steward. Only in Luke is the chief character of parables a rogue, unjust but with a certain pragmatic realism which makes him not unattractive. And only Luke has these parables which do not so much illustrate the situation as encourage to a particular kind of action.

Just as it is possible and attractive to see the parable of the rich fool as taking up a hint in the Book of Ecclesiasticus, so we are drawn to see this parable as a mirror image of the earlier sketch of a fair-minded judge in the same book:

> He does not ignore the orphan's supplication,
>   nor the widow's as she pours out her complaint.
> Do the widow's tears not run down her cheeks,
>   as she accuses the man who is the cause of them?
>
> ECCLESIASTICUS 35:14–15

In both passages there are the widow and the judge, and in both the widow wins through by her perseverance in her plea. But in Luke the judge is represented almost as the personification of injustice, for throughout the biblical tradition 'orphans and widows' are the personification of helpless vulnerability, to protect whom must be the first object of any system of justice. In addition Luke has remoulded the judge to be one of his own lively characters. This is the more audacious because he makes the person whom one is tempted to allegorise as God into a mixed character who does the right thing for the wrong reason. Another delightfully brazen touch of realism in the judge's ruthless assessment of his self-interest is the risk from the widow: this is often translated as if she will come and 'outface' him or 'pester him'; in fact the normal meaning of the word is 'hit in the face'. She will come and give him a clip on the ear or a black eye!

The day of the Lord

The tailpiece of this parable about perseverance in prayer attaches it to the important previous scenario of the day of the Son of Man which will finally come so suddenly. It is almost as though Luke, having noted that nothing was said about prayer in that section, decided to tack this on. During the time of the church, and the persecutions which go with it, persevering prayer will be vital.

The Pharisee and the tax collector

Not only perseverance but the right attitude in prayer will be vital. Tax collectors like Zacchaeus are by nature outcasts, so the object of Luke's special attention: no matter how roguish they are, all sinners need to do in order to win acceptance is repent, like the prodigal son, to acknowledge their fault and turn to the Lord. This is precisely the point of difference between the two characters, as in the prodigal son. As in that story, but more simply, the characters are painted with deft touches, the simple, contrite tax collector and the oily, complacent Pharisee. Luke even dares to say that he prays 'to himself' rather than to God; no doubt one could understand this as meaning *sotto voce*, but the double meaning is there! He may have raised his eyes piously to heaven, but Luke does venture to give the tactful hint that he can also spare a sidelong glance at 'this tax collector here'. The delicious irony of the Pharisee's prayer is that we all know it to be humbug. Throughout the gospel the Pharisees have been presented precisely as avaricious, unjust, an 'adulterous generation' and hypocritical about their fasting and tithing.

That Luke is not necessarily wide of the mark is shown by Rabbi Nechonias' unfortunate prayer (about AD70): 'I thank you, Lord my God, that you have set my lot among those who frequent the synagogue rather than those who sit on street corners. I run my course for the life of the world to come, while they are heading for the abyss.' There seems nothing left to ask for.

All this contrasts with the straightforward, genuine directness of the tax collector's prayer, the perfect example of simplicity and repentance.

Prayer

God, be merciful to me, a sinner.

65 Luke 18:15–30

Two approaches to Jesus

At this point in the travel narrative Luke rejoins the narrative of Mark and Matthew with two fiercely contrasting stories.

The little children

Each of the evangelists has his own lesson to tell in this story. Mark's story is a picture of Jesus' humanity, gentleness and open welcome. He is angry with the disciples for trying to send the children away, and, to make the point of his warmth even clearer, embraces the children and lays his hands upon them. For Matthew it is a lesson in conversion. He inserts 'whoever does not *change and become* like little children', so it is a matter of the spiritual dispositions of children. Rather than any such imagined quality as the innocence or guilelessness of children, he must mean the openness and simplicity of children before the Father in heaven.

Luke has yet another lesson. There is no interest in the spiritual qualities of the candidate for the kingdom, for he says they 'even brought babies to him', using a word which indicates a newborn babe. His interest, therefore, is in the helplessness of the candidate; the candidate can contribute nothing at all. No one can earn entry into the kingdom. This passage, then, joins those which surround it: in the previous passage the tax collector in prayer can only plead his lack of qualities and his guilt. In the following passage we are told that no human being can earn entry into the kingdom.

The rich ruler

For this passage Luke uses Mark's story, but by the smallest changes makes its message uncompromisingly severe. In Mark it is a warm, vibrant scene. The man shows his eagerness and good intentions by coming running up to Jesus and doing him reverence. Jesus responds with affection – he 'looks at him and loves him' (NIV). And, although the man chokes (the normal meaning of the Greek word) over the requirement to sell what he has, he goes away sad. Matthew makes the scene more touching still by calling him a 'young man' and by removing the slight wariness of Jesus at being called 'good'.

But Luke hardens the scene. There is no sign of youth and little of eagerness. No running up, no reverence, merely a question, possibly hostile or at any rate distant. The man has become 'one of the rulers', a magistrate or perhaps a president of the synagogue. Perhaps this is to accommodate him to Luke's own more distinguished audience – the gospel is addressed to 'your Excellency' Theophilus – or perhaps to link him to those who had been habitually opposing Jesus. It puts him from the beginning on the side of the Pharisee rather than the tax collector. Correspondingly, there is no sign of affection from Jesus. His demands are more absolute or even unyielding. He insists that the ruler sell '*everything* you own' (imitating the disciples, all of whom in Luke leave *everything* when they come to follow Jesus) and not merely give, but *distribute* it, scatter it abroad, among the poor. Then, although the ruler does have the decency to be 'overcome with sadness', Luke does not let him go away, but keeps him there to hear Jesus' virtual condemnation of his position. Now we see why he has encountered such hard treatment: he not merely has many possessions, as in Mark; he is exceedingly wealthy – one might almost say 'stinking rich'.

The eye of the needle

The final change in Luke is perhaps the most important. Not only does he keep the wealthy ruler on stage; instead of addressing the disciples alone, all reference to the immediate audience is removed, and Jesus addresses the whole message to the ruler and to everyone else without distinction. It is an uncompromising message. There is no escape in the old legend that by 'the eye of the needle' Jesus means a small gate in Jerusalem; no such gate is known to have existed. It is the same sort of uncompromising statement as that only those who 'hate' their dearest relatives can enter the kingdom. Wealth is a positive bar, and only through the power of God can any be saved.

Prayer

May I realise, Lord, how helpless I am. I can only put obstacles in your way, never earn your kingdom. Help me at least to sweep away the obstacles.

66 Luke 18:31–34

A prophecy of the Passion

As Jesus and his disciples approach Jerusalem, there comes this almost agonising moment of the prophecy of the Passion, which the disciples fail to understand.

The three prophecies in Mark

This prophecy must be seen against the background of Mark's three formal prophecies of the Passion. Mark stakes out the second half of his gospel, starting immediately after Peter's confession at Caesarea Philippi, by Jesus' three prophecies of his Passion, the reiteration becoming ever more explicit and ever more painful. Each time the disciples fail to understand, and indeed show their disregard by squabbling about their own position and precedence. Luke has only this single prophecy, but the threat of the coming Passion looms just as dominantly through the theme of the great journey to Jerusalem, an ever-present reality, ever since Jesus, Moses and Elijah are seen conversing about it at the transfiguration. Luke does not, then, repeat the prophecy three times, but the emphasis on the inability of the disciples to understand is nevertheless heavy, expressed with three dull thuds in the single verse 34.

The scandal of the cross

Familiarity with the Christian symbol of the cross has blunted our perception of the shocking nature of this event. It was a punishment refined by the Romans and reserved for slaves. After the preliminaries, which could be more or less brutal, the victim was simply nailed up naked and left to die, exposed both to the unforgiving heat of the sun and the insults and contempt of passers-by. Crucifixion took place normally beside a road for maximum publicity. After the major slave revolts of Rome, the approach roads were lined with thousands of dead and dying bodies, hanging there. Jesus was crucified beside the main road from Jerusalem to the coast.

The brutality of the business may be judged from the fact that during the siege of Jerusalem in AD70, the Roman besiegers nailed any escapees to the trees of the Mount of Olives till there were none left free. They amused themselves by nailing them up in odd positions. Even the orator

Cicero, not the most squeamish of Romans, describes crucifixion as a most digusting punishment.

In the first two centuries of Christianity, while the memory of crucifixion still lingered, realistic images of Jesus crucified were never attempted. Instead the cross was represented bejewelled, to show the glorification of the cross. It is hardly surprising that the crucified Christ was 'to the Jews an obstacle they cannot get over, to the Gentiles foolishness' (1 Corinthians 1:23).

Why crucifixion?

This foolishness and disgrace must, therefore, be explained. Two avenues of explanation are used here – first, that Jesus knew about it beforehand and went willingly, indeed voluntarily, to this death; second, that it was destined by the will of God, expressed in the scriptures. Luke especially insists that 'it was necessary' that Jesus should suffer, and that each move towards the crucifixion was destined to take place. Thus now Jesus describes in detail the events of his Passion, exactly as they would occur.

It is likely that the details of the prophecy were clarified after the event. How much did Jesus know? He must have known that his proclamation of the kingship of God had set him on a collision course with the authorities at Jerusalem and that they would not be able to tolerate his message. He must also have known that his Father would not desert him. On the other hand, it is hard to believe that the disciples, having heard three detailed descriptions of the Passion and resurrection, still reacted not only with cowardice but also with surprise when it actually occurred. The detailing of the events is a way of showing that Jesus knew just what he was doing, and willingly accepted the consequences.

Prayer

Lord Jesus, you knew beforehand that you were to be brutally rejected, and yet you still carried through your mission. Grant me courage to carry on in difficulties and trust in your saving help.

67 Luke 18:35–43

Jesus heals Bartimaeus

After this ominous prophecy of the Passion, the air is full of the threat of the coming events. Jericho is the first place apart from Jerusalem to be mentioned since Samaria in 17:11. It is the obvious last place before Jerusalem, less than a day's walk from the city up the Wadi Qilt, which featured in the story of the good Samaritan. This serves as a reminder of how close the city now is, a sort of prelude to Jesus' arrival. In order to locate the following story of Zacchaeus in Jericho Luke changes the location of the Bartimaeus incident, putting it at Jesus' entrance to Jericho instead of when Jesus is leaving the town. This is the last of Jesus' miracles of healing.

Son of David

This is the first time in Luke that Jesus has been hailed as son of David. At the annunciation Mary had been told that Jesus would inherit the throne of his father David, and another reminder was given by his birth at Bethlehem, the city of David. Since then, his descent from David has never been mentioned. Perhaps this Jewish title was of less interest to Luke's Gentile audience. In the story of Jesus as told by the other synoptic evangelists, however, it has an important role as a messianic title, for the royal Messiah was to be son of David. There are constant messianic overtones to Jesus' ministry, simply through his proclamation of the kingship of God through his miracles and his teaching. Nevertheless, Jesus would not allow his disciples to proclaim him as Messiah, 'until after the Son of Man had risen from the dead' (Mark 9:9). This was because they were so slow to understand the real nature of his mission.

There were in Judaism many different hopes and expectations current about the Messiah. He would bring the sovereignty of God to perfection, but how? Would he be a warlord who would free Israel from the Roman yoke? Would he bring fire and judgement to the world, separating the wheat from the chaff? Would he ensure that the law of God was observed to the last jot and tittle? Would he bring abundance and plenty to enable every man to luxuriate in milk and honey under his own fig tree? That he would bring God's sovereignty to perfection by his own suffering and death was never part of the conception of the Messiah.

That would involve the rejection of God's Messiah by God's own people, their failure to recognise the fulfilment of the promises for which they had waited so long, and this could surely not even be envisaged. The disciples, too, were slow to appreciate what was the nature of Jesus' messiahship. So Jesus was hesitant about the use of the title of Messiah, until the real nature of his mission would be forced upon them by its climax and conclusion.

Within this pattern it is significant that now at last Jesus is finally hailed publicly as 'son of David', just as he is physically going up the last ascent to Jerusalem, where the nature of his messiahship will be made known by the Passion and resurrection. Now at last he makes no move to silence Bartimaeus, and surely accepts his cry of 'Son of David!' as an expression of the faith which saves him.

Bartimaeus

At this stage, therefore, the miracle of opening the eyes of the blind has special significance. It symbolises the opening of the eyes of understanding which is about to take place with the revelation of the suffering Messiah at Jerusalem. It also somehow has the air of a special celebration, summing up Jesus' miracles of healing. So many features which have occurred in previous miracles are present here too. There is the persistence in prayer shown by Bartimaeus' repeated cry, despite the scolding of those who heard him. Luke also stresses his helplessness. In Mark, as soon as Jesus tells the bystanders to call Bartimaeus to him, Bartimaeus flings off his cloak, leaps up and comes to Jesus; in Luke's account he has to be led to Jesus. The only contribution which he makes himself is faith, the acknowledgement that Jesus has power to save him (and 'save' is again used in an unrestricted sense, suggesting not merely the restoration of sight, but the saving of the whole person). Finally there is that characteristically Lukan outburst of joyful thanks and praise to God by the whole people of God present.

Prayer

Son of David, have pity on me!

68 Luke 19:1–10

Zacchaeus

As the story of Bartimaeus sums up Jesus' miracles of healing, so the story of Zacchaeus sums up the welcome Jesus gives to sinners. The story comes only in Luke, and two interesting balancing stories have been suggested for it. Particularly telling are Jesus' two final sayings. First, that even Zacchaeus, the despised tax collector, is a son of Abraham. This takes us right back to John the Baptist's message of repentance: to the claim of his listeners that they were anyway children of Abraham, John replies that God can raise up children of Abraham from these very stones. Now even the rankest outcast is seen to be granted this status by his repentance. Second, it is another instance of Jesus coming to save what was lost, which has been stressed so heavily in the three parables of the lost sheep, the lost coin and the lost son. Now Jesus voices the principle in terms reminiscent of that early saying, 'It is not those that are well who need the doctor, but the sick' (5:31).

The story is told with typical Lukan zest. The scene is set, with Jesus going peacefully through Jericho, that wonderfully fertile city of palm trees, deliciously irrigated by the Spring of Elisha (2 Kings 2:19–22), the first known site of agriculture and the oldest city in the world (it has a stone tower some 8,000 years old). Zacchaeus himself has that mild eccentricity which is the mark of many of Luke's characters: it is not every head tax collector who would shin up the nearest sycamore tree, just as not every master would congratulate his crafty steward on cheating him out of his money. The lack of regard for his dignity partners the same lack of care for appearances in the father of the prodigal son. One never quite knows what Luke's characters will get up to next. Jesus, needless to say, is not the least fazed by seeing this dignified character clinging to the branches. The lively dialogue is also a feature of Luke's stories.

The generosity of Zacchaeus' little speech remains in character: he is, after all, a financier and used to dealing with figures, so is exact about them. He does not promise to make himself destitute, but promises to give a neat half of his goods to the poor. Is this the scale of donation which we are to consider ideal from the rich to the poor? The disciples, when they are called, forsake 'everything'. But in Acts Ananias and

Sapphira incur their dire penalty not for holding something back but for lying to the Spirit about having done so (Acts 5:3). The fourfold restitution to those he has wronged is also generous, for the law demanded that 'the person must retore in full the amount owed, with one-fifth added' (Numbers 5:7). Zacchaeus' promise goes far beyond this.

But of course the most important feature is the repentance of the chief tax collector. Tax collectors, as we have often seen, were notoriously outcasts from decent, religious society because they were working for the Romans, playing a part in their oppression of the Jews; but this is the first time we have met one of their leaders, who would earn an intensification of that hate and contempt.

Parallels

Luke may also intend us to see in this story of the repentance of a sinner a balance with another sinner, the woman who wept on Jesus' feet at the house of Simon in Luke 7:36–50. This would be in accordance with Luke's careful pairing of men and women: both are sinners who welcome and embrace Jesus in repentance.

On the other hand there is also perhaps a contrast between Zacchaeus and the rich ruler of Luke 18:15–30 (see p. 140). Both are described by the same word as 'wealthy'. Both are men of position, the one an *archon* (= ruler), the other an *architelones* (= chief tax collector). There the similarity ends and the contrast begins, for Zacchaeus responds where the rich ruler fails. The rich ruler is held back by his wealth from following Jesus, and cannot face distributing his goods to the poor. Zacchaeus does precisely this to repair his previous injustice.

Prayer

Lord, I suppose we, each of us, have something of which we are ashamed, which would make us outcasts from your company. Grant me profound repentance, a real turning back to you from sin, and an adherence to you, that I too may be a child of Abraham.

69 Luke 19:11–27

The parable of the pounds

This final parable story is often read in the light of the parallel story in Matthew. Matthew has the parable of the talents as one of his five parable stories about the impending last judgement. Luke's story is commonly seen as a version of the same story, with a few variations. For instance, the sums of money are less gigantic. It is difficult to give equivalents of ancient monetary values in an age when there were no cars, washing machines or holidays to the Bahamas to buy, but Matthew's talent is equivalent to the annual tribute paid by a small province of the empire to Rome, so a gigantic sum, whereas Luke's *mna* (often translated 'pound') is more like half a year's wages for an agricultural worker. A second obvious difference is that Luke includes the dimension that the master is not simply a man going on a business trip or on holiday, but is a nobleman going to secure a kingdom. The historical allusion is surely to King Herod's son Archelaus, who went to Rome to secure the kingdom of Judea, which he did successfully, despite an embassy of the Jews which followed him to prevent it (they were quite right, and he was so incompetent that he was deposed after ten years in AD6). The question is whether this historical background is merely a literary decoration or whether it is the whole point which has transformed the story.

The importance of the political dimension in the story itself may be gauged from two factors: the successful servants are given charge not of more money but of cities; that is, they participate in the new king's rule. Furthermore, the final incident in the story is the punishment, not of the timid servant but of the objectors, who are slaughtered forthwith. Some weight must also be given to the introduction to the story, which gives the reason for the parable as that 'they thought that the kingdom of God was going to show itself then and there'; so, somehow or other, the kingdom should be central.

The return of the king

The whole question is when the king is reckoned to gain his kingdom. Is it at the end of the world? In this case the parable is a warning to use one's abilities to good advantage in view of the final judgement, a warning against the final judgement, much like Matthew's parable. On the other hand the special features of the story answer better to a different scenario: the moment when Jesus receives his kingdom is at the Passion and resurrection. This is already indicated in the introduction: they thought that the kingdom of God was going to show itself then and there. From now onwards in the gospel story the emphasis is on the achievement of the kingdom, at the entry into Jerusalem and on the cross, as well as at the resurrection. After this he will give apostolic authority in the Christian community to those who are faithful. This corresponds to the authority of the good servants over ten or five cities. The servant who merely wrapped his money in a cloth is not (as in Matthew's story) punished; he merely has his money taken away and is not given authority. The corresponding authority is given to others. The punishment falls on those who wanted the kingdom denied to this king, and they are surely the leaders of the Jews.

Luke's scheme of history has two parts: after the life of Jesus, climaxing in his death and resurrection, his mission is carried on by his apostles in the power of the Spirit, as described in the second volume of Luke's history, Acts. There is, so to speak, a second chance, and many of the Jews take it and are converted to Christianity. But the leaders still reject it, and they are the 'enemies' who would not have the king rule over them.

It must be admitted that there are still puzzling features in the story. Why does the timid slave accuse the king of being so exacting, a charge which the king accepts? And what is the point of the protest of the bystanders?

Prayer

Lord, banish laziness, slackness and lack of interest from me. Make me aware of what I can do for your kingdom, of the tasks you have entrusted to me, and help me to respond wholeheartedly to your offer.

70 Luke 19:28-38
Jesus' royal entry into Jerusalem

Jesus' entry into Jerusalem is a point of high significance. It is already so in Mark, but in Luke this significance is further heightened by the previous story. The long and single-minded journey to Jerusalem since 9:51 has focused attention on this moment. The immediately preceding parable about journeying to receive the royal dignity has especially prepared for this event. Hardly any other place-name has intruded into the story (Samaria once, and Jericho), and now at the end it is reinforced that he is 'going up to Jerusalem' (19:28).

The preparations

The story of the acquisition of the colt is full of mystery, a supreme example of the authority of Jesus. We are not told of any preparation for this, such as that the owners of the colt knew Jesus or had been warned. They simply yield unquestioningly when they are told, 'The Lord has need of it' (RSV). The mystery is intensified in that neither they nor the reader know who this 'Lord' is. The word used can mean either 'the master' in the sense of an earthly owner or (as frequently in Luke) the Lord God. This ambiguity is surely deliberate. The fact that it is important that no one has yet ridden the colt is a further hint of the sacredness of the moment, for it indicates that the mount, like a sacred sacrificial victim, had never been subjected to any common use.

The solemnity of the occasion is increased by two scriptural allusions which would spring immediately to mind. Entry riding on such a colt is the fulfilment of the prophecy in Zechariah 9:9 of the king who comes in peace: 'Look, your king is approaching... humble and riding on a donkey, on a colt, the foal of a donkey.' This motif of peace is stressed twice more in the story, by the cries of those who welcomed him (v. 38) and by Jesus himself in his lament (v. 42). His entry into Jerusalem was meant not to condemn but to save Jerusalem – if the city had been open to this. The second allusion is even more portentous: by his mention of the descent of the Mount of Olives (v. 37). Luke reminds the reader of the awesome scene of Zechariah 14, the day of the Lord, when the Lord comes to Jerusalem with all his holy ones from the Mount of Olives.

The entry

The actual historical scene could have been quite simple. It was not necessarily a grand triumphal procession which any onlooker would have recognised as Jesus' royal entry. Pilgrims went up for the great feasts such as the Dedication of the Temple singing Psalm 118 and waving palm branches. There would have been great crowds by the time they came to the gates of Jerusalem. Neither Mark nor Luke indicate a massive retinue: Mark has only 'those who went in front and those who followed' (how many were they?), and Luke's 'the whole group of disciples' gives no indication of number. So the significance of their entry among the pilgrims – though none the less real – may have been seen only later, when the disciples looked back on the events.

There are some little touches by which Luke shows his understanding of the meaning of the event. First, they kept strewing their cloaks under him as he went forward, which is reminiscent of the acclaim of Jehu as king in 2 Kings 9:13; this they did, crying 'Jehu is king'. Luke also stresses the kingship of Jesus by a slight adjustment to the psalm, the addition of the word 'the king'. They cry, 'Blessed is he who is coming *as king* in the name of the Lord.' In Mark it is only after the psalm verse that 'the coming kingdom of David our father' is mentioned.

A final adjustment made by Luke to the entry is the touching echo of the song of the angels at Bethlehem. 'Peace in heaven and glory in the highest heavens' echoes 'Glory to God in the highest heaven, and on earth peace for those he favours', but with a tragic difference: despite Luke's constant emphasis that Jesus' message is 'the gospel of peace', 'the word of peace', there is no promise here that Jesus' entry will in fact bring peace to Jerusalem.

Prayer

Blessed is he who is coming as king in the name of the Lord. Peace in heaven and glory in the highest.

71 Luke 19:39–44
Lament over Jerusalem

The sadness of Jesus at Jerusalem's refusal to accept him is a recurrent theme in Luke. We have seen it already at the halfway point of the great journey (13:34–35, see p. 119). It will recur again in the reply to the women who mourn for Jesus on the way to execution (23:28–31). Perhaps the most tragic feature is the echo and reversal of the Benedictus. Zechariah had foretold the salvation of Israel in similar terms. Israel would be saved 'from our *enemies*' (1:71, 74) when God comes 'to visit us… to guide our feet into the *way of peace*' (1:78–79). But instead, Jerusalem fails to recognise the visitation from on high and so the *way to peace* (19:42). Consequently it will be the *enemies* who surround her (19:43) and besiege her.

The siege of Jerusalem

A question of course immediately arises, whether, in the words of Jesus' prophecy on this occasion, Luke is making use of his knowledge of the siege of Jerusalem some 40 years later. It is certainly not impossible or unacceptable in theory that Luke should have clarified the words by his knowledge of what actually happened. This would give valuable clues to the date of writing of the gospel. In fact this avenue is disappointingly closed. None of the gospel mentions of the fate of Jerusalem contains details which need to be culled from what eventually happened. The details of the siege are given by Josephus at some length, and none of them is clearly reflected in the gospel passages. It was the concern of the gospel writers far more to show the theological import of the sack of Jerusalem, that the fate of Jerusalem was the fulfilment not only of Jesus' prophecies but also the prophecies of the Old Testament. So the fate of Jerusalem is described in the stock prophetic language used by the prophets to describe the sack of any town. For instance, there was not a fortification built all round Jerusalem (this would have taxed even the Romans' skill in engineering), and the dashing of 'children inside your walls to the ground' is a clear reminiscence of Psalm 137:9.

Jerusalem and the Jews

The great difficulty for Luke, as for Paul, was to explain how it was that the promises of God to his chosen people had been fulfilled. How was it that the Jews as a whole had not accepted Christ, but had rejected the fulfilment of their national hopes? Had God forgotten or deserted his people? Both writers were concerned chiefly with Christians sprung from non-Jewish stock, but they both toiled over the mysterious failure of the Jews, how it was that the focus of Christianity had moved from the Jews to the Gentiles, and what the status of the Jews now was.

It is against this background that Luke's attitude to the Jews must be seen. In the infancy narratives he stresses strongly that John the Baptist and Jesus are the fulfilment precisely of Jewish hopes: the parents of both children are models of Jewish piety, perfect examples of the poor and helpless favoured by the God of Israel. Jesus, in his opening sermon at Nazareth, shows that he has come to fulfil the prophecies. Throughout the gospel a clear distinction is made between the people and their leaders. The former are responsive to Jesus and are treated sympathetically; the latter unfavourable and heavily criticised. Later, in Acts, Luke is at pains to point out that always some of the Jews responded to the message of Christ and were converted, despite the continued opposition of their leaders. The first Christian community at Jerusalem is represented as the ideal community, marked by prayer, fraternity and harmony. It is as part of this presentation that Jerusalem features in the gospel. The gospel begins in Jerusalem, and the pilgrimage to the climax at Jerusalem occupies the latter part of the gospel. It is the scene of the resurrection appearances. It is the hinge-point from which the gospel spreads all over the known world. In the course of his journeys Paul is constantly returning there to confirm his message.

At the mid-point of the story, therefore, the final phase of Jesus' ministry, Jesus himself comes to Jerusalem. It should have been the hinge of all his mission, the enthusiastic centre and promoter of his work. Its failure to respond is a large part of the tragedy of Jesus.

Prayer

Lord, I am your favoured child, just as the Jews were, chosen and fostered through all time. Grant that I may respond to your call and follow you in the road of my peace.

Luke 19:45-48

72

Jesus in the temple

This is a passage where the full impact of Luke's message can be seen only by comparison to the account given by the other evangelists; there are staggering differences in the account of these events. Luke's is not simply an abbreviated account; it is a radically different one.

The purging of the temple

Mark's account of the 'purging of the temple' is a statement of the bankruptcy of Judaism. In a prophetic action Jesus 'rubbishes' the temple, upsetting those who did business there and finally declaring it a 'den of thieves'. In itself this was only a symbolic action. It is impossible to believe that Jesus raged in the temple, creating widespread havoc, for a close watch for disturbances was kept not only by the temple police but by the Roman guard as well. He would have been arrested before he got very far. The meaning of this demonstration is given by Mark through the little story of the cursing of the fig tree. Mark often 'sandwiches' one event between two halves of another, in order that they may react on and interpret one another. In this case the fig tree obviously stands for Israel, so that its barrenness is a sign of the barrenness of Israel.

Furthermore, the prominence of Jesus' word against the temple, 'Destroy this temple and in three days I will rebuild it', in the Passion narrative confirms that Jesus' hostile attitude to and threat against the temple were the real reasons why the leaders of the Jews wanted him removed from the scene. He had caused upset in the temple once, and the chief priests and Sadducees were not prepared to risk it happening again, particularly at the big feast of Passover, when the whole of Jerusalem would be thronged with pilgrims. As the high priest so succinctly indicates, if this happened the Romans would come and take away their power, on the grounds that they were incompetent to control the people. What made it worse was Jesus' link with John the Baptist, who was still reverenced by the people.

Luke and Jesus the teacher in the temple

Luke transforms this scene. Instead of Jesus taking action on four different groups of people, those buying and selling, changing money, selling doves and transporting (Mark 11:15-16), in Luke he merely begins driving out those who were selling. This is merely a preliminary, and the accent is on their replacement: 'He taught in the temple every day.' He clears out the sellers in order that he may teach, and day after day. The full extent of this is seen at the end of Jesus' ministry in Jerusalem: 'All day long he would be in the temple teaching… and from early morning the people thronged to him in the temple to listen to him' (21:37-38). These two statements form a bracket round Jesus' Jerusalem activity, emphasising his continuous teaching office; his messianic teaching is the core of his activity in Jerusalem. He makes the temple his regular platform.

Significantly, however, Luke also abbreviates the scriptural quotation from Isaiah given by Mark, 'My house will be called a house of prayer for all peoples.' By removing the final three words, 'for all peoples', Luke deletes the suggestion of the destined inclusion of the Gentiles. For Luke the temple serves as the centre of teaching for Jesus and of prayer for the early Christian community of Jerusalem, but thereafter its usefulness is at an end. Stephen's great speech in Acts 7 against the temple signals its end as a sacred sphere. It is no longer the centre of prayer and true worship.

The beginning of the end

This scene constitutes the spark which ignites the fire of determination to get rid of Jesus. The chief priests and the lawyers burn to get rid of him, in marked contrast to the people (and Luke twice uses the word, *laos*, which designates the sacred people of God), who hung on his words. The chief priests were the principal authorities in the temple, and also largely the secular powers in Jerusalem. In Luke the cause of their implacable hostility is not any rubbishing of the temple, but is Jesus' continuous preaching.

Prayer

Lord, we use often enough your saying, 'My house will be a house of prayer' of our own churches. Grant me there to listen to your voice in words and in silence, in beauty and in wonder.

73 Luke 20:1-8

A challenge to the authority of Jesus

Throughout the gospel Jesus has been represented as a teacher. From the beginning the authority of his teaching has been shown also by his authority as a healer. Now it is as a teacher that his authority is challenged by the leaders of the temple. This is different from Mark's story, where the challenge was to his authority to purge or renew the temple. In Luke (in the previous scene) he has done little of this, but on the other hand he has cleared the temple so that he may teach daily in it. So in Mark the challenge occurs simply when he comes back into the temple and is walking around – as though they took the first opportunity of meeting him again. In Luke Jesus has been engaged on a stable ministry of preaching and proclaiming the good news in the temple, rivalling the temple teachers with his prophetic authority. It is to his teaching authority that the challenge is made.

A rabbinic controversy

The controversy takes a recognisable form. The first challenge is in fact a question: who 'ordained' Jesus? At the end of rabbinic training, when a rabbi reckons that he has taught his pupil all he knows, and the pupil is ready to teach, the rabbi confers authority by the imposition of hands on the pupil's head. No doubt some such transfer of authority existed already in Jesus' day. The continuity of the oral tradition of teaching the law was already important: the oral tradition was held to stem from Moses himself, no less than the written text. It is, then, a question of the chain of authority.

A feature of Jesus' teaching

Jesus replies to the question with a counter-question. Such a form of controversy is not unknown in the rabbinic texts, and indeed in other philosophical discussion, but it seems to have been a special feature of Jesus' speech. Several of the gospel controversies or discussions between Jesus and his opponents proceed in four steps:

1. A question to Jesus from his opponents
2. Jesus' counter-question
3. Unsatisfactory answer from the opponents
4. Jesus silences his opponents

This form is used, for instance, in the discussion on divorce (not given in Luke) and on the tribute coin. It enables Jesus to challenge his opponents to think further and to question their assumptions. Often, also, Jesus' final answer widens their horizons and shocks them by going beyond what they had ever envisaged. Thus on divorce Jesus refers them back, beyond the petty rules of how and when divorce is permitted, to the original purpose of the sexes, the union of two in one flesh. On the coin of tribute he is asked a question which is intended as a merely political booby-trap. He couples to his straightforward answer the demand that they should also give to God 'what belongs to God' – rather more than they had asked!

Two details

There are two special points of interest in the story. The first is the demonstration of the respect in which John the Baptist was held. From the rest of Luke one would have little idea of this. His arrest is narrated before Jesus' baptism, so that he can seem to have been no more than a passing preacher to prepare the way. Mark and Matthew do indeed tell the story of his death, but only as a personal tale of intrigue, malice and indulgence. It is only from the historian Josephus that we know the breadth of his influence, for Josephus says that Herod arrested him for fear of his rousing a revolt among the people. The respect in which he was held obviously outlived him.

Second, the story is instinct with a dreadful irony. In his lament over Jerusalem Jesus has bewailed that they did not recognise the moment of its visitation. Now we see this refusal in action. It is with obvious stubbornness that they refuse to acknowledge what they know in their heart of hearts to be the truth.

Prayer

Grant me openness to the truth, however much it goes against my wishes and personal ideas. Spare me from the stubbornness which prevents me recognising when I am wrong.

74 Luke 20:9–19

The parable of the wicked tenants

Luke follows the line of the parable he found in Mark, with a few touches culled from Matthew and a few added of his own. In Mark this is one of two major story-parables in his gospel (the other being the sower), each of which is strategically placed at a turning point of the gospel; this parable is placed to illustrate the whole of the relationship between Jesus and the Jerusalem authorities which is being played out in the final days of Jesus' ministry. Typical of Luke is the careful crescendo of maltreatment of the messengers: the first is thrashed and sent away empty-handed; the second thrashed, treated shamefully (being shamed is often a Lukan horror, as in the stories of the selfish householder, the unjust judge and the crafty steward) and sent away empty-handed; the third wounded and positively thrown out, all before the final crime.

The vineyard of Israel

To any who know the prophet Isaiah the allusion is obviously to the lovely poem in Isaiah 5:

> My beloved had a vineyard on a fertile hillside.
> > He dug it, cleared it of stones, and planted it with red grapes.
> In the middle he built a tower, he hewed a press there too.
> > He expected it to yield fine grapes: wild grapes were all it yielded.
> And now, citizens of Jerusalem and people of Judah,
> > I ask you to judge between me and my vineyard...
> The vineyard of the Lord of hosts is the house of Israel,
> > and the people of Judah the plant he cherished.
>
> ISAIAH 5:1–3, 7

Perhaps Jesus' story was originally directed against the people of Judah as a whole, rather than against its leaders, reflecting upon their refusal to accept his message, and so the failure of his proclamation of the kingdom. It is possible that originally the rejection was the single point of the parable, with simply a crescendo of stubbornness as increasingly pressing messengers were sent. But, if Jesus understood himself as 'the son', the allegory is obvious. It is made a little more obvious by Matthew and Luke: whereas in Mark, the son is killed and his body thrown out of the vineyard, in Matthew and Luke, he is thrown out first, before being killed. This accords more exactly with the death of Jesus, who was first taken outside the city before being executed. He follows in the line of the prophets who were rejected and maltreated.

But Luke, in particular, has no doubt that it applies directly to the leaders. He makes it explicit that the chief priests and scribes (rather than Mark's indeterminate 'they') recognised that the parable was directed against themselves, and they wanted to lay hands on him in that very moment. But they were deterred by the people (and again Luke uses the technical term which signifies the people of God). In Luke alone they had responded to the threat of the parable with 'God forbid!'

The lesson reinforced

In all three synoptic gospels the lesson of the parable is reinforced by a further quotation from Psalm 118 about the cornerstone. In a fine building, one for which the builders could afford to reject stones, this is a proud stone, properly speaking the head of the corner. A solid and heavy stone, too, as Luke well knows when he illustrates the effects of collision with it, alluding to Isaiah 8:14, where the stone which crushes the opponents is the Lord God himself.

Matthew emphasises constantly in his gospel the failure and total rejection of Israel as a whole. He here adds that the kingdom will be taken away from them and given to another nation which will bear fruit. It is important that Luke omits this comment: for him not all Israel is rejected, but some are saved and only the leaders persist in their rejection.

Prayer

Lord, in your love you send to me messenger after messenger. Let me respond to your love. There is also in the background the fear of being crushed by stubborn refusal to recognise the cornerstone. Give me a fear and reverence for your name.

75 Luke 20:20-26
On paying tribute to Caesar

There follows a pair of controversies between Jesus and his opponents, in which they are trying to catch him out on matters of politics and religion. Mark had put together a neat group of four such tussles, but Luke has already used one of them, the great commandment (10:25-28, see p. 94), perhaps because there the lawyer who puts the question is praised rather than blamed, perhaps because Luke wants to attach to it the story of the good Samaritan.

The trap is set

The object of these questioners is to trap Jesus, and they put to him a good question. It is a religious question as well as a political one, and it contains two different catches, concerning the tribute and the coin. The object was either to discredit or to incriminate this religious leader. They meant to fix him on the horns of a dilemma: either he accepts paying taxes to Caesar and so makes himself liable to the accusation of disloyalty to Jewish nationalism, or he makes himself liable to the accusation of disloyalty to the Roman empire. To pay the tribute implied recognition of the sovereignty of Caesar. When tribute was first imposed on a province of the Roman empire there were frequent revolts, simply because people dislike paying taxes in general and to foreign powers in particular. Judea was no exception; the revolt of Judas the Galilean was still remembered and is enshrined in the gospel. But in Judea there was an additional cause of resentment and controversy. It was deep in the Jewish soul and theology that God alone is king. Therefore to recognise the sovereignty of another and earthly ruler is, at least on the surface, a betrayal of religious loyalty. At the dreadful climax of the trial of Jesus before Pilate in John's gospel, when the leaders of the Jews declare, 'We have no king but Caesar,' they commit the ultimate act of betrayal and hypocrisy.

The second catch concerns use of the coinage itself. The denarius carried an image of the emperor, so ran counter to the prohibition of graven images. The Jews could be very sensitive about this and made out that they were outraged when Pilate had some troops march through Judea carrying their eagle-standards. The coin also had what could be regarded as an idolatrous inscription, describing the emperor as a god and the son of a god. Pilate again fell foul of this difficulty when he had golden inscriptions to the emperor put up on his residence in Jerusalem. Therefore the very use of the coinage could itself be regarded as an act of recognition of false gods. Luke lets the hypocrisy of the opponents of Jesus stand out all the more by making them immediately produce the coin, so to speak, out of their pockets. In Mark they do at least have to go and fetch one.

The trap is sprung

Jesus' reaction to this trap may be considered on two completely different levels. On the level of the tricksters Jesus answers them in their own terms. He shows up their hypocrisy by making them produce the coin which implies their own acceptance of Rome. It is attractive to picture that he uses this coin for his answer, pointing to the two prominent words inscribed on the coin itself: 'Pay Caesar [pointing to the inscription CAES] what belongs to Caesar and God [pointing to the inscription DIV] what belongs to God.' Already on this level Jesus evades their trap and turns the tables on his opponents. He gives them a straight answer, but balances any charge of disloyalty arising from the first half of the answer by adding the second half. His answers often go beyond what the original questioners hoped or foresaw, and here too he goes beyond by urging their loyalty to God, which in itself suggests some defect there.

On a more profound and important level Jesus triumphs over his opponents by cutting through their petty concerns. To him the petty questions of tribal loyalty and political niceties are unimportant. His business is God's kingship. He is not concerned about graven images or the implications of recognition of the emperor, provided that the single essential is observed, to give to God what belongs to God.

Reflection

'Pay Caesar what belongs to Caesar – and God what belongs to God.'
LUKE 20:25

76 Luke 20:27–40

The resurrection of the dead

The question here comes from the Sadducees. They virtually ceased to exist in the Jewish War of AD70, so that we know little about them except what Josephus tells us in his highly schematic presentation of the three parties of the Jews. They formed the priestly aristocracy, theoretically stemming from Zadok, the priest of King David. From their hereditary families were drawn the chief priests and even the high priest. In practice they were, under the Romans, the governing classes. They were traditionalists, rejecting recent developments in theology, such as belief in the resurrection, in spirits and in angels. They seem to have been more interested in the smooth running of the country than in religious matters. Spirits and angels began to bulk large in popular imagination, theology and literature from the return from Babylon onwards, during the so-called Persian period and under Persian influence. Apart from 'the angel of the Lord', angels appear only in the later books of scripture. Belief in the resurrection of the dead dates from even later, being first attested at the time of the Maccabean Revolt in 167BC.

Life after death

The evolution of belief in life after death is fascinating in itself. At the time of the patriarchs and until King David, the dead were thought of as 'gathered to their fathers', as though sinking back into the identity of the ancestral tribe. The same idea still shows itself in the parable of Lazarus 'in the bosom of Abraham'. Later the idea of Sheol prevails, a place somehow under the earth, where the dead live a shadowy and powerless existence, like leaves in the dust, uncomfortable, restless and deprived of God. When the Maccabean martyrs, however, gave their lives in defence of Judaism, belief in a general resurrection of the dead at the end of time comes to view: 'the King of the world will raise us up, since we die for his laws, to live again forever' (2 Maccabees 7:9).

The Sadducees, not accepting this development of two centuries earlier, now attempt to test Jesus by ridiculing it. Their means of doing so is the theological conundrum produced by the levirate law: if one brother dies childless, his brother must marry his wife and raise up a child to continue the original brother's name and line (Deuteronomy 25:5).

Jesus' reply

The reply of Jesus may again be considered on two levels, one immediate and one more profound.

The first is that the Lord is the God of Abraham, the God of Isaac and the God of Jacob. This is a way of using the contemporary literalist exegesis of the scriptures to show that God still *is* the God of these long-past personalities. They still exist, and God never deserts his own. Once he has taken them on he will never leave them. This is a comforting and reassuring thought.

The other level is that they fundamentally misunderstand what is meant by the next world and the resurrection of the dead, if they think that it will be a mere reproduction of this present existence. Luke, who has several times shown a certain reserve towards matrimony, putting it as one of the possible obstacles to the kingdom, here underlines that one of the differences will concern marriage. There will be no marrying, since there will be no death and no need for physical reproduction. But on a more general basis, life will simply be different. To begin with, companionship and love will be different; there will be none of the exclusiveness necessary in marriage. Paul fills this out a little – but not much – in 1 Corinthians 15: 'We shall all be changed.' There will be continuity of personality, but bodies will no longer be physical in the same sense when they are taken up into the sphere of the divine. We must take it literally that 'What no eye has seen and no ear has heard, what the human mind cannot visualise; all that God has prepared for those who love him' (1 Corinthians 2:9, quoting Isaiah 64:3).

Prayer

Lord, God of Abraham, God of Isaac and God of Jacob, there can be no fear of death, as you never desert us. I cannot envisage what this resurrection of the dead will be, but I know that I am safe in your hands.

77 Luke 20:41–44

Christ not only Son but Lord of David

There have been two questions from the representatives of the Jews. After the first we are told that they could not catch him out and were silenced. The second group of questioners is even well enough disposed to praise Jesus, but again they did not dare ask him any more questions. After this Jesus himself takes the initiative to put them a question.

The title 'Son of David' designates Jesus as the fulfilment of the Jewish tradition. The Jews in the first century lived in hope, and a central element of that hope was the fulfilment of the promises to David spoken by God through the prophet Nathan (2 Samuel 7). This we see already in the record of the annunciation, where they are echoed by the words of the angel. David was at once the figure of the ideal king and leader of his people and the figure of the darling of God. His massive sin (adultery with Bathsheba and cover-up murder of her husband Uriah) followed by his wholehearted and prayerful repentance made him a sympathetic and attractive figure with whom any reflective person could identify. His later troubles made him an approachable model for all those who had their own troubles. His leadership of the people into a period of unprecedented prosperity made him also a symbol of gratitude and hope. Thus the designation of the Messiah as 'Son of David' focuses many aspects of Israel's hope.

At first sight it is therefore suprising that Jesus questions this hope: how can the Messiah be son of David? His puzzle needs some explanation. It is, of course, founded on the assumption, taken for granted at the time of Jesus but widely questioned today, that David is the author and singer of the psalms. It also plays on the expression 'my Lord', and understands the two 'Lords' differently: 'The Lord (God) declared to my Lord (the Messiah)…'. Jesus queries how David can call his descendant 'my Lord'. It should be that the descendant calls the ancestor 'Lord', not the other way round. There must therefore be a descendant of David, the Messiah, who is even greater than David himself. He is therefore not simply a descendant of David.

This psalm verse was treasured in the earliest Christian tradition also as an expression of the exaltation of Christ at the resurrection. The vindication of Jesus on the third day was described in several different ways. The empty tomb was only one of these, the appearances of the risen Lord experienced by his disciples another. The inner reality and significance of these had to be described in terms of images, of which 'taking his seat at the right hand' of the Father was a central one. Other images are the exaltation and glorification of Jesus, expressing his sharing in God's glory.

Jesus himself seems to have been slightly hesitant about this title. Perhaps he was cautious about the possible political overtones of kingship. It was, in fact, a title used also by rebel leaders of the time in the hope of gathering support by appeal to the tradition of David. When Peter, at Luke 9:20, hails Jesus as 'the Christ of God' Jesus does not joyfully welcome this recognition. Instead, he chides them, and tells them not to tell anyone; is this acceptance or not? When Bartimaeus twice hails him as son of David (18:38–39), Jesus neither rebukes nor encourages him. Only at the trial before the high priest does he accept the title of Christ, that is, Messiah, and even then he quickly reinterprets it.

The gospels of Matthew and Luke, however, show the full importance of this title. In Matthew Jesus is several times hailed as 'Son of David', and the whole of Matthew 1 is devoted to showing how Jesus came to be incorporated, by divine intervention, into the house of David through Joseph's adoption. Similarly, in Luke's story of the annunciation to Mary, the angel tells her that 'the Lord God will give him the throne of his ancestor David' (1:32). That Jesus was seen as the Messiah is clear also from the title early given – probably with a slight tone of mockery – to his followers at Antioch, 'Christians', or 'followers of the Christ/Messiah'.

Prayer

You are the Christ, the son of the living God. Let me treasure this name of 'Christian', which was given to your followers so early. If it has this tone of mockery, let me feel it an honour to share in your mockery and to follow you with a devotion beyond all reason and all limit.

78 Luke 20:45—21:4
The scribes and the poor widow

The confrontation that has been going on between Jesus and the Jerusalem leaders ends with a contrast between the scribes and a widow. In this Luke follows Mark, who has the same contrast between the two groups. At this point in the gospel Matthew gives a full-scale attack on scribes and Pharisees together (Matthew 23). In his earlier diatribe against the Pharisees and the scribes Luke had made a distinction between the two groups, giving some charges against the Pharisees and some against the scribes. Now he carries on this careful distinction by making his attack on the scribes alone, taking over virtually unchanged the criticisms given in Mark. He has already made sparing use of the Matthean material in Luke 11. The chief criticism here is the self-importance betrayed by their craving for front seats at meals in the synagogue. Luke has already given us an example of the arrogance of the Pharisees in the parable of the Pharisee and the tax collector, and of the importance of prominent positions at table in his warning at 14:8–11. The exact point here is perhaps the self-importance of the lawyers, a danger for teachers at any level!

The final criticism is hypocritical avarice, in which there is a neat contrast with the following section: the scribes swallow up the property of widows, while the poor widow puts all her livelihood into the treasury. In the ancient world widows were the very paradigm of helplessness. In theory in Hebrew society they reverted to the care of their fathers-in-law, but in practice they were often left destitute. In the New Testament there are several mentions of the special care to be taken of them. So to swallow up the property of such people is obviously an extreme case of callous greed, and the widow's gift is obviously an extreme case of generosity. Her two coins are called *lepta*, which literally means 'light' or 'fine', mere wafers of bronze, not unlike the now-discontinued English halfpenny. The 'treasury' was not money for the temple; it appears from the rabbinic literature to have contained a fund for distribution to the poor. It is all the more touching that the widow, herself already destitute, should give money for distribution for other poor people. It is often the poor who are most thoughtful and generous to other people in need.

It was a pious practice in the first century for elderly people to come to Jerusalem and take up residence there for their last years to prepare for death. Perhaps the most famous case at that time was the rich Persian queen, Helen of Adiabene, whose ample tomb is still visible in Jerusalem. Not all were so well off. That widows and their needs were an issue in the earliest Christian community in Jerusalem is made clear from the dispute in Acts 6, which led to the appointment of the seven. The widows of the 'Hellenists' in the Christian community were being overlooked in the distribution of alms in favour of those of the 'Hebrews'. It is not clear exactly who these two parties represent. They possibly refer to two different language groups, possibly two different cultural divisions. At any rate their number and the neglect of them was important enough to require significant community arrangements for them. Luke will have had this in mind when he juxtaposed the two contrasting cases, applying the teaching about God's care for the poor and the danger of wealth which have been so prominent throughout the gospel.

Prayer

Lord, save me from hypocrisy, and especially from making excuses to cover up my own laziness or lack of generosity.

79 Luke 21:5-36

An apocalypse (1): the destruction of Jerusalem

All the synoptic gospels at this stage, just before the final events of Jesus' ministry in Jerusalem, have a long section in which Jesus foretells to his disciples the future trials, and, in highly symbolic language, sketches out the whole future of his community. Mark's version was somewhat differently orientated from Luke's.

Warning signs

In Mark Jesus' prediction of the future is given on the Mount of Olives, looking across the Kidron Valley to Jerusalem. It is still a breathtaking view to see across the valley the shimmering white houses of Jerusalem and the gigantic esplanade or platform which is all that is left of the temple. In Luke the prediction takes place within the temple itself. Jesus takes the temple as his own platform for proclamation. So this prediction is centred on the temple itself rather than simply on the city of Jerusalem. The 'offerings' to which Jesus refers are gone now, but some of the 'fine stonework' remains in the lower courses of the wall. Herodian monumental masonry is unmistakable: huge, perfectly smoothed blocks with delicately bevelled edges to give a play of light on the honey-coloured stone.

The chief import of the first four verses of the discourse is to defuse panic. The drift of Luke's thought is best seen by two deliberate changes he makes from Mark. Mark is concerned about the end of all things; Luke concentrates his attention on the end of Jerusalem. So where Mark has the cosmically threatening 'Tell us when all these things are to be *brought to a conclusion*' (Mark 13:4, a literal translation) and uses the ominous prophetic image of *birthpangs* (13:8), Luke tones these down respectively to 'What sign will there be that it is *about to take place*' and the vaguer 'There will be *terrifying events and great signs* from heaven.' The messianic movements alluded to in verse 8 were particularly frequent after AD44 in Judea, and the build-up to the disastrous Jewish revolt of AD66 must have been clear for all to see.

The persecution of the disciples

It was important that the early church, struggling under persecution even before the siege of Jerusalem (v. 12), should understand that Jesus had foreseen and foretold it all, that none of it was without the will and protection of the Master. In Acts we may see all these predictions being literally fulfilled, as the disciples are arraigned before synagogues and imprisoned, as Paul is brought before governors (Felix and Festus) and kings (Herod Agrippa and Berenice).

Mark had already contained these predictions, but in Luke there is a sharper focus, '*I myself* shall give you an eloquence and a wisdom…' In Mark the sentence was in the theological passive, 'Say whatever is given to you', but here Jesus makes it clear that he himself will be inspiring and guiding them. So in Acts, the Spirit of Jesus is constantly with them as they carry on by their miracles and witness and sufferings the life of Jesus himself in the world. The perseverance to the death which will paradoxically win them their lives (v. 19) has been a keynote of Luke's gospel.

The siege of Jerusalem

Mark had foretold the 'appalling abomination' (Mark 13:14), which is most probably understood as the statue which the Emperor Gaius nearly succeeded in setting up in the temple (he died before arrangements were complete). This was interpreted as one of the signs of the end-time, the catclysm of the last days, so dreadful that 'if the Lord had not shortened that time, *no human being* would have survived' (Mark 13:20). Luke's focus is again limited to the siege of Jerusalem. He includes the name of the city twice (vv. 20, 24), and speaks clearly of slaughter in battle and dispersal of *prisoners of war* to all nations. In fact the Jewish population of Rome was hugely swelled by the prisoners brought there after the capture of Jerusalem to build (among other things) the still-impressive Arch of Titus. For Luke the sack of Jerusalem was theologically important, the fulfilment of Jesus' prophecies of the fate of the city which would not recognise the time of its visitation.

Prayer

If only you had recognised the way to peace!

80 Luke 21:25-38

An apocalypse (II): the coming of the Son of Man

Once the fate of Jerusalem has been foretold, the tone changes and the horizon broadens. The transition from the end of Jerusalem to the wider perspective is smoothly operated: 'And Jerusalem will be trampled down by the Gentiles until *their* time is complete.' He goes on to speak no longer of Jerusalem, but of 'nations' and 'the world'. Luke gives the same awe-inspiring picture of cosmic cataclysm as Mark, in terms of imagery drawn from the prophets of the Old Testament about the day of the Lord, a bewildering chaos of sun, moon and stars. His picture is completed and intensified (v. 26) by the terrified reaction of human beings, utterly bewildered and fainting away at the very expectation of what is about to occur.

But, by contrast, for Christ's disciples, Jesus' audience, it will be a time of hope: as soon as these signs begin they should lift up their heads, for their liberation is near. The signs are the encouraging presage of the approach of the kingship of God. The signs are expressed in terms of prophetic and Old Testament imagery, but we are told that they are as clear as the leaves budding in spring.

The timing of events

The immediate puzzle comes later, with regard to the timing: what can be meant by 'before this generation has passed away, all will have taken place'? Was Jesus wrong? Luke wrote these words some half-century after the time of Jesus' ministry, when the generation addressed by Jesus had surely passed away. It is hard to believe that he (and also Mark and Matthew) would have included them if they had already been proved wrong. Some clue of Luke's view may be gleaned from 9:27: in his version of Mark 9:1 he leaves out the last three words – 'There are some standing here who will not taste death till they see the kingdom of God *come with power.*' So we may deduce that they will see the kingdom of God, but not with power. Similarly, in Luke's version of the trial scene at 22:69, Jesus stresses the immediacy: '*From now on*, the Son of Man will be seated at the right hand of the Power.' It must be, therefore, that Luke sees the Passion and resurrection as somehow the accomplishment of the kingship of God. This is why the theme of Jesus' own kingship is so strongly stated at the time of the Passion and resurrection. The accomplishment of God's kingship is not to be understood as something that happens in a single moment; it comes in stages, with several decisive moments before the final crisis.

The cares of life

Luke's concern is seen strongly from the conclusion to his discourse. He has frequently shown his wary concern for the distractions of wealth and business interests. Now (v. 34) he emphasises particularly the pleasures of food and drink as a distraction, as exemplified in the drunkenness of the steward in 12:45. Distraction is very operative, for the stress is on the suddenness and unexpectedness of the arrival of the day. Once again Luke stresses his message of perseverance in prayer. Now that the expectation of a speedy coming of the triumphant Christ has cooled, it is all the more important to encourage perseverance in their vocation. But Luke uses traditional language and images, which already occur in 1 Thessalonians 5:2–3. One fascinating little verbal detail is the image of the trap being sprung. The same letters in Aramaic can be translated either 'birth pangs' or 'trap'. So 1 Thessalonians speaks of birth pangs and Luke of a trap, both perhaps representing a different translation of the original Aramaic words of Jesus.

Prayer

Keep me alert to the coming of your kingdom, at cockcrow, noon or evening. I do not expect it to come for me in one swoop. You offer it to me again and again in the circumstances of life. Let me embrace it each time, till I finally see the kingship of God come in glory.

81 Luke 22:1-6

Judas betrays Jesus

This passage begins the Passion narrative, the climax of the gospel. The gospels have been described as 'Passion narratives with extended introductions', and here everything comes to fulfilment. The earliest tradition of Christian proclamation was, as we see in Paul, centred on Jesus' death and resurrection, and it has been suggested that Mark's Passion narrative is the earliest piece of continuous writing in the gospels, taken over by Mark from an earlier source. This opinion now seems less likely, and it is more probable that Mark himself put together the sections of the narrative. In some ways Luke is closer to Mark in the Passion narrative than anywhere else. On the other hand this gospel does have clear distinctions from Mark, which will add up to quite a different pattern. The gospel of John similarly has its own reading of the Passion story, and there are some distinct similarities between Luke and John as opposed to Mark and Matthew. But again, the gospel writers were not mere chroniclers; rather they show by their narratives the lessons for Christians which they see in the events of Jesus' suffering and death.

The betrayal

All kinds of motives have been suggested for Judas' action, the most widespread being that he was a thief and cared only for money (as suggested by John 12:6). His nationalist name, the same as that of the great leader Judas the Maccabee, has prompted the suggestion that he had hoped Jesus would be a nationalist military leader and that he 'shopped' him on finally discovering that he had no such intentions. Recently it has even been suggested that, far from betraying Jesus, he really 'handed him over' in good faith to further Jesus' own plans. Luke and John 13:27 are not interested in Judas' psychology, and attribute the action to Satan, who enters into Judas. This is the moment to which Luke had looked forward when, at the end of the temptation story, he had said that the devil left Jesus until the opportune moment.

The failure of Jesus

It has been asked how Jesus could have made the mistake of choosing as one of the twelve foundation stones of the new Israel a disciple who would betray him. Not that he was very successful in choosing stalwart, reliable, quick learners who understood his message and persevered in their support for him! Nor, for that matter, did he succeed in founding the renewed kingship of God which he came to proclaim. Part of the tragedy of his death is that when he hung on the cross his mission was in tatters; when he died his mission should have died with him. Part of the vindication of his unquestioning obedience to his Father was that against all human likelihood the twelve (or the eleven) were strengthened by his Spirit to establish the new Israel.

Luke's insistence that Jesus taught daily in the temple makes a betrayal slightly strange: if they wanted to arrest Jesus, they had had plenty of opportunity to do so. On the other hand, if, as Luke insists twice, they wanted to do it 'apart from the crowd', they would presumably wish to avoid an arrest in the temple, where a guide would be needed to find Jesus among the hordes of pilgrims assembled for Passover. Josephus (who constantly exaggerates numbers) gives a normal figure of over one million pilgrims.

The arresting party

The Pharisees disappear entirely from the scene during the Passion in both Mark and Luke. They were not prepared to take their opposition to the stage of blood. The arrest will be on the initiative of the temple authorities. According to Luke, Judas' pact was made with the chief priests and the *strategoi*, normally a military office. John 18:3 mentions a *speira* at the arrest; this would normally be a detachment of Roman auxiliaries, but it could also be native troops of the province. There is nothing to show definitely that the Romans were involved in the process from the beginning, and throughout the Passion story Luke at least is eager to play down Roman involvement.

Prayer

The deeper the companionship, Lord, the easier it is for me to betray you. By your friendship you lay yourself open. Grant that I may respond to this trust.

82 Luke 22:7-13

Preparations for the Passover supper

The Passover festival

The Passover festival now begins to have major importance in the gospel, being mentioned repeatedly, in almost every verse of this section. The word 'Passover' does not have an equivalent meaning to the Hebrew word *pesach*; it was coined by that most brilliant and original of English translators, William Tyndale, first appearing in 1530. It was not, as it is in Christianity, the greatest festival of all in the year, but was one of the three great feasts which all faithful Jews would, if possible, celebrate at Jerusalem. It commemorated the liberation of the Hebrews from slavery in Egypt and the covenant by which they became God's people in the desert. It was therefore the foundation festival of the people.

From the ritual of the meal one can see that it could have been built on an older festival of pastoral nomads, possibly connected with moon worship, since it was celebrated at the full moon, the first full moon after the spring equinox (now 21 March). It has all the features of a meal of nomads: unleavened bread, roast rather than boiled meat (to save on water and cooking pots), herbs rather than the vegetables of a sedentary people. At the beginning of spring each year a tribe of nomadic pastors would move from their winter to their summer pastures. This was the meal before their departure, when they sacrificed a prime animal from the flocks to win the favour of the gods and turn away evil spirits. This sacred meal was 'baptised' to commemorate the greatest trek of all, the Exodus, when the Egyptians were eventually forced into letting their Hebrew slaves go.

Later, when Israel became sedentary and planted crops, this pastoral feast was combined with the agricultural feast of the first cutting of corn. The keynote of this was the purity of a fresh beginning, expressed in the jettisoning of all last year's leaven and the eating of unleavened bread for a whole week. Both these elements contribute to the Christian meaning of the festival.

The date of the last supper

The Christian Eucharist, the commemoration of the last supper, has the character of a paschal meal. The synoptic gospels all speak of the preparation for a paschal supper, and Jesus speaks explicitly of 'the room for me to eat the Passover'. But the gospel of John, which makes particular use of the symbolism of Jesus as the paschal lamb, places his death on the day *before* Passover, at the hour when the paschal lambs were slaughtered. There are, then, three possibilities: either one of the two chronologies is incorrect, or Jesus celebrated the paschal meal by a different calendar (such as that used in Qumran), or the last supper was not a paschal meal. In this case it could be classified as a fellowship meal with a paschal character.

The preparations

Jesus' sending of two disciples is very similar to the mission to fetch a mount for his entry into Jerusalem. There is the same air of mystery and of authority. We are not told of any preparatory arrangements. The man with the water-pot would be easily recognised; it was almost unthinkable that a man should carry a water-pot. I have never seen such a thing in my visits to the region. It was, and still is, women's work! He simply seems to know and to respond to the instructions. Jesus is seen as the authoritative prophet, who knows beforehand what will happen, and whose instructions are obeyed to the letter. This prescience is part of Jesus' foreknowledge of the whole course of events of the Passion. With the great influx of pilgrims into Jerusalem for the festival, there was no doubt a thriving business in renting out rooms for groups of non-residents, but on this occasion the process does not give the impression of a commercial transaction.

Luke gives more detail than the other gospels about the envoys, naming them Peter and John. In Acts these work together as a pair of envoys, sent down together to Samaria to confirm their reception into the Christian community.

Prayer

Lord, your paschal meal is so solemn and so sacred that even the preparations have their solemnity. Grant me to prepare myself with due seriousness for your eucharistic banquet.

83 Luke 22:14-20

The institution of the Eucharist

Three preliminary remarks must be made. This section makes no attempt to describe the paschal meal with all its ritual. In fact we know little about the ritual of the meal at this time and can only reconstruct it from much later texts. But the gospel account is concerned only with the Eucharist, not with the meal on which it was probably built. The story is a liturgical text, an account to justify the eucharistic practice of the author's own day by Jesus' action. This is shown by the words, 'Do this in remembrance of me,' which legitimate and indeed command the continuance of the rite. It is classic for a liturgical text to include the justification for the performance of the rite. Second, there is a fascinating trace of the earliest tradition of church life. The account of the institution is given also by Paul (1 Corinthians 11:23–26) as part of the tradition which he learnt by heart and passed on to his converts. Careful observation reveals a pattern of small differences between the accounts given by Mark/Matthew and by Luke/Paul. The former has more trace of Semitic culture, the latter of Greek. So it may be that the former tradition was handed down through the Semitic churches, the latter through the Greek-speaking churches. Third, some manuscripts of this section give a shorter text than others, verses 19b–20 being absent from the western tradition; we shall opt for the view that the whole section comes from Luke.

The scene

Luke is clearly using his predecessors, Mark and probably Matthew, but he makes a deliberate change in the order of events. Why? First, he removes all mention of Judas' treachery from this scene, and replaces it with Jesus' declaration of his ardent yearning to eat this paschal meal with his disciples. He wants to concentrate on the climactic nature of this moment and to avoid distracting from its peace by the disharmony of betrayal. Second, he puts before the account of the institution a double emphatic declaration that Jesus will not eat the pasch or drink the cup again until the kingdom of God comes. Then immediately Jesus proceeds to give them the bread and the cup; is he suggesting that in some way the kingdom comes at that moment? True, he is not said himself to eat and drink, but the emphasis on the coming of the kingdom is in any case massive.

The covenant

The covenant on Sinai by which God formed a people for himself was sealed by the blood of sacrifice sprinkled over the people. Thereafter in Judaism, each newborn male child was bound into the covenant by circumcision, that is, by 'the blood of the covenant'. Now Jesus declares a new covenant in his own blood. This is the moment of the formation of a new people of God, parallel to God's covenant with Israel in the desert. It is sealed by the blood of Jesus. So Jesus' action and words are prophetic, both giving meaning to and deriving their meaning from the events of the Passion which are to come.

To drink blood was a strong taboo in Judaism. All blood had to be drained from meat before eating. They held that the life of a creature was in the blood, and so it was sacred to, dedicated to, owned by God. Therefore when Jesus, despite this taboo, offers them his blood, he is offering them a share in his life.

'Poured out for you'

The final words of Jesus allude to the song of the suffering servant in Isaiah 53. This poem speaks of a servant of the Lord who gives his life for the sins of others, and, after humiliation and death, is vindicated by God himself. They are a precious sign of his own whole view of the Passion, giving focus to many other sayings, such as 'the Son of Man has come not to be served but to serve.' If this is Jesus' own interpretation of the events, it comes as a climax of his ministry of service. From such a precious touch it is possible to see the orientation and expectation which lies behind so many other events and sayings.

Prayer

Lord, you longed to eat the Passover with your disciples. Keep alive in me the longing to join you in the meal which bespeaks your sacrifice.

84

Luke 22:21-27

Parting instructions (1)

The parting speech by a leader or great figure was a convention both in Greek and in Jewish literature. The most famous example in Greek literature is probably that of Socrates before his voluntary death. In Hebrew famous examples are the final speeches of Moses in the book of Deuteronomy, and, outside the Bible, the *Testaments of the Twelve Patriarchs*, written in the first century, though attributed to the twelve sons of Jacob. Obviously the final hours are a time when the great man's sayings are listened to with most attention, and also a time when the great man naturally makes dispositions for the future. It is not uncommon for this convention to be combined with the convention Luke has already used several times, that of giving important teaching at a dinner (e.g. on forgiveness, at the supper given by Simon the Pharisee).

The betrayer

Mark and Matthew present before the institution of the Eucharist a dramatic little scene which points out Judas as the traitor. Luke defers this till afterwards, perhaps to avoid darkening that event, and reduces it to one saying of Jesus. The emphasis is on the disgrace of the betrayal, not on the personal identity of the betrayer, for to break a shared table fellowship by such a betrayal was sickeningly odious. At the same time Jesus underlines his foreknowledge and the predestined inevitability of his Passion. He is still being represented as the prophet who knows the future and the secrets of human hearts.

The grandeur of service

The central teaching which Jesus gives in this farewell address after the supper concentrates on the role of the leaders in the community. Luke has saved up these two pieces of teaching about discipleship, which occur earlier in the other gospels, in order to give them additional emphasis by their placement at this solemn moment. They are linked by the theme of the kingdom, and teach about the responsibility of playing a leading role in the kingdom. They are given added emphasis by their position. This is the only general teaching in the address. It is flanked by pieces on two contrasting individuals – Judas, who was faithful and later fell away; Peter, who fell away and later returned to strengthen his brethren.

The first subsection is on dominance and ministering. Luke's teaching is all the more impressive because it is gentle. He moderates Mark's harsh presentation, 'those who seem to rule over the nations *dominate* them', for Mark's word means almost 'grind them down, domineer over them'. Instead he introduces a sort of courtly and formal grandeur, with his 'lord', 'king', 'benefactor' (an honorific title often used in the royal courts of the east). Again Luke's cultured and leisured background is visible; we have frequently seen it in his easy use of financial terms and in his warning against the dangers of wealth.

For 'have authority' Luke uses the word which derives from 'make possible', allowing the conception that the real purpose of authority is to open up possibilities, to be a 'facilitator'. Another word frequently used for 'rule' is *arche*, which also means 'beginning'; an authority is one who makes beginnings. Nevertheless, this is not the whole of the Christian concept, which is to be a servant. Here Luke introduces, aptly for the context of a supper, the contrast between those relaxing at table and those serving. One is reminded of the principal scene at the Johannine last supper, when Jesus washes the feet of the disciples – to the horror of Peter. The same word for 'serve' will be used by Luke of those who distribute food to the poor in Acts 6. It is significant that the word 'slave' is not used. There is nothing demeaning or shaming about this service; it is simply a matter of attending to the needs of others before one's own comfort. The emphasis on this nature of Christian service almost suggests a knowledge of future centuries of the Christian church, when, despite such titles as 'minister', a certain grandeur has seemed unavoidably associated with authority in the church.

Prayer

Lord, grant me to understand and put into practice the truth that all ministry in your church is centred on the needs of those to whom we minister. Help me to put myself into their position and see how I can gently guide them to you.

85 Luke 22:28–38

Parting instructions (II)

The second section of general teaching on the disciples remains with the image of kingship. It focuses on the kingship of Jesus, which has been becoming so prominent in the narrative since the story of Bartimaeus. It combines this with the image of the dinner-table, with its promise of feasting in the kingdom.

But Jesus also promises them to sit on thrones as judges in the kingdom. Here the image is of a court, for in the ancient world people did not sit on chairs at the table, but reclined on couches or mats. This same promise occurs in Matthew. Then it will take place at 'the rebirth'. Here there is no mention of that, and one is left wondering when it is to occur. Is Luke envisaging the second coming or an event which is closer? The account of the institution of the Eucharist has already suggested that the kingdom is now in some way being accomplished at the Passion. One possible interpretation of the parable of the pounds (see p. 148) is that Jesus is to return as king in the narrative of Acts, and the moment when he bestows authority on his faithful disciples has occurred already then. In this case Jesus is promising them that they will exercise authority over the new Israel which is even then being created by the new covenant in his blood, namely the community which Luke will chronicle in Acts.

Peter

In each of the gospels a special place is given to Peter. In the synoptic gospels he is the only one of the disciples who has much more than a walk-on part. Peter is constantly the spokesman of the group. At the same time, he is the most prominent failure, and his denial of Jesus at the trial is deeply etched into every Christian mind. Nevertheless, his part in the future of the community is emphasised in each gospel. They may or may not all go back to the same basic saying, but each gospel contains some passage on Peter's position.

He is the first of the disciples to be called by the lakeside. In Mark's story of the empty tomb, forgiveness of Peter and his reconciliation are specially noted by, 'You must go and tell his disciples *and Peter*…' In Matthew, there is no such reconciliation; the last we see or hear of

Peter is his bursting into tears when the cock crows. But his position in the community is assured by the promises of Jesus made at Caesarea Philippi: 'You are Peter and on this rock I will build my community.' John's statement comes in his final chapter at the lakeside, with the triple commission (corresponding to the triple denial) to 'Feed my sheep.'

In Luke, Peter has frequently been given special attention, such as a slight emphasis by having a named part (for example, in arranging the room for the paschal meal). Now Jesus in his prophetic role foretells Peter's denial, but only *after* he has foretold his conversion. The heart of the pronouncement is the promise that Peter will strengthen his brothers. This is perhaps a more active and continuous role even than that of being the foundation-rock as in Matthew. In his final disposition Luke's Jesus makes sure of stressing the organised structure of the community he leaves to carry on his work.

The final testing

The last section of the farewell speech prepares for the sequel. It predicts the full horror of the testing by announcing that the normal conditions of preaching the kingdom are suspended. These were imposed on the missioners in Luke 10, and were perfectly satisfactory then. But now is a time of violence and unprecedented stress.

At the same time reassurance is given by the quotation from scripture: it was all foreseen and willed by God in the expression of his covenant. The little quotation from Isaiah 53, 'He was counted as one of the rebellious', is enough to recall the whole poem, so frequently occurring during the Passion narrative. Allusions to it are contained in the frequent mention of the silence of Jesus ('like a sheep dumb before its shearers'), the mockery, the tomb with the rich. The detailed comparison, however, is only a vehicle for the interpretation of the event as a whole: at his Passion Jesus takes on the sins of all and himself atones for them. This is the meaning contained in each of the detailed allusions.

Reflection

'By the time the cock crows today you will have denied three times that you know me.'
LUKE 22:34

86 Luke 22:39-46
The Mount of Olives

The scene of the agony in the garden as related by Mark has undergone a radical restructuring in Luke. In Mark there were two centres of emphasis, the failure of the disciples and the horror of Jesus. The failure of the disciples is stressed by a typically Markan triple repetition: Jesus comes back to the disciples three times to find them sleeping. This is more important to Mark even than the triple prayer of Jesus, for the second prayer is barely mentioned and the third not at all. However, Jesus' horror and fear at his approaching arrest and torture are fully expressed. The words used for his 'terror and anguish' are very strong, denoting almost that he was stunned and beside himself with fear. The word used for his falling to the ground suggests that he was stumbling and falling repeatedly, almost uncontrollably.

Luke's recasting of the scene

The Lukan emphasis is quite different. Here the triple scene is welded into one. The prayer of Jesus is presented as an example for the disciples to follow, for the whole episode is bracketed by 'Pray, so that you may not be put to the test' at beginning and end. The disciples themselves are to pray, not merely to wait while Jesus goes and prays. The persecution of Jesus in the Passion is an example which the disciples also will undergo, and in the same way his prayer beforehand is a model for them to imitate. There is no mention here of the failure of the disciples, or indeed of their presence at all, though we were told at the beginning that they followed him, and so shared with him in this prayerful scene. When they are finally mentioned – when the prayer of Jesus is finished – there is no blame attached to them. They are 'sleeping for sheer grief': this suggests merely that they were so sad they could no longer stand up.

The Jesus presented is entirely in control, and the emphasis is on his calm and submissive prayer. There is no stumbling or falling to the ground, no bewilderment in the prayer. Instead Jesus kneels calmly down, as Christians will in fervent prayer. He then expresses his prayer only conditionally, 'If it is your will…'. (There again he is a model for disciples, for Paul prays the same phrase before his arrest in Acts 21:14.) At the end of his prayer Jesus stands upright with full dignity.

What, then, of the agony and the sweat? (Verses 43–44 are in fact omitted by some good manuscripts of the gospel.) It is often carelessly said that Jesus sweated drops of blood, and the saying has even become proverbial. But Luke says only that his sweat was '*like* drops of blood falling to the ground'. The comparison may be of size or of flow. A most plausible interpretation which brings all these elements together is based on the word *agon*, which normally means an athletic contest. Jesus is sweating in anticipation of his struggle, as an athlete whose adrenalin is flowing before the start of a race or competition. This reading of the text agrees well with the appearance of a strengthening angel. There is a strikingly similar scene in Daniel 10:15–19: before his great task of prophecy Daniel prostrates himself on the ground through lack of strength, and is comforted and strengthened by an angel.

The Christian tradition

Jesus' prayer before his Passion is reflected in a quite different scene in John 12:27. Here there is virtually only the words of his prayer and an allusion to an angel, no mention of the Mount of Olives, no scene of falling to his knees, no sharing with the disciples. The Johannine Jesus, for whom the cross and resurrection are the moment of glory and exaltation, does not pray to be spared the hour, but embraces it willingly. Similarly, Hebrews 5:7 relates, 'He offered prayers and entreaty, with loud cries and with tears, to the one who had power to save him from death, and so learnt obedience.' The tradition of the prayer of Jesus before his Passion was, therefore, preserved in various forms in different traditions of the early community. Each evangelist presented this as part of his own presentation of the Passion.

Prayer

You sometimes put me, Lord, before trials which seem beyond my strength. Give me confidence in your power and love to guide me through these trials and to share your Passion with you.

87 Luke 22:47–53

The arrest

The number of pilgrims in Jerusalem for the Passover was immense. The polyglot list of peoples who heard the apostles at Pentecost, however, gives the same impression. To celebrate the feast properly pilgrims were supposed to spend the night in Jerusalem, but the numbers were such that the theoretical limits of the city were extended to include the Mount of Olives. It would be no easy task to find Jesus and his small group among all the throngs on the hillside. Mark and Matthew tell us that the place was called Gethsemane, but that means only 'Garden of Oil/Olives', which on a hill covered with olive orchards would not be very specific. Hence the need for Judas to lead the arresting party to the place where Jesus would be.

Jesus continues to be in control of the scene. In Mark and Matthew, after the turmoil of the prayer scene, Jesus regains control of himself and the situation. In Luke's account he never lost it. But it is additionally stressed by two factors. The first is a contrast: the disciples resort to violence, with an excited cry which could be rendered, 'What about our hitting out with a sword?' The question to Jesus and Jesus' silence makes its impression. Jesus by contrast even now continues his mission of healing, as indeed he will continue it right up to the end by his forgiveness of the good thief. Second, Jesus continues his mission of forgiveness. While Judas is still approaching, Jesus offers him a last chance, asking him whether he really intends what he is about to do, and again, with the juxtaposition of 'betray' and 'kiss', stressing the treachery of the deed. Jesus' gentle offer contrasts vividly with Judas' hard refusal. There is surely a contrast here also with the next occasion when Jesus offers repentance: after Peter's denial 'the Lord turned and looked straight at Peter, and Peter remembered the Lord's words…'. Peter repents, but Judas does not.

The hour of darkness

Jesus intimates that the situation is, in one way, beyond human control. There is no hint that human responsibility is suspended, but there are more than human forces at work: 'This is your hour; this is the reign of darkness.' There is a suggestion of the same supernatural forces as at

22:3, when 'Satan entered into Judas'. There are two curious links here with the gospel of John. Throughout that gospel Jesus has been looking forward to his 'hour'. John treats the whole event of the Passion and resurrection as one single moment, the single hour of his Passion and resurrection, which is the moment of his exaltation not only onto the cross, but to his Father, the moment also of his glorification. In Luke the same concept of 'hour' is used, but now it is the hour of his enemies. More similar to the gospel of John is the use of the image of darkness: 'As soon as Judas had taken the piece of bread he went out. It was night,' says John 13:30. This rejoins the imagery of the sons of light and the sons of darkness which is so common in the contemporary texts from Qumran. Indeed, Luke has also used this symbol, for instance in the Benedictus, 'to give light to those who live in darkness and the shadow dark as death'.

The faithful disciples

One most important difference between Luke's presentation of the scene and that of the other synoptic gospels is that there is no mention of desertion by the disciples. For Mark this is the moment of desertion. The ikon of desertion in Mark is, of course, the young man who in order to flee leaves behind the sheet which is his sole covering. The disciples left all to follow Jesus; now he (ludicrously and with some wit) leaves all to escape from Jesus' company. In Luke we have been constantly reminded that the disciples are those who have stayed with Jesus in his trials. This is exemplified in the Passion. There is no word of their flight now, and at the cross 'all his friends', as well as the women, are present (23:49) and faithful to the end.

Prayer

Lord, we all sometimes feel betrayed by those we trust. Grant that I may face them with your gentleness, your spirit of forgiveness and your outgoing offer of friendship.

88 Luke 22:54–65

Peter's denials and the mockery of Jesus

The historical difficulty

There must have been in the tradition various components of the story of Jesus' examination by the Jewish authorities, which the evangelists felt free to dispose and arrange somewhat differently. The gospel of John gives a decision by the council to get rid of Jesus long before, immediately after the raising of Lazarus; when Jesus has been taken into custody there is only an interrogation by Annas, the high priest's father-in-law (though Jesus is so much master of that scene that it should almost be called an interrogation *of* Annas) without any further Jewish trial. Mark and Matthew give a sort of trial, leading up to a verdict of guilt, by the high priest Caiaphas, sandwiched between the elements of Peter's denial of his master. This is a typical 'Markan sandwich', the triple denial of Peter contrasting with Jesus' triple stand against his accusers. The trial is immediately followed by mockery and abuse of Jesus by some unnamed people, presumably members of the council.

What actually happened in that night it is impossible to tell. We cannot re-establish how closely related the tradition was to eyewitness testimony. We do not even know the code of law under which a trial would have occurred. The legal regulations which we do have form a purely theoretical body of law, which was formulated by the successors of the Pharisees at least a century later and was never even envisaged as the law code of any real national judicature. The chief priests and Sadducees who ruled Judea in the time of Jesus had long ceased to exist with the fall of Jerusalem. We do not even know for certain that a legally constituted Sanhedrin existed at this time. Contemporary sources other than the gospels mention only a sort of council of supporters of the king or the high priest, summoned specially on occasion to give moral backing to a decision; this was very different from the Great Sanhedrin which became the decisive body in Judaism after the fall of Jerusalem.

Peter's treachery

Peter's denial of Jesus was the ultimate assertion that Christ's kingship does not rely on human strength. Faced with a mere slip of a girl (this is the sense of the Greek word), the leader of the disciples denies his master, and then twice more, with increasing emphasis, repeats his treachery. By unpicking Mark's pitiless interweaving of Peter's denial with Jesus' steadfastness, Luke is gentler towards Peter, for the contrast is less strongly painted. It also makes a smoother transition from the meeting of the elders to the decision to hand Jesus over, if the denial does not intervene between them. For Luke, in any case, the point of the event is Peter's conversion. Luke increases the pathos of the scene by having Jesus himself nearby, near enough to be in eye contact. Only when Peter has shown his own complete emptiness does Jesus turn to him with a glance which brings about his own conversion, so that he may 'strengthen his brothers', as Jesus prophesied at the supper. Luke also adds a touch to Peter's sorrow: 'he wept *bitterly*'. The contrast with Judas is complete.

The mockery of the prophet

In Luke the maltreatment of Jesus is specifically mockery, with the physical abuse taking second place. It also changes the sense that the mockers are not the presumed dignified members of the Sanhedrin but are those who were guarding Jesus. Jesus has been presented as a prophet throughout the gospel, and now, ironically, his captors use this aspect to mock him. Their sadistic game is given more content, in that they not merely challenge him to prophesy, but, having blindfolded him, they challenge him to identify his strikers. As a prophet neither the blindfold nor his ignorance of them should be a bar to his recognising them. It is especially ironic that they are blind to the fact that his prophecy of Peter's denial has even now just been fulfilled.

Prayer

When I fail you, Lord, and by my infidelity deny that I am your follower, let me respond to your glance and return, so that all my strength comes from you.

89

Luke 22:66—23:1

Jesus before the elders

This interrogation before the elders has a changed character in Luke from the Jewish hearing in Mark. There is no mention of the high priest, nor of Jesus' saying about the temple. This is, of course, because Luke's whole attitude to Jesus in the temple is different from that of Mark. The temple has played an important part in the gospel right from the infancy stories onwards, and will play an important part in the Jerusalem community in the early part of Acts. The temple is the centre of Jesus' royal and messianic activity of teaching, just as it will be the centre of the early Christian community in Jerusalem and the centre to which Paul constantly returns. Far from sweeping the temple away, Jesus has used it as his centre for daily teaching.

Furthermore, the scene cannot any longer be called a 'trial'. There is no evidence, no verdict, and indeed when they bring Jesus before Pilate they merely accuse him as though this scene had never occurred. At this Jewish interrogation Jesus is in control; the leaderless group of 'elders of the people, chief priests and scribes' is no more than a foil to Jesus, enabling him to make two separate confessions or claims, that he is the Christ and that he is the Son of God. Whereas in Mark and Matthew Jesus is silent, in Luke he testifies on his own behalf, so that his own witness gives his opponents their impetus and they stress, 'Why do we need any evidence? We have heard it for ourselves from his own lips.' (22:71)

Jesus the Christ

Each accusation now receives a new prominence. First, the authorities no longer merely ask Jesus whether he is the Christ; they demand that he proclaim it: 'If you are the Christ, tell us!' Then Luke points out the futility of any attempt to convince the authorities: 'If I tell you, you will not believe, and if I question you, you will not answer' – a resignation reminiscent of Abraham's rejection of the rich man's plea in the parable: 'If they will not listen either to Moses or to the prophets, they will not be convinced even if someone should rise from the dead' (16:31). As in the Pilate scene the stress will be upon the Jewish determination to have Jesus executed, so here it is on the stubbornness of Jesus' interrogators and their refusal to accept the truth.

Furthermore, Luke significantly alters Jesus' own interpretation of 'Christ'. To the Markan claim – immediately denounced by the high priest as blasphemy – that they will see the Son of Man sharing the awesome chariot throne of God, Luke makes two changes. It is no longer a matter of sight and in the future. It is a matter of fact and vividly present: not 'you *will see*', but 'from now on the Son of Man *will be seated*...' But significantly, although it is a matter of fact, his interrogators will not see it – presumably through this same stubbornness. Second, there is no 'coming with the clouds of heaven'. The interest is no longer in the second coming or the final judgement. As the second coming has continued to delay, Luke's interest has moved from the future to the present. The emphasis is not on the future coming but on the present exaltation of Christ. The Passion and resurrection are already the moment of the declaration of God's kingship.

So in this scene the Son of Man is presented as entering his glory now, and ready at the right hand of God to receive his faithful, just as he will be ready to welcome the first martyr, Stephen, who sees 'the heaven thrown open and the Son of Man standing at the right hand of God' (Acts 7:56). Throughout the Passion narrative Luke is aware that Jesus in his Passion supports his followers in theirs.

Jesus the Son of God

The second question centres on the title 'Son of God'. This title is no longer joined to that of Christ, but receives a separate value of its own, in accordance with Luke's more developed understanding of the lordship of Christ. Similarly at the annunciation the child is separately predicted as Christ and as Son of God. What is most significant is that all Jesus' opponents confess this dignity of Jesus: 'They *all* said, "So you are the Son of God, then?" He answered, "It is you who say I am."' The whole scene is more a declaration of Jesus' triumph than a humiliating trial.

Reflection

From now on the Son of Man will be seated at the right hand of God.

90 Luke 23:3-5, 13-25

Jesus before Pilate

Luke is always a careful historian. He has noted that Mark gives us no details of any charge preferred against Jesus before Pilate; Pilate just somehow seems to know that Jesus claims to be King of the Jews. Luke shows Jesus' captors giving definite charges. They are, of course, false. But some charges are required, and these are the sort of charges which could have been brought against Jesus on this occasion: subverting the people; preventing the payment of tribute to Caesar; and claiming to be Christ, a king. Luke is always keen to align the persecution of Jesus with that of his followers, to stress that he stands beside his followers in their trials. The charges against Jesus are described in terms similar to the charges preferred against Paul at Thessalonica: turning the whole world upside down, breaking Caesar's edicts, claiming that there is another king, Jesus (Acts 17:6–7). So in his trial before the Roman governor Jesus prefigures his follower Paul in his trial before the Roman magistrates.

Luke is also considerably more cautious than Mark about the Barabbas incident. There is no mention in Luke of any amnesty or regular custom of releasing a prisoner – a Markan detail (Mark 15:6) which is not attested in external history, though there would be a certain appropriateness in the custom of releasing a prisoner at the festival of the release of the Israelites from captivity in Egypt. According to Luke the crowd (or is it the leaders?) simply roar for the release of Barabbas and are not to be put off by the offer of the release of Jesus. The contrast is all the stronger between Jesus, unjustly accused of subversion, and Barabbas, who had in fact been involved in a riot.

The innocent victim

Luke's chief emphasis is, however, on Pilate's recognition of the innocence of Jesus. Three times Pilate declares that he can find no case against this man, and three times the Jewish authorities react by insisting on pressing their case. With each declaration of Jesus' innocence, Pilate embraces a wider circle – first the charge which has been made, then any charge and finally any evil at all.

It is only in Luke that Pilate first (v. 16) suggests that he whip Jesus (a lighter punishment than the vicious flogging of Mark and Matthew), and then actually wants to release him (v. 20). Finally Luke again stresses the responsibility of the Jewish leaders: Pilate 'handed Jesus over to them to deal with as they pleased' (v. 25). The execution is not Pilate's will. He pronounces no sentence; indeed, it is even as though the Jews rather than the Romans actually carried out the execution. This emphatic insistence that the Roman authorities could find no case against Jesus is probably to be seen in the light of the later history of the church: Luke wishes to show that in Roman eyes Christianity is harmless and deserves no persecution.

Pontius Pilate

Pilate was governor of Judea for ten years (AD26–36). He is represented by the Jewish historian Josephus and the Jewish philosopher Philo as an unfeeling tyrant. But those authors are setting out to blacken Pilate's name in order to explain why the peaceable Jews were forced into rebellion a few years later against the Romans. Reading between the lines of Josephus' description of his period of office, it is possible to see that Pilate was well-meaning enough. For instance he constructed an aqueduct to bring much-needed water into Jerusalem, then found himself confronted by a riot when he tried to get the Jerusalem authorities to pay for it. When he mercifully quelled the riot with batons rather than swords, they claimed to be insulted. The Jews simply ran rings round him, and made any helpful initiative on his part look like a deliberate insult aimed against Jewish susceptibilities. Caiaphas was a wily operator, and was high priest for 18 years, a most unusually long period to retain the office; he would know exactly how to twist Pilate's tail. It is easy to understand how Pilate first tried to avoid the responsibility of having Jesus executed and then capitulated into allowing an unjust execution by which the Jews seemed to set such store. Pilate's weakness is reflected in his final pathetic question, 'What harm has he done?'

Prayer

Lord, help me to be fair and just in my dealings with all people, and not to be swayed into injustice by human respect or fear of the powerful.

91 Luke 23:6–12

Jesus before Herod

Jesus had foretold that his followers would be taken for trial before governors and kings, and indeed this happens to Paul, when he is tried before the governors Festus and Felix and the king Agrippa II. The incident of Jesus before Herod shows that Jesus himself leads the way for his followers in being tried before governors and kings. In fact Herod Antipas, tetrarch of Galilee and Perea, was not exactly a king. His father and several others of the Herod family were given the title of king, but he remained only a tetrarch, a negligible difference.

In the other synoptic gospels this Herod, son of King Herod the Great, has already appeared at his own birthday party as the murderer of John the Baptist. Luke omits this incident (the Baptist is quietly shuffled offstage even before Jesus' baptism, 3:19–20). The present encounter has, typically, been prepared by Luke with his mention that Herod was anxious to see Jesus in 9:9.

The Herod incident occurs only in Luke. It takes the place of the mockery by the Roman soldiers. Historically, the referral of Jesus to the ruler of Galilee is not, however, improbable: as an ostentatiously pious Jew, Herod might well have made the pilgrimage to Jerusalem for the feast. His family had a magnificent palace in Jerusalem. At this time according to Roman law a prisoner could be judged in the *forum delicti* or the *forum domicilii*, that is, either where the supposed crime had been committed or where his domicile was – in the case of Jesus this was Galilee. If Pilate wished to be rid of the case, it would have been a neat ploy to refer the prisoner to Herod. This he does as soon as he hears that Jesus' activity has been in Galilee.

Luke's portrait of Herod

It is hard to resist the impression that Herod, with typical Lukan vivacity, is represented as a rather wacky character. His reaction to having Jesus sent to him is excessive: the Greek, literally 'he was too overjoyed' (23:8), almost suggests whoops of joy. The same slightly maniacal overtone is given by the expression used for the interrogation, 'at some length'; there is a hint of excess here. Then, frustrated at Jesus' silence, Herod literally 'makes nothing of him' and descends to the indignity of joining his soldiery in this play-acting mockery.

The 'glittering' cloak in which Jesus was clothed was no doubt drawn from Herod's own wardrobe to add realism to the mockery of Jesus as a king. The same hysterical bonhomie is suggested by the reconciliation this made with Pilate (23:12). Such a reconciliation too is realistic: Herod Antipas acted as an agent for the emperor, keeping him informed of the activities of Roman officials in the area. This was notorious enough for Jesus to call him 'that jackal' (13:32). No one likes someone who reports behind his back to a superior, so it may well be that the cooperation between the two of them healed a breach. The reconciliation also, of course, serves the purpose of showing that even now Jesus brings peace and reconciliation wherever he goes, just as in his healing of the severed ear in Gethsemane.

The silence of the suffering servant

The silence of Jesus to Herod's questioning is a strong rebuke to Herod's intentions. Did Jesus reckon that Herod had not sufficient good will to deserve an answer, since he would take no notice in any case, like the brothers of the rich man in the parable and the Jewish elders who interrogated him? The motif of Jesus silent before his persecutors occurs also in Mark's trial narrative, both before the Sanhedrin (Mark 14:61) and Pilate (15:4–5). Luke has transferred it to the interrogation by Herod. In this silence the gospel writers see a fulfilment of the prophecy of the suffering servant of the Lord, 'like a sheep dumb before its shearers'. This prophecy of the servant of the Lord, whose atoning death leads to his vindication by God and the glory of God, is a theme which runs through the Passion narrative.

Reflection

While the Jews demand miracles and the Greeks look for wisdom, we are preaching a crucified Christ: to the Jews an obstacle they cannot get over, to the Gentiles foolishness, but to those who have been called, whether they are Jews or Greeks, a Christ who is both the power of God and the wisdom of God.
1 CORINTHIANS: 1:22–24

92 Luke 23:26–32

The way to Calvary

The final scenes of Jesus' life interweave loyalty and disloyalty, cruelty and sorrow, crime and forgiveness. In this journey to execution all the responsibility falls on the Jews. Crucifixion was a Roman punishment and must have been carried out by the Romans, rather than the Jews. Nevertheless Luke, more strongly than Mark or Matthew, represents the Jewish authorities as responsible. At the end of the judgement scene, Pilate 'handed Jesus over to them to deal with as they pleased'. Now, immediately afterwards, the phrase 'as they were leading him away', must refer to the Jews and leave them in charge at least of the grim procession to execution. Luke is using the same words as Mark used to refer to the Roman soldiers who had been mocking Jesus, but his omission of that mockery changes the subject from the Roman soldiers to the Jewish leaders who had been demanding the death penalty.

Loyal disciples

This hostility is set against two scenes of loyalty. The first is the discipleship of Simon of Cyrene. Cyrene was an important trading port on the north coast of Africa which – like many trading cities round the Mediterranean world – had an important Jewish population, important enough to be mentioned in several imperial decrees which have come down to us. Jews from Cyrene were present also among the many nations listed at Pentecost. Presumably there they had come up on pilgrimage for the feast, while here the note 'coming in from the country' suggests (but no more) that Simon was now a farmer near Jerusalem. One might guess that his devotion to Jerusalem and to the promises of God brought him to move to Jerusalem.

Luke emphasises the significance of carrying the cross. He has underlined the importance of the Christian carrying the cross *daily* (9:23), and that 'no one can be my disciple without carrying the cross and coming after me' (14:27). Now, with two little touches he shows Simon as a model of such discipleship. He carries the cross specifically '*behind* Jesus'. The tense of the verb used in Greek also indicates that it was not a momentary taking of the cross, but a long-term, lasting situation. Simon was taking on discipleship.

Discipleship is also the relationship implied by the next note, that large numbers of people *followed* him, for the word has regularly been used as the following which is discipleship. The groups mentioned have often been numbered among Jesus' supporters. The *people* have frequently stood in opposition to the leaders as enthusiastically supporting Jesus while the leaders cavil at him, and Luke has made a point of noting the support of the women who followed Jesus and his disciples.

The final lament

On his way to Calvary Jesus pronounces the last and most tragic of the laments for Jerusalem, so that his ministry in Jerusalem is bracketed at beginning and end by his sorrow at their failure to receive the message of peace. It had been prepared by Jesus' sadness as he approached Jerusalem on the great journey (13:34–35). Then the opening bracket of his ministry in Jerusalem was given as Jesus entered the city in 19:41–44. Now as he leaves Jerusalem comes the most solemn of all. It is so full of prophetic allusions and overtones that we are given clearly to understand that Jesus, the last of the prophets, is announcing the fulfilment of the dooms pronounced by so many of the Old Testament prophets against Jerusalem – with the solemn eschatological prophetic phrase, 'the days are coming when…' 'Daughters of Jerusalem' (or 'Zion') was a phrase often used in reproach at the failure of Jerusalem to repent (Isaiah 3:16; 16:1), and in invitations to join in mourning for the devastation of Jerusalem. The blessing on those whose wombs are barren is a dreadful reversal of so much that has been positive in Jewish tradition about the family and the blessing of children, and in particular in Luke about the blessedness of the womb that bore Jesus and the breasts that he sucked. Even worse is the despairing cry, calling the hills and the mountains to hide them from the awesome wrath of God.

Prayer

You have called me, Lord. I have no alternative to the choice of following you faithfully or refusing the call, as Jerusalem refused it. Grant me to respond and to follow your way of peace.

93 Luke 23:33
The crucifixion

There was no need to go into details about the grisly process of fixing to the cross. They were all too familiar to the original readers of the gospels. The spirituality of some ages has found it inspiring to dwell on the physical sufferings of Jesus. Others have found this a morbid distraction. As already pointed out, the early centuries of Christianity represented the triumph of Christ on the cross by a bejewelled cross rather than any realistic figure.

The explanation from scripture

The most obvious feature of the explanation of the shame of the cross was that Jesus was obeying the will of his Father manifested in scripture. This is expressed by the density of scriptural quotations and allusions throughout the Passion narrative, but especially in the account of the crucifixion. The division of Jesus' clothing, the jeering of the leaders, the friends standing at a distance, Jesus' final prayer – all are described in terms which recall passages in scripture. To the modern mind such detailed comparison, the product of the first-century Jewish approach to scripture, may fail to convey the meaning intended, and seem merely a series of fussily engineered coincidences. It is, however, the means of showing, by the exegetical methods of the time, that the scriptures and all the promises were fulfilled in the death of Jesus. Paul draws the threads together in his letter to the Romans, when he writes of the obedience of Christ, the second Adam, undoing the disobedience of the first Adam.

The obedience of Jesus

How, in practical terms, was Jesus' acceptance of his death an act of obedience to his Father? Throughout the gospel story we have seen Jesus as the final prophet, proclaiming and manifesting the kingship of God by his miracles, teaching, authority, forgiveness. He chose a nucleus of disciples whom he formed to follow him. The climax of his teaching was the daily teaching in the temple, at the very centre of the holy city of Jerusalem, God's dwelling on earth. Luke conveys vividly the ardour of his longing to make Jerusalem the centre from which his teaching would spread. Luke shows us that the people (the people of God) responded, but the leaders persisted in their blindness, which caused him so much distress. His obedience was to accept the failure and rejection, not to divert or wilt away from his message at what he knew lay before him. On the merely human level, let alone as a prophet, he would have known that the leaders would not accept this challenge to their authority. Luke stresses his obedience through the noble calm with which he accepts his destiny. From the 'agony' in Gethsemane to the willing resignation of his life into God's hands, Jesus is in charge of his destiny and voluntarily accepting it.

Golgotha

The name means 'skull'. Crucifixion was normally beside a road for maximum publicity, and all the gospels record that the normal *titulus* was affixed to the cross, detailing the alleged crime for which the criminal was being executed. Not only would this increase the shame and agony of the victim; it would also act as a deterrent to others who saw the twisted result of such pretensions. The traditional place, venerated today as Calvary, is just outside the walled city as it then was, beside the road to Joppe (Jaffa) on the coast. There was clearly a slight hill there into the rock of which tomb chambers have been dug. Presumably the place of crucifixion got its name as a knoll of rock in the shape of a skull. Since that time (possibly under Emperor Hadrian) this hill has been quarried away for building stone, leaving only a 'sugar lump' of rock, some 10 metres cubed. This cube seems to have been left because it is flawed by a great vertical cleft down the middle, which makes it useless for building. Pious legend attributes this cleft to the earthquake at the death of Jesus.

Prayer

Lord Jesus, you were obedient in all things to the will of your Father. Grant me the courage to follow your example. When the way is hard and painful, let me remember your steadfast and unflinching obedience, and obey with the same loving devotion which you showed.

94 Luke 23:34–43
The crucified Jesus

The first part of verse 34, 'Father, forgive them; they do not know what they are doing,' is absent in some good manuscripts. Some scholars think they are original and were cut out by some very early editor in an anti-Semitic attempt to obliterate the forgiveness of the Jews (though the executioners were surely Roman). Others think that they form an original saying of Jesus, inserted here later in part of the manuscript tradition. In any case, they form an invaluable glimpse of Jesus practising the forgiveness he taught others, for instance in the Lord's Prayer, and continue to illustrate the divine forgiveness which has featured so importantly in Luke's gospel. When Stephen is being stoned to death, he too makes a similar prayer for his executioners, but addressed to Jesus: 'Lord, do not hold this sin against them.' Here again we see the disciple imitating his master in suffering, and so carrying on the life of Jesus in the Christian community.

It is also a lovely prayer, beginning 'Father', so that Jesus' first words and his last words on Calvary testify to his affection for his Father, and his obedience to him. In semitic thought such a 'bracketing' process qualifies everything between the brackets, so that Jesus' state of mind on Calvary is being characterised as continuously in loving union with the Father.

The mockers

Luke makes a sharp distinction between the people and their leaders. The people merely look on; we shall hear more of their frame of mind later. The leaders mock Jesus, chiding him with being a Messiah who saved others and cannot even save himself. The irony is exquisite, that at the very moment of the completion of his messiahship, when he is indeed saving others at such voluntary cost to himself, he should be reproached with inability to save. This is the central point of the mockery: each of the mockers in turn challenges him to save – the leader, the soldiers and the thief.

The soldiers also join in to make fun of him. They offer him 'vinegar' to quench his thirst. Perhaps the basis of this is offering him a drink of the cheap wine they would have for themselves. It could originally have been a gesture of kindness. But the 'vinegar' is the fulfilment of a psalm verse, describing the mockery of an innocent sufferer. Their mockery of him as 'King of the Jews' (not in Mark or Matthew) is especially significant in view of the declaration of his kingship. This has been becoming clearer and clearer since, at Jericho, on the last stage of the journey to Jerusalem, Bartimaeus hailed him as 'Son of David'. Now the soldiers do not realise how right they are, and their irony brings the declaration of his kingship to a moment of climax.

The two thieves

In Mark and Matthew the two thieves are merely sketched. It is as though they are simply a fulfilment of the scriptural passage, quoted by Luke at the last supper, 'He was counted as one of the rebellious' (22:37). Luke, however, characteristically gives them each a vivid character and a lively dialogue. Luke likes to balance men and women in his stories, and it has been suggested that in their contrast these two men are the male counterpart of the contrasting sisters Martha and Mary. The one thief joins in the taunts. More important, the 'good thief' is the embodiment of repentance and discipleship. He admits not once but twice his own guilt: 'We deserved it: we are paying for what we did.' One might even suggest that perhaps his reasoning is a little too literary and philosophical for his situation, more adapted to Luke's cast of mind than to the circumstances! In Luke's story of the call of the disciples, Peter is not called to be a disciple until he has confessed that he is a sinner. Like Peter, once he has confessed his sinfulness, the good thief is promised the kingdom. Even to the last, Jesus is exercising his mission of reconciling the repentant. To the last, he is opening the kingdom to sinners.

Prayer

Bring me, Lord, to repentance in the end. Make me never too proud to admit my faults. In my own trials let me feel my solidarity with yours, that you may take me to join you in your kingdom.

95 Luke 23:44-49

The death of Jesus

Without introducing any new facts or events Luke gives a different and quite special atmosphere to the death of Jesus. The first striking feature is the calm and peace. The horror has disappeared. In the other synoptic gospels the death of Jesus follows immediately on a general stir around the cross. There is the cry of Jesus, 'My God, my God, why have you forsaken me?', which has been construed as a cry of despair; in fact it is the opening of Psalm 22, a psalm describing the suffering and rejection of the just man, which leads on to his vindication and the glory of God, all of which must be presumed to be present in Jesus' mind. There is the incident of the soldier running for the sponge and the mocking misunderstanding of the Hebrew words *eli, eli* ('My God, my God) as a summons to the prophet Elijah, a traditional figure of liberation from foreign oppression.

In Luke there is none of this. In Mark, the final cry of Jesus is left unexplained; in Luke, it is a prayer of confident trust, again beginning 'Father', and at this dire moment confirming the loving relationship of Jesus with his Father. After he has declared that he is ready, Jesus breathes his last.

The word for breath and spirit is the same in Greek and Hebrew. It is tempting to see in the word used to describe the moment of Jesus' death (literally 'he breathed out') a reference to the Holy Spirit, which will play such an important part in the future of Jesus' community. It is not so pointed as in John, when Jesus literally '*gave up* his spirit [or breath]' at his death. But the overtone may be there, that the moment of Jesus' death is the moment when the Spirit which was to inspire the community became available.

The signs

The significance of the death of Jesus is highlighted by two phenomena: darkness over the earth and the rending of the temple veil. Originally these were perhaps to be understood symbolically, but by adding small details Luke makes sure that they are viewed as real historical events. The darkness at noon must originally be seen as a fulfilment of Amos' prophecy of the day of the Lord, that terrible day of judgement, when

'I shall make the sun go down at noon and darken the earth in broad daylight' (Amos 8:9). It indicated, then, that this day was the fulfilment and completion of God's plan. Luke turns the symbolic dimension into a rational, factual account by giving the explanation 'the sun's light failed', as an eclipse of the sun. The other sign, the rending of the veil of the temple, is also understood in a physical sense, by the addition of the pictorial 'was torn *right down the middle*'. It must originally have had the sense of a symbol of the end of Judaism. This coincides with a tradition mentioned by Josephus that an omen of the destruction of the temple in AD70 was given by the veil which hung over the doorway being mysteriously torn from top to bottom 40 years earlier (signifying an indefinite, long period of preparation, like the 40 years in the desert). This dating would, of course, bring the incident near the date of the crucifixion.

The reactions

Before his death Jesus was mocked by three groups: the leaders of the Jews, the soldiers and the thief. After his death we hear of three groups of his supporters: the centurion who recognises that he was 'an upright man', the crowds and the disciples. In Mark's gospel, the centurion was the first human being to acknowledge Jesus as 'Son of God', and so mark the completion of the revelation of Jesus' personality. In Luke's version, the use of 'upright' is more in line with his sophisticated and philosophical bent.

The reaction of the crowds at the cross is the typical Lukan reaction of repentance and praise, a sense of unworthiness coupled with wonder and gratitude at the glory of God. So the series of conversions is complete, Peter brought back to strengthen his brethren after his failure, the daughters of Jerusalem, the good thief and now the whole gathering of witnesses. These stand for those who will in the future be brought to repentance and conversion by the cross of Jesus. Present also are the two silent groups of disciples, men and women, watching at a distance, so fulfilling Psalm 38:11: 'Friends and companions shun my disease, even the dearest of them *keep their distance*.'

Prayer

Father, into your hands I commit my spirit.

96 Luke 23:50–56

The burial of Jesus

The importance of the burial of Jesus for Luke is first, of course, the preparation for the accounts of the empty tomb and the resurrection, but second – and perhaps of more importance to Luke personally – that the gospel story has come full circle.

Joseph of Arimathea

The story began in Jerusalem with Zechariah, a priest and so a member of the Jewish establishment, who was like Joseph of Arimathea, good and upright, observant of the law in all its particulars. The next establishment figure we met, in the temple, was Simeon, who, again like Joseph, lived in the hope of seeing the kingdom of God. Luke has always been concerned with the salvation of Israel, how it is that the promises of God to Israel can have been fulfilled, although Jesus was rejected. On the whole his solution has been that part, at any rate, of the nation responded to Jesus. There is a sharp distinction between the leaders and the people; the latter accept Jesus eagerly, while the former acrimoniously reject him. Now, however, we see that even the leaders of the Jews were not uniformly hostile to Jesus. Joseph is from the heart of the establishment, from one of the cities of Judea and a member of the council, and yet a good and upright man who had had no part in the reprehensible dealings of the Sanhedrin.

In the slightly later legislation the burial of criminals was in the charge of a council department, the Lower Beth Din (or House of Judgement). Part of the penalty and disgrace of criminal execution was that the body might not be buried by relatives, but was to be placed in a municipal tomb for a year, until it had decayed. The relatives might then collect the bones. It has been suggested that Joseph was the member of this Lower Beth Din charged with this matter, by a happy accident a pious and open member of the council. Even though Joseph was an official, he must ask Pilate for the body. This is additional proof that, despite some appearances in Luke, the execution was a Roman affair, carried out by Romans and under the authority of the Roman governor.

Burial in Jerusalem

To make sense of the accounts it is essential to understand funeral arrangements in Jerusalem. The ground is uniformly rocky. An English-style six-foot burial in the earth is out of the question. At the time of Jesus the normal tomb was an underground stone chamber, reached down a flight of steps. Leading off this stone chamber (perhaps some three metres square) were half a dozen shafts big enough to receive a body. There the body was left till it had perished enough for the bones to be collected and placed in a sarcophagus, a sort of stone box. The accounts of Jesus' burial stress that this tomb was new and hitherto unused. This emphasis is partly out of respect for Jesus (many of the surviving used tombs are insanitary and unattractive), partly in preparation for the discovery of the empty tomb: there was no possibility of mistake over the vanished body.

The observance of correct burial ritual has always been regarded as an important part of respect for the dead. The matter of spices and ointments for burial has produced some confusion in the gospels. In Mark the women are bringing the spices on Easter morning when they find the empty tomb. The disgrace of Jesus being buried without due anointing has, however, already been avoided by the anointing 'for burial' at Bethany two days before the Passover. Luke omits this scene, replacing some of its elements with the story of the sinful woman (7:36–50, see p. 66). It is therefore all the more important that the body should be duly anointed, which does not seem to have been barred by its criminal status. However, due piety also demanded that they rest on the sabbath day, though there seems a little confusion about this. Luke says that the sabbath was already dawning, as though he thought that the sabbath began at dawn, when in fact it begins at sundown of Friday, which we would regard as the previous evening. The solution is perhaps that Luke adopted 'beginning to grow light' from Matthew's account of the discovery of the empty tomb.

Prayer

Lord, your day of rest between your gruesome death and your glorious resurrection is still precious, enabling us to assimilate that moment, and to see that you shared our mortal condition. Grant me to value the peace and special sanctity of that day.

97 Luke 24:1–8

The empty tomb

The Christian faith is founded on the resurrection of Christ, and the experience of the risen Christ in the community. This is the content of the earliest proclamation as conveyed by Paul (e.g. 1 Corinthians 15:3–5). He writes that he *received* this from the Lord and *handed* it *on* – the technical terms of the rabbinic process of tradition. Paul does not mention the empty tomb. It has been suggested that the story of the empty tomb as we have it now, with its stress on time and place, was originally the kernel of a liturgy at the place where the tomb was venerated, just as the story of the institution of the Eucharist was originally (and still is) the kernel of the eucharistic liturgy.

The emphasis in the story as told by Mark was on the wonder of the event, the awe and fear of the women at the explanation of the empty tomb given by the heavenly messenger. This terrified amazement springs from the fact that the resurrection of the dead, which was expected to occur at the end of time, has already now occurred. God has acted in history as he was to act on the last day, and the last time has therefore burst upon them. As so often, Luke's emphasis can best be seen by comparison with the way Mark tells his story.

All Luke's accounts of the resurrection appearances are in Jerusalem. Mark's angel of the tomb directs Peter and the other disciples to Galilee, where they are to see the risen Christ. In Matthew and John 21 there are corresponding appearances in Galilee. Not so in Luke. For him Jerusalem is the pivot to which Jesus journeys for his final ministry and death, where the risen Christ is seen, and from which the kerygma spreads to the ends of the earth. Accordingly, the angelic message is subtly changed. Instead of 'He is going ahead of you *to* Galilee; that is where you will see him, just as he told you' (Mark 16:7, referring to 14:28), the message is, 'Remember what he told you *when he was still in* Galilee' (24:6).

The reality of the risen body

Luke's first emphasis is on the physical reality of the resurrection. Thus he stresses that the tomb was really empty. In Mark the women enter the tomb and first see the angel. They are invited to see 'the place where they laid him' but there is no record that they actually did so, which would be necessary were it a proof text for the emptiness of the tomb. Luke, on the other hand, adds that 'they could not find the body of the Lord Jesus'. It may be also that the dual witness of the two angels is introduced for this purpose, since in Jewish law two witnesses are required for proof. In the same vein, in the story of the appearance to the disciples gathered in the upper room, the physical reality of the risen body of Jesus is shown by his actually eating a piece of grilled fish before their eyes (24:42). In the same way Luke had insisted at the baptism that the Spirit descended 'in a physical form', and will insist at Pentecost that the Spirit descends in the form of tongues of fire.

The proclamation of the risen Christ

The angels give the first glimpse of the proclamation which will echo through the stories of the appearances of the risen Christ and through the pages of Acts: 'The Son of Man was destined to be handed over into the power of sinful men and be crucified, and rise again on the third day.' This is to be the basic form of the message which is at the centre of all the speeches of Peter and Paul in their apostolate, from Jerusalem to Rome. The messengers underline three facets of this. It is all the fulfilment of the will of God expressed in scripture, since it 'was destined' to happen. It is the fulfilment of what was prophesied during Jesus' ministry, since 'they remembered his words'. The diffusion of the message is under the authority of Jesus himself, 'Remember what he told you.'

The stage is almost set for the proclamation of Acts. The risen Christ will himself twice give the example of the proclamation, to the disciples on the way to Emmaus, and to the eleven assembled in the upper room. For their own opportunity to make the proclamation the disciples will have to wait for the advent of the Spirit at Pentecost.

Prayer

Christ is now risen again, from his death and all his pain. Therefore will we merry be and rejoice with him always, alleluia.

98 Luke 24:9-12

The message to the eleven

The story of the finding of the empty tomb occurs in all the gospels, albeit with a range of variations. After that, however, comes a variety of stories, testifying to the appearances of the risen Jesus experienced by various members of the community. The most primitive tradition recorded by Paul in 1 Corinthians (15:3-5) mentioned appearances to Cephas (that is, the Aramaic equivalent of 'Peter'), the twelve, 500 of the brothers at the same time, James and then all the apostles. Apart from these, Matthew and John share a tradition about an appearance to Mary Magdalen (and other women) near the tomb, and Luke and John at least one appearance to the twelve in the upper room. Matthew and the appendix to John have widely differing traditions of an appearance in Galilee, a tradition at which Mark also hints.

There is also a strong tradition of scepticism. This may first of all lie behind the strange notice in Mark 16:8 that the women who went first to the tomb 'ran away' and 'said nothing to nobody, for they were afraid'. As it stands in Greek (as translated above), this verse shows all the features of Mark's personal style (the emphasis on fear and amazement, a double negative and the explanation added with 'for') which occur frequently throughout his gospel and serve as fingerprints of his own composition. But it certainly attests the tradition of non-communication of the message. Luke has the complete reverse, which nevertheless has the same effect. In Luke there is still non-communication of the message, but for an entirely different reason: the women tell the eleven, and they refuse to receive the message. To this is added the single verse about Peter's amazement and incomprehension.

The same need to be persuaded recurs in every story. In Matthew's story of the appearance on the mountain in Galilee, some hang back from doing reverence. In John, both Mary Magdalen and Peter fail at first to recognise the risen Christ. At the appearance in the upper room, 'doubting Thomas' voices the hesitations with explosive vigour. The whole tradition, therefore, is concerned to show that belief in the resurrection was no pushover, but had to be impressed upon the frightened survivors of Jesus' band of followers.

Luke and the women

This is the final instance in Luke where women come out ahead! Throughout the gospel he has shown the sensitivity of women to the divine message, from the contrast between Zechariah and Mary onwards. On the whole there has been a consistent pairing of women with men: Simeon and Anna; the two children raised to life (the one a son with a mother, the other a daughter with a father); the widow and the traveller at midnight both examples for persistence in prayer; all Jesus' friends (male) *and* the women watching on Calvary. Repeatedly also the reader has been reminded of the faithful band of women who looked after Jesus. Above all, Luke has been careful to paint Mary as the model of discipleship, hearing the word of God and keeping it. Now it is the women who are open to the message of the resurrection, and the chosen men who refuse to accept it.

Peter at the tomb

A single verse relates the story of Peter's puzzlement at the tomb. This is perhaps the strongest of all the traditions of failure to believe. (It is omitted in some versions because one stream of the manuscript tradition lacks this verse. But all the three great manuscripts have it.) The story comes again in John, and the same tradition must underlie both versions. In John the failure of Peter is expressed even more strongly. In John the 'beloved disciple' is the expression of love and openness, the ikon of the Christian disciple. He is added to this story as he was added to the story of Peter's denial during the Passion. His belief contrasts with Peter's disbelief. In Luke it is merely blank amazement, the seedbed of belief.

Prayer

Lord, grant me an openness to your word, but also a firm scepticism. Give me a strong faith, but help me to avoid that credulity which reduces your saving truths to silliness and brings contempt upon your generosity.

99 Luke 24:13-53
The road to Emmaus

Of all Luke's brilliantly told stories this is perhaps the most memorable. From the literary point of view its symmetry is superb: it starts and ends in Jerusalem; within this frame the disciples converse at both beginning and end; within this, Jesus first appears and finally disappears; within this, their eyes are first held from recognising him and then finally opened to recognise him. At the centre stands the message of the resurrection and its explanation. The story is told with all Luke's feeling for character: first the disciples are walking along, morose and wrapped up in their own sorrows; then their disappointment explodes into sarcasm, which gradually gives way to warmth, an invitation to the stranger to remain with them, and finally hospitality and eucharistic participation as their confidence returns. The delicacy of the stranger as he gradually draws them out, and the allusiveness of the gesture whose significance they realise in time only to find that he has left them, are finely painted. Especially positive is the contrast between the sad and lonely walk at the start, and the joyful, thronging gathering at the end.

A model of church life

The story provides a model for life in the Christian community in two ways, both the sacraments and instruction. From the sacramental viewpoint there is a remarkable and deliberate parallel with the story in Acts, of Philip and the Ethiopian. There also Luke gives the story of a journey, in which a seemingly chance-comer and stranger explains the gospel message from the scriptures; there follows a sacrament (the Eucharist in the case of the journey to Emmaus; in the case of the Ethiopian, baptism), and finally the stranger disappears. In both cases, therefore, we are given the model of scriptural instruction leading to sacramental participation in the life of Christ. In the case of the meal at Emmaus, it is precisely in the breaking of bread that Christ is recognised, acknowledged and accepted.

In both these cases the model of scriptural instruction is the salient feature. The story functions as a sort of paradigm of the Christian apostolate. The angel at the empty tomb has already given a brief example of this process, but the Emmaus story is far more explicit. By a literary device of Lukan brilliance the travellers tell us again, and more fully, the story of the empty tomb and the reactions to it. Then the risen Christ explains the meaning of what has happened as the fulfilment of the prophecies. Moses and the prophets lead directly to their destined fulfilment in the Passion and the entry into glory which is its consequence. Without this, the events are inexplicable and make no sense. At the end of his gospel, therefore, as in the Old Testament emphasis of the infancy narratives, Luke underlines that the Christ-event is the completion of the promises to Israel.

The prophet in word and deed

Once again, Jesus is presented – not by himself but by the disappointed disciples – as a prophet powerful in word and deed (the evidence of his authority throughout the gospel). It is the task of a prophet not merely to foretell the future, but to interpret the present, to read it through God's eyes. This Jesus now proceeds to do by explaining the recent happenings in the light of the scripture. He is also the model for the Christian evangelist, whose task it will be to show why it was necessary that the Christ should enter into his glory only by passing through suffering and death.

The conclusion of the journey with the Eucharist is also an important indication of the Christian life. That the meal is a Eucharist is suggested by the use of the identical terms at this meal of Jesus with his disciples, not only at the miraculous feeding in the desert, but also at the last supper. At the latter he had charged the disciples to repeat the action in his memory. Now he himself does so, and thereby creates his community, for in this moment the eyes of the disciples are opened, they reach understanding of what has happened and they enter into community with him. The Eucharist is the meeting of the community with the risen Lord, which in itself both brings to faith and creates the community.

Prayer

When all seems dark and disappointing, Lord, bring me your company. If I turn to you and see your way from suffering to glory, you will open my eyes and make me part of your company.

100 Luke 24:36–49
Jesus appears to the eleven

The final scene of the gospel appears to take place still on the Sunday of the resurrection, though it hardly fits that the two disciples should have rushed back the seven miles from Emmaus after the evening meal (steeply uphill!) in time for the final blessing on the outskirts of Bethany. The dramatic unity is more important than the details.

It shows the inner group of the disciples being prepared for their mission. The appearance of the risen Christ provokes the reaction of awed disbelief which is a feature of all the resurrection appearances. One particular Lukan feature is that they are prevented from recognising him by their joy at seeing him; Luke is perhaps the most joyful of the gospels – from the first moment of Jesus' birth rejoicing and singing on earth and in heaven are keynotes. The risen Jesus explains and shows that his body is real: he is not a ghost. He has hands and feet (there is no mention of nail scars either here or in the crucifixion account of Luke) and he eats a piece of fish before their eyes. Yet always the disciples have difficulty in recognising him. Awe and fear is only one component in this. The resurrection was not a mere resuscitation, as the miraculous raisings from the dead in the course of the gospel story (Jairus' daughter, the boy from Nain, Lazarus) seem to have been. It involved transposition into the glorious sphere of God, and this somehow must have had an effect on his appearance.

The risen body

We can perhaps form some cloudy idea of how different the appearance of the risen Christ was, by appeal to Paul. When in 1 Corinthians 15 Paul is teaching about how the risen body will be, he uses the image of the seed, which dies in the ground before fructifying. The transformation is described by Paul in terms of four changes, or three summed up in a fourth. Each is a transference into the sphere and power of God: 'What is sown is perishable, but what is raised is imperishable' (all potential for decay is removed); 'what is sown is contemptible, but what is raised is glorious' (there is no possibility of failure, but all is suffused with the awesome divine glory); 'what is sown is weak, but what is raised is powerful' (with God's own limitless power); 'what is sown is a natural body, and what is raised is a spiritual body' (the inner dynamism of the body is no longer the soul, but then is the Spirit of God). Such a change could well be somehow visible in the physical appearance of the same person, so that his friends would be awestruck from recognising him.

The commission

The scene is closely allied to the account of Christ's appearance in the upper room on the evening of the day of resurrection in John. The chief difference is that Jesus does not now breathe on them his Spirit, for in Luke the Spirit is merely promised now, and its imparting is reserved till Pentecost. There is the same greeting, 'Peace be with you,' and as we have seen, for Luke the gospel is above all a message of peace. Peace was the greeting of the angels at Jesus' birth, and the way of peace in the message of Jesus was what Jerusalem failed to recognise.

The final instructions of the risen Christ to his disciples again, as in all the resurrection appearances in Luke, stress that the key to understanding what has happened lies in the scripture. The angels at the empty tomb had already explained the event by reference to the scripture, and the stranger on the way to Emmaus explained the happenings in Jerusalem in relation to the prophets from Moses onwards. 'It was written': scripture and all the prophecies have been fulfilled in the death and resurrection of Jesus.

The other keynote is that they are to preach repentance. Luke has consistently underlined the need for repentance, and the welcome to sinners given by Jesus and his Father. Repentance will be the final appeal of all the great missionary speeches in Acts, as the apostles carry out this commission. A change of heart is necessary for every approach to Jesus.

Prayer

Lord, grant me to recognise you as you come to me in the word of your church, and give me the change of heart to embrace your way of peace.

101 Luke 24:50–53
The ascension

The timing

Luke is the only gospel writer to mention the ascension, and he describes it twice, once here and once at the beginning of Acts. There is a puzzle about the timing of the event. In the gospel it seems to occur on the day of the resurrection itself, though the time indication is vague ('then'), and it makes a very full day. In Acts it occurs only after 40 days – and these are both by the same author, who is acutely aware that his composition is to be read as a single work in two parallel volumes. It clearly simply was not a problem to him, just as in Acts he can tell the story of Paul's conversion three times, each time with minor and incompatible variations. The Jewish historian Josephus often tells the story of the same event differently in his two major volumes, the *Antiquities of the Jews* and the *Jewish War*.

Forty days in biblical language means a fairly long, indefinite period, often a period of preparation. Israel is 40 years in the desert, preparing to enter the promised land. Elijah remains 40 days in the desert of Horeb, preparing for his mission of preaching. And Jesus himself remains 40 days in the desert, being tested before he begins to proclaim the kingdom. It is therefore eminently fitting that his disciples should be prepared for their mission by Jesus' final instructions over a period of 40 days.

The blessing

The final action of Jesus is a solemn priestly blessing. 'Raising his hands' indicates just such a priestly gesture, but is full of priestly reminiscences. It is used, of course, of Moses raising his hands to ensure victory for the Israelites against the Amalekites. Overtones must be especially present from the blessing of Aaron in Leviticus 9:22, for this is the conclusion of the investiture of the priests, and its immediate realisation is in the manifestation of the power of the Lord as 'a flame leapt out from the Lord's presence'. Just so, the preparation of the disciples for their mission can be seen as a priestly investiture, concluded by the coming of the Spirit at Pentecost in the form of tongues of fire.

'He was taken up into heaven'

To the modern mind this picture raises difficulties about a three-decker universe, the Hebrew conception of a three-layered creation, heaven above, the earth and the underworld beneath. We are too familiar with paintings of a pair of feet still protruding from a cloud and with the question, 'Where is his body now?' The cloud is in fact the symbol of the divinity. The cloud over the tent of meeting or in the temple is always the sign of the presence of God, so that when (in the account in Acts) the cloud takes Jesus from their sight, this is a statement of his being taken up into the Godhead. The immediately following incident of the coming of the Spirit at Pentecost shows that he is being withdrawn merely in order to return in a more powerful mode of presence.

There is a further dimension of the scene which concludes the presentation of Jesus which has been so important in Luke. Throughout the gospel we have seen that Jesus is a prophet in the line of the Old Testament prophets. He is the climax of the messengers sent by God to his people, and as a prophet brings God's promises to a conclusion. The two great prophets of the tradition, Moses and Elijah, were both said to be taken up into heaven at the end of their lives. Now becomes obvious another dimension of the narrative of the transfiguration, when Moses and Elijah were seen speaking to Jesus about his passing (literally 'exodus') which he was to accomplish at Jerusalem (9:31). The most similar to the ascension is the departure of Elijah in a chariot of fire. It is also the most significant, for as Elijah departs his spirit descends upon his successor, Elisha, who then, clothed with this spirit, continues his mission. So the conclusion of the gospel is at the same time a preparation for the further mission which will be chronicled in Acts.

Prayer

Lord, grant me your Spirit, that I may continue your mission. Let me be your presence in the world, guided by your Spirit and faithful to your ways in all I do.

Friends of BRF

I never fail to be amazed by the generosity of our supporters.

BRF is a remarkable charity, but we can only do what we do with the help of our faithful supporters: volunteers, people who pray for us and spread the word about our work, and people who support us financially, both individuals who give donations and legacies, and charitable trusts.

Many of our supporters have become 'Friends of BRF', choosing to make a regular monthly gift to help ensure that our work can be sustained and developed in the coming years. Every single donation, whether occasional or regular, small or large, makes a huge difference and I, along with all my colleagues here at BRF, thank God for each one.

If you'd like to help support Living Faith and our wider ministry, please visit **brf.org.uk/give**, contact a member of the fundraising team by email at **giving@brf.org.uk** or call **01235 462305** to speak to one of us direct.

With heartfelt thanks

Julie

**Julie MacNaughton,
Head of Fundraising MCIOF(Dip)**

 *Enabling all ages to grow in faith*

Anna Chaplaincy
Living Faith
Messy Church
Parenting for Faith

100 years of BRF

2022 is BRF's 100th anniversary! Look out for details of our special new centenary resources, a beautiful centenary rose and an online thanksgiving service that we hope you'll attend. This centenary year we're focusing on sharing the story of BRF, the story of the Bible – and we hope you'll share your stories of faith with us too.

Find out more at **brf.org.uk/centenary**.

To find out more about our work, visit
brf.org.uk

THE PEOPLE'S BIBLE COMMENTARY

Mark

15 The Chambers, Vineyard
Abingdon OX14 3FE
brf.org.uk

Bible Reading Fellowship is a charity (233280)
and company limited by guarantee (301324),
registered in England and Wales

ISBN (boxed set) 978 1 80039 093 5
First published 1996
This edition published 2022
10 9 8 7 6 5 4 3 2 1 0
All rights reserved

Text © Dick France 1996, 2010
This edition © Bible Reading Fellowship 2022
Cover images: detail of Millennium window, St Agatha's Church,
Brightwell-cum-Sotwell, Oxon, photo © Rex Harris; background
© iStock.com/petekarici; gold texture © AmadeyART/stock.adobe.com

The author asserts the moral right to be identified as the author of this work

Acknowledgements
Scripture quotations are taken from The New Revised Standard Version of
the Bible, Anglicised Edition (NRSV), copyright © 1989, 1995 by the Division
of Christian Education of the National Council of the Churches of Christ in the
United States of America, and are used by permission. All rights reserved.

Every effort has been made to trace and contact copyright owners for material
used in this resource. We apologise for any inadvertent omissions or errors, and
would ask those concerned to contact us so that full acknowledgement can be
made in the future.

A catalogue record for this book is available from the British Library

Printed and bound by CPI Group (UK) Ltd, Croydon CR0 4YY

THE PEOPLE'S BIBLE COMMENTARY

Mark

Dick France

Photocopying for churches

Please report to CLA Church Licence any photocopy you make from this publication. Your church administrator or secretary will know who manages your CLA Church Licence.

The information you need to provide to your CLA Church Licence administrator is as follows:

Title, Author, Publisher and ISBN

If your church doesn't hold a CLA Church Licence, information about obtaining one can be found at **uk.ccli.com**

PREFACE TO THE 2010 EDITION

The first issue had no space for a preface, so all the general things I wanted to say about my approach to Mark had to go into the first two readings. Since then I have published a much bigger commentary on Mark (719 pages, on the Greek text!) and an even bigger one on Matthew. But further study has not changed my overall approach to the gospel in any significant way, and I hope readers will still be willing to tackle those first two readings seriously before launching into the text proper. Mark left us a *book*, not a collection of individual readings, and it is only when we appreciate his work as a whole that we have the necessary framework into which the individual parts can be fitted with real understanding.

It is always a pleasure to hear from readers who have found benefit from one's writing. I have been especially pleased that several have told me that they have taken up my suggestion of reading or listening to the whole of Mark's gospel in a single session (either alone or in a group) before tackling the individual readings, and that this has given them a new, and sometimes significantly different, appreciation of Mark's message. I am happy to repeat that recommendation for a new generation of readers.

Enjoy Mark!

Dick France

CONTENTS

Introduction 8

1. A drama in three acts 10
2. Setting the scene 12
3. The forerunner 14
4. What happened at Jesus' baptism 16
5. In the wilderness 18
6. The mission begins in Galilee 20
7. Partners in mission 22
8. Something new in the synagogue 24
9. In the evening 26
10. Keeping on the move 28
11. 'Unclean! Unclean!' 30
12. 'Who can forgive sins?' 32
13. Disreputable company 34
14. Old and new in religion ... 36
15. In the cornfields 38
16. More trouble on the sabbath 40
17. Beside the seaside 42
18. Twelve good men and true? 44
19. How do you explain Jesus? 46
20. 'Blasphemy against the Holy Spirit' 48
21. Insiders and outsiders 50
22. Introducing Mark's chapter of parables 52
23. What is a parable? 54
24. What happened to the seeds? 56
25. The secret 58
26. Spelling it out 60
27. More pregnant sayings 62
28. The dynamics of growth 64
29. From the least to the greatest 66
30. Storm at sea 68
31. A hopeless case 70
32. A short stay in Decapolis 72
33. 'Who touched me?' 74
34. 'Not dead, but sleeping' 76
35. A difficult visit to Nazareth 78
36. The mission is extended 80
37. Jesus and John the Baptist 82
38. The dance of death 84
39. An abortive 'retreat' 86
40. Food in the wilderness 88
41. Panic on the lake 90
42. More healings 92
43. What is purity? 94
44. Putting the cart before the horse 96
45. Clean hands and a pure heart 98
46. Crumbs for the Gentiles 100
47. Another Gentile healed 102
48. Food for the Gentiles too 104
49. Asking for a sign 106
50. Difficult questions on the lake 108

#	Title	Page
51	A blind man cured – by stages	110
52	Peter declares his faith	112
53	A dose of cold water	114
54	Ultimate realities	116
55	The veil is drawn aside	118
56	What about Elijah?	120
57	Why the disciples failed	122
58	Another warning of what is to come	124
59	Who is the greatest?	126
60	'Not one of us'	128
61	Hard sayings	130
62	No place for divorce	132
63	Did Jesus really mean it?	134
64	Whose is the kingdom of God?	136
65	A potential disciple lost	138
66	No hope for the rich?	140
67	The death march	142
68	An inappropriate request	144
69	'Not so among you'	146
70	Another blind man	148
71	The arrival of the king	150
72	A demonstration in the temple	152
73	The fruitless fig tree	154
74	The challenge from officialdom	156
75	Getting rid of the son	158
76	The poll tax	160
77	The God of the living	162
78	The two great commandments	164
79	David's Lord	166
80	A telling contrast	168
81	The temple to be destroyed	170
82	The disciples' question	172
83	The beginning of the birth pangs	174
84	Crisis in Judea	176
85	The climax of judgement	178
86	An unknown day	180
87	A woman to be remembered	182
88	The priests and Judas Iscariot	184
89	The Passover meal	186
90	Startling symbolism	188
91	Trouble ahead	190
92	Gethsemane	192
93	Betrayal and arrest	194
94	Before the Sanhedrin	196
95	The secret is unveiled	198
96	The witness who failed	200
97	Enter Pontius Pilate	202
98	Barabbas	204
99	Homage to the 'king'	206
100	Golgotha	208
101	Mockery	210
102	Alone on the cross	212
103	The end?	214
104	Dead and buried	216
105	'He is not here'	218
106	How did Mark finish his gospel?	220
107	Mark's good news – a retrospective	222

INTRODUCTION

Many members of the first-century churches could not read, and many more could not afford to possess a scroll of their own. So we should think of our New Testament books as intended to be read aloud, when the members of the church were gathered together.

Mark's gospel, the shortest of the four, may well have been intended to be read out in a single session. It takes about an hour and a half to read aloud, and the experience of listening to it (and still more of reading it) in this way is thrilling, as those who have attended Alec McCowan's hugely popular one-man recitations of the gospel will know.

Mark the storyteller

It is when you read Mark's gospel in a single session that you see most clearly what a well-written story it is. Threads of continuity come to light, and there is a skilful build-up (and sometimes release) of tension, comparable to that achieved by some of the best dramatists.

The author must have been a popular communicator. His style is more expansive and vivid than that of the other gospel writers, and he seems to relish a lively scene. His gospel is shorter than the others not because he writes concisely (where he runs parallel with the other gospels, especially Matthew, he is often much more long-winded), but because he has limited his material. While he says much about Jesus' power as a teacher, he offers less of his actual teaching than the other gospels. He writes rather of eager crowds and impressive miracles, of dramatic confrontation with opponents both human and demonic. He allows us to feel the disconcerting impact of Jesus on his often bewildered disciples, and to share with them the experience of having their world turned upside-down by the revolutionary values of the kingdom of God. He presents in all its starkness the paradox of a rejected and executed Messiah, of a Son of God who meets with incomprehension and hostility from the people of God.

It is all intensely moving, as the story forges ahead with breathless urgency towards the inevitable showdown in Jerusalem, where on a small local stage a drama of cosmic proportions is played out.

The trouble is that for most Christian readers it is now all so familiar that it is almost impossible for us to feel the disconcerting and yet exhilarating impact which the story must have had on those who first heard it. Let me urge you, therefore, if you possibly can, to arrange at best to hear Mark's story told in a single session, or, failing that, to set aside an hour and a half and read it through yourself (in a modern version) as if it were a novel, trying to put yourself in the position of those who first heard the story and for whom it was all so powerfully new. When you have done that, you will be in a better position to see the significance of the individual sections as we work through them in this book.

Mark and Peter

Very early Christian tradition tells us that the gospel was written by John Mark of Jerusalem (Acts 12:12), who was later a colleague both of Paul (Acts 12:25; Colossians 4:10; 2 Timothy 4:11) and of Peter (1 Peter 5:13), and that it was when he was Peter's assistant that Mark decided to record the stories about Jesus which Peter was in the habit of telling in his later days in Rome. The early writers are divided as to whether he did this while Peter was still alive (and with his blessing) or after Peter's death in, probably, AD64 or 65. It seems a plausible tradition, and in Mark's action-packed gospel it may well be that we hear at least an echo of the enthusiastic way in which Peter would have told the stories of the man who had changed his own life and outlook so irrevocably.

The value of Mark

In the early centuries of the church's life, Mark's gospel was undervalued. It was felt to be inferior especially to that of Matthew, which had so much more detailed teaching of Jesus and went into greater theological depths. Since they believed that Matthew's gospel was written first, Mark was too easily dismissed as his 'lackey and abridger' (Augustine). It was only with the growth in the 19th century of the belief that Mark was the earliest gospel that this shorter book came into its own. Nowadays most scholars value Mark as the earliest surviving record of the life and teaching of Jesus of Nazareth. Mark's Greek is lively but not very polished, in the style of the popular storyteller, rather than the sophisticated prose of a professional writer. Where a stylist would recommend subordinate clauses, Mark often strings sentences together with a simple 'and', so that the story rattles quite jerkily along. He is particularly fond of moving the action on with 'immediately' (eleven times in chapter 1 alone, though English versions tend to ration them). It is not easy to get bored as you listen to Mark!

Dick France

1

Mark's gospel

A drama in three acts

After a prologue which sets the scene, Mark's story unfolds in three main sections, each of which has a distinct geographical setting:

1:1–13	Prologue (set in 'the wilderness')
1:14—8:21	Act 1: Galilee
8:22—10:52	Act 2: On the way to Jerusalem
11:1—16:8	Act 3: Jerusalem

The different geographical locations of the three acts serve to show the movement of the story towards its conclusion in Jerusalem, but there is much more to the three-act division than that. The story moves through three distinct phases, in terms both of the nature of Jesus' ministry and of the way people react to it, while the geographical movements serve to underline, and in a significant way even to symbolise, this movement of the plot towards its climax.

Galilee and Jerusalem

Few modern readers of the New Testament realise that first-century Palestine was not a simple unity. Galilee, where most of Jesus' story takes place, was in almost every way separate from Judea (and its capital, Jerusalem). Between them stood the hostile territory of Samaria. Their histories had been separate for most of the 1,000 years since the days of a united Israel under David and Solomon, and they lived under different political systems (at the time of Jesus, Pontius Pilate was the Roman governor in Judea, Herod Antipas the Jewish 'king' in Galilee). Galilee was for most of its history more subject to foreign control, and had been dubbed by Isaiah 'Galilee of the Gentiles'. Its Jewish population were regarded by the Judean Jews as both racially suspect and religiously unorthodox. Galileans had their own dialect of Aramaic, and a Galilean Jew in Jerusalem would have been as obviously 'foreign' as an Irishman in London or a Texan in New York.

The plot

Jesus was a Galilean, and it is in Galilee that Mark tells of the warm popular response to his ministry. It is this period of 'success' which dominates Act 1, set in Galilee; Jesus is among his own people. Of course there are doubters and outright opponents even in this part of the story, but it is significant that Mark twice makes the point that these opponents are not local, but have come 'from Jerusalem' (3:22; 7:1).

Act 3 begins with Jesus' arrival, for the first time in Mark's narrative, in Jerusalem, where he is a stranger. Here, by contrast with Act 1, apart from the Galilean disciples who have come with Jesus to Jerusalem and escort him triumphantly into the city, the overall picture is one of darkness and increasing confrontation, leading up to the death of Jesus at the hands of the authorities of the capital. The darkness is relieved by the prediction of resurrection, but it is not in Jerusalem but in Galilee that the risen Lord will again meet his disciples (14:28; 16:7). Between these two sharply opposed scenes, Act 2 forms a bridge in two main ways (apart from the geographical movement from north to south). First, it is punctuated by Jesus' explicit predictions of the fate which awaits him in Jerusalem (8:31; 9:31; 10:33–34), so that the shadow of the cross now falls darkly across the story, and Jesus' determined southward journey becomes a death-march. Second, the focus of his ministry now moves from public preaching and miracles to the private instruction of his disciples, preparing them for what lies ahead, and patiently re-educating them away from facile hopes of glory to the acceptance of the way of the cross, and the whole new scale of values which it entails.

Reading Mark

All this adds up to a deliberate and quite sophisticated shaping of the story which we do well to notice if we are to hear the story of Jesus as Mark (and Peter) told it. To see Jesus in this human dimension of a divided society is to be made even more aware of how he challenges and overturns all human expectations. The kingdom of God does not operate according to the rules of the kingdoms of this world. It is a kingdom in which the last are first and the first last, where greatness is in humble service and where death is the way to life.

Was there ever another drama like this one?

Prayer

Open my eyes, so that I may behold wondrous things out of your law.
PSALM 119:18

2

Mark 1:1–3

Setting the scene

'The wilderness', mentioned four times in verses 1–13 and never again in Mark's gospel, is a pointer to the different focus in these introductory paragraphs. They are set not among human society in Galilee or Judea, but in the uninhabited land around the Jordan. Before the story proper begins, Mark as it were takes us aside into a lonely place to brief us on what it will all be about.

A glimpse behind the scenes

What he offers in his prologue (1:1–13) is a glimpse behind the scenes, to help us to grasp the deeper significance of the human stories which will follow. First a sonorous quotation from the prophetic hopes of the Old Testament leads us via the larger-than-life figure of John the Baptist in the wilderness to ponder the identity of the even greater one whose coming he announced. And there in the wilderness we see heaven opened, and hear the voice of God himself endorsing the mission of his Son. In the wilderness too we see Jesus in the company of Satan and angels. The supernatural dimension to these opening scenes is further reinforced by noticing that Mark, who elsewhere seldom mentions the Spirit of God, here includes three references to him.

All this provides us, the readers, with a privileged access to the real significance of what is to follow, supplying a dimension which we might otherwise easily lose sight of in the hurly-burly of Jesus' public ministry in Galilee, and still more later in Jerusalem.

Good news

When Mark wrote his book, 'gospel' was not the name of a kind of writing, but meant simply 'good news'. That is how Mark labels the story he is about to tell: this is worth hearing! The opening verse sums it up by reminding us of who Jesus is. First, he is the Messiah – and it is worth remembering whenever we read of 'Christ' in the New Testament that it is not just a name but the special title, which surely no Jew could hear without excitement, of the promised deliverer of God's people. And second, he is the 'Son of God', a term which Mark will record at several key points in his story, and which immediately alerts us to expect something more than the biography of an ordinary man.

A voice in the wilderness

So we begin with some words from the Old Testament to alert us to the importance of the story to follow. They are words which take us to the heart of the hope which had grown throughout the Old Testament period that one day God would act decisively to fulfil his purpose for his people.

The quotation from 'Isaiah' in verses 2–3 is in fact a combination of related prophetic texts about 'preparing the way'. Malachi 3:1 speaks of a messenger who will prepare the people for the Lord's coming as judge, while in Isaiah 40:3 a voice in the wilderness proclaims that God is about to come and deliver his people from their long exile. The messenger and the 'voice' are heralds, forerunners of the great day of God's decisive action. It is all about to begin, here in the wilderness.

But the person of whom these prophecies speak is not yet Jesus. Jesus will not appear until verse 9. The forerunner of God is another and slightly earlier prophet, John. Before Jesus even appears on the scene, the drama has begun, and scripture is being fulfilled as a new voice is heard in the wilderness, calling the people of God to repentance, so that they will be ready for the Lord's coming.

We shall meet this extraordinary prophetic figure in the next study.

Prayer

Thank you that this book is 'good news'. Help us to appreciate how important it is, to be excited about it, and to be as eager as Mark was to pass it on to others.

3 Mark 1:4–8

The forerunner

John the Baptist was a more important figure than many Christians today realise. Indeed, in Josephus' history of the Jews in the first century there is more about John than about Jesus. He made a big impact with his 'revivalist' movement down in the Jordan valley, and Jesus several times referred back to him with appreciation. In a sense, Jesus carried on where John left off, and people naturally saw Jesus as John's successor, despite the difference in their styles of ministry.

The prophet of restoration

Just as Old Testament prophets had often called on Israel to return from their backsliding and to live again as the people of God, so now John calls for repentance and for a new start. His rough clothes are modelled on those of Elijah (2 Kings 1:8), and like Elijah he preaches an uncompromising message and calls people to decision. Those who knew the prophecy of Malachi 4:5–6 that Elijah must return to prepare for the coming of the great and terrible day of the Lord would not have been slow to see the connection. Here in the wilderness something of decisive significance is beginning.

As a symbol of their repentance, John baptises those who respond to his message. This was a novel and rather shocking idea, since baptism was the means by which Gentiles who wished to adopt the Jewish religion were admitted to the community of Israel, as 'proselytes'. But these people John is preaching to are Jews! In asking them to be baptised he is in effect declaring that their Jewishness is in itself no guarantee that they are right with God; they too need a new start. As they join him in the water of the Jordan they are enrolling in a new community of the forgiven and restored people of God, a true 'remnant' in whom God's purposes for Israel can be carried forward. Israel is being reborn.

Looking forward

But John does not think that he is himself the one who will effectively restore Israel. He is only the herald, the 'voice in the wilderness'. So he points forward to someone still to come, someone 'more powerful'. John's baptism in Jordan water is merely a symbol of renewal, but the 'more powerful one' will bring the true baptism not with physical water but with the Holy Spirit. Those upon whom the Spirit of God comes will know true inward renewal. That will be the real thing.

So who is the 'more powerful one'? Christians, who know the story already, will answer without hesitation that it is Jesus – and in verse 9, sure enough, Jesus will 'come', as John has predicted. But wait a minute. In Old Testament prophecy the one who will pour out the Spirit in the last days is God himself. And the verses which Mark has quoted from Malachi and Isaiah speak of a herald of the coming of God. So John's language would naturally have been understood by those who heard him (and by John himself?) as referring not to any human figure but to the imminent coming of God to judge and save his people, as the prophets had so often foretold. The fact that it was in the coming of Jesus that his prediction of the 'more powerful one' was fulfilled suggests something amazingly far-reaching about who Jesus is: more than a prophet like John, more even than only a human Messiah. In the coming of Jesus, God comes, for, as Mark has already reminded us, Jesus is himself the 'Son of God'.

For meditation

Who are the true people of God today? If John were to preach among us now, who would respond?

Are there ways in which we focus our attention on the outward and symbolic (like John's baptism with water) rather than on the inward and real?

4 Mark 1:9-11

What happened at Jesus' baptism

The baptism itself is mentioned almost in passing; it is what happened then that Mark wants us to know about. He seems to find no problem in the fact that Jesus, whom Christian theology has always maintained to be sinless, was willing to accept a 'baptism of repentance for the forgiveness of sins'. (Matthew, by contrast, clearly saw this as a problem: see Matthew 3:14–15.) Probably we should see Jesus' acceptance of baptism as his 'vote' for John's programme of a restored Israel, his personal identification with the new community which John's preaching was gathering together. But that is not where Mark's interest lies.

A supernatural revelation

Everything about this little paragraph (except for the baptism itself) is 'larger than life'. Heaven is torn open, the Spirit is seen coming down upon Jesus, and God speaks from heaven affirming that he is indeed the Son of God. Father, Son and Spirit appear briefly together on the earthly stage.

It seems odd that such an open divine endorsement should have left people still uncertain about Jesus in the story that follows. But perhaps we should not see this as a public revelation. Mark tells it entirely from the point of view of Jesus himself, as what he saw and heard, in a voice addressed to him in the second person, not to the crowds by the Jordan. It is Jesus, not the people around, who is being assured of his divine status and mission.

But we, the readers, are let into the secret, so that we, unlike the people who were to hear and see Jesus around the villages of Galilee, have a vital clue to help us understand the significance of the story Mark is going to tell. This is not just any religious teacher, not even another John the Baptist, but the Son of God, equipped for his mission by the power of the Spirit of God. The 'more powerful one' has arrived, but he has come not in the overwhelming splendour of a divine visitation, but in the utterly improbable form of an unknown countryman, 'Jesus from Nazareth of Galilee' – about as unimpressive and obscure a pedigree as you could imagine (especially if you were a Judean)! And he appears not in the corridors of power, but as one among a crowd of penitents on the banks of a muddy river in the wilderness of Judea. God certainly has a surprising and low-key way of changing the world. He does not seem to have absorbed the principles of PR.

Pregnant words

'You are my Son, the Beloved; with you I am well pleased.' A similar formula will be heard again (and again from the mouth of God himself) when Jesus is transfigured on the mountain in 9:7, though at that time it will be addressed not to Jesus but to his disciples. Those who know their Old Testament can find more in these words than a simple declaration of Jesus as Son of God (though that must remain the main point of the heavenly oracle).

They echo God's introduction of his 'servant' in Isaiah 42:1, the servant who is to suffer and die for the sins of the people. They echo Psalm 2:7, where God greets the messianic king as his Son. And they carry a plaintive echo of the words which, in Genesis 22:2, set Abraham on the road which was to lead to the sacrifice of 'your only son, whom you love'. There is rich material here for meditation on what Jesus' mission as Son of God is going to mean to him – and also to his Father. The journey which begins by the Jordan will finish at Golgotha in a sacrifice more far-reaching even than Abraham had steeled himself to offer; but this time the unhappy father will be God himself.

Prayer

Thank you, Lord Jesus, for accepting the servant's mission; thank you, Spirit of God, for the strength to carry it through; thank you, Father, for not withholding your only Son from the ultimate sacrifice. Help us to appreciate what our salvation has cost.

5

Mark 1:12–13

In the wilderness

At this point in the story both Matthew and Luke offer us a blow-by-blow account of Jesus' temptations in the wilderness, with the familiar threefold question and answer between Satan and Jesus. Mark merely mentions that he was being tempted, but that is all. This final scene of the prologue to Mark's drama is not so much the record of an event as a sort of tableau. Here, far from the scenes of ordinary life, and with no other human being in sight, we see ranged against each other the forces which will be active behind the scenes of the story of Jesus. It is an introduction to the dramatis personae, not of the earthly drama but of the spiritual conflict which will underlie it.

Behind the scenes

The initiative is taken not by Satan but by the Spirit of God, whom Jesus has seen descending upon him at the Jordan. It is he who 'drives' Jesus into the wilderness, away from the human companionship of John and his followers. This time of hardship and of spiritual conflict is not an accident, nor even merely a regrettable necessity. It is planned by God, and as Jesus goes through it he will have the support not only of the divine Spirit, but also of angels to look after him. On the other side there is Satan, the arch-enemy of the purposes of God, and the wild beasts, who represent danger and hostility.

So Jesus, newly declared to be Son of God, now faces up to the implications of that role. The world is a battlefield between God and Satan, good and evil, and Jesus' mission will take him into the heart of that battle. He will again and again confront the spiritual forces of evil, most obviously when he must expel them from those who are possessed, but also as they work through the human opposition which will be a constant undertone of his ministry, and which will in the end lead him to the final conflict on the cross.

The wilderness – place of new beginnings

The wilderness in the Old Testament is a place of hardship and of conflict, of testing and of discipline (Deuteronomy 8:2–5). But it is also a place of hope, the place where God first met and married his 'bride'

Israel (Jeremiah 2:2–3), and the place where the marriage must again be restored (Hosea 2:14–15). So it is 'in the wilderness' that the voice of the herald must be heard (Isaiah 40:3), and in the wilderness the amazing creative power of God will again be deployed for the salvation of his people (Isaiah 35). It was for this reason that the community of the Dead Sea Scrolls set up their headquarters not in Jerusalem but 'in the wilderness' down by the Dead Sea (not very far from the place where Mark 1:2–13 is set); this was where they believed that God must begin the process of restoration in the last days.

All this pregnant symbolism underlies Mark's prologue, in which we are taken to the wilderness to be shown the real significance of the very human drama which is now about to unfold. We have been privileged to see what no human eye at the time could see, and we must not forget it as the scene closes in and the story proper begins. This is the long-prophesied time of God's coming to judge and to save his people; the ultimate conflict between good and evil has begun.

For meditation

Do we take seriously enough (a) the spiritual dimension which underlies our earthly lives and (b) the reality of spiritual evil as well as good? What does Mark's way of introducing his gospel tell us about how he thought of the Old Testament in relation to the Christian story? Have we grasped its significance in the same way?

6 Mark 1:14–15

The mission begins in Galilee

The prologue is over. We are no longer 'in the wilderness', but in the real world of ordinary men and women in the villages of Galilee. This is Jesus' home province, though the focus of his mission will prove to be not in the hills around Nazareth but down by the lake, some 20 miles away.

After John – a new beginning

It was in the context of John's revivalist mission by the Jordan that we first met Jesus, but now that mission has come to a sudden end, as Mark will explain more fully later (see 6:17–29). Rather than continue a baptising ministry by the Jordan (with the danger of being seen simply as another John, and thus possibly sharing John's fate), Jesus launches into a new style of mission, with a new message. He will not stay in one place, but will travel around the province, finding people where they are. And as he goes he will preach good news. Mark has already used this term in the first sentence of his book, to sum up what he has to tell about Jesus. Now he uses it twice more in these verses, to sum up the essence of what Jesus himself preached in Galilee. John's message was more negative and preparatory: repent and be baptised ready for the coming of the 'more powerful one'. Now there is 'good news of God' to be heard and to respond to. The reader knows, even if it was not yet clear to spectators at the time, that with the coming of Jesus the 'more powerful one' is already on the scene.

God is king!

The 'slogan' which sums up Jesus' new message is 'the kingdom of God'. In the first three gospels this phrase is constantly on Jesus' lips; it summarises all that he has come to proclaim and to achieve. It is a phrase rich in echoes of the faith of Israel. God is the rightful king of the world, which he has made, and of everyone in it. But the Old Testament also recognises that not all people acknowledge and submit to God's rule, and so the idea also grew that one day God's rule would be more truly established and his purpose for his world brought to fruition. The 'kingship of God' (for that is what the word means, rather than 'kingdom' thought of as a place or a group of people) thus became not only an eternal truth, but also a future hope. And it is that hope which Jesus' message now triggers. No Jew hearing these words could have missed the point. God is now taking control, and he is doing it through the message and the mission of Jesus, the Messiah.

Now, or not yet?

The kingship of God 'has come near'. Is this saying any more than John had already proclaimed, that people must be ready for what God would soon do? Yes, it is: the perfect tense of the verb ('has come near' rather than 'is coming near'), together with the equally strong perfect which precedes it ('The time has been fulfilled') indicates the present rather than the future. God's rule is already breaking in, and it is time to respond now, not in the future, by repentance and faith in the good news which Jesus has now brought. The days of preparation are over: this is the real thing.

For us, 2,000 years later, the urgency of those heady days may seem far away. But the essential Christian message is unchanged. God is king, and all people are now called to submit to his rule. The good news which Jesus brought, and which this book will richly fill out, is now, as it was then, the ultimate reality to which we must respond and which we must declare to those around us.

Prayer

Thank you, Lord, for good news in a world where bad news so often fills the headlines. Help us to value it, both by following Jesus ourselves in repentance and faith and by inviting others to come under your loving rule. May your kingdom come!

7 Mark 1:16–20

Partners in mission

Mark has barely begun his account of Jesus' mission when he tells us that Jesus called others to share it with him. All through the gospel from this point he will tell not merely the story of Jesus, but the story of Jesus and his disciples, as a team. Jesus, whom we have come to recognise as the unique Son of God and the 'more powerful one' predicted by John, nonetheless shares his mission with others. As the gospel goes on they will often prove to be as much an embarrassment as a help, but Jesus will be committed to them, as they will to him. And when he is gone, it will be on them that the ongoing mission will depend.

The inner circle

Later Jesus will select twelve disciples to accompany him on his travels, but the four we meet in this passage will be mentioned at the head of the list, and several times (usually without Andrew) they will be the only ones allowed to share some of Jesus' more private moments (1:29; 5:37; 9:2; 13:3; 14:33). They were, it seems, not merely assistants in the mission, but close companions with whom Jesus could share secrets. Even the Son of God needed human support and sympathy!

As Mark tells the story, the call to these four fishermen to follow Jesus seems to come out of the blue. But John 1:35–42 mentions another meeting of Jesus with Andrew and Simon (and possibly John?), which was apparently earlier than this one. They had already concluded then that Jesus was the Messiah, and so the call now to drop everything and follow him, while it was sudden and drastic in its implications, did not need to be thought about for very long. Quite likely they had been waiting and hoping for it since that meeting down by the Jordan.

Simon and Andrew leave their nets; James and John leave their father and his crew in the boat. With these deft brush-strokes Mark spells out for us what it will really mean for those first disciples to follow Jesus. The safe, predictable, ordinary life of work and family gives place to an itinerant lifestyle, with no visible means of support – and in the end the ignominious failure of abandoning their master to his fate in a Jerusalem garden. Following Jesus has never been a soft option.

Fishing for people

So why did they do it? Of course there are many levels of answer, even if at this stage they may not have been able to articulate them very clearly. But the one thing that Jesus has offered them is a new profession, fishing for people. (Isn't it a pity that the resonant old phrase 'fishers of men' is no longer appropriate in these days of inclusive language? Of course it is correct to include women and children in the catch, but the pun on 'fishermen' does go a bit flat!) Jeremiah 16:16 talked about God sending fishermen to catch people for judgement, but Jesus' fishermen are going to save people from judgement, to catch them for the kingdom of God. Jesus' disciples have been doing it ever since. The Christian gospel is not a cosy reassurance that everybody is entitled to their point of view, and that the only sin is to rock the boat. It is about catching people out of their native waters and transferring them to a whole new life.

For meditation

Have we lost something of the biblical dimensions of discipleship? What have we left for Jesus? Does he matter to us enough for us to take risks for him? Does our understanding of the good news make it natural for us to want to 'catch' others?

8

Mark 1:21–28

Something new in the synagogue

Simon and Andrew lived in Capernaum (1:29), and their home now became Jesus' base for much of his time in Galilee. In 1:21–38 Mark tells us of 24 hours in Capernaum, beginning with the sabbath service in the synagogue and going through to early the next morning, when Jesus will set off for a more widespread mission. Perhaps we are to think of this as a 'typical' day in the life of Jesus and his disciples?

Teaching with authority

All good Jews attended the synagogue on the sabbath, but to be asked to teach was a privilege. Jesus is already gaining a reputation as a teacher, and the reaction of the people in the Capernaum synagogue shows that it was well deserved. The thing which impresses them is his authority, a word which will often occur in the gospels as a characteristic of Jesus' ministry, both in word and in action. Given what we, the readers of the gospel, already know about Jesus from the prologue, this comes as no surprise, but for the people of Capernaum to hear a young man from the obscure hill village of Nazareth teaching with such authority was astonishing. Mark mentions particularly the contrast with the way the scribes taught – learned and judicious no doubt, but essentially second-hand and predictable. Scribes quoted other rabbinic authorities and weighed up traditional arguments, but did not err on the side of originality. But Jesus is different, bold, dynamic, demanding and exhilarating.

Authority in deed as well as word

Verses 23–26 record the first of several stories of exorcism which Mark will tell. He clearly wants us to see this as a central part of Jesus' ministry, and one which testifies to his unique authority. Not that exorcism was a totally new thing; there is evidence that other Jews engaged in it, as Jesus himself recognises in Matthew 12:27. But what is new about Jesus is not only the frequency of such occurrences in his ministry, but also the extraordinary control which he is able to exercise over demonic forces (Mark usually calls them 'unclean spirits', whereas the other gospel writers speak generally of 'demons'). In this story we notice how the spirit immediately recognises Jesus as someone special, 'the Holy One of God', and assumes that his arrival spells disaster for the powers of evil (notice the 'us'); and how Jesus needs no elaborate ritual or magical formulae (as other exorcists usually did), but dismisses the spirit with an almost contemptuous 'Shut up and get out'! No wonder people were astonished, and Jesus' fame began to spread.

For most Christians in the Western world today, the idea of possession by a personal force of evil, and of the expulsion of a demon, leaving the 'host' changed and restored to normality, sounds at best exotic and at worst decidedly suspect. They would much rather not know about it. But there are times even in glossy Western society when the reality of spiritual evil cannot be ignored, and in some other parts of the world witchcraft, voodoo and the occult are part of daily experience. In Jesus' world, and for Mark, the demonic dimension was as real as the divine, and a Messiah who left the forces of evil unchallenged would be of little interest. There is no sphere of life which falls outside his extraordinary authority; there is no predicament into which people may fall from which he cannot rescue them.

Prayer

Thank you, Lord Jesus, that yours is 'the name high over all', that there is no power which can stand against you. Help us gladly to acknowledge your authority in all aspects of our lives, and to know that with you as our Lord there is nothing we need fear.

9 Mark 1:29–34

In the evening

Straight after the first exorcism comes the first healing. The contrast is remarkable. The first was a dramatic confrontation with evil in a very public arena; the second is the healing of a sick woman in private in her own home. But both are part of the work of restoration on which the Messiah has embarked.

In Simon's house

Simon and Andrew came originally from Bethsaida (John 1:44), but now they lived in the important lakeside town of Capernaum, from which they had until recently run their fishing business. When they left their nets to follow Jesus, they had not given up their home, and this was probably the house in which Jesus was based while he was in Capernaum. There seems good reason to believe that it was this same house which was later covered by an octagonal church building of the fifth century, the remains of which may still be seen in Capernaum. It is not many yards away from the synagogue, and here the small group return after the service. The healing of Simon's mother-in-law is reported in quite a matter-of-fact way. Her 'fever' may not have been a very serious complaint, but it receives Jesus' immediate attention. The fact that this is apparently still the sabbath is not commented on, though in 3:1–6 healing on the sabbath will become a very serious issue. But this is a private affair, with no Pharisees around to be offended!

The end of the sabbath

Mark emphasises the time, since the sabbath ended at sunset. As long as it was sabbath good Jews would not carry sick people around, nor would they expect Jesus to heal them. But once the sabbath is over they are free to take advantage of Jesus' presence in town. They have seen his authority in operation in the synagogue, and his reputation as both exorcist and healer is now established. In a close-knit Eastern community the gathering of 'the whole city' (Capernaum's population was about 10,000) around the door may not be too much of an exaggeration!

Notice the careful distinction which Mark draws between physical illness and demon-possession, not only in the description of those who were brought to Jesus, but also in how he dealt with them. Illnesses are 'cured', while demons are 'cast out'. There are a few places in the gospels where the two conditions seem to be run together, but usually the distinction is kept clear. Demon-possession is not an illness, but an invasion, and it is dealt with as such.

Silencing the demons

Mark is particularly interested in how Jesus treats the demons. They are spiritual beings, and so have supernatural knowledge about Jesus (as we have already seen in v. 24). There is no suggestion that what they might say about Jesus would be untrue: 'they knew him'. But Jesus will not let them speak. Perhaps he can well do without testimony from such a dubious source! But we shall see again and again in Mark's story how Jesus is careful to keep an element of secrecy about who he is and what he has come to do; the subject will recur as soon as verses 44–45. He does not want premature publicity, however well-informed its source. He will make himself known in his own good time, and in his own chosen way. In chapter 4 this whole subject of secrecy will be intriguingly explored.

Prayer

Lord Jesus, may we bring our needs and problems to you as the people of Capernaum did, and find in you healing and relief.

10 Mark 1:35–39

Keeping on the move

In these verses we conclude the '24 hours in Capernaum' which began in verse 21. Jesus has been busy teaching, healing, casting out demons and generally making a formidable impression on the people of this seaside town. He has, it would seem, laid a strong foundation for continuing in Capernaum a ministry which has been so successfully begun. Yet early next morning he has disappeared!

Jesus in prayer

He has gone out of the town to find a secluded spot where he can spend time in prayer. To those who have been brought up on the concept of Jesus as God incarnate, it may seem strange that such a person needs to pray at all. But the Jesus of Mark's story, while clearly portrayed as the Son of God, is unequivocally human, and in many ways shares the weaknesses and emotions of the rest of us. It may not be easy for us to envisage just how God incarnate would pray to God his Father (though in 14:32–36 we will have a precious glimpse into even this mystery), but prayer is as important for him as for his disciples.

Not that Mark often portrays Jesus in prayer (it is Luke who tells us more of that). He mentions Jesus' prayer elsewhere only at special turning points in his ministry, and it may be that its mention here indicates an important decision confronting Jesus, regarding the style of ministry that he should develop. Certainly when this prayer is over he is ready to overturn his disciples' natural expectation that he would build on his success in Capernaum, and instead to launch into a much less predictable itinerant ministry. Was it his hours in prayer before dawn which determined this significant choice?

'Let us go on'

There is something deliberately paradoxical about Jesus' response to the disciples' puzzled appeal, once they have tracked him down. 'Everyone [in Capernaum] is searching for you', so this is not the time to indulge in private meditation. There is a job to be done, a well-launched mission to be developed, an eager populace to be satisfied and helped. Yet it is in precisely that situation where his duty seems so obvious to them that Jesus declares his intention to 'go on to the neighbouring towns', to keep moving, and not to become institutionalised in one place, however needy and however receptive. His mission is wider than simply to Capernaum, and those who have chosen to follow him must be prepared to be on the move as well.

There is here a foretaste of the urgency with which Jesus will later send his disciples out in their turn around the villages of Galilee (6:7–11). The message has to be spread. That is what Jesus has 'come out' for ('out' from Capernaum in the early hours of that morning? or 'out' from God who sent him? – Mark, typically, does not say, and leaves it to his readers to draw their own conclusion).

'Proclaiming the message'

The Greek verb denotes acting as a herald, one sent out with news or with a proclamation, often from a king to those over whom he rules. It is the word which has been used of John the Baptist in 1:4, 7 as well as of Jesus himself in 1:14. God has a message for his people, and it is for his appointed heralds to make it clear to all those to whom it applies.

The focus on proclamation here is quite striking in view of the fact that what the people of Capernaum had come looking for was primarily healing and exorcism. Perhaps that is partly why Jesus feels he must move on, lest his task as herald becomes submerged beneath the popular demand for his miraculous power. True, exorcism is mentioned again in verse 39 (for the third time already in Mark's story), but Jesus leaves no doubt where the primary focus of his mission lies.

For meditation

If even Jesus needed to spend precious hours in prayer, what does this suggest for our own sense of priorities? Does Jesus' concern with proclamation rather than healing and exorcism have anything to teach us both with regard to our own spiritual focus and with regard to the church's priorities in its mission?

11 Mark 1:40–45

'Unclean! Unclean!'

The man's complaint may not have been full-scale 'leprosy' as we use the word, but it would be an unpleasant skin disease which was regarded as infectious, and therefore made the sufferer 'unclean'. Such people were forced to live outside normal society. The word that is used for the restoration of a leper is not 'heal', but 'cleanse'. The vital issue is therefore not only the arresting of the disease, but the restoration of the person to 'clean' society. It was in token of this restoration that the person must be examined and pronounced 'clean' by the priest, and the appropriate animal sacrifice made to take away the impurity.

An emotional encounter

Leprosy was regarded as practically incurable, so that the man's approach involves a remarkable statement of faith in the miraculous power of Jesus. What he puts in question is not Jesus' power but his will to help. The phrase 'moved with pity' represents the reading of most of the Greek manuscripts, but there is a significant minority which reads 'moved with anger', and it is so unusual for anger to be attributed to Jesus in such a situation, and so easy to understand how later scribes might wish to change 'anger' to 'pity', that many scholars think that what Mark actually wrote was 'moved with anger' (see NRSV margin).

But why should Jesus be angry? Perhaps over the suggestion that he might not be willing to help? In that case Jesus' indignant reply 'I do choose' follows naturally. Or perhaps he is more generally upset by the condition in which the man's disease has left him. 'Sternly warning him' in verse 43 is another very emotional word, and it seems that Mark goes out of his way to let us see Jesus not as the coolly detached healer but as the warm-blooded man whose 'gut reactions' run the whole gamut of human emotions.

Testimony – right and wrong

Clearly the priest must know about the cleansing, so that the man can be duly restored to society. So Jesus sends the man off to the priest, to offer a 'testimony to them'. This enigmatic phrase will occur again in 6:11 and 13:9, in each case in a hostile setting. Is it then a testimony 'against them', showing the priests that the Jesus whom they will later hound to death is in fact the one through whom God's power has been operating? Or is it more simply that the man's appearance before the priest testifies that he is clear of leprosy? Again Mark leaves the phrase enigmatic.

But other people are not to know what has happened. The note of secrecy in Jesus' mission, which was sounded already in verse 34, is now loud and clear. But this time we begin to see why it was necessary, since the man's disobedience to Jesus' 'gagging order' has a dramatic effect on Jesus' mission. He immediately becomes the object of unwelcome attention, and has to keep out of the public eye. Perhaps it was the prospect of this sort of public response to a miraculous healer that governed Jesus' decision not to return to Capernaum in verse 38. When he does eventually return there in 2:1, the problem of unwelcome publicity will be all the greater.

Prayer

Thank you, Lord Jesus, that you have not only the power but also the will to restore those whose lives are broken.

12 Mark 2:1–12

'Who can forgive sins?'

Who can forget the vivid scene of the crowded house and the bold attempt to get access to Jesus by demolishing the roof of the flat-roofed, single-storey building? Add to that the dramatic impact of the paralysed man standing up and walking off through the crowd with his stretcher, and it is no wonder the people said, 'We have never seen anything like this!' But, vivid as it is, it is not the healing of the paralytic which is the main focus of the story as Mark tells it. Indeed, the healing itself seems to come in as little more than a visual aid to reinforce Jesus' claim in quite a different area, the authority to forgive sins.

Sin and illness

It was a widespread idea in the ancient world (and even today one can still come across it) that physical illness is in some direct way the result of the patient's sin. Jesus never endorsed that idea, and in John 9:2–3 he directly contradicted it. So it is more than a little surprising to hear him tackle an apparently straightforward case of physical paralysis with the declaration 'Your sins are forgiven'.

Perhaps he was aware of something in the man's condition which made his spiritual state of even more pressing concern to him than his immobility. Perhaps there was some psychosomatic element in his paralysis which demanded this approach. But perhaps also Jesus already had an eye not only on the patient himself but also on the scribes in the audience, whose horrified reaction may have been exactly what he aimed to provoke. Their objection, as he must have expected, is not that a declaration of sins is inappropriate to the man's condition, but that it is blasphemous.

'Who can forgive?'

Since sin is an offence against God, only God can, in any ultimate sense, forgive it. The scribes' theology was correct, and Jesus does not dispute it. But instead of apologising or backing off, he defiantly goes on to repeat his outrageous declaration, and even more remarkably, to put his credibility on the line by linking forgiveness with visible healing.

Forgiveness is not a matter of less importance than physical well-being, but it is no doubt easier to say 'Your sins are forgiven' than to say to a crippled man, 'Stand up', since the former is not easily verified, while the failure of the man to get up would lay him open to instant ridicule. So by linking the two together, Jesus uses his undeniable ability to perform the physical miracle as proof that he also has the authority to perform the greater but less verifiable act of forgiving sin.

The authority of the Son of Man

The issue is one of authority. Jesus claims the right to do what only God can do, and proves it by a spectacular instant healing. The crowd are impressed, while the scribes keep their counsel. But with hindsight we can see here the beginning of the confrontation between this unorthodox and exciting new teacher and the guardians of religious orthodoxy, a confrontation which will develop in the rest of this chapter and into chapter 3 to the point where they begin to plot his overthrow.

The unique authority which he claims is as 'the Son of Man', a title used here for the first time in Mark's story, but later to be the basis of some of Jesus' most daring claims, and the only title he is willing to adopt publicly. It derives from the great vision of Daniel 7, of 'one like a son of man' who is destined to share the eternal kingship of God himself. Jesus certainly does not suffer from false modesty!

Prayer

Lord Jesus, healer of bodies and of souls, we bring to you ourselves in all our varied needs, and rejoice in your unique authority to meet them.

13 Mark 2:13–17

Disreputable company

Tax collectors are probably never popular, but in Roman Palestine their reputation stood at an all-time low. In Galilee they represented Herod Antipas, the unpopular half-Jewish ruler, who in turn represented Roman occupation. So a tax collector was a collaborator, and his association with the pagan occupying power made him religiously as well as politically suspect. Moreover, he was paid no salary, since it was assumed that he would collect more than the amount he was obliged to pass on to his superiors and would keep the difference; some tax collectors lived very comfortably as a result. So the linking of 'tax collectors and sinners' would come naturally to a Jewish mind. They formed a sort of underclass, ostracised from decent society.

The call of Levi

Levi is apparently the same person as 'Matthew' in 3:18 (see Matthew 9:9–13, where the same tax collector is called 'Matthew'). In the border town of Capernaum he would probably be employed in collecting customs duties. He is the only disciple whose call is specifically recorded after the initial four fishermen – the inclusion of a tax collector among Jesus' closest associates was remarkable enough to be worth a special mention. Like Peter and his associates, he left his job to be with Jesus; but no doubt his reputation followed him. We can only imagine how the other disciples felt about the inclusion of a tax collector in their select company!

Tax collectors and sinners

But we do not need to imagine what other people thought, because Mark tells us. The horror of the scribes no doubt reflects the general reaction of polite society. Jesus has carried unconventional behaviour to the point of scandal. It was bad enough for Jesus to call a tax collector to follow him, but when that new disciple gathers a houseful of his associates for a party, and Jesus and his other disciples are seen eating with them, that is too much to bear in silence. For to eat with someone is the ultimate mark of acceptance and identification, and no respectable Jew would be seen eating in such company.

Jesus' response is a classic, and highlights the basic difference between his understanding of his own mission and the scribes' idea of holiness. For them, to please God was to keep yourself as pure as possible, and in practice that was bound to mean limiting the places you went and the company you kept. For Jesus, the priority was not to protect his own personal sanctity but to meet people where they were and to offer new hope to those whom society had disowned. By comparing himself with a doctor and the 'sinners' with patients, Jesus distances himself irrevocably from the scribes' concept of the religious life. He has come, as he said later in another tax-collector's house, 'to seek out and to save the lost' (Luke 19:10), and if that means getting his hands dirty, so be it.

For meditation

Who would be the social equivalent in our society to the tax collectors of Roman Palestine? How does our own attitude to them, and the attitude of the church in general, match up to that of Jesus? How good are we at 'calling sinners'?

14 Mark 2:18–22

Old and new in religion

In the Old Testament the annual day of fasting on the Day of Atonement is the only fast laid down for everyone, but it is clear that other fasts were observed by different groups of people, and the Pharisees had by this time developed a much more rigorous scheme involving weekly fasts (see Luke 18:12). John the Baptist was known as an ascetic (1:6; cf. Matthew 11:18), so it is not surprising that his followers had adopted a similar practice. Jesus accepted the value of fasting (Matthew 6:16–18), but did not impose such a scheme on his disciples. So those whose idea of religion focused on self-imposed discipline would naturally see him as less serious in his religious observance, and wanted to know why.

Feasting and fasting

Jesus' reply suggests that something new and exciting is going on, as far as he and his disciples are concerned. It is like a wedding feast, a time for celebration, not for enforced gloom. The party in Levi's house is more appropriate to the new situation of the coming of the kingdom of God than is the old, tired system of self-discipline practised by the Pharisees.

But along with the celebration goes a note of realism. One day the bridegroom will be taken away from them and the party will be over. Here is the first indication in Mark's story that Jesus knew all along that there were dark days ahead and that his ultimate death in Jerusalem would not come as a surprise to him, however little his disciples may have been able to imagine it during these early days of euphoria. At that time fasting will be more appropriate than feasting, though Jesus' allusive words do not add up to a formal régime of fasting for the church to adopt.

New into old won't go

Two further pictures are used to emphasise how different the new situation is and how incompatible with the old. A piece of strong new cloth should not be used to patch a worn cloak, since the old cloth does not have the strength to resist the pull of the new. And there is a power in new wine which is too much for old containers to resist, as many home brewers know to their cost, even in these days of glass bottles.

The leather wineskins of biblical days soon became brittle with age and were no match for the pressure of fermentation.

That is what it is like when you try to contain the effervescent life of the kingdom of God within the traditional patterns of Jewish religion. Something has to give. This is, no doubt, a sad comment on the confrontation which is already developing in this chapter between Jesus and the representatives of the old régime. He is too strong for them to take. The new life of the kingdom of God is increasingly demanding, and creating, a new religious structure to contain it.

The truth illustrated by these two vivid pictures applies not only to first-century Judaism, but has been played out again and again in the history of Christianity too. Traditional forms of religion tend to 'dry up', and when new life comes it has to break out. It needs great wisdom to recognise what is good among the new trends of our own times and to design the right sort of 'wineskins' to contain it.

Prayer

Thank you, Lord Jesus, for the new life you came to bring. Help us not only to enjoy it, but also to channel it in ways which will preserve it intact for those who come after us.

15 Mark 2:23-28

In the cornfields

The sabbath was one of the most distinctive features of Judaism and was guarded with fierce national pride. The Old Testament itself gave little specific guidance as to how it was to be 'kept holy', beyond the general injunction to 'do no work'. But what is work, and are even necessary types of work forbidden? Here was a fertile field for scribal debate and definition, and their rules and regulations, designed to make it easier for people to know when they were and were not breaking the sabbath law, went into ever more meticulous detail. One of their chief complaints against Jesus was that he did not seem to share their enthusiasm for sabbath regulations.

What was wrong?

Plucking a few ears of grain was not in itself illegal (Deuteronomy 23:25). But among the 39 categories of work which the scribes had identified as forbidden on the sabbath were reaping and threshing, and what they were doing was a sort of reaping – and when you add Luke's comment that they rubbed the ears in their hands (Luke 6:1), it was threshing too!

Jesus does not dispute that the sabbath day should be kept holy, nor does he enter into discussion of the precise definition of work which the Pharisees are assuming. His response is at the more fundamental level of what the sabbath was for in the first place and of who has authority to determine how it is observed. He thus undercuts the whole edifice of scribal definitions of 'work' by going back to first principles.

Jesus and the sabbath

His first argument is that if David could flout the law, so can he! This sounds a pretty thin defence, if all that is being asserted is that if the law has been broken once it can be broken again. But the point is not the mere fact that the law was broken before, but rather who it was who broke it. David could do it because he was David, God's anointed king. He came to the high priest on an urgent mission, and the high priest gave him a special dispensation to make use of the consecrated bread (1 Samuel 21:1-6; this may have been on the sabbath, since that was the day the bread was changed, but that is not the point of Jesus' allusion).

The implication is left unspoken, but surely it is that Jesus has a status and authority at least equivalent to that of David.

The second argument builds on this claim to a special authority. It has two parts. First, what is the sabbath for? – not to make life difficult for people, but to be a blessing to them. By hedging it about with regulations the scribes had turned a joyful divine provision into a burden. Second, who has the right to interpret the sabbath? – Jesus ('the Son of Man') is its 'Lord'. Here again we meet that awesome title from the book of Daniel, which is in itself a claim to share the authority of the God who himself instituted the sabbath. But the literal meaning of 'a son of man' is simply a human being, and so Jesus draws also on the first half of his argument. If the sabbath was made for human beings, who better to pronounce on its proper use than the Human Being?

No wonder the Pharisees found Jesus hard to take! Who did he think he was?

For meditation

In the light of Jesus' arguments here, what should be our priorities with regard to keeping one day in seven as a 'holy' day? Is it important for us to try to determine, for ourselves and for others, what is 'work'? If so, how can this be decided?

16 Mark 3:1–6

More trouble on the sabbath

The encounter in the cornfields may have been just a chance meeting which gave rise to an argument. But this time there is certainly nothing accidental about the confrontation in the synagogue. It almost looks as though the man has been 'planted' to provide a test case. At any rate, the Pharisees are watching Jesus with a view to finding evidence against him.

Healing on the sabbath

Healing would normally involve some sort of work (preparing medicine, binding wounds, etc.), and so fell outside the scribes' definition of what could be permitted on the sabbath. The only concession allowed was if there was imminent danger to life, but clearly a 'withered hand' (probably some form of paralysis) could wait until the next day. It might be suggested that the scribal rules would not apply to the sort of healing Jesus normally practised, by a mere word of command, since no 'work' was involved. But a healing was a healing, and the scribal law forbade it. So 'they watched him'.

It looks as though Jesus takes the initiative, since Mark makes no mention of an appeal for help from the man himself. He is aware of what the Pharisees have planned, but he is as eager as they are to get the issue into the open and decides to take the fight to them. The healing will follow in due course, as authoritatively and immediately as usual, but first the principle of sabbath healing needs to be sorted out.

A question of priorities

Jesus' question, like his comments in the cornfield, goes to the heart of what the sabbath is all about. These are not the terms in which the scribes were accustomed to debating sabbath issues. They could discuss with great skill what did and did not constitute work, and how in practice life could be allowed to carry on while still keeping the sabbath 'holy'. But to put the issue in terms as broad and as unlegal as simply 'to do good or to do harm, to save life or to kill' was to shift the debate on to uncomfortably far-reaching grounds, for which their detailed debates had not prepared them. So 'they were silent'.

But Jesus has not merely succeeded in silencing his opponents. He has also again given an important clue to how religious rules such as the sabbath law need to be interpreted. Taken together with his pronouncement in 2:27 that the sabbath was made for humankind, and not humankind for the sabbath, this principle of aiming to 'do good' on the sabbath leaves detailed casuistry (trying to not break the rules) behind, and takes us on to the far more demanding ground of positively looking for the way of keeping the sabbath holy which will most benefit one's fellow human beings. If to 'do good' involves setting aside a scribal ruling, then it is the ruling which must go. So Jesus heals the man's hand.

Mutual rejection

In verse 5, as probably in 1:41, Mark tells us that Jesus was 'angry'. What annoys him this time is clear, the willingness to put the keeping of man-made rules before the well-being of other people. Perhaps also it is the Pharisees' deliberate attempt to incriminate him which annoys him. But they are no less annoyed, partly by his (as they see it) flagrant flouting of the law and partly by the cavalier way in which he has asserted his general principle of 'goodness' over against their concept of holiness, leaving them silenced and humiliated. The healing in itself may not seem like a capital offence, but the last two encounters have revealed an increasingly unbridgeable gulf between Jesus' understanding of religion and theirs. The man is dangerous, and he must be eliminated. It will still take some time, but the wheels are in motion which will ultimately take Jesus to the cross.

Prayer

Help us, Lord Jesus, to see things in your perspective, to put the positive doing of God's will above the mere avoidance of breaking the rules, and so to seek always to 'do good' rather than to keep out of trouble.

17 Mark 3:7–12

Beside the seaside

The 'sea', here as elsewhere in Mark's story, is of course the Lake of Galilee, a large freshwater inland lake, enclosed by hills, and the scene of the thriving fishing industry from which Jesus has already drawn four of his followers. The shore of the lake in the area around Capernaum is the setting for much of the narrative in these early chapters of the gospel. It was a natural gathering ground, which allowed much larger crowds to gather than was possible in the constricted streets of Capernaum itself.

Growing popularity

In contrast with the hostility of the religious establishment is the increasing crowd of ordinary people who are now coming to find Jesus. They have come 'hearing all that he was doing', and no doubt it is his miraculous activity as much as his teaching which is drawing them. But as we have already seen in 1:38, Jesus' primary concern is with his teaching mission, and this is what he is doing with the crowds on the lake shore (2:13). The request for a boat is not only to allow him to escape from the physical pressure of the crowds of people clamouring to be healed, but also to provide him with a more detached 'pulpit' from which he will be able to address the crowd as a whole, as we shall see him doing in 4:1–2.

The list of places from which the people have come is interesting. Naturally they are mainly locals from Galilee, but the other areas mentioned extend not only to the rest of the Jewish territory (Judea, Jerusalem and across the Jordan), but also to the related but distinct people of Idumea (Edom of the Old Testament) and to the more thoroughly non-Jewish people of Tyre and Sidon. These are among the traditional enemies of Israel, and their people would not be seen as fit company for a pious Jew. While Mark will not say much about Jesus' activity among non-Jews until later in his gospel, already we can see that the Messiah of Israel is happy to extend his mission more broadly and that among some of those who could not claim to belong to the 'chosen people' he meets with a better response than he has found among the leaders of the Jews.

Healing and exorcism

As before (1:32, 34) a clear distinction is made between the cure of diseases and the conflict with unclean spirits. But in both areas Jesus' power is extraordinary. A mere touch seems to be enough to secure physical healing, while demonic forces spontaneously recognise his superior authority. This recognition of Jesus by supernatural beings is clearly important to Mark (1:24, 34; cf. 5:7). It is the reluctant testimony of those who have more than human insight that in Jesus they are confronted by a new and altogether overwhelming spiritual power. Such testimony to the uniqueness of Jesus, despite the unwholesome source from which it comes, is real evidence that Jesus truly is the Son of God and confirms the declaration already made by God himself (1:11).

But, important as this testimony is now for Mark's readers, at the time Jesus did not welcome it, and again we hear the command to silence. Jesus prefers as yet to remain incognito, however great his popular following. The time to declare the full extent of his authority as the Son of God has not yet come; it will ring out with full clarity only in 14:61–62, and by that time it will be too late for people to misunderstand the nature of his mission and to try to divert him into a less spiritual role.

Prayer

Thank you, Lord Jesus, that you welcome people from any background and that you meet their needs. May we come to you and find not only the help we want, but also the help we need.

18 Mark 3:13-19

Twelve good men and true?

This was an important moment, the selection, from among the many people who were following Jesus, of the task force on whom the extension of his mission would depend, not only while he himself was still there to supervise them (6:7-13, 30-31) but more importantly after he was gone. This is the foundation on which the Christian church was to be built.

A firm foundation?

Simon, natural leader as he was in many ways, was one day to disown his Lord. James and John, whose nickname suggests at least an unhealthy degree of self-confidence, would need to be publicly humiliated for their crass misunderstanding of Jesus' mission (10:35-45). Most of the others are little more than names to us; they do not seem to have left much of a mark in history. They include one odd combination: Matthew, if he is the same as Levi (2:14), was one whose profession was anathema to patriotic Jews, while the other Simon was a 'Cananaean', the Aramaic term for a zealot, a political activist dedicated to the liberation of his people from the very régime which employed Matthew! And then, appropriately listed right at the end, there is Judas, whose notorious story is laconically indicated by the words 'who betrayed him'.

Not a very inspired choice? But God has always been ready to work through fallible human sources, and to put his treasure in earthen vessels. No doubt most of us, using proper screening and management criteria, could have done a better job. But as God warned Samuel, 'the Lord does not see as mortals see'. So perhaps there is hope for the rest of us after all!

Nowadays such a shortlist might have led to prosecution under sex discrimination legislation. In the social and cultural situation of the time, however, the inclusion of women in this particular task force would have been a quick route to scandal and to the unthinking rejection of Jesus' mission before it had begun, quite apart from the practical problems of a mixed group sharing the conditions of Jesus' itinerant ministry.

The job description

'Apostle' means 'sent', and these twelve men are indeed to be sent out to share in the activities for which Jesus himself has already become famous. They too will proclaim the same message; they too will have authority to cast out demons. It is an awesome responsibility, and one for which this motley group may well have felt ill-equipped. But that is only the second part of their job description. First comes the element on which all the rest depends, 'to be with him'.

They will be with him in the very basic sense that from now on Jesus will be accompanied by this group wherever he goes (except on a few occasions when he will take only the core group of Peter, James and John). They will travel, eat and sleep together, sharing his itinerant existence and his dependence on the hospitality and the gifts of well-wishers. But they will be with him also in the deeper sense that, increasingly as time goes on, he will devote himself to training and instructing them, rebuking their clumsiness, correcting their misunderstandings, patiently preparing them for the role of leadership which they will too soon have to assume. It is only because they have been 'with him' that they will be up to the task.

For meditation

What are the criteria for responsibility and leadership among the followers of Jesus? What have we, and what has the church today, to learn from the way Jesus selected and trained his task force?

19 Mark 3:20–22

How do you explain Jesus?

Mark sometimes likes to enfold one story within another (or to 'sandwich' it) so as to help his readers listen to the one in the light of the other. He has done that in the latter part of chapter 3. Within the story of how Jesus' own family responded to his extraordinary behaviour (3:20–21, 31–35) he has enclosed an altogether more hostile and threatening encounter with some scribes from Jerusalem. What the two stories have in common is that each group is struggling to find ways of making sense of Jesus. They have heard about his remarkable activity, especially about his exorcisms, and, since they cannot simply dismiss the stories as untrue, they need an explanation. Neither group, however, yet believes his claim to be working by the power of God. The alternative explanations they come up with are not very flattering: his family think he is mad, and the scribes accuse him of being in league with the devil!

Familiarity breeds contempt

Most of us must have some sympathy with Jesus' mother and brothers and sisters. To have a member of the family behave in such an unconventional way and become a public spectacle is deeply embarrassing. Unlike the thronging crowds, they cannot believe that someone they have known all his life can be that special. He is making a fool of himself, and, for his own good, he must be stopped. (Incidentally, where NRSV has 'people were saying', the Greek is simply 'they were saying', and the 'they' reads most naturally as the family themselves.)

In verse 21 they set out on this mission, and in verse 31 they will arrive. We shall see then how Jesus responds to their well-meaning scepticism.

In league with Beelzebul

Mark makes a point of the fact that the scribes are not locals (like those of 2:6, 16, 24; 3:6). Now there is an even more threatening note: scribes have come into Galilee from the capital, Jerusalem, to question his activity. We shall meet more scribes from Jerusalem in 7:1, again coming up to Galilee and making trouble for Jesus. These are strong hints of the confrontation which is to come when Jesus eventually leaves Galilee for Jerusalem.

Their accusation is altogether more damaging than the scepticism of Jesus' family, and will sting Jesus into a much more scathing reply. Beelzebul was a popular name for Satan, the chief of the demons. To accuse Jesus of complicity with Beelzebul was to imply that he practised black magic, or worse. Even more than that, the phrase 'He has Beelzebul' probably means also that he is himself possessed by an evil spirit, indeed by the most evil of all. That is how Mark will interpret their accusation in verse 30. So, far from being the deliverer of those in the grip of spiritual evil, he is himself under its control, and his supposed exorcisms are in fact forwarding the purposes of Satan, not defeating them.

In verses 23–30 we will hear Jesus' response to this scandalous accusation. Then in verses 31–35 we will return to the family. The two groups, in contrast with the eager crowds and the committed disciples, represent the failure of some to grasp the significance of what was happening in the ministry of Jesus, and their defensive reaction is that of people who are out of their depth. People can still today be polarised by their responses to Jesus. It is hard to be indifferent about him.

Prayer

Help us, O God, so to grasp the truth about Jesus that we may respond rightly to his challenge, and not resort to contrived explanations, however well meant, which weaken or deny that truth.

20 Mark 3:23–30

'Blasphemy against the Holy Spirit'

For Satan or against him?

In verses 23–27 Jesus offers what might be called a 'common-sense' reply. The scribes' accusation does not make sense. Why should Satan want Jesus to drive out his own demonic forces. That would be to divide and weaken his own power. The sensible interpretation of the exorcisms (whose reality the scribes clearly cannot deny) is that it is a successful assault on Satan (the 'strong man'), not an act of homage to him!

Jesus is the plunderer of the 'strong man's' house, and the fact that he can do so shows that Satan is powerless ('tied up') before him. The conflict which was foreshadowed in 1:12–13 has now been well and truly joined, and Jesus is proving himself the stronger. The kingdom of Satan is giving way before the kingdom of God.

The unforgivable sin

But Jesus does not leave his response at that level of 'sensible' argument. This is more than a polite academic debate. He confronts these scornful scribes with one of the most severe warnings in the Bible. They are in danger of committing, indeed may already have committed, the unforgivable sin.

There is an amazing breadth to verse 28 – any sin or blasphemy may be forgiven. But to appeal to it as a sort of carte blanche is to take it out of context, for its function here is to place in stark contrast the one sin which is declared to be beyond the scope of forgiveness, that of blasphemy against the Holy Spirit.

This saying has caused untold agony to many who have tortured themselves with the fear that they too may have committed the unforgivable sin. In most cases that fear is quite groundless. It derives from the failure to read the text in its context. And Mark has gone out of his way to help us to interpret it correctly, since he adds his own explanatory comment, 'For they had said, "He has an unclean spirit."' He could hardly be more explicit. This is not a vague, general threat to anyone who may have had unholy thoughts. It is directed against the specific charge of the scribes that Jesus was working by the power of Beelzebul.

In so accusing him they were attributing the glorious and manifest work of God to the power of evil, and such a radical perversion of the truth reveals a deliberate hostility against God himself. It is such settled opposition to the work of the divine spirit which Jesus pronounces unforgivable.

This is a far cry from impure thoughts and words, the memory of which some sensitive souls have tortured themselves with. Such people would be better advised to focus their attention on verse 28 rather than on verse 29!

Prayer

Lord, teach us to follow you in all sincerity and truth, and so assure us of the free forgiveness which is your gracious provision in Christ for all who sin and repent.

21 Mark 3:31–35

Insiders and outsiders

Here is the other end of the 'sandwich' which began in verses 20–21; the family have arrived. At the same time, a further layer is added to the sandwich, in that the inner circle of the disciples, whose call was narrated just before the family were introduced, now return to the scene, and in this final tableau of chapter three the two groups are memorably placed in contrast. Mark thus wraps up a comprehensive portrayal of the differing levels of response to Jesus: outright hostility (the scribes), well-meaning scepticism (the family) and enthusiastic commitment (the disciples).

Standing outside

The tableau is carefully constructed. Jesus is in the house, with a crowd of people sitting around him ('in a circle', says the Greek text in verse 34). Here is the group of those who belong. But outside the house, trying to contact Jesus but separated from him, are his family. They do not belong to the group of 'insiders'. The word 'outside' is repeated twice, and in the next chapter the same term will be used with great effect in 4:11 to describe those who are unable to comprehend the secret of the kingdom of God. The family, at this point, remain 'outsiders'.

Mark will tell us no more about Jesus' family in his gospel, though we know from elsewhere in the New Testament and in early Christian records that eventually most if not all of them became members of the Christian movement, and Jesus' brother James even became the leader of the Jerusalem church. But so far they have not been able to overcome the problem of familiarity and to see Jesus as he really is. And so they provide the basis for a striking, almost shocking, pronouncement by Jesus in verses 33 to 35.

The true family

Family love and loyalty were as important in Jewish culture as in any other, and the Old Testament insisted strongly on the honour and responsibility which were due between members of the same family. In 7:9–13 we shall hear Jesus rebuking the scribes for trying to erode that honour. And yet here he seems to treat his own family with scant respect and to claim a closer link with relative strangers than with them.

The links are of a different kind. It is a matter of priority. Jesus has come to call people into the kingdom of God, and those sitting around him in a circle are those who, as far as they are able, have already committed themselves to obey his call. In responding to his teaching they are 'doing the will of God', and that is what matters most of all. As long as Jesus' family are unable to join that movement, the blood relationship must take second place to the new family which is coming into being through Jesus' ministry.

Jesus will teach his disciples later what the cost of true discipleship may be. It is taking up one's cross and losing one's life. Such a total commitment to the kingdom of God will inevitably produce tension with other loyalties, even so sacred a loyalty as that of the family.

So there is pain implicit in this vivid scene. But there is also splendour, the unheard-of privilege of those who 'do the will of God' that they are called Jesus' brother and sister and mother. In belonging to that new family, they find new worth, new identity and a whole new range of brothers and sisters who are committed with them to follow Jesus in the great adventure of the kingdom of God.

For meditation

Is the tension between the two 'families' a significant factor in our discipleship? What are the practical implications of this tension in our own situations? And how real for us is the privilege of belonging to a new family with all who 'do the will of God'?

22 Mark 4

Introducing Mark's chapter of parables

In the middle of both the first and third acts of Mark's drama (see p. 10 for the three acts) we find what seems like an interlude, where we are offered a concentrated collection of Jesus' teaching before the story resumes at its previous breathless pace. In chapter 13 the teaching will be about what is to happen in the future. Here in chapter 4 we will hear Jesus teaching in parables, and will be invited to think about how the 'secret of the kingdom of God' is both revealed and kept secret.

Perhaps Mark as a storyteller feels the need to allow his readers a pause in the action in order to take stock. But in this chapter we are doing much more than marking time. For the conflicts and divisions we have seen in chapters 2 and 3 have raised important questions, and it is time for those questions to be faced directly.

What has happened to the 'kingdom of God'?

The fanfare with which Jesus' public ministry began in 1:14–15 left the reader expecting dramatic developments as the newly declared kingship of God began to be implemented. And sure enough there have been spectacular healings and exorcisms, enthusiastic crowds and the gathering of a committed group of companions to share Jesus' mission. But it has all been at a limited local level, around the small country towns and villages of Galilee, and among the sort of people who do not usually produce the opinion-formers of society.

And, worse, along with the enthusiasts we have seen sceptics and outright opponents of this new movement. The forces of opposition are gathering, particularly among those who hold real power in the region, and the outlook is increasingly ominous. And even among the crowds who are following Jesus, there is the suspicion that their interest is more in miracles and healing than in the coming of the kingdom of God. How long will their enthusiasm last?

All this is deeply perplexing for those who have understood the revolutionary implications of Jesus' announcement of the kingdom of God. How can God's purpose be resisted? How can so dynamic a message meet with such a mixed response? Does this really look like the 'fulfilment of the time' (1:15)?

Teaching in parables

It is with just these questions that the parables of chapter 4 are concerned. They invite us to question our natural assumptions about how God will fulfil his purpose in the world, and they offer us a new perspective. And they lay firmly upon us, as upon those who heard Jesus' teaching at the time, the responsibility to examine our own grasp of the divine purpose and our own response to the searching message of Jesus.

There are in this chapter three 'story-parables' of the sort which the term 'parable' most naturally suggests to the modern reader (4:3–8, 26–29, 30–32). All of them are drawn from agriculture, and all compare the preaching of the kingdom of God with the sowing of seed. But these three little stories are only a part of the rich mixture of pictorial teaching and explanatory comments which this chapter offers, and all of these too are included in the summary statement that 'with many such parables he spoke the word to them' (v. 33). So before we start to look at the parables individually, it will be worth our while in the next study to think a bit more about what parables are and how they work.

Prayer

Help us to accept, Lord, that your way of doing things is not always what we would expect, and to be ready to learn to see things, as far as we may, from your point of view.

23 Mark 4:1–2
What is a parable?

In 3:23 Mark said that Jesus was speaking 'in parables'. But he was not there telling stories of the sort the word 'parable' suggests to us. The Greek word *parabole* is in fact a more general term which includes also riddles, puzzles, epigrams (as in 7:15) and other forms of vivid teaching. A *parabole* is a striking pronouncement, short or long, which leaves the hearers to work out for themselves what it was all about. It is likely to leave them stimulated, exhilarated, challenged, perhaps puzzled, but it will not spoon-feed them with a simple prosaic statement.

And this means that the same parable may have a very different effect on different people. One may be left puzzled or indifferent, while another sees a flash of light and will never be the same again. One may go away bored, while another will be decisively set on a new course of life. One may say politely, 'What an interesting story,' while another will exclaim, 'Yes, of course, I see it all now!' Parables, by their very nature, divide people, because each individual will respond to them differently.

Parables and cartoons

Parables have been helpfully compared with political cartoons in a newspaper. The cartoonist's picture, often without any words, carries a profound comment on current affairs, and at its best may shock a reader into a new assessment of events or even a new political allegiance. But how much you get out of the cartoon depends on how much you bring to it, in terms of your knowledge of what is going on in the world and your awareness of the conventions of cartoon-drawing, as well as sharpness of mind, openness to new ideas and a willingness to think through the implications with the cartoonist.

Parables, like cartoons, will affect different people in different ways, and those who benefit from them will be those who come with a mind prepared. Some will prove to have what it takes; others will not. As we read through this chapter, we shall see that this is precisely why they formed such an suitable vehicle for Jesus' teaching in the situation of mixed responses to the preaching of the kingdom of God which chapters 2–3 have described.

Setting the scene

Jesus is back beside the lake, and again the boat is on hand to give him a detached 'pulpit' from which he can speak more easily to the large number of people. Such a large crowd will have within it people in many different states of readiness and ability to grasp what he has to say. How can so mixed an audience be effectively taught all at once? Surely through stories and pictures, and in such teaching Jesus is the expert. So they, and we, will now hear 'many things in parables'.

For meditation

Jesus is sometimes described as the greatest teacher the world has known. Mark tells us that his typical method of teaching was in parables. What does this have to say to us about the sort of teaching which really communicates, and about what the aim of that teaching should be? How can we learn from Jesus' teaching method in our own attempts to communicate divine truth?

24 Mark 4:3–9

What happened to the seeds?

The parable of the sower draws on the familiar experiences of a Palestinian farmer, even if not every farmer was so unlucky as to have all these types of problem ground on his farm at once. Jesus is not inventing a fantasy scenario, but using a common everyday experience to illustrate the coming of the kingdom of God.

The seeds that failed

In well-ploughed ground much of the seed would fall immediately out of sight and could quickly take root. But where a path had been trodden across the field there was nowhere for the seed to hide, and no soft earth for the roots to penetrate. It was fair game for the birds. In most of Galilee the rock is close to the surface, so that what appears to be good soil proves too shallow to support roots or to retain moisture. The seed could start to grow, but it would not last long in a hot climate. What looked so promising at first would soon be withered.

Even where the soil was deep enough, it might not be unoccupied. Remember our cornfields before selective weedkillers? A well-established growth of weeds was bound to win in the end.

The seeds that succeeded

Translations usually obscure the fact that whereas the first three seeds are each described in the singular, in verse 8 we change to the plural: 'other seeds fell into good soil…', after which three levels of yield are mentioned. So Mark seems to want us to picture six seeds, three which failed and three which succeeded, but to varying degrees.

Commentators argue whether yields of 30, 60 and 100 are just good or totally exceptional and miraculous. It depends whether you are reckoning grains per plant, grains per seed sown, or what. But Genesis 26:12 suggests that we are not here in the realm of fantasy, but of very good crops under the blessing of God.

If you have ears, listen

We shall hear an 'official' explanation of the parable in verses 14–20, and will think more then about why Jesus told the story like this. The careful spelling out of the fate of the individual seeds suggests that he was concerned with more than just the promise that after all the disappointments there will be a good harvest in the end. We are meant to think about the reasons why the first three seeds failed. They will help to explain why the response to the preaching of the kingdom of God has proved to be so varied. It is not that there is anything wrong with the seed, but that those who receive it are already conditioned in different ways. Some are quite unreceptive, others superficial, others preoccupied; and even among those who prove receptive, there are different levels of effectiveness in their response to the message.

For meditation

What do you think those who first heard this parable would have made of it, given the situation which we have seen in chapters 2 and 3? Would it mean the same thing to the crowds and to the disciples? How would it affect both their understanding of what was happening and their personal response? And are those lessons relevant to us in our different situation? If so, how?

25 Mark 4:10–12

The secret

These three verses go to the heart of the problem of the divided response to Jesus and his message. They raise acutely the problem of why, when the same gospel is preached, some believe and others do not. But it is another matter how far they offer an answer!

Explaining the parables

Even the twelve (and the wider group of supporters indicated by 'those who were around him') did not immediately see the point, and had to ask for an explanation. And they will be given an explanation (vv. 14–20). But this will not be in public, but rather 'when he was alone [with them]'. So, as Mark will explain more directly in verses 33–34, there is a division among those who hear Jesus' teaching. For some there is only the parable, and they are apparently unable to understand it without further help. For others there is also the explanation.

So what makes the difference? It is surely significant that those who receive the explanation are those who ask for it. We do not know how wide a circle is represented by 'those who were around him', but they are contrasted with the rest of the crowd, who apparently cannot be bothered to pursue the matter any further. It is those who go on to ask for help who now constitute the 'insiders' as opposed to 'those outside', for whom 'everything comes in parables' – and only in parables. Remember the striking double use of 'outside' in 3:31–32 to contrast Jesus' family with the 'circle' around Jesus. It seems now that the family are only part of a wider group of 'outsiders'.

The secret of the kingdom of God

Secrecy has been a theme of several of the preceding stories, where Jesus ordered people, and especially demons with their supernatural knowledge, not to talk about who he was and what he was doing. This is reserved information, a 'secret' kept for some and not for others. The ability to grasp the significance of the coming of the kingdom of God, and to discern its powerful presence where others can see only a small group of itinerant peasants, is not for everyone.

That, after all, is what the parable of the sower has just illustrated – much of the soil is not capable of producing a crop.

A depressing precedent

Verse 12 is an abbreviated quotation from Isaiah 6:9–10. After his overwhelming vision in the temple, Isaiah was sent to proclaim God's message to his people with the warning that they would not listen, indeed that they were incapable of it. That same incomprehension now faces Jesus in at least part of his audience, and prevents their responding and being saved. The situation is nothing new – indeed the only contrast with Isaiah's experience is that whereas his failure was apparently to be total, in Jesus' case at least there are some to whom the secret is revealed.

The worst bit of verse 12 is the conjunction with which it begins: 'in order that' suggests that God and/or Jesus wants the message to fail. But it is too literalistic to read this as meaning that God is deliberately keeping people out of his kingdom. The point is rather that they are already by their own nature outsiders, and that teaching in parables merely brings out into the open the division which is already there. The sowing of the seed does not ruin the soil – it is rather the condition of the soil which determines the fate of the seed.

But if this passage does not declare God's determination to keep people out of the kingdom of God, neither does it explain how outsiders can become insiders. The disciples to whom the secret has been revealed were once themselves outsiders. How they have made the transition is a question which must be answered from elsewhere, unless it be by the observation that it is they, and not the outsiders, who have come asking questions.

Prayer

When we are confronted by mysteries, O God, help us earnestly to seek the answers from you and to rejoice in what has been revealed, but also to accept that we may not yet be able to understand all your truth.

26 Mark 4:13–20

Spelling it out

Mark will tell us in verse 34 that Jesus explained everything in private to his disciples. In that case, this detailed spelling out of what the imagery of the parable represented must be typical of many other such explanations; but this is the only one Mark has recorded for us. It consists of a sort of 'glossary' of what each scene in the story represents, but still leaves it to us to work out what was the point of telling the story, and what his hearers were intended to do about it. 'Let anyone with ears to hear listen'!

A parable about parables

Verse 13 suggests that to understand this one parable about the sower is the key to understanding other parables too. The intervening verses (10–12) have focused on the divided response which parables, by their very nature, produce, leaving some enlightened and others none the wiser. The parable of the sower, as it is now explained, is precisely about different ways of responding to the message, and shows that some are fruitful soil and some unfruitful. Moreover, it spells out three different types of unproductiveness. All this reinforces the point that the effect of parables depends not only on the message (the seed) being good, but also on the hearers (the soil) being in a condition to receive it. To have understood this is to be on the way to understand how all parables will work, and thus to be alert to the factors in our own and other people's situation which will determine whether the seed can germinate and grow. Those who have ears will hear.

So what does it mean?

It is natural to want to know 'the answer', to have it spelled out in a single, clear moral which all good hearers can put into practice. But parables are, in their very nature, open-ended. The implications of the truths illustrated in the parable of the sower may be different for different people.

Some may come to it as preachers, puzzled and disappointed that the message of the gospel has met with such a mixed response. Probably their situation is close to that of the original disciples, perplexed by the apparently sporadic progress of the kingdom of God. For them the parable conveys both an explanation of why some are so unresponsive, and the encouragement of knowing that along with the bad soil there is also the good, that after the waste there will be the harvest.

Others may need to be challenged as to their own openness to the call of God. For them the call is to examine themselves against the different types of unfruitful ground and to take steps to improve the condition of their own soil.

Some, while not unfruitful, may be only too aware that the best they can do produces only a modest result, while others seem to be spectacularly effective as disciples. For them it is important to realise that within the purpose of God not all good soil is in the hundredfold bracket.

There are, no doubt, many other appropriate ways of reading the story and its explanation. Jesus has given us the template. It is for each of us to fit it to our own situation and questions. Even for the same reader the parable's message and challenge may not always be the same. That is how parables work.

For meditation

What does the parable of the sower mean for you?

27 Mark 4:21-25

More pregnant sayings

Before we come to the two other 'story-parables' of chapter 4, Mark offers us a collection of short sayings which together explore further the nature of revelation and how we must respond to the truth revealed. The language, while full of vivid imagery, is rather mysterious, and the implications of the sayings are not clearly spelled out. The reader is again left to think it out and to come to their own conclusions. In other words, we are here, just as much as in the stories about seed, in the realm of parable.

Let the light shine

The picture in verse 21 is clear enough: a lamp is no use if it is hidden away; it needs to be put where its light can be most effectively seen. So hidden things must be disclosed. Secrets are meant to be divulged (v. 22).

But what does this mean? Is it an exhortation by Jesus to his disciples to share with others the special understanding of the kingdom of God which they have received (v. 11)? But in that case how does it relate to the theme of secrecy which is so prominent in Mark's gospel, and especially to the assumption of verses 11–12 (and indeed of the parable of the sower) that there are some who will not be able to see the light, and that Jesus teaches in parables for just this reason? If everything is to be made plain, why does he himself not use a less ambiguous form of teaching? Perhaps we are to read these verses as a deliberate counter-weight to the apparent exclusivism of verses 11–12. God's ultimate purpose is not concealment but enlightenment.

Or are these verses a promise to the disciples that what at present is still under wraps will one day be brought into the open? Despite the declaration of verse 11, their own understanding is still far from complete, and they must wait with patience for further light to dawn. As in verse 9, the parable formula ('Let anyone with ears to hear listen') again challenges the reader to think through what these enigmatic words might mean in practice.

Listen with care

The basic principle of verses 24–25 is that what you get out depends on what you put in. We have seen already that this is in the nature of parables. Those who come to them with the right background and the right attitude will find them a source of further enlightenment. Those who come with nothing will take away nothing. Indeed, as in capitalist economics, the inequality tends to be compounded rather than corrected. Those who give good measure will receive back not only what they brought, but more as well, while those who start with nothing will finish up with, if possible, even less!

This principle, when applied to the hearing of parables, chimes in with the parable of the sower. The seed which is not well received is lost or withered, while that which finds a good response will grow and multiply. The same message can be received effectually and ineffectually. So be careful how you hear, and don't let the message go in through one ear and out the other.

There is a tension between verses 21–22, with their apparently optimistic expectation that what is hidden will be revealed, and verses 24–25, which reinforce the message of the first part of the chapter that not all who hear will be enlightened. These verses do not offer a simple 'theology of revelation'. But they do offer a clear challenge to the reader to be sure to finish up on the right side of the divide.

Prayer

Lord, save us from carelessness over your truth. Make us good hearers and doers of what we hear. And use us to bring to light for others what at present is hidden from them.

28 Mark 4:26–29

The dynamics of growth

This time we are offered no explanation, beyond the opening phrase, 'The kingdom of God is as if...' Or, to paraphrase it, 'This is how God works out his purpose in the world'. For 'the kingdom of God', remember, means God being king, God in his sovereign power, God taking control. So 'the kingdom of God' is not something which we can achieve, or even promote. It is what God does. And that, of course, is just what this little parable is about.

Watching the seed grow

The account of arable farming given in this parable is simplified almost to the point of caricature. The farmer sows the seed, and then has nothing more to do until he comes back to gather the harvest. Would that it were so easy! What about ploughing and harrowing, fertilisers and weedkillers, drought and storms, birds and vermin? But this is not meant to be a guide to arable farming. It is a picture, simply drawn, to help us understand how God works in his world.

The focus is on the dynamic of growth which the seed has in itself. The farmer knows it will happen, but he neither causes it nor can he explain it. The power of growth is, as it were, built into the seed. So the ground, once it has received the seed, cannot help producing a crop (forget now about the parable of the sower; this is a different parable!). The process is, to use the Greek word at the beginning of verse 28, 'automatic', both in the beginning of the seed's growth and in the predetermined stages through which it passes from the initial shoot to the 'full grain in the head'.

God's initiative

To the disciples, puzzled by the fact that Jesus' powerful proclamation of the kingdom of God does not yet seem to have had the desired effect, the story suggests that they may wait with patient confidence, for the seed is sown and it is sure to grow. But it will grow in God's way and in God's time and can neither be hindered nor hurried.

The moral might seem to be that the proper attitude is one of laid-back optimism with a minimum of effort. Just leave it all to God, and the harvest will be there in the end. If this parable stood alone that might seem a plausible interpretation. But the same Jesus who told it will later send his disciples out with a sense of urgency to summon people to respond to the announcement of the kingdom of God (6:7–12) – as indeed he himself has been doing with a similar sense of urgency (1:38–39).

The point seems rather to be that we should not make the mistake of imagining that we can take over God's work and make him effectively irrelevant. The proclamation is of God's kingship. His subjects undoubtedly have a vital role to play in disseminating it, but it is his power, not theirs, which will bring it to fruition. This is the basis for due humility on the part of his disciples, but also for unshakeable confidence that the promised harvest really will come, because it is God himself who will produce it.

Prayer

Thank you, Lord, that your kingdom is established by your own power, not by our ability. Help us to cooperate in your sovereign work and to have full confidence that in our day, as in the days of Jesus, you will produce the harvest.

29 Mark 4:30–34

From the least to the greatest

Mustard seed

Mustard seed is proverbially tiny (see Matthew 17:20), and yet it produces 'the greatest of all shrubs'. This is not, of course, the puny 'mustard-and-cress' that we grow in little plastic boxes, but a garden herb which in Palestine commonly grew to a height of three metres. Such a spectacular result from such an unpromising beginning is the stuff of which proverbs are made ('Great oaks from little acorns grow'), and provides Jesus with a clear and compelling illustration for what the kingdom of God is like (see the previous study for what this means). Its beginnings may be unimpressive, even virtually invisible – but just you wait and see!

Both supporters and sceptics may have found it hard to see the powerful inbreaking of the kingdom of God in this motley group of villagers trudging around the countryside with their eccentric leader. They were far from the corridors of power. Could such a movement change the world? Looking back, we know the answer, and Jesus' parable warns them not to 'despise the day of small things' (Zechariah 4:10). There is a pervasive sense of the incognito about Jesus' ministry as Mark records it, and he makes no secret of the fact that many (most?) failed to grasp the significance of what was going on in their neighbourhood. For the disciples, who were at least beginning to grasp it, the need was for patience. God's purpose will be worked out in his own time and way. The seed will grow, for that is the nature of seed – and of the kingdom of God.

Rounding it off

Verses 33–34 round off the whole collection of Jesus' teaching in parables by reiterating the pattern we have already seen repeatedly through this chapter. Parables are for everyone; explanations are only for the disciples, in private. This sounds like a device for maintaining the 'secret of the kingdom of God' by keeping the truth away from the wider crowds. It almost sounds as though Jesus doesn't want the people in general to understand.

But Mark adds the interesting rider 'as they were able to hear it'. We are reminded again of the parable of the sower – the effectiveness of the seed depends on how far people are 'able to hear'. As Jesus speaks in parables, there are some who will simply not see the point, and will enquire no further. These are the people for whom 'everything comes in parables' (v. 11), and who will receive no explanation. But if we were right in suggesting that 'those who were around him' (v. 10) include not only the already committed disciples but others who, as a result of hearing the parables, want to know more, it may be that such people too are now among the 'disciples' for whom explanations are said to be available in verse 34.

For meditation

Are we too ready to jump to superficial conclusions about the work of God, or to try to hurry him on? Can you identify places where God is quietly and secretly at work in your own context? How can we best present the message of Jesus 'as people are able to hear'? Does Jesus' pattern of teaching by parable and (private) explanation offer us an appropriate model for our day?

30 Mark 4:35–41

Storm at sea

In 1986 the complete hull of a cedar-wood fishing boat from about the first century AD was discovered buried in the mud by the shore of the Lake of Galilee. It is probably typical of the boats in use in Jesus' time. It is just over 8 metres long by 2.35 metres wide and is quite shallow (1.25 metres in depth); there is a slightly raised area at one end. A dozen or so men would fit into it with not much room to spare. To see that boat, in the kibbutz at Ginosar, is to gain a vivid insight into the several stories which Mark tells which are set on or beside the lake. Such a boat would not be a comfortable place to be in a storm.

What happened on the lake?

The squall was violent enough to scare seasoned fishermen into thoughts of drowning, and yet Jesus was 'asleep on the cushion' (on the raised section at the end of the boat?)! Mark has no inhibitions about portraying Jesus, the Son of God, as also fully human, in his emotions and, as here, in his physical needs. He was apparently exhausted. The disciples' reaction is an intriguing mixture: they clearly expect him to be able to do something about their danger, and yet in their panic wake him with a lack of ceremony which is hardly the way to treat a divine visitor.

Jesus' response is immediate and awesome in its simplicity. A word is enough. He speaks to the wind and waves as if they were living things, rebukes them for their insolence and dismisses them with a peremptory 'Shut up' (the same vivid expression as he used with the unclean spirit in 1:25). Then he turns on the disciples, and they too suffer a rebuke, though a more gentle one. Didn't they realise whom they had on board with them? Have they learned nothing yet from being with Jesus and from seeing his power? True, all his miracles which Mark has recorded so far relate to people (and the demons who have controlled them), rather than to the forces of nature. But surely they could have put two and two together.

What did the disciples learn about Jesus?

The disciples are committed to following Jesus, but as yet have had only veiled indications of just who he is (unless they have been able to hear the testimony of the demons before they were silenced, 3:11). They know that he has amazing powers, but to see him controlling even the wind and sea has added a new dimension to their amazement. Many passages in the Old Testament declare that God alone has the power to control the elements (Job 38:8–11; Psalm 107:23–32, etc.), and now here is Jesus enacting those passages in his own right. This is one more vital new step along the road to grasping the full truth about Jesus (which we, the readers, have been privileged to know ever since the opening verses of the gospel!).

In the mean time, however limited their theological understanding, they are discovering in practice that to follow Jesus is to enter a new realm of possibilities. With Jesus in the boat, what is there to fear?

Prayer

Lord Jesus, help us to discover for ourselves who you are, not only in our minds but also in practical trust and confidence.

31 Mark 5:1–13

A hopeless case

The other (eastern) side of the Lake of Galilee was a very different area, less well-populated and predominantly non-Jewish (hence the presence of a herd of pigs). Mark does not tell us what purpose Jesus may have had in taking his disciples into this unfamiliar territory and in moving (for the first but not the last time) outside Jewish society. Perhaps the idea, as in 6:31, was to secure a time of rest after much public activity. The area where Jesus and his disciples landed was apparently some way from any village and had been taken over by an extraordinarily violent and disturbed man.

'We are many'

Mark indulges his storytelling enthusiasm to the full in describing this wretched creature. His threatening behaviour had made him a social outcast, and he had found a home among the tombs, a suitably macabre setting for a man whose life had become a living death.

But his problem is not traced to mental abnormality, but to an outside influence. He is demon-possessed. The 'unclean spirit' to which his condition is attributed in verse 2 has in verse 9 become a whole army of spirits (a 'legion' properly consisted of 6,000 men), and when they are expelled there are apparently enough of them to take over a herd of 2,000 pigs. Not that we are obliged to calculate simply on one spirit per pig, but the destruction of such a large herd must indicate an extraordinarily powerful demonic force.

It is useless to speculate how the man's condition might have been diagnosed in our own society with its reluctance to admit anything other than physical and human causes. As far as Mark is concerned, this is the most spectacular manifestation of spiritual evil with which Jesus has yet been confronted, and Jesus' confident authority over even so powerful a force of evil brings to a climax the remarkable series of encounters with unclean spirits which have formed so prominent a feature of these early chapters of Mark's gospel.

'Son of the Most High God'

As we have already seen in other such encounters (1:24, 34; 3:11), evil spirits immediately recognise who it is who is now confronting them, and know that their time is up. The terror of the neighbourhood becomes an abject suppliant, as the resident demons beg not to be tormented, and, knowing that they cannot now stay in their 'host', try to negotiate the best terms for withdrawal. The pigs (unclean animals for unclean spirits) are the unfortunate losers in this bizarre piece of bargaining.

For the possessed man it is an amazing deliverance, for Jesus a great victory, for the disciples a spectacular lesson on the authority of their master. The questions which naturally rise in our minds about the apparently cruel fate of the pigs, and the economic loss to their owners, do not seem to trouble Mark at all. No doubt he lived in a less sensitive age, and perhaps he was right not to complicate his story with secondary issues, but modern readers do not find it so easy to pass over such questions (and would not be likely to be helped by the commentator who moralises on verse 17: 'All down the ages the world has been refusing Jesus because it prefers its pigs'!).

For meditation

Jesus! The name high over all,
In hell or earth or sky;
Angels and men before it fall,
And devils fear and fly.
Charles Wesley (1707–88)

32 Mark 5:14–20

A short stay in Decapolis

Decapolis, the area to which Jesus and his disciples had come on the eastern side of the lake, was a semi-independent confederation of Greek towns, owing allegiance to Rome, but with little contact with Jewish culture and religion. Whatever Jesus' purpose in going across to this foreign territory, the stay now had to be cut short after what had happened with 'Legion'.

Jesus is not welcome

There could be no doubt about the cure of the possessed man, and we might have thought that his compatriots would be grateful for his restoration and for the removal of a serious menace from the neighbourhood. But instead 'they were afraid'. The whole event has been too disturbing for them to think in such positive terms. This mysterious Jewish visitor is frightening and will surely prove to be an uncomfortable person to have around. So, no doubt with due deference (you cannot afford to offend a man with such powers), they ask him to go back home. We may also reasonably assume that Jesus was persona non grata with the former owners of the drowned pigs! And Jesus does not argue, but gets straight back into the boat to return to the western shore.

A potential disciple rejected

But what about 'Legion' himself? He owes everything to Jesus, and naturally enough he wants to stay with him. The use of the same phrase 'to be with him' as we saw in 3:14 suggests that he wants to join Jesus' permanent group of disciples, just like the twelve. And what better ambassador for Jesus could you imagine than a man who could give such a spectacular first-hand testimony to what Jesus' unique spiritual authority has done for him?

But Jesus has a more appropriate job for him. He is to stay in his own country and tell his own people about Jesus. Here in Decapolis, where he is known, he will have a more ready hearing than in the foreign territory of Jewish Galilee. It is in his own home and among his own people that he is to spread the news, and that is what he does, with great effect. Later in Mark's gospel Jesus will come back to the same region (7:31—8:10), and the welcome he will then receive no doubt has a lot to do with the testimony of 'Legion' in the meantime.

A breach of secrecy

There is a fascinating contrast between Jesus' desire to avoid publicity in Galilee (see 1:34, 44–45; 3:12 and the deliberately secret nature of his teaching portrayed in chapter 4) and the open encouragement of this man's testimony in Decapolis. There may have been all sorts of reasons for this which we do not now know, but perhaps it was due at least in part to the fact that this was away from Jesus' home area, and especially away from Jewish territory. The sheer practical difficulty posed by too great a popular following (1:45; 2:2) did not apply over here, since Jesus was not staying in the region. And in this Greek area there was no danger that his mission would be hijacked by a misdirected nationalistic enthusiasm for him as the Jewish messiah, a problem which was never far away in Galilee.

Prayer

Lord, help us to know what is the task you have for each of us, and not to assume that it will be the same as for others. And when we know it, may we, like 'Legion', undertake it gladly and effectively.

33 Mark 5:21–34

'Who touched me?'

Here again Mark tells a story within a story. It is as Jesus is on the way to respond to Jairus' request that he is delayed briefly by another remarkable incident. We shall return to Jairus in the next study.

An embarrassing complaint

The 'haemorrhage' was presumably a menstrual disorder. Quite apart from the physical discomfort and weakness which resulted from it, for a Jewish woman it involved the further serious problem that a physical discharge rendered her ritually unclean and therefore unable to take part in normal communal life (see Leviticus 15:25–31). After so many years it must have seemed incurable, and yet she is still determinedly seeking a cure. (It is perhaps not surprising that when Luke, the doctor, tells this story, he does not echo Mark's wry comment on the shortcomings of the medical profession – v. 26!) Now there is a chance of a cure of a different sort, for she knows of Jesus' reputation as a miraculous healer. If only she can touch him.

But the touch of an 'unclean' woman is the last thing a religious teacher would want, as he too would then be made unclean for the rest of the day. So rather than confront him as other people did when they wanted to be healed, she comes up behind him and touches the edge of his cloak, with the hope that even that minimal degree of contact will be enough. And it is!

Unable to hide

But she has not reckoned with Jesus' supernatural knowledge. Among all the jostling crowd he has been aware of a single touch of a different kind, and he is not prepared to let her get away with it in secret.

There is something oddly mechanical about the idea of feeling that 'power has gone out', as if 'power' was a physical substance and a limited commodity to be used with care. Coupled with the woman's expectation that a mere touch on his cloak would be enough to secure healing and her immediate physical sensation of being cured, it gives to this story a different 'feel' from Jesus' other healings. It sounds rather impersonal, even magical (though we shall see in 6:56 that this was not a unique case; cf. Acts 5:15; 19:12 for similarly 'impersonal' cures later). And perhaps it is true that her understanding of how Jesus could heal was of a more 'magical' type and lacked theological sophistication. She would not have been alone in that.

Jesus has, perhaps involuntarily, responded to that limited understanding, but now he wants to put the relationship on a more personal basis. He wants to meet her openly, and she has no choice but to come forward. Yet she receives not the rebuke which she fears but a warm commendation and assurance that her cure is real and permanent. The key word, as so often in the accounts of Jesus' healings, is 'faith'. Rudimentary as it may have been, her faith has established a real relationship with her healer, and on that basis she is to be commended.

For meditation

Put yourself in the woman's place. What would you have learned from this experience? And what might the disciples, as spectators, have learned about 'faith'?

34 Mark 5:21–24, 35–43
'Not dead, but sleeping'

After the unhappy confrontation the last time we heard of Jesus in the synagogue in Capernaum (3:1–6), it is a relief to find that at least one leading member of that institution still holds him in high regard, even if it is under the pressure of urgent personal need.

Faith under pressure

Jairus, like others who meet Jesus in this gospel, seems to have no doubt of the power of Jesus to heal. Even in the face of apparently imminent death, he takes it for granted that if Jesus will lay his hands on his daughter she will be restored and will not die. The only problem is to get him there in time. But the pressure of the crowd, and the delay in dealing with the woman with the haemorrhage, have held Jesus up for too long, and the report comes that the girl has died while he has been on the way. And, of course, death is death; there is no point in 'troubling the teacher any further'.

We are not told what Jairus himself felt when the news came. But Mark uses a conveniently ambiguous word for Jesus' response (v. 36): it could mean either that he 'overheard' the (private) message or that he 'ignored' it. Certainly, he refuses to be put off, and he summons Jairus to continuing faith rather than fear. We can only imagine the turmoil in Jairus' mind as he hurried on with Jesus to his house, on what must surely be a fool's errand.

'Get up, kid!'

Mark does not actually say that the girl was dead – only that everyone else thought she was dead. So it would be possible to take Jesus' words, 'Not dead, but sleeping', as simply a corrective diagnosis: they have mistaken a coma for death, and Jesus will now revive her from her 'sleep'. Matthew allows no such uncertainty: in his account Jairus does not appeal to Jesus until the girl is already dead (Matthew 9:18). And the way Mark tells the story, and the people's reaction, surely suggests that the death was real and the revival therefore a stupendous miracle, not a medical second opinion! In that case we must take Jesus' words not literally but as a way of saying that even death is not the end. 'They laughed at him' because they took his metaphorical words literally, and knew she was really dead.

The restoration of life is a majestic demonstration of Jesus' God-given authority, but the manner in which it is told is delightfully down-to-earth. The ejection of the sarcastic crowd, the small group at the bedside and the simple act of taking the girl's hand are all as far as possible from the showmanship of a magician. The words *Talitha cum* (in the vernacular Aramaic) are remarkably low-key: *talitha* is literally a young sheep or goat but was used colloquially for a child, and *cum* simply means 'Get up'. So 'Get up, kid!' is an idiomatic equivalent. And then there is the delightful final touch – she needs something to eat! But of course, what else would you do for someone just raised from the dead?!

Note again the avoidance of publicity, both in allowing only five people to witness the event and in the strict instructions to keep it secret. Not that one could stop the neighbours talking when they met the dead girl in the street, but they were to be kept guessing as to just what happened and how it was done. Jesus is not in the business of becoming a travelling roadshow; he has more important things to do.

Prayer

Lord, teach us what faith means when human possibilities are exhausted. May we not join the laughter of the crowd, but come into the little room in faith, even when we can have no idea what you are going to do.

35 Mark 6:1–6

A difficult visit to Nazareth

Nazareth was a small, rather insignificant village tucked away in the hills between the lake of Galilee and the Mediterranean, and away from the main centres of population. It was Jesus' home (1:9, 24), but for the whole of his public activity so far he has been based not in Nazareth but in the more populated area down by the lake some 20 miles away. He has recruited his disciples from the lakeside communities and has made his base in Capernaum, where Simon and Andrew lived (and very likely in their home, 1:29).

Familiarity breeds contempt

This is the first time Mark has told us of a visit to Nazareth since Jesus became a public figure. No doubt some news of his activities has found its way back to the village, but it has all been hearsay. Now for the first time they have a chance to hear and to assess the local boy who has been making a name for himself down by the lake.

An invitation to teach in the synagogue was not automatic, but for a distinguished visitor it would be an expected courtesy, and it would naturally be extended to the local boy who has become so well known as a preacher in Capernaum and has now returned home. And apparently they are not disappointed. Mark's verb 'astounded' indicates that they recognise in Jesus something out of the ordinary, and the references to his 'wisdom' (which they can hear for themselves) and his 'deeds of power' (about which they have heard reports) suggest that they are favourably impressed.

And yet they cannot accept him at face value. How can a member of a local family, whom they have watched growing up and whose services they have employed as the village carpenter, turn out so differently from the rest of his family? We have already seen a similar response on the part of Jesus' family themselves (3:20–21, 31–35), and now the whole village shares in their scepticism. The problem, as with his family, is not outright hostility and rejection so much as incomprehension. This sort of thing happens with other people from far away, not with a member of your own close-knit village community. Perhaps there is an element of jealousy or at least the feeling that Jesus has become too big for his boots. And so 'they took offence at him' – the word means more literally 'they stumbled over him'.

A disappointing homecoming

There is a note of pathos in Jesus' comment in verse 4. But it is a realistic observation. People do find it hard to recognise extraordinary qualities and powers in those they know best, and it is not every day that one of your neighbours turns out to be the herald of the kingdom of God, with power to raise the dead. Capernaum, which has known Jesus only as a remarkable preacher and healer, is likely to prove more fertile soil than Nazareth.

But even so it is startling to read that as a result Jesus could not work miracles in Nazareth (though Mark's give-away aside that he did in fact cure 'a few' sick people perhaps suggests that the difference was one of scale rather than of absolute impotence). But we have seen several times already in this gospel the close link between faith and healing. Where there is no faith, where Jesus is not taken seriously, the necessary basis for healing is missing.

It is not often that we read of Jesus being 'amazed'. Other people were amazed by his power, but the only other time the verb is used of Jesus himself is in Matthew 8:10. There he was amazed by the faith of a stranger, here by the lack of faith among his own people.

It looks as though his visit to Nazareth was a short one. We do not know that he ever came back again.

Prayer

Lord, save us from the prejudice which cannot rejoice in your work in those we know best. Give us the faith which can discern your presence even in the places we would least expect it.

36 Mark 6:7–13

The mission is extended

Jesus called the first four disciples in order to make them 'fish for people' (1:17), and he selected the twelve 'to be sent out to proclaim the message' (3:14). Now the time has come for them to take up that task.

The nature of the task

Verses 12–13 give an overview of the disciples' mission. It includes the three main elements which we have seen to be characteristic of Jesus' own ministry so far – preaching, healing and exorcism. So this is not some new pattern of mission, but simply an extension, a multiplication, of what Jesus himself has already been doing. For some time the twelve have 'been with him' (3:14), and now they have his authority to do what he himself does. Not that they are now taking off on their own. It is as his emissaries, under his authority, that they are sent, and in verse 30 they will report back to him as their 'director'.

It is nonetheless remarkable that what we have so far come to think of as the unique authority of Jesus as the Son of God is in fact able to be delegated in this way to his very fallible associates. But of course this is what has been happening ever since. Once Jesus himself was removed from the earthly scene, such a 'delegation of authority' would become essential, but already while he is still around he is willing to trust these 'learners' with an amazing level of responsibility.

As in Jesus' own ministry the authority over unclean spirits features prominently in their 'job description' – more prominently indeed than preaching! And as we have seen already, exorcism is carefully distinguished in verse 13 from the healing of physical illness. What is unusual here is the mention of anointing with oil as apparently a normal method of physical healing. There is no record that Jesus ever anointed the sick. Indeed the only other reference to the practice in the New Testament is in James 5:14 (where again it seems to be accepted as normal). Anointing is in other contexts a symbol of God's blessing, and perhaps it is used by the disciples as a way of assuring their 'patients' of the love and power of the God on whom they depend for healing. When Jesus himself was present, there was no need for such assurance.

Travelling light

The detailed instructions in verses 8–11 emphasise the need to travel light. They are not to take provisions or spare equipment, but to depend on the hospitality offered by well-wishers wherever they go (as indeed Jesus and the whole disciple group are already in the habit of doing). In the Middle East this is not such an impractical programme as it might seem in our society, since hospitality to strangers is a sacred duty. There is the possibility that in some places they may not be welcome (v. 11), but such rejection is clearly exceptional and is to be marked by a vivid gesture of disassociation. If it happens, it will be on account of the startling message they are sent to proclaim ('they refuse to hear you'), and anyone who will not listen to the call to repent in view of the coming of the kingdom of God needs to be shown in no uncertain terms the gravity of their decision.

In one way the situation of the twelve at this time was unique. But there are elements in their commission which apply to all disciples of Jesus through the ages: the privilege of sharing the master's own mission, the authority he gives, the sense of urgency and of the importance of the message of the kingdom of God. In many different settings these are the experience of Christians all over the world today, as they have always been.

Prayer

We are amazed, Lord, at the privilege of sharing your mission. Thank you that with the commission comes the authority to fulfil it. Help us in our day to find the right way to undertake it and to proclaim your message to those around us where we are.

37 Mark 6:14–16

Jesus and John the Baptist

A change of scene

The disciples, sent out on their mission in verses 7–13, will return and report back in verse 30. The intervening space is filled with an unexpected return to the person with whom Mark's story began. We left John the Baptist after his arrest in 1:14, and since that time we have heard nothing of him (except a brief reference to his followers in 2:18); if we have thought about him at all, we have been left to assume that he is languishing in prison, though we have so far been given no clue as to why he has run into trouble. His time of public acclaim is over, and Jesus has become the centre of attention.

So a return to John at this stage is surprising, the more so because in verses 17–29 the focus will be entirely on John, and Jesus will be temporarily out of the picture altogether. Those verses will, no doubt, satisfy our curiosity as to what has happened to John and why, but they seem an unnecessary digression in the story of Jesus.

But the three verses which introduce the 'digression' give us a clue as to why it is here. In verses 14–16 we discover that in popular opinion Jesus was widely seen as a second John the Baptist (the same idea will emerge in 8:28). The close link between their two missions may not be much emphasised in the story proper, for the very good reason that John was already in prison when Jesus began to appear in public. But Mark does not want us to forget the context in which Jesus began his preaching, and in 11:27–33 the parallel between the two men will be an important testimony to the divine authority with which Jesus himself is endowed. And of course the violent end which John has met is an ominous forewarning of what will happen to his successor (as Jesus will himself declare in 9:11–13). So John is not to be forgotten (even though Mark's gift for telling a good story does perhaps lead him to give the story of John's death a prominence which is a bit out of proportion!).

Herod Antipas

The 'Herod' of this story is not Herod the Great (who died soon after Jesus was born), but his son Antipas, who ruled Galilee (as a protégé of the Romans) during the time of Jesus' ministry. It is his bizarre idea that Jesus is John the Baptist returned to life which gives Mark the excuse to tell us the story of John's end.

Herod was not the only one to link the popular preacher and healer Jesus with the equally popular preacher John. The general public, trying to make sense of the Jesus phenomenon, naturally turned to John as a model (and may well have known that John had talked of a 'more powerful' successor to follow him). And John, as we have seen, was above all a prophet, a man who fearlessly proclaimed God's message and was recognised as having a special authority and charisma. We have seen too that John's mission was to some degree modelled on that of Elijah – and Elijah was expected to return to usher in the great day of the Lord. So all this adds up to a potent mixture of ideas all focused now on Jesus, the one through whom God's voice is now being heard.

But for Herod all this talk of prophecy and of John coming back from the dead has a much more sinister ring, because it is he who has been responsible for the execution of the earlier 'prophet', and now he fears that his victim is coming back to haunt him. For a petty ruler whose insecurity has already led him to eliminate one popular leader, this is a frightening prospect. It may well be that Herod would in due course have a hand in the plot to get rid of Jesus (and indeed Mark includes a few references to him and his supporters as opponents of Jesus: 3:6; 8:15; 12:13), but after this brief glimpse of Herod's fear he will not bring him into his narrative again.

For meditation

Herod and the general public illustrate some of the ways popular superstition tried to make sense of Jesus. In what ways do people today try to pigeonhole Jesus, and how can their ideas best be developed or corrected?

38 Mark 6:17–29
The dance of death

In the previous study, we thought about why this story is here and why Mark may have felt it appropriate to insert it into the story of Jesus. But now we shall look at the story of the death of John in its own right. It is, of course, a flashback; we do not know how soon after his arrest John was executed, but it was while Jesus was still publicly preaching in Galilee.

Why John was in prison

The Jewish historian Josephus tells us that Herod executed John because he knew of his popularity and feared that he might become the leader of a rebellion against him. (He also says that such was John's popularity that a subsequent military defeat of Herod's army was explained by popular opinion as divine retribution for his having executed John.) But Mark gives us another and more personal reason, in Herod's annoyance (and bad conscience?) over John's criticism of his marriage to Herodias, and the implacable hostility of Herodias herself. Herod had divorced his wife in order to marry Herodias, and Herodias had left her husband, who was Herod's half-brother. In Jewish law a woman had no right to divorce her husband, and when you add the close family relations involved in this double 'divorce' and remarriage it is no wonder that people were scandalised. John's robust denunciation was, no doubt, in tune with popular opinion, and that made it doubly wounding, and dangerous, for Herod and Herodias.

And yet Herod himself comes across in this story as irresolute, and will not take action until he is forced into a corner. Verse 20 suggests at least an uneasy conscience and even a perverse pleasure in listening to his tormentor. Moreover, knowing that other people thought John to be 'righteous and holy' (and a prophet of God too!), he must at least have been aware of the political danger in eliminating him; perhaps he himself really shared that opinion of John. Without Herodias to act as his Lady Macbeth, he might have hesitated for a long time.

The death of John

Apart from John's bold and uncompromising stand for principle, there is nothing admirable in this story. It is a notorious and sordid example of intrigue and licentiousness at the court of a minor oriental potentate. Mark tells the story vividly and with gusto, but we are mercifully spared the more lurid details with which tradition has invested the story of the princess' dance.

But John himself appears only as a passive victim, summarily executed off the stage in order to appease the anger of the wicked 'queen'. It is a sadly inglorious end to the life of a man who had had such a powerful impact for good on the society of his time, and from whose ministry the mission of Jesus was born.

For meditation

We are left to ponder on the nature of a world where evil can so openly triumph and where virtue and courage, and even the call of God to a prophetic ministry, are no protection against petty self-interest in high places. But it is a salutary reminder at this stage in the story of the Son of God, who will all too soon be setting out determinedly on the road which leads inevitably to Golgotha.

39 Mark 6:30–34

An abortive 'retreat'

This is the only time in Mark's gospel that the Twelve are called 'apostles'. The word means 'those sent out', and it describes well the experience they have just shared as Jesus' emissaries. But having been 'sent out', they now return and report back to the one who sent them, and now that they are back with him they will again be described by their more common name, 'disciples', that is 'learners'. It is the balance between learning and being sent out which will be the secret of their effectiveness as Jesus' task force for mission.

The need for retreat

And now it is time for 'learning' again. They have been through a demanding and exhausting time of mission, and it is time to recharge. Jesus' words in verse 31 could hardly be more emphatic: 'Come away', 'a deserted place', 'all by yourselves', 'rest'. It has been the experience of Christian people down the ages that such a time of withdrawal from the pressures of everyday activity is needed from time to time, even if the 'deserted places' may not always be found by geographical isolation. And the more the pressure of responsibility the greater the need for retreat. Some Christians, governed by the 'Protestant work ethic', have thought of 'rest' as at best a concession to human weakness, to be enjoyed, if at all, only with an underlying sense of guilt. Jesus and his disciples had no such inhibitions!

The retreat is frustrated

Mark has told us several times of the popularity of Jesus among ordinary people, but here is the most remarkable example of it. We might have thought, as no doubt the disciples did, that an escape by boat should secure the privacy they wanted, but so eager were the people to catch up with Jesus again that they set off along the shore, tracking the progress of the boat, and were there waiting for them when they disembarked.

Jesus would have had every excuse for complaining at the invasion of privacy and refusing to be available, but instead we read of his 'compassion', which leads him to drop the plans for a retreat and launch again into an extended period of teaching. We can only guess what the disciples thought of this!

Why this persistence?

In verse 44 we read that the 5,000 who followed Jesus around the lakeshore were 'men' (the word is specifically masculine: Matthew adds 'without women and children'). What motivated so large a group of men to make this impromptu journey to meet Jesus in the wilderness, when they (and their families) could apparently hear him preaching in Capernaum any time? John tells us that after the feeding miracle they tried to 'take Jesus by force to make him king' (John 6:15). Mark is not so explicit, but there are a few hints: 'sheep without a shepherd' (v. 34) is used in 1 Kings 22:17 for an army without a commander, and the division of the crowd into numbered ranks (v. 40) has a military flavour.

It is quite likely, then, that the reason this large male contingent chased him into the wilderness (the traditional place for a nationalistic uprising) was that they had come to the conclusion that he was the charismatic figure they needed to lead them against the Roman occupation, and that it was more than teaching they were looking for. The fact that Jesus will pack the disciples off so hastily in the boat in verse 45 may suggest that they too were in danger of being caught up in the nationalistic fervour. The danger of being hijacked into leading a political insurrection is never far away from Jesus in Mark's gospel, and here it may well be that the issue was coming to a head.

For meditation

What practical guidance may we draw for our own lives from Jesus' intention to take his disciples into a retreat and his response when the plan was foiled?

40 Mark 6:35–44
Food in the wilderness

Bread from heaven

When Israel were hungry in the wilderness under the leadership of Moses, they were given 'bread from heaven' to eat, in the form of manna (Exodus 16). The prophet Elisha once fed a hundred people with a mere 20 loaves (a 'loaf' in these stories is more like what we would call a 'roll', enough for one person at most), and there was still some left over (2 Kings 4:42–44). Now Jesus will perform a miracle on a far greater scale than Elisha's, and the comparison with Moses, the great leader who had made Israel into a nation, must inevitably be made. If it was a charismatic leader they were looking for, surely here was another Moses.

If that was how the 5,000 men saw it, however, it does not seem to have been Jesus' intention, nor is it the message Mark wants his readers to take away from this amazing story. Jesus' motive is 'compassion' for a hungry crowd, not a desire to display divine power or establish a claim to leadership.

Much from little

From the disciples' point of view, this was a lesson in faith (and one which Jesus will later expect them to have learned: 8:17–21). Jesus' challenge to them to provide enough food is ludicrous – the food simply is not available even if they could afford to buy it. The amount they can actually lay their hands on is not enough to feed even the disciple group themselves, let alone their vast crowd of uninvited guests. We can guess their bewilderment and embarrassment when they have to get the crowd sitting down ready for a picnic – of what? But they have to go through with it, and Jesus deliberately involves them all the way through, in preparing the crowd, in serving the food and in gathering up the leftovers (which are far more than there was to start with!). The carefully preserved numbers (five rolls, two fish, twelve baskets, five thousand men) reflect their amazement as they went round with their twelve baskets collecting up the impossible remains. They would never forget any detail of this experience.

A foretaste of the future

Mark's readers can see in this story something else which the disciples could not see at the time. The verbs in verse 41 ('Take', 'bless', 'break', 'give') are the same verbs which will be used at each account of the last supper, where Jesus will institute a memorial meal for Christians to observe in memory of him. Christianity has a shared meal at the centre of its worship, and Christians accustomed to this observance cannot fail to see in this impromptu meal shared beside the lake a foretaste of the eucharistic feast of the kingdom of God. And, having recognised this symbolic dimension, we note with approval that all who ate this meal, small as its provisions had been, were fully satisfied. So it is with the eucharistic bread from heaven.

For meditation

Jesus said to them, 'It was not Moses who gave you the bread from heaven, but it is my Father who gives you the true bread from heaven. For the bread of God is that which comes down from heaven and gives life to the world.' They said to him, 'Sir, give us this bread always.' Jesus said to them, 'I am the bread of life. Whoever comes to me will never be hungry.'

JOHN 6:32–35

41 Mark 6:45-52

Panic on the lake

What Jesus did next

If our speculations about the insurrectionary atmosphere in the wilderness were right, the disciples, fresh from the amazing experience of the loaves and fish, may well have shared the crowd's hopes and enthusiasm, and wanted Jesus to declare himself as the new Moses. But Jesus has no such intention, and instead packs the disciples off as quickly as possible in the boat, away from the excited crowd. As for the crowd themselves, Jesus simply 'dismissed' them. We cannot know how much is hidden behind that little word, but it may well have been one of the supreme tests of Jesus' authority to pacify such a large and eager crowd, and to be able to get away from them by himself.

But for Jesus the priority is prayer. As in 1:35, he needs to get away alone with his Father and to clarify his vision of the task he has come to fulfil. If Jesus needed this, even at a time of such hectic activity, what does that imply for the rest of us?

Meanwhile, out on the lake

It cannot have been much more than three or four miles back by boat to the Capernaum area, but the conditions are so bad that even experienced fishermen are still far out on the lake in the early hours of the morning. Exhausted and frightened, they are in no state to cope with the vision of a human figure walking over the waves in the dim predawn light, and they assume it is a ghost. Once again, Jesus is doing what is impossible, and it is hardly surprising that they cannot recognise him or realise the miracle that is taking place, until he speaks to them.

They have been in a storm on the lake before (4:35–41), but that time they had Jesus with them. Now when he joins them in the boat, again the danger is over, and the storm subsides. But the quelling of the storm is mentioned this time almost as an afterthought, overshadowed by the amazing feat of walking on a stormy lake. Of course there have been attempts to explain away the miracle, by picturing Jesus wading in the surf by the shore or walking on a hidden sandbank. But experienced fishermen would know their lake better than that, and Mark clearly has no doubt that the boat is far from the shore. Following on the equally impossible event of the multiplying of the bread and fish, this is undoubtedly presented to us as a miracle. Certainly that was how the disciples understood it.

Hard hearts?

And yet Mark adds the rather harsh comment that they still did not understand, because their hearts were hardened. We might well wonder whether any of us would have scored any more highly in such circumstances. It is not easy to take miracles for granted, especially where, as in this case, nothing of the sort has happened before. Mark apparently expects them to have learned something from 'the loaves' which would have prepared them also for this quite different encounter with supernatural power. He will return to the theme more fully in 8:14–21, and in the following chapters we shall see again and again how difficult the disciples found it to adapt to the new realities and values of the kingdom of God. But at this point we may have a good deal of sympathy with them: there is a limit to how much impossibility one can absorb in a short time!

Prayer

Lord, make us ready to be surprised by you, and help us not to try to limit you to what we can grasp.

42 Mark 6:53–56

More healings

Once again Mark allows us a brief respite from the breathless series of amazing events. This more general summary of what Jesus was doing in Galilee at this period, like that in 3:7–12, shows us that the relatively few specific miracles which he has included in his story are part of a much more wide-ranging ministry. But general as this summary may be, it still breathes an air of restless activity and excitement. Nothing is ever ordinary when Jesus is around.

Healing at Gennesaret

Capernaum was Jesus' base, and it was probably from there that he and his disciples had set out on their abortive retreat. They return now to Gennesaret, a few miles further down the west shore of the lake. But it is close enough to Capernaum for Jesus to be well known, and immediately the people of this area seize their opportunity to benefit in their turn from the presence of the famous healer.

In this summary Mark makes no mention of either teaching or exorcism, the other main components of Jesus' ministry as he has presented it so far. From the point of view of ordinary people, no doubt, it was the possibility of healing which was the most immediate hope when someone like Jesus came along. And the hope is amply fulfilled: 'all who touched were healed'.

Touching the fringe of his cloak

Perhaps the news of how the woman with the haemorrhage was healed (5:24–34) has got around, and people have concluded that touching Jesus' cloak is the proper way to seek for healing! They clearly believe that his healing power is such that the patient does not need a lengthy personal encounter with Jesus. We might look rather askance at such a 'magical' approach to healing, but presumably we are to understand that those who touched and were healed were motivated by the same sort of faith as Jesus commended in the woman who had pioneered this sort of approach. It is faith, not the technique which is followed, which is the basis of healing. The contrast with Nazareth (v. 5) is striking. Here people may have had little idea of who Jesus really was, but they came to him with real faith, not with the scepticism which we have seen in his fellow-villagers at Nazareth.

For meditation

This little passage offers us the opportunity to pause and reflect on what we have learned so far about Jesus' ministry in Galilee.

Try to put yourself into the place of (a) an ordinary villager in Capernaum or Gennesaret and (b) one of Jesus' disciples, and ask yourself what you would have made of Jesus by this point. What would be the things that most excited and most puzzled you? How much would you have been able to see for yourself of the coming of the kingdom of God, and of Jesus as the Son of God?

43 Mark 7:1–8

What is purity?

The last time we met scribes who had come from Jerusalem to Galilee to confront Jesus (3:22), their arrival spelt trouble. Here again they are a hostile group, a foretaste of the sort of reception Jesus is going to meet when he eventually goes to Jerusalem himself. The issue of purity which they raise is one which will fundamentally divide Jesus from the religious establishment, and it is important enough for Mark to devote a long section directly to the discussion (vv. 1–23), while the stories that follow will illustrate the way Jesus' mission inevitably takes him outside the 'pure' boundaries of Israel, into company which would scandalise the scribes.

The tradition of the elders

Ritual purity, the ways in which it may be lost and the procedure necessary to restore it are major themes in the Old Testament law. Those Jews who wished to remain ceremonially 'clean' (and therefore able to take part in worship and in social activities) had to be careful about whom they encountered, what they ate and touched, and about their own bodily condition.

In the Old Testament the formal washing of hands before eating was prescribed only for priests, but by the time of Jesus the keener type of Jews (particularly the Pharisees) had adopted this as a requirement for themselves and for anyone else they could influence to follow them. Mark's broad-brush comment on Jewish practice in verses 3–4 exaggerates a little, but this is the way things were moving. So surely Jesus, as a professed religious leader, could be expected to be equally strict with his own followers. If he ignored this (recently developed!) 'tradition of the elders' he could not be taken seriously as a religious teacher.

A matter of priorities

We shall hear what Jesus has to say directly about the issue of purity when we come to verse 15. But first he has some more general comments to make on the status of the 'tradition of the elders'. The scribes' question (v. 5) contained a veiled threat, but Jesus launches into a direct and stinging attack on their whole approach to religious observance.

They are 'hypocrites', a word which sometimes in the gospels means what we mean by it – insincere people who put on an act – but also goes further to include those who have got things disastrously out of proportion, who think they are doing the will of God when in fact they are doing just the opposite.

Their 'hypocrisy' is defined in Isaiah's scathing words about his own contemporaries, whose supposed worship was all on the surface and who paid more attention to their own human religious traditions than they did to knowing and loving God himself. The same is true, Jesus implies, of these scribes, who are more concerned to uphold their 'tradition of the elders' than to find out what God really wants from them. Indeed, he goes further: they actually abandon God's declared will and put their own human traditions in its place. Just how they do this will be explored in the next study.

Prayer

Save us, O God, from putting our own or other people's ideas of what is right before what you have revealed to us as your will, and give us the wisdom to discern the difference.

44 Mark 7:9–13

Putting the cart before the horse

'Making void the word of God'

The unexpected accusation which Jesus has launched against the scribes in verse 8 is repeated in different words twice more, in verses 9 and 13. The 'tradition' of which they are so proud, and which they see as the key to living as God requires, in fact has quite the opposite effect and prevents people from living according to God's law. The terms used, 'commandment of God', 'word of God', underline the seriousness of the charge. God has plainly declared his will, and they are undermining it by setting up their own rules and regulations. 'Tradition', which can and should be a helpful guide to how we may apply God's laws to the realities of everyday life, has a dangerous tendency to develop a life of its own, and when it does it becomes an enemy rather than a friend. That is what has happened to the scribes.

An offering to God?

The particular example Jesus chooses to establish his charge involves a complex area of scribal law. The formula 'Corban' (dedicated) was used to set something aside from common use. It became, in theory, the property of God to whom it was dedicated, and so was not available to anyone else. But it is easy to see how this formula could be abused by someone whose motive was not really to give anything to God but to keep it out of the reach of other people. And it seems that this device was being applied, with the consent of the scribes, to family disputes about property.

Respect for parents, and therefore the obligation to provide for them when they were no longer able to look after themselves, was a basic principle of Israelite society, enshrined in the fifth commandment. An aging parent should be able to look forward with confidence to the care and material support of sons and daughters. But a selfish son could apparently declare his property 'Corban', and so remove it from his parents' reach. It seems likely that some device had been contrived to enable him nonetheless to retain the use of it himself even after it had been declared the property of God. The whole system was a fiddle, cynically manipulating the religious ideal of giving to God in the interests of sheer selfishness. And the scribes, apparently, not only connived at it, but even directly forbade the son to give any help to his parents once the formula had been invoked (v. 12). There is a good deal of discussion in the Mishnah about how, if at all, such a vow could be repealed, and in at least some cases the rabbis declared it impossible, even where the son who made the vow had now changed his mind and wanted to help his parents. So much for the fifth commandment!

All this has nothing to do with purity; we shall come back to that issue in the next study. But it shows how easily the scribes' meticulous concern for rules and regulations could end up by not only ignoring but even undermining the 'weightier matters' (Matthew 23:23). Knowingly or not, the same concern for ritual detail which had led them to criticise the eating habits of Jesus' disciples had made them 'hypocrites' with regard to family responsibilities.

For meditation

In what ways are we also in danger of putting the cart before the horse, by focusing on minor externals and forgetting the things that really matter, and by putting our traditions before the word of God?

45 Mark 7:14-23

Clean hands and a pure heart

We now return to the issue which sparked off this sharp dialogue, that of purity. Jesus declares his position by means of a 'parable' (which means here an epigram or a puzzling saying needing interpretation – see our study of chapter 4 on p. 52), which, following the pattern established in chapter 4, he then goes on to explain to his disciples.

Not what goes in but what comes out

The purity laws of the Old Testament were all based on the principle that uncleanness is contracted by touching and eating unclean things. In other words, the impurity is there 'outside' the person and 'comes in', rendering the person unclean. It is this basic principle which Jesus here questions and indeed turns completely on its head. Impurity is already there 'inside', and it 'comes out' in what a person says and does.

It is difficult for us to appreciate what a radical reorientation this pronouncement involves for those brought up in a culture which has never questioned the principle of 'external defilement'. The laws regulating what food is clean or unclean were one of the main distinguishing marks of the Jews and severely limited the social contact they might have with those outside Israel. To observe them carefully was, for many Jews, a matter of patriotic pride as well as religious obligation.

How far did Jesus mean to go?

Of course, it was not the Old Testament food laws that the scribes had questioned Jesus about, but rather the relatively insignificant issue of washing hands before meals (which was not in itself an Old Testament regulation for anyone except priests). But Jesus has deliberately responded in a much more general vein, repudiating not merely the practice of ritual washing, but the whole concept of external defilement on which it and the Old Testament food laws were based. His rather crude depiction of what happens to the food we eat in the first part of verse 19 indicates that food as such cannot be regarded as the source of defilement: it is merely a temporary visitor to the body.

Mark adds at the end of verse 19 his own editorial comment, 'Thus he declared all foods clean.' For Mark, then, the implications of Jesus' 'parable' were clear: the Old Testament food laws no longer apply. The result of this is, of course, to remove at a stroke one of the major obstacles to fellowship between Jew and Gentile, and one which was to be the focus of a lot of controversy in the early years of the church, as we see in the book of Acts, until the Christians eventually came to accept that Jew and Gentile must be accepted on an equal footing in the kingdom of God.

Jesus did not actually say that in so many words, and perhaps that is why some of his followers were so slow to get the point (like Peter in Acts 10:9–16). But it is hard to see what else he could have intended by so general a declaration as verse 15.

Inner purity

Verses 21–23 are a sad commentary on what human nature is capable of. Not that these are the only products of 'the heart', but they are only too familiar. In the light of such 'uncleanness', ritual purity becomes irrelevant. To meditate on these vices (and their corresponding virtues) is to take us to the heart of what true religion is really about.

Prayer

Create in me a clean heart, O God, and put a new and right spirit within me.
PSALM 51:10

46 Mark 7:24–30
Crumbs for the Gentiles

The question of purity, discussed in the first part of this chapter, would have important repercussions for the eventual expansion of the church to contain Gentiles alongside the original Jewish believers. This strange little story illustrates the point, as the Jewish teacher is confronted by a cry for help from an 'unclean' Gentile woman.

An unlikely request

Jesus' attempts to escape from public attention are constantly doomed to failure. Even in Phoenician territory to the north of Galilee, the home of Israel's traditional enemies, he is sought out by someone in need. It is hard to imagine a more inappropriate request, from a traditional Jewish point of view. As a religious teacher Jesus should not have any dealings with a woman or with a Gentile, and the fact that her daughter is possessed by an 'unclean spirit' compounds the problem. Other rabbis would have turned from her in horror.

An unsympathetic response?

Jesus does at least listen to her request. But his first words are far from encouraging, and indeed they sound quite brutal. The woman and her daughter are, apparently, classed as 'dogs'. It is true that the Greek word means a little dog, but that does not help much, as a dog of any size was for the Jews an unclean animal, and the term 'dogs' was a traditional and deliberately offensive Jewish way of describing Gentiles.

It is remarkable that the woman does not give up there and then. The fact that she persists, and in the end is rewarded for her perseverance, may suggest that there was something about the way Jesus said these rough words which indicated that he was hoping for a reply. This is the sort of response which long experience of Jewish–Gentile hostility must have led her to expect from a Jewish teacher, but was he perhaps testing her with this stock answer to see whether she could rise above it? And that is exactly what she does.

A clever reply

Rather than protest against Jesus' use of such an unwelcome term she turns it against him. If we Gentiles are dogs, then even dogs have their rights. They may be second-class citizens, but they too are fed. The children do not eat all the food; there is some left for the dogs.

It is a clever development of Jesus' imagery, but it is more than that. Jesus is the Messiah of Israel, and his mission to Israel is the primary focus of his ministry. The children do indeed have the first priority. But she is perceptive enough to realise that Jesus' mission is broader than that. Perhaps she has seized especially on his word 'first'. If the feeding of the children comes first, what then? Then it will be time for the dogs! Here, in a nutshell, is the pattern of the Christian mission in New Testament times: 'To the Jew first and also to the Greek [i.e. Gentile]' (Romans 1:16).

A happy ending

'For saying that', and thus revealing her grasp of his special situation as Israel's Messiah without abandoning her hope that she as a Gentile also has a claim on his attention, her request is granted. And who is to say that that is not what Jesus intended all along, despite the apparent coldness of his first reply? She has passed the test with flying colours and is rewarded by one of the most remarkable miracles in Mark's story, an exorcism not by face-to-face confrontation but by 'remote control'.

Prayer

Lord, give us the faith to discern your purpose for us, and so to pray on in spite of apparent refusal.

47 Mark 7:31-37

Another Gentile healed

The previous story focused on the question of Jesus' mission to Gentiles as well as Jews. Now we see him continuing in Gentile territory: Sidon, like Tyre, was Phoenician, and Decapolis was the Greek-dominated area to the east of the lake of Galilee (see on 5:14–20). So while the racial origin of the deaf man is not made an issue in this story, we are surely right to assume that again it is a Gentile who benefits from the healing power of the Messiah of Israel. (Matthew at this point, 15:31, tells how the crowds 'praised the God of Israel', which sounds like a Gentile reaction.)

'He makes the deaf to hear'

Deafness and dumbness (or a serious speech impediment: note the expression 'his tongue was released' in verse 35) are complaints which have not yet been mentioned specifically, though they may well have been included in the general summaries of Jesus' healing ministry. To heal such a person would have special significance in the light of Isaiah 35:5–6, where the blessings of the age to come include: 'Then shall the ears of the deaf be unstopped… and the tongue of the speechless sing for joy.' These things are to happen when God comes to save his people – and here they are happening at the hands of Jesus!

Mark tells the story in unusual detail (though he will give a similar account of the healing of a blind man in 8:22–26). Here we read not merely of Jesus touching or speaking to the patient, but more specifically of his touching the organs affected and using saliva as part of the cure (as also in 8:23). This more elaborate method in place of a simple word of healing would of course be particularly appropriate for a deaf man. The use of saliva as a healing agent, which seems strange to us, was quite common in the ancient world, sometimes in a more magical healing ritual, but sometimes in ordinary medical practice.

But there is also an authoritative word of healing, 'Be opened.' The fact that Mark records it in the original Aramaic as well as in Greek (as he did in 5:41) suggests that people remembered this ringing command – and no doubt so did the man himself, as the first word he had ever heard.

The command to silence – again

The fact that the local people have brought the man to Jesus expecting him to cure him indicates that his reputation has spread into this Gentile area. It may well have been quite close to where 'Legion' had been delivered from his demon-possession, and after that incident Jesus had told him to go back and tell people about what had happened (5:19–20). It looks as if he has done so very effectively, and when Jesus reappears in their region they are ready for him. So it is surprising that this time Jesus again tries to avoid publicity, as we have seen him doing several times in Jewish areas. He carries out the cure in private, and afterwards asks the people not to talk about it – and again they take no notice!

Jesus' previous commands to silence seem to have been in order to avoid too much popular enthusiasm among his own people, who might have their own ideas as to what sort of Messiah they wanted him to be. But perhaps by this time even among Gentiles his reputation as a healer is getting out of hand. He has other priorities in his mission, and from this point on we shall hear much less of his healing and much more of his teaching, particularly his private teaching of the disciples. In the long term this, rather than an extended healing campaign, will be what counts for the future.

Prayer

Lord, you have done everything well. You even make the deaf to hear and the mute to speak. Cause us too to hear your voice and to speak of you, so that others may find your saving power.

48 Mark 8:1-9

Food for the Gentiles too

Why another impromptu feast?

Only a page or two ago Mark has told a story of the miraculous feeding of a large crowd of men. Now he tells another story, similar in general outline, but different in detail, particularly in the numbers (4,000 people instead of 5,000 men; seven loaves and a few small fish instead of five and two; seven baskets instead of twelve). Why the repetition? Is Mark so short of material that he has to tell the same story twice?

But of course it is not the same story, and in 8:19-21 Jesus will make the point that there were two such incidents, not just one. So there must be some importance in the fact that Jesus did it twice.

'The dogs eat the children's crumbs'

Perhaps we should find the clue in the fact that since 7:24 Jesus has been moving in Gentile territory. Here he is, apparently, still in the region of Decapolis, from which he and the disciples will return to the Jewish shore of the lake in verse 10. In that case, whereas the crowd of 5,000 whom he fed in 6:35-44 were Jews, these 4,000 are predominantly Gentiles.

Is there a pointer to this deliberate extension of Jesus' ministry outside Israel in the strange dialogue between Jesus and the Gentile woman in 7:27-28? There is bread for the children, but there is also bread for the dogs. The bread which Jesus provided for the large Jewish crowd is now matched by bread for the Gentiles. The scale of the miracle is a little reduced (fewer people fed from a slightly more ample supply, and not so much left over), but we are still in the realm of the impossible. The 'children's crumbs' turn out to be an ample feast after all.

A pointer to the future

This miracle brings us to the end of the short section of Mark's gospel in which he tells of Jesus' ministry among non-Jewish people (7:24—8:9). After this point Jesus will be among Jewish people; when he takes the disciples into Gentile territory again in 8:27 it will not be to conduct a mission among the local people, but to find a quiet place where he can concentrate on teaching his own disciples. When he returns to Jewish territory it will be as the Jewish Messiah that he will eventually come to the Jewish capital and be rejected by the leadership of the Jewish people.

But those who have seen the significance of this little section will know that that is not the end of the story. What Jesus has symbolically enacted by feeding a Gentile crowd as well as a Jewish one will soon become a more lasting reality, as his disciples will, reluctantly and uncertainly at first, but with increasing determination, take the gospel of salvation to all nations. When they look back on this incident, so little understood at the time, they will see in it a mandate for their universal mission. The Messiah of Israel is the Saviour of the world.

Prayer

Lord Jesus, help us to share the breadth of your vision and to know that your blessings are for all people, and not only for our own group.

49 Mark 8:10–13
Asking for a sign

When Jesus left Galilee in 7:24 he had been engaged in sharp debate with the Pharisees and scribes. The dialogue had ended with Jesus making a radical pronouncement about purity which must have left his opponents seething, since he was apparently taking it upon himself to undermine a basic principle of the Old Testament law, and one on which much of their professional expertise depended. So now when he comes back to the Jewish side of the lake they are ready for him.

A sign from heaven

Their request for a sign is on the face of it quite legitimate. Often in the Old Testament, signs (usually some form of miraculous occurrence) were given in order to authenticate one who claimed to have a mission from God. Moses was given 'signs' to perform in order to convince the sceptics (Exodus 4:1–9), and Isaiah invited Ahaz to ask for one (Isaiah 7:10–11). Given the contentious nature of what Jesus has been saying, it might therefore seem wise on the part of the Pharisees to ask for his credentials in the same way. But Mark indicates that their motivation is not a dispassionate search for truth. They have come 'to argue with him', 'to test him'.

The sign they are looking for is one 'from heaven'. It must make it quite clear that he has God's approval and authority. Mark's readers know, of course, that God has already declared that Jesus is his Son, in whom he is well pleased (1:11). The people of these villages, however, have not heard that direct declaration. Even so, might we not expect that they would be convinced by the extraordinary sequence of miraculous happenings which have surrounded Jesus' ministry? Some of those miracles have been very public and have made him the talk of the town. What more can they ask?

No sign for this generation

Perhaps this group of Pharisees has not been personally present at any of these alleged miracles, and they are not prepared to trust to hearsay. Or they may be thinking that even miraculous events may have more than one explanation, just as the scribes in 3:22 attributed Jesus' exorcisms to the power of Satan, not to God. But Jesus' response indicates that their request is not sincere and that no sign would be of any value in the face of determined scepticism. There is to be no sign for this generation.

And with that 'he left them'. Galilee and its religious leaders have seen the last of Jesus. Thus Act 1 of Mark's drama draws to its close. Now Jesus is going away on a journey which will ultimately take him to the even more hostile territory of Judea and to his death in Jerusalem. Galilee has had its opportunity, and Jesus will not go on appealing forever to those who do not want to be convinced. 'This generation' has made its choice.

For meditation

How much 'proof', and of what sort, is it legitimate for us to expect from God? What is the balance between proof and faith? In what circumstances might it be appropriate for us to decide that no further evidence should be offered to those who are not willing to be convinced?

50 Mark 8:14–21

Difficult questions on the lake

Act 1 finishes with an enigmatic little scene on the lake as Jesus and his disciples go away from Galilee. Its connecting theme is bread, but it takes some lateral thinking to follow how the dialogue develops. Bread has, of course, been a prominent motif in recent chapters, the literal bread of the two feeding miracles and the metaphorical bread which is for the children not for the dogs. Mark has already warned us that the disciples have failed to understand 'about the loaves' (6:52), and now that lack of understanding will be more fully exposed.

Bread and yeast

The setting is down to earth enough. The disciples realise that they have set off on their journey with no more than a single small bread roll in the boat. When they hear Jesus talking about yeast they immediately assume that he is commenting on their failure to make proper provision. They are so preoccupied with their problem that they fail to see that Jesus is not talking about literal bread at all. And it is this misunderstanding on their part that gives Jesus the excuse to make some pretty scathing comments of their persistent ability to miss the point.

But what was Jesus talking about when he spoke of yeast? The yeast he refers to is the yeast of the Pharisees and of Herod – an odd combination of parties who had little in common, beyond the fact that in their different ways each was a threat to Jesus and his preaching of the kingdom of God. Pharisees opposed him for theological reasons: he was preaching dangerously radical ideas and undermining their authority. Herod was afraid of what he had heard about him, as we have seen in 6:14–16, as a potential political danger, another populist leader like John the Baptist. But why 'yeast'?

Yeast was a traditional symbol for pervasive influence, sometimes good (Matthew 13:33), usually bad (1 Corinthians 5:6–9). It works unseen until the whole lump of dough is affected. The Pharisees and Herod in their different ways represent the insidious danger of a mistaken attitude to Jesus. Beware of being infected by it. That was probably what he intended the disciples to hear, but their preoccupation with their lack of bread prevented them from hearing it.

Spiritual myopia

Jesus' language in verses 17–18 is extraordinarily strong. It reminds us of the ominous words from Isaiah which he used in 4:12. But there he was talking about 'outsiders', whereas the disciples were those to whom the secret had been revealed. But now it is the disciples themselves who are blind and deaf to the realities of the kingdom of God.

In particular, they have failed to learn the lesson of the two miracles of feeding. His careful reminder of the details of the two stories shows how important these two miracles were. So what is the lesson they have failed to grasp? Is it that with Jesus in the boat they have no need to worry about lack of provisions? If so few loaves fed so many people with so much left over, surely one little roll is more than enough for a group of 13! Perhaps that is all he means, but perhaps also there is the more general criticism that they are still thinking of merely mundane matters when Jesus' mission is on a different level altogether. The feeding miracles did provide literal food indeed, but those who had experienced them ought surely also to be beginning to see that Jesus is more than just a provider of food. 'Do you not yet understand?'

Prayer

Lord, we often fail to understand your purposes and cannot see beyond our own little concerns. Please cure our blindness.

51 Mark 8:22–26

A blind man cured – by stages

Another healing outside Galilee

Bethsaida was across the Jordan at the north end of the lake, not in Galilee but in the neighbouring territory ruled by Herod Philip, adjoining the Decapolis. So this healing occurs in a similar area to that of 7:31–37, and it follows a similar pattern. In each case it is other people who approach Jesus on behalf of the sufferer, asking for a healing touch. In each Jesus deliberately withdraws from the public arena before healing, and then issues a command to silence. Each story goes into unusual detail on the actions performed by Jesus to effect the healing, each involving touching directly the affected organs and the use of saliva.

Blindness – literal and metaphorical

Act 2 of Mark's gospel begins and ends with the healing of a blind man (see 10:45–52 for the second). In between Jesus will devote much of his attention to teaching his disciples, who will again and again show how little they have yet grasped of what Jesus' mission is all about. Their gradual awakening to the radical new dynamics of the kingdom of God is one of the main themes of this central section of the gospel. So it is likely that Mark expected his readers to understand the two healings of blind men which frame the section not only literally but also symbolically. After all, Jesus has just described his disciples as spiritually blind (vv. 17–18). He has also called them deaf (v. 18), and we have seen that the healing of the deaf and dumb man in 7:31–37 is closely parallel to this story. So perhaps the two miracles are to be seen as a pair, important indeed in their literal sense, but also symbolic of the dawning of new understanding in the disciples.

A two-stage healing

The story of the blind man at Bethsaida is unique in the gospels in that when Jesus first lays his hands on the man's eyes the healing is only partial ('people like trees, walking'), and it is only after a second touch that he sees everything clearly. Perhaps it is for this reason that neither Matthew nor Luke includes this story, as they may not have liked the suggestion that at first Jesus was not completely successful. But Mark may have found it particularly appropriate to his purpose, since the restoration of 'sight' to the disciples also proceeded by stages. In 4:11 they were described as privileged to understand the secret of the kingdom of God, but by 8:17-18 they seem no better than the outsiders who cannot grasp the secret. In 8:29 Peter will make a great declaration of faith in Jesus as the Messiah, but three verses later he will reveal that he has still not grasped what Jesus' mission really involves. As the disciples struggle to come to terms with new realities in these three chapters, they will be like the blind man, seeing at first only dimly and still needing further help to get things really clear.

Prayer

Thy blessed unction from above
Is comfort, life, and fire of love;
Enable with perpetual light
The dullness of our blinded sight.
Veni Creator

52 Mark 8:27–30

Peter declares his faith

Caesarea Philippi is the most northerly point of Jesus' journeys, in a remote non-Jewish area in the foothills of the Mount Hermon range. He takes his disciples not to the town itself but into the countryside, and the whole focus of this part of the story is on time spent by Jesus alone with his disciples. He has not come here for public ministry, but for private instruction. And like any good teacher he begins with questions.

What do other people think?

He begins with the easier, more objective question. The disciples have no difficulty in reporting what they have gathered of popular opinion about Jesus. The answer is already familiar to us from 6:14–15, where the same three options – John the Baptist, Elijah or an (unnamed) prophet – were being canvassed. We have thought about the names offered when we looked at that passage (see pp. 82–83). All are variations on the theme 'prophet'. And as far as they go, they are right, for Jesus is a prophet, someone who speaks the word of God to the people of God, and calls them to respond to him.

But is that all there is to be said about Jesus? Is he merely a spokesman for God? And so we come to the second and much more searching question.

What do you think?

It is typical of Peter that he emerges as the spokesman for the disciple group. They have been sharing together the extraordinary experiences of Jesus' teaching and miracles, and no doubt they have already been discussing together what they are to make of it all. It is unlikely that what Peter now says is a brand new idea thought up on the spur of the moment. But it is the first time the truth has been squarely faced, and it is Peter who has the honour, and the responsibility, of giving it open expression.

Jesus is the Messiah. The word would mean different things in detail to different groups of Jews, but to all of them it would have the ring of uniqueness and of finality. The one whose coming has long been foretold has at last arrived. The 'last days' of which the prophets have spoken are upon us. 'The time is fulfilled and the kingdom of God is at hand' (1:15).

So much would be agreed, but what does the coming of the kingdom of God mean? How is the Messiah to fulfil his pivotal role? Is he coming to bring spiritual renewal to God's people or to deliver them from the sovereignty of Rome? It is here that there is too much room for misunderstanding, not to mention vested interests. The word 'Messiah' is a trigger for all sorts of different hopes and fears to be brought into play.

The 'Messianic secret'

Jesus' command to tell no one must have been a terrible deflation after the euphoria which Peter's heady words would induce. But there is too much danger in unguarded talk of 'the Messiah' for Jesus to allow them to use it outside their own small circle. Even the disciples have a long way to go before they understand it themselves, as verses 31–33 will go on to show. So, for the time being, the secret must be kept. It will not be until 14:61–62, in very different circumstances, that Jesus lifts the embargo.

Prayer

Lord, give us the wisdom to know what may be said, and when, and to whom. Save us both from the timidity which will not speak and from unwisely blurting out what must be communicated with care.

53 Mark 8:31–34

A dose of cold water

The command to maintain silence must have been deflating enough, but what follows is far harder to take.

The martyrdom of the Son of Man

The exciting title 'Messiah' is immediately dropped, and Jesus speaks of himself, as he usually does, as the 'Son of Man'. This was a title without the ready-made associations of 'Messiah', and one which therefore Jesus could use to express what he wanted to say about his unique role without the danger of triggering inappropriate hopes of political liberation.

But worse than the change of title is what Jesus actually says about his 'messianic' mission. It is the very opposite of what most Jews would have expected, and surely also of what Peter and the other disciples had in mind. Rather than being an all-conquering hero, he is to be the victim of rejection and assassination. And worse still, those who reject and kill him are to be not the Romans (that would at least have been a noble if futile self-sacrifice), but the leaders of his own people. 'The elders, the chief priests and the scribes' were the three groups who made up the Sanhedrin, the Jewish supreme court; you could not have a more formidable and authoritative listing of the Jewish authorities. And it is this Jewish power-group who will reject and eliminate Israel's Messiah!

Peter gets it wrong

This is too much for Peter, fresh from the exhilaration of his great statement of faith. And the first part of verse 33 suggests that he is speaking also for the other disciples when he takes it upon himself to 'rebuke' Jesus. His protest is entirely natural – but that is just the trouble. He is speaking 'human thoughts', and completely missing the divine perspective. To human thinking, a rejected and assassinated Messiah is sheer nonsense – but it is through such 'nonsense' that God's saving purpose is to be fulfilled (see Paul's comments in 1 Corinthians 1:18–25). To adopt this human perspective is to take the side of Satan.

Take up your cross

And, still worse, it is not only Jesus who must face the cross, but his followers too. When they first responded to Jesus' 'Follow me' they can have had no idea of what this new commitment might involve, but now it is becoming painfully clear that they have joined not a triumphal procession but a funeral cortege. We have become so familiar with the language of 'taking up the cross' that we miss its stark and unpalatable meaning: the funeral is likely to be their own! To follow a martyr Messiah is to accept the risk of martyrdom.

So the shadow of the cross falls firmly across the road to Jerusalem, and several more times Jesus will remind them of it before they reach the capital, where the grim prediction will become only too real a fact. The cross is that of Jesus, but potentially it is also their own. Was this what they had reckoned with when they signed on as disciples of the Messiah?

For meditation

Put yourself in the position of one of the twelve disciples, with all the experiences of chapters 1–8 behind you. How would you have reacted to Peter's confession and to Jesus' response to it? With what thoughts would you have set out on the road to Jerusalem? Would you have set out at all?

54 Mark 8:35—9:1
Ultimate realities

Gaining and losing

Verses 35–37 are hard to translate, since the same Greek word, here translated by 'life' (but sometimes also by 'soul'), means both the fact of being physically alive and not dead and also the real self which is far more than physical life and which survives beyond it. Jesus' words depend on the contrast between these two senses of the same Greek word. To cling to (physical) life may be to forfeit (spiritual) life, while those who lose their (physical) life because of their loyalty to the cause of the gospel will find that their true (spiritual) life is saved and not lost. The ultimate question, then, is which is more worth preserving. In the light of his command to 'take up the cross', it is a real and pressing question for the disciples as they set out for Jerusalem.

A choice of loyalty

The language about the Son of Man 'coming' in glory and in the company of angels is a clear echo of the vision of Daniel 7:13–14, the passage from which Jesus drew his chosen title 'the Son of Man'. In that vision the 'one like a son of man' comes before God and is given eternal and universal sovereignty over all nations. It is a heavenly enthronement scene and is set in a context of universal judgement. So the same 'Son of Man' who will die in Jerusalem is destined after that to be enthroned as judge of all people.

To recognise this will put the disciples' choice in a new perspective. To fail under the more immediate pressure of human opposition is to risk the more ultimate danger of being repudiated by the Judge of all, whom they have chosen to follow and then have denied. When you put it like that, who would want to throw in their lot with 'this adulterous and sinful generation'?

Seeing and believing

Some of those who have taken up their cross to follow the Son of Man may well have to 'taste death' before they see any fruition for their loyalty in this life. For them it will be only the ultimate encounter with the

Son of Man after death which will vindicate their loyalty. But for others there will be something to show for their faithfulness even in this life: they 'will see that the kingdom of God has come with power'.

Jesus does not say when and how they will see it, and interpreters have offered many guesses. There is no reason to imagine that he was referring to his second coming: that is not what he says. Perhaps the kingdom of God will be seen to have come in power in Jesus' own vindication by resurrection after his death; perhaps in his visible ascension to the right hand of power; perhaps in the coming of the Holy Spirit; or in the powerful spread of the gospel among the nations in the decades after Pentecost. Certainly while some of those first disciples were still alive there would be ample evidence, for those with the eyes to see it, that the kingdom of God, planted secretly like a little mustard seed, was now beginning its growth into a great bush. The authority of the Son of Man enthroned at God's right hand would soon be seen in its power and glory.

Prayer

Lord, you know how strongly we are affected by the people and pressures which surround us. Help us to see beyond the immediate, to have the eyes to see the evidence of your power at work in our world, and to see beyond this world to your ultimate power and glory. And so may our loyalty be rightly placed, where it will matter in the end.

55 Mark 9:2-8

The veil is drawn aside

There is a further possible meaning of Jesus' puzzling saying in verse 1 about seeing that the kingdom of God has come with power. For 'some' (only three) of those who heard it would indeed have a more immediate vision of power and glory, a foretaste of what was to come after Jesus' death and resurrection. Mark does not usually link his episodes together with careful notes of time, and perhaps the unusual precision here ('after six days') is meant to alert us to the link between verse 1 and the incident which follows so closely upon it.

A vision of glory

Mark relates this extraordinary vision from the point of view of the three disciples who were privileged to witness it, speaking throughout of what they saw, experienced, heard and felt. After the depressing words at the end of chapter 8, no doubt they needed some encouragement to offset the gloom which must have descended on the disciple group. But this was more than just a timely reassurance. It lifted their understanding of Jesus to new and amazing heights.

We have no way of knowing how such a 'vision' (as Matthew calls it, Matthew 17:9) came about, whether there was anything which a cine-camera could have recorded or whether it was 'all in the mind'. But Mark records it as a shared experience which seemed to Peter real enough to make him think of building physical dwellings for the visionary visitors.

There is no other story like this in the gospels. Jesus' power and authority as the Son of God is displayed in many ways, but always in the form of what appears to be an ordinary human being. But here the veil is briefly drawn aside, and the glory of heaven shines through. No wonder they are bewildered and frightened as they see the dazzling light and Jesus recognisable and yet transformed. Then, just as Jesus had after his baptism (1:11), they hear the voice of God himself identifying Jesus as his Son. In 1:11 God spoke to Jesus himself, but now he speaks to the disciples and calls them to accept his authority and 'listen to him'. After this there can be no choice as to whom they are to follow, whatever the cost.

Elijah and Moses

Elijah and Moses have been long dead, yet here they are 'talking with Jesus'! Elijah, as we have seen, was expected to come back to usher in the day of the Lord, and Moses had left a promise that God would send to his people 'a prophet like me' (Deuteronomy 18:15). So the reappearance of these two worthies from Israel's past marks the time for the fulfilment of God's promises. Moreover, there are other links between these two men and the story of Jesus. Both were men sent by God but rejected by his people. Both had to battle with loneliness and misunderstanding. Both had gone up on a high mountain to meet with God. And these two men, together with Enoch, were famous as the three who had mysteriously disappeared from the earth, Elijah in a chariot of fire and Moses on a mountain where 'no one knows his burial place' (Deuteronomy 34:6).

Peter, James and John probably understood little of this at the time. Peter's strange proposal to erect impromptu shelters on the mountain is perhaps a clumsy attempt to do justice to the presence of such august visitors. Perhaps too he has hopes of 'fixing' this passing experience in physical structures, but if so he is unsuccessful, because soon the whole mind-blowing experience is over, and nothing remains but the memory.

Prayer

Thank you, Lord, for the 'mountaintop' experiences you sometimes allow us to enjoy. Help us to draw strength from them, but not to cling to them, and to know the reality of Jesus' divine glory and authority in the valley as well.

56 Mark 9:9–13

What about Elijah?

There is something bizarre and yet reassuring in the picture of Jesus walking down the mountain in earnest conversation with Peter, James and John, so soon after they have seen him bathed in dazzling light and talking with men long dead. The otherworldly vision is over, and now they must return to ordinary life. But what they have seen on the mountain has left them with a lot to think about.

Sworn to secrecy

Can you imagine how Peter, James and John would have enjoyed telling their story to the others – and what the others might have made of it? But they are not to have the opportunity. If Peter's declaration that Jesus is the Messiah has had to be embargoed, how much more this vision of him as the Son of God. This was not to be a matter of public amazement and speculation. It was 'for their eyes only'.

But this time there is a time limit. The embargo remains until after 'the Son of Man has risen from the dead'. When Jesus talked in 8:31 of his forthcoming death, he had also predicted that he would rise again after three days. The disciples clearly can make nothing of such language, and even after three more such predictions (9:31; 10:34; 14:28) they will still be caught unawares by his physical resurrection.

'Elijah has come'

But for now they have another matter on their minds. When they saw Elijah on the mountain they began to put the pieces together, and realised that this had something to do with the coming of the last days. But how does it all fit? Are the scribes right that Elijah must come first? If so, where is he? Was this vision perhaps all that his promised coming would amount to? Or is he still waiting in the wings?

Yes, says Jesus, the scribes are right (and indeed it was not their idea: they got it from Malachi 4:5–6!). But what they and the disciples have failed to realise is that that prophecy has already been fulfilled, in the coming of John the Baptist as the 'Elijah' of the last days (see comments on his Elijah image, on 1:4–8, pp. 14–15). Not that Jesus names John the Baptist here, but the reference to what 'they did to him' is a clear allusion to the story of the death of John which Mark has told in 6:17–29. And in John's fate Jesus sees a foreshadowing of his own: if 'Elijah' has been treated like that, surely the Son of Man must expect no better response. He too must 'go through many sufferings and be treated with contempt'.

So even on the way down from the mountain of glory the shadow of the cross still falls. The Son of God who has shone on the mountain is the same as the Son of Man who will suffer on the cross, but who will also rise from the dead. Is it any wonder that the disciples are finding it all too hard to grasp?

Prayer

Lord, help us to grasp as much as you want us to grasp of your truth and to trust you where we do not yet understand.

57 Mark 9:14–29
Why the disciples failed

After the splendour of the mountaintop comes a sad contrast, a story of human distress and of the failure of faith. This will be the last time Mark tells of an exorcism by Jesus, but he tells this story as much to explain why the disciples failed to help the possessed boy as to display yet again Jesus' total mastery over the powers of evil. It is a lesson about faith and prayer rather than just another miracle of Jesus.

Demon possession and physical illness

We have noted repeatedly that Mark uses different language for demon-possession and exorcism from that which he uses for physical illness and its cure. The two are different situations and are not to be confused. But the vivid description of the physical suffering of the boy in this story (vv. 18, 20, 22) is so similar to what we know as an epileptic fit that it is often rather unthinkingly referred to as the story of 'The epileptic boy'.

There is no doubt that Mark understands it as a case of demon possession, both in his description of the problem and in the way Jesus confronts and expels the unclean spirit in verses 25–26. Our knowledge of ancient medical thinking is not full enough for us to say how widely epilepsy (sometimes known in pagan circles as 'the divine illness') was taken to be a spiritual rather than a purely physical affliction. Knowledge of brain function was very limited, and it would be quite understandable if the symptoms of epilepsy were attributed to a supernatural force. But Mark does not use any word meaning 'epilepsy', and we are on safer ground if we take it to be, as Mark describes it, a case of demon possession which had severe physical and behavioural repercussions.

The disciples' failure

While Jesus and the three disciples have been away, the rest of the group have found themselves confronted by a situation which they could not cope with. When Jesus had sent them out in 6:7 their commission was specifically to have 'authority over the unclean spirits' and they were then able to 'cast out many demons' (6:13) without having Jesus with them. So why have they not been able to do the same now? Was that authority given them only for the specific occasion of the mission in chapter 6? There is no indication that this was so. Or was there something uniquely demanding about this particular case which lifted it out of the normal run of exorcisms? Both symptoms and exorcism are indeed described in unusually lurid detail, but it is not easy to see why one demon should be more resistant to the delegated authority of Jesus than another.

The disciples themselves are taken by surprise: 'Why could we not cast it out?' Jesus' reply is equally surprising. He does not specify what 'this kind' are, but it is strange that prayer is the key to 'this kind' rather than to all exorcisms, and even more strange that he implies that the disciples had not in fact prayed about this case. One might have expected that to be normal.

Faith and prayer

So is the point perhaps that after their earlier successes they have become blasé and have assumed that they have been given an automatic guarantee of success, instead of turning to God for the authority which is needed in this (and every) case? Those who have been for some time in Christian ministry are too easily prone to taking God's work for granted. The whole story is thus a salutary reminder that there is nothing automatic about spiritual conflict. Even the twelve must depend not on their status as Jesus' chosen agents but on the power which comes through prayer.

The key word again is 'faith'. It is 'faithlessness' that Jesus complains of (v. 19), and 'faith' which is the essential condition of deliverance (vv. 23–24). It is the faith of the disciples which has proved inadequate, as they have failed to pray.

Prayer

'Lord, I believe. Help my unbelief!'

58 Mark 9:30-32

Another warning of what is to come

In this brief paragraph we find several of the key themes which run through the middle section (Act 2) of Mark's story, as Jesus and his disciples make their way from Galilee towards Jerusalem. We may therefore take it as an opportunity to remind ourselves of how the drama is developing.

Private teaching

Jesus' attempts to avoid public notice have been a repeated feature of the story since chapter 1. But this time we are given the reason for it. It is because he is teaching his disciples. During the time in Galilee the disciples have learned along with the crowds, with further private explanation added from time to time. But now the time has come to focus more narrowly on the little group who will be the key to the continuation of Jesus' mission when he himself is no longer there. So in Act 2 there is relatively little public activity, and Jesus and his disciples travel together as a small group. And as they go, he teaches them many things to do with the kingdom of God. They have many new things to grasp while he is still there to teach them, and the time is short.

The shadow of the cross

The shock statement with which Jesus has launched the journey towards Jerusalem in 8:31 is repeated here and again in more detail in 10:33-34. This awful new dimension to their understanding of Jesus' mission is thus relentlessly kept before their reluctant minds. The heady days of public acclaim and popularity in Galilee are over, and Jesus is on his way to martyrdom. And that means that it will not be very long before they must learn to manage without him. But above all they must learn to recognise that the death which he so unequivocally predicts is not to be an unfortunate accident, but is the very goal of his ministry. What it will achieve is so far left unexplained, though later he will spell it out for them (10:45; 14:22-25). And again there is that tantalising hint that for Jesus, death will not be the end, but he will rise again after three days. All this is so new and so stunning, that even with constant repetition it will take them all their time even to begin to grasp it.

'They did not understand'

Already Jesus has complained at the disciples' failure to understand (8:17–21). This failure is a repeated theme of these chapters. Immediately after each of the three predictions of his death we come down to earth with a bump as the disciples reveal in various ways their complete lack of sympathy with the new values of the kingdom of God (8:32; 9:33–34; 10:35–37). And each time Jesus patiently (or not so patiently, 8:33!) puts them right.

Everything is so new and unexpected, and so contrary to conventional human thinking, that it needs a complete programme of re-education to accustom the disciples to the radical and paradoxical values of the kingdom of God. And much of it they would rather not learn. The little note in verse 32 that 'they were afraid to ask him' indicates not so much that Jesus was difficult to approach, but rather that they had enough of an inkling of what he was talking about to know that they would rather not hear it spelled out!

Prayer

Lord, be patient with our slowness to grasp your truth, and lead us on to new understanding. And when you need to teach us things we would rather not hear, give us the courage to face up to them.

59 Mark 9:33-37

Who is the greatest?

Lines of authority

In a newly formed group of colleagues with an important task, it is natural to want to clarify the lines of authority. So far, of course, Jesus has been the focal authority of the group, but if they are going to lose him it will surely be vital to establish a clear pecking order. So they feel the need to decide between themselves 'who is the greatest'. Any management consultant would have urged them to do so.

The issue comes up repeatedly in the gospels, and will be tackled more fully in 10:35-45. But already it seems that the disciples are beginning to be aware that Jesus looks at this question of status rather differently. When he wants to know what they have been talking about, they refuse to reply – for all the world like a group of naughty schoolboys who have been caught misbehaving by the teacher.

Greatness in service

'The first will be last' was something of a slogan of Jesus' teaching. It will be stated more definitively in 10:31, and its implications for leadership in the disciple group will be spelled out more fully in 10:42-45. Here it is stated with devastating simplicity. Rather than looking for greatness, they should be eager to be at the bottom of the pile. Rather than aiming to dominate others, they should aspire to be the servant of all. The object of their ambition should be not influence and authority but usefulness. The greatest is the least and the leader is the dogsbody.

That is not the way most people think. Such an attitude is not even respected. It is not noble but demeaning. The people who get things done are the aggressive and ruthless, and people respect the leadership of those who assert themselves. Jesus' upside-down principle of greatness would be dismissed by most people, then and now, as at best whimsical and unrealistic.

The example of a child

Jesus, good teacher as he is, reinforces his startling pronouncement with a visual aid. The child symbolises the 'least'. Children are at the bottom of the authority structure of society. They are expected to do as they are told and have no self-determination. They are to be looked after, not to be looked up to. They are all too easily overlooked and exploited by adult society. And they long for the day when they in their turn will be grown up and able to tell others what to do.

But for Jesus the child represents the one who matters in the kingdom of God. Anyone who wants to share the values of Jesus must welcome and respect the little one as much as (or more than?) the great. The last are to be first. For behind the vulnerable figure of the child stands Jesus himself, and behind Jesus stands 'the one who sent me'. Remember Jesus' words in Matthew 25:40: 'Just as you did it to one of the least of these… you did it to me.'

For meditation

In what ways should we as followers of Jesus challenge the accepted ideas of our society about status and leadership? How far are we ourselves conditioned by the assumption that 'the first shall be first'?

60 Mark 9:38–41
'Not one of us'

John the son of Zebedee was one of the 'Sons of Thunder' (3:17) and here he lives up to his name. In 10:35–40 he and his brother James will show even more blatantly how far they have yet to go to grasp the values of the kingdom of God.

Building barriers, not bridges

The issue here is cliquishness. It is natural for most groups of people to develop a sense of group identity and to erect barriers to define who does and who does not belong. And for a religious group, whose concern is properly with truth and orthodoxy, this is an even more natural tendency. The history of religion is all too often the history of drawing lines of demarcation, of secessions and expulsions, of schism and of closing ranks. It is characteristic of many religious people to be sure that 'I am right and you are wrong' and to insist that 'what is not done my way should not be done at all'.

So it was natural for John to conclude that a man who was casting out demons (apparently successfully) but who did not belong to the disciple group was not to be tolerated. He was using Jesus' name, but he was not one of Jesus' disciples. He was at best a fellow-traveller, at worst a charlatan. But in any case he was 'not one of us'.

A more welcoming approach

The existence of such a character need not surprise us. Exorcism was a recognised (if not widespread) practice among the Jews. Jesus refers to other Jewish exorcists apparently with approval in Matthew 12:27, and we meet others in Acts 19:13–16. And Jesus will not allow John to write this man off. Whatever his background, he is engaged in good work. He is on the side of good against evil.

Jesus reinforces this open attitude with a series of comments in verses 39–41 on the approach to people who are 'not one of us'. The disciple group may find support from unexpected quarters, and they should welcome and not repel it. There are people out there who may not themselves wear the name of Christ on their sleeve, but who in the end will prove to be supporters and not opponents. Such people 'will by no means lose their reward'.

For or against

The refreshingly open-minded attitude of this section is summed up in the formula: 'Whoever is not against us is for us.' John would no doubt have preferred to invoke the saying in Matthew 12:30 (again in a context of exorcism), 'Whoever is not with me is against me'. On either formula there is no room for neutrality, but what a difference of atmosphere between the open, welcoming attitude of this verse and the exclusivism of the other. In different circumstances there may be a place for either, but we should beware of the natural tendency to jump to the negative conclusion when faced with an 'outsider' who may in fact turn out to be 'for' rather than 'against'.

Prayer

Thank you, Lord, that you welcome us. Help us to welcome others in your name.

61 Mark 9:42–50

Hard sayings

These verses contain a collection of sayings, probably originally independent of each other, which are linked by catchwords: stumbling, fire, salt. They draw out some of the demands and the perils of discipleship, and warn against an easy, lax approach which refuses to take the kingdom of God seriously.

Verse 42

The child of verses 36–37 and the donor of the cup of water in verse 41 are examples of the 'little ones' whom a careless disciple may cause to stumble. Such people are easily ignored or pushed aside. But if a disciple's attitude or actions makes it harder for them to find their place in the kingdom of God, that is a serious matter, so serious that even drowning would be better than the fate such behaviour deserves.

Verses 43–48

But 'stumbling' may be caused not only by someone else but by something in our own lives. The disciple who is 'tripped up' by his or her own hand, foot or eye would be better off without the offending part of the body. The hand, foot and eye are probably to be taken as symbolic of areas of personality or behaviour which may prevent us from fulfilling our calling as disciples. Bad habits and bad company may make it impossible for us to live the life of the kingdom of God. If that is the case, let them be cut out before it is too late. The alternative is hell, 'Gehenna', the name of the rubbish tip outside Jerusalem where refuse was thrown out and burned. The chilling words 'their worm never dies and the fire is not quenched', drawing on the picture of the rubbish tip, make it luridly clear how much is at stake. Here is Jesus at his most severe, an important corrective to the 'cuddly' image of Jesus which is sometimes presented.

Verse 49

This verse is a puzzle. Perhaps it draws on the Old Testament ritual in which salt was added to sacrifices, and so pictures the disciple as a living sacrifice to God. Or perhaps it suggests that fire which can destroy (as in verses 43–48) can also be used to purify and preserve, as salt does, so that a disciple's painful experience may bring salvation in the end. But it remains obscure.

Verse 50

Here are two more sayings involving salt. Salt was used by the rabbis as a metaphor for wisdom, and Paul uses it similarly in Colossians 4:5–6. A disciple's life and words should contribute to the 'flavour' of life by their wisdom and suitability. But if we lose our Christian distinctiveness the 'salt' goes out of our discipleship, and we cease to be of any value to those around us. A life without Christian wisdom is as unpalatable, and as liable to go bad, as food without salt. But where Christian 'saltiness' is maintained, it will avoid conflict and promote peace with one another.

These verses form a strange and rather incoherent section of the gospel, but one which is full of provocative nuggets of thought by which we can test the seriousness and effectiveness of our own discipleship.

Prayer

Lord, save us from the casual and uncaring approach to the kingdom of God which puts our own and other people's discipleship at risk.

62 Mark 10:1–9

No place for divorce

Divorce – now and then

In a society in which divorce has become normal and accepted, Jesus' robust condemnation of it comes as a shock. But the same was true in his own day. While Jewish authorities debated the grounds for divorce, no one questioned that divorce as such was permissible. After all, had not Moses given explicit directions to regulate it (Deuteronomy 24:1–4)? Some taught that the 'something objectionable' mentioned in Deuteronomy 24:1 meant adultery and nothing more, while others (and their view was inevitably the more popular among Jewish men) taught that it could cover even quite trivial matters like bad cooking or even not being pretty enough. The casual approach that prevailed is summed up in Josephus' laconic comment in his autobiography: 'At this time I divorced my wife, since I did not like her behaviour.' The main difference from our own situation was that in Jewish law a man could divorce his wife with a minimum of fuss, but the woman could not divorce her husband.

Going back to first principles

Jesus' first response to the question is to establish the legal basis for divorce in the Old Testament. There is only one relevant legal text, and that is the one they quote. But in fact they do not quote it exactly, since Deuteronomy 24:1–4 does not in fact explicitly 'allow divorce', but rather regulates what may and may not happen once a divorce has been officially recognised and the woman has remarried. Moses certainly assumes divorce, and it may be argued that this implies that he 'allows' it. That was the basis on which the whole Jewish approach to divorce rested. But it would be going too far to claim that Moses either commanded or approved divorce; he merely regulated the aftermath. That is what Jesus means by describing his regulations as 'because of the hardness of your hearts' – they were a concession to human weakness, not a statement of the way things ought to have been.

So Jesus turns their attention instead not to the concession but to the original statement of God's intention for marriage in the first two chapters of Genesis. The key concept is that a man and a woman form 'one flesh', by entering into a new and exclusive union in place of their previous parental links. Marriage, in other words, is not just a contract for mutual convenience (and therefore able to be terminated when it ceases to suit the parties), but the creation of a new and indivisible unit of man and woman as 'one flesh'.

Marriage is forever

If that is how God intended marriage to be, it is not for human beings to tamper with it. 'What God has joined together, let no one separate.' There it is, God's standard for marriage stated simply, clearly, unequivocally and without a hint of any basis for divorce. Divorce is, quite simply, against the will of God.

The boldness of Jesus' statement is breathtaking. In Matthew's version (5:32; 19:9) there is an escape clause, 'except on the ground of unchastity', but in Mark and Luke (16:18) it is entirely unqualified. In the next study we shall return to the question of how we are to live with this absolute demand in the real world and of how the standard set out in Genesis relates to the concession allowed in Deuteronomy, but for now it is important that we do not seek to evade the uncompromising call to lifelong fidelity in marriage. The moment we begin to think about exceptions and concessions (and, as Matthew's 'escape clause' reminds us, we cannot avoid doing so in dealing with real people in a real world), this simple clarity is lost, and we are in danger of treating as normal what is in fact the betrayal of God's plan for marriage. Jesus insists instead that we go back to the way God meant it to be, and draw our standards from there.

Prayer

Forgive us, Lord, for our eagerness to find the easy way out and our fear of facing up to your full demand. Restore to us and to our society the vision of marriage as you meant it to be.

63 Mark 10:10–12

Did Jesus really mean it?

As in 7:17 and in chapter 4 a startling pronouncement is followed by the disciples asking Jesus to explain it. Surely he could not really want to sweep away the whole possibility of divorce (which Moses apparently allowed) at one go? So what did he mean?

Divorce and remarriage

But the explanation which follows in no way weakens the demand made in verse 9. Rather it spells out in more practical detail what are its radical implications. Divorce followed by remarriage is tantamount to adultery, since it violates the 'one flesh' union. If the divorce was not permissible, clearly neither is the remarriage: you cannot be married to two people at once.

It is sometimes suggested that Jesus' words apply only to the remarriage which follows on a divorce, and that Jesus does not condemn a divorce if the parties then remain unmarried. In terms of the precise words of verses 11–12 this is a possible interpretation, but it flies in the face of the absolute prohibition of divorce in verse 9, where the issue of remarriage had not yet been raised. In any case, in Jewish society at the time it would have made no sense to talk of divorce without the right to remarry: divorce was precisely the setting free of a formerly married person to marry again. So it is not the remarriage as such which is the focus of Jesus' condemnation, but the breaking of the one-flesh union, whether or not another marriage follows.

(Mark, alone among the gospels, envisages in verse 12 a wife divorcing her husband as well as vice versa. While this was impossible in Jewish law it was allowed in Roman law, and Mark, if he was writing in Rome, may have included this logical extension of the principle for the sake of those around him.)

Biblical ideals in the real world

Mark therefore offers us an unqualified and total rejection of divorce by Jesus. Marriage is 'till death us do part'. But divorces do in fact happen, and Moses had already provided legislation to deal with what follows from a divorce. Are we then to say that Moses was wrong even to countenance the possibility? According to Jesus he provided for divorce 'because of your hardness of heart' – and human hearts are still hard, and marriages do break down. Should those who follow Jesus simply close their eyes to this reality? Or should they sadly accept that Jesus' ideal teaching, wonderful as it is, simply does not fit the way things are?

There is a way between these two extremes, but it is a difficult one to define and to practise without inconsistency. It is to insist both that God's standard is absolute and that divorce can never be good, and also that in a world which is characterised by human weakness and failure it must be possible to find ways of coping with a broken marriage (as Moses found that he had to). In that case divorce and remarriage, while it can never be good, may be the least bad of the options available. It may thus be the right thing to do in the circumstances, but can never cease to be a cause for regret and sorrow that God's standard for marriage has been violated. Perhaps it is this reluctant recognition of the realities of human failure which led Matthew to include his clause allowing divorce in the case of 'unchastity'.

But if, reluctantly, we come to this conclusion, it is a very different matter from accepting the verdict of society that divorce is 'okay', and assuming that Jesus' words are an unworkable ideal. They are not. They are the way God expects marriage to be, and woe betide the church and society once that clear standard is allowed to fade into only an unreachable ideal. Divorce and remarriage can never be more than the outworking of human weakness, a recognition of failure.

For meditation

How has it been possible for society to move so far from the clear teaching of Jesus, and how can the church now both witness to God's purpose for marriage and also offer appropriate pastoral help to those whose marriages are in trouble?

64 Mark 10:13-16

Whose is the kingdom of God?

The 'kingdom of God' is mentioned twice in these verses and three times more in verses 23-25. The phrase, as we have seen, means 'God's rule', and what the disciples are being forced to face in this series of incidents are some of the radically different ways in which life must be lived under God's sovereignty as compared with the conventions of human society. The programme of re-education for the disciples which has been under way since Caesarea Philippi is now coming to its climax as Jesus draws nearer to Jerusalem, and one blow after another to the disciples' unthinking assumptions leaves them, and us, reeling before the values of the kingdom of God which seem to turn all our natural expectations upside down.

Do not stop them

It was the custom for children to be brought to the elders for blessing on the Day of Atonement, and perhaps that was the occasion for this incident. Or perhaps this was something less formal: people wanted Jesus to touch and bless their children, just as they wanted him to heal those who were ill.

But the disciples are not happy with this. Perhaps they feel that it is beneath the master's dignity to be worried with children, or perhaps, aware of the great threats hanging over Jesus, they want to protect him being troubled and distracted by lesser concerns. Jesus has better things to do than to be stopping to bless children.

After the lesson the disciples have already been taught in 9:36-37 you would think they would have a clearer understanding of Jesus' sense of priorities, but old prejudices die hard and, for the adult male, children are not a priority. So again (they must be getting used to this!) they get a good telling off from Jesus, and once again he proceeds to turn their values upside down.

Children and the kingdom of God

Jesus makes two separate comments relating to children and the kingdom of God.

First, the kingdom of God belongs to 'such as these'. In the light of 9:33–37 we are probably right not to take this as referring exclusively, or even mainly, to children as such. 'Such as these' means rather those in the childlike position, the weak, vulnerable, unnoticed members of society, the people who are easily marginalised by a macho disciple, the 'little ones' of 9:42. Not that this excludes children, of course; it was because they were keeping actual children away from him that Jesus said it. But it is wider than that. The kingdom of God 'belongs to' such people in the sense that they are the ones who most naturally fit into it. The God who 'has brought down the powerful from their thrones and lifted up the lowly' (Luke 1:52) rejoices to have such people as his subjects, and it is from them, not from the self-important, that we can best learn how to serve him.

Second, in order to enter God's kingdom, to become his true subjects, we must receive it 'as a little child'. The child is dependent and knows it. What the child receives from grown-ups is not earned or fought for. The child's empty hand receives simply and gratefully. That is how we must receive God's kingship and the blessings it brings to those who know they cannot deserve his grace, but simply enjoy it.

Prayer

Lord, make us more like children in our relationship with you, and more ready to welcome and value those whom society does not regard as important.

65 Mark 10:17-22

A potential disciple lost

The man who had everything

From the disciples' point of view this man must have seemed the ideal recruit. He was an earnest seeker for eternal life, with a good moral record (v. 20). According to Matthew he was a young man and according to Luke a ruler. And he was very rich. Any religious movement would go to great lengths to gain such an adherent, and here he was making contact of his own accord. If ever there was a case for the red-carpet treatment, this must be it.

But instead Jesus sends him away with his tail between his legs. Whatever can he be thinking of? What is the kingdom of God all about if it is not interested in such a recruit as this? We shall consider the disciples' amazed reaction in the next study, but first we must listen to the dialogue between Jesus and the rich enquirer.

What is 'good'?

His address to Jesus as 'Good Teacher' is probably mere politeness, but Jesus takes it as an opportunity to raise a fundamental issue. The man's opening question seems to assume that eternal life is to be 'earned' by doing good things. Like many people today, he perhaps thinks of salvation as like sitting an examination and coming up with high enough marks to pass. Jesus' unexpected response turns the spotlight away from doing good things to the one true focus of goodness, which is in God himself. (To read Jesus' words, as some do, as implying that he himself is not good, and therefore not God, is to take them completely out of context. The discussion is about eternal life, not about who Jesus is.)

Jesus first offers him the ten commandments (or rather that part of them which relates to how we treat other people, without the commandments touching on our relationship with God). But this is all familiar ground, and if that was all the man wanted to be told he would not have come to Jesus with his urgent question. Despite his (no doubt sincere) claim to have kept the commandments, he is not satisfied: there must be something more. Jesus may well have been hoping for such a response, as it shows that the man is aware of a dimension to salvation which is more than just keeping rules. So far, so good, and the comment that Jesus 'loved him' suggests that his response has struck the right note; he is ready for the 'something more'.

Sell and give; come and follow

The 'one thing lacking' is a bombshell. It cuts away the whole basis of the man's life and status, his reputation and his security. Jesus' searching demand penetrates his defences and exposes where his priorities really lie. He is not ready for the kingdom of God.

Which of us would have done any better? Of course preachers are usually careful to point out (rightly) that Jesus does not seem to have demanded such a radical renunciation of all his disciples, and many have gratefully concluded that this man must have had a particular problem with money and that Jesus would not say the same to the rest of us who (we trust) are not tempted in the same way. If that is what you think, here are some wise words from a commentator: 'That Jesus did not command all his followers to sell all their possessions gives comfort only to the kind of people to whom he would issue that command.'

We hear no more about this rich man. We may wonder whether he ever did find his way to eternal life.

Prayer

Lord, most of us play at being disciples for most of the time. Help us to face up to what following you really means for us and to put first things first.

66 Mark 10:23–31

No hope for the rich?

The eye of a needle

The disciples are shocked, and Jesus does nothing to soothe their feelings, but rather makes things worse by the stark statement, twice repeated, that the way into the kingdom of God is hard for the wealthy. In a society which regarded affluence as a sign of God's blessing, this was crazy talk. And then, to make matters worse, Jesus says that it is not only hard, but impossible – unless, that is, a camel really can go through the eye of a needle!

Some commentators, in a misguided attempt to turn the impossible into the extraordinarily difficult, have suggested that 'the eye of a needle' was the name of a small door through which it might be just possible to envisage a camel being squeezed if it offloaded all its baggage. There is no evidence to support this 19th-century notion, and it has the effect both of destroying Jesus' proverbial image (the rabbis also used an elephant going through the eye of a needle as a figure for what is totally impossible) and of making nonsense of the disciples' reply. They at least understood Jesus to mean what he said, that it was impossible.

By human standards it is indeed impossible: the conflict between God and Mammon for our loyalty is a deadly one. But dealing with the impossible is God's speciality. Take it out of the realm of human endeavour, and there is hope after all. For what Jesus is talking about is the kingdom of God (the phrase is repeated three times to make sure we don't miss it), and in the kingdom of God everything is the other way up, and the impossible is possible.

Losses and gains

Peter's comment in verse 28 sounds very smug: 'At least we are all right!' But Jesus takes him quite seriously. Yes, true discipleship has meant for them, as it would have meant for the rich man, the loss of material security. But no one who puts the kingdom of God first will in the end be a loser. There will be recompense on a grand scale, not only in the age to come, but even here in this age. The experience of becoming a member of the new family (remember 3:31–35?) will compensate a hundredfold for all that has been forfeited.

But there are two stings in the tail. The first is the word 'persecutions', slipped in at the end of the list of earthly gains; it is not all joy for the disciple. The second is the formula about the first being last and the last first. It would be possible to take these words as simply a positive statement of the disciples' privilege: by making themselves 'last' they have in fact become 'first', while those like the rich man who have clung to their status have become the last. But in view of the discussions about precedence within the disciple group which we have already seen (9:33–35) and will soon meet in a yet sharper form (10:35–45), it may well be that this is also a gentle rebuke to Peter: 'Yes, you have done well to give up so much for me, but don't imagine that even that now guarantees you the top rank in the kingdom of God!'

For meditation

'Many who are first will be last, and the last will be first.' In what ways can this slogan be seen as summing up the lessons learned by the disciples in the last couple of chapters? And how should it apply to our own attitudes in relation to the values of the kingdom of God?

67 Mark 10:32-34

The death march

'Were you there…?'

Verse 32 is one of the most vivid pieces of descriptive writing in Mark's gospel, and seems to preserve the impression of someone who was there at the time, who was himself part of the tableau this verse presents. Peter seems the most obvious candidate.

The scene is 'on the road', a phrase which has become a familiar theme in this part of the gospel with its restless onward movement (8:27; 9:33; 10:17; 10:52). The goal is Jerusalem, now directly named in verses 32 and 33 (it was there only by implication in 8:31 and 9:31) – and we already know from 3:22 and 7:1 what sort of reception Jesus can expect in Jerusalem. Yet for all that Mark allows us to see Jesus striding purposefully ahead on the road, leading the way impatiently towards what he knows is his own death. But his eagerness is not shared by his disciples, who are perhaps slowly beginning to realise that he means what he has said about what lies ahead. They follow him 'amazed', while an apparently larger group of fellow-travellers are quite simply 'afraid'. The contrast between the determined leader and the reluctant followers is striking, the more so when we remember that it is his death, not theirs, which is the immediate prospect.

A third prediction of what lies ahead

And so we come to the third of Jesus' direct predictions of what is to happen when they get to Jerusalem. It agrees with the others, but this time he goes into more detail. His death is to follow an official trial and condemnation, and to the death itself are now added the shame and humiliation of the mocking, spitting and flogging which will precede it. Jesus is fully aware of the horror which lies ahead and does not want his disciples to be taken by surprise when it all happens.

And yet Jesus again describes himself by the majestic title 'the Son of Man', the figure who in Daniel 7:13–14 is destined to receive the homage of all people and to rule over the whole world forever. The paradox of using such a title to speak of such abuse and suffering is extraordinary, and lends added pathos to his words.

This time there is also a further note added, that Jesus' condemnation and death, while it will begin with the Jewish authorities (the chief priests and scribes) will also involve the Gentiles, the Roman occupying forces in whose hands the death penalty officially rests. It is not clear whether the mocking, spitting, flogging and killing are to be understood here as the action of the Jewish leaders or of the Gentiles, but in the event it will make little difference, since both groups will be equally involved (14:65–66; 15:15–20).

But at the end of this terrible litany of suffering and rejection comes again the simple, unexplained note, 'after three days he will rise again'. To those who understand, it makes all the difference, but to the disciples at the time it probably remained a puzzle, as it had been in 9:10.

Prayer

Lord, sometimes to follow where you lead is a bewildering and frightening business. Even when we are afraid help us still to follow, as your disciples did on the road to Jerusalem.

68 Mark 10:35–40

An inappropriate request

The two 'Sons of Thunder' (3:17) have appeared from time to time along with Peter as the small group with whom alone Jesus has shared and will share some of his most private moments (1:29; 5:37; 9:2; 14:33). The three of them with Andrew were the first disciples called to follow Jesus (1:16–20), and they are mentioned together at the head of the list of the twelve in 3:16–17. So they can reasonably think of themselves as leaders in the group. But it has been Peter who has taken the lead and acted as spokesman for the group on several occasions. James and John may well have begun to feel overshadowed and decided that it was time to assert their position. Hence this bizarre approach to Jesus.

Sitting in the top seats

The request for the seats beside Jesus in his glory could hardly have come at a more incongruous moment. He has just spoken not of glory but of humiliation, rejection and death. Perhaps they have picked up the words about rising again and are beginning to see that there may be some 'glory' beyond that death. Or, perhaps more likely, they may have simply fastened on the title 'the Son of Man', with its associations of glory in the Old Testament, and filtered out the less welcome parts of what Jesus has said about how the mission of the Son of Man is to be achieved. For whatever reason, they do seem to have put their foot in it rather seriously, and Jesus is not slow to point out to them the unwelcome implications of their request.

Death and glory

The glory is to be real enough, but the way to it is through suffering, which Jesus refers to as a cup to be drunk and a baptism to be endured. If they want to share the glory, they must share the suffering too. Jesus' question in verse 38 sounds rhetorical, and it is a surprise to find that it is answered at all, let alone that it is answered positively. The glib assurance of their reply 'We are able' is breathtaking, but perhaps it betrays not so much a conscious claim to be ready and able to share all that Jesus will undergo as a still inadequate grasp of what he has been talking about.

One day they will indeed suffer in their turn, James as one of the first Christian martyrs (Acts 12:2) and John, according to tradition, as a prisoner on the isle of Patmos. But that suffering will not in itself earn them the places of honour they covet. 'Promotion' in the kingdom of God is not won by aggressive self-presentation or even by martyrdom. It is for God, not us, to determine how its 'honours' are distributed. In the light of this chapter so far, we may be sure that it will not be on the sort of basis that human society takes for granted. It will be the little ones who will be the greatest in the kingdom of God.

For meditation

It is easy to pour scorn on the crass self-assertion of James and John. But how far have we, after 2,000 years to absorb the values of the kingdom of God, yet managed to escape from the world's concepts of status and importance?

69 Mark 10:41–45
'Not so among you'

At first sight you might imagine that the indignation of the other ten against James and John sprang from a holy disapproval of their failure to grasp the principles of the kingdom of God. But a much less flattering explanation suggests itself when we note that Jesus' stern words in verses 42–44 are addressed not to James and John, but to the other ten, who apparently deserve a rebuke no less than the two brothers. Their anger, then, probably arose from the much more unspiritual cause of their annoyance that the other two had got in first, and tried to steal a march on them by claiming the top seats in advance!

Rulers and great ones

By now we are familiar with Jesus' reversal of the world's ideas of greatness and leadership. But this is the most powerful statement yet of the contrast between the way society operates and the way it is in the kingdom of God. It is specifically 'the Gentiles' whom Jesus singles out for comparison, but the desire to impose your authority on everyone else is not an exclusively Gentile trait! Perhaps he mentions them specifically because under Roman occupation the Jews had less opportunity to be 'lords' and 'tyrants', and resented the domineering attitude of their imperial overlords.

But all this is quite the opposite of the way the kingdom of God operates, where greatness is in service and the slave is master. 'It is not so among you' could be written as a motto over all this part of the gospel. The disciples are learning, painfully, that this new movement into which they have come does not work like other human movements. It is an alternative society, in which the first are last and the last first. Wherever we see the stratifications and divisions which human society takes for granted we need to remind ourselves, 'not so among you'.

The supreme model

It was the destiny of the 'Son of Man' that 'all peoples, nations and languages should serve him' (Daniel 7:14). Yet Jesus, the Son of Man in whom Daniel's prophecy is fulfilled, came not to be served but to serve. And in serving he would also fulfil another great prophecy of the Old

Testament, the portrait of God's suffering servant in Isaiah chapters 42 and 53, one who was to be God's chosen, anointed with his Spirit and sent to fulfil his mission of mercy and judgement, and yet who would accomplish this mission by suffering and death, dying for the sins of his people.

The words 'to give his life a ransom for many' echo the language of Isaiah 53:10–12. This is about as close as Jesus will get in Mark's gospel to spelling out why his death is necessary, and what it is intended to achieve. The words are brief and allusive, but they point unmistakably to that great passage Isaiah 52:13—53:12 in which the Christian church has ever since seen a clear blueprint for what Jesus would achieve on the cross: 'He was wounded for our transgressions, crushed for our iniquities; upon him was the punishment that made us whole, and by his bruises we are healed; the Lord has laid on him the iniquity of us all.'

All this is a model for our imitation, not of course in his specific role of being a ransom for many – only he could do that, and it need never be done again – but in the utter neglect of self-interest which enabled him to choose death 'for many' rather than the glory which was his due.

For meditation

Read again Isaiah 52:13—53:12, and think about what it meant for Jesus to fulfil that vision. And then reflect that in this he is a model for us!

70 Mark 10:46–52

Another blind man

Act 2, which began with the healing of a blind man (8:22–26) now comes to its close with another. The treatment of the disciples' spiritual blindness which has been such a prominent feature of the intervening chapters will now give way to the rapidly unfolding events which follow on Jesus' arrival in Jerusalem. The time of preparation is over, and the last act is about to begin.

Last stop before Jerusalem

Jericho, in the Jordan valley, is the last town to be passed by the pilgrim on the way to Jerusalem. The steep desert road will lead up from here into the hills where the capital stands. For the first time in Mark's story, Jesus is about to come to the city of David, the site of the great temple which has been for a thousand years the focus of Israel's relationship with their God. By now the disciple group has gathered a large crowd of fellow-travellers, all going up to Jerusalem for the Passover festival. They are impatient to be there, and have no desire to be detained by a mere blind beggar; they tell him, roughly, to be quiet.

From darkness to light

But this man, like the children in 10:13, is one of the 'little ones', the people who matter in the kingdom of God. Despite the crowd, Jesus hears his shouts and stops. And the whole cavalcade stops with him, such is Jesus' authority. Now, following Jesus' lead, they change from rough rejection to encouraging acceptance, and the man has his wish granted. He stands before Jesus.

The cure is told simply, in an almost matter-of-fact way. The theme is familiar: it is faith which is the key to healing, faith which in this case has been demonstrated by his persistence in drawing Jesus' attention despite the crowd's rebuff, and by his simple assumption that Jesus, the 'teacher', has the authority to restore his sight. It is interesting that he twice addresses Jesus as 'Son of David': it is as the Messiah, Son of David, on his way to the city of David, that Jesus has the authority to heal. This title, here used by the blind man for the first time in Mark's gospel, will be taken up with enthusiasm by the crowds when they get to Jerusalem (11:10).

'On the way'

If we were right in concluding that the two stories of the healing of blind men have a symbolic dimension, there is special significance in the way this story ends. That the man, now able to see and therefore to travel, wants to join Jesus on his journey to Jerusalem is not in itself very surprising, but Mark's addition of the phrase 'on the way' suggests more. We read in Acts (9:2; 19:9, 23; 24:14, 22) that the early Christian movement was sometimes known as 'The Way', and this seems to have been one of their favourite terms for themselves. Does Mark then use the term here to indicate that once our spiritual blindness is cured the next step is to set out, with Jesus and his disciples, on the 'way' of discipleship?

Prayer

Lord, Son of David, give us the faith to know that you can meet our need, the persistence not to be put off, and the determination to follow you 'on the way'.

71 Mark 11:1–11

The arrival of the king

Passover time

It is important to remember that in the week or two leading up to Passover large numbers of pilgrims would be arriving in Jerusalem, which at this time of the year had to accommodate something like six times its normal population. Jesus and his disciples would not be the only pilgrims coming up the road from Jericho. This was the way most Galilean pilgrims would arrive. So the crowd who 'went ahead and followed' (v. 9) would be mainly from Galilee. The excited shouts of verses 9 and 10 are not those of the people of Jerusalem, but of northerners, like Jesus and his disciples, arriving for the festival. The verdict of the people of Jerusalem will be given later, and it will be very different: 'Crucify him!' (15:11–15).

A deliberate messianic gesture

Act 3 begins with the long-heralded arrival of Jesus in the capital city, for the first (and last) time in Mark's story. And he does it in style. This is the only time Jesus is recorded as riding rather than walking. He has walked more than 100 miles, and surely does not need a ride so close to his journey's end. But among so many pilgrims on foot a mounted person will be conspicuous. And those who know their prophetic scriptures will immediately recognise what he is enacting: 'Lo, your king comes to you [Jerusalem]; triumphant and victorious is he, humble and riding on a donkey' (Zechariah 9:9).

So far Jesus has not allowed his disciples to talk openly about him as the Messiah. Even now it is in act rather than in words that the claim is made, and it will not be until 14:61–62 that he will himself state his messianic identity in so many words. But the time has now come to begin to call people to decision.

The event has been carefully prepared. In a village a mere two miles from the gates of Jerusalem a donkey (presumably belonging to a local supporter of Jesus) is ready to be collected, and at the given password his disciples are allowed to take it for Jesus' use. The apparently spontaneous provision of a 'red carpet' of clothes and branches may well have been orchestrated by the disciples, for all these people have already been travelling together up the long road from Jericho (10:46). The arrival has been deliberately staged to make a point.

The kingdom of David

The shouts of the pilgrim crowd show that they have not missed the point. They have understood the acted allusion to Zechariah 9:9. Jerusalem's king is coming into his capital, and he comes to re-establish the long-lost kingdom of David. It was David who first set up his capital in Jerusalem, and it was his descendants who had reigned there until the Babylonians destroyed it 600 years earlier. Since then there had been no Davidic king on the throne in Jerusalem, but now the 'Son of David' (10:47–48) is coming. The messianic hopes of all the prophets, that one day God would set up a new king like David to restore the fortunes of his people, are all coming to fruition.

So Jesus, the prophet from the north, throws down the gauntlet to the authorities of the capital city. Will they recognise in this popular but already suspect teacher from Galilee 'the one who comes in the name of the Lord'?

For meditation

'Hosanna' means 'Save us', though it had also come to be used as simply a shout of praise. What sort of 'salvation' do you think the crowds were looking for? How would their hopes relate to what Jesus had in fact come to do?

72 Mark 11:11–18

A demonstration in the temple

Mark has carefully interwoven two themes here, as the scene shifts repeatedly between the temple and a fig tree on the Bethany road, thus: verse 11, temple; verses 12–14, fig tree; verses 15–19, temple; verses 20–25, fig tree; verse 27, temple (which will then be the setting until the end of chapter 12). We have noted before Mark's tendency to 'sandwich' stories in this way, and when he does so it is usually because he wants us to notice a connection between them. We shall consider what that connection is in the next study, and we shall leave the fig tree until then. For now, we must focus on the temple.

The national sanctuary

There were many synagogues but only one temple. Since Solomon's time this had been the focus of national religion, and more, a symbol of Israel's national identity. Surrounding the sanctuary itself was a vast complex of buildings and courtyards covering some 30 acres. The buildings were massive and magnificent ('He who has not seen Herod's temple has not seen a beautiful building', said the rabbis), and were the focus of intense national pride and patriotism. Anyone who treated the temple with disrespect could expect to be fiercely opposed, and might well be killed.

Jesus first of all visited the temple, as any visitor to the city would (v. 11). He 'looked around at everything' but did nothing on this first day. This was probably more than simply sightseeing. When Jesus comes back next day he will be ready to take decisive action, and this first visit may well have been the opportunity for planning his next move, or, as the crime-writers would say, 'casing the joint'.

Holy violence

The stalls of the traders were set up before the Passover in the 'Court of the Gentiles', the huge open area surrounding the inner courts and the sanctuary itself. This was a place of general concourse, not a worship area as such, though it was the closest that a non-Jewish visitor was allowed to get to the sanctuary. The stalls were set up with the approval of the temple authorities and fulfilled the useful, indeed necessary, purpose of enabling visitors to change their money into the special coinage needed for temple offerings, and to buy the animals needed for sacrifice. But to Jesus they were a symbol of debased worship and a distraction from the prayer which all nations should be able to offer in God's house.

He apparently cleared them out single-handed, such was his personal authority (together with the element of surprise?). It was a gesture which not surprisingly excited the implacable hostility of the temple authorities. So why did he do it?

It was more than a spontaneous expression of his disgust at the misuse of a holy place. Like the entry to Jerusalem the previous day, it was a defiant gesture, embodying a messianic claim. Those who saw it might have thought of Malachi 3:1–4, which speaks of the Lord suddenly coming in judgement to his temple and purifying the descendants of Levi. Or they might remember the prophecy that in the day when God restores his people 'there shall no longer be traders in the house of the Lord' (Zechariah 14:21). The restoration of the temple was one of the tasks the Messiah was expected to perform, and here was Jesus setting about it with a will. He left the temple authorities with little choice: if they did not accept his claim, they must oppose such a flagrant attack on their authority to the death.

For meditation

Is what Jesus did in the temple an encouragement for his followers to use violence? If so, when and for what reasons? If not, what is the difference?

73 Mark 11:19–25

The fruitless fig tree

A pointless display of power?

Interwoven with Jesus' attack on the traders in the temple is the story of his cursing and destruction of a fig tree because it had no fruit. Jesus' other miracles save life and restore health, but this one seems quite out of character. It is apparently wantonly destructive and serves no useful purpose.

But by linking it with the story of Jesus' demonstration in the temple, Mark suggests that, even if in itself it achieved no good, its value is to be seen rather in what the fate of the fig tree symbolises. The temple has proved to be equally barren and disappointing, and can expect a similar fate. In chapter 13 Jesus will take up the theme of the temple's destruction more fully.

Leaves and fruit

So how does the fig tree represent the temple? It was all leaves and no fruit, show without substance, promise without performance. The disappointment of the hungry traveller on reaching a promising tree and finding it empty represents God's disappointment with his people's worship. (See Micah 7:1; Jeremiah 8:13 for exactly the same imagery.) What happened to the fig tree is what may also be expected to happen to the temple whose outward show hides an empty performance.

Mark does rather complicate matters, however, by his comment that in any case 'it was not the season for figs' – so how could the poor tree be blamed for not having any? Figs are not harvested until June, but at Passover season in Jerusalem the fig trees have begun to come into leaf, and at that time there are early green figs already on the trees. They are not very palatable so early in the year, but can be eaten if there is nothing else (I have tried them!). But this tree, for all its show of leaves, did not even have any of these early figs to offer.

Have faith in God

By his placing of the story, then, Mark has suggested its symbolic dimension. But the lesson which is explicitly drawn out from it is not about the temple, but about the sheer power which Jesus has shown in the complete withering up of the tree in a mere 24 hours. It is this, rather than any underlying symbolism, which has aroused Peter's amazement, and the suggestion is that such an act of power must be unique.

Not at all, says Jesus. You can do even more amazing things if you have faith in God. Throwing a mountain into the sea is not on the face of it any more useful a miracle than destroying a fig tree, but it is undeniably spectacular; it represents what is from a human perspective impossible. But it is not impossible for God. So it all depends on faith, which is the secret to experiencing the power of God in answer to prayer.

Verses 22–24 have an unqualified sound which many rightly find uncomfortable. Does Jesus really mean that we can have just whatever we like, so long as we believe it? Why then have so many 'believing' prayers remained unanswered? But this is to treat faith as a magical formula, rather than what it really is, a relationship of trust in a heavenly Father. If that relationship is real, there will be no room for selfish or inappropriate prayers.

Prayer

Lord, give us the faith which can ask and receive according to your will – and so may you not find us unfruitful.

74 Mark 11:27–33

The challenge from officialdom

Jesus is back in the Court of the Gentiles, the ideal place for gathering a crowd for teaching, but a place on which he has already stamped his authority in a different way when he drove out the traders. After so public a challenge to the powers that be, he can hardly have expected to return there without facing official sanctions, and now he is confronted by a very high-level delegation: the chief priests, scribes and elders were the three groups who made up the Sanhedrin, the supreme Jewish religious council. It was their responsibility to maintain orthodoxy in matters of religion, and Jesus is definitely under investigation.

By what authority?

'These things' must refer primarily to what Jesus has just done in the temple courtyard. This, and his dramatic entry to the city, are his only public actions yet recorded in Jerusalem, and the two symbolic acts together do in fact add up to what looks like an outrageous claim – unless it is true. Anyone who throws his weight about in this way must expect to be called to account. What right has he to assume such a high-profile role, and one which by implication is a challenge to the existing authorities? So their question is a fair one: who has given him authority to behave like this?

Jesus' reply looks like a clever cop-out. He hinges his reply to their question on their first replying to his and makes sure that the question he asks them is one they will not want to answer. They know very well what they think about John the Baptist, of course: he was a charlatan who got what he deserved. But they dare not say so publicly, because that is not how ordinary Jews felt about John. So Jesus is let off the hook, and the encounter ends in a stalemate.

John and Jesus

But while Jesus has indeed cleverly got out of a tight corner, his reply was not merely a smart debating ploy. By bringing John the Baptist into the discussion he has in fact made, by implication, an important claim. For the logic of his reply is that whatever conclusion they come to about John's authority must also apply to his own. So just as other people have interpreted Jesus as a second John the Baptist (6:14; 8:28), Jesus himself now endorses that view. If John came with authority 'from heaven', Jesus' authority is no less. And the way people have responded to John's preaching is likely to determine the way they respond to Jesus as well. As in 9:12–13 Jesus linked John's fate with his own, so now he also links himself to John's heaven-sent authority.

So Jesus' answer to the officials' question is clear: his authority, like John's, is 'from heaven'. But he will not give them the satisfaction of hearing him say so in so many words, for any such explicit claim would be sure to be used against him (as indeed it will be when eventually he declares himself openly to the Sanhedrin in 14:61–64).

Prayer

Lord, may our prejudices not keep us from recognising your authority and gladly living under it, even when it means accepting that we may have been wrong.

75 Mark 12:1–12

Getting rid of the son

In the last study we heard Jesus' claim, by implication, to divine authority for what he was doing. Now the same claim is made, this time in the form of a fictional story with a transparent meaning. His opponents know exactly what he means (v. 12), but they can do nothing about it yet.

The tenants of the vineyard

The tenants were under contract to supply a fixed proportion of each year's produce to the absentee landowner, but rent collectors were no more popular then than now. Of course there is an element of exaggeration, even of burlesque, in the violence with which the tenants treated the messengers, and still more in their naive assumption that if they killed the son and heir they would somehow gain a right to the property. But this is not a depiction of real life; it is a story meant to convey a message.

What the story means

A Jewish audience, hearing a story about a vineyard which failed, would surely think of Isaiah's famous allegory of Israel as God's vineyard, which disappointed him by producing only 'wild grapes' (Isaiah 5:1–7). So the vineyard is Israel, and the owner is God. When the Jerusalem authorities 'realised that he had told this parable against them' (v. 12), they recognised the allegory and saw themselves and their predecessors in the role of the defaulting tenants. The servants, then, are the prophets, who often enough in the Old Testament suffered rejection and even death for faithfully calling God's people back to their true allegiance.

So who is the son, whose death is the climax of the story and will provoke the landowner to take decisive action against the tenants? Jesus does not say, but then he surely does not need to. This is as near as he will get to making a public claim to be the Son of God until his ringing declaration before the Sanhedrin in 14:62. He comes to them, then, with the authority of his Father (as he has just implied in 11:27–33), and presents them with one last chance to respond to God's call. By killing him, they will be sealing their own fate, and the vineyard will be given to 'others'.

The rejected stone

Jesus leaves it at that, and does not offer any interpretation of the story (though one is given in Matthew 21:43). Instead he adds a quotation from Psalm 118:22, about the rejected stone. What is rejected by human valuation may prove to be the very thing which God has chosen. The rejected stone becomes the cornerstone; the rejected Son will be the Lord of all. The message is clear enough. In setting themselves against Jesus they are taking the opposite side to God, and in the end those who oppose God cannot win. Jesus has no illusions about his coming death, but he can also see beyond it, to when 'the Lord's doing' will overturn all human attempts to hijack the kingdom of God.

For meditation

In what ways may we be in danger of setting ourselves against God's purpose and refusing him the produce which is his due? Has this parable any warning for us?

76 Mark 12:13–17
The poll tax

A loaded question

When the Romans deposed Archelaus, the son of Herod, from his kingship in Judea and imposed direct rule from Rome, one of the most resented by-products was the imposition of a poll tax on all adult Jewish males, to be paid to the Roman state. Some patriots could not accept that the people of God should pay tax to a pagan king, and a serious armed revolt against the poll tax took place in AD6. That was not many years ago, and the poll tax still rankled; it was one of the main targets of the later Zealot revolt, and already a strong nationalist movement was growing again.

Jesus, as a Galilean, was not subject to this Judean tax. But to ask him, as a respected visiting teacher, to comment on it was a clever move. If he approved the tax he would immediately lose much popular support; if he opposed it he could be denounced to the Romans as a troublemaker. So they had good grounds for hoping that they could 'trap him in what he said'.

The significance of the coin

Jesus' first move is to ask them to show him a denarius, the Roman coin which was used for paying the poll tax. This apparently unnecessary request is in fact a clever way of discrediting his questioners. The silver denarius carried on it a portrait of the emperor and an inscription in which he was described as 'Son of God'. Both the 'graven image' and the wording were offensive to Jews, and the Romans, recognising this, had sensibly arranged for copper coins to be minted for everyday use in Palestine which had no such portrait. Yet those who have come to Jesus with this political question can produce a denarius on the spot. If they are carrying the emperor's (idolatrous) coinage about with them, they can have no grounds for refusing to pay his taxes!

God and the emperor

But to show up the hypocrisy of his questioners is not in itself to answer the question, and it is an important one (and one which, in principle, applies to many other situations where a conflict of loyalties may arise between human government and our duty to God). So Jesus goes on to make his memorable pronouncement (more familiar in its traditional version, 'Render to Caesar…') which balances the duty to the emperor with the duty to God.

His words are enigmatic enough to allow him to escape the 'trap'. He throws back to the questioners the obligation to think out what are the limits of loyalty to God and to the state, and depending on your answer to that you might see Jesus as either opposing or supporting the payment of poll tax. But the important thing about Jesus' reply is that it assumes that there is room for both loyalties at the same time. According to the Zealot ideology loyalty to God ruled out submission to the Roman state, and obedience to Rome was rebellion against God. But for Jesus there is room for both.

Of course it is true that in the real world there will sometimes be a conflict between our religious and our political duty, as many Christians under despotic regimes know to their cost. Jesus gives us no clue here as to how such a conflict may be resolved. But what he does offer is the important principle that such conflict is the exception rather than the rule and that in normal circumstances it is possible to be both a faithful disciple and a loyal citizen.

Prayer

Lord, make us equally eager to serve you and to play our part as citizens of the society in which you have set us, and where the two seem to come into conflict, help us to see clearly what are 'the things that are God's'.

77 Mark 12:18–27
The God of the living

The Pharisees have failed to 'trap' Jesus. So now it is time for the Sadducees to try. They were a separate party within the Jewish hierarchy, and at many points were in opposition to the Pharisees, but they seem to be at one with them on the need to silence this radical new teacher. While the Pharisees believed in life after death, the Sadducees rejected this as a new and unfounded teaching, and so now they test Jesus to find out how he will line up on this controversial issue.

Another trick question

So they set Jesus up with a trick question. It depends on the Old Testament regulation (Deuteronomy 25:5–6) which provided for the wife of a man who died childless to become the wife of his brother and so to 'raise up children for his brother' – and thus to provide him the only form of immortality the Sadducees would recognise. This legislation was still in force, at least in theory, at the time of Jesus, and so it was theoretically possible for the same woman to be the wife of seven brothers, though their story is more likely a fictional case designed to pour scorn on the idea of an afterlife. But of course the issue is a real one for anyone who believes in life after death, since many people are in fact married more than once, whether because of death or divorce, and in such cases the idea of reunion after death can pose a problem.

'Like angels in heaven'

There are two levels to the question – first, that of married relations after death; second, the more fundamental issue of whether there is life after death at all. Jesus deals with both levels in turn.

But first he exposes the basis of their scepticism: they are ignorant both of scripture and of the power of God. Their outlook is limited to human logic and human possibilities, and so cannot cope with the concept of life after death which necessarily falls outside their current experience. In this they are typical of the secular thinking which we know so well today, which has no room for anything beyond our immediate experience.

So the answer to the first level of the question is that we must not picture life in heaven as being just the same as life on earth. Where there is no death there is no need for procreation, and so the exclusive relationship within which procreation takes place is no longer appropriate: 'they neither marry nor are given in marriage'. This is not to say that there is no love, but there is no need for the exclusiveness and jealousy which are an essential part of married life on earth. We may hope that Jesus speaks not of something lost, but of something gained in heaven.

Why there must be life after death

The underlying issue of what happens when we die is dealt with in a very compressed argument in verses 26–27. It depends on the character of God, and of the relationship into which he enters with those who are privileged to be his people. When God identified himself to Moses as the God of Abraham, Isaac and Jacob (Exodus 3:6), those three worthies had already been dead for several centuries. Could God, the living God, enter into a solemn covenant with Abraham and his descendants only to see it end in death? Could he describe himself as the God of someone who was now nothing more than a memory? God's covenant cannot be so easily broken, nor his 'steadfast love' so temporary. It is an obscurely brief argument, but behind it lies a satisfying theology of life and not death and of the faithfulness of God, which makes no sense without a resurrection to eternal life.

Prayer

Lord, give us the boldness to reach beyond the limitations of our human experience and to believe even where we cannot yet see.

78 Mark 12:28-34

The two great commandments

This is another tricky question, since an unwise answer could expose Jesus to the charge of not valuing some other aspect of the Old Testament law. To find a commandment in the Old Testament which really does sum up all the rest calls for great wisdom. But the atmosphere this time is not so hostile as before, and the questioner, who is already aware that Jesus is worth listening to (v. 28), is quite prepared to concede that he has given a good answer.

God and my neighbour

The first commandment selected by Jesus would come as no surprise. Deuteronomy 6:4-5 had already been singled out as the basic requirement of the law, and was recited daily by all pious Jews. What is creative about Jesus' reply is that he links with it a less prominent commandment from Leviticus 19:18, 'You shall love your neighbour as yourself.' And the result is to cover the full scope of the law, which is concerned not only with our duty to God but with how we treat other people. The first four of the ten commandments deal with our duty to God, and the other six with our duty to our neighbour. When you think about it, there is not much in the Old Testament law which does not come under one or other of these headings.

And the key word in both texts is 'love'. Love goes behind the outward acts which the law commands to include also the attitude and motive for doing them. This will become a key theme of Christian teaching as it develops in the New Testament: 'love is the fulfilling of the law' (Romans 13:8-10; 1 Corinthians 13, etc.).

'Not far from the kingdom of God'

The scribe immediately catches the point. He admires the comprehensiveness of Jesus' answer, but he also recognises the new perspective which it offers. In practice what concerned the scribes from day to day was mainly the practical implementation of the law, particularly its ritual requirements, the 'whole burnt offerings and sacrifices'. It was easy for this to get so much out of proportion that the underlying purpose was forgotten, and the 'love' element became a casualty. Jesus has redressed the balance, and the scribe can immediately see the liberating force of this new summary of the law. It is putting first things first, and putting the 'burnt offerings and sacrifices' in their place.

Such a clear sense of priorities shows that the scribe and Jesus are fighting on the same side. For the kingdom of God is about love rather than burnt offerings and sacrifices. Once the man has recognised that, he is not far from the kingdom of God. We do not know whether he became a disciple, but surely his attitude to his scribal duties could never be the same again.

There can be no answer to such a far-reaching pronouncement which was so obviously 'right'. Jesus' teaching is in a different league from normal scribal debate. No wonder that from now on 'no one dared ask him any question'!

For meditation

How wide-ranging are the implications of Jesus' summary of the law? How can we love God with all our heart, soul, mind and strength? And what does it mean to love our neighbours as ourselves? How far have my attitudes and actions today matched up to these commandments?

79 Mark 12:35-37
David's Lord

Now that all his questioners have been silenced, it is time for Jesus to take the initiative and in his turn to pose a tricky question. But instead of putting his opponents on the spot, he goes straight on to answer his own question. Or rather he answers it with another question, which is then left hanging in the air. We readers, like the crowds in the Jerusalem temple, are left to work out for ourselves what his rhetorical question implies.

The issue is, on the face of it, a purely 'academic' discussion about what is the right terminology to describe the Messiah. But in view of the increasingly strong hints we have seen in Mark's story, we may be sure that many of Jesus' hearers understood that it was not messiahship in the abstract that he was talking about, but his own mission. He may not yet have openly called himself the Messiah, but his actions and teaching have left little doubt that he saw himself in that light.

The Son of David

The blind man at Jericho appealed to Jesus as 'Son of David', and the pilgrim crowds escorting Jesus into Jerusalem were expecting him to bring in 'the coming kingdom of our ancestor David'. Jews at that time had a variety of ideas about the 'Messiah', the one whom God was going to send as his agent in the last days. But one element which almost all of them would have had in common would be the hope that in some sense the kingdom of David would be restored. 'Son of David' was a title calculated to arouse messianic excitement.

It was also a title which early Christians had no hesitation in applying to Jesus. Matthew in particular emphasises and defends Jesus' role as Son of David, and Paul takes it for granted as basic to the Christian gospel (Romans 1:3). Yet here is Jesus questioning the title and apparently repudiating it. So what is going on?

More than a son

Jesus' argument, drawn from Psalm 110:1, is about status. If, as both Jesus and his audience would naturally assume, the psalm was written by the great David himself, then there is someone whom even that supreme king referred to as his 'Lord'. Yet that person cannot be God, since in the psalm he is addressed by God. That person must then be the Messiah, still to come in the future to bring to completion the work which David has begun. (This too would be common ground: the psalm was understood to be about the future Messiah.)

In that case the Messiah is not merely another David, still less someone who, as his son, is under his authority. Rather he is David's 'Lord', or, as the hymn-writer puts it, 'Great David's greater Son'. So the trouble with the title 'Son of David' is not that it claims too much, but that it claims too little.

The wrong vibes

Another problem with the title 'Son of David' was that for most Jews it would carry an inevitably nationalistic and political overtone. David was a great warrior, whose victories established the greatest empire Israel ever possessed. Now Israel was again under foreign rule, as it had been under the Philistines before David took over. So a 'Son of David' must have as his primary task the restoration of Israel's fortunes, and that could only mean armed rebellion against Rome. Is it any wonder then that Jesus found it necessary to question the title? It would, in the wrong hands, commit him to a mission very different from what he had come to do.

So, as usual, Jesus is in the business of asking people to reconsider their fundamental assumptions and not to limit him and his mission to what they have been expecting and hoping for.

Prayer

Lord, help us to realise that your agenda may not be the same as ours and to be prepared to accept your lordship on your terms, not ours.

80 Mark 12:38–44

A telling contrast

In these verses a scathing attack on the hypocrisy of the religious professionals is followed by an example of true piety. The example, however, is not of a prominent religious figure, but of a poor widow whom everyone (and especially the scribes?) would overlook. Truly, the first shall be last and the last first.

The first shall be last (verses 38–40)

Not all scribes were as bad as this, of course, as we have just seen in verses 28–34. But the pattern of outward show combined with inner corruption is an occupational hazard of religious professionals, now as much as then. 'Let anyone who is without sin cast the first stone.'

We all like to be noticed and to be respected by others. But there are some who go out of their way to achieve this, just as the 'great ones' among the Gentiles lord it over others (10:42). And when it is those in a position of religious leadership who do this, it is particularly inappropriate. But it is still worse when their real behaviour does not match their pretensions, when they prey on the vulnerable and cover up their greed by a show of piety. Such hypocrisy on the part of 'religious' people rightly draws the scorn of those who are able to see through the pretence. The words are strong, but the scenario is not imaginary. The history of the Christian church offers us conspicuous examples of such hollow profession, and no doubt there have been, as there are now, plenty of less prominent but no less pathetic examples.

The last shall be first (verses 41–44)

It is a relief to turn to someone quite the opposite, someone who had no desire to be noticed and who would have been as surprised as Jesus' disciples must have been if she had heard what Jesus said to them about her. She was a person of no importance, and she knew it. But she loved God and gave the little she had to him.

Contributing to the temple funds was a very public business. A row of 13 large collecting boxes were lined up in the Court of the Women (the point in the temple beyond which only men could go), and people could and did go there to watch. And no doubt many of those who put money into the boxes were not at all reluctant to be seen and made sure that the size of their donation was clearly visible. Jesus' comment to his disciples is typical of what he has been teaching them on the way to Jerusalem about the values of the kingdom of God. The natural human perspective is to welcome and make much of the big donor and to treat the poor widow with at best a condescending greeting. But in the kingdom of God, her total dedication counts for far more than an easily spared fortune.

For meditation

In my church, and among my own personal acquaintance, who are the people I most respect and admire? Are they the ones Jesus would put first? What can we do to develop the values of the kingdom of God within our own congregations?

81 Mark 13:1–2

The temple to be destroyed

The temple has been the scene of most of Jesus' activity and teaching since he arrived in Jerusalem. Now he leaves it, never to return, and as he leaves he utters words which must have shocked his disciples profoundly. No wonder that yet again some of them will have to ask him to explain privately what he means (vv. 3–4).

Herod's temple

The original temple, built by Solomon, was destroyed by the Babylonians in the sixth century. Its replacement, built towards the end of the sixth century, survived until the time of Herod the Great, who began the process of replacing the old structure with a magnificent complex of buildings worthy of the nation's capital. By the time of Jesus' public ministry, the replacement was still not complete, but already it was one of the architectural wonders of the world. The huge, finely dressed stones which make up the lower part of the Western Wall in Jerusalem today give only a hint of the magnificence of the temple itself; they are only a part of the substructure, the huge artificial platform on which the temple proper stood. Of the temple buildings themselves not a trace survives (as Jesus predicted).

Not one stone upon another

Jesus' Galilean disciples are, understandably, awestruck by what they see. There is nothing to match this in their Galilean towns and villages. But Jesus is impressed not by the appearance of the temple, but by what he knows will soon be its fate. The 'house of God' is to be utterly destroyed. A generation later, when the Romans conquered Jerusalem in AD70, his prediction would be literally fulfilled.

Jesus was not the first to utter such an oracle against the temple. Micah in the eighth century (Micah 3:12) and Jeremiah in the sixth (Jeremiah 26) had said the same – and then too it had proved true when the Babylonians came. But such an unpopular and 'unpatriotic' message had nearly cost Jeremiah his life, and Jesus' words are not likely to have been any more popular. If there was one thing on which almost all Jews could agree, it was the importance and the sanctity of the temple. It was God's house, and its destruction was unthinkable. Anyone who spoke against it was speaking against God and against Israel. As we shall see later, Jesus' words against the temple stuck in people's minds and were ready to be used against him (14:58; 15:29). Whatever you thought of the rest of his teaching and actions, an attack on the temple was unforgivable.

A symbol of a new order

But this was not the first time Jesus had provoked such anger. When he drove the traders out of the Court of the Gentiles (11:15–18) it was an expression of his repudiation of what the temple had become, and Mark, by interweaving that story with the cursing of the fruitless fig tree, has heightened the sense of doom. This temple, with all its magnificent stones, was merely a 'temple made with hands', and what God was now preparing through the ministry of Jesus was a new temple 'not made with hands' (14:58). The old order, focused on a single nation and its national shrine in the capital city, was soon to give way to a new order in which all nations would indeed find their house of prayer (11:17), not in a single building but in a faith community which would transcend all racial and political boundaries.

The disciples would understand very little of this at the time, but Jesus has sown a seed which will one day lead to a radically new understanding of what it means to be the people of God, in which there will be no place for this old temple made with hands.

Prayer

Lord, may we be impressed not by outward show and magnificence, but by holiness and truth. Teach us not to cling to the wrong things, but to be open to new ways as we follow you.

82 Mark 13:3–4

The disciples' question

It may seem out of proportion to devote a whole study to one question. But the interpretation of the chapter which follows is controversial, and the question to which the following discourse (vv. 5–37) provides the answer is an important key to understanding it. So to think first about the opening question gives us the opportunity also to gain an overview of the discourse as a whole.

An interlude in the drama

We have seen that in the middle of Act 1 Mark has placed a lengthy section of teaching (4:1–34) to give the reader the opportunity to think about the implications of the story which has been unfolding so rapidly up to that point. Now in the middle of Act 3 we have a similar 'pause for breath'. From 11:1 onwards the confrontation between Jesus and the Jerusalem authorities has been building up to a climax, and in chapter 14 we shall witness the inevitable result in the arrest and trial of Jesus. But first in chapter 13 we can sit quietly with Jesus and the original four disciples on the Mount of Olives, looking across the Kidron Valley to the temple buildings, and listen to Jesus speaking about what is soon to come.

It is in the temple that Jesus has acted and taught in such a way that he has antagonised the authorities, and his alleged attack on the temple will be a central element in his trial and condemnation. So it is appropriate that it is the future fate of the temple, with all that that implies, which is the starting point for this vision of what is to come. But interpreters do not agree on how far the rest of the chapter remains focused on the coming destruction of the temple, and how far it moves off into a more distant future.

What are 'these things'?

The question in verse 4 picks up directly from Jesus' startling pronouncement in verse 2. They want to know when the temple will be destroyed and how they may know when that time is coming. The question therefore does not suggest that there is anything more on the agenda than the event Jesus has predicted in verse 2.

The problem is that some of the language in the later part of the chapter speaks of what seems to be a more ultimate crisis, when the sun and moon are darkened and the Son of Man is seen coming in clouds. And when Matthew relates the same discourse in chapters 24–25 of his gospel, it is considerably expanded to include explicit language about the 'coming' (*parousia*, a technical term not used in Mark) of the Son of Man and about the final judgement, while the disciples' question in Matthew asks not only about the destruction of the temple but also about 'the sign of your coming and of the end of the age'. There is no such language here in Mark, but is it possible that Mark understood 'all these things' to include more than just the events associated with the destruction of the temple?

A minority view

This is where interpreters take different positions. Some think that chapter 13 is all about the destruction of the temple, while others think that much of it (and particularly verses 24–27) is about the second coming of Jesus. The author of these notes holds a view between these two positions: I believe that the bulk of the discourse, including verses 24–27, is a direct answer to the disciples' question and refers to the destruction of the temple, which will happen within 'this generation' (v. 30), but that from verse 32 onwards a new note is introduced by speaking of a different 'day and hour', the time of Jesus' return to earth at some indefinite time in the future.

Since many would not agree with my interpretation, I thought it right to draw attention to its minority status at this point. I cannot argue the case here, but I trust that the notes which follow will help to explain why I understand the chapter in this way.

For meditation

Try to imagine how you, as a first-century Galilean fisherman, would have reacted to what Jesus said in verse 2. What questions would be uppermost in your mind? What would you think would be the implications of the loss of the temple? What sort of assurances, and warnings, would you need from Jesus?

83 Mark 13:5–13

The beginning of the birth pangs

The theme which runs through these verses is 'not yet'. They have asked for a 'sign' of the coming events, and Jesus replies by talking about things which are not as yet signs of the destruction of the temple. These are all necessary preliminaries, but 'the end is still to come'. This note of warning against getting excited too soon is in sharp contrast to the wording of verse 14, 'But when you see…' That will be the time to take action, but all the events described in verses 5–13, however dramatic they may seem, are no more than preliminary skirmishes.

Impostors

When Jesus himself is gone, the disciples will need to be on their guard against impostors. History confirms this need, as the Christian church has been visited by a long succession of people claiming to represent Jesus and trying, often by proclaiming the imminent end of the world, to gain influence over gullible believers. The warning will be repeated in verses 21–22, so the problem is clearly important. It is not clear just how their claim 'I am' relates to the destruction of the temple. Perhaps they will claim that they have come to fulfil Jesus' prophecy and to offer a new alternative to the doomed temple and its worship.

Wars, earthquakes and famines

Another easy mistake would be to imagine that when catastrophic events happen in the world this is the sign that Jesus' prophecy is to be fulfilled. But there have been few ages of history which have not seen their share of 'wars and rumours of wars', of earthquakes and famines. Such news fills our newspapers still today. There were certainly plenty of wars, earthquakes and famines in the middle years of the first century, but when the disciples hear of them they are not to take them as signs of 'the end'. At most they are 'the beginning of the birth pangs' – but who knows how long the labour will be?

Opposition and persecution

Another recurrent feature of this interim period will be the experience of opposition and persecution. This too is not peculiar to the middle years of the first century. At many times during the first three centuries the Christian church faced the hostility of the Roman state. Ever since then Christians in various times and places have faced persecution, sometimes from the state, sometimes from local pressure groups, sometimes, it must be admitted, from other Christian groups and power structures.

The opposition Jesus describes is both Jewish ('councils' [literally Sanhedrins], 'synagogues') and Gentile ('governors and kings'). But it will not be a purely negative experience; rather it will provide the opportunity for 'testimony', and for the good news to be proclaimed to all nations. Mark has included in his gospel increasing hints of the expansion of the 'Jesus movement' outside the bounds of Israel, and here is a clear indication that the good news is to reach all people, even if the means is through the Christian experience of persecution. The Holy Spirit, directing the disciples' words, will ensure that the opportunity is not lost.

The road of discipleship is not going to be easy, either in the days before the destruction of the temple or in the long centuries to follow when the experience of hostility will be ever present. But even when the whole world seems to be against them, they have the assurance that it is worth going on, for at the end of the road of endurance there is salvation for those whose suffering has been incurred 'because of me' (v. 9), 'because of my name' (v. 13). Those who follow Jesus on the way of the cross can expect no less.

Prayer

Lord, help us to endure. May we be less concerned with calculating 'the end' than with being faithful witnesses to the good news here and now, whatever it may cost.

84 Mark 13:14–23

Crisis in Judea

In AD70 the Romans captured Jerusalem and destroyed the temple and much of the city. That was the crucial turning point in the war of Jewish independence which began in AD66, even though resistance dragged on until the fall of Masada in AD73. Before Jerusalem fell, it endured a long and terrible siege, and it is that period which forms the background to Jesus' warnings in these verses.

The desolating sacrilege

In 167BC the Syrian king Antiochus desecrated the temple in Jerusalem by setting up in it an idolatrous statue. It was that assault on the Jewish religion which sparked off the great Maccabean revolt. In the book of Daniel Antiochus' statue is referred to as 'the abomination which desolates' (Daniel 9:27; 11:31; 12:11). Jesus here predicts that in some way that dreadful event will be re-enacted, and when it is, that will be the time to take action, because his prediction of the destruction of the temple is about to be fulfilled. Just how it will be re-enacted the reader is left to 'understand' in the light of events, and it is not easy for us to be sure what Jesus had in mind. Perhaps he was thinking of the time just before the Roman siege began when the Zealot troops took over the sanctuary as a military headquarters, or perhaps of the bringing of the idolatrous Roman standards into the city when it was captured.

The horrors of the siege

The Roman siege will be a time of unparalleled suffering (as indeed the graphic account by the contemporary Jewish historian Josephus makes clear), and those who have the opportunity to escape must use it urgently. It will be hard to get away in time, and those encumbered by young children or by pregnancy will be particularly vulnerable. If it occurs in winter, when weather conditions may be severe and the roads impassable, the suffering will be even greater. This is a portrayal of a national disaster of the first order.

But even in that time of disaster, God will not be absent. The fall of the city and the destruction of the temple, which might seem to be the triumph of a pagan power over the God of Israel, will take place only within the will of God, and the length and severity of that time of suffering remains under his control. For while the fate of Jerusalem is to be seen as God's judgement on a fruitless people, the city contains also those who are God's 'elect' (see also verse 27), his true people through whom his purpose for Israel is still to continue beyond the disaster. For their sake the suffering will be limited.

A time of confusion

At such a time people search for answers, for some meaning in the chaos of events. And so it will be the perfect opportunity for those who wish to make an impression. 'False messiahs and false prophets' are usually waiting in the wings for such an opportunity, and they can be very plausible, especially when, as Jesus warns here, they can appeal to 'signs and omens' as proof of their bona fides. The signs (such as Jesus himself has refused to provide, 8:11–12) are presumably miraculous occurrences: we are warned often enough in the Bible that not all apparent miracles are indications that the person who performs them comes with God's authority. Still today even the elect, the true people of God, are too easily taken in by 'signs and wonders'. But for them it is not the spectacular claims and actions of these impostors which should count, but the words of Jesus: 'I have already told you everything.'

Prayer

In times of confusion and of conflicting claims, give us the wisdom to perceive where your hand is at work and to hold fast by your word.

85 Mark 13:24–31

The climax of judgement

So far Jesus has spoken of preliminary events and of the siege of the city, but without specifically talking of the destruction of the temple – which is what the disciples had asked him about. The words 'But in those days, after that suffering…' seem to be about to bring us to that climax, but instead we read of heavenly portents and the Son of Man coming in clouds. Most interpreters think that here Jesus has moved unaccountably to speak of the end of the world and of his own second coming, only to return awkwardly in verse 30 to events which will occur within 'this generation'. I beg to differ!

Cosmic imagery for political events

The words of verses 24–25 are drawn from Isaiah 13:10 and 34:4, where the subject is not the end of the world but the fall of pagan powers, Babylon and Edom. This language was for Isaiah a vivid way of speaking of the political disruption of the familiar world order, to be followed not by the end of everything, but by a new order; history will continue. Jesus' use of this language is therefore appropriate for the fall of Jerusalem, the end of the old order under which the purpose of God has been focused on a single city. The change to a new structure of authority is effectively, if extravagantly, conveyed by the cosmic language of Old Testament prophecy.

A new focus of authority

In place of the old regime comes a new ruler, the Son of Man. We have seen earlier (8:38) that when Jesus used this title for himself he was drawing on the vision of Daniel 7:13–14, the vision of 'one like a son of man' who comes in clouds to the throne of God and is given dominion over all nations forever. When Jerusalem loses its central place in the purpose of God, the Son of Man will enter into his destined kingship and will gather in his elect (see vv. 20, 22) not merely from the people of Israel, but 'from the four winds'. Hitherto God's purpose has been focused on a national group, the 'chosen people' of Israel, with their capital in Jerusalem. Now, as Jerusalem loses its supremacy, an international people of God, the people of the Son of Man, will be gathered. It is through the people of Jesus that God's purpose will then go forward.

'This generation will not pass'

Already Jesus has said that while some of his disciples are still alive they will see that the kingdom of God has come with power (9:1), and in 14:62 he will again speak, using the language of Daniel 7:13–14, of a mighty reversal which will be seen by those who have rejected him. The climax is fast approaching, and it will all happen within this generation. It will come as inevitably as summer follows spring. Just as the leaves on the fig tree are a sign, so Jesus' disciples will be able to recognise the events he has spoken of and be ready for the dramatic change which is coming. Unlike other people in Jerusalem, they need not be taken by surprise, for what Jesus predicts will surely happen.

Thus, in highly coloured language drawn from the Old Testament, Jesus has answered the disciples' question, 'When will this [the destruction of the temple] be?' It will be within the living generation. And by his choice of prophetic texts, Jesus has given them important clues for understanding the cataclysmic events which they and other Jews are soon to experience. What to others will seem to be the end will prove for the followers of Jesus to be a decisive new beginning, the reign of the Son of Man.

For meditation

If you had been a Jewish disciple of Jesus in the first century, what would have been the significance for you of the destruction of the temple? How would you have been able to relate it to Jesus' enthronement as the Son of Man? And what has all this to say to a modern Gentile Christian?

86 Mark 13:32-37

An unknown day

A change of subject

So far Jesus has been talking in colourful language but with firm conviction of when a specific event, the destruction of the temple, will take place. His definite prediction that it will take place within 'this generation' is underscored with the assurance that they can trust his words, which 'will never pass away'. It is therefore surprising to read now of a day which Jesus does not claim to know and which is known to no one but God himself. Whereas he has spoken of signs which the disciples may observe as the fall of the temple comes near, he now speaks of a day which comes without warning and for which they must be ready at any time. The change of atmosphere is startling. What 'day' or 'hour' is this that he now speaks of in such different terms?

Verse 32 sounds like a change of subject: 'But about that…' No single 'day' or 'hour' has been mentioned so far in this chapter. Jesus has spoken of 'those days' (v. 24) and 'these things' (vv. 29, 30; see also v. 4), but what 'day' is this which, unlike 'these things', cannot be dated? It is at this point, I believe, that Jesus has moved from talking about the destruction of the temple (as a near and datable event) to the day of his own future return in judgement (at an unknown and unpredictable time). There is little enough in the words of this chapter to make the reference clear, but when we compare this little paragraph with the much longer parallel section in Matthew (24:36 onwards) and with language about the second coming in other parts of the New Testament, this seems the most likely interpretation.

Reserved information

Jesus usually speaks with such authority and certainty that it is a shock to hear him say that there is something which he does not know. True, the order in which he lists those who do not know – people, angels, the Son – has the effect of placing him above the angels and next only to the Father. He is the highest authority next to God, but he is still ignorant on this one point, the time of his own triumphant return. This must be, from the point of view of Christian orthodoxy, a limitation imposed by his incarnation: while living a human life on earth he is subordinate to the Father in knowledge as well as in authority.

Don't be caught out

If the Son does not know, then certainly we do not. Those who devote long hours to trying to puzzle out from the prophets a timetable for the end of the world are wasting their time. It is unknown, and it is meant to be unknown. So the only appropriate response is not calculation but constant readiness. The little parable of the slaves left in charge while their master is away makes the point simply and clearly. We must always be ready, so that we will not be found asleep on duty.

Just how we are to be ready is not spelled out. No one can live on constant red alert. But while life consists mainly of the ordinary and the humdrum, and while the round of work and leisure, waking and sleeping must go on, it is healthy for us to remember that wherever in that cycle we may be our stewardship should be always open to scrutiny. Responsibilities postponed may prove to have been left too long.

Prayer

Lord, help us to live day by day as citizens of heaven, alert to your voice and ready for your coming.

87 Mark 14:1–9

A woman to be remembered

It is now time to return from the interlude of teaching on the Mount of Olives back to the doomed city. The lines of confrontation have been sharply drawn since Jesus arrived in chapter 11, and now the climax of the drama is fast approaching. Mark sets the scene with an elaborate 'sandwich'. In verses 1 and 12 he reminds us that the setting is the Passover festival; in verses 1–2 and 10–11 he introduces us to those who at this sacred time are plotting Jesus' death; but within this framework he has set a powerful little story (vv. 3–9) which gives us a further insight into how Jesus himself is preparing for what he knows is soon to happen. In this study we concentrate on the story of the anointing of Jesus. In the next we shall return to the priests and Judas.

What a waste!

Bethany, a village just over the hill from Jerusalem, was where Jesus and his disciples had found lodgings for their visit to the crowded city (11:11–12). An unnamed woman (John tells us it was Mary, the sister of Martha and Lazarus) performs an extravagant act of devotion by anointing Jesus' head with extremely expensive ointment. A single flask of ointment which could have been sold for nearly a year's wages must surely have been a family heirloom. To break open the jar and pour the whole lot over the head of this visitor was incredibly wasteful, and people are not slow to protest. There were so many more productive ways in which such a valuable possession could have been used. This is sheer irresponsibility.

A matter of priorities

Jesus has often spoken in favour of the poor, and indeed has demanded of a rich man that he sell all his possessions and give the proceeds to the poor. So why does he not join in condemning this woman's squandering of such a valuable resource? It is a matter of priorities. To help the poor is good, but on this particular occasion to 'waste' the ointment on Jesus is better, for it is a unique opportunity. Her extravagant gift is a symbolic act of deep significance and an example to be remembered. There is room in the kingdom of God both for the careful stewardship of resources for the sake of those in need, and, on occasion, for spontaneous and uncalculating devotion. True discipleship embraces not only scrupulous accountancy but also reckless exuberance. There is 'a time to gather… and a time to throw away' (Ecclesiastes 3:5–6).

Death and good news

So what is so special about anointing Jesus with expensive ointment? It is 'a good service', not only because it beautifully expresses her devotion but also because, whether or not she knows it, she is pouring the ointment on what will in a few days be a hastily buried corpse, lacking the proper treatment with aromatic spices (see 16:1). Her act thus brings Jesus' death firmly into the picture, and Jesus himself welcomes its symbolism. He has come to Jerusalem to die, and his disciples must not be allowed to forget it. But that death is foreshadowed not in bleak horror and despair, but in the rich smell of a sumptuous ointment. There is something almost bizarre in speaking about burial and 'good news' in the same breath, but that is how Jesus' death will be. It will be proclaimed with joy in the whole world, and when it is, this woman's spontaneous act will be part of the story. What a wonderful way to be remembered!

For meditation

In what ways may it be right for us to be extravagant in our service to Christ? Would you have joined the scolding in verse 5?

88 Mark 14:1-2, 10-11

The priests and Judas Iscariot

The plot against Jesus

We have had plenty of indications of how the religious authorities are reacting to Jesus. Even as far back as 3:6 they were plotting his death. Now he is in Jerusalem, within their grasp, and the time has come. But the same Passover festival which has brought Jesus to Jerusalem has also brought thousands of other pilgrims to the temple, and many of them already know Jesus and are his enthusiastic supporters – as the pilgrim crowds have demonstrated when they escorted him into the city with shouts of Hosanna. To make an open move against Jesus would be likely to provoke a riot.

During the day, Jesus spent his time in the temple, very publicly. The only answer, then, is to try to arrest him at night, when there are no crowds of supporters around. But how do you find one among 100,000 Passover visitors? The city was far too small for the crowds who came at festival time, and the visitors spread out to the surrounding villages or camped on the hillsides around the city. They must find inside information of where Jesus and his disciples are staying.

The informer

And that is where Judas comes in. His betrayal of Jesus consists first in his willingness to tell the authorities where the disciple group may be found at night, and indeed, as we shall see, to lead them there in person and identify Jesus so that they can arrest him. This is the service they most need from him, and it is for this that he is to be well paid. We shall see also, however, that when Jesus is brought to trial the high priest will be well informed about the sort of things Jesus has been saying about himself and his mission. Since most of the relevant sayings have been uttered in private to the disciples, it seems likely it is Judas who has fed the authorities with appropriate evidence which they can use against Jesus when the time comes.

Why did he do it?

It has always seemed incredible that a man who has devoted a year or more of his life to following Jesus could suddenly turn against him in this way. Few have been able to believe that a cash payment would alone be enough to motivate such a radical decision. Beyond that we are in the area of conjecture.

One interesting fact is that Judas' name, Iscariot, may indicate that he came from a town, Keriot, in southern Judea. If so, that would probably mean that he was the only non-Galilean among the twelve. So he may have come to feel out of place in this Galilean movement, and the more so when the group has come down to Judea and the Galilean crowds have welcomed 'their' prophet into the capital. So perhaps there is an element of racial prejudice in Judas' decision.

But it is likely that there is a more fundamental reason than that. As they have journeyed towards Jerusalem, Jesus has again and again made it plain to his disciples that he has no intention, as many had hoped, of leading a movement to restore Israel's national independence; his mission is not to lead his people to victory but to be rejected and die. Peter's remonstrance against such an idea (8:32) would have been echoed by the other disciples, and they have followed him reluctantly and with bewilderment.

If Judas originally joined the movement for motives of high-minded patriotism, he will have watched with dismay as Jesus has stubbornly rejected any such mission. And now in Jerusalem Jesus has made matters worse by actually attacking the temple itself, the very symbol of national pride, and daring to predict its destruction. Judas' desertion would then have been the result of disillusionment: this is not the sort of movement he had thought he was joining. His approach to the priests would then be partly an attempt to save his own skin while there is still time; but it might also arise from a genuine conviction that Jesus has embarked on a dangerous and unpatriotic course and must be stopped before he does any more harm.

For meditation

If you think you are standing, watch out that you do not fall.

89 Mark 14:12–21

The Passover meal

Old Passover and new

Jesus died at the festival of Passover, and it was at a Passover meal on the night before he died that he instituted the central act of Christian worship, the Lord's supper. The Passover is itself a commemorative meal, celebrating Israel's original liberation from slavery in Egypt. It was through this act of God, and under the leadership of Moses, that Israel became a nation. Now a new Passover meal, under a new leader, marks the foundation of a people of God which is no longer national but international, the people of the new covenant.

And at the heart of the Passover ritual is death, the death of the lamb, whose blood on the doorposts kept safe the houses of the Israelites when the firstborn of Egypt were being killed. Now blood will again be shed, the blood not of a sacrificial lamb but of the Son of God, by whose death 'many' will be saved.

The last supper

In the light of all this symbolism of the Passover, and its significance for what is now taking place, it is no wonder that Jesus has made careful preparations for this last meal with his disciples. The meeting with the man carrying a jar of water is not a coincidence, but, like the finding of the donkey for the ride into Jerusalem, has been planned in advance, for the room is already prepared and waiting for them. There is at least one houseowner in Jerusalem who can be relied on to help Jesus even in these threatening days. Here the group who have spent so much time together in the last year or two will share a last meal together, and Jesus wants to make sure that it is a special occasion. In years to come they will remember and pass on every detail of it, as they 'do this in remembrance of me' (1 Corinthians 11:23–26).

The cuckoo in the nest

But first there is an important matter to be dealt with. The group of twelve is soon to be cruelly broken up, and Jesus does not want the rest of them to be taken by surprise. They must be made to realise that there is a traitor among them and that Jesus himself knows it, even though he will do nothing to stop him. He tells them clearly that one of the twelve will betray him, but does not say which one it will be. If he had identified the traitor no doubt Peter and the others would have made sure that Judas did not leave the room to go about his deadly business. By not identifying Judas, Jesus, not for the only time, deliberately lets slip an opportunity to prevent the course of events which will bring him to the cross. This is what he has come to Jerusalem for, and he will not now try to avoid it.

The disciples' anguished question, 'Surely, not I?', is probably not just a rhetorical question. After the bewildering experiences of recent weeks, and their constant failure to be in tune with Jesus' way of thinking, probably none of them could be quite sure that he would not let the side down in the end. But the form of the question is one which, as the grammarians say, 'expects the answer no'; none of them can really believe that he would fall so low. Mark does not say whether Judas asked the same question, in the same form. I wonder!

Prayer

Lord, may we bring you our fears and our failures as well as our faith and our love for you, secure in the knowledge that you know us better than we know ourselves.

90 Mark 14:22–25

Startling symbolism

The Passover meal consisted of a series of courses interspersed by cups of wine (four in all), and for each course and each cup there were appropriate words of blessing and explanation repeated by the head of the family. Jesus, as head of the 'family' of his disciples, also utters blessings and adds words of explanation, but his explanations are startlingly new and disturbing. This is a Passover with a difference!

This is my body; this is my blood

Whatever else the disciples may yet have understood, they cannot miss the essential point that Jesus is enacting before them his own death. Even if they have not yet taken his predictions seriously, there can now be no doubt that he has meant what he has said. His body is about to be broken and his blood poured out. The bread and wine are thus symbols of death.

But in inviting them to eat the bread and drink the wine, Jesus is adding another level to the symbolism. The death he is enacting is to be one in which they are in some way to participate. The broken body and shed blood are to be food and drink for his people. The imagery is shocking: are Christians to be cannibals? But by now we know better than to assume that Jesus' sayings are always to be taken dead literally. Eating and drinking are the basis of life, and Jesus is to be the basis of the disciple's life. The bread and wine which symbolise his death are the disciple's sustenance, for his death is the source of our life.

A covenant... for many

The words over the cup are full of Old Testament echoes. At Mount Sinai, when Israel came out of Egypt to become a nation under Moses, God made a covenant with them, and it was this covenant which was the basis of their status as God's chosen people. It was sealed with the blood of sacrifices, and Moses proclaimed 'See the blood of the covenant...' (Exodus 24:8). Now another sacrifice will seal a new covenant, and the people of God will be reborn. And the words 'for many' are an echo of Isaiah 53:11–12 (as we have already seen in 10:45), the prophecy of the servant of God whose mission it is to suffer and die for the salvation of his people. So the death that Jesus is about to undergo is not a mistake or a disaster, but the means to the salvation of his people, the people of the new covenant.

Looking forward

Verses 22–24 speak of death, but that death is not the end, and in verse 25 Jesus is already looking forward beyond the cross to the new life of the kingdom of God. This is his last meal and his last drink on earth, but soon there will be new wine to enjoy. Jesus is thinking probably of the messianic banquet which all Jews looked forward to enjoying in the last days. That time is now fast approaching, and soon Jesus and his disciples will be able to celebrate together.

So the final Passover meal is in fact but a foretaste of what is to come. There will be death tomorrow, but through that death there will be life forever. As Christians today share the bread and wine of the Lord's supper, they do so with due solemnity indeed, for it is their Lord's death which they are remembering, but also with thanksgiving (which is what 'eucharist' means) for the life which that death has achieved.

For meditation

In what ways might it enrich our understanding of our worship at the Holy Communion if we were able to enter more fully into the experience and understanding of the disciples at that last supper in Jerusalem?

91 Mark 14:26–31

Trouble ahead

The sense of impending disaster was already strong at the Passover meal, as Jesus not only enacted symbolically his own imminent death but also predicted that one of his twelve closest associates would turn against him. But in these verses which follow the account of the meal the screw is turned even tighter: not only one of them, but all, will desert him in the end!

The Mount of Olives

The Mount of Olives is the hillside which faces Jerusalem across the narrow valley of the Kidron. Many Passover pilgrims would be camping out in this area. Bethany, where Jesus has been staying since coming to Jerusalem, is on the other side of the hill, but for this night he is not going back to Bethany, but staying closer to the city. Gethsemane is the name of a plot of land, probably an olive orchard, on the slope opposite the city, and this is where (as Judas already knows) Jesus and his disciples are going for the night. The 'hymn' referred to in verse 26 will be the Hallel psalm traditionally sung at the Passover season. With that their Passover meal is over, and they go out to face the terrible events for which Jesus has so long been preparing them.

The scattering of the sheep

But all that preparation has not been enough. Jesus knows that they will not be able to stand the pressure which is soon to come upon them all. He knows it because he knows them too well. But he knows it also because the prophecy of Zechariah (that same book from which he drew the model for his triumphant ride into Jerusalem) has predicted it. Throughout these final hours in Jerusalem there is a recurrent theme of the fulfilment of prophecy. These are not random, unscripted events, but the outworking of a pattern long ago perceived and set down by God's spokesmen for the last days. Among Zechariah's prophecies the vision of a rejected and stricken shepherd is one of the most memorable, and Jesus knows that that is to be his role.

The disciples are not yet so clear-sighted. All of them (except Judas, presumably, who has already gone about his business) believe that they will be able to stand the strain. Their loyalty is unquestioned, but its strength is as yet untested, and when the test comes it will fail. Peter, as usual, is both the spokesman for the group and the man who is confident in his own loyalty and strength of character. But his reward for such gallantry is to be given his own personal prediction of betrayal; before many hours have passed the cock will crow, and he will remember.

Back to Galilee

Yet among this overwhelming sense of gloom and foreboding, Jesus' mind is still, as it was at the Passover meal (v. 25), not only on the more immediate future, but on the ultimate outcome. Beyond the cross, he can see the resurrection; beyond the rejection and death in Jerusalem is the triumphant return to Galilee. There, in the familiar hills, he looks forward to a rendezvous with the eleven disciples, who will have put their temporary failure behind them and will be ready for a new beginning, back in the province where it all began so hopefully all those months ago. It is astonishing that a man who knows he is about to die can speak so calmly of a new beginning, and his disciples seem still to be quite unable to grasp what he is talking about. But by now we should be getting used to being astonished by Jesus!

Prayer

Lord, you know us better than we know ourselves. Keep us from being too confident in our own resources, and help us instead to listen to you and to find our strength in you.

92 Mark 14:32–42

Gethsemane

Here we are on holy ground, privileged to join Peter, James and John in sharing one of the most poignant and personal moments in Jesus' life on earth. More than once Mark has told us about Jesus praying, but now we come closer and hear the actual words of the Son of God as he pleads with his Father. And they are astonishing words.

Jesus in distress

After the apparently calm way in which Jesus has spoken repeatedly to his disciples about the fate which awaits him in Jerusalem, it is sobering to witness now his extreme agitation as the time comes closer and the prospect becomes more real. Some Christians have mistakenly pictured Jesus as a sort of superman whose humanity was only skin-deep and who sailed untroubled through the experiences of life, and death, on earth. Mark will not allow any such fantasy. Jesus is well aware of what is soon to happen to him, and the prospect horrifies him.

It is a mark of the depth of his suffering, and of the reality of his human character, that in this time of crisis he wants and needs human companionship. Peter, James and John are there not merely as spectators, but for the support they ought to be able to give to Jesus in his distress.

Remove this cup

Before they fell asleep the disciples heard enough to know the gist of Jesus' prayer. They heard and remembered the confident way in which Jesus addressed God by the familiar term 'Abba', a degree of closeness to God which other Jews at that time did not presume to claim. But even more memorably they heard the Son of God, whose clear predictions of his coming suffering and death they had had to come to terms with, now pleading to be 'let off the hook'. The 'cup' was an Old Testament image for destined suffering and judgement (remember 10:38); now that Jesus looks into it he is appalled by what he sees.

We cannot hope to enter fully into the thoughts and emotions of the Son of God as he comes face to face with what his Father has called him to undergo. Many a hero has resolutely faced physical death, but there is more to Jesus' revulsion than that. We have been given some clues in his words about the purpose of his death: 'a ransom for many' (10:45), 'blood poured out for many' (14:24), the role of the servant of God who dies for the sins of his people. We shall see something of the horror of what this means in Jesus' cry from the cross in 15:34.

But with the horror goes the acceptance of the Father's will, all the more amazing because Jesus now knows just what it will mean: 'Not what I want, but what you want.'

The flesh is weak

In contrast with Jesus' hard-won readiness to suffer is the disciples' total unreadiness. Exhausted by the bewildering pace of events, they cannot even stay awake to give Jesus the support he needs. Yet they need to pray for themselves (v. 38) as well as for him. In a few moments they will be, almost literally, caught napping.

Prayer

'Abba, Father, not what I want but what you want.'

93

Mark 14:43-52

Betrayal and arrest

The arrest of Jesus is carried out by an armed 'crowd', not specifically described as either soldiers or police, but sent out with the authority of 'the chief priests, the scribes, and the elders'. Mark has used this full listing of the component groups of the Sanhedrin before when he wishes to emphasise the official nature of the opposition to Jesus (8:31; 11:27; see also 14:53). This is not a Roman action, but the Sanhedrin exercising its delegated power to control the internal affairs of the Jewish community, and so it will be to the Sanhedrin, not to the Roman governor, that Jesus will be taken.

The kiss of Judas

Judas has fulfilled his bargain and has brought the arresting party through the darkness to the right one among the many pilgrim groups camping out on the Mount of Olives. His final, famous act of betrayal, to identify Jesus with a kiss, seems hardly necessary, since Jesus has become a well-known figure during the last few days as he has taught publicly in the temple, but perhaps in the darkness the Jerusalem crowd might find it hard to single out the right man among these Galilean strangers.

Who is in charge?

Jesus apparently offers no resistance when he is arrested, and when 'one of those who stood near' attempts to fight for him he does not seem to encourage the attempt. His rebuke in verse 48 is addressed to the arresting party, but it implies that there is no place for weapons to be used on either side. He is not a desperado but a peaceful religious teacher.

So Jesus is the unresisting victim of an armed crowd. And yet there is a tone of authority in his rebuke, and his final words, 'Let the scriptures be fulfilled,' show that he has not been taken by surprise and is now ready for what is to come. If Jesus had wished to avoid arrest, he need not have gone to Gethsemane that night. He is being arrested because that is what he has accepted as the Father's will, not because he is helpless.

The scattering of the sheep

Jesus' prediction in verse 27 is now fulfilled. Perhaps the disciples feel they have little option: if Jesus does not wish to resist his arrest, what else is there for them to do? The language, however, is not of an orderly withdrawal, but of panic-stricken flight to save their own skins, and the vivid little story of the naked young man shows that they had reason to be afraid. Bewildered by the way things have developed since they came to Jerusalem, demoralised by Judas' desertion and now thrown by Jesus' determination not to resist arrest, they quickly turn and run. We can only guess what would be going through their minds as they disappear among the trees.

For meditation

Think how the arrest of Jesus must have seemed to the various people in Gethsemane that night: the armed crowd, Judas, the disciples, the young man who ran away.

94 Mark 14:53–61

Before the Sanhedrin

Mark carefully sets the scene at the high priest's house on a double stage: Jesus before the full council of the Sanhedrin (v. 53; note again the full listing of the dignitaries) and Peter out in the courtyard among the servants (v. 54). As the spotlight falls first on the one stage and then (vv. 66–72) on the other, we shall see a striking contrast between the two men under pressure.

False testimony

Mark clearly does not want us to think of this as a fair and impartial trial. The aim is, quite simply, 'to put him to death'. The verdict is already decided, and the only problem is how to find suitable evidence to support it. But it seems that the authorities are anxious to ensure that due process of law is seen to have been carried out. Jewish law demanded that a defendant should have the right to be heard and that any evidence for the prosecution must be sustained by two independent witnesses under cross-examination. There is in this case, apparently, no shortage of willing witnesses, but their act has not been adequately prepared, and under cross-examination they fail to establish their charges: 'their testimony did not agree'.

A new temple

The failure to agree is surprising when we notice the one specific charge which Mark records and declares to be false (vv. 57–59). Jesus' cavalier attitude to the temple has been one of the main reasons for the hostility of the Jerusalem authorities. In both words and actions he has declared his belief that it is no longer fulfilling its purpose as the focus of Israel's religious life. In the hearing of his disciples, if not more openly, Jesus has actually predicted that the temple will soon be totally destroyed (13:2), and Judas will by now have had time to pass on this incriminating statement to the authorities. True, as far as our records go, Jesus has not said that he will himself destroy the temple or that it will be replaced with another, but the charge is sufficiently close to the tenor of his words and deeds to be a damaging one, if only they could get their 'witnesses' to agree on the words he has used. We shall see in 15:29 that this charge against Jesus stuck in the popular mind, even if it could not be made to stand up in court.

But while Mark records the charge as, technically, false, he does not want us to miss its theological significance. By including the phrases 'made with hands' and 'not made with hands', he underlines the contrast which is important throughout the New Testament between a religion based on external, man-made structures and a religion of the heart and life, between a community which finds its focus in a building and one which knows no such restriction. While they failed in their charge, these witnesses in fact spoke truer than they knew.

No case to answer?

Jesus' silence may be purely pragmatic: there is, as yet, no case to answer and therefore no need to exercise his right to speak in his own defence. When it is time to speak he will not be reluctant to do so. But his silence infuriates the high priest, and leaves him with no choice but to invite the prisoner to incriminate himself.

But Mark may also want us to remember what Isaiah said about the servant of the Lord: 'He was oppressed, and he was afflicted, yet he did not open his mouth; like a lamb that is led to the slaughter, and like a sheep that before its shearers is silent, so he did not open his mouth' (Isaiah 53:7).

Prayer

Lord, as you faced injustice and dishonour for us, may we be prepared also to be abused for you. Help us to know when to speak and when to be silent.

95 Mark 14:61–65

The secret is unveiled

'Are you the Messiah?'

The high priest's question is not so much a change of subject as it may seem. To claim, as Jesus is alleged to have claimed, the right to replace the temple was, in effect, to claim to be the Messiah, since the Messiah was expected to restore the temple. But by phrasing it as directly as this, the high priest goes to the heart of the question of Jesus' authority to act and speak in so radical a way.

And by linking the title of Messiah with that of 'Son of God' ('Son of the Blessed One' is a Jewish way of saying the same thing without pronouncing the sacred name of God), the high priest takes up the even more audacious claim which Judas must have told him about (12:6; 13:32), and which the three disciples may not have been able to keep secret when they came down from the mountain (9:7,9). So here is a chance for Jesus to clear up any doubt about who he thinks he is.

An open confession

While Jesus might still have been mistaken for a political liberator, he kept his role as Messiah a secret. But now, on trial for his life before the nation's leaders, no such misunderstanding is possible. The moment has come for Jesus to reveal publicly who he is, and he does it in a ringing declaration which goes far beyond the terms of the high priest's question. The 'I am' is clear enough, but Jesus does not leave it at that.

When Peter first hailed Jesus as the Messiah, Jesus immediately went on to speak of himself instead as the Son of Man (8:29–31). Now he does the same thing, but this time instead of speaking of the suffering of the Son of Man, he speaks of his glory. He uses again the words of Daniel 7:13, the vision of the 'one like a son of man coming with the clouds of heaven' to be enthroned in the presence of God as lord of all nations forever. Combined with this are the words of Psalm 110:1 (see above on 12:35–37) about sitting at God's right hand. The two prophecies together declare that the prisoner in the dock is none other than God's designated king, and those who now presume to sit in judgement over him will live to see it. Here, as in 8:38—9:1 and in 13:26, 30, Jesus expects the vision of Daniel to be visibly fulfilled within the generation (see comments on those passages for how this may have been fulfilled).

Blasphemy

To claim to be the Messiah was not in itself blasphemous – if it was true! But Jesus' judges have decided in advance that it is not true, and combined with his presumptuous language about sitting at God's right hand it is more than enough for a verdict. Witnesses are now irrelevant; they have heard it for themselves. This is what they have been trying for, and the solemn court proceedings now degenerate into cruel parody. There was a belief that the Messiah would be identified by his ability to recognise those who touched him when blindfolded. It is not hard to imagine the gusto with which they put this pretender to the test.

For meditation

Compare the authority of the Sanhedrin with the authority of Jesus, the Son of Man. If you had been there as a member of the Sanhedrin, what would you have made of verse 62, uttered by a helpless prisoner on trial for his life?

96 Mark 14:66-72

The witness who failed

We noted that in verses 53–54 Mark has set up this part of his drama on a double stage. The effect is to allow us to watch a tale of two witnesses. So far the spotlight has been on Jesus, called upon to testify to his divine calling in the highest court in the land, and he has done so decisively and with courage. Now we return to the courtyard where Peter sits among the servants. How will he match up to the test?

At least he was there

Before we rake over Peter's notorious failure, we should notice that he is by now the only disciple who is anywhere near Jesus. Jesus' prediction that all the disciples would desert him (v. 27) has been literally fulfilled (v. 50), all except for Peter. Peter, who had the temerity to contradict Jesus and to insist on his own loyalty to death (vv. 29–31), has so far proved as good as his word. He is in the high priest's courtyard, and he is alone. This dogged loyalty will make his ultimate failure look all the more miserable, but at least we should give him the credit for having come so far. Only Peter denied Jesus – but only Peter had put himself in a position to face the test.

The turning of the screw

In the three challenges to Peter there is a steady increase in the pressure put upon him. First comes a private challenge from just one servant girl, which is relatively easily brushed off. Then she makes her suspicions public, and that is more serious. But a further denial still does not get Peter off the hook, and the whole group come back at him with the additional evidence of his telltale Galilean accent. So Peter has to resort to drastic measures to escape the net which seems to be closing round him: 'He began to curse, and he swore an oath.' The Greek verb 'curse' normally has an object: it is to curse someone, not just to utter profanities. Did Peter actually go to the length of uttering a curse upon Jesus, to make it clear that he could not be his follower? Mark does not make it explicit, but that is the natural implication of the word he uses.

The cock crows

Under the pressure of the moment Peter has apparently forgotten all about Jesus' warning and his own brash self-confidence on the Mount of Olives before Jesus was arrested. The crowing of the cock brings it all back, and Peter breaks down. We can imagine the self-disgust which the memory would evoke, the utter sense of failure and humiliation. But worse than that is the knowledge that he has betrayed the man who has come to mean more to him even than his own family. And worse still, this man is the Son of God. Peter, who was so proud to confess Jesus as his Messiah at Caesarea Philippi, has fallen right into the trap which Jesus had warned him of immediately afterwards: 'Those who are ashamed of me and of my words in this adulterous and sinful generation...' (8:38). No wonder he wept.

But this is not the last time we shall hear of Peter. When Jesus has risen from the dead he will send a message to 'his disciples and Peter' (16:7). For this special disciple there is not only a special failure, but also a special message from the master he has betrayed. His tears of sorrow are the prelude to restoration. There is hope even for a Peter. (It is interesting to notice the difference between Peter and Judas, both traitors, but one whose treachery under the pressure of the moment was not an irrevocable disaster.)

Prayer

Lord, you know that the flesh is weak. Help us not so much to condemn Peter as to learn from his experience.

97 Mark 15:1–5

Enter Pontius Pilate

It was one thing for a Jewish court to decide on the death penalty, but quite another to implement it. Under the direct Roman rule which had now been imposed in Judea the right to pronounce the death penalty was reserved to the Roman governor alone. So to achieve an execution they must secure a conviction also before Pontius Pilatus, the prefect of Judea. And that was not necessarily going to be easy.

Pontius Pilatus

The man who represented Roman power in Judea through the time of Jesus' public activity was a mean-minded and brutal official, by no means typical of Roman government at its best. Contemporary records mention no less than five occasions on which his insensitive handling of situations led to serious unrest among his Jewish or Samaritan subjects, three times resulting in a massacre while a fourth was narrowly averted. In the end, some years after Jesus appeared before him, he was removed from office for misgovernment. So the Jewish authorities could certainly not count on an official rubber stamp on their verdict. It was not in Pilate's character to be nice to the Jews.

'King of the Jews'

To tell Pilate that Jesus claimed to be the Messiah and the Son of God, or that he had committed blasphemy, would not cut much ice. These were not crimes against the state and would be of little interest to a pagan governor. But the title Messiah was easily translated into a title with a much more sinister political ring to it, 'King of the Jews'. It was on the charge of claiming this title, then, that the Jewish leaders brought their prisoner before the governor early in the morning, and it would be under this title that, before many hours had passed, Jesus would hang on the cross.

'Have you no answer?'

The silence of Jesus which had so exasperated the high priest is now repeated before Pilate, and Mark emphasises it even more strongly. True, Jesus does respond to the first question, 'Are you the King of the

Jews?', but his answer gives little away: 'You say so'! This phrase occurs a number of times in the gospels, and it seems generally to be a guarded 'Yes' – guarded in the sense that while the words used are in a real sense correct, they are easily misunderstood. Jesus is the King of the Jews: that was what he had enacted when he rode into Jerusalem. But he is a king on a much wider stage than merely Jewish national politics, the Son of Man who will soon be seated at the right hand of God as sovereign over all nations. To turn this sublime destiny into a local political intrigue, as surely Pilate must have understood by the phrase 'King of the Jews', was to miss the point completely. So Jesus' answer probably means 'That is how you put it, but the truth is very different from what you are thinking.'

And after that he has no more to say. His next words will be the terrible cry from the cross. Had he wished, he could have mounted a strong and probably convincing defence, and Pilate might well have held out against the Jewish pressure. But again Jesus refuses the opportunity to deflect the course of events which he knows to be his Father's will.

For meditation

Think how easy it is for people to miss the point about Jesus. What are the sort of ways in which people today jump to wrong conclusions about him? How would you explain Jesus' kingship to someone who did not have a background knowledge of the Old and New Testaments?

98 Mark 15:6–15
Barabbas

The insurrection

Barabbas was not just a common criminal. He was a 'rebel', who had been involved in an 'insurrection'. We have no other record of this particular uprising against the Roman occupation, but it need not surprise us: several such incidents are recorded in the turbulent years between the imposition of Roman rule and the final and catastrophic revolt in AD66 which led to the destruction of the temple. And Barabbas was, probably, the leader of this earlier revolt, since it is he whom the crowd now want to have released. He was, therefore, a patriotic leader, a popular hero, of the sort many may well have hoped that Jesus would agree to become. He has the popular support of a Robin Hood.

The amnesty

Pilate is a pragmatist. He has apparently been sufficiently impressed by Jesus to feel that he is not a political danger and so is trying to avoid sentencing an innocent man. But the pressure from the crowd is building up, and the last thing a governor wants is a rioting crowd at the sensitive time of the Passover festival. So the traditional amnesty seems a convenient way to avoid an unnecessary conviction. Why not substitute this newly accused 'King of the Jews' for the other nationalist leader. The fact that Jesus is as yet uncondemned and therefore needs no amnesty, while Barabbas is a convicted criminal, does not seem to bother him.

Unfortunately, he has miscalculated. It is Barabbas whom the people of Jerusalem recognise as their sort of hero. This supposed 'King of the Jews' is a stranger from Galilee, and he has shown no inclination to take up the patriotic cause. They are not to be fobbed off with a pseudo-revolutionary.

'Crucify him'

People sometimes express surprise that a crowd who welcomed Jesus with shouts of 'Hosanna' only a few days before could so quickly turn against him. But that is to miss the point completely. Those who welcomed Jesus into the city were the Passover pilgrims arriving with him from Galilee, and Mark has given us no reason to think that the people of Jerusalem joined in the celebrations; indeed Matthew makes it clear that they took a very different view of this Galilean prophet (Matthew 21:10–11). But the crowd outside the governor's headquarters early on this festival morning are the people of Jerusalem, and they have no doubt which 'king' they want: not this Galilean teacher but their own Barabbas, who has already proved his patriotic credentials through 'the insurrection'.

What is surprising and chilling, however, is to hear a Jewish crowd calling for the barbaric Roman punishment of crucifixion to be imposed on any Jew, however unwelcome his political stance. But they have been under Roman rule long enough to know that this is the way the Romans deal with sedition: whether it is Barabbas or Jesus, this will be the fate of the one who is not released. And the chief priests are determined to be rid of Jesus, even if this cruel form of execution is the only way to do it. So let him be crucified.

Pilate is not a man of principle, and he gives way to the pressure. He adds his own characteristically sadistic touch by having the condemned man flogged before execution, a brutal flogging with leather thongs which was often in itself fatal.

For meditation

He was wounded for our transgressions, crushed for our iniquities; upon him was the punishment that made us whole, and by his bruises we are healed.
ISAIAH 53:5

99 Mark 15:16–20

Homage to the 'king'

In the hands of the Romans

Even among the Jewish people Jesus has been subjected to cruelty and abuse both from the members of the Sanhedrin and from their (Jewish) guards (14:65). But now he is in the hands of the Romans, and they too will have their turn. For them there is not the same religious motive of horror at his 'blasphemy'. But for a group of bored soldiers of the occupying forces it would be a welcome diversion to have in their power the so-called 'King of the Jews'. If, like many Romans at the time, they had no great love for the Jewish people and their strange religion, it would come naturally to poke fun at a popular Jewish leader and religious teacher, now out of favour. And a group of ordinary soldiers would do it with no great refinement or delicacy.

'Hail, King of the Jews'

It may not be much of an exaggeration to say that 'the whole cohort' (which would at full strength be 600 men) gathered together for a mock parade before the 'King'; none of them would want to miss the fun. Clearly a king must have the proper symbols of royalty, and so they are provided. The 'purple cloak' is probably a soldier's red cape made to do duty for the imperial purple, and the 'reed' with which they strike him would represent the royal sceptre. For a crown, they improvise a coronet made of 'thorns' (perhaps the long spikes that grow at the base of a date-palm leaf), to imitate the crowns worn by oriental rulers which had rays like those of the sun. And in this parody of splendour they kneel and pay homage to the captive 'king'.

But sheer mockery is not enough for them, and the homage degenerates into horseplay. Following so soon after a severe flogging the physical pain must have been extreme, and the humiliating appearance of the bedraggled 'king' would only add to their enjoyment. So Jesus' words on the way to Jerusalem are coming to literal and terrible fulfilment: 'They will hand him over to the Gentiles; they will mock him, and spit upon him, and flog him, and kill him.' Now it is all happening. Jesus himself has become the passive focus of a relentless course of events which will soon bring him inevitably to the cross.

What sort of a king?

For the soldiers, no doubt, the situation was simple enough. Here was a man who had had the foolhardiness to challenge the might of Rome and to attempt to lead his people to liberation. He had failed, as all such insurgents were bound to fail, and now he must accept the consequences. The label 'King of the Jews' said it all.

But there is a telling irony in Mark's account. None of this is true of Jesus. Others may have wanted him to be such a 'king', but he has consistently set himself against the role of the popular liberator. Yet here is he, who repudiated such a kingship, condemned to suffer for it, while Barabbas, who hoped to be just such a leader, is going free. And yet Jesus is a king as well, the Son of Man who is to be enthroned at the right hand of God, with a universal sovereignty which makes any mere Jewish kingship look very pale. And that kingship is to be over all nations: the one whom the Gentile soldiers are mocking is not merely the king of the Jews, but their king as well.

Prayer

Help us to offer you true homage, Lord, and hasten the time when all nations will recognise and worship you as their true king.

100 Mark 15:21–27
Golgotha

Crucifixion was a particularly cruel form of execution reserved normally for slaves and for political insurgents. The Roman writer Cicero called it 'the most cruel and revolting punishment' and the Jewish historian Josephus called it 'the most pitiable of deaths'. A crucified person would hang in agony for hours, sometimes days, before finally dying. And it was a horribly public form of execution, designed as a deterrent to passersby. Human nature being what it is, Golgotha, the public gibbet, would be a place where many would gather.

Carrying the cross

It was probably the cross-beam which was carried, normally by the criminal himself, to be fixed to an upright post on arrival at the place of execution. After the flogging and the ill-treatment by the soldiers Jesus is in no state to carry the beam himself, and a stranger who just happens to be in the wrong place at the wrong time is given the dubious honour. Jesus had talked about his disciples taking up their own cross and following him, but now there are no disciples to be found to carry his cross.

But Mark curiously mentions the names of Simon's two sons. Is this perhaps because they would be known to his readers? If so that means that even if Simon was a complete stranger at the time, his family later became members of the church. Was it this day's forced labour which set Simon's family on a new course? (One of the sons may perhaps have been the 'Alexander, son of Simon' whose funeral inscription was found in a tomb near Jerusalem, probably belonging to a Jewish family from Cyrene.)

Crucifixion

The narcotic drink to dull the pain was kindly meant, but Jesus refuses it, determined to undergo the ordeal in full consciousness. Mark gives no details of the fastening to the cross. He mentions rather the offer of drugged wine and the casting of lots for Jesus' clothes because in these minor details of the scene Christians had come to recognise the fulfilment of scripture: see Psalms 22:18 and 69:21, two psalms from which several echoes are found in the Passion story.

Mark's mention of nine o'clock in the morning is a problem, since John 19:14 has Jesus still before Pilate at noon, and the other gospels more easily agree with that timing. For Mark Jesus remained alive on the cross for at least six hours, for the others probably not much more than three hours. John's detailed account inspires confidence, and Mark may have confused the time of the trial with that of the crucifixion.

In bad company

The 'bandits' may well have been some of Barabbas' associates in 'the insurrection', since the same term is used by Josephus to describe political insurgents. So Jesus, who has refused the temptation to lead a political movement, dies in the company of revolutionaries. And the placard above his head bears the title which was used against him at his trial and was the basis of his condemnation, 'The King of the Jews'. We have thought before of the irony of Jesus being executed under such a title. The presence of the two freedom fighters on either side of him merely compounds the irony, and it underlines the depth of popular, and indeed official, misunderstanding of what Jesus' mission has been all about.

For meditation

If you had been an uninvolved passerby at Golgotha that day, what would you have seen and felt? Would you have had any idea of the significance of what was happening? Why did God allow it to be like this?

101 Mark 15:29–32

Mockery

Rejection

When Jesus foretold his coming suffering in Jerusalem he included along with his physical suffering and death the prospect of being 'rejected' (8:31). For the disciples this must surely have been one of the most terrible and incomprehensible aspects of his predictions. How could the Messiah of Israel be rejected by the very people God is sending him to save?

In these few verses that rejection is graphically portrayed. We have seen the mockery of the Gentile soldiers, but perhaps that could be excused – they knew no better. But now it is Jews who join the mocking chorus. And they are Jews of all classes, the ordinary passersby (v. 29), the religious authorities (v. 31) and even the patriots who hang on the crosses beside him (v. 32). And there is not a disciple in sight.

Paradoxical truth

As the proverb says, 'There's many a true word spoken in jest.' The titles which are now thrown at Jesus in mockery are ones in which we, Mark's readers, can see with hindsight some of the most vital truths about Jesus and why he was there on the cross.

He is the 'destroyer and rebuilder of the temple'. There is, they assume, no prospect of that now that he has been hung up to die. But we have seen already that one result of Jesus' death on the cross will be to hasten the end of the old temple and to set in motion the formation of a new temple, 'not made with hands', to take its place. Even as he dies, this drastic change in the divine purpose will be vividly symbolised in the tearing of the temple curtain (v. 38).

He claimed to be 'the Messiah, the King of Israel', but now that he is dying his pretensions have, they suppose, been shown to be hollow. And yet Jesus has been teaching his disciples that his suffering and death is in fact at the centre of his messianic mission. It is not failure, but his crowning achievement. It is the route he must take to his future glory, seated at the right hand of God, where he will be the king not only of Israel but of all nations. All this we have learned already, if we have listened to Jesus' private teaching of his disciples. But those who are standing by the cross have no inkling of this truth.

He is the one who claimed to save others, yet he cannot save himself. But the cross is in fact the very means of that salvation, to die as a ransom for many, to shed his 'blood of the covenant' for many. If Jesus could have 'saved himself', by avoiding the cross (the temptation he fought and overcame in Gethsemane), he would in fact have forfeited his ability to save others.

But to see these depths in the meaning of Jesus' crucifixion you need to have absorbed his startling teaching, so extraordinary that even his closest disciples have not yet been able to grasp it. No wonder the bystanders at the cross knew nothing of it, and used as mocking insults the very truths on which Jesus' mission depended.

'As it is written'

Several times we have heard Jesus say or imply that what is going to happen to him is in fulfilment of the scriptures (8:31 'must'; 9:12; 14:21, 27, 49). As he has tried to explain why he must die, he has echoed the words of Isaiah 53 (10:45; 14:24). Now Mark again draws in the testimony of Psalm 22, which he has already alluded to in verse 24. A central theme of that psalm is the mockery endured by the godly sufferer, and in verse 29 he again echoes that psalm: 'All who see me mock at me; they make mouths at me, they shake their heads' (Psalm 22:7). Soon we shall hear Jesus himself expressing his deepest agony in the words of that same psalm (v. 34). The scriptures are indeed being fulfilled.

Prayer

Sometimes it causes me to tremble, tremble, tremble;
Were you there when they crucified my Lord?

102 Mark 15:33–36
Alone on the cross

If to overhear Jesus praying in Gethsemane was to tread on holy ground, surely here we venture into the Holy of Holies, as we hear the only words of Jesus on the cross which Mark has recorded. Indeed, these are the only words of Jesus in this gospel after his enigmatic 'You say so' before Pilate. Through the crowd's hostility, his condemnation and flogging, the soldiers' mockery and the extreme pain of being hung on the cross, Jesus has been a silent, passive victim. But now he breaks his silence in one powerful, appalling cry of desolation, which so impressed itself on those who heard it that they remembered and passed it on in the original Aramaic.

In the dark

Darkness at midday cannot have been caused by a natural eclipse of the sun at Passover time, because then the moon is full. However it was caused, it is an expression of God's anger, as in Amos 8:9 and in the plagues of Egypt (Exodus 10:22). It is also a symbol of the darkness into which Jesus himself now enters, the darkness of abandonment by his Father.

The words are the opening line of Psalm 22, and the whole psalm, as we have seen, spells out the agony of the godly sufferer, at the mercy of his mocking enemies. But the words Jesus draws from that psalm are perhaps, for him, the most terrible of all. For the Son of God to be abandoned by his Father is the ultimate, unthinkable horror. This is, significantly, the only time in all the gospels when Jesus does not use the term 'Father' to address God in prayer. A darkness has come between them.

It would be impertinent for us to try to penetrate the nature of the relationship between Jesus and his Father in order to analyse what such a separation might mean. But Jesus' own words about giving his life as a ransom for many perhaps take us as far as we dare go, by reminding us of the role of the servant of God: 'The Lord has laid on him the iniquity of us all.' We may well believe that when Jesus shrunk from the cross in Gethsemane it was the prospect of this sin-bearing rather than only the physical suffering of the cross which appalled him. And now it has happened, and he is alone, abandoned not only by his earthly friends but even by his Father.

Enter Elijah?

After the numbing mystery of Jesus' words the reaction of the bystanders is a pathetic anticlimax. They hear the name 'Eloi, Eloi' and mistake it for Elijah. Elijah, as we have seen, was expected to return in the last days, and some Jews came to think of him as a sort of heavenly superman figure who would be available to rescue God's people in times of extreme need. But probably the crowd at Golgotha take this idea no more seriously than the great titles they have already flung against Jesus on the cross, and the attempt to give Jesus a drink to keep him going until Elijah comes will merely have added to the ribald humour of the occasion.

For meditation

Read Psalm 22, and think why these words may have come to Jesus' mind at such a time.

103 Mark 15:37–41

The end?

The death of Jesus

Most victims of crucifixion lingered on in pain for many hours and gradually lost consciousness. Jesus' death is very different. Now that he has borne the ultimate horror of his Father's withdrawal from him, his work is done, and his death comes suddenly and with a loud cry. It is as if he is deliberately letting go. John 19:30 tells us that that loud cry was one of triumph, 'I have done it!'

The temple had two great curtains, one covering the entrance to the Holy Place, where only the priests could go to offer incense, and one separating off the Holy of Holies, into which only the high priest could go and that only once a year with the sacrifice of atonement. It is not clear which of these curtains was now torn apart, but in either case the symbolism is powerful: the way which was previously closed is now thrown open, and there is free access to the holy place. The violent destruction also points forward to what will happen to the temple as a whole a generation later. With the death of Jesus, its whole sacrificial ritual has become obsolete. The fact that the huge curtain, some 60 feet high, is torn from the top to the bottom suggests that this is not a human act.

A Gentile's testimony

The centurion, a middle-ranking Roman soldier roughly equivalent to our NCO, would be in charge of the execution squad. While the Jewish crowd have been insulting Jesus, this man has been watching him, and what he has seen and heard has moved him to a very different perception to theirs. We do not know what it was about how Jesus died that so impressed him, but his verdict is in striking contrast to their rejection of Jesus' claims. Perhaps he has heard something of Jesus' alleged claim to be 'the Son of God' in a special sense, or perhaps he is simply talking in his natural pagan way about 'a son of God', a good and pious man. Whatever was in his mind, for Mark this is the crowning testimony to the truth of Jesus' claim so powerfully proclaimed before the Sanhedrin. And it is in full accord with Mark's love of paradox that it is in the moment of Jesus' ultimate humiliation and death that he receives this glowing tribute, and that even then it is not from his own people but from one of the pagan occupying forces.

The witnesses

Mark gives no hint that any of the male disciples were around to see Jesus die, but there were some supporters on the edge of the crowd. The men have run away, and the women take over. It is they who are at the centre of the rest of the story. They form an important chain of witness, as these same women will watch first Jesus' death then his burial (v. 47), and it will be they who discover that the tomb is empty and to whom the message of the resurrection is entrusted (16:1–8). So there can be no mistake, no allegations about Jesus not being really dead or about going to the wrong tomb. The same group of women have witnessed the whole thing, and it is on their testimony that the church will forever depend.

For meditation

We have this hope, a sure and steadfast anchor of the soul, a hope that enters the inner shrine behind the curtain, where Jesus, a forerunner on our behalf, has entered, having become a high priest forever... We have confidence to enter the sanctuary by the blood of Jesus, by the new and living way that he opened for us through the curtain (that is, through his flesh).
HEBREWS 6:19–20; 10:19–20

104 Mark 15:42–47
Dead and buried

The sabbath

The Jewish day began and ended at sunset. So the evening of that Friday would be the beginning of the sabbath. The desire to bury the body of Jesus before the sabbath began was partly due to the convention that it was not proper for the body to remain publicly exposed on the sabbath day (or indeed after sunset on any day, Deuteronomy 21:23). But there was also the practical concern that the 'work' involved in taking down a body and preparing it for burial would be against accepted sabbath law. It may have been because of the short time available before sunset that Joseph, for all his care, apparently omitted to provide the customary spices for the burial (see 16:1).

The Romans had no such scruples, and clearly expected the crucified men to remain on the crosses through the sabbath day; they might well still not be dead by the end of it. Hence Pilate's surprise that Joseph could be contemplating burying Jesus a mere few hours after he was crucified. Crucified men did not normally die as quickly as that. But in any case, the Romans would not be concerned about burial, since one of the more shameful aspects of crucifixion was that the corpses were normally simply thrown on the ground unburied, unless their families took them away. Joseph is asking something quite unusual in proposing to provide proper burial for this criminal.

Joseph of Arimathea

Who was this brave man who, when none of the male disciples were there to take action, took it upon himself to ask for Jesus' body? It was surely a brave act, since even though a dead Jesus could no longer be a potential revolutionary leader, to be linked publicly with a crucified 'rebel' was politically dangerous. And of course Joseph was a Jew, and a highly respected one at that. Yet here he is publicly taking the part of the man whom his own Sanhedrin has so recently thrown out as a blasphemer.

He was 'waiting expectantly for the kingdom of God'. So were many Jews, of course, but for Mark the Christian writer to describe him in these terms suggests that, even if he was not a 'signed-up' disciple of Jesus, he was recognised by the church as 'one of us'. Perhaps at this stage he was like the scribe of 12:34, 'not far from the kingdom of God'. But the fact that he was remembered in the Christian stories of Jesus suggests that he was later, if not already, identified as one of Jesus' followers – though we need not believe the medieval legend which brings him to Glastonbury as a Christian missionary! If so, this is an important hint that Jesus' followers were not all from the fisherman class. Indeed, a man who could provide a rock-cut tomb just outside the city of Jerusalem must have been a very wealthy man.

The tomb of Jesus

The visitor to Jerusalem can still visit dozens of rock-hewn tombs in and around the city, some of them still with a large stone to roll across the low entrance. Many of them are multiple tombs with spaces for a considerable number of bodies. Perhaps that is why all the other gospels mention that this was a new tomb, with no other bodies, so that there was no possibility of mistake when the tomb was declared to be empty. But in any case Mark makes sure we know that the women who are going to find it empty are the same ones who 'saw where the body was laid'. There is no mistake. We cannot now be sure just where the tomb of Jesus was, but they knew well enough.

So at the end of chapter 15 Jesus is a corpse, wrapped up in tight linen grave-clothes, placed in a tomb and guarded by a great stone. You cannot get much more final than that.

Prayer

Thank you, Lord, for the example of the 'lesser' characters in the gospel story like Joseph. May we too be ready for any special task we may be called on to perform in your service.

105 Mark 16:1-8

'He is not here'

All four gospels tell about the finding of the empty tomb early on Sunday morning. The details do not all agree – how many women; which women; the stone already gone or an angel rolling it back; how many angels and where were they; and just what did they say? But these are not the central features of the story, and we can hardly be surprised to find a certain amount of variation in the way a story of such a mind-blowing event was told and passed down. The main points are not in question.

The tomb is empty

The women, who had seen the body laid there on Friday evening, and who have come expecting to find it still there so that they can complete the burial rites, are specifically invited to look at the place where it should have been. Whatever the explanation, the simple fact is that there is no body.

The message of resurrection

If we may judge by the parallel accounts in the other gospels, the young man in white is an angel (white, shining clothes are a feature of stories of angels appearing in the Bible; see also Luke 24:4, and the mention that these men in dazzling clothes were angels in 24:23). He is too well informed to be a passerby who has just happened to look into the open tomb, and attempts to identify him as any of the disciples are purely speculative and in any case do not tally with his message, which is specifically addressed to the disciples. He is a heavenly messenger sent to explain to them why the tomb is empty. Perhaps, after Jesus' predictions that he would rise again, they should have needed no angelic messenger; but even his closest disciples seem not to have grasped what he meant.

The promise of reunion

But the empty tomb is not an end in itself. It is for the disciples the promise of a living Jesus and of a new beginning with him. Just as the original mission began and flourished in Galilee, so now it is to Galilee that they must go to meet their risen Lord. Jerusalem, with all its terrible memories, is to be left behind. A new chapter is about to begin.

The message is the same as that which Jesus has already given to the disciples in 14:28, but at that stage they were hardly in a position to take it in. Now that all hope seems to have gone, it is repeated as the dawn of new hope. It is the promise not just that they will rally again and the cause will not die. It is much more specific than that: 'You will see him'!

And the message is not merely to the disciples, but to 'his disciples and Peter'. We can readily imagine what those words would mean to the disciple whom we last saw weeping in failure and despair in the high priest's courtyard.

The women run away

We can well understand the women's 'terror and amazement'. To go to a tomb looking for a body and to find there a living angel instead of the body would unnerve the strongest of us. What is not so easy to grasp is their fear and their silence. The message they have been given is one of hope and joy, and they have been specifically commissioned to pass it on to the disciples. Does Mark want us to believe that their fear and their silence were only temporary, and that in due course they plucked up courage and delivered the message? Perhaps, but he does not say so. Few books can finish in a more mystifying and unsatisfying way. Unless of course that is not the end – see the next study!

For meditation

If Christ has not been raised, your faith is futile… If for this life only we have hoped in Christ, we are of all people most to be pitied.
1 CORINTHIANS 15:17, 19

He is risen indeed. Hallelujah!

106 Mark's gospel

How did Mark finish his gospel?

In the last study I referred to 16:8 as the end of Mark's gospel. But in older Bibles twelve further verses used to be printed after 16:8. Modern versions, however, either do not print these 'verses 9–20' as part of the text of the gospel at all or indicate in some way that their status is suspect. With very few exceptions, modern scholars agree that verses 9–20 are not part of the original gospel of Mark. In many early manuscripts and versions these verses are either absent altogether or marked as of doubtful authority. In some early texts an alternative ending appears, either on its own or together with verses 9–20.

Is this the end?

So how did Mark finish his gospel? Did he really intend to leave it hanging in the air at verse 8, with the message entrusted to the women but not delivered and with the puzzling comment that they said nothing to anyone? Many scholars think that he did, that the book is deliberately open-ended, leaving readers to make up their own minds about the riddle of the empty tomb rather than spelling it all out for them. Others feel that that is a very 'modern' (or better 'postmodern'?) way of thinking and that an early Christian like Mark is likely to have been more concerned with making the gospel message clear and explicit than with achieving a teasing literary effect. In any case, the angel's message in verse 7 is explicit enough – all that is lacking is an account of how it was fulfilled.

If this latter view is right, and 16:8 was not intended to be the end of the story, we have two options. Either Mark intended to go on, but was prevented from finishing his book (and one can only guess what might have prevented him: sudden illness; a knock at the door from the secret police?). Or he did finish it, and the original end is lost, perhaps through a leaf being torn off the scroll. Matthew, whose account is so closely parallel to Mark's up to this point, goes on to record a meeting of Jesus with the eleven disciples in Galilee, as the angel has predicted (Matthew 28:16–20), and perhaps Mark originally had a similar ending with one or more appearances of the risen Jesus to his disciples.

Filling the gap

We do not know, and guesses are not helpful. But the feeling that 16:8 cannot be the intended end is supported by the fact that the 'shorter' and 'longer' endings began to circulate with the gospel probably some time in the second century. These endings were added because early readers of Mark felt something important was missing. The 'shorter ending' rounds it all off succinctly, while the 'longer ending' consists of a more substantial collection of traditions about the risen Jesus drawn from the other gospels, particularly Luke, and from early Christian preaching. The language and style of both endings is clearly different from that of Mark.

There is not much in these later endings which is new or surprising. The one section which is not paralleled elsewhere in the New Testament is the alleged words of Jesus in verses 15–18, with their promise of 'signs' including 'speaking in new tongues' and protection from venomous snakes and poisons. 'Speaking in tongues' was, of course, a feature of some of the early churches, as we know especially from 1 Corinthians 12 and 14. And in Acts 28:3–6 there is an account of Paul surviving the bite of a poisonous snake (though no indication that this was a regular occurrence, still less something to be deliberately encouraged). But it is not wise to base one's understanding of Christian discipleship and mission on this later addition to Mark's gospel.

For meditation

If you had been Mark, would you have finished your story at 16:8? What would be missing? Was there really any need for someone to add on a further 'ending'? In what sense, if at all, is it appropriate to think of either or both of the later endings as scripture?

107 Mark's gospel

Mark's good news – a retrospective

Now that we have reached the end of Mark's story, it is worth while to pause and ask what we have learned from it.

We have learned at least, I hope, to appreciate Mark as a lively, interesting and skilful writer. If you haven't yet had the opportunity to read Mark's whole gospel at one go, why not find time to do it now, and see how the various episodes and teaching which we have been looking at all come together into an enthralling and powerful story? As you do so, you will notice again the special emphases and interests which make this not just another gospel, but in a very distinctive way Mark's gospel.

But Mark did not write his book to tell us about himself. It is the good news about Jesus, the Messiah, the Son of God (1:1). So what have we learned about Jesus?

It has been a book full of surprises. Jesus is a man of contrasts and of paradox. He attracts both enthusiastic crowds and implacable enemies. He preaches a kingdom of God which is coming with power and yet which is as easily overlooked as a grain of mustard seed. He acts with miraculous power and controls the elements of nature, and yet we see him as weak and vulnerable, sharing our emotions of frustration, anger and the fear of death. He is revealed on the mountain as a majestic, other-worldly being, and yet we see him unrecognised, mocked and humiliated. He is declared by God's own voice to be his beloved Son, and yet he is one of us, sharing the full range of human experience. He is the Son of Man, destined to reign in glory over all the world – and yet also destined to be rejected by his own people, to suffer and to die. He has a unique relationship with God as his Father ('Abba'), and yet on the cross he cries out to a God who has abandoned him.

To follow such a master, as Mark clearly longs that we should, is sure to be an equally paradoxical experience, at once exhilarating and humbling, enlightening and bewildering. It is an experience of losing life in order to gain it. As we walk with Jesus' closest disciples through this story we share their excitement as the secret of the kingdom of God is gradually revealed to them, and yet their embarrassment when Jesus declares them to be still as blind as ever. They struggle to keep up with the new values and ideas which he insistently places before them, but again and again they are wrong-footed. They are discovering, sometimes painfully, a whole new world in which the last are first and the first last, the greatest are the lowest and the leader is the servant. They are summoned to take up their cross and follow Jesus, but the end of the road is glory. So we, Mark's readers, are called to join them 'on the road', a road where there is little that is familiar or secure, but a road which leads to life. The road begins with the summons 'Follow me, and I will make you fish for people,' but it seems to end at Golgotha – until we hear the angel's message to the eleven disciples through a few frightened women: 'He is going ahead of you; you will see him.'

What a book! What a Messiah! What a calling to follow him!

 *Enabling all ages to grow in faith*

Anna Chaplaincy
Living Faith
Messy Church
Parenting for Faith

100 years of BRF

2022 is BRF's 100th anniversary! Look out for details of our special new centenary resources, a beautiful centenary rose and an online thanksgiving service that we hope you'll attend. This centenary year we're focusing on sharing the story of BRF, the story of the Bible – and we hope you'll share your stories of faith with us too.

Find out more at **brf.org.uk/centenary**.

To find out more about our work, visit
brf.org.uk

THE PEOPLE'S BIBLE COMMENTARY
Matthew

15 The Chambers, Vineyard
Abingdon OX14 3FE
brf.org.uk

Bible Reading Fellowship is a charity (233280)
and company limited by guarantee (301324),
registered in England and Wales

ISBN (boxed set) 978 1 80039 093 5
First published 2001
This edition published 2022
10 9 8 7 6 5 4 3 2 1 0
All rights reserved

Text © John Proctor 2001, 2022
This edition © Bible Reading Fellowship 2022
Cover images: detail of Millennium window, St Agatha's Church,
Brightwell-cum-Sotwell, Oxon, photo © Rex Harris; background
© iStock.com/petekarici; gold texture © AmadeyART/stock.adobe.com

The author asserts the moral right to be identified as the author of this work

Acknowledgements
Scripture quotations from The New Revised Standard Version of the Bible, Anglicised Edition (NRSV), are copyright © 1989, 1995 by the Division of Christian Education of the National Council of the Churches of Christ in the United States of America, and are used by permission. All rights reserved.

Scripture quotations from The Revised Standard Version of the Bible (RSV) are copyright © 1946, 1952, 1971 by the Division of Christian Education of the National Council of the Churches of Christ in the United States of America, and are used by permission. All rights reserved.

Every effort has been made to trace and contact copyright owners for material used in this resource. We apologise for any inadvertent omissions or errors, and would ask those concerned to contact us so that full acknowledgement can be made in the future.

A catalogue record for this book is available from the British Library

Printed and bound by CPI Group (UK) Ltd, Croydon CR0 4YY

THE PEOPLE'S BIBLE COMMENTARY

Matthew

John Proctor

Photocopying for churches

Please report to CLA Church Licence any photocopy you make from this publication. Your church administrator or secretary will know who manages your CLA Church Licence.

The information you need to provide to your CLA Church Licence administrator is as follows:

Title, Author, Publisher and ISBN

If your church doesn't hold a CLA Church Licence, information about obtaining one can be found at **uk.ccli.com**

PREFACE

This commentary was written with churches and church people in mind. Some Christians have followed it in their daily Bible reading. Others have used it to help them lead Bible study. Preachers have turned to it, as they think about their sermons for Sunday. All of that is exactly what we hoped for when BRF asked me to write this commentary. It is a joy to know that it is being reissued. I hope it will help many people to grasp the good news of Jesus and to follow it in their own living.

There are some excellent big commentaries on Matthew's gospel, some stretching to several volumes. I have learned a lot from these. Yet for many people a big commentary would be no help at all – they would find it too costly or too heavy. So this much smaller commentary aims to digest the insight into Matthew that specialists can give, and to reflect on Matthew's message for today. What does it mean in the 21st century to hear the good news, to welcome God's kingdom and to be a disciple of Jesus? What can we receive from this gospel for Christian living in our times and among our neighbours?

God has surely given us four gospels for a good reason. Each of the four is unique. They tell of the same Lord, but in different ways. Each has its own angles and emphases, as it shares the message of Jesus. Here are some of Matthew's:

- Roots and continuity were important to Matthew. He wanted to connect the Christian good news with the past, with the story of God's work in the Old Testament. He believed that history pointed forward to Jesus, and that the New Testament story is rooted in the Old. To read Matthew is to be reminded of a God who works through the generations, and to think again about our own debt to the past.

- Matthew's gospel follows a sandwich pattern. Word and deed alternate. Blocks of Jesus' teaching are interleaved with blocks of action, with reports of things he did and people he met. Action and teaching mesh with one another, and in the mesh is a message. Belief in Jesus and practical Christian living are linked. True Christian living should be an integrated whole, where faith and conduct nourish one another.

- Matthew is a demanding gospel. It takes Christian commitment seriously – commitment to Jesus, to discipleship, to high standards of conduct, to one another. To read with care is likely to be a searching experience. Yet Matthew was realistic. He knew that Christians are fragile, vulnerable and fallible. His gospel urges us to be patient with one another, and to find gentle ways of supporting each other in the church and in the Christian life.

- Matthew is a gospel of hope. He believed in the lordship of Jesus Christ, in Jesus' authority and presence in the church's mission, and in his coming to judge the world. To follow Jesus is to be in his company, under his command and within his care. Matthew wrote to give Christians confidence as they served Jesus in a complex world and in difficult times. We may read this gospel, and share its message, with that same aim. We too can be confident in the Christ who is with us always, whose word and presence we proclaim and enjoy.

Some people who use this commentary may worship in churches that use the Revised Common Lectionary. This calendar of Bible readings runs over three years of Sundays. In Year A of the three-year cycle – starting in Advent 2022, 2025, 2028 and so on – most of the gospel readings come from Matthew. Roughly half of this gospel will be read in main Sunday services, but it is not followed in precise gospel order, because we cover the sweep of the gospel story from Jesus' birth to resurrection in the four months from December to Easter. This involves a very selective approach to gospel readings in these months. The rhythm of the church year, rather than the flow of Matthew's text, sets the tone and context for these.

Once we come into the weeks after Trinity Sunday, from June to November, however, the gospel readings run steadily through Matthew from chapters 7 to 25, sometimes skipping a slice but always moving forward. Many of Matthew's main themes figure plain and large: miracles and mission, preaching and parables, crisis and controversy, fellowship and following. For churches who want to trace the movement and message of a big biblical book, the Revised Common Lectionary offers a great deal. Listen to Matthew's gospel in worship, and live by it through the year.

John Proctor

CONTENTS

Introduction 9

1	Lines of introduction 20	30	Workers for the harvest 79
2	Child of God 22	31	News cast 81
3	Worship from afar 24	32	Sheep among wolves 83
4	Threat and preservation 26	33	Getting perspective 85
5	Stream of renewal 28	34	Pouring cold water 88
6	Immersed into new responsibility 30	35	Sign language 90
		36	More than a prophet 92
7	Probed and proven 32	37	Missing generation 94
8	Making waves 34	38	The gentle yoke of Jesus 96
9	Honours list (1) 36		
10	Honours list (2) 38	39	Against the grain 98
11	Taste and see 40	40	Just healing 100
12	Right now 42	41	Crooked thinking 102
13	Fresh perspectives 44	42	Opposing matters 104
14	An honourable estate 46	43	Moment of opportunity 106
15	Coping with hostility 48		
16	Cover your faith 50	44	Family gathering 108
17	When you pray… 52	45	Grains of truth 110
18	Long-term investment 54	46	Turning a blind eye 112
19	Neighbours and God 57	47	Grounds for hearing 114
20	Taking it seriously 59	48	Tangled growth 116
21	For a whole people 61	49	Majesty in miniature 118
22	Faith from afar 63	50	Treasure new and old 120
23	Lifting the burden 65	51	No local hero 122
24	Open agenda 67	52	Pointer to the Passion ... 124
25	Tossed by storms 69	53	Table in the wilderness 126
26	Walking free 71		
27	Party spirit 73	54	Steps of faith 128
28	Daughters of faith 75	55	Clean hands and a pure heart (1) 130
29	Completing the circle 77		

#	Title	Page
56	Clean hands and a pure heart (2)	132
57	Crossing the frontier	134
58	Signing off	136
59	Rising opposition	138
60	Rock formation	140
61	Solemn departure	143
62	Mountaintop experience	145
63	Facing suffering	147
64	The costs of belonging	149
65	Reception class	151
66	Searching question	153
67	Restoring presence	155
68	Forgive us our debts	157
69	Calling for commitment	159
70	Kingdom people	161
71	Valuing the kingdom	163
72	Vintage rewards	165
73	Servant king	167
74	Compassion road	169
75	Coming king	171
76	Turning the tables	173
77	Hollow hopes	175
78	Pause for thought	177
79	Rejected and raised	179
80	I cannot come to the banquet	181
81	Maker's mark	183
82	Life to come	185
83	Love the Lord	187
84	Grief and anger	189
85	Leading questions	191
86	Religious audit	193
87	Division and desolation	195
88	Looking ahead	197
89	Panic, pressure and patience	199
90	Time to run	201
91	Day of darkness	203
92	Wait, wake and work	205
93	Out of oil	207
94	Hidden talent	209
95	Judged by Christ	212
96	Anointed for burial	214
97	The trap is sprung	216
98	Body language	218
99	Struck and scattered	220
100	Garden of tears	223
101	Swords and a kiss	225
102	The Jewish trial	228
103	No friend of mine	230
104	Bitter end	232
105	The Roman trial	234
106	Road to the cross	237
107	Around the cross	239
108	The shaking of the foundations	241
109	Sharing our death	243
110	The place where he lay	245
111	Appearance and disappearance	247
112	With you forever	249

INTRODUCTION

Jesus of Nazareth has a strong claim to be the most influential person who ever lived. Two thousand years after his own time, hundreds of millions of people in every part of the world are glad to be known as Christians, as his friends and followers. The life he lived, the things he said and did, how he died and what happened afterwards, make a remarkable story. Christians have always wanted to know about Jesus, to understand the Lord who launched our faith.

Why write gospels?

That is why we have gospels. Probably they arose something like this. For a few years after Jesus' time, people remembered what he had said and done. Memories were good in the ancient Middle East, as they have to be in any culture where paper is expensive. But the people who remembered gradually died out, and Christians wanted a record of Jesus that they could keep. So about a generation after Jesus' lifetime, the gospels started to appear.

That is very approximate. Nobody really knows when Matthew was written. Guesses vary from about AD40 to AD100. Many scholars come down in the middle of that range, between about 60 and 90. Around that time, the record of Jesus' life that we call Matthew's gospel was put to paper.

Global or local?

For whom was the gospel written? Two answers are popular today. One says that Matthew (and Mark, Luke and John) always meant their gospels to be widely read. The church of that day was spread across much of southern Europe, western Asia and northern Africa. There were good communications between various Christian centres. The gospels were bound to travel. The gospel writers believed that Jesus' story was worth telling and wanted to preserve it for their own generation and those who would follow. From very early on, the four gospels belonged to the whole church.

A second approach suggests that the four gospels were written for Christians in different local areas. Each of the writers was trying to help the Christians he knew best. So each gospel is angled differently, to reflect the needs and circumstances of the writer's own local church. If we follow that sort of tack, we may try to read between the lines of each gospel to find out about the needs and situation of the first readers, as well as about Jesus himself.

There is some truth in both those theories. The early Christians were interested in Jesus. They thought his life was important. They wanted to preserve their memories of him, so others could know about him too. Jesus is the main focus of the whole gospel story and of Christian faith. But the four gospels do have different selections of material and different emphases. They are portraits, not engineers' drawings. To some extent they each reflect their own author's perspectives on Jesus and the questions and concerns of four different groups of early Christians.

Why read four gospels?

So I take a positive approach to the gospels. I value the material they contain, and I believe they give a true picture of Jesus. But none of them gives the whole truth. All of the gospel writers had to choose what to include and how to present it. Let me mention four reasons why it is helpful to have several gospels.

- **Selection:** Some material in other gospels is not in Matthew. For example, Matthew only shows Jesus making one journey to Jerusalem, at the end of his ministry. Jesus goes with grim foreboding, expecting to suffer. His enemies there act quickly and harshly against him, very soon after he arrives. That sequence of events is easier to understand if we connect it to John's gospel, which shows Jesus making several visits to Jerusalem. By the time of the last Passover visit he was known in the city and was a marked man. Both he and his enemies were ready for trouble. The accounts in two different gospels mesh together, to give a fuller and clearer picture of Jesus' career.

- **Order:** Some material in Matthew is in a different order in other gospels. For example, much of the teaching in Matthew 5—7 (the sermon on the mount) is scattered through Luke. Matthew seems to have a tendency to collect material on a similar theme and include it in one place in his gospel. There is something similar in Matthew 8 and 9, which shows a series of miracles in quick succession, whereas in Mark the same material is spread more widely, across Mark 1—5.

- **Detail:** Some material in Matthew is briefer than in other gospels. Mark reports action at length. Matthew cuts to the main point. Compare Mark 5:21-43 with Matthew 9:18-26, for example. Mark shows

each scene very closely and clearly; Matthew makes an impact by moving swiftly from one incident to the next.
- **Angle:** Some material in Matthew is told a bit differently in other gospels. Look at the comment on Matthew 26:26–30, for example. Jesus' words at the last supper vary a little as we move from one gospel to another. The main lines of the incident are very clear, but each gospel has its own emphasis and angle.

So for many reasons it is helpful to have four different gospels. But in some vitally important ways they are closely similar, both in broad outline and even in some fine details. Why is this? Why in particular are Matthew, Mark and Luke so very like each other at so many points?

Identify your sources

Most people who study the gospels think Matthew knew Mark's gospel, or something very like it. The two gospels have a great deal of material in common. Most of that material – indeed all of it after Matthew 13 – is in the same order, and much of it has similar wording. So the thought that Matthew knew and used Mark, and adapted Mark's material into his own gospel, has become widespread in modern study of the gospels.

However, a lot of Matthew's material is missing from Mark. About half of that extra material, almost all of it sayings of Jesus, is very like parts of Luke's gospel. This raises the suspicion that Matthew and Luke both had the same source for this stuff. This source has been named 'Q', which is the first letter of the German word for 'source', and a suitably mysterious title for a shadowy body of material about which we really know very little indeed.

Everything in the two paragraphs above is sensible guesswork; we cannot be certain. Matthew, like many a modern journalist, does not identify his sources. Even so, something like the above may very well explain Matthew as we now have it. But as we read Matthew, it is important to hear the way he tells the story of Jesus, to listen for his own emphases, and trace his own plan.

Matthew's plan

Have you ever been in an old building that was converted from one use to another during its lifetime? Both the original design and the later modifications contribute to the ground plan and the shape of the rooms. Some people think that has happened to Matthew. At any rate there seem to be two plans, dovetailed into each other.

The 'Jesus began' plan

The first three or four chapters of Matthew are a sort of preface to the main action. Jesus is born; later on he is baptised and tempted. Then he is ready to start his ministry, and at 4:17 it says, 'From then on Jesus began to preach.' The gospel then shows Jesus making God's kingdom known, in word and action, in and around Galilee.

Gradually we see a very mixed response arising, and there is a hint that serious difficulties may be emerging, when we read in 11:20, 'Then he began to speak against the places which had not heeded his word.'

Opposition now starts to sharpen, and at 16:21 we realise where this will lead: 'From then on Jesus began to show his disciples that he must go to Jerusalem, suffer and die.'

By using the word 'began' as a milestone, we have found the route the gospel takes. By that plan, Matthew's gospel has twelve chapters about the mission of Jesus in Galilee (4—16), and twelve chapters leading to the Passion of Jesus in Jerusalem (16—27). Once we pass chapter 16, the story is drawn to the cross like a moth to a lamp. Opposition steadily advances, the moment of destruction is inevitable, and there is a deepening mood of sorrow and fear. Only at the very end does hope return, with Easter and resurrection and a completely new beginning.

The 'Jesus finished' plan

The first plan has picked out the action of the gospel – what Jesus did. The second plan picks out what Jesus said. The words 'When Jesus had finished these sayings' come five times in Matthew (7:28; 11:1; 13:53; 19:1; 26:1). Each one ends a major block of teaching, the five great sermons of Matthew's gospel. Each of the blocks has a main theme running right through:

- Chapters 5—7, the sermon on the mount, about practical living.
- Chapter 10, about mission and evangelism.
- Chapter 13, a long string of parables about God's kingdom.
- Chapter 18, about Christian community and relationships.
- Chapters 24 and 25, about the future.

So the teaching and action are interspersed, like a giant multi-decker sandwich. Each section of teaching connects with the action around it, and carries the story forward.

Why two plans? Many people answer something like this. Mark used the first plan: half of his gospel is about Jesus' mission in Galilee, and half is about Jesus' journey to Jerusalem and his suffering and death there. Matthew adopted Mark's plan. But Matthew also knew a good deal of Jesus' teaching, most of which Mark had missed (including the so-called 'Q' material), and wanted to highlight this. So the second plan, overlaid on the first, draws attention to Jesus as teacher. The church remembers and trusts the Lord who lived, died and rose again. The church also values and follows what he taught. Both aspects are important to Matthew.

Who was Matthew?

Jesus had a follower called Matthew, a former tax collector, whom he had called and who belonged to the circle of twelve disciples. We meet this man at Matthew 9:9, and there is an ancient tradition that his personal reminiscences of Jesus have come into this gospel. But did he actually write it? Many people think it would be odd if Matthew, who was one of the twelve, copied from Mark, who was not.

Matthew's gospel also shows a close acquaintance with Jewish religious lore and custom, and tax collectors were not very religious Jews. Some of the style in the gospel seems to be much more like that of a Jewish religious teacher. So could Matthew the tax collector be the source for some of the information, but someone else be the writer? And is there a trace of that writer – rather like a film director appearing for a moment in the film – in Jesus' saying about the 'scribe trained for the kingdom' (13:52)? None of the other gospels has this saying, but the writer of Matthew feels it describes his own calling, and is glad to include it.

If we take that approach, whom shall we mean when we say 'Matthew': the tax collector, or the writer of the gospel? I shall use the name 'Matthew' to refer to the person who wrote the gospel, and to the way he tells the story of Jesus.

Matthew and Judaism

In many ways, Matthew is the most Jewish of the gospels. It shows a strong acquaintance with Jewish customs and laws (for example, 5:23; 17:24; 23:5). It stresses how the ancient law of the Old Testament is fulfilled in the teaching of Jesus (5:17), and how the prophecies come to fulfilment in his life and work (1:23; 12:17). In some sections it presents Jesus as a new Moses (see comment on 2:13–23, pp. 26–27).

Yet Matthew also includes some sharp criticism of Jewish leaders. This is clearest in chapter 23. We also read that 'the kingdom of God will be taken away from you and given to a people that produces the fruits of the kingdom' (21:43). Some of Israel's ancient privileges are being taken over by the community that Jesus is founding. So Matthew's gospel is very Jewish in its background and atmosphere, but it also tells of Judaism being split by the coming of Jesus. At the start of Matthew's gospel, we see Jesus' mission focused on Israel. But Israel divides: there is a core of opposition among the nation's leaders, yet many of the ordinary people are warm and receptive. Although Matthew does not directly mention this, the Christian gospel made great strides among the Jewish people in the years after the resurrection, as the church began to grow. But it was never accepted by the nation's official leadership.

Matthew's church

The strong Jewish flavour to Matthew's writing suggests that he was writing for a Jewish audience, probably for a group of Jewish people who had accepted and believed in Jesus. Matthew saw this faith as a true fulfilment of their ancient Jewish heritage. Prophecy and law found focus and completion in Jesus. Jesus was Israel's Messiah, and God's ancient purpose was being carried forward through him.

Yet Matthew's first readers may have had very awkward relations with some of their neighbours, who did not share their beliefs. Jews who had accepted Jesus would have been suspect, seen as a fringe group within Israel. That may be the reason Matthew included so much controversial material, involving disputes and criticism between Jesus and his opponents. All the gospels show some of this, but it is clearest in Matthew, and it may have been especially relevant to his readers' own situation. (The comments at the start of chapter 23 discuss this point further.)

But Matthew did not expect Christianity to stay within a Jewish horizon. He was convinced that the church's mission should include Gentiles too. Jesus sometimes met Gentile people during his mission in Galilee. When he saw their faith, he recognised and welcomed it. Those contacts were a hint of what was ahead. Once Jesus is risen, the horizon is the world. After the resurrection the Christian message spreads out to all the nations.

Matthew and Christian living

Three major emphases stand out when we compare Matthew with other gospels.

- Matthew's is the only gospel to use the word 'church' (16:18; 18:17). He shows very clearly that Jesus is gathering and shaping a community.

- There is a lot of material in Matthew about practical living. Jesus' teaching about lifestyle and relationships has a very prominent place. Matthew obviously believes that faith must show itself in everyday life.

- Matthew includes a great deal of Jesus' teaching about judgement. God weighs and measures the way people live. Faith that does not show itself in deeds is hollow, and will never be able to bluff God. God is rich in forgiveness, but that does not give Christians the right to be casual or complacent about how we live.

So Matthew's Christianity is church-centred: we belong to one another. It is practical: we aim to express our faith in love and action. And it is serious: we trust God's mercy, but we must not be careless and complacent in the service we offer.

Text and translation

Have you ever noticed a footnote in your Bible saying, 'Some manuscripts have…' or 'Other ancient authorities read…'? We do not have the original manuscript of any book of the Bible. Thank God, the early Christians copied out the biblical books, by hand. But some of the first copies got lost, decayed or were destroyed in persecutions. So when we want to find out what Matthew wrote, we use the earliest copies we have. But these manuscripts come from several generations after Matthew's own time.

These manuscripts do not agree with each other precisely. That can always happen with copying by hand. Where we meet disagreements in wording, we have to work out as well as we can which version is original – what Matthew actually wrote. Very rarely those differences affect a whole verse – included in some manuscripts, missing from others. Examples are 6:13; 16:2–3; 17:21; 18:11; and we now doubt whether those five verses were actually written by Matthew. Yet much, much more often we have no serious disagreements in the manuscripts:

what we read in our 21st-century English Bibles is based on a very solid knowledge of what Matthew wrote in the first century.

Matthew did not write in English. He used Greek, though not exactly the language spoken in Greece today. In some places it has been hard to translate the Greek into English, and English Bibles show different meanings. One example is in 28:17: the last few words could mean 'but they doubted' or 'but some of them doubted'. Were all the disciples hesitant, or just a few of them? We do not know. That sort of problem is occasionally to be expected when we use a very old piece of writing. It is hard to know fully and exactly what the ancient language meant. But most of the time we can be confident in our modern translations. In our day, as for the last 2,000 years, Christians are happy to use the four gospels because they were written close to the time and place where Jesus lived, and give us the best information we have about his life and work.

Matthew's good news

So Christians read Matthew as an introduction to Jesus. That was Matthew's main motive, to present Jesus clearly and helpfully, so that his readers would understand and trust Jesus. The word gospel means 'good news', about Jesus and about the life he invites people to live.

So listen to the teaching of Jesus in Matthew, take it seriously, and try to apply it in your own life. Value your Christian relationships with the brothers and sisters who help you to follow this way. And treasure above all your relationship with Jesus who is 'with you always, to the end' (Matthew 28:20).

The Bible quotations included in the commentary are usually taken from the New Revised Standard Version; occasionally I have used a translation or paraphrase of my own.

Some further reading on Matthew

A lot has been written about Matthew's gospel in recent years, and I have learned much from these books. This list aims to give credit for that. It also suggests books that might help you to explore Matthew further.

Longer commentaries on Matthew

These are the current editions of the four big commentaries from which I learned most while writing this commentary in 1999–2000.

- D.A. Carson, *Matthew, Expositor's Bible Commentary (Revised Edition)* (Zondervan, 2017).
- W.D. Davies and D.C. Allison, *The Gospel According to St Matthew, International Critical Commentary* (on the Greek text; three volumes) (T&T Clark, 1988–97). Abridged as *Matthew, A Shorter Commentary* (Bloomsbury, 2005).
- D.A. Hagner, *Matthew, Word Biblical Commentary*, two volumes (Zondervan, 2015).
- U. Luz, *Matthew, Hermeneia Commentary*, three volumes (Fortress, 2001–07).

If I were writing now, I might also have turned to the following, among a host of informative recent commentaries.

- J.K. Brown and K. Roberts, *Matthew, Two Horizons NT Commentary* (Eerdmans, 2018). Discusses how we might use Matthew in theology and Christian living.
- W. Carter, *Matthew and the Margins* (Continuum, 2001). Interprets Matthew against the realities of politics and empire in the ancient world.
- R.T. France, *The Gospel of Matthew, New International Commentary on the NT* (Eerdmans, 2007). Outstandingly clear, shrewd and careful.
- E.M. Wainwright, *Habitat, Human, and Holy: An eco-rhetorical reading of the gospel of Matthew, Earth Bible Commentary* (Sheffield Phoenix, 2017). Jesus' gospel in and for God's created world.

Shorter commentaries on Matthew

For those who want a shorter commentary, here are a variety of approaches.

- W. Barclay, *The Gospel of Matthew, The New Daily Study Bible*, two volumes (revised edition, St Andrew Press, 2001). Very accessible in style, although now dating a little.
- R.T. France, *Matthew, Tyndale New Testament Commentary* (IVP, 1985). Explains the meaning of the text. Very clear, careful and well-informed.
- Pope Francis, *The Gospel of Matthew: A spiritual and pastoral reading* (Orbis, 2020). Straightforward in style, serious in approach and intended to help a wide range of church people.
- I.H. Jones, *The Gospel of Matthew, Epworth Commentary* (Epworth Press, 1994). Part of a series designed for Methodist preachers.
- S.M. Uytanlet and K.-K. Kwa, *Matthew: A pastoral and contextual commentary, Asia Bible Commentary* (Langham, 2017). Perspectives from east Asia.
- T. Wright, *Matthew for Everyone*, two volumes (SPCK, 2002). Like Barclay, part of a series on the whole New Testament, and very accessible to non-specialists.

Other books on Matthew

Those who want a thematic introduction to Matthew, to help with a formal study programme, might wish to explore one of the following.

- I. Boxall, *Discovering Matthew: Content, interpretation, reception* (SPCK, 2014).
- U. Luz, *The Theology of the Gospel of Matthew* (Cambridge University Press, 1995).
- E.M. Wainwright, *Matthew: An introduction and study guide – the Basileia of the heavens is near at hand* (Bloomsbury, 2017). Asks how we respond to Matthew amid the questions of today.

By way of acknowledgement

I was greatly helped on the divorce passage in Matthew 19 by D. Instone-Brewer, *Divorce and Remarriage in the Bible* (Eerdmans, 2001); and on Matthew 11 by G. Theissen, *The Gospels in Context* (T&T Clark, 1992). I also used some major German commentaries, by H. Frankemölle, A. Sand and W. Wiefel.

1

Matthew 1:1–17

Lines of introduction

The scenery on a stage helps you to enjoy the play. Action makes more sense, a story carries more impact, if you can see where the events are set. The scenery can sharpen your hearing and tune your mind to the author's intentions and concerns. These opening verses of Matthew's gospel lay out the scenery. Matthew presents Jesus against the background of the Old Testament. There were clues, longings, promises, running through the Old Testament, that had come to life in Jesus. The very first verse of the gospel names some of them: 'Jesus the Messiah, son of David, son of Abraham'.

Son of Abraham

Abraham was the great forefather of the Jewish people. Jesus was born a Jew, spent most of his life among Jewish people and rarely travelled outside Jewish territory. He thought, taught, argued and prayed in a Jewish way. We understand Jesus properly only if we understand him as a Jew.

Yet God had called Abraham for a wider purpose: 'in you all the families of the earth shall be blessed' (Genesis 12:3). Abraham is an international figure. The promise to Abraham is that Israel's God will do great things for the whole world. From this small people, a blessing will flow outward to the nations. To call Jesus 'son of Abraham' means that he is heir to this promise. He has blessing to share with the world.

Messiah, son of David

Jesus is also called 'son of David'. David was remembered as Israel's most successful king, who made the nation peaceful and prosperous. But that had been long ago. The Jews had grown hungry for a new David, a leader to make them great again and give them fresh hope. So the title 'son of David' is not just about ancestry. It is a job description. Through Jesus the kingly power of God will be made known in Israel. That is why he was called 'Messiah'. The word means 'anointed', a person marked out by God for a special task. In Greek – the language Matthew wrote – the word for 'anointed' is our word 'Christ'. Jesus Christ was God's anointed leader, a new David, the shepherd king who would show the loving rule of God.

Undulating path

The long genealogy (vv. 2–16) is divided into three sections of 14 names each (v. 17). At the very start is Abraham (vv. 2, 17). The next marker in the sequence, ending the first main section, is the name of 'David the king' (vv. 6, 17). Then the second major landmark is the 'deportation to Babylon' (vv. 11, 12, 17), when many thousands of Jews were led across the desert to exile.

This is a roll of honour. It reflects the whole Old Testament story of Israel's long journey of faith and the patient goodness of God. Yet it is no whitewash. David and the exile are the milestones on the road, marking triumph and tragedy, fortune and failure. Jesus came to a nation with a patchy record. He stepped into real human history, the mixture of grief and glory that the world still experiences today.

Mothers with a message

The genealogy is mainly a list of fathers. Only five mothers are mentioned. Four have unusual stories to tell. Tamar (v. 3) acted the part of a prostitute to claim the protection of the family into which she had married (Genesis 38). Rahab (v. 5) was a prostitute in Jericho who helped two Jewish spies (Joshua 2). Ruth (v. 5) was a foreigner who came into Israel's line through a complex story of bereavement and famine. 'The wife of Uriah' (v. 6) was Bathsheba, whose husband David murdered to conceal his adultery with her (2 Samuel 11); yet she later became the mother of King Solomon. These are not ideal Jewish mothers. Possibly all were Gentiles. Their circumstances and their conduct were unusual, and even irregular. Yet they underline the element of grace, that God can take human life as it is – often untidy, sometimes perverse and odd – and fill it with the rich promise of love and hope. They hint too that the fifth mother, Mary (v. 16), will also give birth amid unexpected circumstances. So Jesus comes out of Israel, for the world. He is born to be king, yet from a turbulent and tangled heritage. He is Mary's son and God's Messiah, a figure of perplexity and a child of promise.

Prayer

We praise you, God of Israel and our God, for the long reach and far horizon of your purpose, and for the breadth and generosity of your love. Through Jesus Christ our Lord. Amen

2

Matthew 1:18–25

Child of God

The long line of ancestry has run from Abraham down to Joseph. Yet the genealogy ends with a novel and intriguing turn of phrase: instead of the repeated 'was father of', the last link in the chain is that Joseph was 'husband of Mary, of whom Jesus was born' (1:16). We discover the reason for that wording in this next passage, in verses 18–25.

Joseph was not the father of Jesus, at least not biologically. No human father was involved in Jesus' conception: he was 'born of the Virgin Mary'. The life in him came directly from God. Matthew – and indeed Joseph himself – knew perfectly well that this is not the normal order of things; that's why Joseph wanted to break the engagement when he first heard of Mary's pregnancy (vv. 18–19).

Father-in-law

Matthew tells this section of the gospel from Joseph's point of view. He is said to be 'a righteous man' (v. 19), anxious to avoid a marriage that seemed compromised from the start, yet unwilling to make more trouble than necessary about calling the plans off. A dream helped to settle his fears (v. 20), so that he, a 'son of David', married Mary and gave his name and his family line to her child (vv. 24–25). Legally he became the father of Jesus. He protected mother and child through the hazards ahead (2:13–25). He taught Jesus his own trade (13:55; compare Mark 6:3). He seems to have died before Jesus launched into public ministry, but, so far as we can tell, his work was lovingly and faithfully done.

In a name

The child's name, Jesus, is a loaded word (v. 21). In Hebrew it is written Joshua, and means 'God to the rescue'. There had been an earlier Joshua who led the people of Israel, centuries before, into the land God had promised them. So Jesus too would make hopes become real. He would be God to the rescue. He would offer the Jewish people a new era, filled with freedom and forgiveness.

As the prophets foretold

A quotation from Isaiah helps to explain the virgin birth (vv. 22–23, from Isaiah 7:14); it had been predicted this way, we hear, seven centuries earlier. Yet no one – so far as we can tell – had taken the Isaiah text in quite that way until Jesus came. Isaiah seemed to be speaking of a young woman, perhaps a girl on the threshold of marriage, who would soon be pregnant with her first child. Then Matthew heard a fuller meaning in those ancient words, as a description of the birth of Jesus. He found fresh life in an old prophecy; but he also took up the hopes that had always been seen in it.

For this text from Isaiah 7 is about a prince, a royal leader for Israel. To connect these words to Jesus is to mark him out as a kingly figure, a new David. But he was more than a king. Isaiah's prophecy spoke of Emmanuel, which is Hebrew for 'God is with us'. In Jesus the creative power and love of God took human flesh, personally and directly. Through Jesus, in a unique and immediate way, God comes to be with his people.

Worth taking seriously

For many people, even some church people, the whole idea of Jesus' virgin birth seems a fantasy. But the evidence should not be sneezed at. Two positive points may be made.

First, the Jewish people read Isaiah for centuries without expecting a virgin birth. Matthew turned to Isaiah, not primarily because he spotted ideas in the text that others had missed, but because it fitted the facts he had to tell. The scripture did not teach him his story; it resonated with what he already knew.

Second, Matthew and Luke tell the Christmas story in very different ways in their two gospels. Yet at the heart of it all they match, and confirm one another's material, as two very different witnesses to the same event: that Jesus was 'conceived by the Holy Spirit and born of the Virgin Mary'.

So Jesus, son of the Jewish people, carried in his humanity the life and presence of Israel's God. The hopes of the prophetic scriptures took flesh in him. Joseph and Mary's love nurtured the Son of God.

Prayer

Lord Jesus Christ, we praise you that you lived the life of God in our human flesh, truly one of us, yet not merely one of us.

3

Matthew 2:1–12

Worship from afar

Matthew's first chapter has told of a Jewish king, born of Jewish descent, according to the promises of Jewish scriptures. That raises an intriguing question. Has Israel not got a king already? If so, what will the old king and the new have to do with each other?

The gospel begins to answer that question by telling us (v. 1) that 'in the time of King Herod… Jesus was born in Bethlehem of Judea'. Herod was a notoriously ruthless king, with grand ambitions and a paranoid fear of any possible rival. The reader expects an ugly clash. Yet this clash comes about in an unexpected way, as light and worship stream into the story from two quite new directions.

Travelling light

The word 'magi' means possessors of mysterious wisdom or hidden knowledge. They are 'wise men', not 'kings', and the text does not mention how many they were, only that they gave three gifts. Here they represent the wealth and wisdom of the Gentile world, the deep yearning and generous worship of the nations beyond Israel, coming to greet God's royal Messiah.

As the magi represent the praise of the Gentiles, the leading of the star suggests that even creation worships. The lights of heaven rise to greet the birth of the Christ, to hail the coming of God's creative love in human flesh. The nations and the skies are moved to worship. How will Israel and her king respond?

We two kings

Herod hears of the child's birth from the magi (v. 2), and apparently wishes to worship too (v. 8). But his deeper reaction is hostile and fearful. He is disturbed and troubled, he gathers his religious leaders for advice, and his plans for action are discreet and devious. Threat, foreboding and danger are in the air, and no one (except the magi, v. 12) does anything to thwart or divert the king. Gentiles can see the reality of Christ's birth, yet Israel seems curiously unaware, while her leader tries to destroy him.

For those who know the gospel story, there are uncomfortable similarities with the events of the Passion. Jesus is called 'king of the Jews' (v. 2; 27:37). Israel's leaders gather against him (v. 4; 27:1). There are secret plots (v. 7; 26:4, 14–16). The end of the gospel is foreshadowed in its beginning. Yet even now the wrath of men does not achieve all it plans. God is in control (v. 12), and Jesus' life is secure in his hands.

Threads of prophecy

Much of Matthew's gospel is like woven cloth. As the lines of the story lead forward, across them run strands from scripture. The narrative is dense with echoes of and allusions to Old Testament themes.

The direct quotation in verse 6, from Micah 5:2, presents Jesus as a new David, born at Bethlehem to be shepherd king for God's people – and that royal theme will be important right through Matthew. Yet surely in this chapter we hear also an echo of Isaiah 60, which speaks of light rising in Israel and Gentiles gathering with gifts: a new era has come, an age of light and hope. Psalm 72 tells of Israel's ideal king, to whom the nations will bring worship and gifts. Numbers 24:17 prophesies the coming of a messianic figure, as the rising of a new star.

Matthew (who knew the Hebrew scriptures better than we do) would have been well aware of these echoes and of the hints they conveyed. His tapestry is rich and whole precisely because of this intersecting weave. He shows us meaning in the story by the light of the scriptures.

But is it all i-magi-nation?

So how could these events have actually happened? For myself, I am intrigued by some Iranian traditions which seem to match this story from the other end of the journey; impressed by some recent and serious astronomical enquiry into the nature of a planetary conjunction in 7BC and of a comet in 5BC; and inclined to think that improbable events become a little more probable when God's Son is born.

This account of a wandering star and visiting foreign academics strikes some modern people as far-fetched and incredible. If that is your view, don't overlook the points of Matthew's story: that the coming of Jesus is important enough for nations and creation to honour him, for tyrant thrones to tremble and for all the glories of scripture to be recalled.

For thought

The hinge of all history hangs on the door of a Bethlehem stable.
Anonymous

4

Matthew 2:13–23

Threat and preservation

This sombre story displays the shadowy side of human power. Herod shows with awful clarity that kings of his ilk fall far short of God's ideal. Israel needs a new kind of ruler. So Jesus is preserved, kept safe from the anger and harshness of the Herod family, so that the true rule of God might one day be seen and known in him.

Directed by dreams

Joseph is portrayed in these chapters as a dreamer (1:20; 2:13, 19, 22). God helped him turn his fears into action by shaping and speaking through his dreams. This may be another echo of the Old Testament. There was another Joseph, long before (Genesis 37—50), whose dreams helped to preserve the Jewish people in hard times. Matthew may be hinting that the story of Jesus breathes new life into that episode. Jesus lives out and sums up the history of his people, as he too is kept safe in Egypt.

Leader to liberty

That first period in Egypt, more than a thousand years before, ended with the Exodus. Moses, the leader and lawgiver chosen by God, brought the Jewish people across the desert to the promised land. In these chapters of Matthew, the parallels between Jesus' story and that of Moses come thick and fast. Both were threatened at birth by an evil king (2:12-15; Exodus 2) and came out of Egypt to Israel (2:21; Exodus 12—13). Both passed through water (3:13-17; Exodus 14) and spent time in the desert (4:1-11; Exodus 16—17). To climax this set of parallels, both taught Israel from a mountain top (Matthew 5; Exodus 20). The links are not all precise. Jesus is not exactly a new Moses. Yet he is destined to be a new leader, a lawgiver and liberator for all in Israel who will follow him. Ancient hopes and dreams will take fresh form. There will be a new journey to freedom.

Fulfilment formula

Three times in this section Matthew includes a scripture quotation, underlining the varied ways in which his story of Jesus 'fulfils' the Old

Testament. Verse 15 is taken from Hosea 11:1, which recalls Israel's special relationship with God, as a child guided by a loving Father. Jesus gives fresh vitality and meaning to that relationship: God's love focuses on him with a special intimacy, yet through him many others are able to call God 'Father'.

Verse 18 is from Jeremiah 31:15, remembering the distress of the Jewish exile in Babylon, six centuries before Jesus. The misery inflicted then by a foreign army has come again through Herod. While kings like Herod rule, the agony of exile is still present and the people still need release.

The snippet at the end of verse 23 is a mystery. Nothing in the Old Testament reads quite like this, and we do not know which text Matthew had in mind. However, Isaiah 11:1 is a strong possibility – a passage about a coming ruler, a 'branch' from David's line. The Hebrew for branch is '*nezer*', a resonance with the name 'Nazareth'. When Jesus goes there, this reflects his royal potential.

Innocents of Bethlehem

The killing of the children of Bethlehem was a dreadful atrocity for which there are no quick or comforting explanations. They had done nothing to deserve it. The era into which Jesus was born was as bitter and brutal as our own. Innocent people got hurt; justice was not always honoured; rulers could be ruthless and proud. That reality remains, and the suffering continues. Yet when the adult Jesus deliberately faced the harshness, in his own crucifixion, he showed that even wrath and violence cannot overcome or extinguish the love of God.

Destination Galilee

Herod died in 4BC, and the worst of his sons, Archelaus, inherited Judea, the area around Jerusalem and Bethlehem. Galilee, in the north, was a calmer place. Here Jesus grew up and began his ministry.

For reflection

Wherever we see refugees, violent rule and untimely death, we are in touch with the gospel story. We can pray, and we may be able to offer practical help. If we serve Jesus, these things concern us.

5

Matthew 3:1–12

Stream of renewal

The story leaps forward. Matthew does not tell us how far, although it is clear from other gospels that Jesus was about 30 years old when he started his public ministry.

Voice in the wilderness

John comes suddenly on to the scene. The story has not mentioned him until now. He comes as a man with a message. We have heard of Jesus the king. Now John proclaims the kingdom, the rule and realm of God. It is near, he says, and so people must respond, urgently and deliberately (v. 2). Lives must be made new, commitments be reviewed, patterns of behaviour changed, quarrels mended, neighbours loved, hearts set right with the ways of God.

The gospel describes John (v. 3) with words drawn from Isaiah 40:3. This Old Testament passage told of the ending of Israel's exile; it was a word of comfort and freedom, of rejoicing and hope. God would travel ahead of his people and lead them into a fuller experience of goodness and grace. This is John's message too. He echoes the summons of Isaiah. He speaks as a roadmaker, preparing the way, calling the Jewish people to the path where they will discover in new ways the leadership and love of God.

Town and country

John lives rough (v. 4). He is an outsider, whose dress and diet label him as a figure on the fringe of society. He resembles the Old Testament prophet Elijah (1 Kings 17; 2 Kings 1:8), who also appears in the desert, lives a rough and remote life, and yet shakes the whole land with the force of his message.

For John gathers a crowd. His fame spreads and people from the towns of Judea flock to him. His message of fresh beginnings, of lives turned into new directions, of water that washes away the past and rinses clean for God, proved highly attractive. Many in Israel brought their desires and aspirations to live a better and more godly life down to the Jordan, and plunged into the current of John's renewal movement.

Yet John remains a man on the edge. There is no obvious link between his activity and the worship and sacrifice practised at the Jerusalem temple. It almost seems that he is deliberately critical and subversive about what is available there. He offers prayer, preaching and signs of God's grace, far away from the main centre and recognised leaders of Israel's religion. There will surely be a collision when the two parties meet.

Troubler of Israel

We shall have to say more about the Sadducees and Pharisees at 16:1 and 5:20 respectively. They correspond roughly to the 'chief priests and scribes' of 2:4. Here John greets them sharply and aggressively, as threats and potential traitors to the renewal for which he strives (vv. 7–12). As he speaks, three fresh aspects of his message come into view.

- **John divides the nation.** His challenge splits Israel into two. Birth rights are not enough: there must be deeds to match. There is an uncomfortable separation in view.
- **John expects judgement.** His language is urgent and dramatic. He senses that through his preaching and in his own time the searching judgement of God is at work.
- **John looks for someone greater to come.** He believes that God will do a greater work than he has done, that the Holy Spirit will flow in Israel, mightier than all his preaching and baptism. There is a 'stronger one' coming who will make God's people clean and whole. Both the renewing and the divisive aspects of John's ministry will be carried forward with fresh power and fuller purpose.

Preparing the way

So Matthew presents John as the herald and forerunner for Jesus. He announces the kingdom (v. 2) in the very same words that Jesus will use (4:17). He prepares the way (v. 3) that the Lord will take. He tells of a 'stronger one' to come, through whom the Holy Spirit will refresh and stir Israel's life. The stage is set for the stronger one to appear.

Prayer

God, let me be a roadmaker for Jesus, living and speaking so that hearts will open to his life and power.

6

Matthew 3:13–17

Immersed into new responsibility

When the adult Jesus steps into the gospel story, he comes first to ask for baptism (v. 13). He comes from Galilee, where he has grown up, to ally himself with the movement of renewal and hope that John has launched. The values and vision that John has been preaching will be the launching pad for his own ministry.

We have been led to look for a strong man of the Spirit, but Jesus does not make a dramatic entrance. He does not stride powerfully across the earth; he approaches humbly. The Spirit will come upon Jesus through his baptism. He will indeed be strong. Yet, as elsewhere in his ministry, his strength comes through apparent weakness, and his service touches others through his gentleness and humility.

The right way round

As Jesus approaches John, there is a brief conversation between them; only Matthew of the four gospels mentions this exchange. John raises a question: he tries to prevent what Jesus is doing. 'Why should you need to receive baptism?' he asks (v. 14). Surely that is for sinners (3:6). Things should be the other way round: Jesus should baptise John.

Jesus replies that this is the way to 'fulfil all righteousness' (v. 15). Accepting baptism is the right thing for him to do. Matthew's gospel portrays Jesus as constantly concerned for what is right. Here at the start it is important that he identify with the people he comes to serve, that he show his solidarity with them and immerse himself in their hopes and needs.

In baptism Jesus embarks deliberately on a long and hard path of righteousness. He commits himself, willingly and obediently, to God's mission for the sake of his people. In this way he will bring about 'all righteousness', for others as well as himself, as he carries forward the just and loving purpose of God.

Vision and voice

Matthew describes only very briefly what Jesus sees and hears at his baptism, but the words are filled with meaning and promise.

The Spirit comes upon him. John has already spoken of the 'stronger one' baptising with the Spirit. Now Jesus receives the Spirit, not as an exclusive personal possession, but so that he may share the Spirit's life with those he serves, that he may cleanse and flood other people's lives with God's goodness.

The picture of the Spirit descending as a dove, as Jesus rises from the water, hints at the creation story in Genesis 1:2. The Spirit of God hovered over the face of the waters, bringing life out of the depths. Now the Spirit hovers again, breathing fresh life into the world through Jesus. A new work of creation is happening. Through the coming ministry of Jesus, the world will be renewed from within.

The voice from above, 'This is my Son, the beloved, in whom I am well pleased' (v. 17), echoes the Old Testament, casting Jesus – it seems – in three important roles. The first echo, 'my Son', is from Psalm 2:7, where God greets Israel's anointed king. 'In whom I am well pleased' recalls Isaiah 42:1, and portrays Jesus as God's servant, the same servant figure who is graphically described in Isaiah 53 as suffering to make others whole. Finally, 'the beloved one' takes the reader to Genesis 22, and shows Jesus in the part of Isaac, the child of promise who is taken to sacrificial death.

Counting the cost

Three times, then, the text shows Jesus as the apple of God's eye, giving God pleasure and serving God's purpose. Yet in two of these motifs we see the awful cost of his ministry. He will be a suffering Messiah, a sacrificed Son, a Servant King.

How fully did Jesus see all this as he looked forward to his work for God? We cannot know for sure, but some points are very clear. Jesus found through his baptism a deeper assurance of his Father's presence and power. It gave him a calm confidence, a vocation to mission and service. Perhaps he also heard a warning that what he would achieve for God would not be easily gained; it would come at a cost. For it seems that he had begun to understand the costly path ahead, when he tested his vocation in the desert – as the next portion of the gospel shows.

Prayer

Lord Jesus Christ, may our baptism in your name assure us of God's love and beckon us without fear to follow your path of service.

7

Matthew 4:1–11

Probed and proven

The spiritual 'high' of baptism does not last. The Holy Spirit leads Jesus into the desert for a time of testing (v. 1). The scene is strange, for the Spirit urges Jesus forward, and the evil one waits to tempt him. From one point of view this is a period of proving, as Jesus clarifies in his own mind the way in which his vocation and service must develop. From another angle this is a vulnerable moment, a time when Jesus' ministry could be skewed and distorted before it starts.

This spell of withdrawal, of rural isolation from the normal routines and contacts of human life, may seem to offer the stillness of calm retreat. But the desert is a rough, hard place – a battleground. Here Jesus might be driven back from following God's way; or it could be a place of advance, of consolidation and assurance in his Father's calling and love. From our Christian perspective it seems impossible that Jesus could have succumbed and fallen. But if we think too quickly along these lines, we miss the sharpness, the reality and the attraction of the choices he had to face.

Naming the opposition

Jesus' mysterious opponent is named in three different ways. 'Devil' (v. 1) and 'Satan' (v. 10) are really the same word. One is Greek, the other Hebrew. Both mean 'opponent', 'slanderer' or 'accuser' – the person who stands opposite you in a courtroom, challenges your integrity and tries to destroy your good name. This period in the wilderness challenges the integrity of Jesus' relationship with God, and threatens his good name and title as God's Servant Son.

The third word is 'tempter' (v. 3) – one who tries, tests and probes the quality of his target. Ultimately that probing becomes a proving: it reveals and confirms the quality and commitment that are in Jesus.

If you really are who you say you are...

Matthew's account has three temptations. Each of them explores – and undermines – the relationship that Jesus has with his Father. The baptism brought a word of assurance, 'This is my Son' (3:17). The tempter turns that assurance into a question, 'If you are the Son of God' (vv. 3, 6).

The first temptation asks Jesus to use his relationship with God to meet his own needs, and satisfy his hunger (vv. 2–4). Jesus replies that obeying God's word is even more basic for life than bodily food. Following God's commands will nourish him as fully as he needs (John 4:34). The Spirit has not been given him for his own comfort, but to bring mercy and love to others.

The second trial invites Jesus to prove God's love with a stunt that would be spectacular but entirely useless (vv. 5–6). If he leapt off the temple tower and landed without injury, then he would know – and so might others – that God was looking after him. Jesus responds that God is not to be dealt with in that way. It is not our business to stress-test God's love, but to trust and follow God's will.

The third test suggests that Jesus mix his commitment to God with some hard-headed realism (vv. 8–9). If he wants influence over people and nations, let him honour the devil, who rules them. Jesus does not pause to question the limits, nature and intention of that rule. He speaks about the heart of his commitment, that God alone is worthy of worship, loyalty and service. Jesus has no right or desire to dilute or compromise that claim.

Signposts from scripture

In all three temptations Jesus quotes the Old Testament to justify his resistance. All three texts come from Deuteronomy (8:3; 6:16; 6:13), from chapters that look back on Israel's exodus journey as a period of testing by God. Jesus is tried as Israel was tried. The values and priorities that God taught her then will shape and direct his life – not for himself alone, but for his people. He enters into Israel's history, that he may lead her to God's destiny. He becomes as she was, that she may know the nearness to God that he enjoys.

Yet scripture can be misused, and then it can mislead. The devil quotes scripture too (v. 6; from Psalm 91:11–12). A text without a context is a pretext. Put another way, if our use of a verse or passage leads us away from the main tenor and emphasis of the Bible, it is probably doing us more harm than good.

For thought and prayer

'Tested as we are, yet without sin' (Hebrews 4:15). Temptations, even those that make us feel ashamed and afraid, are situations that Jesus understands and can help us to handle.

8

Matthew 4:12–25

Making waves

The end of the beginning

These verses bring the overture of the gospel to an end. John is arrested (v. 12) – we do not hear why – and Jesus withdraws to Galilee, possibly to avoid danger himself. He bases himself 20 miles from Nazareth, at Capernaum, a fishing town on the northern shore of the Sea of Galilee. His active ministry is poised to begin.

At this point Matthew inserts another fulfilment quotation, to emphasise that Jesus' arrival in Galilee is a coming of light, hope and gladness. Isaiah 9, from where verses 15–16 are drawn, looks forward to a prince of David's line whose rule will give Israel security and joy. Thus the royal theme, which was so prominent in the birth stories, is underlined once again as Jesus begins his work. The kingdom of God is indeed at hand.

The region is called 'Galilee of the Gentiles' (v. 15; from Isaiah 9:1); indeed the area had been racially mixed in Old Testament times. In Jesus' day it was predominantly Jewish, but was surrounded by a number of Gentile communities. So although Jesus worked mostly among Jewish people (see 10:5–6), Matthew's choice of Old Testament text suggests that the effects of this activity will ripple out much more widely (28:18–20).

Kingdom come

'From that time Jesus began…' (v. 17). A new phase of the gospel is under way. Many people think that Matthew divides his gospel into two main sections, one of mission and the other of passion, using this sentence and the one like it at 16:21. (For more detail, see the section 'Matthew's plan' in the Introduction, pp. 11–12.)

'Jesus began to proclaim…' He repeats the message John had proclaimed (see 3:2). Times are changing. God is at work. People should amend their lives and get ready to join in. But there is more here than the continuation of John's ministry. There will be a different emphasis to what Jesus does. A powerful and gentle mercy will be at work through him. His words and deeds will display the loving rule of God. Jesus will reach needs and griefs that John did not – as the verses ahead will show.

Networking for God

The first followers of Jesus accept a sketchy job description: 'Follow me, and I will make you fish for people' (v. 19). They come with little prior warning (John 1:37–42 indicates some earlier contact; even so, this encounter by the seashore is still rather abrupt). They join an enterprise with no premises, no pension scheme and no obvious business plan. Even the uncertainties and dangers of the fishing trade look better than this.

There must have been something magnetic about Jesus. From any perspective he was a charismatic and compelling personality, able to inspire and influence others. He chooses disciples – the word means 'learners' – who will watch what he does and eventually do it themselves (10:1–5). They will be the core of his renewal movement, the community within a community, the heart of Israel's new life, the inner family with whom he will be at home. Jesus did not want to work alone. He wanted others to learn from him and live the life of the kingdom with him.

These encounters at the lakeside remind us that the Christian life often gives a person new directions and new tasks. That still applies today: we do not choose how much of ourselves to give to Christ. There is a serious note in his call that is sometimes urgent, demanding and quite unexpected.

Circuit of mercy

So Jesus goes around Galilee, telling the kingdom and showing its power. Verses 23–25 are only a summary. The chapters ahead give more detail, of his teaching in chapters 5—7, and of his varied healings in chapters 8—9. But the impression is already clear and powerful. He has taken time to be ready. He is marked out by God and anointed with the Spirit (3:16–17). He has understood his vocation and carefully distanced himself from the temptations of preservation, presumption and power (4:1–11). Now his time has come. Light shines in Galilee (vv. 15–16), bright, warm and strong.

For thought and prayer

Jesus is still the light of the minds that know him, the life of the souls that love him, and the strength of the wills that serve him.

9

Matthew 5:1–12

Honours list (1)

Hillside preacher

Jesus has been mobbed by an excited and expectant throng (4:25). Now he begins to share his own expectations, the vision for human community, relationships, lifestyle and attitudes that excites him, the way that he wants his followers to live. He climbs to a place where he can be heard, and people come to sit around him (v. 1).

The sermon on the mount, as we now call it, runs through chapters 5, 6 and 7. It is one of five major blocks of teaching in Matthew, with its beginning and its end point (7:28—8:1) clearly indicated.

Most of the material in these chapters appears in Luke too: quite a lot comes in the shorter 'Sermon on the Plain' (Luke 6:17–49), but other snippets are spread throughout Luke. So no one knows for sure whether the whole sermon was delivered on a single occasion or whether Matthew is responsible for gathering it together. Certainly it has an inspiring, searching (and daunting) vision for human living. And if the present order of the material owes something to Matthew, the heart of the vision surely comes from Jesus. This is the teaching on lifestyle that he wanted his friends to follow.

Family rule

Two themes run all the way through the sermon.

- It speaks of God as Father, a figure of love and care, who knows, notices and guides his children. This idea comes many times (5:9, 16, 45, 48; 6:1, 4, 6, 9, 14, 18, 32; 7:11).
- It is about the kingdom of God, God's loving rule. We have heard (4:17, 23) that Jesus came preaching the kingdom. This sermon fills out the detail: here is what it means to enter, experience and enjoy God's good and holy reign. The kingdom is mentioned many times over (5:3, 10, 19–20; 6:10, 33; 7:21).

The 'when' of the kingdom is not at all straightforward. Jesus often talks as if the kingdom is ahead, a distant destination to aim and strive for (5:20). Yet the sermon is itself actually about kingdom living, life that reflects God's character and concerns here and now (5:48). So this kingdom is both now and not yet, here and not fully here, arrived and still on its way. The kingdom is like seed – already filled with life, but still to show its full potential.

Hallowing the humble

The sermon begins with blessing – as if Jesus looks around him and rejoices in the people he sees. These are the ones on whom God's favour rests. They should be joyful, for God is at work among them and within them. They are not great in themselves, but they are people whose lives are open for the blessing of God.

The eight 'beatitudes' (the word is Latin for 'blessings') come in verses 3–10, one per verse. Verses 11–12 repeat at greater length the point made in verse 10, and conclude the whole section. The point of the beatitudes is not to select eight different groups of people and to offer eight different reasons why God should bless them. It is a broad-brush sketch of the followers of Jesus, a pen-picture of the kind of people whose lives reflect the kingdom of God and who enjoy the blessings of that kingdom.

The picture offers an unusual view of human living. These are not the regular patterns of behaviour that make for power, progress and popularity. Something deeper than mere worldly fortune is involved. This is Christian character and conduct, the sort of outlook and behaviour that God honours, the kind of human life in which the joy and goodness of God will be at home.

Tip of the iceberg

Most of the blessings look ahead: 'they *will* be comforted… they *will* inherit…' (vv. 4–5). The blessing is now, but the perspective is future. These people are favoured by God, but they do not yet see the full glory of his love. God has much more to show and to give them. 'Theirs is the kingdom of heaven' (vv. 3, 10), but the full reality of the kingdom is only beginning to be seen.

For thought and prayer

Through our lives and by our prayers, your kingdom come.
Iona Community

10 Matthew 5:1–12

Honours list (2)

Old, yet ever new

The beatitudes are striking, but not entirely new. Jesus regularly used Old Testament teaching, sometimes giving it a thrust or angle of his own. So verse 5 reflects Psalm 37:11, for example, and verse 8 reflects Psalm 24:3–4. There is an important link to Isaiah 61, which speaks of good news to the poor and broken-hearted (61:1) and comfort to mourners (61:2); they will be filled beyond their dreams (61:6), and God will turn their shame into rejoicing (61:7). In a similar way Matthew's beatitudes tell of blessing to the poor in spirit (v. 3), comfort to mourners (v. 4), the hungry being filled (v. 6), and people who were scorned bursting out in joy (vv. 11–12). The same issues and hopes are present in Isaiah and in Matthew. Interestingly, Isaiah 61 is the scripture that Jesus read in the Nazareth synagogue, at the start of his ministry, as his 'mission statement'. Only Luke (4:16–21) records that episode, but here we see how Jesus' first teaching in Matthew's gospel, from the same period of his life, draws on the same material.

Mission of hope

So the beatitudes outline Jesus' mission in Israel. He came as herald of God, moved by God's Spirit, to bring good news to the distressed, hope in place of sorrow, a future of promise in place of a difficult and bitter past. He came to people whose lives had been hard, and he wanted to give them a keener and deeper awareness of God's healing love. He sensed that God was stirring in him, that new hopes and prospects were dawning through what he did. He called this 'the kingdom of God'. The blessings Jesus offered were for people who would receive and respond, who brought nothing but their weakness and their hopes, people with whom he could share the love and renewing power of God. These people were indeed blessed. God would use them to spread his grace, and would show them his glory.

Poor, yet making many rich

So what do these blessings say about the Christian life? Who are the people for whom they speak? What is the profile sketched out by Jesus? We work through the beatitudes, verse by verse.

Blessing comes to the poor in spirit (v. 3). They have no inflated opinion of themselves, their achievements or their worth, but look to God as their strength and hope.

Blessed people are able to grieve (v. 4). They are hurt, not only by their own misfortune, but by others' wounds too. They will sorrow for God to be better known in their land.

Kingdom living is not pushy (v. 5). It doesn't rush to grasp and grab at every opening, but takes its turn in the confidence that – though sometimes slow – God is always sure.

Godly people care deeply about what is right, for others as well as for themselves (v. 6). They feel hollow and dry when people are wronged.

Compassion – to notice, help, and support a person in need – is a regular mark of the kingdom (v. 7).

God rejoices in a pure heart, whose motives are genuine, with no hidden deceit or dishonesty (v. 8).

It is blessed to spread peace, bring divided people together, defuse anger and help others to be calm (v. 9).

Finally, true Christian living can lead to persecution (vv. 10–12). Goodness of this kind is not normal; it comes from close association with Jesus. That sometimes bothers other people and makes them resentful. There may be little the Christian can do but to bear the burden and rejoice in the Lord.

Now and then

Life in ancient Galilee was very hard. Following the beatitudes was not easy then, any more than now. But people who take Christ's beatitudes seriously are still liable to find his blessing, in ways that may surprise them. We shall think more about how we follow this teaching as we read Matthew 7:13–29 (pp. 59–60).

For thought and prayer

Can you remember when you last heard or said, 'God bless you'? Those words really mean, 'May God make you a person whose life is ripe for blessing, the kind of person described in the beatitudes.'

11 Matthew 5:13–16

Taste and see

Blessed people make a difference. When lives are lived as Jesus teaches, the world is a better place. Other people notice, and feel the benefit. Jesus described this influence in two ways – salt and light.

Spread around

Salt helps food to taste good; it stops meat going rotten. So Christians bring out the best in other people; they help to keep the world wholesome. Yet if they lose the taste of Christ, they're completely useless (v. 13). Perhaps that's a sermon you've heard many times; it reflects common experience and it seems to fit the text. Jesus intended his followers to nourish the world, to sharpen the rich flavours of creation. They would not only be good people themselves; they would help to bring out the wholeness and vitality God had put in others.

Salt losing saltiness seems odd to us. Our table salt cannot lose its saltiness: it's pure, so it's salty all through. But in Jesus' time salt was dug from the ground around desert lakes, and the mixture contained various other crystals too. If the salt got washed out, the residue was indeed fit for nothing except to be used as gravel.

Good salt, however, makes food healthier and tastier. Of course, salt only works if it gets around. It has to circulate. So Christians work best as salt for the world if they are involved in it – if they look on daily work as part of their Christian service, if they spend time with neighbours and relatives as well as with church friends, if they have time to be normal as well as to be religious.

Christians should be 'salt, not honey' (Helmut Thielicke). There is an honest tang about wholesome Christian integrity: salt is clean rather than cosy, whereas honey coats everything, however sour and rough the flavour, with the same artificial film of sweetness, which can leave a sickly taste behind. Agreeing to everything, trying to be all things to all people, can strain us beyond credibility. Being ourselves, where we are and as we are, is what Jesus asks of us.

Light programme

Light is a common theme in the Bible. In the beginning God said, 'Let there be light' (Genesis 1:3). God himself is light (Psalm 27:1; 67:1). The Old Testament spoke of Jerusalem as a light for the whole world. Glory would shine out to beckon the nations, and they would come in peace to worship the God of Israel (Isaiah 2:1–4; Isaiah 60). Jesus echoed this hope when he spoke of 'a city built on a hill' (v. 14). Jerusalem stood on a ridge: the Jews 'went up' to it year by year on pilgrimage. The life of the Jewish people was meant to be a visual aid for the world, a lighthouse to gather many peoples to God.

Now Jesus puts this responsibility before his followers. He wants them to be radiant with God's goodness. He kindles afresh within Israel the hope of what Israel might be.

Borrowed light

So when Christians read the teaching of Jesus today, we enter into a world of hope that was first Jewish. Jesus invited his hearers to take up the role and heritage God had for Israel. He, above all people, made that heritage real: it focused on him in a unique way. Then, through him, it has spread wider, as millions of Gentiles (non-Jews, including me and possibly you) have come to faith in Jesus. We have joined – as adopted brothers and sisters, as light-bearers for God – the ancient family of faith that started with the Jews.

The situation is complex, of course. Many Jewish people have not joined the Jesus movement. That is one reason why Matthew wrote his gospel, to show how this movement, which started among the Jews, both spread beyond Judaism and missed a lot of people inside. That is still the situation today. What, then, becomes of the prophecy about light spreading out from Israel? Two answers:

- The prophecy is being fulfilled. The spread of faith in Jesus has drawn many from around the world to worship Israel's God. So we can call Jesus 'the light of the world' (John 8:12; 9:5).
- Yet the task is still going on. There is still plenty of darkness in God's world. Jesus still invites his followers to be luminous with the light we borrow from him. Our actions – our 'good works' (v. 16) – should help other people to see what God is like. Light (like salt) often works best when it works gently and gradually.

Prayer

May the light of Christ shine for us and through us, gently and clearly, even when we are not aware of it.

12 Matthew 5:17–20

Right now

Fuller meaning

These verses help us to understand the six paragraphs ahead, to the end of chapter 5. In all six of them Jesus mentions something that 'was said to the people of old' and then offers a fresh approach of his own. The key idea in all of this is the word 'fulfil' (v. 17).

Matthew has already written of Jesus 'fulfilling' Old Testament prophecies (1:23; 4:15 and so on). The life of Jesus brought a new perspective to some prophetic texts. He gave their original meaning a new lease of life; he acted them out in a new way. The old meaning of a prophecy – kingship, for example – was not rubbed out, but Jesus took the text beyond its old meaning to something greater and fuller.

In the sermon on the mount, the same thing happens to Israel's ancient law. 'I have come not to abolish, but to fulfil,' says Jesus (v. 17). He takes the commands of the Jewish law and uses them to point to something beyond. He is concerned for the deeper intentions of God that lie behind the law. His teaching does not ignore the old law, but gives it a new dignity and importance.

Still in place

So these verses help Matthew's readers to understand the link between their Christian faith and the Jewish way of life in which many of them had grown up. Christians have not discarded the Jewish law. It is powerful and permanent (v. 18). Christians should not speak as if the law can simply be ignored. It is important to follow the standards it teaches (v. 19). However, the way in which Jesus outlines those standards is fresh and controversial. That is the point of verse 20 – but first a word about the two Jewish groups mentioned there, the scribes and the Pharisees.

Legal eagles

The Pharisees were a strong, widespread and influential group of pious Jewish lay people. They placed great emphasis on observing the Jewish law, carefully and devotedly, and they tried to encourage others to do the same. They were known for their attention to detail. Scribes were scholars of the Jewish law who knew it well, who spent time and effort in understanding what it meant and explaining how it should be followed. Obviously scribes and Pharisees had important concerns in common, and there would surely be many who belonged to both groups.

These groups clashed with Jesus because he seemed careless about some issues that mattered to them. He claimed that God was working through him, yet he apparently ignored important legal concerns. He broke some of the rules. Scribes and Pharisees – some of them, at least – could not believe that God would honour such a maverick, and they complained about Jesus and to him. We shall read often, throughout the gospel, of arguments and angry words.

(The sections of the Introduction entitled 'Matthew and Judaism' and 'Matthew's church', pp. 13–14, explore this issue more fully.)

Righter than right

Jesus has told his followers to value the Jewish law and observe the standards it teaches (vv. 18–19). Now he says that to enter the kingdom, they must do better than the scribes and Pharisees (v. 20).

The scribes and Pharisees could not be beaten in matters of detail; they were the experts. However, the approach Jesus takes is not one of greater detail, but of greater depth. His teaching will be different in style to the finely tuned law codes of the Pharisees and scribes. He will go behind the law, to the intention of God. He will look inside the law, to the attitudes of the human heart. He will reach around the law, and gather it into a double love command, for God and neighbour.

Yet as Jesus does this, the people who follow a traditional approach – scribes and Pharisees – will feel that he speaks against the law. They will think that he scorns and devalues it because he does not handle it in their way. So, as we move to the paragraphs ahead, which outline the 'better righteousness' Jesus expects of his followers, the reader is forewarned: first, to realise that Jesus is not departing from the law, but deepening it; second, that there will be clashes between these two kinds of teaching, which take such different approaches to deciding what is right.

For thought and prayer

Is there any part of your life where you are committed to God in detail, but need to discover a greater depth in your service and love?

13

Matthew 5:21–26, 33–37

Fresh perspectives

The six paragraphs in 5:21–48 are known as the 'Six Antitheses'. In each of them Jesus takes an idea or command from the Old Testament and looks at the issue in a new way. 'You have heard that it was said... but I say to you...' is his typical introduction. This approach was not usual in Judaism of the day. Teachers of the law tended to approach the scriptures by using the teaching of their predecessors. The sense of fresh authority in Jesus' words is rather different.

The ingredients of murder

This first antithesis (vv. 21–26) begins with the command not to kill, the sixth of the ten commandments from Exodus 20.

Jesus does not look on murder as a rare and unique wrong, a sin like no other. It is the extreme case of a much more common failing. When we nurse and cherish resentment and anger, when we speak with scorn and contempt of a neighbour, when we think of another person as mere low-life, not deserving of common courtesy – this, says Jesus, is the stuff of which murder is made. This kind of attitude can occasionally, and sadly, lead to the taking of life. Whether in an individual heart or in the prejudice and collective memory of a community, this outlook lowers our boundaries of self-control. It blinds us to our proper responsibility for mutual concern and protection. If we live like this, we bring ourselves under the judgement of God.

So Jesus speaks about the importance of settling quarrels. When we worship – and especially when we take Communion – we should put our lives under audit. If we are nursing grudges or contributing to feuds and disputes, we may not be properly ready for meeting with God (vv. 23–24). If we learn to settle angry disagreements sooner rather than later, we limit the damage they cause, in time and in eternity (vv. 25–26).

Direct speech

The second and third antitheses belong together, so it is convenient to study the fourth antithesis here (vv. 33–37). This is about truth, the relationship between what we say and what we do. The introductory line (v. 33) summarises various texts in the Jewish law (Leviticus 19:12; Deuteronomy 23:21–23). Vows to God are important and should be kept.

Jesus extends that demand to every promise we make and every undertaking we give. Oaths may seem to make some of our truth-telling solemn and important, but the result is that other things we say get devalued. Never think, says Jesus, that God is not involved. Everything we see and touch involves God. It is simpler to tell the truth without needing the support of an oath – to mean what we say and to do what we say. It is wrong to complicate our speech more than this.

Courts of the Lord?

I once had to testify in court on behalf of the church. The clerk of court approached me hesitantly, Bible in hand: 'Will you take the oath?' Should a Christian do this?

Obviously a Christian should be committed to honest speech at all times. Some Christians think that this regular commitment is enough even in court, and they testify without taking an oath. Others reckon the oath a useful way of showing the court – and reminding themselves – that they intend to speak the truth, plainly and directly.

The point of Jesus' teaching is that we are 'on oath' all the time. So far as truthfulness and sincerity are concerned, all Christian speech is 'on the record'. If we learn that habit in regular daily life, it will be likely to sustain us in any crises and dilemmas we meet, where truthfulness seems an awkward and unattractive choice. People who are trustworthy make a difference: others start trusting and copying them.

Inside view

So Jesus is shifting the emphasis in the ancient law. When he speaks of murder, he goes inside the law to the motives and attitudes that shape the action. When he talks about truth, he uses the ancient command as a signpost that points beyond truthful oaths to a simple and total habit of truthful speech.

For thought and prayer

God of truth and love, give me a truthful tongue and a healing heart. Teach me the habit of honesty and the art of reconciliation. In the name of Jesus Christ. Amen

14 Matthew 5:27–32

An honourable estate

The second and third antitheses belong together. Both concern relations between men and women. Respect, protection, loyalty and self-discipline should shape the way we treat one another.

One thing leads to another

The command not to commit adultery is the seventh of the ten commandments (Exodus 20:14). The approach Jesus takes is similar to his teaching about the murder command. He goes behind the action itself to the attitude and motivation. Adultery comes, says Jesus, not as a bolt from the blue, but as one of a chain of events. One thing leads to another. For a man to look at a woman 'desiring or imagining a sexual relationship with her' (D. Hagner) is often the first link in the chain. Jesus calls that inner intention – selfish, demeaning and impatient as it is – 'adultery in the heart'.

Jesus speaks about strategies of avoidance. Temptations sometimes come without prior warning, but we do not have to make them welcome. The strong language of verses 29–30 means, 'Avoid situations that will lead you into serious sin.' It is better to make sacrifices in our routine or lifestyle than to shipwreck our character and faith – quite apart from the other people who might get hurt.

Responsible relationships

Women of Jesus' time were at a disadvantage, socially and legally, liable to be the weaker party in a situation of pressure, and suspect in a situation of scandal. Jesus tells men to respect women, to allow a woman the integrity of her own person and personality, and to take proper responsibility for their own conduct as men.

Of course society has changed since Jesus' time, and in many settings men and women mix easily and equally. Responsibility for right relationships must be taken on both sides. That is not to say that women must be more responsible and men may be less so; we all owe one another the security that comes from full and fair respect.

To have and to hold

Jesus begins in verse 31 with a command from Deuteronomy 24:1–4. In Old Testament society, where men had most of the power, this law offered some limited protection to a divorced woman. There had to be a reason for the divorce, she had to be given a legal document, and the husband could not reclaim her later. Jesus again goes inside the law, to its aim and purpose, which were to protect the marriage bond and particularly to protect the wife. He tells men to honour their marriage vows, to accept the responsibility and permanence of their commitment.

This approach offered better security to the woman than was sometimes the way in Judaism. As long as she remained faithful, she could not be thrown aside for a trivial reason, or for a younger or prettier candidate. This created more scope for marriage to be a partnership of dignity and trust.

(The phrase 'except… unchastity' is unique to Matthew's gospel. See comment on Matthew 19:9, p. 160.)

Hurts and dreams

Marriage has become a very fragile institution in our time. Plenty of people, including many Christians, have to pick up the pieces of their own (and their children's) self-confidence when a home divides. Perhaps our pastoral responsibility for one another includes the following issues.

- Taking our own vows seriously. Being patient when problem spells arise. Seeking help if (or better before) real damage occurs.
- Being gentle with friends who limp away from collapsed marriages. We cannot know how difficult it was, nor how hard they tried to hold it together. They need friends to listen rather than judge.
- Offering careful marriage preparation to young adults.
- Helping teenagers to realise that sex is meant to be respected as well as enjoyed. It was designed to happen within lifelong committed relationship.
- Learning to forgive one another (and ourselves) as deeply as God forgives us.

Prayer

May God, in whom are purity, pleasure and peace, help us to love and cherish the people he gives us.

15 Matthew 5:38–48

Coping with hostility

Striking out

The command about eyes and teeth, from Exodus 21:24, concerns compensation for personal injury. This apparently rough law aimed to limit the amount of revenge that was exacted, to prevent vengeance turning into vendetta. Apparently, by the time of Jesus people often paid compensation in cash.

The change Jesus makes is to move from measured and limited retaliation to non-retaliation. He tells his followers not to seek revenge for physical injury, for seizure of property or for loss of time and dignity. The Christian does not insist on personal rights or struggle to avenge every wound. We are prepared to be hurt and exploited, rather than to hurt and exploit others.

The illustrations – of a demeaning insult, a poor man being humiliated in court, a soldier's demand – give the impression of a society where might is right, where harsh men rule and good people get hurt. Jesus says, 'Don't join in. Show a different way.'

How literally should Christians take these commands today? Should a Christian contest an unjust redundancy or resist a mugging? Probably we should, if the struggle is going to do any good, and if we can see it through without behaving just like our opponents. The issue Jesus highlights is that when we think of our rights, our protection and our dues, we may become bitter, aggressive and vindictive, and repay aggression in its own coin – tit for tat, like for like, eye for eye, tooth for tooth. Sometimes there is no middle way: the only Christian way is the path of non-resistance.

Just like God

The Old Testament does not actually say 'and hate your enemy' (v. 43), although neighbour love always seems easier when we can limit its reach to include chiefly people of our own sort. This paragraph in Matthew stretches the command to include everybody – even, indeed especially, the people who make life hard for us. Pray for them, do them a good turn, treat them decently, surprise them with the love of Christ. There are two motives.

The first is to be like God (vv. 45, 48). God sends good weather to just and unjust people alike. The rain and the sunshine fall on every garden in town, not only on the land that belongs to righteous people. Followers of Jesus should be complete and open in their care, just as God is.

The second motive is to be different (vv. 46–47). There is nothing unusual about loving our friends and greeting those who are good to us. Everybody does that. Christians will be salt and light in the world only if they show a better way, if they extend their love and care to the people they do not like.

Loving enemies can be difficult; some enemies do not want our love. Then we have to be content with 'praying for our persecutors' (v. 44). But if we want genuine chances to meet old enemies with kindness and friendship, we shall probably be able to find them.

Peaceful protest?

A man I regarded highly was a conscientious objector during World War II. As one of a very large company of Christians, across the world, he applied this teaching of Jesus to public issues and believed that a Christian should decline to share in military action. Another Christian friend, of deep and generous faith, reckoned it his duty to serve in the forces during that same war, but quickly became involved in Christian efforts at reconciliation and friendship when the war ended.

There is no agreed solution of this issue. We live in a fallen world. Many people think that the best way to uphold justice and protect the weak is to resist aggression and to fight where necessary. Christians who think like this may still be gentle and calm in their personal relationships. They may also try to exert an influence for good, when decisions are taken about how and where to use force. Others feel that armed force always causes more trouble than it solves, and that Jesus' teaching should be received and obeyed, simply and directly, in every sphere of life.

The language of being 'perfect' (v. 48) sets a high, indeed an impossible, standard. Yet we need to aim high if we are to bear suffering with the grace of Christ, and to meet hate with love in his name.

For thought and prayer

Where could you start handling disagreements and disputes in a different, and more Christlike, way?

16 Matthew 6:1–6, 16–18

Cover your faith

This section has three short paragraphs. Each is arranged in a similar way, and each has a similar message: there should be modesty in the way we practise our faith.

Better righteousness

Verse 1 is a heading for the whole section: 'Beware of practising your piety before others.' Matthew's Greek word for 'piety' is 'righteousness', the same word used in 5:20. The antitheses of 5:21–48 were about right relationships; these verses are about right religious observance.

Religion that we make obvious to other people is liable to get overlooked by God. God prefers that there be privacy in our service. We should not use our piety to seek respect or honour from other people, but should be content to serve and honour God for his own sake – to give service simply because it is worth giving, rather than because anyone will notice.

This principle affects three areas of religious life: charitable and religious giving (vv. 2–4); prayer (vv. 5–6); and fasting (vv. 16–18).

Private account

'Do not let your left hand know what your right hand is doing' (v. 3). This is the knack of giving so that only the recipient finds out what has been given, and even the recipient may not know where it came from. There is privacy and secrecy in our giving, and contentment in knowing that the money is being well used. God shares the secret with us, and will surely honour the gift.

Prayer cell

Prayer should be private too (vv. 5–6). Jesus is not opposing the idea of meeting for prayer. This is about individual prayer. The point is that it should be truly individual, between the believer and God. Prayer is not a spectator sport. If we need to pray alone, we should find a place where we can be alone. God will be there, seeing clearly what we do, and will recognise and reward the faith and intentions we bring.

(The pattern of prayer Jesus gives, the words we call the Lord's Prayer, are in 6:7–15: see next reading.)

Fast track

Jews in the time of Jesus fasted at certain main festivals. Some Pharisees (see Luke 18:12) adopted a weekly pattern of fasts to express their devotion. Jesus does not condemn this. Indeed, he seems to assume that his followers will fast, but he urges them to fast inconspicuously. There should be nothing in their appearance or behaviour to advertise what they are doing (vv. 16–18).

Fasting is not (so far as I can see) much discussed in Christian circles these days. Perhaps we all fast on the quiet, in obedience to Matthew 6. Or has the church largely lost sight of this tradition, and forgotten that we might be able to deepen our love for God through voluntary self-discipline?

Faith in acting

All three paragraphs urge Christians not to be like 'hypocrites'. The word meant a stage actor, whose real self was concealed, who pretended to be someone different. To give, pray and fast chiefly in order to be noticed is a piece of hypocrisy. It looks as if it's being done for God, but the real target is human praise.

The best and truest reward of real piety is that it receives what it wants. People who give want the money to be well used for God; those who pray want their prayers to be part of God's good purpose; believers who fast want that sacrifice to bear fruit in godly living. These results often come about in ways that only God fully knows, which we shall not discover this side of eternity.

Shining lights

So how does secret religion square with lights that shine so that others may see (5:16)? The shining is righteous action, 'good works' (5:16), whereas 6:1–18 is about righteous observance. The seeds of prayer and faith that we sow, we should hide. The fruit that we bear, other people will notice anyway.

Prayer

Lord Jesus Christ, hallow our desires and shape our habits, so that we may serve chiefly out of love for you.

17 Matthew 6:7–15

When you pray…

The Lord and the prayer

This is the church's model prayer, pattern for all our Christian praying from the earliest times until now. This prayer comes from Jesus. The mix of ideas – the Fatherhood of God, the coming of the kingdom, the emphasis on forgiveness – matches the message of Jesus as we find it elsewhere in the gospels. Here, in the form of a prayer, are the issues and concerns that mattered most deeply to him.

Some prayers use grand and stirring language. This prayer has depth and glory through its brief and direct way of approaching God. There is nothing casual or irreverent here, but there is nothing elaborate either. This clear, compact yet profoundly worshipful style of prayer is typical of Jesus, who knew God deeply and intimately, and could speak of faith plainly and simply.

The disciples and the prayer

This is a prayer for disciples. Jesus has spoken to his friends as 'children of their Father in heaven' (5:9, 45, 48). This prayer begins from within that family circle, and says 'Our Father'. The prayer is plural – 'we, us, our'. This prayer represents a group – the church – that serves God together. There is a strong reminder that we, as disciples, should reflect God's forgiveness in our own forgiving (vv. 14–15). Only a community committed to good relationships can do that.

Heaven and earth

'Our Father in heaven' is the prayer's point of entry. It comes into God's presence in confidence, as one of the family, yet knowing that God sees and rules a larger family and a wider world than ours. To draw near to God is to enter a broad panorama of grace and love, and to see our own concerns against that greater background.

After meeting God as 'our Father in heaven', the prayer yearns for heaven to touch earth, and for earth to be like heaven. The Christian prays that God's name would be hallowed, God's kingdom come and God's will be done, on earth as truly as in heaven. May God's praise, power and purpose be known among us. Yet even while we pray, our own daily worship hallows God's name, our faith rejoices to serve God, and our obedience seeks to follow God's will. Today's service is part of the dawning of God's kingdom on earth.

Today and tomorrow

More than that, today's requests are part of the church's longing for that kingdom. The second half of the prayer concerns everyday struggles. Yet it sees the claims and pressures of every new day – our need for provision, pardon and power – against the grand horizon of the kingdom's coming.

- Bread is a regular physical need, but also a signpost and foretaste of the great family banquet in God's nearer presence, the kingdom company for which the church hopes and prays.
- Forgiveness concerns the current account of sins we accumulate daily, but also looks ahead to God's great and final judgement, when all the richness of God's forgiving love will be tasted, deep and full.
- Temptation is a daily reality, and the Christian prays not to succumb. (Realistically that should often be a prayer to be spared the battle.) Yet even everyday temptation is part of the great tussle between good and evil, whose final outcome is in the hands of God.

Hopeful and practical

So this is a hopeful prayer. It is also a practical prayer, seeing the daily horizon, the struggle to get to tomorrow. The two perspectives fuse – today and eternity, daily concerns and kingdom hopes. The prayer brings them together. We hope now, and we serve the world ahead; we live now, and we long for what we cannot yet see. Hope and practicality, confidence and obedience, faith and service, shape our praying and our being – until we see God face to face.

(You may have missed the 'kingdom, power and glory'. This line is not in the oldest manuscripts, and was not in Matthew's original wording. It got added later, as the prayer was used in the churches.)

For thought and prayer

Pray the Lord's Prayer, in the words you know best. Pause to reflect on each line. If you take a long time on any line, then stop. Let that be your prayer for today. Come back to the rest another time.

18 Matthew 6:19–34

Long-term investment

Matthew 6:1–18 was about piety; these verses are about property. One theme remains the same – an invitation to trust God. In 6:1–18, can we trust God enough to pray, give and fast secretly? Then, here, can we trust God enough to use our money in ways that serve the kingdom?

Making a pile

Instinctively we stack up resources against a rainy day. It is practical, and also biblical: be like an ant, work hard for winter (Proverbs 6:6–8). Jesus does not say, 'Do not work.' He does say, 'Do not accumulate for its own sake. Do not invest in the wrong place.' Anything stored on earth is fragile – liable to damp, decay and declining markets. Heaven is a better place to invest. Treasure there is secure, not subject to the ravages of bugs and burglars.

For we tend to invest our emotional energy in the place where our material resources are stored. We give ourselves to the causes to which we are already committed (v. 21). Only people who invest in God's kingdom are likely to get really involved in God's kingdom.

So how does one invest in heaven? The answer appears to be, 'Follow the teaching of the sermon on the mount – even if it costs us financially or materially.' What is given or lost for Jesus' sake, in situations where the path of Christian duty is plain but costly, is not really lost: it is securely invested.

What you see is what you give

People in Jesus' time did not think of the eye as a window, but as a lamp, radiating light from inside the body. If your lamp, says Jesus, is generous in outlook – if your eye lights cheerfully, sincerely and kindly on opportunities for giving and sharing – then there is bright and generous light within (v. 22). If, on the other hand, the eye is mean and tight in its outlook, that suggests a dull and narrow-sighted personality. So our vision, our ability to spot occasions for kindness and generosity, is a sign of our inner self.

Silver service

Obviously no servant can take orders from two bosses. Wires get hopelessly crossed. In the end, the servant has to choose which master should take priority (v. 24).

So there is no effective way to serve the constant call of mammon (the word means 'wealth') and the way of God. They regularly lead in different directions. Mammon is only concerned with the level of our bank account; God always has other things in mind. There is only one sensible way to handle the situation: decide which one to follow, and stick with that decision.

Worried, of Galilee

All these challenges would concern many who heard Jesus. 'What if I take him seriously?' they would say. 'How will I survive? How will my basic needs be met?' Jesus explains himself in three ways.

- First, he looks at nature (vv. 26, 28–30). Birds find food and the grass is clothed with colourful flowers. They do not worry, but God provides for them. So neither need you worry. God cares for you even more than for them.
- Second, Jesus reflects for a moment on worry (v. 27). Anxiety by itself never achieves anything. Experience can teach us that.
- Third, Jesus asks his friends to consider what is really important. Life is more than food and clothing (v. 25). To forget this is a faithless outlook. God, who controls the great issues of life, can surely provide for his children's everyday needs (v. 32).

The main thing

So the passage leaves the reader with one major concern (v. 33) – to seek God's kingdom, to come into its way of working, and to follow its pattern of right living. Jesus has not given an exact plan for the Christian use of money. He has encouraged his followers to use their money with heaven in mind, to put God first in material matters, confident that those who honour God need not fear. The last verse (v. 34) is more than homespun wisdom. The point is not just that tomorrow is another day. Tomorrow is God's day, a day to taste God's faithfulness, love and care. That is our reason not to worry.

Prayer

Lord, show us ways of investing in your kingdom that will help us to invest our hearts there too.

19 Matthew 7:1–12

Neighbours and God

The theme running through these verses is relationships with people around us and with God.

Clarity begins at home

We are often ready to form opinions on the people we deal with. 'Be careful' is the warning here. Of course, Jesus expected people to use their common sense: there is a place for discernment, for dealing wisely and appropriately with the different people we meet (7:6, 15–20). But we need to deal humbly and patiently too. Critical gossip, comment that demeans and destroys, interference without love, and opinion without knowledge – all of this is ruled out.

Jesus' story about specks and logs (vv. 3–5) sounds like a memory of the carpenter's shop: eyes sting and stream as the dust flies around. The story applies, of course, to judging: we have to deal with our own failings first. Clarity begins at home: the one person whose faults we can tackle is ourself. Maybe later, our experience will leave us in a position to offer help to others (v. 5). But the main point is to avoid judgements we are not in a position to make. In particular we should avoid trying to take over God's role. True assessment of a person's faith and worth is a judgement only God can make.

Pearls in the pigsty

Verse 6 probably concerns people who are hostile and antagonistic to us and our faith and simply want us to get out of their hair. In that sort of situation, we should go. We shall not convince them of the worth and wisdom of the gospel; they will just discredit and despise us. There is a time to break contact – and give God a chance to approach these people in a different way at another time.

Child benefit

Christians deal not only with neighbours and with our own failings. We have a bond with God and access to God in prayer. Ask, seek, knock. Keep in the habit; keep contact; for God answers when people call and gives good things when his children ask (vv. 7–11).

The line of argument in verses 9–11 is very similar to that in 6:26 and 6:28–30. The aim is to reassure followers of Jesus who are troubled or pressured. The atmosphere is pastoral, comforting, encouraging, showing how the disciple's relationship with God gives help and strength for earthly trials. Jesus appeals to ordinary experience (birds and flowers in 6:26–30, family relationships here), then raises his hearers' sights beyond the ordinary to God. 'How much more' will God answer and provide for trusting children (6:26, 30; 7:11).

The sermon on the mount put many strenuous demands before the followers of Jesus, both in Jesus' own time and among Matthew's first readers, and it continues to challenge everyone who reads the gospel today. Yet it is not simply a list of instructions, God's wish-list for human behaviour. It is much more intimate than that.

This is family talk, for people who are learning to trust God as Father with the same hope and confidence that Jesus himself had. This is for people who love and serve as sons and daughters, who are able to live in the assurance that they are guarded and supported by the love of God.

This is also kingdom teaching, about heaven's power touching earth. There is a new world dawning. Followers of Jesus are invited to look at the kingdom from the inside, to taste its joys even now, to live with faith and to trust without fear. They are indeed blessed (5:3–12).

Good as gold

The formula, 'Do to others as you would have them do to you' (v. 12) has been called the Golden Rule. Ideas like this are found in many religions and philosophies. It is basic to human understanding, that this is how life ought to be.

We hear that this sentence sums up the commands of the Old Testament: 'for this is the law and the prophets'. It also seems to summarise Jesus' sermon, so that the sermon is an outline of how to follow the Golden Rule. This simple rule – so short and so profound, so basic to how life ought to be – would be realised in full measure if only people would follow the sermon on the mount.

Prayer

Lord God, show us how to shift the barriers to our own vision, encourage us to knock confidently on your door, and so teach us to treat other people as we would like to be treated.

20 Matthew 7:13-29

Taking it seriously

This final half-chapter of the sermon is mostly emphasis, with four graphic reminders that the teaching of the sermon is vital. This is the stuff of life, the way to live life, the way to find life.

Routes and fruits

There are two routes through life (vv. 13–14). The route outlined in the sermon is tough, arduous and unpopular, but it leads to life. Jesus never pretended that his teaching was easy. Yet he often spoke about life: we become most truly and deeply human, we find the wholesome and enduring life that God gives, when we commit ourselves to the pattern of living that Jesus taught.

Verses 15–20 present the church with an acid test for any new movement or leader that emerges: what fruits are being produced? Is there anything solid, dependable and wholesome to show for this? That may not be immediately obvious: even good fruit takes time to ripen.

Fine words and foundations

Before we move on to miracles and healings in chapters 8 and 9, verses 21–23 remind the church that mighty works cannot be the core of our Christian living. Without the bread and butter of daily righteousness, even our best achievements for Christ count for little.

There is one major difference between the two builders in verses 24–27: both hear Christ's words, but only one acts upon them. To hear and not to do is to build an insecure life: eventually the storms of misfortune or persecution or final judgement will leave us empty and ruined. However, a life built on habitual obedience is built solidly, with good hopes of withstanding the pressures ahead.

Strange authority

So these four paragraphs are like nails, fixing the teaching of Jesus' sermon firmly to our minds, giving us reasons for returning again and again to this material, to measure our lives against its wisdom.

Yet the sermon can stick in the memory by itself. Many of its phrases have come into our regular speech: salt of the earth (5:13); light under a bushel (5:15); blow your own trumpet (6:2); turn the other cheek (5:39); wolf in sheep's clothing (7:15). No wonder that Jesus' hearers found him a teacher of unusual power and authority.

Here and now

There are still questions about interpretation for today. 'Did Jesus mean all this literally?' people ask. Or is there an element of graphic exaggeration in some of his teaching? Is he provoking people to think, by overstating his case? Perhaps Jesus was deliberately teaching a high ideal, so that people would realise how much they needed God's mercy.

Another view is that Jesus meant this only for unusually devoted individuals; you could not expect most people to live like this. So while many Christians may observe some of the sermon in private life, you could not extend these principles to the conduct of public affairs.

How do we respond ourselves? We need to keep several things in mind:

- This is teaching for disciples of Jesus. We read it as his followers. What we do with Jesus' teaching is not a matter of theory alone, but should be worked out in our relationship with Jesus himself.
- This is teaching for the whole church. We are all involved in working out how to follow. I long to see Christians take time to help each other discover how to obey Christ in a changing world. Some of this we shall only do well if we do it together.
- This is teaching for Christian contribution in society. It is good news for the world, a sign of God's love and of hope, when people seek to live in this way. That is what it means to be salt. For the salt to do its job, we must be in touch with the life our neighbours lead, but prepared to be different if necessary.
- This teaching is part of the gospel. Only the good news of Christ crucified and risen will make it at all possible for us to obey from the heart. Often his teaching will seem out of our reach, but it should not be out of our mind. When we turn to the cross for forgiveness, that forgiveness should send us back to the sermon on the mount. The world is still meant to see Christ's pattern of life in us.

Prayer

Christ be our light, that we may shine for you.

21 Matthew 8:1–4

For a whole people

Mercy moving through

We have read in 4:23–25 of Jesus going around Galilee, telling the kingdom and showing its power. Chapters 5—7 have given detail of that kingdom teaching. Now, through chapters 8 and 9, come a series of miracles, showing in different ways how Jesus expressed the power and mercy of God. Jesus was applauded for the authority of his teaching (7:29). Now we shall see that same authority in his deeds.

These two chapters have nine miracle stories altogether. To run the whole sequence without a break would be splendid in its effect, but almost overpowering, like a fast-moving firework show that leaves you exhilarated but breathless. So it is helpful that Matthew presents the nine incidents in three separate groups, with three stories in each. The groups are 8:1–15; 8:23—9:8; and 9:18–33. In the gap after each of the groups there are short sections that help the reader to digest the material. These include summaries of what has happened and scripture quotations to show the meaning of the events.

Following and fuming

Each of these intervals also has a short episode involving Jesus and his disciples. Jesus has already called disciples (4:18–22), and the sermon on the mount was intended for them. But we have more to learn about them. Who will be called next? What sort of person might be suitable? What else will Jesus teach them? Is there a special task he has in mind for them? These two chapters develop the theme of discipleship.

They also warn us of coming conflict. The incidents in chapters 8 and 9 spread mercy far and wide. Jesus meets many sorts of misfortune, many desperate and disappointed people, with the hope and wholeness of God. Yet the reactions of those who watch are sometimes quite unpleasant. By the end of the series (9:33–34), people have become very polarised: the crowds are excited and enthusiastic while the Pharisees are sour and sceptical. So these chapters give the impression of clouds gathering on the horizon. The sun may be shining now, but there is a storm brewing in the distance.

Restoring touch

The condition called 'leprosy' in the Bible probably included a number of different skin diseases. These may have varied quite a lot in their physical severity. But the physical symptoms were not the only problem. For leprosy led to social isolation, exclusion from a lot of normal community life, for fear the disease would be passed on. A leper was treated as an unclean outsider.

Jesus touches the man (v. 3). His hand reaches across the gulf between clean and unclean, not with the risk that he will contract uncleanness himself, but to pass on his own cleanness, the wholeness and purity of the kingdom of God. This is a physical healing, but also a social healing. Jesus refuses to treat the man as an outsider. He treats him as an insider and he brings him inside.

Jesus wants to heal the man (v. 3). There is nothing accidental about what he is doing. God's creation is bruised and broken, and Jesus acts to restore it. Jesus sends the man to the local priest (v. 4). Priests acted as public health officers in Israel. They had to inspect and certify suspected cases of leprosy, and when a sufferer recovered it was the priest's duty to check and confirm the recovery (Leviticus 14). Certain animal sacrifices would then be offered, to mark the person's return to normal society. So Jesus tells the man not to broadcast his news himself, but to have his cure checked in the proper manner. He should offer the due sacrifice to let his neighbours know what has happened. So Jesus is working within the requirements of the law. He respects the leaders of Judaism. Will they respect him?

All-round wholeness

This first miracle shows what a complex and diverse thing healing is. Body, mind, emotions, faith, relationships – all are bound up together, and when any one is damaged the others are liable to suffer too. That means that healing of any sort always has a knock-on effect. It produces a fuller wholeness than it seemed to be aiming for. So the church's pastoral care has a greater potential for healing and wholeness than we often realise.

Prayer

May we love God, and receive God's love, with our heart, soul, mind and strength.

22 Matthew 8:5–13

Faith from afar

Hope of healing

Capernaum had been Jesus' base for his travels around Galilee (4:13), so he was well known there. The centurion was probably not a Roman legionary; he belonged to the security force kept by Herod Antipas, the ruler of Galilee. He was a Gentile. The sick person was either his son or his servant (v. 6) – the word Matthew uses can mean either. The parallel story in Luke (7:1–10) suggests it was a servant, while a similar story in John (4:46–54) features a son. Whatever the relationship, this tough and travelled soldier is disturbed by the boy's illness and comes to seek help.

Not in the race

Jesus seems willing to come (v. 7). It is difficult to know whether this was a direct offer, or a question: 'Shall I come and heal him, then?' At any rate, the remark touched a tender spot. It was not regular practice for Jews and Gentiles to mix socially, and the centurion knows that it would be odd to have a Jewish preacher in his home. But he does not think it necessary for Jesus to come. Jesus can heal with a word, from a distance: 'Only say the word, and he will be healed' (v. 8).

Holy orders

The centurion explains why he is so confident (v. 9). He can recognise authority in Jesus. He himself has the authority to instruct his soldiers and his servants, and they do what he tells them. But he realises that he is a man *under* authority. His authority comes from higher up in the army. He is who he is because of the power that operates through him. Now he sees the same sort of authority in Jesus, authority that comes from higher up and gives real power to command. If only Jesus would say the word, distance would not be a problem: the healing would surely take place.

Beyond expectation

Jesus is amazed (v. 10). This is not the sort of faith he is used to. Not even Jews have worked him out as plainly as this. No one, but no one, has seen as clearly as this centurion has that God's power is working in Jesus and that mighty works are flowing because God is in charge.

So this Gentile, this man of faith from outside the people of faith, becomes a sign of the breadth of God's grace. This is just the first instalment of a great movement of God. The promise to Abraham, that all the families on earth would be blessed through him (Genesis 12:3), seems suddenly alive. When the kingdom comes in all its fullness, it will be a grand international banquet with guests from all round the world (v. 11).

Then, sadly, the darker side of that future comes into view (v. 12). As Gentiles flock into the kingdom, as the world gathers to the gospel of Jesus, many Jews will turn away and never come back. For them the rise of the Christian church will be an offence; its attraction to Gentiles will compound that offence. By Matthew's time the trend will be obvious, that a gulf is forming between Gentiles who are drawn to the gospel from afar and the many Jews who are missing out.

Faith that works

Finally this is a story of faith. This man from outside Israel, who preferred that Jesus stay outside his house, saw the inside of God's purpose with astonishing clarity. He saw the authority in Jesus and he trusted that authority to work for him. That is faith: seeing that God is at work in Jesus, and asking Jesus to touch our lives with his love. That is enough. 'According to your faith be it done for you' (v. 13).

Outside chance

Both miracles so far have been about outsiders: the leper was outside normal society, and the soldier was outside Israel. Jesus finds people, and finds faith in people, who are not at the centre of things. So when we get pushed to the edge, excluded or caused to feel unworthy by what is happening around us, we are not out of range of Jesus' love. We may still pray and we may expect answers.

Prayer

Lord, I am not worthy to receive you. But only say the word and I shall be whole.

23 Matthew 8:14–17

Lifting the burden

Mother's day

The first snippet of this passage (vv. 14–15) has just enough detail to make it a story. It has characters, a sequence of actions and a plot. The healing is simply told, in six movements. Three are actions of Jesus: he came, he saw, he touched. Then three things happen in response: the fever left, she got up, she served. Yet we can read between the lines of this report and sense the anxiety caused by the fever. There is a buzz as Jesus arrives, and the hope that he can do something to help; then relief spreads as the life of the home returns calmly and gradually to normal.

If the previous two healings were of outsiders, this is very much an inside job. Jesus is among the people who know him best. Simon Peter's house at Capernaum seems to have been Jesus' retreat now that he had moved away from his own home town. Though unmarried himself, Jesus understood family life and shared in it. Yet he had also placed heavy demands on this family: calling Peter away to discipleship would have strained relationships and possibly caused some financial difficulty.

Jesus was not easy company; you never knew what he would plan next. But this is a moment when the healing love of Jesus touches a home that has given him much. Surely in church families, when the demands of Christian service ask much of us, we may also ask Jesus to be present at times of crisis and fear, helping us to handle the burden, carrying it with us and lifting its weight.

Servant signs

Matthew has completed the first group of three miracle stories, and there is an interval before the next group begins in 8:23. The evening encounter (v. 16) was probably at Capernaum (compare Mark 1:21–34), and the scene contributes to Matthew's story in two ways. First, it stresses that the healings Matthew reports are only a sample from a much wider range of activity. Second, it leads into a scripture quotation from Isaiah 53:4, which Matthew introduces with another fulfilment formula (as at 2:15).

Isaiah 53 is a famous Old Testament chapter. It describes a figure it calls the 'servant', who will suffer for others, who will be hurt and broken to make other people whole. So – as Jesus takes away the burdens of others – Matthew's quotation links his healing ministry to the servant passage in Isaiah. This connection hints that the work of Jesus will be costly. His love for Israel will not be cheaply delivered. The opposition that will emerge in these chapters will eventually exact a heavy price from Jesus himself.

Pictures of wholeness

This use of Isaiah 53 also helps to show the purpose of the miracles themselves, for the servant passage is at the heart of a journey to freedom. Throughout chapters 40 to 66 of Isaiah, the story is of Israel coming out of exile, back home to God. Her release comes through suffering, through the pain and humiliation of the strange figure called the servant. He seems to represent Israel's own struggles, and also to represent God's love to her.

So as Jesus wears the mantle of the servant, that is a sign of freedom coming, of a people brought back to themselves and to God. His healings are important for their own sake, as deeds of love and care for people of faith and need. Yet as part of Jesus' servant ministry, the healings point to something greater and fuller still. They are visual aids, signs of a nation made whole.

Blind people in Israel will see, and Israel herself will see God more clearly. Lame people will walk, and Israel will walk more confidently and surely with God. Lepers will be drawn back into society, and Israel – who has lived long with the bitter memory of exile, who has felt discarded by her neighbours and even by God – will be gathered again into the joy of the kingdom.

In the home where Jesus lodged, a woman has been healed. Surely the nation where he belongs is also offered his hand, full with the healing and wholeness of the love of God.

For thought and prayer

The church continues the servant work of Jesus, helping people to find their way home to God. That is sometimes costly work. Pray for patience, courage and love, as you serve in the footsteps of Jesus.

24 Matthew 8:18–22

Open agenda

To boldly go

We are still in the interval before the second group of miracle stories. The scene is beside the Sea of Galilee. This freshwater lake, about twelve miles by eight, marked the border of the land of Galilee. Around the western edge, both on the lakeside and in the hills and valleys that led back from the shore, was the land where Jesus belonged, where most of the gospel is set. On the eastern bank was the territory of the Decapolis, more Greek than Jewish. So when Jesus takes a boat to cross the lake (v. 18), he is not only avoiding the crowds, but is also heading into strange country (8:28). For some Galileans, whose lives had been sheltered and local, the far shore would be a world away. Following Jesus suddenly feels challenging and uncertain. Discipleship will not be a comfortable cruise but a voyage into the unknown.

Ready, steady… maybe

These two short encounters with potential disciples contrast with the earlier calling of Peter and his friends (4:18–22). On that earlier occasion Jesus had taken the initiative, and the response was swift and sure. They left their nets and followed. Even if the new disciples had private fears, they were willing to go.

Here the pattern is reversed. When Jesus speaks he seems to warn rather than invite, to push the enquirers back rather than beckon them forward. He probes their inhibitions and reservations, testing whether they are really ready to follow.

To the scribe (v. 19), whose religious commitment has revolved around books, a man who has laboured to learn the Hebrew scriptures and has loved that work, Jesus sets the demands of the open road. Can he cope with sleeping rough, not knowing quite what each day will bring? Or would he prefer a regular seat in the library? We do not know what his answer was.

Throwing a lifeline

On the face of it, verse 22 is an outrageous saying. Was Jesus really telling the man to miss his father's funeral? Burial of parents was a sacred duty, part of honouring one's father and mother. What possible reason could there be for not taking part? On the other hand, if the father had just died – and in such a hot climate the funeral would be the same day – it is odd that the young man had time to seek Jesus out. So both sides of this brief encounter are difficult to understand.

Obviously Jesus wanted to stress the urgency of his own mission, and the young man was inclined to hesitate. Beyond that we do not know quite what was going on. It is just possible that the father was not dead, so that the young man is saying, 'I'll come later, when I'm my own master.'

Whatever the precise circumstances, Jesus realises that a person who is held too tightly by family ties will never get away. There will always be some excuse. Jesus himself has had to make the break out of Nazareth. So Jesus' word, 'Leave the dead to bury the dead', is a challenge. If the family have shown no interest in Jesus, it is time for the young man to face that fact. He is discovering God's kingdom, he is coming alive in a new way, and they are not. Hanging around for one more family event will not solve anything. He must either stay or go. If he is serious about discipleship, he must follow Jesus when the chance presents itself.

In the looking-glass

Jesus' call to commitment can be a mirror in which we see ourselves. Jesus confronts the bookish scribe with the uncertainties of an outdoor life. He presses a conscientious son to face the question of whether he could ever bear to leave home.

If you or I consider some new kind of Christian service, Jesus' question might be, 'Which aspect of this are you going to find hardest to handle?' The answer to that question might show whether or not we are cut out for the task. Along the way it could show us our own commitment: what we can handle is not just what we can do, but what we are willing to put up with.

Prayer

Teach me, O Lord, to serve thee as thou deservest: to give and not to count the cost, to fight and not to heed the wounds, to toil and not to seek for rest, to labour and not to ask for any reward, save that of knowing that I do thy will.

Ignatius Loyola (1491–1556)

25 Matthew 8:23–34

Tossed by storms

Here are two storms: one on open water, the other – equally wild – in the recesses of human personality. Jesus has healed physical diseases (8:1–15). Now he brings peace to a rough sea and to troubled minds.

Raging sea

Jesus, who has nowhere settled to lay his head (8:20), has the inner peace to sleep anywhere (v. 24). Meanwhile the disciples are alarmed and afraid. Some of them fish this water: they know its moods; their fear is informed by experience. This boat is on the point of capsizing with the loss of all on board. Then Jesus rises. He asks about their faith, and he calms the sea.

This story is about faith. 'Little faith' (v. 26) is faith that has embarked on the voyage of discipleship but is not properly aware of Jesus' power. It is fearful faith (as in 6:30). Matthew's readers would have pictured themselves in the disciples' situation. The tossing of the boat would remind them of the church's trials, its doubts, struggles and persecutions. But even in trials, Jesus is 'with you always' (28:20). The church is often a people of 'little faith', but never a people alone.

'What sort of person is this?' (v. 27). This is someone who can cross stormy waters and bring order and peace, who can quell raging seas, who can bring his community through danger to the further shore. In Jesus, the God of creation (Genesis 1:2), of Exodus (Exodus 14) and of Israel's praise (Psalm 107:29) is at work.

Storms within

The two sad people in verse 28 live on the burial ground. Death is around them, and something has died inside them – the peace and balance to live a happy human life. They challenge Jesus, calling him God's Son (v. 29) – as if their troubled minds can recognise the approach of God's goodness, and fear to tangle with him. For his work is premature: he brings God's healing love to a troubled world as an advance instalment of the wholeness of the kingdom. He brings the power of Israel's God to this Gentile land, before the church's Gentile mission is properly begun. In every sense he is ahead of time (v. 29).

The pigs seem odd (vv. 30–32). No other gospel incident has anything like this. For a Jew, pigs expressed the impurity of the Gentile world; these were unclean animals, forbidden for Jews to keep or eat. Yet even they cannot contain the disturbing forces released from the two people. The flight of the pigs suggests that Jesus is fighting a greater evil than anything regulated by the Jewish purity system. He has larger concerns than laws can measure.

Finally Jesus is asked to leave (vv. 33–34). He is viewed as a strange and dangerous magician. Goodness can be uncomfortable if it brings hope and joy to people we prefer to avoid.

For clear minds

A lot of human disorders in scripture are described as caused by demons (for example, 8:16, 28, 31, 33). Two responses to this are common among church people. Some feel very aware of a world of evil forces around them, and identify very easily with these biblical stories. Other folk are sceptical, and dislike reading of 'demon possession'; they feel that such ailments would be diagnosed by clinical psychiatry nowadays. I come somewhere between these two viewpoints.

To the first group mentioned, I make several brief points. Good and evil were polarised around the ministry of Jesus. His own spiritual power enabled him to discern and address human disorder very acutely and effectively. None of us is as sharply aware of spiritual forces as he was. Only Christians with considerable pastoral experience, well informed by responsible psychology, should claim discernment in such matters. Discretion, training and accountability are vital; most of us will not seek deep involvement.

None the less, whatever language we use to describe them, 'the mystery of evil and the web of malevolent causation behind it remain' (D. Hagner). We may surely pray for the power and love of Jesus to penetrate the mystery of psychological disorder, as readily as we pray for friends with physical illness. Mental health, like physical health, is a spiritual issue – by which I mean that it matters to God.

For thought and prayer

Pray for anyone you know who lives with storms, for whom distress is a bleak horizon, for whom peace of mind would be another world.

26 Matthew 9:1–8

Walking free

Four themes are woven together in this story: physical healing, forgiveness, opposition and authority.

First movement

This is first of all a healing story about a man who could not walk, about faith (of the friends who brought him and perhaps of the sick man too), and about the thrill of heading for home – on his feet! 'Stand up, take up your bed and go,' says Jesus, and the invalid actually walks away. It seems straightforward, direct and powerful. Yet this impressive storyline is almost totally overshadowed by other concerns.

Which is easier?

Sin is the root problem in human living; there will be no final wholeness, no full view of God's kingdom, unless sin's work is undone. But there is no simple link between a person's sin and any illness or misfortune that person might suffer. It is not that straightforward. Some people around Jesus spoke as if the link were obvious (John 9:2–3), but Jesus never supported that idea.

So why does Jesus talk about forgiveness, when people expect him to heal (v. 2)? We do not know. There may have been some personal reason why this man needed to hear those words: this is a town Jesus knows (v. 1), and he may know these people. But no such reason is mentioned. We have to connect to Matthew's message in other ways.

Forgiveness was always going to be important in Matthew's gospel. Jesus came to save his people from their sins (1:21). Forgiveness is a sign of the kingdom (6:10, 12). So as Jesus travels through Galilee showing the kingdom by mighty deeds, we expect him to bring forgiveness.

'Is it easier,' Jesus asks, 'to speak a word of forgiveness or a word of healing?' (v. 5). Obviously forgiveness is easily spoken, whereas healing requires action. So Jesus heals the man – the more difficult task – to prove that he is entitled to offer forgiveness. He shows he can forgive, by showing that he can heal. But which is really easier – to heal a limb, or to draw the poison of the world's sin on the cross? Which was the more difficult for Jesus in Galilee? Healing had made him many friends.

Forgiveness started to make him enemies. In the long run, forgiveness will become the bigger issue.

Heart dis-ease

For the first time Jesus has to confront some of Israel's religious teachers. These scribes seem to have had their opinions written on their faces. Their hearts were uneasy. Blasphemy (v. 3) means insulting God. It was an insult to God, they thought, for Jesus to forgive sins. That was God's job, and no one else should try to claim it.

On this occasion the opposition peters out, and the encounter finishes without serious trouble. Once the lame man walks, Jesus has shown his credibility. The sceptics will be back before long, but for the moment they are silent. The story ends with loud praise to God for the authority that is in Jesus.

Authority from God

We have seen Jesus' authority already – in teaching (7:29), in healing (8:9), and now in forgiveness (9:6, 8). Jesus offers on earth the pardon that only God can truly give. He forgives as 'Son of Man' (v. 6).

'Son of Man' is a riddle. Perhaps Jesus meant it to be. It could be a roundabout way of saying 'I'. That fits Matthew 8:20, for example. However, there is a figure in Daniel 7:13–14 called the Son of Man, a human figure who rises to receive great authority from God. He rules with God and for God. Some Jews in the time of Jesus were starting to connect this figure in Daniel with their hopes for a Messiah.

When Jesus said 'Son of Man' in Matthew 9:6, some people might have heard only 'I'. But since he is talking about authority, I reckon that Jesus had Daniel at the back of his mind. He was hinting, for those with ears to hear, that Daniel 7 helped him to see his own mission: he shared, in a unique way, the authority and kingly rule of God.

Fullness and freedom

The theme of authority is important throughout Matthew. So is forgiveness: Christians need to receive and share it. We often learn most about Jesus' authority through forgiving and being forgiven.

Prayer

Lord, release me, where I need it, to enjoy being forgiven, and to forgive truly and finally.

27 Matthew 9:9–17
Party spirit

This is the second interval in Matthew 8 and 9, the buffer zone before the next group of miracle stories begins in 9:18. The material here is mainly about the purpose of Jesus' activity.

Duty free

The call of Matthew the tax collector is very similar to the earlier call of the fishermen (4:18–22), and a contrast to the last two encounters with hopeful disciples (8:19–22). There was a frontier near Capernaum, dividing the Galilee of Herod Antipas from his brother Philip's territory to the north-east. A tax office there could levy dues on goods that were moving through. But Matthew himself moves out. He just leaves, simply, decisively and instantly, and follows Jesus.

Many people have asked if Matthew the tax collector is the Matthew behind the gospel. That is certainly possible. It could have been the tax collector's civil service mind that produced the orderly, arranged feel of Matthew's gospel. Another possibility is that this Matthew was the source of much material for the gospel. He remembered Jesus' words and deeds and handed his memories on. But he may not have compiled and written the gospel in the form we now have. For more detail, see the section 'Who was Matthew?' in the Introduction (p. 13).

Responding to an invitation

Shared meals were important occasions in the time of Jesus. People who ate together felt they belonged together. Pharisees used meals to meet with like-minded friends, to express their devotion to God through the careful observance of food and purity laws. It seemed odd to them that Jesus ate with 'tax collectors and sinners' (v. 11).

Taxation is never popular, especially when the system allows the collector to keep a slice of the takings. Taxation in the Holy Land was doubly suspect because it involved dealing with Gentiles and Gentile money, and it supported a system which was ultimately under Gentile control. Tax collectors were despised. So it seemed odd when Jesus, a religious man, visited Matthew's house for dinner. This was a company of rather irreligious Jews, different in their outlook from the zeal and care of Pharisaic faith. What business has Jesus got, eating with them? What could they have in common?

Jesus' answer has three punchlines. 'These people need me,' he says. 'Sick people need a doctor; others don't.' Second, he quotes scripture, from Hosea 6:6. There are times for showing the favour and mercy of God in ways that do not follow strict legal expectations. You can keep the rules and miss the point, if you're not careful. Finally Jesus talks about his own target audience. He comes to people who need the forgiveness of God and know it – not to those who think they don't.

Feasting and fasting

John the Baptist is in prison (4:12), and his followers are concerned that Jesus' friends have not copied John's earnest discipline (v. 14). They seem more at home in the dining-room than the desert, and ignore the regular fasts that mean so much to some Jews (see comment on 6:16–18, p. 51).

Jesus uses the Old Testament idea that God's love for Israel is like a bridegroom's for his bride. The kingdom ministry of Jesus is like a wedding feast. It marks the arrival of God's love in a new and intimate way. Fasting would be out of place: you should feast when you celebrate. But the sunlight also casts a shadow: the bridegroom will be taken away, and that will be a time for gloom and grief. The gospel is beginning to show us the suffering ahead.

The two sayings in verses 16 and 17 shed light on the incident in 9:1–8, as well as on today's portion. Jesus brings something genuinely new to Israel, and must not be pushed into old ways. The kingdom requires patterns of conduct and friendship that are flexible enough to contain its potent new wine. The righteousness of the scribes and the Pharisees cannot hold it.

In our church life today, we still need ways of meeting which celebrate the generosity and promise of the gospel, events that bring people of different backgrounds cheerfully together, occasions to remind us all that we are welcomed and loved – even though we don't deserve it.

Prayer

Lord Jesus Christ, you are the unseen guest at every meal we take. May we eat and meet in the gladness of your love.

28 Matthew 9:18–26

Daughters of faith

Here is one miracle story nested within another, like layers of a Russian doll. We are only able to see the whole of the outer layer when we have read through the inner layer and picked up the outer story again. This sandwich pattern is found a number of times in Mark's gospel, with these two incidents (Mark 5:21–43) and in several other places. If Matthew is using Mark, then he has shortened this passage from 23 verses to nine. That is typical of much of Matthew's work. The stories are told briefly and crisply, the essential points are well made, but much of Mark's graphic detail is missing.

Urgent summons

After the challenges from scribes and Pharisees (9:3, 11), it is remarkable that a leader of the local synagogue (for that is what 'ruler' will mean here) should come to Jesus so freely and humbly. His daughter has just died, but surely – he believes – something can still be done for her (v. 18). So the story moves quickly from introduction through request to response. There is a sense of urgency. As Jesus and his friends follow the man home, the reader's mind runs ahead of them: what will happen when they get there?

Healing touch

Suddenly and abruptly the story breaks. There is another encounter, and Jesus pauses (v. 22). The woman's ailment would have made her ritually unclean, and that surely explains some of the fear and apprehension that led her to touch Jesus from the back. She may have often been treated as a marginal and dirty figure in society, and learned not to risk another insult or rebuff. Yet there is an urgent confidence that drives her to seek Jesus' help. She touches the corner of his garment from the back: that will be enough. And it was.

In the house

Funerals happened quickly in the Holy Land (they still do). Music was playing and a weeping crowd had gathered by the time Jesus got there (v. 23). When he said that the child was only asleep, they could not take him seriously. However, he was not denying the reality of the situation but looking beyond it. God could do more than they could see. Privately, calmly, he raised the girl to life.

Words of hope

These two stories are filled with faith. The ruler's enquiry at the beginning, 'But come… and she will live' (v. 18), sets the tone, and Jesus' word to the woman as he leaves her and moves on, 'Your faith has made you well' (v. 22), confirms the mood. These two people recognise that God is powerfully at work through Jesus, and have the confidence to act on that belief. This is the faith the centurion expressed (8:8–13). It is the faith the disciples found hard to grasp – they had 'little faith' (8:26). The same faith is here, not 'little', but big enough to reach out confidently towards Jesus.

The woman was healed. But the word also means 'save'. '"If I touch his cloak I shall be saved"… "Your faith has saved you." And from that moment she was saved' (vv. 21–22). Matthew's readers would have heard the double meaning. There was certainly physical healing, but the words resonated with the promise of a greater and more permanent salvation. 'Believe and be saved' – this they understood for themselves. Years after the earthly life of Jesus, they could still experience his salvation. They could have faith, by trusting in the gospel of Jesus. They could enjoy the sure love of God that lasts forever, to death and beyond.

Life out of death

There are only a few accounts in the gospels of people being brought back from death to life. Apart from this incident, there are two (Luke 7:11–16; John 11:1–44). These three people would all die again. Yet their resurrections give advance notice of the great resurrection, the decisive breach that Jesus would himself make in the boundary wall of life. When we read that Jairus' daughter 'rose' (v. 25), we start to glimpse that hope. Jesus will rise, and in him the faithful dead will find their eternal life. They will be saved through their faith in him. Death will truly be 'sleep' and there will be glad waking beyond.

Prayer

Lord Jesus Christ, give us faith in the power of your love and hope in the victory of your resurrection, that we may live in trust and die in peace.

29 Matthew 9:27–35

Completing the circle

Seeing the king

The blind men shout from a distance, calling Jesus 'Son of David'. This is new. Matthew connects Jesus and David at the very beginning (1:1), but no one in the story has called Jesus by this title until now. The title hails Jesus as Israel's Messiah. He is their promised anointed leader, who will usher in an age of hope, and his healings are signs of that hope appearing. Strangely, Jesus does nothing until he is in the house. There the blind men approach him again, and he heals them. As we saw before, faith is a vital factor (v. 29). The privacy of the house provides opportunity for Jesus to speak with the men, to probe the faith behind their excited shouting. But there may be another reason for his seeking privacy.

'Son of David' was a dangerous slogan. The Jewish people had rulers already, who would scarcely welcome a rival king. Jesus was not a violent revolutionary, and did not wish to be seen as one, either by eager nationalists or by the current political powers. So he speaks with the two men out of public view, and urges them to keep quiet (v. 30). If they want to call him David's son, they should not shout about it. In the end they were too exuberant to be silent – but their enthusiasm may have created some danger for Jesus.

Fresh sounds

A mute man receives the gift of speech (vv. 32–33). The incident is described briefly. The sounds and voices that rise from the encounter are reactions, the opinions that Jesus has provoked among bystanders. In this last of the miracle stories, the contrast is very marked indeed.

Some rejoice in the freshness and promise of what Jesus does, in the hope and new dawn they find in his coming. Others, who cannot connect him with their own religious patterns and practice, react very differently: 'He must be in league with evil, fighting the devil with his own weapons.' Jesus will counter this accusation later (12:22–30). For the moment the gospel moves on, leaving the reader aware of a widening and potentially damaging gulf.

Rounding off

Finally the circle closes. Verse 35 echoes 4:23, and brings this circuit of Galilee, these chapters of teaching and healing, to a close. Several themes have come into view.

- The number and variety of the miracles show God's mercy and power at work in Jesus. Often it is weak, helpless or marginalised people who find help. God is not limited by human status.
- The various sorts of healing fit Old Testament expectations and hopes, as Matthew's story will indicate before long (11:2–6). The work Jesus does shows that he is God's true Messiah.
- Many of the individual stories have a message for the church that reads them, in Matthew's day and in ours – about faith, salvation, resurrection, peace, and so on. They are 'transparent', as one writer puts it: you start seeing your own experience through them.
- There has been sharpening controversy in these chapters. Jesus is not an easy figure to grasp or control. His mercy does not fit traditional patterns, and some people cannot understand that.
- Discipleship has been a recurrent theme. The disciples have often been in the background, but never far away. Chapter 10 will show us more of their work.

Some people today wonder what to make of these miracle stories. It all seems so irregular, as if it cuts against nature. But for Matthew these incidents point to the wholeness of nature: the creator is restoring his handiwork and ending the dominance of illness and suffering. These healings speak of mercy in a world that is too often hindered and blinkered by misfortune. There is a smell of the future about them. They hint at the final purposes of God, and link all that to the coming of Jesus, in whom God was truly 'with us' in flesh and in love. They invite us to discover more of the loving power of Jesus in our own lives.

Prayer

Lord, show me how to bring your restoring love to broken places, in my own life and around me.

30 Matthew 9:36—10:4
Workers for the harvest

A new phase of mission

The second main block of teaching in Matthew, sometimes called the 'Mission Charge', fills the next chapter. Jesus is preparing his twelve apostles to go out on mission. They have followed him, listened to his words and watched his deeds. Now he sends them out to make God's kingdom known by word and deed, just as he has done. So another horizon opens – the church's mission.

Matthew's first readers know that Jesus' own career as missionary has ended, long before their time. He is still with his people (28:20), but no longer present in the flesh. His mission has now become their mission. So this passage in the gospel, showing the disciples taking up the task from Jesus, will be unusually 'transparent' for Matthew's church. They will see themselves in it. They will expect their own experiences to be illuminated by this material.

Today's section is a transition in the gospel, leading into chapter 10, opening the way for the instruction Jesus will give to the twelve.

Shepherd concern

Jesus looks at the crowds, as he did when he began the sermon on the mount (5:1). On that earlier occasion he spoke of blessing. This time he sees a people straying (v. 36). Surely many of them are still open and ready for the blessing of God, but Jesus is grieved: they seem to have no direction, no strong spiritual leadership and care. They are a people 'harassed and helpless'.

Several Old Testament passages speak of sheep without a shepherd. Most (for example, Ezekiel 34:5 or Zechariah 10:2) reflect situations where Israel's spiritual leaders have not given the guidance they should. That matches the picture we are beginning to see in Matthew, where there is a deep gulf in outlook between Jesus and the scribes and Pharisees. If they are at the helm, Jesus feels that the people will never receive his kingdom message.

So Jesus makes other plans. The picture changes, from wandering sheep to ripened crops (v. 37). Elsewhere in Matthew the image of harvest is used for God's last judgement, with the solemn picture of wheat and weeds being separated from one another (13:24–30). But the picture of a harvest seems to be used very positively in this verse. There is good fruit to gather, and rewarding work to be done. Now we meet the people who will do it.

Authority to serve

We met several of these men earlier, when they were called. Jesus may well have started to form an inner circle among his followers some time before this. That could fit the impression given in Matthew 10:1. Now he commissions them for a new kind of work.

The number twelve is heavy with meaning. Israel had twelve tribes, descended from twelve patriarchs, the fathers of the nation. Now Jesus appoints a new leadership patterned after the old tradition, a new core for Israel, promising a revival of her life from within. The twelve are sent out as shepherds, for a responsible ministry of care and guidance. By what right and strength will they do this? The two key words are 'apostles' and 'authority'.

The authority of Jesus was an important theme in the last few chapters (7:29; 8:8–13; 9:6–8). He has spoken and acted with authority. Now he passes it on, authority to heal and overcome evil. We are not told precisely how he passes it on – other than by the words of commission throughout chapter 10. Certainly the authority seems to work (Mark 6:12–13, 30). The twelve will preach and heal as he has done (10:7–8).

Only in verse 2, after receiving authority, are the twelve called 'apostles'. The idea has a Jewish background. It means a messenger of a special kind. An apostle is an agent, commissioned and trusted by a senior and more powerful person, sent to carry out the master's business. This requires wisdom, responsibility and initiative, and also loyalty to the master's policy and wishes.

The mission of the church continues the mission of Jesus. The basis on which the twelve were sent remains the basis for all our Christian work, for our pastoral care, our mission and our leadership. We work for the Lord and are committed to following his purpose, ahead of our own preferences.

Prayer

Lord God, let your church be truly apostolic, obedient to your sending, faithful in your service.

31 Matthew 10:5–15

News cast

The 'fishing for people' (4:19) is about to begin. The apostles of Jesus are going out as messengers of the kingdom of God. These verses give them instruction about what to do.

Broadcast

This is a mission to Jewish people. Jesus himself has worked mostly among Jews in Galilee, and his disciples should stick to Jewish communities. Israel are the lost sheep (v. 6) for whom Jesus grieves (9:36). The time for wider international mission will come, but is not yet.

Matthew's gospel reminds his readers – and us – that Christianity comes from a Jewish stock. Jesus came in fulfilment of Israel's ancient hopes, bringing fresh energy and vision to a long tradition. The church celebrates a gospel that was given to Israel first, a message that is faithful to Israel's history and heritage. (See the section 'Matthew and Judaism' in the Introduction, pp. 13–14.)

So the disciples are to preach the kingdom and show its presence, as Jesus has done. Signs will support the preaching, and preaching will explain the signs. God is stirring in Israel. This message of God's kingdom fits the Jewish audience that Jesus has in view. The idea of God as king was an old and honoured belief among Jews. Jesus was speaking in language they could grasp – and was bringing the reality of the kingdom within reach.

Supporting cast

The missionaries are not to take a lot of equipment. This will be a simple venture, unsophisticated in style. They should not trouble themselves with money, either by taking any with them (v. 9) or by accepting payment for what they do (v. 8). 'Labourers deserve their food' (v. 10) and they should expect to get food and lodging on the road – but without money changing hands in either direction. They are not to act as beggars, but should accept hospitality in the communities they visit.

When they arrive in a place (v. 11), they should seek out a known sympathiser, someone who is already inclined to support the work of Jesus, and lodge with that person until they leave town and move on.

In Jewish society, with its tradition of close national solidarity, a request for lodging would not be strange. Even so, the kingdom message would divide people. Some homes and villages would not be welcoming.

Cast out?

The style of the mission is straightforward. The preachers should go from house to house, and greet people as they go, bringing a word of peace to each place (v. 12). We should think of houses as grouped, often around open yards, with extended families gathering from work in farms or crafts. Many a place would prove 'worthy', and welcome the news of God's kingdom. Others, however, would have no interest or pleasure in what they heard: the greeting of 'peace' would find no place in which to rest, and would leave with the one who gave it.

A shadow side to the good news comes into view here. The kingdom is an urgent message. It is near. You cannot ignore God's reign, and you cannot remain the same once you have heard and seen it. Places that turn away will be the worse for that decision. The cities of Sodom and Gomorrah were notorious Old Testament examples of disobedience and judgement (Genesis 19:24–28), but even they never heard this word of the kingdom (v. 15). What a catastrophe it would be, to be really near and then to resist and reject the good news!

Cast of thousands

So what of the church's mission today? Matthew 10 fits a society with a solid faith tradition, where there is fresh and important news to bring. The message must be shared. It is immediate, alive, urgent, a movement of God not to be missed.

If we find mission heavy going, that is partly because there is less of a faith tradition into which we can speak: our Western society is becoming very secular. It may also be because we overlook the sheer life and vigour of the gospel, the passion that fired the first Christians and that sparked the spread of their faith. Their style was simple but the grace and mercy in their message were rich and full.

Prayer

Lord, please give us a love for the communities around us, and the ability to make the kingdom known by word and action.

32 Matthew 10:16–23

Sheep among wolves

The church's mission will not be all smooth progress and sunny days. There will be opposition and rejection, and some of it will be harsh and painful. Today's verses give warning of dangers ahead.

Serpents and doves

Verse 16 is like a headline across the coming section, sketching the attitude the apostles must adopt if they are to survive and serve when the going gets tough.

In 9:36 the 'sheep' were the nation of Israel, seen as a wandering and wounded flock. In this verse the disciples are sheep, and the point is that sheep are vulnerable. When they are in open country and unprotected, they cannot defend themselves. The disciples will meet threats and even violence. Some of the people they encounter will be 'wolves' – brutal, deceitful, malicious.

There is no sure way of preventing other people's wolfishness. Sheep have to keep their eyes open and their minds clear; they must be 'wise as serpents'. But they should keep their integrity too; they must not be wolves themselves. They need to be above reproach, people whose conduct is always true and fair. They must be prudent and pure, shrewd and honest. They have to live the good news if they are to tell it.

Governors and kings

The next verses speak of arrest and harassment, first by the religious authorities of a local synagogue, then before the civil judgement of Jewish kings and Roman governors. 'Be careful,' says Jesus (v. 17). Do not invite danger. But if serious trouble does come, the advice he gives is 'not to think beforehand what you will say', but to depend on God's Spirit for words when the time comes (vv. 19–20). Even a court appearance can be an occasion for witness.

These few verses seem also to look across to a broader horizon, to the church's mission among the nations. Christians who heard them, even in Matthew's time, would find their own trials mirrored here. Two thousand years on, persecution of Christians remains a live issue.

Brothers and sisters in various lands value this passage, with its promise of the Spirit's help, very highly indeed. They deserve our prayers.

Brothers and fathers

It takes a rare toughness to cope with the force of the legal and judicial system when your only crime is faith. It is surely even more hurtful to face hatred in the family. But when a person changes faith and leaves an old family tradition behind, that may be seen as betrayal. Relatives feel personally degraded and insulted, and strong reactions can result (v. 21). There will be times, says Jesus, when all the world seems against you (v. 22). It is still worth hanging on: there is a finish line, and salvation beyond it.

Unfinished business

The first half of verse 23 is clear: when one community reacts strongly against the gospel, move to the next. There is a job to be done, and it is right to get on with it. But the second half is very difficult to interpret.

One understanding might be that however long the world endures, the church's mission will never be finished. It is like painting the Forth Bridge: you just keep going. Mission to Israel still remains an unfinished task, just like mission to the rest of the world.

However, we may see more of the original meaning of the saying if we connect the 'coming of the Son of Man' to the destruction of Jerusalem in AD70 (see also comments on 24:29–35, pp. 203–204). That event catastrophically disrupted Israel's life, and ended an era of Christian evangelism within Israel. So while there was still time, the task of preaching the kingdom to Jews was an urgent one.

Still biting

A minister I know remembers the sermon text at his ordination: 'I am sending you out like lambs into the midst of wolves' (Luke 10:3). Looking back on his home mission work, serving in the name of the church but outside the walls of the church, he says it was a well-chosen text. There can be real discomfort in speaking, living and being recognised as Christian. Both wisdom and innocence are still required of us.

Prayer

Pray for Christians – possibly including yourself – whose faith causes them pressure, hurt and hardship.

33 Matthew 10:24–33

Getting perspective

The apostles' mission will be dangerous. They will be hated, hurt and harassed, for Jesus' sake. Can they cope? Have they strength to bear the burdens, stamina to go the distance and nerve to face the opposition? These verses offer encouragement for the task, with a blend of challenge and comfort.

Do not be afraid

The middle section, verses 26–31, is chiefly comfort. The words 'Do not be afraid' (vv. 26, 28, 31) recur like the chorus of a song. Jesus gives his followers three reasons to keep fears in their place.

- **Open secret (vv. 26–27):** When Christians get discouraged, we may lose sight of God's purpose and forget what a grand message the gospel is. These verses are about the power of God's truth. The message of the kingdom is not going to remain a secret. One day the whole world will know that God is king. It is a mighty privilege to start spreading that message already, to let people know the way things really are. This is the truth that fills heaven and renews the earth. It is worth sharing without fear.

- **Body and soul (v. 28):** This verse is about God's judgement. God holds the future and controls human destiny. Final power never lies with persecutors. Judgment is in God's hands, and God weighs a person's whole life, for good or ill. Even if persecution ends in death, it cannot kill the soul. Christians should revere God – that is the right kind of fear. But we do not need to fear people who oppose and obstruct God's work; their power is very limited.

- **Parting shot (vv. 29–31):** These verses describe God's clear-sighted love that notices sparrows falling in the street and can count the hairs on our head. Now, says Jesus, understand the depth and detail of God's care. You matter more than sparrows. God is concerned for far more than your hairstyle. Nothing can happen to you to take you outside God's love.

These are Jesus' reasons for not being afraid. God guards the future: his truth and judgement will prevail. God guards the present: his care and love are sure. Let Christians proclaim God's truth, respect his judgement and trust his love.

The one we follow

Now we come to the challenging material. This urges the disciples to take their relationship to Jesus seriously, and not to be afraid of admitting that they follow him.

- **Teacher and pupil (vv. 24–25):** Jesus himself attracted opposition in his ministry. 'He casts out demons by the prince of demons,' people said (9:34, RSV), and they linked him with Beelzebul, the ruler of the world of evil. We shall hear this accusation again, and Jesus will make a vigorous response to it (12:22–30). For the moment he reminds his friends that they are serving his cause, copying his activity, and working under his leadership. They should not be alarmed or surprised to be treated as he was.

- **Earth and heaven (vv. 32–33):** Verses 24–25 said that if the apostles serve Jesus, their relationship with other people will be just like his. Verses 32–33 say that their relationship with God will be like his too. For he will speak to God about them and call them his friends (v. 32). If, on the other hand, they do not admit to being his followers – and so avoid the risks of discipleship – they will miss out on the bond that he has with God (v. 33). Christianity is a personal relationship, not only with Jesus but with God too. You cannot have one without the other.

Calm and courage

I personally have not faced opposition as severe as this chapter describes. But I know that Christian witness is still a difficult task in almost every part of the world. It needs courage to let our own relationship with Jesus be known to others. Certainly there is a time and a place for discretion (7:6; 10:16–17: 'be careful'). There are also times when we should acknowledge clearly whose we are and whom we serve. God's kingdom is still worth telling, and God's love can still be trusted. If Jesus is real to us, we need not be afraid to say so.

Prayer

Lord Jesus Christ, let my life make you known, through my silence and my speech, in ways that will help others to believe in you.

34 Matthew 10:34–42

Pouring cold water

This last part of the Mission Charge could dampen the zeal of many an aspiring Christian and, indeed, of more seasoned believers. It asks about loyalty and about commitment, but speaks also of costly discipleship and the abundant love of God.

Families at war

The first part of the passage picks up from verses 32–33, which were about acknowledging Jesus in front of other people. The language of verse 34 is stark, to stress the point. Jesus did indeed come to bring peace, but the peace of the kingdom can be costly. The call of Jesus can split families when some want to follow and others resist. Jesus quotes the Old Testament (vv. 35–36; from Micah 7:6) and describes the division that faith can bring to some families as the cut of a sword through human flesh. The person who is always inhibited by family opinions and pressures will never take the kingdom seriously enough (v. 37). There is no easy peace in the service of Jesus.

Commitment for life

Verse 38 continues the rhythm of verse 37, but gives an alarming new twist to the warnings. Taking up the cross is a picture of death – grisly, humiliating, ugly and painful death. To take up the cross is to commit oneself to that path, to turn aside from the route of personal pleasure and interest, into the way of humble, self-denying and demanding service. The way of the cross has no comfortable guarantees.

Taking up the cross is a description of Christian commitment. It is not about personal problems – 'the crosses we bear' – although personal distress is an important biblical theme elsewhere. This is about a deliberate choice to follow a crucified man, whatever the cost, because he deserves our loyalty and love. The surprise of the gospel is that in giving ourselves, we receive ourselves (v. 39). Christ asks nothing that he cannot repay – as the next verses confirm.

Doors open for God

The idea of the apostles as Jesus' envoys, which we met at 10:1–4, explains verse 40. They come in his name, under his instructions, on his business. To offer them help and hospitality is like offering it to him. And as the apostles are Jesus' envoys, he is God's envoy. He represents God, advances God's kingdom, and acts in God's love and power. Helping someone who does Jesus' work is like helping God.

So people who support the work of the missionaries will indeed be rewarded. To offer lodging, or even the refreshment of cold water, to people engaged on Jesus' work is a gift to God, and a gift that God will cheerfully repay. Those who spread the good news of the kingdom may feel very vulnerable. In 10:16 they are called 'sheep among wolves'; in 10:42 they are 'little ones'. But all their ways and all their days are under the eye and the love of God.

Mission improbable?

Much of this chapter seems far away from our life, our era and our church situation. This teaching comes from a time when the new wine of the kingdom was heady and hot. Even then it was intended primarily for roving missionaries. What, then, can we make of it? How do you translate it into your age and place? Two points in response.

First, Christianity involves commitment and we should not pretend, to ourselves or to new Christians, that it is easy. The faith will slip like water through our fingers if we start thinking it is a soft gospel. It can sometimes be very tough indeed. Material like Matthew 10 both challenges our complacency and offers real comfort to Christians who face particular pressure and opposition just now.

Second, this material speaks about the sort of situation where Christian witness may be painful. Whoever we are and wherever we live, that pain could affect and involve us. Even where the church is comfortable now, the cost of Christian witness in any society or era is not really under our control. Matthew 10 is a resource to keep against the day when the heat is turned up. None of us should say, 'It will never be like that here.'

For thought and prayer

It is not foolish to give what you cannot keep to gain what you cannot lose.
Jim Elliot (1927–56)

35 Matthew 11:1–6

Sign language

The next couple of chapters show a rising tide of opposition to Jesus. Many people did not understand what he was doing and some did not like it. Within these chapters Jesus speaks a number of times about seeing properly. What he is doing is clear enough, for those who have eyes to see (11:4, 25; 13:10–17). He is showing the work and life of God. Today's passage invites people to look.

Words from a sentence

John the Baptist's own preaching had got him into trouble and into prison. This happened when John criticised King Herod Antipas for dumping his first wife and marrying his sister-in-law (Luke 3:19–20). John was doubtless a stern and sharp critic, and the king decided to shut him up. So John lay in prison. His horizons were narrow, but his hopes remained. He had spoken of one who would come after him (3:11–12). Now he wanted to know what to make of the rumours he had heard about Jesus (vv. 2–3). Was Jesus the coming one, or was there something more to look forward to?

We simply do not know what was in John's mind, and what particular concerns were behind his question. Had he expected a sterner messiah, with more judgement and less mercy than he found in Jesus? Had he hoped for something more sudden than the mission tour of Galilee that Jesus had undertaken? Had prison so demoralised him that he needed to be assured and encouraged? Or did he just want to know more about what he could not see? We cannot be sure.

Seeing is believing

Jesus does not give a direct answer to John's question, but his meaning seems straightforward enough. Watch what's happening (v. 4). Look at the healing, the newness, the wholeness that is coming to battered and troubled folk. That should be sign enough that Jesus represents the active mercy of God. But this answer has another level of meaning coded within it.

For the signs to which Jesus draws attention are mentioned in scripture, in Isaiah's prophecy. Isaiah 35 speaks about Israel coming home, and rejoices in the hope of blind people seeing, the deaf hearing, the lame leaping and the dumb speaking. Isaiah 61 (which also influenced the beatitudes of 5:3–12) looks forward to the work of God's anointed: God's Spirit rests on him; he will bring good news to the poor. Now Jesus turns hopes into happenings, and invites people to see not only the signs but also the scriptures, not only the healings but the hopes as well, not only the marvels but the meaning too. This is a time of renewal. Ancient promises are coming to fulfilment. This is a movement that will bring Israel back to God. Jesus is the Messiah on whom God's Spirit rests.

So this short exchange, at the start of Matthew 11, reflects the long sequence of miracles from chapters 8 and 9 and underlines the point made there, for example at 8:17 and 27. This is messianic activity, fulfilling hopes and dreams from long ago. Healings are good in themselves, but these events do not stand on their own. They have a place within the pattern of God's purpose. They carry a message about the one who does them.

Signs and blunders

'Blessed is anyone who takes no offence at me,' says Jesus (v. 6). He has already faced jealous criticism (9:34), and others too would miss the point of what he was doing. Some would take offence. There would be people unable – or unwilling, or unprepared – to recognise what they saw in Jesus, groups who would act and react against him. So Jesus ends his answer to John by hinting that there is conflict coming. He will not be a comfortable or easy presence in Israel. In his way he will be as divisive a figure as John has been, both a healer and an irritant within Israel's life. There will be choices to make. The blessing that he brings will come only to those who want it.

Answering back

Two thousand years on, Jesus still attracts questions. Christians tell his story and live his life, as our way of answering the questions people bring. Many still discover him as the answer to their deepest hopes. And some still take offence.

Prayer

Lord Jesus Christ, help us to know you as a figure of liberty and wholeness. Help us to live by your love, so that others may discover your healing power.

36 Matthew 11:7–15

More than a prophet

The question in yesterday's passage was, 'What does John think of Jesus?' Today's section turns the question round: 'What does Jesus think of John?' The answer is that Jesus thinks very highly of him. He respects John for the quality of his work, and also for the vital role that John had in preparing for his own ministry. John was a prophet, a spokesman for God, and a very good one too. He was also a sign that times were changing and a new phase in God's purposes was dawning.

Reeds and robes

Of course people did not go to the wilderness to admire the vegetation (v. 7); they went to hear John. And John was not dressed in soft royal robes (v. 8). All that is obvious. But there may be another layer, a hint of satire in the words of Jesus. For the reed-man is Herod. There is a reed on some of Herod's coins, a symbol of his territories in the Jordan valley and beside the Sea of Galilee. It may be that the coinage gave Herod a nickname as a flexible fellow, a man easily swayed. He switched his capital city from Sepphoris to Tiberias; he exchanged one wife for another; he could trim and twist his loyalties to the gusts of political fortune. There was no inner firmness in the man.

But John is different. He was straight and consistent in his ministry, firm in his faith and conviction, committed to God even though it cost him dearly. He is different in every way from the king who holds him in prison. He has no wealth or rich clothing, but his trust in God gives him an inner toughness. This man was worth travelling to the desert to see and hear. He is a real and worthy prophet. But he is something more too.

Voice from the boundary

When Jesus speaks of John as 'more than a prophet', he thinks of John's role in the coming of God's kingdom. Promises have come to fulfilment through John's ministry. So as Jesus describes John, he looks first backward and then forward, to the ancient prophets and to the coming kingdom.

'The law and the prophets spoke their message until John came' (v. 13). The Old Testament was a long era of promise, a period when

God dealt with Israel in love and care, yet an age that looked forward to fuller and more intimate knowledge of God. Jesus uses words from the last Old Testament prophet, Malachi, to explain John's role. John was a messenger, making way for the coming of God (v. 10; from Malachi 3:1). He was a figure like Elijah, turning the nation to God's ways and preparing them to meet God's holy presence (v. 14; from Malachi 4:5).

So John stood at the hinge between Old Testament and New, the latest of the prophets and the herald of the kingdom. No one did a more important or better piece of work for God than John the Baptist (v. 11). He ushered the kingdom in. He was its announcer and forerunner. Yet once the kingdom comes, John's work is completely overshadowed. A fuller grace is at work than he knew. Something much bigger is happening (v. 11).

Verse 12 is difficult. It probably means, 'The kingdom of heaven presses strongly forward, and people press forward to grasp it.' John has launched something forceful that has a vigour and energy of its own, through the love and power of God at work in Jesus. Many people respond with enthusiasm and commitment, although others will be cautious and sceptical (11:16–19).

Tuning in

There are hints in this chapter about seeing properly. In verse 15 the metaphor changes to hearing. 'Listen,' says Jesus. Understand that John's whole ministry is pointing to something much bigger than himself. God is present, in Jesus.

God still stirs, in our times. As times change, God may work in new ways. Christians should listen, to be sensitive to what God is doing. But all the work of God in every age is an echo of his greatest work – the coming of Jesus. There we see God's kingly rule and fatherly care. There we see the hope of the gospel and the generous love of the Lord who brought it among us.

Prayer

Lord Jesus Christ, let me speak for you and listen to you, that my days may be a time of your grace.

37 Matthew 11:16–24

Missing generation

Blind spot

'What you see is what you get' is a slogan of our times. But we do not always live that way. Sometimes we see clearly, but we decline to take real notice of the things we observe because they could lead us to conclusions and commitments we prefer to avoid.

Jesus met precisely that sort of response. His deeds were 'the deeds of the Messiah' (11:2), but still he said, 'Blessed is anyone who takes no offence at me' (11:6). John's preaching was powerful and important (11:7–14), but still the invitation has to come, 'Let anyone with ears listen!' (11:15). For some people were offended by what they saw, and some were determined not to hear. So verses 16–24 are about excuses, evasiveness and resistance.

No time to dance

Have you ever tried to play with children when they are bored and cannot lift themselves out of it? Whatever you try falls flat. That's the picture here (vv. 16–17). Someone is trying to start a tune, and nothing catches on. The children do not want to dance, but they do not want to sing a sad song either. Nothing will suit them, neither foot-tapping rhythms nor the slow strains of a folk lament. The children are bored and nothing will stir them.

That, says Jesus, is how some people greet God's messengers. For the preachers had different styles. John followed a simple lifestyle, without beer or banquets, and people said, 'What a dull, unbalanced fellow. He must be possessed by something odd' (v. 18). Then Jesus came, living a very different life, welcoming friendship and hospitality, and the same people shook their heads: 'Just look at the company he keeps. What an undisciplined character!' (v. 19).

Excuses are easy to find at first, but eventually they wear thin. Grumbling at everything is a childish attitude. That is no way to approach a serious issue like faith. Yet, in the end, God's wisdom will show itself, plainly and truly, by its effects (v. 19). Jesus and John have achieved much for God, and that is what really matters.

Urban priorities

These Galilean 'cities' were busy communities, but were not very big by our standards – more like large villages or small market towns. They had their share of sceptical and suspicious people. So when Jesus visited, and people gathered for healing (8:16), many of the townsfolk did not turn a hair.

Jesus grieves over the places that reject his message (vv. 20–24). He compares them with rebellious towns of Old Testament times. Tyre had been intoxicated with her own wealth (Ezekiel 26—28). Sodom was a lawless place (Genesis 19). But they never had a chance to see the signs of the gospel or to welcome the arrival of God's kingdom. Their evil was of a lesser kind, so even they would fare better in God's judgement than towns which shut their eyes to Jesus. The places that were first to hear would be last in God's reckoning, if they took no notice of what they heard.

These verses repeat the point made at 10:15. Jesus expected his ministry to bring a time of crisis and judgement to Israel. His message was challenging rather than cosy. He warned people to be ready, to respond, to be on the right side. He wanted people to 'repent' (4:17; 11:20–21), to follow the path of kingdom loyalty and lifestyle. God's kingdom would be durable, and those who found it would have nothing to fear. But those who missed out on the kingdom, who saw nothing because the lenses of their minds were closed, would realise one day how hollow their excuses really were.

Excuse me

The Christian message often encounters excuses – from outsiders who resist getting drawn in; and from Christians, when we are content with a shallow and superficial faith. Only God can really deal with the human heart and help a person to get beyond excuses to commitment. But all of us have a responsibility here: to be honest with God about our own attitude, and to live credible Christian lives, so that neighbours find in us reasons to believe in Jesus, not excuses to avoid him.

Prayer

Lord Jesus Christ, help me to grow away from poor excuses, into the richness of faith.

38 Matthew 11:25–30

The gentle yoke of Jesus

Here is the other side of the coin. The previous passage was full of gloom and warning. Now come warmth and invitation. Jesus has attracted opposition and misunderstanding, but he has also found people who want to follow, and he welcomes them into the love and friendship of God. Like so much in Matthew's gospel, these verses are 'transparent': they have a proper place in the gospel story, but they also leap beyond the story and beckon the reader. 'You come to Jesus as well,' they seem to say. 'Discover the pattern of life he offers his friends. Enjoy the security and peace that come through trusting him.'

Jesus appears here as a uniquely important figure, the only person who truly knows God, and the one who brings others to God. Yet he is also a humble man: he is gentle and lowly; he offers an easy yoke to his followers; children understand his truth. That paradox runs right through Matthew and, indeed, through all the gospels. It is the mystery of Jesus himself: he was humble yet mighty, accessible to little people yet himself a person of greatness and majesty.

Through the eyes of a child

The Old Testament suggests that learned and clever people can miss the mark in their dealings with God, but that God's law is a lamp to humble folk (Isaiah 29:14; Psalm 19:7). That same thing may happen when people encounter Jesus. He knows God like a son knows a father. The people who respond to him he calls 'little children', and he gathers them into his own special relationship with God. Others have turned away – sophisticated and sure of themselves, yet not really open to the kingdom.

The picture of children playing was used in verses 16–17: bored and weary children can be difficult company. But here in verse 25 children are a pattern to copy. For children are often trusting and straightforward, firm in their loyalty, and receptive to love. Their minds are not cluttered by prejudice, cleverness and pride. These are the sort of people – those who can be humble, open and child-like – who will discover the secrets of the kingdom of God. This teaching is very like the beatitudes (5:3–12). The poor in spirit and pure in heart are truly blessed. They find it easiest to follow Jesus, and they get to know him most deeply.

Rest for the weary

Jesus offers relief to tired people, and rest to the troubled and weary. Here is a pattern of life that is bearable and wholesome; here is the promise of refreshment and renewed strength. But in Jesus' own time these words carried other resonances and hopes. They echo the invitation wisdom gives, in Proverbs 1—3, to come and enjoy the life of God. So Jesus speaks as God's wisdom, the creative power of God in human flesh.

Jesus offers an 'easy yoke' (v. 30). A yoke was not always easy to bear. It was part of the harness of a working animal, and meant load and toil. In some Old Testament texts the word refers to Israel's experience of heavy-handed foreign rule. Jews also used the word 'yoke' to describe the discipline of the Jewish law – which could be applied in burdensome ways. But Jesus speaks of an alternative 'yoke', the loving rule of God that will not chafe and destroy. The 'yoke' of Jesus, his teaching of the law, is bearable rather than oppressive. He interprets the law in different ways from the Pharisees (for example, 12:1–14).

So Jesus speaks of a pattern of life, of discipleship, that is indeed a 'yoke'. It is a path of service, involving commitment, discipline and hard work. But it is not a hurtful or unnatural yoke. It is lined with mercy. It is shaped by the loving wisdom of God, not by human anger. It fits especially well on the child-like in heart.

These words in verses 28–30 are used in some churches as an invitation to Communion. Although Communion was not the setting where they were first spoken, they suit the occasion well. For Communion is not a stopping place; it is a refreshment station on our journey of discipleship. The yoke of Jesus is for the rhythm and routine of Christian living, that we may follow without fear and serve without strain.

For thought and prayer

Can you still come to Communion like a child, receptive and trustful, expecting God to refresh and teach you, ready to be surprised by God's grace and love?

39 Matthew 12:1–8

Against the grain

Chapter 12 is full of arguments. The first two stories, in verses 1–14, concern the Jewish sabbath. The Jews kept one day each week as a holy day for God. There were rules to ensure that you observed the sabbath properly, and – as often happens with systems of laws – some of the rules had become quite detailed.

Eyeing the ears

A few raw grains of wheat would scarcely fill the stomach. They might just take the edge off midday hunger. This was not a real meal. Nor was it theft. Jews were permitted to pluck a few ears from a neighbour's field (Deuteronomy 23:25). But even this counted as work, so far as the Pharisees were concerned. Harvesting corn, and threshing it to separate grain from husk, were disallowed on the sabbath (Exodus 20:10; 34:21). The behaviour of Jesus' disciples aroused comment and indignation. If he was a religious teacher, it was odd that his followers did not conduct themselves in a careful and law-abiding way. They seemed not to bother about obedience in the way that Pharisees did. What can Jesus say to justify his friends' conduct?

Prophet, priest and king

The answer Jesus gives is surprising. He does not say (as we might have done), 'It's only a very small matter. This is not real work. It's the spirit of the law that counts.' He does not discuss (as the Pharisees might have expected) detailed interpretation of ancient laws. He makes a bigger point. He talks about his own ministry, what he is doing as God's Messiah, and the new age of opportunity that he has brought. He uses Old Testament examples to make the point.

Jesus refers first (vv. 3–4) to an incident from 1 Samuel 21:1–6. David was running for his life, and he and his men were tired and hungry. They were given holy bread by the priests, bread that had been dedicated to God for use in worship. Now Jesus is a new David, another king-to-be in Israel. He also has a vital mission to carry out, that overshadows the normal sensitivities of religious and ceremonial law. Let no one stand in his way.

Jesus' second point (vv. 5–6) refers to the regular practice of Jewish priests. There were sacrifices and offerings to be made on the sabbath (for example, see Numbers 28:9–10), and the priests had to ensure that all was done properly. They needed to work on the sabbath. The temple, the place where heaven touches earth and Israel meets with God, warranted a break with the normal sabbath pattern. Yet Jesus is greater than the temple. The kingdom of heaven touches earth in his ministry. People meet the mercy and power of God in what he does. The normal restrictions and patterns of everyday law need not all apply to him. Something more important is happening.

Thirdly (v. 7), Jesus cites a text from the prophets, from Hosea 6:6. Mercy matters more than sacrifice. The active compassion that God shows in Jesus takes precedence over the laws that shape holy days. Jesus brings the ancient prophet's hope to life. Indeed he fulfils the whole direction of the prophetic scriptures (5:17). He brings a new era of messianic intention and action.

Lord's day

The short controversy ends with a flourish. 'The Son of Man is lord of the sabbath' (v. 8). Jesus is in charge. His purpose, his activity, his mission, are important enough to make the sabbath holy. He does not need the protection of detailed laws to secure his holiness. The days he lives and the deeds he does are holy in themselves. Whatever serves his cause surely hallows the sabbath.

Trading places

The Christian Sunday is not the same as the Jewish sabbath – although it conserves much from that older tradition. So how should we use it, and what should be done to protect it? Is it just a day for faith, family and friendship, or might shift-work, sports or even shopping have a place there too? Customs have changed a lot. How do Christians respond?

This passage in Matthew suggests that one question above all should guide a Christian: does my use of Sunday enhance and advance the work of Jesus and the spread of his mercy, love and good news?

Prayer

Lord Jesus Christ, help me to keep every day as holy as I can, by living in ways that please and honour you, whatever I am doing.

40 Matthew 12:9–21
Just healing

This second sabbath incident revolves around the healing of a withered hand. But we hear little about the person who is healed. Nothing is said about faith or salvation. Those points have been well made through chapters 8 and 9, and now Matthew's story has moved on. This chapter emphasises the opposition that emerges and the way that Jesus responds to it.

The dead hand

Healing counted as work. Indeed it can be hard work – ask any doctor! So Jewish law did not allow healing on the sabbath, unless there was a danger to life. Here is Jesus in the synagogue, the local centre of scriptural and legal knowledge, and some people challenge him (v. 10). Is he going to heal? Is this allowed?

Jesus is quick to explain himself. The answer he gives is less complicated than in the previous incident. There is no recourse to the Old Testament, no complex piling up of points. He makes one single comparison. If a sheep falls into a ditch on the sabbath, the farmer will drag it out as soon as possible. Concern for the animal's health, for the distress and waste that delay could cause, will lead to prompt action. Surely, says Jesus (v. 12), a person is a more deserving case than a sheep. We ought to relieve suffering. There is no point in delay and every reason to act immediately. So it is lawful to heal on the sabbath.

Jewish rabbis of the time actually discussed how much help should be given to a stranded animal on the sabbath. But Jesus is not really joining their debate. He is more direct. This is what people do, he argues. They act quickly to avoid serious harm. And he is equally straightforward in his healing. He is concerned for human need and pain, and acts wherever he can make a difference. If law fails to see that, then it is a dead hand, stifling the work of love.

The incident ends with a little conference among the Pharisees about how to get rid of Jesus (v. 14). For the first time in Matthew, the possibility of the cross comes into view. A withered hand has indeed been restored, but we are beginning to see a widening rift within Israel, that will not be healed.

Gentle for the Gentiles

Jesus retreated once before, in order to avoid sharp opposition (4:12). He does not seek controversy, nor excess publicity (v. 16; compare 8:4; 9:30). For the moment, he wants time and opportunity to extend his ministry among receptive people.

Matthew quotes the Old Testament in verses 18–21, the longest quotation anywhere in the gospel. It comes from Isaiah 42, a chapter which has already figured in a smaller way at 3:17 (see comment there, p. 31) and will echo again in the transfiguration story at 17:5. Matthew has a particular reason for putting these verses here, for we have just read of a threat to Jesus' life. But God's purpose will not fail. Jesus will accomplish his task. Graciously, steadily, persistently and successfully, he will carry God's work through to its destination. So these verses from Isaiah offer a wide-angle view of the course of Matthew's gospel, where it is leading and how it will get there.

Jesus is the servant of God. God's Spirit rests upon him (v. 18) from his baptism (3:16–17). He will not court controversy; his messianic style will not be aggressive and arrogant (v. 19; compare v. 15). He will be sensitive in his dealing with vulnerable, hurting and discouraged people (v. 20; compare 11:29). And in all that he does, there will be a wider horizon. He will spread the mercy and justice of God to Gentile nations, and give them reason to hope and rejoice (vv. 18, 21; compare 8:11).

This quote gives Matthew's readers a moment of insight into what is going on behind the scenes of the story. The controversies will continue. Jesus will not avoid them. He will eventually suffer and die. But the lamp of the gospel will not be snuffed out. The deliberate gentleness of Jesus may seem oddly unmessianic to some. Yet his ministry will restore withered and broken lives to wholeness and launch a message to take to the world. Out of the tragedy of his cross will come resurrection and international mission (28:18–20).

For thought and prayer

Can gentleness ever be a successful strategy in a world where so many people are sharp – in mind, tongue and deed? These verses suggest that it can. But it may be a costly path to follow. Review your relationships and dealings with people: is there anywhere where you should be gentler than you have been?

41 Matthew 12:22–30

Crooked thinking

The scripture quotation in 12:18–21 sets the stage for this next incident. The main point of the Isaiah text is that Jesus is filled with God's Spirit and doing God's work. Now, immediately afterwards, people ask about whose power really drives him. Is it God's, or someone else's?

Matthew's story has been leading this way for a while. In 9:27 and 9:34 we read of two very different views about Jesus: is he Son of David, or agent of the devil? Again in 10:25 Jesus spoke of being tarred with the title 'Beelzebul', the prince of demons. So this very direct clash is not unexpected. We are ready for Jesus to respond.

Talk of the devil

Matthew does not describe the miracle in much detail (v. 22). The point of this incident is to show how trouble and controversy arise and how Jesus explains himself. The healing leads, apparently very quickly, to clear sight and ready speech for the individual concerned. But can the people around see properly for themselves? What have they got to say? Have they really noticed what and who is at work among them?

The crowds are enthusiastic; they sense messianic activity (see comment on 9:27, p. 77). Yet the Pharisaic voices strike a discordant note; they cannot believe that Jesus is inspired by God. They see him as a maverick, a lone ranger. He sits light to their laws, so they cannot take him seriously. If there is superhuman power in his life, it must be a devilish power.

Power points

Jesus shows that his accusers' thinking is topsy-turvy. Their logic does not make sense. His response has five stages: two arguments (vv. 25–26, 27); two conclusions (vv. 28, 29); and a challenge (v. 30).

- **No inside job (vv. 25–26):** Jesus cannot be inspired by the devil in his mission of healing, because he is actually attacking the devil's territory. He is loosening the grip of evil on human lives. Evil power would surely not work against itself. Any kingdom or community that fights itself will quickly dissolve and collapse. Satan's kingdom could not go on standing if it were battling against its own successes.

- **Fair play (v. 27):** Some other Jewish writings of this era also mention exorcism. There were people who could do this – although it appears that Jesus was unusually prolific, that others did not exorcise on the same scale as he did. So Jesus asks his accusers if they would recognise other exorcisms as God's work. If they would, why do they challenge him? They should be more consistent.
- **Whose kingdom? (v. 28):** This first conclusion takes up from the previous point. The number, variety and power of Jesus' signs come from a very intimate relationship with God. He is inspired by God's Holy Spirit, as a sign of God's kingdom, an indication that the loving rule of God is at work in him.
- **Right of entry (v. 29):** This second conclusion moves on from the first. The Spirit of God gives Jesus power over evil. The only way a burglar can ransack a house is by first tying up the householder and securing a clear entry to the property. So, implies Jesus, the reason he makes inroads into the realm of evil and releases people from suffering and fear is that he has already overcome the devil. In his temptations (4:1–11) Jesus proved himself stronger than the powers of evil, and claimed the right to serve as God's Spirit-filled Son.

So Jesus is the man in control. He is not possessed by any evil power. But he himself has the right to push back the boundaries of evil, to release people held in its clutches and to spread the clean and holy power of God's kingdom.

No soft options

Finally Jesus poses a hard choice (v. 30). This group of hearers has come close enough to recognise what is going on in his ministry. Now they should decide. If they will not support what Jesus is doing, they are actually turning against him and making his work more difficult.

For thought and prayer

The cause of Jesus is a power struggle, for the victory of gentleness and wholeness over the damaging harshness of suffering and evil. Do not be afraid to take sides.

42 Matthew 12:31–37
Opposing matters

Limits of forgiveness

Verses 31 and 32 are hard to understand. The great Christian thinker Augustine reckoned them the most difficult in the Bible, and many readers since have been puzzled and disturbed by this awkward saying. We shall try to make sense of the words, by connecting them to the storyline in Matthew.

This passage continues the theme of yesterday's portion. Pharisees have accused Jesus of acting as an agent of the devil (12:24), and he has not only defended himself but has challenged them. It is time for them to make their minds up about him. If they are unwilling to recognise the Holy Spirit's work in him, then they are standing in the way of God's kingdom (12:30).

The hard saying in verses 31–32 takes up from there. People may start by criticising Jesus thoughtlessly, without understanding what they do. But once they understand that God's Holy Spirit is at work in him, and then deliberately oppose this work – 'thoughtfully, wilfully and self-consciously rejecting the work of the Spirit, even though there can be no other explanation of Jesus' exorcisms' (D.A. Carson) – they are turning their backs on the mercy of God. When people sense that the powers of God's kingdom are at work, and then shut their hearts against that work, they 'undercut the very possibility of experiencing God's salvation' (D. Hagner). They have seen what God's love looks like, and decided it is not for them. There is no way home from this sort of position, other than retreat.

The inner life

Our outer appearance and actions can sometimes reveal a great deal about our inner self. A nurse or doctor will 'hear' the movement of a person's heart by taking a pulse. We can read the tiredness in a friend's mind when we see a drawn face or dull eyes. In exactly the same way, we learn a great deal about a person's inner feelings and attitudes by listening to what they say. What is inside becomes visible on the outside. Good trees bear good fruit; if you do not get decent fruit, then you must have a poor-quality tree (v. 33). What is in the heart comes out of the mouth (v. 34). A good person's heart is like a treasure chest of good things, where it is easy to select kind, fair and true words to speak (v. 35), whereas the people who speak harshly about Jesus are actually saying more about themselves than about him. Jesus invites them to look inside and reflect on what they find.

Counting words

Verses 36 and 37 link together the two paragraphs above. God judges our words, our casual, everyday, instinctive speech – because the words show what is inside us. People of integrity and love, where the goodness of God is active within, will show that inner self to God – in a thousand ordinary ways. God will see the reflection of his own love, and will welcome what he sees. But the person who speaks deliberately and maliciously against Jesus, and persists in that opposition, is showing God a heart that wants nothing to do with the kingdom. They should not be surprised to find that their words count against them.

Do not be afraid

This passage has sometimes given rise to serious pastoral problems. Verses 31 and 32, and their parallels in Mark 3:28–29 and Luke 12:10, have caused perplexity and distress to some sensitive Christians, who look back fearfully across their own lives in case they have committed sins God cannot forgive.

The wisest pastors deal gently with such worried souls. For their very fear and sorrow come from belief in Jesus. They realise how important he is, and they do not want to reject or spurn his love. If they ever did reject him, they have not persisted in that course, but have found a way back to a different and more positive attitude. Theirs may have been a temporary sin, but it is not the 'eternal sin' of which we read in Mark 3:29. It was well written of such a troubled person, 'If you repent, then you have the Spirit' (Ulrich Zwingli); the very fact that you are seriously concerned shows that this is not your problem.

Prayer

Lord God, when I am careless or cruel in my dealings, remind me that you see and hear what I do; and when I feel the weight of my own sin, assure me of the openness and depth of your forgiveness.

43 Matthew 12:38–45

Moment of opportunity

Asking the impossible

Jesus has performed many healings and exorcisms. Why ask for another sign? (v. 38). Had these people not seen enough of his activity already? What difference would one more incident make?

The point seems to be that they have seen, but have not been receptive to what they saw. The controversy began at 12:24 – 'he casts out demons by the prince of demons'. Jesus' opponents are suspicious of his exorcisms. So they ask if he could perform a different sign to show quite clearly that God is with him, a sign which will not allow any other interpretation or leave any room for doubt.

Of course, signs are not like that. Strange or unusual deeds can usually be understood in more than one way. We interpret the signs we see according to the ideas and prejudices of our hearts (12:34). So Jesus did not perform signs simply to impress people or to prove himself. Signs do not prove God. They invite faith and show grace, but only to those who are ready to believe and receive.

'For God all things are possible' (19:26). But we come near to asking the impossible if we ask God to show us something convincing, when we do not actually want to be convinced. When I hear people today say, 'I'd believe if only…', I sometimes wonder if they would.

Hard to swallow

There would, however, be one great sign, to Israel and to the world. It would be a sign of life, to show how God can overcome suffering and death. It would echo the story of the prophet Jonah, who was gulped down and then vomited back up by a giant fish (Jonah 1:17; 2:10). For Jesus too would be lost from view in the tomb, and then emerge to life again (v. 40). Death would not consume or destroy him. Here would be one final majestic sign, to show the meaning of all the signs Jesus had done, to show the power and strength of his love, and to beckon people to the vitality and hope of his good news.

Yet even the resurrection requires a response. The evidence is firm enough to support Christian belief, but not enough to force people into faith. Signs show where the road is, but we still have to follow it for ourselves.

Voices from afar

The ministry of Jesus was a moment of unparalleled opportunity. There was never a better time to see the grace of God at work (vv. 41–42). So from the vantage point of eternity it would seem very odd indeed that many rejected him. In Old Testament times, the people of Nineveh listened to Jonah's preaching (Jonah 3:5). The Queen of Sheba came to hear King Solomon teach (1 Kings 10:1–3). They were Gentiles, they had no obvious reason for heeding Israel's God and they had seen nothing of Jesus, but they responded to what they heard. Yet when Jesus comes to Israel as a greater prophet than Jonah, a mightier king and a wiser and holier teacher than Solomon, he meets resistance and resentment. Surely there will be Gentile voices, from the past and from far away, to criticise the generation that refuses him.

Occupied territory

Like so many of Jesus' parables, this last story (vv. 43–45) has a second layer of meaning lurking beneath the surface. On the face of it, the story suggests that religion must be a positive thing. If we merely try to avoid sin, without energetically embracing a positive goodness, we shall be vacant territory for all sorts of other evils – pride, bitterness, resentment, meanness, selfishness. Christian commitment has to be active.

But that may not have been the original meaning of the story. Jesus reminds his opponents that their generation has experienced the cleansing and releasing power of God's Holy Spirit – in his own healings and exorcisms. But the very removal of evil creates a dangerous situation for Israel. It presents them with a sharp choice. They could welcome the work of God's Holy Spirit. Or they could slip into greater and deeper evil, if they reject and resist the grace they have seen in Jesus.

For thought and prayer

Spiritual opportunities can be dangerous for us too. When we learn something fresh and new about Christ, we cannot make a neutral response; we cannot stand still. Ask God for wisdom and courage to take the chances you are given for growth and advance in the Christian life.

44 Matthew 12:46–50

Family gathering

Man apart

We have heard nothing about Jesus' home and family life since chapter 2. He is operating away from home, moving from place to place, and using Simon Peter's house at Capernaum as an occasional base. He has gathered some followers, but has also attracted suspicion and criticism. He already seems a vulnerable, threatened and isolated figure (see 10:25; 11:19; 12:14).

He is a man apart. Yet he is not a man alone. He is shaping a community, forming a company of people where the life of God will be known in fresh ways. It takes a visit from his natural family to show, in stark and even hurtful ways, just how much he values his followers.

Outer circle

Mary is here, but Joseph is not mentioned, and it may be that he had died by this time. There were at least four brothers, for 13:55–56 mentions James, Joseph, Simon and Judas and also some sisters. Indeed, two of the letters in the New Testament come from two of these brothers, James and Jude. But there is no indication in Matthew's story that the brothers are men of faith at this stage.

In fact, the reverse may be true. Mark says (3:20–21) that Jesus' family were concerned about his balance of mind and had come to restrain him. That detail is missing in Matthew's version, but when we meet the family 'standing outside' we realise that they do not belong to Jesus' inner group. They address him from a distance, from the edge of the crowd, while his followers are much closer.

Family likeness

The question in verse 48 must have sounded cruel and harsh to Jesus' relatives. He sees his truest family not as the people he comes from, but as those who come with him. The family likeness is not determined by DNA and genes, by the similarities of face or form that show the parent in the child. The really important family likeness concerns what people do: it is a likeness of lifestyle and habit, of commitment and action.

This family likeness comes from God. Members of the family of faith show by doing God's will that they are God's children. That is the mark of true sons and daughters (21:28–31). It was the way that Jesus lived (John 5:19), and is also his family's way.

That does not mean, though, that Christians should ignore the needs and welfare of relatives. Jesus was very critical of people who used religion as an excuse to neglect elderly parents (15:4–6), and a similar warning comes later in the New Testament (1 Timothy 5:8, 16).

Sister actions

Jesus spoke of 'brother and sister and mother' (v. 50). Judaism of that time usually stressed male leadership in religion, and women were often overlooked as people whose faith and commitment need not be taken very seriously. Jesus broke with that pattern. He respected women and the faith they showed, and he wanted them among his followers as full members of his community.

The church as family

Some Christian churches talk much about family, in an effort to strengthen and support the parents and young children in the congregation. 'Family worship' means that services are planned and led with parents and children in mind, and many other church activities have these same households in view. That pastoral concern is important, but it can sometimes be emphasised in ways that cause hurt.

Not all Christians belong to neat or easy families. Many live alone, and not all of them by choice. If 'family' always means two parents and 2.4 children, it leaves a lot of people out. More importantly, it misses the really big point that the church is a new, large, inclusive and very mixed and untidy family, united in Christ, committed together to doing the will of God, and knit tight in active love. That's real good news, a pattern of community life and love to enrich and shape the whole of our living – a home that is open for all to belong to and for all to enjoy.

For thought and prayer

Pause to realise – especially if following Jesus is tough at the moment – that he counts you among his family. What can you do to treat other Christians as brothers and sisters?

45

Matthew 13:1–9

Grains of truth

Jesus often used words to draw pictures, and then employed these word-pictures to illustrate and explain his message about God's kingdom. We have already seen some of this, in 7:13–27 and 9:16–17, for example. But now the word 'parable' appears for the first time. This chapter is full of parables; but also it is a chapter about parables – what they are, how they work and what they achieve.

Beach mission

The Sea of Galilee was a mainstay of the local economy. It was full of fish, and a circle of small towns stood around it. When Jesus went out along the beach, he would find people at their work. He sat down among them, like a rabbi sitting to preach in a synagogue (as in Luke 4:20). But the sheer numbers who gathered obliged him to push out from the shore in a boat and use it as a floating pulpit. One can imagine people fanning out around a little bay, with Jesus a few yards away on the water.

Plain and perplexing

Strictly speaking, the word 'parable' means 'comparison' – one thing put down beside another so that people can see how they match. But there was an ancient Hebrew word, *mashal*, that could mean a parable but could also refer to a much wider variety of sorts of saying. A *mashal* could be a mystery or riddle, a proverb, a story with a meaning, as well as a comparison of one thing with another.

The parables of Jesus often begin, 'The kingdom of God is like…' as in 13:24; that is obviously a comparison. But his stories also seem to reflect the mysterious aspect of the *mashal* tradition.

This story about a sower, for example (vv. 3–8), appears simple and accessible. None of the towns in Galilee was big by our standards: people lived near the land, and would understand farmers and fields very well. Yet there is a perplexing aspect to this parable too. It does not really explain what it is about. It leaves the reader – as it would have left its first hearers – with work to do. People would find themselves starting to think. Then the story would take a grip on them as they tried to puzzle it out.

Scattered success

What – on earth – is this about? Is Jesus provoking attention by sketching a picture of a careless farmer, who scatters his precious grain all over the place instead of spreading it on the best of the soil? Or is Jesus describing the mixed fortunes that regularly follow the sowing of seed? The process is rather random, and you cannot always tell which of the grains will grow.

There is a strong positive climax at the end (v. 8). The lavish fruitfulness of the last batch of seed exceeds all normal expectations. But the story takes a long time to get there; the farmer's hopes are frustrated over and again. So does the story make its impact through the long sequence of failed sowings, or because of this eventual success? Is it really about final plenty? Or about the patchy and discouraging process that came first?

Easy listening?

Jesus was easy to listen to, but hard to hear. He was a master teacher. These parables were so ordinary that people would remember them. But the stories had an elusive quality too, like mercury, gleaming with light but constantly slipping out of your hand.

So responsible hearing required hard work. The stories had to be kept in mind, allowed to rub around the hearer's mind for a long time, like grit in an oyster, until grit became gospel and the puzzle turned into a rich pearl. 'Use your ears,' said Jesus. He meant not just physical hearing, but inner hearing too, holding on to the story until the good news of God's kingdom lodges firmly in a person's heart and life.

Dwelling place

Learning the truth of the gospel needs effort and patience. The love of Jesus is big enough to deserve that commitment. Sometimes we can only grow when we make room for his teaching to dwell in our minds and shape our lives. Then we start to hear his word in fresh and deeper ways.

Prayer

God of mystery and majesty, help us to cherish your word in our hearts, that we may truly hear and see, and may turn afresh to you. Through Jesus Christ our Lord. Amen

46 Matthew 13:10–17

Turning a blind eye

This is difficult material. It appears so different from the open teaching style that Jesus often adopted. Did he really mean to prevent people understanding? This strangeness has prompted a suggestion that these words did not come from Jesus at all, but were added to the story some years later to explain why the gospel had not spread very well. But the substance of what is here fits fairly well with a number of other things Jesus said, and could very well have come from him. We consider what he might have meant, a section at a time.

Stating secrets

The followers of Jesus had begun to understand how God's kingdom was working in him. For them the parables were fresh shafts of light. A 'mystery' is hidden and impenetrable – until an interpreter comes, who can unveil it and explain it to others. Jesus' teaching had begun to open the mystery of God's work for his friends to understand and follow (vv. 10–11).

But for people who knew nothing of God's coming kingdom, parables seemed opaque and obscure (vv. 12–13). We need not think that Jesus meant people to remain in this condition. 'Seek and you will find,' he said (7:7–8). But there were those who had not found and showed little desire to seek. Indeed Jesus said that his message would be like a closed book to sophisticated and self-sufficient people (11:25–27). So his parables left people with a responsibility: either to brush the message aside or to dwell on it until its truth became clear and compelling.

Taking leave of their senses

The quotation in verses 14 and 15 comes from Isaiah 6:9–10. As part of God's call to the prophet, these verses warned Isaiah that many in Israel would ignore and resist his ministry. Jesus used these verses to point out that many of his hearers, too, would prefer not to understand. For them the message would be too threatening, too disturbing and demanding, to be worth the risk of proper hearing. Clarity would be too costly; they would rather stay in darkness and silence. But two hopes lighten the gloom.

First, there can be a difference between the words we use and the effect we want them to have. A sports coach or musical conductor may say in apparent frustration, 'You people will never get this right', as a challenge to greater earnestness and application. The actual words are negative, but the intention is positive. So Isaiah – and Jesus too – could use words of gloom and sorrow with the positive hope that there would be a responsive remnant, people who would make the effort to grasp the message, whose hearts and minds would be open to God's word. That remnant is the second hopeful element in Isaiah's text. He calls it 'the holy seed' (Isaiah 6:13), the same image that Jesus used to describe the rich promise of God's kingdom, despite many setbacks and disappointments.

Vantage point

Even though hearers are responsible for what they do with the message, just to be allowed to hear is a gift of God (v. 16). Response is a duty, but revelation is a gift. The disciples of Jesus have a special place in history. They can see Jesus' deeds (11:4) and hear his words. They are watching the fulfilment of Israel's hopes, and this is a moment for which many in Old Testament times longed and yearned (v. 17). The disciples have not yet fully understood, but they are on the way. This is indeed a blessing, the unveiling of a mystery.

Long division

Since the end of chapter 9, Matthew's story has portrayed a mixed reception to Jesus' mission in Israel (9:34; 10:17; 11:20; 12:10). Many are unreceptive, swayed by other pressures, suspicious and sceptical of what Jesus brings. So this portion of chapter 13 has an important role. It helps the reader to interpret the advancing story, to see behind the varied attitudes of the people. The text from Isaiah in verses 14–15 is a reminder that God's word has not always been well received in the past. Yet the confident words of verses 16–17 speak of God doing a new thing. Here is – for those who will respond – a moment of fresh promise and rich harvest.

Prayer

Thank you, God, for the privilege of hearing your good news. Help us to value it. Through Jesus Christ our Lord. Amen

47 Matthew 13:18-23

Grounds for hearing

Because the disciples have been given a special moment of opportunity (13:16), Jesus stresses that they must listen (v. 18). The parable concerns them: it is about people who hear and what they do with the message afterwards. Indeed the interpretation of the parable begins by striking exactly that note: 'When anyone hears the word of the kingdom and...' (v. 19). So these verses offer a challenge to every reader: what are we doing with the gospel; which of the four groups in the story matches our response most closely?

Soil types

The four soils where the seed landed are typical of people and the different receptions they give the word. One person simply does not grasp what is said. Another reacts brightly for a while, but lacks the solidity to stand up to persecution and pressure. A third has too many competing concerns and ambitions, is too tightly bound to material possessions, and so finds no real room for nurturing the message until it shapes heart and life. Only the fourth hears, understands and bears fruit – in deeds and a renewed life. It is typical of Jesus (7:21–27) and a long Jewish tradition (for example, Micah 6:8) that hearing and doing belong together. Jesus' words were always intended to affect the way people lived.

Old, old story

The parable of the sower has come to us in three phases: the parable itself (13:3–9); the middle section (13:10–17) about sight and blindness; then the explanation of the parable. N.T. Wright (in *Jesus and the Victory of God*, SPCK, 1996) shows how this structure is curiously similar to an Old Testament passage from Daniel 2. That too speaks of a God who reveals mysteries (2:28–30), of a strange story, in this case a dream (2:31–36), and of its interpretation (2:37–47). The three slices are admittedly not in the same order. But the similarity is quite detailed.

In Daniel, as in Matthew, the mystery involves several phases – the earlier parts of the story ending in waste and the last phase showing the triumph of the kingdom of God. In both passages God's kingdom involves the revelation of a mystery; only some are given to understand it; it rises amid alien powers, and eventually triumphs after setback and opposition. So Jesus stands within an older Jewish tradition, telling a veiled story. Yet he now proclaims the moment when God's kingdom appears. Still there is opposition, setback and delay, but there is also the prospect of abundant fruit.

What's in a name?

We call this the 'parable of the sower', but by the end of the story the sower is almost a forgotten character. His work is done, and the emerging results are the real focus of interest. That brings us back to the question posed in the comments on 13:1–9: is this about failures or about fruitfulness, about plentiful harvest or patchy harvest? The 'parable of the soils' might be a better title, if we think the main emphasis is on the differences in the ways that people respond: they react differently just as portions of a field give different yields.

Or we might call it the 'parable of the seed', if we reckon that the chief point is the eventual harvest. One Old Testament echo suggests that the stress should be on these final results. Isaiah 55 speaks of God's word not returning to him fruitless, but producing seed and bread (55:10–11), and triumphing over thorns and briars (55:13). So in Jesus' story, the word triumphs, to produce a full and lasting crop. But the name 'parable of the sower' should not be dismissed completely. This whole section is about Jesus himself. This is a parable about a man who teaches in parables. Jesus himself is the sower. In his ministry, God's kingdom has arrived. But it grows and advances gradually and quietly, like seed rising up to harvest.

Spring of life

Jürgen Moltmann, in *Jesus Christ for Today's World* (SCM Press, 1994), points out that the gospel parables frequently describe growth and harvest. They picture a world laden with potential, where it is always springtime and fresh promise is bursting to the surface all around. This is the kingdom of God, the spiritual environment in which we are invited to live the Christian life.

Prayer

God of life, let us live as people of hope and expectancy, bearing fruit that will endure, rejoicing in your rich provision for us in Jesus Christ. Amen

48 Matthew 13:24–30, 36–43

Tangled growth

This is the first of six parables beginning, 'The kingdom is like…' (vv. 24, 31, 33, 44, 45, 47). They expand on the story of the sower, to give a fuller insight into how God's rule grows. Like the parable of the sower, this story has an explanation attached. But the explanation is not given straight away – there is a pause before the meaning is unveiled.

Creative suspense

The interval between parable (vv. 24–30) and interpretation (vv. 36–43) achieves two purposes. First, it reminds Matthew's readers that Jesus did not give instant answers, nor explain his material to everyone. Parables were intended to stimulate thought and to lead to response. Because of their cryptic style, the parables were always potentially divisive, sharpening the interest of those who wanted to follow Jesus, puzzling any who did not. Second, the gap creates room and time for us as readers to think about the meaning of this parable for ourselves. It draws us into the story, and into the crowd who were themselves trying to understand what Jesus intended.

Weeding between the lines?

Tares are a mongrel form of wheat, with smaller leaves, suitable for chicken feed but quite unfit for human consumption. A few tares would be almost inevitable in a field of sown corn. But when a disconcertingly large quantity is discovered, the first thought is to weed them out immediately (v. 28). However, that would be risky if the roots were tangled, for then the corn would be uprooted too (v. 29). So the farmer follows another plan. He lets both crops grow together and will separate them when they are fully grown (v. 30).

Spelling it out

The explanation falls neatly into two sections. Verses 37–39 are like a little dictionary. They define the meaning of each of the words in the parable. Then verses 40–43 tell a new and parallel story, of the coming judgement of God, as the destination to which the parable points.

These verses bring out a number of themes that are important in Matthew, emphases that occur again and again: Jesus as Lord and judge of the world; judgement that divides and rewards people according to what they have done; the call to be 'righteous' (v. 43). The parable itself ended (v. 30) with an echo of the judgement preaching of John the Baptist (3:12; Luke 3:17), which Jesus had himself taken up. The explanation of the parable stresses and explains this theme. But what Matthew must have seen, and the first hearers may not, is the view from after the resurrection. The coming judge, whose power now spans the whole world, is Jesus himself.

Putting evil in its place

Following the parable of the sower, which showed a very mixed response to Jesus' kingdom preaching, this parable of the wheat and tares has offered a broader understanding of the complex mystery of good and evil. There is an 'enemy' whose malicious work is spread wide in the world. But evil has a limited span of life: in God's good time it will be finally and fully destroyed. The kingdom may seem hampered and blocked by much opposition and ungodliness, but God's eventual victory is certain and sure.

There is no call here for panic measures to separate good from evil, for there is no easy and practical way of drawing a line between them. The church must wait. Jesus may have deliberately taken a different approach from some Jewish groups of his time. Groups such as Pharisees and Essenes were keen to form pure religious community, where all the members would be godly and righteous, and where contact with outsiders might be rather limited. Jesus was more open. He was in no hurry to put a firm and permanent boundary around his own group of followers. God knows who is serving the kingdom, and in due time God will judge truly and rightly.

In the meantime, Christians are called to be 'salt of the earth' (5:13), influencing its life, attracting others to Christ, and playing our part in the energetic and certain growth of the gospel – which is graphically illustrated in our next passage.

Prayer

May God grant us the persistence to do our work, and the patience not to try to do God's. For Jesus Christ's sake. Amen

49 Matthew 13:31-35

Majesty in miniature

The two short parables in verses 31–33 balance the picture of the wheat and tares in verses 24–30, and together the three stories help to expound the parable of the sower. The sower spoke of a piecemeal, even apparently erratic, set of responses to the word of the kingdom, but still looked forward to an abundant final harvest. The wheat and the tares showed how good and evil must live side by side for the moment; there are serious difficulties to be endured before God's final triumph comes into view. These next two little comparisons tell of the promise and power the kingdom has within it; their focus is on the sureness and scale of the coming glory.

Growth point

The mustard seed was tiny indeed, but could grow to be a sizeable shrub, expanding far beyond its original scale. Its usefulness in the parable is not in the initial smallness alone, nor in the great destiny, but in the way that one is already stored and stirring within the other. There is a massive contrast, but also a close correspondence, between start and finish. Jesus invites his disciples to look beyond the difficulties and opposition of their own day. These small beginnings have immeasurable power within them, to lead to a glorious end.

Jesus stretches his illustration beyond its natural scope. The mustard plant was big for a vegetable, but it scarcely counted as a tree. Yet Jesus echoes an Old Testament text which describes God's coming rule as a great cedar (Ezekiel 17:22–24). He appears to be suggesting, 'Nature has no proper match for the remarkable growth of the kingdom; it will surpass all the scales and parallels available.' And by alluding yet again to the scriptures, he roots his own vision in the history of God's dealings with Israel. He is no maverick. The nation's whole tradition of faith and grace is coming to focus in him.

Lifting power

In a couple of other places (Luke 15:3–10; 18:1–14) we find a pair of parables together, one about a man and the other about a woman. Jesus was rather unusual among Jewish teachers, in welcoming women into his circle of followers and learners. His teaching reflects the work and world of women as well as of men.

The yeast parable (v. 33) is not an exact parallel to the mustard seed. Nothing is said directly about the smallness of the yeast. But Jesus points to the hiddenness of the rising process (see wording in RSV, or NRSV footnote). The effect is invisible, yet almost explosive. Three measures of flour makes more than 50 large loaves – enough for quite a crowd. Perhaps this short word-picture hints at an incident to come (see 14:15–22).

The word 'hidden' is picked up in a couple of other places in the next few lines, at verses 35 and 44. The kingdom is growing in a quiet and concealed fashion, and the cryptic language of the parables is part of that growth. But when the hidden suddenly comes into our view, we should grasp it as surely and strongly as we can, like treasure turned up in a field.

Hiding secrets

Matthew's gospel often stresses the fulfilment of scripture in Jesus' life and work (as in 8:17; 12:15–21, for example). The quotation from Psalm 78:2 in verses 34–35 speaks of secret things being brought to light. The parables have the capacity to reveal the kingdom. Yet even when they are brought into the light, they remain hidden; there are people who cannot grasp their truth. These parables both reveal and conceal; they explain and they exclude. So the crowds have work to do in weighing the stories in their minds. But as the gospel moves on, it moves indoors to the privacy of 'the house' (13:36) where Jesus will teach his disciples.

Forward movement

Jesus' vision of God's kingdom is dynamic. It has an inner power. It reaches, quietly and yet surely, for a splendid and spectacular future. It is obscure now, like the parables themselves. Though small amid the world's doubt and opposition, it will shine in God's good time with the greatness and grandeur of heaven.

Prayer

Lord God, when everything around us seems to cloud and obscure your love, give us calm and confident faith, to wait and watch for the coming growth of your work. Through Jesus Christ our Lord. Amen

50 Matthew 13:44–52

Treasure new and old

So far, the parables in this chapter have spoken of the kingdom's struggles, and of its certain growth. They trace what God is doing. Now come three short, punchy stories that urge us to join in.

Doing business with God

It must be every farmer's dream to turn up a hoard of gold coins beneath the blade of the plough (v. 44). In the Holy Land, territory that had often been fought over, there was always a chance. A former tenant might have hidden valuables in the ground before fleeing or going out to war.

Historians have puzzled over the legal background. Would it be lawful to cover treasure up and then buy the field, without telling the owner? Certainly that question could have been in Jesus' mind. Perhaps he told the parable with a twinkle in his eye, to stir people into thinking about such an odd and dubious tale. But his main point is at the end of this little story: the kingdom is so important, it is worth everything you have to make sure you secure it.

That matches exactly the parable of the pearl merchant (vv. 45–46). Again the story is about a single treasure which turns a businessman into a lover. Suddenly he can no longer simply buy and sell. Here is something so precious that he must possess it. And so he is possessed by it; he gives himself to make sure he gets it. This is not commerce; it is commitment.

Matthew has already shown his readers a couple of times that Christians must not be preoccupied by property and possessions (6:19–34; 10:9–10). These two little stories, with their line about 'selling everything', remind us that seeking and serving God's kingdom may involve material sacrifices. Commitment to Christ includes the commitment of our wealth.

Coming to the surface

A drag-net was long, and hung from floats a few feet beneath the surface of the water. It could be positioned by two boats and then hauled in by ropes to the shore. The sifting of the catch was an everyday job, but Jesus uses it as a picture of God's great day of judgement (vv. 47–48).

An explanation is given with the parable, rather like the one that followed the wheat and the tares (13:37–43). But the focus here is sharper: nothing is said about waiting; there is only one point, the final sorting out. The emphasis is on the down-side of judgement (vv. 49–50). Alongside the two little treasure parables, which stress the excitement of finding the kingdom, this strikes a solemn warning. It is vital to be 'righteous', to be like soil that welcomes the gospel seed, to grasp the kingdom when the opportunity arises and to serve it faithfully from then on.

The first time I worked carefully through Matthew, I was struck by its solemnity. This gospel presents discipleship seriously. Every one of the five long discourses ends with a parable about judgement and reward (see also 7:13–27; 10:41–42; 18:23–35; 25:31–46). 'Don't be casual,' Matthew seems to be saying. 'Don't take the kingdom for granted. Take it seriously.'

Wealth to share

The disciples have been given privileged insights into the parable material (13:11, 36). They still need to 'hear' (13:18, 43) and to respond earnestly and actively (vv. 44–46). But their nearness to Jesus gives them a special role. They have been able to understand, and now they can share that understanding with others. They will have a teaching role in the church to come.

So when Jesus says, 'Have you understood?' he goes on to speak of the 'scribe trained for the kingdom' – someone who knows the ancient scripture, and can use it to proclaim and explain the freshness of God's kingdom. Treasure is to be grasped (v. 44), but also shared (v. 52). The kingdom message is to be passed on, in a way that shows its firm base in God's past work.

So the disciples' task is threefold: to grasp the message of the kingdom; to live by its truth, as people whose lives will be judged; and to share its message.

For reflection

The gospel still needs teachers whose message is up-to-date and yet is firmly grounded in ancient scripture. There is just a suspicion (see the section 'Who was Matthew?' in the Introduction, p. 13) that 13:52 is Matthew's own 'signature', his hopes and ideals for his own teaching ministry. Could it also be yours?

51 Matthew 13:53–58

No local hero

This passage is a counterpart to 12:46–50. There Jesus gathered his new family, the followers who wanted to serve God with him. Theirs was the company where he felt he belonged, where he could find sympathy and support, whereas in today's passage he goes back to the district where he grew up. The people there – quite understandably – recall him and relate to him as a member of his old family. No wonder that this was not a very easy or happy encounter.

Moving on

Each of the five major blocks of teaching in Matthew has a very clear ending: 'When Jesus had finished…' (v. 53; compare 7:28 and 11:1, for example). Matthew lets his readers know that they are returning to the action of the gospel. But the parable chapter has sharpened our expectations: will people understand; will they grasp the kingdom; what sort of ground will the seed fall upon?

The next couple of chapters show some very varied reactions to Jesus and his cause. Many people show faith and give praise, but there is hostility too, and the prospect that Jesus will die a martyr's death begins to come into view. By the time we meet the next concentrated instalment of teaching in chapter 18, it has become clear that there will be a painful clash ahead.

More questions than answers

Jesus moves on from the lakeside to the western hills of Galilee. It seems (although it does not say directly) that he comes to his own home village of Nazareth, and teaches during sabbath worship in the synagogue. Nazareth was a small place, off the main routes – the sort of tight rural community where people knew one another well. Jesus' old neighbours remembered his upbringing among them, and a number of his relatives still lived in the area.

There are six questions in a row in verses 54–56. These begin with amazement (v. 54) and end in disbelief, disdain and disapproval (v. 57). The people in Nazareth know plenty about Jesus. 'Where did he get all this from?' is a question they feel they should be able to answer.

They cannot believe that there might be another aspect to Jesus' life, something about him that they do not understand. The same sort of question crops up in another setting, in John 6:42.

Carpenter's house

Joseph was a skilled craftsman. The word used in verse 55 commonly means 'carpenter, woodworker', but it can also refer to a small building contractor, who made houses out of mudbrick and wood.

Jesus' brothers are named, and his sisters are mentioned, for the only time in this gospel. These may have been younger sons and daughters of Joseph and Mary. However, many Christians throughout the church's history have wondered about another explanation: either that these were Joseph's children by an earlier marriage, or that they were actually Jesus' cousins, children of the other Mary who appears at Matthew 27:56. None of these suggestions can really be ruled out.

A number of these relatives later believed in Jesus and took leading roles in the spread of the Christian faith after the resurrection. On this occasion, however, they offer him little support.

Fortunes of a prophet

There are other ancient sayings to roughly this effect, that an emerging public figure receives scant applause on home ground (v. 57). This particular proverb surfaces in all four gospels (Mark 6:4; Luke 4:24; John 4:44), though not always in exactly the same setting. In the end, Jesus acknowledges his former neighbours' lack of faith, which has prevented him accomplishing much in Nazareth.

So the visit ends on a note of disappointment. But a more disturbing and distressing shadow is about to fall, for Jesus has described himself as a prophet, a spokesman for God. John the Baptist too is a prophet (11:9; 14:5), and we are just about to hear of John's imprisonment and death (14:3–12). It seems that a prophet's eventual fate may be a good deal worse than home-town scepticism.

Prayer

Holy Spirit of God, teach me to see the goodness you have put in my neighbours. Give me grace to rejoice when friends show gifts I had never noticed. And when people are unimpressed by me, help me not to get angry, nor to give up what I ought to be doing. For Jesus Christ's sake. Amen

52 Matthew 14:1–12

Pointer to the Passion

This is one of the few passages in the gospel that is not directly about Jesus, one of few scenes where he is not on stage. John was a man of spiritual depth and great courage, who deserves much credit for his ministry. But in all four gospels he is far more than a prophet (11:9). He is the forerunner whose work launches and prepares for the work of Jesus. Jesus has spoken of him with warmth and honour (11:10–19). The preaching of the two men had a lot in common (3:2; 4:17). So when John comes to such an ugly and undeserved end, the reader may rightly fear what will become of Jesus.

Troubled tetrarch

The 'Herod' of this passage is Herod Antipas. His father, Herod the Great, was the king who had tried to kill Jesus at birth, and had himself died a year or two later, in 4BC. Antipas ruled a third of his father's lands – Galilee, and Perea on the east bank of Jordan – under the permission and power of the Roman Empire, until AD39. He was known as 'tetrarch', which means 'ruler of a quarter', but was not allowed to use the title 'king'; that was Rome's way of reminding him who was really in charge.

Herod was disturbed to hear of the attention Jesus was attracting and the signs he was performing. Although Herod had recently executed John the Baptist, here was a new prophet creating just the same sort of stir as John had done. Like so many others (13:13, 54–58), Herod completely fails to understand Jesus. But before we return to Jesus, and hear of his response to Herod's interest (14:13), Matthew explains how John died.

Man in a corner

Herod had switched wives, abruptly and illegally. John criticised him for it, and Herod threw John into jail (see comment on 11:2–3, p. 90). But once John was locked up, Herod himself was trapped. He wanted to kill John and silence him forever, but he was afraid of popular opinion (v. 5). There was a corner of his own conscience, too, that was disturbed by John and would not have been comfortable with the idea of putting him to death (Mark 6:20). Herod had no easy room for manoeuvre.

Dance of death

According to the Jewish historian Josephus, writing about AD100, John died at the desert fortress of Machaerus, high on a mountain-side east of the Dead Sea. Archaeologists digging at Machaerus have found the remains of two separate large dining-rooms, which would match the indications (clearer in Mark 6:14–29 than here) that men and women dined separately on festive occasions.

The whole affair seems sordid and demeaning. The dancing princess is simply used by the adults around her. Her mother Herodias comes across as a cynical opportunist. And Herod – the host who should be in control, the man responsible for law and order – is totally spineless, cornered by 'his oaths and his guests' (v. 9) into an action that lacks any trace of justice or dignity.

But John is dead. His active ministry is over, although the memory of what he has said and done will not be easily quietened. Herod himself could not shake off the memory of that murky night (vv. 1–2), and (again from Josephus) his public image and popularity never quite recovered from this episode.

Matthew's gospel says a good deal about the pressure and persecution that frequently come to God's prophets (5:12; 21:33–39; 23:29–39). In a few chapters' time, it makes a direct link between the death of John the forerunner and the fate that is waiting for Jesus (17:12–13). For the moment, those connections are not underlined. But Jesus would surely have realised, when he heard of John's death (v. 12), that his own work could become increasingly difficult.

For thought and prayer

Dangers always arise when power is not linked to principle, and when people use public office for their own pride and pleasure. Criticism is sometimes a right Christian response – as it surely was when John challenged Herod Antipas.

But quick and thoughtless criticism is unlikely to be helpful. More regular, more constructive, are the commitments that Christians have to pray for our rulers, and to offer respect, support and obedience whenever we properly can. We should pray too that in every generation people of faith and integrity will come into public life, to serve God and neighbour there.

53 Matthew 14:13-21

Table in the wilderness

Alone with a crowd

Jesus withdraws to a lonely place. But the wording of verse 13 is not very clear. Has he just heard of John's death (14:12)? Or has he heard of Herod's concern about his own ministry (14:1-2), so that he feels the need to avoid an ugly confrontation (as at 4:12 and 12:15)?

Surely Jesus wanted to reflect and pray about the growing atmosphere of conflict and danger around his ministry. It appears (from Mark 6:45 and John 6:1) that he went to the area around Bethsaida on the north-east shore of the Sea of Galilee, just out of Antipas' territory. Jesus did not lack courage. But he did not want to provoke a needless and premature clash. He may already have realised that he would finish his work in Jerusalem (Luke 13:33).

Jesus is pursued by eager, needy people. They come for healing, but the remoteness of the place, and the time taken to get there, lead quickly to another concern: where will they get food?

Dinner in the desert

The word 'evening' (v. 15) has a pretty broad span, starting in mid-afternoon. But there would be little food available in the small, unwalled hamlets and local farmsteads. 'You give them something to eat,' seems mysterious, and even perverse. John 6:6 says that Jesus was testing the disciples, but Matthew's writing style is very compressed, and he does not dwell on this sort of detail.

The resulting expansion of food is spectacular indeed. Bread and fish were the staple foods in Galilee, and there was plenty to be shared that day. Matthew's first readers might have thought back to the Old Testament, to Moses with the manna and quails (Exodus 16; Numbers 11). But the clearest echoes in the story are of a lesser-known passage, Elisha's bread miracle in 2 Kings 4:42-44.

As well as looking back, the episode points ahead. Israel looked forward to a great banquet with God (Isaiah 25:6-9; see also Matthew 8:11), and this desert feeding would suggest to some that Jesus was ushering in those days of prosperity and hope. Some other popular leaders in this era, so-called messiahs, had also promised signs and gathered excited crowds in the desert. No wonder, then, that Jesus was hailed as a 'king' (John 6:14–15). But again he stepped aside (Matthew 14:23). God's kingdom was growing under his leadership (13:31–33), but he was not the sort of king many people wanted.

Lord's supper

The language of verses 18–19 matches Matthew's account of the last supper (26:20–29): 'When evening came... he took bread, blessed, broke, and gave to the disciples.' The earliest Christians told the story of this feeding in ways that showed a clear connection to the last supper, and so to their own sharing of bread and wine in Holy Communion. Jesus nourishes his church spiritually at his table, as surely as he fed his first followers in the lonely hills of Galilee.

But the connection works the other way round too. Matthew's story suggests that Jesus is already gathering and tending the community that will become the Christian church. He has been harried by Pharisees, cold-shouldered in Nazareth, and growled at by Herod. As many in Israel turn against him, Jesus starts to shape a new community, a people within a people, and feeds them in a way that already foreshadows the Christian Eucharist.

But what really...

But what actually happened? Could Jesus really multiply bread and fish? Certainly Matthew believed it; the feeding is mentioned again (16:9), in a way that shows he thought it true. The other gospels include it – only this miracle, apart from the resurrection, comes in all four. The numbers five and two (v. 17) have no obvious symbolic meaning – which tends to suggest that they were remembered from the event.

C.S. Lewis (in his book *Miracles*) links this feeding to our belief in God as creator. We know that God can multiply fish in the sea and corn in the field, although we are accustomed to God doing this gradually. But when God comes in human flesh, just occasionally he shows this creative power as if it were accelerated, compressed into Jesus' ministry of care and compassion (v. 14).

Prayer

To God who is known in creation and compassion, in humility and humanity, be praise and glory, now and always. Amen

54 Matthew 14:22–36

Steps of faith

This passage has two messages, entwined around one another. The first concerns who Jesus is. These verses present him in a new and fresh light, and show the disciples growing in faith and understanding. The second message is pastoral, about faith and how it operates. It invites Christians to see ourselves as the disciples in the boat, or even as Peter struggling to stay afloat, and to place our trust in Jesus. For Matthew, the two messages go together: because Jesus is Lord of the storms, he is worth trusting in our own times of turbulence and fear.

The action takes place at night. If the first 'evening' (14:15) was the slight cooling of the afternoon sun (see comment on 14:15, p. 126), this second 'evening' (v. 23) must be the deep dusk of falling night. 'Early in the morning' (v. 25) refers to the last few hours of the night, from about 3 o'clock onwards.

Presence in the storm

This is the second sea miracle in Matthew (the other being 8:23–27). When the wind blew through the steep valleys around the Sea of Galilee, the waters could get rough and rowing would be hard. Then Jesus comes, portrayed here in ways that speak simply and directly of the presence of God.

He walks on the sea, as only God can do (Job 9:8; Psalm 77:19). He greets his friends, saying, 'It is I' (v. 27): the words echo the 'I am' of God's presence in Exodus 3:14. His 'Fear not' (v. 27) recalls Isaiah 43:1–2: 'Fear not… you are mine… when you pass through the waters I shall be with you.' This is truly Emmanuel, God with his people (1:23).

Wading for God

In the next few chapters there are several places where Peter takes the lead among the disciples (15:15; 16:16, 22; 17:4, 24; 18:21; 19:27), and most of these episodes are mentioned only in Matthew. This gospel, in particular, shows Peter emerging from the group of disciples as spokesman, venturer, even as leader. During these chapters, which foreshadow the life of a new community called the church, we meet the man who will become its first leader.

Here Peter emerges from the group, and quite literally goes overboard for Jesus (vv. 28–29). He comes over as impulsive, committed and enthusiastic, but also as fragile, ordinary and vulnerable. Many Christians find him an attractive character for that reason. We see something of ourselves in his undulating spiritual pilgrimage, his blend of devotion and disaster. Here Jesus calls him, 'You of little faith' (v. 31; the same word used at 6:30 and 8:26). Peter is not faithless, but his faith is faulty, patchy, not complete or secure.

Yet Jesus trusted Peter, and went on doing so, even after Peter's threefold denial on the night before the crucifixion. You do not need to be perfect, or have an armour-plated Christian faith, to hold office in the church. Doubts are allowed (see 28:17). But it helps to be honest with God – and with yourself – about your failures.

Faith finding solid ground

For the disciples as a group, this experience was a moment of growth in their faith and understanding. The incident ends with, 'Truly you are the Son of God' (v. 33), which is a stronger and clearer ending than their 'What sort of man is this?' of 8:27. They do not know Jesus nearly as well as he knows them. But their eyes are starting to open.

Contagious mercy

Gennesaret is an area of flat land stretching back a few miles from the north-west shore of the Sea of Galilee (v. 34). Again Jesus encounters a throng of needy people, but the whole episode is summarised in just a couple of sentences. There is scarcely any detail, only this: Jesus appears as a pious Jew, wearing a robe with a tasselled hem (Deuteronomy 22:12), and that is what people touch to find healing (v. 36). In the crowd there may be all kinds of unclean people. But when they touch Jesus, he does not become impure too. The influence flows the other way. Jesus communicates the wholeness and mercy of God (8:3; 9:20–22), for the healing of others.

But matters of purity were important to Jews, and our next passage centres on just this issue: what makes a person truly clean?

Prayer

Pray for any people you know who are struggling to stay afloat, who feel insecure and unsupported, that they may know the steady hand of Jesus reaching to them and holding them up.

55 Matthew 15:1–9

Clean hands and a pure heart (1)

There were many debates in Judaism about interpretation of the nation's ancient law. Jesus got involved in these, in the sermon on the mount. He spoke about 'righteousness that exceeds that of the scribes and Pharisees' (5:20) and, in the 'Six Antitheses' (5:21–48), Matthew shows him dealing with a number of legal questions.

Since that sermon, ill-feeling has been rising. Scribes and Pharisees have become a regular irritant in Jesus' ministry (9:3, 11, 34; 12:2, 24, 38), while his popularity has made him a serious nuisance, so far as they are concerned. He strikes them as dangerously lax, teaching his followers to live an irresponsible and irreligious life (9:14; 12:2). So this clash is no surprise. But there is a sinister feel about it.

Questioners come from Jerusalem (vv. 1–2); Jesus' reputation has evidently spread. He answers back quite aggressively at his questioners (vv. 3–9). Once before, he felt seriously threatened by Pharisaic anger, and moved out of danger (12:14–15). After this incident he will move on again (15:21).

The whole episode (15:1–20) unfolds in three scenes. The first (vv. 1–9) shows Jesus in discussion with scribes and Pharisees.

Honour your elders

Pharisees wanted to live by the biblical ideal that Israel was a 'priestly kingdom and a holy nation' (Exodus 19:6). So they tried to import some of Israel's priestly laws into daily life, so that home and table would express in a small way the holiness of the temple. The priestly duty of handwashing before temple service (Exodus 30:17–21) was one of these laws. To observe it at every meal was a 'tradition of the elders' (v. 2), handed down from one generation of Pharisees to another. But Jesus' disciples do not follow this pattern. 'Why not?' the visitors ask.

Jesus defends his disciples. He counterattacks on the issue of tradition, which had been the basis for his opponents' question. 'Your tradition,' he says, 'violates a basic command of scripture' (vv. 3–6).

Jesus refers to the practice called *korban*, the making of vows. It was possible to assign property to the temple, and call this a vow to God (Deuteronomy 23:21–23), without actually losing one's right of ownership. A tight-fisted person could adopt this device in order to protect wealth, and could avoid having to help needy neighbours or support elderly parents. So it was possible to use a biblical law about vows to break the command to honour father and mother (Exodus 20:12).

Lips and lives

It is all too easy to say one thing and to do or desire something else. Our words may be very godly, but what we really want, and how our motives work out in action, might be rather different. That, according to Jesus, is the problem with the scribes and Pharisees. Tradition has taken over. Building on scripture, tradition has actually eclipsed and obscured the real force that is in scripture. Their words sound grand; the real character of their religion is not.

The quotation in verses 8 and 9 is from Isaiah 29:13, in a chapter which speaks of God leading Israel from blindness to sight (Isaiah 29:10, 18). Sight is an important theme in Matthew. Jesus offers people a fresh view of the presence of God, but those who persist in blindness (15:14) he regards with suspicion verging on despair.

Open table

There were some big differences between Jesus' approach to religion and that of the Pharisees. He was not committed as they were to the idea of tradition. When he taught, he did not start with the sayings of other teachers, from a generation or two earlier. His 'I tell you…' (8:11; 12:36) was much more direct. He showed a great personal authority. He reflected for himself on the Old Testament, and on the work of God in his own times and ministry.

Jesus appeared casual and careless to some of his opponents. He was not bound by other people's custom. But this freedom allowed him to be very open in personal relationships. With Jesus, meals were an occasion for showing the wide mercy and care of God (as at 9:9–17), not for expressing a strict and exclusive purity.

For thought and prayer

May God grant us wisdom to see when our tradition diverges from truth, or destroys trust, or causes more trouble than it is worth. For Jesus Christ's sake.

56 Matthew 15:10–20

Clean hands and a pure heart (2)

The discussion about purity continues. The opponents slip out of view, as Jesus turns first to the crowd (vv. 10–11), then privately to his disciples (vv. 12–20). He wants to deepen his disciples' understanding and also to give the crowds – many of them people without fixed opinions – a chance to respond to his teaching. Although Jesus' clashes with scribes and Pharisees become more painful as the gospel goes on, the crowds remain supportive (see 21:46). Only very late in the gospel does their attitude change.

Which matters more – input or output?

Thus far Jesus has met his opponents' question by counter-attack. In stressing tradition, he said, they stand on very shaky ground. Now he answers directly the question they raised: why don't his disciples wash as the Pharisees do? Here – very briefly, and to be expanded later – is the nub of his argument.

Food and purity laws attend to what goes into the mouth, what a person eats and drinks: only if input is pure will the person be pure as well. Jesus disagrees. True purity, he says, is not known by the mouth's input, but by its output (v. 11). Our speech shows the quality of our inner self – sometimes with the utmost clarity (12:33–37).

Blind guides

In the final phase of this long conversation, Jesus is talking with his disciples. There are two parts: the first (vv. 12–14) refers again to the scribes and Pharisees; the second (vv. 15–20) will explain at greater length the brief saying in verse 11.

'The Pharisees took offence' (v. 12) – presumably at the attitude to purity that Jesus had just stated (v. 11). He is unmoved by their anger. If they are not rooted in God's purpose, their faith will lack staying power; they will be like tares amid the wheat (13:24–30, 36–43). They objected to his healing of a blind man (12:22–24), but they are the truly blind ones. They cannot help others to find the way of God, because they cannot see it for themselves. In spiritual matters we can rarely lead other people into wisdom we have not first made our own.

Teaching to digest

Verses 15–20 clarify the little saying in verse 11. Peter calls it a 'parable' (v. 15), meaning that it is a riddle, a cryptic and perplexing statement (see comment on 13:3, p. 110). So Jesus explains himself.

Food, which goes into our mouth, does not contaminate a person, because it is digested and then goes to waste. It does not become a permanent part of what we are. But what comes out of our mouth comes from the heart, and reveals our true nature. It is the heart that gives rise to all sorts of wrong actions, and these actions make for real uncleanness.

This list (v. 19) includes several of the ten commandments (Exodus 20). Jesus mentioned the fifth command in verse 4. Now come the sixth, seventh, eighth and ninth. All of them express the love for neighbour that Jesus regarded as such an important standard of human behaviour (7:12; 22:39).

Finally the discussion ends where it began. 'Why don't your disciples wash their hands?' (15:2). 'Because eating with unwashed hands does not make a person unclean' (v. 20). The ceremony really doesn't matter. It does not touch the roots of real uncleanness in the human heart.

Side by side

It is interesting to compare Matthew's version of this conversation with Mark's. For example, Mark includes some words of explanation (7:2–4) which Matthew's audience would not need. Matthew has some sharp words about Jesus' opponents, which might have been especially relevant to his readers and their situation (vv. 12–14). The summing up in Matthew 15:20 is not as sweeping a statement as the last few words in Mark 7:19. These differences may reflect the different groups and settings in which the two gospels were written. But the very broad and deep similarities between the two accounts come from Jesus, from the impact he made and the teaching he gave.

For thought and prayer

Focusing on outward conformity is a constant danger for religious people. We feel safe with regular and respectable conduct. Unusual people, who break tradition and sit lightly to custom and convention, are less likely to impress us. Ask God to help you recognise true purity of heart in the people around you. Then welcome that, whatever their personality or style.

57 Matthew 15:21–28

Crossing the frontier

This incident is one of the most puzzling in the gospels. Why was Jesus so slow to respond to the woman's appeal? And why, after refusing at first, did he eventually help? A number of suggestions have been made. We come to them after working through the passage itself.

Lying low

Galilee was a small province, and we have already seen Jesus moving out of range when Herod became curious (14:13). After his latest clash with scribes and Pharisees, he goes up into the high ground of northwest Galilee and crosses into lands that belong to Tyre and Sidon. These were port cities, on the coast that is now southern Lebanon, and their territory stretched a few miles inland, to the edge of the Galilean hills. We may picture Jesus pausing for a few days in a highland village, to gain peace and perspective on his work and its effect. Even there his reputation has gone ahead of him.

A woman comes for help. Mark (7:26) calls her a 'Syro-Phoenician' – she belongs to the local area. Matthew writes 'Canaanite' (v. 22), stressing that she is a Gentile; that is the issue around which the whole story will revolve. The conversation has four movements.

Four movements to mercy

'Son of David,' she says (v. 22), hailing him as the Jewish Messiah. Some Jewish traditions thought of the Messiah as a miracle-worker and healer, and she has latched on to this hope. Her daughter is desperately ill, and she needs help. But Jesus does nothing.

Then the disciples join in. 'Send her away' (v. 23). That could mean either 'Refuse her' or, possibly, 'Do what she asks.' Only then does Jesus respond. He speaks of 'the lost sheep of the house of Israel' (v. 24) as his proper mission field.

The woman is not a Jew, but she persists (v. 25). Still Jesus seems reluctant to get involved. Children's bread should not be thrown to dogs. His mission is to the children of Israel, to God's chosen family of faith (v. 26), and he seems unprepared to spread his work.

Eventually the woman breaks through. Even if Gentiles are 'dogs', a dog may come near enough to the table to gather up the crumbs that spill, and so share the same food as the family. So finally Jesus commends her 'great faith' (v. 28), and her daughter is healed.

Who's listening?

Different readers respond in different ways to this story. Some see the woman pushing Jesus to do something he had not intended to, opening his mind, and expanding his vision of what his mission could be. He had a narrow Jewish perspective (as in 10:6), and it took her persistence and stubbornness to shake him out of it. He healed her daughter, but she taught him what it meant to be God's Son – not just a Jewish Saviour, but a man for others too.

A different approach would observe that Jesus had already worked among Gentiles (see comments on 8:5–13 and 8:28–34). He was impressed by the centurion's faith, surpassing anything he met in Israel (8:10). And in this meeting with the Canaanite woman, it is faith that settles the matter. So another way of reading the story is to see Jesus as the person pushing the conversation to its eventual destination, testing the woman by his hesitancy, to show the quality of her faith. Does she really recognise that 'salvation is from the Jews' (John 4:22)? Is she ready to trust another nation's grace?

Ahead of her time

As you think about the passage, you may want to keep two things in mind.

First, the New Testament is clear that the gospel is for the whole world. But it comes to the world through God's long work of preparation within Israel. Only after the cross and resurrection was the good news fully released to the Gentile nations. This Phoenician woman has come to faith ahead of time. She has pressed into the kingdom from outside, a first-fruit of a great harvest ahead, a sign and pioneer of the gathering of the nations. She is – in more ways than one – an exceptional believer.

Second, recall that Jesus told a parable about a woman's persistent prayers (Luke 18:1–8). He admired faith that was unyielding and determined, the sort of trust that could hold up even when tested.

For reflection

Prayer sometimes has to be persistent and determined, to gain all that God has for us.

58 Matthew 15:29–39
Signing off

The incidents earlier in this chapter have shown Jesus adopting an unconventional attitude to the Jewish law, and extending his grace beyond the fringes of Israel. He has spoken as a loyal Jew, emphasising scripture (15:1–20) and the special place of the chosen nation (15:21–28). Yet his work will eventually strain to breaking point his relationship with the leaders of his own people. Matthew 16 will begin Jesus' long pilgrimage to Jerusalem and the cross. From then on there will be less emphasis on signs, and more on suffering. The last couple of sections of Matthew 15 conclude his ministry in Galilee.

Mountain of mercy

Mark 7:31 suggests that Jesus went to the Decapolis, Gentile land southeast of the Sea of Galilee. But this passage in Matthew is not directly parallel to Mark's, and is not specific about place. We only hear that Jesus went to a hillside near the sea, and sat down as if to teach (v. 29). Then, as people brought sick and disabled friends, he healed them. This is almost the last of Matthew's short 'healing summaries'. Others were at 4:23–25; 8:16–17; 9:35–36; 14:13–14, 34–36; two more snippets follow, at 19:2 and 21:14. This account is distinctive, for it ends on a note of glad gratitude to God (v. 31). God is at work in Jesus, and God is to be praised for Jesus.

Second sitting

This feeding (vv. 32–38) is told in a very similar way to the previous feeding of 5,000 (14:13–21), although the dialogue at the start between Jesus and his disciples is not identical (vv. 32–34). The numbers involved are different too – seven loaves, 4,000 people and seven baskets picked up afterwards. Yet once we get to the feeding itself, the two accounts stay closely in step (vv. 35–38; 14:19–21). Once again there is a strong resonance with Matthew's account of the last supper, and so with the church's Holy Communion service.

Some readers of the Bible think that these two accounts go back to a single incident, that Jesus would not have done this sort of thing more than once. But it becomes clear, in a few verses' time (16:7–12), that

Matthew thinks of two separate feedings. The early Christians remembered and spoke of two feedings. And they told of these feedings in words that also recalled the last supper. So they remembered, when they shared bread and wine, the power and provision of their Lord.

Homecoming to God

Some careful scholars have found echoes of Israel's Old Testament hopes in these verses.

- Crowds of people come together on a hillside, like pilgrims going up to Mount Zion, in Jerusalem (Isaiah 2:2–4).
- The healings reflect the hopes of Isaiah 35:5–6, a chapter which ends with the redeemed of the Lord coming in praise to Zion.
- There may also be an echo of Isaiah 29. God judges shallow and stubborn hearts (29:13, quoted at Matthew 15:8–9), but brings healing and hope to the needy (Isaiah 29:18).
- There is a banquet, like the promise of Isaiah 25:6–9, a feast for peoples from far and near on the mountain of God.

If these connections were in Matthew's mind, then he is hinting that an age of promise has come, and that prophecies are fulfilled. Jesus is God's great meeting point, the new gathering place for the faithful. 'Something greater than the temple is here' (12:6). The nations will come to him, to learn of Israel's God. That hint becomes clear and compelling at the very end of Matthew's gospel, when good news goes out to reach the world (28:18–20). In Jesus God is known, God is with us, and the world may come to God.

Going out alone

After many have been fed, Jesus leaves. Magadan (v. 39) is a mystery. There was a lakeside town called Magdala; perhaps Magadan was near there, but we do not know for sure. There are uncertainties ahead too, as the coming chapter will bring testing, warning and sorrow. The gospel is beginning to move towards the cross.

Prayer

For the mercy of God in Jesus Christ, seen by those who knew him in flesh, shared with us who trust him in faith, be thanks and praise to Israel's God, now and evermore. Amen

59 Matthew 16:1–12
Rising opposition

Noblest foe-men

Sadducees appear, for the first time since 3:7, to question Jesus. They were a much smaller group than the Pharisees, and were based in Jerusalem. This group of a few wealthy families controlled the religious and economic life of the temple, monopolised the succession of Jewish high priests, and wielded a good deal of judicial and political influence. By comparison with the Pharisees, they appear as rather worldly ecclesiastics; but they had a great deal more clout.

It is curious to meet Sadducees in Galilee. However, some rich Jerusalem families had big agricultural estates in the northern part of the Holy Land. So possibly some Sadducees heard of Jesus through local contacts or when visiting their property.

Colours of day

Verses 1–4 include a large 'textual variant': some of the most ancient copies of Matthew that we have omit most of verses 2 and 3. A footnote in your Bible may mention this. We really do not know whether Matthew wrote those two verses or not. (The verse numbering does not help; it was inserted long after Matthew's time.)

If we left out verses 2–3, then what remained of 16:1–4 would be very similar to 12:38–39. But one small difference here is the word 'to test him' (v. 1), which makes this interrogation seem like devilish work – for Jesus' temptation by Satan was also called a 'testing' (4:1).

If the 'missing verses', 2–3, are included in this little dialogue, then they make the point that even Jesus' opponents should have spotted what God was doing through him. They can read the sky when they have to, but cannot read the marks of the kingdom of heaven. They are perverse in asking 'a sign from heaven' (v. 1), for they ignore the signs they already have of God's activity on earth.

Crumbs of comfort

If ever a conversation starts off like ships passing in the night, with no point of contact or even of real hearing, here it is (vv. 5–12). It seems more typical of some of the misunderstandings in John's gospel (such as 3:1–16 or 4:7–26), than of Matthew. The two halves of the conversation begin at the same time, and both mention bread, but they set off in opposite directions.

'Beware of the yeast of the Pharisees and Sadducees,' says Jesus (v. 6), meaning his opponents' influence and teaching.

Meanwhile it occurs to the disciples that they meant to bring bread and had not done so. They respond as if Jesus were asking about the supply of sandwiches (v. 7).

So Jesus calls them 'little faith people' (v. 8; as at 8:26; 14:31). Their faith is real, but it does not always connect very well with experience. They should have realised that he can supply hungry people when he has to. They have seen him do that twice. He would not need to worry about a few loaves, if his friends were in need (vv. 9–10).

'You should have understood,' says Jesus, 'that I wasn't using the word "yeast" literally.' Finally he says again, 'Beware of the yeast of the Pharisees and Sadducees' (v. 11), and this time his friends realise that he means the opponents' teaching.

Of course Jesus knew what he was doing. Often the best teachers work by provoking their hearers to think. The best-remembered lessons can be those which were a struggle to grasp. The conversation with the disciples converges in the end, and they eventually understand what Jesus means. The teaching of his enemies could have a yeast-like effect, expanding to fill the minds that absorbed it, influencing habits and outlook. So Jesus warns his disciples that much is at stake. Are they prepared to listen to him as their teacher, and follow his view when it differs from more popular or respectable opinion?

For thought and prayer

Most of us are shaped by the thinkers and attitudes we follow. In Matthew's gospel one of the most vital tasks of the church is to heed and pass on the teaching Jesus has given (28:20). This gospel reminds us to weigh everything that invites our loyalty against his words and outlook. The teaching of Jesus is still a solid basis and a wise guide for living, for people who are ready to take it seriously.

60 Matthew 16:13–19
Rock formation

Jesus' relationship to the leaders of his own nation is under strain. There are hints already that he is shaping the community which will become the Christian church. Now we start to see this community more clearly, and hear of Jesus' own plans and desires for its life.

Question time

The zig-zag movement around Galilee continues. Caesarea Philippi is in the far north of the area, out of Herod's territory. Again we get the impression that Jesus wants some quiet time with his disciples. His opinion poll (v. 13) receives a range of answers. All of them cast Jesus as a prophet, returned to minister to God's people.

When Jesus asks for the disciples' view, then Simon Peter's ringing affirmation (v. 16) confirms and expands what they began to see before (14:33). Peter recognises Jesus as much more than just a spokesman for God. For him, Jesus is Israel's promised Messiah, bringing the life and presence of God to his people with new depth and power.

First base

Although verses 13–16 are also in Mark and Luke, the next snippet (vv. 17–19) appears only in Matthew. It makes several points:

- Simon's faith is a gift of God. Only God gives that sort of insight.
- From now on, Simon will be called 'Peter', the rock-man. There is a word-play in Matthew's Greek: *petra* means 'stone' and *Petros* is 'Peter'. And in Aramaic, the language most Jews spoke, the link is even more direct. The name given to Simon is *Kepha*, the exact word that means 'stone'.
- On this rock Jesus will build the community he is shaping. Peter and the faith he has declared will be the base on which the church will grow and stand.
- Forces of evil will not destroy the church. It will have the life and strength to prevail against all assaults and trials.

- Peter will lead the church as it opens the kingdom of God, drawing many in, but also 'binding and loosing', setting out the way that believers should live. (See also comment on 18:18, p. 156.)

Splintered rock?

I am writing this as a Reformed Christian in the cordial hospitality of a Roman Catholic college. The church is divided, and our understanding of these very verses reflects some of these divisions.

- There is an old-established view in the Greek-speaking churches, going right back to the third century, that the 'rock' is Peter's faith, and that he stands for the typical Christian believer.
- The idea that the 'rock' is Jesus, whom Peter has just confessed, comes from the great African theologian Augustine (about AD400), and was taken up strongly by the 16th-century Reformers.
- The understanding that Peter himself is the 'rock', and that his authority has been handed down to his successors, the popes, has been held by many Roman Catholics since the fifth century.

Digging in the Bible

So what is the text saying? I think the word-play on Peter's name is important – it does suggest that Simon Peter himself is the 'rock'. Then there is an echo of an Old Testament passage, Isaiah 51:1–2, which describes Abraham and Sarah, the father- and mother-figures of Israel, as the rock and quarry from whom the nation's life was cut. They were founders and prototypes of faith, who could hand on to others the heritage of grace and trust into which God had drawn them. That is Peter's position: the prototype Christian believer, the new Abraham of the Christian church, the rock of a new community.

Finally, it is important to me that Jesus does not say 'churches'. The church is one, even though it has been hard to live by that ideal. All Christians – whether or not we take Communion together, and however we interpret Matthew 16 – belong to the one family of faith that started to find its identity in the far reaches of Galilee when Peter said, 'You are the Christ, the Son of the Living God.'

Prayer

Give thanks for the firmness of God's purpose, for the faith God has given the church, and for the promise that no evil will destroy this worldwide fellowship, in which Jesus is known as Son of God.

61

Matthew 16:20–28

Solemn departure

'Don't tell anyone,' says Jesus (v. 20). He is keen not to be misunderstood by the crowds, careful not to give opponents any grounds for acting against him. He did not want the wrong kind of acclaim (see also comments on 9:27–31 and 14:13–21, pp. 77, 126–127). The disciples too would have to learn that his kingdom involved suffering and a cross.

New direction

'From that time on, Jesus began...' (v. 21) matches the wording of 4:17. That earlier text led the way into the Galilean ministry; this verse points the road out of Galilee to Jerusalem and crucifixion. If the stretch from 4:17 to 16:20 is Jesus' mission, then 16:21 onwards is his passion, his long journey to the cross. From Caesarea Philippi in the extreme north of the land, the movement is southwards, with a consistent focus on the holy city.

Unexpected rejections

Jesus' words (v. 21) are solemn and shocking. The earlier hints of trouble brewing have not seemed as harsh as this. Jerusalem is far from these Galilean hills and shores, and rejection so bitter and final by the central authorities of his own people seems a wretched and worthless end for God's Messiah. All Peter's loyalty and emerging faith rises up in protest and pain (v. 22).

Then suddenly the rock-man feels himself reduced to dust (v. 23). His attitude is wrong. His perspective is human, not godly. He is an obstacle in Jesus' path. He is the summons of Satan, beckoning Jesus aside from the way he must take, like the enticing words of temptation in chapter 4.

What about Peter's statement of faith, from just a few verses ago? Was it real? Surely it was, but it was fragile too. Peter, like the other disciples, was a person of 'little faith' (16:8), keen to believe, though not always alert to what faith means in practice. His failure here does not rub out his earlier gain. In the realm of faith, as with so many other activities, progress can be slow and painful. Growth often leads to new challenge, to fresh struggle and to deeper learning.

The 'must' that Jesus speaks (v. 21) is a deliberate commitment to a path laid out for him. In his own prayers, in his reflection on scripture, in his sense of God's calling, has come the conviction that he must suffer and die in the service of the kingdom. Yet he also believes that God will prove faithful, that he will be vindicated, that beyond death will be life. Along this road he takes his followers.

Following hard

Verses 13–20 showed the church's faith, its privilege and final triumph; here we see the hard way of discipleship along which faith must walk. Jesus called his friends to costly obedience. Matthew's readers would realise that they too were summoned to a life of demanding service. And so are we.

Verses 24–25 are very similar to 10:38–39 (see also comments there, p. 88). 'Carrying the cross' will mean different things for different people – it depends on our circumstances. But whoever we are, and whatever the life we lead, we have not signed up for a cost-free Christianity. Faithful service is always likely to involve sacrifice, which may be unpredictable, inconvenient and intrusive. Jesus asks us for a basic decision to put him ahead of our own interests or desires. Only then will we 'find our life', in time and eternity.

Kingdom coming

Verse 27 offers assurance to fearful disciples. The Christian road has a destination. It is not just a journey of suffering. Faithful following will be gloriously and lastingly worthwhile. Jesus will honour the commitment his disciples make to him.

Verse 28 is difficult. It seems to suggest that the 'Son of Man coming in his kingdom' will happen soon. Could it refer to the fall of Jerusalem in AD70? If this was seen as God's judgement on the city that condemned Jesus, it might also point to his vindication and heavenly glory. But see further on chapters 24 and 25 for much material on Christ's coming and judgement.

For reflection

Carrying the cross means directing yourself to Jesus as your model for living... Self-denial means knowing Christ alone, instead of yourself, and watching him... rather than looking at the road.
Ulrich Luz

62 Matthew 17:1–9
Mountaintop experience

Jesus has spoken of the hard road he must take to the cross, and of his coming heavenly glory. Now comes an advance vision of that glory. He talked of founding a new community. Here he also stands honourably within Israel's ancient heritage of faith. In it all he receives the backing and approval of heaven. This transfiguration invites the disciples (and the reader) to follow Jesus without fear.

Speaking for the past

A riot of biblical connections link Moses and Elijah to one another and to Jesus (v. 3):

- One represents the law and the other the prophets – the two main portions of ancient scripture.
- Both were 'mountain men'. They met God on Mount Sinai – Moses amid cloud and glory, so that his face glowed with mysterious light (Exodus 24:9–17; 34:29–35); Elijah when the burdens of his ministry crushed him, yet God gave him assurance and encouragement (1 Kings 19).
- Both are, in different ways, forerunners for Jesus. Moses spoke of a coming prophet like himself (Deuteronomy 18:15–18), and Matthew has shown how Jesus takes up this mantle of Moses (see comment on 2:13–23, pp. 26–27). Elijah was expected by the Jews as road-maker for the coming of God (Malachi 4:5–6; Luke 1:17), to bring reconciliation and peace to the nation. He stands for the dawning of promise, the coming fulfilment of Israel's hopes.

Together these two great figures bring the witness of the Old Testament to endorse the Messiah of the New. Both of them point to Jesus – Moses as pattern, and Elijah as herald.

Voice of God

Peter's offer (v. 4) is unnecessary, though well-meant. We cannot freeze-frame our deep experiences of God. Nor can we add anything to the sight of God's radiance. There are times, in worship and in our walk with Christ, when it is best simply to wait, to enjoy the presence of the Lord, and to relish this awareness of his greatness and love. Pray for those occasions, by all means. But do not try to preserve them. Let them be sufficient in themselves to sustain your journey ahead.

The cloud both reveals and conceals. God is present, in 'cloud and majesty and awe'. God's voice repeats the words of 3:17 (at Jesus' baptism; see comment there, pp. 30–31). Jesus is God's anointed king, the sacrificial Son and the servant who will bring God's justice and victory to the waiting nations. The final command, 'Listen to him' (as at Deuteronomy 18:15), casts Jesus in the role of a new Moses. All the promise of the past rests on him as he goes humbly to the cross.

Quietly down

The three disciples fall to the ground and, as Jesus gently raises them to their feet, the vision has gone: they are there with him, alone (v. 8). As they walk down to join the others, Jesus presses them to say nothing of the experience – for the present. (Similar silence commands come at 8:4; 9:30; 12:16; 16:20.) Spreading their memories of this moment would cause confusion and trouble. Only after the resurrection will Jesus' glory be properly understood.

Gate of glory

By any reckoning the transfiguration is something of a mystery. What did the disciples see and how did they know it? What was Jesus expecting, and how did the experience help him? And how can heaven be revealed on earth?

Perhaps we are not going to find complete answers. There is majesty here that we cannot fathom. C.S. Lewis suggests (in *The Great Divorce*) that the stuff of heaven is not nebulous, elusive and shadowy, but firmer and more solid than our own world. We cannot yet know the full glory and grandeur of God. The depth and density in God's being are presently beyond us. The disciples were allowed a brief and special vision. Yet the transfiguration is a glimpse of things to come, for the whole church. For Christ is risen (v. 9), and all who love him will one day see him as he truly is (1 John 3:2).

Prayer

God of time and eternity, all heaven praises you. Accept our praise for all we have known of you, and for all you have yet to show us. Through Jesus Christ our Lord. Amen

63 Matthew 17:10–20
Facing suffering

This section could have been called 'Down to Earth'. However splendid the mountain view, you must eventually come back to the valley. As Jesus and his friends make their way down, suffering comes into sight, in two ways. First Jesus speaks about John the Baptist's suffering and his own. Then they meet a needy family, desperate for help. If the high-spots of our Christian life can help us to face the cost of our own discipleship and the needs of our neighbour, then they are high-spots indeed; if not, perhaps we should be a little suspicious of what they seem to offer.

Elijah incognito

The appearance of Elijah raises the question (v. 10; see comment on 17:1–3, p. 145), 'Is Elijah going to come back, then? Does the transfiguration give a new angle on that hope?' Jesus' reply is positive, but rather disturbing: 'Yes, the tradition is right. Elijah is meant to come, as a preacher of righteousness in Israel, just as the scriptures say.' But Elijah has come and the nation did not recognise him. It was John – the rough desert prophet – who took the role of Elijah (11:14). He had a strong popular appeal, but the religious leaders of the nation were not impressed (21:25, 32), and Herod killed him. 'They did to him whatever they pleased' (v. 12). His work was not given the attention or respect it deserved.

Then Jesus warns his friends that the Son of Man – Jesus himself – will suffer as well. Jesus' first direct prediction of his passion and death was at 16:21, and as the warning is repeated a number of times in these chapters (17:12, 22–23; 20:18–19, 28), it casts a shadow over this long journey to Jerusalem.

Son of God, Son of Man

This little conversation meshes with what has come before, to complete an interesting pattern:

Jesus as Son of God	*Silence command*	*Jesus will suffer as Son of Man*
16:13–19	16:20	16:21–28
17:1–8	17:9	17:10–13

Twice over, words of triumph are followed by words of tribulation – splendour by suffering. What holds all this together is that Jesus, the suffering earthly Son of Man, will also come as the glorious heavenly Son of Man (16:27). The glory of the transfiguration is not just a mist of summer, doomed to vanish in the heat of suffering. Both transfiguration and cross are the real Jesus. He is the Son of God, now ascended in glory. He is also the Lord who walked as one of us and died our death, sharing the pain and perplexity of human living. He has known the agony; he is no stranger to hurt and distress.

Helpless for healing

It is a fearful and desperate business to watch a sick child and be unable to heal or help. The father of this boy unloads his pain and fear before Jesus (vv. 14–16).

Jesus heals the child (v. 18). The verse says, 'The demon came out of him'; you may like to read the comment on 8:23–34 ('For clear minds', p. 70), on the issue of demon involvement. But verse 17 is strange: it seems that Jesus too has been drawn into the distress, and is frustrated that his disciples' faith has been unable to overcome it. Yet again the disciples are 'little faith people' (as at 6:30; 8:26; 14:31; 16:8). They have faith that 'understands and assents, but which does not trust God totally' (J.P. Meier). If only they had the tiniest quantity of true faith, it would have the expansive power of a mustard seed (13:31–32), and then obstacles would move before them.

(Note: verse 21, about prayer and fasting, is not in the earliest copies of Matthew, and is left out of most modern Bibles. But it may still have something to teach us.)

For prayer

Pray for children who suffer, for parents who fear for them and suffer with them, and for people whose work is to share the caring and try to help.

64 Matthew 17:22–27

The costs of belonging

These two snippets have a common focus: the community of Jesus and its relationship to the central religious life of Israel.

Pilgrim people

'As they were gathering in Galilee' (v. 22) is the assembling of pilgrims before a journey. Many Jews, from around the Holy Land and from much further afield, travelled to Jerusalem for the annual Passover festival. Jesus and his friends are about to set off. We see the company moving on from Galilee at 19:1.

At the start of the journey, Jesus warns them that this will be no ordinary Passover (vv. 22–23). The disciples hear his sombre words, not with sharp contradiction (16:22), nor just with quiet understanding (17:12–13), but this time with deep sorrow.

Many church buildings include a large wooden cross as a focus for the eyes and thoughts of the congregation. In the looming shadow of his own crucifixion, Jesus will speak to his friends about how to be church (ch. 18), about the care, trust and mutual commitment they need, to live as his family.

Count me in

But first comes a question about whether Jesus and his company are committed to the religious life of the Jewish people. The temple tax required each adult male Jew to make an annual payment of half a shekel – about two days' wages. Although not compulsory, it was viewed as a patriotic duty. Capernaum was Peter's home town and was Jesus' base, if not his fixed abode. So the local collectors ask whether Jesus will pay or not (v. 24).

Jesus speaks about freedom. God is a Father to his people and does not tax them. The kingdom is a realm where God gives generously and God's people respond with their grateful and glad commitment. Any sort of compulsory religious tax, the collection of an obligatory and measured slice of income, is a poor reflection of that relationship. This may also be the reason Jesus attacked the money-changers in the temple (21:12–13). Money should not block or control people's access to God.

But Jesus will not cause unnecessary offence. He tells Peter to pay the tax – with a curious little saying about a coin in a fish's mouth.

Gold-fish

This saying (v. 27) is rather like the parable about treasure in the field (13:44). Routine daily work yields an extraordinary return. Some people think that Jesus was telling Peter to do a day's fishing, and so earn enough to pay the tax. But the language is very specific – 'cast a hook, and take the first fish that comes' – and that suggests an unusual find.

So did Peter simply have an uncommonly good fishing expedition? Or did he manage to do what others have occasionally done, and hook a fish that had picked up a coin dropped in the water? Whatever Jesus meant, this little saying matches a regular theme of the gospels. With Jesus, creation acquires a new generosity – bread and fish for thousands, water becoming rich wine (John 2), miraculous shoals of fish (Luke 5; John 21), provision from God (Matthew 6:31–33). The kingdom is about glimpses of light and generosity breaking through from heaven. And this fish saying points to an event on the limits of normality, 'a significant crack in ordinary experience… to enable us to glimpse… the dawning of the kingdom of God' (R. Bauckham, in *Gospel Perspectives*, Vol. 6, ed. D. Wenham and C. Blomberg, Sheffield Academic Press, 1986). God, for whose temple the tax was gathered, provides the wealth for his children to pay.

For reflection

While writing this, I spoke with a friend who was promoting local development in a remote part of South America. For some of our neighbours, in many areas of the world, creation seems to have lost its generosity. Crops fail, health is hard to sustain and medicine difficult to afford, children grow weak, nature's resources are scarce. Christians may, in a small way, be copies of Christ if we will help others to discover and enjoy the wealth that God has put in his world. Let us thank God for the missions and relief organisations who help that to happen, on behalf of us all.

65 Matthew 18:1–9

Reception class

Chapter 18 is the fourth block of teaching in this gospel, and the theme is Christian community. Jesus speaks with his friends about their life together. Matthew is the only gospel to use the word 'church' (16:18; 18:17); for him the church is a strong, caring family.

Trouble with the ranks

Twice on this journey to Jerusalem, Jesus has to contend with his disciples' ambition (also at 20:20–28). As his own thoughts are drawn repeatedly to his coming suffering, his friends have not really grasped what it should mean for them too to take up the cross (16:24). So when they ask about rank and importance in the kingdom of heaven, Jesus leads their thoughts in a very different direction.

Small world

The word 'child' crops up repeatedly in the first few verses. Jesus calls a young child into the company and then says, 'This is how you have to be, to receive the wealth and dignity of God's kingdom.' The disciples, who are so concerned about position and precedence, must turn their attitudes right around and become like children.

So what was it about children that Jesus meant? Many answers have been suggested: children are innocent, gentle, uncomplicated, eager, expectant, receptive, humble, and so on. While all that is surely true (if not for every child all the time), it may miss the point. For children did not have much status in the ancient world; they were not thought very important. Jesus counters that view later (19:13–15), but here he uses it to explain the attitude that Christians should adopt.

The child-like attitude is to reckon ourselves truly unimportant, as 'less than the least of all God's people' (Ephesians 3:8), and genuinely to 'count others better than ourselves' (Philippians 2:3, RSV). Then we shall be small enough to know the greatness of God. Then we shall be 'great in the kingdom of heaven' (v. 4). Then we shall be generously open to Christ's other 'children' (v. 5), and in receiving them we shall be blessed by the presence of Christ himself.

Steps to stop stumbling

The first paragraph was about 'children'. The two words that appear next are 'little ones' (18:6, 10, 14), and 'stumble' or 'stumbling block' (six times in vv. 6–9). The nearest English equivalent to 'stumbling block' is probably 'banana skin'. But in these verses there is a moral aspect to making someone stumble: it is a wrong thing to do if it leads them astray and interrupts their walk with Christ.

The 'little ones' are other Christians, the people who are called 'children' in the preceding verses. Christians should recognise one another as fragile and vulnerable, as people to treat carefully. It is a fearful and serious matter, says Jesus, to drag a fellow Christian down. He warns his followers to be very careful of the effect our behaviour may have on others.

Strong language

Jesus makes his point forcibly and colourfully. A 'millstone' (v. 6) was the heavy top stone of a corn-grinding mill, that needed a donkey to drag it round. Jesus says it would be better to be sunk in the ocean by such a weight than to cause a 'little one' to fall. And it would be better to lose a hand or foot or eye than to be led by our own actions or desires into losing our faith (vv. 7–9).

What this means, so far as I can see, is taking care about how we live, and being watchful not to damage someone else's Christian life, or indeed our own. It is easy to be casual about conduct and lifestyle: 'Everyone has different ways of living these days... I'm an individual, I'll work it out for myself... God will forgive, that's his job.' This text urges a different approach.

Adrian Plass discusses these verses in his *View from a Bouncy Castle* (Fount, 1991). He tells of a woman who changed her regular commuting arrangement and started taking a different train. She was developing a friendship with a man who travelled with her, that looked as if it might encroach on her marriage. So without great guilt or anger, but decisively and calmly, she stopped seeing him. That's probably not your problem. But your Christian life is a precious thing too, and is worth making an effort to protect.

Prayer

May God grant us vigilance, common sense and a humble heart. For Jesus Christ's sake. Amen

66 Matthew 18:10–14

Searching question

One of the tragedies of church life, in almost every congregation, is the number of people who used to be heavily involved and have now stopped coming. Sometimes people fall suddenly out of the fellowship, as abruptly and visibly as mud flung off a wheel. Others drift away gradually: almost without anyone noticing, their enthusiasm for Christian worship and service seems to wane and wither. Matthew's gospel sets that issue within the much broader commitment that we have to care for one another's Christian lives, and to support and sustain one another in our walk with God.

Looking down

Looking down upon other people, despising those whom we find difficult to get on with or who are very different from ourselves, is a real temptation even in the Christian church. It is often easier to keep company with like-minded Christians of easy personality than to be genuinely receptive in spirit (18:5) to all the people of Christ. Verse 10 urges us to overcome that barrier, for the hosts of heaven look down in love on all Christ's 'little ones', rejoicing in our faith, not put off by our awkwardness, and glad when we love one another.

(Note: verse 11 is not in the earliest copies of Matthew, and was probably not written by Matthew. It comes from Luke 19:10, and may have been written into some copies of Matthew 18 because it connects so well with the story of the lost sheep in the following verses.)

Love that en-folds us

Jesus told a parable about a lost sheep in Luke 15:1–7, to explain his own habit of spending time with people who seemed far away from God. He wanted to help them find their way back. Here in Matthew is a very similar story, but with a different purpose to its telling. It urges the church to give time and effort to seek wandering Christians, and to help them back into the fold.

There is a lively debate about why two very similar stories are used in two rather different ways. Did the early Christians use a parable of Jesus that was originally about himself, and give it a different twist, so that it applied to their own church life? Or did Jesus, like many an itinerant preacher, use the same story more than once, for rather different purposes? Either way, the church is to do what Jesus did, and seek the wanderer in patience and love.

Some people wander away because of 'stumbling blocks' (18:6–9). They make a serious mistake and then find it hard to hang on to their Christian commitment. Or somebody else leads them off the tracks and they are not confident enough to make their own way back. Whatever has happened, none of us has the right to 'despise' (v. 10), and many of us may have a part in the gentle friendship, help and prayer that lead the wanderer back. It could have been – perhaps it once was, or it could yet be – us.

Searching question

The searching question is at the start of verse 12: 'What do you think?'

Is it not risky to leave 99 sheep on their own in the open country? This is not the cautious approach of percentage farming. Is there not a trace of favouritism in rejoicing more over one that returned than over 99 that did not stray? What balanced and sensible community does that?

Again Jesus is using picture-language to make a point that could be stated a good deal more plainly. The church is not like any other community. People are more than percentages. Every one is important. This is a community where the last, the least and the lost can be first, favoured and found.

What do you think?

For prayer

Thank God for the people who have helped you to find the way of Christ, and to stay on the Christian road thus far.

Pray for the people who look to you for guidance, leadership and example.

Pray for anyone you know who has dropped out of church life, that they will come into contact with friends who can help them back.

67 Matthew 18:15–20

Restoring presence

Many a church has occasionally to deal with serious breaches of good conduct and trust within its fellowship, and there are times when no comfortable or tidy resolution can be found. In some situations the safety of young or fragile people requires firm and careful action (as 18:6–9 suggests). But when responsible adults fall out we can often reach for reconciliation and try to restore a measure of trust. The advice in this section of Matthew 18 has a similar aim.

The word 'child' ran through verses 2–5; then in verses 6–14 Christians were 'little ones'. Now Matthew's word is 'brother' (twice in v. 15, then in vv. 21 and 35), properly translated in some modern versions as the inclusive 'brother or sister'. Church is family: even in times of dispute, we belong to one another.

Falling out

Verses 12–14 urge the church to restore the person who has wandered away. But what do you do when there is deep hurt and tension within a local fellowship, so that people no longer feel confident to worship or work together? First, try to settle it privately (v. 15). Talk it over. You might turn out to be wrong, and find more good in the other person than you expected. Or you might be listened to. Either result would be a gain for you and for the whole congregation.

If the first stage leads nowhere, one or two other people can be drawn in (v. 16), primarily to listen, possibly also to advise, and to bring some balance and perspective to a stubborn disagreement. The reference to 'two or three witnesses' comes from the Old Testament (Deuteronomy 19:15), where a person could not be judged on the word of one witness alone.

A third stage involves the whole congregation (v. 17). This passage seems to assume that a local church will be small enough, and well-enough known to one another, to be able to help. Perhaps any company small enough to be damaged by a personal dispute also has a responsibility for helping to sort the problem out. The last resort seems to be exclusion of the offending party. But that need not be the end of the matter, for there is always the hope of restoration (18:12–14).

Binding rules

Verse 18 is very similar to 16:19. What was said of Peter there now applies to the whole church. 'Binding and loosing' probably means taking decisions about right and wrong, about how Christians should behave, and about what sort of practical commitment to godly living we owe one another.

The church has a duty to its members, especially when disputes seem insoluble, to offer the security of guidance and judgement. When the church accepts that responsibility with good conscience and care, then God honours and backs what we do. The considered guidance of our brothers and sisters comes to us as from God; only a very solemn matter indeed would justify our ignoring that wisdom.

Not on our own

Verses 19–20 support and encourage the church as it takes up the duty of verses 17–18. Even in a small fellowship, if Christians can pray in agreement and common concern, God answers the desires of their praying and stands with them in what they seek to do. Jesus – Emmanuel, God with us – is a dynamic presence, constantly moving the church forward in fresh hope, like the bright and tender company of God on the exodus journey (Exodus 13:21–22; 33:14).

In this together

While it may be rare for the three-stage procedure (18:15–17) to be followed right through, I have known the first stage – frank and private conversation – to produce a surprising growth in understanding and trust. One would need to be deeply concerned about an issue, and feel that a lot was at stake, to go much further than that.

The ability of the church to handle difficulties of this kind appears to depend on three things: faith – a grain is enough (17:20); fellowship – the readiness of Christians to pray and act together (18:19); and forgiveness – a heart that can let go of personal grudges, without keeping the score (18:21–35). Even to say the Lord's Prayer together requires a forgiving spirit (6:14–15).

Prayer

God of peace and light, may our churches be places where quarrels can be settled, where prayer draws us together, and where love can grow. Through Jesus Christ our Lord. Amen

68 Matthew 18:21–35

Forgive us our debts

As so often, especially in Matthew, Peter speaks out. He pursues an issue from the earlier verses. 'Suppose a fellow Christian offends me, and we sort it out. Then it happens again. How many times must I forgive? How far does Christian forgiveness stretch?'

Counting out

Peter offers a first bid, of seven. To forgive the same person the same fault seven times could well test our calm and courtesy. Seven times can seem quite a lot of forgiving, if we have to do it. Yet Jesus puts that figure in a very different perspective. 'Not seven,' he says. 'Many more times than that.'

Jesus' reply means either 'seventy-seven', or 'seventy times seven'. But exact numbering was not what he intended. He was taking the Christian duty of forgiveness right out of the realm of arithmetic. We are to stop counting, and simply get used to forgiving, for the forgiveness of God is loving and limitless.

Pass it on

Each of the five major blocks of teaching in Matthew ends with a solemn parable about judgement. The point in this parable (vv. 23–35) is that if we cannot pass on the forgiveness of God, we may find our own experience of it turning out to be hollow.

The parable pictures a king summoning his administrators to collect the proceeds of their work (v. 23). Galilee may have known just such a summons, after Herod Antipas visited Rome about AD29, and Jesus could be using that piece of news in his parable. A talent represented about 20 or 30 years' wages, the equivalent of a large mortgage. So the first servant's debt was astronomical (v. 24). No normal sum would be as large as this. The debt is utterly unpayable and the situation has gone far beyond recovery.

Yet the debt that could not be paid is pardoned (v. 27), and the servant goes free. Then he meets one of his subordinates, whose accounts are also out of balance (v. 28). A denarius is a day's wage, so this is a much smaller sum. But the servant treats his colleague harshly, and has him locked up until friends and family can settle the account (v. 30). He is totally unwilling to pass on his master's pardon to his fellow servant. The upshot is that the king withdraws the forgiveness he originally granted, and the story ends in bitterness and misery (vv. 31–34).

Copies of Christ

'So also...' says verse 35. We shall not enjoy the forgiveness of God unless we share it. We have not really grasped it unless we can pass it on. The church has to copy Jesus in its pastoral care (18:12–14), and also in its willingness to forgive.

Unless we can forgive, we shall not know real security and acceptance with one another (18:5, 10). We shall not be very good at seeking the wanderer (18:12–14). Our grievance procedures (18:15–17) will be harsh, with no sense of reconciliation about them. Yet when forgiveness flavours all we do together, then the church is a very special kind of community – truly the people of Christ.

Should you ever...

Should you ever not forgive? Are some deeds so bad that you cannot forgive? I can think of three limits that must operate in practice.

- If a person is unrepentant – say someone swindles us in business and is quite proud of having done so – we cannot really offer forgiveness and expect a positive response. But we may owe it to ourselves to forgive inwardly, before we are eaten up by annoyance.
- Jesus himself did not create unnecessary opportunities for people to sin against him – he dodged Herod, for example. There is nothing wrong with a proper caution when dealing with people who have hurt us or let us down badly.
- Some kinds of serious offence – for example, criminal actions against another person – do such severe damage that there is no satisfactory way for the people concerned to go on living, working or even worshipping together. Even then, wise Christian friends may have a role in helping all parties to find their separate ways and to live with the memories. We remain, even after unspeakable hurts, a family that cares for all its members.

Prayer

Forgive us our sins, as we forgive those who sin against us.

69 Matthew 19:1–9
Calling for commitment

Jesus sets out for Jerusalem, travelling down the east side of the Jordan (v. 1). The concentrated instruction of chapter 18 is over, but teaching continues about the way Jesus' followers should live. In the Christian community, marriage and children are valued (19:1–15), commitment will often involve sacrifice (19:16–30), and some worldly values become strangely irrelevant (20:16, 27).

Designed for life

In Jewish society of this time, only the husband could initiate a divorce action. Deuteronomy 24:1 allowed divorce for 'a matter of indecency' and there were various opinions about what sort of grounds would fit this law. Stricter teachers believed that the law only applied to adultery. Others, freer in their interpretation, permitted divorce 'for any cause' (v. 3) that the husband thought fit. So Pharisees come to test Jesus. What sort of grounds will he recognise?

Jesus does not answer directly, but speaks first about marriage as part of God's design for human life. God made us male and female (v. 4); as male and female we bear God's image (Genesis 1:27). So when man and woman leave the parental home to marry, they forge a firm and solid unit, becoming 'one flesh' together (v. 5; Genesis 2:24). This bond is not meant for breaking (v. 6), either by the couple themselves or by intrusion on someone else's part.

Emergency exit

The Pharisees reply that Jesus has missed their concern (v. 7). He has not mentioned the divorce provision in Deuteronomy 24. So Jesus speaks about that text as God's allowance for human weakness. It was not God's first and ideal plan for our life (v. 8), but was a safeguard, to regulate and restrain our hardness of heart. It does allow divorce, but as an emergency exit – when the other partner has effectively ended the marriage already by forming another sexual relationship (v. 9).

So Jesus draws his teaching back towards God's first ideal: marriage should be treated as permanent. The exit is for emergencies only. Divorce is an obituary, not an opportunity – a sad recognition that the marriage bond is already broken, not a card up a husband's sleeve to be played as desired. Thus Jesus answers the original question (v. 3) by supporting the stricter view within Judaism. Some who read the gospels wonder, however, if his view was even stricter than this.

Just one exception

The divorce sayings in Matthew (5:32, 19:9) include the phrase 'except for unchastity'. Adultery is the one valid ground for divorce. Yet Mark (10:11–12) and Luke (16:18) do not mention this. So was Jesus so totally opposed to divorce that he would not support it even after unfaithfulness? If so, Jesus was stricter than any of his contemporaries, and perhaps the exception clause was then inserted by Matthew to match the teaching of Jewish rabbis.

However, it may be more probable that Jesus, like most Jews of his time, simply assumed that adultery ended marriage. If he did not actually say 'except for unchastity', he may well have taken this exception for granted, and the words in Matthew spell this meaning out.

Believing makes a difference

Divorce as a subject touches many raw nerves. The church can make three important contributions.

- We believe in marriage – as Jesus did. Marriage is meant to last, as one of the building blocks of human living. We urge people who marry to embark on it carefully and thoughtfully – as well as joyfully.
- We believe in forgiveness as pattern for all our relationships, and we try to practise it in church life. Married life too depends on willing and practical forgiveness in the small disagreements and irritations, not only in the major crises. Coping with divorce often involves some serious forgiving too – not least in forgiving oneself.
- We believe that God's love reaches out to us not just when we prosper in faith and fortune, but also when we come badly unstuck. Our pastoral care can reflect that sort of love, for Christ's sake.

For reflection

Marriage is a demanding and serious vocation. The next verses point out that single life can be testing too. Whatever our pattern of relationships, we need the daily grace of God if we are to be faithful to our commitments, and to the people who share them with us.

70 Matthew 19:10–15

Kingdom people

Verses 10–12 continue the discussion about marriage that started at verse 3. Then comes one of the most memorable and moving incidents in the gospels, as children are brought to Jesus for him to put a hand of blessing upon them.

Single-minded

The disciples' rather sceptical comment in verse 10 reflects the impact of Jesus' teaching on marriage. He has raised expectations, supported women's need for security and protection, and assigned to men much more commitment and responsibility than was customary. Marriage is a bond and one is bound by it, is his view. Suddenly the scales seem to be tilting, levelling out the rights and roles of husband and wife. No longer is it a man's world.

'Who is going to want a deal as tough as that?' say the disciples. 'It would be better not to marry' (v. 10). Jesus takes them at their word. 'Do you really mean that?' is his response. 'Not everyone can live up to that sort of commitment' (v. 11). The single vocation is not something that everyone can handle.

Jesus goes on to talk about 'eunuchs' (v. 12), applying that word in a broader way to mean people who do not marry and start a family, but live a single life. Some are made that way by nature: for whatever reason, they cannot seriously consider marrying. Some have been badly hurt by other people, and would now find it impossible to form a healthy marriage relationship. A third group deliberately adopt a single lifestyle because of the opportunities it will allow them for serving God's kingdom.

Perhaps Jesus was thinking of himself in the third group, and explaining why he lived the way he did. But he was also challenging the disciples. Commitment to singleness is a good choice, if made by the right people for the right reasons. But not everyone can or should take this path (v. 12). In any case, people who grumble about the binding ties of marriage may not be very well prepared for commitment to singleness.

Child allowance

Jesus has encountered children a number of times already in Matthew. For example, he has healed children (9:18–26; 15:21–28; 17:14–20), and used a child to illustrate God's kingdom (18:2–5). Yet strangely the disciples still think he might be averse to children's company (v. 13). In the event he turns out to be very welcoming. He overrules the disciples, and the children come to him (vv. 14–15).

'Of such is the kingdom.' The kingdom is for lowly people, who do not think too highly of their own place or position in the world. To children that often comes more easily than to adults. It is not so hard for them to enjoy God's grace, for they are used to receiving, to living by the plans and provision of others. Of course, children have much to learn. But adults sometimes have much to unlearn, habits of thought and behaviour that make it harder for us to grasp God's love and follow his leading. A child comes without that luggage.

So children are welcome in the kingdom, to enjoy the love of Jesus and to help older people to enjoy it too. The story ends as it began, that children were brought for blessing and Jesus indeed blessed them. The last are becoming first (19:30; 20:16).

Children's church?

This story is sometimes used as an argument for infant baptism. I doubt very much if Matthew (or Jesus) intended it to be. The story is both simpler and more far-reaching than that. But it certainly encourages churches to take children seriously, as worshippers and learners of Christ and as people who have something to teach the rest of us. Children remind us not just of how we were but of how we could be.

A leader of Christian work among children recently said, 'I want our churches to be places where children are noticed, valued and protected.' Jesus would have agreed.

Prayer

Pray for children you know, and for their steady growth, in body, mind and faith. Pray for your church, that within its fellowship children may both receive and contribute. Pray for yourself, for an open and child-like spirit in your walk with God.

71 Matthew 19:16-26
Valuing the kingdom

This incident, where Jesus tests the commitment of an eager enquirer, is reminiscent of 8:18-22. There are also a number of connections to the sermon on the mount, so that this passage brings a lot of the teaching of the sermon into focus. Keeping God's commands (5:21-47), being perfect (5:48), handling wealth (6:19-34) and squeezing through a narrow gate (7:13) all crop up in 19:18-24. The man in this episode has been described as a living illustration of Matthew 6:24, trying to serve the two masters of God and money.

Path to perfection

Matthew says that the man was young (v. 20) and rich (v. 22). Luke 18:18 calls him a ruler. He wants to gain the life of heaven and taste the blessings that only God can give. Jesus, however, talks about the kingdom in a different way. The man asks to 'have life' (v. 16), and Jesus tells him to 'enter life' (v. 17). We gain heaven by committed pilgrimage, not as an asset to drop into our investment portfolio.

Then Jesus directs the man to the chief commands of the Old Testament (vv. 18-19): to five of the ten commandments (Exodus 20:12-16), plus the command about neighbour love (Leviticus 19:18). The man knows these well, and supposes that he keeps them – although the reader, who has read through the sermon on the mount, will not be so sure. Loving neighbours, respecting life, staying faithful – these are hard targets (5:21-30, 43-47).

But the man is keen to move the discussion on. There must be something else, he says (v. 20). What is it? So Jesus challenges him. If he wants to be 'complete, perfect, whole' (v. 21), there is for him only one way forward: to share all his wealth among the poor. At this point the conversation subsides into thoughtful silence (v. 22), and we are left to wonder – about him, and about ourselves.

Money makes the world go blind

Jesus accepted hospitality (Luke 10:38) and the help of monied friends (Luke 8:3). But he and his disciples travelled light, and his teaching on wealth carries a sharp edge. Whatever we have, and whatever we give time and effort to, can come between us and God.

The young man in this story seems a superficial character, not really recognising the nature of the Old Testament law, and yet hoping to leapfrog into the kingdom. His wealth has clouded his vision. That, says Jesus, is always the danger. It may push this present world around, but money finds it desperately hard to wriggle into God's coming kingdom (vv. 23–24).

The camel is a fine long-distance runner on sand, but a total non-starter when it comes to sliding through narrow openings. Jesus seems to have found its irregular shape splendidly bizarre (see also 23:24), and here he offers the ridiculous picture of using a camel to thread a needle. All the probabilities are stacked against success. Rich Christians need a special kind of grace and wisdom, to steward humbly and generously what they have been given. (See also comments on 6:19–34, pp. 54–55.)

Possible with God

The disciples are amazed (v. 25). They presumably thought that a large fortune was a sign of blessing. If the rich cannot make it, who can? Humanly speaking, it is never possible, says Jesus. No one comes into the kingdom on their own resources alone. It always depends upon God, who is able to save all sorts of people, often in ways we would not expect (v. 26).

The discussion then runs on to Peter's question (v. 27). The rich young man's problem was an unwillingness to make sacrifices. But the twelve have given up a lot. So, Peter asks Jesus, can they assume that they will be alright? See the next page.

For reflection and prayer

Money is a bad master. We only keep money in its proper place, as a good servant, if we are ready to plan our giving, sharing, saving and spending with Jesus Christ plainly in mind. When the offering is dedicated in church, can you dedicate to God the money you still have in your pocket and in the bank, as well as what you have given? Acknowledge inwardly that this money too is for God's use. You are the manager. Christ is the Master.

72 Matthew 19:27—20:16
Vintage rewards

The two parts of this section speak, in different ways, about the same issue. Work for God can be tough: what will God give in return?

God is no one's debtor

Peter's question (v. 27) arises from the conversation with the rich young man. The twelve have made big sacrifices. Will they squeeze into eternal life? So Jesus speaks of a new world coming (v. 28).

He had chosen twelve disciples to represent the new life of Israel (see comments on 10:1–4, pp. 79–80). Now he looks forward, and recalls the hopes of scripture. As Daniel prophesied the glory of the Son of Man, when kingship will be entrusted to God's holy people (Daniel 7:9, 13–14, 27), so Jesus' followers will share in his authority. They will make his glory and power known in Israel. A foretaste of the fulfilment of these words came in the period after Pentecost. The twelve – who were witnesses of the resurrection – preached to the Jewish people the good news that Christ was risen. (But see also comments on chapters 24 and 25, pp. 197–213.)

Jesus then talks about sacrifices. God asks nothing that he cannot repay many times over (v. 29). Many Christians give up much to follow Christ or serve his church: comfort, material prospects, friendships, home. Sometimes those sacrifices are foreseen and planned; on other occasions they come unexpectedly and painfully. God still honours what people offer him, and he still gives eternal life – yet not always in the way anyone expects (v. 30), as the next parable shows.

Clocking on

Jesus pictures the owner of a big vineyard recruiting day labourers to pick the harvest. Many rural people had little or no land of their own, and needed casual work. A denarius was a typical day's pay, although it would buy only limited sustenance for a big family. Wages were paid daily, as the law prescribed (Deuteronomy 24:14–15); some families lived literally from hand to mouth.

Time is reckoned by a twelve-hour clock, from dawn to dusk. The first group of workers agree for the standard daily amount, and set to work (v. 2). Other teams of workers start later in the day, and there is an element of suspense about how they will be paid. 'I will pay you whatever is right,' says the master to the second group (v. 4), but we never hear what that will be. The hiring of the third, fourth and fifth groups heightens that uncertainty. How will they all be rewarded?

Settling up

The last group are paid first, and receive the normal sum for a whole day's work (vv. 8–9). We then skip over the three middle groups, and watch the first group rubbing their hands in anticipation. If this is the hourly rate, they will surely do nicely. But they too get just one denarius (v. 10).

So some grumbling follows. 'Favouritism, unfairness, injustice, idleness' – we can almost hear the rising tide of resentment and dismay. The master's reply makes two points. First, 'You got what you agreed; that's fair' (v. 13). And second, 'It's my money, and if I want to be generous with it, that's up to me' (v. 15).

Thinking it over

Jesus did not offer the parable as a regular management technique. He knew the master's behaviour was odd. This was part of his teaching method, to help the parable stick in hearers' minds. God is odd, by human standards. God does not always do what we expect or would do ourselves.

This brings us back to the last being first and the first last. The kingdom will bring glorious rewards that completely overshadow the sacrifices it demands of us (19:29). But if we think of those rewards as a right, we have some fresh learning to do (20:16). God will not leave himself in our debt, but nor will he come under our direction. Grace is not measured by hours of service, it is always a gift.

It is always good to see senior Christians, who have done much in their lives, coming alongside young people or newcomers to the faith in a pew or a queue, without any fuss about status or rank. Happy is the church where people mingle on truly level terms; that is one way of preparing for heaven.

Prayer

Teach us, Lord, the art of cheerful giving – of our service, our substance, our selves – for the sake of your kingdom.

73 Matthew 20:17-28
Servant king

Progress to passion

The pilgrim journey to Jerusalem, which started at the beginning of chapter 19, is moving towards its destination. For the fourth time Jesus tells his friends very plainly of his coming death (the other occasions were 16:21; 17:12 and 17:22–23). This is the most specific prediction of what will happen, and the first time the word 'crucify' is mentioned.

Crucifixion was a Roman punishment, though never inflicted upon Roman citizens. It was a humiliating and miserably extended form of killing. The victim was suspended from a rough wooden cross by nails through wrists and feet, and was then left until he was overtaken by pain, exhaustion and death. This is the way Jesus will die.

What might have led Jesus to expect a criminal's death? There are four likely factors. First, he knew what had happened to John the Baptist. Second, he had long been aware of growing opposition to his ministry. Third, he felt drawn, as part of his calling from God, to come to Jerusalem as prophet and challenge the leadership of his people. Fourth, there was deeply embedded in Israel's scripture the thought of one suffering for many (v. 28), a destiny which Jesus sensed as his own.

Eyes on the podium

A number of women (27:55) had joined Jesus' Passover pilgrimage, including the mother of James and John. Her sons are already part of the inner circle of Jesus' disciples (17:1), and all three of them hope for higher things still. Might they become Jesus' chief lieutenants when he is revealed as king?

Jesus must have groaned inwardly. Had they never listened? He responds by speaking of the 'cup' he must drink. In the Old Testament the image of a cup describes the bitter anger of God (Psalm 75:8; Isaiah 51:17, 22), and the suffering it brings. In Gethsemane Jesus speaks again of drinking a cup from God (26:39), and at the last supper this cup represents his shed blood (26:27–28). All of this suggests that the 'cup' means his coming suffering.

So James and John will suffer too. James died by the sword in AD44 (Acts 12:2). We think that John lived into old age, but he endured a good deal along the way. And their mother was one of the faithful witnesses who saw Jesus raised on to a throne (Matthew 27:55–56) very different from the one she first had in mind.

A different greatness

The anger of the twelve looks to be a concern for their own places in the pecking order, rather than any support for Jesus' view. So he gathers them and talks about his style of leadership. Gentile rulers were strong on ceremony, dignity and pride. People quailed with terror when presenting petitions to the Roman Emperor. The Christian pattern must be very different.

The word 'servant' (v. 26) commonly meant someone who waited at table, bringing food and drink to others. A 'slave' (v. 27) was another person's property, with no rights, choices or freedom of his or her own. We have heard of Christians being 'like children' (18:3); this idea matches and meshes with that one. It is a position without status, indeed the last place in human rank and importance.

Yet the Lord took that last place, and died the slaves' death so that his people might live God's life. He lived out, in his journey to the cross, the lesson he taught. And his suffering was purposeful: it was a 'ransom for many' (v. 28). The same word 'ransom' is used to describe the Exodus (Deuteronomy 7:8), where the main emphasis is on God's power releasing his people. But a closer link to verse 28 is Isaiah 53:10–12, in the chapter about a servant whose suffering brings healing and hope to many.

Jesus is the humble servant. He is the suffering servant. His service is our example for Christian living. It is also a sign that suffering borne for God need not be fruitless or futile, but may be far-reaching in the good it does and the grace it brings to others.

For thought

Jesus' servant life and death put into perspective the disciples' concern for status in the church. Do you exercise any responsibility in your church? Pause to think about how you reflect the servant style of Jesus in the way you carry out that task. Then pray for grace to be consistent and humble as you continue in serving.

74 Matthew 20:29–34

Compassion road

Approaching the end

The pilgrim journey is nearing its completion. Jesus and his friends have travelled southwards along the east bank of the Jordan. Then they would have crossed the river a few miles north of the Dead Sea, and come to Jericho, a sizeable town in the valley. From Jericho a steep uphill road led south-west to Jerusalem, about 15 miles away. As the group moved out of the town, and set off into the hills, they attracted quite a crowd (v. 29).

Royal mercy

The two blind people needed to shout. Someone must have told them that Jesus was coming by, and they had heard of his power. But they could not see him. So shouting was the only way to make contact, and no one was going to shut them up (vv. 30–31).

'Son of David' is an unusual greeting, cropping up in just a few of the miracle incidents (9:27; 12:23; 15:22). It is a royal title. These blind people think of Jesus as a new king. But their kingly hope is more than a political notion. Loaded into it are the promises and expectations that God's Messiah will be a figure of mercy, a worker of wonders, who sets suffering people free from their distress. Sight for blind eyes is the hope of Isaiah 35:5, linked by Jews to the ministry of God's Spirit-anointed Messiah (see Matthew 11:4–5). Similarly in Isaiah 42:7, sight comes through the work of God's servant (Matthew 12:18–21). Jesus takes that double role, servant and king, humble and afflicted for his people, yet mighty and majestic in what he brings them from God.

Son of promises

Many names and titles are used for Jesus in Matthew's gospel:

- Jesus is Son of Man (20:18), a human figure, vulnerable as we are, destined to suffer and to pass through suffering to glory.
- In this passage he is Son of David, a name which stresses all he can do for God's people Israel.

- He is Son of God, revealing his Father's will and presence on earth (3:17; 17:5).
- He is Emmanuel, God with us (1:23; 28:20).
- Yet for many he remains only the son of a carpenter (13:55). They do not see. But the two blind people at Jericho see very clearly.

Asking and following

Nothing is said in this episode about faith. The way the blind people speak to Jesus is sign enough that they recognise God's work in him. They see spiritually, even though they cannot see physically. So they ask for 'open eyes', and Jesus gives them their sight. Then they join the crowd that is following him to Jerusalem (v. 34). There ought always to be a link between vision and discipleship. But how clearly will Jerusalem see?

Threshold of the city

This incident prepares the way for Jesus' entry to Jerusalem. There were many healings and wide public acclaim earlier in the gospel. But for the last few chapters Matthew has concentrated our attention on the teaching Jesus has given his friends. Little has been said about miracles since he set his face to Jerusalem at 16:21. The main focus has been on the coming church and its life.

This encounter at Jericho, reminiscent of an earlier healing at 9:27–31, resets the focus of the gospel story. Again Jesus is in contact with the public, with the wider Jewish community. As he approaches the capital city, this incident shows him as one who gathers a crowd, as Son of David, and as a healer whose praise cannot be silenced. All these themes will recur in the next few verses (21:8–9, 14–16).

Prayer

Lord Jesus Christ, light of the minds that know you, life of the souls that love you, and strength of the wills that serve you, help us so to know you that we may truly love you, so to love you that we may fully serve you, whose service is perfect freedom. Amen
Augustine of Hippo (354–430)

75

Matthew 21:1–11

Coming king

Jesus has reached Jerusalem, the destination to which he has been moving since chapter 16. As he approaches the city, crowds greet him with loud acclaim.

Humble, riding on an ass

The road from Jericho runs into Jerusalem from the east. Bethphage was within a mile of the city wall, and counted as part of the city limits. From Bethphage the way led over the Mount of Olives, and down across the Kidron Valley to the city proper.

Matthew has not mentioned yet that Jesus had friends at Bethany, a village near Bethphage. So the fetching of the donkey has the feel of a royal command, as if the king commandeers any animal he needs. But it much more likely reflects an agreement with a sympathetic local contact. Even so, there is a curiously cryptic feel to the matter – almost like something out of a spy novel – and it may be that Jesus was even now being careful about how and where he attracted attention. Mark and Luke only mention one donkey, but John speaks of a 'young donkey', and Matthew's story indicates that the mother came too, to steady the young animal in unfamiliar surroundings.

So (v. 5) Jesus fulfils the prophecy of Zechariah 9:9. There are a number of links to Zechariah in Matthew's Passion account, to chapters of Zechariah that tell of a coming king and of a shepherd rejected by the Jewish people. Here Jesus comes as king of peace, riding royally into the city, yet showing a quiet and lowly spirit. He is not on a great war-horse, but on a donkey's colt. He is a meek and gentle Messiah (5:5; 11:29), accessible to humble people (21:14–16).

Loud hosannas

'Hosanna' is Hebrew and means, 'Come and save us!' The words are from Psalm 118:25, which was one of the regular Passover hymns. It speaks of a righteous one coming to the 'gate of the Lord' (118:20), and of a stone that is rejected by men and raised by God (118:22). Jesus comes now to enter city gates where he will indeed be rejected and raised (Matthew 21:42).

The spreading of garments and branches is a real celebrity welcome. When Jehu became king over Israel (2 Kings 9:13), garments were spread before him. Much nearer to the time of Jesus, just a couple of centuries back, is an incident recorded in the Apocrypha, when the Jewish freedom-fighter Simon Maccabeus was greeted with 'palms and psalms' (1 Maccabees 13:51). Simon had driven out a foreign force, and went on to cleanse the city ceremonially to make it fit again for the worship of God. Jesus too will cleanse God's house, not from foreign pollution but from the way his own people have misused it. The freedom he offers will be very different from anything that military action could bring.

Shaken – if not stirred

Matthew suggests a contrast between the sympathetic crowd (v. 9) and the ripple of alarm that runs through the city (v. 10). Jerusalem was perturbed by Jesus' arrival once before (2:3), and he will be no easy company for many there. He is a prophet, coming to speak for God, and prophets do not always bring words of comfort. He is from Galilee, a stranger who will find much to disturb him here.

In our worship

This account of Jesus coming into Jerusalem has been used in Christian worship in two rather different ways. The regular tradition in Britain is to read the story on Palm Sunday, a week before Easter. We celebrate Jesus as the king who comes in peace, to die and yet to rise and reign. We join the crowd and sing their songs. Then as Holy Week goes on we follow the gospel accounts through the solemnity of Maundy Thursday and the grim darkness of Good Friday to the light of Easter morning. We travel alongside the story.

There is another tradition, in some continental European churches, of reading in the Advent season about Jesus' coming to Jerusalem. The worshippers wait, as if they were in Jerusalem, to receive the Lord who comes to search and test his people. During the lead-up to Christmas we examine and hallow ourselves, in order to celebrate Christ's coming to earth. As a temple of living stones, we invite his cleansing, his challenging and renewing presence among us.

For reflection and prayer

Let me be your donkey, Lord.
Dom Hélder Câmara (1909–99)

76 Matthew 21:12-17

Turning the tables

Falling market

The Jerusalem temple courts covered a vast area, roughly 400 yards by 300, with a high perimeter wall. The main buildings were in the centre, but the bulk of the space – called the Court of the Gentiles – was open to the sky, and available for people to move about and talk in. It was probably in this area that the traders were operating. The temple tax could only be paid in Tyrian coinage, which had no human images on it. If tax had been collected in other currency, then money-brokers would change it into Tyrian. Other dealers sold sacrificial animals, which had been approved by the temple authorities as blemish-free and fit for offering to God.

Jesus' action is abrupt and aggressive. It cannot have caused a widespread disturbance, for soldiers were stationed nearby at festival times and would have intervened quickly if there were major trouble. But those who caught the brunt of Jesus' wrath must have found it a fierce enough affair. What bothered him so much?

Crooked shepherds

Certainly Jesus was offended at the extent to which money surrounded and affected the work of the temple. He had already taken a dim view of the temple tax (17:24–26). Nor would he welcome the official monopoly on sacrificial animals at inflated prices. 'The legitimate and necessary operation of the temple was supported by a maze of intrigue, nepotism and corruption' (M. Bockmuehl, *This Jesus*, T&T Clark, 1994), and the wealth that accrued to the high priestly families would have been resented by many ordinary Jews. Jesus already felt that God's flock had no true spiritual leadership (9:36; 10:6), and the temple trade convinced him afresh that the people were being fleeced rather than fed (compare Ezekiel 34:1–6).

Clouds gathering

So Jesus is not opposed to the temple itself, but his action is a protest about how it works – profit is obscuring the importance of prayer. Verse

13 combines two Old Testament passages, Isaiah 56:7 and Jeremiah 7:11. The Jeremiah chapter came from a time of crisis and threat, and warned the people of Judah not to place a casual confidence in their temple. It would not be any help, if their life was not right with God.

That may give another clue to Jesus' thoughts, for he too predicted the fall of the temple (24:2). He took the view (as did some other Jews) that the temple would have a limited lifespan. It was not doing what God expected, and God would one day bring it down and replace it with something more worthy. So Jesus' temple protest is an acted symbol of trouble ahead, a signpost and a token of a coming great destruction.

Healing and praise

Jesus the king of peace has acted fiercely and forcefully. Yet he remains accessible, a man of mercy, healing the sick and receiving the praise of children. The approachable style of his ministry involves no tax or toll. He remains the gentle Christ, to whom the burdened and broken may turn (11:29).

High priests and scribes come to investigate (v. 15). Last time they checked up on Jesus, he was almost killed (2:4). We have heard of them on the way to Jerusalem (16:21; 20:18), and their arrival now is a portent of danger ahead. At the moment their protest makes little impact; but they will surely be back again. Meanwhile Jesus retires to his lodging at Bethany, a couple of miles outside the city.

Counter culture

How do we translate this incident into our time? Does it mean (some Christians ask) that a church should not sell fairly traded goods from developing countries after Sunday worship? Is a church bookstall ruled out too?

I think the issue is more about attitude than rules. Certainly this episode suggests that money should not dominate our church life; that Christian giving should be genuinely a gift – not a levy; that church life should be as fully open to poor people as to rich; and that even the best-organised and most carefully budgeted church may learn from the simplicity and spontaneity of children's praise (v. 16).

Prayer

Lord Jesus Christ, cleanse us and our worship from all that obscures your love.

77 Matthew 21:18-22
Hollow hopes

Fruitless tree

The withered fig tree stands stark and alone among all the gospel miracles. Only this miracle is destructive. The others are positive and creative – healings, providing food, and so on. They make the world a fuller place. This incident takes something away. So what is it about?

The time of year is odd. The new spring figs would not be due for another month. All you would expect in early April would be small green figs, or old figs left over from winter. One writer points out that in a hot climate certain fruit trees occasionally burst into leaf at the wrong time, and look as if they are bearing fruit, though in fact they are empty. Whether that takes us nearer to knowing what happened, I am not sure. But it does help to show the meaning of the incident. This tree looked fruitful, but was not. It was worth Jesus' while to go to it, but it had nothing for him. Its fruitfulness was just a show.

House of disappointment

The tree, then, had the same problem as the temple. It promised more than it could deliver. The temple offered itself as a place of light and hope. Jerusalem was looked on as the 'navel of the world', the supply line of its life from God. Yet Jesus saw the temple – Jerusalem's religious heart – as sadly introverted. For him, the temple was a tree with no fruit, a dry oasis, efficient in securing its own preservation yet weak in presenting free and joyful grace to pilgrim and enquirer.

So Jesus' words against the tree indicate his feelings about the temple. It has no life worth preserving, no goodness to nourish people with, and will surely come under the withering judgement of God. Jesus takes his place in the succession of Jewish prophets who spoke critically against their own people and their nation's religious life, often at considerable personal risk. Jeremiah had called the leaders and life of Jerusalem a basket of rotten figs (Jeremiah 24), and Jesus takes a fairly similar view.

Note: Mark (11:11-21) shows this link between tree and temple more clearly than Matthew. The temple cleansing and the cursing of the tree are interwoven in Mark's account. But they stand side by side in Matthew, and there appears to be a close connection.

Motive prayer

The shrivelling of the fig tree leads into a conversation about prayer. The wording of verse 21 is fairly similar to 17:20, but the place where it is said gives fresh edge to the remark. 'Say to this mountain,' here sounds as if it means the temple mount. Faith could shift even this major landmark. Faith could be a stronger force than the temple. The temple may not stand forever, but prayer can draw on the power of God to fulfil all that faith desires.

So the incident about the fig tree seems to be used in two ways. On one hand, the tree is an emblem of the temple, and its perishing foreshadows the temple's own fall. On the other hand, it illustrates the power of faith and prayer. Though these sound like different issues, the two messages converge. For the temple ought to be a house of prayer (21:13); it is not, and it will fall. Yet Jesus invites his friends to pray confidently. His example and his community offer a fruitful place of prayer, with open access to the power and love of God.

Praying with 'L' plates

Many other texts in the gospels speak of answered prayer. See, for example, Matthew 7:7–11; 17:20; 18:19; John 14:13; 15:7; 16:23–24. It sounds very easy and straightforward. But prayer can be a difficult business to understand and practise. We cannot simply tell God how things ought to be.

I have no quick fix to offer, but I think these texts in Matthew offer some help. One point from chapter 18 may be worth repeating here: the word 'you' in 21:21–22 is plural. Learning to pray, growing in faith, listening to God, and dealing with the answers, are often better done by Christians together. Solitary prayer is a precious gift. So is praying with friends.

Prayer

Give me the faith which can remove
And sink the mountain to a plain;
Give me the child-like praying love,
Which longs to build Thy house again.
Charles Wesley (1707–88)

78 Matthew 21:23-32
Pause for thought

Now follow several pieces of teaching given by Jesus in the temple during the days before the cross. He proves admirably nimble in the cut-and-thrust of debate, and all this teaching is directed, in one way or another, against the religious leaders of Jerusalem. This first conversation is with 'chief priests and elders'. Strictly there was only one high priest, but he was supported by a cluster of senior temple officials, and this will be the group involved here. The 'elders' are lay members of the Jewish ruling council, the Sanhedrin.

Questioning authority

'What right have you got to do these things?' is the first move in the exchange (v. 23). These men are responsible for the temple. Jesus has caused a disturbance and is attracting attention. So they want to rein him in. But he wrong-foots them by answering their question with another one (vv. 24–25), which puts them in a quandary, and they pause to confer.

They cannot reply that John the Baptist was led by God, or Jesus will ask why they themselves took so little notice of John. Nor can they criticise John's ministry, for that would cost them popular support. So they stall, and in return Jesus declines to answer their question (v. 27). There the conversation might have stopped, except that Jesus now moves to take the initiative with one of his parables.

The lost shall be first

Jesus told a very famous parable about two sons (Luke 15:11–32). This story (vv. 28–32) is much shorter and quite subtle. One son seems an awkward, rebellious fellow, but eventually goes to work on the farm. The other sounds loyal and industrious, but does not do what he promises. What you see is not necessarily what you get. Minds can be changed. People can act in ways you did not expect.

That, says Jesus, is what happened with John the Baptist's ministry. Religious people, who appeared committed to God, did not respond. Yet many from the edges of society – unlikely people, you would think – believed John and started a new walk with God. That is the obvious application of the parable. But there is another angle, which pulls the whole of today's passage together. It is about people who change their mind.

Room to reconsider

Jesus' counter-question (v. 25) was not asked just to be awkward. He wanted people to think again about their attitude to him. For Jesus' own authority was linked to John's. The two men were similar in style, outlook and aim. They believed that God was doing a new thing in Israel, that the kingdom was coming and that people should set their lives in order (3:2; 4:17). The two ministries were closely linked. If people respected John, they would be more likely to listen to Jesus.

But these opponents in the temple had not thought well of John. So Jesus tells his parable (vv. 28–32), in order to give them space to re-think. He invites them to act their part as Israel's religious leaders, to perform what they profess. 'Even when you saw, you did not change your mind and believe' (v. 32). But there is still time. If the shaft of this parable strikes home, if the questioners can review their opinion about John, then perhaps they can take Jesus seriously too.

The way home

A good parable has hidden layers. As the story rolls around in the mind, fresh meaning comes to the surface – rather like a cough sweet with a honey centre that seeps out as you suck. People would think about Jesus' words as they walked home, and would suddenly see the link to their own lives. Some hearers that day might have thought poorly of John and been critical of Jesus. Yet here was a fresh opportunity, a chance to reconsider, to respond positively to Jesus, to find their way into the kingdom of God.

Not everyone in the Sanhedrin remained hostile to Jesus. Two of its members gave him an honourable burial (27:57–60; John 19:38–42). I wonder how many others came to think highly of him.

But the very first question about authority has been left hanging. Where does Jesus get his authority from? The next couple of parables offer an answer.

For reflection

Do you meet situations where changing your mind would be a sign not of weakness, but of wisdom?

79 Matthew 21:33-46

Rejected and raised

This parable answers the question about Jesus' authority. He is the latest in a line of messengers from God, reminding the Jewish people of the love and loyalty they owe to God. Yet he is more than just one of the line. He represents God more intimately and directly than any prophet. They were servants; he is the Son.

Payment in kind

The fig tree incident portrayed the temple as a fruitless tree. This time there is fruit in plenty, but the tenants keep it all. The picture is of a commercial vineyard, laid out by a landowner, then worked by tenants, who pay part of their harvest as rental. There is a clear resonance with Isaiah 5. That passage calls Israel a well-built vineyard, which does not bear fruit for God. All it produces is injustice and oppression. That, says Jesus, is the problem again. The tenants, who administer the nation's religious life on God's behalf, yield little by way of goodness. Prophets have brought this message before, and were treated roughly (for example, 2 Chronicles 24:21; Jeremiah 38:6). This time the owner has sent his son.

The tenants kill the son to get the owner off their back once and for all. If he has no one to leave the land to, they hope to gain it by default (v. 38). In fact the people around Jesus know very well that the reverse would happen (v. 41). The owner would install new tenants, whom he could trust to pay properly.

Rising s(t)on(e)

Of course, Jesus knows he is on collision course with the powers of the land. He himself is the owner's son, who will be thrown out of the vineyard and killed. So he ends the parable with a text (v. 42; from Psalm 118:22-23) which switches the illustration from son to stone, and from dying to rising. In biblical Hebrew, the word for son is *ben*, and stone is *eben*. Jesus spotted that word-play and shared it with his audience. The rejected stone will be raised up high. The crucified son will be the capstone of the new household of God.

So Jesus' death will be a turning point in Israel's history. The people who have him killed will lose their tenure and trust. The nation's religious leaders will be displaced, and God's favour will settle on others. A people reshaped and renewed by God will bring the fruit of obedient service (v. 43). Then Jesus, as God's honoured stone, will be a figure for all to reckon with. In him the power of God's kingdom will be known (v. 44, drawing on Daniel 2:44–45).

Home ground

The temple leaders take the parable personally (v. 45). Some rich Jerusalem families owned country estates themselves. They would know about collecting rent, and what to do if tenants were slow to pay. They could see the owner's point of view. But the parable has put the boot on the other foot. These men were used to owning; Jesus casts them as tenants. He points out, too, that their lease is running out. They have not been faithful to their trust. They have used their position to make themselves rich, but have not given God his due.

Building a people

Matthew's gospel outlines how the Christian church emerged from within the life of the Jewish people. There are three main themes:

- **Fulfilment:** This gospel stresses fulfilment of the Old Testament (for example, 1:23; 5:17). Jesus, his teaching and his community are a faithful and sure expression of Israel's heritage and hope. The Old is being realised in the New.
- **Foundation:** God is building Israel's life around a new centre. Peter is the rock (16:18) of a new temple, made of living stones, with Jesus himself in the place of headship and honour (v. 42).
- **Forfeit:** Matthew portrays the leadership of Israel not only as self-serving and unfaithful, but as hopelessly out of touch with their own flock (21:26, 46). The crucifixion will be a turning point. There will be judgement, change and new fruitfulness (v. 43).

For reflection

Perhaps passages like this offer a sober warning to those who lead our churches. Even the best need to be vigilant and self-aware. Position, responsibility, habit, can all cloud a person's vision and take focus away from God. If you are a leader, will you search your own heart? If you are not, please pray for those you know who are.

80 Matthew 22:1–14

I cannot come to the banquet

The last parable pictured the temple leadership as tenants who would not pay the master's rent. This story casts them as wedding guests who decline to turn up on the day.

Absent friends

In some countries a wedding in a rich family can last a week. The marriage of a king's son is more than just a social event. It is an occasion for leading citizens of the realm to show support for the prince and his future among them. Casual refusal would be more than rude, it would be a first sign of rebellion, as if to say, 'We will not have this man to rule over us.'

The sending of one group of servants after another (vv. 3–4) matches the last parable, that of the vineyard. Verse 3 uses the same word twice over: 'to *invite* those who had been *invited*'. These guests know what is expected of them. Like the son of 21:30, or the tenants of 21:34–38, they are going back on their word. Once refusal turns to murder, the king responds fiercely and promptly (v. 7). And there the parable could end. But it continues.

Out and about

The feast is ready to start, but all the places at table are empty. So the king sends servants out again. They go to the thoroughfares (v. 9): the word means the place where a town road runs out into the country. They search the streets and open land and gather everyone they can find, to fill the hall.

Thus far the parable is very similar to a story in Luke 14:16–23. The message is that Israel's leaders miss out, and a new people is gathered in, roughly as in the parable of the vineyard (21:33–43). The newcomers might be the wayward and lowly in Israel (21:31–32), or even Gentiles (8:11–12). Grace lands in some unexpected places. There is more joy in heaven over unlikely people who come to God than over supposedly righteous people who turn away from his love. God's grace is free, but it does require a response. That point is made over again in verses 11–14, which seems to be a sort of postscript to the larger parable.

Dress for the occasion

The final scene (vv. 11–14) is unexpectedly severe. The king has a man thrown out because he is not wearing good clothes. That may seem unrealistic. After all, the guests have not had much time to go home and change. But the parable does not work in that tightly connected way. This last instalment has a message of its own – that we should respond to God's love with the fullest commitment we can. 'Wearing a wedding garment' (v. 11) means being properly ready to enjoy God's kingdom. The invitation to the kingdom is open, but God does expect a serious response. God wants people who will be glad to enjoy his company, honour his Son and learn of his love.

Three-course message

So there are three messages here, in the three stages of the parable.

- Those in Israel who scorn and ignore Jesus are in danger of missing out on God's grace (vv. 1–7).
- God gathers a new people. The church arises as a mixed and motley company (vv. 8–10).
- The gospel requires committed response (vv. 11–13).

Looking at Luke, majoring on Matthew

Matthew's version of this parable is rather longer than Luke's, either because Jesus used the story in varied ways, or because the two gospel writers have adapted it differently. The verses that come in Matthew alone are verses 7 and 11–13. Both these snippets emphasise the solemnity and, indeed, the severity of God. God is rich in mercy, but is not to be trifled with. Verse 7 in particular, with its talk of a burning city, might have made Matthew's first readers think of the fall of Jerusalem. We will hear much more about this in a couple of chapters' time.

For thought

The one thread that runs right through this complex parable is the word 'wedding'. God's banquet is indeed to be taken seriously, but is also spectacularly joyful. The kingdom is a place of rich love, full life, and holy laughter.

81 Matthew 22:15–22

Maker's mark

The discussions in the temple courts began with a challenge to Jesus (21:23–27). There were three parables in a row, all questioning the temple leaders' commitment to God (21:28—22:14). Next come three challenges to Jesus, from different quarters (22:15–40), before he takes the initiative himself (22:41) and the discussion ends.

Test question

By any reckoning this is a cunning question (vv. 16–17). We do not know anything about the Herodians, except that '-ians' is a Latin word-ending meaning 'supporters of'. The Pharisees were pious lay Jews, serious in their commitment to the law. They use honeyed words as a challenge to Jesus (v. 16): 'You're a plain speaker. You won't mind what people think of you. You just state your opinion.' They hope to draw him into an indiscretion.

The problem was money. Israel was occupied land. There were taxes on agricultural yield, and a personal 'poll tax'. That is why the Romans took a census (Luke 2:1–5), to count how much tax they could levy. Israel was also a nation with a keen sense of God's majesty. So paying tax in Roman coin was a threefold burden: no one likes paying taxes; Israel hated foreign rule; and the image on the coin was regarded as idolatry, breaking the command about graven images (Exodus 20:4–6).

So if Jesus supported paying tax, he could be criticised as unpatriotic. But if he opposed tax-paying, he could be reported as a troublemaker and rebel. The question has no right answer. Either reply is wrong. 'Yes' is religiously offensive. 'No' is politically dangerous.

Other side of the coin

One denarius per year, a day's wage, was the standard levy. This is the coin given to Jesus, and he asks his questioners to name the head on it. It is Caesar's. Jesus' next reply is sharp, but serious and searching too (v. 21).

The coin is Caesar's property. It bears his image. So they should give to Caesar what is his. The verb 'give' or 'render' means repaying a debt, settling what is owed, returning something to where it belongs. It is all right to give back to Caesar what belongs to him. It is his money, his stuff. Pay your taxes in the normal way. That is half of Jesus' answer.

The other side of the matter is that God should receive his due. Israel must offer God the worship and service he deserves. This is no limited tax bill, but a completely open cheque. There is only one proper way of responding to God's generosity – with the worship, love and service of our whole lives.

Costly commitment

So Jesus leaves his questioners with two challenges. First, what are they giving to God of themselves, their devotion and their obedience? Second, they must think whether their duty to God gets in the way of civic duty. Probably they would go on paying. Jews had been paying taxes to foreign governments for centuries. But that would be their own decision. In principle there is nothing wrong with returning to the state money it has minted, to support work it must do. In practice that always needs to sit within a greater loyalty and love.

What about us? Should Christians be obedient citizens and pay our taxes with an honest and ready heart? 'In general, yes, we should,' is the answer from this passage – unless and until it clashes with our commitment to God. That 'unless' is the reason we honour many Christians, all through history, who have suffered for their commitment to God and to right. In our own era there are Christians who confess Christ openly in lands where that is a crime, who defy unjust public policies, who support human rights, and who resist tyranny. They do it because they believe that Caesar's rights are limited, and that God's are not.

Think about your image

'Whose image is on the coin?' leads on to the question, 'In whose image have you and I been made?' We carry the maker's mark. We bear God's image. Our life and first loyalty belong to God.

Father, please give me
love to serve others, in my service to you,
courage to stand apart from others, in my stand for you,
and wisdom to know which to choose, day by day.
Through Jesus Christ our Lord. Amen

82 Matthew 22:23-33

Life to come

Once again, men confront Jesus with a thorny question. The last discussion, on tax, concerned Israel's relationship to her colonial lords. This next question is strictly within the realm of religion. Jews disagreed about resurrection. What happened to faithful people when they died? Could they expect any afterlife with God? Pharisees said 'Yes', Sadducees said 'No' (v. 23). What will Jesus say?

One bride for seven brothers

The Sadducees' argument is put forward in biblical terms. The ancient Jewish law obliged a young widow's nearest male relative – normally her late husband's brother – to marry her (Deuteronomy 25:5-6). This offered the woman some protection, and gave her a fresh opportunity of becoming a mother. It also preserved her husband's memory, and kept his land and property within the family. This custom drives the plot of the book of Ruth, many centuries before Christ, but there is not much evidence of it being practised in New Testament times.

So the Sadducees sketch a rather improbable scenario, with a woman marrying seven brothers in turn, producing children with none of them and eventually outliving them all. So none of the seven has a stronger claim on her than his brothers do: none fathered a child by her; none lived with her to the end of her life. To which of them will she belong in the afterlife? Of course, the tale is designed to make belief in resurrection look ridiculous. Who could possibly take seriously a doctrine that produces riddles of this kind?

A greater world

Jesus replies that *he* takes resurrection seriously. The Sadducees' perspective is too narrow. They have not been biblical enough (v. 29). Jesus' direct answer is that the woman will be married to none of the brothers in the resurrection. Heaven is not that sort of place.

Some Christians would find Jesus' answer alarming. Will our closest personal relationships on earth count for nothing in heaven? Does Jesus mean that Christianity is really anti-marriage, so that the pure life of heaven will require us all to be single? Once our minds run along those lines, then, like the Sadducees, we are taking too narrow a view. Whatever heaven is like, it will not erase the goodness of earth but will gather it into the radiance of God's greater glory. Heaven will not be a poorer place than earth, but a richer, fuller, stronger, brighter place. If we insist on squeezing heaven into our earthly patterns of thought, it will simply not fit. That is where the Sadducees went wrong.

God of the living

Jesus now reaches for scripture himself. The Sadducees recognised the authority of the law, the first five books of the Old Testament, whereas Pharisees worked with a much wider range of scriptures. The two groups disagreed on resurrection partly because it was most clearly taught in books that the Sadducees did not use very much. Here Jesus manages to meet the Sadducees on their own ground, to produce an original argument and to explain his own views on resurrection.

He quotes (v. 32) from God's words to Moses in Exodus 3:6. By Moses' time the three patriarchs Abraham, Isaac and Jacob were long dead. Yet God says, 'I am their God.' Though dead to human eyes, they are alive to God. God's relationship with them is not past and over, but present and active. Those who live by faith will die to God, and will rise to new and lasting life with God.

Clearer view

Christians believe in resurrection, not just because Christ taught it but also because Christ himself rose from the grave. We see more clearly, because of his resurrection, that God's power is greater than the power of death. We celebrate Easter, and in our Easter faith is hope and confidence for those who have died in Christ. We need not think of heaven as unrelated to the experience of earth. Jesus' words speak of real people, who have lived on earth, now living in the presence of God. But the vexing tangles of earth will not always help us to understand the radiant clarity of heaven.

For thought and prayer

Thank God for the people you have known who died in faith. Thank God for people whom you have seen face weakness with courage. Thank God for our Easter faith. Pray for grace that you may live to God, live in hope, and live by faith in Jesus.

83 Matthew 22:34–46

Love the Lord

Here are two short pieces of teaching, one about the Jewish law, the other about the Jewish Messiah.

Top of the orders

A challenge comes from Pharisees. They put to Jesus a question common in Jewish legal debate: 'Which is the greatest command in the law?' Jesus replies by quoting Deuteronomy 6:5, the command to love God with our whole selves. Deuteronomy says, 'with heart, soul and strength'; Matthew says, 'heart, soul and mind'; and slightly different versions come in Mark and Luke. The meaning is the same: all that we are, and all that we can be, is ours to give to God in obedience, service and praise.

Jesus then sets a second command beside the first – to love our neighbour as we love ourselves (Leviticus 19:18). This was a common technique among Jewish teachers. To explain an issue fully, they would string together scripture verses that had an important word in common. Loving God is the great command, but it does not stand alone because we are not made to be solitary people.

The command in Leviticus is very practical. It sums up a paragraph about helping weak people, about fair dealing and honest speech, and it means, 'Give your neighbour the consideration you would like to receive in their situation. Give a neighbour's interests and rights the respect you give your own.'

One breath for God

Verse 40 does not quite mean that two commands are all you need. But it does claim that everything in the ancient Jewish law leads towards those two commands and fills out their detail. Only Matthew words the verse in this way, reflecting his concern to relate Christian teaching to the ancient Jewish law (compare 5:17). And as followers of Jesus today, God still calls us to shape our life by these two great commandments – simple to say without even taking a breath, but utterly absorbing to live out, claiming every breath we take.

Royal issue

Jesus now takes the initiative in the discussion (v. 41), and introduces a new topic. He puts a question, and the Pharisees give the standard answer. 'The Messiah is son of David,' they say (v. 42). Jesus does not reject that answer, but he expands it. 'Son of David' is a true answer; the Messiah will be a royal figure, a ruler in Israel. But this is not the whole truth. Jesus invites the Pharisees to explore a text with him.

Psalm 110 is headed 'Psalm of David', and it says, 'The Lord [the Hebrew word for God] said to my lord, "Sit at my right hand…"'

Jesus assumes that this psalm is talking about the Messiah: who else would sit at God's right hand? Then he points out how the psalm speaks with respect and humility, calling the Messiah 'my lord'. These are not the tones a senior ancestor would normally use of a young relative. The Messiah must be much more than David's son. His destiny, nature and rank far surpass David's. Israel's Christ is indeed a royal figure, but he is far greater than any human royalty.

Bigger picture

The first encounter asked Jesus to shrink the law to a narrow focus (v. 36). In this second exchange Jesus asks the Pharisees to expand their vision of messiahship to a broader horizon. The Messiah is indeed a special person, but he is more than a person. There is something profoundly God-like about him that no human title can fully describe. On a previous occasion when Jesus talked about identity, he accepted Peter's confession, 'Son of God' (16:14–16). This time he leaves broad hints, but in the presence of enemies he does not make outright claims. The time for that will come later (26:63–64).

Moving to crisis

The discussion is over (v. 46). Jesus came to the temple as Son of David (21:9, 15). Now he leaves his enemies with the thought that he is much greater than this. From here onwards the gospel moves steadily towards a harsh collision. Jesus' opponents will pursue him again. He himself talked of a burning city (22:7), and will speak in the next chapters about God's judgement on Jerusalem.

For thought and prayer

People need to love and be loved. Never be frightened to tell God that you love him, and to rejoice that God loves you.

84 Matthew 23
Grief and anger

This chapter is one of the most difficult in Matthew, and this page discusses some general points about it before we go on to read it, a section at a time, in the pages ahead.

Bridge of sorrows

Chapter 23 is a bridge in the development of Matthew's story. It spans across from the controversies of 21 and 22 to the teaching in 24 about the destruction of Jerusalem, and to the arrest, trial and cross in 26 and 27. It spells out how polarised Jesus and his opponents have become, and shows with painful clarity how far they are from reconciliation and how inevitable are the crises and calamities ahead.

Only Matthew

The matching sections of Mark and Luke are shorter than this. Hardly any material in Matthew 23 has a parallel in Mark, although quite a lot is in Luke, mostly in Luke 11:39–51. Many writers think that Matthew has assembled a quantity of critical comment that Jesus made about his opponents, and has included it all together here because it carries the storyline forward so effectively.

Others pursue that approach even further. They reckon Matthew had a reason for assembling this critical material about scribes and Pharisees. They suggest that his own church was at odds with the Jewish leadership of his time, and that Christians were being elbowed out of Judaism. So this material expresses Matthew's own viewpoint, his unease and anger at the church's troubles in his own time.

I reckon it quite possible that Matthew gathered material. Like all this gospel's blocks of teaching, the chapter has a single consistent theme. But I am inclined to trace the main thrust of this criticism back to Jesus. The gospels record some very sharp differences of opinion. Jesus' style and approach differed quite widely from the formality and legal focus of the Pharisees' piety.

Hard words

If we judge the language of this chapter by modern Western standards, it seems very harsh. But these words relate more easily to the customs of their own time and place. Polemic (argument between different groups and parties) was pretty sharp in the first century: 'one's opponents were, as a rule, blind, foolish, impious, hypocritical' (Davies and Allison). This polemic does not aim to be balanced. It does not pick out the best points in Pharisaism. It intentionally draws attention to division, dispute and difficulty.

The same sort of thing is found elsewhere in first-century Judaism, for example in the Dead Sea Scrolls and the writings of Josephus. It is plentiful in the Old Testament prophets. Jews could speak to Jews in this way when serious questions of loyalty, faith or tradition were at stake. That leads on to the next issue.

Matthew the Jew

As the Jewish people have spread through the world, over the last 2,500 years or so, they have met appalling hostility and cruelty in many lands and times. The horror of the Holocaust in the 1940s has moved many Christians to reflect on Christian anti-Semitism across the years, and to do all they can to prevent any re-emergence of that spirit in our own day. We are rightly suspicious of anything anti-Semitic. So what about Matthew 23?

This material was surely not intended by Matthew (nor by Jesus) as anti-Semitic, although it has been used in that way since. Matthew was a Jewish Christian, a member therefore of a small but significant group within Judaism, trying to explain and justify his church's faith by writing a gospel. That gospel naturally shows some of the pressures and conflicts that have arisen, reasons why Christianity has diverged from other streams within Judaism. But Matthew would never have thought of Christianity (or himself) as un-Jewish. Open to Gentiles, yes; but un-Jewish, no. Matthew 23 is polemic, but it was not written as racist polemic.

Take to heart

Some Christians have used this text to fuel anti-Jewish prejudice. There is surely a truer approach. Matthew 23 shows some of the faults into which religion – even well-meaning religion – can fall. If we listen to it with ourselves in mind, we may be humbled and challenged.

85

Matthew 23:1–12

Leading questions

This section speaks of the servant lifestyle that Christians should adopt, along lines we have already met in 20:24–28. It targets especially those who teach and guide others in faith, and so offers a checklist for how leadership is exercised in the church.

Sitting still

Matthew has pointed out several times that the Jerusalem crowds were more receptive to Jesus than were some of their teachers and leaders (21:15–16, 26, 46). Here Jesus talks to the crowds and criticises the scribes and Pharisees, men who studied the law and encouraged others to observe it.

'Sitting on Moses seat' (v. 2) means exercising a teaching role within Israel, interpreting the directions and duties of the ancient law and applying it to people's needs and lives. 'Do whatever they teach' (v. 3) is difficult. It could be saying, 'When they teach the law truly, then take it seriously.' For Jesus valued the law, though he disagreed sorely with some of its interpreters. Or it could be rather ironic: 'You are welcome to observe what they say – but you really must avoid what they do!'

Either way, Jesus' criticism (v. 4) is that these teachers expect too much from others. Their legal rulings cut deep into daily life, yet they show little awareness of the practical effect these teachings have. Jesus, by contrast, offers an easy and bearable yoke (11:28–30).

The preachers who are heard most clearly today are usually those who know their people well and who share the burdens of their lives. A preacher may live largely among fellow Christians, but must still be sensitive to the pressures and perplexities facing Christian people who live and work in less sympathetic or supportive places.

Showing up

Most people enjoy attracting the good opinions and attention of others. We easily forget that good opinions and attention are worth little unless they have been patiently earned and can be accepted humbly. 'Phylacteries' (v. 5) are small leather boxes containing scripture texts, that were strapped to the forehead and arm (Deuteronomy 6:8). The 'tassels' were blue cords that hung from the four corners of a Jew's robe (Numbers 15:38–39). Perhaps a modern Christian equivalent would be carrying a large and well-worn Bible, in the hope that people will notice our piety and learning.

The word 'rabbi' (v. 7) appears here for the first time in Matthew. Literally it means 'my great one', 'my master', and was applied to Jewish teachers from about Jesus' time onwards. Enjoying titles and places of honour, basking in public regard and revelling in social opportunity are not ideal character traits in a religious leader. The deepest work is sometimes done by those who are noticed the least.

Levelling down

In the Christian community, no one is any greater than the rest. All are brothers and sisters under the sheltering fatherhood of God. All of us are learners, following the one teacher, Jesus Christ (vv. 8–10). The church has found these verses hard to take literally. Concern for responsible leadership has proved hard to manage without names, offices and titles. So what does Matthew 23 ask of those who carry one or other of these?

- It asks those of us called 'Father' or 'Mother' to be rightly childlike in spirit, to serve like an older brother or sister who is caring for younger ones while our heavenly Father is out of sight.
- Teachers must carry on learning of Christ, and in particular should learn from the Christian experience of the people we teach.
- Any among us who are thought great must work hard to sustain the virtue of humility.

Authority in the church is always loaned and delegated, held on trust rather than owned and possessed. Leadership is a temporary role. In heaven there will be no ranks, only worshippers. Dignity and achievement are found in some unlikely places, often among people who work steadily at a humble task and expect little in return, except the satisfaction of knowing that their work is worthwhile.

Prayer

Lord, help me to take pleasure in applauding the successes of others, in learning from the people around me, in sharing the burdens of friends. Through Jesus Christ our Lord. Amen

86 Matthew 23:13–28

Religious audit

Jesus' public teaching in Matthew opens with a series of beatitudes (5:3–12), declaring the blessings of God's kingdom on people who are poor in spirit, meek and pure in heart. His public teaching ends here in chapter 23, with seven woes. Jesus grieves that his opponents are so far from the kingdom, so alien to it in the way they behave and think. The woes stand as if facing the beatitudes, like two avenues of great trees, at either end of the gospel.

There is something similar in the Old Testament, in Deuteronomy 27 and 28. When Israel came into the promised land and committed herself afresh to God, she was to recite the blessings and curses of God's covenant from opposite mountain-sides. Matthew writes of a new covenant, of God's covenant with Israel, renewed in the death of Jesus (26:28). He knows of many who have come into that new covenant, and of others who have resisted and resented the good news. These markers of blessing and woe are invitation and lament, challenge and warning, bright hope and bitter sorrow.

Roughly speaking, two of these seven woes are about the scribes' and Pharisees' activity, two about their teaching, and two about their character. The seventh (23:29–33) we leave till later.

Unmaking converts

The first two woes (vv. 13 and 15, leaving aside v. 14, which is not in the earliest manuscripts) concern the kingdom. The Pharisees will not enter themselves, they discourage others from doing so, and they make strenuous efforts to win people to their own religious views without bringing them any nearer to God.

The issue here is spiritual growth. Are we serious in trying to get nearer to Christ? How do we react when someone else shows more enthusiasm for the gospel than we have – do we try to rein them back? Do our efforts to win people really help them to open their lives to God, or simply draw them into our habits and prejudices?

Hard to swallow

The next two woes are about finely tuned legal teaching, rules that seem splendidly detailed but which miss such great and obvious truths that they are almost useless. The third woe (vv. 16–22) is about oaths. Jesus has already taught that simple and consistent truthfulness is better than elaborate oath-taking (5:33–37). Now he attacks the idea that oaths could be split into two categories – those you needed to keep, and others you did not. His point of view is much more direct. Promises that sound serious should be seriously kept; there is no honest or godly way of getting round that.

The fourth woe (vv. 23–24) is about putting first things first, letting the most important matters in religion and life be those we take the most seriously. If we spend so much effort on the finer points of church affairs that we never take time to 'stir one another up to love and good works' (Hebrews 10:24), we could be in danger of swallowing the same camel.

Beneath the surface

The fifth and sixth woes are about the falsity of life that looks religious on the outside but lacks a deep vein of goodness within. Jesus knows that the Pharisees were careful to wash eating and drinking vessels. But he says that they themselves are like half-washed cups (vv. 25–26). Their formal and dutiful piety, he says, camouflages flaws in their practical and personal lifestyle. If they are so zealous for cleanliness, let them clean up their own lives, on the inside.

The sixth woe (vv. 27–28) compares Jesus' opponents to a painted tomb – either a white-marked grave, so that passers-by did not tread on impure land, or possibly an elaborately decorated and wealthy tomb. The point is the same in either case. The clarity and apparent innocence of the markings conceal the grim decay of death.

My family once bought a tin of peas that looked fine outside but had an insect inside. It must have flown in at the critical moment, after the peas were poured in and before the lid was clamped on top. It was there to greet us, very dead, when we opened the can. We have not much enjoyed tinned peas since. What is there within your life, or mine, that could put someone off the Christian faith?

Prayer

Search me, O God, and know my heart. See if there is any wicked way in me. And lead me in the way everlasting.
PSALM 139:23–24

87

Matthew 23:29-39

Division and desolation

The last woe (23:29-33) is the harshest of the seven. It tells of martyrdom and crucifixion, of hatred and violence, of jealous and angry faith, and of the ugly consequences of rivalry and fear. Yet as it runs into the final verses of the chapter, righteous anger mingles with tears, and desperate grief speaks one last word of compassion and love.

Trail of death

Verses 29-32 take up a theme from the vineyard parable (21:34-39). God sent prophets to Israel across the centuries, and many of them were treated harshly and cruelly. Finally God has sent his Son, and in his coming the whole tangled history will be summed up in both grace and judgement.

If Jesus' opponents honour the tombs of prophets, he says, let them examine their own attitude. They are – at least in spirit – the heirs of those who did the damage, who resisted the message the prophets brought. For God's final and greatest prophet stands among them, and they resent him and his word. There will be an awful 'fulfilment' (v. 32) of this shadow side of Israel's tradition, in the wrath that will be measured out to Jesus.

No meeting place

Yet still God's gospel will go out to Israel. Christian messengers will bring the word but will not always be well received. There will be a solid core of resistance among the religious leadership of the nation (v. 34). Finally and climactically, the events of 'this generation' (v. 36), in the lifetime of Jesus' hearers, will sum up a long history of conflict and gather to a focus the judgement of God.

Abel was the first godly martyr in the Bible (Genesis 4). 'Zechariah' (v. 35) may refer to 2 Chronicles 24:20-22, regarded as the last martyrdom of the Old Testament. (In the Hebrew Bible, Chronicles comes last.) The death of Jesus, and the harassment of his followers, will bring this history to a head, and 'this generation' will feel the recoil.

Yearning love

Jesus holds out his arms in sorrow for opportunity lost. He had longed to gather Jerusalem into the gentle grasp of God's kingdom. Like the sheltering wings of a mother hen, he had tried to reach out in love (v. 37). But love had met with refusal, and is now moving on.

The temple was seen as God's dwelling place, the house where God was known in an intimate way (23:21). Now Jesus speaks of an awful vacuum, of the temple becoming empty and desolate (v. 38), a sort of anti-Emmanuel, the house of God's absence.

The last verse turns again to Psalm 118, to the words that greeted Jesus when he came into the city (21:9). Now the wheel has turned full circle, and his time in the temple is over. As the glory of God once left the city before (Ezekiel 11:23), Jesus too steps away and pauses on the Mount of Olives (24:1–3). One day he will be known again as king. But before that day dawns, tumultuous and terrible days will come.

Passage of time

These verses expect the summing up of Israel's history in Jesus' own generation. But that history, stretching through the Old Testament, contains both light and shadow, faith and unfaith. Jesus himself is the culmination of Israel's faithfulness, the godly prophet *par excellence*. The opposition that eventually engineers his death is the completion of Israel's unfaithfulness, of the strand of disobedience that runs through her scriptures. So this passage at the end of Matthew 23 speaks to its own time, and also to ours. Do remember:

- The distinction Matthew has often shown us between the crowds and their leaders. Jesus and the movement he launched found a good reception among many Jews.
- If God's public judgement on Israel's leaders came in the fall of Jerusalem in AD70, then it is over.
- This passage is also about you and me, about the dangers of bitterness in religion, and the terrible consequences of trying too hard to defend God. We are not immune.

For reflection

A wise friend once told me, 'When I take Holy Communion, I ask God to show me if I have gone badly awry in my faith, if I have seriously misunderstood God's call and love.'

88

Matthew 24:1–3

Looking ahead

Starting to teach

The last verse of chapter 23 closed a circle: it echoed 21:9, and drew Jesus' time in the temple to an end. Now he moves out of the temple to a new venue. The Mount of Olives was just outside the city wall of Jerusalem, on the east side, looking across the Kidron Valley to the temple buildings. Jesus sits down – the position in which a rabbi taught – with his disciples around him. This is the fifth great sermon of Matthew's gospel: it runs to the end of chapter 25.

Crumbling securities

The temple was famed for its grandeur, size and light-coloured, gleaming stone. The Mount of Olives was an ideal place from which to view it. The disciples' first comment (v. 1) sounds like the admiration of pilgrims. But Jesus' words cut grimly and abruptly into their awe (v. 2): it will not last; it will be shattered. What has made him think this?

First, he has a sense of history. This prediction carries forward the teaching in the last three chapters. The rejection of the Son will mean the loss of the vineyard. The wedding guests refuse to banquet with God, and murder the messengers who summon them; that will cost them their city. The temple has failed to deliver; Jesus' demonstration there was an acted symbol of trouble ahead. The lives of the martyrs will be charged to the generation that kills the Son.

Second, he reads the political mood. Israel was impatient under foreign rule. There was a series of small but bloody uprisings in the first century. A little sober foresight could trace the likely consequences. Under Rome, Israel found it hard to live at peace but would surely fail badly if she went to war.

Third, he knows the scripture. Past prophets had spoken of God's judgement against Jerusalem (for example, Jeremiah 7:12–15; 9:11). The city was not overshadowed by a cosmic insurance policy, but was sustained only by its people's covenant obedience. When that obedience reached a low ebb, then the covenant was a positively dangerous relationship.

Thinking positively

Jesus looked ahead and saw gloom and sadness for Jerusalem. But he was also a man of hope. He believed that God's power and love would one day be known on earth in a much fuller way than even he had shown. His parables of growth look forward with great confidence. So although this chapter tells of catastrophe, it also reflects a belief that time is in God's hands. The disaster ahead is part of a bigger purpose of salvation and judgement, of righteousness, hope and love.

If you look at a range of mountains, the highest peaks may appear interleaved with the nearer and lower hills. It is hard to sort out the separate layers when viewing from far away. A map-maker finds that sort of thing annoying, and wants to fix accurate distances and positions. However, for a prophet, the nearer and more immediate purposes of God can be a foretaste, assurance and meaningful anticipation of God's greater and final work. A prophet can revel in the merging of two horizons.

There is a similar merging in some biblical texts that look forward. A conviction that God controls the final outcome of all things, and an awareness of God's work in the foreseeable future, merge into one forward view. It is right that the two do hold together, that the God of the ages is known as the God who acts in time. History is the place where eternity is made known.

Posing problems

The disciples' question (v. 3) weaves two issues together. Two horizons merge and fuse in their minds.

- 'When will all this be?' is a fair follow-on to verse 2, and is a reasonable and predictable question.
- 'What will be the sign of your coming?' picks up 23:39, that one day people would again see Jesus coming in the name of the Lord. Again that is an understandable reaction.

The disciples seem to assume that the fall of the city will be a sign of the presence of Jesus. It will surely also be a time of great change in history, the turning of an era.

For reflection and prayer

God of the ages, please teach your church to meet the uncertainties of time without fear, and to greet the certainties of eternity in faith. Through Jesus Christ our Lord. Amen

89 Matthew 24:4–14
Panic, pressure and patience

Matthew's gospel looks back, at the life of Jesus and at the disciples' desire to understand him. But for Matthew's first readers, and for Christians ever since, this chapter has been much more than history. It looks forward from the time of Jesus, and describes events to come. Christians through the ages have asked when all this will arise: 'Are these verses speaking of our days?' This part of the chapter urges Jesus' disciples – and Matthew's readers, and us – to be patient. Panic is not a Christian virtue.

False alarm

There were several small rebellions in Israel in the generation after Jesus. During the period from AD30 to 66, the temperature was rising, and nationalism was becoming restless and increasingly militant. Leaders emerged who attracted groups of followers and promised signs and wonders. So far as we know, none of them actually claimed to be God's anointed, but their style and appeal drew the loyalty and hopes of many. None of them succeeded.

When the news is filled with disaster, it is tempting to think that the world is shifting, that present troubles will be worse than any before and will allow no return to normality. Where communication is poor, such thoughts and rumours can carry an eerie power. Herod Antipas went to war with an eastern neighbour in the late 30s, there was an earthquake in Syria in 37, in 40 the Roman emperor outraged the Jews by trying to place his statue in the Jerusalem temple, and there was a long famine in the region in the mid-40s. To a church expecting the fulfilment of Jesus' words, such events could be unsettling.

But any alarm would be false. Many Jews expected a time of suffering – sometimes called 'messianic woes' – before God's purposes came to fruition. Jesus shares that view. The church should see these distresses as the very first 'birth pangs' (v. 8), indications that there is new life ahead, but not yet signs of its urgent coming.

Church under pressure

In its early centuries, Christianity was a vulnerable minority faith, liable to bouts of harassment and persecution. In Judea itself there were three prominent executions in the first generation: Stephen, about AD33 (Acts 6—7); James Zebedee in 44 (Acts 12:2); and James the brother of Jesus, leader of the Jerusalem church, in 62. In such an environment, many ordinary Christians are likely to have come under pressure. The temptation to fall away will have been strong (vv. 9–10).

Yet even in those years, when the mother church in Jerusalem and Judea was under such strain, the faith was spreading wide (v. 14). In well under a generation it reached Rome, from where roads radiated across Europe. The New Testament shows us part of that spread, but there is much more about which we have only slight and sketchy information – the movement eastwards, for example.

Home truths

You will see that I connect this chapter to events in the Holy Land in the decades after AD30. Jesus' words relate most naturally to his own land and people, and I think Matthew and his first readers were either in the land itself, or sufficiently near it – Syria perhaps – to be affected by the mood there. But these verses also carry wisdom for the church in every age and place.

Christianity is a hopeful faith. We believe that the God of Jesus Christ is Lord of time and eternity, God of the future as surely as of the past. We cannot help being hopeful. But Christians have often found difficulty in balancing hope with patience, in walking the narrow ridge between over-enthusiasm and exhaustion. Panic, prophets and persecution still tempt.

Panic leads us into burn-out – we run out of energy. False prophets beckon us into byways – to invest our faith in some wayward discovery or futuristic timetable. Persecution pushes us into backsliding – we lose ground as Christians because it is hard to hold on.

These verses urge a steady calm. This is a long-distance journey. Let us run with perseverance the race that is set before us (Hebrews 12:2). Out of the turbulence of his world, God is working in creative love to bring new life to birth. Through the trials of the church, God is spreading the gospel to the nations. We may rightly travel in hope.

For reflection

I do not know what the future holds, but I do know who holds the future.

Anonymous

90 Matthew 24:15–28
Time to run

The start of this section is sharp and urgent. Previous verses have been cautious and cool: 'Keep watch, look out, not yet.' Suddenly here is something to react to.

Tainted temple

The key sign is 'the desolating sacrilege' (v. 15). This odd phrase comes from the visions and prophecies in Daniel 7—12. The main event they cover is the defiling of the Jerusalem temple by the Syrian king, Antiochus Epiphanes, about 200 years before Christ. He set up an altar to the Greek god Zeus, on top of the sacrificial altar in the temple. This is what Daniel calls 'the abomination that makes desolate' (Daniel 9:27; 11:31; 12:11). For the Jews this was a ruinous defilement of the temple's life, robbing the building of its role and reverence.

So this phrase in Matthew 24 surely refers to something improper and unworthy in the temple. Jesus speaks of its being defiled and compromised. Exactly what Jesus meant, and how much detail he foresaw of the events ahead, is difficult to know for certain. Perhaps the linking of word to fulfilment became clear to the early Christians only as events unfolded. A possible 'match' to this text came in AD67–68. The Zealots, Jewish freedom fighters, adopted the temple as their headquarters, and violently and aggressively disrupted some of its life and worship.

If verse 15 describes this occupation of the temple, then the verses that follow speak of the distresses of the Jewish War, which ran to a bloody end in the early 70s. Meanwhile Matthew's aside – 'let the reader understand' – suggests that the link to Daniel will be taken up again.

Hard times

The next verses urge the Christians in the Jerusalem area to run for the country. Times will be hard and conditions harsh. The language of verses 17 to 18 – 'Don't even run indoors or go back for a coat' – may be deliberately graphic and stark. But the point is clear. Once the temple is tainted, it is no time to hang around. The writing is on the wall. It is far better to flee for safety.

Many Jerusalem Christians migrated at this time to Pella, beyond the Jordan, apparently in response to a prophetic message. These verses may be that message: the church acted on its memory and record of the words of Jesus. The letter of James, which may well come out of Jerusalem a few years before this, also urges Christians to avoid 'conflicts and disputes' (James 4:1). Many Christians did not join the war. They were a peaceful group. They opposed rebellion, and reckoned it was not their battle.

There is a warning about 'winter or sabbath' (v. 20). Wintry weather, with rivers running high, would make hasty travel almost impossible. Sabbath travel would be resented by Jewish neighbours, and indeed the Christians themselves may have been reluctant to do this. Verse 21 refers again to Daniel (12:1). These will be terrible days, but they are under God's sight, and they will come to an end (v. 22).

Distractions and deceptions

The warnings in verses 23–28 match those of the previous section (24:4–5, 11). Even in times of fear and flight, the Christians should not be taken in by flimsy claims and wild rumour. They will not need to hunt for the work of Jesus. When it comes, no mistake will be possible. As when vultures gather round a corpse, you will not need to ask what is happening.

Forward look

I have suggested (p. 197) why Jesus might have foreseen the fall of the temple. He must also have spent time learning from the book of Daniel. He had the vision to prophesy a crisis in the temple and to warn his friends to flee. And amid all the words of chaos, he retained a sense that God would vindicate him and his cause.

For reflection and prayer

Many people in our times have to live through refugee experiences like those described here: urgent flight; concern for weak relatives; unpredictable weather; longing for it to end. Many kinds of troubles make people run. Ethnic rivalry, political power struggles, religious conflicts, revolutions and those who try to crush them can all cause fearsome consequences for humble and ordinary people. Pray for refugees, wherever you hear of them in the world today.

91

Matthew 24:29–35

Day of darkness

As if time had stopped

Verse 29 is the awful climax of this prophecy. All the lights go out. The earth is shrouded in darkness and cold. The skies shiver and fall. A dreadful gloom covers every horizon. Every certainty and landmark is gone, as if the end of all things has come.

This language of cosmic collapse and falling skies describes the fall of the city. This was the city on which God had set his love in a unique way. For it to come to destruction, fire and slaughter, for Jerusalem to be reduced to ruins, for the nation to lose past, present and future in one awful bloody disaster, cannot be spoken of in measured and easy words. This is like the end of the world.

Kingdom coming

Yet in a grim and awful irony, this dreadful event reveals the kingdom and Lordship of Jesus. This was the city whose leaders resisted and crucified him, whose temple drew and devoured the wealth of God's people, the city against which he had spoken in sadness and dreadful finality. Even this awful destruction is a sign that he is Lord. That moment in the book of Daniel when God confirms the authority and rule of the Son of Man is acted out once again, as the words of Jesus against the city run to fulfilment (v. 30; from Daniel 7:13). The 'tribes of the land', the people of Israel, weep at the fall of the city (v. 30). Yet the word of Jesus goes out across the world (v. 31).

These words and pictures burst the bounds of normal experience. Here is one of time's most bitter days, when the fragility and futility of the world, its judgement and its sorrow, are tasted to the full – truly a sign of the end of all things. Yet it will come to the generation to which Jesus speaks (v. 34).

Green shoots

The illustration Jesus uses is common experience (v. 32). A greening tree is a sign of summer ahead. Buds, leaves and shoots are nature's clock. They carry the promise of the year running forward to its next stage. So with the sequence of events in Matthew 24: the defiling of the temple and the need to flee (24:15–22) show that the fall of Jerusalem is near (vv. 29–31).

For the person reading Matthew, the fig tree is already a symbol of the fruitless temple and of coming ruin (21:18–19). Now that sign is coming to fulfilment. The short fig-tree parable in chapter 24 is a solemn reminder of a falling temple and of the city running into serious trouble. This will come within a generation (v. 34), under the sure word that Jesus has spoken (v. 35).

Yet as people observe the fig tree, and trace from Jesus' prophecy that one event leads to another, they should also look further forward. The fall of Jerusalem is the shadow of a greater day ahead, a time when all humanity will know the authority of Jesus. 'But of that day and hour, no one knows' (v. 36).

Certain yet not clear

You will see that I have applied these verses to the fall of the city, but as a foreshadowing of that final day which the church knows as the second coming of Christ. Yet these are verses on which the wisest interpreters do not entirely agree. This chapter is unusually difficult territory, and there are two good reasons why.

First, Matthew's chapter differs in places from the parallel material in Mark and Luke. All three aimed to record the teaching of Jesus in ways that would be helpful to their own readers. They select and arrange rather differently, and this may arise in part from how near they were to the events described. This is Jesus' teaching about the future, written down by people who were living through it.

Second, we have already mentioned (at 24:1–3) the issue of merging horizons. When events lead towards and foreshadow one another, we may expect difficulty in fixing a precise perspective. Understanding God's future is always hard, and Christians in our own day have wasted energy trying to work out dates and details. This chapter urges care and confidence. We must not panic (24:6). We should not trust leaders who try to take the place of Christ (24:24). We need not hunt high and low to locate God's activity (24:26).

For reflection

Wise discipleship involves a balance of calm scepticism (24:26) and confident faith (24:35). Pray for both.

92 Matthew 24:36–51
Wait, wake and work

There is a shift of focus between 24:34 ('all these things') and verse 36 ('but about that day'). Up to 24:34, the main emphasis of the chapter is on the stresses and distresses that will afflict the church in its first generation. After verse 36 there is a wider view of the church waiting and serving until the final judgement of Christ. The parables that follow, here and in chapter 25 – though they surely spoke to the first generation of the church – have something to say to Christians in every age.

Flood warning

The theme that runs to the end of chapter 24 is of normal life being abruptly interrupted. God's timetables are not easily read. His plans can take the world by surprise. The disciples' last question in 24:3, 'What will be the sign of the end of the age?' does not have a direct answer. The events that usher time to its final destination, the processes by which the kingdoms of this world become the kingdom of our God and his Christ, are not easily discerned.

The story of Noah (Genesis 6—9) is an account of normal life being utterly submerged by the intervention and judgement of God. The message here is that we should not take God for granted. The world is not so fully under our control as we often imagine (vv. 37–39). However usual business may appear to be, there is a greater issue that should always concern and shape the church. How ready are we?

Crime watch

The picture in verses 42–44 is of Jesus coming quietly and unexpectedly, like a thief in the night. When a householder expects a burglary, it is well to stay awake. A burglar who knows we are asleep has the advantage of surprise. The only way to prevent that is to be constantly on the alert. This parable is about living the sort of spiritual life that is vigilant, involved, alive to the work of God in our world. It speaks against a dozy, careless and casual faith. Again, do not take God for granted. Do not drift or despair. Patience, persistence, prayer – these are basics of Christian readiness.

Service charge

The next parable (vv. 45–51) has a particular message for Christian leaders, and it may be that Jesus had the twelve in mind. But it applies to any Christian whose responsibilities involve other people. The point is simple: be faithful to your work, keep at it, do it properly, treat other people with care and respect. That is readiness. The church does not need to run to and fro looking for Jesus (24:23–28). Steady commitment to the work of God, to love and care, to faithful responsibility and patient service, is the way to honour Christ.

Apparently Martin Luther was once asked what he would do if he thought Christ would come back the next day. He replied that he would get on with today's work as normal. Daily life, regular activity, faithful duty, may be all the readiness Christ expects of us. So how do we do our work? Is it work with which Christ can be pleased, and do we go about it in ways that honour him?

Ready, steady

As in so many aspects of belief, we need balance in our Christian hope. The history of the church is littered with disappointed people who thought the coming of the Lord was near. Some dropped normal responsibilities, some travelled to out-of-the-way places to greet the coming, some flamed with zeal and then burned rapidly low. But God is not a railway company, and the gospel is not a timetable.

The opposite fault is to lose hope. It does not all depend on us. God holds the issues of time in his hands: the God who created will complete; the God who commands will judge; the God who sent Christ will save through Christ. 'Fog in Channel. Continent cut off,' said one newspaper headline of a century ago. We may feel as if the cloudiness in our vision and faith pushes God to a distance. But God is there, as solid and as near as ever, seeing through the mist with purpose and love.

Prayer

May the God of hope fill us with all joy and peace in believing, that by the power of the Holy Spirit we may be filled with hope.
From ROMANS 15:13

93 Matthew 25:1–13

Out of oil

The last parable was a call to patient readiness, to the sort of faithful service that will not be surprised or embarrassed by the unexpected coming of the Lord. This parable of the ten maidens gives the other side of that same message. The time will come when it is too late to repair or restore what we have neglected to do and to be for Christ. Sudden retrieval of the situation may not be possible. As with a lot of human activity, you need to get ready when you have the chance. Then, even if the timing of God catches us by surprise, it need not find us unprepared.

A Jewish wedding

We have already met the idea of Jesus as God's bridegroom, come to claim his people (9:15; 22:2). Here he again appears as the bridegroom, but before he does we have an inside view of some Jewish wedding customs. In Britain it is often the bride who keeps everyone waiting. In first-century Jewish culture it appears that the wedding started when the groom and his company arrived. These girls with their lanterns appear to be all set to give the wedding party a ceremonial escort, as a sort of guard of honour.

Beyond that, the details of the situation are not fully clear. Why did the groom not come until nightfall? Had the girls left their lamps burning constantly, or did they try to light them up when the bridegroom came? Why could the wise girls not share what they had? Why are the foolish girls shut out so abruptly at the end – is that realistic?

As so often with parables, the detail is not all meant to be interpreted, nor is it all realistic. There is a main thread, about readiness, and that is what the reader or hearer should take away. We should take the opportunities we have, and respond faithfully and readily to the love and call of Christ, as we hear them. That is the only sure way to be ready for what is ahead.

The parable teaches that readiness is really an individual matter. We can help one another in the Christian life, but ultimately we have each to take responsibility for our own spiritual life and service. Commitment to Christ is one of the things that no one else can take on for us.

Time lapse

This parable and the previous one both feature a delay. The wicked servant (24:48) expects a delay, and then finds himself overtaken by the master's sudden arrival. The foolish girls seem not to reckon on a long wait, and are caught out when things move slowly.

The church has to be committed to the long haul, but also to make every day's activity fit for Christ. Church history may last much longer than we can foresee. But God is never so slow that we can afford to be slack in our service. It is that balance again, between hope that is ready and hope that is not afraid to wait.

Pictures of today

People who preach on parables sometimes try to be creative, in updating the story to fit something from our own society or experience. A modern parallel may help hearers to get their minds inside the message of the biblical story.

By all means think of your own examples. This story works because weddings are both quite structured and a bit unpredictable. That affects everyone, from guests to caterers to musicians to photographers. Can you weave something out of those threads? Jesus had an inventive mind and used stories from his own culture to explain the message of God's eternal kingdom. Good preachers should not be afraid to do the same.

For reflection and prayer

Time is more important than all eternity. Here you can prepare for the Lord. There you cannot.
Anonymous, from the Middle Ages

Lord Jesus Christ, may your church be ready to meet your coming, with the lamps of faith burning sure and strong. Give us the bright eyes of hope, the steady gaze of faith and the caring look of love.

94 Matthew 25:14–30
Hidden talent

This is the third parable in a row about waiting for someone to appear. Three servants are entrusted with their master's cash, to invest and do business until he returns. As with the ten virgins, this parable is about right and wrong responses: five virgins were wise and five foolish. Here it is two against one: two servants are active and successful, while the third is an ineffective and unhappy figure.

A similar parable occurs in Luke's gospel (19:11–27). There are many differences of detail, and it is hard to know whether it is the same story or not. Did Jesus tell it more than once, in different ways? Or were details adjusted as different groups of Christians used the story? Certainly the parable fits well in this part of Matthew, and connects with the material around. It provides a lesson on Christian stewardship and service in the face of the coming judgement of Christ. It urges Christians to be diligent, energetic and confident in working for God, and in seeking to advance God's kingdom.

Capital gains

The parable pictures a wealthy businessman entrusting slaves with large sums of money while he travels. While many slaves in the ancient world had very harsh lives, some rose to high positions in their owner's household and exercised considerable responsibility. That is the picture here. These slaves are expected to be active stewards, managers and entrepreneurs.

The first two slaves act with alacrity and judgement, and make solid gains for their master (vv. 16–17). He responds with praise and enthusiasm: 'Enter into the joy of your master' (vv. 21, 23). The slaves are promoted, no longer simply to work for the master but to share his friendship. The thought that faithful Christians will be gathered into the eternal joy of Christ is peeping through the parable: the 'application is creeping into the telling of the story' (R.T. France). Thus far, all seems to be well.

Losing interest

The third servant has an unsatisfactory tale. Fear of his master or lack of confidence in his own ability paralysed him, and he took the easiest route available, involving no risk, no imagination and no work.

The master is not impressed. The servant could surely have done better. Even a bank deposit would have produced some visible return. So his one talent is passed on to the servant who started with five, and he himself is thrown out of the security of the master's house.

Parable of application

Christian obedience is meant to be active. The church is not called simply to be, but to obey. We are meant to apply ourselves and achieve something for Christ. To sustain our own faith and Christian outlook is right. But we are Christians not just for our own spiritual survival, but in order to serve God, and to use the gifts and opportunities God has given us.

The English language has adopted a word from this story: talent, which originally meant a weight of silver. We use it nowadays to mean a personal gift, ability or skill. Here are two thoughts from the story.

- A talent is a very large sum. Personal abilities are precious: though often given for nothing, they are rarely developed without great effort. Treasure what you have been given. Treat it as valuable. And let us also value one another's gifts. Many people are far more gifted than they realise, but lack of opportunity or the doubts of others have choked the gift and now they lack confidence to launch out. Part of the privilege of being church is that we believe in one another, and we encourage and enable the talents of each, for the good of all and the glory of God.

- The talents in the story 'belong to someone else' (R.V.G. Tasker, *Matthew*, Tyndale New Testament Commentary, IVP, 1961). A Christian is steward and servant. Our lives and abilities are to be used for God, not just for ourselves. Whatever your calling – secular employment, voluntary service, family care, church duty – if it is worthwhile work, and you can do it honestly and effectively, then be proud to do it as service to Christ.

For prayer

Pause to reflect on what you have been given: abilities, time, friendships, energy. Then consciously and deliberately offer yourself to Christ, not just as a bundle of talents but as a loving disciple and willing servant. Ask that your life may be truly effective for him.

95 Matthew 25:31–46

Judged by Christ

This solemn and humbling passage is a dramatic display of Jesus Christ in judgement. As Son of Man he has authority over the nations (Daniel 7:13–14). Here he exercises that authority with all-seeing eye, tender heart and frighteningly powerful word.

Division according to kind(ness)

Strictly, verses 32–33 are the only part of the passage that is really a parable: 'as a shepherd separates the sheep from the goats'. It seems at first rather similar to the parables of the wheat and tares, and the net, in Matthew 13. What is very different here is the explanation that follows, of the division and judgement of the two groups.

Judgement is based on deeds of mercy to the 'least of these who are members of my family' (v. 40). It is all very practical, concerned with the basic requirements for human survival – food and water, warmth and shelter, and the provision of practical help and supplies to the sick and prisoners. But who are the 'members of my family'? Two opinions exist.

The least of my people

One view is that these are all poor people, of any race or religion. The whole human race is judged by its response to people in need. Christ is present everywhere, in the face and form of poverty and suffering, and even the simplest act of relief can be service to him. Jesus' teaching on neighbour love is not only the heart of the Jewish law (7:12; 22:39), but is also the standard by which the true humanity of every person and nation will be tested.

A second view connects the parable to other material in Matthew. Jesus speaks of his followers as his 'brother, sister and mother' (12:50). The 'little ones' are members of the church (18:6). In a verse that hints at the teaching of this present scene, the 'little one' is helped as a disciple of Jesus (10:42). So, it is suggested, the 'least of these' are Christians, and this separation of sheep and goats is the judgement of the nations according to their treatment of Christ and his followers.

Able writers on Matthew are evenly divided between these two views. Where does that leave us?

Right responses

The issue with all Jesus' teaching is not just what we think but what we do. Matthew's gospel is clear that Christians will be judged, that faith should be expressed in obedient and loving behaviour, and that we should not confine our love to the people we like (5:43–47; 7:21–23). Those teachings push us to take this judgement scene seriously, to weigh our own lives by the marks of kindness mentioned here, and to love others genuinely and generously for Christ's sake – wherever we find them.

Some people ask how grace and faith fit into this picture. Does not this passage tell of judgement by works? Yes, it does, but faith ought to produce good works. That was the message of the last parable, about the talents: faith should aim to be active for God; otherwise it loses the right to count as faith. Then this parable fills out that picture: the main thing faith should do is to care, practically, sympathetically and readily. Jesus Christ is 'God with us'. He cares for us despite our own 'little faith'. He also leads and teaches us to serve the needs of others. Here is the grace of Jesus Christ, alive within the Christian and touching the world through the care given in his name.

Suffering shepherd

This is the end of the last great block of teaching. Jesus is moving on.

- The shepherd who divides sheep and goats is the same one who looked lovingly upon God's wandering sheep (9:36). Now he goes to his last and greatest act of care.
- The Son of Man who will one day sit in heavenly power (v. 31) will first hang in humiliation and pain (26:2).
- The Christ who identifies with the naked and the prisoner, with the famished and thirsty, with the weak, estranged and despised, is the Christ who will be subjected to all this himself.
- The Lord who speaks judgement now goes to bear it.

For reflection

Jesus Christ invites us to know him in his weakness, that we may serve him in our neighbours' needs.

96

Matthew 26:1–13

Anointed for burial

The teaching is over (v. 1), and we return to the unfolding events of Holy Week. As we enter the Passion story, all the lines start to converge, to gather our thoughts and expectations. It is like a well-designed garden, where every stretch of path directs the visitor's eye to a distant central tree. Each of four short scenes (26:2–16) points us in the same direction – to the cross.

Time for sacrifice

Passover is at hand – the Jewish springtime festival that celebrated the people's rescue from Egypt over a thousand years before. Again Jesus predicts his coming death (v. 2), as he did on the journey to Jerusalem. Matthew's story does not yet show us that Jesus himself will be the great Passover sacrifice. That will come later. But we do see that he goes to death knowingly and willingly. He accepts obediently the 'must' (16:21) that is the destiny and plan of God.

On the quiet

Once again (as at 2:4) religious leaders of the nation gather, and again Jesus' life will come under threat. Caiaphas was high priest from about AD18 to 36. He must have been a politically skilful man, for he had difficult responsibilities to balance. His father-in-law Annas, who is mentioned in Luke and John, and had served as high priest from AD6 to 15, was still an influential background figure.

The leaders plan to 'arrest Jesus by stealth' (v. 4). This contrasts with the theme of Jesus' innocence, which will be important in the coming trial. But only by a quiet capture would they avoid a riot. Jesus has won the sympathy of many in the festal crowd, and direct action against him would be very risky.

Praise flowing freely

The woman's action seems to be entirely her own initiative (v. 7). It is demonstrative, lavish, devoted, intimate and moving. It also proved somewhat embarrassing, though not necessarily for the reasons that would apply in our culture.

The disciples start reckoning the cost involved. Their explanation sounds quite creditable. After all, Jesus has encouraged people to sell and give (19:21). But they miss the point. Worship has a value of its own that cannot be easily rated and measured. This act of worship is uniquely precious: the poor will always be there (Deuteronomy 15:11), but Jesus will not.

He senses the cross looming over him, and accepts this woman's worship as a kind of funeral ceremony (v. 12). As dead bodies were buried with spices and perfume, so Jesus receives this myrrh as a burial anointing ahead of time. He goes forward from now as the anointed one, named as the Christ and marked out for death by the silent worship of an unnamed woman. In the reading of the gospel, her action has become known across the world (v. 13). Her memorial of the Christ, and his of her, lead the church's worship towards his coming death.

The lines that converge on the cross are of many kinds. Jesus' steady commitment to God sits strangely beside the worldly cunning of the priests. The generosity of the woman's worship contrasts with Judas' actions in the next short scene. Sin and sacrifice, deceit and devotion, generosity and greed, all come together at the place where the love of God meets the suffering of earth.

Worthy worship

Worship in most of our churches is quite well planned and controlled. The woman's action at Bethany was unexpected, unusual, lavish and emotional. We use the order of a service to help worshippers offer their whole selves to God. This woman's worship seems to have been more spontaneous. So perhaps this passage invites some gentle reflection on how we worship. How much room ought we to leave, even occasionally, for the unscripted praise of the heart?

Jesus sees no clash of loyalties either between costly and committed worship and care for the poor. When we worship gladly and gratefully, God can deepen our love for others in ways that will affect all our living. Good praise is practical: it produces good practice.

For prayer

Give thanks that God accepts the worship of your life, as you are – your prayer and practical service, your thoughts and emotions, the order of your life, and your spontaneity.

97 Matthew 26:14–25

The trap is sprung

Matthew's narrative moves on two parallel tracks. On one hand is the priests' desire to have Jesus arrested, and their scheming to that end. The other movement is the path taken by Jesus as he goes with his friends to the Passover table, then out to the garden (26:30, 36). The go-between from one line to another is Judas Iscariot.

Man of mystery

I cannot read the mind of Judas. There is too much darkness to see clearly: the darkness of deceit, the darkness of death and the darkness of our limited knowledge. Had he expected Jesus to be a different kind of leader, and was his betrayal the reaction of a disillusioned man? Was he trying in some perverse and ill-judged way to force Jesus into more aggressive action, by putting him in a tight corner? Had his facility with money (John 12:6) caused him to be just too eager for one lucrative opportunity – as a person's greatest strengths may sometimes be the cause of great sins? However tangled his motives, his name has now become a byword for treachery, and one cannot help thinking that he should have known better. Nothing is unforgivable, but for some actions there is no real excuse.

So Judas watched for an opportunity (v. 16). What he eventually betrayed was the meeting place, the garden where Jesus and his disciples would go after the meal. That gave the priests their opportunity to take Jesus quietly, to try him quickly and to have the matter in the hands of the Romans soon after dawn. The popular tumult they feared (26:5) never came. Events moved too rapidly for that.

The figure of 30 silver coins is mentioned only in this gospel. It echoes an Old Testament text (Zechariah 11:12–13) which Matthew takes up later (27:3–10). Judas' request for payment (explicit only in Matthew) contrasts with the free and generous worship of the woman at Bethany. Clear light and deep shadow set one another in sharp relief.

Setting out

The whole Passover festival lasted a week. This 'first day of Unleavened Bread' was the day for the festal meal. Once again (as at 21:2–3) there seems to be a prior arrangement, this time concerning the room. Even so, the story suggests that Jesus is in command. He knows; he arranges; he orders. As Judas seeks a moment of 'opportunity' (v. 16), Jesus prepares deliberately for his 'time' (v. 18), the critical hour to which he has long been drawn, and which now comes very near. The disciples go off to the city to prepare the room and meal as they are bidden.

Tension at table

The little group take their places at the Passover table, but the atmosphere is strained. As Jesus speaks of betrayal, the disciples search their own hearts. They have stumbled and misunderstood often enough, but to betray Jesus would be far worse. The word about dipping in the dish (v. 23) may be enough to alert Judas. Jesus knows his secret. He asks his own sad question (v. 25), there is a terrible moment as he feels Jesus looking right into him, and we do not see him leave.

Only Judas calls Jesus 'Rabbi' (v. 25). The other disciples say 'Lord' (v. 22). The different name seems to set Judas apart from the group. This is the language an outsider would use.

Destiny and despair

There is tension in this whole matter. Jesus' destiny is inevitable. This is the road he must take. But the people who bring him there, and especially Judas, remain responsible for what they do. Though the cross was God's purpose, some of the human deeds that caused it were very ungodly. It is easy 2,000 years later to say 'them'. But these people were not so different from us. Many of their faults were common human failures. It was not just *for* our sins that Jesus died; it was also *by* our sins that he died.

Even if there is no excusing Judas, to be caught without excuse is not his plight alone. Many of us have been there over one issue or another. The forgiveness of Christ is broad enough to cover even the most wretched sins. Judas' final misery – who knows? – may have been that he could not believe that.

Prayer

May God forgive what we have been, sanctify what we are, and direct what we shall be. Through Jesus Christ our Lord. Amen

98 Matthew 26:26–30

Body language

The last supper of Jesus has spoken powerfully and profoundly to Christians through 2,000 years. The church across the centuries is welcomed in Holy Communion to the quiet intimacy of the upper room, to sit as friends of Jesus and witness as if for the first time the holy words and actions. There are four records of these words in the New Testament. Many of us will know Paul's account best (1 Corinthians 11:23–26). Matthew's version, though very similar, also has a slant and power of its own.

Given for you

Jesus presides among his friends, and he shapes the course of events. Only in Gethsemane will he be overtaken by his enemies. His four actions with the bread – 'took, blessed, broke and gave' – recall his two feeding miracles (14:19; 15:36). This meal also will be for the feeding of many. With the cup too, he takes, blesses and gives. Matthew shows the two actions, with bread and cup, as parallel: the same giving, twice over, of the signs of body and blood.

In a Jewish animal sacrifice, the blood was drained away. The flesh and blood were separated by death. So the elements Jesus shares with his friends speak of sacrifice, of the separating of flesh and blood, of life laid down as worship and gift. His dying is a new Passover. He is, though the words are not used, the Lamb of God. There are other Old Testament resonances too.

- **Covenant:** God's covenant with Israel was sealed with the sprinkling of blood (Exodus 24:8). So now that ancient covenant ceremony is re-enacted, by the shedding of Jesus' blood.
- **Hope:** This is, although Matthew does not actually say so, a new kind of covenant. Jeremiah (31:31–34) wrote of God remaking his covenant, and covering his people with forgiveness.
- **Suffering:** Here is a reminder of Jesus' servant ministry. The words 'poured out for many' echo Isaiah 53:12. The Lord gives his life 'as ransom for many' (Matthew 20:28).

Parted from you

There is a finality in this meeting of friends. They will never gather this way again. The bond they have shared is being broken by death. There is anticipation in Jesus' words, but no mention of his friends continuing the meal or commemorating him. He looks forward to a new meeting, in 'my Father's kingdom'. He expects to die, and yet he looks forward to sharing in the great feast of God, and to a greater fellowship that time and tribulation will not break.

Shared among you

Christians rejoice to share this feast, week after week and year after year. There are many aspects on which we may reflect. Matthew's account of the last supper suggests a number.

- **Covenant:** The bread and wine speak of the depth of God's commitment to us, and of the bond forged at the cross of Christ. Holy Communion draws Christians into relationship with Christ and with each other.
- **Forgiveness:** Only Matthew's version actually says 'for the forgiveness of sins'. Jesus shared bread and wine with disciples who would desert and deny him. We come to Communion not because we deserve to, but because we do not; to the God whose pardon is clear and complete, for Christ has died.
- **Separation:** If we celebrate Communion at special gatherings – synods, conferences and so on – we may be well aware that this group will never reassemble in exactly the same form. But in any local church, on any Sunday, the company who gather at the Lord's Table may never be all together again. Life – and death – move people on. Communion is a sacrament of parting, of fragile and fleeting life. Yet it is a chance to share, in time, a taste of eternity. We do this together as a signpost to the life where there will be no more parting and no more pain.
- **Service:** Jesus and his company close with a Passover hymn, and go to the Mount of Olives (v. 30). For Jesus that will be a place of painful wrestling and costly commitment. Communion is not simply a withdrawal. It is also a sacrament of discipleship, beckoning us forward to the trials, decisions and service we undertake for God.

99 Matthew 26:31-36
Struck and scattered

The Mount of Olives (26:30) was a sizeable wooded ridge, a place where Jesus might hope to find some peace. Gethsemane (v. 36) means 'oil-press'. John (18:1-2) tells us it was a garden – perhaps a small olive grove – and that Jesus and the disciples often met there. According to ancient tradition it is on the lower slopes of the Mount, not far from the city wall.

Shepherd and flock

The eleven disciples have searched their own thoughts, for fear they might betray Jesus (26:22). They will not betray; but they will come under strain they cannot bear (v. 31). The arrest of Jesus will scatter them to the winds, like sheep without care or leadership, spread aimlessly across the hills.

Jesus had wanted to give the people of Israel a shepherd's care (9:36). He was able to gather a 'little flock' (Luke 12:32) around himself. Now he will be struck down, so that even the little flock will disintegrate for a while. Then afterwards he will be raised up. The scattered flock will be gathered again. Their leader will call them, and go ahead of them, as a shepherd walks in front of the sheep (v. 32). In resurrection he will meet them in Galilee (28:16), to lead his people into new places under his ever-watchful care.

Cock-sure

As so often before (see comment on 14:28-31, pp. 128-129), Peter is the first disciple to speak (v. 33). Not for the first time, his comments are wishful rather than wise. He wants to support Jesus all the way, but he completely underestimates both the severity of the coming trials and his own frailty and inexperience. He is a man out of place, a sailor in the city, an eager follower who cannot understand that the master has to take this journey on his own.

Jesus' words seem harsh (v. 34). The reader will take them seriously, but Peter cannot. He refuses to believe Jesus. 'Peter, crowing like a proud cock, rebuts Jesus' (Davies and Allison). He is impulsive and indignant, and the other disciples follow his lead. We shall start to see in Gethsemane how much stamina they really have (26:40–45).

As the little procession moves on to the hillside, Jesus' words 'this night' (vv. 31, 34) suggest an atmosphere more sinister than mere physical darkness. The shadows are dense and disturbing. There is evil abroad.

Shepherd and king

A couple of Old Testament episodes echo in these verses, one very clear, the other so faint that we might be imagining it.

- The faint echo is from 2 Samuel 15. David faces a rebellion by his son Absalom, and flees Jerusalem for a period. He makes his way over the Mount of Olives. Like Jesus in Gethsemane, he grieves bitterly, but lays himself open to the will of God (15:25–26, 30). Like Jesus, he has a turncoat supporter who ends up hanging himself (15:12; 17:23). So Jesus too is a king under attack, a new David harried and hunted by Israel. A major difference is that David's loyal friends stuck with him (15:21; 18:1), and helped to get him out of trouble. Jesus' friends, despite all their confident claims, could not.

- The second and stronger resonance is in Matthew 26:31: 'I will strike the shepherd, and the sheep will be scattered.' This quote comes from Zechariah 13:7. A number of texts from this prophet figure in Matthew's Passion chapters – about a peaceful king, a stricken shepherd, 30 silver coins and the Mount of Olives as a place of crisis and judgement.

There are many links to the Old Testament in all four gospels, and Matthew surpasses the other three in the way that he emphasises these links. I am sure the fertile mind at the root of it all is Jesus himself. He knew the Jewish scriptures and understood his own work in relation to them. Son of Man, servant, shepherd – these were his links and his ideas. The early Christians, Matthew among them, rejoiced to follow the lead Jesus had given and to tell his story against an Old Testament background.

For reflection and prayer

Give thanks for the unfolding of God's purposes through the years, for the complex tapestry God weaves, yet with one design – love – and with one focus – Jesus Christ.

> Let us keep our eyes fixed on Jesus, the author and finisher of our faith.
> HEBREWS 12:2

100

Matthew 26:36–46

Garden of tears

For Jesus, Gethsemane was a garden of stillness, and of terrible turbulence. The night was quiet, but his spirit was tense and perturbed. His resolve and his relationship with the Father were tested to the limit. Yet he rose from his prayers a man deliberate and determined not simply to submit to fate, but to carry through his Father's will and work. He had been tried and had not drawn back.

With three disciples

Once again Jesus takes Peter, James and John, the same friends who witnessed the transfiguration (17:1–9). This experience too is about sonship, and the cross, and God's will. At the transfiguration in the light of the mountaintop the disciples saw Jesus, as he went towards the cross, as Son of God. Here in the darkness of the garden it is Jesus who understands, with fresh clarity and immediacy, that sonship and crucifixion will belong together.

If it be possible

Jesus has seen the Passion coming from far away. But as he looks the experience in the face, he is sharply aware of the awful cost involved. The 'cup' is his suffering (see comment on 20:20–23, pp. 167–168). Jesus expects this, but he cannot embrace it. He would rather God's will did not lead him this way, would rather he could express and exercise his role as Son without the cross.

Gethsemane is not cowardice, nor even natural strain showing in a tired and committed personality. Gethsemane is such a very intense experience because something more than physical suffering is involved. The suffering will be spiritual too. Up to now, Jesus' Sonship has been both a task for God and a tie, a bond, to God. Now, in finishing the task, he will break the tie. He has taken the role of servant, the bearer of the sins of others; that is where the cost lies. To be a sin-bearer will mean separation and alienation from God, and dreadful darkness (27:46).

Jesus returns in prayer to words and ideas he has often used: 'Father' (v. 39), 'thy will be done' (v. 39), 'pray not to succumb to temptation' (v. 41). His own Lord's Prayer has within it words and concerns that shape his approach to God, even out of deep distress. A well-formed prayer habit is the resource he brings to this crisis. He is speaking to the God he knows.

Man alone

Gethsemane is a pivot in the gospel story. This is the moment when action becomes passion. Here Jesus becomes isolated from his friends, a man entirely on his own. He goes to the garden 'with them' (v. 36), but they cannot stay awake 'with him' (vv. 38, 40). They drift away, first into sleep (v. 40), then into the night (v. 56), and he passes into the hands of his enemies.

Up to this point, Jesus has been in control of the group, giving the lead, expressing his own will. From now on he is subjected to a very different will, by men who hate and hurt him. His transition point is the will of God (vv. 39, 42), which leads him from power into passion, from initiative into humiliation, from control to the cross. Jesus goes forward into that will – of his Father and of his enemies – willingly, knowingly and obediently (vv. 45–46).

Watch and pray

In Jesus' last great sermon, he taught that the church should be a people alert, spiritually 'on watch', ready to meet the crisis of judgement (24:42–44). But here Jesus himself keeps watch alone. Gethsemane, and indeed the whole Passion story, is a kind of compression of many of the troubles and persecutions in Matthew 24. Jesus keeps watch, he is handed over to trial, others fall away around him, and yet he stays faithful to the end. The path that the church must take, and the pressures they must bear, he takes and bears first. He goes through crisis alone, that his people may be able to go through it after him and with him.

For reflection and prayer

Gethsemane was not a public event. There are depths of Jesus' experience we cannot probe. But Gethsemane tells us that there is no uncharted territory. In our costly decisions; in our bitterest loneliness; in our wrestling with God; if friends should fail us – in all of this, Jesus has been there, and he understands, and we do not need to go through it alone.

101 Matthew 26:47–56

Swords and a kiss

The one I shall kiss

The armed contingent comes from 'the chief priests and elders of the people' (v. 47), the group we have already seen acting against Jesus (26:3–5, 14–16; see comment on 21:23, p. 177). These were the men who held power in Jerusalem. The Pharisees, who had given Jesus a good deal of trouble in Galilee, scarcely appear in these chapters.

The arresting party intend to capture Jesus on his own. They have no interest in rounding up the disciples. Jesus was not a typical rebel or guerrilla. His strength lay in his knowledge of God, not in an armed human following.

So finally Jesus is 'handed over' (26:45), as he said he would be (17:22; 20:18; 26:2). Judas is called 'the one who hands over' (26:46, 48) – sometimes translated 'traitor' or 'betrayer' – but he is also the man who fulfils what Jesus prophesied. He picks Jesus out of the group with a kiss. Again he calls him 'Rabbi', which is not a disciple's greeting (v. 49; see comments on 26:25, p. 217). Jesus acknowledges Judas as 'friend', but that need not be a very intimate term, as its earlier use in Matthew shows (20:13; 22:12). The kiss cannot really conceal the barrier of distrust between the two men.

Violence breeds

John's gospel identifies Peter as the swordsman among the disciples. He was the disciple who had been keenest to support and stick by Jesus (26:33, 35), and he is the first to fight back when Jesus is arrested. His hasty blow must have come very near to killing the other man (v. 51). But Jesus will have none of it.

'Tit for tat' is often the way human life works. People who use violence generally reap violence in return. Peter is just following the usual pattern. But Jesus has already taught his friends to take a different path, to break the spiral of violence, to reply to anger with peace (5:38–42). Because violence breeds, it also breaks those who use it (v. 52), and Jesus does not want this sort of support.

Even in the grip of his enemies, Jesus commands the situation. He retains his poise, his penetrating facility with words, his ability to think clearly under challenge, his trust in God. He is committed to the path laid out for him in scripture (v. 54), to live out the roles of the suffering servant (26:28) and stricken shepherd (26:31). He does not want or need powerful defence, either from earth or heaven (v. 53).

Like a band of robbers

Jesus called the temple 'a den of robbers' (21:13). Now the temple police come armed, as if Jesus is the bandit (v. 55). 'Could you not have arrested me in the temple?' he asks. He was an easy enough target, surely. Of course they did not act against Jesus there, because of his popularity. A dark hillside is a much better and more discreet opportunity. But his challenge strikes home. Banditry is their role, and it seems to be their rule of operation.

Running out

The disciples show up badly, as Jesus said they would (26:31). For a while they were able to obey and follow (26:19, 30), but eventually they can only sleep and scatter (26:45, 56). Two of them stand out from the group.

- Judas has taken his own deliberate and fateful line of action, a course that will finally destroy him (26:14, 25, 47; 27:3–6).
- Then there is Peter, constantly overreaching himself (26:33, 35, 51, 58), until he breaks down in tears (26:75).

Christians often stumble. We mistake and misjudge many situations. We are often fearful, like the ten men who melted into the dark. We are sometimes foolhardy, like Peter. But we should pray to be kept from the deep and sustained falsehood of a Judas. The time may come when, for weakness or lack of wisdom, we cannot act for Christ. But let us at least avoid – at almost any cost – acting against him.

For reflection and prayer

There are some pressures and pains to which the proper Christian response cannot be either fight or flight: either would amount to abandoning our discipleship.
Alexander Sand

Lord Jesus Christ, please give me the courage and patience to be steadfast and calm when I ought to be. Share with me your inner peace and strength, when I need it most. Amen

102 Matthew 26:57–68

The Jewish trial

Matthew's gospel has two trial scenes, this one before the Jewish Sanhedrin and the second before the Roman governor Pontius Pilate. The Sanhedrin was the chief ruling body of the Jewish people, and had very wide legal powers. Only the Romans, however, could carry out the death penalty.

The two authorities had different concerns. What counted with the Roman governor was peace and order. The Sanhedrin was different: it was a religious court as well as a political body. So although the two trials face the same issue – Jesus' claim to be the Jewish Messiah – they deal with it in different ways. For the Romans, a man calling himself king is a potential threat to peace. With the Jews, the main issue turns out to be blasphemy.

It is odd to have a trial at night. This hearing may have been an initial investigation, to prepare a case against Jesus. Then a more formal sitting of the Sanhedrin followed the next morning (27:1–2).

Two good men and true?

A capital charge required at least two witnesses (Deuteronomy 17:6). The impression is that the court cast about for adequate testimony, and paid more regard to haste than truth. The stress on falsehood (v. 60) emphasises that Jesus is innocent and does not deserve to die.

Eventually two witnesses report that Jesus declared himself able to demolish and rebuild the temple (v. 61). Jesus never says exactly this in the gospels. Matthew 24:2 is a distant approximation. John 2:21 is much closer, though with the aside that 'he was speaking of the temple of his body'. But his words and deeds have evidently been interpreted by the witnesses to produce a very serious charge.

Jesus' restraint may simply be shrewd (v. 63). The testimony is off-target, but if he tries to explain or clarify, that will only make the situation worse. Yet his silence hints, for the sharp-eyed reader, that he is fulfilling the servant's role (Isaiah 53:7) – a suggestion that will become much stronger later.

Uttering the unthinkable

With the temple charge not settled one way or the other, the trial takes another tack. The high priest challenges Jesus (v. 63): his question almost exactly matches Peter's earlier confession of faith (16:16). Jesus' first cryptic reply (v. 64) corresponds to the English expression, 'You said it!' But he continues with words and images that are far from cryptic and that bring together two Old Testament texts.

- Psalm 110:1 pictures Messiah sitting at God's right hand.
- Daniel 7:9–14 shows the Son of Man coming with clouds.

So Jesus does not just accept the title 'Messiah'. He associates himself with the glory, majesty and power of God. Though being judged, he speaks as Judge. Questioned under authority, he asserts higher authority. Facing his nation's leaders, he claims to be their true leader.

Blasphemy and blows

Blasphemy had a pretty broad scope – anything that expressed contempt for the sacred. Jesus' words come far outside acceptable limits. The court is outraged. They hear what he says as a gross affront – to decency, to reverence and to God. The high priest tears his robes in disgust (v. 65). There may be a touch of irony here: high-priestly robes were not supposed to be torn (Leviticus 21:10). In rejecting the Messiah, the high priest denies his own role.

The court moves quickly to decision, and the final scene is ugly and cruel. Jesus is blindfolded (Luke 22:64): that is why they ask who has hit him (26:68). Again he fulfils the prophecy of the suffering servant, who was spat upon, insulted and beaten (Isaiah 50:6). More poignantly, Jesus acts out his own teaching about not resisting evil and aggression (5:38–42). Even here, in the face of scorn, he remains Israel's true teacher, in whom God's way is truly known.

For reflection and prayer

Jesus has been caught and cornered, physically and legally. There will be no way out, only a painful way through. Yet we may read this part of the gospel with thanksgiving that the Lord came through this for us. And as part of our response, we may act to oppose injustice wherever we can.

103 Matthew 26:69–75
No friend of mine

Peter's denial is one of the best-known stories in the gospels. He is no worse than the other ten disciples, who fled. But Peter's headstrong personality means that his failures are generally more dramatic and conspicuous than other people's. God does not love Peter any less for that. God can do business with honest failure.

Waiting to see

Peter follows the arresting party through the dark lanes and streets. He manages to get access to the outer yard of the high priest's house, where the hearing is being held. Now he waits to see how things will turn out (26:58). It is the best support he can give Jesus, but he must be tired, fearful and apprehensive. He sits among strangers, and tries to look as if he belongs there.

You were with him

Three times over, Peter is challenged, and three times he denies that he knows Jesus. The incidents escalate from one to the next. Each is more public and open than the one before. The stakes seem to rise, and so too does the intensity of Peter's denial. His mood gets more and more desperate, his words become less and less controlled, as the night wears on and one awkward conversation follows another.

- The first accusation is made by one person, directly to Peter himself. His answer is simple and straightforward (vv. 69–70).
- The second challenge comes from one person again, but her question draws a group into the conversation. Peter replies 'with an oath' (vv. 71–72).
- The third time a number of people confront Peter together. His accent gives him away. He 'starts cursing and swearing', and blusters his way through another refusal (vv. 73–74).

Meanwhile the reader has been counting, and recalling what Jesus said earlier (26:34).

Cock-crow and tears

Straight away after the third denial, the cock crows. It is Luke (22:61) who tells us that Jesus turned round and looked at Peter. Matthew simply mentions how Peter remembered that Jesus had said this would happen. Suddenly Peter cannot contain himself. It is all too much for him – the pace of events, dark sayings about death, Judas' deceit, Jesus' arrest, his own tiredness, and now this wretched failure. The sheer tragedy and helplessness of the situation engulf him, and he runs out to hide, alone with his sorrow and shame.

The strange purposes of grace

There are a number of ironies and surprises in these verses. It is bitter indeed that just when the high priest challenged Jesus (26:64) in almost the very words with which Peter had once confessed his faith, Peter should deny he ever knew Jesus.

There is a subtle mockery in the words, 'You were with Jesus' (vv. 69, 71). For Peter had tried to stay awake with Jesus and there too he had drifted away from his best intentions. 'Could you not stay awake with me?' (26:38, 40). He could not.

It is ironic that while Jesus is taunted and goaded to prophesy (26:68), one of his prophecies is fulfilled through Peter's threefold denial.

Finally, it is strange and marvellous that God should choose a man who gets into such a miserable mess to be the church's first leader, first evangelist, pioneer missionary to the Gentiles, and one of the earliest martyrs for the gospel. Our church, yours and mine, is built on the rock of faith, not on the rock of perfect holiness and virtue. That could be God's way of reminding us not to think too highly of ourselves. It could also be God's assurance that however many disasters and tangles we manage to make, there is still a place for us in his will and work.

For reflection and prayer

In the times when tiredness and tension prove too much for you, when tears take over, when you aim high and sink low, remember Peter. God used him, loved him and stood by him.

104

Matthew 27:1–10

Bitter end

There are two short paragraphs in this section. The first is a phase in the trial of Jesus, a process which is now starting to move rapidly towards the cross. But before we follow the legal process to the next stage, Matthew interrupts the sequence to tell of the death of Judas.

Case conference

This short account of a meeting of the Sanhedrin (vv. 1–2) is really just a link in the chain. We have already heard of the hearing they have given Jesus, of his claim to be the Messiah, and of the reaction he provoked. The outcome of this morning meeting simply confirms the view that he ought to die. Now they will need to put their case to Pilate, and secure his co-operation.

Pilate was 'Prefect of Judea' from AD26 to 36, appointed by Rome and answerable there. History has given us a good deal of information about him apart from what is in the gospels. The overall impression is of an awkward and unreasonable man. He was a tough governor, inclined to use a firm hand, but without a sure touch or good judgement.

So Jesus is 'handed over', passed from hand to hand like a parcel: first by Judas to the high priests (26:15); then by the Sanhedrin to the Roman authorities (27:2), and finally by Pilate to the soldiers who crucify him (27:26). This handing over to the Gentiles fulfils what Jesus had said would happen (20:19). But before we go forward to the final stage, we step aside from the main line of the story.

Innocent blood

Once again we see Matthew's technique of putting light alongside shadow. Interrupting the trial of Jesus to show the remorse and death of Judas highlights Jesus as an innocent man. The relentless process of hearings and crucifixion is unjust and unfair. That same theme will return again in the coming verses (27:19, 25, 54).

Matthew's inclusion at this stage of the death of Judas enables him not to interrupt the story ahead. Jesus is the central character, and his cross and resurrection must command full attention. In fact Judas may not have died as soon as this.

The Bible records a handful of suicides – Samson, Saul, Ahithophel. In different ways these incidents speak for themselves. The death of Judas tells of bitter and unbearable remorse, of the terrible loneliness of a man who could not live with his own deed. Scripture makes no further comment about the morality involved. There is no word of judgement against Judas here, beyond what Jesus has already given (26:24).

Scripture does, however, affirm that life is a good and precious gift from God. The small number of extreme cases in the Bible – and all of them are extreme – have rightly led the church to advise strongly and consistently against suicide. But there is more we may do than teach. Many people in our society live with grave remorse, and may for various reasons consider taking their own life. Some, of course, go through with it. Skilled pastoral care, patient sympathy and practical support may often be asked of us, from people who have to live with deep misery, and also from their relatives.

Tapestry of texts

The main burden of verses 9–10 is to link Judas' death to the Old Testament. This is the last of Matthew's famous fulfilment quotations. The purchase of the field is mentioned also in Acts 1:18–19, again with the name 'Blood Acre' (although the Acts account of Judas' death is rather different). The scripture texts come from Zechariah 11:12–13 (30 pieces of silver), from Jeremiah 18 and 19 (a potter and a burial ground), and possibly from Jeremiah 32 (the purchase of a field). Matthew has plaited the texts together, seeing in each a foreshadowing of one aspect of this incident. Thus, he says to the reader, even this painful ending finds its place in the purpose of God.

For prayer

God of mercy, we pray:
For those who live with shame: may they know your forgiveness.
For those who live with sin: grant them amendment of life.
For those who live with sorrow: bring them your comfort.
For those who hate themselves: give them loving friends.
Through Jesus Christ our Lord. Amen

105

Matthew 27:11–26

The Roman trial

Pontius Pilate is involved all through this scene, and is responsible for the final outcome. At the very end it is 'the governor's soldiers' (v. 27) who take Jesus away. Yet Pilate seems strangely and unusually indecisive. Against this background of indecision, Matthew highlights the determination of the Jewish leaders.

First questions

Jesus' claim to be Messiah fell foul of the Jewish court as a religious blasphemy. Here the Jewish leaders present the same material to Pilate, but with a fresh twist. The Messiah is a royal figure. So Jesus claims to be 'king of the Jews', and that is politically dangerous. It marks him out as a revolutionary, a prince pretender.

Pilate asks Jesus if he is king of the Jews. Jesus replies briefly, but not directly (v. 11): 'You said it.' He is a king, though not the kind Pilate thinks. When Pilate presses him further, he stays silent, as he did during the Jewish trial. Pilate is amazed, and perhaps scornful. Jesus cannot have appeared a very threatening character.

This man or Barabbas

The custom of releasing a prisoner at feast-time is known in some ancient lands, although we have no other knowledge of this from the Holy Land. Barabbas was a rebel, a violent man (Luke 23:19), presumably awaiting crucifixion. Giving the crowd a choice strikes Pilate as a good way out of an awkward situation. He can save face without having to decide whether Jesus of Nazareth is guilty or not. And if the Jewish leaders have charged Jesus out of envy, then rejecting their request will be one more petty gain in the power-play of colonial administration (v. 18). Pursuing a compromise instead of taking a decision is often a risky strategy. It can rebound badly. None the less, Pilate finds this an attractive option. As we wait to hear which way the choice will fall, Pilate is called aside.

Warned in a dream

Only Matthew mentions Pilate's wife (v. 19). She is a counterpart to the soldiers at the cross (27:54) – a sympathetic Gentile. For Matthew, dreams can be God's postal service (as in 1:20—2:22). Romans too took them seriously. Pilate's handwashing (v. 24) suggests that he himself is unsettled by his wife's message, but her intervention is too late to affect the trial. The matter is in the hands of the crowd.

People's choice

For the first time in Matthew, the crowd turns against Jesus. It is difficult to tell how big this crowd was. They may not have been the same people who cheered Jesus into the city, for example. Matthew stresses that they were led into their choice, persuaded by the chief priests and elders. The shouting against Jesus gets louder, and Pilate eventually realises that he has been pushed into a bad decision.

The end of the matter

Washing one's hands of something has become a casual proverb. But there was nothing casual about Pilate's mood that day. I suspect he was haunted by what his wife had said, confused by the strange calm of his prisoner, and rather ashamed of the mess he had made of the case. The hand-washing is a desperate but futile attempt to rid himself of guilt and responsibility.

Pilate's final reply to the crowd is, 'You see to it' (v. 24). 'It's your responsibility.' The high priests used exactly the same expression to Judas (27:4). As with Adam and Eve in Genesis 3, none of the main actors will accept the blame. So the people bear the burden (v. 25). Matthew highlights Jewish responsibility for the death of Jesus more than the other gospels do. But the people's responsibility should be qualified in several ways: that the high priests led them; that Pilate let them; and that God still loves them. There is nothing in the crucifixion story to warrant anti-Jewish feeling today. (There is further comment on this at Matthew 23, p. 190.)

Finally Jesus is beaten. A Roman whip was made of knotted leather straps, sometimes with pieces of metal or bone driven through the leather. This is the start of the degrading experience of crucifixion. A beaten man would not take so long to die.

For reflection

'Crucified under Pontius Pilate' means that the Son of God was subjected to the jealousy, folly and stubbornness of human power. Pray for people who suffer today through the abuse of power.

106 Matthew 27:27–34
Road to the cross

The trial is over. Suddenly it is very certain what is coming next. Events have moved with frightening speed to this point. Now that the prisoner has been found guilty, the execution will follow without any delay. Jesus is weak and badly hurt from the beating he has been given, a soft target for the callous mockery of Pilate's soldiers.

A soldiers' joke

Jesus was taunted and spat upon after his Jewish trial (26:67–68). After the Roman trial the same sort of thing happens again. This seems to be a more elaborate mockery than the earlier episode; certainly Matthew describes it more fully.

Pilate normally lived at Caesarea on the coast, but at festival times he came to Jerusalem with a strong contingent of soldiers to contain any trouble among the crowds. The mockery takes place in his headquarters, with 'the whole cohort' (v. 27) taking part. A cohort was about 600 men, and would have been second-grade soldiers, Syrian auxiliaries rather than the élite legionaries. The men who were off duty gathered around for a bit of cynical sport.

The scene is a shallow copy of a king's coronation. A soldier's red cloak does duty for a royal robe, Jesus is crowned with a wreath of thorns and a reed is put into his right hand as if it were a sceptre of kingly authority and power. The whole thing is a sarcastic humiliation. It mocks Jesus personally. Perhaps the soldiers were also mocking the Jewish nation: is this the best king they can produce – a broken, beaten, poor village carpenter? The irony is really the other way round. These soldiers make sport of the man who will judge the whole world. They laugh at him now, but one day his authority will overshadow every human empire.

As he did before, Jesus remains silent. Yet these events fill out his earlier words (20:19). He goes to death as a prophet. He also dies as a king, ironically acclaimed with the same title given him at birth (2:2). Gentiles kneel to mock him, as the wise men once knelt in worship (2:11). He leaves Jerusalem as he came into it (21:9), to the sound of royal greetings. The cross will become a throne, and through his suffering the power of his love will be known.

Led out to die

The vertical stake of the cross would already have been in place, with a slot for the cross-bar to be dropped into. The condemned man had to carry his own cross-beam to the place of crucifixion. But Jesus was so weak from the beating that a passer-by was pressed into service (v. 32). Roman soldiers could press anyone to carry a load for a set distance (5:41). But there was never another load like this.

Simon came from Cyrene in north Africa, in what is now Libya. He may have been a Jew whose family had settled in Africa, but who was in Jerusalem for the festival. It appears (Mark 15:21) that his two sons were known to Mark's readers, and so Simon himself may have been a Christian too. It is intriguingly possible that he is 'Simeon called Black' (Acts 13:1), the first of many black African Christians.

Seeing and tasting death

Golgotha is Aramaic for 'skull'. The sinister name fits the atmosphere of the day, of cheapened life and stark death. Someone offers Jesus a drink of wine mixed with gall, a sour toxic stuff (v. 34). This may be yet another stage in the taunting and mockery, pretending to offer a drink, but giving only bitter acid. Or it could be a kindly gesture, an opportunity for Jesus to take poison and spare himself some of the lingering pain ahead. Jesus refuses the drink. Then they nail him to the cross.

Prayer

Thanks be to thee, my Lord Jesus Christ, for all the benefits thou hast won for me, for all the pains and insults thou hast borne for me. O most merciful Redeemer, Friend and Brother, may I know thee more clearly, love thee more dearly, and follow thee more nearly, day by day. Amen

Richard of Chichester (1197–1253)

107 Matthew 27:35–44

Around the cross

The four gospels describe the scene at the cross in varied ways. Matthew and Mark's accounts are closely similar, Luke is rather different and John is different again. Some well-known features of the story come in only one of the four gospels. For example, only Luke (23:39–43) mentions the penitent thief. Only John (19:20–22) tells us that the inscription on the cross was in three languages, and that the Jewish leaders tried to get Pilate to change its wording.

As we think about the various differences, we may want to keep three points in mind.

- The four gospels agree on the main aspects of the story: Jewish trial, Roman trial, crucifixion, death, burial and resurrection. They match in many smaller details too: for example, the group of women followers looking on, the soldiers dicing for Jesus' clothing, Joseph burying the body.
- The gospel writers had to be selective. We should expect some variation between one gospel and another.
- We should aim to read each gospel on its own terms, and hear its distinctive tones and themes. They all help us to experience the atmosphere of the crucifixion, but in different ways. Matthew's main emphasis in this section is the sheer desolation and loneliness of the cross. Jesus is a man utterly on his own.

When they had crucified him

Crucifixion involved driving nails through the victim's wrists into a wooden beam. Then the beam was attached to the vertical stake of the cross, and the victim's feet were secured, probably again by nailing. Matthew says little about the physical aspects – everyone in the ancient world knew that crucifixion was horribly and excruciatingly painful.

The victim would be stripped naked, or nearly so. Any articles of clothing he had would fall to the soldiers who executed him. So the men raffled Jesus' garments, while they waited for his death (vv. 35–36). It was a day's work – normal, nasty, necessary. The title above Jesus' head labelled him a rebel, and this was how rebels died.

The foolishness of God

Either side of Jesus are 'bandits', men who have lived on the edge of society (v. 38). Whether they were driven by hunger and need, or were pursuing rebel aspirations, or belonged to an armed gang of thieves, we cannot tell. Whatever they have been and done has caught up with them. Jesus dies among criminals, keeping the company of 'sinners' right to the end (9:10–13).

In these hours on the cross, Jesus becomes a target for taunts and jibes from all sides. People can stare at him and scorn him as they choose. The Roman soldiers had their jest with him earlier. Now he is mocked by fellow Jews. Everyone seems to be involved: clerics and criminals – the highest and lowest in the land – and ordinary passers-by too. They scoff at his words (v. 40), his deeds (v. 42), his faith in God (v. 43). They look on him, they think of him, as a complete fool – humiliated, hanging, helpless, hopeless. Only later will the world discover that 'God's foolishness is wiser than human wisdom, and God's weakness is stronger than human strength' (1 Corinthians 1:25).

As it is written

Even in dying, Jesus fulfils scripture. There are three echoes of Psalm 22: passers-by shake their heads (22:7); 'If he trusts God, let God rescue him' (22:8); men cast lots for his clothing (22:18). This psalm was a prayer, a desperate prayer by a faithful believer, out of the depths of hurt and humiliation. Matthew shows the psalm coming to life again through the suffering of Jesus. The life and death of Jesus are a magnet, drawing out the meaning of ancient scripture. And the Old Testament is like a bank of floodlights, illuminating Jesus, showing his life in the light of God's long purpose.

For reflection and prayer

We may not know, we cannot tell, what pains he had to bear, but we believe it was for us he hung and suffered there.
C.F. Alexander (1818–95)

108 Matthew 27:45–54
The shaking of the foundations

Matthew's account takes us into both the personal experience of the crucifixion – how it impacted on Jesus himself – and its meaning – what the cross achieved. The death of Jesus has opened up a new era in history, a fresh age of hope.

Darkness at noon

Dark covers the land 'from the sixth hour to the ninth' – from roughly noon until 3 o'clock. Matthew does not mention any natural explanation. That is not his concern. The accent in these verses is on the power and strangeness of the signs. Surely God is at work. Yet the earth is not bright with greeting: it is wrapped in gloom.

There is no light in the sky. There seems also to be a thick veil of darkness over Jesus' own spirit, blocking any awareness of his Father's presence. His loneliness now becomes a total separation, from human support and from heaven too. Jesus feels utterly forsaken. Only here does he say 'My God' (v. 46). Everywhere else in the gospel, he says 'Father'. This is the separation that he has dreaded, the path he shrank from in Gethsemane (26:36–46) – the time when his faith and his Father seem utterly remote. This is the cost of bearing human sin – a fracture in the bond that links Father and Son, a cross in the very heart of God.

The words Jesus calls out come from the first line of Psalm 22. This psalm was echoed several times in earlier verses (27:35–44). It speaks of miserable loneliness, of a helpless and empty sense of forsakenness. But it also speaks in faith, that when God seems far away, even then only God can really help. Jesus' faith on the cross is not the comfortable faith of knowing that God is near and all is well. It is the faithfulness that hangs on to God even when it has no sense at all that God is still there to hang on to.

Last breath

Eli is Aramaic for 'my God', but some bystanders mishear or misunderstand and think that Jesus is calling for Elijah (v. 47). Elijah did not die, he was taken up into heaven (2 Kings 2), and many Jews expected him to return as an advance sign of the coming of God. But Jesus looked on John the Baptist as God's latter-day Elijah (see comments on 17:1–13, pp. 145–147). He was not calling on Elijah from the cross, and Elijah did not come to rescue him.

The sponge soaked in vinegary wine (v. 48) appears to be a small act of kindness, to ease the dreadful thirst of crucifixion. But then the time for kindness is over. Jesus lifts his voice in one last great cry, and 'gives up the ghost'. His breath is gone. His work is done.

Judgement and resurrection

The Jerusalem temple had two great curtains. One hung across the entrance to the main central building, the other covered the innermost shrine, the Holy of Holies. The tearing of either (v. 51) would be a mark of judgement, another warning of the destruction that Jesus prophesied. If the innermost curtain were the one torn – as Hebrews 10:19–20 suggests – this would also signal that God's presence is no longer shut away. Because Jesus has died, access to God is free and open.

When Jesus was born, a new light in the sky welcomed his coming. When he dies, creation groans, as if with the pain of childbirth, breaking open into new life. Rocks split. Graves open – not by any means unusual during an earth tremor. Only Matthew mentions the rising of the 'dead saints', and his account leaps forward here to speak of the aftermath of the resurrection. Because Christ is raised, the faithful dead shall rise too. Matthew's story expresses with graphic clarity the hope to which New Testament letters look forward (1 Corinthians 15:20–21; 1 Thessalonians 4:14). God has not forsaken Jesus: out of death comes new life.

God squad

As at the start of the gospel (2:2), Gentiles recognise Jesus (v. 54). These soldiers do not have a carefully formed faith. They simply sense that God is present in this man. For them, even the darkness has brought a kind of light.

For reflection

We only understand the cross if we feel both the darkness and the light, the absence of God from Jesus, and the presence of God in Jesus. Where was God on Golgotha? Nailed to a tree.

109 Matthew 27:55–66
Sharing our death

The burial completes Matthew's long account of Jesus' crucifixion. It seals and certifies death. Jesus has shared our human dying. But his story will not end there: the burial and the guarding of the tomb set out the stage for the next act – for resurrection.

Faithful women

This is almost the first time Matthew has mentioned women among the group that followed Jesus. Mary came from Magdala, a lakeside town in Galilee. Only in Luke (8:2) do we hear about Jesus healing her 'of seven demons'. There was another Mary, who was 'mother of James and Joseph'. There was also the mother of James and John Zebedee, who had hoped for great things from Jesus (20:20–21). The male disciples have scattered, but these women have found the courage and commitment to wait at the cross. The two Marys are last to leave the tomb (v. 61), and first to come back to it (28:1). They are the last witnesses of Jesus' burial and the first of his resurrection. At this key moment in history, they are the nucleus of the church, the thin thread of its continuing faithfulness to Jesus.

Rich man's grave

A long day is drawing to an end, from the trial 'in the morning' (27:1), to this burial as the sun sinks towards evening. Jews believed that even a condemned man deserved a decent burial (Deuteronomy 21:22–23), but it was not common for a crucified criminal to be laid in a private grave.

Joseph was a rich man, and a follower of Jesus' teaching. Mark and Luke mention that he was a member of the Jewish ruling council, an exception to the steady opposition the nation's leaders had shown Jesus. John (19:38) says that Joseph had kept his discipleship secret until now, but this burial would surely make his loyalty obvious. Still, this was the last service he could offer Jesus and, cost what it might, it was a challenge he had to meet.

The tomb was fresh, never previously used (v. 60). It was a cave in a rock face, and had been cut ready for Joseph's own death. A heavy stone, the shape of a coin or a cheese, would be rolled across the front. The last act of worship – as it seemed at the time – was over.

As secure as possible

The alliance of chief priests (mostly Sadducees) and Pharisees is unusual. Their acting on the sabbath is stranger still. But these were tense times. Jesus had caused enough trouble already. It would be important to prevent even a whispered rumour of resurrection. The disciples might start some odd stories if they could spirit Jesus' body away. With that concern in mind, the Jewish leaders ask Pilate to post a guard. Only Matthew mentions this incident, and he takes it up again in the light of Easter Day (28:11–15). As before, he emphasises the Jewish leaders' deliberate and determined opposition to Jesus.

Yet rarely can a security operation that seemed so easy have gone so badly wrong. We start to sense trouble ahead when Pilate says, 'Make it as secure as you can' (v. 65). But how secure can you be with the Son of God? Despite the stone, the seal and the soldiers, the only certainty is that God will have the last word.

Holy ground

The Church of the Holy Sepulchre in Jerusalem is built above the tomb where Christians believe Jesus was buried. This site has a good historical claim to be the right place. The evidence goes back a very long way. But Jesus' death hallows more than just one spot. He goes before us in human death. He stays beside us in our dying, and waits to meet us on the other side. The dust of our humanity and the earth to which it returns have been shared by Jesus, so that we may share his risen life.

Prayer

Thank you, God, that death is not unknown territory. You have been there in Jesus. When our life nears its end, may his cross give us courage and his resurrection give us hope. Amen

110 Matthew 28:1–7
The place where he lay

None of the gospels describes the resurrection itself. No one saw it happen. The first sign was an empty tomb, an open grave.

Light dawning

It is early on the Sunday morning. Jesus was crucified on Friday. Saturday was the sabbath, the Jewish rest day, and now the sabbath is over there is opportunity for travel and activity. The faithful women who watched where Jesus was buried come back to visit the tomb. Mark (16:1–3) says they brought spices to anoint the body, and they wondered how they would shift the great stone. But Matthew concentrates on the strangeness of what meets them. He is keen to accentuate (more than Mark) the supernatural aura of this event.

The earthquake, the angel, the paralysis that grips the guards – all this is the stuff of theophany, of God's appearing on earth. We overhear echoes of the God of Sinai (Exodus 19:18) and of ancient visions (Daniel 10:8–9). The angel's radiant white clothing is like the splendour of Jesus' Transfiguration (17:1–8). This place is rich with symbols of the glory of God. Here is the dawn, not just of a new day, but of a new era and a new creation.

Fearing and fearing not

When God comes near, when earth is changed by his presence, people get frightened. When things happen beyond normal human experience and control, fear quickly asserts its presence. Sometimes fear is a proper response. But so often in the Bible we hear the words 'Fear not'. At Jesus' birth, on a stormy sea, on a mountaintop, comes the simple command, 'Do not be afraid' (1:20; 14:27; 17:7). The mystery of God is laden with grace and rich with promise.

There is irony in the guards' fearful collapse (v. 4). They had been posted to keep the dead body securely in the tomb, and now they are like dead men themselves. Armed secular power cannot contain and limit the power of Jesus Christ – as the witness of persecuted Christians across the ages has shown.

But the women are told, 'Do not be afraid.' They came seeking Jesus 'who was crucified' (v. 5). Their eyes are still blinkered by death. It is too soon to grasp that he could be alive. But 'he has been raised, as he said' (v. 6). The tomb he occupied is empty. And they are ordered to bear witness to what they have seen (v. 7). They will be 'apostles to the apostles'.

The women must go and tell the male disciples what they have heard and seen. A woman's testimony counted for comparatively little in that society. But these were the witnesses God used to let the church hear the gospel. Jesus had promised to meet his friends in Galilee (26:32), to go ahead of them there like a shepherd leading his flock. He is going to keep that promise (v. 7). They will see him in Galilee, in the place where he first called them and spoke of God's kingdom. In Galilee, where he healed and taught, he will commission his friends to start again, to share his mission and to reach the world.

Celebration

Christians celebrate Easter – not just once a year, but every week. We worship on a Sunday because this is the day of resurrection, a weekly reminder that we live in a new era. The great brooding powers of death and decay have been disturbed. The normal physical order has been interrupted by the God of life. Christians rejoice in hope, because Christ is risen. We praise him for his cross, and we know him as risen Lord. The empty tomb is full with possibility and power. We live, even now, in the light of Easter morning.

For reflection and prayer

If Christ has not been raised, our faith is futile, and we are the most pitiable people in the world. But the truth is that Christ has been raised. Thanks be to God, who gives us the victory through our Lord Jesus Christ.

From 1 CORINTHIANS 15:17–20, 57

111 Matthew 28:8–15

Appearance and disappearance

Two groups of people leave the graveyard, each with a story to pass on. There is quite a contrast between them. The women race to tell Jesus' friends about what they have seen and heard (v. 8). Their feet are light and their hearts are leaping with joy, whereas the soldiers go with heavy and dragging steps, shame-faced, embarrassed and worried, to report the failure of their mission.

Living Lord

The empty tomb was an important sign of mysterious and mighty powers at work. The angel's words sent the women running off, 'with fear and great joy'. But their meeting with Jesus is the vital moment of this whole experience. They have seen the place where he was (28:6). They have heard the promise of where he will be (28:7). Now suddenly he is there, with them, so solid that he can be touched and held. Fear and joy are overtaken by love, awe, worship and praise.

Once again the beginning and end of the gospel meet. The combination of great joy leading into worship is exactly what was said about the wise men (2:10–11). The wise men worshipped Jesus at the start of his earthly life. These women are the first to worship him in his risen power.

Jesus' message underlines what the angel has said. The women should not fear, but should go and tell the eleven disciples to make their way to Galilee, to meet Jesus there. There is one important word that makes quite a difference. Jesus speaks of 'my brothers'. Though these male disciples have scattered and fled, he still counts them among his spiritual family, as people he relies on to do his will (12:46–50). He still trusts them, includes them and values them.

So the women go as witnesses. Their story, their sight of Jesus, will show the men the way forward so that they can see him too. As so often in the gospels, one follower's testimony leads someone else to Jesus and to faith. People help one another towards their own encounter with the Lord. Christians who speak naturally and positively about what Christ means in their lives can still inspire others to find out too.

Missing person

The guards' short journey and report is less positive. They 'tell everything that has happened' (v. 11), but in truth they do not know half of it. They get a substantial bonus payment for failing in their task. They were sent to prevent grave robbery, but the eventual tale is that the grave was robbed. And if anyone asks why they are so sure about their story, they can say they were asleep. All very dubious – but perhaps the best that could be thought of in the circumstances.

Sadly, Matthew tells his readers, that is the story many Jews have heard and believed, right up to the time the gospel was written (v. 15). The people's leaders have opposed Jesus in life and death; now they discredit his resurrection. But Israel as a whole nation is not completely set against him. There is a group of believing women, eleven 'brothers', and a rich man who buried the body. These are just the tip of the iceberg, a small selection of the followers Jesus already has, and the first visible instalment of a large Jewish church which will grow through the decades ahead.

Risen indeed

This episode with the guards is the first indication that the Christian church's faith in resurrection will be hard for the world to believe. Right down to our own day, there have been many thoughtful enquirers who have tested the evidence and asked seriously whether any other explanation fits the facts. So far as I can see, nothing comes near.

Suppose, for example, the disciples had stolen the body. That would mean that for years they preached and spread the faith, being persecuted and some martyred, and none of them ever let on – all for something they knew was a hoax. That really does not make sense.

Easter was incomparable. There is no natural and everyday explanation that fits. Something unique is here, an extraordinary event, the power of God breaking through human death. He is not here. He is risen.

For reflection

The church did not make Easter. Easter made the church. So how is Easter – the message and presence of the risen Christ – shaping, influencing and inspiring your church and your Christian life?

112 Matthew 28:16–20
With you forever

This 'Great Commission' is one of the most famous passages in the Bible. Christians through 2,000 years have read these verses as the church's marching orders, our mandate for mission, a task that is always ahead of us.

Whole gospel

The word 'all' comes up four times in just a few verses. Jesus has all authority. He sends his followers to all nations, to pass on all that he has taught. And he will be with them through all time.

There is no time or place outside Jesus' reach or care. There is no limit to his involvement in his people's lives. The details of Christian obedience may alter as times change, but the serious call to practical discipleship goes on. Jesus still wants committed people. There are four words in these verses that describe what his followers do.

- **Learn (v. 16):** The word disciple means 'learner', someone who listens, watches and copies Jesus.
- **Worship (v. 17):** A church that honours Jesus, that makes his life, death and resurrection the regular focus of our praise, will always be likely to grow in faith and love.
- **Doubt (v. 17):** 'They (or some of them) doubted'. This is the word used when Peter tried to walk on water, and fell in (14:31). Not all Christians are successful and confident. Most of us are hesitant and cautious. Jesus often invites us to step beyond our inhibitions. But he never discards us because of our fears or failures.
- **Keep (v. 20):** This is the other side of learning. Followers take Jesus' teaching seriously, and try to keep his commands.

End of the story

These few verses weave together threads that have been clear and strong throughout Matthew. Each of the five great sermons in the gospel is reflected in this final commission.

- Matthew 5—7. The sermon on the mount showed Jesus as the great Teacher. His teaching is practical, involving lifestyle, relationships, wealth, words. Making disciples (28:19) means passing on the practice of the faith, helping people to act out what Jesus has taught.
- Matthew 10 was the Mission Charge. Jesus sent his friends out to gather the Jewish people, like a scattered flock of sheep (9:36; 10:6). At the end of the gospel, he is still the great Shepherd, going ahead of his friends to Galilee (26:31–32; 28:7). But this time the flock is greater. The church is sent to reach the world.
- Matthew 13 is the parable chapter. This small company of Jesus' followers will be like seed, like yeast, changing the world with their faith.
- Matthew 18 teaches about Jesus' community, the church. The sign of baptism (28:19) marks this community. It is the family sign, the badge of belonging, a call to be committed to Jesus and to one another.
- Matthew 24—25 looked forward to the end of the age. Until then Jesus will be with his friends (28:20), guiding and helping them as they do his work. He has authority as Son of Man, to be Lord and Judge over all the nations (28:18).

Story without end

So the Lord dies, and rises. His work runs on and reaches out. This is the end of Matthew's gospel. It is also a new beginning, of a worldwide mission. It is the next chapter in a continuing story. For the Jesus who came as 'God with us' (1:23) will still be 'with you forever' (28:20), in the spreading life of his church.

At the start of the gospel Jesus was called 'son of David, son of Abraham' (1:1), a new king and a child born to reach the nations. At the end he fulfils all that destiny. His royal authority touches the whole world (28:18–20). His story goes on, until now it includes you and me. Like his first followers, we are sent – to serve, to share, to spread and to show the love and life of Jesus Christ.

Prayer

Lord Jesus Christ, Lord of every far horizon and of every faithful heart, take our small service and weave it into your grand purpose. For your honour and glory we pray. Amen

The Bible is at the heart of BRF's work, and this special anniversary collection is a celebration of the Bible for BRF's centenary year. Bringing together a fantastically wide-ranging writing team of authors, supporters and well-wishers from all areas of BRF's work, this resource is designed to help us go deeper into the story of the Bible and reflect on how we can share it in our everyday lives. Including sections which lead us through the Bible narrative as well as thematic and seasonal sections, it is the perfect daily companion to resource your spiritual journey.

The BRF Book of 365 Bible Reflections
With contributions from BRF authors, supporters and well-wishers
Edited by Karen Laister and Olivia Warburton
978 1 80039 100 0 £14.99

brfonline.org.uk

Prayer is at the heart of BRF's work, and this special illustrated anniversary collection is a celebration of prayer for BRF's centenary year. It can be used in a range of different settings, from individual devotions to corporate worship. Including sections on prayers of preparation, seasonal prayers, and themed prayers for special times and hard times, it is the perfect daily companion to resource your spiritual journey.

The BRF Book of 100 Prayers
Resourcing your spiritual journey
Martyn Payne
978 1 80039 147 5 £12.99

brfonline.org.uk

'Lord Jesus Christ, Son of God, have mercy on me.' This ancient prayer has been known and loved by generations of Christians for hundreds of years. It is a way of entering into the river of prayer which flows from the heart of God: the prayer of God himself, as Jesus continually prays for his people and for the world he loves. Simon Barrington-Ward teaches us how to use the Jesus Prayer as a devotional practice, and opens up the Bible passages that are crucial to understanding it.

The Jesus Prayer
BRF Centenary Classics
Simon Barrington-Ward
978 1 80039 087 4 £14.99

brfonline.org.uk

The BRF Centenary Prayer

Gracious God,
we rejoice in this centenary year
that you have grown BRF
from a local network of Bible readers
into a worldwide family of ministries.
Thank you for your faithfulness
in nurturing small beginnings
into surprising blessings.
We rejoice that, from the youngest to the oldest,
so many have encountered your word
and grown as disciples of Christ.
Keep us humble in your service,
ambitious for your glory
and open to new opportunities.
For your name's sake
Amen

Friends of BRF

I never fail to be amazed by the generosity of our supporters.

BRF is a remarkable charity, but we can only do what we do with the help of our faithful supporters: volunteers, people who pray for us and spread the word about our work, and people who support us financially, both individuals who give donations and legacies, and charitable trusts.

Many of our supporters have become 'Friends of BRF', choosing to make a regular monthly gift to help ensure that our work can be sustained and developed in the coming years. Every single donation, whether occasional or regular, small or large, makes a huge difference and I, along with all my colleagues here at BRF, thank God for each one.

If you'd like to help support Living Faith and our wider ministry, please visit **brf.org.uk/give**, contact a member of the fundraising team by email at **giving@brf.org.uk** or call **01235 462305** to speak to one of us direct.

With heartfelt thanks

Julie

**Julie MacNaughton,
Head of Fundraising MCIOF(Dip)**

Registered with
FUNDRAISING
REGULATOR

 *Enabling all ages to grow in faith*

Anna Chaplaincy
Living Faith
Messy Church
Parenting for Faith

100 years of BRF

2022 is BRF's 100th anniversary! Look out for details of our special new centenary resources, a beautiful centenary rose and an online thanksgiving service that we hope you'll attend. This centenary year we're focusing on sharing the story of BRF, the story of the Bible – and we hope you'll share your stories of faith with us too.

Find out more at **brf.org.uk/centenary**.

To find out more about our work, visit
brf.org.uk